Stanley Gibbons Stamp

PART 9
Portugal & Spain
(also covering Portuguese and Spanish Colonies)

6th edition 2011

Stanley Gibbons Ltd
London and Ringwood

By Appointment to Her Majesty The Queen
Stanley Gibbons Ltd, London
Philatelists

1st edition 1980
2nd edition 1984
3rd edition 1991
4th edition 1996
5th edition 2004
6th edition 2011

Published by Stanley Gibbons Ltd
Editorial, Publications Sales Offices
and Distribution Centre:
7 Parkside, Christchurch Road, Ringwood,
Hants BH24 3SH

© Stanley Gibbons Ltd 2011

Copyright Notice

The contents of this Catalogue, including the numbering system and illustrations, are fully protected by copyright. No part of this publication may be reproduced, stored in a retrieval system, or transmitted in any form or by any means, electronic, mechanical, photocopying, recording or otherwise, without the prior permission of Stanley Gibbons Limited. Requests for such permission should be addressed to the Catalogue Editor. This Catalogue is sold on condition that it is not, by way of trade or otherwise, lent, re-sold, hired out, circulated or otherwise disposed of other than in its complete, original and unaltered form and without a similar condition including this condition being imposed on the subsequent purchaser.

British Library Cataloguing in
Publication Data.
A catalogue record for this book is available from the British Library.

Errors and omissions excepted. The colour reproduction of stamps is only as accurate as the printing process will allow.

ISBN-10: 0-85259-798-3
ISBN-13: 978-0-85259-798-9

Item No. R2838-11

Printed by Burlington

Stanley Gibbons Foreign Catalogue Parts 2–22

ABOUT THIS EDITION

The Stanley Gibbons Part 9 Portugal and Spain catalogue is the only one published in English that contains all the stamps of Portugal, Spain, French and Spanish Andorra and all the Portuguese and Spanish Colonies in one book.

Since the last edition, detailed and up-to-date new issue listings have been added:
- Portugal (listed up to October 2009)
- Spain (July 2010)
- Azores (July 2010)
- Madeira (May 2010)
- Spanish Andorra (March 2010)
- French Andorra (March 2010)

The Colonies of both Spain and Portugal are covered in detail up to their independence. The machine labels of both Portugal and Spain have been updated and listed up to 2006 (Spain) and 2010 (Portugal).

A useful and informative "Guide to Entries", and an index to countries covered have been included for the first time to aid collectors stamps in using this catalogue.

Updated Portugal and Spain design indexes will aid the collector in identifying and cataloguing their stamps.

Pricing has been thoroughly revised and brought up to date throughout the catalogue, there has been a steady rise in prices, with notable increases in the Portuguese Colonies.

The first supplement to this catalogue appeared in *Gibbons Stamp Monthly* for April 2011.

Hugh Jefferies
Clare de la Feuillade
Barbara Hawkins
Michael Mayall

SPECIALIST SOCIETIES

Portuguese Philatelic Society
Secretary: John Swan
26 The Crescent
Whitley Bay
Tyne and Wear
NE26 2JG
Website: www.pps-uk.net
Email: john.swan9@btopenworld.com

International Society for Portuguese Philately
Secretary: Clyde J. Homen
1491 Bonnie View Road
Hollister
CA 95023-5117
USA
Email: cjh1491@sbcglobal.net

Spanish Study Circle
Hon. Secretary: Mrs. J. F. Richardson
16 Fairfield Avenue
Luton
LU2 7ER
Email: djr@luton.myzen.co.uk

STAMPS ADDED

SPAIN
379, 388b, 391c

PORTUGAL
2429, 2433, 2437a, 2437ab, 2439a, 2440ba, 2440c, 2440ca, 2444

Stanley Gibbons Holdings Plc

Stanley Gibbons Limited, Stanley Gibbons Auctions
399 Strand, London WC2R OLX
Telephone: +44 (0)207 836 8444
Fax: +44 (0)207 836 7342
E-mail: enquiries@stanleygibbons.co.uk
Internet: www.stanleygibbons.com
for all departments, Auction and Specialist Stamp Departments.
Open Monday–Friday 9.30 a.m. to 5 p.m.
Shop. Open Monday–Friday 9 a.m. to 5.30 p.m. and Saturday 9.30 a.m. to 5.30 p.m.

Stanley Gibbons Publications
7 Parkside, Christchurch Road, Ringwood, Hampshire BH24 3SH.
Telephone: +44 (0)1425 472363
(24 hour answer phone service)
Fax: +44 (0)1425 470247,
E-mail: info@stanleygibbons.co.uk
Publications Mail Order.
FREEPHONE 0800 611622
Monday–Friday 8.30 a.m. to 5 p.m.

Gibbons Stamp Monthly and Philatelic Exporter
7 Parkside, Christchurch Road, Ringwood, Hampshire BH24 3SH.
Subscriptions. +44 (0)1425 481031
Fax: +44 (0)1425 470247
E-mail: sboyle@stanleygibbons.co.uk

Stanley Gibbons (Guernsey Office)
18–20 Le Bordage, St Peter Port, Guernsey GY1 1DE.
Telephone: +44 (0)1481 708270

Fraser's
(a division of Stanley Gibbons Ltd)
399 Strand, London WC2R OLX
Autographs, photographs, letters and documents
Telephone +44 (0)207 836 8444
Fax: +44 (0)207 836 7342
E-mail: info@frasersautographs.co.uk
Internet: www.frasersautographs.com
Monday–Friday 9 a.m. to 5.30 p.m. and Saturday 10 a.m. to 4 p.m.

Stanley Gibbons Publications Overseas Representation

Stanley Gibbons Publications are represented overseas by the following:

Australia
Renniks Publications PTY LTD
Unit 3 37-39 Green Street
Banksmeadow, NSW 2019
Australia
Tel: +612 9695 7055
Website: www.renniks.com

Belgium
N.V. deZittere (D.Z.T.)/Davo
Heuvelstraat 106
3390 Tielt (Brabant), België
Tel: +32 16772673
E-mail: dzt@dezittere.be
Website: www.dezittere.be

Canada
Unitrade Associates
99 Floral Parkway, Toronto,
Ontario M6L 2C4, Canada
Tel: +1 416 242 5900
Website: www.unitradeassoc.com

Denmark
Samlerforum/Davo
Ostergade 3, DK7470, Karup
Denmark
Tel: +45 97102900
Website: www.samlerforum.dk

Finland
Davo C/o Kapylan
Merkkiky Pohjolankatu 1
00610 Helsinki, Finland
Tel: +358 9 792851
E-mail: jarnosoderstrom@kapylanmerkki.fi

France
ARPHI/Davo
Rue de Jouy 58, 78220 Viroflay, France
Tel: +33 130242162
E-mail: info@arphi.net

Germany
Schaubek Verlag Leipzig
Am Glaeschen 23,
D-04420 Markranstaedt,
Germany
Tel: +49 34 205 67823
Website: www.schaubek.de

India
Trustin Philatelic.
96, Richmond Raod.
Bangalore 560 025.
India
Contact Person: Mr. Ramesh Salvi
Tel: +9180 222 11 555 / 222 97 516
Hand Phone : +9180500 49500
Email: trustin@vsnl.net

Italy
Ernesto Marini S.R.L.
V. Struppa, 300, Genova, 16165,
Italy
Tel: +3901 0247-3530
Website: www.ernestomarini.it

Japan
Japan Philatelic
PO Box 2, Suginami-Minami,
Tokyo 168-8081,
Japan
Tel: +81 3330 41641
Website: www.yushu.co.jp

Netherlands
Uitgeverij Davo BV
PO Box 411, Ak Deventer, 7400
Netherlands
Tel: +315 7050 2700
Website: www.davo.nl

New Zealand
House of Stamps
PO Box 12, Paraparaumu,
New Zealand
Tel: +61 6364 8270
Website: www.houseofstamps.co.nz

New Zealand
Philatelic Distributors
PO Box 863
15 Mount Edgecumbe Street
New Plymouth 4615, New Zealand
Tel: +6 46 758 65 68
Website: www.stampcollecta.com

Norway
SKANFIL A/S
SPANAV. 52 / BOKS 2030
N-5504 HAUGESUND, Norway
Tel: +47-52703940
E-mail: magne@skanfil.no

Saudi Arabia
Arabian Stamp Centre
PO Box 54645, Riyadh, 11524
Saudi Arabia
Fax: +966 1 419 1379
Website: www.ArabianStamps.com

Singapore
C S Philatelic Agency
Peninsula Shopping Centre #04-29
3 Coleman Street, 179804, Singapore
Tel: +65 6337-1859
Website: www.cs.com.sg

Sweden
Chr Winther Sorensen AB
Box 43, S-310 20 Knaered, Sweden
Tel: +46 43050743
Website: www.ifsda.org/i/dealer.
php?mid=2100&asscd=SE

USA
Filatco
Inc. 5054 Lee Hwy, Arlington VA 22207
USA
Tel: +1 703 538 2727
Fax: +1 703 538 5210
Website: www.filatco.com

We have catalogues to suit every aspect of stamp collecting

Our catalogues cover stamps issued from across the globe - from the Penny Black to the latest issues. Whether you're a specialist in a certain reign or a thematic collector, we should have something to suit your needs. All catalogues include the famous SG numbering system, making it as easy as possible to find the stamp you're looking for.

Catalogues published by Stanley Gibbons include:

1 Commonwealth & British Empire Stamps 1840–1970 (113th edition, 2011)

Stamps of the World 2011
- Volume 1   A–Chil
- Volume 2   Chin–Geo
- Volume 3   Ger–Ja
- Volume 4   Je–New R
- Volume 5   New S–Sor
- Volume 6   Sou–Z

Commonwealth Country Catalogues
- **Australia and Dependencies** (6th edition, 2010)
- **Bangladesh, Pakistan & Sri Lanka** (2nd edition, 2011)
- **Belize, Guyana, Trinidad & Tobago** (1st edition, 2009)
- **Brunei, Malaysia & Singapore** (3rd edition, 2009)
- **Canada** (3rd edition, 2008)
- **Central Africa** (2nd edition, 2008)
- **Cyprus, Gibraltar & Malta** (2nd edition, 2008)
- **East Africa with Egypt and Sudan** (2nd edition, 2010)
- **Eastern Pacific** (2nd edition, 2011)
- **Falkland Islands** (4th edition, 2010)
- **Hong Kong** (3rd edition, 2010)
- **India (including Convention and Feudatory States)** (3rd edition, 2009)
- **Indian Ocean** (1st edition, 2006)
- **Ireland** (4th edition, 2008)
- **Leeward Islands** (1st edition, 2007)
- **New Zealand** (4th edition, 2010)
- **Northern Caribbean, Bahamas & Bermuda** (2nd edition, 2009)
- **St. Helena & Dependencies** (3rd edition, 2007)
- **Southern Africa** (2nd edition, 2007)
- **West Africa** (1st edition, 2009)
- **Western Pacific** (2nd edition, 2009)
- **Windward Islands and Barbados** (1st edition, 2007)

Foreign Countries
2   **Austria & Hungary** (7th edition, 2009)
3   **Balkans** (5th edition, 2009)
4   **Benelux** (6th edition, 2010)
5   **Czechoslovakia & Poland** (6th edition, 2002)
6   **France** (7th edition, 2010)
7   **Germany** (9th edition, 2011)
8   **Italy & Switzerland** (7th edition, 2010)
9   **Portugal & Spain** (6th edition, 2011)
10 **Russia** (6th edition, 2008)
11 **Scandinavia** (6th edition, 2008)
12 **Africa since Independence A-E** (2nd edition, 1983)
13 **Africa since Independence F-M** (1st edition, 1981)
14 **Africa since Independence N-Z** (1st edition, 1981)
15 **Central America** (3rd edition, 2007)
16 **Central Asia** (4th edition, 2006)
17 **China** (7th edition, 2006)
18 **Japan & Korea** (5th edition, 2008)
19 **Middle East** (7th edition, 2009)
20 **South America** (4th edition, 2008)
21 **South-East Asia** (4th edition, 2004)
22 **United States of America** (7th edition, 2010)

Thematic Catalogues
Stanley Gibbons Catalogues for use with **Stamps of the World**.
- **Collect Aircraft on Stamps** (2nd edition, 2009)
- **Collect Birds on Stamps** (5th edition, 2003)
- **Collect Chess on Stamps** (2nd edition, 1999)
- **Collect Motor Vehicles on Stamps** (1st edition 2004)

Great Britain Catalogues
- **Collect British Stamps** (61st edition, 2010)
- **Great Britain Concise Stamp Catalogue** (25th edition, 2010)
- Volume 1   **Queen Victoria** (15th edition, 2008)
- Volume 2   **King Edward VII to King George VI** (13th edition, 2009)
- Volume 3   **Queen Elizabeth II Pre-decimal issues** (11th edition, 2006)
- Volume 4   **Queen Elizabeth II Decimal Definitive Issues – Part 1** (10th edition, 2008)
   Queen Elizabeth II Decimal Definitive Issues – Part 2 (10th edition, 2010)
- Volume 5   **Queen Elizabeth II Decimal Special Issues** (3rd edition, 1998 with 1998 99 and 2000/1 Supplements)

Other publications
- **Asia Simplified Volume 1** (1st edition, 2010)
- **Antarctica (including Australian and British Antarctic Territories, French Southern and Antarctic Territories and Ross Dependency)** (1st edition, 2010)
- **Collect Channel Islands and Isle of Man Stamps** (26th edition, 2010)
- **Commonwealth Simplified**
- **Great Britain Numbers Issued** (3rd edition, 2008)
- **Enjoy Stamp Collecting** (7th edition, 2006)
- **How to Identify Stamps** (4th edition, 2007)
- **North America Combined** (1st edition, 2010)
- **Philatelic Terms Illustrated** (4th edition, 2003)
- **United Nations (also including International Organizations based in Switzerland and UNESCO)** (1st edition, 2010)
- **Western Europe Simplified**

Visit stanleygibbons.com to find out more about our full range of philatelic literature

Stanley Gibbons Publications
7 Parkside, Christchurch Road, Ringwood, Hampshire BH24 3SH
UK: 0800 611 622 Int: +44 1425 363 | orders@stanleygibbons.co.uk
www.stanleygibbons.com

Contents

General Philatelic Information and Guidelines to the Scope of Stanley Gibbons Foreign Catalogues	viii	
Abbreviations	xv	
Features Listing	xvi	
International Philatelic Glossary	xviii	
Guide to Entries	xxii	

PORTUGAL	**1**
Machine Labels	84
Stamp Booklets	91
Design Index	93
ANGOLA	**100**
Portuguese Congo	111
AZORES	**113**
Stamp Booklets	126
Angra	126
Horta	126
Ponta Delgada	127
British Post Office on São Miguel	127
CAPE VERDE ISLANDS	**128**
British Post Office at St. Vincent	134
MACAO	**134**
Machine Labels	160
Stamp Booklets	160
British Post Office in Macao	160
MADEIRA	**161**
A. Madeira	161
B. Funchal	162
C. Madeira	162
Stamp Booklets	170
British Post Office in Madeira	170

MOZAMBIQUE	**171**
Inhambane	182
Kionga	183
Lourenço Marques	183
Mozambique Company	185
Nyassa Company	191
Quelimane	193
Tete	193
Zambezia	193
PORTUGUESE COLONIES AND OVERSEAS TERRITORIES	**195**
General Issues	**195**
A. African Colonies	195
B. General Issues	195
PORTUGUESE GUINEA	**196**
PORTUGUESE INDIA	**204**
British India Post Office at Damão	214
ST. THOMAS & PRINCE ISLANDS	**214**
TIMOR	**223**
East Timor (United Nations Transitional Administration)	229
SPAIN	**231**
Machine Labels	362
Stamp Booklets	364
Fiscal Stamps used for Postage	365
Postal Tax Stamps	365
Design Index	366
Carlist Issues	371
Civil War, 1936-39	371
British Post Offices in Spain	**379**
CAPE JUBY	**380**
CUBA	**382**
A. Cuba and Puerto Rico	382
B. Separate Issues for Cuba	383
British Post Offices in Cuba	**385**
ELOBEY, ANNOBON AND CORISCO	**386**

FERNANDO POO	**387**
British Post Offices in Fernando Poo	392
IFNI	**393**
MARIANA ISLANDS	**398**
PHILIPPINES	**399**
Filipino Revolutionary Government	403
PUERTO RICO	**404**
British Post Offices in Puerto Rico	406
RIO MUNI	**408**
SPAINISH GUINEA	**411**
Spanish Territories of the Gulf of Guinea	412
SPANISH MOROCCO	**418**
SPANISH POST OFFICES IN MOROCCO AND TANGIER	**424**
A. Morocco	424
B. Tangier	425
SPANISH SAHARA	**427**
A. Rio de Oro	427
B. La Agüera	429
C. Spanish Sahara	429
SPANISH WEST AFRICA	**437**
ANDORRA	**438**
I. French Post Offices	438
Stamp Booklets	467
II. Spanish Post Offices	467
Machine Labels	482
Index	**483**

vii

General Philatelic Information and Guidelines to the Scope of Stanley Gibbons Foreign Catalogues

These notes reflect current practice in compiling the Foreign Catalogue.

The *Stanley Gibbons Stamp Catalogue* has a very long history and the vast quantity of information it contains has been carefully built up by successive generations through the work of countless individuals. Philately itself is never static and the Catalogue has evolved and developed during this long time-span. These notes apply to current policy – some of the older listings were prepared using slightly different criteria – and we hope you find them useful in using the catalogue.

THE CATALOGUE IN GENERAL

Contents. The Catalogue is confined to adhesive postage stamps, including miniature sheets. For particular categories the rules are:
(a) Revenue (fiscal) stamps or telegraph stamps are listed only where they have been expressly authorised for postal duty.
(b) Stamps issued only precancelled are included, but normally issued stamps available additionally with precancel have no separate precancel listing unless the face value is changed.
(c) Stamps prepared for use but not issued, hitherto accorded full listing, are nowadays footnoted with a price (where possible).
(d) Bisects (trisects, etc.) are only listed where such usage was officially authorised.
(e) Stamps issued only on first day covers and not available separately are not listed but priced (on the cover) in a footnote.
(f) New printings, as such, are not listed, though stamps from them may qualify under another category, e.g. when a prominent new shade results.
(g) Official and unofficial reprints are dealt with by footnote.
(h) Stamps from imperforate printings of modern issues which also occur perforated are covered by footnotes or general notes, but are listed where widely available for postal use.

Exclusions. The following are excluded:
(a) non-postal revenue or fiscal stamps;
(b) postage stamps used fiscally;
(c) local carriage labels and private local issues;
(d) telegraph stamps;
(e) bogus or phantom stamps;
(f) railway or airline letter fee stamps, bus or road transport company labels;
(g) cut-outs;
(h) all types of non-postal labels;
(i) documentary labels for the postal service, e.g. registration, recorded delivery, airmail etiquettes, etc.;
(j) privately applied embellishments to official issues and privately commissioned items generally;
(k) stamps for training postal officers;
(l) specimen stamps.

Full listing. "Full listing" confers our recognition and implies allotting a catalogue number and (wherever possible) a price quotation.

In judging status for inclusion in the catalogue broad considerations are applied to stamps. They must be issued by a legitimate postal authority, recognised by the government concerned, and must be adhesives valid for proper postal use in the class of service for which they are inscribed. Stamps, with the exception of such categories as postage dues and officials, must be available to the general public, at face value, in reasonable quantities without any artificial restrictions being imposed on their distribution.

We record as abbreviated Appendix entries, without catalogue numbers or prices, stamps from countries which either persist in having far more issues than can be justified by postal need or have failed to maintain control over their distribution so that they have not been available to the public in reasonable quantities at face value. Miniature sheets and imperforate stamps are not mentioned in these entries.

The publishers of this catalogue have observed, with concern, the proliferation of "artificial" stamp-issuing territories. On several occasions this has resulted in separately inscribed issues for various component parts of otherwise united states or territories. Stanley Gibbons Publications have decided that where such circumstances occur, they will not, in the future, list these items in the SG catalogue without first satisfying themselves that the stamps represent a genuine political, historical or postal division within the country concerned. Any such issues which do not fulfil this stipulation will be recorded in the Catalogue Appendix only.

For errors and varieties the criterion is legitimate (albeit inadvertent) sale over a post office counter in the normal course of business. Details of provenance are always important; printers' waste and fraudulently manufactured material is excluded.

Certificates. In assessing unlisted items due weight is given to Certificates from recognised Expert Committees and, where appropriate, we will usually ask to see them.

New issues. New issues are listed regularly in the Catalogue Supplement in *Gibbons Stamp Monthly*, then consolidated into the next available edition of the Catalogue.

Date of issue. Where local issue dates differ from dates of release by agencies, "date of issue" is the local date. Fortuitous stray usage before the officially intended date is disregarded in listing.

Catalogue numbers. Stamps of each country are catalogued chronologically by date of issue. Subsidiary classes (e.g. postage due stamps) are integrated into one list with postage and commemorative stamps and distinguished by a letter prefix to the catalogue number.

The catalogue number appears in the extreme left column. The boldface type numbers in the next column

Information and Guidelines

are merely cross-references to illustrations. Catalogue numbers in the *Gibbons Stamp Monthly* Supplement are provisional only and may need to be altered when the lists are consolidated. Miniature sheets only purchasable intact at a post office have a single MS number; sheetlets – individual stamps available – number each stamp separately. The catalogue no longer gives full listing to designs originally issued in normal sheets, which subsequently appear in sheetlets showing changes of colour, perforation, printing process or face value. Such stamps will be covered by footnotes.

Once published in the Catalogue, numbers are changed as little as possible; really serious renumbering is reserved for the occasions when a complete country or an entire issue is being rewritten. The edition first affected includes cross-reference tables of old and new numbers.

Our catalogue numbers are universally recognised in specifying stamps and as a hallmark of status.

Illustrations. Stamps are illustrated at three-quarters linear size. Stamps not illustrated are the same size and format as the value shown unless otherwise indicated. Stamps issued only as miniature sheets have the stamp alone illustrated but sheet size is also quoted. Overprints, surcharges, watermarks and postmarks are normally actual size. Illustrations of varieties are often enlarged to show the detail.

CONTACTING THE CATALOGUE EDITOR

The editor is always interested in hearing from people who have new information which will improve or correct the Catalogue. As a general rule he must see and examine the actual stamps before they can be considered for listing; photographs or photocopies are insufficient evidence. Neither he nor his staff give opinions as to the genuineness of stamps.

Submissions should be made in writing to the Catalogue Editor, Stanley Gibbons Publications, 7 Parkside, Christchurch Road, Ringwood, Hants BH24 3SH. The cost of return postage for items submitted is appreciated, and this should include the registration fee if required.

Where information is solicited purely for the benefit of the enquirer, the editor cannot undertake to reply if the answer is already contained in these published notes or if return postage is omitted. Written communications are greatly preferred to enquiries by telephone or e-mail and the editor regrets that he or his staff cannot see personal callers without a prior appointment being made.

The editor welcomes close contact with study circles and is interested, too, in finding local correspondents who will verify and supplement official information in overseas countries where this is deficient.

We regret we do not give opinions as to the genuineness of stamps, nor do we identify stamps or number them by our Catalogue.

TECHNICAL MATTERS

The meanings of the technical terms used in the Catalogue will be found in *Philatelic Terms Illustrated*, published by Stanley Gibbons (Price £14.95 plus postage).

1. Printing

Printing errors. Errors in printing are of major interest to the Catalogue. Authenticated items meriting consideration would include background, centre or frame inverted or omitted; centre or subject transposed; error of colour; error or omission of value; double prints and impressions; printed both sides; and so on. Designs *tête-bêche*, whether intentionally or by accident, are listable. *Se-tenant* arrangements of stamps are recognised in the listings or footnotes. Gutter pairs (a pair of stamps separated by blank margin) are excluded unless they have some philatelic importance. Colours only partially omitted are not listed, neither are stamps printed on the gummed side.

Printing varieties. Listing is accorded to major changes in the printing base which lead to completely new types. In recess-printing this could be a design re-engraved, in photogravure or photolithography a screen altered in whole or in part. It can also encompass flat-bed and rotary printing if the results are readily distinguishable.

To be considered at all, varieties must be constant.

Early stamps, produced by primitive methods, were prone to numerous imperfections; the lists reflect this, recognising re-entries, retouches, broken frames, misshapen letters, and so on. Printing technology has, however, radically improved over the years, during which time photogravure and lithography have become predominant. Varieties nowadays are more in the nature of flaws and these, being too specialised for a general catalogue, are almost always outside the scope. We therefore do not list such items as dry prints, kiss prints, doctor-blade flaws, blanket set-offs, doubling through blanket stretch, plate cracks and scratches, registration flaws (leading to colour shifts), lithographic ring flaws, and so on. Neither do we recognise fortuitous happenings like paper creases or confetti flaws.

Overprints (and surcharges). Overprints of different types qualify for separate listing. These include overprints in different colours; overprints from different printing processes such as litho and typo; overprints in totally different typefaces, etc.

Overprint errors and varieties. Major errors in machine-printed overprints are important and listable. They include overprint inverted or omitted; overprint double (treble, etc.); overprint diagonal; overprint double, one inverted; pairs with one overprint omitted, e.g. from a radical shift to an adjoining stamp; error of colour; error of type fount; letters inverted or omitted, etc. If the overprint is handstamped, few of these would qualify and a distinction is drawn.

Varieties occurring in overprints will often take the

ix

form of broken letters, slight differences in spacing, rising spacers, etc. Only the most important would be considered for footnote mention.

Sheet positions. If space permits we quote sheet positions of listed varieties and authenticated data is solicited for this purpose.

2. Paper

All stamps listed are deemed to be on "ordinary" paper of the wove type and white in colour; only departures from this are mentioned.

Types. Where classification so requires we distinguish such other types of paper as, for example, vertically and horizontally laid; wove and laid bâtonné; card(board); carton; cartridge, enamelled; glazed; GC (Grande Consommation); granite; native; pelure; porous; quadrillé; ribbed; rice; and silk thread.

Our chalky (chalk-surfaced) paper is specifically one which shows a black mark when touched with a silver wire. This and other coatings are easily lost or damaged through immersion in water.

The various makeshifts for normal paper are listed as appropriate. They include printing on: unfinished banknotes, war maps, ruled paper, Post Office forms, and the unprinted side of glossy magazines. The varieties of double paper and joined paper are recognised.

Descriptive terms. The fact that a paper is hand-made (and thus probably of uneven thickness) is mentioned where necessary. Such descriptive terms as "hard" and "soft"; "smooth" and "rough"; "thick", "medium" and "thin" are applied where there is philatelic merit in classifying papers.

Coloured, very white and toned papers. A coloured paper is one that is coloured right through (front and back of the stamp). In the Catalogue the colour of the paper is given in italics, thus

black/*rose* = black design on rose paper.

Papers have been made specially white in recent years by, for example, a very heavy coating of chalk. We do not classify shades of whiteness of paper as distinct varieties. There does exist, however, a type of paper from early days called toned. This is off-white, often brownish or buffish, but it cannot be assigned a definite colour. A toning effect brought on by climate, incorrect storage or gum staining is disregarded here, as this was not the state of the paper when issued.

Safety devices. The Catalogue takes account of such safety devices as varnish lines, grills, burelage or imprinted patterns on the front or moiré on the back of stamps.

Modern developments. Two modern developments also affect the listings, printing on self-adhesive paper and the tendency, philatelic in origin, for conventional paper to be reinforced or replaced by different materials. Some examples are the use of foils in gold, silver, aluminium, palladium and steel; application of an imitation wood veneer; printing on plastic moulded in relief; and use of a plastic laminate to give a three-dimensional effect. Examples also occur of stamps impregnated with scent; printed on silk; and incorporating miniature gramophone records.

3. Perforation and Rouletting

Perforation gauge. The gauge of a perforation is the number of holes in a length of 2 cm. For correct classification the size of the holes (large or small) may need to be distinguished; in a few cases the actual number of holes on each edge of the stamp needs to be quoted.

Measurement. The Gibbons Instanta gauge is the standard for measuring perforations. The stamp is viewed against a dark background with the transparent gauge put on top of it. Though the gauge measures to decimal accuracy, perforations read from it are generally quoted in the Catalogue to the nearest half. For example:

Just over perf.
12¾ to just under perf. 13¼ = perf. 13
Perf. 13¼ exactly, rounded up = perf. 13½
Just over perf.
13¼ to just under perf. 13¾ = perf. 13½
Perf. 13¾ exactly, rounded up = perf. 14

However, where classification depends on it, actual quarter-perforations are quoted.

Notation. Where no perforation is quoted for an issue it is imperforate. Perforations are usually abbreviated (and spoken) as follows, though sometimes they may be spelled out for clarity. This notation for rectangular stamps (the majority) applies to diamond shapes if "top" is read as the edge to the top right.

P 14: perforated alike on all sides (read: "perf. 14").

P 14×15: the first figure refers to top and bottom, the second to left and right sides (read: "perf. 14 by 15"). This is a compound perforation. For an upright triangular stamp the first figure refers to the two sloping sides and the second to the base. In inverted triangulars the base is first and the second figure refers to the sloping sides.

P 14-15: perforation measuring anything between 14 and 15: the holes are irregularly spaced, thus the gauge may vary along a single line or even along a single edge of the stamp (read: "perf. 14 to 15").

P 14 irregular. perforated 14 from a worn perforator, giving badly aligned holes irregular spaced (read "irregular perf. 14").

P *comp(ound)* 14×15: two gauges in use but not necessarily on opposite sides of the stamp. It could be one side in one gauge and three in the other, or two adjacent sides with the same gauge (Read: "perf. compound of 14 and 15"). For three gauges or more, abbreviated as "P 14, 14½, 15 or compound" for example.

P 14, 14½: perforated approximately 14¼ (read: "perf. 14

Information and Guidelines

or 14½"). It does not mean two stamps, one perf. 14 and the other perf. 14½. This obsolescent notation is gradually being replaced in the Catalogue.

Imperf: imperforate (not perforated).

Imperf × P 14: imperforate at top and bottom and perf 14 at sides.

P 14 × *imperf* = perf 14 at top and bottom and imperforate at sides.

Such headings as "P 13 × 14 (vert) and P 14 × 13 (horiz)" indicate which perforations apply to which stamp format – vertical or horizontal.

Some stamps are additionally perforated so that a label or tab is detachable; others have been perforated suitably for use as two halves. Listings are normally for whole stamps, unless stated otherwise.

Other terms. Perforation almost always gives circular holes; where other shapes have been used they are specified, e.g. square holes; lozenge perf. Interrupted perfs are brought about by the omission of pins at regular intervals. Perforations have occasionally been simulated by being printed as part of the design. With few exceptions, privately applied perforations are not listed.

Perforation errors and varieties. Authenticated errors, where a stamp normally perforated is accidentally issued imperforate, are listed provided no traces of perforation (blind holes or indentations) remain. They must be provided as pairs, both stamps wholly imperforate, and are only priced in that form.

Stamps merely imperforate between stamp and margin (fantails) are not listed.

Imperforate-between varieties are recognised, where one row of perfs has been missed. They are listed and priced in pairs:

Imperf between (horiz pair): a horizontal pair of stamps with perfs all around the edges but none between the stamps.

Imperf between (vert pair): a vertical pair of stamps with perfs all around the edges but none between the stamps.

Where several of the rows have escaped perforation the resulting variety is listable. Thus:

Imperf vert (horiz pair): a horizontal pair of stamps perforated top and bottom; all three vertical directions are imperf – the two outer edges and between the stamps.

Imperf horiz (vert pair): a vertical pair perforated at left and right edges; all three horizontal directions are imperf – the top, bottom and between the stamps.

Straight edges. Large sheets cut up before issue to post offices can cause stamps with straight edges, i.e. imperf on one side or on two sides at right angles. They are not usually listable in this condition and are worth less than corresponding stamps properly perforated all round. This does not, however, apply to certain stamps, mainly from coils and booklets, where straight edges on various sides are the manufacturing norm affecting every stamp. The listings and notes make clear which sides are correctly imperf.

Malfunction. Varieties of double, misplaced or partial perforation caused by error or machine malfunction are not listable, neither are freaks, such as perforations placed diagonally from paper folds. Likewise disregarded are missing holes caused by broken pins, and perforations "fading out" down a sheet, the machinery progressively disengaging to leave blind perfs and indentations to the paper.

Centering. Well-centred stamps have designs surrounded by equal opposite margins. Where this condition affects the price the fact is stated.

Type of perforating. Where necessary for classification, perforation types are distinguished. These include:

Line perforation from one line of pins punching single rows of holes at a time.

Comb perforation from pins disposed across the sheet in comb formation, punching out holes at three sides of the stamp a row at a time.

Harrow perforation applied to a whole pane or sheet at one stroke.

Rotary perforation from the toothed wheels operating across a sheet, then crosswise.

Sewing-machine perforation. The resultant condition, clean-cut or rough, is distinguished where required.

Pin-perforation is the commonly applied term for pin-roulette in which, instead of being punched out, round holes are pricked by sharp-pointed pins and no paper is removed.

Punctured stamps. Perforation holes can be punched into the face of the stamp. Patterns of small holes, often in the shape of initial letters, are privately applied devices against pilferage. These "perfins" are outside the scope. Identification devices, when officially inspired, are listed or noted; they can be shapes, or letters or words formed from holes, sometimes converting one class of stamp into another.

Rouletting. In rouletting the paper is cut, for ease of separation, but none is removed. The gauge is measured, when needed, as for perforations. Traditional French terms descriptive of the type of cut are often used and types include:

Arc roulette (percé en arc). Cuts are minute, spaced arcs, each roughly a semicircle.

Cross roulette (percé en croix). Cuts are tiny diagonal crosses.

Line roulette (parcé en ligne or en ligne droite). Short straight cuts parallel to the frame of the stamp. The commonest basic roulette. Where not further described, "roulette" means this type.

Rouletted in colour or coloured roulette (percé en lignes colorees or en lignes de coleur). Cuts with coloured edges, arising from notched rule inked simultaneously with the printing plate.

Saw-tooth roulette (percé en scie). Cuts applied zigzag fashion to resemble the teeth of a saw.

Serpentine roulette (percé en serpentin). Cuts as sharply wavy lines.

Zigzag roulettes (percé en zigzags). Short straight cuts at angles in alternate directions, producing sharp

xi

points on separation. U.S. usage favours "serrate(d) roulette" for this type.

Pin-roulette (originally *percé en points* and now *perforés trous d'epingle*) is commonly called pin-perforation in English.

4. Gum

All stamps listed are assumed to have gum of some kind; if they were issued without gum this is stated. Original gum (o.g.) means that which was present on the stamp as issued to the public. Deleterious climates and the presence of certain chemicals can cause gum to crack and, with early stamps, even make the paper deteriorate. Unscrupulous fakers are adept in removing it and regumming the stamp to meet the unreasoning demand often made for "full o.g." in cases where such a thing is virtually impossible.

Until recent times the gum used for stamps has been gum arabic, but various synthetic adhesives – tinted or invisible-looking – have been in use since the 1960s. Stamps existing with more than one type of gum are not normally listed separately, though the fact is noted where it is of philatelic significance, e.g. in distinguishing reprints or new printings.

The distinct variety of grilled gum is, however, recognised. In this the paper is passed through a gum breaker prior to printing to prevent subsequent curling. As the patterned rollers were sufficient to impress a grill into the paper beneath the gum we can quote prices for both unused and used examples.

Self-adhesive stamps are issued on backing paper from which they are peeled before affixing to mail. Unused examples are priced as for backing paper intact. Used examples are best kept on cover or on piece.

5. Watermarks

Stamps are on unwatermarked paper except where the heading to the set says otherwise.

Detection. Watermarks are detected for Catalogue description by one of four methods:
(1) holding stamps to the light;
(2) laying stamps face down on a dark background;
(3) adding a few drops of petroleum ether 40/60 to the stamp laid face down in a watermark tray; or
(4) by use of the Stanley Gibbons Detectamark, or other equipment, which works by revealing the thinning of the paper at the watermark. (Note that petroleum ether is highly inflammable in use and can damage photogravure stamps.)

Listable types. Stamps occurring on both watermarked and unwatermarked papers are different types and both receive full listing.

Single watermarks (devices occurring once on every stamp) can be modified in size and shape as between different issues; the types are noted but not usually separately listed. Fortuitous absence of watermark from a single stamp or its gross displacement would not be listable.

To overcome registration difficulties the device may be repeated at close intervals (a multiple watermark), single stamps thus showing parts of several devices. Similarly a large sheet watermark (or all-over watermark) covering numerous stamps can be used. We give informative notes and illustrations for them. The designs may be such that numbers of stamps in the sheet automatically lack watermark; this is not a listable variety. Multiple and all-over watermarks sometimes undergo modifications, but if the various types are difficult to distinguish from single stamps notes are given but not separate listings.

Papermakers' watermarks are noted where known but not listed separately, since most stamps in the sheet will lack them. Sheet watermarks which are nothing more than officially adopted papermakers' watermarks are, however, given normal listing.

Marginal watermarks, falling outside the pane of stamps, are ignored except where misplacement causes the adjoining row to be affected, in which case they are footnoted.

Watermark errors and varieties. Watermark errors are recognised as of major importance. They comprise stamps intended to be on unwatermarked paper but issued watermarked by mistake, or stamps printed on paper with the wrong watermark. Watermark varieties, on the other hand, such as broken or deformed bits on the dandy roll, are not listable.

Watermark positions. Paper has a side intended for printing and watermarks are usually impressed so that they read normally when looked through from that printed side.

Illustrations in the Catalogue are of watermarks in normal positions (from the front of the stamps) and are actual size where possible.

Differences in watermark position are collectable as distinct varieties. In this Catalogue, however, only normal sideways watermarks are listed (and "sideways inverted" is treated as "sideways"). Inverted and reversed watermarks have always been outside its scope: in the early days of flat-bed printing, sheets of watermarked paper were fed indiscriminately through the press and the resulting watermark positions had no particular philatelic significance. Similarly, the special make-up of sheets for booklets can in some cases give equal quantities of normal and inverted watermarks.

6. Colours

Stamps in two or three colours have these named in order of appearance, from the centre moving outwards. Four colours or more are usually listed as multicoloured.

In compound colour names the second is the predominant one, thus:

orange-red = a red tending towards orange;

red-orange = an orange containing more red than usual.

Standard colours used. The 200 colours most used for stamp identification are given in the Stanley Gibbons Colour Key. The Catalogue has used the Key as a standard for describing new issues for some years. The names are also introduced as lists are rewritten, though exceptions are made for those early issues where traditional names have become universally established.

Determining colours. When comparing actual stamps with colour samples in the Key, view in a good north daylight (or its best substitute: fluorescent "colour-matching" light). Sunshine is not recommended. Choose a solid portion of the stamp design; if available, marginal markings such as solid bars of colour or colour check dots are helpful. Shading lines in the design can be misleading as they appear lighter than solid colour. Postmarked portions of a stamp appear darker than normal. If more than one colour is present, mask off the extraneous ones as the eye tends to mix them.

Errors of colour. Major colour errors in stamps or overprints which qualify for listing are: wrong colours; one colour inverted in relation to the rest; albinos (colourless impressions), where these have Expert Committee certificates; colours completely omitted, but only on unused stamps (if found on used stamps the information is footnoted).

Colours only partially omitted are not recognised.

Colour shifts, however spectacular, are not listed.

Shades. Shades in philately refer to variations in the intensity of a colour or the presence of differing amounts of other colours. They are particularly significant when they can be linked to specific printings. In general, shades need to be quite marked to fall within the scope of this Catalogue; it does not favour nowadays listing the often numerous shades of a stamp, but chooses a single applicable colour name which will indicate particular groups of outstanding shades. Furthermore, the listings refer to colours as issued: they may deteriorate into something different through the passage of time.

Modern colour printing by lithography is prone to marked differences of shade, even within a single run, and variations can occur within the same sheet. Such shades are not listed.

Aniline colours. An aniline colour meant originally one derived from coal-tar; it now refers more widely to colour of a particular brightness suffused on the surface of a stamp and showing through clearly on the back.

Colours of overprints and surcharges. All overprints and surcharges are in black unless otherwise in the heading or after the description of the stamp.

7. Luminescence

Machines which sort mail electronically have been introduced in recent years. In consequence some countries have issued stamps on fluorescent or phosphorescent papers, while others have marked their stamps with phosphor bands.

The various papers can only be distinguished by ultraviolet lamps emitting particular wavelengths. They are separately listed only when the stamps have some other means of distinguishing them, visible without the use of these lamps. Where this is not so, the papers are recorded in footnotes or headings. (Collectors using the lamps should exercise great care in their use as exposure to their light is extremely dangerous to the eyes.)

Phosphor bands are listable, since they are visible to the naked eye (by holding stamps at an angle to the light and looking along them, the bands appear dark). Stamps existing with and without phosphor bands or with differing numbers of bands are given separate listings. Varieties such as double bands, misplaced or omitted bands, bands printed on the wrong side, are not listed.

8. Coil Stamps

Stamps issued only in coil form are given full listing. If stamps are issued in both sheets and coils the coil stamps are listed separately only where there is some feature (e.g. perforation) by which singles can be distinguished. Coil strips containing different stamps *se-tenant* are also listed.

Coil join pairs are too random and too easily faked to permit of listing; similarly ignored are coil stamps which have accidentally suffered an extra row of perforations from the claw mechanism in a malfunctioning vending machine.

9. Booklet Stamps

Single stamps from booklets are listed if they are distinguishable in some way (such as watermark or perforation) from similar sheet stamps. Booklet panes, provided they are distinguishable from blocks of sheet stamps, are listed for most countries; booklet panes containing more than one value *se-tenant* are listed under the lowest of the values concerned.

Lists of stamp booklets are given for certain countries and it is intended to extend this generally.

10. Forgeries and Fakes

Forgeries. Where space permits, notes are considered if they can give a concise description that will permit unequivocal detection of a forgery. Generalised

Information and Guidelines

warnings, lacking detail, are not nowadays inserted since their value to the collector is problematic.

Fakes. Unwitting fakes are numerous, particularly "new shades" which are colour changelings brought about by exposure to sunlight, soaking in water contaminated with dyes from adherent paper, contact with oil and dirt from a pocketbook, and so on. Fraudulent operators, in addition, can offer to arrange: removal of hinge marks; repairs of thins on white or coloured papers; replacement of missing margins or perforations; reperforating in true or false gauges; removal of fiscal cancellations; rejoining of severed pairs, strips and blocks; and (a major hazard) regumming. Collectors can only be urged to purchase from reputable sources and to insist upon Expert Committee certification where there is any doubt.

The Catalogue can consider footnotes about fakes where these are specific enough to assist in detection.

PRICES

Prices quoted in this Catalogue are the selling prices of Stanley Gibbons Ltd at the time when the book went to press. They are for stamps in fine condition for the issue concerned; in issues where condition varies they may ask more for the superb and less for the sub-standard.

All prices are subject to change without prior notice and Stanley Gibbons Ltd may from time to time offer stamps at other than catalogue prices in consequence of special purchases or particular promotions.

No guarantee is given to supply all stamps priced, since it is not possible to keep every catalogued item in stock. Commemorative issues may, at times, only be available in complete sets and not as individual values.

Quotations of prices. The prices in the left-hand column are for unused stamps and those in the right-hand column are for used.

Prices are expressed in pounds and pence sterling. One pound comprises 100 pence (£1 = 100p).

The method of notation is as follows: pence in numerals (e.g. 10 denotes ten pence); pounds and pence up to £100, in numerals (e.g. 4·25 denotes four pounds and twenty-five pence); prices above £100 expressed in whole pounds with the "£" sign shown.

Unused stamps. Prices for stamps issued up to the end of the Second World War (1945) are for lightly hinged examples and more may be asked if they are in unmounted mint condition. Prices for all later unused stamps are for unmounted mint. Where not available in this condition, lightly hinged stamps are often available at a lower price.

Used stamps. The used prices are normally for stamps postally used but may be for stamps cancelled-to-order where this practice exists.

A pen-cancellation on early issues can sometimes correctly denote postal use. Instances are individually noted in the Catalogue in explanation of the used price given.

Prices quoted for bisects on cover or on large piece are for those dated during the period officially authorised.

Stamps not sold unused to the public but affixed by postal officials before use (e.g. some parcel post stamps) are priced used only.

Minimum price. The minimum catalogue price quoted is 10p. For individual stamps prices between 10p and 95p are provided as a guide for catalogue users. The lowest price charged for individual stamps purchased from Stanley Gibbons Ltd. is £1.

Set prices. Set prices are generally for one of each value, excluding shades and varieties, but including major coulour changes. Where there are alternative shades, etc, the cheapest is usually included. The number of stamps in the set is always stated for clarity.

Where prices are given for *se-tenant* blocks or strips, any mint set price quoted for such an issue is for the complete *se-tenant* strip plus any other stamps included in the set. Used set prices are always for a set of single stamps.

Repricing. Collectors will be aware that the market factors of supply and demand directly influence the prices quoted in this Catalogue. Whatever the scarcity of a particular stamp, if there is no one in the market who wishes to buy it it cannot be expected to achieve a high price. Conversely, the same item actively sought by numerous potential buyers may cause the price to rise.

All the prices in this Catalogue are examined during the preparation of each new edition by expert staff of Stanley Gibbons and repriced as necessary. They take many factors into account, including supply and demand, and are in close touch with the international stamp market and the auction world.

GUARANTEE

All stamps are guaranteed genuine originals in the following terms:

If not as described, and returned by the purchaser, we undertake to refund the price paid to us in the original transaction. If any stamp is certified as genuine by the Expert Committee of the Royal Philatelic Society, London, or by B.P.A. Expertising Ltd, the purchaser shall not be entitled to make claim against us for any error, omission or mistake in such certificate. Consumers' statutory rights are not affected by this guarantee.

The establishment Expert Committees in this country are those of the Royal Philatelic Society, 41 Devonshire Place, London W1N 1PE, and B.P.A. Expertising Ltd, P.O. Box 137, Leatherhead, Surrey KT22 0RG. They do not undertake valuations under any circumstances and fees are payable for their services.

Abbreviations

Printers

A.B.N. Co.	American Bank Note Co, New York.
B.A.B.N.	British American Bank Note Co. Ottawa
B.D.T.	B.D.T. International Security Printing Ltd, Dublin, Ireland
B.W.	Bradbury Wilkinson & Co, Ltd.
Cartor	Cartor S.A., La Loupe, France
C.B.N.	Canadian Bank Note Co, Ottawa.
Continental	Continental Bank Note Co. B.N. Co.
Courvoisier	Imprimerie Courvoisier S.A., La-Chaux-de-Fonds, Switzerland.
D.L.R.	De La Rue & Co, Ltd, London.
Enschedé	Joh. Enschedé en Zonen, Haarlem, Netherlands.
Harrison	Harrison & Sons, Ltd. London
P.B.	Perkins Bacon Ltd, London.
Questa	Questa Colour Security Printers Ltd, London
Walsall	Walsall Security Printers Ltd
Waterlow	Waterlow & Sons, Ltd, London.

General Abbreviations

Alph	Alphabet
Anniv	Anniversary
Comp	Compound (perforation)
Des	Designer; designed
Diag	Diagonal; diagonally
Eng	Engraver; engraved
F.C.	Fiscal Cancellation
H/S	Handstamped
Horiz	Horizontal; horizontally
Imp, Imperf	Imperforate
Inscr	Inscribed
L	Left
Litho	Lithographed
mm	Millimetres
MS	Miniature sheet
N.Y.	New York
Opt(d)	Overprint(ed)
P or P-c	Pen-cancelled
P, Pf or Perf	Perforated
Photo	Photogravure
Pl	Plate
Pr	Pair
Ptd	Printed
Ptg	Printing
R	Right
R.	Row
Recess	Recess-printed
Roto	Rotogravure
Roul	Rouletted
S	Specimen (overprint)
Surch	Surcharge(d)
T.C.	Telegraph Cancellation
T	Type
Typo	Typographed
Un	Unused
Us	Used
Vert	Vertical; vertically
W or wmk	Watermark
Wmk s	Watermark sideways

(†) = Does not exist
(−) (or blank price column) = Exists, or may exist, but no market price is known.
/ between colours means "on" and the colour following is that of the paper on which the stamp is printed.

Colours of Stamps

Bl (blue); blk (black); brn (brown); car, carm (carmine); choc (chocolate); clar (claret); emer (emerald); grn (green); ind (indigo); mag (magenta); mar (maroon); mult (multicoloured); mve (mauve); ol (olive); orge (orange); pk (pink); pur (purple); scar (scarlet); sep (sepia); turq (turquoise); ultram (ultramarine); verm (vermilion); vio (violet); yell (yellow).

Colour of Overprints and Surcharges

(B.) = blue, (Blk.) = black, (Br.) = brown, (C.) = carmine, (G.) = green, (Mag.) = magenta, (Mve.) = mauve, (Ol.) = olive, (O.) = orange, (P.) = purple, (Pk.) = pink, (R.) = red, (Sil.) = silver, (V.) = violet, (Vm.) or (Verm.) = vermilion, (W.) = white, (Y.) = yellow.

Arabic Numerals

As in the case of European figures, the details of the Arabic numerals vary in different stamp designs, but they should be readily recognised with the aid of this illustration.

Features Listing

An at-a-glance guide to what's in the Stanley Gibbons catalogues

Area	Feature	Collect British Stamps	Stamps of the World	Thematic Catalogues	Commonwealth and British Empire Stamps and country catalogues)	Comprehensive Catalogue, Parts 1-22 (including Commonwealth	Great Britain Concise	Specialised catalogues
General	SG number	√	√	√		√	√	√
General	Specialised Catalogue number							√
General	Year of issue of first stamp in design	√	√	√		√	√	√
General	Exact date of issue of each design					√	√	√
General	Face value information	√	√	√		√	√	√
General	Historical and geographical information	√	√	√		√	√	√
General	General currency information, including dates used	√	√	√		√	√	√
General	Country name	√	√	√		√	√	√
General	Booklet panes					√	√	√
General	Coil stamps					√		√
General	First Day Covers	√					√	√
General	Brief footnotes on key areas of note	√	√	√		√	√	√
General	Detailed footnotes on key areas of note					√	√	√
General	Extra background information					√	√	√
General	Miniature sheet information (including size in mm)	√	√	√		√	√	√
General	Sheetlets					√		
General	Stamp booklets					√	√	√
General	Perkins Bacon "Cancelled"					√		
General	PHQ Cards	√					√	√
General	Post Office Label Sheets						√	
General	Post Office Yearbooks	√					√	√
General	Presentation and Souvenir Packs	√					√	√
General	*Se-tenant* pairs	√				√	√	√
General	Watermark details - errors, varieties, positions					√	√	√
General	Watermark illustrations	√				√	√	√
General	Watermark types	√				√	√	√
General	Forgeries noted					√		√
General	Surcharges and overprint information	√	√	√		√	√	√
Design and Description	Colour description, simplified		√	√				
Design and Description	Colour description, extended	√				√	√	√
Design and Description	Set design summary information	√	√	√		√	√	√
Design and Description	Designer name					√	√	√
Design and Description	Short design description	√	√	√		√	√	√

xvi

Features Listing

Area	Feature	Collect British Stamps	Stamps of the World	Thematic Catalogues	Comprehensive Catalogue, Parts 1-22 (including Commonwealth and British Empire Stamps and country catalogues)	Great Britain Concise	Specialised catalogues
Design and Description	Shade varieties				√	√	√
Design and Description	Type number	√	√		√	√	√
Illustrations	Multiple stamps from set illustrated	√			√	√	√
Illustrations	A Stamp from each set illustrated in full colour (where possible, otherwise mono)	√	√	√	√	√	√
Price	Catalogue used price	√	√	√	√	√	√
Price	Catalogue unused price	√	√	√	√	√	√
Price	Price - booklet panes				√	√	√
Price	Price - shade varieties				√	√	√
Price	On cover and on piece price				√	√	√
Price	Detailed GB pricing breakdown	√			√	√	√
Print and Paper	Basic printing process information	√	√	√	√	√	√
Print and Paper	Detailed printing process information, e.g. Mill sheets				√		√
Print and Paper	Paper information				√		√
Print and Paper	Detailed perforation information	√			√	√	√
Print and Paper	Details of research findings relating to printing processes and history						√
Print and Paper	Paper colour	√	√		√	√	√
Print and Paper	Paper description to aid identification				√	√	√
Print and Paper	Paper type				√	√	√
Print and Paper	Ordinary or chalk-surfaced paper				√	√	√
Print and Paper	Embossing omitted note						√
Print and Paper	Essays, Die Proofs, Plate Descriptions and Proofs, Colour Trials information						√
Print and Paper	Glazed paper				√	√	√
Print and Paper	Gum details				√		√
Print and Paper	Luminescence/Phosphor bands - general coverage	√			√	√	√
Print and Paper	Luminescence/Phosphor bands - specialised coverage						√
Print and Paper	Overprints and surcharges - including colour information	√	√	√	√	√	√
Print and Paper	Perforation/Imperforate information	√	√		√	√	√
Print and Paper	Perforation errors and varieties				√	√	√
Print and Paper	Print quantities				√		√
Print and Paper	Printing errors				√	√	√
Print and Paper	Printing flaws						√
Print and Paper	Printing varieties				√	√	√
Print and Paper	Punctured stamps - where official				√		
Print and Paper	Sheet positions				√	√	√
Print and Paper	Specialised plate number information						√
Print and Paper	Specimen overprints (only for Commonwealth & GB)				√	√	√
Print and Paper	Underprints					√	√
Print and Paper	Visible Plate numbers	√			√	√	√
Print and Paper	Yellow and Green paper listings				√		√
Index	Design index	√			√	√	

xvii

International Philatelic Glossary

English	French	German	Spanish	Italian
Agate	Agate	Achat	Agata	Agata
Air stamp	Timbre de la poste aérienne	Flugpostmarke	Sello de correo aéreo	Francobollo per posta aerea
Apple Green	Vert-pomme	Apfelgrün	Verde manzana	Verde mela
Barred	Annulé par barres	Balkenentwertung	Anulado con barras	Sbarrato
Bisected	Timbre coupé	Halbiert	Partido en dos	Frazionato
Bistre	Bistre	Bister	Bistre	Bistro
Bistre-brown	Brun-bistre	Bisterbraun	Castaño bistre	Bruno-bistro
Black	Noir	Schwarz	Negro	Nero
Blackish Brown	Brun-noir	Schwärzlichbraun	Castaño negruzco	Bruno nerastro
Blackish Green	Vert foncé	Schwärzlichgrün	Verde negruzco	Verde nerastro
Blackish Olive	Olive foncé	Schwärzlicholiv	Oliva negruzco	Oliva nerastro
Block of four	Bloc de quatre	Viererblock	Bloque de cuatro	Bloco di quattro
Blue	Bleu	Blau	Azul	Azzurro
Blue-green	Vert-bleu	Blaugrün	Verde azul	Verde azzuro
Bluish Violet	Violet bleuâtre	Bläulichviolett	Violeta azulado	Violtto azzurrastro
Booklet	Carnet	Heft	Cuadernillo	Libretto
Bright Blue	Bleu vif	Lebhaftblau	Azul vivo	Azzurro vivo
Bright Green	Vert vif	Lebhaftgrün	Verde vivo	Verde vivo
Bright Purple	Mauve vif	Lebhaftpurpur	Púrpura vivo	Porpora vivo
Bronze Green	Vert-bronze	Bronzegrün	Verde bronce	Verde bronzo
Brown	Brun	Braun	Castaño	Bruno
Brown-lake	Carmin-brun	Braunlack	Laca castaño	Lacca bruno
Brown-purple	Pourpre-brun	Braunpurpur	Púrpura castaño	Porpora bruno
Brown-red	Rouge-brun	Braunrot	Rojo castaño	Rosso bruno
Buff	Chamois	Sämisch	Anteado	Camoscio
Cancellation	Oblitération	Entwertung	Cancelación	Annullamento
Cancelled	Annulé	Gestempelt	Cancelado	Annullato
Carmine	Carmin	Karmin	Carmín	Carminio
Carmine-red	Rouge-carmin	Karminrot	Rojo carmín	Rosso carminio
Centred	Centré	Zentriert	Centrado	Centrato
Cerise	Rouge-cerise	Kirschrot	Color de ceresa	Color Ciliegia
Chalk-surfaced paper	Papier couché	Kreidepapier	Papel estucado	Carta gessata
Chalky Blue	Bleu terne	Kreideblau	Azul turbio	Azzurro smorto
Charity stamp	Timbre de bienfaisance	Wohltätigkeitsmarke	Sello de beneficenza	Francobollo di beneficenza
Chestnut	Marron	Kastanienbraun	Castaño rojo	Marrone
Chocolate	Chocolat	Schokolade	Chocolate	Cioccolato
Cinnamon	Cannelle	Zimtbraun	Canela	Cannella
Claret	Grenat	Weinrot	Rojo vinoso	Vinaccia
Cobalt	Cobalt	Kobalt	Cobalto	Cobalto
Colour	Couleur	Farbe	Color	Colore
Comb-perforation	Dentelure en peigne	Kammzähnung, Reihenzähnung	Dentado de peine	Dentellatura e pettine
Commemorative stamp	Timbre commémoratif	Gedenkmarke	Sello conmemorativo	Francobollo commemorativo
Crimson	Cramoisi	Karmesin	Carmesí	Cremisi
Deep Blue	Blue foncé	Dunkelblau	Azul oscuro	Azzurro scuro
Deep bluish Green	Vert-bleu foncé	Dunkelbläulichgrün	Verde azulado oscuro	Verde azzurro scuro

International Philatelic Glossary

English	French	German	Spanish	Italian
Design	Dessin	Markenbild	Diseño	Disegno
Die	Matrice	Urstempel. Type, Platte	Cuño	Conio, Matrice
Double	Double	Doppelt	Doble	Doppio
Drab	Olive terne	Trüboliv	Oliva turbio	Oliva smorto
Dull Green	Vert terne	Trübgrün	Verde turbio	Verde smorto
Dull purple	Mauve terne	Trübpurpur	Púrpura turbio	Porpora smorto
Embossing	Impression en relief	Prägedruck	Impresión en relieve	Impressione a relievo
Emerald	Vert-eméraude	Smaragdgrün	Esmeralda	Smeraldo
Engraved	Gravé	Graviert	Grabado	Inciso
Error	Erreur	Fehler, Fehldruck	Error	Errore
Essay	Essai	Probedruck	Ensayo	Saggio
Express letter stamp	Timbre pour lettres par exprès	Eilmarke	Sello de urgencia	Francobollo per espresso
Fiscal stamp	Timbre fiscal	Stempelmarke	Sello fiscal	Francobollo fiscale
Flesh	Chair	Fleischfarben	Carne	Carnicino
Forgery	Faux, Falsification	Fälschung	Falsificación	Falso, Falsificazione
Frame	Cadre	Rahmen	Marco	Cornice
Granite paper	Papier avec fragments de fils de soie	Faserpapier	Papel con filamentos	Carto con fili di seta
Green	Vert	Grün	Verde	Verde
Greenish Blue	Bleu verdâtre	Grünlichblau	Azul verdoso	Azzurro verdastro
Greenish Yellow	Jaune-vert	Grünlichgelb	Amarillo verdoso	Giallo verdastro
Grey	Gris	Grau	Gris	Grigio
Grey-blue	Bleu-gris	Graublau	Azul gris	Azzurro grigio
Grey-green	Vert gris	Graugrün	Verde gris	Verde grigio
Gum	Gomme	Gummi	Goma	Gomma
Gutter	Interpanneau	Zwischensteg	Espacio blanco entre dos grupos	Ponte
Imperforate	Non-dentelé	Geschnitten	Sin dentar	Non dentellato
Indigo	Indigo	Indigo	Azul indigo	Indaco
Inscription	Inscription	Inschrift	Inscripción	Dicitura
Inverted	Renversé	Kopfstehend	Invertido	Capovolto
Issue	Émission	Ausgabe	Emisión	Emissione
Laid	Vergé	Gestreift	Listado	Vergato
Lake	Lie de vin	Lackfarbe	Laca	Lacca
Lake-brown	Brun-carmin	Lackbraun	Castaño laca	Bruno lacca
Lavender	Bleu-lavande	Lavendel	Color de alhucema	Lavanda
Lemon	Jaune-citron	Zitrongelb	Limón	Limone
Light Blue	Bleu clair	Hellblau	Azul claro	Azzurro chiaro
Lilac	Lilas	Lila	Lila	Lilla
Line perforation	Dentelure en lignes	Linienzähnung	Dentado en linea	Dentellatura lineare
Lithography	Lithographie	Steindruck	Litografía	Litografia
Local	Timbre de poste locale	Lokalpostmarke	Emisión local	Emissione locale
Lozenge roulette	Percé en losanges	Rautenförmiger Durchstich	Picadura en rombos	Perforazione a losanghe
Magenta	Magenta	Magentarot	Magenta	Magenta
Margin	Marge	Rand	Borde	Margine
Maroon	Marron pourpré	Dunkelrotpurpur	Púrpura rojo oscuro	Marrone rossastro
Mauve	Mauve	Malvenfarbe	Malva	Malva
Multicoloured	Polychrome	Mehrfarbig	Multicolores	Policromo
Myrtle Green	Vert myrte	Myrtengrün	Verde mirto	Verde mirto
New Blue	Bleu ciel vif	Neublau	Azul nuevo	Azzurro nuovo
Newspaper stamp	Timbre pour journaux	Zeitungsmarke	Sello para periódicos	Francobollo per giornali

International Philatelic Glossary

English	French	German	Spanish	Italian
Obliteration	Oblitération	Abstempelung	Matasello	Annullamento
Obsolete	Hors (de) cours	Ausser Kurs	Fuera de curso	Fuori corso
Ochre	Ocre	Ocker	Ocre	Ocra
Official stamp	Timbre de service	Dienstmarke	Sello de servicio	Francobollo di
Olive-brown	Brun-olive	Olivbraun	Castaño oliva	Bruno oliva
Olive-green	Vert-olive	Olivgrün	Verde oliva	Verde oliva
Olive-grey	Gris-olive	Olivgrau	Gris oliva	Grigio oliva
Olive-yellow	Jaune-olive	Olivgelb	Amarillo oliva	Giallo oliva
Orange	Orange	Orange	Naranja	Arancio
Orange-brown	Brun-orange	Orangebraun	Castaño naranja	Bruno arancio
Orange-red	Rouge-orange	Orangerot	Rojo naranja	Rosso arancio
Orange-yellow	Jaune-orange	Orangegelb	Amarillo naranja	Giallo arancio
Overprint	Surcharge	Aufdruck	Sobrecarga	Soprastampa
Pair	Paire	Paar	Pareja	Coppia
Pale	Pâle	Blass	Pálido	Pallido
Pane	Panneau	Gruppe	Grupo	Gruppo
Paper	Papier	Papier	Papel	Carta
Parcel post stamp	Timbre pour colis postaux	Paketmarke	Sello para paquete postal	Francobollo per pacchi postali
Pen-cancelled	Oblitéré à plume	Federzugentwertung	Cancelado a pluma	Annullato a penna
Percé en arc	Percé en arc	Bogenförmiger Durchstich	Picadura en forma de arco	Perforazione ad arco
Percé en scie	Percé en scie	Bogenförmiger Durchstich	Picado en sierra	Foratura a sega
Perforated	Dentelé	Gezähnt	Dentado	Dentellato
Perforation	Dentelure	Zähnung	Dentar	Dentellatura
Photogravure	Photogravure, Héliogravure	Rastertiefdruck	Fotograbado	Rotocalco
Pin perforation	Percé en points	In Punkten durchstochen	Horadado con alfileres	Perforato a punti
Plate	Planche	Platte	Plancha	Lastra, Tavola
Plum	Prune	Pflaumenfarbe	Color de ciruela	Prugna
Postage Due stamp	Timbre-taxe	Portomarke	Sello de tasa	Segnatasse
Postage stamp	Timbre-poste	Briefmarke, Freimarke, Postmarke	Sello de correos	Francobollo postale
Postal fiscal stamp	Timbre fiscal-postal	Stempelmarke als Postmarke verwendet	Sello fiscal-postal	Fiscale postale
Postmark	Oblitération postale	Poststempel	Matasello	Bollo
Printing	Impression, Tirage	Druck	Impresión	Stampa, Tiratura
Proof	Épreuve	Druckprobe	Prueba de impresión	Prova
Provisionals	Timbres provisoires	Provisorische Marken. Provisorien	Provisionales	Provvisori
Prussian Blue	Bleu de Prusse	Preussischblau	Azul de Prusia	Azzurro di Prussia
Purple	Pourpre	Purpur	Púrpura	Porpora
Purple-brown	Brun-pourpre	Purpurbraun	Castaño púrpura	Bruno porpora
Recess-printing	Impression en taille douce	Tiefdruck	Grabado	Incisione
Red	Rouge	Rot	Rojo	Rosso
Red-brown	Brun-rouge	Rotbraun	Castaño rojizo	Bruno rosso
Reddish Lilac	Lilas rougeâtre	Rötlichlila	Lila rojizo	Lilla rossastro
Reddish Purple	Poupre-rouge	Rötlichpurpur	Púrpura rojizo	Porpora rossastro
Reddish Violet	Violet rougeâtre	Rötlichviolett	Violeta rojizo	Violetto rossastro
Red-orange	Orange rougeâtre	Rotorange	Naranja rojizo	Arancio rosso
Registration stamp	Timbre pour lettre chargée (recommandée)	Einschreibemarke	Sello de certificado lettere	Francobollo per raccomandate
Reprint	Réimpression	Neudruck	Reimpresión	Ristampa
Reversed	Retourné	Umgekehrt	Invertido	Rovesciato

International Philatelic Glossary

English	French	German	Spanish	Italian
Rose	Rose	Rosa	Rosa	Rosa
Rose-red	Rouge rosé	Rosarot	Rojo rosado	Rosso rosa
Rosine	Rose vif	Lebhaftrosa	Rosa vivo	Rosa vivo
Roulette	Percage	Durchstich	Picadura	Foratura
Rouletted	Percé	Durchstochen	Picado	Forato
Royal Blue	Bleu-roi	Königblau	Azul real	Azzurro reale
Sage green	Vert-sauge	Salbeigrün	Verde salvia	Verde salvia
Salmon	Saumon	Lachs	Salmón	Salmone
Scarlet	Écarlate	Scharlach	Escarlata	Scarlatto
Sepia	Sépia	Sepia	Sepia	Seppia
Serpentine roulette	Percé en serpentin	Schlangenliniger Durchstich	Picado a serpentina	Perforazione a serpentina
Shade	Nuance	Tönung	Tono	Gradazione de colore
Sheet	Feuille	Bogen	Hoja	Foglio
Slate	Ardoise	Schiefer	Pizarra	Ardesia
Slate-blue	Bleu-ardoise	Schieferblau	Azul pizarra	Azzurro ardesia
Slate-green	Vert-ardoise	Schiefergrün	Verde pizarra	Verde ardesia
Slate-lilac	Lilas-gris	Schieferlila	Lila pizarra	Lilla ardesia
Slate-purple	Mauve-gris	Schieferpurpur	Púrpura pizarra	Porpora ardesia
Slate-violet	Violet-gris	Schieferviolett	Violeta pizarra	Violetto ardesia
Special delivery stamp	Timbre pour exprès	Eilmarke	Sello de urgencia	Francobollo per espressi
Specimen	Spécimen	Muster	Muestra	Saggio
Steel Blue	Bleu acier	Stahlblau	Azul acero	Azzurro acciaio
Strip	Bande	Streifen	Tira	Striscia
Surcharge	Surcharge	Aufdruck	Sobrecarga	Soprastampa
Tête-bêche	Tête-bêche	Kehrdruck	Tête-bêche	Tête-bêche
Tinted paper	Papier teinté	Getöntes Papier	Papel coloreado	Carta tinta
Too-late stamp	Timbre pour lettres en retard	Verspätungsmarke	Sello para cartas retardadas	Francobollo per le lettere in ritardo
Turquoise-blue	Bleu-turquoise	Türkisblau	Azul turquesa	Azzurro turchese
Turquoise-green	Vert-turquoise	Türkisgrün	Verde turquesa	Verde turchese
Typography	Typographie	Buchdruck	Tipografia	Tipografia
Ultramarine	Outremer	Ultramarin	Ultramar	Oltremare
Unused	Neuf	Ungebraucht	Nuevo	Nuovo
Used	Oblitéré, Usé	Gebraucht	Usado	Usato
Venetian Red	Rouge-brun terne	Venezianischrot	Rojo veneciano	Rosso veneziano
Vermilion	Vermillon	Zinnober	Cinabrio	Vermiglione
Violet	Violet	Violett	Violeta	Violetto
Violet-blue	Bleu-violet	Violettblau	Azul violeta	Azzurro violetto
Watermark	Filigrane	Wasserzeichen	Filigrana	Filigrana
Watermark sideways	Filigrane couché liegend	Wasserzeichen	Filigrana acostado	Filigrana coricata
Wove paper	Papier ordinaire, Papier uni	Einfaches Papier	Papel avitelado	Carta unita
Yellow	Jaune	Gelb	Amarillo	Giallo
Yellow-brown	Brun-jaune	Gelbbraun	Castaño amarillo	Bruno giallo
Yellow-green	Vert-jaune	Gelbgrün	Verde amarillo	Verde giallo
Yellow-olive	Olive-jaunâtre	Gelboliv	Oliva amarillo	Oliva giallastro
Yellow-orange	Orange jaunâtre	Gelborange	Naranja amarillo	Arancio giallastro
Zig-zag roulette	Percé en zigzag	Sägezahnartiger Durchstich	Picado en zigzag	Perforazione a zigzag

Guide to Entries

Ⓐ Country of Issue – When a country changes its name, the catalogue listing changes to reflect the name change, for example Cambodia was formerly known as Kampuchea, the stamps in Part 21 South East Asia are all listed under Cambodia, but spilt into Kampuchea and then Cambodia. When a country spilts, for example Czechoslovakia split into Czech Republic and Slovakia, there will be a listing for Czechoslovakia and then separate sections for Czech Republic and Slovakia.

Ⓑ Currency – Details of the currency, and dates of earliest use where applicable, on the face value of the stamps.

Ⓒ Country Information – Brief geographical and historical details for the issuing country.

Ⓓ Illustration – Generally, the first stamp in the set. Stamp illustrations are reduced to 75%, with overprints and surcharges shown actual size.

Ⓔ Illustration or Type Number – These numbers are used to help identify stamps, either in the listing, type column, design line or footnote, usually the first value in a set. These type numbers are in a bold type face – **123**; when bracketed (**123**) an overprint or a surcharge is indicated. Some type numbers include a lower-case letter – **123a**, this indicates they have been added to an existing set. New cross references are also shown in bold.

Ⓕ Date of issue – This is the date that the stamp/set of stamps was issued by the post office and was available for purchase. When a set of definitive stamps has been issued over several years the Year Date given is for the earliest issue. Commemorative sets are listed in chronological order. Stamps of the same design, or issue are usually grouped together, for example one of the French Marianne definitive series' was first issued in 2002 but includes stamps issued to the end of 2004.

Ⓖ Number Prefix – Stamps other than definitives and commemoratives have a prefix letter before the catalogue number.
Their use is explained in the text: some examples are A for airmail, E for East Germany or Express Delivery stamps.

Ⓗ Footnote – Further information on background or key facts on issues.

Ⓘ Stanley Gibbons Catalogue number – This is a unique number for each stamp to help the collector identify stamps in the listing. The Stanley Gibbons numbering system is universally recognized as definitive.
Where insufficient numbers have been left to provide for additional stamps to a listing, some stamps will have a suffix letter after the catalogue number (for example 214a). If numbers have been left for additions to a set and not used they will be left vacant.
The separate type numbers (in bold) refer to illustrations (see **E**).

Ⓙ Colour – If a stamp is printed in three or fewer colours then the colours are listed, working from the centre of the stamp outwards (see **R**).

Ⓚ Design line – Further details on design variations

Ⓛ Key Type – Indicates a design type on which the stamp is based. These are the bold figures found below each illustration, for example listed in Cameroun, in the Part 7 Germany catalogue is the Key type A and B showing the ex-Kaiser's yacht *Hohenzollern*. The type numbers are also given in bold in the second column of figures alongside the stamp description to indicate the design of each stamp. Where an issue comprises stamps of similar design, the corresponding type number should be taken as indicating the general design. Where there are blanks in the type number column it means that the type of the corresponding stamp is that shown by the number in the type column of the same issue. A dash (–) in the type column means that the stamp is not illustrated. Where type numbers refer to stamps of another country, e.g. where stamps of one country are overprinted for use in another, this is always made clear in the text.

Ⓜ Coloured Papers – Stamps printed on coloured paper are shown – e.g. "brown/*yellow*" indicates brown printed on yellow paper.

Ⓝ Surcharges and Overprints – Usually described in the headings. Any actual wordings are shown in bold type. Descriptions clarify words and figures used in the overprint. Stamps with the same overprints in different colours are not listed separately. Numbers in brackets after the descriptions are the catalogue numbers of the non-overprinted stamps. The words "inscribed" or "inscription" refer to the wording incorporated in the design of a stamp and not surcharges or overprints.

Ⓞ Face value – This refers to the value of each stamp and is the price it was sold for at the Post Office when issued. Some modern stamps do not have their values in figures but instead shown as a letter, shown as a letter, for example Great Britain use 1st or 2nd on their stamps as apposed to the actual value.

Ⓟ Catalogue Value – Mint/Unused. Prices quoted for pre-1945 stamps are for lightly hinged examples.

Ⓠ Catalogue Value – Used. Prices generally refer to fine postally used examples. For certain issues they are for cancelled-to-order.

Prices
Prices are given in pence and pounds. Stamps worth £100 and over are shown in whole pounds:

Shown in Catalogue as	Explanation
10	10 pence
1.75	£1.75
15.00	£15
£150	£150
£2300	£2300

Prices assume stamps are in 'fine condition'; we may ask more for superb and less for those of lower quality. The minimum catalogue price quoted is 10p and is intended as a guide for catalogue users. The lowest price for individual stamps purchased from Stanley Gibbons is £1.
Prices quoted are for the cheapest variety of that particular stamp. Differences of watermark, perforation, or other details, often increase the value. Prices quoted for mint issues are for single examples. Those in *se-tenant* pairs, strips, blocks or sheets may be worth more. Where no prices are listed it is either because the stamps are not known to exist (usually shown by a †) in that particular condition, or, more usually, because there is no reliable information on which to base their value.
All prices are subject to change without prior notice and we cannot guarantee to supply all stamps as priced. Prices quoted in advertisements are also subject to change without prior notice.

Ⓡ Multicoloured – Nearly all modern stamps are multicoloured (more than three colours); this is indicated in the heading, with a description of the stamp given in the listing.

Ⓢ Perforations – Please see page x for a detailed explanation of perforations.

xxii

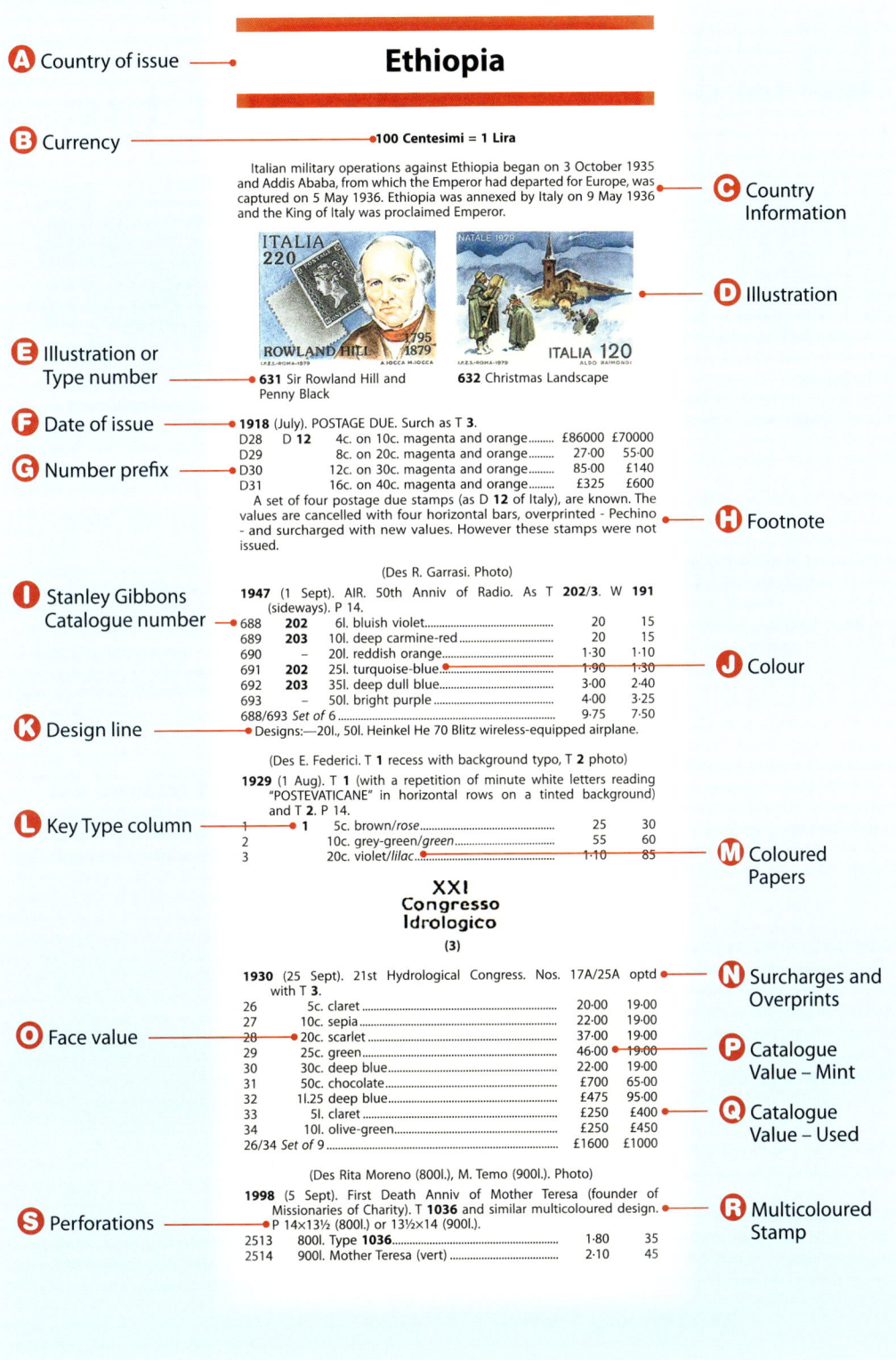

About Us

Our History
Edward Stanley Gibbons started trading postage stamps in his father's chemist shop in 1856. Since then we have been at the forefront of stamp collecting for over 150 years. We hold the Royal Warrant, offer unsurpassed expertise and quality and provide collectors with the peace of mind of a certificate of authenticity on all of our stamps. If you think of stamp collecting, you think of Stanley Gibbons and we are proud to uphold that tradition for you.

399 Strand
Our world famous stamp shop is a collector's paradise, with all of our latest catalogues, albums and accessories and, of course, our unrivalled stockholding of postage stamps.
www.stanleygibbons.com   shop@stanleygibbons.co.uk   +44 (0)20 7836 8444

Specialist Stamp Sales
For the collector that appreciates the value of collecting the highest quality examples, Stanley Gibbons is the only choice. Our extensive range is unrivalled in terms of quality and quantity, with specialist stamps available from all over the world.
www.stanleygibbons.com/stamps   shop@stanleygibbons.co.uk   +44 (0)20 7836 8444

Stanley Gibbons Auctions and Valuations
Sell your collection or individual rare items through our prestigious public auctions or our regular postal auctions and benefit from the excellent prices being realised at auction currently. We also provide an unparalleled valuation service.
www.stanleygibbons.com/auctions   auctions@stanleygibbons.co.uk   +44 (0)20 7836 8444

Stanley Gibbons Publications
The world's first stamp catalogue was printed by Stanley Gibbons in 1865 and we haven't looked back since! Our catalogues are trusted worldwide as the industry standard and we print countless titles each year. We also publish consumer and trade magazines, Gibbons Stamp Monthly and Philatelic Exporter to bring you news, views and insights into all things philatelic. Never miss an issue by subscribing today and benefit from exclusive subscriber offers each month.
www.stanleygibbons.com/shop   orders@stanleygibbons.co.uk   +44 (0)1425 472 363

Stanley Gibbons Investments
The Stanley Gibbons Investment Department offers a unique range of investment propositions that have consistently outperformed more traditional forms of investment, from capital protected products with unlimited upside to portfolios made up of the world's rarest stamps and autographs.
www.stanleygibbons.com/investment   investment@stanleygibbons.co.uk   +44 (0)1481 708 270

Fraser's Autographs
Autographs, manuscripts and memorabilia from Henry VIII to current day. We have over 60,000 items in stock, including movie stars, musicians, sport stars, historical figures and royalty. Fraser's is the UK's market leading autograph dealer and has been dealing in high quality autographed material since 1978.
www.frasersautographs.com   sales@frasersautographs.co.uk   +44 (0)20 7557 4404

stanleygibbons.com
Our website offers the complete philatelic service. Whether you are looking to buy stamps, invest, read news articles, browse our online stamp catalogue or find new issues, you are just one click away from anything you desire in the world of stamp collecting at stanleygibbons.com. Happy browsing!
www.stanleygibbons.com

Thinking of selling all or part of your collection?

Contact us today in order to make the most of strong auction realisations in the current market

- Reach over 200,000 potential buyers
- The largest philatelic audience in the UK
- Unrivalled expertise in the field of philately
- 100% exceptional clearance rate
- Download each catalogue for FREE

- We can offer featured write-ups about any auction in GSM
- Confidence and trust make Stanley Gibbons Auctions the first port of call for people selling their collections
- Auctions hosted on www.stanleygibbons.com, offering massive worldwide exposure

Consignments are always considered for auction
Contact us today to get the best price for your collection

All World, specialised and one vendor sales

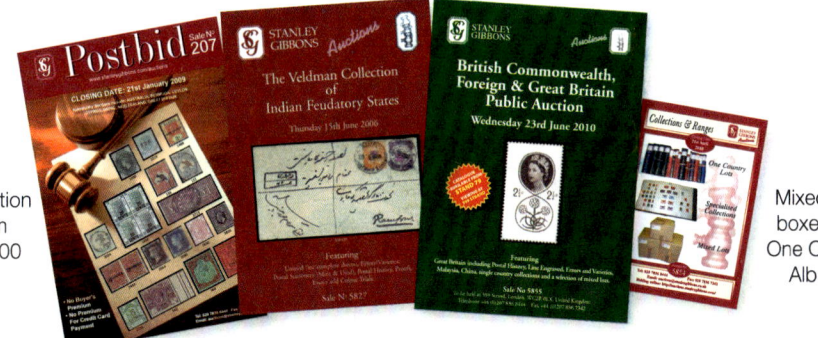

Postal auction lots from £5 - £5,000

Mixed lots, boxes and One Country Albums

Est 1856
STANLEY GIBBONS

Stanley Gibbons Auction Department
399 Strand, London WC2R 0LX
Contact Ryan Epps or Steve Matthews on Tel: +44 (0)20 7836 8444
Fax: +44 (0)20 7836 7342 | Email: auctions@stanleygibbons.co.uk
www.stanleygibbons.com/auctions

The Archive has everything from the first edition of the Monthly Journal in 1890 to the December 2009 issue of Gibbons Stamp Monthly.

Covering all of the articles, illustrations, notes and more. If it was in the magazine, then it's on the digital archive.

Just think of all of those great articles you can rediscover or read for the first time. You will have access to over 40,000 pages.

Gibbons Stamp Monthly exactly how *you* want it...

NEW and EXCLUSIVE

You can have every issue of GSM since 1890 at your fingertips to search, browse, print and store as you choose, when you choose, with the **Gibbons Stamp Monthly Digital Archive**

If you're passionate about collecting, you really don't want to be without it – the **GSM DIGITAL ARCHIVE**. It is the perfect complement to the hobby of kings.

You'll have private access to **a complete library of information on almost anything you can think of from the world of stamp collecting**. The Archive is an absolute treasure trove of facts, articles, images and commentary on everything from specific topics like Machins to High Value Keyplates to more general fields such as King George VI – and it spans 120 years of these riches.

In short, it is **GSM exactly how you want it** – without it taking up vast amounts of space, getting dog-eared or in the wrong order. At your leisure and at the touch of a button or click of a mouse, you'll be able to view front covers, contents lists, articles, correspondence, book reviews, illustrations, notes and jottings from 120 years of Gibbons Stamp Monthly, with **full search and full browse capabilities built in**.

You can be the editor of the world's most important stamp magazine. You will have access to over **40,000 pages worth of the most useful and interesting philatelic material available**, delivered to you in a convenient, easy to use, searchable, digital format.

This is the exclusive GSM Archive, covering all articles, features, editorial and other content right from the first issue of the Monthly Journal, Gibbons Stamp Weekly & Gibbons Stamp Monthly – from 1890 up to 2009.

Build your own library of information on any topic you can think of by saving articles to your own archive or **print them off and store them physically** if you choose.

With full unlimited printing capabilities available, you are not confined to reading the articles on your computer screen.

The NEW & EXCLUSIVE Gibbons Stamp Monthly Archive is available now.
The full 5 DVDs (+ bonus disc) are available to you for just £199.95 or, looking at it another way, just 20p per magazine! You can even pay in 3 equal instalments if that makes it easier for you.
Get *your* copy today – **JUST £199.95**
Prices correct as of November 2010 and subject to change.

Call us today on FREEPHONE **0800 611 622** *(UK)*
or +44 1425 472 363 *(International)* to secure your copy
www.stanleygibbons.com | Email: orders@stanleygibbons.co.uk

THE WORLD OF STAMP COLLECTING IN YOUR HANDS

- The UK's biggest selling stamp magazine • Consistently over 150 pages per issue
- Written by stamp collectors for stamp collectors • Monthly colour catalogue supplement
- Philatelic news from around the world • Dedicated GB stamp section
- Regular offers exclusively for subscribers

FREE SAMPLE

For your **FREE** sample, contact us by:

Telephone: +44(0)1425 472 363
Email: orders@stanleygibbons.co.uk
Post: Stanley Gibbons Limited, 7 Parkside, Christchurch Road, Ringwood, Hampshire, BH24 3SH

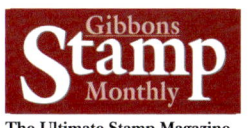

The Ultimate Stamp Magazine

For more information please visit
www.gibbonsstampmonthly.com

NEW LOOK
FOR OUR 399 STRAND STORE

The New 399 Strand
More space | Better displays
Interactive information | A better shop for you

**Come and experience it for yourself!
The new look home of stamp collecting**

Following months of renovations in advance of the London 2010 show, the new look 399 Strand has officially re-opened its doors to provide you with an exciting new shopping and browsing experience.

The retail area has been expanded to allow you much more space, better, clearer displays and to allow dedicated seating areas for stamp viewing and helpful, interactive information points. The famous stamp counter will remain and the shop will continue to offer an unrivalled range of philatelic items, coupled with the expertise you expect from our dedicated team of philatelic specialists.

399 Strand – The only choice for valuations, auctions, investments, gifts and a range of premium collectibles.

We look forward to seeing you!

Thousands of high quality modern issues added to stock following the acquisition of N&M Haworth in August 2010. **Visit us in store to find out more.**

399 Strand, London WC2R 0LX | Tel: +44 (0)20 7836 8444
Email: orders@stanleygibbons.co.uk
www.stanleygibbons.com

Portugal

1853. 1000 Reis = 1 Milreis
1912. 100 Centavos = 1 Escudo
2002. 100 Cents = 1 Euro

PRINTERS. All Portuguese stamps were printed at the Mint, Lisbon, unless otherwise stated.

REPRINTS. Reprints of some of the following issues were made in 1864, 1885 and 1905 as indicated in footnotes.
These can generally be distinguished as follows:—
  1864 reprints are on thin white paper with white gum, the originals having brownish gum.
  1885 reprints are on stout very white paper, usually ungummed but sometimes with white gum having yellowish spots. When perforated they are generally perf 13½ with large clean-cut holes producing sharp pointed teeth. Some also exist perf 12½ and these are indicated in the footnotes.
  1905 reprints are on creamy white paper of ordinary quality with shiny white gum, all perf 13½.
  Reprints can be further differentiated by colour variations and they are often printed from new dies which differ slightly from those used for the originals.

Queen Maria II
24 July 1833-13 Nov 1853

1 (No. 1)

In No. 2 the head appears smaller, with greater space between diadem and circle, and pendant hair is shortened to one curl pointing left.

2   3   4

(T **1/13** des and eng F. de Borja Freire. Typo and embossed)

1853 (July). Imperf.
1	1	5r. red-brown (1 July)	£4500	£1300
2		5r. red-brown (worn die)	£4500	£1500
3	2	25r. greenish blue (1 July)	£2500	45·00
4		25r. blue (shades)	£1400	29·00
		a. Double impression	£8000	£2750
5		25r. deep blue	£1400	29·00
6	3	50r. yellow-green (21 July)	£5500	£1500
7		50r. blue-green	£11000	£2750
		a. Double impression	£27000	£12000
8	4	100r. pale lilac (2 July)	£47000	£3000
9		100r. lilac	£47000	£3000

The 5r. (both Nos. 1 and 2), 25r. and 100r. are found on thin paper.
All values were reprinted in 1864, 1885 and 1905 and they can be distinguished as follows:—
  5r. The 1864 reprint has a defect in the neck which makes the Adam's apple appear very large: later reprints differ in colour and by the absence of the pendant curl.
  25r. The background burelage and the upper and lower right-hand corners are very blurred in the 1864 reprint instead of being sharp; in the later reprints the central oval is fully ¾ mm from the frame at sides instead of less than ½ mm in the originals.
  50r. The 1864 and 1885 reprints show a small break in the upper right diagonal line of the frame, while the engraver's initials (F.B.F.), which are clearly visible in the lower part of the bust on the originals, no longer show; the 1905 reprints do not have the frame break but the initials are distinct.
  100r. The 1864 reprints show the small vertical lines at top and bottom at each side much heavier than in the originals; the later reprints are only distinguishable by the paper, gum and shades.
  In connection with the International Philatelic Exhibition at Lisbon in 1953 held on the occasion of the stamp centenary, all values were reprinted on thick paper without gum and with the dates "1853" and "1953" printed on the back in two lines.

King Pedro V
13 Nov 1853-11 Nov 1861

5r. Seven dies differing in the position, etc., of the ornaments round the frame, in the number of pearls round the circle, the shape of the letters and numerals "5" and in other points.
25r. Two dies: in (1) the pearls do not touch the outer oval, and the letters "R" of "CORREIO" are closer together than in (2)

1855 (Jan)–56. Head with straight hair. Imperf.
10	5	5r. red-brown	£14000	£1400
10a		5r. orange-brown (worn plate)	£15000	£1900
11	6	25r. blue (1)	£1500	38·00
12		25r. blue (2)	£1800	44·00
13	7	50r. yellow-green (4.56)	£750	£110
14		50r. blue-green	£1200	£150
		a. Double impression	£3250	£1300
15	8	100r. lilac (1.56)	£1200	£150

All values were reprinted in 1885 and 1905. In each case the 25r. is Type (1).

(a) Single lines   (b) Double lines

1856–58. As T **5/6** but head has curly hair. Imperf.
16	5	5r. red-brown (10.5.56)	£650	£130
16a		5r. orange-brown	£650	£130
17		5r. yellow-brown	£700	£200
18		5r. bistre-brown	£650	£130
18a		5r. brown	£650	£120
19		5r. black-brown	£650	£140
20	6	25r. blue (a) (4.56)	£15000	85·00
21		25r. blue (b) (8.56)	£600	22·00
21a		25r. deep blue (b)	£600	22·00
22		25r. pale rose (b) (8.1.58)	£450	8·75
23		25r. deep rose (b)	£450	8·75

There are three types of the blue 25r., and four of the red, one being common to both.
The 5r. and 25r. blue (b) were reprinted in 1864 and the 5r., 25r. blue (a) and (b) and 25r. rose (b) in 1885 and 1905.

King Luis
11 Nov 1861—19 Oct 1889

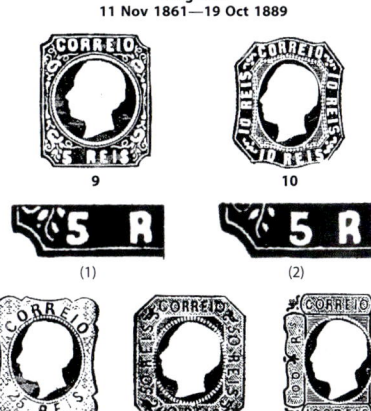

9   10

(1)   (2)

11   12   13

1

PORTUGAL

1862–64. Imperf.
24	**9**	5r. brown (1) (9.62)	£200	39·00
25		5r. deep brown (1)	£200	39·00
26		5r. brown (2)	£250	44·00
27		5r. deep brown (2)	£250	44·00
		a. Double impression	£1200	£650
28	**10**	10r. pale orange-yellow (15.3.63)	£225	70·00
29		10r. orange-yellow	£225	70·00
30	**11**	25r. pale rose (1.7.62)	£160	7·00
31		25r. deep rose	£160	7·00
32	**12**	50r. yellow-green (15.4.64)	£1100	£120
33		50r. blue-green	£1200	£140
34	**13**	100r. dull lilac (15.4.64)	£1300	£140

For No. 34 *percé en croix*, see No. E1 of Madeira.
All values were reprinted in 1885 and all except the 25r. in 1905.

15 Straight label

    (1) 15r. (2)   (1) 80r. (2)

Two types of the 15r. and 80r. with figures spaced as shown. Similar varieties of spacing occur on other values (including two more of the 15c. but they are less prominent than those illustrated.

(Des and eng F. A. de Campos. Typo and embossed)
1870–84.

A. Unsurfaced paper
(a) P 12½

69	**15**	5r. black (1.1.71)	80·00	8·25
70		10r. yellow (15.1.71)	£110	43·00
71		10r. orange-yellow	£110	43·00
72		10r. blue-green (7.79)	£550	£350
72a		10r. pale green (6.80)	£190	45·00
73		10r. yellow-green (6.80)	£190	45·00
74		15r. fawn (1) (2.8.75)	£150	43·00
75		15r. fawn (2)	£150	43·00
76		20r. bistre (4.71)	£110	38·00
77		20r. pale bistre	£110	38·00
78		20r. olive-bistre	£110	38·00
79		25r. carmine (11.70)	43·00	5·50
80		25r. rose	43·00	5·50
81		25r. pale rose	43·00	5·50
82		25r. rose-pink	43·00	5·50
83		50r. pale green (2.71)	£225	65·00
84		50r. green	£225	65·00
85		50r. deep green	£225	65·00
86		50r. dull blue (5.79)	£475	80·00
87		50r. blue	£475	80·00
88		80r. yellow-orange (1) (10.71)	£225	45·00
89		80r. orange (1)	£225	45·00
90		80r. orange-vermilion (1)	£225	45·00
91		80r. orange-vermilion (2)	£275	60·00
92		100r. pale mauve (15.4.71)	£170	33·00
93		120r. dull blue (15.12.71)	£425	£110
94		120r. bright blue	£425	£110
95		150r. pale blue (1.1.76)	£500	£180
96		150r. dull blue	£500	£180
97		150r. bright blue	£500	£180
98		150r. yellow (5.80)	£1000	£200
99		240r. pale dull lilac (9.73)	£2250	£1600
100		300r. lilac (1.1.76)	£500	£200
101		1000r. black (10.6.84)	£475	£140

Stamps perf 12½ may be found on pelure paper or with the paper ribbed on front or back.

(b) P 13½ (1875)

102	**15**	5r. black	£100	12·00
103		10r. yellow	£130	50·00
104		10r. orange-yellow	£130	50·00
105		10r. blue-green	£1000	£475
106		10r. yellow-green	£180	43·00
107		10r. pale green	£180	43·00
108		15r. fawn (1)	£225	90·00
109		15r. fawn (2)	£225	90·00
110		20r. bistre	£150	45·00
111		20r. pale bistre	£150	45·00
112		20r. olive-bistre	£150	45·00
113		25r. rose	42·00	6·00
114		25r. pale rose	42·00	6·00
115		50r. green	£225	60·00
116		50r. deep green	£225	60·00
117		50r. dull blue	£475	80·00
118		50r. blue	£475	80·00
119		80r. orange-buff (1)	£250	65·00
120		80r. orange-vermilion (1)	£250	65·00
121		80r. orange-buff (2)	£300	85·00
122		100r. grey-lilac	£250	75·00
123		120r. deep blue		£6000
124		150r. dull blue	£1100	£450
125		150r. bright blue	£1100	£450
126		150r. yellow	£275	£120
127		300r. lilac	£375	£140
128		1000r. black (10.6.84)	£450	£140

14 Curved label

(Des and eng C. Wiener. Typo and embossed)
1866–67. Imperf.

35	**14**	5r. black (5.10.66)	£170	14·50
		a. Double impression	£450	£325
36		10r. yellow (9.66)	£350	£225
37		10r. orange-yellow	£350	£225
38		20r. bistre (10.8.66)	£275	£100
39		25r. pale rose (1.67)	£350	12·00
40		25r. rose	£350	12·00
41		50r. green (20.2.67)	£375	£110
42		50r. yellow-green	£375	£110
43		80r. orange (1.9.66)	£375	£110
44		80r. pale orange	£375	£110
45		100r. dull purple (20.2.67)	£450	£170
46		120r. blue (28.7.66)	£475	£110
47		120r. deep blue	£475	£110
		a. Double impression	£1200	£750

Some values show variations in the setting of the figures of value, but these are rather minute, and very difficult to describe, and none are so distinct as the two varieties mentioned in the perforated stamps of the same type.

The 240r. previously listed is now known to have come from reprints made in 1885.

Stamps *percé en croix* or rouletted 8 were used only in Madeira and are listed under that heading.

All values were reprinted in 1885 and 1905.

    (1) 5r. (2)   (1) 100r. (2)

Two types of 5r. and 100r. with figures spaced as shown. Similar varieties of spacing occur in other values, but most of these are less prominent than those illustrated.

1867–70. P 12½.

52	**14**	5r. black (1) (5.11.67)	£180	65·00
53		5r. black (2)	£180	65·00
54		10r. yellow (1.9.67)	£375	£160
55		10r. orange-yellow	£375	£160
56		20r. bistre (4.69)	£450	£170
57		25r. pale rose (9.9.67)	£100	11·50
58		25r. deep rose	£100	11·50
59		50r. pale green (1.7.68)	£375	£160
60		50r. green	£375	£160
		a. Linen-surfaced paper	£550	£160
61		80r. orange (9.67)	£375	£160
62		100r. deep lilac (1) (3.69)	£375	£160
63		100r. pale mauve (2)	£375	£160
64		120r. blue (5.11.67)	£450	£110
65		120r. deep blue	£450	£110
66		120r. sky-blue	£450	£110
67		240r. pale dull lilac (15.2.70)	£1500	£700
68		240r. reddish lilac	£1500	£700

No. 60a is only known used in the Azores.
All values were reprinted in 1885 perf 12½ and 13½ and in 1905.

PORTUGAL

(c) P 14 (1872)

129	**15**	5r. black	£350	£200
130		10r. yellow	£650	£425
131		25r. rose	£650	41·00
132		80r. orange (1)	£1700	£1200
133		100r. pale mauve	£2000	£1200

The perfs 13½ and 14 are quite distinct.

(d) P 11

133*a*	**15**	5r. black	£200
133*b*		10r. yellow	£200
133*c*		20r. bistre	£200
133*d*		25r. rose	£200
133*e*		50r. green	£225
133*f*		80r. orange (1)	£225
133*g*		120r. dull blue	
133*h*		240r. pale dull lilac	

The 5, 10, 20, 25 and 80r. are known *imperf* but only the 25r. is known used.

(1) 　　　　　　(2)

Two types of the 20r. rosine with figures spaced as shown

B. Chalk-surfaced paper (1882–84)
(a) P 12½

134	**15**	10r. bright yellow-green	£190	43·00
135		10r. deep yellow-green	£190	43·00
136		15r. fawn (1)	£170	49·00
137		15r. fawn (2)	£170	49·00
138		15r. yellow-brown (1)	£170	49·00
139		15r. yellow-brown (2)	£170	49·00
140		15r. red-brown (1)	£170	49·00
141		15r. red-brown (2)	£170	49·00
142		20r. pale bistre	£150	38·00
143		20r. deep carmine (1) (24.12.84)	£500	85·00
143*a*		20r. deep carmine (2)	£500	85·00
144		20r. rosine (1)	£500	85·00
145		20r. rosine (2)	£500	85·00
146		80r. yellow (1)	£200	35·00
147		80r. yellow (2)	£200	35·00
148		80r. pale orange (1)	£180	28·00
149		80r. pale orange (2)	£180	28·00
150		80r. orange (1)	£180	28·00
151		80r. orange (2)	£180	28·00
151*a*		80r. orange-vermilion (1)	£180	28·00
152		80r. orange-vermilion (2)	£180	28·00
153		100r. mauve-pink	£100	16·00
155		150r. yellow	£190	22·00
156		300r. bright mauve	£180	45·00
157		300r. purple	£180	45·00

(b) P 13½

158	**15**	10r. bright yellow-green	£200	55·00
159		10r. deep green	£200	55·00
161		15r. fawn (2)	£180	49·00
163		15r. red-brown (2)	£180	49·00
164		15r. grey-brown (2)	£180	49·00
165		20r. pale bistre	£200	49·00
166		20r. rosine (1)	£550	£130
167		20r. rosine (2)	£550	£130
169		80r. pale orange (1)	£225	45·00
170		80r. pale orange (2)	£225	45·00
171		80r. orange (1)	£225	45·00
172		80r. orange (2)	£225	45·00
173		100r. mauve-pink	£250	65·00
174		150r. yellow	£225	55·00
175		300r. dull violet	£225	70·00
176		300r. bright mauve	£225	70·00

Reprints of T **15**: In 1885 all values except the 20r. carmine on unsurfaced paper perf 13½, also the 5, 10, 15, 20, 25, 50, 120, 150, 240 and 1000r. perf 12½, most being gummed. In 1885–93 the 20r. carmine on chalk-surfaced paper but without gum perf 13½ and 12½. In 1905 all values except the 20r. carmine.

N **16**　　　　　N **17**

(Des and eng F. A. de Campos (2r.), E. C. A. Gneco (2½r.). Typo)
1876 (1 July)–**94**. NEWSPAPER.

A. Unsurfaced paper
(a) P 12½

N177	N **16**	2r. black (15.7.84)	36·00	24·00
N178	N **17**	2½r. grey-green	22·00	2·00
N179		2½r. olive	22·00	2·00

(b) P 13½

N180	N **16**	2r. black (15.7.84)	33·00	21·00
N181	N **17**	2½r. grey-green	22·00	2·00
N182		2½r. olive	22·00	2·00

(c) P 11½

N183	N **17**	2½r. olive (1886)	£250	42·00

B. Chalk-surfaced paper. P 11½ (1887)

N184	N **17**	2½r. olive	19·00	1·70
N185		2½r. olive-ochre	19·00	1·70
N186		2½r. yellow-brown	38·00	4·00
N187		2½r. brown	19·00	1·70

C. Enamel-surfaced paper. P 11½

N188	N **17**	2½r. olive-yellow (1894)	19·00	1·70

Although the 2r. was issued for making up small amounts on telegrams, and the 2½r. was nominally for use on newspapers, both values were available for franking ordinary correspondence, and were often so used.
The 2r. was reprinted in 1885–93 perf 12½, and 13½ on chalk-surfaced paper and also perf 13½ on unsurfaced paper; in 1905 it was reprinted on unsurfaced paper. The 2½r. was reprinted in 1885 and 1905.

16　　　　　　17

17a　　　　　　18

Two types of the 5r.
(1) Space to right of eye shaded.
(2) White space to right of eye down the cheek.

(Des and eng P. Gomes da Silva. Typo)
1880–82.

A. Unsurfaced paper
(a) P 12½

178	**16**	5r. black (1) (6.80)	43·00	6·00
179		5r. black (2)	43·00	6·00
180	**17**	25r. bluish grey (1.80)	£475	44·00
181	**17a**	25r. grey (4.80)	44·00	5·50
182		25r. purple-grey	44·00	5·50
183		25r. purple-brown	44·00	5·50
184	**18**	50r. blue (1.81)	£475	22·00

(b) P 13½

185	**16**	5r. black (1)	43·00	6·00
186		5r. black (2)	43·00	6·00
187	**17**	25r. bluish grey	£475	44·00
188	**17a**	25r. grey	44·00	5·50
189		25r. purple-grey	44·00	5·50
190		25r. purple-brown	44·00	5·50
191	**18**	50r. blue	£475	22·00

All values also exist on thin paper.

B. Chalk-surfaced paper (1882)
(a) P 12½

192	**16**	5r. black (2)	£250	80·00

(b) P 13½

193	**16**	5r. black (2)	£225	80·00

All values were reprinted in 1885 and 1905. The 1885 reprints are perf 13½ but the 5r. also exists perf 12½, all gummed.

19　　　　　20　　　　　21

3

PORTUGAL

(Centre eng E. Mouchon, frame eng V. Alves. Typo)
1882–86. Unsurfaced paper.

(a) P 12½

194	20	25r. brown (1.2.82)	55·00	4·25
195		25r. pale brown	55·00	4·25
196		25r. purple-brown	55·00	4·25
197	21	50r. pale blue (15.6.82)	80·00	4·75
198		50r. deep blue	80·00	4·75

(b) P 13½

199	20	25r. brown	55·00	5·50
200		25r. pale brown	55·00	5·50
201		25r. purple-brown	55·00	5·50
202	21	50r. blue	80·00	10·50
203		50r. pale blue	80·00	10·50
204		50r. deep blue	80·00	10·50

(c) P 11½

205	19	5r. black (1.3.83)	75·00	18·00
206	20	25r. brown (1886)	46·00	3·75
206a		25r. pale brown (1886)	46·00	3·75
206b		25r. purple-brown (1886)	46·00	3·75

22   23

(Centre eng E. Mouchon, frame eng V. Alves. Typo)
1882–87. Chalk-surfaced paper.

(a) P 12½

207	19	5r. drab (1.3.83)	50·00	5·25
208		5r. grey	48·00	4·75
209		5r. grey-black	48·00	4·75
210	22	10r. yellow-green (15.7.84)	75·00	6·00
211		10r. green	75·00	6·00
212	20	25r. brown (1.2.82)	42·00	3·75
213		25r. pale brown	42·00	3·75
214		25r. purple-brown	42·00	3·75
215	21	50r. blue (15.6.82)	80·00	5·25
216	24	500r. black (5.84)	£650	£425
217		500r. magenta (1.7.87)	£400	85·00

(b) P 13½

218	19	5r. drab	55·00	11·00
219		5r. grey	55·00	11·00
220		5r. grey-black	55·00	11·00
221	22	10r. green	£100	11·00
222	20	25r. brown	55·00	5·25
223		25r. pale brown	55·00	5·25
224		25r. purple-brown	55·00	5·25
225	21	50r. blue	75·00	16·00
226		50r. deep blue	75·00	16·00
227	23	500r. magenta	£950	£650

24   25

(Centre eng E. Mouchon, frame eng A. Gneco (T **24**)
or V. Alves (others). Typo)
1886–89. Chalk-surfaced paper. P 11½.

228	19	5r. grey-black (1888)	25·00	2·30
229		5r. black	19·00	1·70
230	22	10r. blue-green	55·00	6·00
231		10r. pale green	55·00	6·00
232	24	20r. rosine	65·00	26·00
233	20	25r. purple-brown	49·00	3·75
234	25	25r. magenta (7.87)	44·00	4·50
235		25r. rosy mauve (1887)	44·00	4·50
		a. Imperf (pair)	£180	£225
236	21	50r. blue	65·00	4·50
237		50r. pale blue	65·00	4·50
238		50r. deep blue	65·00	4·50

Reprints of T **19/25**: In 1885–93 the 5, 10, 20, 25 (T **20** and **25**) and 50r. perf 13½ on chalk-surfaced paper but without gum; also the 5, 10 and 50r. perf 12½ on chalk-surfaced paper without gum; the 500r. magenta perf 13½ on gummed paper. In 1900 the 5r. and 25r. (T **25**) perf 11½. In 1905 all values (both types of 25r.) except the 500r. black.

King Carlos
19 Oct 1889–1 Feb 1908

26   PROVISORIO   PROVISORIO
        (27)   (28)

(Head eng M. D. Neto, frame eng J. S. de Carvalho e Silva. Typo)
1892–94. Chalk-surfaced paper, or enamel-surfaced paper (E).

(a) P 12½

239	26	10r. rosy mauve	42·00	8·25
240		10r. rosy mauve (E) (1894)	£400	65·00
241		15r. brown	44·00	9·00
242		20r. lavender	50·00	13·50
242a		20r. lavender (E)	£2500	£850
243		50r. bright blue	50·00	14·50
244		50r. grey-blue	50·00	14·50
245		75r. carmine	£100	12·00
246		75r. carmine (E) (1894)	£350	44·00
247		80r. pale green	£160	80·00
248		100r. brown/*buff* (15.3.93)	95·00	9·50
250		150r. carmine/*rose* (1.8.93)	£375	£160
252		200r. blue/*blue* (1.8.93)	£250	65·00

(b) P 13½

253	26	10r. rosy mauve	50·00	12·00
254		10r. rosy mauve (E) (1894)	55·00	12·00
255		15r. brown	50·00	13·50
256		15r. brown (E) (1894)	42·00	6·00
257		20r. lavender	75·00	18·00
258		50r. bright blue	£150	19·00
259		50r. grey-blue	£150	19·00
260		75r. carmine	£275	45·00
261		75r. carmine (E) (1894)	£350	44·00
262		80r. pale green	£130	80·00
263	26	100r. red-brown/*pale brown*	£150	19·00
264		100r. brown/*yellow*	£150	19·00
265		150r. carmine/*rose*	£250	80·00
266		200r. blue/*blue*	£275	£110
267		300r. blue/*pale brown* (1.8.93)	£275	£110

(c) P 11½

268	26	5r. yellow	18·00	3·00
269		5r. buff	18·00	3·00
270		5r. brown-orange	18·00	3·00
271		5r. pale orange (E) (1894)	18·00	3·00
272		10r. dull magenta	£2500	70·00
273		10r. rosy mauve (E) (1894)	55·00	3·00
274		25r. deep green	60·00	4·25
275		25r. deep green (E) (1894)	60·00	4·25
276		25r. green (E) (1894)	40·00	3·00
277		50r. pale blue	80·00	9·00
278		50r. pale ultramarine	80·00	9·00
279		75r. carmine	£475	20·00
281		100r. brown/*buff*	£550	25·00

The 50, 100 and 350r. were reprinted in 1900 perf 11½ and all values in 1905.

1892 (27 July). Nos. *229/30* optd with T **27/8** respectively.

282	19	5r. black	24·00	13·50
283	22	10r. blue-green	24·00	13·50

The above were reprinted in 1905.

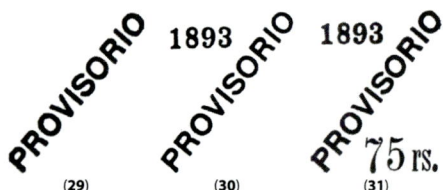

(29)   (30)   (31)

1892 (1 Oct)–**93.** Various stamps optd with T **29**.

A. Chalk surfaced paper

(a) P 11½ or 12½ (T 15)

284	19	5r. black (C.)	21·00	10·50
285	22	10r. blue-green (C.)	24·00	14·50
286	15	15r. fawn (1) (1.1.93)	31·00	18·00
287		15r. fawn (2) (C.)	31·00	18·00
288		15r. yellow-brown (1) (C.)	31·00	18·00
289		15r. red-brown (2) (C.)	42·00	24·00
290	24	20r. rosine	60·00	34·00

4

291	25	25r. rosy mauve (1.11.92)	21·00	8·25
		a. Perf 12½*	£700	£110
292	21	50r. blue (C) (1.2.93)	£120	95·00
293	15	80r. pale orange (1) (1.2.93)	£150	£140
294		80r. pale orange (2)	£150	£140

(b) P 13½

295	15	15r. fawn (2) (C)	42·00	34·00
296		15r. red-brown (2) (C)	42·00	34·00

B. Unsurfaced paper
(a) P 12½

297	15	15r. fawn (1) (C)	27·00	24·00
298		15r. fawn (2) (C)	30·00	22·00
299		15r. chocolate (1) (C)	30·00	22·00
300		15r. chocolate (2) (C)	30·00	22·00

(b) P 13½

301	15	15r. fawn (1) (C)	£950	£550

*No. 291a is only known overprinted.
All values were reprinted in 1905.

1893 (3 Aug–Dec). Various stamps optd. Chalk-surfaced paper. P 11½ or 12½ (T **15**).

(a) Optd with T **30**

302	19	5r. black (C)	35·00	32·00
303	22	10r. blue-green (C) (28.12)	33·00	29·00
		a. "1863" for "1893"	£400	£400
		b. "1938" for "1893"	£375	£350
304	24	20r. rosine	55·00	47·00
305	25	25r. rosy mauve	£150	£150
		a. Opt inverted	£500	£500
306	21	50r. blue	£150	£150
307	15	80r. pale orange (1)	£150	£140
		a. Orange (1)	£150	£140
308		80r. pale orange (2)	£150	£140
		a. Opt double	£900	£900
		b. Orange (2)	£150	£140

(b) Surch as T **31**

309	25	20r. on 25r. rosy mauve	75·00	65·00
310	15	50r. on 80r. pale orange (1)	£180	£150
		a. Orange (1)	£180	£150
311		50r. on 80r. pale orange (2)	£180	£150
312		75r. on 80r. pale orange (1)	£100	£150
		a. Orange (1)	£225	£180
313		75r. on 80r. pale orange (2)	£100	£100
		a. Orange (2)	£100	£100

Nos. 303a/b occur on positions 19 and 7 respectively in the setting of 25; each setting was used six times in the sheet.
All values were reprinted in 1900 perf 11½ and again in 1905.

32 Prince Henry in his Caravel and Family Motto

33 Prince Henry directing Movements of his Fleet

34 Symbolical of Prince Henry's Studies

(Des after paintings by J. V. Salgado, T **32/3** litho; T **34** recess. Giesecke & Devrient, Leipzig)

1894 (4 Mar). 500th Birth Anniv of Prince Henry the Navigator. P 14.

314	32	5r. orange	5·50	1·20
315		10r. rosy lake	5·50	1·20
316		15r. brown	14·50	4·50
317		20r. lilac	14·50	5·25
318	33	25r. green	13·50	1·70
319		50r. blue	43·00	9·00
		a. Aniline blue	85·00	15·00
320		75r. carmine-rose	85·00	19·00
		a. Aniline carmine	85·00	15·00
321		80r. pale green	85·00	22·00
322		100r. brown/buff	65·00	18·00
323	34	150r. rose-red	£190	44·00
324		300r. blue/bright buff	£225	60·00
325		500r. deep purple/bluish	£500	£120
326		1000r. black/buff	£850	£180
314/326 Set of 13			£2000	£475

35 St. Anthony's Vision

36 St. Anthony preaching to the Fishes

37 St. Anthony ascending into Heaven

38 St. Anthony, from picture in Academy of Fine Arts, Paris

39

(Des A. M. Ramalho (T **35/7**), C. Reis (T **38**). T **38** eng on wood M. D. Neto. Recess Mint. Others litho Companhia Nacional Editora, Lisbon)

1895 (13 June). *700th Birth Anniv of St. Anthony (Patron Saint).* With a prayer in Latin printed on the back. P 12×11½ and also P 11½.

327	35	2½r. black	6·00	2·00
328	36	5r. orange	6·00	2·00
329		10r. mauve	17·00	11·00
330		15r. brown	20·00	11·00
331		20r. grey-lilac	20·00	12·00
332		25r. purple and green	17·00	2·00
333	37	50r. brown and blue	42·00	31·00
334		75r. brown and rosine	70·00	55·00
335		80r. brown and pale green	85·00	80·00
336		100r. black and chocolate	75·00	43·00
337	38	150r. rosine and bistre	£250	£150
338		200r. blue and bistre	£225	£160
339		300r. slate and bistre	£325	£225
340		500r. brown and green	£650	£475
341		1000r. deep lilac and green	£1100	£600
327/341 Set of 15			£2750	£1800

(Des and eng E. Mouchon. Typo)

1895 (1 Nov)–**1905**. Numerals of value in carmine (Nos. 354 and 363/4) or black (others).

(a) P 11½

342	39	2½r. pale grey	50	20
343		5r. pale orange-brown	50	20
		a. Brown-orange	50	20
		b. Pale orange	50	20
		c. Orange	50	20
344		10r. pale green	70	25
		a. Yellow-green	70	25
345		15r. green (1.1.99)	70·00	4·00
346		15r. chocolate	£140	5·50
347		20r. deep lilac	90	55
348		25r. blue-green	£100	35
349		25r. carmine (1.1.99)	55	20
		a. Deep carmine	30	20
350		50r. blue	£140	65
		a. Deep blue	£140	65
351		50r. ultramarine (7.05)	75	35
		a. Pale ultramarine	75	35
		ab. "50" omitted	12·00	15·00
		ac. "50" misplaced	6·00	6·50
352		65r. steel blue (1.7.98)	80	45
353		75r. rose	£170	6·75
		a. Carmine	£170	6·75
354		75r. brown/yellow (7.05)	2·20	1·00
355		80r. mauve	2·75	1·60
356		100r. blue/bright blue	1·30	60
		a. Dull blue/azure	1·30	60
357		115r. orange-brown/pink (1.7.98)	6·50	4·50
358		130r. sepia/cream (1.7.98)	4·50	2·20
359		150r. purple-brown/straw	£225	£100
360		180r. slate/pale pink (1.7.98)	29·00	13·50
361		200r. purple/pale pink	27·00	3·75
		a. Dull purple/pale pink	6·25	1·00
362		300r. blue/pink	5·00	3·00
363		500r. black/azure (1.7.96)	12·50	6·75
342/363 Set of 22			£1000	90·00

(b) P 12½

364	39	500r. black/azure	£150	35·00

Other errors and varieties are of clandestine origin.

Nos. 365/74 are vacant.

PORTUGAL

40 Departure of Fleet

41 Arrival at Calicut

42 Embarkation at Rastello

43 Muse of History

44 Da Gama and Camoens and *São Gabriel* (flagship)

45 Archangel Gabriel, Patron Saint of the Expedition

46 The Flagship *São Gabriel*

47 Vasco da Gama

(Des **40** R. Gameiro. **41** M. P. de Faria Luna. **42** S. Correia Belem. **43**, **45**, **47** J. Vaz. **44** J. J. G. Coelho. **46** J. R. Cristino da Silva. Recess Waterlow)

1898 (1 Apr). Vasco da Gama Commemoration. Fourth Centenary of Discovery of Route to India. P 12½ to 16.

378	**40**	2½r. blue-green	1·90	55
379	**41**	5r. vermilion	1·90	55
380	**42**	10r. dull purple	12·00	2·30
381	**43**	25r. yellow-green	8·25	65
382	**44**	50r. deep blue	17·00	4·25
383	**45**	75r. red-brown	65·00	17·00
384	**46**	100r. bistre-brown	50·00	17·00
385	**47**	150r. yellow-brown	£110	44·00
378/385		*Set of 8*	£250	85·00

D 48 Da Gama received by the Zamorin of Calicut

D 49

(Des C. M. Miranda da Costa, eng J. S. de Carvalho e Silva. Typo Mint)

1898 (1 May). POSTAGE DUE. Value in black. P 11½×12.

(a) Unsurfaced paper

D386	D **48**	5r. black	5·00	3·50
D387		10r. magenta	6·25	4·00
D388		20r. orange	10·50	4·50
D389		50r. slate	80·00	9·00

(b) Chalk-surfaced paper

D390	D **48**	100r. carmine/rose	£120	65·00
D391		200r. brown/buff	£130	90·00

(Des and eng J. S. de Carvalho e Silva. Typo)

1904 (1 Jan–Mar). POSTAGE DUE. P 11½.

D392	D **49**	5r. brown	85	80
D393		10r. dull orange	4·25	1·30
D394		20r. dull mauve (23 Mar)	12·00	5·75
D395		30r. green	8·50	4·25
D396		40r. deep lilac	9·75	4·25
D397		50r. carmine	65·00	7·25
		a. Rose	65·00	7·25
D398		100r. blue	14·50	9·50
D392/398		*Set of 7*	£100	30·00

The above may be found on white or on toned paper (20r. white only).

See also Nos. D484/501 and D578/94.

King Manoel II
1 Feb 1908–5 Oct 1910

48

49

(Des and eng D. A. do Rego. Typo)

1910 (1 Jan). P 14×15.

390	**48**	2½r. lilac	40	35
391		5r. black	40	35
392		10r. grey-green	70	40
393		15r. pale purple-brown	3·75	2·50
394		20r. carmine	1·40	1·10
395		25r. chocolate	85	25
396		50r. indigo-blue	2·30	95
397		75r. yellow-brown	14·00	7·75
398		80r. French-grey	4·25	3·25
399		100r. brown/*green*	16·00	4·00
400		200r. deep green/*salmon*	9·00	6·50
401		300r. black/*azure*	11·50	7·25
402	**49**	500r. chocolate and olive	21·00	18·00
403		1000r. black and indigo	48·00	38·00
390/403		*Set of 14*	£125	85·00

The white paper of this issue is glazed and slightly chalk-surfaced.

REPUBLIC
5 October 1910

(50)

1910 (1 Nov)–**12**. Optd with T **50**, in red or green (G.).

404	**48**	2½r. lilac	45	30
405		5r. black	45	30
		a. Bisected (2½r.) (on piece) ('12)		
406		10r. grey-green	4·50	1·50
407		15r. pale purple-brown	1·60	1·20
408		20r. carmine (G.)	6·25	2·75
409		25r. chocolate	1·20	45
410		50r. indigo-blue	8·75	3·25
		a. Bright blue	8·75	3·25
411		75r. yellow-brown	15·00	6·75
412		80r. French-grey	4·50	3·50
413		100r. brown/*green*	2·75	1·40
414		200r. deep green/*salmon*	3·25	3·00
415		300r. black/*azure*	5·75	5·00
416	**49**	500r. chocolate and olive	16·00	13·50
417		1000r. black and indigo	40·00	30·00
404/417		*Set of 14*	£100	70·00

A coarse provisional printing of the 2½, 5 and 25r. exists on chalk-surfaced paper, and of the 25r. on enamelled paper.

It is believed that the inverted and double overprint varieties formerly listed are clandestine productions.

1911 (Jan). POSTAGE DUE. Optd with T **50**, in red or green (G.).

D418	D **49**	5r. brown	80	70
D419		10r. dull orange	80	70
D420		20r. dull mauve	2·10	1·80
D421		30r. green	2·00	70
D422		40r. deep lilac	2·10	70
D423		50r. carmine (G.)	8·75	6·75
D424		100r. blue	9·25	7·25
D418/424		*Set of 7*	20·00	15·00

All values are known with overprint inverted.

PORTUGAL

REPUBLICA (51)   **REPUBLICA** (52)

REIS 15 REIS (53)   **R^s 500 R^s** (54)   **1$000** (55)

1911 (1 Oct)–**12.** Postage and Postage Due stamps of 1898 optd as T **51** or **52** respectively, or surch in addition as T **53/5**.

441	40	2½r. blue-green	75	30
		a. Opt inverted	25·00	22·00
		b. Opt double	31·00	28·00
442	D 48	5r. grey-black	1·70	75
		a. Chalk-surfaced paper	4·25	3·50
		b. Opt double, one inverted	26·00	20·00
		c. Value and "CONTINENTE" omitted		
		d. Bisected (2½r.) (on piece) ('12)		
443		10r. magenta	2·10	1·20
		a. Chalk-surfaced paper	4·75	3·75
444	41	15r. on 5r. vermilion	1·30	60
		a. Surch inverted	18·00	16·00
445	D 48	20r. pale orange	7·75	5·00
		a. Chalk-surfaced paper	10·50	6·50
446	43	25r. yellow-green	90	45
447	44	50r. deep blue	4·50	2·10
448	45	75r. red-brown	65·00	47·00
449	47	80r. on 150r. yellow-brown	8·00	6·25
450	46	100r. bistre-brown	8·00	3·75
		a. Opt inverted	50·00	43·00
451	D 48	200r. brown/buff	£180	£110
		a. Opt double	£150	£150
452		300r. on 50r. slate	£130	65·00
453		500r. on 100r. carmine/rose	70·00	36·00
		a. Surch inverted	£225	£160
		b. Surch doubled	£225	£160
454	42	1000r. on 10r. dull purple	90·00	55·00
441/454	Set of 14 (cheapest)		£550	£325

The 200r. and 500r. are on chalk-surfaced paper.

CHARITY TAX STAMPS. Stamps bearing C numbers issued between 1911 and 1928 were for compulsory use on internal letters on certain days of the year as an additional postal tax for public charities. Other values in some of the types were for use on telegrams only.

ASSISTENCIA
(C **56**)

1911 (4 Oct). CHARITY TAX. No. 406 optd with Type C **56** horizontally.
C455		10r. green (R.)	13·00	3·50

1911 (Oct)–**12.** 1898 issue of Madeira optd with T **51**, or surch in addition as T **53** or **55**, and used in Portugal.

455		2½r. blue-green (1.12)	17·00	13·50
456		15r. on 5r. vermilion (1.12)	3·75	3·75
		a. Surch inverted	22·00	19·00
457		25r. yellow-green (12.11)	7·50	7·25
458		50r. deep blue (12.11)	17·00	13·50
459		75r. red-brown (10.11)	17·00	8·25
		a. Opt inverted	65·00	55·00
		b. Opt double	80·00	70·00
460		80r. on 150r. yellow-brown (1.12)	18·00	16·00
		a. Surch inverted	85·00	75·00
461		100r. bistre-brown (12.11)	60·00	13·50
		a. Opt inverted	£225	£190
462		1000r. on 10r. dull purple (1.12)	60·00	38·00
455/462	Set of 8		£190	£100

Very few of these stamps were sent to Madeira.

56 Ceres

(Des C. Fernandes, Eng S, de Carvalho e Silva. Typo)

1912–20. New Currency. Ceres type with imprint below design. Chalk-surfaced paper (thick, medium or thin).

(a) P 15×14

463	56	¼c. olive-brown (4.12)	21·00	1·10
464		½c. black (4.12)	21·00	1·10
465		1c. green (shades) (2.12)	19·00	1·10
466		1½c. brown (7.12)	39·00	5·00
467		2c. carmine (8.12)	39·00	2·75
468		2½c. violet (shades) (5.12)	34·00	1·10
469		5c. blue (shades) (2.12)	39·00	2·20
470		7½c. yellow-brown (6.12)	£100	6·75
471		8c. slate (8.12)	£170	13·50
472		10c. chestnut (8.12)	£250	2·75
473		15c. brown-purple (8.12)	£300	21·00
474		20c. chocolate/green (8.12)	26·00	2·75
		a. Pale brown/green	26·00	2·75
475		20c. chocolate/buff (1920)	27·00	7·25
476		30c. brown/rose (8.12)	£190	18·00
477		30c. brown/yellow (3.17)	18·00	3·50
478		50c. orange/salmon (8.12)	26·00	2·20
479		50c. orange/yellow (1918)	29·00	2·20
480		1E. green/azure (shades) (8.12)	29·00	2·20
463/80	Set of 18 (cheapest)		£1200	85·00

(b) P 12×11½

481	56	14c. indigo (9.20)	3·50	2·40
482		20c. chocolate/buff (1.20)	£800	£200
483		50c. orange/salmon (10.20)	£225	34·00

The ¼c., ½c., 1c., 2½c. and 5c. also exist on glazed non-chalky paper.

See also Nos. 484/577, 702/25 and 813/34.

1912 (4 Oct). CHARITY TAX. No. 465 optd with Type C **56** diagonally.
C484	56	1c. green (R.) (shades)	9·50	3·00

C **57** "Lisbon"   C **58** "Charity"

(Des A. Pina. Litho)

1913 (8 June). CHARITY TAX. Lisbon Festival. P 12×11½.
C485	C **57**	1c. green	1·80	1·30

1915 (18 Mar). POSTAGE DUE. Value in centavos. P 11½.

(a) Chalk-surfaced paper

D484	D **49**	½c. brown	4·00	3·00
D485		1c. orange	4·00	3·00
D486		2c. maroon	4·00	3·00
D487		3c. green	4·00	3·00
D488		4c. lilac	4·00	3·00
D489		5c. red	8·00	5·75
D490		10c. blue	9·50	5·75
D484/490	Set of 7		35·00	22·00

(b) Unsurfaced paper

D491	D **49**	½c. pale brown	90	85
D492		1c. yellow	90	85
D493		2c. pale maroon	90	85
D494		3c. pale green	90	85
D495		4c. lilac	90	85
D496		5c. carmine	90	85
D497		10c. pale blue	1·10	1·00
D491/497	Set of 7		6·00	5·75

(c) Pelure paper (unsurfaced)

D498	D **49**	1c. orange	1·10	1·00
D499		3c. bluish green	1·10	1·00
D500		4c. pale lilac	1·10	1·00
D501		5c. red	1·10	1·00
D498/501	Set of 4		4·00	3·75

(Des P. Guedes. Eng J. A. Pedroso. Typo)

1915 (4 Oct). CHARITY TAX. For the Poor. P 12.
C486	C **58**	1c. rose-red	50	45
		a. Thick carton paper	1·50	85

See also No. C669.

1917–26.

(a) Unsurfaced wove paper (thick, medium or thin). P 15×14 (1917–21)

484	56	¼c. olive brown	95	30
		a. Thick carton paper	36·00	7·25
485		½c. black	1·00	30
		a. Thick carton paper	36·00	7·25
		b. Bluish paper (1920)	95	55
486		1c. green (shades)	1·90	55
		a. "CORREIC" for "CORREIO"	£700	£700
487		1c. brown	35	30
		a. Thick carton paper	30·00	7·50

PORTUGAL

488		1½c. brown	10·50	4·50
489		1½c. green (shades)	55	30
490		2c. carmine (shades)	10·50	3·75
491		2c. yellow-orange	65	30
		a. Orange-yellow	65	30
492		2½c. lilac	90	30
493		3c. carmine (shades)	60	30
494		3c. pale blue (1.4.21)	£200	80·00
495		3½c. yellow-green (shades) (4.18)	55	30
496		4c. yellow-green (8.19)	55	30
		a. Thick carton paper	30·00	7·50
497		5c. deep blue (shades)	10·50	1·00
498		5c. yellow-brown	2·20	50
499		6c. claret (shades) (1.20)	85	50
		a. Thick carton paper	22·00	7·50
500		7½c. yellow-brown	19·00	3·75
501		7½c. deep blue	1·10	55
502		8c. slate	14·00	2·00
503		10c. chestnut	25·00	1·60
504		12c. slate-blue (1.20)	2·20	1·20
505		15c. purple-brown (shades)	3·25	1·30
506		20c. chocolate (1.20)	£120	13·50
507		30c. grey-brown	£200	42·00
508		36c. red (5.21)	7·75	3·50
509		60c. blue (6.21)	7·75	3·50
510		80c. dull claret (6.21)	2·75	1·70
511		90c. cobalt (6.21)	10·00	6·00
512		1E. lilac (4.21)	£275	£140
484/512 Set of 29			£850	£250

(b) Unsurfaced paper. P 12×11½ (1920–26)

513	56	¼c. olive-brown	60	35
514		½c. black	60	35
		a. Thick carton paper	14·00	2·10
515		1c. pale brown	35	30
		a. Thick carton paper	70·00	23·00
516		1½c. green	45	30
517		2c. yellow-orange	1·80	40
		a. Thick carton paper	£110	14·50
		b. Orange-yellow	1·80	40
		ba. Thick carton paper	£110	14·50
518		2c. pale yellow (6.24)	1·40	65
519		2c. chocolate (11.26)	3·25	2·75
520		2½c. lilac	7·75	2·20
521		3c. carmine	55	40
522		3c. blue (shades) (1.4.21)	35	30
523		4c. yellow-green	35	30
		a. Thick carton paper	£150	29·00
524		4c. yellow-orange (11.26)	2·75	2·10
525		5c. yellow-brown	2·00	55
526		5c. olive-brown (3.23)	85	50
527		6c. claret (shades) (1.4.21)	1·40	65
		a. Thick carton paper	1·60	90
528		6c. chocolate (11.24)	1·70	65
529		7½c. deep blue	55	30
530		8c. slate	65	65
531		8c. blue-green (6.22)	1·10	70
532		8c. salmon (11.24)	1·20	65
533		10c. brown-red	35	30
		a. Thick carton paper	43·00	3·50
534		12c. deep blue-green (4.21)	85	55
535		13½c. grey-blue	2·20	1·60
536	56	14c. purple (6.21)	1·00	85
		a. Thick carton paper	£250	£180
537		15c. jet-black (4.23)	85	45
538		16c. ultramarine (9.24)	1·70	90
		a. Pale blue (1926)	1·70	90
539		20c. chocolate (9.20)	1·00	70
		a. Thick carton paper	60·00	11·00
540		20c. deep blue-green (9.23)	85	55
541		20c. drab (7.24)	1·20	65
542		24c. greenish blue (5.21)	1·00	65
543		25c. rose-pink (4.23)	85	45
544		25c. pale drab (9.26)	5·25	2·75
545		30c. grey-brown (5.21)	85	50
546		30c. deep brown (10.24)	16·00	4·75
547		32c. deep blue-green (10.24)	2·40	1·40
548		36c. red (shades) (5.21)	3·00	65
549		40c. blue (9.23)	2·10	1·10
		a. "CORREIC" for "CORREIO"	£350	£275
550		40c. sepia (4.24)	1·40	55
		a. "CORREIC" for "CORREIO"	95·00	70·00
551		40c. emerald-green (11.26)	2·50	1·70
552		48c. carmine-pink (8.24)	13·50	6·00
553		50c. yellow (4.21)	3·00	1·10
554		60c. blue (6.21)	2·75	1·10
555		64c. cobalt (9.24)	16·00	8·75
556		75c. brown-rose (9.23)	27·00	10·00
557		80c. brown-red (6.21)	50·00	13·00
558		80c. lilac (8.24)	2·40	90
559		90c. cobalt (6.21)	3·00	1·10
560		96c. dull carmine (3.23)	70·00	45·00
561		1E. lilac (4.21)	6·75	3·50
562		1E.10 yellow-brown (6.21)	6·75	3·25
563		1E.20 apple green (6.21)	3·75	2·10
564		2E. deep grey-green (6.21)	£100	10·00
513/564 Set of 52			£375	£140

(c) Glazed paper. P 12×11½ (1923–26)

565	56	1E. deep blue (11.23)	7·50	2·20
566		1E. slate-purple (5.24)	7·00	2·50
567		1E.20 yellow-buff (7.24)	£110	65·00
568		1E.50 slate-purple (9.23)	30·00	7·75
569		1E.50 pale lilac (5.24)	33·00	7·25
570		1E.60 blue (11.24)	47·00	8·75
571		2E. grey-green (7.24)	80·00	8·25
572		2E.40 sage-green (3.26)	£425	£250
573		3E. pink (5.26)	£425	£225
574		3E.20 bronze-green (12.24)	90·00	23·00
575		5E. turquoise-green (shades) (8.24)	90·00	16·00
576		10E. rose (8.24)	£350	90·00
577		20E. turquoise-blue (12.24)	£700	£300
565/577 Set of 13			£2000	£900

The "CORREIC" error occurs on position 23 of the sheet of 100 for the 1c., and on position 14 of the sheet of 180 for the 40c.

New printings on whiter paper from slightly retouched plates were issued in 1930 (see Nos. 813/34).

P 59

(Des A. Quaresma. Eng G. A. Santos. Typo)

1920 (Dec)–**22**. PARCEL POST. P 12.

P578	P 59	1c. pale chocolate	55	45
P579		2c. orange	55	45
P580		5c. pale brown	55	45
P581		10c. red brown	55	45
P582		20c. lavender-blue	75	45
P583		40c. deep carmine	75	45
P584		50c. black	1·10	80
P585		60c. blue (5.21)	1·00	80
P586		70c. brown (6.21)	6·25	3·00
P587		80c. pale blue (5.21)	6·50	4·75
P588		90c. violet (11.21)	6·75	3·50
P589		1E. pale green	7·00	4·25

Glazed paper

P590	P 59	1E. pale green (?)	11·00	3·25
P591		2E. pale lilac (5.22)	20·00	5·25
P592		3E. olive (7.22)	37·00	6·00
P593		4E. bright ultramarine (7.22)	80·00	10·50
P594		6E. grey-lilac (7.22)	£110	7·00
P595		10E. deep brown (7.22)	£170	12·50
P578/595 Set of 18			£450	60·00

1921 (Dec)–**27**. POSTAGE DUE. P 11½.

D578	D 49	½c. grey-green (7.22)	80	55
D579		4c. grey-green (1.27)	80	55
D580		8c. grey-green (12.23)	80	55
D581		10c. grey-green (9.22)	80	55
D582		12c. grey-green (6.22)	90	65
D583		16c. grey-green (12.23)	90	65
D584		20c. grey-green (6.22)	90	65
D585		24c. grey-green	90	65
D586		32c. grey-green (12.23)	1·40	90
D587		36c. grey-green (6.22)	2·50	1·80
D588		40c. grey-green (12.23)	2·50	1·80
D589		48c. grey-green (12.23)	1·60	1·00
D590		50c. grey-green (6.22)	1·60	1·00
D591		60c. grey-green	1·60	1·00
D592		72c. grey-green (6.22)	1·60	1·00
D593		80c. grey-green (12.23)	12·00	10·50
D594		1E.20 grey-green	5·50	5·50
D578/594 Set of 17			30·00	27·00

60 Presidents of Portugal and Brazil and Airmen Gago Coutinho and Sacadura Cabral

(C 61)

PORTUGAL

(Litho Waterlow)

1923 (30 Mar). Portugal–Brazil Trans-Atlantic Flight. P 14.

578	**60**	1c. deep brown	20	1·10
579		2c. orange	20	1·10
580		3c. blue	20	1·10
581		4c. yellow-green	20	1·10
582		5c. yellow-brown	20	1·10
583		10c. red-brown	20	1·10
584		15c. black	20	1·10
585		20c. green	20	1·10
586		25c. carmine	20	1·10
587		30c. terra-cotta	1·00	2·75
588		40c. chocolate	70	1·10
589		50c. yellow	60	1·30
590		75c. bright purple	60	1·40
591		1E. deep blue	60	2·75
592		1E.50 olive-grey	1·10	3·50
593		2E. deep green	1·30	8·75
578/593 Set of 16			7·00	28·00

1924 (4 Oct). CHARITY TAX. Surch with Type C **61**.

| C594 | C **58** | 15c. on 1c. rose-red | 2·50 | 1·10 |

62 Camoens at Ceuta

63 Saving the *Lusiad*

(Des Alberto de Sousa. Eng G. Fairweather (2E.40 to 20E.), J. Harrison (others). Recess Waterlow)

1924 (11 Nov). 400th Birth Anniv of Camoens (poet). Value in black. P 14.

600	**62**	2c. blue	35	35
601		3c. orange	35	35
602		4c. slate	35	35
603		5c. yellowish green	35	35
604		6c. carmine	35	35
605	**63**	8c. orange-brown	35	35
606		10c. slate-violet	35	35
607		15c. olive-green	35	35
608		16c. deep claret	40	40
609		20c. red-orange	50	40
610	–	25c. slate-violet	50	40
611	–	30c. brown	50	40
612		32c. deep grey-green	1·40	1·40
613		40c. royal blue	50	45
614		48c. black-lake	2·10	2·30
615		50c. orange-red	2·50	1·50
616		64c. green	2·50	1·50
617		75c. deep lilac	2·75	1·50
618		80c. yellow-brown	1·90	1·50
619		96c. deep carmine	1·90	1·50
620		1E. deep turquoise	1·60	1·20
621		1E.20 red-brown	9·25	6·75
622		1E.50 vermilion	2·50	1·50
623		1E.60 indigo	2·50	1·50
624		2E. olive-green	9·25	6·25
625		2E.40 green/*green*	8·00	4·25
626		3E. blue/*azure*	2·75	1·40
		a. Value double	£160	£200
627		3E.20 black/*turquoise*	2·75	1·30
628		4E.50 black/*yellow*	8·50	5·50
629		10E. brown/*rose*	15·00	11·00
630		20E. violet/*mauve*	18·00	11·00
600/630 Set of 31			90·00	60·00

Designs: Vert—25c. to 48c. Luis de Camoens; 50c. to 96c. First Edition of *Lusiad*; 20E. Monument to Camoens. Horiz—1E. to 2E. Death of Camoens; 2E.40 to 10E. Tomb of Camoens.

65 Branco's house at S. Miguel de Seide

67 Camilo Castelo Branco

(Des Alberto de Sousa. Recess Waterlow)

1925 (26 Mar). Birth Centenary of Camilo Castelo Branco (novelist). Value in black. P 12½.

631	**65**	2c. orange	40	25
632		3c. green	40	25
633		4c. blue	40	25
634		5c. scarlet	40	25
635		6c. purple	40	25
636		8c. sepia	40	25
637	A	10c. light blue	40	25
638	**67**	15c. olive-green	45	35
639	A	16c. red-orange	55	50
640		20c. violet	55	50
641	**67**	25c. carmine	55	50
642	A	30c. bistre	55	50
643		32c. green	1·70	1·50
644	**67**	40c. black and green	1·20	95
645	A	48c. brown-lake	4·50	5·00
646	B	50c. blue-green	1·20	95
647		64c. chestnut	4·75	5·00
648		75c. slate	1·40	1·00
649	**67**	80c. brown	1·40	1·10
650	B	96c. carmine	2·40	2·30
651		1E. lilac	2·20	2·30
652		1E.20 apple-green	2·50	2·30
653	C	1E.50 deep blue/*blue*	46·00	22·00
654	**67**	1E.60 deep blue	9·00	5·75
655	C	2E. green/*green*	10·50	6·25
656		2E.40 scarlet/*orange*	£100	50·00
657		3E. carmine/*blue*	£130	65·00
658		3E.20 black/*green*	60·00	50·00
659	**67**	4E.50 black and scarlet	25·00	5·75
660	C	10E. brown/*buff*	26·00	6·00
661	D	20E. black/*orange*	27·00	6·00
631/661 Set of 31			£450	£225

Designs: Horiz—A, Branco's study. Vert—B, Teresa de Albuquerque; C, Mariana and João da Cruz; D, Simão de Botelho. Types B/D show characters from Branco's *Amor de Peredicao*.

Nos. 379/80 surcharged "VASCO DA GAMA/1924-1925/ 2$00" were issued in 1926 for voluntary use on registered mail in aid of a memorial to Vasco da Gama, but they had no franking value.

C **71** Muse of History

D **72**

(Des R. Gonçalves. Typo Litografia Lusitana)

1925 (8 Apr). Portuguese Army in Flanders, 1484 and 1918. P 11.

(a) CHARITY TAX

C662	C **71**	10c. carmine	1·80	1·60
C663		10c. green	1·80	1·60
C664		10c. ultramarine	1·80	1·60
C665		10c. brown	1·80	1·60

(b) POSTAGE DUE

| D662 | D **72** | 20c. yellow-brown | 95 | 75 |

Nos. C662/5 were in use on 8 and 9 April 1925, 10 and 11 November 1925, and from 9 to 15 December 1928. If one was not affixed in addition to the ordinary rate of postage, the postage due stamp (No. D662) was used to collect the deficiency and the fine.

C **73** Monument to De Pombal

C **74** Planning Reconstruction of Lisbon

C **75** Marquis de Pombal

(Des H. Fleury. Eng J. A. C. Harrison. Recess Waterlow)

1925 (8 May). CHARITY TAX. Marquis de Pombal commemoration. Value and "CONTINENTE" in black. P 12½.

C666	C **73**	15c. blue	1·80	1·10
C667	C **74**	15c. blue	1·80	1·10
C668	C **75**	15c. blue	65	55

Nos. C666/8 were in use from 8 to 13 May 1925 and from 5 to 15 May of 1926 to 1929. The postage due stamps used in default were Nos. D663/5. Stamps of this issue of the Portuguese Colonies were used indiscriminately in Portugal.

PORTUGAL

MULTA
(D **76**)

1925 (8 May). POSTAGE DUE. Types C **73/5** optd with Type D **76**.
D663	C **73**	30c. blue	1·90	1·60
D664	C **74**	30c. blue	1·90	1·60
D665	C **75**	30c. blue	1·90	1·60

In Oporto, the corresponding 15c. stamps of St. Thomas and Prince were handstamped "PORTEADO" separately or in pairs, for use as Postage Due Stamps.

1925 (4 Oct). CHARITY TAX. For the Poor. P 12.
C669	C **58**	15c. carmine-red	95	95

76 Afonso I, First King of Portugal, 1140

77 Battle of Aljubarrota

(Des E. A. R. da Costa. Eng G. Harrison and N. Broad. Recess De La Rue)

1926 (13 Aug). First Independence issue. Designs as T **76/7** (dated 1926). Centres in black. P 14.
671	**76**	2c. orange-red	40	40
672	–	3c. blue	40	40
673	**76**	4c. green	40	40
674	–	5c. sepia	40	40
675	**76**	6c. brown-orange	40	40
676	–	15c. myrtle-green	40	40
677	**76**	16c. deep blue	1·40	1·10
678	**77**	20c. violet	1·40	1·10
679	–	25c. scarlet	1·40	1·10
680	**77**	32c. deep green	1·50	1·30
681	–	40c. brown	1·00	75
682	–	46c. carmine	6·50	5·00
683	–	50c. olive-bistre	6·50	5·00
684	–	64c. myrtle-green	9·00	6·50
685	–	75c. red-brown	9·00	6·25
686	–	96c. vermilion	13·50	10·50
687	–	1E. deep violet	13·50	11·00
688	**77**	1E.60 deep greenish blue	18·00	15·00
689	–	3E. purple	50·00	43·00
690	–	4E.50 olive-green	70·00	55·00
691	**77**	10E. carmine	£110	85·00
671/691	Set of 21		£300	£225

Designs: Horiz—3, 5, 15, 46c. Monastery of D. João I. Vert—25, 40, 50, 75c. Philippa de Vilhena arms her sons; 64c., 1E. Don João IV, 1640; 96c., 3E., 4E.50. Independence Monument, Lisbon.

These stamps were issued for compulsory use on certain days instead of the regular issue, and the receipt from the sale was intended to create a fund for a number of objects, notable among which was the purchase of a War Museum.

(78)

79 Ceres

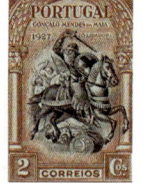
80 Gonçalo Mendes da Maia

1926 (20 Nov). Independence Commemoratives as last surch as T **78**, with bar or bars obliterating old value. Centres in black.
692	–	2c. on 5c. sepia	2·00	1·80
693	–	2c. on 46c. carmine	2·00	1·80
694	–	2c. on 64c. myrtle-green	2·30	2·10
695	–	3c. on 75c. red-brown	2·30	2·10
696	–	3c. on 96c. vermilion	3·50	2·75
697	–	3c. on 1E. deep violet	3·00	2·50
698	**77**	4c. on 1E.60 deep greenish blue	23·00	17·00
699	–	4c. on 3E. purple	8·50	7·00
700	–	6c. on 4E.50 olive-green	8·50	7·00
701	**77**	6c. on 10E. carmine	8·75	7·00
692/701	Set of 10		60·00	45·00

(Eng E. Meronti. Typo De La Rue)

1926 (2 Dec). Ceres type redrawn without imprint below design. P 14.
702	**79**	2c. chocolate	20	20
703		3c. bright blue	20	20
704		4c. orange	20	20
705		5c. grey-brown	20	20
706		6c. chestnut	20	20
707		10c. vermilion	20	20
708		15c. black	45	20
709		16c. bright ultramarine	45	20
710		25c. grey	45	20
711		32c. green	95	55
712		40c. emerald-green	80	20
713		48c. rose	2·00	1·40
714		50c. orange-yellow	3·25	3·00
715		64c. blue	3·25	3·00
716		80c. violet	6·25	75
717		96c. carmine	4·25	1·90
718		1E. plum	19·00	1·60
719		1E.20 yellow-brown	19·00	1·60
720		1E.60 deep blue	4·50	75
721		2E. green	28·00	1·60
722		3E.20 sage-green	12·00	1·60
723		4E.50 yellow	12·00	1·60
724		5E. bistre-brown	£150	5·75
725		10E. scarlet	17·00	3·25
702/725	Set of 24		£275	29·00

(Des A. de Sousa (**80**), A. R. Gameiro (horiz designs), A. de Morais (others). Eng G. Harrison. Recess De La Rue)

1927 (29 Nov). Second Independence issue. Designs as T **80**. Centres in black. P 14.
726	**80**	2c. light brown	40	20
727	–	3c. blue	40	20
728	**80**	4c. orange	40	20
729	–	5c. sepia	40	20
730	–	6c. chestnut	40	20
731	–	15c. agate	90	65
732	–	16c. deep blue	1·90	80
733	**80**	25c. slate	2·10	1·50
734	–	32c. myrtle green	4·75	2·40
735	–	40c. green	1·30	95
736	**80**	48c. carmine-red	20·00	16·00
737	–	80c. deep lilac	14·50	11·00
738	–	96c. vermilion	30·00	22·00
739	–	1E.60 deep turquoise-blue	31·00	23·00
740	–	4E.50 ochre	44·00	34·00
726/740	Set of 15		£125	£110

Designs: Horiz—3, 15, 80c. Guimarães Castle; 6, 32c. Battle of Montijo. Vert—5, 16c., 1E.60, João das Regras; 40, 96c. Brites de Almeida; 4E.50, João Pinto Ribeiro.

The note after No. 691 also applies to this set.

C **81** Hurdler

D **82**

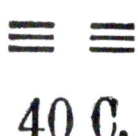
(**83**)

(Des J. Alves. Litho)

1928 (22 May). Olympic Games.
(a) CHARITY TAX. P 12
C741	C **81**	15c. black and dull red	6·00	3·50

(b) POSTAGE DUE. P 12×11½
D741	D **82**	30c. black and pale carmine	3·00	2·75

No. C741 was in use from 22 to 24 May 1928, in default of which the postage due was charged.

1928 (Oct)–**29**. Stamps of 1917–26 surch as T **83**. P 12×11½.
742	**56**	4c. on 8c. salmon (2.29)	85	50
743		4c. on 30c. grey-brown (2.29)	85	50
744		10c. on ¼c. olive-brown	85	50
745		10c. on ½c. black (R.) (12.28)	1·10	65
		a. Perf 15×14	32·00	20·00
		b. Perf 15×14. Thick carton paper	30·00	25·00
		c. Perf 15×14. Bluish paper	1·80	95
746		10c. on 1c. brown (*shades*) (11.28)	1·10	65
		a. Perf 15×14	£140	90·00
747		10c. on 4c. yellow-green (11.28)	85	65
		a. Perf 15×14	£400	£200
		b. Perf 15×14. Thick carton paper	£500	£375
748		10c. on 4c. yellow-orange (11.28)	85	55
749		10c. on 5c. olive-brown	85	55

PORTUGAL

750		15c. on 16c. ultramarine (12.28)	2·10	1·20
751		15c. on 16c. blue (12.28)	2·10	1·20
752		15c. on 20c. chocolate (11.28)	65·00	50·00
753		15c. on 20c. drab (11.28)	85	50
754		15c. on 24c. greenish blue (12.28)	4·00	2·50
755		15c. on 25c. rose-pink (12.28)	85	50
756		15c. on 25c. pale drab (12.28)	85	50
757		16c. on 32c. deep blue-green (1.29)	1·60	1·20
758		40c. on 2c. orange-yellow	85	50
		a. Thick carton paper	£375	£275
759		40c. on 2c. pale yellow (1.29)	8·25	5·00
760		40c. on 2c. chocolate	85	50
761		40c. on 3c. blue (shades)	85	55
762		40c. on 50c. yellow (11.28)	85	50
763		40c. on 60c. blue (11.28)	1·60	1·10
		a. Perf 15×14	18·00	12·50
764		40c. on 64c. cobalt (11.28)	1·60	1·20
765		40c. on 75c. dull rose (1.29)	1·70	1·40
766		40c. on 80c. lilac (1.29)	1·20	80
767		40c. on 90c. cobalt (1.29)	8·25	5·00
		a. Perf 15×14	21·00	14·00
768		40c. on 1E. slate (glazed) (12.28)	1·60	1·20
769		40c. on 1E.10 yellow-brown (11.28)	1·60	1·20
770		80c. on 6c. claret (shades)	1·60	1·10
		a. Thick carton paper	5·75	5·00
771		80c. on 6c. chocolate	1·60	1·10
772		80c. on 48c. carmine-pink	2·30	1·70
773		80c. on 1E.50 pale lilac (3.29)	3·50	1·90
774		96c. on 1E.20 apple-green (12.28)	7·00	4·00
775		96c. on 1E.20 yellow-buff (12.28)	6·75	4·50
776		1E.60 on 2E. deep grey-grn (2.29)	70·00	45·00
777		1E.60 on 2E. grey-green (glazed) (2.29)	75·00	50·00
778		1E.60 on 3E.20 bronze-grn (2.29)	19·00	11·50
779		1E.60 on 20E. turquoise-blue (2.29)	27·00	15·00
742/779 Set of 38			£250	£190

84 Storming of Santarém

CORREIO

(86) Revalidado

1$60

(87)

(Des A. de Sousa (6, 32, 96c.), A. R. Gameiro (3, 5, 15, 40, 80c., 1E.), A. de Morais (others). Eng G. Harrison. Recess De La Rue)

1928 (27 Nov). Third Independence issue. Designs as T **84** (dated 1928). Centres in black. P 14.

780		2c. light blue	60	35
781	**84**	3c. green	60	35
782	–	4c. lake	60	35
783	–	5c. olive	60	35
784	–	6c. red-brown	60	35
785	**84**	15c. slate	1·20	1·10
786	–	16c. purple	1·20	1·10
787	–	25c. bright ultramarine	1·20	1·10
788	–	32c. green	6·25	5·75
789	–	40c. sepia	1·20	1·10
790	–	50c. vermilion	18·00	8·50
791	**84**	80c. grey	18·00	11·00
792	–	96c. scarlet	35·00	23·00
793	–	1E. mauve	60·00	44·00
794	–	1E.60 indigo	23·00	17·00
795	–	4E.50 yellow	24·00	22·00
780/795 Set of 16			£180	£130

Designs: Vert—2, 25c., 1E.60, Gualdim Pass; 6, 32, 96c. Joana de Gouveia; 4E.50, Matias de Albuquerque. Horiz—4, 16, 50c. Battle of Roliça; 5, 40c., 1E. Battle of Atoleiros.
The note after No. 691 also applies to this set.

1929. Stamps of 1917–26 optd with T **86.** P 12×11½.

805	**56**	10c. brown-red	85	50
		a. Chestnut. Perf 15×14	£550	£450
806		15c. black (R.)	85	50
807		40c. sepia	1·20	90
808		40c. emerald-green	1·10	65
810		96c. dull carmine	10·50	6·75
811		1E.60 blue	43·00	27·00
		a. Double overprint	£200	£180
		b. Thin paper	35·00	
805/811 Set of 6			55·00	36·00

1929 (May). Telegraph stamp surch for postage as T **87**. P 12×11½.

812		1E.60 on 5c. red-brown	27·00	17·00
		a. Surch double		
		b. Thin transparent paper	90·00	65·00

1930 (Mar–Dec). Lisbon reissue (with imprint below design). Wove paper. P 12×11½.

813	**56**	4c. orange (Sept)	50	40
814		5c. sepia	50	40
815		6c. brown-red (Apr)	50	40
816		10c. scarlet (Aug)	50	40
817		15c. black	2·50	50
818		25c. olive-drab	95	45
819		25c. deep blue-green (Aug)	95	45
820		32c. deep blue-green	95	45
821		40c. green	3·50	75
823		50c. buff	3·50	1·20
824		50c. brown-red (Sept)	3·50	1·20
826		75c. carmine (Aug)	3·00	1·30
827		80c. myrtle (Aug)	3·00	1·30
829		1E. lake (Apr)	8·25	1·30
830		1E.20 chocolate (Dec)	6·00	1·40
831		1E.20 indigo (Aug)	5·50	1·40
833		2E. bright mauve (Aug)	36·00	10·50
834		4E.50 orange-yellow (Dec)	£100	65·00
813/834 Set of 18			£160	80·00

This issue was printed at the Mint, Lisbon, new plates from the original dies being used for the previously issued denominations. The stamps can be distinguished by much whiter paper and white gum. Some of the figures of value have a much bolder appearance.

88 Camoens' Poem *Lusiad* **89** St. Anthony's Birthplace **90** Dom Nuno Alvares Pereira

(Des P. Guedes. Eng A. Fragoso. Typo)

1931 (Mar)–**38**. P 14.

835	**88**	4c. yellow-brown	45	20
836		5c. sepia	45	20
837		6c. slate-grey (4.31)	45	20
838		10c. mauve	45	30
839		15c. black	45	30
840		16c. light blue	2·30	1·00
841		25c. green	5·75	55
841*a*		25c. light blue (7.34)	6·75	65
841*b*		30c. deep blue-green (6.33)	3·50	65
842		40c. vermilion	11·50	20
843		48c. chestnut (4.31)	2·30	1·60
844		50c. brown	55	20
845		75c. carmine (4.31)	9·75	1·80
846		80c. emerald	80	25
846*a*		95c. carmine (6.33)	31·00	10·00
847		1E. claret (4.31)	60·00	25
848		1E.20 olive-green (4.31)	4·00	1·60
849		1E.25 deep blue	3·75	35
849*a*		1E.60 blue (6.33)	60·00	6·75
849*b*		1E.75 blue (4.38)	1·20	35
850		2E. mauve	1·40	35
851		4E.50 orange (4.31)	3·00	40
852		5E. yellow-green	3·00	40
835/852 Set of 23			£200	25·00

(15c. des and die-eng A. Fragoso; typo. 25c. des A. Lima and die-eng Zimbarra; 75c. to 4E.50, des and die-eng J. Alves; litho)

1931 (13 June). 700th Death Anniv of St. Anthony. T **89** and similar designs. P 12.

853		15c. deep reddish purple	1·60	45
		a. "CORRFIO" for "CORREIO"	19·00	17·00
854		25c. myrtle green and green	1·80	45
855		40c. deep brown and buff	1·60	45
856		75c. brown-rose	55·00	22·00
857		1E.25 greenish slate and pale blue	£100	46·00
858		4E.50 slate-purple and dull mauve	55·00	5·50
853/858 Set of 6			£200	75·00

Designs: Vert—25c. St. Anthony's baptismal font; 40c. Lisbon Cathedral; 75c. St. Anthony; 1E.25, Santa Cruz Cathedral, Coimbra. Horiz—4E.50, The Saint's tomb, Padua.
No. 853a occurs on position 50 in the sheet of 100.

(Des and eng A. Fragoso. Typo)

1931 (1 Nov). Fifth Death Centenary of Nuno Alvares Pereira. P 12×11½.

859	**90**	15c. black	1·90	1·70
860		25c. green (black figures)	10·00	1·70
861		40c. orange	5·25	95
862		75c. carmine	44·00	38·00
863		1E.25 grey-blue and blue	50·00	33·00
864		4E.50 light green and chocolate	£275	85·00
859/864 Set of 6			£375	£150

11

PORTUGAL

D 91

(92)

(Des and eng R. Araújo. Typo)

1932 (14 July)–**33**. POSTAGE DUE. P 11½×12.

D865	D **91**	5c. buff	1·20	90
D866		10c. blue	1·20	90
D867		20c. pink	2·50	1·30
D868		30c. greenish blue	2·75	1·30
D869		40c. emerald	2·75	1·30
D870		50c. grey	3·75	1·30
D871		60c. carmine-pink (30.8.32)	7·50	3·50
D872		80c. maroon	14·00	7·25
D873		1E.20 bronze-green (9.3.33)	23·00	18·00
D865/873 Set of 9			55·00	30·00

1933 (Sept–Oct). Surch as T **92**.

865	**90**	15c. on 40c. orange (Sept)	1·30	75
866		40c. on 15c. black	6·25	3·50
867		40c. on 25c. green (black figures)	1·60	1·20
868		40c. on 75c. carmine	13·50	8·00
869		40c. on 1E.25 grey-blue and blue	13·50	6·00
870		40c. on 4E.50 light green & choc	13·50	6·00
865/870 Set of 6			45·00	18·00

(93)

1933 (Oct). Nos. 853/858 surch as T **93**.

871		15c. on 40c. deep brown and buff	1·70	75
872		40c. on 15c. deep reddish purple	3·50	1·60
		a. "CORRFIO" for "CORREIO"	26·00	18·00
873		40c. on 25c. myrtle green and green	3·00	75
874		40c. on 75c. brown-rose	13·50	8·00
875		40c. on 1E.25 greenish slate & pale blue	13·50	8·00
876		40c. on 4E.50 slate-purple & dull mauve	13·50	8·00
871/876 Set of 6			45·00	25·00

94 President Carmona

95

96 Queen Maria

(Des and eng A. Fragoso. Typo)

1934 (28 May). P 11½×12.

877	**94**	40c. violet	35·00	50

(Des A. Negreiros. Eng A. Fragoso. Typo)

1934 (July). Colonial Exhibition. P 11½×12.

878	**95**	25c. sepia	7·50	1·90
879		40c. scarlet	36·00	60
880		1E.60 blue	75·00	20·00
878/880 Set of 3			£100	20·00

(Des A. Negreiros. Eng R. Araújo. Centre embossed, frame typo)

1935 (1 June). First Portuguese Philatelic Exhibition. P 11½×12.

881	**96**	40c. bright scarlet	2·40	40

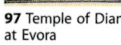
97 Temple of Diana at Evora

98 Prince Henry the Navigator

99 "All for the Nation"

100 Coimbra Cathedral

P **101**

(Des and eng G. Santos (T **97**), A. Fragoso (T **98**).
T **99** des A. Negreiros, eng A. Fragoso. T **100**
eng Institut de Gravure, Paris. Typo)

1935–41. P 11½×12 or 12×11½ (1E.75).

882	**97**	4c. black (22.6.35)	85	30
883		5c. blue (22.6.35)	90	30
884		6c. chocolate (1.1.36)	1·40	50
885	**98**	10c. emerald-green (without accent) (11.35)	13·50	30
		a. With accent on "E" of "PORTUGUÉSA"	13·00	25
886		15c. brown-red (with accent) (5.6.35)	55	30
		a. Without accent on "E" of "PORTUGUESA"	5·00	90
887	**99**	25c. blue (29.8.35)	12·50	65
888		40c. brown (26.12.35)	4·25	20
889		1E. carmine (20.11.35)	20·00	75
890	**100**	1E.75 blue (20.11.35)	£140	1·90
890a	**99**	10E. slate (4.41)	46·00	4·50
890b		20E. greenish blue (4.41)	60·00	3·25
882/890b Set of 11 (cheapest)			£275	10·00

In the first Printing of the 10c. there is no accent on the "E" of "PORTUGUESA"; in the second and third printings the letter is accented. 34 examples in the sheet of 100 of the first printing of the 15c. have the "E" without accent; all positions in the second printing have the accented letter.

(Des A. Negreiros. Die eng A. Fragoso. Typo)

1936 (Jan–Nov). PARCEL POST. P 12×11½.

P891	P **101**	50c. drab	1·10	95
P892		1E. yellow-brown	1·10	95
P893		1E.50 violet	1·10	95
P894		2E. claret	4·75	1·00
P895		2E.50 olive-green	4·75	1·00
P896		4E.50 maroon (Jan)	12·50	1·00
P897		5E. bright violet	18·00	1·20
P898		10E. orange	23·00	2·50
P891/898 Set of 8			60·00	9·00

These were later made valid for use on all classes of mail.

102 Shield and Propeller

(Des A. Negreiros. Eng G. Santos. Typo)

1936 (Nov)–**41**. AIR. P 12×11½.

891	**102**	1E.50 deep blue	1·40	45
892		1E.75 orange-red	2·10	50
893		2E.50 rosine	2·20	50
893a		3E. blue (17.3.41)	31·00	17·00
893b		4E. green (17.3.41)	40·00	25·00
894		5E. bright carmine-lake	3·50	1·70
895		10E. brown-lake	6·50	1·80
895a		15E. orange (17.3.41)	30·00	11·00
896		20E. purple-brown	17·00	4·00
896a		50E. maroon (17.3.41)	£325	£120
891/896a Set of 10			£425	£175

103 Symbol of Medicine

104 Gil Vicente

(O **105**)

PORTUGAL

(Des A. Duarte de Almeida. Typo)

1937 (24 July). Centenary of Medical and Surgical Colleges at Lisbon and Oporto. P 11½×12.
| 897 | **103** | 25c. pale blue | 19·00 | 1·40 |

(Des R. R. Gameiro. Eng A. Fragoso. Typo)

1937. 400th Death Anniv of Gil Vicente (poet). P 11½×12.
| 898 | **104** | 40c. sepia (29 July) | 36·00 | 30 |
| 899 | | 1E. scarlet (Aug) | 4·50 | 30 |

1938 (June). OFFICIAL. Optd with Type O **105**.
| O900 | **99** | 40c. brown | 90 | 20 |

  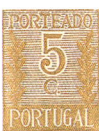

106 Grapes   **107** Cross of Avis   D **108**

(Des J. Rocha. Die-eng G. A. Araújo. Typo)

1938. Wine and Raisin Congress. P 11½.
900	**106**	15c. bright violet (8.11.38)	2·50	95
901		25c. brown (27.10.38)	5·00	2·40
902		40c. magenta (24.10.38)	17·00	50
903		1E.75 light blue (11.11.38)	55·00	40·00
900/903 Set of 4			70·00	40·00

(Des A. Lima. Die-eng G. A. Araújo. Typo)

1940 (27 Jan). Portuguese Legion. P 11½×12.
904	**107**	5c. buff	80	35
905		10c. violet	80	35
906		15c. light blue	80	35
907		25c. brown	44·00	1·50
908		40c. green	70·00	60
909	**107**	80c. yellow-green	3·75	1·00
910		1E. scarlet	£100	5·75
911		1E.75 dark blue	17·00	4·00
904/911 Set of 8			£200	13·00
MS911a 155×170 mm. Nos. 904/11 (sold at 5E.50)			£700	£1200

(Des A. Duarte de Almeida. Eng G. Santos. Typo)

1940 (1 Feb)–**65**. POSTAGE DUE.

(a) P 14
D912	D **108**	5c. bistre-brown	95	60
D913		10c. bright lilac	80	50
D914		20c. carmine	80	50
D915		30c. bright violet	80	50
D916		40c. magenta	80	50
D917		50c. greenish blue	80	50
D918		60c. emerald-green	80	50
D919		80c. scarlet	80	50
D920		1E. brown	1·60	50
D921		2E. mauve	2·50	1·10
D922		5E. yellow-orange	20·00	14·00
D912/922 Set of 11			28·00	18·00

(b) P 12½ (Dec 1955–1965)
D923	D **108**	10c. bright lilac	50	25
D924		20c. rose-lilac	50	25
D925		30c. bright violet (1957)	50	25
D926		40c. magenta	50	25
D927		50c. greenish blue	50	25
D928		60c. green (1959)	50	25
D929		80c. scarlet (1959)	50	25
D930		1E. brown	50	25
D931		2E. mauve	70	60
D932		5E. orange (1965)	£250	£180
D923/932 Set of 10			£250	£180

109 Portuguese World Exhibition   **110** Statue of King João IV

111 Monument of Discoveries, Belém   **112** King Afonso Henriques

(Des Martins Barata (**109**), H. Franco (**110**), Maria Keil de Amaral (**111**), A. de Sousa (**112**). Eng Pedroso (**109**, 111/12) and Renato Araújo (all). Recess Bank of Portugal)

1940 (4 June–1 Dec). Portuguese Centenaries. P 12×11½ (T **109**). 11½×12 (**110**/2).
912	**109**	10c. maroon (24 Oct)	45	35
913	**110**	15c. greenish blue (1 Dec)	45	35
914	**111**	25c. grey-olive (July)	2·20	45
915	**110**	35c. yellow-green (1 Dec)	2·00	60
916	**112**	40c. bistre-brown	4·75	30
917	**109**	80c. purple (24 Oct)	9·75	55
918	**111**	1e. scarlet (July)	23·00	2·40
919	**112**	1e.75 ultramarine	13·50	4·00
912/919 Set of 8			55·00	8·00
MS919a 160×229 mm. Nos. 912/9. (sold at 10E.)			£325	£500

113 Sir Rowland Hill   **114** Fish-woman of Nazaré   **115** Caravel

(Des P. Guedes. Die-eng A. Fragoso. Typo)

1940 (12 Aug). Centenary of First Adhesive Postage Stamps. P 11½×12.
920	**113**	15c. brown-purple	50	25
921		25c. brown-red	50	25
922		35c. green	50	25
923		40c. claret	90	25
924		50c. bluish green	36·00	6·25
925		80c. light blue	3·50	1·80
926		1E. scarlet	43·00	5·75
927		1E.75 deep blue	9·75	5·50
920/927 Set of 8			90·00	16·00
MS928 160×152 mm. Nos. 920/7 (sold at 10E.)			£150	£300

(Des R. R. Gameiro (4c., 5c., 10c, 15c., 1E., 2E.); A. Duarte de Almeida (others). Die-eng G. Santos (4c., 40c., 2E.); G. A. Araújo (5c., 25c.); Renato Araújo (10c.); M. Norte (15c.); A. Fragoso (80c., 1E., 1E.75). Typo)

1941 (4 Apr). As T **114** (costumes). P 11½.
932		4c. blue-green	40	30
933		5c. red-brown	40	30
934		10c. purple	5·50	1·70
935		15c. yellow-green	40	40
936		25c. purple	4·50	90
937		40c. green	40	30
938		80c. light blue	7·25	3·25
939		1E. scarlet	21·00	2·50
940		1E.75 blue	22·00	7·25
941		2E. red-orange	85·00	38·00
932/941 Set of 10			£125	50·00
MS941a 163×146 mm. Nos. 932/41. (sold at 10E.)			£250	£250

Designs:—5c. Woman from Coimbra; 10c. Vine-grower of Saloio; 15c. Fish-woman of Lisbon; 25c. Woman of Olhão; 40c. Woman of Aveiro; 80c. Shepherdess of Madeira; 1E. Spinner of Viana do Castelo; 1E.75, Horsebreeder of Ribatejo; 2E. Reaper of Alentejo.

(Des Martins Barata. Die-eng G. A. Araújo. Typo)

1943–49. P 14.
942	**115**	5c. black	35	20
943		10c. chestnut	35	20
944		15c. grey	35	20
945		20c. violet	35	20
946		30c. brown-purple	35	20
947		35c. blue-green	40	20

PORTUGAL

948	50c. purple		40	20
948a	80c. green (4.49)		6·75	60
949	1E. carmine		14·00	20
949a	1E. dull lilac (27.12.48)		4·25	35
949b	1E.20 carmine (4.49)		6·75	45
949c	1E.50 olive-green (7.49)		55·00	55
950	1E.75 indigo		40·00	20
950a	1E.80 yellow-orange (7.49)		60·00	5·25
951	2E. purple-brown		3·00	20
951a	2E. blue (1.49)		8·75	65
952	2E.50 rose-red		4·75	20
953	3E.50 greenish blue		20·00	70
953a	4E. orange (7.49)		90·00	3·75
954	5E. brown-red		2·75	35
954a	6E. yellow-green (7.49)		£170	6·00
954b	7E.50 deep green (3.49)		60·00	5·50
955	10E. blue-grey		5·00	35
956	15E. emerald-green		55·00	1·60
957	20E. grey-olive		£200	95
958	50E. red		£550	1·50
942/958 *Set of 26*			£1200	25·00

116 Labourer

117 Mounted Postal Courier

118 Felix Avellar Brotero

(Des M. Costa and A. D. de Almeida. Typo)

1943 (Oct). First Congress of Agricultural Science. P 11½×12.

959	**116**	10c. blue	1·50	50
960		50c. carmine	2·40	55

(Des A. de Sousa. Eng A.Fragoso. Typo)

1944. Third National Philatelic Exhibition, Lisbon. P 11½×12.

961	**117**	10c. chocolate (26 May)	50	25
962		50c. violet (20 May)	50	25
963		1E. carmine-red (22 May)	6·00	1·10
964		1E.75 deep dull blue (20 May)	6·00	2·50
961/964 *Set of 4*			12·00	3·75
MS964a 82×121 mm. Nos. 961/4 (sold at 7E.50)			70·00	£350

(Des Martins Barata. Eng G. A. Araújo (10c., 1E.75). M. Norte (50c., 1E.). Typo)

1944 (23 Nov). Birth Bicentenary of Avellar Brotero (botanist). T **118** and similar vert design. P 11½×12.

965	**118**	10c. deep brown	45	25
966	–	50c. deep green	2·20	25
967		1E. carmine-red	14·50	2·20
968	**118**	1E.75 deep blue	11·00	4·50
965/968 *Set of 4*			25·00	6·50
MS968a 144×195 mm. Nos. 965/8 (sold at 7E.50)			85·00	£200

Design:—50c., 1E. Brotero's Statue, Coimbra.

120 Vasco da Gama

121 President Carmona

(Des M. Barata. Eng M. Farré (50c., 2E.), R. G. Godbehear (1E.75, 3E.50), E. T. Dawson (others). Recess Bradbury, Wilkinson)

1945 (29 July). Portuguese Navigators. T **120** and similar vert designs. P 13×13½.

969		10c. chocolate	45	25
970		30c. brown-orange	45	25
971		35c. green	95	40
972		50c. olive	2·75	45

973		1E. red	7·25	1·10
974		1E.75 blue	9·25	3·25
975		2E. black	11·00	3·75
976		3E.50 carmine	22·00	6·50
969/976 *Set of 8*			50·00	12·00
MS976a 167×173 mm. Nos. 969/76 (sold at 15E.)			75·00	£200

Portraits:—10c., Gil Eanes; 30c. João Gonçalves Zarco; 35c. Bartolomeu Dias; 1E. Pedro Alvares Cabral; 1E.75, Fernão de Magelhães (Magellan); 2E. Frey Gonçalo Velho; 3E.50, Diogo Cão.

(Photo Courvoisier)

1945 (12 Nov). P 11½.

977	**121**	10c. violet	60	35
978		30c. red-brown	60	35
979		35c. blue-green	55	35
980		50c. olive-green	1·20	35
981		1E. brown-red	24·00	2·20
982		1E.75 blue	20·00	6·00
983		2E. maroon	£120	8·00
984		3E.50 greenish slate	80·00	12·00
977/984 *Set of 8*			£225	25·00
MS984a 136×98 mm. Nos. 977/84 (sold at 15E.)			£325	£350

122

123 Almourol Castle

(Des M. Barata. Eng G. A. Araújo. Typo)

1945 (27 Dec). Naval School Centenary. P 11½×12.

985	**122**	10c. light green	65	25
986		50c. deep grey-green	85	25
987		1E. carmine-red	7·25	1·40
988		1E.75 royal blue	7·75	4·50
985/988 *Set of 4*			16·00	5·00
MS988a 115×134 mm. Nos. 985/8 (sold at 7E.50)			75·00	£200

(Des C. Telmo. Eng K. Bickel. Recess Courvoisier)

1946 (1 June). Portuguese Castles. T **123** and similar designs. P 11½.

989		10c. purple (Silves)	40	35
990		30c. purple-brown (Leiria)	65	35
991		35c. grey-olive (Feira)	90	35
992		50c. grey (Guimarães)	1·50	35
993		1E. carmine (T **123**)	50·00	1·90
994		1E.75 blue (Lisbon)	32·00	3·75
995		2E. blue-green (Braganza)	£100	6·50
996		3E.50 reddish brown (Ourém)	46·00	8·50
989/996 *Set of 8*			£225	20·00
MS996a 135×102 mm. 1E.75, grey-blue/*buff* (block of 4) (sold at 12E.50)			£275	£450

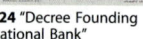
124 "Decree Founding National Bank"

125 Madonna and Child

(Des Martins Barata. Eng Renato Araújo. Recess Bank of Portugal)

1946 (19 Nov). Centenary of Bank of Portugal. P 12×11½.

997	**124**	50c. indigo	1·20	40
MS997a 156×144 mm. No. 997 (block of four) (sold at 7E.50)			£250	£350

(Des Martins Barata. Eng M. Ferré. Recess Bradbury, Wilkinson)

1946 (8 Dec). Tercentenary of Proclamation of St. Mary of Castile as Patron Saint of Portugal. P 13½.

998	**125**	30c. slate	75	35
999		50c. dull green	50	35
1000		1E. carmine	5·00	1·70
1001		1E.75 blue	8·00	3·25
998/1001 *Set of 4*			13·00	5·00
MS1001a 108×158 mm. Nos. 998/1001 on bluish grey paper (sold at 7E.50)			90·00	£200

PORTUGAL

126 Caramulo Shepherdess **127** Surrender of the Keys of Lisbon

(Des Mello e Castro. Photo Courvoisier)

1947 (1 Mar). As T **126** (regional costumes). P 11½.
1002	10c. mauve	40	25
1003	30c. brown-red	40	25
1004	35c. olive-green	80	25
1005	50c. chocolate	1·30	25
1006	1E. rose-red	29·00	1·00
1007	1E.75 ultramarine	31·00	6·25
1008	2E. blue	£110	7·25
1009	3E.50 blackish green	75·00	25·00
1002/1009	Set of 8	£225	25·00
MS1009*a* 135×98 mm. Nos. 1002/9 (sold at 15E.)		£325	£400

Designs:—30c. Malpique timbrel player; 35c. Monsanto flautist; 50c. Woman of Avintes; 1E. Maia field labourer; 1E.75, Woman of Algarve; 2E. Miranda do Douro bastonet player; 3E.50, Woman of the Azores.

(Des Martins Barata. Eng Renato Araújo. Recess Waterlow)

1947 (13 Oct). 800th Anniv of Recapture of Lisbon from the Moors. P 12½.
1010	**127**	5c. blue-green	40	30
1011		20c. carmine	65	30
1012		50c. violet	95	30
1013		1E.75 blue	11·50	7·50
1014		2E.50 reddish brown	16·00	9·50
1015		3E.50 black	31·00	20·00
1010/1015	Set of 6		55·00	35·00

128 St. João de Brito **130** "Architecture and Engineering"

(Des Martins Barata. Eng Renato Araújo. Recess Bank of Portugal)

1948 (28 May). Birth Tercentenary of St. João de Brito. T **128** and similar vert design. P 11½×12.
1016	**128**	30c. deep dull green	40	35
1017	–	50c. blackish brown	40	35
1018	**128**	1E. bright carmine	16·00	2·50
1019	–	1E.75 blue	20·00	4·25
1016/1019	Set of 4		30·00	7·00

Design:—50c., 1E.75, St. João de Brito (*different*).

(Des Cottinelli Telmo. Eng Renato Araújo. Recess Bank of Portugal)

1948 (28 May). Exhibition of Public Works and National Congress of Engineering and Architecture. P 13½×12½.
1020	**130**	50c. claret	1·60	45

131 King João I **132** Statue of Angel **133** Hands and Letter

(Des P. Guedes. Photo Courvoisier)

1949 (6 May). Portraits, as T **131**, of the Avis Dynasty and its supporters. P 11½.
1021	10c. violet and buff	75	35
1022	30c. blue-green and buff	75	35
1023	35c. blackish green and olive	1·50	35
1024	50c. blue and light blue	2·40	35
1025	1E. lake and brown-red	2·50	35
1026	1E.75 violet-black and grey	45·00	18·00
1027	2E. blue and grey-blue	28·00	3·00
1028	3E.50 chocolate and sepia	90·00	33·00
1021/1028	Set of 8	£150	50·00
MS1028*a* 136×98 mm. Nos. 1021/8 (sold for 15E.) (27.8.49)		£100	£120

Portraits:—30c. Queen Philippa; 35c. Prince Fernando; 50c. Prince Henry the Navigator; 1E. Nun' Alvares; 1E.75, João da Regras; 2E. Fernão Lopes; 3E.50, Afonso Domingues.

(Des M. Barata. Eng K. Seizinger. Recess J. Enschedé)

1949 (20 Dec). Sixteenth Congress of the History of Art. P 12½×14.
1029	**132**	1E. red-brown	18·00	30
1030		5E. olive-brown	4·75	55

(Des C. da Costa Pinto. Eng R. Araújo. Recess De La Rue)

1949 (29 Dec). 75th Anniv of Universal Postal Union. P 13×13½.
1031	**133**	1E. deep rose-lilac	55	25
1032		2E. deep blue	1·60	35
1033		2E.50 bottle green	9·25	1·60
1034		4E. lake-brown	25·00	6·00
1031/1034	Set of 4		30·00	7·50

134 Our Lady of Fatima **135** Saint and Invalid **136** G. Junqueiro

(Des M. Barata. Eng R. Araújo. Recess Bank of Portugal)

1950 (13 May). Holy Year. P 11½×12.
1035	**134**	50c. deep green	1·10	40
1036		1E. reddish brown	5·00	45
1037		2E. blue	10·50	3·25
1038		5E. deep reddish lilac	£160	44·00
1035/1038	Set of 4		£150	42·00

(Des M. Barata. Eng R. Araújo. Recess Bank of Portugal)

1950 (30 Oct). 400th Death Anniv of San Juan de Dios. P 11½×12.
1039	**135**	20c. violet	75	35
1040		50c. carmine	1·20	45
1041		1E. olive-green	2·75	60
1042		1E.50 orange	35·00	5·25
1043		2E. blue	28·00	4·00
1044		4E. reddish brown	80·00	12·50
1039/1044	Set of 6		£140	20·00

(Des P. Guedes. Litho)

1951 (2 Mar). Birth Centenary of G. Junqueiro (poet). P 13½.
1045	**136**	50c. brown	9·00	55
1046		1E. deep blue	2·75	50

137 Fisherman **138** Dove and Olive Branch

(Des D. Rebelo. Litho)

1951 (9 Mar). Fisheries Congress. P 13½.
1047	**137**	50c. green/*buff*	8·50	85
1048		1E. purple/*buff*	2·00	20

(Des M. Barata. Litho)

1951 (11 Oct). Termination of Holy Year. T **138** and horiz portrait inscr "ANO. SANTO. 1951". P 13½.
1049	**138**	20c. brown and buff	85	40
1050		90c. olive-green and yellow	20·00	2·75
1051	–	1E. maroon and pink	18·00	45
1052		2E.30 slate-green and pale blue	22·00	3·25
1049/1052	Set of 4		55·00	6·00

Portrait:—1E., 2E.30, Pope Pius XII.

PORTUGAL

139 Fifteenth-Century Colonists   **140** Revolutionaries

(Des M. Barata. Litho)

1951 (24 Oct). Fifth Centenary of Colonization of Terceira. Azores. P 13½.
| 1053 | **139** | 50c. blue/*flesh* | 5·50 | 75 |
| 1054 | | 1E. brown/*buff* | 2·75 | 70 |

(Des D. Rebelo. Litho)

1951 (22 Nov). 25th Anniv of National Revolution. P 13½.
| 1055 | **140** | 1E. purple-brown | 15·00 | 40 |
| 1056 | | 2E.30 indigo | 11·50 | 2·00 |

141 Coach of King João VI   **142** "N.A.T.O."

(Des C. da Costa Pinto. Recess Bradbury, Wilkinson)

1952 (8 Jan). National Coach Museum. T **141** and similar horiz designs inscr "MUSEU NACIONAL DOS COCHES". P 13×13½.
1057	–	10c. purple	40	30
1058	**141**	20c. olive	40	30
1059	–	50c. blue-green	1·20	30
1060	–	90c. emerald	4·75	2·40
1061	–	1E. orange	2·10	35
1062	–	1E.40 carmine-rose	11·00	6·50
1063	**141**	1E.50 lake-brown	9·75	3·50
1064	–	2E.30 blue	6·25	3·25
1057/1064 *Set of 8*			30·00	15·00

Designs:—10, 90c. Coach of King Felippe II; 50c., 1E.40, Coach of Papal Nuncio to João V; 1E., 2E.30, Coach of King José.

(Des C. da Costa Pinto. Litho)

1952 (4 Apr). Third Anniv of North Atlantic Treaty Organization. P 12½.
1065	**142**	1E. green and blackish green	16·00	65
		a. Imperf (pair)		
1066		3E.50 grey and royal blue	£500	34·00

143 Hockey Players   O **144**

(Des Martins Barata. Litho)

1952 (28 June). 8th World Roller-skating Hockey Championship. P 13½.
| 1067 | **143** | 1E. black and deep blue | 6·00 | 35 |
| 1068 | | 3E.50 black and purple-brown | 10·50 | 3·50 |

(Des Martins Barata. Litho)

1952 (Sept)–**75**. OFFICIAL. No value. P 12½.
| O1069 | O **144** | (1E.) black and stone | 90 | 15 |
| O1070 | | (1E.) black & yellow-ochre (1975) | 1·00 | 35 |

On No. O1069 "CORREIO DE PORTUGAL" is in stone on a black background, on No. O1070 it is in black on the yellow-ochre background.

144 Prof. G. Teixeira   **145** Marshal Carmona Bridge

(Des P. Guedes. Litho Litografia Nacional, Oporto)

1952 (25 Nov). Birth Centenary of Prof. Gomes Teixeira (mathematician). P 14.
| 1069 | **144** | 1E. cerise and pink | 1·50 | 35 |
| 1070 | | 2E.30 deep blue and pale blue | 11·50 | 6·50 |

(Des V. R. Camelo. Litho)

1952 (10 Dec). Centenary of Ministry of Public Works. T **145** and similar horiz designs. P 12½.
1071		1E. red-brown/*stone*	1·20	40
1072		1E.40 deep purple/*stone*	20·00	7·25
1073		2E. deep green/*stone*	12·50	4·50
1074		3E.50 indigo/*stone*	21·00	6·25
1071/1074 *Set of 4*			50·00	16·00

Designs:—1E.40, 28th May Stadium; 2E. Coimbra University; 3E.50, Salazar Barrage.

146 St. Francis Xavier   **147** Medieval Knight   **148** St. Martin of Dume

(Des M. Lapa. Eng Pais Ferreira. Recess Bank of Portugal)

1952 (23 Dec). Fourth Death Centenary of St. Francis Xavier. P 13½.
1075	**146**	1E. turquoise-blue	1·00	40
1076		2E. deep claret	2·75	80
1077		3E.50 dull ultramarine	38·00	18·00
1078		5E. deep lilac	75·00	6·50
1075/1078 *Set of 4*			£100	22·00

(Des Martins Barata. Litho)

1953 (10 Jan)–**71**. P 12½.
1079	**147**	5c. bronze-green/*yellow*	40	20
1080		10c. deep violet-grey/*pink*	40	20
1081		20c. orange/*yellow*	40	20
1081*a*		30c. reddish purple/*buff* (22.11.55)	50	20
1082		50c. black	40	20
1083		90c. green/*yellow*	29·00	1·10
		a. Thin paper (1967)	25·00	1·10
1084		1E. lake-brown/*pink*	70	20
1085		1E.40 rose-red	29·00	1·60
		a. Thin paper (1967)	29·00	1·60
1086		1E.50 brown-red/*yellow*	90	20
1087		2E. greenish black	1·40	20
1088		2E.30 blue	45·00	1·30
		a. Thin paper (1967)	35·00	1·50
1089		2E.50 greenish black/*pink*	2·50	25
1089*a*		2E.50 olive-green/*yellow*	2·50	25
1090	**147**	5E. purple/*yellow*	2·50	25
1091		10E. deep turquoise-blue/*yellow*	11·00	35
1092		20E. orange-brown/*yellow*	22·00	50
1093		50E. lilac	15·00	70
1079/93 *Set of 18*			£150	7·25

After Nos. 1083, 1085 and 1088 had been off sale for some time they were reprinted in 1967 to enable complete sets to be sold. Besides being on thinner paper these reissues can be distinguished by their gum which is appreciably whiter.

(Des M. Lapa. Litho Litografia de Portugal, Lisbon)

1953 (26 Feb). Fourteenth Centenary of Landing of St. Martin of Dume on Iberian Peninsula. P 13½.
| 1094 | **148** | 1E. black and grey | 2·50 | 35 |
| 1095 | | 3E.50 sepia and yellow | 20·00 | 8·25 |

149 G. Gomes Fernandes   **150** Club Emblems, 1903 and 1953

(Des P. Guedes. Litho Litografia Maia, Oporto)

1953 (28 Mar). Birth Centenary of G. Gomes Fernandes (fire-brigade chief). P 13.
| 1096 | **149** | 1E. reddish purple and cream | 1·50 | 35 |
| 1097 | | 2E.30 blue and cream | 20·00 | 8·75 |

PORTUGAL

(Des C. da Costa Pinto. Litho)
1953 (15 Apr). 50th Anniv of Portuguese Automobile Club. P 12½.
| 1098 | **150** | 1E. deep green and pale green | 1·20 | 40 |
| 1099 | | 3E.50 sepia and buff | 21·00 | 8·50 |

151 Princess St. Joan   **152** Queen Maria II

(Des M. Barata. Litho Litografia Nacional, Oporto)
1953 (14 May). Fifth Centenary of Birth of Princess St. Joan. P 14½.
| 1100 | **151** | 1E. black and pale green | 2·75 | 35 |
| 1101 | | 3E.50 deep blue and light blue | 21·00 | 10·00 |

(Des M. Barata. Photo Enschedé)
1953 (3 Oct). Centenary of First Portuguese Postage Stamps. P 14×13.
1102	**152**	50c. brown-lake and gold	40	35
1103		1E. chocolate and gold	40	35
1104		1E.40 slate-purple and gold	4·00	1·40
1105		2E.30 Prussian blue and gold	7·50	3·25
1106		3E.50 deep blue and gold	7·50	3·25
1107		4E.50 deep bluish green and gold	13·00	2·40
1108		5E. deep olive and gold	15·00	2·10
1109		20E. reddish violet and gold	£110	12·50
1102/1109	Set of 8		£140	22·00

153   **154**

(Des Martins Barata. Litho)
1954 (22 Sept). 150th Anniv of Trade Secretariat. P 13½.
| 1110 | **153** | 1E. greenish blue and light blue | 1·10 | 25 |
| 1111 | | 1E.50 sepia and buff | 4·75 | 1·00 |

(Des C. da Costa Pinto. Litho)
1954 (15 Oct). People's Education Plan. P 13½.
1112	**154**	50c. greenish blue & turquoise-blue	60	25
1113		1E. red and pink	60	25
1114		2E. deep green and green	55·00	1·70
1115		2E.50 reddish brn & yellow-brn	47·00	2·40
1112/1115	Set of 4		95·00	4·00

155 Cadet and College Banner   **156** Father Manuel da Nobrega

(Des C. da Costa Pinto. Litho)
1954 (17 Nov). 150th Anniv of Military College. P 13½.
| 1116 | **155** | 1E. brown and dull yellow-green | 2·50 | 35 |
| 1117 | | 3E.50 deep blue & dull yellow-grn | 11·00 | 4·25 |

(Des Martins Barata. Eng Professor Baiardi. Recess Enschedé)
1954 (17 Dec). Fourth Centenary of São Paulo. P 14×13.
1118	**156**	1E. red-brown	1·20	40
1119		2E.30 deep blue	95·00	37·00
1120		3E.50 deep dull green	25·00	4·50
1121		5E. deep green	80·00	7·25
1118/1121	Set of 4		£180	45·00

157 King Sancho I, 1154–1211   **158** Telegraph Poles   **159** A. J. Ferreira da Silva

(Des Antonio Lino. Recess Bradbury, Wilkinson)
1955 (17 Mar). Portuguese Kings. Various vert portraits as T **157**. P 13½×13.
1122		10c. purple (Afonso I)	45	35
1123		20c. grey-green	45	35
1124		50c. deep turquoise-blue (Afonso II)	55	35
1125		90c. bluish green (Sancho II)	8·00	2·20
1126		1E. lake-brown (Afonso III)	2·10	40
1127		1E.40 carmine (King Diniz)	16·00	5·50
1128		1E.50 brown-olive (Afonso IV)	5·25	1·70
1129		2E. orange-red (Pedro I)	18·00	6·50
1130		2E.30 deep ultram (King Fernando)	14·50	4·25
1122/1130	Set of 9		60·00	18·00

(Des C. da Costa Pinto. Litho)
1955 (16 Sept). Centenary of Electric Telegraph System in Portugal. P 13½.
1131	**158**	1E. brown-lake and ochre	1·10	35
1132		2E.30 deep turquoise-bl & dull grn	42·00	6·25
1133		3E.50 blue-green and olive-yellow	41·00	4·75
1131/1133	Set of 3		80·00	10·00

(Des C. da Costa Pinto. Litho)
1956 (3 May). Birth Centenary of Ferreira da Silva (teacher). P 13½.
| 1134 | **159** | 1E. deep blue, slate-blue and azure | 95 | 35 |
| 1135 | | 2E.30 deep green, emer & pale grn | 25·00 | 7·75 |

160 Steam Locomotive, 1856   **161** Madonna and Child

(Des F. George. Litho)
1956 (28 Oct). Centenary of Portuguese Railways. T **160** and similar horiz design. P 13½.
1136	**160**	1E. olive-green and blackish green	85	35
1137	–	1E.50 greenish bl & turquoise-grn	19·00	80
1138	–	2E. chestnut and bistre	50·00	2·20
1139	**160**	2E.50 brown and deep brown	70·00	3·00
1136/1139	Set of 4		£125	5·75

Design:—1E.50, 2E. Class 2500 electric locomotive, 1956.

(Des M. Barata. Litho)
1956 (8 Dec). Mothers' Day. P 13×13½.
| 1140 | **161** | 1E. sage-green and deep dull green | 85 | 20 |
| 1141 | | 1E.50 pale olive-brown and brown | 2·10 | 40 |

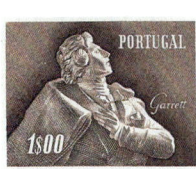

162 Almeida Garrett (writer) (after Barata Feyo)   **163** Cesario Verde

(Des and eng F. Lorber. Recess State Printing Works, Vienna)
1957 (7 Mar). Almeida Garrett Commemoration. P 13½×14.
1142	**162**	1E. deep brown	1·20	35
1143		2E.30 deep lilac	70·00	17·00
1144		3E.50 deep green	24·00	1·80
1145		5E. carmine-red	£130	16·00
1142/1145	Set of 4		£200	30·00

17

PORTUGAL

(Des J. Gil. Litho)
1957 (12 Dec). Cesario Verde (poet) Commemoration. P 13½.
1146	163	1E. brown, buff and yellow-olive	65	25
1147		3E.30 black, olive and dull green	3·25	1·80

164 Exhibition Emblem   **165** St. Elizabeth

(Des J. de A. Negreiros. Litho)
1958 (7 Apr). Brussels International Exhibition. P 13½.
1148	164	1E. red, blue, yellow and green	55	25
1149		3E.30 red, blue, yellow and brown	2·75	2·00

(Des Martins Barata from bas-reliefs by Barata Feyo. Photo Harrison)
1958 (10 July). St. Elizabeth and St. Teotonio Commemoration. T **165** and similar vert portrait. P 14½×14.
1150	165	1E. brown-lake and cream	45	30
1151	–	2E. bottle green and cream	85	60
1152	165	2E.50 reddish violet and cream	7·25	1·30
1153	–	5E. reddish brown and cream	12·00	1·60
1150/1153	Set of 4		18·00	3·50

Portrait:—2E., 5E. St. Teotonio.

166 Institute of Tropical Medicine, Lisbon   **167** Liner

(Des A. Duarte de Almeida. Litho)
1958 (4 Sept). Sixth International Congress of Tropical Medicine. P 13½.
1154	166	1E. deep green and drab	3·25	40
1155		2E.50 blue and bluish grey	13·00	2·20

(Des J. de Moura. Litho)
1958 (27 Nov). Second National Merchant Navy Congress. P 13½.
1156	167	1E. light brown, yellow-brn & sepia	7·50	40
1157		4E.50 bluish vio, lavender & deep bl	10·50	3·50

168 Queen Leonora   **169** Arms of Aveiro

(Des C. da Costa Pinto. Litho)
1958 (17 Dec). 500th Birth Anniv of Queen Leonora. P 13½.
1158	168	1E. turquoise, bistre, chestnut & blk	45	25
1159		1E.50 turquoise, bistre, blue & blk	6·50	1·00
1160		2E.30 turquoise, bistre, grn & blk	5·75	2·10
1161		4E.10 turquoise, bistre, grey & blk	5·75	2·10
1158/1161	Set of 4		17·00	5·00

(Des A. Duarte de Almeida. Litho)
1959 (30 Aug). Millenary of Aveiro. P 13½.
1162	169	1E. dull purple, grey, gold, silver and greenish yellow	2·10	40
1163		5E. deep green, grey, gold, silver and pink	22·00	3·00

170   **171** "Doorway to Peace"

(Des C. da Costa Pinto. Litho)
1960 (2 Mar). Tenth Anniv of North Atlantic Treaty Organization. P 12½.
1164	170	1E. black and reddish lilac	55	35
1165		3E.50 black-green and grey	5·25	2·75

(Des A. Negreiros. Litho)
1960 (7 Apr). World Refugee Year. P 13½.
1166	171	20c. yellow, blk, greenish yell & brn	25	20
1167		1E. yellow, black, pale green & blue	80	20
1168		1E.80 yellow, black and green	1·70	1·40
1166/1168	Set of 3		2·50	1·50

172 Glider   **173** Padre Cruz (after M. Barata)

(Des M. Morais. Litho)
1960 (2 May). 50th Anniv of Portuguese Aero Club. T **172** and similar horiz designs. Multicoloured. P 13½.
1169		1E. Type **172**	40	35
1170		1E.50 Light monoplane	1·30	45
1171		2E. Airplane and parachutes	2·10	1·10
1172		2E.50 Model glider	3·75	1·60
1169/1172	Set of 4		7·00	3·25

(Des J. P. Roque. Litho)
1960 (18 July). Death Centenary of Padre Cruz. P 13½.
1173	173	1E. brown	70	35
1174		4E.30 greenish blue	13·50	10·00

174 University Seal   **175** Prince Henry's Arms

(Des A. Cardoso. Litho)
1960 (18 July). 400th Anniv of University of Evora. P 13½.
1175	174	50c. deep ultramarine	40	25
1176		1E. red-brown and yellow	60	25
1177		1E.40 claret	4·25	2·40
1175/1177	Set of 3		5·00	2·50

(Des J. P. Roque. Photo Courvoisier)
1960 (4 Aug). Fifth Centenary of Death of Prince Henry the Navigator. T **175** and similar vert designs inscr "1460–1960". Multicoloured. P 13½.
1178		1E. Type **175**	55	35
1179		2E.50 15th-century Caravel	4·75	55
1180		3E.50 Prince Henry the Navigator	6·00	2·10
1181		5E. Motto	15·00	1·20
1182		8E. 15th-century Barketta	6·25	1·20
1183		10E. Map showing Sagres	21·00	3·00
1178/1183	Set of 6		50·00	7·75

PORTUGAL

175a Conference Emblem   176 Emblems of Prince Henry and Lisbon

(Des R. Rahikainen. Litho)

1960 (16 Sept). Europa. P 13½.
| 1184 | 175a | 1E. light blue and blue | 45 | 35 |
| 1185 | | 3E.50 rose-red and brown-lake | 5·25 | 3·00 |

(Des S. Rodrigues. Litho)

1960 (17 Nov). Fifth National Philatelic Exhibition, Lisbon. P 13½.
| 1186 | 176 | 1E. ultramarine, black and olive | 60 | 35 |
| 1187 | | 3E.30 ultramarine, black & light bl | 8·75 | 5·50 |

177 Portuguese Flag   178 King Pedro V

(Des M. Rodrigues. Litho)

1960 (20 Dec). 50th Anniv of Republic. P 13½.
| 1188 | 177 | 1E. red, green, orange and black | 50 | 15 |

(Des A. Duarte de Almeida. Eng Baiardi. Recess Enschedé)

1961 (3 Aug). Centenary of Lisbon University Faculty of Letters. P 13×12½.
| 1189 | 178 | 1E. deep bluish green and sepia | 75 | 30 |
| 1190 | | 6E.50 sepia and deep blue | 5·00 | 1·40 |

179 Arms of Setubal   180

(Des C. da Costa Pinto. Litho)

1961 (24 Aug). Centenary of Setubal (city). P 12×11½.
| 1191 | 179 | 1E. multicoloured | 80 | 30 |
| 1192 | | 4E.30 multicoloured | 29·00 | 9·00 |

(Des M. Rodrigues. Litho)

1961 (18 Sept). Europa. P 13½.
1193	180	1E. pale blue, blue and deep blue	35	35
1194		1E.50 pale green, green & deep grn	2·00	1·80
1195		3E.50 pink, red and lake	2·30	2·10
1193/1195 Set of 3			4·50	4·00

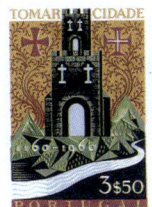  

181 Tomar Gateway   182 National Guardsman   183 St. Gabriel

(Des C. da Costa Pinto. Litho)

1962 (26 Jan). Eighth Centenary of Tomar. T **181** and similar vert designs. P 11½×12.
| 1196 | | 1E. multicoloured | 35 | 25 |
| 1197 | | 3E.50 multicoloured | 2·10 | 1·70 |

Design:—1E. As T **181** but without ornamental background.

(Des J. Resende. Litho)

1962 (20 Feb). 50th Anniv of National Republican Guard. P 13.
1198	**182**	1E. multicoloured	35	25
1199		2E. multicoloured	3·50	1·20
1200		2E.50 multicoloured	3·25	1·00
1198/1200 Set of 3			6·75	2·00

(Des C. da Costa Pinto. Litho)

1962 (24 Mar). St. Gabriel Commemoration (Patron Saint of Telecommunications). P 13.
| 1201 | **183** | 1E. chocolate, green & yellow-olive | 1·00 | 30 |
| 1202 | | 3E.50 olive-grn, choc & yellow-ol | 1·10 | 60 |

184 Scout Badge and Tents   185 Children with Ball

(Des G. Camarinha. Litho)

1962 (11 June). 18th International Scout Conference (1961). P 13½.
1203	**184**	20c. multicoloured	35	25
1204		50c. multicoloured	40	25
1205		1E. multicoloured	85	30
1206		2E.50 multicoloured	5·75	75
1207		3E.50 multicoloured	2·75	75
1208		6E.50 multicoloured	1·70	1·30
1203/1208 Set of 6			10·00	3·25

(Des Maria Keil. Litho)

1962 (10 Sept). Tenth International Paediatrics Congress, Lisbon. T **185** and similar horiz designs. Centres in black. P 13½.
1209		50c. yellow and grey-green	35	25
1210		1E. yellow and pale bluish grey	1·30	25
1211		2E.80 yellow and orange-brown	4·25	2·10
1212		3E.50 yellow and reddish purple	7·75	2·75
1209/1212 Set of 4			12·00	4·75

Designs:—50c. Children with book; 1E. Inoculating child; 3E.50, Weighing baby.

186 Europa "Honeycomb"   187 St. Zenon (the Courier)

(Des F. Kradolfer. Litho)

1962 (17 Sept). Europa. "EUROPA" in gold. P 13½.
1213	**186**	1E. ultramarine, light blue and blue	40	35
1214		1E.50 deep green, light green & grn	2·00	1·30
1215		3E.50 brown-purple, pink & claret	2·30	2·00
1213/1215 Set of 3			4·50	3·50

(Des J. M. da Costa. Litho)

1962 (1 Dec). Stamp Day. Saint in yellow and pink. P 13½.
1216	**187**	1E. black and claret	35	30
1217		2E. black and grey-green	1·60	1·10
1218		2E.80 black and bistre	2·75	2·75
1216/1218 Set of 3			4·50	4·00

188 Benfica Emblem and European Cup   189 Campaign Emblem

(Des A. Bual. Litho)

1963 (5 Feb). Benfica Club's Double Victory in European Football Cup Championships (1961–62). P 13×13½.
| 1219 | **188** | 1E. red, brown-red, gold & black | 1·20 | 30 |
| 1220 | | 4E.30 chestnut, sepia, gold & blk | 2·10 | 1·90 |

19

PORTUGAL

(Des J. A. Manta. Litho)

1963 (21 Mar). Freedom from Hunger. P 13½.
1221	**189**	1E. gold, blue, black and pale grey......	35	30
1222		3E.30 gold, green, blk & yell-ol............	2·00	1·60
1223		3E.50 gold, crimson, blk & pale red......	2·20	1·60
1221/1223 Set of 3			4·50	3·00

190 Mail Coach

191 St. Vincent de Paul

(Des C. da Costa Pinto. Litho)

1963 (7 May). Paris Postal Conference Centenary. P 12×11½.
1224	**190**	1E. deep blue, light blue and grey......	35	20
1225		1E.50 brown, yellow-brn, pk & bis........	3·00	75
1226		5E. deep red-brown, lilac and light orange-brown....................................	1·30	60
1224/1226 Set of 3			4·50	1·25

(Des after bas-relief by Maria Monsaraz. Photo Harrison)

1963 (10 July). Death Tercentenary of St. Vincent de Paul. Inscriptions in gold. P 13½×14½.
1227	**191**	20c. ultramarine and light blue............	35	35
1228		1E. indigo and light grey......................	55	35
1229		2E.80 black and green...........................	6·50	2·75
		a. Gold (inscr) omitted.....................	£225	£150
1230		5E. blue-grey and magenta..................	5·75	2·00
1227/1230 Set of 4			12·00	5·00

192 Mediaeval Knight

193 Europa "Dove"

(Des C. da Costa Pinto. Litho)

1963 (13 Aug). 800th Anniv of Military Order of Aviz. P 12.
1231	**192**	1E. multicoloured	35	25
1232		1E.50 multicoloured	1·00	40
1233		2E.50 multicoloured	2·00	1·40
1231/1233 Set of 3			3·00	2·00

(Des P. Guilherme. Litho)

1963 (16 Sept). Europa. P 13½.
1234	**193**	1E. drab, light blue and black..............	50	35
1235		1E.50 drab, green and black.................	4·25	2·00
1236		3E.50 drab, vermilion and black..........	6·25	3·00
1234/1236 Set of 3			15·00	5·00

194 "Supersonic Flight"

195 Pharmacist's Jar

(Des P. Guilherme. Litho)

1963 (1 Dec). Tenth Anniv of T.A.P. Airline. P 13½.
1237	**194**	1E. light blue and deep blue................	30	25
1238		2E.50 light yellow-grn & black-grn.......	2·10	1·00
1239		3E.50 light orange and brown-red.......	2·50	1·80
1237/1239 Set of 3			4·50	3·00

(Des J. A. Manta. Litho)

1964 (9 Apr). 400th Anniv of Publication of *Coloquios dos Simples* (Dissertations on Indian herbs and drugs) by Dr. G. d'Orta. P 13½.
1240	**195**	50c. brown, black and bistre................	80	35
1241		1E. reddish pur, blk & Venetian red....	80	35
1242		4E.30 slate-blue, black and grey...........	7·00	5·75
1240/1242 Set of 3			8·00	6·00

196 Bank Emblem

197 Sameiro Shrine (Braga)

198 Europa "Flower"

(Des C. da Costa Pinto. Litho)

1964 (19 May). Centenary of National Overseas Bank. P 13½.
1243	**196**	1E. yellow, yellow-olive & deep bl......	35	30
1244		2E.50 yellow, yellow-olive & grn..........	4·00	1·60
1245		3E.50 yellow, yellow-olive & brn..........	3·50	1·70
1243/1245 Set of 3			7·50	3·00

(Des J. P. Roque. Litho)

1964 (5 June). Centenary of Sameiro Shrine. P 13½.
1246	**197**	1E. olive-yellow, light brn & crm.........	35	25
1247		2E.50 olive-yellow, light brown & brn..	3·00	1·10
1248		5E. olive-yell, grey-grn & dp ultram...	3·50	1·70
1246/1248 Set of 3			6·50	3·00

(Des G. Bétemps. Litho)

1964 (14 Sept). Europa. P 13½.
1249	**198**	1E. deep blue, light blue and blue......	1·00	35
1250		3E.50 brown, orange-brn & brn-pur.....	8·00	2·50
1251		4E.30 bronze-grn, lt yell-grn & grn......	9·50	4·75
1249/1251 Set of 3			15·00	7·00

199 Sun and Globe

200 Olympic "Rings"

201 E. Coelho (Founder)

(Des S. Rodrigues. Litho)

1964 (12 Oct). International Quiet Sun Years. P 13½.
1252	**199**	1E. bistre, green, yellow and black......	45	25
1253		8E. orange-red, green, yellow & blk....	2·20	1·60

(Des S. Rodrigues. Litho)

1964 (1 Dec). Olympic Games. Tokyo. P 13½.
1254	**200**	20c. multicoloured	35	30
1255		1E. multicoloured	45	35
1256		1E.50 multicoloured	2·50	1·60
1257		6E.50 multicoloured	4·50	3·00
1254/1257 Set of 4			7·00	4·75

(Des J. Gil. Litho)

1964 (28 Dec). Centenary of *Diario de Noticias* (newspaper). P 13½.
1258	**201**	1E. multicoloured	95	20
1259		5E. multicoloured	11·50	1·60

202 Traffic Signals

203 Dom Fernando (second Duke of Braganza)

(Des P. Guilherme. Litho)

1965 (15 Feb). First National Traffic Congress, Lisbon. P 13½.
1260	**202**	1E. bistre-yellow, red and green..........	40	35
1261		3E.30 green, red & bistre-yellow..........	10·00	5·25
1262		3E.50 red, bistre-yellow & green..........	6·50	2·50
1260/1262 Set of 3			15·00	7·50

PORTUGAL

(Des J. Manta. Litho)

1965 (16 Mar). 500th Anniv of Braganza. P 13½.
1263	203	1E. Venetian red and black	40	25
1264		10E. deep bluish green and black	4·50	1·20

204 Angel and Gateway

205 I.T.U. Emblem

(Des C. da Costa Pinto. Litho)

1965 (27 Apr). 900th Anniv of Capture of Coimbra from the Moors. P 11½×12.
1265	204	1E. multicoloured	35	35
1266		2E.50 multicoloured	3·00	2·40
1267		5E. multicoloured	3·75	3·00
1265/1267 Set of 3			6·50	5·50

(Des A. Cardoso. Litho)

1965 (17 May). Centenary of International Telecommunications Union. P 13½.
1268	205	1E. yellow-olive and olive-brown	35	35
1269		3E.50 brown-purple & olive-green	2·40	2·00
1270		6E.50 slate-blue and apple-green	2·75	1·80
1268/1270 Set of 3			5·00	4·00

206 C. Gulbenkian

207 Red Cross Emblem

(Des C. da Costa Pinto. Litho)

1965 (20 July). Tenth Anniv of Death of Calouste Gulbenkian (oil industry pioneer and philanthropist). P 13½.
1271	206	1E. multicoloured	1·00	20
1272		8E. multicoloured	1·10	75

(Des M. Rodrigues. Litho)

1965 (17 Aug). Centenary of Portuguese Red Cross. P 13½.
1273	207	1E. red, green and black	40	35
		a. Green omitted*		
1274		4E. red, olive and black	6·50	3·25
1275		4E.30 red, Venetian red and black	18·00	11·50
1273/1275 Set of 3			20·00	16·00

*In this variety the deeper green overlay is omitted and this includes the imprint at foot of design.

208 Europa "Sprig"

209 North American F-86 Sabre

(Des H. Karlsson. Litho)

1965 (27 Sept). Europa. P 13½.
1276	208	1E. light blue, black and blue	55	35
1277		3E.50 flesh, sepia & brown-lake	13·50	2·40
1278		4E.30 apple-green, black & green	24·00	11·50
1276/1278 Set of 3			35·00	13·00

(Des P. Guilherme. Litho)

1965 (20 Oct). 50th Anniv of Portuguese Air Force. P 13½.
1279	209	1E. red, green and olive	45	25
1280		2E. red, green & light purple-brown	2·20	1·00
1281		5E. red, green and slate-blue	4·50	2·75
1279/1281 Set of 3			6·50	3·50

210

211 Monogram of Christ

(Des J. A. Manta. Litho)

1965 (1 Dec). 500th Birth Anniv of Gil Vicente (poet and dramatist). T **210** and similar vert designs depicting characters from Vicente's poems. P 13½.
1282		20c. multicoloured	25	20
1283		1E. multicoloured	70	20
1284		2E.50 multicoloured	4·75	80
1285		6E.50 multicoloured	2·30	1·10
1282/1285 Set of 4			7·25	2·00

(Des S. Rodrigues. Litho)

1966 (28 Mar). International Committee for the Defence of Christian Civilisation Congress, Lisbon. P 13½.
1286	211	1E. bluish violet, gold & yell-blk	40	20
1287		3E.30 black, gold & lt greyish pur	10·00	5·50
1288		5E. black, gold and brown-lake	7·50	3·00
1286/1288 Set of 3			15·00	8·00

212 Emblems of Agriculture, Construction and Industry

213 Giraldo the "Fearless"

(Des P. Guilherme. Litho)

1966 (28 May). 40th Anniv of National Revolution. P 13½.
1289	212	1E. black, slate-blue & light grey	45	35
1290		3E.50 blksh brn, bis-brn & lt bis	4·50	2·10
1291		4E. deep maroon, brn-lake & pink	4·50	1·70
1289/1291 Set of 3			8·75	3·75

(Des C. da Costa Pinto. Litho)

1966 (8 June). 800th Anniv of Reconquest of Evora. P 13½×13.
1292	213	1E. multicoloured	55	25
1293		8E. multicoloured	1·80	1·00

214 Salazar Bridge

215 Europa "Ship"

(Des A. N. de Almeida. Litho)

1966 (6 Aug). Inauguration of Salazar Bridge, Lisbon. T **214** and similar design. P 13½.
1294	214	1E. red and gold	45	25
1295		2E.50 ultramarine and gold	2·50	1·40
1296		2E.80 ultramarine and silver	3·25	2·50
1297		4E.30 myrtle-green and silver	3·50	2·50
1294/1297 Set of 4			8·75	6·00

Design: Vert—2E.80, 4E.30, Salazar Bridge (different view).

(Des G. and J. Bender. Litho)

1966 (26 Sept). Europa. P 11½×12.
1298	215	1E. multicoloured	60	35
1299		3E.50 multicoloured	19·00	3·00
1300		4E.30 multicoloured	19·00	4·75
1298/1300 Set of 3			35·00	7·50

PORTUGAL

216 C. Pestana (bacteriologist)   **217** Bocage   D **218**

(Des C. da Costa Pinto. Litho)

1966 (1 Dec). Portuguese Scientists. T **216** and similar vert portraits. Portraits in deep brown and bistre; background colours given. P 13½.

1301	20c. grey-green		25	15
1302	50c. yellow-orange		25	15
1303	1E. olive-yellow		35	15
1304	1E.50 cinnamon		50	15
1305	2E. orange-brown		2·75	25
1306	2E.50 pale green		3·00	70
1307	2E.80 salmon		4·75	2·50
1308	4E.30 light slate-blue		6·25	4·75
1301/1308 Set of 8			16·00	8·00

Scientists:—50c. E. Moniz (neurologist); 1E. A. P. Coutinho (botanist); 1E.50, J. C. da Serra (botanist); 2E. R. Jorge (hygienist and anthropologist); 2E.50, J. L. de Vasconcelos (ethnologist); 2E.80, M. Lemos (medical historian); 4E.30, J. A. Serrano (anatomist).

(Des L. Dourdil. Litho)

1966 (28 Dec). Birth Bicentenary (1965) of Manuel M. B. du Bocage (poet). P 11½×12.

1309	**217**	1E. black, pale green & light bistre	25	15
1310		2E. black, pale green & orange-brn	1·60	70
1311		6E. black, pale green and light grey	2·10	1·30
1309/1311 Set of 3			3·50	1·75

1967 (Feb)–**84**. POSTAGE DUE. Litho. P 12×11½ (40, 50E.) or 11½×12 (others).

D1312	D **218**	10c. red-brown, greenish yellow and orange	15	10
D1313		20c. mar, greenish yell & ochre	15	10
D1314		30c. red-brown, greenish yellow and orange-yellow	15	10
D1315		40c. maroon, greenish yellow and light bistre	15	10
D1316		50c. indigo, pale blue and bright blue	20	10
D1317		60c. deep olive, pale blue and light greenish blue	20	10
D1318		80c. indigo, pale blue & new blue	20	10
D1319		1E. indigo, pale blue & ultram	20	10
D1320		2E. deep olive, pale apple green and yellow-green	20	15
D1321		3E. deep yellowish green, pale yellow-green and bright yellowish green (1975)	45	15
D1322		4E. myrtle green, pale yellow-green & blue-green (1975)	45	20
D1323		5E. chocolate, pale mve & clar	35	20
D1324		9E. deep lilac, pale lilac and violet (1975)	45	25
D1325		10E. deep purple, pale lavender grey and purple (1975)	45	25
D1326		20E. maroon, pale lavender-grey and purple (1975)	1·30	35
D1327	D **218**	40E. deep rose-lilac, pale lavender grey and deep magenta (24.9.84)	3·00	1·40
D1328		50E. maroon, pale lavender-grey and bright purple (24.9.84)	3·75	1·60
D1312/1328 Set of 17			10·50	4·75

218 Cogwheels

219 Adoration of the Virgin

(Des O. Bonnevalle. Litho)

1967 (2 May). Europa. P 13.

1312	**218**	1E. Prussian blue, black & light blue	60	35
1313		3E.50 lake-brown, blk & lt salmon	15·00	1·90
1314		4E.30 bronze-grn, blk & lt yell-grn	21·00	3·75
1312/1314 Set of 3			30·00	5·00

(Des J. P. Roque. Litho)

1967 (13 May). 50th Anniv of Fatima Apparitions. T **219** and similar vert designs. Multicoloured. P 11½×12.

1315	1E. Type **219**	20	15
1316	2E.80 Fatima Church	95	90
1317	3E.50 Virgin of Fatima	60	45
1318	4E. Chapel of the Apparitions	70	55
1315/1318 Set of 4		2·25	1·80

220 Roman Senators   **221** Lisnave Shipyard

(Des J. A. Manta. Litho)

1967 (1 June). New Civil Law Code. P 13.

1319	**220**	1E. lake and gold	20	15
1320		2E.50 Prussian blue and gold	3·25	1·80
1321		4E.30 deep grey-green and gold	2·75	1·80
1319/1321 Set of 3			5·50	3·00

(Des L. F. de Abreu. Litho)

1967 (23 June). Inauguration of Lisnave Shipyard, Lisbon. T **221** and similar horiz design. P 13½.

1322	**221**	1E. multicoloured	20	20
1323		2E.80 multicoloured	4·00	1·90
1324	**221**	3E.50 multicoloured	3·00	1·80
1325		4E.30 multicoloured	3·75	2·00
1322/1325 Set of 4			10·00	5·50

Design:—2E.80, 4E.30, Section of ship's hull and location map.

222 Serpent Symbol   **223** Flags of EFTA Countries

(Des J. A. Manta. Litho)

1967 (8 Oct). Sixth European Rheumatological Congress, Lisbon. P 13½.

1326	**222**	1E. multicoloured	20	20
1327		2E. multicoloured	1·90	1·00
1328		5E. multicoloured	3·00	2·00
1326/1328 Set of 3			4·75	3·00

(Des L. F. de Oliveira. Litho)

1967 (24 Oct). European Free Trade Association. P 13½.

1329	**223**	1E. multicoloured	35	35
1330		3E.50 multicoloured	2·40	2·00
1331		4E.30 multicoloured	4·75	4·50
1329/1331 Set of 3			7·00	6·00

224 Tombstones   **225** Bento de Goes

PORTUGAL

(Des J. A. Manta. Litho)
1967 (27 Dec). Centenary of Abolition of Death Penalty in Portugal. P 13½×13.
1332	224	1E. yellow-olive	20	20
1333		2E. red-brown	2·10	1·30
1334		5E. green	3·75	3·00
1332/1334 Set of 3			5·50	4·00

(Des D. Rebelo. Eng A. Lucas. Recess)
1968 (14 Feb). Bento de Goes Commemoration. P 12×11½.
1335	225	1E. indigo, deep purple-brown and olive-green	95	20
1336		8E. deep purple, olive-green and orange-brown	2·50	1·00

226 Europa "Key" **227** "Maternal Love"

(Des H. Schwarzenbach. Litho)
1968 (29 Apr). Europa. P 13½×13.
1337	226	1E. multicoloured	60	35
1338		3E.50 multicoloured	16·00	2·75
1339		4E.30 multicoloured	24·00	5·00
1337/1339 Set of 3			35·00	7·50

(Des Maria Keil. Litho)
1968 (26 May). 30th Anniv of the Organisation of Mothers for National Education (OMEN). P 13½.
1340	227	1E. black, red-orange & pale drab	35	25
1341		2E. black, red-orange & pale pink	2·75	1·00
1342		5E. black, red-orange & pale blue	5·25	2·75
1340/1342 Set of 3			7·75	3·50

228 "Victory over Disease" **229** Vineyard, Girão

(Des L. Filipe de Abreu. Litho)
1968 (10 July). 20th Anniv of World Health Organization. P 12½.
1343	228	1E. multicoloured	35	35
1344		3E.50 multicoloured	2·20	1·10
1345		4E.30 multicoloured	12·00	8·50
1343/1345 Set of 3			13·00	9·00

(Des C. da Costa Pinto. Litho)
1968 (17 Aug). Lubrapex 1968 Stamp Exhibition. Madeira. "Pearl of the Atlantic". T **229** and similar multicoloured designs. P 12×11½ (horiz) or 11½×12 (vert).
1346		50c. Type 229	25	20
1347		1E. Firework display	30	15
1348		1E.50 Landscape	60	20
1349		2E.80 J. Fernandes Vieira (liberator of Pernambuco)	3·50	2·50
1350		3E.50 Embroidery	2·75	1·60
1351		4E.30 J. Gonçalves Zarco (navigator)	12·00	11·50
1352		20E. *Musschia aurea* (wrongly inscr "MUSCHIA AUREA")	7·75	2·20
1346/1352 Set of 7			25·00	16·00

The 2E.80 to 20E. are vert designs.
Nos. 1346/52 have tri-lingual captions (Portuguese, French and English) printed on the back.

230 Pedro Alvares Cabral (from medallion) **231** Colonnade

(Des J. P. Roque. Eng A. Lucas (1E., 3E.50). Litho (6E.50) or recess (others))
1969 (30 Jan). 500th Birth Anniv of Pedro Alvares Cabral (explorer). T **230** and similar designs. P 12½×12 (3E.50) or 12×12½ (others).
1353		1E. blue	40	20
1354		3E.50 reddish purple	6·25	3·50
1355		6E.50 multicoloured	4·50	3·50
1353/1355 Set of 3			10·00	6·50

Designs: Vert—3E.50, Cabral's arms. Horiz—6E.50, Cabral's fleet (from contemporary documents).
Issued with descriptive captions on the backs of the stamps similar to Nos. 1346/52.

(Des L. Gasbarra and G. Belli. Litho)
1969 (28 Apr). Europa. P 13½.
1356	231	1E. multicoloured	60	35
1357		3E.50 multicoloured	17·00	3·50
1358		4E.30 multicoloured	26·00	5·75
1356/1358 Set of 3			40·00	9·00

232 King Joseph I **233** ILO Emblem

(Des J. P. Roque. Litho)
1969 (14 May). Centenary of National Press. P 11½×12.
1359	232	1E. multicoloured	20	20
1360		2E. multicoloured	1·70	95
1361		8E. multicoloured	1·60	1·30
1359/1361 Set of 3			3·00	2·00

(Des J. A. Manta. Litho)
1969 (28 May). 50th Anniv of International Labour Organization. P 13.
1362	233	1E. multicoloured	25	20
1363		3E.50 multicoloured	3·00	1·00
1364		4E.30 multicoloured	4·00	3·25
1362/1364 Set of 3			6·50	4·00

234 J. R. Cabrilho (navigator and coloniser) **235** Vianna da Motta (from painting by C. B. Pinheiro)

(Des J. P. Roque. Litho)
1969 (16 July). Bicentenary of San Diego, California. P 11½×12.
1365	234	1E. bronze-green, pale yell & grn	20	20
1366		2E.50 brown, pale brown and blue	2·50	1·00
1367		6E.50 blackish brn, pale grn & brn	3·25	1·90
1365/1367 Set of 3			5·50	2·75

Issued with descriptive captions on the reverse in three languages.

1969 (24 Sept). Birth Centenary of Jose Vianna da Motta (concert pianist) (1968). Litho. P 12.
1368	235	1E. multicoloured	1·20	20
1369		9E. multicoloured	1·70	1·30

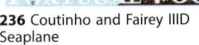

236 Coutinho and Fairey IIID Seaplane **237** Vasco da Gama

PORTUGAL

(Des C. da Costa Pinto. Litho)
1969 (22 Oct). Birth Centenary of Gago Coutinho (aviator). T **236** and similar horiz design. Multicoloured. P 12×12½.
1370		1E. Type **236**	35	15
1371		2E.80 Coutinho and sextant	3·75	2·10
1372		3E.30 Type **236**	3·50	3·00
1373		4E.30 Coutinho and sextant	3·50	3·00
1370/1373 Set of 4			16·00	7·50

(Des J. M. Barata. Litho)
1969 (30 Dec). 500th Birth Anniv of Vasco da Gama. Multicoloured designs as T **237**. P 12×11½ (1E., 2E.80) or 11½×12 (others).
1374		1E. Type **237**	35	25
1375		2E.80 Arms of Vasco da Gama	4·75	3·75
1376		3E.50 Route map (horiz)	3·50	1·70
1377		4E. Vasco da Gama's fleet (horiz)	3·25	1·40
1374/1377 Set of 4			11·00	6·50

Issued with descriptive captions on the backs of the stamps, similar to Nos. 1346/52.

238 "Flaming Sun"

239 Distillation Plant and Pipelines

(Des L. le Brocquy. Litho)
1970 (4 May). Europa. P 13½.
1378	**238**	1E. pale cream and deep blue	60	25
1379		3E.50 pale cream and red-brown	16·00	2·10
1380		4E.30 pale cream and olive-green	23·00	6·25
1378/1380 Set of 3			35·00	8·00

(Des A. Lino. Litho)
1970 (5 June). Inauguration of Porto Oil Refinery. T **239** and similar square design. P 13½.
1381	**239**	1E. deep blue and light grey-blue	25	20
1382	–	2E.80 black and light bluish green	3·50	2·75
1383	**239**	3E.30 blackish olive & lt yell-olive	2·75	2·20
1384	–	6E. deep brown & light yellow-brn	2·50	1·90
1381/1384 Set of 4			8·00	6·25

Design:—2E.80, 6E. Catalytic cracking plant and pipelines.

240 Marshal Carmona (from sculpture by L. de Almeida)

241 Station Badge

(Eng A. Lucas. Recess and litho)
1970 (1 July). Birth Centenary of Marshal Carmona. T **240** and similar horiz designs. Head and inscriptions in black. P 12×12½.
1385		1E. olive-green	25	10
1386		2E.50 bright blue and red	2·20	90
1387		7E. slate-blue	2·50	1·70
1385/1387 Set of 3			4·75	2·50

Nos. 1386/7 differ from T **240** in background ornamentation.

(Des A. de Matos e Silva. Litho)
1970 (29 July). 25th Anniv of Plant-Breeding Station. P 12×12½.
1388	**241**	1E. multicoloured	30	10
1389		2E.50 multicoloured	1·80	70
1390		5E. multicoloured	2·20	90
1388/1390 Set of 3			3·75	1·50

242 Emblem within Cultural Symbol

243 Wheel and Star

(Des A. Garcia. Litho)
1970 (16 Sept). Expo 70. T **242** and similar vert designs, each incorporating the Expo symbol. Multicoloured. P 13.

(a) POSTAGE
1391		1E. Compass	25	15
1392		5E. Christian symbol	2·00	1·70
1393		6E.50 Symbolic initials	4·75	4·00

(b) AIR. Inscr "Correio Aéreo"
1394		3E.50 Type **242**	90	45
1391/1394 Set of 4			7·00	5·50

Issued with descriptive captions on the backs of the stamps, as Nos. 1346/52.

(Des C. da Costa Pinto. Litho)
1970 (7 Oct). Cities' Centenaries. T **243** and similar horiz designs. Multicoloured. P 12×11½.

(a) Covilha
1395		1E. Type **243**	30	20
1396		2E.80 Ram and weaving frame	3·50	3·00

(b) Santarém
1397		1E. Castle	20	15
1398		4E. Two knights	2·30	1·30
1395/1398 Set of 4			5·50	4·25

244 Great Eastern (cable ship) laying Cable

245 Harvesting Grapes

(Des D. N. Simões. Litho Litografia Nacional, Oporto)
1970 (21 Nov). Centenary of Portugal–England Submarine Telegraph Cable. T **244** and similar square design. P 14.
1399	**244**	1E. black, violet-blue & bright green	30	15
1400		2E.50 black, brt blue-grn & pale buff	2·50	70
1401	–	2E.80 multicoloured	4·00	3·25
1402	–	4E. multicoloured	2·50	1·30
1399/1402 Set of 4			8·25	4·75

Design:—2E.80, 4E. Cable cross-section.

(Des C. da Costa Pinto. Litho)
1970 (30 Dec). Port Wine Industry. T **245** and similar horiz designs. Multicoloured. P 12×11½.
1403		50c. Type **245**	15	10
1404		1E. Harvester and jug	25	10
1405		3E.50 Wine-glass and vine	95	25
1406		7E. Wine-bottle and casks	1·60	80
1403/1406 Set of 4			2·50	1·00

246 Mountain Windmill, Bussaco Hills

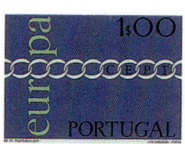
247 Europa Chain

PORTUGAL

(Des C. da Costa Pinto. Litho)

1971 (24 Feb). Portuguese Windmills. T **246** and similar vert designs. P 13.

1407	20c. red-brown, black & pale olive-sepia	15	10
1408	50c. red-brown, black and pale blue	20	10
1409	1E. reddish purple, black & pale ol-grey	30	10
1410	2E. lake, black and dull mauve	1·00	35
1411	3E.30 chocolate, black & yellow-brn	3·50	2·50
1412	5E. chocolate, black and pale green	3·25	1·20
1407/1412	Set of 6	7·50	4·00

Windmills:—50c. Beira Litoral Province; 1E. "Saloio" type, Estremadura Province; 2E. St. Miguel, Azores; 3E.30, Porto Santo, Madeira; 5E. Pico, Azores.

Issued with tri-lingual descriptions on the reverse.

(Des H. Haflidason. Litho Litografia Nacional, Oporto)

1971 (3 May). Europa. P 14.

1413	**247**	1E. light green, blue and black	45	30
1414		3E.50 light yellow, lake-brn & blk	12·00	1·10
1415		7E.50 buff, yellow-olive and black	17·00	2·75
1413/1415	Set of 3		25·00	3·75

248 F. Franco   **249** Pres. Salazar

(Des A. Duarte. Eng A. Lucas. Recess)

1971 (7 July). Portuguese Sculptors. T **248** and similar horiz designs. P 13 (4E.) or 11½×12 (others).

1416	20c. black	15	10
	a. Perf 13	3·50	55
1417	1E. brown-lake	35	10
1418	1E.50 yellow-brown	85	60
1419	2E.50 blue	1·20	55
	a. Perf 13	1·20	55
1420	3E.50 cerise	1·50	90
1421	4E. deep bluish green	4·00	2·50
1416/1421	Set of 6	7·25	4·25

Designs:—1E. A. Lopes; 1E.50, A. da Costa Mota; 2E.50, R. Gameiro; 3E.50, J. Simões de Almeida (the Younger); 4E. F. dos Santos.

(Des P.O. Art Dept. Eng A. Lucas. Recess)

1971 (27 July). Pres. Antonio Salazar Commemoration. P 13.

1422	**249**	1E. brown, yellow-olive & orange	25	10
		a. Perf 12	£130	4·75
1423		5E. brown, brown-purple & orange	2·30	80
1424		10E. brown, blue and orange	3·50	1·60
		a. Perf 12	23·00	2·30
1422/1424	Set of 3		5·50	2·00

250 Wolframite   **251** Town Gate

(Des P.O. Art Dept. Litho)

1971 (24 Sept). First Spanish-Portuguese-American Congress of Economic Geology. T **250** and similar horiz designs, showing minerals. Multicoloured. P 11½.

1425	1E. Type **250**	15	10
1426	2E.50 Arsenopyrite	2·50	60
1427	3E.50 Beryllium	90	55
1428	6E.50 Chalcopyrite	1·70	80
1425/1428	Set of 4	4·75	1·75

(Des A. Cardoso. Litho Litografia Nacional, Oporto)

1971 (7 Oct). Bicentenary of Castel Branco. T **251** and similar multicoloured designs. P 14.

1429	1E. Type **251**	15	15
1430	3E. Town square and monument	1·80	90
1431	12E.50 Arms of Castel Branco (horiz)	1·60	90
1429/1431	Set of 3	3·25	1·75

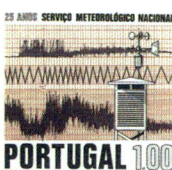 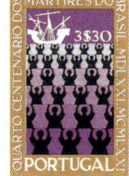

252 Weather Equipment   **253** Drowning Missionaries

(Des L. Chaves. Litho)

1971 (29 Oct). 25th Anniv of Portuguese Meteorological Service. T **252** and similar horiz designs. Multicoloured. P 13.

1432	1E. Type **252**	20	10
1433	4E. Weather balloon	3·00	1·40
1434	6E.50 Weather satellite	2·00	1·00
1432/1434	Set of 3	4·75	2·25

(Des J. Manta. Litho Litografia Maia, Oporto)

1971 (24 Nov). 400th Anniv of Martyrdom of Brazil Missionaries in 1570. P 13½.

1435	**253**	1E. black, bright blue and grey	15	10
1436		3E.30 black, purple and ochre	2·75	1·90
1437		4E.80 black, green and yell-olive	2·75	1·90
1435/1437	Set of 3		5·00	3·50

254 Man and his Habitat   **255** Clerigos Tower, Oporto

(Des L. F. de Abreu. Litho)

1971 (22 Dec). Nature Conservation. T **254** and similar horiz designs. Multicoloured. P 11½.

1438	1E. Type **254**	15	10
1439	3E.30 Horses and tree ("Earth")	90	60
1440	3E.50 Birds ("The Atmosphere")	90	55
1441	4E.50 Fishes ("Water")	3·50	2·10
1438/1441	Set of 4	5·00	3·00

PHOSPHOR BANDS. From 1975, stamps were issued with bands of phosphor printed on the front for use with postal mechanisation equipment. These bands can be seen by holding the stamp at an angle to the light and looking along it.

(Des P.O. Art Dept. Litho)

1972 (1 Mar)–**81**. T **255** and similar horiz designs. Unlettered paper (Nos. 1449p, 1451p) or paper lettered and dated on reverse (others). P 12½ (Nos. 1442/57) or 13 (others).

1442	5c. grey, black and green (5.9.73)	30	15
1443	10c. blk, grey-ol & greenish bl (18.9.74)	20	15
1444	30c. sepia, yellow-brown and greenish yellow (18.9.74)	20	15
1445	50c. grey-blue, yell-orge & blk (6.12.72)	2·00	10
	p. One phosphor band (3.11.75)	55	10
1446	1E. black orange-brown & turq-grn	1·20	10
	p. One phosphor band (1977)	2·00	25
	pa. Unlettered paper (1978)	55	10
1447	1E.50 yellow-brown, dp cobalt & blk	1·60	10
	a. Unlettered paper (1981)	75	10
1448	2E. black, ochre & dp claret (18.9.74)	3·25	10
	p. One phosphor band (3.11.75)	3·75	15
	pa. Unlettered paper (1978)	60	10
1449	2E.50 brown, orge-brn & grey (5.9.73)	1·70	10
	p. One phosphor band (1978)	55	10
1450	3E. yellow, black & yell-brn (6.12.72)	3·25	10
	p. One phosphor band (1976)	90	10
1451	3E.50 myrtle green, yellow-orange and brown (5.9.73)	2·30	10
	p. One phosphor band (1979)	55	10
1452	4E. black, yellow & deep blue	1·00	10
1453	4E.50 black, ochre & emer (18.9.74)	1·50	10
1454	5E. dp green, olive-sep & blk (18.9.74)	9·25	10
1455	6E. bistre, emerald and black (18.9.74)	3·75	25
	p. One phosphor band (3.11.75)	40·00	80
1456	7E.50 black, yellow-orange and grey green (18.9.74)	2·10	20
	p. One phosphor band (1977)	4·25	25

25

PORTUGAL

1457	8E. bistre, black & myrtle grn (5.9.73)	2·75	15
	p. One phosphor band (1976)	7·25	15
	pa. Unlettered paper (1978)	3·00	15
1458	10E. multicoloured (6.12.72)	1·30	15
	p. One phosphor band (1977)	5·50	15
	pa. Unlettered paper (1978)	1·60	15
1459	20E. multicoloured (6.12.72)	8·75	55
1460	50E. multicoloured	9·25	40
	a. Unlettered paper (1978)	4·25	40
1461	100E. multicoloured	10·00	95
	a. Unlettered paper (1978)	14·00	1·30
1442/1461 Set of 20 (cheapest)		55·00	4·25

Designs: As T **255**—5c. Aguas Livres aqueduct, Lisbon; 10c. Lima bridge; 30c. Monastery interior, Alcobaca; 50c. Coimbra University; 1E.50, Belém Tower. Lisbon; 2E. Domus Municipalis. Braganza; 2E.50, Castle, Vila da Feira; 3E. Misericord House, Viana do Castelo; 3E.50, Window, Tomar Convent; 4E. Gateway, Braga; 4E.50, Dolmen of Carrazeda; 5E. Roman temple, Evora; 6E. Monastery, Leca do Balio; 7E.50, Almourol Castle; 8E. Ducal Palace, Guimarães. 31×22 mm—10E. Cape Girao. Madeira; 20E. Episcopal garden, Castelo Branco; 50E. Town Hall. Sintra; 100E. Seven Cities' Lake, São Miguel, Azores.

The lettered paper has minute continuous inscriptions printed on the reverse, over the gum, made up of the date of printing and the letters "C.T.T.". Where values exist with more than one year date, the price quoted is for the cheapest sort.

260 Football   **261** Marquis de Pombal

(Des L. F. de Abreu. Litho Litografia Nacional, Oporto)

1972 (26 July). Olympic Games, Munich. T **260** and similar horiz designs. Multicoloured. P 14×13½.

1476	50c. Type **260**	15	10
1477	1E. Running	20	10
1478	1E.50 Show jumping	55	25
1479	3E.50 Swimming	1·20	50
1480	4E.50 Sailing	1·80	1·40
1481	5E. Gymnastics	3·50	1·50
1476/1481 Set of 6		6·50	3·50

(Des Post Office Art Dept. Litho Litografia Maia, Oporto)

1972 (28 Aug). Pombaline University Reforms T **261** and similar vert designs. Multicoloured. P 13.

1482	1E. Type **261**	20	10
1483	2E.50 "The Sciences" (emblems)	2·10	1·20
1484	8E. Arms of Coimbra University	2·20	1·60
1482/1484 Set of 3		4·00	2·50

256 Arms of Pinhel   **257** Heart and Pendulum

(Des J. Candido. Litho)

1972 (29 Mar). Bicentenary of Pinhel's Status as a City. T **256** and similar multicoloured designs. P 13.

1464	1E. Type **256**	25	10
	a. Perf 11½×12½	£100	4·25
1465	2E.50 Balustrade (vert)	2·30	55
1466	7E.50 Lantern on pedestal (vert)	1·80	80
1464/1466 Set of 3		4·00	1·25

(Des A. Garcia. Litho Litografia de Portugal)

1972 (24 Apr). World Heart Month. T **257** and similar vert designs. P 13.

1467	1E. red and slate-lilac	25	15
1468	4E. red and dull green	3·50	1·60
1469	9E. red and brown	2·40	1·00
1467/1469 Set of 3		5·50	2·50

Designs:—4E. Heart in spiral; 9E. Heart and cardiogram trace.

262 Tomé de Sousa   **263** Sacadura Cabral, Gago Coutinho and Fairey IIID Seaplane

(Des C. da Costa Pinto. Litho Litografia de Portugal)

1972 (5 Oct). 150th Anniv of Brazilian Independence. T **262** and similar vert designs. Multicoloured. P 13.

1485	1E. Type **262**	20	15
1486	2E.50 José Bonifacio	1·10	40
1487	3E.50 Dom Pedro IV	1·10	45
1488	6E. Dove and globe	2·10	1·00
1485/1488 Set of 4		4·00	1·75

(Des P.O. Art Dept. Litho)

1972 (15 Nov). 50th Anniv of First Flight from Lisbon to Rio de Janeiro. T **263** and similar horiz design. Multicoloured. P 11½×12½.

1489	1E. Type **263**	15	10
	a. Perf 13	50·00	1·70
1490	2E.50 Route map	1·20	70
1491	2E.80 Type **263**	1·50	1·10
1492	3E.80 As 2E.50	1·90	1·60
	a. Perf 13½	£160	50·00
1489/1492 Set of 4		4·25	3·25

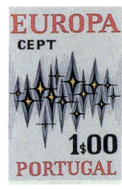

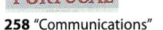

258 "Communications"   **259** Container Truck

(Des P. Huovinen. Litho)

1972 (1 May). Europa. P 13.

1470	**258**	1E. multicoloured	50	20
1471		3E.50 multicoloured	9·75	65
1472		6E. multicoloured	16·00	2·30
1470/1472 Set of 3			24·00	2·75

(Des L. Carrolo. Litho Litografia Nacional, Oporto)

1972 (17 May). 13th International Road Transport Union Congress, Estoril. T **259** and similar vert designs. Multicoloured. P 13.

1473	1E. Type **259**	25	20
1474	4E.50 Roof of taxi	2·50	1·50
1475	8E. Motor coach	2·30	1·30
1473/1475 Set of 3		4·50	3·50

264 Camoens   **265** Graph and Computer Tapes

PORTUGAL

(Des D. Costa. Litho Litografia Maia, Oporto)

1972 (27 Dec). 400th Anniv of Camoens' *Lusiads* (epic poem). T **264** and similar horiz designs. P 13.

1493	1E. yellow, brown and black	25	15
1494	3E. grey-blue, apple-green and black	1·60	95
1495	10E. pale cinnamon, brown-pur & blk	2·30	1·10
1493/1495	Set of 3	4·75	1·90

Designs:—3E. "Saved from the Sea"; 10E. "Encounter with Adamastor".

(Des J. Candido. Litho Litografia Nacional, Oporto)

1973 (11 Apr). Portuguese Productivity Conference, Lisbon. T **265** and similar square designs. Multicoloured. P 14.

1496	1E. Type **265**	20	10
1497	4E. Computer scale	1·60	85
1498	9E. Graphs	1·60	80
1496/1498	Set of 3	3·00	1·50

266 Europa "Posthorn"

267 Pres. Medici and Arms

(Des L. F. Anisdahl. Litho)

1973 (30 Apr). Europa. P 13.

1499	**266**	1E. multicoloured	75	30
1500		4E. multicoloured	18·00	1·40
1501		6E. multicoloured	20·00	2·40
1499/1501		Set of 3	35·00	3·50

(Des P.O. Art Dept. Eng A. Lucas. Recess and litho)

1973 (16 May). Visit of Pres. Medici of Brazil. T **267** and similar horiz design. Multicoloured. P 11½.

1502	1E. Type **267**	20	15
1503	2E.80 Pres. Medici and globe	1·00	85
1504	3E.50 Type **267**	1·10	80
1505	4E.80 As 2E.80	1·10	85
1502/1505	Set of 4	3·00	2·25

268 Child Running

269 Transport and Weather Map

(Des L. F. de Abreu. Litho)

1973 (28 May). "For the Child". T **268** and similar vert designs. P 13.

1506	1E. royal blue, new blue and brown	20	10
1507	4E. maroon, cerise and lake-brown	1·90	85
1508	7E.50 orange, pale ochre and brown	2·30	1·50
1506/1508	Set of 3	3·75	1·25

Designs:—4E. Child running (to right); 7E.50, Child jumping.

(Des P.O. Art Dept. Litho)

1973 (25 June). 25th Anniv of Ministry of Communications. T **269** and similar horiz designs. Multicoloured. P 13.

1509	1E. Type **269**	15	10
1510	3E.80 "Telecommunications"	65	40
1511	6E. "Postal Services"	1·50	90
1509/1511	Set of 3	2·00	2·25

270 Child and Written Text

271 Electric Tram-car

(Des L. Correia, Litho)

1973 (24 Oct). Bicentenary of Primary State School Education. T **270** and similar multicoloured designs. P 13.

1512	1E. Type **270**	25	10
1513	4E.50 Page of children's primer	2·10	65
1514	5E.30 "Schooldays" (child's drawing) (horiz)	1·80	95
1515	8E. "Teacher and children" (horiz)	4·75	2·00
1512/1515	Set of 4	8·00	3·25

(Des A. Alves. Litho Litografia Maia, Oporto)

1973 (7 Nov). Centenary of Oporto's Public Transport System. T **271** and similar multicoloured designs. P 13 (7E.50) or 13½ (others).

1516	1E. Horse-drawn tram-car (31½×31½ mm)	30	10
1517	3E.50 Double-decker bus (31½×31½ mm)	2·75	1·90
1518	7E.50 Type **271**	3·00	1·60
1516/1518	Set of 3	5·50	3·25

272 League Badge

273 Death of Nuno Gonçalves

(Des Post Office Art Dept. Litho)

1973 (28 Nov). 50th Anniv of Servicemen's League. T **272** and similar vert designs. Multicoloured. P 13.

1519	1E. Type **272**	20	15
1520	2E.50 Servicemen	3·00	85
1521	11E. Awards and Medals	2·10	90
1519/1521	Set of 3	4·75	1·50

(Des Post Office Art Dept. Litho)

1973 (19 Dec). 600th Anniv of Defence of Faria Castle by the Alcaide, Nuno Gonçalves. T **273**.

1522	**273**	1E. slate-green and orange-yellow	30	15
1523		10E. dull purple and orange-yellow	2·75	1·50

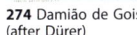
274 Damião de Gois (after Dürer)

275 "The Exile" (A. Soares dos Reis)

(Des P.O. Art Dept. Litho)

1974 (5 Apr). 400th Death Anniv of Damião de Gois (scholar and diplomat). T **274** and similar vert designs. Multicoloured. P 12.

1524	1E. Type **274**	20	10
1525	4E.50 Title-page of *Chronicles of Prince Dom João*	3·00	80
1526	7E.50 Lute and "Dodecahordon" score	1·80	80
1524/1526	Set of 3	4·50	1·50

(Des P.O. Art Dept. Litho)

1974 (29 Apr). Europa. P 13.

1527	**275**	1E. bronze-grn, dp bl & yell-olive	90	30
1528		4E. bronze-grn, carm & orge-yell	21·00	1·40
1529		6E. bronze-green, myrtle-grn & lt bl	25·00	1·80
1527/1529		Set of 3	40·00	3·00

276 Light Emission

277 "Diffusion of Hertzian Radio Waves"

PORTUGAL

(Des P. Guilherme. Litho Litografia Nacional, Oporto)

1974 (26 June). Inauguration of Satellite Communications Station Network. T **276** and similar horiz designs. P 14.

1530	1E.50 deep olive	25	20
1531	4E.50 deep blue	1·80	90
1532	5E.30 bright purple	2·50	1·30
1530/1532	Set of 3	4·00	2·00

Designs:—4E.50, Spiral waves; 5E.30, Satellite and Earth.

(Des N. Cavalcanti. Litho)

1974 (4 Sept). Birth Centenary of Guglielmo Marconi (radio pioneer). T **277** and similar horiz designs. Multicoloured. P 12.

1533	1E.50 Type **277**	20	10
1534	3E.30 "Radio Waves Across Space"	2·50	1·10
1535	10E. "Radio Waves for Navigation"	1·90	80
1533/1535	Set of 3	4·00	1·75

278 Early Post-boy and Modern Mail Van

279 Luisa Todi

(Des L. F. de Abreu. Litho Litografia Maia, Oporto)

1974 (9 Oct). Centenary of Universal Postal Union. T **278** and similar horiz designs. Multicoloured. P 13½.

1536	1E.50 Type **278**	15	10
1537	2E. Hand with letters	90	15
1538	3E.30 Sailing packet and modern liner	70	25
1539	4E.50 Dove and airliner	1·40	65
1540	5E.30 Hand and letter	1·40	75
1541	20E. Steam and electric locomotives	3·00	1·60
1536/1541	Set of 6	6·75	3·00
MS1542	106×147 mm. Nos. 1536/41 (sold at 50E.)	8·75	7·50

(Des F. George. Litho)

1974 (30 Oct). Portuguese Musicians. T **279** and similar vert designs. P 12.

1543	1E.50 bright purple	20	15
1544	2E. red	1·40	35
1545	2E.50 light brown	1·00	25
1546	3E. indigo	1·50	50
1547	5E.30 deep grey-green	1·20	80
1548	11E. crimson	1·30	80
1543/1548	Set of 6	6·00	2·50

Designs:—2E. João Domingos Bomtempo; 2E.50, Carlos Seixas; 3E. Duarte Lobo; 5E.30, João de Sousa Carvalho; 11E. Marcos Portugal.

280 Arms of Beja

281 "The Annunciation"

(Des J. de Moura. Litho Litografia de Portugal)

1974 (13 Nov). Bimillenary of Beja. T **280** and similar horiz designs. Multicoloured. P 13½.

1549	1E.50 Type **280**	25	10
1550	3E.50 Inhabitants of Beja through the ages	3·00	1·50
1551	7E. Moorish arches	3·25	1·70
1549/1551	Set of 3	5·75	2·75

(Des A. de Mattos e Silva. Litho Litografia Maia, Oporto)

1974 (4 Dec). Christmas. T **281** and similar square designs. Multicoloured. P 13½.

1552	1E.50 Type **281**	20	10
1553	4E.50 "The Nativity"	4·00	80
1554	10E. "The Flight into Egypt"	3·50	1·10
1552/1554	Set of 3	6·75	1·75

282 Rainbow and Dove

283 Egas Moniz

(Des V. Ribeiro. Litho)

1974 (18 Dec). Portuguese Armed Forces' Movement of 25th April. P 12.

1555	**282** 1E.50 multicoloured	15	15
1556	3E.50 multicoloured	4·00	1·90
1557	5E. multicoloured	3·00	1·10
1555/1557	Set of 3	6·50	2·75

(Des P. O. Art Dept. Recess)

1974 (27 Dec). Birth Centenary of Professor Egas Moniz (brain surgeon). T **283** and similar vert designs. P 11½×12.

1558	1E.50 bistre-brown & yellow-orange	35	15
1559	3E.30 dull orange and reddish brown	3·00	80
1560	10E. grey and dull ultramarine	6·00	1·00
1558/1560	Set of 3	8·50	1·50

Designs:—3E.30, Nobel Medicine and Physiology prize medal, 1949; 10E. Cerebral angiograph, 1927.

284 Portuguese Farmer and Soldier

285 Hands and Peace Dove

(Des J. A. Manta. Litho)

1975 (21 Mar). Portuguese Cultural Progress and Citizens' Guidance Campaign. P 12.

1561	**284** 1E.50 multicoloured	25	10
1562	3E. multicoloured	2·50	85
1563	4E.50 multicoloured	3·50	1·40
1561/1563	Set of 3	5·50	2·00

(Des L. F. de Abreu. Litho)

1975 (23 Apr). First Anniv of Portuguese Revolution. T **285** and similar square designs. Multicoloured. P 13½.

1564	1E.50 Type **285**	20	10
1565	4E.50 Hands and peace dove	3·50	90
1566	10E. Peace dove and emblem	4·25	1·50
1564/1566	Set of 3	7·00	2·00

Nos. 1564/6 were issued with captions on the reverse, under the gum.

PHOSPHOR BANDS. See note below No. 1441.

286 "The Hand of God"

287 "The Horseman of the Apocalypse" (detail of 12th-century manuscript)

(Des Q. Lapa. Litho)

1975 (13 May)–**76**. Holy Year. T **286** and similar square designs. Multicoloured. P 13½.

1567	1E.50 Type **286**	20	15
	p. One phosphor band (1976)	29·00	80
1568	4E.50 Hand with cross	4·25	1·30
1569	10E. Peace dove	5·75	1·50
1567/1569	Set of 3	9·00	2·50

PORTUGAL

(Des P.O. Art Dept. Litho)

1975 (26 May)–**76**. Europa. T **287** and similar square design. Multicoloured. P 13½.
1570	1E.50 Type **287**	1·20	15
	p. One phosphor band (1976)	75·00	2·00
1571	10E. "Fernando Pessoa" (poet) (A. Negreiros)	55·00	1·90

288 Assembly Building   **289** Hiking

(Des P.O. Art Dept. Litho Litografia de Portugal)

1975 (2 June). Opening of Portuguese Constituent Assembly. P 13½.
1572	**288** 2E. black, vermilion and lemon	45	10
1573	20E. black, bright emerald and lemon	7·50	1·80

(Des V. Ribeiro. Litho)

1975 (4 Aug)–**76**. 36th International Camping and Caravanning Federation Rally. T **289** and similar horiz designs. Multicoloured. P 13½.
1574	2E. Type **289**	1·10	15
	p. One phosphor band (1976)	8·50	45
1575	4E.50 Swimming and boating	3·25	1·40
1576	5E.30 Caravanning	2·40	1·40
1574/1576 Set of 3		6·00	2·50

290 Planting Tree   **291** Lilienthal Glider and Modern Space Rocket

(Des L. F. de Abreu. Litho)

1975 (17 Sept)–**76**. 30th Anniv of United Nations. T **290** and similar horiz designs. Multicoloured. P 13½.
1577	2E. Type **290**	55	10
	p. One phosphor band (1976)	13·50	75
1578	4E.50 Releasing peace dove	1·80	80
1579	20E. Corn harvesting	4·75	1·60
1577/1579 Set of 3		6·50	2·00

(Des J. L. Tinoco. Litho)

1975 (26 Sept)–**76**. 26th International Astronautical Federation Congress. Lisbon. T **291** and similar multicoloured designs. P 13½.
1580	2E. Type **291**	70	15
	p. One phosphor band (1976)	10·50	40
1581	4E. "Apollo"–"Soyuz" space link	2·30	1·10
1582	5E.30 R H. Goddard, R. E. Pelterie, H. Oberth and K. E. Tsiolkovsky (space pioneers)	1·50	1·10
1583	10E. Astronaut and spaceships (70×32 mm)	5·75	1·60
1580/1583 Set of 4		9·25	3·50

292 Surveying the Land   **293** Symbolic Arch

(Des P.O. Art Dept. Litho)

1975 (19 Nov). Centenary of National Geographical Society, Lisbon. T **292** and similar horiz designs. Multicoloured. P 12×12½.
1584	2E. Type **292**	35	10
1585	8E. Surveying the sea	2·30	90
1586	10E. People and globe	3·50	1·50
1584/1586 Set of 3		5·50	2·00

(Des J. Rodrigues. Litho Litografia Maia, Oporto)

1975 (28 Nov). European Architectural Heritage Year. T **293** and similar square designs. One phosphor band. P 13½.
1587	2E. grey, deep turq-bl & Prussian bl	35	25
1588	8E. grey and carmine	4·00	1·10
1589	10E. multicoloured	4·50	1·90
1587/1589 Set of 3		8·00	2·25

Designs:—8E. Stylised building plan; 10E. Historical building being protected from development.

294 Nurse in Hospital Ward   **295** Pen-nib as Plough Blade

1975 (30 Dec). International Women's Year. T **294** and similar horiz designs. Multicoloured. One phosphor band. P 13½.
1590	50c. Type **294**	30	15
1591	2E. Woman farm worker	1·10	40
1592	3E.50 Woman office worker	1·40	90
1593	8E. Woman factory worker	2·10	1·50
1590/1593 Set of 4		4·50	2·50
MS1594 104×115 mm. Nos. 1590/3 but without phosphor bands (sold at 25E.)		5·50	4·50

(Des A. Alfredo. Litho)

1976 (6 Feb). 50th Anniv of National Writers Society. One phosphor band. P 12.
1595	**295** 3E. deep blue and orange-red	50	10
1596	20E. rose-red and bright blue	5·25	1·60

296 First Telephone Set   **297** "Industrial Progress"

(Des J. Cândido. Litho)

1976 (10 Mar). Telephone Centenary. T **296** and similar horiz design. One phosphor band. P 12×12½.
1597	3E. black, yellish grn & dull yell-grn	1·10	15
1598	10E.50 black, vermilion and rose	4·25	1·20

Design:—10E.50, Alexander Graham Bell.

(Des P.O. Art Dept. Litho)

1976 (7 Apr). National Production Campaign. T **297** and similar horiz design. P 12½.
1599	50c. Venetian red	35	10
1600	1E. grey-green	55	20

Design:—1E. Consumer products.

298 Carved Olive-wood Spoons   **299** Stamp Designing

(Des P.O. Art Dept. Litho)

1976 (3 May). Europa. T **298** and similar horiz design. Multicoloured. One phosphor band. P 12×12½.
1601	3E. Type **298**	3·75	50
1602	20E. Gold ornaments	75·00	7·25

(Des P.O. Art Dept. Litho Litografia Nacional, Oporto)

1976 (29 May). Interphil 1976 International Stamp Exhibition, Philadelphia. T **299** and similar horiz designs. Multicoloured. One phosphor band. P 14.
1603	3E. Type **299**	35	10
1604	7E.50 Postage stamp being hand cancelled	1·30	85
1605	10E. Stamp printing	2·20	90
1603/1605 Set of 3		3·50	1·50

PORTUGAL

300 King Fernando promulgating Law

301 Athlete with Olympic Torch

(Des P.O. Art Dept. Litho)

1976 (2 July). 600th Anniv of "Sesmarias" (uncultivated land) Law. T **300** and similar horiz designs. Multicoloured. One phosphor band. P 12×11½.

1606	3E. Type **300**	25	15
1607	5E. Plough and farmers repelling hunters...	1·90	60
1608	10E. Corn harvesting	2·75	1·00
1606/1608 Set of 3		4·50	1·50
MS1609 230×150 mm. Nos. 1606/8 but without phosphor bands (sold at 30E.)		6·00	£100

(Des V. Graca. Litho Litografia Maia, Oporto)

1976 (16 July). Olympic Games, Montreal. T **301** and similar horiz designs. Multicoloured. One phosphor band. P 13½.

1610	3E. Type **301**	35	15
1611	7E. Women's relay	1·90	1·50
1612	10E.50 Olympic flame	2·50	1·40
1610/1612 Set of 3		4·25	2·75

302 "Speaking in the Country"

303 Azure-winged Magpie (*Cyanopica cyanea*)

(Des P. Barbosa and L. Domingues. Litho)

1976 (15 Sept). Anti-illiteracy Campaign. T **302** and similar horiz designs symbolising communication. Multicoloured. One phosphor band. P 12.

1613	3E. Type **302**	65	15
	a. Perf 13½	30·00	75
1614	3E. "Speaking at Sea"	65	15
	a. Perf 13½	85	25
1615	3E. "Speaking in Town"	65	15
	a. Perf 13½	30·00	75
1616	3E. "Speaking at Work"	1·60	15
	a. Perf 13½	85	25
1613/1616 Set of 4		3·25	55
1613a/1616a Set of 4		60·00	1·90
MS1617 145×104 mm. Nos. 1613/16 but without phosphor bands (sold at 25E.)		18·00	16·00

(Des P.O. Art Dept. Litho)

1976 (30 Sept). "Portucale 77" Thematic Stamp Exhibition, Oporto (1st issue). Portuguese Flora and Fauna. T **303** and similar vert designs. Multicoloured. One phosphor band (3, 5, 7E.) P 11½×12.

1618	3E. Type **303**	35	10
1619	5E. Lynx (*Lynx pardina*)	1·50	50
1620	7E. Portuguese laurel cherry (*Prunus lusitanica*) and blue tit	1·60	1·10
1621	10E.50 Wild carnation (*Dianthus broteri*) and lizard	1·80	1·30
1618/1621 Set of 4		4·75	2·75

See also Nos. 1673/**MS**1679.

304 "Lubrapex" Emblem and Exhibition hall

305 Bank Emblem

(Des J. Vidal. Litho)

1976 (9 Oct). Lubrapex 1976 Luso-Brazilian Stamp Exhibition. T **304** and similar vert design. Multicoloured. One phosphor band. P 13½.

1622	3E. Type **304**	45	15
1623	20E. "Lubrapex" emblem and "stamp"	3·00	2·00
MS1624 180×142 mm. Nos. 1622/3 but without phosphor bands (sold at 30E.)		5·00	5·00

(Des A. de Jesus Mendes. Litho)

1976 (29 Oct). Centenary of National Trust Fund Bank. One phosphor band (3E., 7E.). P 12×11½.

1625	**305**	3E. multicoloured	15	10
1626		7E. multicoloured	2·75	1·20
1627		15E. multicoloured	4·00	1·40
1625/1627 Set of 3			6·25	2·25

306 Sheep grazing

307 "Liberty"

(Des C. Dourado. Litho Litografia Nacional, Oporto)

1976 (24 Nov). Water Conservation. Preservation of Humid Zones. T **306** and similar horiz designs. Multicoloured. One phosphor band (Nos. 1628/30). P 14.

1628	1E. Type **306**	55	10
1629	3E. Marshland	1·10	40
1630	5E. Sea trout	3·00	55
1631	10E. Mallards	4·25	1·10
1628/1631 Set of 4		8·00	2·00

(Des P.O. Art Dept. Litho)

1976 (30 Nov). Consolidation of Democratic Institutions. One phosphor band. P 13½.

| 1632 | **307** | 3E. grey, light green and vermilion | 90 | 25 |

308 Examining Child's Eyes

309 Hydro-electric Power

(Des J. Vidal. Litho)

1976 (13 Dec). World Health Day. Detection and Prevention of Blindness. T **308** and similar horiz designs. Multicoloured. One phosphor band. (3E., 5E). P 13½.

1633	3E. Type **308**	35	15
1634	5E. Welder wearing protective goggles	2·40	35
1635	10E.50 Blind person reading Braille	2·50	1·50
1633/1635 Set of 3		4·75	2·75

(Des J. L. Tinoco. Litho Litografia Nacional, Oporto)

1976 (30 Dec). Uses of Natural Energy. T **309** and similar horiz designs, Multicoloured. One phosphor band (Nos. 1636/8). P 14.

1636	1E. Type **309**	30	20
1637	4E. Fossil fuel (oil)	60	25
1638	5E. Geo-thermic sources	1·00	35
1639	10E. Wind-power	1·70	1·00
1640	15E. Solar energy	3·75	1·70
1636/1640 Set of 5		6·50	3·00

310 Map of Member Countries

311 Bottle inside Human Body

PORTUGAL

(Des A. Mendes. Litho)

1977 (28 Jan). Admission of Portugal to the Council of Europe. One phosphor band. P 12×11½.
| 1641 | **310** | 8E.50 multicoloured | 1·60 | 1·60 |
| 1642 | | 10E. multicoloured | 1·80 | 1·70 |

(Des A. Garcia. Litho)

1977 (4 Feb). Tenth Anniv of Portuguese Anti-Alcoholic Society. T **311** and similar horiz designs. Multicoloured. One phosphor band (Nos. 1643/4). P 13½.
1643	3E. Type **311**	30	10
1644	5E. Broken body and bottle	1·10	55
1645	15E. Sun behind prison bars and bottle	3·00	1·60
1643/1645 Set of 3		3·75	2·00

312 Forest

313 Exercising

(Des L. F. Abreu. Litho)

1977 (21 Mar). Natural Resources. Forests. T **312** and similar horiz designs showing forest scenes. Multicoloured. One phosphor band (Nos. 1646/8). P 13½.
1646	1E. Type **312**	30	20
1647	4E. Cork oaks	95	35
1648	7E. Logs and trees	2·00	1·60
1649	15E. Trees by the sea	2·00	1·70
1646/1649 Set of 4		4·75	3·50

(Des C. D. Leitão. Litho)

1977 (13 Apr). International Rheumatism Year. T **313** and similar horiz designs. One phosphor band. P 12×12½.
1650	4E. yellow-orange, chestnut & blk	35	15
1651	6E. ultramarine, greenish bl & blk	1·50	1·10
1652	10E. rosine, mauve and black	1·40	95
1650/1652 Set of 3		2·75	1·90

Designs:—4E. Rheumatism victim, 10E. Group exercising.

314 Southern Plains

315 John XXI Enthroned

(Des P.O. Art Dept. Litho)

1977 (2 May). Europa. T **314** and similar horiz design. Multicoloured. One phosphor band. P 12×12½.
1653	4E. Type **314**	70	15
1654	8E.50 Northern terraced mountains	4·50	1·00
MS1655 148×95 mm. Nos. 1653/4, each×3	55·00	33·00

No. **MS**1655 has no phosphor bands.

(Des P.O. Art Dept. Litho)

1977 (20 May). Seventh Death Centenary of Pope John XXI. T **315** and similar vert design. Multicoloured. One phosphor band (4E.). P 13½.
| 1656 | 4E. Type **315** | 30 | 20 |
| 1657 | 15E. Pope as doctor | 80 | 65 |

316 Compass

317 Child and Computer

(Des P.O. Art Dept. Litho)

1977 (8 June). Camões Day. One phosphor band. P 12.
| 1658 | **316** | 4E. multicoloured | 35 | 20 |
| 1659 | | 8E.50 multicoloured | 1·50 | 1·40 |

(Des J. L. Tinoco. Litho)

1977 (20 July). Permanent Education. T **317** and similar horiz designs. Multicoloured. One phosphor band. P 12×12½.
1660	4E. Type **317**	55	20
1661	4E. Flautist and dancers	55	20
1662	4E. Farmer and tractor	55	20
1663	4E. Students and atomic construction	55	20
1660/1663 Set of 4		2·00	70
MS1664 148×96 mm. Nos. 1660/3 but without phosphor bands (sold at 20E.)	7·50	8·25

318 Pyrite

319 Alexandre Herculano

(Des L. Dias. Litho)

1977 (4 Oct). Natural Resources. The Subsoil. T **318** and similar horiz designs. Multicoloured One phosphor band (Nos. 1665/7). P 12×11½.
1665	4E. Type **318**	35	15
1666	5E. Marble	1·10	45
1667	10E. Iron ore	1·20	60
1668	20E. Uranium	3·25	1·60
1665/1668 Set of 4		5·25	2·50

(Des P.O. Art Dept. Eng A. Cardoso. Recess and litho)

1977 (19 Oct). Death Centenary of Alexandre Herculano (writer and politician). One phosphor band (4E.). P 13½.
| 1669 | **319** | 4E. multicoloured | 40 | 15 |
| 1670 | | 15E. multicoloured | 2·00 | 70 |

320 Early Steam Locomotive and Peasant Cart (ceramic panel, J. Colaço)

321 Poviero (Northern coast)

(Des P.O. Art Dept. Litho)

1977 (4 Nov). Centenary of Railway Bridge over River Douro, T **320** and similar horiz design. Multicoloured. One phosphor band. P 12×11½.
| 1671 | 4E. Type **320** | 40 | 20 |
| 1672 | 10E. Maria Pia bridge (Eiffel) | 3·00 | 2·20 |

(Des A. Alves, Litho)

1977 (19 Nov). Portucale 77 Thematic Stamp Exhibition (2nd issue). T **321** and similar horiz designs depicting Portuguese coastal fishing boats. Multicoloured. One phosphor band (Nos. 1673/7). P 12×11½.
1673	2E. Type **321**	55	15
1674	3E. Sea-going rowing boat, Mar	40	15
1675	4E. Rowing boat from Nazaré	40	20
1676	7E. Caicque from Algarve	60	35
1677	10E. Tunny fishing boat, Xavega	1·20	75
1678	15E. Buarcos fishing boat	1·60	1·10
1673/1678 Set of 6		4·25	2·50
MS1679 148×104 mm. Nos. 1673/8 (sold at 60E.)	6·00	5·00

No. **MS**1679 has no phosphor bands.

322 "The Adoration"
(Maria do Sameiro A. Santos)

323 Medical Equipment and Operating Theatre

31

PORTUGAL

(Des P.O. Art Dept. Litho)

1977 (14 Dec). Christmas. T **322** and similar designs showing children's paintings. Multicoloured. One phosphor band (Nos. 1680/2). P 12×11½ (horiz) or 11½×12 (vert).

1680	4E. Type **322**	40	15
1681	7E. "Star over Bethlehem" (Paula Maria L. David)	1·40	50
1682	10E. "The Holy Family" (Carla Maria M. Cruz) (vert)	1·60	75
1683	20E. "Children following Star" (Rosa Maria M. Cardoso) (vert)	3·50	1·60
1680/1683	Set of 4	6·25	2·75

I II

Two types of 30E.:
 I. Forge defined by quarter circle.
 II. Forge defined by half circle.

(Des. P.O. Art Dept. Litho)

1978 (15 Feb)–**84**. T **323** and similar horiz designs.

(a) Size 22×17 mm. Two phosphor bands. P 12½

1684	50c. dull blue-green, black and carmine (24.1.79)	15	10
1685	1E. deep grey-blue, dull orange and black (24.1.79)	15	10
1686	2E. dull ultramarine, grey-green and red-brown (2.1.80)	15	10
1687	3E. brown-ochre, yellow-olive and black (2.1.80)	15	10
1688	4E. sage green, chalky blue and light brown	20	15
1689	5E. chalky blue, grey-green and bistre-brown	20	15
1690	5E.50 deep brown, buff and yellow-olive (2.1.80)	25	15
1691	6E. bistre-brown, yellow & bronze-grn	25	15
1692	6E.50 bright blue, royal blue and yellow-olive (2.1.80)	25	15
1693	7E. black, brownish grey and light dull blue	25	15
1694	8E. brown-ochre, red-brown and slate (2.1.80)	25	15
1694a	8E.50 orange-brown, black and yellow-brown (13.6.81)	40	15
1695	9E. orange-yellow, red-brown and black (2.1.80)	35	15
1696	10E. brown-ochre, black and deep blue-green (24.1.79)	35	15
1697	12E.50 slate-blue, brown-red and black (16.3.83)	45	15
1698	16E. chestnut, black and violet (14.9.83)	2·75	45

(b) Size 30×21 mm. No phosphor bands. P 13½

1699	20E. multicoloured	70	15
	a. Two phosphor bands (1984)	6·25	20
1700	30E. multicoloured (I) (2.1.80)	1·10	45
	a. Type II (22.2.80)	1·00	50
1701	40E. multicoloured (24.1.79)	90	40
1702	50E. multicoloured (2.1.80)	1·30	30
1703	100E. multicoloured (24.1.79)	2·20	65
1703a	250E. multicoloured (16.3.83)	5·75	1·00
1684/1703a	Set of 22	16·00	5·00

Designs:—1E. Old and modern kitchen equipment; 2E. Telegraph key and masts, microwaves and dish aerial; 3E. Dressmaking and ready-to-wear clothes; 4E. Writing desk and computer; 5E. Tunny fishing boats and modern trawler; 5E.50, Manual and mechanical weaver's looms; 6E. Plough and tractor; 6E.50, Early monoplane and, B.A.C. One Eleven jetliner; 7E. Hand press and modern printing press; 8E. Carpenter's hand tools and mechanical tool; 8E.50, Potter's wheel and modern ceramic machinery; 9E. Old cameras and modern cine and photo cameras; 10E. Axe, saw and mechanical saw; 12E.50, Navigation and radar instruments; 16E. Manual and automatic mail sorting; 20E. Hand tools and building site; 30E. Hammer, anvil, bellows and industrial complex; 40E. Peasant cart and lorry; 50E. Alembic, retorts and modern chemical plant; 100E. Carpenter's shipyard, modern shipyard and tanker; 250E. Survey instruments.

The phosphor bands are at right angles, along the top and left or right of the stamp.

Type I of the 30E. was officially withdrawn before issue, the redrawn version (Type II) being placed on sale instead. However some small local post offices had inadvertently sold the original version and so it was made generally available in 1982.

324 Mediterranean Soil   **325** Pedestrian on Zebra Crossing

(Des P.O. Art Dept. Litho)

1978 (6 Mar). Natural Resources. The Soil. T **324** and similar horiz designs. Multicoloured. One phosphor band (Nos. 1704/6). P 12×11½.

1704	4E. Type **324**	40	20
1705	5E. Rock formation	60	25
1706	10E. Alluvial soil	1·60	90
1707	20E. Black soil	3·25	1·30
1704/1707	Set of 4	5·25	2·25

(Des A. Sena da Silva. Litho)

1978 (19 Apr). Road Safety. T **325** and similar horiz designs. One phosphor band (Nos. 1708/12). P 12×11½.

1708	1E. chalky blue, black and pale orange	20	20
1709	2E. chalky blue, black and blue-green	45	20
1710	2E.50 chalky blue, black and new blue	75	20
1711	5E. chalky blue, black and vermilion	1·60	25
1712	9E. chalky blue, black and ultramarine	3·75	85
1713	12E.50 chalky blue and black	4·50	2·20
1708/1713	Set of 6	10·00	3·50

Designs:—2E. Motor cyclist; 2E.50, Children in back of car; 5E. Driver in car; 9E. View of road from driver's seat; 12E.50, Road victim ("Don't drink and drive").

326 Roman Tower of Centum Callas, Belmonte   **327** Roman Bridge, Chaves

(Des A. Cardoso. Litho)

1978 (2 May). Europa. T **326** and similar horiz design. Multicoloured. P 12×12½.

1714	10E. Type **326**	1·50	35
1715	40E. Belém Monastery, Lisbon	6·00	1·80
MS1716	111×96 mm. Nos. 1714/5, each×2 (sold at 120E.)	27·00	16·00

(Des R. da Silva. Litho)

1978 (14 June). 19th Centenary of Chaves (Aquae Flaviae). T **327** and similar vert design. Multicoloured. One phosphor band (5E.). P 13½.

1717	5E. Type **327**	55	20
1718	20E. Inscribed tablet from bridge	3·25	1·40

328 Running   **329** Pedro Nunes

(Des P.O. Art Dept. Litho)

1978 (24 July). Sport for All. T **328** and similar horiz designs. Multicoloured. One phosphor band (Nos. 1719/20). P. 12.

1719	5E. Type **328**	25	15
1720	10E. Cycling	55	35
1721	12E.50 Swimming	1·10	95
1722	15E. Football	1·10	1·10
1719/1722	Set of 4	2·75	2·25

PORTUGAL

(Des P.O. Art Dept. Litho)

1978 (9 Aug). Fourth Death Centenary of Pedro Nunes (cosmographer). T **329** and similar horiz design. Multicoloured. One phosphor band (5E.). P 12×11½.
1723	5E. Type **329**	30	10
1724	20E. Nonio (navigational instrument) and diagram	1·70	55

(Des L. De Freitas. Litho)

1979 (21 Feb). Portuguese Emigrants. T **335** and similar horiz designs. Multicoloured. One phosphor band (5E.). P 12×11½.
1742	5E. Type **335**	25	10
1743	14E. Emigrants at airport	85	65
1744	17E. Man greeting child at railway station	1·60	1·40
1742/1744 Set of 3		2·25	1·75

330 Trawler, Crates of Fish and Lorry   **331** Post Rider

336 Traffic   **337** NATO Emblem

(Des L. Dias. Litho)

1978 (15 Sept). Natural Resources. Fishes. T **330** and similar horiz designs. Multicoloured. One phosphor band (Nos. 1725/6). P 12×11½.
1725	5E. Type **330**	35	15
1726	9E. Trawler and dockside cranes	90	25
1727	12E.50 Trawler, radar and lecture	1·40	1·10
1728	15E. Trawler with echo-sounding equipment, and laboratory	2·50	1·60
1725/1728 Set of 4		4·50	2·75

(Des D. Simões. Litho)

1979 (14 Mar). Fight against Noise. T **336** and similar square designs. Multicoloured. One phosphor band (Nos. 1745/6). P 13½.
1745	4E. Type **336**	60	25
1746	5E. Pneumatic drill	90	20
1747	14E. Loud hailer	1·70	75
1745/1747 Set of 3		2·75	1·00

(Des J. L. Tinoco. Litho)

1978 (30 Oct). Introduction of Post Code. T **331** and similar horiz designs. Multicoloured. One phosphor band. P 12×11½.
1729	5E. Type **331**	45	20
1730	5E. Pigeon with letter	45	20
1731	5E. Sorting letters	45	20
1732	5E. Pen nib and post codes	45	20
1729/1732 Set of 4		1·50	70

(Des P.O. Art Dept. Litho)

1979 (4 Apr). 30th Anniv of North Atlantic Treaty Organization. One phosphor band. P 12×11½.
1748	**337**	5E. bright blue, bright rose-red and chestnut	45	10
1749		50E. bright blue, bistre-yellow and rose-red	3·75	3·00
MS1750 120×100 mm. Nos. 1748/9, each×2			8·25	5·25

No. **MS**1750 has no phosphor bands.

332 Symbolic Figure   **333** Sebastião Magalhães Lima

338 Door-to-door Delivery   **339** Children playing Ball

(Des J. Vidal. Litho)

1978 (7 Dec). 30th Anniv of Declaration of Human Rights. T **332** and similar horiz design showing symbolic figure. P 12×11½.
1733	14E. multicoloured	70	50
1734	40E. multicoloured	2·50	1·40
MS1735 120×100 mm. Nos. 1733/4, each×2		7·75	5·25

(Des P.O. Art Dept. Litho)

1978 (7 Dec). 50th Death Anniv of Magalhães Lima (journalist and pacifist). One phosphor band. P 12×11½.
| 1736 | **333** | 5E. multicoloured | 45 | 20 |

(Des P.O. Art Dept. Litho)

1979 (30 Apr). Europa. T **338** and similar horiz design. Multicoloured. P 12×11½.
1751	14E. Postal messenger delivering letter in cleft stick	1·10	50
	p. One phosphor band	12·50	9·75
1752	40E. Type **338**	2·20	1·10
	p. One phosphor band	16·00	10·50
MS1753 119×103 mm. Nos. 1751/2, each ×2		16·00	8·25

No. **MS**1753 has been reported with grey (inscription) missing.

Forgeries of Nos. 1751/2p have been produced by overprinting fake phosphor bands on genuine plain stamps. The forged bands are about ½ mm. narrower than the genuine ones and are slightly misplaced. They are best detected by a U.V. lamp under which the forgeries react with a strong yellow colour.

334 Portable Post Boxes and Letter Balance   **335** Emigrant at Railway Station

(Des L. Chaves. Litho)

1978 (20 Dec). Centenary of Post Museum. T **334** and similar horiz designs. Multicoloured. One phosphor band (Nos. 1737/9). P 12×11½.
1737	4E. Type **334**	65	15
1738	5E. Morse equipment	45	20
1739	10E. Printing press and Portuguese stamps of 1853 (125th anniv)	1·60	30
1740	14E. Books, bookcases and entrance to Postal Library (centenary)	2·75	1·90
1737/1740 Set of 4		5·00	2·25
MS1741 120×99 mm. Nos. 1737/40 but without phosphor bands (sold at 40E.)		7·00	5·75

(Des J. L. Tinoco, Litho)

1979 (1 June). International Year of the Child. T **339** and similar horiz designs. Multicoloured. One phosphor band (Nos. 1754/6). P 12×12½.
1754	5E.50 Type **339**	45	35
1755	6E.50 Mother, baby and dove	45	10
1756	10E. Child eating	55	50
1757	14E. Children of different races	1·10	1·00
1754/1757 Set of 4		2·25	1·75
MS1758 110×104 mm. Nos. 1754/7 but without phosphor bands (sold at 40E.)		5·00	4·00

340 Saluting the Flag   **341** Pregnant Woman

33

PORTUGAL

(Des O. Batista. Litho)
1979 (8 June). Camões Day. One phosphor band. P 12×12½.
1759	**340** 6E.50 multicoloured	50	20
MS1760	148×125 mm. No. 1759×9	5·50	4·00

(Des F. Vidal, Litho)
1979 (6 July). The Mentally Handicapped. T **341** and similar horiz designs. Multicoloured. One phosphor band (6E.50). P 12×12½.
1761	6E.50 Type **341**	45	10
1762	17E. Boy sitting in cage	1·00	65
1763	20E. Face, and hands holding hammer and chisel	1·50	1·00
1761/1763	Set of 3	2·50	1·50

342 Children reading Book

343 Water Cart, Caldas de Monchique

(Des L. F. de Abreu. Litho)
1979 (25 July). 50th Anniv of International Bureau of Education. T **342** and similar horiz design. Multicoloured. One phosphor band (6E.50). P 12×12½.
1764	6E.50 Type **342**	45	10
1765	17E. Teaching a deaf child	2·40	1·30

(Des A. Cardoso. Litho)
1979 (15 Sept). Brasiliana 79 International Stamp Exhibition. Portuguese Country Carts. T **343** and similar horiz designs. Multicoloured. One phosphor band (Nos. 1766/8). P 12×12½.
1766	2E.50 Type **343**	25	25
1767	5E.50 Wine sledge, Madeira	25	25
1768	6E.50 Wine cart, Upper Douro	40	20
1769	16E. Covered cart, Alentejo	1·10	95
1770	19E. Cart, Mogadouro	1·60	1·30
1771	20E. Sand cart, Murtosa	1·70	55
1766/1771	Set of 6	4·75	3·00

344 Aircraft flying through Storm Cloud

345 Antonio José de Almeida

(Des M. Chaves, Litho)
1979 (21 Sept). AIR. 35th Anniv of TAP (national airline). T **344** and similar horiz design. Multicoloured. P 12×11½.
1772	16E. Type **344**	1·40	65
1773	19E. Aircraft and sunset	1·60	1·10

(Des V. Santos. Litho)
1979 (4 Oct). Republican Personalities (1st series). T **345** and similar vert designs. One phosphor band (Nos. 1774/6). P 12½×12.
1774	5E.50 magenta, grey & carmine	45	15
1775	6E.50 bright rose-red, grey & carmine	45	10
1776	10E. light brown, grey & carmine-verm	65	10
1777	16E. deep grey-blue, grey & carmine	1·40	75
1778	19E.50 olive-green, grey & car-verm	1·80	1·30
1779	20E. deep claret, grey & carmine-verm	2·00	65
1774/1779	Set of 6	6·00	2·75

Designs:—6E.50, Afonso Costa; 10E. Teófilo Braga; 16E. Bernardino Machado; 19E.50, João Chagas; 20E. Elias Garcia.
See also Nos. 1787/92.

346 Family Group

347 "The Holy Family"

(Des J. L. Tinoco. Litho)
1979 (26 Oct). Towards a National Health Service. T **346** and similar horiz design. Multicoloured. One phosphor band (6E.50). P 12×12½.
1780	6E.50 Type **346**	45	10
1781	20E. Doctor examining patient	1·80	65

(Des P.O. Art Dept. Litho)
1979 (5 Dec). Christmas. Tiles. T **347** and similar horiz designs. Multicoloured. One phosphor band (Nos. 1782/3). P 12×12½.
1782	5E.50 Type **347**	50	35
1783	6E.50 "Adoration of the Shepherds"	50	30
1784	16E. "Flight into Egypt"	1·50	1·10
1782/1784	Set of 3	2·25	1·50

348 Rotary Emblem and Globe

349 Jaime Cortesão

(Des V. Graça. Litho)
1980 (22 Feb). 75th Anniv of Rotary International. T **348** and similar horiz design. Multicoloured. P 12×11½.
1785	16E. Type **348**	1·60	90
1786	50E. Rotary emblem and torch	3·50	2·40

(Des J. Cândido. Litho)
1980 (19 Mar). Republican Personalities (2nd series). T **349** and similar horiz designs. One phosphor band. P 12×11½.
1787	3E.50 orange and light brown	35	15
1788	5E.50 dull yellow-green, yellow-olive and brown-olive	45	25
1789	6E.50 bright lilac and deep reddish violet	45	25
1790	11E. orge-yell, brownish grey, slate & blk	2·20	1·30
1791	16E. deep yellow-ochre & yell-brn	1·20	80
1792	20E. pale turquoise-green, violet-blue and grey-blue	1·20	55
1787/1792	Set of 6	5·25	3·00

Designs:—3E.50, Alvaro de Castro; 5E.50, António Sérgio; 6E.50, Norton de Matos; 16E. Teixeira Gomes; 20E. José Domingues dos Santos.

350 Serpa Pinto

351 Barn Owl (*Tyto alba*)

(Des J. P. Roque. Litho)
1980 (14 Apr). Europa. T **350** and similar vert design. Multicoloured. One phosphor band (16E). P 11½×12.
1793	16E. Type **350**	1·10	55
1794	60E. Vasco da Gama	2·75	1·30
MS1795	107×110 mm. Nos. 1793/4, each×2	9·25	3·25

No. **MS**1795 has no phosphor bands.

(Des J. A. Cardoso. Litho)
1980 (6 May). Protection of Species. Animals in Lisbon Zoo. T **351** and similar horiz designs. Multicoloured. One phosphor band. P 12×11½.
1796	6E.50 Type **351**	30	10
1797	16E. Red fox (*Vulpes vulpes*)	1·20	80
1798	19E.50 Wolf (*Canis lupus signatus*)	1·50	85
1799	20E. Golden eagle (*Aquila chrysaetus*)	1·50	80
1796/1799	Set of 4	4·00	2·25
MS1800	109×107 mm. Nos. 1796/9 but without phosphor bands	5·00	4·00

The margin of No. **MS**1800 is inscribed for "London 1980" international stamp exhibition.

PORTUGAL

352 Luis Vaz de Camões   **353** Pinto in Japan

(Des J. P. Roque. Eng J. Carvalho. Recess and litho)

1980 (9 June). 400th Death Anniv of Luis Vaz de Camões (poet). One phosphor band. P 12.
1801	**352**	6E.50 multicoloured	55	15
1802		20E. multicoloured	1·40	65

Nos 1801/2 were each issued with a *se-tenant* stamp-size label showing an extract from *The Lusiads* (6E.50) or *Sonnets* (20E.).

(Des L. de Freitas. Litho)

1980 (30 June). 400th Anniv of Fernão Mendes Pinto's *A Peregrinação* (*The Pilgrimage*). T **353** and similar horiz design. Multicoloured. One phosphor band. P 12×11½.
1803	6E.50 Type **353**	45	10
1804	10E. Sea battle	1·30	75

354 Lisbon and Statue of St. Vincent (Jerónimos Monastery)   **355** Caravel

(Des A. Cardoso. Litho)

1980 (17 Sept). World Tourism Conference, Manila, Philippines. T **354** and similar horiz designs. Multicoloured. One phosphor band. P 12×12½.
1805	6E.50 Type **354**	45	20
1806	8E. Lantern Tower, Évora Cathedral	65	35
1807	11E. Mountain village and "Jesus with Top-hat" (Mirando do Douro Cathedral)	1·40	75
1808	16E. Caniçada dam and "Lady of the Milk" (Braga Cathedral)	1·90	1·00
1809	19E.50 Aveiro River and pulpit from Santa Cruz Monastery, Coimbra	2·20	1·10
1810	20E. Rocha beach and ornamental chimney	1·70	80
1805/1810 *Set of 6*		7·50	3·75

(Des S. Rodrigues. Litho)

1980 (18 Oct). Lubrapex 80 Portuguese–Brazilian Stamp Exhibition, Lisbon. T **355** and similar horiz designs. Multicoloured. One phosphor band. P 12×11½.
1811	6E.50 Type **355**	45	10
1812	8E. Nau	1·20	60
1813	16E. Galleon	1·70	80
1814	19E.50 Early paddle-steamer with sails	2·20	85
1811/1814 *Set of 4*		5·00	2·00
MS1815	132×88 mm. Nos. 1811/14 but without phosphor bands (sold at 60E.)	8·75	7·50

356 Lightbulbs   **357** Duke of Bragança and Open Book

(Des V. Graça. Litho)

1980 (31 Oct). Energy Conservation. T **356** and similar horiz design. Multicoloured. One phosphor band. P 12.
1816	6E.50 Type **356**	45	10
1817	16E. Speeding car	2·50	90

(Des A. Cardoso, Litho)

1980 (19 Dec). Bicentenary of Academy of Sciences, Lisbon. T **357** and similar horiz design. Multicoloured. One phosphor band. P 12×11½.
1818	6E.50 Type **357**	40	10
1819	19E.50 Uniformed academician, Academy and sextant	1·90	90

358 Cigarette contaminating Lungs   **359** Head and Computer Punch-card

(Des V. Graça. Litho Litografia Maia, Oporto)

1980 (19 Dec). Anti-Smoking Campaign. T **358** and similar horiz design. Multicoloured. One phosphor band. P 13½.
1820	6E.50 Type **358**	40	10
1821	19E.50 Healthy figure pushing away hand with cigarette	2·40	1·40

(Des J. L. Tinoco. Litho Litografia Maia, Oporto)

1981 (28 Jan). National Census. T **359** and similar horiz design. Multicoloured. One phosphor band. P 13½.
1822	6E.50 Type **359**	45	25
1823	16E. Houses and punch-card	1·70	1·30

360 Fragata, River Tejo   **361** "Rajola" Tile from Setúbal Peninsula (15th century)

(Des A. Alves. Litho)

1981 (23 Feb). River Boats. T **360** and similar horiz designs. Multicoloured. One phosphor band. P 12×12½.
1824	8E. Type **360**	40	30
1825	8E.50 Rabelo, River Douro	40	25
1826	10E. Moliceiro, Aveiro River	55	30
1827	16E. Barco, River Lima	95	60
1828	19E.50 Carocho, River Minho	1·00	60
1829	20E. Varino, River Tejo	1·00	55
1824/1829 *Set of 6*		4·00	2·25

(Des P.O. Art Dept. Litho)

1981 (16 Mar). Tiles (1st series). One phosphor band. P 12.
1830	**361** 8E.50 multicoloured	95	15
MS1831	146×102 mm. No. 1830×6	6·50	80

See also Nos. 1843/**MS**1844, 1847/**MS**1848, 1862/**MS**1864, 1871/**MS**1872, 1885/**MS**1886, 1893/**MS**1894, 1902/**MS**1904, 1914/**MS**1915, 1926/**MS**1927, 1935/**MS**1936, 1941/**MS**1943, 1952/**MS**1953, 1970/**MS**1971, 1972/**MS**1973, 1976/**MS**1978, 1983/**MS**1984, 1993/**MS**1994. 2020/**MS**2021 and 2031/**MS**2033.

362 Agua Dog   **363** "Agriculture"

(Des A. Cardoso. Litho)

1981 (16 Mar). 50th Anniv of Kennel Club of Portugal. T **362** and similar horiz designs. Multicoloured. One phosphor band (Nos. 1832/6). P 12.
1832	7E. Type **362**	55	30
1833	8E.50 Serra de Aires	55	30
1834	15E. Perdigueiro	1·00	30
1835	22E. Podengo	1·90	80
1836	25E. Castro Laboreiro	2·40	1·40
1837	33E.50 Serra da Estrela	2·75	1·00
1832/1837 *Set of 6*		8·25	3·50

35

PORTUGAL

(Des A. Alves. Litho)

1981 (30 Apr). May Day. T **363** and similar horiz design. Multicoloured. One phosphor band. P 12×12½.
1838	8E.50 Type **363**	45	10
1839	25E.50 "Industry"	1·80	1·20

364 Dancer and Tapestry   **365** St. Anthony Writing

(Des T. de Mello. Litho Litografia Maia, Oporto)

1981 (11 May). Europa. T **364** and similar vert design. Multicoloured. One phosphor band. P 13½.
1840	22E. Type **364**	1·60	65
1841	48E. Painted boat prow, painted plate and shipwright with model boat	3·25	1·70
MS1842	108×109 mm. Nos. 1840/1, each ×2	13·00	6·50

(Des P.O. Art Dept. Litho)

1981 (13 June). Tiles (2nd series). Horiz design as T **361**. Multicoloured. One phosphor band. P 12.
1843	8E.50 Tracery-pattern tile from Seville (16th century)	95	15
MS1844	146×102 mm. No. 1843×6	6·25	5·00

(Des J. Vidal. Litho)

1981 (13 June). 750th Death Anniv of St. Anthony of Lisbon. T **365** and similar horiz design. Multicoloured. One phosphor band (8E.50). P 12.
1845	8E.50 Type **365**	55	15
1846	70E. St. Anthony giving blessing	4·75	2·50

(Des P.O. Art Dept. Litho)

1981 (28 Aug). Tiles (3rd series). Vert design as T **361**. Multicoloured. Two phosphor bands. P 12.
1847	8E.50 Arms of Jaime, Duke of Bragança (Seville, 1510)	95	15
MS1848	146×102 mm. No. 1847×6	6·00	5·00

The phosphor bands are at right angles, along the left and top of the stamp.

366 King João II and Caravels   **367** Dom Luiz, 1862

(Des L. de Freitas. Litho)

1981 (28 Aug). 500th Anniv of King João II's Accession. T **366** and similar horiz design. Multicoloured. One phosphor band. P 12×11½.
1849	8E.50 Type **366**	55	15
1850	27E. King João II on horseback	3·25	1·10

(Des A. Cardoso. Litho)

1981 (28 Oct). 125th Anniv of Portuguese Railways. T **367** and similar horiz designs. Multicoloured. One phosphor band. P 12×11½.
1851	8E.50 Type **367**	90	25
1852	19E. Pacific steam locomotive, 1925	2·75	1·30
1853	27E. Alco 1500 diesel locomotive, 1948	2·75	1·40
1854	33E.50 Alsthom BB 2600 electric locomotive, 1974	3·25	1·20
1851/1854	Set of 4	8·75	4·00

368 "Perrier" Pump, 1856   **369** "Virgin and Child"

(Des J. Cardoso. Litho)

1981 (18 Nov). Portuguese Fire Engines. T **368** and similar horiz designs. Multicoloured. One phosphor band. P 12×12½.
1855	7E. Type **368**	95	25
1856	8E.50 Ford fire engine, 1927	85	25
1857	27E. Renault fire pump, 1914	2·40	1·30
1858	33E.50 Ford Snorkel combined hoist and pump, 1978	3·75	1·40
1855/1858	Set of 4	7·25	2·75

(Des P.O. Art Dept. Litho)

1981 (16 Dec). Christmas. Crib Figures. T **369** and similar vert designs. Multicoloured. One phosphor band. P 12½×12.
1859	7E. Type **369**	1·20	40
1860	8E.50 "Nativity"	95	40
1861	27E. "Flight into Egypt"	2·50	1·50
1859/1861	Set of 3	4·25	2·00

(Des P.O. Art Dept. Litho)

1981 (16 Dec). Tiles (4th series). Horiz design as T **361**. Multicoloured. Two phosphor bands. P 12.
1862	8E.50 "Pisana" tile, Lisbon (16th century)	95	20
MS1863	146×102 mm. No. 1862×6	6·00	5·00
MS1864	120×102 mm. Nos. 1830, 1843, 1847 and 1862	6·75	5·75

No. 1862 has the phosphor bands at right angles, along the left and bottom of the stamp.

370 St. Francis with Animals   **371** Flags of E.E.C. Members

(Des J. Tinoco. Litho)

1982 (20 Jan). 800th Birth Anniv of St. Francis of Assisi. T **370** and similar vert design. Multicoloured. One phosphor band. P 12½×12.
1865	8E.50 Type **370**	50	30
1866	27E. St. Francis helping to build church	2·75	1·90

(Des A. Santos. Litho)

1982 (24 Feb). 25th Anniv of European Economic Community. One phosphor band. P 12½×11½.
1867	**371** 27E. multicoloured	1·70	1·00
MS1868	155×88 mm. No. 1867×4	6·75	5·75

372 Fort St. Catherina, Lighthouse and Memorial Column   **373** Sagres I (cadet barque)

(Des A. Cardoso. Litho Litografia Maia, Oporto)

1982 (24 Feb). Centenary of Figueira da Foz City. T **372** and similar horiz design. Multicoloured. One phosphor band. P 13½×13.
1869	10E. Type **372**	60	10
1870	19E. Tagus bridge, shipbuilding yard and trawler	2·30	1·20

(Des P.O. Art Dept. Litho)

1982 (24 Mar). Tiles (5th series). Horiz design as T **361**. Multicoloured. Two phosphor bands. P 12×11½.
1871	10E. Italo-Flemish pattern tile (17th century)	95	20
MS1872	146×102 mm. No. 1871×6	6·75	5·00

The phosphor bands are at right angles, along the left and bottom of the stamp.

(Des J. Tinoco. Litho)

1982 (24 Mar). Sporting Events. T **373** and similar horiz designs. Multicoloured. One phosphor band (Nos. 1873/4). P 12×12½.
1873	27E. Type **373** (Lisbon sailing races)	2·00	1·10
1874	33E.50 Roller hockey (25th world championships)	2·75	1·80
1875	50E. "470" class racing dinghies (world championships)	4·00	1·90
1876	75E. Football (World Cup Football Championship, Spain)	6·25	2·20
1873/1876	Set of 4	13·50	6·25

374 Edison Gower Bell Telephone, 1882   **375** Embassy of King Manuel to Pope Leo X

(Des J. Brandão. Litho)

1982 (14 Apr). Centenary of Public Telephone Service. T **374** and similar vert design. Multicoloured. One phosphor band. P 11½×12.
1877	10E. Type **374**	55	10
1878	27E. Consolidated telephone, 1887	1·80	1·40

(Des J. P. Roque. Litho)

1982 (3 May). Europa. One phosphor band. P 12×11½.
1879	**375** 33E.50 multicoloured	2·75	1·10
MS1880	140×114 mm. No. 1879×4	13·00	6·50

376 Pope John Paul II and Shrine of Fatima   **377** Dunlin (*Calidris alpina*)

(Des J. Candido. Litho Litografia Maia, Oporto)

1982 (13 May). Papal Visit. T **376** and similar horiz designs. Multicoloured. One phosphor band. P 14.
1881	10E. Type **376**	55	10
1882	27E. Pope and Sameiro Sanctuary	2·50	1·50
1883	33E.50 Pope and Lisbon Cathedral	3·00	1·50
1881/1883	Set of 3	5·50	2·75
MS1884	138×78 mm. Nos. 1881/3, each ×2	12·00	5·75

(Des P.O. Art Dept. Litho)

1982 (11 June). Tiles (6th series). Horiz design as T **361**. Multicoloured. Two phosphor bands. P 12½.
1885	10E. Altar front panel depicting oriental tapestry (17th century)	95	20
MS1886	146×102 mm. No. 1885×6	6·00	5·00

The phosphor bands are at right angles, along the left and bottom of the stamp.

(Des A. da Conceição. Litho)

1982 (11 June). Philexfrance 82 International Stamp Exhibition, Paris. Birds. T **377** and similar vert designs. Multicoloured. One phosphor band. P 12.
1887	10E. Type **377**	55	15
1888	19E. Redcrested pochard (*Netta rufina*)	2·20	80
1889	27E. Greater flamingo (*Phoenicopterus ruber*)	2·50	1·10
1890	33E.50 Black-winged stilt (*Himantopus himantopus*)	2·75	1·60
1887/1890	Set of 4	7·25	3·25

PORTUGAL

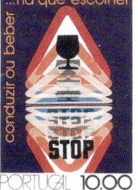

378 Dr. Robert Koch   **379** Wine Glass and Stop Sign

(Des J. Tinoco. Litho)

1982 (27 July). Centenary of Discovery of Tubercle Bacillus. T **378** and similar horiz design. Multicoloured. One phosphor band. P 12.
1891	27E. Type **378**	2·00	1·50
1892	33E.50 Lungs	2·30	1·60

(Des P.O. Art Dept. Litho)

1982 (22 Sept). Tiles (7th series). Horiz design as T **361**. Multicoloured. Two phosphor bands. P 12.
1893	10E. Polychromatic quadrilobate pattern, 1630/40	95	15
MS1894	146×102 mm. No. 1893×6	6·00	5·00

The phosphor bands are at right angles, along the left and bottom of the stamp.

(Des A. Santos. Litho)

1982 (22 Sept). "Don't Drink and Drive". One phosphor band. P 11½×12.
1895	**379** 10E. multicoloured	70	15

380 Fairey IIID Seaplane *Lusitania*   **381** Marquis de Pombal

(Des C. Dinis. Litho)

1982 (15 Oct). Lubrapex 82 Brazilian–Portuguese Stamp Exhibition, Curitiba. T **380** and similar horiz designs. Multicoloured. One phosphor band (Nos. 1896/8). P 12×11½.
1896	10E. Type **380**	45	30
1897	19E. Dornier Do-J Wal flying boat *Argus*	2·10	1·00
1898	33E.50 Douglas DC-7C "Seven Seas" airliner	2·50	1·00
1899	50E. Boeing 747-282B jetliner	2·75	1·30
1896/1899	Set of 4	7·00	3·25
MS1900	155×98 mm. Nos. 1896/9	8·00	6·50

(Des L. F. de Abreu. Litho)

1982 (24 Nov). Death Bicentenary of Marquis de Pombal (statesman and reformer). One phosphor band. P 12×11½.
1901	**381** 10E. multicoloured	70	15

(Des P.O. Art Dept. Litho)

1982 (15 Dec). Tiles (8th series). Horiz design at T **361**. Multicoloured. Two phosphor bands. P 12.
1902	10E. Monochrome quadrilobate pattern, 1670/90	95	15
MS1903	146×102 mm. No. 1902×6	6·00	5·00
MS1904	101×121 mm. Nos. 1871, 1885, 1893 and 1902	6·00	5·00

No. 1902 has the phosphor bands at right angles, along the left and bottom of the stamp.

382 Gallic Cock and Tricolour

(Des A. Santos. Litho)

1983 (5 Jan). Centenary of French Alliance (French language-teaching association). One phosphor band. P 12.
1905	**382** 27E. multicoloured	2·00	1·00

37

PORTUGAL

383 Lisnave Shipyard

(Des A. Magalhães. Litho)

1983 (5 Jan). 75th Anniv of Port of Lisbon Administration. One phosphor band. P 12½.
| 1906 | 383 | 10E. multicoloured | 70 | 15 |

384 Export Campaign Emblem   **385** Midshipman and *Vasco da Gama* (frigate), 1782

(Des J. Cândido. Litho)

1983 (28 Jan). Export Promotion. One phosphor band. P 12×11½.
| 1907 | 384 | 10E. multicoloured | 70 | 15 |

(Des A. Cardoso, Litho)

1983 (23 Feb). Naval Uniforms. T **385** and similar square designs. Multicoloured. One phosphor band. P 13½.
1908	12E.50 Type **385**	1·00	15
	a. Imperf×p 13½. Booklets	1·80	1·70
	ab. Booklet pane. Nos. 1908a/11a	11·00	9·00
1909	25E. Seaman and *Estefânia* (steam corvette), 1845	1·70	40
	a. Imperf×p 13½. Booklets	2·75	2·75
1910	30E. Marine sergeant and *Adamastor* (cruiser), 1900	2·30	75
	a. Imperf×p 13½. Booklets	3·00	3·00
1911	37E.50 Midshipman and *João Belo* (frigate), 1982	2·50	90
	a. Imperf×p 13½. Booklets	3·75	3·50
1908/1911 Set of 4		6·75	1·90

386 WCY. Emblem   **387** Portuguese Helmet (16th century)

(Des A. Santos. Litho)

1983 (23 Feb). World Communications Year. T **386** and similar vert design. Multicoloured. One phosphor band. P 11½×12.
| 1912 | 10E. Type **386** | 55 | 25 |
| 1913 | 33E.50 W.C.Y. emblem (different) | 2·30 | 1·40 |

(Des P.O. Art Dept. Litho)

1983 (16 Mar). Tiles (9th series). Horiz design as T **361**. Multicoloured. Two phosphor bands. P 12.
| 1914 | 12E.50 Hunter killing white bull (tile from Saldanha Palace, Lisbon, 17/18th century) | 1·10 | 20 |
| MS1915 146×102 mm. No. 1914×6 | | 7·25 | 6·25 |

The phosphor bands are at right angles, along the left and bottom of the stamp.

(Des A. M. Oliveira. Litho)

1983 (6 Apr). Expo XVII Council of Europe Exhibition. T **387** and similar horiz designs. Multicoloured. One phosphor band (Nos. 1916/20). P 12×11½.
1916	11E. Type **387**	1·20	35
1917	12E.50 Astrolabe (16th century)	95	35
1918	25E. Portuguese caravels (from 16th century Flemish tapestry)	2·00	65
1919	30E. Carved capital (12th century)	2·30	70
1920	37E.50 Hour glass (16th century)	2·10	1·20
1921	40E. Detail from Chinese painting (16/17th century)	2·50	1·10
1916/1921 Set of 6		10·00	4·00
MS1922 115×120 mm. Nos. 1916/21		16·00	9·75

388 Egas Moniz (Nobel Prize winner and brain surgeon)

(Des J. Tinoco. Litho Litografia Maia, Oporto)

1983 (5 May). Europa, One phosphor band. P 12½.
| 1923 | **388** | 37E.50 multicoloured | 2·75 | 1·00 |
| MS1924 140×114 mm. No. 1923×4 | | 14·50 | 8·25 |

389 Passenger in Train

(Des A. Santos. Litho)

1983 (16 May). European Ministers of Transport Conference. One phosphor band. P 12½.
| 1925 | **389** | 30E. greenish blue, royal blue and silver | 3·00 | 1·00 |

(Des P.O. Art Dept. Litho)

1983 (16 June). Tiles (10th series). Horiz designs at T **361**. Multicoloured. Two phosphor bands. P 12.
| 1926 | 12E.50 Tiles depicting birds (18th century) | 1·10 | 20 |
| MS1927 146×102 mm. No. 1926×6 | | 7·25 | 6·25 |

The phosphor bands are at right angles, along the left and bottom of the stamp.

390 Mediterranean Monk Seal (*Monachus monachus*)   **391** Assassination of Spanish Administrator by Prince John

(Des V. Lages. Litho)

1983 (29 July). Brasiliana 83 International Stamp Exhibition, Rio de Janeiro. Marine Mammals. T **390** and similar horiz designs. Multicoloured. One phosphor band (Nos. 1928/30). P 12×11½.
1928	12E.50 Type **390**	1·00	35
1929	30E. Common dolphin (*Delphinus delphis*)	3·75	60
1930	37E.50 Killer whale (*Orcinus orca*)	3·25	1·60
1931	80E. Humpback whale (*Megaptera novaeangliae*)	5·75	1·50
1928/1931 Set of 4		12·50	3·50
MS1932 133×81 mm. Nos. 1928/31		14·50	12·50

(Des L. de Freitas. Litho)

1983 (14 Sept). 600th Anniv of Independence. T **391** and similar square design. Multicoloured. One phosphor band. P 13½.
| 1933 | 12E.50 Type **391** | 1·00 | 25 |
| 1934 | 30E. Prince John proclaimed King of Portugal | 3·50 | 1·60 |

(Des P.O. Art Dept. Litho)

1983 (19 Oct). Tiles (11th series). Horiz design as T **361**. Multicoloured. Two phosphor bands. P 12.
| 1935 | 12E.50 Flower pot by Gabriel del Barco (18th century) | 1·10 | 20 |
| MS1936 146×102 mm. No. 1935×6 | | 7·00 | 5·75 |

The phosphor bands are at right angles, along the left and bottom of the stamp.

PORTUGAL

392 Bartolomeu de Gusmão and Model Balloon, 1709

393 "Adoration of the Magi"

(Des J. Tinoco. Litho)

1983 (9 Nov). Bicentenary of Manned Flight. T **392** and similar horiz design. Multicoloured. One phosphor band. P 12×11½.
1937	16E. Type **392**	75	15
1938	51E. Montgolfier balloon, 1783	2·75	1·20

(Des P.O. Art Dept. Litho)

1983 (23 Nov). Christmas. Stained Glass Windows from Monastery of Our Lady of Victory, Batalha. T **393** and similar vert design. Multicoloured. One phosphor band. P 12½.
1939	12E.50 Type **393**	70	25
1940	30E. "The Flight into Egypt"	3·00	1·20

(Des P.O. Art Dept. Litho)

1983 (23 Nov). Tiles (12th series). Horiz design as T **361**. Multicoloured. Two phosphor bands. P 12.
1941	12E.50 Turkish horseman (18th century)	1·10	20
MS1942	146×102 mm. No. 1941×6	7·00	5·75
MS1943	120×102 mm. Nos. 1914, 1926, 1935 and 1941	6·00	5·00

No. 1941 has the phosphor bands at right angles, along the left and bottom of the stamp.

394 Siberian Tiger (*Panthera tigris*)

395 Fighter Pilot and Hawker Hurricane Mk II, 1954

(Des J. P. Roque. Litho)

1984 (18 Jan). Centenary of Lisbon Zoo. T **394** and similar horiz designs. Multicoloured. One phosphor band. P 12×11½.
1944	16E. Type **394**	1·80	25
	a. Strip of 4. Nos. 1944/7	7·00	7·00
1945	16E. Cheetah (*Acinonyx jubatus*)	1·80	25
1946	16E. Blesbok (*Damaliscus albifrons*)	1·80	25
1947	16E. White rhino (*Ceratotherium simum*)	1·80	25
1944/1947	Set of 4	6·50	90

Nos. 1944/7 were printed together in *se-tenant* strips of four, both horizontally and vertically, within sheetlets of 16 stamps.

(Des A. Cardoso. Litho)

1984 (15 Feb). Air Force Uniforms. T **395** and similar square designs. Multicoloured. One phosphor band. P 13½.
1948	16E. Type **395**	80	10
	a. Imperf×p 13½. Booklets	3·00	2·75
	ab. Booklet pane. Nos. 1948a/51a	16·00	
1949	35E. Pilot in summer uniform and Republic F-84G Thunderjet, 1960	2·50	80
	a. Imperf×p 13½. Booklet	5·50	5·50
1950	40E. Paratrooper in walking-out uniform and Nord 2501D Noratlas military transport plane, 1966	2·50	85
	a. Imperf×p 13½. Booklets	5·50	5·25
1951	51E. Pilot in normal uniform and Vought A-70 Corsair II bomber, 1966	3·00	1·20
	a. Imperf×p 13½. Booklets	6·00	5·75
1948/1951	Set of 4	8·00	2·50

(Des P.O. Art Dept. Litho)

1984 (8 Mar). Tiles (13th series). Horiz design as T **361**. Multicoloured. Two phosphor bands. P 12.
1952	16E. Coat of arms of King José I (late 18th century)	1·10	20
MS1953	146×102 mm. No. 1952×6	7·25	6·25

The phosphor bands are at right angles, along the left and bottom of the stamp.

396 "25" on Crate

397 National Flag

(Des L. F. Alves. Litho)

1984 (3 Apr). Events. T **396** and similar multicoloured designs. One phosphor band. P 11½×12 (51E.) or 12×11½ (others).
1954	35E. Type **396** (25th International Lisbon Fair)	2·50	85
1955	40E. Wheat, rainbow and globe (World Food Day)	2·20	85
1956	51E. Hand holding stylised flower (15th World Congress of Rehabilitation International) (vert)	3·00	1·20
1954/1956	Set of 3	6·75	2·50

(Des L. Duran. Litho)

1984 (25 Apr). Tenth Anniv of Revolution. One phosphor band. P 13½.
1957	**397** 16E. multicoloured	1·40	20

398 Bridge

399 "Panel of St. Vincent"

(Des J. Larrivière and J. Cândido. Litho)

1984 (2 May). Europa. Two phosphor bands. P 12.
1958	**398** 51E. multicoloured	3·00	1·50
MS1959	140×114 mm. No. 1958×4	14·00	8·25

(Des P.O. Art Dept. Litho)

1984 (9 May). Lubrapex 84 Portuguese–Brazilian Stamp Exhibition, Lisbon. T **399** and similar horiz designs. Multicoloured. One phosphor band (1960/2). P 12.
1960	16E. Type **399**	70	25
1961	40E. "St. James" (altar panel)	3·25	90
1962	51E. "View of Lisbon" (painting)	4·00	1·20
1963	66E. "Head of Youth" (Domingos Sequeira)	4·25	1·60
1960/1963	Set of 4	11·00	3·50
MS1964	110×111 mm. Nos. 1960/3	12·50	9·75

400 Fencing

401 Gil Eanes (explorer)

(Des J. Tinoco. Litho)

1984 (5 June). Olympic Games, Los Angeles, and 75th Anniv of Portuguese Olympic Committee. T **400** and similar horiz designs. Multicoloured. Two phosphor bands (1965/7). P 12.
1965	35E. Type **400**	2·40	70
1966	40E. Gymnastics	2·75	90
1967	51E. Running	3·25	1·30
1968	80E. Pole vaulting	3·50	1·30
1965/1968	Set of 4	11·00	3·75
MS1969	90×92 mm. 100E. Hurdling	9·75	8·25

The phosphor bands are at right angles, along the left and bottom of the stamps.

39

PORTUGAL

(Des P.O. Art Dept. Litho)

1984 (18 July). Tiles (14th series). Horiz design as T **361**. Multicoloured. Two phosphor bands. P 12.

1970	16E. Pictorial tile from Pombal Palace, Lisbon (late 18th century)		1·10	20
MS1971	146×102 mm. No. 1970×6		7·25	6·25

The phosphor bands are at right angles, along the left and bottom of the stamp.

(Des P.O. Art Dept. Litho)

1984 (3 Aug). Tiles (15th series). Horiz design as T **361**. Multicoloured. Two phosphor bands. P 12.

1972	16E. Four art nouveau tiles (late 19th century)		1·10	20
MS1973	146×102 mm. No. 1972×6		7·25	6·25

The phosphor bands are at right angles, along the left and bottom of the stamp.

(Des L. de Abreu. Litho)

1984 (24 Sept). Anniversaries. T **401** and similar horiz design. Multicoloured. One phosphor band. P 12×11½.

1974	16E. Type **401** (550th anniv of rounding of Cape Bojador)		55	10
1975	51E. King Pedro IV of Portugal and I of Brazil (150th death anniv)		3·25	1·30

(Des P.O. Art Dept. Litho)

1984 (17 Oct). Tiles (16th series). Horiz design as T **361**. Multicoloured. Two phosphor bands. P 12.

1976	16E. Grasshoppers and wheat (R. Bordalo Pinheiro) (19th century)		1·10	20
MS1977	146×102 mm. No. 1976×6		7·25	6·25
MS1978	120×102 mm. Nos. 1952, 1970, 1972 and 1976		6·00	5·00

The phosphor bands are at right angles, along the left and bottom of the stamp.

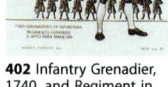

402 Infantry Grenadier, 1740, and Regiment in Formation

403 Calçada R. dos Santos Kiosk

(Des A. Cardoso. Litho)

1985 (23 Jan). Army Uniforms. T **402** and similar square designs. Multicoloured. One phosphor band (1979/81). P 13½.

1979	20E. Type **402**		80	25
	a. Imperf×p 13½. Booklets		1·90	1·90
	ab. Booklet pane. Nos. 1979a/82a		14·00	
1980	46E. Officer, Fifth Cavalry, 1810, and cavalry charge		3·25	85
	a. Imperf×p 13½. Booklets		3·75	3·75
1981	60E. Artillery corporal, 1891, and Krupp 9 mm. gun and crew		3·25	1·00
	a. Imperf×p 13½. Booklets		4·00	3·75
1982	100E. Engineer in chemical protection suit, 1985, and bridge-laying armoured car		3·75	1·50
	a. Imperf×p 13½. Booklets		4·25	4·25
1979/1982	Set of 4		10·00	3·25

(Des P.O. Art Dept. Litho)

1985 (13 Feb). Tiles (17th series). Horiz design as T **361**. Multicoloured. Two phosphor bands. P 12.

1983	20E. Detail of panel by Jorge Barrados in Lisbon Faculty of Letters (20th century)		1·10	20
MS1984	146×102 mm. No. 1983×6		6·75	5·75

The phosphor bands are at right angles, along the left and bottom of the stamp.

(Des Maluda. Litho)

1985 (19 Mar). Lisbon Kiosks. T **403** and similar vert designs. Multicoloured. Two phosphor bands. P 11½×12.

1985	20E. Type **403**		1·20	25
	a. Strip of four. Nos. 1985/8		5·00	5·00
1986	20E. Tivoli kiosk, Avenida da Liberdade		1·20	25
1987	20E. Porto de Lisboa kiosk		1·20	25
1988	20E. Rua de Artilharia Um kiosk		1·20	25
1985/1988	Set of 4		4·25	90

Nos. 1985/8 were issued together in *se-tenant* strips of four within the sheet.

404 Flags of Member Countries   **405** Profiles

(Des A. Santos. Litho)

1985 (10 Apr). 25th Anniv of European Free Trade Association. One phosphor band. P 12×11½.

1989	**404** 46E. multicoloured		1·90	80

(Des A. Santos. Litho)

1985 (10 Apr). International Youth Year. One phosphor band. P 12.

1990	**405** 60E. multicoloured		2·40	1·10

406 Woman holding Adufe (tambourine)   **407** Knight on Horseback

(Des J. Tinoco. Litho)

1985 (6 May). Europa. One phosphor band. P 12.

1991	**406** 60E. multicoloured		4·25	1·70
MS1992	140×114 mm. No. 1991×4		18·00	8·25

(Des P.O. Art Dept. Litho)

1985 (19 June). Tiles (18th series). Horiz design as T **361**. Multicoloured. Two phosphor bands. P 12.

1993	20E. Detail of panel by Maria Keil on Avenida Infante Santo (20th century)		1·10	20
MS1994	146×102 mm. No. 1993×6		6·75	5·75

The phosphor bands are at right angles, along the left and bottom of the stamp.

(Des L. de Abreu. Litho)

1985 (5 July). Anniversaries. T **407** and similar horiz designs. Multicoloured. One phosphor band. P 12×11½.

1995	20E. Type **407** (600th anniv of Battle of Aljubarrota)		90	15
1996	46E. Queen Leonor and hospital (500th anniv of Caldas da Rainha thermal hospital)		2·75	90
1997	60E. Pedro Reinel (500th anniv of first Portuguese sea-chart)		3·00	1·50
1995/1997	Set of 3		6·00	2·25

408 Farmhouse, Minho   **409** Aquilino Ribeiro (writer)

(Des J. Tinoco. Litho)

1985 (20 Aug)–**89**. Architecture. T **408** and similar horiz designs. Two phosphor bands. P 12.

1998	50c. black, olive-bistre and greenish blue (8.3.89)		15	15
1999	1E. black, olive-yellow and yellowish green (8.3.89)		15	15
2000	1E.50 black, apple green and emerald (15.3.88)		15	15
2001	2E.50 blackish brown, pale orange and turquoise-blue (10.3.86)		15	15
2002	10E. black, dull purple and rose-pink (6.3.87)		25	20

2003	20E. blackish brown, chrome yellow and olive-yellow		40	15
2004	22E.50 blackish brown, new blue and ochre (10.3.86)		40	20
2005	25E. blackish brown, yellow & turq-grn		45	15
2006	27E. black, yellow-ol & lemon (15.3.88)		65	15
2007	29E. black, greenish yellow and salmon (8.3.89)		65	15
2008	30E. black, greenish blue and yellow-brown (5.3.88)		65	15
2009	40E. black, yellow & turq-grn (6.3.87)		90	25
2010	50E. black, turquoise-blue & ochre		1·00	20
2011	55E. black, olive-yell & bl-grn (15.3.88)		1·00	20
2012	60E. black, yellow-orange and dull blue (6.3.87)		1·30	40
2013	70E. black, greenish yellow and dull orange 6.3.87)		1·30	40
2014	80E. blackish brown, sage green and red (10.3.86)		1·50	45
2015	90E. blackish brown, olive-yellow and blue-green (10.3.86)		1·70	45
2016	100E. blackish brown, chrome yellow and pale blue		2·00	50
2017	500E. black, bluish grey and greenish blue (8.3.88)		8·50	3·00
1998/2017 Set of 20			20·00	6·75

Designs:—50c. Saloia house, Estremadura; 1E. Beira inland house; 1E.50, Ribatejo house; 2E50, Trás-os-montes houses; 10E. Minho and Douro coast house; 22E.50, Alentejo houses; 25E. Sítio house, Algarve; 27E. Beira inland house (*different*); 29E. Trás-os-montes house; 30E. Algarve house; 40E. Beira inland house (*different*); 50E. Beira coast house; 55E. Trás-os-Montes house (*different*); 60E. Beira coast house (*different*); 70E. South Estremadura and Alentejo house; 80E. Estremadura house; 90E. Minho house; 100E. Monte houses, Alentejo; 500E. Terraced houses, East Algarve.

The phosphor bands are at right angles, along the left and bottom of the stamps.

Nos. 2018/19 are vacant.

(Des P.O. Art Dept. Litho)

1985 (20 Aug). Tiles (19th series). Horiz design as T **361**. Multicoloured. Two phosphor bands. P 12.
2020	20E. Head of woman by Querubim Lapa (20th century)		1·10	20
MS2021	147×101 mm. No. 2020×6		6·75	5·75

The phosphor bands are at right angles, along the left and bottom of the stamp.

(Des L. Duran. Litho)

1985 (2 Oct). Anniversaries. T **409** and similar vert design. Multicoloured. One phosphor band. P 11½×12.
2022	20E. Type **409** (birth centenary)		95	10
2023	46E. Fernando Pessoa (poet, 50th death anniv)		2·40	85

410 Berlenga National Reserve

411 "Nativity"

(Des J. P. Roque. Litho)

1985 (25 Oct). National Parks and Reserves. T **410** and similar horiz designs. Multicoloured. One phosphor band (2024/6). P 12.
2024	20E. Type **410**		55	10
2025	40E. Estrela Mountains National Park		2·40	90
2026	46E. Boquilobo Marsh National Reserve		3·00	1·10
2027	80E. Formosa Lagoon National Reserve		3·25	1·20
2024/2027 Set of 4			8·25	3·00
MS2028	100×68 mm. 100E. S. Jacinto Dunes National Reserve		7·75	6·50

The miniature sheet also commemorates "Italia '85" International Stamp Exhibition, Rome.

1985 (15 Nov). Christmas. T **411** and similar vert design showing illuminations from *Book of Hours of King Manoel I*. Multicoloured. Two phosphor bands. P 11½×12.
2029	20E. Type **411**		60	10
2030	46E. "Adoration of the Three Wise Men"		2·40	90

(Des P.O. Art Dept. Litho)

1985 (15 Nov). Tiles (20th series). Horiz design as T **361**. Multicoloured. Two phosphor bands. P 12.
2031	20E. Detail of panel by Manuel Cargaleiro (20th century)		1·10	20
MS2032	146×102 mm. No. 2031×6		10·50	6·25
MS2033	120×102 mm. Nos. 1983, 1993, 2020 and 2031		6·75	5·75

The phosphor bands are at right angles, along the left and bottom of the stamp.

412 Post Rider

413 Map and Flags of Member Countries

(Des A. Santos. Litho)

1985 (13 Dec). No value expressed. One phosphor band. P 13½.
2034	**412**	(–) apple green and yellowish green	1·10	15

No. 2034 was sold at the current first class inland letter rate. This was 22E.50 at time of issue but the stamp remained on sale during subsequent rate increases.

(Des A. Santos (20E.). Spanish Ptg Wks (57E.50). Litho)

1986 (7 Jan). Admission of Portugal and Spain to the European Economic Community. T **413** and similar horiz design. Multicoloured. One phosphor band. P 12×11½.
2035	20E. Flags of Portugal and Spain uniting with flags of other members		80	25
2036	57E.50 Type **413**		3·00	1·30

See also No. **MS**2056.

414 Feira Castle

415 Globe and Dove

(Des J. Tinoco. Litho)

1986 (18 Feb). Castles (1st series). T **414** and similar horiz design. Multicoloured. One phosphor band. P 12.
2037	22E.50 Type **414**		1·20	20
	a. Booklet pane. No. 2037×4		5·50	
2038	22E.50 Beja Castle		1·20	20
	a. Booklet pane. No. 2038×4		5·50	

The stamps in the booklet panes are arranged in two vertical pairs, with a coat of arms in the gutter between.

See also Nos. 2040/1, 2054/5, 2065/6, 2073/4, 2086/7, 2093/4, 2102/3 and 2108/9.

(Des J. Cândido. Litho)

1986 (18 Feb). International Peace Year. Two phosphor bands. P 12.
2039	**415**	75E. multicoloured	3·25	1·40

(Des J. Tinoco. Litho)

1986 (10 Apr). Castles (2nd series). Horiz designs as T **414**. Multicoloured. One phosphor band. P 12.
2040	22E.50 Bragança castle		1·20	20
	a. Booklet pane. No. 2040×4		5·50	
2041	22E.50 Guimarães Castle		1·20	20
	a. Booklet pane. No. 2041×4		5·50	

The stamps in the booklet panes are arranged in two vertical pairs, with a coat of arms in the gutter between.

416 Benz Three-wheeler (1886)

417 Allis Shad

PORTUGAL

(Des Quadricula. Litho)
1986 (10 Apr). Centenary of Motor Car. T **416** and similar horiz design. Multicoloured. One phosphor band. P 12.
2042	22E.50 Type **416**	1·50	15
	a. Pair. Nos. 2042/3	2·50	2·50
2043	22E.50 Daimler motor carriage (1886)	1·50	15

Nos. 2042/3 were issued together in *se-tenant* pairs within the sheet.

(Des J. P. Roque. Litho)
1986 (5 May). Europa. One phosphor band. P 12.
2044	**417** 68E.50 multicoloured	3·75	1·60
MS2045	140×114 mm. No. 2044×4	19·00	9·75

418 Alter   **419** Comet

(Des L. de Abreu. Litho)
1986 (22 May). Ameripex 86 International Stamp Exhibition, Chicago. Thoroughbred Horses. T **418** and similar horiz designs. Multicoloured. One phosphor band. P 12×11½.
2046	22E.50 Type **418**	80	25
2047	47E.50 Lusitano	2·75	95
2048	52E.50 Garrano	3·00	1·30
2049	68E.50 Sorraia	3·25	1·50
2046/2049	Set of 4	8·75	3·50

(Des J. Tinoco. Litho)
1986 (24 June). Appearance of Halley's Comet. Sheet 100×68 mm. P 12.
MS2050	**419** 100E. multicoloured	15·00	12·50

420 Diogo Cão (navigator) and Monument   **421** Hand writing on Postcard

(Des L. de Abreu. Litho)
1986 (28 Aug). Anniversaries. T **420** and similar horiz designs. Multicoloured. One phosphor band. P 12.
2051	22E.50 Type **420** (500th anniv of second expedition to Africa)	80	15
2052	52E.50 Passos Manuel (Director) and capital (150th anniv of National Academy of Fine Arts, Lisbon)	2·10	95
2053	52E.50 João Baptista Ribeiro (painter and Academy Director) and drawing (150th anniv of Portuguese Academy of Fine Arts, Oporto)	2·10	95
2051/2053	Set of 3	4·50	1·75

(Des J. Tinoco. Litho)
1986 (18 Sept). Castles (3rd series). Horiz designs as T **414**. Multicoloured. One phosphor band. P 12.
2054	22E.50 Belmonte Castle	1·20	25
	a. Booklet pane. No. 2054×4	5·50	
2055	22E.50 Montemor-o-Velho Castle	1·20	25
	a. Booklet pane. No. 2055×4	5·50	

The stamps in the booklet panes are arranged in two vertical pairs, with a coat of arms in the gutter between.

1986 (3 Oct). Europex 86 Stamp Exhibition, Lisbon. Sheet 127×91 mm. Multicoloured. Litho. P 12.
MS2056	Nos. 2035/6, each×2	8·00	6·50

(Des L. Duran. Litho)
1986 (24 Oct). Anniversaries. T **421** and similar vert designs. Multicoloured. Two phosphor bands. P 12.
2057	22E.50 Type **421** (centenary of Portuguese postcards)	1·10	20
2058	47E.50 Guardsman and houses (75th anniv of National Republican Guard)	2·00	95
2059	52E.50 Calipers, globe and banner (50th anniv of Order of Engineers)	2·20	1·00
2057/2059	Set of 3	4·75	1·75

422 Seasonal Mill, Douro   **423** Houses on Stilts, Tocha

(Des L. Duran. Litho)
1986 (7 Nov). Lubrapex 86 Portuguese–Brazilian Stamp Exhibition, Rio de Janeiro. Water Mills. T **422** and similar horiz designs. Multicoloured. One phosphor band (2060/2). P 12.
2060	22E.50 Type **422**	80	30
2061	47E.50 Seasonal mill, Coimbra	1·80	1·10
2062	52E.50 Overshot bucket mill, Gerez	2·40	1·20
2063	90E. Permanent stream mill, Braga	3·00	1·10
2060/2063	Set of 4	7·25	3·25
MS2064	140×114 mm. Nos. 2060/3	12·00	8·25

(Des J. Tinoco. Litho)
1987 (16 Jan). Castles (4th series). Horiz designs as T **414**. Multicoloured. One phosphor band. P 12.
2065	25E. Silves Castle	1·20	20
	a. Booklet pane. No. 2065×4	5·50	
2066	25E. Évora-Monte Castle	1·20	20
	a. Booklet pane. No. 2066×4	5·50	

The stamps in the booklet panes are arranged in two vertical pairs, with a coat of arms in the gutter between.

(Des C. Rocha. Litho)
1987 (10 Feb). 75th Anniv (1986) of Organized Tourism. T **423** and similar horiz designs. Multicoloured. Two phosphor bands. P 12.
2067	25E. Type **423**	80	25
2068	57E. Fishing boats, Espinho	2·75	1·20
2069	98E. Fountain, Arraiolos	3·50	2·00
2067/2069	Set of 3	6·25	3·00

424 Hand, Sun and Trees   **425** Bank Borges and Irmão Agency, Vila do Conde (Alvaro Siza)

(Des C. Calvet. Litho Litografia Maia. Oporto)
1987 (20 Mar). European Environment Year. T **424** and similar horiz designs. One phosphor band. Multicoloured. P 12½×12.
2070	25E. Type **424**	80	30
2071	57E. Hands, flower and map of Europe	2·00	1·10
2072	74E.50 Hand, sea, purple dye murex shell, moon and rainbow	3·25	1·40
2070/2072	Set of 3	5·50	2·25

(Des J. Tinoco. Litho)
1987 (10 Apr). Castles (5th series). Horiz designs as T **414**. Multicoloured. One phosphor band. P 12.
2073	25E. Leiria Castle	1·20	20
	a. Booklet pane. No. 2073×4	5·50	
2074	25E. Trancoso Castle	1·20	20
	a. Booklet pane. No. 2074×4	5·50	

The stamps in the booklet panes are arranged in two vertical pairs, with a coat of arms in the gutter between.

(Des J. Tinoco. Litho)
1987 (5 May). Europa. Architecture. Two phosphor bands. P 12.
2075	**425** 74E.50 multicoloured	3·00	1·60
MS2076	140×114 mm. No. 2075×4	15·00	8·25

426 Cape Mondego   **427** Souza-Cardoso (self-portrait)

PORTUGAL

(Des Maluda. Litho)

1987 (12 June). Capex 87 International Stamp Exhibition, Toronto. Lighthouses. T **426** and similar vert designs. Multicoloured. Two phosphor bands. P 12.
2077	25E. Type **426**	1·00	35
	a. Strip or block of four. Nos. 2077/80	4·00	
2078	25E. Berlenga	1·00	35
2079	25E. Aveiro	1·00	35
2080	25E. Cape St. Vincent	1·00	35
2077/2080	Set of 4	3·75	1·25

Nos. 2077/80 were issued together in *se-tenant* strips and blocks of four within the sheet.

(Des A. Pimentel. Litho)

1987 (27 Aug). Birth Centenary of Amadeo de Souza-Cardoso (painter). Two phosphor bands. P 12.
| 2081 | **427** | 74E.50 multicoloured | 2·40 | 1·10 |

428 Clipped 400 Reis Silver Coin   **429** Dias's Fleet leaving Lisbon

(Des L. de Abreu. Litho)

1987 (27 Aug). 300th Anniv of Portuguese Paper Currency. Two phosphor bands. P 12.
| 2082 | **428** | 100E. multicoloured | 3·25 | 1·00 |

(Des L. de Abreu. Litho)

1987 (27 Aug)–**88**. 500th Anniv of Bartolomeu Dias's Voyages (1st issue). T **429** and similar horiz design. Multicoloured. One phosphor band. P 12.
2083	25E. Type **429**	1·20	20
	a. Pair. Nos. 2083/4	2·10	2·10
	b. Imperf×p 12. Booklets (3.2.88)	1·50	1·10
	ba. Booklet pane. Nos. 2083b, 2084a, 2099a and 2100a		
2084	25E. Ships off coast of Africa	1·20	20
	a. Imperf×p 12. Booklets (3.2.88)	1·50	1·10

Nos. 2083/4 were issued together in *se-tenant* pairs within the sheet, each pair forming a composite design.
See also Nos. 2099/2100.

430 Library   **431** Records and Compact Disc Player

(Des L. de Abreu. Litho)

1987 (27 Aug). 150th Anniv of Portuguese Royal Library, Rio de Janeiro. Two phosphor bands. P 12.
| 2085 | **430** | 125E. multicoloured | 3·75 | 1·60 |

(Des J. Tinoco. Litho)

1987 (15 Sept). Castles (6th series). Horiz designs as T **414**. Multicoloured. One phosphor band. P 12.
2086	26E. Marvão Castle	1·20	20
	a. Booklet pane. No. 2086×4	5·50	
2087	25E. St. George's Castle, Lisbon	1·20	20
	a. Booklet pane. No. 2087×4	5·50	

The stamps in the booklet panes are arranged in two vertical pairs, with a coat of arms in the gutter between.

(Des J. Machado. Litho)

1987 (9 Oct). Centenary of Gramophone Record. Sheet 140×114 mm containing T **431** and similar horiz design. Multicoloured. P 12.
| MS2088 75E. Type **431**; 125E. Early gramophone | 12·00 | 9·75 |

432 Angels around Baby Jesus, Tree and Kings (José Manuel Coutinho)   **433** Lynx

1987 (6 Nov). Christmas. T **432** and similar horiz designs showing children's paintings. Multicoloured. Two phosphor bands. P 12.
2089	25E. Type **432**	1·10	25
2090	57E. Children dancing around sunburst (Rosa J. Leitão)	2·10	1·00
2091	74E.50 Santa Claus flying on dove (Sónia Alexandra Hilário)	2·30	1·30
2089/2091	Set of 3	4·75	2·25
MS2092 140×114 mm. Nos. 2089/91. P 12½×12	6·75	5·25

(Des J. Tinoco. Litho)

1988 (19 Jan). Castles (7th series). Horiz designs as T **414**. Multicoloured. One phosphor band. P 12.
2093	27E. Fernandine walls, Oporto	1·10	20
	a. Booklet pane. No. 2093×4	5·00	
2094	27E. Almourol castle	1·10	20
	a. Booklet pane. No. 2094×4	5·00	

The stamps in the booklet panes are arranged in two vertical pairs, with a coat of arms in the gutter between.

(Des J. Projecto. Litho)

1988 (3 Feb). Iberian Lynx (*Lynx pardina*). T **433** and similar horiz designs. Multicoloured. Two phosphor bands. P 12.
2095	27E. Type **433**	1·40	35
	a. Strip or block of four. Nos. 2095/8	6·25	
2096	27E. Lynx carrying rabbit	1·40	35
2097	27E. Pair of lynxes	1·40	35
2098	27E. Mother with young	1·40	35
2095/2098	Set of 4	5·00	1·25

Nos. 2095/8 were issued together in *se-tenant* strips and blocks of four within the sheet.

434 King João II sending Pêro da Covilhã on Expedition   **435** 19th-century Mail Coach

(Des L. de Abreu. Litho)

1988 (3 Feb). 500th Anniv of Voyages of Bartolomeu Dias (2nd issue) (2099/2100) and Pêro da Covilhã (2101). T **434** and horiz designs as T **429**. Two phosphor bands (2101), one band (others). P 12.
2099	27E. Dias's ships in storm off Cape of Good Hope, 1488	1·00	25
	a. Pair. Nos. 2099/2100	1·80	1·80
	b. Imperf×p 12. Booklets	2·50	2·75
2100	27E. Contemporary map	1·00	55
	a. Imperf×p 12. Booklets	2·50	2·75
2101	105E. Type **434**	3·25	1·50
2099/2101	Set of 3	4·75	2·00

For booklet pane, see No. 2083ba.

(Des J. Tinoco. Litho)

1988 (15 Mar). Castles (8th series). Horiz designs as T **414**. Multicoloured. Two phosphor bands. P 12.
2102	27E. Palmela Castle	1·10	20
	a. Booklet pane. No. 2102×4	5·00	
2103	27E. Vila Nova de Cerveira Castle	1·10	20
	a. Booklet pane. No. 2103×4	5·00	

The stamps in the booklet panes are arranged in two vertical pairs, with a coat of arms in the gutter between.

(Des L. Duran and C. Leitão. Litho)

1988 (21 Apr). Europa. Transport and Communications. Two phosphor bands. P 12.
| 2104 | **435** | 80E. multicoloured | 4·25 | 1·70 |
| MS2105 139×112 mm. As No. 2104×4 but with cream background | 16·00 | 9·75 |

43

PORTUGAL

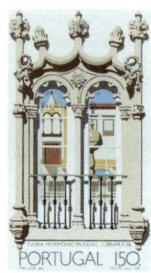

436 Map of Europe and Monnet

437 Window reflecting Cordovil House and Fountain

(Des A. Santos. Litho)

1988 (9 May). Birth Centenary of Jean Monnet (statesman). Europex 88 Stamp Exhibition. Two phosphor bands. P 12.
| 2106 | **436** | 60E. multicoloured | 1·90 | 1·10 |

(Des Maluda. Litho)

1988 (13 May). U.N.E.S.C.O. World Heritage Site: Évora. Lubrapex 88 Stamp Exhibition. Sheet 112×139 mm. P 13×12½.
| **MS**2107 | **437** | 150E. multicoloured | 10·50 | 9·25 |

(Des J. Tinoco. Litho)

1988 (1 July). Castles (9th series). Horiz designs as T **414**. Multicoloured. Two phosphor bands. P 12.
2108	27E. Chaves Castle	1·10	25
	a. Booklet pane. No. 2108×4	5·25	
2109	27E. Penedono Castle	1·10	25
	a. Booklet pane. No. 2109×4	5·25	

The stamps in the booklet panes are arranged in two vertical pairs, with a coat of arms in the gutter between.

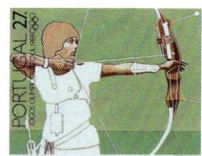

438 "Part of a Viola" (Amadeo de Souza-Cardoso)

439 Archery

(Des P.O. Art Dept. Litho)

1988 (23 Aug). 20th-Century Portuguese Paintings (1st series). T **438** and similar vert designs. Multicoloured. Two phosphor bands. P 11½×12.
2110	27E. Type **438**	80	30
2111	60E. "Acrobats" (Almada Negreiros)	2·00	1·00
2112	80E. "Still Life with Viola" (Eduardo Viana)	2·30	1·20
2110/2112	Set of 3	4·50	2·25
MS2113	138×112 mm. Nos. 2110/12	7·50	6·25

See also Nos. 2121/**MS**2125, 2131/**MS**2134, 2148/**MS**2152, 2166/**MS**2169 and 2206/**MS**2210.

(Des J. Cândido. Litho)

1988 (16 Sept). Olympic Games, Seoul. T **439** and similar horiz designs. Multicoloured. Two phosphor bands (2114/17). P 12.
2114	27E. Type **439**	1·00	30
2115	55E. Weightlifting	1·90	1·10
2116	60E. Judo	2·00	1·10
2117	80E. Tennis	2·50	1·10
2114/2117	Set of 4	6·50	3·25
MS2118	114×67 mm. 200E. Dinghies (39×30 mm)	12·50	11·50

440 "Winter" (House of the Fountains, Coimbra)

441 Braga Cathedral (900th anniv)

(Des L. Cândido. Litho)

1988 (18 Oct). Roman Mosaics of 3rd Century. T **440** and similar horiz design. Multicoloured. One phosphor band. P 12.
| 2119 | 27E. Type **440** | 70 | 30 |
| 2120 | 80E. "Fish" (Baths, Faro) | 2·40 | 1·10 |

(Des P.O. Dept. Litho)

1988 (18 Nov). 20th-Century Portuguese Paintings (2nd series). Vert designs as T **438**. Multicoloured. Two phosphor bands. P 11½×12.
2121	27E. "Internment" (Mário Eloy)	80	20
2122	60E. "Lisbon Houses" (Carlos Botelho)	1·90	80
2123	80E. "Avejão Lírico" (António Pedro)	2·20	1·10
2121/2123	Set of 3	4·50	1·90
MS2124	140×114 mm. Nos. 2121/3	7·50	6·25
MS2125	139×144 mm. Nos. 2110/12 and 2121/3. P 12.	13·00	10·50

(Des C. Santos. Litho)

1988 (20 Jan). Anniversaries. T **441** and similar horiz designs. Multicoloured. Two phosphor bands. P 12.
2126	30E. Type **411**	1·00	40
2127	55E. Caravel, Fischer's lovebird and S. Jorge da Mina Castle (505th anniv)	1·70	80
2128	60E. Sailor using astrolabe (500th anniv of South Atlantic voyages)	2·40	1·30
2126/2128	Set of 3	4·50	2·25

Nos. 2127/8 also have the "India 89" Stamp Exhibition, New Delhi, emblem.

442 "Greetings"

443 Flags in Ballot Box

(Des L. Duran. Litho)

1989 (15 Feb). Greetings Stamps. T **442** and similar horiz design. Multicoloured. Two phosphorescent bands. P 12.
| 2129 | 29E. Type **442** | 80 | 20 |
| 2130 | 60E. Airplane distributing envelopes inscribed "with Love" | 1·30 | 70 |

(Des P.O. Dept. Litho)

1989 (15 Feb). 20th-Century Portuguese Paintings (3rd series). Vert designs as T **438**. Multicoloured. Two phosphor bands. P 11½×12.
2131	29E. "Antithesis of Calm" (António Dacosta)	80	15
2132	60E. "Unskilled Mason's Lunch" (Júlio Pomar)	1·90	90
2133	87E. "Simumis" (Vespeira)	2·20	1·20
2131/2133	Set of 3	4·50	2·00
MS2134	139×111 mm. Nos. 2131/3	7·50	6·25

(Des J. Brandão. Litho)

1989 (8 Mar). Third Direct Elections to European Parliament. Two phosphor bands. P 12.
| 2135 | **443** | 60E. multicoloured | 1·90 | 1·10 |

444 Boy with Spinning Top

445 Cable Railway

(Des A. Pimentel. Litho)

1989 (26 Apr). Europa. Children's Games and Toys. T **444** and similar horiz design. Multicoloured. Two phosphor bands. P 12.
| 2136 | 80E. Type **414** | 2·50 | 1·50 |
| **MS**2137 | 138×112 mm. 80E.×2, Type **444**; 80E.×2, Spinning tops | 8·75 | 7·25 |

PORTUGAL

(Des J. Tinoco. Litho)

1989 (22 May). Lisbon Transport. T **445** and similar multicoloured designs. Two phosphor bands (2138/41). P 12.

2138	29E. Type **445**	80	25
2139	65E. Electric tram-car	2·30	95
2140	87E. Santa Justa lift	2·40	1·30
2141	100E. Cacilheiro (bus)	2·75	1·30
2138/2141	Set of 4	7·50	3·50
MS2142	100×50 mm. 250E. Double decker (ferry) (39×29 mm)	11·00	10·00

446 Gyratory Mill, Ansião

(Des Isabel Botelho. Litho)

1989 (14 June). Windmills. T **446** and similar horiz designs. Multicoloured. Two phosphor bands. P 12.

2143	29E. Type **446**	80	25
	a. Imperf×p 13½. Booklets	1·50	1·50
	ab. Booklet pane. Nos. 2143a/46a	9·75	
2144	60E. Stone mill, Santiago do Cacém	2·30	95
	a. Imperf×p 13½. Booklets	2·50	2·50
2145	87E. Post mill, Afife	2·40	1·40
	a. Imperf×p 13½. Booklets	2·75	2·75
2146	100E. Wooden mill, Caldas da Rainha	2·75	1·40
	a. Imperf×p 13½. Booklets	3·00	3·00
2143/2146	Set of 4	7·50	3·50

447 Drummer Boy

(Des L. Duran and C. Leitão. Litho)

1989 (7 July). Bicentenary of French Revolution and "Philexfrance 89" International Stamp Exhibition, Paris. Sheet 111×139 mm. P 12.

MS2147	**447** 250E. multicoloured	11·00	10·00

(Des P.O. Art Dept. Litho)

1989 (7 July). 20th-Century Portuguese Paintings (4th series). Vert designs as T **438**. Two phosphor bands. P 11½×12.

2148	29E. new blue, dull blue-green and black	75	30
2149	60E. multicoloured	1·90	1·10
2150	87E. multicoloured	2·30	1·40
2148/2150	Set of 3	7·00	2·75
MS2151	139×111 mm. Nos. 2148/50	7·50	6·25
MS2152	138×144 mm. Nos. 2131/3 and 2148/50. P 12	13·00	10·50

Designs:—29E. "046-72" (Fernando Lanhas); 60E. "Spirals" (Nadir Afonso); 87E. "Sim" (Carlos Calvet).

448 Luis I (death centenary) and Ajuda Palace, Lisbon
449 *Armeria pseudarmeria*

(Des L. Duran and C. Leitão. Litho)

1989 (18 Oct). National Palaces (1st series). T **448** and similar horiz design. Multicoloured. Two phosphor bands. P 12.

2153	29E. Type **448**	45	20
2154	60E. Queluz Palace	1·80	1·10

See also Nos. 2211/14.

(Des L. de Abreu. Litho)

1989 (17 Nov). Wild Flowers. T **449** and similar vert designs. Multicoloured. Two phosphor bands. P 12.

2155	29E. Type **449**	70	20
	a. Imperf×p 13½. Booklets	1·40	1·40
	ab. Booklet pane. Nos. 2155a/8a	9·75	
2156	60E. *Santolina impressa*	1·70	80
	a. Imperf×p 13½. Booklets	2·20	2·20
2157	87E. *Linaria lamarckii*	2·10	1·20
	a. Imperf×p 13½. Booklets	2·75	2·75
2158	100E. *Limonium multiflorum*	2·50	1·60
	a. Imperf×p 13½. Booklets	3·50	3·25
2155/2158	Set of 4	7·00	3·50

450 Blue and White Plate
451 João Gonçalves Zarco

(Des P.O. Art Dept. Litho)

1990 (24 Jan). Portuguese Faience (1st series). T **450** and similar horiz designs. Multicoloured. Two phosphor bands (2159/64). P 12.

2159	33E. Type **450**	80	30
2160	33E. Blue and white plate with man in centre	80	30
2161	35E. Vase decorated with flowers	95	35
2162	60E. Fish-shaped jug	1·50	95
2163	60E. Blue and white plate with arms in centre	1·50	95
2164	60E. Blue and white dish with lid	1·80	1·10
2159/2164	Set of 6	6·75	3·50
MS2165	112×140 mm. 250E. Plate with crown in centre	9·50	8·50

See also Nos. 2221/**MS**2227 and 2262/**MS**2268.

(Des P.O. Art Dept. Litho)

1990 (14 Feb). 20th-Century Portuguese Paintings (5th series). Vert designs as T **438**. Multicoloured. Two phosphor bands. P 11½×12.

2166	32E. "Aluenda-Tordesillas" (Joaquim Rodrigo)	65	30
2167	60E. "Painting" (Luis Noronha da Costa)	2·00	1·00
2168	95E. "Painting" (Vasco Costa)	2·75	1·40
2166/2168	Set of 3	5·25	2·50
MS2169	138×111 mm. Nos. 2166/8	9·00	7·50

(Des L. F. de Abreu. Litho)

1990 (6 Mar)–**94**. Portuguese Navigators. T **451** and similar horiz designs. Two phosphor bands or no bands. P 12×11½.

2170	2E. deep carmine-red, bright rose and black (P)	15	15
2171	3E. deep turq-green, turq-blue and black (29.4.94)	15	10
2172	4E. brown-purple, pale Venetian red and black (6.4.93)	15	10
2173	5E. red-brown, grey and black (P)	20	15
2174	6E. deep yellow-green, yellowish green and black (P) (3.6.92)	20	15
2175	10E. Indian red, orange-red and black (29.4.94)	15	10
2176	32E. dp yellow-green, yell-brn & blk (P)	90	15
2177	35E. rosine, rose and black (P) (6.3.91)	85	15
2178	38E. dp brt bl, new bl & blk (P) (3.6.92)	90	30
2179	42E. slate-green, grey and black (6.4.93)	90	20
2180	45E. olive-green, sage green and black (29.4.94)	70	35
2181	60E. bistre-yellow, bright purple and black (P) (6.3.91)	1·60	60
2182	65E. lake-brown, yellow-olive and black (P) (6.3.91)	1·60	50
2183	70E. bright violet, light mauve and black (6.4.93)	1·50	45
2184	75E. yellowish green, yellow and black (29.4.94)	1·30	75
2185	80E. light orange, red-brown and black (P) (6.3.91)	2·10	85
2186	100E. rose-carmine, yellow-orange and black (P)	2·75	1·00
2187	200E. emerald, brt ol-yell & blk (6.4.93)	3·75	1·10
2188	250E. royal blue, light blue-green and black (P) (6.3.91)	5·75	2·30
2189	350E. verm, salmon-pk & blk (P) (3.6.92)	7·00	2·75
2170/2189	Set of 20	30·00	11·00

45

PORTUGAL

Designs:—3E. Pedro Lopes de Sousa; 4E. Duarte Pacheco Pereira, 5E. Tristão Vaz Teixeira; 6E. Pedro Álvares Cabral, 10E. João de Castro; 32E. Bartolomeu Perestrelo; 35E. Gil Eanes; 38E. Vasco da Gama; 42E. João de Lisboa; 45E. João Rodrigues Cabrilho; 60E. Nuno Tristão ; 65E. João da Nova; 70E. Fernão de Magalhães (Magellan); 75E. Pedro Fernandes de Queirós; 80E. Diogo Gomes; 100E. Diogo de Silves; 200E. Estêvão Gomes; 250E. Diogo Cão; 350E. Bartolomeu Dias.

Nos. 2174, 2177/8, 2181/2, 2185 and 2188/9 have the phosphor bands at right angles, along the left and bottom edges. No. 2173 exists with the bands on opposite vertical sides or at right angles.

No. 2190 is vacant.

452 Score and Singers

453 Santo Tirso Post Office

(Des J. Tinoco. Litho)

1990 (6 Mar). Anniversaries. T **452** and similar multicoloured design. Two phosphor bands. P 12.

| 2191 | 32E. Type **452** (centenary of *A Portuguesa* (national anthem)) | 75 | 25 |
| 2192 | 70E. Students and teacher (700th anniv of granting of charter to Lisbon University) (vert) | 2·50 | 1·30 |

(Des C. Leitão. Litho)

1990 (11 Apr). Europa. Post Office Buildings. T **453** and similar horiz design. Multicoloured. Two phosphor bands. P 12.

| 2193 | 80E. Type **453** | 2·50 | 1·40 |
| MS2194 | 139×111 mm. 80E.×2, Type **453**; 80E.×2, 19th-century Mail Coach Office | 9·75 | 6·25 |

454 Stamping Letter

455 Street with Chairs under Trees

(Des J. Martins Barata. Litho)

1990 (3 May). "Stamp World London 90" International Stamp Exhibition and 150th Anniv of the Penny Black. Sheet 111×140 mm. P 12×11½.

| MS2195 | **454** 250E. multicoloured | 13·00 | 11·50 |

(Des A. Botelho. Litho)

1990 (5 June). Greetings Stamps. T **455** and similar horiz designs. Multicoloured. Two phosphor bands. P 12.

2196	60E. Type **455**	1·70	90
	a. Imperf×p 13½. Booklets	2·40	2·30
	ab. Booklet pane. Nos. 2196a/9a	9·50	
2197	60E. Hand holding bouquet out of car window	1·70	90
	a. Imperf×p 13½. Booklets	2·40	2·30
2198	60E. Man with bouquet crossing street	1·70	90
	a. Imperf×p 13½. Booklets	2·40	2·30
2199	60E. Woman with bouquet behind pillar box	1·70	90
	a. Imperf×p 13½. Booklets	2·40	2·30
2196/2199 Set of 4		6·00	3·25

456 Camilo Castelo Branco (writer)

457 Barketta

(Des A. Modesto. Litho)

1990 (11 July). Death Anniversaries. T **456** and similar horiz design. Multicoloured. Two phosphor bands. P 12.

| 2200 | 65E. Type **456** (centenary) | 1·30 | 90 |
| 2201 | 70E. Brother Bartolomeu dos Mártires (Bishop of Braga, 400th anniv) | 1·90 | 1·10 |

(Des C. Santos. Litho)

1990 (21 Sept). 15th-century Explorers' Ships. T **457** and similar horiz designs. Multicoloured. Two phosphor bands. P 12.

2202	32E. Type **467**	55	25
	a. Imperf×p 13½. Booklets	1·10	1·10
	ab. Booklet pane. Nos. 2202a/5a	7·50	
2203	60E. Caravel-built fishing boat	1·60	80
	a. Imperf×p 13½. Booklets	1·80	1·80
2204	70E. Nau	1·80	1·10
	a. Imperf×p 13½. Booklets	2·00	2·00
2205	95E. Caravel	2·20	1·40
	a. Imperf×p 13½. Booklets	2·50	2·40
2202/2205 Set of 4		5·50	3·25

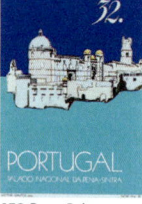
458 Pena Palace

459 Carneiro

(Des P.O. Art Dept. Litho)

1990 (21 Sept). 20th-Century Portuguese Paintings (6th series). Vert designs as T **438**. Multicoloured. Two phosphor bands. P 11½×12.

2206	32E. "Dom Sebastião" (Costa Pinheiro)	55	30
2207	60E. "Domestic Scene with Green Dog" (Paula Rêgo)	1·80	1·10
2208	95E. "Homage to Magritte" (José de Guimarães)	2·75	1·30
2206/2208 Set of 3		4·50	2·40
MS2209 138×112 mm. Nos. 2206/8		4·50	2·40
MS2210 138×145 mm. Nos. 2166/8 and 2206/8. P 12.		13·00	10·50

No. **MS2210** also commemorates "Lubrapex 90" Portuguese–Brazilian Stamp Exhibition.

(Des V. Santos. Litho)

1990 (11 Oct). National Palaces (2nd series). T **458** and similar vert designs. Multicoloured. Two phosphor bands. P 12.

2211	32E. Type **458**	75	25
2212	60E. Vila Palace	1·60	80
2213	70E. Mafra Palace	1·70	1·10
2214	120E. Guimarães Palace	2·10	1·40
2211/2214 Set of 4		5·50	3·25

(Des P.O. Art Dept. Litho)

1990 (7 Nov). Tenth Death Anniv of Francisco *Sá Carneiro* (founder of Popular Democratic Party and Prime Minister, 1980). Two phosphor bands. P 12.

| 2215 | **459** 32E. black and light olive-sepia | 70 | 25 |

460 Steam Locomotive No. 02, 1887

461 Greater Flamingoes

(Des D. Botelho. Litho)

1990 (7 Nov). Centenary of Rossio Railway Station, Lisbon. T **460** and similar horiz designs. Multicoloured. Two phosphor bands (2216/19). P 12.

2216	32E. Type **460**	75	25
2217	60E. Steam locomotive No. 010, 1891	1·60	80
2218	70E. Steam locomotive No. 071, 1916	1·70	1·10
2219	95E. Electric locomotive, 1956	2·10	1·40
2216/2219 Set of 4		5·50	3·25
MS2220 112×80 mm. 200E. Station clock (39×29 mm)		7·50	7·50

(Des P.O. Art Dept. Litho)

1991 (7 Feb). Portuguese Faience (2nd series). Horiz designs as T **450**. Multicoloured. Two phosphor bands (2221/6). P 12.

2221	35E. Barrel of fish and plate (Rato factory, Lisbon)	70	25
2222	35E. Floral vase (Bica do Sapato factory)	70	25
2223	35E. Gargoyle (Costa Briozo factory, Coimbra)	70	25

2224	60E. Dish with leaf pattern (Juncal factory)..		1·30	70
2225	60E. Coffee pot (Cavaquinho factory, Oporto)		1·30	70
2226	60E. Mug (Massarelos factory, Oporto)		1·30	70
2221/2226 Set of 6			5·50	2·50
MS2227 114×140 mm. 250E. Plate with portrait in centre (Miragaia factory, Oporto)			8·25	8·00

(Des J. Projecto. Litho)

1991 (6 Mar). European Tourism Year. T **461** and similar horiz designs. Multicoloured. Two phosphor bands (2228/9). P 12.

2228	60E. Type **461**	1·20	90
2229	110E. European chameleon	2·30	1·70
MS2230 112×104 mm. 250E. Red deer (39×31 mm)		7·25	7·00

462 "Eutelsat II" Satellite   **463** Caravel

(Des P. Vidigal. Litho)

1991 (11 Apr). Europa. Europe in Space. T **462** and similar horiz design. Multicoloured. Two phosphor bands. P 12.

2231	80E. Type **462**	2·50	2·00
MS2232 140×112 mm. 80E.×2, Type **462**; 80E.×2, "Olympus I" satellite		8·50	5·75

(Des P.O. Art Dept. Litho)

1991 (27 May). 16th-century Explorers' Ships. T **463** and similar horiz designs. Multicoloured. Two phosphor bands. P 12.

2233	35E. Type **463**	55	30
	a. Imperf×p 13½. Booklets	1·20	1·20
	ab. Booklet pane. Nos. 2233a, 2234a, 2235a and 2236a	7·50	
2234	75E. Port view of nau	1·80	85
	a. Imperf×p 13½. Booklets	2·00	1·90
2235	80E. Stern view of nau	1·90	1·00
	a. Imperf×p 13½. Booklets	2·00	2·00
2236	110E. Galleon	2·20	1·10
	a. Imperf×p 13½. Booklets	2·30	2·30
2233/2236 Set of 4		6·00	3·00

464 "Isabella of Portugal and Philip the Good" (anon)

(Des P.O. Art Dept. Litho)

1991 (27 May). "Europalia 91 Portugal" Festival, Belgium. Sheet 140×112 mm. P 12½.
MS2237 **464** 300E. multicoloured .... 10·50 9·50

465 Emerald and Diamond Bow   **466** Antero de Quental (writer)

(Des P.O. Art Dept. Litho)

1991 (8 July). "Royal Treasures" Exhibition, Ajuda Palace (1st issue). T **465** and similar vert designs. Multicoloured. Two phosphor bands. Litho. Imperf×p 13½ (70E.) or 12 (others).

2238	35E. Type **465**	55	35
2239	60E. Royal sceptre	1·60	70
2240	70E. Sash of the Grand Cross	1·80	95
	a. Booklet pane. No. 2240×5	9·00	
2241	80E. Hilt of sabre	1·90	1·00
2242	140E. Crown	2·40	1·20
2238/2242 Set of 5		7·50	3·75

No. 2240 was issued only in booklets.
See also Nos. 2270/4.

(Des L. Duran. Litho)

1991 (2 Aug). Anniversaries. T **466** and similar horiz design. Multicoloured. Two phosphor bands. P 12.

2243	35E. Type **466** (death centenary)	60	20
2244	110E. Arrival of expedition and baptism of Sonyo prince (500th anniv of first Portuguese missionary expedition to the Congo)	2·40	1·20

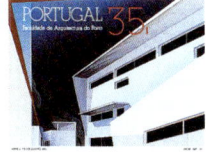 

467 Faculty of Architecture, Oporto University (Siza Vieira)   **468** King Manoel I creating Public Post, 1520

(Des A. Pessegueiro. Litho)

1991 (4 Sept). Architecture. T **467** and similar horiz designs. Multicoloured. Two phosphor bands. P 12.

2245	35E. Type **467**	55	20
2246	60E. Torre do Tombo (Arsénio Cordeiro Associates)	1·40	50
2247	80E. River Douro railway bridge (Edgar Cardoso) and Donna Maria bridge	1·70	1·00
2248	110E. Setúbal-Braga highway	2·10	1·10
2245/2248 Set of 4		5·25	2·50

(Des L. Duran. Litho)

1991 (9 Oct). History of Communications in Portugal. T **468** and similar horiz designs. Multicoloured. Two phosphor bands (2249/51). P 12.

2249	35E. Type **468**	60	25
2250	60E. Woman posting letter and telegraph operator (merging of posts and telegraph operations, 1881)	1·20	65
2251	80E. Postman, mail van and switchboard operator (creation of Posts and Telecommunications administration, 1911)	1·50	85
2249/2251 Set of 3		3·00	1·50
MS2252 140×111 mm. 110E. Modern means of communications (introduction of priority mail service, 1991)		2·75	2·30

469 Show Jumping   **470** Peugeot 19 Victoria (1899)

(Des F. Telechea. Litho)

1991 (9 Oct). Olympic Games, Barcelona (1992) (1st issue). T **469** and similar horiz designs. Multicoloured. Two phosphor bands. P 12.

2253	35E. Type **469**	60	25
2254	60E. Fencing	1·30	55
2255	80E. Shooting	1·60	90
2256	110E. Dinghies	2·10	1·10
2253/2256 Set of 4		5·00	2·50

See also Nos. 2295/MS2299.

(Des C. Leitão. Litho)

1991 (15 Nov). Caramulo Automobile Museum. T **470** and similar horiz designs. Multicoloured. Two phosphor bands. P 12.

2257	35E. Type **470**	55	25
2258	60E. Rolls Royce 40/50 Silver Ghost (1911)	1·30	55
2259	80E. Bugatti Type 35B (1930)	1·60	95
2260	110E. Ferrari 195 Inter coupe (1950)	2·10	1·10
2257/2260 Set of 4		5·00	2·50
MS2261 140×111 mm. 70E.×2, Mercedes Benz 380K (1934); 70E.×2, Hispano-Suiza H6B (1924)		6·00	4·50

No. MS2261 also commemorates "Phila Nippon 91" International Stamp Exhbition, Tokyo.
See also Nos. 2275/MS2279.

PORTUGAL

(Des P.O. Art Dept. Litho)

1992 (24 Jan). Portuguese Faience (3rd series). Horiz designs as T **450**. Multicoloured. Two bands (2262/7). P 12.
2262	40E. Jug (Viana do Castelo factory)	65	35
2263	40E. Plate with flower design ("Ratinho" faience, Coimbra)	65	35
2264	40E. Dish with lid (Estremoz factory)	65	35
2265	65E. Decorated violin by Wencislau Cifka (Constância factory, Lisbon)	1·30	65
2266	65E. Figure of man seated on barrel (Cavaquinho factory, Oporto)	1·30	65
2267	65E. Figure of woman (Fervença factory, Oporto)	1·30	65
2262/2267 Set of 6		5·25	2·75
MS2268	112×140 mm. 260E. Political figure by Rafael Bordalo Pinheiro (Caldas da Rainha factory) (44×38 mm)	5·25	5·00

471 Astrolabe (Presidency emblem)

472 Portuguese Traders

(Des L. Coelho. Litho)

1992 (24 Jan). Portuguese Presidency of European Community. Two phosphor bands. P 12.
2269	**471**	65E. multicoloured	1·50	1·00

(Des V. Santos. Litho)

1992 (7 Feb). "Royal Treasures" Exhibition, Ajuda Palace (2nd issue). Vert designs as T **465**. Multicoloured. Two phosphor bands. Imperf×p 13½ (65E.) or 12 (others).
2270	38E. Coral diadem	55	35
2271	65E. Fabergé clock	1·40	75
	a. Booklet pane. No. 2271×5	7·00	
2272	70E. Gold tobacco box studded with diamonds and emeralds by Jacqumin	1·30	65
2273	85E. Royal sceptre with dragon supporting crown	1·40	90
2274	125E. Necklace of diamond stars by Estêvão de Sousa	1·80	1·10
2270/2274 Set of 5		5·50	3·25

No. 2271 was issued only in booklets.

(Des C. Leitão. Litho)

1992 (6 Mar). Oeiras Automobile Museum. Horiz designs as T **470**. Multicoloured. Two phosphor bands. P 12.
2275	38E. Citroën 5CV Type C Torpedo (1922)	55	25
2276	65E. Rochet Schneider 12h.p. tourer (1914)	1·40	65
2277	85E. Austin Seven tourer (1933)	1·60	85
2278	120E. Mercedes Benz 770 saloon (1938)	2·00	1·10
2275/2278 Set of 4		5·00	2·50
MS2279	140×111 mm. 70E.×2, Renault 10/14 Limousine (1911); 70E.×2, Ford Model T runabout (1927)	6·00	4·50

(Des L. Duran. Litho)

1992 (24 Apr). 450th Anniv of First Portuguese Contacts with Japan (1st issue). T **472** and similar horiz design showing details of painting attributed to Kano Domi. Multicoloured. Two phosphor bands. P 12.
2280	38E. Type **472**	60	30
2281	120E. Portuguese visitors with gifts	1·90	1·30

See also Nos. 2342/4.

473 Portuguese Pavilion

474 Cross-staff

(Des V. Santos. Litho)

1992 (24 Apr). Expo 92 World's Fair, Seville. Two phosphor bands. P 12.
2282	**473**	65E. multicoloured	1·00	75

(Des J. Tinoco. Litho)

1992 (9 May). Nautical Instruments (1st series). T **474** and similar horiz designs. Multicoloured. Two phosphor bands. P 12.
2283	60E. Type **474**	95	45
2284	70E. Quadrant	1·30	70
2285	100E. Astrolabe	1·50	70
2286	120E. Compass	1·80	1·10
2283/2286 Set of 4		5·00	2·50
MS2287	140×112 mm. Nos. 2283/6	6·00	5·00

See also Nos. 2318/21.

475 Royal All Saints Hospital, Lisbon

(Des L. Duran (38E.), J. Tinoco (70E.), A. Pessegueiro (120E.). Litho)

1992 (11 May). Anniversaries. T **475** and similar horiz designs. Multicoloured. Two phosphor bands. P 12.
2288	38E. Type **475** (500th anniv of foundation)	70	40
2289	70E. Lúcia, Francisco and Jacinta (75th anniv of apparitions of Our Lady at Fátima)	1·20	90
2290	120E. Crane and docks (centenary of Port of Leixões)	2·00	1·20
2288/2290 Set of 3		3·50	2·25

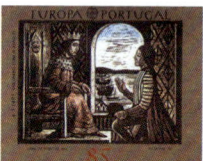
476 Columbus with King João II

477 Columbus soliciting Aid of Isabella

(Des L. de Freitas (2291), A. Major and D. Sheaff (**MS**2292). Litho)

1992 (22 May). Europa. 500th Anniv of Discovery of America by Columbus. P 12.

(a) Two phosphor bands
2291	**476**	85E. multicoloured	2·40	1·80

*(b) Six sheets, each 111×91 mm, containing horiz designs as T **477** reproducing scenes from United States 1893 Columbian Exposition issue*
MS2292 Six sheets. (a) 260E. brown and black (Type **479**); (b) 260E. deep turquoise-blue and black (Columbus sighting land); (c) 260E. deep reddish purple and black (Landing of Columbus); (d) 260E. blackish lilac and black (Columbus welcomed at Barcelona); (e) 260E. black (Columbus presenting natives); (f) 260E. black ("America", Columbus and "Liberty")	41·00 29·00

478 Black-headed Gull flying over contaminated River

479 Running

(Des J. Projecto. Litho)

1992 (12 June). Second United Nations Conference on Environment and Development, Rio de Janeiro. T **478** and similar horiz design. Multicoloured. One phosphor band. P 12.
2293	70E. Type **478**	1·10	55
	a. Horiz pair. Nos. 2293/4	2·75	2·75
2294	120E. River kingfisher and butterfly beside clean river	1·90	1·10

Nos. 2293/4 were issued together in horizontal *se-tenant* pairs within the sheet, each pair forming a composite design.

(Des J. Tinoco. Litho)

1992 (29 July). Olympic Games, Barcelona (2nd issue). T **479** and similar vert designs. Multicoloured. Two phosphor bands (2295/8). P 12.

2295 38E. Type **479** ... 55 35
2296 70E. Football ... 1·30 65
2297 85E. Hurdling ... 1·50 75
2298 120E. Roller hockey ... 1·70 1·00
2295/2298 *Set of* 4 ... 4·50 2·50
MS2299 140×112 mm. 250E. Basketball ... 4·50 4·25

No. **MS**2299 also commemorates "Olymphilex 92" Olympic Stamps Exhibition, Barcelona.

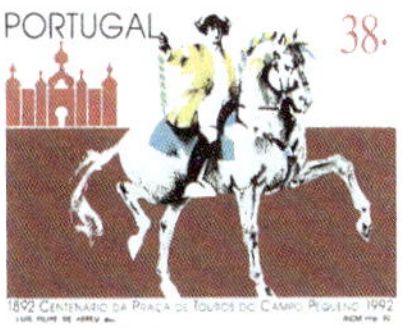

480 Bullfighter on Horse

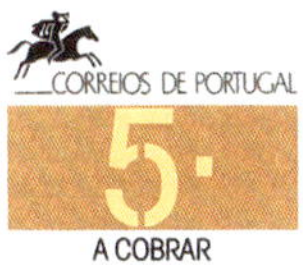

D **481**

(Des Maluda (**MS**2304), L. de Abreu (others). Litho)

1992 (18 Aug). Centenary of Campo Pequeno Bull Ring, Lisbon. T **480** and similar multicoloured designs. Two phosphor bands (2300/3). P 12.

2300 38E. Type **480** ... 55 30
2301 65E. Bull charging at horse ... 1·30 60
2302 70E. Bullfighter attacking bull ... 1·40 85
2303 155E. Bullfighter flourishing hat ... 1·90 1·30
2300/2303 *Set of* 4 ... 4·50 2·75
MS2304 140×113 mm. 250E. Entrance to ring (35×50 mm) ... 4·50 4·25

(Des A. Santos. Litho)

1992 (7 Oct)–**93**. POSTAGE DUE. P 12×11½.

D2305 D **481** 1E. greenish blue, royal blue and black ... 10 10
D2306 2E. bright apple green, blue-green and black ... 10 10
D2307 5E. lemon, brown-ochre and black ... 10 10
D2308 10E. carmine-red, red-orange and black (9.3.93) ... 20 10
D2309 20E. yellowish green, violet and black (9.3.93) ... 35 10
D2310 50E. chrome-yellow, yellow-green and black (9.3.93) ... 80 45
D2311 100E. salmon, brown-red and black (9.3.93) ... 1·50 1·00
D2312 200E. bright magenta, bright violet and black ... 3·00 1·90
D2305/2312 *Set of* 8 ... 5·50 3·50

For similar design but inscribed "CTT CORREOS" see Nos. D2445/8.

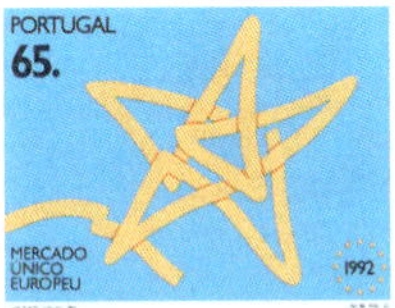

482 Star

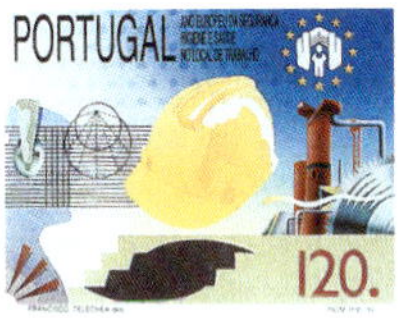

483 Industrial Safety Equipment

(Des L. Coelho. Litho)

1992 (4 Nov). European Single Market. Two phosphor bands. P 12.

2313 **482** 65E. multicoloured ... 1·10 75

(Des F. Telechea. Litho)

1992 (4 Nov). European Year of Health, Hygiene and Safety in the Workplace. Two phosphor bands. P 12.

2314 **483** 120E. multicoloured ... 2·00 1·50

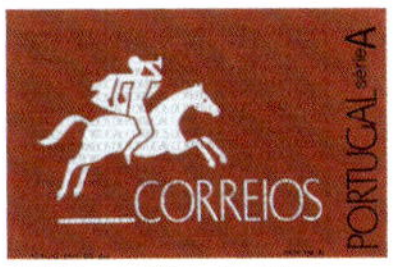

484 Post Office Emblem

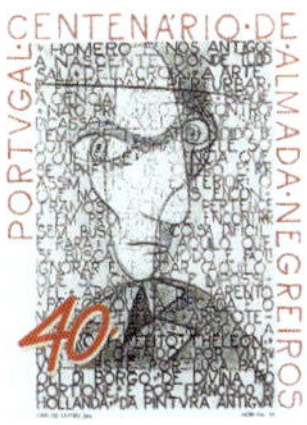

485 Graphic Poem

(Des A. Santos. Litho)

1993 (4 Jan). No value expressed. P 12×12½.

2315 **484** (–) brown-red and black ... 75 35

No. 2315 was sold at the current first class inland letter rate. This was 42E. at time of issue.

(Des C. Leitão. Litho)

1993 (9 Mar). Birth Centenary of José de Almada Negreiros (artist and poet). T **485** and similar vert design. Multicoloured. P 12.

2316 40E. Type **485** ... 70 35
2317 65E. *Trawlers* (painting) ... 1·10 85

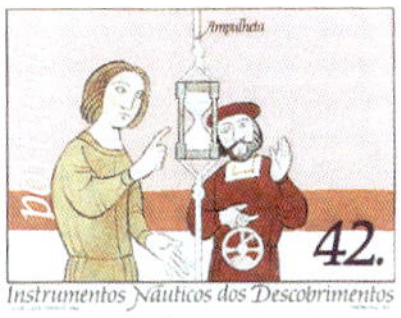

486 Sand Clock

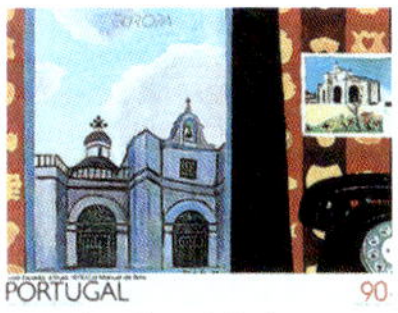

487 View from Window

(Des J. Tinoco. Litho)

1993 (6 Apr). Nautical Instruments (2nd series). T **486** and similar horiz designs. Multicoloured. P 12.

2318 42E. Type **466** ... 55 25
2319 70E. Nocturlabe ... 1·10 65
2320 90E. Kamal ... 1·70 90
2321 130E. Back-staff ... 2·10 1·00
2318/2321 *Set of* 4 ... 5·00 2·50

(Des C. Leitão. Litho)

1993 (5 May). Europa. Contemporary Art. T **487** and similar horiz design showing untitled paintings by José Escada. Multicoloured. P 12.

2322 90E. Type **487** ... 2·00 1·40
MS2323 140×112 mm. 90E.×2, Type **487**; 90E.×2, Body parts ... 10·00 6·50

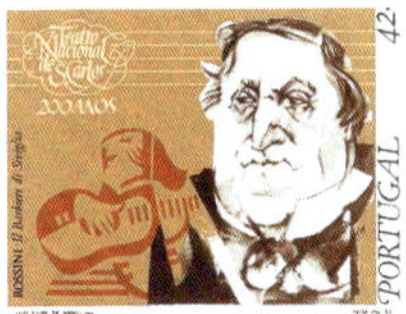

488 Rossini and *The Barber of Seville*

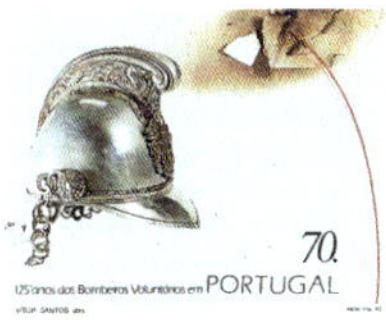

489 Fireman's Helmet

(Des L. de Abreu. Litho)

1993 (21 June). Bicentenary of San Carlos National Theatre, Lisbon. T **488** and similar horiz designs. Multicoloured. P 12.

2324 42E. Type **488** ... 55 35
2325 70E. Verdi and *Rigoletto* ... 1·20 65
2326 90E. Wagner and *Tristan and Isolde* ... 1·50 90
2327 130E. Mozart and *The Magic Flute* ... 2·30 1·00
2324/2327 *Set of* 4 ... 5·00 2·50
MS2328 140×112 mm. 300E. Exterior of theatre (39×29 mm) ... 5·25 5·00

(Des V. Santos. Litho)

1993 (21 June). 125th Anniv of Association of Volunteer Firemen of Lisbon. P 12.

2329 **489** 70E. multicoloured ... 1·30 80

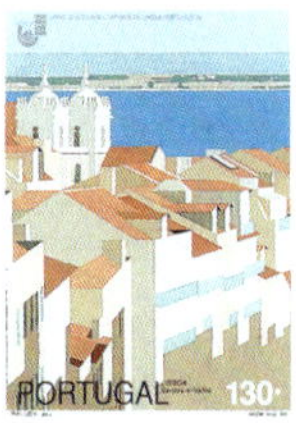

490 Santos-o-Velho, Lisbon

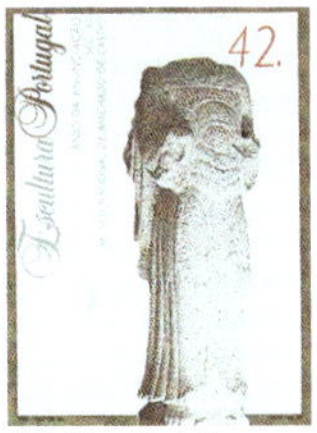

491 "Angel of the Annunciation" (from Oporto Cathedral)

(Des Maluda. Litho)

1993 (30 July). Union of Portuguese-speaking Capital Cities. P 12.

2330 **490** 130E. multicoloured ... 2·10 1·30
MS2331 140×112 mm. No. 2330×4 ... 8·50 7·00

PORTUGAL

(Des V. Santos. Litho)

1993 (18 Aug). Sculptures (1st series). T **491** and similar multicoloured designs. P 12.

2332	42E. Type **491**	55	25
2333	70E. "St. Mark" (Cornelius de Holanda) (horiz)	1·30	65
2334	75E. "Madonna and Child"	1·60	70
2335	90E. "Archangel St. Michael"	1·70	75
2336	130E. "Count of Ferreira" (Soares dos Reis)	2·10	1·10
2337	170E. "Construction" (Hélder Batista)	2·40	1·30
2332/2337 Set of 6		8·50	4·25

MS2338 112×140 mm. 75E. Marble bust of Agrippina the Elder; 75E. "Virgin of the Annunciation" (Master of the Royal Tombs); 75E. "The Widow" (Teixeira Lopes); 75E. "Love Ode" (Canto da Maya) .... 5·25 4·25
See also Nos. 2380/**MS**2386 and 2466/**MS**2472.

492 Road Tanker and Freight Train   **493** Japanese Man with Musket

(Des L. Duran and F. Espinho. Litho)

1993 (6 Sept). International Railways Congress, Lisbon. T **492** and similar horiz designs. Multicoloured. P 12.

2339	90E. Type **492**	1·20	70
2340	130E. Train and traffic jam	2·00	1·10
MS2341	140×112 mm. 300E. Electric train	4·75	4·50

(Des C. Leitão. Litho)

1993 (22 Sept). 450th Anniv of First Portuguese Contacts with Japan (2nd issue). T **493** and similar horiz designs. Multicoloured. P 12.

2342	42E. Type **493**	55	40
2343	130E. Portuguese missionaries	2·75	1·50
2344	350E. Traders carrying goods	4·50	2·40
2342/2344 Set of 3		7·00	3·75

494 Peniche Trawler   **495** Rural Post Bag, 1800

(Des A. Alves. Litho)

1993 (1 Oct). Trawlers (1st series). T **494** and similar horiz designs. Multicoloured. P 12.

2345	42E. Type **494**	55	25
	a. Imperf×p 11½. Booklets	90	90
	ab. Booklet pane. Nos. 2345a, 2346a, 2347a and 2348a	5·75	
2346	70E. Peniche type trawler	1·00	55
	a. Imperf×p 11½. Booklets	1·30	1·30
2347	90E. *Germano 3* (trawler)	1·60	75
	a. Imperf×p 11½. Booklets	1·50	1·50
2348	130E. *Estrela I* (trawler)	2·00	1·00
	a. Imperf×p 11½. Booklets	1·90	1·80
2345/2348 Set of 4		4·50	2·25

See also Nos. 2392/5.

(Des C. Leitão. Litho)

1993 (9 Oct). Post Boxes. T **495** and similar vert designs. Multicoloured. P 12.

2349	42E. Type **495**	55	30
2350	70E. 19th-century wall-mounted box for railway travelling post office	1·00	55
2351	90E. 19th-century pillar box	1·60	70
2352	130E. Modern multi-function post box	2·00	1·00
2349/2352 Set of 4		4·75	2·25

MS2353 140×112 mm. 300E. 19th-century box for animal-drawn post wagons .... 4·75 4·50

496 Imperial Eagle   **497** Knot

(Des J. Projecto. Litho)

1993 (9 Oct). Endangered Birds of Prey. T **496** and similar vert designs. Multicoloured. P 12.

2354	42E. Type **496**	55	30
2355	70E. Eagle owl	1·20	70
2356	130E. Peregrine falcon	2·75	1·10
2357	350E. Hen harrier	4·50	2·40
2354/2357 Set of 4		8·00	4·00

(Des A. Santos. Litho)

1993 (3 Nov). 40th Anniv of Brazil–Portugal Consultation and Friendship Treaty. P 12.

2358	**497** 130E. multicoloured	2·00	1·20

498 Arms   **499** Stylized Map of Member Nations

(Des V. Santos. Litho)

1993 (9 Dec). 850th Anniv of Zamora Conference (recognizing Afonso I as King of Portugal). Sheet 106×114 mm. P 12.

MS2359 **498** 150E. multicoloured .... 2·75 2·75

(Des C. Leitão. Litho)

1994 (27 Jan). 40th Anniv of Western European Union. P 12.

2360	**499** 85E. multicoloured	1·30	85

500 Olympic Rings as Torch Flame   **501** Oliveira Martins (historian)

(Des J. Machado. Litho)

1994 (27 Jan). Centenary of International Olympic Committee. T **500** and similar horiz design. Multicoloured. P 12.

2361	100E. Type **500**	2·30	1·10
	a. Pair. Nos. 2361/2	2·75	2·75
2362	100E. "100" and rings	2·30	1·10

Nos. 2361/2 were issued together in *se-tenant* pairs within sheets of eight stamps and one label showing Baron de Coubertin (founder).

(Des J. Manta. Litho)

1994 (21 Feb). Centenaries. T **501** and similar horiz design. Multicoloured. P 12.

2363	45E. Type **501** (death)	70	30
2364	100E. Florbela Espanca (poet, birth)	1·30	80

502 Map and Prince Henry

(Des L. Duran and C. Leitão. Litho)
1994 (4 Mar). 600th Birth Anniv of Prince Henry the Navigator. P 12.
2365   502   140E. multicoloured................................. 2·00   1·10

503 Dove

504 Mounted Knight and Explorer with Model Caravel

(Des A. Alves. Litho)
1994 (22 Apr). 20th Anniv of Revolution. P 12.
2366   503   75E. multicoloured.................................... 1·00   60

(Des L. de Abreu. Litho)
1994 (5 May). Europa. Discoveries. T **504** and similar horiz design. Multicoloured. P 12.
2367   100E. Type 504 .... 1·60   1·10
MS2368 140×112 mm. 100E.×2, Type **504**; 100E.×2, Millet and explorer with model caravel............ 8·75   6·50

505 Emblem

506 Footballer kicking Ball and World Map

(Des GAT. Litho)
1994 (15 May). International Year of the Family. P 12.
2369   505   45E. vermilion, black and brown-lake.... 65   25
2370   140E. vermilion, black and deep grey-green... 1·90   1·10

(Des J. Machado. Litho)
1994 (7 June). World Cup Football Championship, U.S.A. T **506** and similar horiz design. Multicoloured. P 12.
2371   100E. Type **506**.. 1·40   70
2372   140E. Ball and footballers' legs................... 2·00   1·00

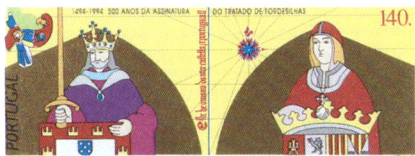
507 King João II of Portugal and King Fernando of Spain

(Des V. Santos. Litho)
1994 (7 June). 500th Anniv of Treaty of Tordesillas (defining Portuguese and Spanish spheres of influence). P 12.
2373   507   140E. multicoloured................................ 2·00   1·10

508 Music

(Des H. Cajate. Litho)
1994 (1 July). Lisbon, European Capital of Culture. T **508** and similar horiz designs. Multicoloured. P 12.
2374   45E. Type **508**.. 50   35
2375   75E. Photography and cinema................... 1·20   70
2376   100E. Theatre and dance............................... 1·50   1·10
2377   140E. Art.. 1·90   1·50
2374/2377 Set of 4 .... 4·50   3·25
MS2378 140×112 mm. Nos. 2374/7........................... 5·75   5·75

509 Emblem

510 Falconer, Peregrine Falcon and Dog

(Des C. Leitão. Litho)
1994 (16 Aug). Portuguese Road Safety Year. P 12.
2379   509   45E. rosin, emerald and black................... 65   30

(Des V. Santos. Litho)
1994 (16 Aug). Sculptures (2nd series). Multicoloured designs as T **491**. P 12.
2380   45E. Carved stonework from Citânia de Briteiros (1st century) (horiz)................. 60   25
2381   75E. Visigothic pilaster (7th century)......... 80   45
2382   80E. Capital from Amorim Church (horiz)..... 1·00   60
2383   100E. Laying Christ's body in tomb (attr. João de Ruão) (Monastery Church of Santa Cruz de Coimbra) (horiz)................. 1·20   70
2384   140E. Carved wood reliquary (Santa Maria Monastery, Alcobaça) (horiz).................. 1·80   1·00
2385   180E. Relief of Writers (Leopoldo de Almeida) (Lisbon National Library) (horiz)... 2·40   1·20
2380/2385 Set of 6 .... 7·00   3·75
MS2386 112×140 mm. 75E. Queen Urraca's tomb (Santa Maria Monastery, Alcobaça); 75E. Count of Ourém's tomb (Colegiada de Ourém Church); 75E. João de Noronha and Isabel de Sousa's tomb (Santa Maria Church, Óbidos); 75E. Mausoleum of Admiral Machado dos Santos (Alto de São João Cemetery, Lisbon).. 4·75   4·00
The stamps in the miniature sheet are all horizontal in format.

(Des J. Projecto. Litho)
1994 (16 Sept). Falconry. T **510** and similar horiz designs showing a peregrine falcon in various hunting scenes. Multicoloured. P 12.
2387   45E. Type **510**.. 50   25
2388   75E. Falcon chasing duck.............................. 90   50
2389   100E. Falconer approaching falcon with dead duck.. 1·20   70
2390   140E. Falcons... 1·60   1·00
2387/2390 Set of 4 .... 3·75   2·25
MS2391 97×121 mm. 250E. Hooded falcon on falconer's arm.. 3·75   3·75

511 Maria Arminda

512 19th-century Horse-drawn Wagon

(Des A. Alves. Litho)
1994 (16 Sept). Trawlers (2nd series). T **511** and similar horiz designs. Multicoloured. P 12.
2392   45E. Type **511** 50   25
            a. Imperf×p 11½. Booklets........................ 95   80
            ab. Booklet pane. Nos. 2392a, 2393a, 2394a and 2395a............................. 6·00
2393   75E. *Bom Pastor*.. 1·20   50
            a. Imperf×p 11½. Booklets........................ 1·50   1·30
2394   100E. Aladores trawler with triplex haulers...... 1·30   70
            a. Imperf×p 11½. Booklets........................ 1·80   1·60
2395   140E. *Sueste*.. 1·70   1·00
            a. Imperf×p 11½. Booklets........................ 1·80   1·60
2392/2395 Set of 4 .... 4·25   2·25

(Des C. Pinto. Litho)
1994 (10 Oct). Postal Transport. T **512** and similar horiz designs. Multicoloured. P 12.
2396   45E. Type **512**.. 60   25
2397   75E. Travelling Post Office sorting carriage No. C7, 1910.. 1·00   50

PORTUGAL

2398	100E. Mercedes mail van, 1950	1·20	70
2399	140E. Volkswagen mail van, 1950	1·60	95
2396/2399	Set of 4	4·00	2·25
MS2400	140×112 mm. 250E. DAF truck, 1983	3·50	3·00

No. 2398 is dated "1910" in error.

513 Electric Multiple Unit, Sintra Suburban Railway

(Des L. Duran, C. Leitão and L. Oliveira. Litho)

1994 (10 Oct). Modern Electric Locomotives (1st series). T **513** and similar horiz designs. Multicoloured. P 12.

2401	45E. Type **513**	50	25
2402	75E. Locomotive Series No. 5611-7 (national network)	95	55
2403	140E. Lisbon Underground train	1·70	95
2401/2403	Set of 3	2·75	1·50

See also No. 2465.

514 Medal   **515** St. Philip's Fort, Setúbal

(Des N. Fischer. Litho)

1994 (31 Oct). 150th Anniv of Montepio Geral Savings Bank (45E.) and World Savings Day (100E.). T **514** and similar horiz design. Multicoloured. P 12.

2404	45E. Type **514**	65	30
2405	100E. Coins and bee	1·20	65

(Des C. Leitão. Litho)

1994 (7 Nov). Pousadas (hotels) in Historic Buildings. T **515** and similar horiz designs. Multicoloured. P 12.

2406	45E. Type **515**	50	25
2407	75E. Obidos Castle	1·20	50
2408	100E. Convent of Lóios, Évora	1·30	70
2409	140E. Santa Marinha Monastery, Guimarães	1·60	95
2406/2409	Set of 4	4·25	2·25

 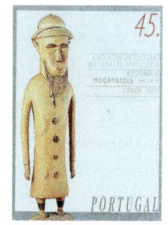

516 Businessman and Tourist   **517** Statuette of Missionary, Mozambique

(Des L. Duran. Litho)

1994 (7 Nov). American Society of Travel Agents World Congress, Lisbon. P 12.

2410	**516** 140E. multicoloured	1·80	95

(Des V. Santos. Litho)

1994 (17 Nov). Evangelization by Portuguese Missionaries. T **517** and similar multicoloured designs. P 12.

2411	45E. Type **517**	50	25
2412	75E. "Child Jesus the Good Shepherd" (carving), India	1·20	50
2413	100E. Chalice, Macao	1·30	70
2414	140E. Carving of man in frame, Angola (horiz)	1·60	95
2411/2414	Set of 4	4·25	2·25

518 Africans greeting Portuguese   **519** Battle Scene (detail of tile panel, Hall of Battles, Fronteira Palace, Lisbon)

(Des L. Duran and C. Pinto. Litho)

1994 (17 Nov). 550th Anniv of First Portuguese Landing in Senegal. P 12.

2415	**518** 140E. multicoloured	1·80	95

(Des L. Duran, C. Leitão and L. Oliveira. Litho)

1994 (1 Dec). 350th Anniv of Battle of Montijo. Sheet 63×83 mm. P 12.

MS2416	**519** 150E. multicoloured	2·20	2·20

520 Adoration of the Wise Men   **521** Great Bustard (*Otis tarda*)

(Des J. Tinoco. Litho)

1994 (8 Dec). Christmas. Sheet 140×111 mm. P 12.

MS2417	**520** 150E. multicoloured	2·20	2·20

(Des J. Projecto. Litho)

1995 (22 Feb). European Nature Conservation Year. T **521** and similar horiz designs. Multicoloured. P 12.

2418	42E. Type **521**	90	55
2419	90E. Osprey (*Pandion haliaetus*)	1·50	1·10
2420	130E. Schreiber's green lizard (*Lacerta schreiberi*)	1·70	1·40
2418/2420	Set of 3	3·75	2·75
MS2421	140×112 mm. Nos. 2418/20. P 12½×12	4·50	5·00

 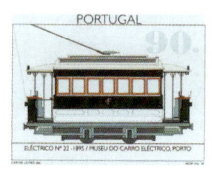

522 St. John and Sick Man   **523** Electric Tramcar No. 22, 1895

(Des L. de Abreu. Litho)

1995 (8 Mar). 500th Birth Anniv of St. John of God (founder of Order of Hospitallers). P 12.

2422	**522** 45E. multicoloured	65	30

(Des C. Leitão. Litho)

1995 (8 Mar). Centenaries of Trams and Motor Cars in Portugal. T **523** and similar horiz design. Multicoloured. P 12.

2423	90E. Type **523**	1·20	55
2424	130E. Panhard and Levassor Phoenix motor car (1895)	1·50	95

524 Bread Seller   D **525**

PORTUGAL

1995 (20 Apr)–**99**. 19th-century Itinerant Trades. T **524** and similar vert designs. Multicoloured. P 11½×12.

2425	1E. Type **524** (Bread seller)	10	10
2426	2E. Laundry woman (12.3.97)	10	10
2427	3E. Broker (20.3.96)	10	10
2428	5E. Broom seller (12.3.97)	10	10
2429	10E. Fish seller (20.3.98)	10	10
2431	20E. Spinning-wheel and spoon seller	20	10
2432	30E. Olive oil and vinegar seller (12.3.97)	30	20
2433	40E. Seller of indulgences (20.3.96)	40	30
2434	45E. General street trader	50	30
	a. Booklet pane. No. 2434×10	5·50	
2435	47E. Hot chestnuts seller (20.3.96)	40	25
	a. Booklet pane. No. 2435×10	5·50	
2436	49E. Clothes mender (12.3.97)	55	40
	a. Booklet pane. No. 2436×10	6·50	
2437	50E. Fruit seller	70	40
2437a	50E. Pottery seller (20.3.98)	65	45
	ab. Booklet pane. No. 2437a×10	7·00	
2438	51E. Knife grinder (26.2.99)	45	30
2439	75E. Whitewasher	90	60
	a. Booklet pane. No. 2439×10	10·00	
2440	78E. Cloth seller (20.3.96)	90	45
	a. Booklet pane. No. 2440×10	9·75	
2440b	80E. Carrier/messenger boy (12.3.97)	95	55
	ba. Booklet pane. No. 2440b×10	10·00	
2440c	85E. Goose seller (20.3.98)	1·00	70
	ca. Booklet pane. No. 2440c×10	11·00	
2440d	86E. Bread seller (26.2.99)	80	55
2440e	95E. Coachman (26.2.99)	90	65
2441	100E. Mussels seller (20.3.96)	1·30	65
2441a	100E. Milk seller (26.2.99)	1·00	70
2442	210E. Basket seller (26.2.99)	2·10	1·40
2443	250E. Water seller (26.2.99)	2·75	1·60
2444	250E. Pastry seller (20.3.98)	2·75	1·60

The booked panes all have a perforated margin around the pane edge.

Numbers have been left for additions to this series.

(Des A. Santos. Litho)

1995 (20 Apr)–**96**. POSTAGE DUE. P 12×11½.

D2445	D **525**	3E. multicoloured	20	10
D2446		4E. multicoloured	20	10
D2446a		5E. multicoloured (24.5.96)	10	10
D2447		9E. multicoloured	45	10
D2447a		10E. scarlet, reddish orange and black (24.5.96)	15	10
D2447b		20E. multicoloured (24.5.96)	25	20
D2448		40E. multicoloured	80	65
D2449		50E. multicoloured (22.5.96)	90	60
D2450		100E. reddish orange, scarlet and black (24.5.96)	1·30	90
D2445/D2450 Set of 9			4·00	2·50

For similar design but inscr "CORREIOS DE PORTUGAL" see Nos. D2305/12.

526 Emblem

528 "St. Antony holding Child Jesus" (painting)

527 Evacuees from Gibraltar arriving at Madeira

(Des B2 Design Studio. Litho)

1995 (5 May). 50th Anniv of United Nations Organization. T **526** and similar horiz design. Multicoloured. P 12.

2449	75E. Type **526**	90	55
2450	135E. Clouds and emblem	1·60	1·00
MS2451	140×111 mm. No. 2449/50, each×2	5·50	5·00

(Des L. Duran and C. Leitão. Litho)

1995 (5 May). Europa. Peace and Freedom. Portuguese Neutrality during Second World War. T **527** and similar horiz design. Multicoloured. P 12.

2452	95E. Type **527**	2·00	1·20
2453	95E. Refugees waiting at Lisbon for transatlantic ship and Aristides de Sousa Mendes (Portuguese Consul in Bordeaux)	2·00	1·20

(Des Ana Bela Silva (45E.), N. Russo (75E.), V. Santos (135E.). Litho)

1995 (13 June). 800th Birth Anniv of St. Antony of Padua (Franciscan preacher). T **528** and similar multicoloured designs. P 12.

2454	45E. Type **528**	1·40	35
2455	75E. St. Antony with flowers (vert)	2·50	85
2456	135E. "St. Antony holding Child Jesus" (statue)	4·00	1·60
2454/2456 Set of 3		7·00	2·50
MS2457	96×110 mm. 250E. "St. Antony holding Baby Jesus" (18th-century Madeiran statue)	17·00	10·00

529 Carpenters with Axes and Women with Water, 1395

530 Coronation

(Des L. Duran and A. Magalhães. Litho)

1995 (4 July). 600th Anniv of Fire Service in Portugal. T **529** and similar horiz designs. Multicoloured. P 12.

2458	45E. Type **529**	50	25
2459	80E. Fire cart and men carrying barrels of water, 1834	1·00	55
2460	95E. Merryweather steam-powered fire engine, 1867	1·10	70
2461	135E. Zoost fire engine No. 1 (1908)	1·50	1·00
2458/2461 Set of 4		4·00	2·25
MS2462	Two sheets, each 120×100 mm. (a) 4×45E. Dutch fire engine, 1701; (b) 4×75E. Picota fire engine, 1780, and Portuguese fire cart, 1782	5·25	5·75

(Des C. Leitão. Litho)

1995 (4 Aug). 500th Anniv of Accession of King Manoel I. P 12.

2463	**530**	45E. olive-sepia, pale olive-yellow and carmine-red	55	30
MS2464	112×140 mm. No. 2463×4		2·50	2·50

(Des L. Duran and C. Pinto. Litho)

1995 (1 Sept). Modern Electric Locomotives (2nd series). Horiz design as T **513**. P 12.

2465	80E. multicoloured	95	55
	a. Booklet pane. No. 2465×4	5·25	

Design:—80E. Electric railcar.

The booklet pane has its upper and lower edges imperforate, giving stamps with one side imperf.

(Des V. Santos. Litho)

1995 (27 Sept). Sculptures (3rd series). Vert designs as T **491**. Multicoloured. P 12.

2466	45E. "Warrior" (castle statue)	45	25
2467	75E. Double-headed fountain	95	55
2468	80E. "Truth" (monument to Eça de Quelrós by António Teixeira Lopes)	95	55
2469	95E. First World War memorial, Abrantes (Ruy Gameiro)	1·10	65
2470	135E. "Fernão Lopes" (Martins Correia)	1·60	1·00
2471	190E. "Fernando Pessoa" (Lagoa Henriques)	2·10	1·30
2466/2471 Set of 6		6·50	4·00
MS2472	112×140 mm. 75E. "Knight" (from Chapel of the Ferreiros); 75E. "King José I" (J. Machado de Castro), Commerce Square, Lisbon; 75E. "King João IV" (Francisco Franco), Vila Viçosa; 75E. "Vimara Peres" (Barata Feyo), Oporto Cathedral Square	3·75	3·25

531 "Portugal's Guardian Angel" (sculpture, Diogo Pires)

532 Queiroz

PORTUGAL

(Des L. Duran and C. Leitão. Litho)

1995 (9 Oct). Art of the Period of Discoveries (15th–16th centuries). T **531** and similar multicoloured designs. P 12.

2473	45E. Type **531**	45	25
2474	75E. Reliquary of Queen Leonor (Master João)	95	55
2475	80E. "Don Manuel" (sculpture, Nicolas Chanterenne)	95	55
2476	95E. "St. Anthony" (painting, Nuno Gonçalves)	1·10	65
2477	135E. "Adoration of the Three Wise Men" (painting, Grão Vasco)	1·90	1·00
2478	190E. "Christ on the Way to Calvary" (painting, Jorge Afonso)	2·10	1·30
2473/2478	Set of 6	6·75	4·00
MS2479	140×112 mm. 200E. "St. Vincent" (polyptych, Nuno Gonçalves)	2·50	2·00

(Des J. Manta. Litho)

1995 (27 Oct). 150th Birth Anniv of Eça de Queiroz (writer). P 12.

| 2480 | **532** 135E. multicoloured | 1·50 | 1·00 |

533 Archangel Gabriel

534 Airbus Industrie A340/300

(Des L. de Abreu. Litho)

1995 (14 Nov). Christmas. T **533** and similar vert designs. Multicoloured. P 12.

(a) With country name in silver at foot

| 2481 | 80E. Type **533** | 1·40 | 1·00 |
| **MS**2482 | 112×140 mm. No. 2481×4 | 6·50 | 5·00 |

(b) With country name omitted

| 2483 | 80E. Type **533** | 1·30 | 1·00 |
| **MS**2484 | 112×140 mm. No. 2483×4 | 6·25 | 6·25 |

A little under one third of the printing had the country name omitted.

(Des C. Leitão and A. Santos. Litho)

1995 (14 Nov). 50th Anniv of TAP Air Portugal. P 12.

| 2485 | **534** 135E. multicoloured | 1·50 | 1·00 |

535 King Carlos I of Portugal

(Des J. Tinoco. Litho)

1996 (1 Feb). Centenary of Oceanographic Expeditions. T **535** and similar horiz design. Multicoloured. P 12.

| 2486 | 95E. Type **535** | 1·10 | 65 |
| 2487 | 135E. Prince Albert I of Monaco | 1·60 | 1·20 |

536 Books

537 João de Deus (poet and author of reading primer)

(Des J. Tinoco. Litho)

1996 (29 Feb). Anniversaries. T **536** and similar horiz design. Multicoloured. P 12.

| 2488 | 80E. Type **536** (bicentenary of National Library) | 95 | 55 |
| 2489 | 200E. Hand writing with quill pen (700th anniv of adoption of Portuguese as official language) | 2·20 | 1·40 |

(Des C. Leitão and L. Duran. Litho Litografia Maia, Oporto)

1996 (12 Apr). Writers' Anniversaries. T **537** and similar horiz design. Multicoloured. P 12.

| 2490 | 78E. Type **537** (death centenary) | 95 | 55 |
| 2491 | 140E. João de Barros (historian, philosopher and grammarian, 500th birth) | 1·50 | 1·00 |

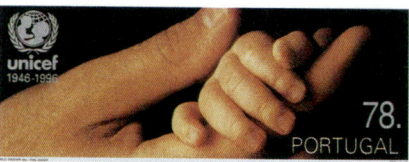
538 Holding Child's Hand

(Des N. Fischer. Litho)

1996 (12 Apr). 50th Anniv of United Nations Children's Fund. T **538** and similar horiz design. Multicoloured. P 12.

2492	78E. Type **538**	1·00	55
	a. Booklet pane. Nos. 2492×2 and 2493×2	4·50	
2493	140E. Children of different races	1·60	95

The outer edges of the booklet pane are imperforate, giving stamps with one side imperf.

539 Helena Vieira da Silva (artist, self-portrait)

540 Match Scene

(Des L. Duran. Litho)

1996 (3 May). Europa. Famous Women. P 12.

| 2494 | **539** 98E. multicoloured | 1·70 | 1·20 |
| **MS**2495 | 140×112 mm. No. 2494×3 | 5·50 | 6·50 |

(Des A. Santos. Litho Litografia Maia, Oporto)

1996 (7 June). European Football Championship, England. T **540** and similar horiz design. Multicoloured. P 12.

2496	78E. Type **540**	1·00	55
2497	140E. Match scene (*different*)	1·70	95
MS2498	140×112 mm. Nos. 2496/7. P 13½	2·75	2·50

541 Caravel and Arms

(Des L. Duran and C. Leitão. Litho Litografia Maia, Oporto)

1996 (7 June). 500th Death Anniv of João Vaz Corte-Real (explorer). T **541** and similar design. P 12.

| 2499 | 140E. Type **541** | 1·70 | 1·00 |
| **MS**2500 | 90×127 mm. 315E. Close-up of caravel in Type **541** (39×30 mm) | 4·25 | 4·25 |

542 Wrestling

543 Hilário and Guitar

54

PORTUGAL

(Des J. Tinoco. Litho Litografia Maia, Oporto)

1996 (24 June). Olympic Games, Atlanta. T **542** and similar horiz designs. Multicoloured. P 12.

2501	47E. Type **542**	50	25
2502	78E. Show jumping	95	55
2503	98E. Boxing	1·10	65
2504	140E. Running	1·50	95
2501/2504	Set of 4	3·50	2·25

MS2505 96×110 mm. 300E. Athletes at starting block .... 4·00 4·00

No. **MS**2505 also commemorates "Olymphilex'96" sports stamp exhibition.

(Des C. Leitão. Litho Litografia Maia, Oporto)

1996 (1 July). Death Centenary of Augusto Hilário (fado singer). P 12.

2506	**543**	80E. multicoloured	95	55

544 António Silva (actor)

545 King Afonso V

(Des B2 Design Studio. Litho Litografia Maia, Oporto)

1996 (7 Aug–Sept). Centenary of Motion Pictures. T **544** and similar horiz designs. Multicoloured. P 12.

2507	47E. Type **544**	50	25
2508	78E. Vasco Santana (actor)	90	55
2509	80E. Laura Alves (actress)	90	55
2510	98E. Aurélio Pais dos Reis (director)	1·10	55
2511	100E. Leitão de Barros (director)	1·10	65
2512	140E. António Lopes Ribeiro (director)	1·60	90
2507/2512	Set of 6	5·50	3·25

MS2513 Two sheets, each 112×140 mm. (a) Nos. 2507/9; (b) Nos. 2510/12 .... 6·50 5·50

MS2514 141×111 mm. Nos. 2507/12 (11 Sept) .... 6·50 5·75

(Des C. Leitão. Litho)

1996 (7 Aug). 550th Anniv of Alphonsine Collection of Statutes. P 12.

2515	**545**	350E. multicoloured	3·75	2·20

546 Perdigão

547 Aveiro

(Des J. Tinoco. Litho)

1996 (19 Sept). Birth Centenary of José de Azeredo Perdigão (lawyer and Council of State member). P 12×11½.

2516	**546**	47E. multicoloured	65	40

(Des C. Pinto. Litho Litografia Maia, Oporto)

1996 (27 Sept). District Arms (1st series). T **547** and similar horiz designs. Multicoloured. P 12.

2517	47E. Type **547**	55	25
2518	78E. Beja	90	60
2519	80E. Braga	90	60
2520	98E. Bragança	1·10	65
2521	100E. Castelo Branco	1·10	75
2522	140E. Coimbra	1·60	1·00
2517/2522	Set of 6	6·00	3·50

MS2523 Two sheets, each 140×112 mm. (a) Nos. 2517/19; (b) Nos. 2520/22 .... 7·00 6·50

See also Nos. 2579/**MS**2585 and 2648/**MS**2654.

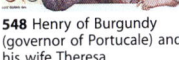

548 Henry of Burgundy (governor of Portucale) and his wife Theresa

549 Rojões (Pork dish)

(Des L. Duran. Litho)

1996 (9 Oct). 900th Anniv of Foundation of County of Portucale by King Afonso VI of Leon and Castille. P 12.

2524	**548**	47E. multicoloured	65	40

(Des A. Santos. Litho Litografia Maia, Oporto)

1996 (9 Oct). Traditional Portuguese Dishes (1st series). T **549** and similar horiz designs. Multicoloured. P 12.

2525	47E. Type **549**	60	35
2526	78E. Boticas trout	90	50
2527	80E. Oporto tripe	90	50
2528	98E. Baked cod with jacket potatoes	1·10	55
2529	100E. Aveiro eel	1·10	70
2530	140E. Peniche lobster	1·70	90
2525/2530	Set of 6	5·50	3·75

See also Nos. 2569/2574.

550 Lisbon Postman, 1821

551 King Manuel I in Shipyard

(Des C. Pinto. Litho)

1996 (9 Oct). 175th Anniv of Home Delivery Postal Service. T **550** and similar vert designs. Multicoloured. P 12.

2531	47E. Type **550**	55	25
2532	78E. Postman, 1854	90	65
2533	98E. Rural postman, 1893	1·10	70
2534	100E. Postman, 1939	1·10	70
2535	140E. Modern postman, 1992	1·60	1·00
2531/2535	Set of 5	4·75	3·00

(Des C. Possolo. Litho Litografia Maia, Oporto)

1996 (12 Nov). 500th Anniv (1997) of Discovery of Portugal–India Sea Route by Vasco da Gama (1st issue). T **551** and similar horiz designs. Multicoloured. P 13½.

2536	47E. Type **551**	70	35
2537	78E. Departure from Lisbon	1·30	70
2538	98E. Fleet in Atlantic Ocean	1·50	85
2539	140E. Sailing around Cape of Good Hope	1·70	1·00
2536/2539	Set of 4	4·75	2·50

MS2540 141×113 mm. 315E. "Dream of King Manuel I" (illustration from Poem IV of *The Lusiads* by Luís de Camões) .... 4·25 4·25

See also Nos. 2590/**MS**2596 and 2665/**MS**2680.

552 "Banknote"

553 East Timorese Couple

(Des L. de Abreu. Litho)

1996 (12 Nov). 150th Anniv of Bank of Portugal. P 12.

2541	**552**	78E. multicoloured	90	55

(Des J. Brandão. Litho Litografia Maia, Oporto)

1996 (12 Nov). Rights of People of East Timor. Award of 1996 Nobel Peace Prize to Don Carlos Ximenes Belo and José Ramos Horton. P 12.

2542	**553**	140E. multicoloured	1·50	1·10

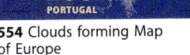

554 Clouds forming Map of Europe

555 Portuguese Galleon

PORTUGAL

(Des J. Tinoco. Litho)

1996 (2 Dec). Organization for Security and Co-operation in Europe Summit Meeting, Lisbon. Sheet 95×110 mm. P 12.
MS2543 554 200E. multicoloured .... 3·00 3·00

(Des C. Santos. Litho Litografia Maia, Oporto)

1997 (12 Feb). Sailing Ships of the India Shipping Line. T **555** and similar horiz designs. Multicoloured. P 12.
2544	49E. Type **555**	50	35
2545	80E. *Principe da Beira* (nau)	1·20	75
2546	100E. Bow view of *Don Fernando II e Glória* (sail frigate)	1·20	95
2547	140E. Stern view of *Don Fernando II e Glória*	1·50	1·10
2544/2547 Set of 4		4·00	2·75

556 Youth with Flower   **557** Arms

(Des J. Tinoco. Litho Litografia Maia, Oporto)

1997 (20 Feb). "No to Drugs – Yes to Life" (anti-drugs campaign). P 12.
2548	**556**	80E. multicoloured	90	60
		a. Imperf × p 12. Booklets	1·10	75
		ab. Booklet pane. No. 2548a×5	5·75	

(Des A. Santos. Litho Litografia Maia, Oporto)

1997 (12 Mar). Bicentenary of Managing Institute of Public Credit. P 12.
2549 **557** 49E. multicoloured 65 40

558 Desman eating Worm   **559** Moorish Girl guarding Hidden Treasure

(Des J. Projecto. Litho)

1997 (12 Mar). The Pyrenean Desman (*Galemys pyrenaicus*). T **558** and similar vert designs. Multicoloured. P 12.
2550	49E. Type **558**	70	40
	a. Block or strip of 4. Nos. 2550/3	3·25	
2551	49E. Diving	70	40
2552	49E. With wet fur	70	40
2553	49E. Cleaning snout	70	40
2550/2553 Set of 4		2·50	1·40

Nos. 2550/3 were issued together in *se-tenant* blocks and strips of four stamps within the sheet.

(Des Celeste Maia. Litho Litografia Maia, Oporto)

1997 (5 May). Europa. Tales and Legends. P 12.
2554 **559** 100E. multicoloured .... 1·70 1·40
MS2555 140×107 mm. No. 2554×3 .... 6·50 6·25

560 Surfing   **561** Night Attack on Santarém Fortress

(Des F. Tellechea. Litho Litografia Maia, Oporto)

1997 (29 May). Adventure Sports. T **560** and similar horiz designs. Multicoloured. P 12.
2556	49E. Type **560**	55	35
2557	80E. Skateboarding	95	65
2558	100E. In-line skating	1·10	85
2559	140E. Paragliding	1·50	1·10
2556/2559 Set of 4		3·75	2·50
MS2560	134×113 mm. 150E. B.M.X. cycling; 150E. Hang-gliding	4·00	3·00

(Des L. de Freitas. Litho Litografia Maia, Oporto)

1997 (9 June). 850th Anniv of Capture from the Moors of Santarém and Lisbon. T **561** and similar vert design. Multicoloured. P 12.
2561	80E. Type **561**	85	65
	a. Pair. Nos. 2561/2	1·60	1·60
2562	80E. Victorious King Afonso riding past Lisbon city walls	85	65
MS2563	140×113 mm. Nos. 2561/2, each×2	4·25	4·00

Nos. 2561/2 were issued together in *se-tenant* pairs within the sheet.

562 Fróis with Japanese Man   **563** Indian Children and José de Anchieta

(Des C. Leitão and L. Duran (2564), Posts and Telecommunications, Macao (2565), M. Morita (2566). Litho Litografia Maia Oporto)

1997 (9 June). 400th Death Anniv of Father Luis Fróis (author of *The History of Japan*). T **562** and similar multicoloured designs. P 12.
2564	80E. Type **562**	1·20	75
2565	140E. Father Fróis and church (vert)	1·60	1·10
2566	140E. Father Fróis and flowers (vert)	1·60	1·10
2564/2566 Set of 3		4·00	2·75

(Des C. Possolo. Litho Litografia Maia, Oporto)

1997 (9 June). Death Anniversaries of Missionaries to Brazil. T **563** and similar vert design. Multicoloured. P 12.
2567	140E. Type **563** (400th)	1·50	1·00
2568	350E. António Vieira in pulpit (300th)	4·00	2·75

(Des A. Santos. Litho Litografia Maia, Oporto)

1997 (5 July). Traditional Portuguese Dishes (2nd series). Horiz designs as T **549**. Multicoloured. P 12.
2569	10E. Scalded kid, Beira Baixa	10	10
2570	49E. Fried shad with bread-pap, Ribatejo	55	35
2571	80E. Lamb stew, Alentejo	90	60
2572	100E. Rich fish chowder, Algarve	1·10	80
2573	140E. Sword fillets with maize, Madeira	1·60	1·10
2574	200E. Stewed octopus, Azores	2·20	1·60
2569/2574 Set of 6		5·75	4·00

564 Centre of Oporto   **565** Couple before Clerk

(Des A. Alves. Litho Litografia Maia, Oporto)

1997 (5 July). "Lubrapex 97" Portuguese–Brazilian Stamp exhibition, Oporto. UNESCO World Heritage Site. Sheet 121×85 mm. P 12.
MS2575 **564** 350E. multicoloured .... 4·25 4·25

(Des A. Santos. Litho)

1997 (19 July). 700th Anniv of Mutual Assurance in Portugal. P 12.
2576 **565** 100E. multicoloured .... 1·20 80

PORTUGAL

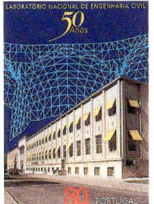 

566 Laboratory, Lisbon

567 King Dinis and Arms of Portugal and King Fernando IV and Arms of Castile and Leon

(Des A. Santos. Litho)

1997 (29 Aug). 50th Anniv of National Laboratory of Civil engineering. P 12.
2577	**566**	80E. multicoloured	90	50

(Des J. Guedes. Litho)

1997 (12 Sept). 700th Anniv of Treaty of Alcanices (defining national frontiers). P 12.
2578	**567**	80E. multicoloured	90	50

568 Évora

569 Chart by Lopo Homem-Reinéis, 1519

(Des J. Guedes. Litho Litografia Maia, Oporto)

1997 (17 Sept). District Arms (2nd series). T **568** and similar horiz designs. Multicoloured. P 12.
2579		10E. Type **568**	10	10
2580		49E. Faro	55	30
2581		80E. Guarda	80	55
2582		100E. Leiria	1·20	65
2583		140E. Lisbon	1·40	1·00
2584		200E. Portalegre	2·10	1·30
2579/2584 Set of 6			5·50	3·50
MS2585 Two sheets each 140×112 mm. (a) Nos. 2579, 2581 and 2583; (b) Nos. 2580, 2582 and 2584			5·00	2·75

(Des V. Santos. Litho)

1997 (9 Oct). Portuguese Charts. T **561** and similar horiz designs. Multicoloured. P 12.
2586		49E. Type **569**	45	25
2587		80E. Chart by João Freire, 1546	95	70
2588		100E. Planisphere by Diogo Ribeiro, 1529	1·10	75
2589		140E. Chart showing Tropic of Capricorn (anon), 1630	1·40	95
2586/2589 Set of 4			3·50	2·25
MS2590 139×112 mm. Nos. 2586/9			4·50	4·50

 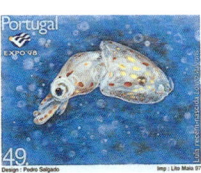

570 Queen Maria I and Mail Coach

572 Squid (*Loligo vulgaris*)

571 Erecting Landmark Monument, Quelimane

(Des J. Tinoco. Litho)

1997 (9 Oct). Bicentenary of State Postal Service. P 12.
2591	**570**	80E. multicoloured	90	50

(Des C. Possolo. Litho Litografia Maia, Oporto)

1997 (5 Nov). 500th Anniv of Discovery of Portugal–India Sea Route by Vasco da Gama (2nd issue). T **571** and similar horiz designs. Multicoloured. P 13½.
2592		49E. Type **571**	50	35
2593		80E. Arrival of fleet at Mozambique	90	50
2594		100E. Arrival of fleet in Mombasa	1·10	80
2595		140E. King of Melinde greeting Vasco da Gama	1·50	1·00
2592/2595 Set of 4			3·50	2·50
MS2596 140×113 mm. 315E. Vasco da Gama on beach at Natal			4·00	4·00

(Des P. Salgado. Litho Litografia Maia, Oporto)

1997 (5 Nov). Expo '98 World's Fair, Lisbon (1st issue). Ocean Life. T **572** and similar horiz designs. Multicoloured. P 12.
2597		49E. Type **572**	50	35
2598		80E. Rock lobster (*Scyllarus arctus*) larva	95	65
2599		100E. Adult *Pontellina plumata* (crustacean)	1·10	80
2600		140E. Senegal sole (*Solea senegalensis*) larva	1·40	1·20
2597/2600 Set of 4			3·50	2·75
MS2601 110×150 mm. 100E. *Calcidiscus leptoporus*; 100E. *Tabellaria sp.* colonies			2·50	2·50

See also Nos. 2611/**MS**2615 and 2621/2641.

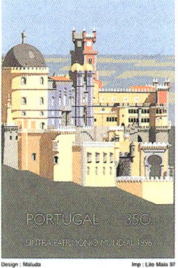 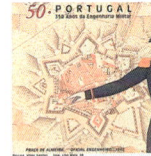

573 Sintra

574 Officer and Plan of Almeida Fortress, 1848

(Des Maluda. Litho Litografia Maia, Oporto)

1997 (5 Dec). UNESCO World Heritage Site. Sintra. "Indepex 97" International Stamp Exhibition, New Delhi. Sheet 112×140 mm. P 12.
MS2602	**573**	350E. multicoloured	4·25	4·25

(Des V. Santos. Litho Litografia Maia, Oporto)

1998 (28 Jan). 350th Anniv of Portuguese Military Engineering. T **574** and similar horiz designs. Multicoloured. P 12.
2603		50E. Type **574**	50	30
		a. Imperf×p 12. Booklets	95	90
		ab. Booklet pane. Nos. 2603a, 2604a, 2605a and 2606a	5·25	
2604		80E. Officer and plan of Miranda do Oduro Fortress, 1834	1·10	65
		a. Imperf×p 12. Booklets	1·20	1·10
2605		100E. Officer and plan of Monção Fortress, 1797	1·30	70
		a. Imperf×p 12. Booklets	1·40	1·40
2606		140E. Officer and plan of Elvas Fortress, 1806	1·50	1·10
		a. Imperf×p 12. Booklets	1·60	1·60
2603/2606 Set of 4			4·00	2·50

 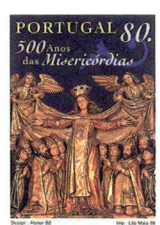

575 Ivens and African Scene

576 Adoration of the Madonna (carving)

(Des J. Tinoco. Litho)

1998 (28 Jan). Death Centenary of Roberto Ivens (explorer). P 12.
2607	**575**	140E. multicoloured	1·50	1·00

PORTUGAL

(Des B2 Design Studio. Litho Litografia Maia, Oporto)

1998 (20 Feb). 500th Anniv of Holy Houses Misericórdia (religious social relief order). T **576** and similar multicoloured designs. P 12.

2608	80E. Type **576**	90	50
2609	100E. Attending patient (tile mural)	1·00	85

577 Aqueduct over Alcântara

578 Vasco da Gama Bridge

(Des C. Leitão. Litho)

1998 (20 Feb). 250th Anniv of Aqueduct of the Free Waters (from Sintra to Lisbon). Sheet 155×110 mm. P 12.

MS2610	**577** 350E. multicoloured	4·25	4·25

(Des P. Salgado. Litho Litografia Maia, Oporto)

1998 (20 Mar). "Expo '98" World's Fair, Lisbon (2nd issue). Ocean Life. Horiz designs as T **572**. Multicoloured. P 12.

2611	50E. Crab (*Pilumnus* sp.) larva	50	25
2612	85E. Monkfish (*Lophius piscatorius*) larva	1·10	55
2613	100E. Gilthead sea bream (*Sparus aurata*) larva	1·20	70
2614	140E. Medusa (*Cladonema radiatum*)	1·40	1·00
2611/2614	Set of 4	3·75	2·25
MS2615	112×140 mm. 110E. Bioluminescent protozoan (*Noctiluca miliaris*); 110E. Dinoflagellate (*Dinophysis acuta*). P 12.	2·50	2·50

(Des C. Leitão. Litho)

1998 (29 Mar). Opening of Vasco da Gama Bridge (from Sacavém to Montijo). P 12.

2616	**578** 200E. multicoloured	2·00	1·60
MS2617	125×85 mm. As No. 2616 but with background extended to edges	2·30	2·20

579 Coloured Balls

580 Seahorse

(Des J. Machado. Litho Litografia Maia, Oporto)

1998 (30 Apr). 150th Anniv of Oporto Industrial Association. P 12.

2618	**579** 80E. multicoloured	90	50

(Des C. Leitão. Litho)

1998 (13 May). International Year of the Ocean. Centenary of Vasco da Gama Aquarium. T **580** and similar horiz design. Multicoloured. P 12.

2619	50E. Type **580**	70	35
2620	80E. Angelfish and shoal	95	75

581 Diver and Astrolabe

582 Revellers before Statues of St. Antony of Padua, St. John and St. Peter

(Des P. Oliveira and J. Sarmento (2621/6, MS2628a, 2636/41), H. Cayatte Studio (MS2627, MS2628b), P. Salgado (others). Litho SNP Cambec, Melbourne, Australia (2630/41) or Litografia Maia, Oporto (others))

1998 (21 May). "Expo '98" World's Fair, Lisbon (3rd issue). P 12.

*(a) The Ocean. T **581** and similar horiz designs. Multicoloured*

2621	50E. Type **581**	50	25
2622	50E. Caravel	50	25
2623	85E. Fishes and coral reef (inscr "oceanário")	90	55
2624	85E. Underwater exploration equipment observing fishes	90	55
2625	140E. Mermaid and sea anemones	1·70	1·00
2626	140E. Children with hands on globe	1·70	1·00

*(b) Miniature sheets. Designs as T **581***

MS2627	154×116 mm. 50E. Portuguese Pavilion; 85E. Pavilion of the Future; 85E. Oceanarium; 140E. Knowledge of the Seas Pavilion; 140E. Pavilion of Utopia	6·25	6·25
MS2628	Two sheets, each 147×90 mm. (a) Nos. 2621/6; (b) 80E. Postal mascot; stamps as in No. MS2627	7·25	
MS2629	148×151 mm. Nos. 2597/MS2601 and 2611/MS2615	14·50	

No. **MS**2628a/b were also sold together, with the sheet prices removed from the margins, in a folder priced at 1750E.
No. **MS**2629 was also sold, with the sheet price removed from the margin, in a folder priced at 1750E.

(c) Coil stamps. As Nos. 2611/MS2615 (but with Latin names removed) and 2621/6. Size 29×23 mm. Self-adhesive. P 11½

2630	50E. As No. 2612	85	55
	a. Strip of 6. Nos. 2630/5	2·50	
2631	50E. Bioluminescent protozoan (as in No. MS2615)	85	55
2632	50E. As No. 2611	85	55
2633	50E. As No. 2613	85	55
2634	50E. Dinoflagellate (as in No. MS2615)	85	55
2635	50E. As No. 2614	85	55
2636	85E. Type **581**	1·50	90
	a. Strip of 6. Nos. 2636/41	4·75	
2637	85E. As No. 2624	1·50	90
2638	85E. As No. 2626	1·50	90
2639	85E. As No. 2622	1·50	90
2640	85E. As No. 2623 (but inscr "Portugal e os Oceanos")	1·50	90
2641	85E. As No. 2625	1·50	90

The designers' names and printer's imprints have been removed from Nos. 2630/41.
Nos. 2630/5 and 2636/41 respectively were issued in *se-tenant* coils of 50 (85E.) or 100 (50E.) stamps. Strips of six were made available to collectors at Post Offices and the Philatelic Bureau.

(Des L. de Abreu. Litho Litografia Maia, Oporto)

1998 (21 May). Europa. National Festivals. P 12.

2642	**582** 100E. multicoloured	1·50	1·20
MS2643	140×108 mm. No. 2642×3	5·00	5·75

583 Marie Curie

584 Ferreira de Castro and Illustration to *The Jungle*

(Des C. Leitão. Litho)

1998 (1 June). Centenary of Discovery of Radium. P 12.

2644	**583** 140E. multicoloured	1·40	90

(Des L. de Abreu. Litho Litografia Maia, Oporto)

1998 (10 June). Birth Centenary of José Ferreira de Castro (writer). P 12.

2645	**584** 50E. multicoloured	60	35

585 Untitled Painting

586 Adam (Michelangelo) (detail from Sistine Chapel ceiling)

(Des V. Santos. Litho Lithografia Maia, Oporto)

1998 (10 June). Death Centenary of Bernardo Marques (artist). P 12.

2646	**585** 85E. multicoloured	90	65

(Des J. Tinoco. Litho Litografia Maia, Oporto)

1998 (18 June). Juvalex '98 Stamp exhibition. 50th Anniv of Universal Declaration of Human Rights. Sheet 90×55 mm. P 12.

MS2647	**586** 315E. multicoloured	3·50	3·50

PORTUGAL

587 Glass Production

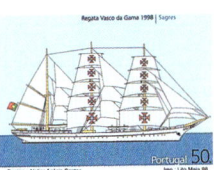
588 *Sagres II* (cadet barque), Portugal

590 Modern Mail Van

591 Globe and Flags of Participating Countries

(Des J. Guedes. Litho Litografia Maia, Oporto)

1998 (23 June). District Arms (3rd series). Horiz designs as T **568**. Multicoloured. P 12.

2648	50E. Vila Real	50	35
2649	85E. Setubal	1·30	80
2650	85E. Viana do Castelo (150th anniv of elevation to city)	1·30	80
2651	100E. Santarém	1·40	80
2652	100E. Viseu	1·40	80
2653	200E. Oporto	2·00	1·20
2648/2653	Set of 6	7·00	4·25
MS2654	Two sheets, each 140×113 mm. (a) Nos. 2648, 2650 and 2653; (b) Nos. 2649 and 2651/2	8·25	9·00

(Des J. Machado. Litho Litografia Maia, Oporto)

1998 (7 July). 250th Anniv of Glass Production in Marinha Grande. T **587** and similar horiz designs. Multicoloured. P 12.

2655	50E. Type **587**	50	25
2656	80E. Heating glass and finished product	95	65
2657	100E. Bottles and factory	1·00	70
2658	140E. Blue bottles and glass-maker	1·90	1·00
2655/2658	Set of 4	4·00	2·25

(Des A. Santos. Litho Litografia Maia, Oporto)

1998 (31 July). Vasco da Gama Regatta. T **588** and similar horiz designs. Multicoloured. P 12.

2659	50E. Type **588**	50	30
2660	85E. *Asgard II* (Irish cadet brigantine)	1·20	60
2661	85E. *Rose* (American replica)	1·20	60
2662	100E. *Amerigo Vespucci* (Italian cadet ship)	1·30	80
2663	100E. *Kruzenshtern* (Russian cadet barque)	1·30	80
2664	140E. *Creoula* (Portuguese cadet schooner)	2·00	1·10
2659/2664	Set of 6	6·75	3·75

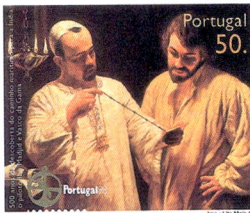
589 Da Gama with Pilot Ibn Madjid

(Des C. Possolo. Litho Litografia Maia, Oporto)

1998 (4 Sept). 500th Anniv (1997) of Discovery of Portugal–India Sea Route by Vasco da Gama (3rd issue). T **589** and similar horiz designs. Multicoloured. P 13½.

2665	50E. Type **551**	75	45
	a. Sheetlet. Nos. 2665/76	9·25	
2666	50E. As No. 2537	75	45
2667	50E. As No. 2538	75	45
2668	50E. As No. 2539	75	45
2669	50E. Type **571**	75	45
2670	50E. As No. 2593	75	45
2671	50E. As No. 2594	75	45
2672	50E. As No. 2595	75	45
2673	50E. Type **589**	95	60
2674	50E. *São Gabriel* (flagship) in storm	75	45
2675	50E. Fleet arriving at Calicut	75	45
2676	50E. Audience with the Samorin of Calicut	75	45
2677	80E. As No. 2674	1·00	70
2678	100E. As No. 2675	1·10	75
2679	140E. As No. 2676	1·40	90
2665/2679	Set of 12	10·50	6·25
MS2680	140×112 mm. 315E. King of Melinde listening to Vasco da Gama	4·00	4·00

Nos. 2665/76 were issued together in *se-tenant* sheetlets of 12 stamps.

No. 2673 was also issued together with Nos. 2677/9 in sheets of 16, each value occurring in a separate block of four with the blocks separated by gutters.

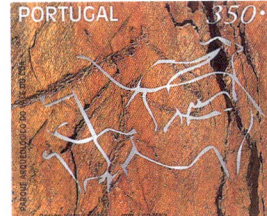
592 Cave Paintings

593 Male and Female Figures

(Des V. Santos. Litho Litografia Maia, Oporto)

1998 (9 Oct). Bicentenaries of Inauguration of Lisbon–Coimbra Mail Coach Service and of Re-organization of Maritime Mail Service to Brazil. T **590** and similar horiz design. Multicoloured. P 12.

2681	50E. Type **590**	50	35
2682	140E. Mail coach and *Postilhão da América* (brigantine)	1·80	1·10

(Des J. Machado. Litho Litografia Maia, Oporto)

1998 (18 Oct). Eigth Iberian–American Summit of State Leaders and Governors, Oporto. Sheet 90×55 mm. P 12½.

MS2683	**591** 140E. multicoloured	1·70	1·60

(Des N. Fischer. Litho Litografia Maia, Oporto)

1998 (23 Oct). Archeological Park, Côa Valley. Sheet 140×113 mm. P 13½.

MS2684	**592** 350E. multicoloured	4·25	4·25

1998 (5 Nov). Health Awareness. P 12.

2685	**593** 100E. multicoloured	1·20	80

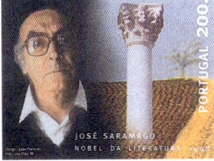
594 Saramago

595 Knife Grinder

(Des J. Machado. Litho Litografia Maia, Oporto)

1998 (15 Dec). José Saramago (winner of Nobel prize for Literature, 1998). Sheet 140×114 mm. P 12.

MS2686	**594** 200E. multicoloured	2·40	2·40

DENOMINATION. From No. 2687 Portugal stamps are denominated both in Escudos and in Euros.

(Des J. Tinoco. Litho)

1999 (26 Feb). 19th-Century Itinerant Trades. Booklet stamps. T **595** and similar horiz design. Multicoloured. Self-adhesive. Die-cut perf 11½.

2687	51E. Type **595**	50	35
2688	95E. Coachman	1·20	80

The stamps are peeled directly from the booklet covers and cannot therefore be collected as separate panes.

Numbers have been left for possible additions to this series.

596 Flags of European Union Members and Euro emblem

597 Kangaroos and Galleon

PORTUGAL

(Des J. Machado. Litho)
1999 (15 Mar). Introduction of the Euro (European currency). P 12.
2696 **596** 95E. multicoloured .... 1·20 95

(Des C. Possolo. Litho Litografia Maia, Oporto)
1999 (19 Mar). "Australia 99" International Stamp Exhibition, Melbourne. The Portuguese in Australia. T **597** and similar horiz designs. Multicoloured. P 12.
2697 140E. Type **597** .... 1·40 90
    a. Horiz pair. Nos. 2697/8 .... 2·50 2·50
2698 140E. Galleon and aborigines .... 1·40 90
MS2699 137×104 mm. 350E. Motifs of Nos. 2688/9 (79×30 mm) .... 4·25 4·00
    Nos. 2697/8 were issued together in horizontal *se-tenant* pairs within the sheet, each pair forming a composite design.

598 Norton de Matos   599 Almeida Garrett

(Des J. Brandão. Litho Litografia Maia, Oporto)
1999 (24 Mar). 50th Anniv of Candidature of General José Norton de Matos to Presidency of the Republic. P 12.
2700 **598** 80E. multicoloured .... 1·10 70

(Des J. Tinoco. Litho)
1999 (24 Mar). Birth Bicentenary of João Baptista Almeida Garrett (writer). P 12.
2701 **599** 95E. multicoloured .... 1·20 75
MS2702 130×105 mm. **599** 210E. multicoloured .... 2·50 2·40

600 Breguet 16 Bn2 *Patria*   601 Carnation

(Des L. Duran and A. Santos. Litho)
1999 (25 Apr). 75th Anniv of Sarmento de Beires and Brito Pais's Portugal–Macao Flight. T **600** and similar horiz designs. Multicoloured. P 12.
2703 140E. Type **600** .... 1·60 1·00
2704 140E. De Havilland D.H.9 biplane .... 1·60 1·00
MS2705 137×104 mm. Nos. 2694/5 .... 3·25 3·25

(Des L. Duran (51E.), J. Machado (80E.). Litho)
1999 (25 Apr). 25th Anniv of Revolution. T **601** and similar horiz design. Multicoloured. P 12.
2706 51E. Type **601** 50 30
2707 80E. National Assembly building (78×29 mm) 90 60
MS2708 140×108 mm. Nos. 2706/7 .... 1·60 1·60

602 Council Emblem   603 Wolf and Iris (Peneda-Gerês National Park)

(Des C. Leitão. Litho)
1999 (5 May). 50th Anniv of Council of Europe. P 12.
2709 **602** 100E. multicoloured .... 1·40 1·10

(Des J. Sarmento and P. Oliveira. Litho Litografia Maia, Oporto)
1999 (5 May). Europa. Parks and Gardens. P 12.
2710 **603** 100E. multicoloured .... 1·40 1·20
MS2711 154×109 mm. No. 2710x3 .... 5·25 6·50

604 Marquis de Pombal   605 Harbour

(Des J. Tinoco. Litho)
1999 (13 May). 300th Birth Anniv of Marquis de Pombal (statesman and reformer). T **604** and similar horiz designs, Multicoloured. P 12.
2712 80E. Type **604** 90 70
MS2713 170×135 mm. 80E. Head of Marquis and part of statue; 210E. Hand holding quill .... 3·50 2·75

(Des J. Sarmento. Litho Litografia Maia, Oporto)
1999 (24 June). "Meeting of Cultures". Return of Macao to China. T **605** and similar multicoloured designs. P 12.
2714 51E. Type **605** 50 30
2715 80E. Dancers 90 55
2716 95E. Procession of the Madonna 95 80
2717 100E. Ruins of St. Paul's Basilica .... 1·20 80
2718 140E. Garden with bust of Luis Camões (horiz) .... 1·60 95
2714/2718 Set of 5 .... 4·75 3·00

 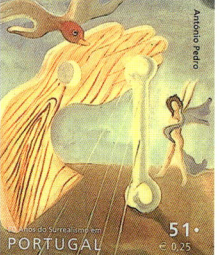

606 De Havilland D.H.82A Tiger Moth   607 Portion by António Pedro

(Des J. Rodrigues and A. Costa. Litho Litografia Maia, Oporto)
1999 (1 July). 75th Anniv of Military Aeronautics. T **606** and similar horiz designs. Multicoloured. P 12.
2719 51E. Type **606** 50 30
2720 51E. Supermarine Spitfire V6 fighter 50 30
2721 85E. Breguet Bre XIV A2 .... 1·20 65
2722 85E. SPAD VII-C1 .... 1·20 65
2723 95E. Caudron G-3 .... 1·40 75
2724 95E. Junkers Ju 52/3m .... 1·40 75
2719/2724 Set of 6 .... 5·50 3·00
MS2725 150×117 mm. Nos. 2719/24 .... 6·25 6·50

(Des V. Santos. Litho Litografia Maia, Oporto)
1999 (2 July). 50th Anniv of Surrealism (modern art movement) in Portugal. T **607** and similar vert designs showing details by artist named of collective painting "Cadavre exquis". Multicoloured. P 13½.
2726 51E. Type **607** 45 30
2727 80E. Vespeira 90 65
2728 95E. Moniz Pereira 95 70
2729 100E. Fernando de Azevedo .... 1·00 70
2730 140E. António Domingues .... 1·50 1·00
2726/2730 Set of 5 .... 4·25 3·00
MS2731 175×153 mm. Nos. 2726/30 forming a composite design of complete picture .... 4·75 5·25
    No. MS2731 is inscribed with the "Philexfrance 99" International Stamp Exhibition emblem on the sheet margin.

608 Passenger Train on Bridge   609 Heinrich von Stephan (founder)

PORTUGAL

(Des J. Sarmento. Litho Litografia Maia, Oporto)

1999 (29 July). Inauguration of Railway Section of the 25th of April Bridge over River Tagus, Lisbon. T **608** and similar horiz design. Multicoloured. P 12.

2732	51E. Type **608**	50	30
2733	95E. Passenger train on bridge (*different*)	1·20	75
MS2734	Two sheets, each 140×110 mm. (a) 350E. Close-up of part of Type **608** (79×30 mm); (b) 350E. Close-up of part of No. 2733 (79×30 mm)	8·25	8·00

(Des L. Duran. Litho)

1999 (21 Aug). 125th Anniv of Universal Postal Union. T **609** and similar horiz design. Multicoloured. P 12.

2735	95E. Type **609**	95	70
2736	140E. Globe, letter and keyboard	1·40	90
MS2737	140×98 mm. 315E. Combination of motifs in Nos. 2735/6 (79×29 mm)	3·75	3·50

610 Egg Packs

611 Portuguese Troops and Moslem Ships

(Des A. Santos. Litho Litografia Maia, Oporto)

1999 (30 Aug). Convent Sweets (1st series). T **610** and similar horiz designs. Multicoloured. P 12.

2738	51E. Type **610**	50	30
2739	80E. Egg pudding	85	50
2740	95E. Angel's purses	95	65
2741	100E. Abrantés straw	1·60	70
2742	140E. Viseu chestnuts	1·80	1·10
2743	210E. Honey cake	2·20	1·60
2738/2743	Set of 6	7·00	4·25

See also Nos. 2785/2790.

(Des L. F. de Abreu. Litho)

1999 (3 Sept). 750th Anniv of King Afonso III's Conquest of the Algarve. P 12.

2744	**611**	100E. multicoloured	1·20	75

612 Câmara Pestana (bacteriologist)

613 José Diogo de Mascarenhas Neto (first General Mail Lieutenant)

(Des J. Machado. Litho Litografia Maia, Oporto)

1999 (20 Sept). Medical Anniversaries. T **612** and similar horiz designs. Multicoloured. P 12.

2745	51E. Type **612** (death centenary)	50	30
2746	51E. Ricardo Jorge (founder of National Health Institute, 60th death anniv)	50	30
2747	80E. Francisco Gentil (oncologist, 35th death anniv)	85	65
2748	80E. Egas Moniz (neurosurgeon, 125th birth anniv)	85	65
2749	95E. João Cid dos Santos (surgeon, 23rd death anniv)	1·00	70
2750	95E. Reynaldo dos Santos (arteriography researcher, 30th death anniv (2000))	1·00	70
2745/2750	Set of 6	4·25	3·00

(Des L. Duran. Litho Litografia Maia, Oporto)

1999 (9 Oct). Bicentenary of the Provisional Mail Rules (re-organization of postal system). P 12.

2751	**613**	80E. multicoloured	90	55

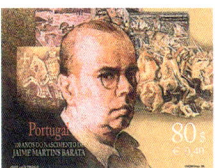
614 Barata, Stamps and Mural

615 Wise Men following Star (Maria Gonçalves)

(Des J. Tinoco. Litho)

1999 (9 Oct). Birth Centenary of Jaime Martins Barata (artist and stamp designer). P 12.

2752	**614**	80E. multicoloured	90	55

(Des F. Galamba. Litho)

1999 (19 Nov). Christmas. National Association of Art and Creativity for and by Handicapped Persons. T **615** and similar horiz designs with artists name in brackets. Multicoloured. P 12.

2753	51E. Type **615**	45	30
2754	95E. Father Christmas delivering presents (Marta Silva)	95	65
2755	140E. Father Christmas (Luis Farinha)	2·00	95
2756	210E. The Nativity (Maria Gonçalves)	2·40	1·30
2753/2756	Set of 4	5·25	2·75

616 Macanese Architecture

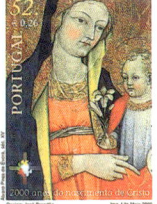
617 Macao Coat of Arms

(Des C. Marreiros. Litho)

1999 (19 Nov). Portuguese–Chinese Cultural Mix in Macao. Sheet 138×90 mm. P 12.

MS2757	**616**	140E. black and bright scarlet	1·80	1·80

(Des C. Marreiros. Litho)

1999 (19 Dec). Macao Retrospective. Sheet 138×90 mm. P 12.

MS2758	**617**	350E. multicoloured	4·50	4·50

618 "Madonna and Child" (Álvaro Pires of Évora)

619 Astronaut and Space Craft

(Des J. Brandão. Litho Litografia Maia, Oporto)

2000 (15 Feb). Birth Bimillenary of Jesus Christ. P 12.

2759	**618**	52E. multicoloured	80	40

(Des J. Tinoco. Litho Litografia Maia, Oporto)

2000 (18 Feb). The Twentieth Century (1st issue). Conquest of Space. P 12.

2760	**619**	86E. multicoloured	1·10	65

See also Nos. **MS**2768 and 2819/2826.

620 Golden eagle

621 Crowd and Suffragettes

61

PORTUGAL

(Des J. Projecto. Litho)

2000 (2 Mar). Birds (1st series). T **620** and similar horiz designs. Multicoloured.

(a) Sheet stamps. Ordinary gum. P 12×11½

2761	52E. Type **620**		50	35
2762	85E. Great crested grebe		90	65
2763	90E. Greater flamingo		90	70
2764	100E. Northern gannet		1·60	80
2765	215E. Green-winged teal		2·75	1·60

(b) Booklet stamps. Self-adhesive. Die-cut perf 11½

2766	52E. As No. 2761		55	35
2767	100E. As No. 2764		1·00	80
2761/2767 Set of 7			7·25	4·75

Nos. 2766/7 are peeled directly from the booklet covers and cannot therefore be collected as separate panes.

See also Nos. 2832/2839.

(Des J. Tinoco. Litho Litografia Maia, Oporto)

2000 (15 Mar). The Twentieth Century (2nd issue). Three sheets, 190×220 mm, containing T **621** and similar multicoloured designs. P 12.

MS2768 (a) 52E. Type **621** (Human Rights); 52E. Fashion through the century (59×29 mm); 52E. Windmills, electricity pylon and birds (ecology) (59×29 mm); 52E. early airplanes, car, steam locomotive and ship (transport); 52E. Modern airplane, boat and train (transport); 52E. As No. 2760; 52E. Space shuttle on launch pad (conquest of space) (b) 52E. Marcel Proust and Thomas Mann (novelists), James Joyce (writer), Franz Kafka (novelist), Fernando Pessoa (poet), Jorge Luis Borges and Samuel Beckett (writers) (literature) (49×29 mm); 52E. Achille-Claude Debussy, Igor Stravinsky, Arnold Schöenberg, Béla Bartók, George Gershwin (composers), Charlie Parker (saxophonist) and William (Bill) Evans (pianist) (music) (49×29 mm); 52E. Performers (theatre); 52E. Auditorium and performers (theatre) (59×29 mm); 52E. Sculptures and paintings (art) (49×29 mm); 52E. Abstract art (29×29 mm); 52E. Charlie Chaplin on left (cinema) (49×29 mm); 52E. Woody Allen on left (cinema and television) (29×29 mm); 52E. Old and modern buildings (architecture); 52E. Modern buildings (architecture); 52E. Front and aerial views of modern buildings (architecture) (c) 52E. Edmund Husserl, Ludwig Wittgenstein and Martin Heidegger (philosophy); 52E. Jules Poincaré, Kurt Gödel and Andrei Kolmogorov (mathematics); 52E. Max Planck, Albert Einstein and Niels Bohr (physics) (49×29 mm); 52E. Franz Boas (anthropologist), Levi Strauss (clothing manufacturer) and Margaret Mead (anthropologist) (social science and medicine); 52E. Sigmund Freud (neurologist) and Alexander Fleming (bacteriologist) (social science and medicine) (29×29 mm); 52E. Christiaan Barnard performing operation (organ transplant surgeon) (medicine); 52E. Office workers, Joseph Schumpeter and John Keynes (economics); 52E. Circuit boards (technology); 52E. Fibre optics (technology) (29×29 mm); 52E. Binary code, Alan Turing (mathematician) and John Von Neuman (mathematician) (information technology and telecommunications); 52E. Guglielmo Marconi (physicist) and satellite aerials (information technology and telecommunications); 52E. Binary code and satellite (information technology and telecommunications) (29×29 mm) .... 22·00 20·00

No. **MS**2768 consists of horizontal strips and blocks, some of which form horizontal composite designs.

No. **MS**2768 were issued together in a presentation wallet.

In addition to No. **MS**2768 these miniature sheets were also available in a stapled presentation album issued on 15 March 2000, with the sheets separated from the booklet by a line of roulettes.

622 Member's Flags forming Stars

623 Native Indians

(Des L. Duran. Litho)

2000 (23 Mar). Portuguese Presidency of European Union Council. P 12.

2769	**622**	100E. multicoloured	1·50	1·20

(Des L. de Abreu. Litho Litografia Maia, Oporto)

2000 (11 Apr). 500th Anniv of Discovery of Brazil. T **623** and similar horiz designs. Multicoloured. P 12.

2770	52E. Type **623**		60	40
2771	85E. Native Indians watching Pedro Álvares Cabral's fleet		1·10	75
2772	100E. Ship's crew and sails		1·60	95
2773	140E. Native Indians and Portuguese sailors meeting		1·80	1·30
2770/2773 Set of 4			4·50	3·00
MS2774 140×140 mm. Nos. 2770/3			5·00	3·50

624 "Building Europe"

625 Pope John Paul II and Children

(Des J.-P. Cousin. Litho)

2000 (9 May). Europa. P 12.

2775	**624**	100E. multicoloured	2·00	1·70
MS2776 154×109 mm. No. 2775×3			6·25	7·75

(Des L. Duran. Litho Litografia Maia, Oporto)

2000 (12 May). Papal Visit to Portugal. Beatification of Jacinta and Francisco Marto (Children of Fatima). P 12.

2777	**625**	52E. multicoloured	75	45

626 Draisienne Bicycle, 1817

627 Slices of Tomar

(Des L. Duran. Litho)

2000 (22 May). "The Stamp Show 2000" International Stamp Exhibition, London. Centenary of International Cycling Union. Bicycles. T **626** and similar horiz designs. Multicoloured. P 12.

2778	52E. Type **626**		55	40
2779	85E. Michaux, 1868		1·60	75
2780	100E. Ariel, 1871		1·20	95
2781	140E. Rover, 1888		1·90	1·30
2782	215E. BTX, 2000		3·00	1·90
2783	350E. GT, 2000		4·50	3·25
2778/2783 Set of 6			11·50	7·75
MS2784 140×112 mm. Nos. 2778/83			12·50	12·00

(Des A. Santos. Litho Litografia Maia, Oporto)

2000 (30 May). Convent Sweets (2nd series). T **627** and similar horiz designs. Multicoloured. P 12.

2785	52E. Type **627**		55	40
2786	85E. Rodrigo's present		1·60	75
2787	100E. Sericaia		1·20	95
2788	140E. Ló bread		1·90	1·30
2789	215E. Grated bread		3·00	1·90
2790	350E. Royal paraíso cake		4·50	3·25
2785/2790 Set of 6			11·50	7·75

628 Fishing Boat and Fishes

(Des Filipa Mata. Litho)

2000 (31 May). Fishermen's Day. P 12.

2791	**628**	52E. multicoloured	75	45

PORTUGAL

629 Portuguese Landscapes

(Des J. Machado. Litho Litografia Maia, Oporto)

2000 (1 June). EXPO 2000 World's Fair, Hanover, Germany. Humanity–Nature–Technology. T **629** and similar horiz design. Multicoloured. P 12.
2792	100E. Type **629**	1·20	90
MS2793	140×113 mm. 350E. Portuguese Pavilion, Hanover (39×30 mm)	4·00	4·00

630 Statue and Assembly Hall   **631** Fishermen and Boat

(Des J. Machado. Litho)

2000 (2 June). 25th Anniv of Constituent Assembly. P 12.
2794	**630**	85E. multicoloured	1·10	75

(Des L. Duran. Litho)

2000 (24 June). Cod Fishing. T **631** and similar horiz designs. Multicoloured. P 12.
2795	52E. Type **631**	55	40
2796	85E. Fishing barquentine and fisherman at ship's wheel	1·10	75
2797	100E. Three fishermen and boat	1·20	90
2798	100E. Fisherman and dories on fishing schooner	1·20	90
2799	140E. Fisherman rowing and fishing barquentine	1·90	1·20
2800	215E. Fisherman and fishing schooner	2·75	1·90
2795/2800	Set of 6	8·00	5·50
MS2801	140×112 mm. Nos. 2795/2800	9·50	5·50

632 De Queiroz   **633** Running

(Des L. de Abreu. Litho Lithografia Maia, Oporto)

2000 (16 Aug). Death Centenary of Eça de Queiroz (author). P 12.
2802	**632**	85E. multicoloured	1·10	75

(Des L. de Abreu. Litho)

2000 (15 Sept). Olympic Games, Sydney. T **633** and similar horiz designs. Multicoloured. P 12.
2803	52E. Type **633**	55	40
2804	85E. Show jumping	1·10	75
2805	100E. Dinghy racing	1·20	90
2806	140E. Diving	1·70	1·20
2803/2806	Set of 4	4·00	3·00
MS2807	140×112 mm. 85E. Fencing; 215E. Beach volleyball	4·50	4·25

Nos. 2803/**MS**2807 were wrongly inscribed "Sidney".

634 Airplane and Runway   **635** Writing Letter on Computer

(Des C. Leitão. Litho)

2000 (15 Sept). Inauguration of Madeira Airport Second Runway Extension. P 12.
2808	**634**	140E. multicoloured	1·90	1·30
MS2809	110×80 mm. 140E. multicoloured	1·90	2·00

(Des L. Duran. Litho)

2000 (15 Sept). 50th Anniv of Snoopy (cartoon character created by Charles Schulz). Postal Service. T **635** and similar horiz designs. Multicoloured. P 12.
2810	52E. Type **635**	55	40
2811	52E. Posting letter	55	40
2812	85E. Driving post van	1·10	75
2813	100E. Sorting post	1·40	90
2814	140E. Delivering post	1·90	1·20
2815	215E. Reading letter	2·40	1·90
2810/2815	Set of 6	7·50	5·00
MS2816	140×112 mm. Nos. 2810/15	9·25	9·75

636 Drawing, Telescope and Sextant   **637** Carolina Michaëlis de Vasconcellos (teacher)

(Des L. Duran. Litho)

2000 (10 Nov). 125th Anniv of Lisbon Geographic Society. T **636** and similar horiz design. Multicoloured. P 12.
2817	85E. Type **636**	1·10	75
	a. Horiz pair. Nos. 2817/18	2·75	1·90
2818	100E. Sextant and drawing	1·40	1·00

Nos. 2817/18 were issued together in *se-tenant* horizontal pairs within the sheet, each pair forming a composite design.

(Des J. Tinoco. Litho Litografia Maia, Oporto)

2001 (20 Feb). The Twentieth Century (3rd issue). History and Culture. T **637** and similar horiz designs. Multicoloured. P 12.
2819	85E. Type **637**	1·00	80
	a. Sheetlet of 8. Nos. 2819/26 plus 4 labels	9·75	8·75
2820	85E. Miguel Bombarda (doctor and politician)	1·00	80
2821	85E. Bernardino Machado (politician)	1·00	80
2822	85E. Tomás Alcaide (lyricist)	1·00	80
2823	85E. José Régio (writer)	1·00	80
2824	85E. José Rodrigues Miguéis (writer)	1·00	80
2825	85E. Vitorino Nemésio (scholar)	1·00	80
2826	85E. Bento de Jesus Caraca (scholar)	1·00	80
2819/2826	Set of 8	7·00	5·75

Nos. 2819/26 were issued together in *se-tenant* sheetlets of eight stamps and four labels.

638 Athletics   **639** Decorated Dish

(Des J. Tinoco. Litho)

2001 (1 Mar). World Indoor Athletics Championship, Lisbon. T **638** and similar horiz designs. Multicoloured. P 12.
2827	85E. Type **638**	1·10	85
2828	90E. Pole vault	1·10	90
2829	105E. Shot put	1·40	95
2830	250E. High jump	3·25	2·20
2827/2830	Set of 4	6·00	4·50
MS2831	122×100 mm. 350E. Hurdles	4·75	4·75

(Des J. Projecto. Litho)

2001 (6 Mar). Birds (2nd series). Horiz designs as T **620**. Multicoloured.
(a) Sheet stamps. Ordinary gum. P 12×11½
2832	53E. Little bustard	60	45
2833	85E. Purple swamphen	95	75
2834	105E. Pratnicole	1·20	90
2835	140E. Black-shouldered kite	1·60	1·30
2836	225E. Egyptian vulture	2·75	2·10

63

PORTUGAL

(b) Self-adhesive gum. Litho Enschedé. Die-cut perf 11½×12
(i) Size 25×21 mm

2837	53E. As No. 2832	75	45
2838	105E. As No. 2834	1·30	1·00

(ii) Sheet stamps. Size 48×22 mm

2839	85E. Purple swamphen	1·30	85
2832/2839	Set of 8	9·50	7·00

Nos. 2837/8 are available both in booklets of ten which are peeled directly from the booklet covers and cannot therefore be collected as separated panes and also in sheets of 100 stamps.

No. 2839 is inscribed "CorreioAzul" and is only available in sheetlets of 50 stamps.

(Des L. Duran. Litho Litografia Maia, Oporto)

2001 (28 Mar). Arab Artefacts. T **639** and similar horiz designs. Multicoloured. P 12.

2840	53E. Type **639**	60	40
2841	90E. Painted tile	1·10	80
2842	105E. Carved stone tablet and fortress	1·40	95
2843	140E. Coin	2·40	1·30
2844	225E. Carved container	3·00	2·00
2845	350E. Jug	4·25	3·25
2840/2845	Set of 6	11·50	7·75

640 Coastal Environment (Angela M. Lopes)   **641** Statue, Building Façade and Stained Glass Window

2001 (10 Apr). "Stampin' the Future". Winning entries in Children's International Painting Competition. T **640** and similar multicoloured designs. Litho. P 12.

2846	85E. Type **640**	1·00	75
2847	90E. Earth, Sun and watering can (Maria G. Silva) (vert)	1·10	80
2848	105E. Marine life (João A. Ferreira)	1·20	95
2846/2848	Set of 3	3·00	2·25

(Des L. Duran. Litho)

2001 (19 Apr). Centenary of National Fine Arts Society. T **641** and similar horiz designs. Multicoloured. P 12.

2849	85E. Type **641**	1·00	75
2850	105E. Painting and woman holding palette and brush	1·20	1·00
MS2851	105×80 mm. 350E. "Hen with Chicks" (detail) (Girão)	4·75	4·75

642 Congress in Session   **643** Fishes

(Des L. Duran. Litho Litografia Maia, Oporto)

2001 (25 Apr). 25th Anniv of Portuguese Republic Constitution. P 12.

2852	**642** 85E. multicoloured	1·10	80

(Des J. Machado. Litho)

2001 (9 May). Europa. Water Resources. P 12.

2853	**643** 105E. multicoloured	1·70	1·40
MS2854	140×110 mm. No. 2853×3	5·50	6·50

644 Couple and Heart   **645** Open Book

(Des J. Machado. Litho Litografia Maia, Oporto)

2001 (16 May). Greetings Stamps. T **644** and similar vert designs. Multicoloured. P 12.

2855	85E. Type **644**	1·10	85
2856	85E. Birthday cake	1·10	85
2857	85E. Glasses	1·10	85
2858	85E. Bunch of flowers	1·10	85
2855/2858	Set of 4	4·00	3·00
MS2859	91×110 mm. Nos. 2855/8	4·25	4·00

(Des A. Santos. Litho)

2001 (23 May). Porto, European City of Culture. T **645** and similar horiz designs. Multicoloured. P 12.

2860	53E. Type **645**	60	45
2861	85E. Bridge and Globe	1·10	70
2862	105E. Grand piano	1·20	95
2863	140E. Stage curtain	1·60	1·30
2864	225E. Picture frame	2·75	2·10
2865	350E. Firework display	4·00	3·25
2860/2865	Set of 6	10·00	7·75
MS2866	140×110 mm. Nos. 2861/6	12·00	11·00

646 Campaign Cannon, 1773   **647** Brown Bear

(Des A. Santos. Litho Litografia Maia, Oporto)

2001 (7 June). 150th Anniv of Military Museum, Lisbon. T **646** and similar horiz design. Multicoloured. P 12.

2867	85E. Type **646**	1·10	80
2868	105E. 16th-century armour	1·40	1·10
MS2869	140×112 mm. 53E. Pistol of King José I, 1757; 53E. Cannon on carriage, 1797; 140E. Cannon "Tigre", 1533; 140E. 15th-century helmet	5·00	4·50

(Des Sofia Martins. Litho Litografia Maia, Oporto)

2001 (11 June). Lisbon Zoo. T **647** and similar horiz designs. Multicoloured. P 12.

2870	53E. Type **647**	55	40
2871	85E. Emperor tamarin	1·00	75
2872	90E. Green iguana	1·00	85
2873	105E. Jackass penguin	1·30	1·00
2874	225E. Toco toucan	2·75	2·10
2875	350E. Giraffe	4·00	3·25
2870/2875	Set of 6	9·50	7·50
MS2876	140×112 mm. 85E. Indian elephant (29×38 mm); 85E. Grevy's zebra (29×38 mm); Lion (29×38 mm); White rhinoceros (29×38 mm)	8·00	6·50

648 Emblem   **649** Azinhoso Pillory

(Des P. C. Sampaio. Litho Litografia Maia, Oporto)

2001 (6 Sept). 47th Lion's European Forum, Oporto. P 12.

2877	**648** 85E. multicoloured	1·10	75

(Des L. Duran. Litho)

2001 (19 Sept). Pillories. T **649** and similar horiz designs. Multicoloured. P 12.

2878	53E. Type **649**	60	45
	a. Sheetlet of 16. Nos. 2878/85, each×2	9·00	
2879	53E. Soajo	60	45
2880	53E. Bragança	60	45
2881	53E. Linhares	60	45
2882	53E. Arcos de Valdevez	60	45
2883	53E. Vila de Rua	60	45
2884	53E. Sernancelhe	60	45
2885	53E. Frechas	60	45
2878/2885	Set of 8	4·25	3·25

Nos. 2878/85 were issued together in *se-tenant* sheetlets of sixteen stamps.

PORTUGAL

650 Faces   **651** Disney

(Des L. Duran. Litho Litografia Maia, Oporto)

2001 (9 Oct). United Nations Year of Dialogue among Civilizations. P 12.
| 2886 | **650** | 140E. multicoloured | 1·60 | 1·20 |

(Des Walt Disney Company. Litho)

2001 (18 Oct). Birth Centenary of Walt Disney (artist and film producer). T **651** and similar horiz designs. Multicoloured. P 12.
| 2887 | 53E. Type **651** | 65 | 50 |

MS2888 160×132 mm 53E. Huey, Dewey and Louie, and 15th-century Mudéjares tile; 53E. Mickey Mouse and 16th-century tiles forming coat of arms; 53E. Minnie Mouse and 17th-century religious allegory tiles; 53E. Goofy and 18th-century tiles of birds; 53E. Type **651**; 53E. Pluto and 19th-century tile design by Rafael Bordalo Pinheiro; 53E. Donald Duck and 19th-century tiles; 53E. Scrooge McDuck and 20th-century "Querubim Lapa" tiles; 53E. Daisy Duck and 20th-century tile designs by Manuel Cargaleiro .... 8·00   7·00

652 Royal Police Guard, 1801   **653** Chinese Junk

(Des A. Santos. Litho)

2001 (22 Oct). Bicentenary of National Guard. T **652** and similar horiz designs. Multicoloured. P 12.
2889	53E. Type **652**	60	50
2890	85E. Lisbon Municipal Guard bandsman, 1834	1·00	75
2891	90E. Infantry helmet, 1911 and modern guardsman	1·00	80
2892	105E. Mounted division helmet of 1911 and modern guardsmen	1·20	95
2893	140E. Guardsmen with motorcycle and car	1·60	1·20
2894	350E. Customs and Excise officer and boat	4·25	3·00
2889/2894	Set of 6	8·75	6·50

MS2895 117×90 mm. 225E. Mounted division helmet and guardsman of 1911 .... 3·00   3·00

(Des V. Santos and C. Leitão. Litho)

2001 (8 Nov). Ships. T **653** and similar horiz design. Multicoloured. P 12.
2896	53E. Type **653**	65	50
	a. Pair. Nos. 2896/7	1·40	1·25
2897	53E. Portuguese caravel	65	50

Nos. 2896/7 were issued together in *se-tenant* pairs throughout the sheet.
Stamps in similar designs also issued by China.

New Currency. 100 cents = 1 Euro

654 1c. Coin   **655** Horse-rider

(Des A. Santos. Litho Litografia Maia, Oporto)

2002 (2 Jan). New Currency. T **654** and similar horiz designs. Multicoloured. P 12.
2898	1c. Type **654**	10	10
2899	2c. 2c. coin	10	10
2900	5c. 5c. coin	15	10
2901	10c. 10c. coin	20	15
2902	20c. 20c. coin	45	35
2903	50c. 50c. coin	1·10	90
2904	€1 €1 coin	2·50	1·80
2905	€2 €2 coin	4·75	3·50
2898/2905	Set of 8	8·50	6·25

(Des L. Duran. Litho Litografia Maia, Oporto)

2002 (2 Jan). No value expressed. P 13½.
| 2906 | **655** | A (28c.) multicoloured | 65 | 50 |

No. 2906 was sold at the current first class inland letter rate.

D **656** "0.01"   **657** European Bee-eater

(Des A. Santos. Litho)

2002 (2 Jan). POSTAGE DUE. Type D **656** and similar horiz designs. Multicoloured. P 12×11½.
D2907	1c. Type D**656**	10	10
D2908	2c. "0.02"	10	10
D2909	5c. "0.05"	15	10
D2910	10c. "0.10"	30	25
D2911	25c. "0.25"	60	50
D2912	50c. "0.50"	1·30	95
D2913	€1 "1"	2·50	2·00
D2907/2913	Set of 7	4·50	3·50

(Des J. Projecto)

2002 (26 Feb). Birds (1st series). T **657** and similar multicoloured designs.

(a) Litho Mint, Lisbon
(i) Sheet stamps. Ordinary gum. P 12 × 11½
2914	2c. Type **657**	10	10
2915	28c. Little tern	70	50
2916	43c. Eagle owl	1·00	80
2917	54c. Pin-tailed sandgrouse	1·30	95
2918	60c. Red-necked nightjar	1·40	1·10
2919	70c. Greater spotted cuckoo	1·70	1·30

(ii) Sheet stamp. Self-adhesive gum. Size 49×23 mm
| 2920 | 43c. Little tern (*different*) | 1·30 | 85 |

(iii) Booklet stamps. Self-adhesive gum. Size 29×24 mm. Die-cut perf 11½×11
| 2921 | 28c. As No. 2919 | 75 | 55 |
| 2922 | 54c. As No. 2916 | 1·30 | 1·00 |

(b) Sheet stamps. Self-adhesive gum. Litho Enschedé. Size 27×23 mm. Die-cut perf 11½×12
2923	28c. As No. 2919	1·00	70
2924	54c. As No. 2916	1·70	1·10
2914/2924	Set of 11	11·00	8·00

Nos. 2921/2 are peeled directly from the booklet covers and cannot therefore be collected as separate panes.
No. 2924 is inscribed "CorreioAzul" and is only available in sheet of 50 stamps.
See also Nos. 2988/2992b and 3105/3109.

658 De Góis

(Des L. Duran. Litho Litografia Maia, Oporto)

2002 (26 Feb). 500th Birth Anniv of Damião de Góis (writer). P 12.
| 2925 | **658** | 45c. multicoloured | 1·10 | 80 |

659 Loxodromic Curve, Ship and Globe   **660** Children and Flower

65

PORTUGAL

(Des L. Duran. Litho)

2002 (6 Mar). 500th Birth Anniv of Pedro Nunes (mathematician). T **659** and similar horiz designs. Multicoloured. P 12.

2926	28c. Type **659**		65	50
2927	28c. Nonius (navigational instrument)		65	50
2928	€1.15 Portrait of Nunes		2·75	2·10
2926/2928 Set of 3			3·50	2·25
MS2929 140×105 mm Nos. 2926/8			4·25	4·00

(Des L. Duran. Litho)

2002 (12 Mar). America. Youth, Education and Literacy. T **660** and similar horiz designs. Multicoloured. P 12.

2930	70c. Type **660**		1·60	1·30
2931	70c. Children, book and letters		1·60	1·30
2932	70c. Children and pencil		1·60	1·30
2930/2932 Set of 3			4·25	3·50

661 Refracting Telescope and Polytechnic School Observatory, Lisbon

662 Square and Compass

(Des A. Santos. Litho Litografia Maia, Oporto)

2002 (23 Apr). Astronomy. T **661** and similar horiz designs. Multicoloured. P 12.

2933	28c. Type **661**		65	50
2934	28c. 16th-century astrolabe and Colégio dos Nobres, Lisbon		65	50
2935	43c. Quadrant and Solar Observatory, Coimbra		1·00	80
2936	45c. Terrestrial telescope and King Pedro V.		1·00	80
2937	45c. Cassegrain telescope and King Luis		1·00	80
2938	54c. Earth, refracting telescope and Observatory, Ajuda		1·30	1·00
2939	€1.15 Cassegrain telescope and Saturn		2·75	2·10
2940	€1.75 Zeiss projector and planets		4·00	3·25
2934/2940 Set of 8			11·00	8·75
MS2941 140×111 mm. 70c. 18th-century armillary sphere; 70c. 19th-century theodolite			3·75	3·75

(Des L. Duran. Litho Litografia Maia, Oporto)

2002 (9 May). Bicentenary of Grande Oriente Lusitano (Masonic Grand Lodge). P 12.

2942	**662**	43c. multicoloured	1·10	80

663 Clown

664 *Scabiosa nitens*

(Des E. Aires. Litho Litografia Maia, Oporto)

2002 (9 May). Europa. Circus. P 12.

2943	**663**	54c. multicoloured	2·00	1·60
MS2944 140×110 mm No. 2943×3. P 12½			6·25	7·75

(Des P. Salgado. Litho)

2002 (20 May). Flowers of Azores. T **664** and similar horiz designs. Multicoloured. P 12.

2945	28c. Type **664**		65	50
2946	45c. *Viburnum tinus subcordatum*		1·00	75
2947	54c. *Euphorbia azorica*		1·20	95
2948	70c. *Lysimachia nemorum azorica*		1·60	1·30
2949	€1.15 *Bellis azorica*		2·75	2·10
2950	€1.75 *Spergularia azorica*		4·00	3·25
2945/2950 Set of 6			10·00	8·00
MS2951 120×121 mm. €1.15 *Azorina vidalli*; €1.75 *Senecio malvifolius*			6·75	6·50

665 General Dynamics F-16 Fighting Falcon

666 Gymnastics

(Des Sofia Martins. Litho)

2002 (1 July). 50th Anniv of Portuguese Air Force. T **665** and similar horiz designs. Multicoloured. P 12.

2952	28c. Type **665**		65	50
2953	43c. Sud Aviation SA 300 Puma helicopter		1·00	80
2954	54c. Dassault Dornier Alpha Jet A		1·20	95
2955	70c. Lockheed C-130 Hercules transport aircraft		1·60	1·30
2956	€1.25 Lockheed P-3P Orion reconnaissance aircraft		2·75	2·20
2957	€1.75 Fiat G-91 fighter aircraft		4·00	3·00
2952/2957 Set of 6			10·00	7·75
MS2958 140×112 mm. €1.15 Four airplanes; €1.75 Aerospatiale Epsilon TB 30			7·25	7·00

(Des J. Tinoco. Litho)

2002 (8 Aug). Sports and Sports Anniversaries. T **666** and similar horiz designs. Multicoloured. P 12.

2959	28c. Type **666** (50th anniv of Portuguese Gymnastic Federation)		60	50
2960	28c. Walking race		60	50
2961	45c. Basketball		1·00	80
2962	45c. Handball		1·00	80
2963	54c. Roller hockey (sixth Women's World Roller Hockey Championship, Paços de Ferriera)		1·20	95
2964	54c. Fencing (World Fencing Championship, Lisbon)		1·20	95
2965	€1.75 Footballers (World Cup Football Championship, Japan and South Korea)		3·75	3·00
2966	€1.75 Golf		3·75	3·00
2959/2966 Set of 8			11·50	9·50
MS2967 140×110 mm. €1 Footballer and part of football; €2 Torsos and legs of two players			7·00	5·75

No. **MS**2967 was inscribed for "PHILAKOREA 2002" International Stamp Exhibition, Seoul, in the margin.

667 Globe And Emblem

669 Portrait and Symbols of Industry and Agriculture

668 Anniversary Emblem

(Des C. Letão. Litho Litografia Maia, Oporto)

2002 (9 Sept). 13th World International Economic Association Congress. P 12.

2968	**667**	70c. multicoloured	1·60	1·20

(Des J. Machado. Litho)

2002 (30 Sept). 150th Anniv of Ministry of Public Works, Transport and Housing. T **668** and similar horiz designs. Multicoloured. P 12×12½.

2969	43c. Type **668**		1·00	75
MS2970 144×123 mm. 43c.×6, Ship and oil terminal; Locomotive; Aeroplane; Bridge and city skyline; Factories; Houses			6·50	5·00

(Des V. Santos. Litho)

2002 (9 Oct). 150th Anniv of Technical Education. P 12.

2971	**669**	43c. multicoloured	1·00	75

PORTUGAL

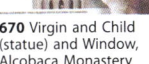

670 Virgin and Child (statue) and Window, Alcobaça Monastery

671 1870 Dress Uniform

673 1853 5r. Stamp and Queen Donna Maria II

674 *Orchis italica*

(Des J. Brandão and P. Fulardo. Litho Litografia Maia, Oporto)

2002 (7 Nov). UNESCO World Heritage Sites. T **670** and similar multicoloured designs. P 12.

2972	28c. Type **670**	60	50
2973	28c. Lion (statue) and embossed ceiling, Jerónimos Monastery	60	50
2974	43c. Column capitals, Guimarães	95	75
2975	43c. Cherub (statue) and vineyards, Alto Douro	95	75
2976	54c. Corbel, lake and vineyards, Alto Douro (80×30 mm)	1·20	95
2977	54c. Houses and statues, Guimarães (80×30 mm)	1·20	95
2978	70c. Carved arch and statue, Jerónimos Monastery (80×30 mm)	1·60	1·20
2979	70c. Nave and tomb, Alcobaça Monastery (80×30 mm)	1·60	1·20
2972/2979 Set of 8		7·75	6·00

MS2980 Four sheets, each 141×114 mm. (a) €1.25 Door and statue, Alcobaça Monastery; (b) €1.25 Double doors, Jerónimos Monastery; (c) €1.25 Arches, Guimarães; (d) €1.25 Grapes, Alto Douro ...... 12·00 9·75

(Des A. Santos. Litho Litografia Maia, Oporto)

2003 (22 Feb). Bicentenary of Military College, Luz. T **671** and similar vert designs. Multicoloured. P 12.

2981	20c. Type **671**	40	35
2982	30c. 1806 uniform	65	50
2983	43c. 1837 parade uniform	95	75
2984	55c. 1861 uniform (rear view)	1·20	95
2985	70c. 1866 dress uniform	1·60	1·30
2986	€2 1912 cavalry cadet uniform	4·50	3·50
2981/2986 Set of 6		8·25	6·50

MS2987 141×114 mm. €1 1802 uniform; €1 1948 Porta Guião dress uniform ...... 4·75 4·00

(Des J. Projecto. Litho)

2003 (7 Mar). Birds (2nd series). Square designs as T **657**. Multicoloured.

(a) Ordinary gum. P 12×11½

2988	1c. Green woodpecker	10	10
2989	30c. Rock dove	70	50
2990	43c. Blue thrush	1·00	75
2991	55c. Sub-alpine warbler	1·30	95
2992	70c. Black-eared wheatear	1·60	1·20

(b) Self-adhesive gum. Size 27×33 mm. Die-cut perf 11½×12

2992a	30c. No. 2989	75	50
2992b	43c. No. 2990 (50×23 mm)	1·00	80
2992c	55c. No. 2991	1·80	1·20
2988/2992c Set of 8		7·50	5·50

No. 2992b is inscribed "CorreioAzul".

672 People forming Mobility Symbol

(Des E. Aires. Litho Litografia Maia, Oporto)

2003 (12 Mar). European Year of the Disabled. T **672** and similar horiz designs. Multicoloured. P 13½.

2993	30c. Type **672**	75	50
2994	55c. People forming head shape	1·30	95
2995	70c. As No. 2994 but with eyes, ears and mouth pink	1·60	1·20
2993/2995 Set of 3		3·25	2·25

(Des E. Aires. Litho)

2003 (13 Mar). 150th Anniv of First Postage Stamp (1st issue). T **673** and similar horiz designs showing 1853 stamps. Multicoloured. P 12.

2996	30c. Type **673**	65	50
2997	43c. 25r. stamp and coin	95	75
2998	55c. 50r. stamp and portrait	1·20	95
2999	70c. 10r. stamp and arms	1·60	1·20
2996/2999 Set of 4		4·00	3·00

(Des P. Salgado. Litho)

2003 (29 Apr). Orchids. T **674** and similar vert designs. Multicoloured. P 12.

| 3000 | 46c. *Aceras anthropophorum* | 1·00 | 80 |
| 3001 | 46c. *Dactylorhiza maculata* | 1·00 | 80 |

MS3002 Two sheets, each 113×140 mm. (a) 30c. Type **674**; 30c. *Orphrys tenthredinifera*; 30c. *Ophrys fusca fusca*; 30c. *Orchis papilionacea*; 30c. *Barlia robertiana*; 30c. *Ophrys lutea*; 30c. *Dactylorhiza ericetorum*. (b) 30c. *Orchis champagneuxii*; 30c. *Orchis morio*; 30c. *Serapias cordigera*; 30c. *Orchis coriophora*; 30c. *Ophrys bombyliflora*; 30c. *Ophrys vernixia*; 30c. *Orphrys speculum*; 30c. *Ophrys scoplopax*; 30c. *Anacamptis pyramidalis* ...... 14·00 11·00

675 Jazz Festival (João Machado)

676 Lawyer and Union Seal

(Des J. Brandão. Litho)

2003 (5 May). Europa. Poster Art. T **675** and similar vert designs. Multicoloured. P 12×12½.

| 3003 | 55c. Type **675** | 1·60 | 1·20 |
| 3004 | 55c. Woman wearing swimsuit ("Espimho") (Fred Kradolfer) | 1·60 | 1·20 |

MS3005 140×113 mm. Nos. 3004/5 ...... 3·25 3·50

(Des E. Aires. Litho Litografia Maia, Oporto)

2003 (13 May). International Lawyer's Congress, Lisbon. T **676** and similar horiz designs. Multicoloured. P 12×12.

3006	30c. Type **676**	65	50
3007	43c. Lawyers, arms and Court building	95	75
3008	55c. Medieval lawyer, Bishop and legal document	1·20	95
3009	70c. Lawyer's union presidential medal and female lawyer	1·60	1·20
3006/3009 Set of 4		4·00	3·00

MS3010 140×113 mm. €1 Lawyer wearing red robe and seal; €2 Seal, painted plaque and bishop ...... 7·00 5·50

677 "150" and Stamp (Viseu)

678 Championship Emblem

67

PORTUGAL

(Des L. Duran and C. Leitão. Litho Enschedé)

2003 (23 May–9 Oct). 150th Anniv of Portuguese First Stamp (1st issue). Itinerant Exhibition. P 14×13½.
3011	**677**	30c. multicoloured	80	50
3012		30c. multicoloured (21.7.03)	80	50
3013		30c. multicoloured (9.10.03)	80	50
3011/3013	Set of 3		2·00	1·25

See also Nos. **MS**3047.

(Des A. Santos. Litho Enschedé)

2003 (28 May). European Football Championship 2004, Portugal (1st issue). T **678** and similar horiz designs. P 14×13½.
3014	**678**	30c. multicoloured	70	50
3015		43c. multicoloured	1·00	75
3016		47c. multicoloured	1·10	85
3017		55c. multicoloured	1·30	95
3018		70c. multicoloured	1·60	1·20
3014/3018	Set of 5		5·25	3·75
MS3019	140×109 mm. 55c.×4, Parts of championship emblem		5·25	4·25

See also Nos. **MS**3072, 3073/3074, 3084/3087, 3089/3104, 3110/3117, 3119/3128 and **MS**3147.

679 Open-topped Car

680 Ricardo do Espirito Santo Silva

(Des V. Santos. Litho)

2003 (24 June). Centenary of Portuguese Automobile Club. T **679** and similar horiz designs. Multicoloured. P 12.
3020		30c. Type **679**	65	50
3021		43c. Club engineer riding motorcycle	95	75
3022		€2 Racing cars	4·50	3·50

(Des J. Brandão. Litho)

2003 (9 July). 50th Anniv of Ricardo do Espirito Santo Silva Foundation. T **680** and similar vert designs. Multicoloured. P 13½.
3023		30c. Type **680**	60	50
3024		30c. 18th-century inlaid chess table	60	50
3025		43c. Cutlery box, 1720–1750	95	75
3026		43c. 15th-century silver tray	95	75
3027		55c. 18th-century wooden container	1·20	95
3028		55c. Ming dynasty ceramic box	1·20	95
3023/3028	Set of 6		5·00	4·00
MS3029	140×112 mm. €1 17th-century cupboard; €1 18th-century tapestry		7·00	5·50

681 "Bay of Funchal"
(W. G. James) (1839)

(Des V. Leitão and V. Santos. Litho Litografia Maia, Oporto)

2003 (30 Aug). Museums of Madeira. T **681** and similar horiz designs. Black (No. **MS**3034) or multicoloured (others). P 13½.
3030		30c. Type **681**	60	50
3031		43c. Nativity (straw sculpture, Manuel Orlando Noronha Gois)	1·00	75
3032		55c. "O Largo da Fonte" (Andrew Picken) (1840)	1·30	95
3033		70c. "Le Départ" (Martha Teles) (1983)	1·50	1·20
3030/3033	Set of 4		4·00	3·00
MS3034	140×112 mm. €1. Vicente Gomes da Silva (photograph); €2 Jorge Bettencourt (photograph)		6·75	5·25

682 Curved Shape containing "EXD"

(Des Brandia and Novodesign. Litho Enschedé)

2003 (17 Sept). ExperimentaDesign2003 (design exhibition). Sheet containing T **682** and similar curved designs. Either black (30c.) or black and carmine (others). Self-adhesive. Die-cut perf 11.
3035		30c. Type **682**	65	50
		a. Strip of 4. Nos. 3035/8	1·70	
		b. Sheetlet of 12. Nos. 3035/46	12·00	
3036		30c. "EXD" centrally	65	50
3037		30c. "EXD" bottom	65	50
3038		30c. "EXD" left	65	50
3039		43c. As No. 3038 but design reversed	95	75
		a. Strip of 4. Nos. 3039/42	2·50	
3040		43c. As No. 3037 but design reversed	95	75
3041		43c. As No. 3036 but design reversed	95	75
3042		43c. As No. 3035 but design reversed	95	75
3043		55c. As No. 3035	1·20	90
		a. Strip of 4. Nos. 3043/6	3·25	
3044		55c. As No. 3036	1·20	90
3045		55c. As No. 3037	1·20	90
3046		55c. As No. 3038	1·20	90
3035/3046	Set of 12		10·00	7·75

Nos. 3035/46 were perforated in curved shapes as T **682** and were issued in horizontal *se-tenant* strips of four stamps within sheetlets of 12.

683 Queen Maria II

684 St. John's Well, Vila Real

(Litho (30c., €1), litho and holography (€2.50) or litho and embossed (€3))

2003 (19 Sept–12 Dec). 150th Anniv of First Portuguese Stamp (2nd issue). Four sheets each 140×112 mm containing T **683** and similar multicoloured designs. P 12.
MS3047	(a) 30c. Type **683**; 30c.×4 No. 2996×4 (25.9); (b) €1 Queen Maria II and euro coins (90×40 mm) (12.12); (c) €2.50 Seal and postal marks (80×30 mm) (23.9); (d) €3 King Pedro V, 1853 25r. stamp and Queen Maria II (80×30 mm)		18·00	15·00

(Des Sofia Martins. Litho)

2003 (1 Oct). America. Fountains. T **684** and similar horiz designs. Multicoloured. P 12.
3048		30c. Type **684**	60	50
3049		43c. Fountain of Virtues, Porto	95	75
3050		55c. Fountain, Giraldo Square, Évora	1·20	95
3051		70c. Senora da Saúde fountain, St. Marcos de Tavira	1·50	1·20
3052		€1 Town fountain, Castelo de Vide	2·20	1·70
3053		€2 St. Andreas fountain, Guarda	4·25	2·40
3048/3053	Set of 6		9·50	6·75

685 Jose I engraved Glass Tumbler (18th-century)

686 Persian Medicine Jar and Roman Dropper

68

PORTUGAL

(Des Sofia Martins. Litho)

2003 (9 Oct). Glass Production. T **685** and similar vert designs. Multicoloured. P 12.

3054	30c. Type **685**	60	50
3055	55c. Maria II engraved tumbler (19th-century)	1·20	95
3056	70c. Blue glass vase (Carmo Valente) (20th-century)	1·50	1·20
3057	€2 Bulbous vase (Helena Matos) (20th-century)	4·25	3·50
3054/3057	Set of 4	6·75	5·50
MS3058	140×112 mm €1·50 Stained glass window (detail) (Fernando Santos) (19th-century)	3·50	2·75

(Des V. Santos. Litho)

2003 (23 Oct). Medicine and Pharmacy. T **686** and similar horiz designs. Multicoloured. P 12.

3059	30c. Type **686**	60	50
3060	43c. Ceramic bottle and jar	95	75
3061	55c. Pestle and mortar	1·20	95
3062	70c. Still and glass bottle	1·50	1·20
3059/3062	Set of 4	3·75	3·00

687 Drawing Board and Chair (Jose Epinho)   **688** Championship emblem

(Des J. Brandão and P. Falardo. Litho)

2003 (3 Nov). Contemporary Design. T **687** and similar multicoloured designs. P 12.

3063	43c. Type **687**	95	75
3064	43c. Telephone point (Pedro Silva Dias) (vert)	95	75
3065	43c. Tea trolley (Cruz de Carvlho)	95	75
3066	43c. Tap (Carlos Aguiar)	95	75
3067	43c. Desk (Daciano da Costa)	95	75
3068	43c. Knives (Eduardo Afonso Dias)	95	75
3069	43c. Stacking chairs (Leonor and Antonio Sena da Silva)	95	75
3070	43c. Flask (Carlos Rocha) (vert)	95	75
3071	43c. Chair (Antonio Garcia) (vert)	95	75
3063/3071	Set of 9	7·75	6·00

(Des A. Santos. Litho Enschedé)

2003 (28 Nov). European Football Championship 2004, Portugal (2nd issue). Sheet 150×165 mm containing T **688** and similar horiz designs. P 14×13½.

MS3072 30c.×10 Type **688**; Municipal stadium, Aveiro; Dr. Magalhaes Pessoa stadium, Leiria; Luz stadium, Lisbon; D. Afonso Henriques stadium, Guimaraes; Municipal stadium, Coimbra; Bessa stadium, Porto; Dragao stadium, Porto; Algarve stadium, Faro-Loulé; José Alvalade stadium, Lisbon ... 12·00 6·00

689 Kinas

2004 (Mar). European Football Championship 2004, Portugal (3rd series). Mascot. T **689** and similar horiz design. Multicoloured. Self adhesive. Litho. Die-cut perf 11½.

(a) Ordinary post

| 3073 | 45c. Type **689** | 95 | 80 |

(b) AIR

| 3074 | €1·75 Kinas and football | 3·75 | 3·00 |

No. 3073 was inscribed "CorreioAzul". No. 3074 was inscribed "Airmail Priority".

 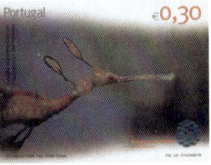

690 King Joao IV and Vila Vicosa   **691** Seadragon (*Phyllopteryx taeniolatus*)

(Des L. Duran. Litho Enschedé)

2004 (19 Mar). 400th Birth Anniv of King Joao IV. T **690** and similar horiz design. Multicoloured. P 14×13½.

3075	45c. Type **690**	95	80
	a. Pair. Nos. 3075/6	3·25	2·75
3076	€1 King Joao standing	2·20	1·80

Nos. 3075/6 were issued in horizontal *se-tenant* pairs within the sheet, each pair forming a composite design.

(Des H. Soares. Litho Enschedé)

2004 (22 Mar). Lisbon Oceanarium. T **691** and similar horiz designs. Multicoloured. P 14×13½.

3077	30c. Type **691**	60	50
3078	45c. Magellanic penguin (*Spheniscus magellanicus*)	95	75
3079	56c. Hypsypops rubicundus	1·20	95
3080	72c. Sea otter (*Enhydra lutris*)	1·60	1·30
3081	€1 Grey nurse shark (*Carcharias taurus*)	2·10	1·70
3082	€2 Atlantic puffin (*Fratercula artica*)	4·25	3·50
3077/3082	Set of 6	9·50	7·75
MS3083	140×112 mm. €1·50 Macaroni penguin (*Eudyptes chrysolophus*) (80×30 mm)	3·50	2·75

692 Foot kicking Ball   **693** Portugal

(Des A. Santos. Litho Walsall)

2004 (30 Mar–27 May). European Football Championship 2004, Portugal (4th series). Official Match Ball. T **692** and similar circular designs. Multicoloured.

(a) Self-adhesive. Die-cut perf 6

3084	10c. Type **692**	25	15
3085	20c. Ball right	45	35
3086	30c. Ball and line	70	50
3087	50c. Ball and goal post	1·10	85
3084/3087	Set of 4	2·25	1·50
MS3088	104×104 mm. Nos. 3084/7 (27·5)	4·25	2·30

(b) Size 24×24 mm. Ordinary gum. P 13½

MS3088 105×105 mm. As. Nos. 3084/7

(Des A. Santos. Litho Walsall)

2004 (6 Apr). European Football Championship 2004, Portugal (5th series). Participating Teams. T **693** and similar horiz designs showing Kinas (mascot) and country flags. Multicoloured. P 13.

3089	30c. Type **693**	70	55
	a. Sheetlet. Nos. 3088/3104	12·00	
3090	30c. France	70	55
3091	30c. Sweden	70	55
3092	30c. Czech Republic	70	55
3093	30c. Greece	70	55
3094	30c. UK	70	55
3095	30c. Bulgaria	70	55
3096	30c. Latvia	70	55
3097	30c. Spain	70	55
3098	30c. Switzerland	70	55
3099	30c. Denmark	70	55
3100	30c. Germany	70	55
3101	30c. Russia	70	55
3102	30c. Croatia	70	55
3103	30c. Italy	70	55
3104	30c. Netherlands	70	55
3089/3104	Set of 16	10·00	8·00

Nos. 3089/3104 were issued in *se-tenant* sheetlets of 16 stamps.

PORTUGAL

(Des J. Projecto. Litho)
2004 (15 Apr). Birds (3rd series). Horiz designs as T **657**. Multicoloured.

(a) Ordinary gum. P 12×11½
3105	30c. Red crossbill	60	50
3106	45c. Red-rumped swallow	95	75
3107	56c. Golden oriole	1·20	95
3108	58c. Crested lark	1·30	1·00
3109	72c. Crested tit	1·60	1·30
3105/3109	Set of 5	5·75	4·50

(b) Self-adhesive gum. Size 28×23 mm. Die-cut perf 12
3109a	30c. No. 3105	60	50
3109b	45c. No. 3106 (50×23 mm)	95	75
3109c	56c. No. 3107	1·20	95

No. 3109b is inscribed "Correio Azul".

694 "Moliceiros" Boat (Aveiro)   **695** Carnations

(Des A. Santos. Litho Enschedé)
2004 (20 Apr). European Football Championship 2004, Portugal (6th series). Host Cities. T **694** and similar horiz designs. Multicoloured. P 14×13½.
3110	30c. Type **694**	65	55
3111	30c. University tower (Coimbra)	65	55
3112	30c. Don Afonso Henriques (statue) (Guimaraes)	65	55
3113	30c. Castle (Leiria)	65	55
3114	30c. Tower (Faro/Loulé)	65	55
3115	30c. Bom Jesus (Braga)	65	55
3116	30c. Torre di Belem (Lisbon)	65	55
3117	30c. D. Luís I Bridge (Porto)	65	55
3110/3117	Set of 8	4·50	4·00

(Des maisdesign. Litho Walsall)
2004 (25 Apr). 30th Anniv of 25 April (Carnation revolution). P 13×13½.
3118	**695**	45c. multicoloured	1·00	80

696 Dr. Magalhaes Pessoa Stadium, Leiria   **697** Stylized Figures

(Des A. Santos. Litho Enschedé)
2004 (28 Apr). European Football Championship 2004, Portugal (7th series). Stadiums. T **696** and similar horiz designs Multicoloured. P 14×13½.
3119	30c. Type **696**	65	55
3120	30c. Municipal stadium, Coimbra	65	55
3121	30c. Municipal stadium, Braga	65	55
3122	30c. Bessa stadium, Porto	65	55
3123	30c. Luz stadium, Lisbon	65	55
3124	30c. D. Afonso Henriques stadium, Guimaraes	65	55
3125	30c. Algarve stadium, Faro-Loulé	65	55
3126	30c. José Alvalade stadium, Lisbon	65	55
3127	30c. Dragao stadium, Porto	65	55
3128	30c. Municipal stadium, Aveiro	65	55
3119/3128	Set of 10	5·75	5·00

(Des A. Santos. Litho Enschedé)
2004 (3 May). European Union. T **697** and similar horiz designs. Multicoloured. P 14×13½.
3129	30c. Type **697** (EU parliamentary elections)	70	50
3130	56c. EU emblem and new members' flags (80×30 mm) (new members)	1·20	90
MS3131	140×111 mm. €2 Original members' flags (80×30 mm)	4·75	4·00

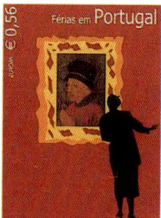 

698 Picture Gallery   **699** Bells of Early Telephone

(Des J. Machado. Litho Enschedé)
2004 (10 May). Europa. Holidays. T **698** and similar vert designs. Multicoloured. P 13½×14.
3132	56c. Type **698**	1·50	1·20
3133	56c. Beach	1·50	1·20
MS3134	141×112 mm. Nos. 3132/3	4·50	3·50

(Des E. Aires. Litho Enschedé)
2004 (17 May). Centenary of Telephone Line from Porto to Lisbon. T **699** and similar vert designs. Multicoloured. P 13½×14.
3135	30c. Type **699**	60	50
3136	45c. Insulator	95	75
3137	56c. Fibre optic cable	1·20	95
3138	72c. Video telephone	1·60	1·30
3135/3138	Set of 4	4·00	3·00
MS3139	140×112 mm. €1.×2, No. 3135; No. 3138	6·75	4·00

700 Flower (illustration, Maimonides' Mishneh Torah)   **702** Stamps

701 Henri Delaunay Trophy

(Des J. Brandão. Litho Enschedé)
2004 (20 May). Jewish Heritage. T **700** and similar vert designs. Multicoloured. P 13½×14.
3140	30c. Type **700**	60	50
3141	45c. Star of David (illustration, Cervera Bible)	95	75
3142	56c. Menorah (illustration, Cervera Bible)	1·20	95
3143	72c. Menorah (carved tablet)	1·60	1·30
3144	€1 Illustration, Abravanel Bible	2·10	1·70
3145	€2 Prophet (statue, de Cristo Convent, Tomar)	4·25	3·50
3140/3145	Set of 6	9·50	7·75
MS3146	140×112 mm. €1.50 Shaaré Tikvá Synagogue (centenary)	3·50	2·75

(Des A. Santos. Litho Walsall)
2004 (27 May). European Football Championship 2004, Portugal (8th series). Sheet 140×112 mm. Multicoloured. P 13½×13.
MS3147	**701**	€1 multicoloured	2·40	2·00

(Des Carlos Leitão. Litho Enschedé)
2004 (18 June). 50th Anniv of Portuguese Philatelic Federation. T **702** and similar horiz design. Multicoloured. P 14×13½.
3148	30c. Type **702**	75	50
MS3149	111×79 mm €1.50 Seal	3·50	2·75

PORTUGAL

703 Footballers Past and Present
(½-size illustration)

(Des A. Santos Litho Cartor)

2004 (18 June). 50th Anniv of Union of European Football Associations (UEFA). Sheet 141×85 mm. P 13×13½.

| MS3150 | 703 | €1 multicoloured | 2·40 | 1·90 |

704 Hurdler   **705** Swimmer

(Des A. Santos. Litho Enschedé)

2004 (13 Aug). Olympic Games, Athens 2004. T **704** and similar horiz design. Multicoloured. P 14×13½.

| 3151 | 30c. Type **704** | 65 | 50 |
| 3152 | 45c. High jump | 1·10 | 75 |

(Des A. Santos. Litho Enschedé)

2004 (2 Sept). Paralymic Games, Athens 2004. T **705** and similar vert design. Multicoloured. P 13½×14.

3153	30c. Type **705**	60	50
3154	45c. Wheelchair racer	95	75
3155	56c. Cyclist	1·20	95
3156	72c. Runner	1·50	1·30
3135/3156	Set of 4	4·00	3·25

706 Pedro Homem de Melo

(Des V. Santos. Litho Enschedé)

2004 (6 Sept). Birth Centenary of Pedro Homem de Melo (folklorist). Sheet 140×112 mm. P 14×13½.

| MS3157 | 706 | €2 multicoloured | 4·75 | 4·00 |

707 Museum Façade
(½-size illustration)

(Des J. Brandao and P. Falardo. Litho Enschedé)

2004 (5 Oct). Inauguration of Bélem Palace Museum (President of the Republic's Museum). T **708** and similar horiz design. Multicoloured. P 14×13½.

| 3158 | 45c. Type **708** | 1·00 | 75 |
| MS3159 | 140×112 mm. €1 Museum interior | 2·40 | 1·90 |

708 Quim and Manecas   **709** Third-century Sarcophagus
(José Stuart Carvalhais)   and Mosaic

(Des Silva. Litho Enschedé)

2004 (8 Oct). Comic Strips. T **708** and similar horiz designs. Multicoloured. P 14×13½.

3160	30c. Type **708**	60	50
3161	45c. Guarda Abila (Julio Pinto and Nuno Saraiva)	95	75
3162	56c. Simao Infante (Raul Correia and Eduardo Teixeira Coelho)	1·20	95
3163	72c. A Pior Banda du Mondo (José Carlos Fernandes)	1·50	1·30
3160/3163	Set of 4	3·75	3·25
MS3164	141×111 mm. 50c.×4, O espiao Acacio (Relvas); Jim del Monaco (Louro and Simoes); Tomahawk Tom (Vitor Peon); Pitanga (Arlndo Fagundes)	4·75	4·00

(Des E. Aires. Litho Enschedé)

2004 (15 Oct). Viticulture. T **709** and similar horiz designs. Multicoloured. P 14×13.

3165	30c. Type **709**	70	50
	a. Pair. Nos. 3165/6	2·00	1·75
3166	45c. Mosaic and 12th-century tapestry	1·10	75
3167	56c. Man carrying grapes (14th-century missal) and grape harvesting (15th-century Book of Hours)	1·30	95
	a. Strip of 3. Nos. 3167/9		
3168	72c. Grape harvesting and "Grupo de Leao" (Columbano Bordalo Pine)	1·70	1·30
3169	€1 "Grupo de Leo" and 20th-century stained glass window	2·30	1·70
3165/3169	Set of 5	6·50	4·75
MS3170	140×115 mm. 50c.×4, Fields, grapes and mechanical harvester; Harvester and amphora; Barrels in cellar, steel vats and barrels; Barrels, bottling and glass of wine	4·50	4·00

Nos. 3165/6 were issued in horizontal se-tenant pairs and 3167/9 in horizontal strips of three stamps within the sheet, each pair and strip forming a composite design.

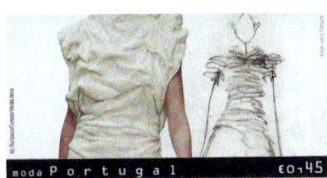

710 Ruched Dress (Alexandra Moura)
(²/₃-size illustration)

(Des Sofia Martins, V. Marques and L. Duran. Litho)

2004 (10 Nov). Fashion. Sheet 190×200 mm containing T **710** and similar horiz designs. P 14×13.

MS3171 45c.×10, Type **710**; Poncho (Ana Salazar); Boned and laced dress (Filipe Faisca); Ribboned skirt (J. Branco and L. Sanchez); Wrap-over dress (Antonio Tenente); Frilled front (Luis Buchinho); White top and skirted pants (Osvaldo Martins); Magenta dress with red attachments (Dino Alves); Silk-edged coat (Alves and Goncalves); Sequinned halter necked dress (Fatima Lopes) .... 11·00 8·50

The stamps of No. MS3171 each have a 13-stamp size label showing the outfit designer attached at either left or right.

711 "Adoration of the Magi"   **712** "Entrudo", Lazarim,
(Jorge Afonso)   Lamego

(Des V. Santos. Litho Cartor)

2004 (19 Nov). Christmas. T **711** and similar horiz designs. Multicoloured. P 13×13½.

3172	30c. Type **711**	60	50
3173	45c. "Adoration of the Magi" (16th-century Flamenga school)	95	75
3174	56c. "Escape into Egypt" (Francisco Vieira)	1·20	95
3175	72c. "Nativity" (Portuguese school)	1·50	1·30
3172/3175	Set of 4	3·75	3·25
MS3176	140×112 mm. €3 "Nativity" (detail) (Josefa de Obidos) (50×35 mm)	6·75	5·50

71

PORTUGAL

(Des C. Leitao. Litho)

2005 (17 Feb). Masks. T **712** and similar horiz designs. Multicoloured.

(a) Ordinary gum. P 12

3177	10c. Type **712**		20	15
3178	30c. "Festa dos Rapazes", Salsas, Bragança....		60	50
3179	45c. "Festa do Chocalheiro" Mougadouro, Bragança		90	75
3180	57c. "Cardador", Vale de Ilhavo		1·20	1·00
3181	74c. "Festa dos Rapazes", Avelada, Bragança		1·60	1·30

(b) Self-adhesive gum. Die-curt perf 11

3182	30c. As No. 3178 (29×24 mm)		1·10	50
3183	45c. As No. 3179 (48×23 mm)		1·60	80
3184	57c. As No. 3180 (29×24 mm)		2·10	1·00
3177/3184 Set of 8			8·25	5·50

No. 3183 is inscribed "Correio Azul".

713 Subway Train and Tram **714** Sortelha

(Des E. Aires. Litho)

2005 (17 Mar). Public Transport. T **713** and similar horiz designs. Multicoloured. P 12½.

3185	30c. Type **713**		60	50
3186	50c. Locomotive and tram		1·00	85
3187	57c. Hovercraft		1·20	1·00
3188	€1 Coach		2·10	1·70
3189	€2 Train		4·25	3·50
3185/3189 Set of 5			8·25	6·75

Nos. 3185/9 form a composite design.

(Des A. Santos. Litho Enschedé)

2005 (28 Apr). Historic Villages (1st issue). T **714** and similar horiz designs. P 14×13½.

(a) Sheet stamps

3190	30c. Type **714**		65	50
	a. Sheetlet of 12. Nos. 3190/201			
3191	30c. Idanha-a-Velha		65	50
3192	30c. Castelo Novo		65	50
3193	30c. Castelo Rodrigo		65	50
3194	30c. Piodao		65	50
3195	30c. Linhares		65	50
3196	30c. Transcoso		65	50
3197	30c. Monsanto		65	50
3198	30c. Almeida		65	50
3199	30c. Belmonte		65	50
3200	30c. Marialva		65	50
3201	30c. Castelo Mendo		65	50

(b) Booklet stamps

3202	30c. Buildings and coast, Linhares		65	50
	a. Booklet pane. Nos. 3202 and 3214		1·75	1·25
3203	30c. Roof tops, Transcoso		65	50
	a. Booklet pane. Nos. 3203 and 3215		1·75	1·25
3204	30c. Church, Marialva		65	50
	a. Booklet pane. Nos. 3204 and 3216		1·75	1·25
3205	30c. Castle and houses, Castelo Rodrigo		65	50
	a. Booklet pane. Nos. 3205 and 3217		1·75	1·25
3206	30c. Buildings and terrace, Almeida		65	50
	a. Booklet pane. Nos. 3206 and 3218		1·75	1·25
3207	30c. Houses, Castelo Mendo		65	50
	a. Booklet pane. Nos. 3207 and 3219		1·75	1·25
3208	30c. Rooftops, Sortelha		65	50
	a. Booklet pane. Nos. 3208 and 3220		1·75	1·25
3209	30c. Balcony, Belmonte		65	50
	a. Booklet pane. Nos. 3209 and 3221		1·75	1·25
3210	30c. Rooftops, Monsanto		65	50
	a. Booklet pane. Nos. 3210 and 3222		1·75	1·25
3211	30c. Ruins, Idanha-a-Velha		65	50
	a. Booklet pane. Nos. 3211 and 3223		1·75	1·25
3212	30c. Tower, Castelo Novo		65	50
	a. Booklet pane. Nos. 3212 and 3224		1·75	1·25
3213	30c. Rooftops, Piodao		65	50
	a. Booklet pane. Nos. 3213 and 3225		1·75	1·25
3214	57c. Castle, Linhares		1·30	1·00
3215	57c. Castle walls, Transcoso		1·30	1·00
3216	57c. Bells, Marialva		1·30	1·00
3217	57c. Church, Castelo Rodrigo		1·30	1·00
3218	57c. Walls, Almeida		1·30	1·00
3219	57c. Rooftops, Castelo Mendo		1·30	1·00
3220	57c. Column, Sortelha		1·30	1·00
3221	57c. Castle walls, Belmonte		1·30	1·00
3222	57c. Tower, Monsanto		1·30	1·00
3223	57c. Doorway, Idanha-a-Velha		1·30	1·00
3224	57c. Rooftops, Castelo Novo		1·30	1·00
3225	57c. Building façade, Piodao		1·30	1·00
3190/3225 Set of 36			28·00	20·00

Nos. 3190/201 were issued in se-tenant sheetlets of 12 stamps. The booklet consists of 12 pages each containing an example of a 30c. and a 57c. stamp interleaved with 12 illustrated pages describing the villages.

The booklets could only be obtained from the philatelic centre.

715 "A Beira-Mar" **716** Cozido a Portuguesa (stew)

(Des A. Santos. Litho)

2005 (28 Apr). 150th Birth Anniv of Jose Malhoa (artist). T **715** and similar horiz designs. Multicoloured. P 14×13½.

3226	30c. Type **715**		60	50
3227	45c. "As Promessas"		95	80
MS3228 93×117 mm. €1.77 "Conversa com o Vizinho"			3·75	2·75

(Des A. Santos. Litho Enschedé)

2005 (5 May). Europa. Gastronomy. T **716** and similar horiz design. Multicoloured. P 14×13½.

3229	57c. Type **716**		1·50	1·20
MS3230 125×95 mm. 57c.×2, Bacalhau assado com batatas a murro (cod and potatoes) ×2			6·50	5·25

717 Paul Harris (founder) **718** 19th-century Open Carriage (Carrinho de Passeio)

(Des V. Marques. Litho)

2005 (20 May). Centenary of Rotary International. P 14×13½.

3231	717	74c. multicoloured	1·50	1·30
MS3232 125×95 mm. **717** €1.75 multicoloured			3·75	3·00

(Des J. Brandao and P. Falardo. Litho Enschedé)

2005 (23 May). Centenary of National Coach Museum, Lisbon. T **718** and similar horiz designs. Multicoloured. P 14×13½.

3233	30c. Type **718**		60	50
3234	30c. 19th-century closed carriage (Carruagem de Porto Covo)		60	50
3235	45c. 17th-century carriage (Coche Francisca Saboia)		95	80
3236	45c. 18th-century small carriage ("Das Plumas")		95	80
3237	57c. 18th-century sedan chair		1·20	1·00
3238	74c. 18th-century coach (Coches dos oceanos)		1·60	1·30
3233/3238 Set of 6			5·50	4·50
MS3239 125×100 mm. €1.75 Queen Amelia			3·75	3·00

719 Pegoes Aqueduct, Tomar **720** Man and Cat (Raphael Bordallo Pinheiro)

72

PORTUGAL

(Des V. Santos. Litho)

2005 (7 June). Cultural Heritage. T **719** and similar vert designs. Multicoloured. P 12.

3240	5c. Type **719**	10	10
3241	30c. Chalice (1581)	60	50
3242	45c. Stained glass, De Christo convent, Tomar	95	80
3243	57c. Turret, Angra, Azores	1·20	1·00
3244	€1 Ship	2·10	1·70
3245	€2 St. Vincente de Fora church, Lisbon	4·25	3·50
3240/3245	Set of 6	8·25	7·00
MS3246	112×140 mm. Crucifix, Tesauro da Sé, Lisbon	3·00	2·75

2005 (8 June). Historic Villages (2nd issue). 12 sheets, each 60×150 mm containing horiz designs as T **714**. P 14×13½.

MS3247 (a) Nos. 3202 and 3214; (b) Nos. 3203 and 3215; (c) Nos. 3204 and 3216; (d) Nos. 3205 and 3217; (e) Nos. 3206 and 3218; (f) Nos. 3207 and 3219; (g) Nos. 3208 and 3220; (h) Nos. 3209 and 3221; (i) Nos. 3210 and 3222; (j) Nos. 3211 and 3223; (k) Nos. 3212 and 3224; (l) Nos. 3213 and 3225 ... 19·00 14·00

(Des A. Santos. Litho Enschedé)

2005 (12 June). Caricaturists. T **720** and similar vert designs. Multicoloured. P 13½×14.

3248	30c. Type **720**	75	50
3249	30c. Bearded man (Sebastiao Sanhudo)	75	50
3250	30c. Soldier (Celso Herminio)	75	50
3251	30c. Man wearing glasses (Leal da Camara)	75	50
3252	30c. Man holding broken pencil (Francisco Valenca)	75	50
3253	30c. Man smoking (Stuart Carvalhais)	75	50
3254	30c. Guarda Ricardo (Sam Samuel Torres de Carvalho))	75	50
3255	30c. Almada Negreios (Joao Abel Manta)	75	50
3256	30c. Man tie (Augusto Cid)	75	50
3257	30c. Head and pencil (Antonio Atunes)	75	50
3258	30c. Ze Povinho (Raphael Bordallo Pinheiro)	75	50
3248/3258	Set of 11	7·50	5·00

Nos. 3248/58 were issued in se-tenant sheetlets of 11 stamps and one stamp size label.

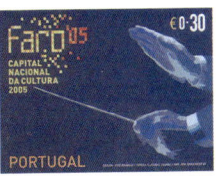
721 Conductor's Hands

722 Coastline and Bell

(Des J. Brandao and Tereza Olazabal Cabral. Litho Enschedé)

2005 (15 June). Faro—National Cultural Capital 2005. T **721** and similar horiz designs. Multicoloured. P 14×13½.

3259	30c. Type **721**	60	50
3260	45c. Ancient pot	95	80
3261	57c. Shell	1·20	1·00
3262	74c. Hands	1·60	1·30
3259/3262	Set of 4	4·00	3·25

(Des A. Santos. Litho)

2005 (7 Aug). Tourism. T **722** and similar horiz designs. Multicoloured. P 14×13½.

(a) Lisbon

3263	45c. Type **722**	95	75
3264	48c. Monument and tram	1·00	85
3265	57c. Tram, rooftops and cupola	1·40	1·00

(b) Porto e Norte

3266	45c. Ceramic rooster, valley and church	95	75
3267	48c. Church, bay and wine glass	1·00	85
3268	57c. Wine glass, seafront and yachts	1·40	1·00
3263/3268	Set of 6	6·00	4·75

Nos. 3262/3 and 3265/7, respectively, each form a composite design.

723 Harvesting Bark from protected Cork Trees

724 "50" and UN Emblem

(Des J. Projecto. Litho)

2005 (19 Aug). Environmental Protection. T **723** and similar horiz designs. Multicoloured. P 12.

3269	30c. Type **723**	60	50
3270	45c. Fire prevention officers	90	75
3271	57c. Buçaco Forest	1·20	1·00
3269/3271	Set of 3	2·50	2·00
MS3272	95×95 mm. €2 Chestnut trees (Serra de S. Mamede)	4·00	3·25

(Des V. Marques. Litho)

2005 (21 Sept). 50th Anniv of United Nations Membership. T **724** and similar horiz designs. Multicoloured. P 12.

3273	30c. Type **724**	60	50
3274	45c. Dove (International Day of Peace)	90	75
3275	57c. Child (UNESCO–Children at Risk)	1·20	1·00
3276	74c. Albert Einstein (International Year of Physics)	1·50	1·30
3273/3276	Set of 4	3·75	3·25

725 Sundial, St John the Baptist Church, São João das Lampas

726 Pen Nib

(Des V. Marques. Litho)

2005 (3 Oct). Annular Solar Eclipse–3rd October 2005. T **725** and similar vert designs. Multicoloured. P 12½×12.

3277	45c. Type **725**	95	75
3278	€1 Portable sundial, 1770	2·00	1·70
MS3279	125×135 mm. €1.20×3, Partial eclipse, Lisbon; Annulus, Bragança; Partial eclipse, Faro	7·50	6·00

(Des E. Aires. Litho)

2005 (13 Oct). Communications. T **726** and similar horiz designs. Multicoloured. P 12×12½.

3280	30c. Type **726**	60	50
3281	45c. Radio microphone	90	75
3282	57c. Television camera	1·20	1·00
3283	74c. Globe and @ (internet)	1·50	1·30
3280/3283	Set of 4	3·75	3·25
MS3284	Two sheets, each 125×90 mm. (a) €1.10 Newspaper; €1.55 Radio studio. (b) €1.10 Television studio; €1.55 "http://www"(internet)	10·50	10·00

727 Fisherman and Boats, Aldeia da Carrasqueira

728 Multipurpose Ship

(Des Sofia Martins. Litho)

2005 (18 Oct). Fishing Villages. T **727** and similar horiz designs. Multicoloured. P 12½×12.

3285	30c. Type **727**	60	50
	a. Horiz pair. Nos. 3285/6	1·50	
3286	30c. Moorings and pier, Aldeia da Carrasqueira	60	50
3287	30c. Boat, Tai O, Hong Kong	60	50
	a. Horiz pair. Nos. 3287/8	1·50	
3288	30c. Wrapped fish, Tai O	60	50
3285/3288	Set of 4	2·00	1·50

Nos. 3285/6 and 3287/8, respectively were issued in horizontal *se-tenant* pairs within the sheet, each pair forming a composite design. Stamps of the same design were issued by Hong Kong.

(Des V. Marques. Litho)

2005 (8 Nov). Modernisation of the Navy. T **728** and similar horiz designs. Black. P 12×12½.

3289	45c. Type **728**	90	75
3290	57c. Hydro-oceanographic ship	1·20	1·00
3291	74c. Patrol vessel	1·50	1·30
3292	€2 Submarine	4·00	3·25
3289/3292	Set of 4	6·75	5·75

73

PORTUGAL

729 Alvaro Cunhal, Women and Children   **730** Building

(Des V. Santos. Litho)

2005 (10 Nov). Alvaro Barreirinhas Cunhal (politician and writer) Commemoration. T **729** and similar horiz design. Multicoloured. P 12½×12.
3293	30c. Type **729**		1·00	50
MS3294	112×104 mm. €1 Alvaro Cunhal and girl		1·80	1·80

(Des J. Machado. Litho Enschedé)

2005 (15 Nov). Serralves Foundation. T **730** and similar multicoloured designs. P 14×13½ (**MS**3301) or 13½×14 (others).
3295	30c. Type **730**		60	50
3296	45c. "Projected Shadow of Adami" (Lourdes de Castro)		90	75
3297	48c. Building façade		1·00	85
3298	57c. Trowel (Claes Oldenburg Cooseje van Bruggen)		1·20	95
3299	74c. Hand and painting		1·50	1·30
3300	€1 Path, hedges and lawn		2·00	1·70
3295/3300	Set of 6		6·50	5·50
MS3301	Two sheets, each 125×150 mm. (a) 30c. As No. 3297 (horiz); 45c. Path; 45c. Columns and balustrade; 45c. Tower; 45c. Canal and evergreens (b) €1 Museum building (80×30 mm); €1 Museum displays (80×30 mm); €1 Parkland		10·50	8·25

731 Futebol Clube do Porto Emblem and Player (1993)

(Des Atelier Acacio Santos. Litho)

2005 (25 Nov). Football Clubs' Centenaries. T **731** and similar horiz designs showing emblem and player. Multicoloured. P 12×12½.
3302	N (30c.) Type **731**		60	50
3303	N (30c.) Sport Lisboa e Benefica (2004)		60	50
3304	N (30c.) Sporting Clube de Portugal (2006)		60	50
3302/3304	Set of 3		1·50	1·25
MS3305	Three sheets, each 125×96 mm. (a) €1 Porto Football Club emblem and trophy; (b) €1 Sport Lisboa e Benefica emblem, player, stadium and trophy; (c) €1 Anniversary emblem		6·75	1·70

Nos. 3302/4 were for use on letters weighing 20 grams or less.

732 Scenes of Devastation

(Des J. L. Tinoco. Litho Enschedé)

2005 (25 Nov). 250th Anniv of Earthquake–31 October 1755. T **732** and similar horiz designs. Multicoloured. P 14×13½.
3306	45c. Type **732**		90	75
3307	€2 Aftermath		4·00	3·25
MS3308	80×80 mm. €2.65 Survivors (40×30 mm)		5·25	4·25

733 Children's Party   **734** Rain Clouds

(Des E. Aires. Litho)

2006 (7 Feb). Greetings Stamps. T **733** and similar horiz designs. Multicoloured.

(a) Sheet stamps. P 12×12½
3309	N (30c.) Type **733**		60	50
3310	N (30c.) Girl and couples		60	50
3311	N (30c.) Mother, father and baby		60	50
3312	N (30c.) Conductor		60	50
3313	N (30c.) Couple about to kiss		60	50

(b) Size 40×29 mm. Booklet stamps. Imperf×p 12½ (2 sides)
3314	N (30c.) As No. 3309		60	50
	a. Booklet pane. Nos. 3314/18		6·00	
3315	N (30c.) As No. 3310		60	50
3316	N (30c.) As No. 3311		60	50
3317	N (30c.) As No. 3312		60	50
3318	N (30c.) As No. 3313		60	50
3309/3318	Set of 10		5·50	4·50

Nos. 3314/18 form a composite design.

(Des C. Leitao. Litho)

2006 (1 Mar). Masks (2nd series). Horiz designs as T **712**. Multicoloured. Self-adhesive gum. Die-cut perf 11.
3319	N "Festa dos Rapazes", Salsas, Bragança (29×24 mm)		60	50
3320	A Lazarim carnival, Bragança (29×24 mm)		90	75
3321	E "Dia de Ano Novo", Mogadouro, Bragança (29×24 mm)		1·20	1·00
3319/3321	Set of 3		2·50	2·00

No. 3320 is inscribed "Correio Azul".
No. 3319 was for use on normal domestic mail, up to 20 grams, No. 3320 was for domestic first class (blue) mail and No. 3321 was for European mail.

(Des J. Machado. Litho)

2006 (22 Mar). Water. T **734** and similar horiz designs. Multicoloured. P 12.
3322	N Type **734**		60	50
3323	N Glass of water		60	50
3324	A Water from tap		90	75
3325	A Water turbines		90	75
3326	E Yacht		1·20	1·00
3327	E Flower		1·20	1·00
3322/3327	Set of 6		5·00	4·00

Nos. 3322/3 were for use on normal domestic mail, up to 20 grams, No. 3324/5 were for domestic first class (blue) mail and No. 3326/7 were for European mail.

 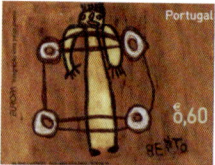

735 Baptising   **736** Enclosed Figure (Bento Luz)

(Des Teresa Olazabal Cabral and J. Brandão. Litho)

2006 (5 Apr). 500th Birth Anniv of Saint Francis Xavier. T **735** and similar horiz designs. Multicoloured. P 12½×12.
3328	45c. Type **735**		95	75
3329	€1 Preaching		2·00	1·70
MS3330	85×125 mm. €2.75 Saint Francis Xavier (painting)		4·50	3·25

2006 (9 May). Europa. Integration. Winning Entries in ANACED (association for art and creativity by and for people with disabilities) Painting Competition. T **736** and similar horiz designs. Multicoloured. P 12½×12.
3331	60c. Type **736**		1·30	1·00
MS3332	125×95 mm. 60c.×2, Figure in wheelchair (David Fernandes); Aliens and humans from many nations (Ana Sofia, Renarto, Jose Luis and Alcidia)		2·50	2·00

PORTUGAL

737 Romulo de Carvalho (science writer)

738 Players' Legs

(Des Teresa Olazabal Cabral and J. Brandão. Litho)
2006 (15 May). Birth Centenaries. T **737** and similar vert designs. Multicoloured. P 12.

3333	€1 Type **737**	2·00	1·70
3334	€1 Agostinho da Silva (philosopher)	2·00	1·70
3335	€1 Thomaz de Mello (artist)	2·00	1·70
3336	€1 Humberto Delgado (politician)	2·00	1·70
3337	€1 Lopes-Graca (composer and musician)	2·00	1·70
3333/3337	Set of 5	9·00	7·50

(Des Atelier Acacio Santos)
2006 (23 May). UEFA Under-21 Football Championships, Portugal. Sheet 125×65 mm. P 12×12½.

| MS3338 | **738** €2.75 multicoloured | 5·50 | 4·50 |

739 Players   **739a** Mozart (etching)

(Des Atelier Acacio Santos. Litho)
2006 (7 June). World Cup Football Championships, Germany. T **739** and similar horiz designs. Multicoloured. P 12.

3339	45c. Type **739**	90	4·75
3340	€1 Players (different)	2·00	1·70
MS3341	125×85 mm. €2.40 Emblem and trophy	5·00	4·00

(Des Elizabete Rolo and J. Brandao. Litho)
2006 (7 June). 250th Birth Anniv of Wolfgang Amadeus Mozart (composer). Etchings by Giovanni Antonio Sasso. T **739a** and similar horiz design. Multicoloured. P 12.

| 3341a | 60c. Type **739a** | 1·20 | 1·00 |
| MS3341b | 90×115 mm. €2.75 Mozart facing right | 5·50 | 4·50 |

740 Dunes

741 Oceanus (mosaic)

(Des J. Machado. Litho)
2006 (17 June). International Year of Deserts and Desertification. T **740** and similar horiz designs. Multicoloured. P 12.

| 3342 | 30c. Type **740** | 60 | 50 |
| 3343 | 60c. Dead and live trees | 1·20 | 1·00 |

(Des J. Brandao and P. Falardo. Litho)
2006 (21 June). Roman Heritage. T **741** and similar horiz designs. Multicoloured. P 12.

3344	30c. Type **741**	60	50
3345	45c. Temple, Évora	90	75
3346	50c. Pátera de Lameira Larga	1·00	85
3347	60c. Two headed statue ("Herma Bifronte")	1·20	1·00
3344/3347	Set of 4	3·25	2·75
MS3348	125×95 mm. €2.40 Seahorse (mosaic)	5·00	4·00

(Des C. Leitao. Litho)
2006 (29 June). Masks (3rd series). Horiz designs as T **712**. Multicoloured. Ordinary gum. P 12.

3349	3c. Owl (Lazarim carnival, Bragança)	10	10
3350	5c. Scarecrow, "Festa dos Rapazes", Baçal, Bragança	10	10
3351	30c. As No. 3319 ("Festa dos Rapazes", Salsas, Bragança)	60	50
3352	45c. As No. 3320 (Lazarim carnival, Bragança)	90	75
3353	60c. As No. 3321 ("Dia de Ano Novo", Mogadouro, Bragança)	1·20	1·00
3354	75c. Devil ("Dia dos Diabos", Vinhais, Bragança)	1·50	1·30
3349/3354	Set of 6	4·00	3·25

Nos. 3355/3356 and Type **742** are vacant.

743 Flags

744 Picture of a Young Woman (Domenico Ghirlandaio)

(Des J. Machado. Litho Cartor)
2006 (12 July). Tenth Anniv of Community of Portuguese Speaking Countries (CPLP). Sheet 125×65 mm. P 12½×13.

| MS3357 | **743** €2.85 multicoloured | 6·00 | 4·75 |

(Des J. Brandao and P. Falardo. Litho Cartor)
2006 (18 July). 50th Anniv of Calouste Gulbenkian Foundation. T **744** and similar multicoloured designs. P 12.

3358	30c. Type **744**	60	50
3359	45c. Brooch (René Lalique)	90	75
3360	60c. Tiles (Turkish c. 1573)	1·20	1·00
3361	75c. "Flora" (sculpture) (Jean Baptiste Carpeaux) and Roman medallion	1·50	1·30
3362	€1 Jade jar	2·00	1·70
3363	€2 "Calouste Gulbenkian" (C. J. Watelet)	4·00	3·25
3358/3363	Set of 6	9·00	8·00
MS3364	125×95 mm. 30c.×4, Statues (art); Books (education); Spectroscope (science); Mother and child (charity)	2·50	2·00

Nos. 3358/63 when laid together form a composite design. The stamps of No. **MS**3364 form a composite design.

745 José Gomes Ferreira School, Lisbon (Raul Hestnes Ferreira)

746 Early Camera and Crew

(Des J. Machado. Litho)
2006 (21 Aug). Contemporary Architecture. T **745** and similar horiz designs. Multicoloured. P 12.

3365	30c. Type **745**	60	50
3366	30c. Borges & Irmao Bank, Vila do Conde (Álvaro Siza)	60	50
3367	30c. Matosinhos City Council (Alcino Soutinho)	60	50
3368	30c. Casa das Artes, Porto (Eduardo Souto Moura)	60	50
3369	30c. University campus, Santiago (Nuno Portas/CEFAUP)	60	50
3370	30c. Escola Superior de Comunicação Social (ESCS), Lisbon (Carrilho da Graça)	60	50
3371	30c. Plan for Alto do Restelo, Lisbon (Teotónio Pereira, Nuno Portas, Pedro Botelho and Joao Paciência)	60	50
3372	30c. Order of architects, Lisbon (Manuel Graça Dias and Egas JoséVieira)	60	50
3373	30c. St. Mary's church, Forno, Marco de Canaveses (Alvaro Siza)	60	50
3374	30c. Bairro da Bouca, SAAL, Porto (Álvaro Siza)	60	50
3365/3374	Set of 10	5·50	4·50

PORTUGAL

(Des Atelier Acacio Santos. Litho)
2006 (4 Sept). 50th Anniv of First Television Broadcast in Portugal. T **746** and similar horiz design. Multicoloured. P 12.
3375	30c. Type **746**	60	50
3376	60c. Modern camera	1·20	1·00

747 Ponte de Alcântara

(Des Atelier Acacio Santos. Litho)
2006 (14 Sept). Bridges. T **747** and similar horiz design. Multicoloured. P 12.
3377	30c. Type **747**	60	50
3378	52c. Ponte de Vila Real de Sto. António	1·10	90

Stamps of similar design were issued by Spain.

748 Grapes and Terraces

(Des E. Aires. Litho)
2006 (14 Sept). 250th Anniv of Douro Wine Demarcated Region. Sheet 125×95 mm. P 12.
MS3379	**748**	€2.40 multicoloured	5·00	4·00

749 Capros aper   **750** "a"

(Des P. Salgado and V. Marques. Litho)
2006 (7 Oct). Fish. T **749** and similar horiz designs. Multicoloured. P 12.
3380	30c. Type **749**	60	50
3381	45c. Anthias anthias	90	75
3382	60c. Lepadogaster lepadogaster	1·20	1·00
3383	75c. Gobiusculus flavescens	1·50	1·30
3384	€1 Coris julis	2·00	1·70
3385	€2 Calliomymus lyra	4·00	3·25
3380/3385	Set of 6	9·50	8·00

MS3386 Two sheets, each 125×115 mm. (a) 80c.×2, Macroramphosus scolopax; Echiichthys vipera. (b) 80c.×2, Thalassoma pavo; Blennius ocellaris ... 7·00 5·50

(Des Sofia Lucas. Litho Cartor)
2006 (9 Oct). School Correspondence. T **750** and similar horiz design. Multicoloured. P 12.
3387	N Type **750**	60	50
3388	N "c, g, d"	60	50

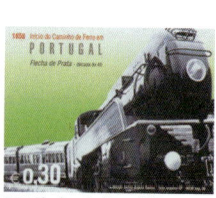 

751 Flecha de Prata (Silver Arrow)   **752** "A Cidade de Gale"

(Des B. Marques and A. Santos (€1.60) or A. Santos (others). Litho)
2006 (28 Oct). 150th Anniv of National Railways. T **751** and similar horiz designs. Multicoloured. P 12.
3389	30c. Type **751**	60	50
3390	45c. Sud-Express	90	75
3391	60c. Foguette	1·20	1·00
3392	€2 Alfa Pendular	4·00	3·25
3389/3392	Set of 4	6·00	5·00

MS3393 125×95 mm. €1.60 Blessing first train (80×30 mm) ... 3·25 2·50

(Des V. Marques. Litho)
2006 (30 Oct). 500th Anniv of Portuguese in Ceylon. T **752** and similar vert design. Multicoloured. P 12.
3394	30c. Type **752**	60	50
3395	75c. "O Livro das Plantas e Todas as Fortalezas"	1·50	1·30

MS3396 125×95 mm. €2.40 As No. 3394 ... 5·00 4·00

753 16th-century Tiles   **754** Laundress wearing Scarves ("Lavadeira") (Minho)

(Des José Brandão and Paulo Falardo. Litho Cartor)
2007 (15 Feb). In Search of Arab Lisbon. T **753** and similar horiz designs. Multicoloured. P 12½×13½.
3397	30c. Type **753**	60	50
3398	45c. 9th-century limestone carving	90	75
3399	52c. Neo-Arab door	1·00	90
3400	61c. Neo-Arab interior, National Film Library	1·20	1·00
3401	75c. Casa Alentejo	1·50	1·20
3402	€1 Palacete Ribeiro da Cunha	2·00	1·60
3397/3402	Set of 6	6·50	5·00

MS3403 130×95 mm. €2.95 11th-century Islamic jug.. 6·00 4·75

(Des Vasco Maques. Litho Cartor)
2007 (28 Feb). Regional Costume. T **754** and similar horiz designs. Multicoloured. P 12½×13½.
3404	30c. Type **754**	60	50
	a. Sheetlet. Nos. 3404/13	6·50	
3405	30c. Bride wearing gold chains ("Noiva") (Minho)	30	50
3406	30c. Cape ("Capa de Honras") (Tras-os-Montes)	60	50
3407	30c. Embroidered tunic ("Pauliteiro") (Tras-os-Montes)	60	50
3408	30c. Fisherman's jersey ("Camisola de Pescador") (Douro Litoral)	60	50
3409	30c. Straw cape ("Coroça") (Beiras/Tras-os-Montes)	60	50
3410	30c. Embroidered apron and skirts ("Saias de Nazaré") (Estremadura)	60	50
3411	30c. Horseman wearing red waistcoat ("Campino") (Ribatejo)	60	50
3412	30c. Floral apron and skirt ("Camponesa") (Algarve)	60	50
3413	30c. Cape with fur collar ("Capote") (Alentejo)	60	50
3414	30c. Hooded cloak ("Capote e Capelo") (Azores)	60	50
	a. Sheetlet. Nos. 3414/17	2·75	
3415	30c. Short jacket, white shirt and red sash ("Camponés") (Beira Litoral)	60	50
3416	30c. Striped dress and red cape ("Viloa") (Madeira)	60	50
3417	30c. Smoked blouse, apron and embroidered cloak ("Camponesa") (Ribatejo)	60	50
3404/3417	Set of 14	7·50	6·50

Nos. 3404/13 and 3414/17, respectively were issued in *se-tenant* sheetlets of ten or four stamps with enlarged margins.

755 "Carreaux Diamants"   **756** "D. Jo'o i Reforça a Casa dos Contos" (painting by Jaime Martins Barata)

(Des Francisco Galalimba. Litho Cartor)
2007 (16 Mar). Manuel Cargaleiro (artist and ceramist). T **755** and similar horiz designs. Multicoloured. P 12½×13½.
3418	30c. Type **755**	60	50
3419	45c. "Composizione Floreale"	90	75
3420	52c. "Decorção Mural"	1·20	1·00
3418/3420	Set of 3	2·50	2·00

PORTUGAL

(Des José Brandão and Paulo Falardo. Litho Cartor)

2007 (17 Mar). Bicentenary of European Court of Auditors. T **756** and similar horiz designs. Multicoloured. P 12½×13½.
3421	30c. Type **756**		60	50
3422	61c. Creation of Court of Auditors (painting by Almada Negreiros)		1·20	1·20
3423	€2 Headquarters of the Court, 1954–1989		4·00	3·25
3421/3423	Set of 3		5·25	4·50
MS3424	95×125 mm. €2.95 "The Auditor" (tapestry)		6·00	4·75

757 Pen, Flag and Stars

758 Ox-drawn Carriage

(Des Vasco Maques Litho Cartor)

2007 (23 Mar). 50th Anniv of Treaty of Rome. P 13½×12½.
3425	**757**	61c. multicoloured	1·20	1·00

(Des Atelier Acácio Santos. Litho)

2007 (30 Mar)–**09**. Public Transport. T **758** and similar horiz designs. Multicoloured.

(a) Ordinary gum. P 12
3425a	6c. Electric car (1927) (12.9.08)	10	30
3425b	20c. Bus (1957) (9.2.09)	40	30
3426	30c. Type **758**	60	50
3426a	31c. Oldsmobile taxi (1928) (12.9.08)	60	45
3426b	32c. Triple unit electric car (1957) (9.2.09)	65	50
3427	45c. Horse-drawn tram facing right ("Americano") (1872)	90	70
3427a	47c. Tram (1926) (12.9.08)	1·00	60
3427b	47c. Carruagem ML7 (1959) (9.2.09)	1·00	75
3428	50c. Horse-drawn tram facing left ("Americano") (1873)	1·00	80
3429	61c. Electric tram (Elétrico No. 22) (1895)	1·20	95
3429a	67c. Coach (1944) (12.9.08)	1·40	70
3429b	68c. Bus No. 207 (1960) (9.2.09)	1·30	1·30
3430	75c. Electric tram (Elétrico No. 283) (1901)	1·50	1·20
3430a	80c. Electric car (1911) (12.9.08)	1·60	75
3430b	80c. Trolley bus (1961) (9.2.09)	1·60	1·20

(b) Size 30×22 mm. Self-adhesive gum. Die-cut perf
3436	N	As No. 3426 (30.5)	60	50
3436a	N	Oldsmobile taxi (1928)	60	45
3436b	N	(32c.) Triple unit electric car (1957) (As No. 3426b) (9.09)	65	50
3437	A	Tram with driver (Elétrico No. 22) (1895) (30.5)	90	75
3437a	A	Tram (1928) (inauguration of electrical traction company, Estoril)	90	70
3437b	A	(47c.) Carruagem ML7 (1959) (As No. 3427b) (9.09)	1·00	75
3438	E	Tram with driver (Elétrico No. 283) (1901) (30.5)	1·20	1·00
3438a	E	Coach (1944) (inauguration of coach company, Carris)	1·30	1·00
3438a	E	(67c.) Bus No. 207 (1960) (As No. 3429b) (9.09)	1·40	70
3425a/3438a		Set of 24	20·00	15·00

No. 3436 was for use on normal domestic mail, up to 20 grams, No. 3437 was for domestic first class (blue) mail and No. 3438 was for European mail.
Numbers have been left for possible additions to this series.
No. 3436b was for use on normal domestic mail, up to 20 grams, No. 3437b was for domestic first class (blue) mail and No. 3438b was for European mail.

759 Castelo do Bode Dam

760 Robert Baden Powell (founder)

(Des FIL CGD and Atelier Acácio Santos. Litho Cartor)

2007 (17 Apr). Dams. T **759** and similar horiz designs. Multicoloured. P 12½×13½.

(a) Size 40×30 mm
3445	30c. Type **759**	60	50

(b) Size 80×30 mm
3446	30c. Aguieira	60	50
3447	61c. Valeira	1·20	1·00
3448	75c. Alto Lindoso	1·50	1·20
3449	€1 Castelo do Bode extended	2·00	1·60
3445/3449	Set of 5	5·00	4·00

No. 3445 was also available with a stamp size label.

(Des Hulton-Deutsch and Corbis. Litho Cartor)

2007 (9 May). Europa. Centenary of Scouting. T **760** and similar horiz designs. Multicoloured. P 12½×13½.
3450	61c. Type **760**	1·30	1·00
MS3451	125×95 mm. 61c.×2, Compass; Scouts reading map	2·50	2·00

The stamps of No. **MS**3451 form a composite design.

(Des João Machado. Litho)

2007 (31 May). Contemporary Architecture. Horiz designs as T **745**. Multicoloured. P 12.
3452	30c. ESAD, Caldas da Rainha (Vitor Figueiredo)	60	50
3453	30c. Pavilion, Lisbon (Álvaro Siza)	60	50
3454	30c. VTS Tower, Lisbon Port (Gonçalo Byrne)	60	50
3455	30c. Casa dos 24, Porto (Fernando Távora)	60	50
3456	30c. José Saramago Library, Loures (Fernando Martins)	60	50
3457	30c. Documentation and Information Centre of President of the Republic, Lisbon (Carrilho da Graça)	60	50
3458	30c. Art Centre, Sines (Aires Mateus)	60	50
3459	30c. Municipal building, Braga (Eduardo Souto Moura)	60	50
3460	30c. Centre for Visual Arts, Coimbra (Joõ Mendes Ribeiro)	60	50
3461	30c. Maritime Museum, Ílhavo (ARX Portugal)	60	50
3452/3461	Set of 10	5·50	4·50
MS3462	125×95 mm. €1.85 Pavilion, Lisbon (Álvaro Siza) (different) (Lisbon Architecture Triennale 2007)	3·75	3·00

The stamps and margins of No. **MS**3462 form a composite design.

761 Catamarans

762 Castelo de Guimaraes

(Des João Machado. Litho)

2007 (12 June). ISAF World Sailing Championships. T **761** and similar horiz designs showing stylized craft. Multicoloured. P 12.
3463	61c. Type **761**	1·20	1·00
3464	61c. Two yachts, sail nos. '23' and '105'	1·20	1·00
3465	75c. Yacht, sail no. '75'	1·30	1·10
3466	75c. Two yachts, sail nos. '34' and '16'	1·30	1·10
3463/3466	Set of 4	4·50	3·75
MS3467	125×95 mm. €2.95 As No. 3465	6·00	4·75

The stamp and margin of No. **MS**3467 form a composite design.

(Des Atelier Acácio Santos. Litho)

2007 (14 June). Seven Marvels of Portugal. T **762** and similar horiz designs. Multicoloured. P 12.
3468	30c. Type **762**	60	50
	a. Sheetlet. Nos. 3468/74 plus label	4·00	
3469	30c. Palácio de Mateus, Vila Real	60	50
3470	30c. São Francisco church, Porto	60	50
3471	30c. Torre dos Clérigos church, Porto	60	50
3472	30c. Clock tower, University of Coimbra	60	50
3473	30c. Ruins, Conimbriga, Condeixa-a-Nova	60	50
3474	30c. Batalha monastery	60	50
3475	30c. Convent of Christ, Tomar	60	50
	a. Sheetlet. Nos. 3475/81 plus label	4·00	
3476	30c. Almourol castle, Vila Nova da Barquinha	60	50
3477	30c. Alcobaça monastery,	60	50
3478	30c. Obidos castle	60	50
3479	30c. Basilica and convent of Mafra	60	50
3480	30c. Marvão castle	60	50

77

PORTUGAL

3481	30c. Blockhouses, Monsaraz	60	50
3482	30c. Vila Viçosa Ducal palace	60	50
	a. Sheetlet. Nos. 3482/8 plus label	4·00	
3483	30c. Roman temple, Evora	60	50
3484	30c. Palácio Nacional da Pena, Sintra	60	50
3485	30c. Palacio Nacional da Queluz, Sintra	60	50
3486	30c. Mosteiro dos Jerónimos, Lisbon	60	50
3487	30c. Torre de Belem, Lisbon	60	50
3488	30c. Sagres fortress, Vila do Bispo	60	50
3468/3488 Set of 21		10·00	9·00

Nos. 3468/74, 3475/81 and 3482/8, respectively were issued in *se-tenant* sheetlets of seven stamps and one label.

763 *Ponte* (Amadeo de Souza Cardoso) **764** Building and Stars

(Des Atelier Acácio Santos. Litho)

2007 (25 June). Exhibits from Berado Museum Collection. T **763** and similar multicoloured designs. P 12.

3489	45c. Type **763**	90	75
3490	61c. *Les Baigneuses* (Niki de Saint Phalle) (vert)	1·20	1·00
3491	61c. *Le Couple* (Oacar Dominguez) (vert)	1·20	1·00
	a. Sheetlet. Nos. 3941/4		
3492	61c. *Café Man Ray* (Man Ray) (vert)	1·20	1·00
3493	61c. *Néctar* (Joana Vasconcelos) (vert)	1·20	1·00
3494	61c. *Head* (Jackson Pollack) (vert)	1·20	1·00
3495	€1 *Interior with Restful Paintings* (Roy Lichtenstein) (vert)	2·00	1·60
3496	€2 *Femme dans un Fauteuil* (Pablo Picasso) (vert)	4·00	3·25
3489/3496 Set of 8		10·00	9·50

Nos. 3941/4 were issued in *se-tenant* sheetlets of four stamps with enlarged margins.

(Des João Machado. Litho)

2007 (1 July). Portugal—Presidency of European Union. T **764** and similar horiz design. Multicoloured. P 12 (irregular indentation on each vert side).

3497	61c. Type **764**	1·20	1·00
MS3498	125×95 mm. €2.45 As No. 3497 but direction of stars reversed	4·50	4·50

The indentation in the vertical perforations forms the shape of a cross when viewed across the sheet.

765 SMC Nacional 500cc., 1935 **766** Globe

(Des Atelier Acácio Santos. Litho)

2007 (4 July). Motorcycles. T **765** and similar horiz designs. Multicoloured. P 12 (irregular indentation on each vert side).

3499	30c. Type **765**	60	50
3500	52c. Famel Fougete, 1959	1·00	90
3501	61c. Vilar Cucciolo, 1955	1·20	1·00
3502	€1 Casal Carina, 1969	2·00	1·60
3499/3502 Set of 4		4·25	3·50
MS3503	125×95 mm. 61c.×4, Qimera Alma, 1952; Cinal Pachancho, 1958; SIS Sachs V5, 1965; Casal K287, 1985	5·00	4·00

The stamps of No. MS3467 form a composite background design. The indentation in the vertical perforations forms the shape of a cross when viewed across the sheet.

(Des Atelier Acácio Santos. Litho)

2007 (7 July). Declaration of Winning Entries in New Seven Wonders of the World Competition—Lisbon 2007. Sheet 125×95 mm. P 12.

MS3504 **766**	€2.95 multicoloured	6·00	4·75

The stamp and margin of No. MS3467 form a composite design.

767 Raul Maria Pereira and Postal Building, Peru **768** José Valentim Fialho de Almeida

(Des Francisco Galamba. Litho)

2007 (10 Aug). 130th Birth Anniv of Raul Maria Pereira (artist and architect). P 12.

3505 **767**	75c. multicoloured	1·50	1·20

Stamp of a similar design was issued by Peru.

(Des Andre Carrilho and Francisco Galamba. Litho)

2007 (12 Aug). Personalities. T **768** and similar vert designs. Multicoloured. P 12.

3506	45c. Type **768** (writer) (150th birth anniv)	90	75
3507	45c. Columbano Bordalo Pinheiro (Columbano) (artist) (150th birth anniv)	90	75
3508	45c. Adolfo Correia da Rocha (Miguel Torga) (writer) (birth centenary)	90	75
3506/3508 Set of 3		2·25	2·00

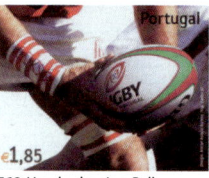 

769 Hands clasping Ball **770** *Horus*, 1953

(Des Atelier Acácio Santos. Litho Cartor)

2007 (22 Aug). Rugby World Cup, France. Sheet 125×95 mm. P 12.

MS3509 **769**	€1.85 multicoloured	3·75	3·00

The stamp and margin of No. MS3509 form a composite design.

(Litho Cartor)

2007 (5 Sept). Portuguese Artists. Nadir Afonso. T **770** and similar horiz designs. Multicoloured. P 12.

3510	30c. Type **770**	60	50
3511	45c. *Veneza*, 1956	90	75
3512	61c. *Procissao em Veneza*, 2002	1·20	1·00
3510/3512 Set of 3		2·25	2·00

771 Jacaranda **772** Torre de Menagem, Arzila

2007 (25 Sept). Plants and Animals from the Americas. T **771** and similar multicoloured designs. P 12.

3513	30c. Type **771**	60	50
3514	30c. Potatoes	60	50
3515	30c. Maize	60	50
3516	45c. Cocoa	90	75
3517	61c. Turkeys (inscr 'Peru')	1·20	1·00
3518	75c. Passion fruit	1·50	1·20
3513/3518 Set of 6		5·00	4·50
MS3519	125×95 mm. €1.85 Humming bird and passion fruit (horiz)	3·75	3·00

The stamp and margin of No. MS3519 form a composite design.

2007 (26 Sept). Architecture. T **772** and similar vert design. Multicoloured. P 12.

3520	30c. Type **772**	60	50
3521	75c. Castelo de Silves, Portugal	1·50	1·20

Stamps of a similar design were issued by Morocco.

PORTUGAL

773 National Flag
774 Children and Globe (Sofia Fiteire Passeira)

(Des Joao Machado. Litho)

2007 (5 Oct). Symbols of the Republic. Flags. T **773** and similar horiz designs showing flags. Multicoloured. P 12 (irregular indentation on each vert side) (3522).
3522	30c. Type **773**	60	50

MS3523 95×125 mm. 30c.×5, As Type **773**; President of the Republic; National Assembly; Azores; Madeira ... 3·00 2·50

The indentation in the vertical perforations forms the shape of a cross when viewed across the sheet.
The stamps and margins of No. **MS**3523 form a composite background design.

2007 (9 Oct). School Correspondence. Children's Paintings. T **774** and similar horiz designs. Multicoloured. P 12 (irregular indentation on each vert side).
3524	N Type **774**	60	50
3525	N Girls and flowers (Ines Filipa Navrat)	60	50
3526	N Globe enclosed in hands (Maria Correira Borges)	60	50
3524/3526	Set of 3	1·50	1·25

The indentation in the vertical perforations forms the shape of a cross when viewed across the sheet.
Nos. 3524/6 were for use on domestic mail weighing 20 grams or less.

775 Fallow Deer (*Cervus dama*)
776 Courtyard, Centro Ismali, Lisbon

(Des José Projecto and Atelier Acácio Santos. Litho Cartor)

2007 (16 Oct). Mafra National Park. T **775** and similar horiz designs. Multicoloured. P 12.
3527	30c. Type **775**	60	50
3528	45c. Wild boar (*Sus scrofa*)	90	75
3529	61c. Fox (*Vulpes vulpes*)	1·20	1·00
3530	75c. Red deer (*Cervus elaphus*)	1·50	1·20
3531	€1. Eurasian eagle owl (*Bubo bubo*)	2·00	1·25
3532	€2. Bonelli's eagle (*Hieraaetus fasciatus*)	4·00	2·50
3527/3532	Set of 6	9·50	7·50

No. **MS**3533 has been left for miniature sheet not yet received.

(Litho Cartor)

2007 (7 Nov). 50th Anniv of Ismaili Community in Portugal. T **776** and similar horiz design. Multicoloured. P 12.
3533	N Type **776**	60	50
3534	I Aerial view of courtyard	1·50	1·20

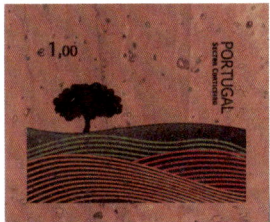

777 Cork Tree

2007 (28 Nov). Cork Production. Self-adhesive gum. Die-cut perf 12½.
3535	**777**	€1 multicoloured	2·00	1·25

No. 3535 was made of cork applied to a paper backing.
No. 3535 was also issued with a *se-tenant* half stamp size label.

778 Motorcycle ridden by Ruben Faria
779 Royal Family and Entourage

(Des Rita Rodrigues)

2008 (5 Jan). 30th Anniv of Dakar Rally. Lisbon—Dakar Rally, 2007. Sheet 126×95 mm containing T **778** and similar horiz designs. Multicoloured. P 12.
MS3536 30c. Type **778**; 45c. Motorcycle ridden by Helder Rodrigues; 75c. Car driven by Carlos Sousa; €1.25 Lorry driven by Rainer Weigart ... 5·50 4·25
The stamps and margins of No. **MS**3536 form a composite design.

(Des J. L. Tinoco. Litho Cartor)

2008 (22 Jan). Bicentenary of Portuguese Royal Family's Arrival in Brazil. T **779** and similar horiz design. Multicoloured. P 12 (irregular indentation on each vert side).
3537	N Type **779**	60	45
	a. Pair. Nos. 3537/8	2·25	
3538	I King João VI	1·50	1·20

Nos. 3537/8 were issued in horizontal *se-tenant* pairs within the sheet, each pair forming a composite design.
The indentation in the vertical perforations forms the shape of a cross when viewed across the sheet.

780 Family
781 Woodland

(Des João Machado)

2008 (12 Mar). Infertility Awareness Campaign. P 12 (irregular indentation on each vert side).
3539	**780** 30c. multicoloured	60	45

The indentation in the vertical perforations forms the shape of a cross when viewed across the sheet.

(Des F. Galamba)

2008 (25 Mar). International Year of Planet Earth. T **781** and similar horiz designs. Multicoloured. P 12 (irregular indentation on each vert side).
3540	30c. Type **781**	60	45
3541	45c. Clouds	90	70
3542	61c. Volcano erupting	1·20	95
3543	75c. Under water	1·50	1·20
3540/3543	Set of 4	3·75	3·00

The indentation in the vertical perforations forms the shape of a cross when viewed across the sheet.

782 Throw
783 Father Antonio Vieira

(Des Elizabete Fonseca and Acácio Santos)

2008 (7 Apr). Sporting Events (1st issue). European Judo Championships. T **782** and similar horiz design. Multicoloured. P 12 (irregular indentation on each vert side).
3544	30c. Type **782**	60	45
3545	61c. Throw (different)	1·20	95

MS3546 125×95 mm. 45c. As Type **782** but including competition emblem; €2 As No. 3545 but including competition emblem ... 3·00 2·00
See also Nos. 3553/**MS**3556 and 3559.

PORTUGAL

(Des Andre Carrilho. Litho Cartor)

2008 (18 Apr). Personalities. T **783** and similar vert designs. Multicoloured. P 12 (irregular indentation on each horiz side).
3547	30c. Type **783** (Jesuit and writer) (400th birth anniv)	60	45
3548	30c. Jose Maria Mascarenhas Relvas (politician) (150th birth anniv)	60	45
3549	30c. Aureliano de Mira Fernandes (mathematician) (50th death anniv)	60	45
3550	30c Ricardo Jorge (physician and humanist) (150th birth anniv)	60	45
3551	30c. Maria Elena Vieira da Silva (artist) (birth centenary)	60	45
3552	30c. Manoel Candido Pinto de Oliveira (film director) (birth centenary)	60	45
3547/3552 Set of 6		3·00	2·25

The indentation in the horizontal perforations forms the shape of a cross when viewed across the sheet.

784 Runners   **785** Envelope Rider

(Des Joao Machado)

2008 (30 Apr). Sporting Events (2nd issue). Olympic Games, Beijing. T **784** and similar horiz designs. Multicoloured. P 12 (irregular indentation on each vert side).
3553	30c. Type **784**	60	45
3554	30c. Cyclists	60	45
3555	75c. Long jumper	1·50	1·20
3552/3555 Set of 3		2·50	1·90
MS3556 125×95 mm. 75c.×4, Show jumper; Rower; Marksman; Gymnast		6·00	4·50

The stamps and margins of No. **MS**3556 form a composite design.
The indentation in the vertical perforations forms the shape of a cross when viewed across the sheet.

(Des Luiz Duran Litho Cartor)

2008 (9 May). Europa. The Letter. T **785** and similar horiz design. Multicoloured. P 12 (irregular indentation on each vert side).
3557	61c. Type **785**	1·20	95
MS3558 125×95 mm. 61c.×2, As Type **785**; Postvan, envelope and bull		2·40	1·90

The stamps of No. **MS**3558 form a composite design.
The indentation in the vertical perforations forms the shape of a cross when viewed across the sheet.

786 Athletes (Illustration reduced. Actual size 80×30 mm)   **787** Mother, Child and Teacher

(Des Tulio Coelho)

2008 (9 May). Sporting Events (3rd issue). European Triathlon Championship, Lisbon. P 12 (irregular indentation on each vert side).
3559	**786** €2 multicoloured	4·00	3·00

The indentation in the vertical perforations forms the shape of a cross when viewed across the sheet.

(Des Alain Corbel)

2008 (2 June). The Rights of the Child. Right to Education. T **787** and similar vert designs. Multicoloured. P 12 (irregular indentation on each horiz side).
3560	30c. Type **787**	60	45
3561	45c. Teacher and pupils	90	70
3562	61c. Children reading	1·20	95
3563	75c. Child reading with parents	1·50	1·20
3560/3563 Set of 4		3·75	3·00
MS3564 95×125 mm. €2.95 Boy hugging '4'		6·00	4·50

The indentation in the horizontal perforations forms the shape of a cross when viewed across the sheet.

788 Players   **789** Esposende

(Des Joao Machado. Litho Cartor)

2008 (5 June). Euro 2008—European Football Championships, Austria and Switzerland. T **788** and similar vert design. Multicoloured. P 12 (irregular indentation on each horiz side).
3565	30c. Type **788**	60	45
3566	61c. Goal keeper catching ball and player	1·20	95
MS3567 125×95 mm. €1.20 Players heading ball; €1.66 Players tackling		5·75	4·50

The indentation in the horizontal perforations forms the shape of a cross when viewed across the sheet.

(Des A. Santos and H. Soares. Litho Cartor)

2008 (19 June). Lighthouses. T **789** and similar multicoloured designs. P 12 (irregular indentation on each horiz side) (vert) or 12 (irregular indentation on each vert side) (horiz).
3568	30c. Type **789**	60	50
3569	30c. Penedo da Saudade	60	50
3570	30c. Cabo Sardao (horiz)	60	50
3571	30c. Cabo da Roca (horiz)	60	50
3572	30c. Torre do Bugio (horiz)	60	50
3573	30c. Leça	60	50
3574	30c. Montedor	60	50
3575	30c. Santa Marta	60	50
3576	30c. Cabo de São Vicente (horiz)	60	50
3577	30c. Cabo Espichel	60	50
3568/3577 Set of 10		5·50	5·00

790 Calidris alba (sanderling)   **791** Vanwall 57 VW5 driven by Stirling Moss, 1958

(Des Nunu Farinha. Litho Cartor)

2008 (23 June). International Polar Year. T **790** and similar horiz designs. Multicoloured. P 12 (irregular indentation on each vert side).
3578	30c. Type **790**	60	45
3579	52c. Alca torda (razorbill)	1·00	85
3580	61c. Oceanites oceanicus (Wilson's storm-petrel)	1·20	95
3581	€1 Sterna paradisea (arctic tern)	2·00	1·60
MS3582 125×95 mm. €2.95 Phoca hispida (ringed seal) and Ursus maritimus (polar bear) (80×30 mm)		6·00	4·50

(Des Vasco Marques. Litho Cartor)

2008 (11 Sept). 50th Anniv of Formula I Grand Prix in Portugal. T **791** and similar horiz designs. Multicoloured. P 12 (irregular indentation on each vert side).
3583	31c. Type **791**	60	45
3584	67c. Cooper T53 driven by Jack Brabham, 1960	1·40	1·10
3585	80c. Cooper driven by Mark Haywood, 2005	1·60	1·20
3586	€2 McLaren M26 driven by Bobby Vernon Roe	4·00	3·00
3583/3586 Set of 4		7·00	5·00
MS3587 125×95 mm. €2.45 F1 Grand Prix, 1960 (80×30 mm)		5·00	3·75

The indentation in the horizontal perforations forms the shape of a cross when viewed across the sheet.

792 Symbols of Information Technology

2008 (15 Sept). Information Technology 'E-School' Programme. Sheet 125×95 mm. P 12 (irregular indentation on each vert side).
MS3588 **792** multicoloured .... 6·00 4·75
The indentation in the horizontal perforations forms the shape of a cross when viewed across the sheet.

793 Metal Work   **794** Vases (17th century)

(Des José Brandão. Litho Cartor)

2008 (19 Sept). Centenary of Group CUF. T **793** and similar multicoloured designs. P 12 (irregular indentation on each vert side).
3589   31c. Type **793** 60 45
3590   67c. Textiles .... 1·40 1·10
3591   €1 Naval construction .... 2·00 1·60
3592   €2 Chemicals .... 4·00 3·00
3589/3592 Set of 4 .... 7·25 7·00
MS3593 125×95 mm. €2.45 Alfredo da Silva (founder) (vert) .... 5·00 4·00
The indentation in the horizontal perforations forms the shape of a cross when viewed across the sheet.

(Des Folk Design)

2008 (26 Sept). Pharmaceutical Ceramics. T **794** and similar multicoloured designs. P 12 (irregular indentation on each vert side).
3594   31c. Type **794** 60 45
3595   47c. Bottle (18th century) .... 1·00 80
3596   67c. Vases (17th—18th century) .... 1·40 1·10
3597   80c. Vases (19th century) .... 1·60 1·20
3594/3597 Set of 4 .... 4·00 3·25
MS3598 125×95 mm. €2.45 Pharmacy (17th—18th century) .... 5·00 4·00
The indentation in the horizontal perforations forms the shape of a cross when viewed across the sheet.

795 Vineyard, Dão Region   **796** Centenary of First 'Executivo Republicano Camarário', Lisbon

(Des Atelier Acácio Santos)

2008 (2 Oct). Centenary of Demarcated Wine Regions. T **795** and similar horiz designs. Multicoloured. P 12 (irregular indentation on each vert side).
3599   31c. Type **795** 60 45
       a. Pair. Nos. 3599/600............................. 1·25
3600   31c. Barrels, Dão 60 45
3601   31c. Vineyard, Vinhos Verdes 60 45
       a. Pair. Nos. 3601/2 .... 1·25
3602   31c. Terraces, Vinhos Verdes 60 45
3603   31c. Vines, Colares 60 45
       a. Pair. Nos. 3603/4 .... 1·25
3604   31c. Barrels, Colares 60 45
3605   31c. Vineyard, Bucelas 60 45
       a. Pair. Nos. 3605/6 .... 1·25
3606   31c. Barrels, Bucelas 60 45
3607   31c. Barrels, Moscatel de Setúbal.............. 60 45
       a. Pair. Nos. 3607/8 .... 1·25
3608   31c. Vineyard, Moscatel de Setúbal.......... 60 45
3599/3608 Set of 10 .... 5·50 4·50
The indentation in the horizontal perforations forms the shape of a cross when viewed across the sheet.
Nos. 3599/600, 3601/2, 3603/4, 3605/6 and 3607/8, respectively, were issued in horizontal *se-tenant* pairs within the sheet, Nos. 3599/600, 3601/2, 3605/6 each forming a composite design.

(Des Vasco Marques. Litho Cartor)

2008 (5 Oct). Republican Ideas. T **796** and similar horiz designs. Multicoloured. P 12 (irregular indentation on each vert side).
3609   31c. Type **796** 60 45
3610   31c. Republican school 60 45
3611   47c. Industrialization .... 1·00 80
3612   47c. Housing .... 1·00 80
3613   57c. State modernization .... 1·20 95
3614   67c. Civil register .... 1·30 1·00
3615   67c. Public health .... 1·40 1·10
3616   80c. Civic participation .... 1·50 1·20
3609/3616 Set of 8 .... 8·00 6·00
MS3617 125×95 mm. €2.95 Rail—road link project over River Tejo (80×30 mm) .... 6·00 4·75
The indentation in the horizontal perforations forms the shape of a cross when viewed across the sheet.

797 Olive Grove   **798** Rainbow and Symbols of Communication (Érica Bluemel Potocarrero)

(Des Susana Brito and José Brandão)

2008 (7 Oct). Olive Oil Production. T **797** and similar horiz designs. Multicoloured. P 12 (irregular indentation on each vert side).
3618   31c. Type **797** 60 45
3619   47c. Early harvesters .... 1·00 80
3620   57c. Early milling .... 1·20 95
3621   67c. Mill stones .... 1·40 1·10
3622   80c. Oil storage .... 1·60 1·20
3623   €2 Ready for consumption .... 4·00 3·00
3618/3623 Set of 6 .... 8·00 6·75
MS3624 125×95 mm. €1.85 Hands holding olives .... 3·75 3·00
The indentation in the horizontal perforations forms the shape of a cross when viewed across the sheet.

2008 (9 Oct). School Correspondence. Childrens Drawings. T **798** and similar horiz designs. Multicoloured. P 12 (irregular indentation on each vert side).
3625   31c. Type **798** 60 45
3626   47c. Girl and symbols of communication (Eloisa Pereira) .... 1·00 80
3627   67c. Postman (João Mario Martins Branco)... 1·40 1·10
3625/3627 Set of 3 .... 2·75 2·00

799 Ponte 25 de Abril, Lisbon   **800** Mesoamerican Bas Relief and Ceramic Plate

(Des Atelier Acácio Santos)

2008 (16 Oct). Bridges. T **799** and similar horiz designs showing bridges. Multicoloured. P 12 (irregular indentation on each vert side).
3628   31c. Type **799** 60 45
3629   47c. Arrábida, Porto .... 1·00 80
3630   57c. Arade, Portimão .... 1·20 95
3631   67c. Mosteirô, Cinfães .... 1·40 1·10
3632   80c. Amizade, Vila Nova de Cerveira .... 1·60 1·20
3633   €1 Sta Clara, Coimbra .... 2·00 1·60
3628/3633 Set of 6 .... 7·00 5·50
MS3634 125×95 mm. €1.85 Ponte 25 de Abril (80×30 mm) .... 3·75 3·00
The indentation in the horizontal perforations forms the shape of a cross when viewed across the sheet.
No. 3628 was also available with a *se-tenant* stamp size label which could be personalised with the addition of a photograph or logo.

(Des L. Duran. Litho Cartor)

2008 (23 Oct). European Year of Intercultural Dialogue. T **800** and similar horiz designs. Multicoloured. P 12 (irregular indentation on each vert side).
3635   31c. Type **800** 60 45
3636   47c. Asian mask and Greek head .... 1·00 80
3637   67c. Moorish window and feathered headdress .... 1·40 1·10
3638   80c. African mask and Chinese lion headdress .... 1·60 1·20
3635/3638 Set of 4 .... 4·00 3·00

PORTUGAL

801 *Waiting for Success* (Henrique César de Araújo Pousão)

802 Euro Coins

(Des Francisco Galamba. Litho Cartor)

2009 (27 Jan). Personalities. T **801** and similar multicoloured design. P 12 (irregular indentation on each vert (3639) or horiz side (3640)).
3639	32c. Type **801** (artist) (150th birth anniv)......	65	50
3640	32c. Soeiro Pereira Gomes (writer) (birth centenary) (horiz)..............	65	50

(Des João Machado. Litho Cartor)

2009 (28 Jan). Tenth Anniv of Euro. T **802** and similar horiz design. Multicoloured. P 12 (irregular indentation on each vert side).
3641	47c. Type **802**	1·00	75
3642	€1 '€'...	2·00	1·50

803 Finches

803b Guitarist (ceramic statue)

(Des Elisabete Rolo and Jose Brandao. Litho Cartor)

2009 (12 Feb). Birth Bicentenary of Charles Darwin (naturalist and evolutionary theorist). T **803** and similar multicoloured designs. P 12 (irregular indentation on each vert (horiz stamps) or horiz side (MS3649)).
3643	32c. Type **803**	65	50
3644	32c. Iguana..	65	50
3645	68c. Orchid...	1·40	1·00
3646	68c. Diana monkey..	1·40	1·00
3647	80c. Platypus...	1·60	1·20
3648	80c. Skull and fossils.......................................	1·60	1·20
3643/3648	Set of 6...	6·50	4·75
MS3649	125×95 mm. €2.50 *Charles Darwin* (George Richmond) (vert)..................	5·50	3·75

(Des Elisabete Rolo and Jose Brandao)

2009 (26 Feb). African Heritage in Portugal. T **803b** and similar horiz designs. Multicoloured. P 12 (irregular indentation on each vert side).
3649a	32c. Type **803b**	65	50
3649b	47c. Trumpeter (altarpiece, St Auta (detail))...	1·00	75
3649c	57c. Three children (Conrado Roza)..............	1·10	75
3649d	68c. Woman...	1·40	1·00
3649e	80c. Woman's head (ceramic).......................	1·60	1·20
3649f	€2 Three musicians (painted wood)..............	4·25	3·00
3649a/3649f	Set of 6		
MS3649g	125×95 mm. €2.50 Musicians (Joaquim Marques)..............	4·50	3·00

Type **803a** is vacant.

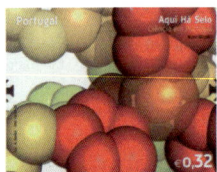
804 CotA-lacase Enzyme (Nuno Micaêlo)

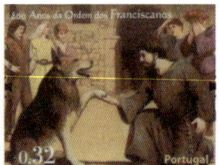
805 St. Francis and Dog

(Litho Cartor)

2009 (4 Mar). Aquihaselo. Winning Designs in Painting Competition. T **804** and similar horiz design. Multicoloured. P 12 (irregular indentation on each vert side).
3650	32c. Type **804**	65	50
3651	32c. Multiplication (Sa de Miranda School pupils)...................................	65	50

(Des Carlos Barahona. Litho Cartor)

2009 (11 Mar). 800th Anniv of Franciscan Order. T **805** and similar multicoloured designs. P 12 (irregular indentation on each vert (3652) or horiz side (MS3653)).
3652	32c. Type **805**	65	50
MS3653	125×95 mm. Size 31×40 mm. 50c. St. Francis kneeling; €2 Pope Innocent III giving blessing (vert)..............	5·50	4·00

806 Álvares Pereira

807 Eclipse of the Moon (3rd March 2007) Sequence

(Des Tulio Coelho. Litho Cartor)

2009 (26 Apr). Canonization of Nuno De Santa Maria (Álvares Pereira). P 12 (irregular indentation on each vert side).
3654	**806**	32c. multicoloured..	65	50

(Des Elizabete Fonseca. Litho Cartor)

2009 (8 May). Europa. Astronomy. T **807** and similar horiz design. Multicoloured. P 12 (irregular indentation on each vert side).
3655	68c. Type **807**	1·40	1·00
MS3656	125×95 mm. 68c.×2, European Southern Observatory's 'Very Large Telescope', Chile; As Type **807**...............	2·75	2·10

The stamps and margins of No. **MS**3657 form a composite design. The indentations in the vertical perforations form the shape of a cross when viewed across the sheet.

808 Iznik Mosque Lamp (Turkey)

809 Sanctuary

(Des Antonio Magalhaes. Litho Cartor)

2009 (12 May). Ceramics. T **808** and similar horiz design. Multicoloured. P 13×13½.
3657	32c. Type **808**	65	50
3658	68c. Ceramic Jar (Portugal)............................	1·40	1·00

Stamps of a similar design were issued by Turkey.

(Des Antonio Magalhaes)

2009 (17 May). 50th Anniv of Cristo Rei Sanctuary, South Bank of the River Tagus, near Lisbon. T **809** and similar multicoloured designs. P 12 (irregular indentation on each horiz side).
3659	32c. Type **809**	65	50
3660	68c. Christ (statue)...	1·40	1·00
MS3661	125×95 mm. €2.48 Head of Christ, bridge and Lisbon (80×31 mm).................	5·00	3·75

The indentations in the horizontal perforations form the shape of a cross when viewed across the sheet.

810 Bebinca das Sete Colinas (layered pudding) (India)

811 'Ensino' (training)

PORTUGAL

(Des Helder Soares. Litho Cartor)

2009 (5 June). Flavours of Lusophone (Portuguese speaking countries). T **810** and similar multicoloured designs. P 12 (irregular indentation on each vert (horiz stamps) or horiz side (**MS**3649)).

3662	32c. Type **810**	65	50
3663	32c. Leitoa num ar de Sarapatel (meat dish) (Brazil)	65	50
3664	68c. Caldeirada de cabrito (goat stew) (Angola)	1·40	1·00
3665	68c. Balcalhau, pao, vinho e azeite (cooked dried cod, bread, wine and olive oil)	1·40	1·00
3666	80c. No caldeiro a tempura (stew and tempura) (Asia)	1·60	1·20
3667	80c. Do cozido a Cachupa (slow boiled stew of corn, beans, vegetables, spices and marinated pork or tuna) (Cape Verde Islands)	1·60	1·20
3662/3667	Set of 6	6·50	5·00
MS3668	125×95 mm. €1.85 Balcalhau, pao, vinho e azeite (detail) (vert)	3·75	2·75

(Des Helder Soares. Litho Cartor)

2009 (16 June). The Lusitanian Horse. T **811** and similar vert designs. Multicoloured. P 12 (irregular indentation on each horiz side).

3669	32c. Type **811**	65	50
3670	32c. 'Equitacao de Trabalho' (working)	65	50
3671	57c. 'Toureio' (bullfighting)	1·20	90
3672	68c. 'Alta Escola' (schooling)	1·40	1·00
3673	80c. 'Atrelagem de Competicao' (Cape Verde Islands)	1·60	1·20
3669/3673	Set of 5	5·00	3·75
MS3674	125×95 mm. €2.50 'Alter-Real'	5·00	3·75

812 Alfonso Henriques (statue)

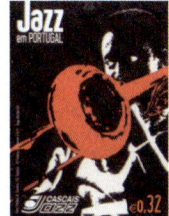
813 Trumpeter (Cascais Jazz)

(Des Elizabete Fonseca. Litho Cartor)

2009 (24 June). 900th Birth Anniv of Alfonso Henriques (Afonso I, first king of Portugal). T **812** and similar horiz design. Multicoloured. P 12 (irregular indentation on each vert side).

3675	32c. Type **812**	65	50
MS3676	95×125 mm. €3.07 On horseback	6·00	4·50

The indentations in the vertical perforations form the shape of a cross when viewed across the sheet.

(Des Adelino Insua, Carlos Barradas, Garizo do Carmo, João Machado, Pedro Morais and Sinais de Fumo)

2009 (26 June). Jazz in Portugal. T **813** and similar multicoloured designs. P 12 (irregular indentation on each vert (horiz stamps) or horiz side (**MS**3683)).

3677	32c. Type **813**	65	50
3678	47c. Trees and musicians as keyboard (Estoril Jazz Festival–Jazz On A Summer Day)	1·00	75
3679	57c. Saxophonist walking in street on instruments (Jazz in August, Calouste Gulbenkian Foundation)	1·20	90
3680	68c. Saxophonist (European Jazz Festival, Oporto)	1·40	1·00
3681	80c. Trumpeter (different) (Guimaraes Jazz Festival)	1·60	1·20
3682	€1 Fish playing saxophone (Seixal Jazz Festival)	2·00	1·50
3677/3682	Set of 6	6·50	4·75
MS3683	125×95 mm. €3.16 Hot Club of Portugal quartet	6·25	4·75

814 Pao de Centeio (rye bread)

815 Antonio Pedro

(Des Elizbete Fonseca and Atelier Acácio Santos . Litho Cartor)

2009 (28 July). Bread. T **814** and similar horiz designs showing loaves of bread. Multicoloured. P 12 (irregular indentation on each vert side.

3684	32c. Type **814**	65	50
3685	32c. Quartos (quartered)	65	50
3686	47c. Regueifa (Arabic bread)	1·00	75
3687	68c. Chouriço (bread with sausage)	1·40	1·00
3688	68c. Testa ('brow' bread)	1·40	1·00
3689	80c. Mealhada (bread from Mealhada)	1·60	1·20
3684/3689	Set of 6	6·00	4·50

Nos. 3690/3691 are vacant.

(Des Whitestudio)

2009 (1 Sept). Birth Centenary of António Pedro da Costa (actor, writer and painter). T **815** and similar horiz design. Multicoloured. P 12 (irregular indentation on each vert side).

3692	32c. Type **815**	65	50
MS3693	125×95 mm. €3.16 Facing right	6·25	4·75

816 Building Façade, 1841

817 Pandion haliaetus (Osprey)

(Des Folk Design)

2009 (17 Sept). Belém Palace. T **816** and similar horiz designs. Multicoloured. P 12 (irregular indentation on each vert side).

3694	32c. Type **816**	65	50
3695	47c. Pintura das Sobreporta (painting over doorway)	1·00	75
3696	57c. Copper and silver writing equipment	1·20	90
3697	68c. Satyrs (bas relief)	1·40	1·00
3698	80c. Gold Room, detail of the ceiling molding	1·60	1·20
3699	€1 Floral allegory	2·00	1·50
3694/3699	Set of 6	7·00	5·25
MS3700	125×95 mm. €2.50 Salas das Bicas (fountain room)	5·50	3·75

(Des Atelier Acacio Santos)

2009 (21 Sept). Raptors. T **817** and similar vert design. Multicoloured. P 13½.

3701	32c. Type **817**	65	50
	a. Pair. Nos. 3701/2	2·50	1·75
3702	80c. Haliaeetus albicilla (White-tailed eagle)	1·60	1·20

Stamps of a similar design were issued by Iran.

818 Coffee (smell)

819 Adelaide Cabete

(Des Joao Machado or Atleier Acacio Santos (**MS**3708). Litho or litho and embossed (**MS**3708) Cartor)

2009 (2 Oct). Stamps and the Senses. Birth Bicentenary of Louis Braille (inventor of Braille writing for the blind) (**MS**3718). T **818** and similar multicoloured designs. P 12 (irregular indentation on each vert side).

3703	32c. Type **818**	65	50
3704	68c. Ice lolly (taste)	1·40	1·00
3705	80c. Glasses (vision)	1·60	1·20
3706	€1 Paint (touch)	2·00	1·50
3707	€2 File (Hearing)	4·00	3·00
3703/3707	Set of 5	8·50	6·50
MS3708	135×105 mm. €2.50 Louis Braille	5·00	3·75

No. **MS**3708 is embossed with Braille letters.

PORTUGAL

(Des Folk Design)

2009 (5 Oct). Women of the Republic. T **819** and similar vert designs. Multicoloured. P 12 (irregular indentation on each horiz side).
3709	32c. Type **819**	65	50
3710	32c. Maria Veleda	65	50
3711	57c. Ana de Castro Osorio	1·20	90
3712	68c. Angelina Vidal	1·40	1·00
3713	80c. Carolina Beatriz Angelo	1·60	1·20
3714	€1 Carolina Michaelis	2·00	1·50
3709/3714	Set of 6	6·50	5·00
MS3715	125×95 mm. €1.15×2, Virginia Quaresma; Emilia de Sousa Costa	4·50	3·50

820 Children (Martina Marques Teixeira Santos)

821 Santa and Hearts

(Des Antonio Magalhaes. Litho Cartor)

2009 (9 Oct). School Correspondence. Children's Drawings. T **820** and similar horiz designs. Multicoloured. P 12 (irregular indentation on each vert side).
3716	32c. Type **820**	65	50
3717	47c. 'Lets recycle to improve the world' (Joel Filipe Silva Carmo)	1·00	75
3718	68c. Post boxes and recycle bins (Manuel Pedro A. B. Paiva Martins)	1·40	1·00
3716/3718	Set of 3	2·75	2·00

(Des Joao Machado. Litho Cartor)

2009 (21 Oct). Christmas. T **821** and similar horiz designs. Multicoloured. P 12 (irregular indentation on each horiz side).
3719	32c. Type **821**	65	50
3720	47c. Santa delivering letter through window	1·00	75
3721	68c. Christmas tree and Santa	1·30	1·00
3722	80c. Santa and reindeer	1·60	1·20
3719/3722	Set of 4	4·00	3·00
MS3723	125×95 mm. 50c. Santa riding reindeer on rocker; €1 Stocking containing Santa and parcels	3·00	2·20

MACHINE LABELS

A **1**

FRAMA LABELS. From 19 May 1981 gummed labels in design A, printed in red on paper with a blue security underprint and ranging in vlaue from 50c. to 999E.50, were available from six automatic machines, with further machines in use later. The number in the bottom frame indicates the machine.
  001, Portimao (1 September 1981)
  002, Terreiro do Paco, Lisbon (2 December 1981)
  003, Faro (1 September 1981)
  004, Santa Maria, Lisbon
  005, Vila Real de Santo, António (1 September 1981)
  006, Albufeira (1 September 1981)
  007, Lagos (1 September 1981)
  008, Lisbon Airport (1 December 1985)
  009, Funchal, Maderia (15 January 1986)
  010, Restauradores, Lisbon (15 July 1987)
Machine No. 4 was withdrawn from use in November 1985, No. 5 in December 1985, No. 2 in July 1987, Nos. 1, 3, 6 and 7 in April 1988 and Nos. 8, 9 and 10 in February 1990.

From 1990 onwards automatic machines of various makes were installed throughout the country, all dispensing labels from 1 to 9999E. in 1E. steps. The different designs are grouped according to type of machine.

B. KLUSSENDORF

All Klussendorf designs have every fifth label numbered on the back.

B **1** Post Rider

(Des A. Santos. Typo Unipress, Germany)

1990 (5 Sept). Type B **1**. Brown and brown-ochre. Two phosphor bands.
Fixed values   5.9.90 32, 60, 70, 95E.
              10.5.91 35, 60, 80, 110E.
              1.1.92 38, 65, 70, 120E.
              9.3.93 40, 70, 90, 130E.

B **2** Caravelle

(Des Ana Bela Silva. Typo Enschedé)

1992 (9 Oct). Ships. As Type B **2**. Black, new blue and grey-brown. Simulated perforation holes.
Fixed values   9.10.90 38, 65, 70, 120E.
              9.3.93 40, 70, 90, 130E.
              1.3.95 40, 75, 95, 135E.
              1.3.96 45, 75, 95, 140E.
              1.1.97 45, 80, 100, 140E.
                National (75E.), International (350E.)
              1.3.98 50, 80, 100, 140E.
                National (75E.), International (350E.)
              25.10.99 50, 85, 95, 100, 140E.
                National (80E.), International (350E.)
              1.1.00 50, 85, 90, 100, 140E.
                National (85E.), International (350E.)
  Labels overprinted "Correio Azul" are available at the national and international rate.

(Des Ana Bela Silva. Typo Enschedé)

1993 (9 Oct). Ships. Design as Type B **2** showing a Portuguese Nau. Black, turquoise and grey. Simulated perforation holes.
Fixed values   9.10.93 40, 70, 90, 130E.
              1.3.95 40, 75, 95, 140E.
              1.3.96 45, 75, 95, 140E.
              1.1.97 45, 80, 100, 140E.
                National (75E.), International (350E.)
              1.3.98 50, 80, 100, 140E.
                National (75E.), International (350E.)
              25.10.99 50, 85, 95, 100, 140E.
                National (80E.), International (350E.)
              1.1.00 50, 85, 90, 100, 140E.
                National (85E.), International (350E.)
  Labels overprinted "Correio Azul" are available at the national and international rate.

(Des Ana Bela Silva. Typo Enschedé)

1995 (20 Apr). Ships. Design as Type B **2** showing a Galleon. Black, yellow-orange and light blue. Simulated perforation holes.
Fixed values   20.4.95 40, 75, 95, 135E.
              1.3.96 45, 75, 95, 140E.
              1.1.97 45, 80, 100, 140E.
                National (75E.), International (350E.)
              1998 50, 80, 100, 140E.
                National (75E.), International (350E.)
              1999 50, 85, 95, 100, 140E.
                National (80E.), International (350E.)
              2000 50, 85, 90, 100, 140E.
                National (85E.), International (350E.)
  Labels overprinted "Correio Azul" are available at the national and international rate. These labels were also issued without the numbering on the back and in paler colours on the following dates; 1 Jan 1997, 1 Jan 1998, 25 Oct 1999 and 1 Jan 2000.

PORTUGAL

B **3** Flamingo

(Des J. Projecto. Litho The Mint, Lisbon)

2000 (5 Sept). Birds. Design as Type B **3**. Multicoloured. Simulated perforations (right-hand side).
Fixed values   5.9.00 50, 85, 100, 140E.
                 National (85E.), International (350E.)

C. CROUZET

All Crouzet labels are self-adhesive.

C **1** Espigueiro, North Portugal

(Des V. Santos. Litho French State Ptg Wks, Paris)

1991 (15 Nov). Design as Type C **1**. New blue, green and olive-yellow.
Fixed values   15.11.91 35, 75, 140E. 40, 75, 170E.
                 National (75E.), International (350E.)
Labels overprinted "Correio Azul" are available at the national and international rate.

1992 (1 July). Design as Type C **1** but with simulated perforation holes.
Fixed values   1.7.92 38, 70, 155E. 40, 75, 170E.
                 National (75E.), International (350E.)
Labels overprinted "Correio Azul" are available at the national and international rate.

C **2** Monocyclist

(Des V. Santos. Litho French State Ptg Wks, Paris)

1992 (9 Oct). Mechanical Toys. Design as Type C **2**. Bright scarlet, new blue and lemon.
Fixed values   9.10.92 38, 70, 155E.
                 9.3.93 40, 75, 170E.
                 1.9.94 National (75E.), International (350E.)
                 1994 40, 75, 180E.
                 1995 40, 75, 190E.
Labels overprinted "Correio Azul" are available at the national and international rate.

1995 (15 Feb). Design as Type C **2** showing pecking chickens. Turquoise-green, rose-red and greenish yellow.
Fixed values   15.2.95 40, 70, 190E.
                 National (75E.), International (350E.)
Labels overprinted "Correio Azul" are available at the national and international rate.

1995 (13 June). Design as Type C **2** showing pecking chickens. Turquoise-green, rose-red and greenish yellow. Simulated perforation holes.
Fixed values   13.6.95 40, 75, 190E.
                 National (75E.), International (350E.)
                 1.3.96 45, 75, 200E.
                 National (75E.), International (350E.)
                 1.1.97 45, 80, 200E.
                 National (75E.), International (350E.)
                 1.1.98 45, 80, 200E.
                 National (80E.), International (350E.)
Labels overprinted "Correio Azul" are available at the national and international rate.

1997 (8 Jan). Design as Type C **2** showing pecking chickens. Smaller design (?? x ?? mm). Turquoise-green, rose-red and greenish yellow. Simulated perforation holes.
Fixed values   8.1.97 45, 75, 95, 200E.
                 National (75E.), International (350E.)
                 1.1.98 50, 85, 100, 210E.
                 1.1.99 50, 95, 140, 210E.
                 National (80E.), International (350E.)
Labels overprinted "Correio Azul" are available at the national and international rate.

1999 (7 Aug). Design as Type C **2** showing pecking chickens. Face values in Portuguese Escudo and in euros. Simulated perforation holes.
Fixed values   7.8.99 50E./25c., 85E./42c., 95E./47c., 100E./50c., 140E./70c.
                 National (80E./40c.), International (350E./€1.75)
                 Jan 2000 50E./25c., 85E./42c., 90E./??c., 100E./50c., 140E./70c.
                 National (85E./40c.), International (350E./€1.75)
Labels overprinted "Correio Azul" are available at the national and international rate.

C **3** Wooden Bird

(Des V. Santos. Litho)

1995 (9 Oct). Mechanical Toys. Design as Type C **3**. Multicoloured. Simulated perforation holes.
Fixed values   9.10.95 45, 75, 95, 200E.
                 National (75E.), International (350E.)
                 1.8.99 50, 85, 95, 100, 140E.
                 National (80E.), International (350E.)
Labels overprinted "Correio Azul" are available at the national and international rate.

1996 (18 Dec). Mechanical Toys. Designs as Type C **3** showing wooden bird additionally inscr "Felix Azul". Multicoloured. Simulated perforation holes.
Fixed values   18.12.96 45, 75, 95, 200E.
                 National (75E.), International (350E.)
Labels overprinted "Correio Azul" are available at the national and international rate.
These labels were only available between 18 December 1996 and 7 January 1997.

1999 (7 Aug). Mechanical Toys. Designs as Type C **3** showing wooden bird. Face values in Portuguese Escudos and in euros. Multicoloured. Simulated perforation holes.
Fixed values   7.8.99 50E./25c., 85E./52c., 95E./47c., 100E./50c., 140E./50c.
                 National (80E./40c.), International (350E./€1.75)
                 Jan 2000 50E./25c., 85E./52c., 90E./??c., 100E./50c., 140E./50c.
                 National (85E./??c.), International (350/€1.75)
Labels overprinted "Correio Azul" are available at the national and international rate.

C **4** Exhibition Emblem

(Des F. Rego. Litho)

1997 (9 Oct). Design as Type C **4** showing the exhibition emblem for "Expo '98" International Philatelic Exhibition, Lisbon. Multicoloured. Face values in black. Simulated perforation holes.
Fixed values   9.10.97 45, 80, 100, 140E.
                 National (75E.), International (350E.)
                 1.1.99 50, 95, 100, 140E.
                 National (80E.), International (350E.)
Labels overprinted "Correio Azul" are available at the national and international rate.

PORTUGAL

1997 (9 Oct). Design as Type C **4** showing "Expo '98" exhibition emblem. Multicoloured. Face values in blue. Simulated perforation holes.
Fixed values   9.10.97 45, 80, 100, 140E.
                National (75E.), International (350E.)

1999 (7 Aug). Design as Type C **4** showing "Expo '98" exhibition emblem. Multicoloured. Face values in Portuguese Escudos and in euros. Simulated perforation holes.
Fixed values   7.8.99 50E./25c., 85E./42c., 95E./47c., 100E./50c., 140E./70c.
                National (80E./40c.), International (350E./€1.75)
                Jan 2000 50E./25c., 85E./42c., 90E./??c., 100E./50c., 140E./70c.
                National (85E./??c.), International (350E./€1.75)

Labels overprinted "Correio Azul" are available at the national and international rate.

C **5** The Knife Grinder

(Des J. L. Tinoco. Litho)

1999 (26 Feb). Design as Type C **5**. Multicoloured. Simulated perforations (right-hand side).
Fixed values   26.2.99 50, 95, 100, 140E.
                National (80E.), International (350E.)

Labels overprinted "Correio Azul" are available at the national and international rate.

1999 (7 Aug). Design as Type C **5**. Multicoloured. Face values in Portuguese Escudos and in euros.
Fixed values   7.8.99 50E./25c., 85E./42c., 95E./47c., 100E./50c., 140E./70c.
                National (80E./40c.), International (350E./€1.75)
                Jan 2000 50E./25c., 85E./42c., 90E./??c., 100E./50c., 140E./70c.
                National (85E./??c.), International (350E./€1.75)

Labels overprinted "Correio Azul" are available at the national and international rate.

C **6** Green-winged Teal

(Des J. Projecto. Litho)

2000 (5 Sept). Birds. Design as Type C **6**. Multicoloured. Face values in Portuguese Escudos and euros. Simulated perforation hole (right-hand side).
Fixed values   5.9.00 50E./25c., 95E./47c., 100E./50c. 140E./70c.
                National (85E./42c.), International (350E./€1.75)
                2001 50E./25c., 90E./??c., 105E./??c., 140E./70c.
                National (85E./42c.), International (350E./€1.75)
                2002 27c., 45c., 46c., 54c., 70c.
                National (47c.), International (€1.75)

Labels overprinted "Correio Azul" are available at the national and international rate.

C **7** The Euro

(Des A. Santos. Litho)

2002 (1 Mar). Design as Type C **7**. Multicoloured. Simulated perforations (right-hand side).
Fixed values   1.3.02 27, 46, 54, 70c.
                National (43c.), International (€1.75)
                2003 30, 46, 47, 55, 70c.
                National (43c.), International (€1.75)

Labels overprinted "Correio Azul" are available at the national and international rate.

C **8** Emblem

(Des A. Santos. Litho)

2003 (29 Apr). European Football Championship 2004, Portugal. Design as Type C **8**. Multicoloured. Simulated perforations (right-hand side).
Fixed values   29.4.03 30, 47, 55, 70c.
                National (43c.), International (€1.75)

Labels overprinted "Correio Azul" are available at the national and international rate.

C **9** Emblem

(Des A. Santos. Litho)

2004 (2 Feb). European Football Championship 2004, Portugal. Design as Type C **9**. Multicoloured. Simulated perforations (right-hand side).
Fixed values: 2.2.04 30, 45 (National), 48, 56, 72c, €1.75 (International)

Labels overprinted "Correio Azul" were at the national and international rate.

C **10** Heart

(Des V. Santos)

2004 (12 July). Tenth Anniv of International Year of the Family. Design as Type C **10**. Multicoloured. Simulated perforations (right-hand side).
Fixed values: 12.7.04 30, 45 (National), 48, 56, 72c, €1.75 (International)

Labels overprinted "Correio Azul" were at the national and international rate.

C **11** Stylized Person and Heart Rate

(Des C. Leitao)

2005 (14 Feb). Campaign for the Prevention of Heart Disease. Design as Type C **11**. Multicoloured. Simulated perforations (right-hand side).
Fixed values: 14.2.05 30, 45 (National), 48, 57, 74c, €1.75 (International)

Labels overprinted "Correio Azul" were at the national and international rate.

PORTUGAL

C **12** Cat

(Des V. Matos)

2005 (18 July). Domestic Animals. Designs as Type C **12** showing different pets. Design as Type C **12**. Multicoloured. Simulated perforations (right-hand side).
Fixed values: 14.2.05 30, 45 (National), 48, 57, 74c., €1.75 (International) (Type C **12** and Parrot)
Labels overprinted "Correio Azul" were at the national and international rate.

C **13** Wind Turbines

(Des J. Machado)

2006 (22 May). Alternative Energy. Design as Type C **13**. Multicoloured. Simulated perforations (right-hand side).
Fixed values: 22.5.06 30, 45 (National), 52, 60, 74c., €1.80 (International)
Labels overprinted "Correio Azul" were at the national and international rate.

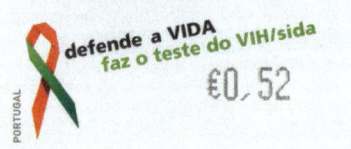

C **14** Campaign Emblem

(Des V. Marques)

2006 (20 Oct). AIDS Awareness Campaign. Design as Type C **14**. Multicoloured. Simulated perforations (right-hand side).
Fixed values: 20.10.06 30, 45 (National), 48, 52, 60, 75c., €1.80 (International)
Labels overprinted "Correio Azul" were at the national and international rate.

C **15** Children playing

(Des L. Duran)

2007 (28 May). Child Protection Campaign. Design as Type C **15**. Multicoloured. Simulated perforations (right-hand side).
Fixed values: 28.5.07 30, 45 (National), 48, 52, 60, 75c., €1.80 (International)
Labels overprinted "Correio Azul" were at the national and international rate.

C **16** European Flag and Stylized People

2007 (9 Oct). European Year of Equal Opporunities. Design as Type C **16**. Multicoloured. Simulated perforations (right-hand side).
Fixed values: 9.10.07 30, 45 (National), 52, 61, 75c., €1.85 (International)
Labels overprinted "Correio Azul" were at the national and international rate.

C **17** Fireman's Helmet

(Des R. Rodrigues)

2008 (30 May). Volunteer Fire Department. Design as Type C **17**. Multicoloured. Simulated perforations (right-hand side).
Fixed values: 30.5.08 30, 45 (National), 52, 61, 75c., €1.85 (International)
Labels overprinted "Correio Azul" were at the national and international rate.

C **18** Emblem

(Des F. Galamba)

2008 (31 Oct). 50 Years of the Portuguese Blood Institute. Design as Type C **18**. Multicoloured. Simulated perforations (right-hand side).
Fixed values: 31.10.08 30, 45 (National), 52, 61, 75c., €1.85 (International)
Labels overprinted "Correio Azul" were at the national and international rate.

C **19** Recycling Emblem

(Des E. Aires)

2009 (15 Apr). Recycling. Design as Type C **19**. Multicoloured. Simulated perforations (right-hand side).
Fixed values: 15.4.09 32, 47 (National), 54, 57, 68, 80c., €1.85 (International)
Labels overprinted "Correio Azul" were at the national and international rate.

C **20** Recycling Emblem

(Des J. Machado)

2009 (9 Oct). Campaign for Healthy Eating. Design as Type C **20**. Multicoloured. Simulated perforations (right-hand side).
Fixed values: 9.10.09 32, 47 (National), 54, 57, 68, 80c., €1.85 (International)
Labels overprinted "Correio Azul" were at the national and international rate.

PORTUGAL

C **21** Emblem

2010 (11 May). European Year for Combating Poverty. Design as Type C **21**. Multicoloured. Simulated perforations (right-hand side).
Fixed values: 11.5.10 32, 47 (National), 54, 57, 68, 80c., €1.85 (International)
Labels overprinted "Correio Azul" were at the national and international rate.

D. OLIVETTI

D **1** Travelling Post Office (1950s)

(Des Ana Bela Silva. Litho The Mint, Lisbon)

1995 (14 Nov). Design as Type D **1**. Vermilion and black. Simulated perforation holes.
Fixed values 14.11.95 40, 75, 95, 135E.
1.3.96 45, 75, 94, 140E.
1.3.97 45, 80, 100, 140E.
National (75E.), International (350E.)
1.3.98 50, 80, 100, 140E.
National (75E.), International (350E.)
25.10.99 50, 85, 95, 100, 140E.
National (80E.), International (350E.)
1.1.00 50, 85, 90, 100, 140E.
National (85E.), International (350E.)
Labels overprinted "Correio Azul" are available at the national and international rate.

D **2** Exhibition Emblem

(Des F. Rego. Litho The Mint, Lisbon)

1997 (9 Oct). Design as Type D **2** showing the exhibition emblem for "Expo '98" International Philatelic Exhibition, Lisbon. Multicoloured. Simulated perforation holes.
Fixed values 9.10.97 45, 80, 100, 140E.
National (75E.), International (350E.)
1.3.98 50, 80, 100, 140E.
National (75E.), International (350E.)
25.10.99 50, 85, 95, 100, 140E.
National (80E.), International (350E.)
1.1.00 50, 85, 90, 100, 140E.
National (85E.), International (350E.)
Labels overprinted "Correio Azul" are available at the national and international rate.

E. MULTIPLE MACHINES

E **1** Fish

(Des Marta Caralho. Litho)

1998 (29 Apr). "Expo '98" International Philatelic Exhibition, Lisbon. Multicoloured. Simulated perforation holes.
(a) AMIEL (Automatic Electronic Printing Machine) (with $ in face value)
Fixed values 29.4.98 50, 85, 100, 140E.
National (85E.), International (350E.)
(b) AMIEL (Automatic Electronic Printing Machine) (with dot in face value)
Fixed values 22.3.99 50, 85, 95, 100, 140E.
National (80E.), International (350E.)
(c) AMIEL (Automatic Electronic Printing Machine) (face values in Portuguese Escudos and in euros)
Fixed values 21.2.00 50E./25c., 85E./42c., 90E./45c., 100E./50c., 140E./70c.
National (85E./42c.), International (350E./€1.75)
Jan 2001 50E./25c., 90E./??c., 105E./??c., 140E./70c.
National (85E./42c.), International (350E./€1.75)
(d) SMD (Multipost and Distribution System)
Fixed values 29.4.03 50, 85, 100, 140E.
National (80E.), International (350E.)
(e) SMD (Multipost and Distribution System) (face values in Portuguese Escudos and in euros)
Fixed values 13.3.00 50E./25c., 85E./42c., 90E./45c., 100E./50c., 140E./70c.
National (85E./42c.), International (350E./€1.75)
Jan 2001 50E./25c., 90E./45c., 105E./??c., 140E./70c.
National (85E./42c.), International (350E./€1.75)
Labels overprinted "Correio Azul" are available at the national and international rate.

E **2** Horses and Carriage

(Des C. Leitao. Litho)

1998 (15 May). Design as Type E **2**. Multicoloured. Simulated perforations (right-hand side).
(a) AMIEL (Automatic Electronic Printing Machine)
Fixed values 15.5.98 50, 85, 100, 140E.
National (80E.), International (350E.)
(b) AMIEL (Automatic Electronic Printing Machine) (face values in Portuguese Escudos and in Euros)
Fixed values 21.2.00 50E./25c., 85E./42c., 90E./45c., 100E./50c., 140E./70c.
National (85E./42c.), International (350E./€1.75)
Jan 2001 50E./25c., 90E./45c., 105E./50c., 140E./70c.
National (85E./42c.), International (350E./€1.75)
Jan 2002 27, 45, 46, 54, 70c.
National (43c.), International (€1.75)
(c) SMD (Multipost and Distribution System) (face values in Portuguese Escudos)
Fixed values 15.5.98 50, 85, 100, 140E.
National (80E.), International (350E.)
(d) SMD (Multipost and Distribution System) (face values in Portuguese Escudos and in euros)
Fixed values 13.3.00 50E./25c., 85E./42c., 90E./45c. 100E./50c., 140E./70c.
National (85E./42c.), International (350E./€1.75)
Jan 2001 50E./25, 90E./45c., 105E./??c., 140E./70c.
National (85E./42c.), International (350E./€1.75)
Labels overprinted "Correio Azul" are available at the national and international rate.

E **3** Dinosaurs

(Des J. Projecto. Litho)

1999 (9 Nov). Dinosaurs. Designs as Type E **3** all showing different dinosaurs. Multicoloured. Simulated perforations (right-hand side).

(a) AMIEL (Automatic Electronic Printing Machine)
Fixed values   9.11.99 50, 95, 100, 140E.
              National (80E.), International (350E.)

(b) AMIEL (Automatic Electronic Printing Machine) (face values in Portuguese Escudos and in Euros)
Fixed values   21.2.00 50E./25c., 85E./42c., 90E./45c., 100E./50c., 140E./70c.
              National (85E./42c.), International (350E./€1.75)
              Jan 2001 50E./25c., 90E./45c., 105E./50c., 140E./70c.
              National (85E./42c.), International (350E./€1.75)
              Jan 2002 27, 45, 46, 54, 70c.
              National (43c.), International (€1.75)

(c) SMD (Multipost and Distribution System) (face values in Portuguese Escudos)
Fixed values   9.11.99 50, 95, 100, 140E.
              National (80E.), International (350E.)

(d) SMD (Multipost and Distribution System) (face values in Portuguese Escudos and in euros)
Fixed values   13.3.00 50E./25c., 85E./42c., 90E./45c., 100E./50c., 140E./70c.
              National (85E./42c.), International (350E./€1.75)
              Jan 2001 50E./25c., 90E./45c., 105E./50c., 140E./70c.
              National (85E./42c.), International (350E./€1.75)
              Jan 2002 27, 45, 46, 54, 70c.
              National (43c.), International (€1.75)

Labels overprinted "Correio Azul" are available at the national and international rate.

E **4** The Euro

(Des A. Santos. Litho)

2002 (1 Mar). The Euro Currency. Design as Type E **4**. Multicoloured. Simulated perforations (left-hand side).

(a) AMIEL (Automatic Electronic Printing Machine) (with dot in face value)
Fixed values   1.3.02 27, 45, 46, 54, 70c.
              National (43c.), International (€1.75)

(b) AMIEL (with comma in face value)
Fixed values   1.3.02 27, 45, 46, 54, 70c.
              National (43c.), International (€1.75)
              2003 30, 46, 47, 55, 70c.
              National (43c.), International (€1.75)

(c) SMD (Multipost and Distribution System)
Fixed values   1.3.02 27, 45, 46, 54, 70C.
              National (43c.), International (€1.75)
              2003 30, 46, 47, 55, 70c.
              National (43c.), International (€1.75)

(d) e-post
Fixed values   1.3.02 27, 45, 46, 54, 70c.
              National (43c.), International (€1.75)
              2003 30, 46, 47, 55, 70c.
              National (43c.), International (€1.75)

Labels overprinted "Correio Azul" are available at the national and international rate.

E **5** Emblem

(Des A. Santos. Litho)

2003 (29 Apr). European Football Championship 2004, Portugal. Design as Type E **5**. Multicoloured. Simulated perforations (right-hand side).

(a) AMIEL (Automatic Electronic Printing Machine) (with dot in face value)
Fixed values   29.4.03 30, 46, 47, 55, 70c.
              National (43c.), International (€1.75)

(b) AMIEL (with comma in face value)
Fixed values   29.4.03 30, 46, 47, 55, 70c.
              National (43c.), International (€1.75)

(c) SMD (Multipost and Distribution System)
Fixed values   29.4.03 30, 46, 47, 55, 70c.
              National (43c.), International (€1.75)

(d) e-post
Fixed values   29.4.03 30, 46, 47, 55, 70c.
              National (43c.), International (€1.75)

Labels overprinted "Correio Azul" are available at the national and international rate.

E **6** Emblem

2004 (2 Feb). European Football Championship 2004, Portugal. Design as Type E **6**. Multicoloured. Simulated perforations (right-hand side).

(a) AMIEL (Automatic Electronic Printing Machine) (with dot in face value)
Fixed values: 2.2.04 30, 45 (National), 48, 56, 72c, €1.75 (International)

(b) AMIEL (with comma in face value)
Fixed values: 2.2.04 30, 45 (National), 48, 56, 72c, €1.75 (International)

(c) SMD (Multipost and Distribution System)
Fixed values: 2.2.04 30, 45 (National), 48, 56, 72c, €1.75 (International)

(d) e-post
Fixed values: 2.2.04 30, 45 (National), 48, 56, 72c, €1.75 (International)

Labels overprinted "Correio Azul" were at the national and international rate.

E **7** Heart

(Des V. Santos)

2004 (12 July). Tenth Anniv of International Year of the Family. Design as Type E **7**. Multicoloured. Simulated perforations (right-hand side).

(a) AMIEL (Automatic Electronic Printing Machine) (with dot in face value)
Fixed values: 12.7.04 30, 45 (National), 48, 56, 72c., €1.75 (International)

(b) AMIEL (with comma in face value)
Fixed values: 12.7.04 30, 45 (National), 48, 56, 72c., €1.75 (International)

(c) SMD (Multipost and Distribution System)
Fixed values: 12.7.04 30, 45 (National), 48, 56, 72c., €1.75 (International)

(d) e-post
Fixed values: 12.7.04 30, 45 (National), 48, 56, 72c., €1.75 (International)

Labels overprinted "Correio Azul" were at the national and international rate.

E **8** Stylized Person and Heart Rate

PORTUGAL

(Des C. Leitao)

2005 (14 Feb). Campaign for the Prevention of Heart Disease. Design as Type E **8**. Multicoloured. Simulated perforations (right-hand side).

(a) AMIEL (Automatic Electronic Printing Machine) (with dot in face value)
Fixed values: 14.2.05 30, 45 (National), 46, 48, 57, 74c., €1.75 (International)

(b) AMIEL (with comma in face value)
Fixed values: 14.2.05 30, 45 (National), 46, 48, 57, 74c., €1.75 (International)

(c) SMD (Multipost and Distribution System)
Fixed values: 14.2.05 30, 45 (National), 46, 48, 57, 74c., €1.75 (International)

(d) e-post
Fixed values: 14.2.05 30, 45 (National), 46, 48, 57, 74c., €1.75 (International)

Labels overprinted "Correio Azul" were at the national and international rate.

E **9** Guinea Pig

(Des V. Matos)

2005 (18 July). Domestic Animals. Designs as Type E **9** showing different pets. Multicoloured. Simulated perforations (right-hand side).

(a) AMIEL (Automatic Electronic Printing Machine) (with dot in face value)
Fixed values: 18.7.05 30, 45 (National), 46, 48, 57, 74c., €1.75 (International) (Type E9, Dog)

(b) AMIEL (with comma in face value)
Fixed values: 18.7.05 30, 45 (National), 46, 48, 57, 74c., €1.75 (International) (Type E9, Dog)

(c) SMD (Multipost and Distribution System)
Fixed values: 18.7.05 30, 45 (National), 46, 48, 57, 74c., €1.75 (International) (Type E9, Dog)

(d) e-post
Fixed values: 18.7.05 30, 45 (National), 46, 48, 57, 74c., €1.75 (International) (Type E9, Dog)

Labels overprinted "Correio Azul" were at the national and international rate.

E **10** Solar Panels

(Des J. Machado)

2006 (22 May). Alternative Energy. Design as Type E **10**. Multicoloured. Simulated perforations (right-hand side).

(a) AMIEL (Automatic Electronic Printing Machine) (with dot in face value)
Fixed values: 22.5.06 30, 45 (National), 48, 52, 60, 75c., €1.80 (International)

(b) AMIEL (with comma in face value)
Fixed values: 22.5.06 30, 45 (National), 48, 52, 60, 75c., €1.80 (International)

(c) SMD (Multipost and Distribution System)
Fixed values: 22.5.06 30, 45 (National), 48, 52, 60, 75c., €1.80 (International)

(d) e-post
Fixed values: 22.5.06 30, 45 (National), 48, 52, 60, 75c., €1.80 (International)

Labels overprinted "Correio Azul" were at the national and international rate.

E **11** Campaign Emblem

(Des V. Marques)

2006 (20 Oct). AIDS Awareness Campaign. Design as Type E **11**. Multicoloured. Simulated perforations (right-hand side).

(a) AMIEL (Automatic Electronic Printing Machine) (with dot in face value)
Fixed values: 20.10.06 30, 45 (National), 48, 52, 60, 75c., €1.80 (International)

(b) AMIEL (with comma in face value)
Fixed values: 20.10.06 30, 45 (National), 48, 52, 60, 75c., €1.80 (International)

(c) SMD (Multipost and Distribution System)
Fixed values: 20.10.06 30, 45 (National), 48, 52, 60, 75c., €1.80 (International)

(d) e-post
Fixed values: 20.10.06 30, 45 (National), 48, 52, 60, 75c., €1.80 (International)

Labels overprinted "Correio Azul" were at the national and international rate.

E **12** Children playing

(Des L. Duran)

2007 (28 May). Child Protection Campaign. Design as Type E **12**. Multicoloured. Simulated perforations (right-hand side).

(a) AMIEL (Automatic Electronic Printing Machine) (with dot in face value)
Fixed values: 28.5.07 30, 45 (National), 48, 50, 61, 75c., €1.85 (International)

(b) AMIEL (with comma in face value)
Fixed values: 28.5.07 30, 45 (National), 48, 50, 61, 75c., €1.85 (International)

(c) SMD (Multipost and Distribution System)
Fixed values: 28.5.07 30, 45 (National), 48, 50, 61, 75c., €1.85 (International)

(d) e-post
Fixed values: 28.5.07 30, 45 (National), 48, 50, 61, 75c., €1.85 (International)

Labels overprinted "Correio Azul" were at the national and international rate.

E **13** European Flag and Stylized People

2007 (9 Oct). European Year of Equal Opportunities. Design as Type E **13**. Multicoloured. Simulated perforations (right-hand side).

(a) AMIEL (Automatic Electronic Printing Machine) (with dot in face value)
Fixed values: 9.10.07 30, 45 (National), 50, 52, 61, 75c., €1.85 (International)

(b) AMIEL (with comma in face value)
Fixed values: 9.10.07 30, 45 (National), 50, 52, 61, 75c., €1.85 (International)

(c) SMD (Multipost and Distribution System)
Fixed values: 9.10.07 30, 45 (National), 50, 52, 61, 75c., €1.85 (International)

(d) e-post
Fixed values: 9.10.07 30, 45 (National), 50, 52, 61, 75c., €1.85 (International)

Labels overprinted "Correio Azul" were at the national and international rate.

E **14** Fireman's Helmet

PORTUGAL

(Des R. Rodrigues)

2008 (30 May). Volunteer Fire Department. Design as Type E **14**. Multicoloured. Simulated perforations (right-hand side).

(a) *AMIEL (Automatic Electronic Printing Machine) (with dot in face value)*
Fixed values: 30.5.08 30, 45 (National), 50, 52, 61, 75c., €1.85 (International)

(b) *AMIEL (with comma in face value)*
Fixed values: 30.5.08 30, 45 (National), 50, 52, 61, 75c., €1.85 (International)

(c) *SMD (Multipost and Distribution System)*
Fixed values: 30.5.08 30, 45 (National), 50, 52, 61, 75c., €1.85 (International)

(d) *e-post*
Fixed values: 30.5.08 30, 45 (National), 50, 52, 61, 75c., €1.85 (International)

Labels overprinted "Correio Azul" were at the national and international rate.

E **15** Emblem

(Des F. Galamba)

2008 (31 Oct). 50 Years of the Portuguese Blood Institute. Design as Type E **15**. Multicoloured. Simulated perforations (right-hand side).

(a) *AMIEL (Automatic Electronic Printing Machine) (with dot in face value)*
Fixed values: 31.10.08 31, 47 (National), 55, 57, 67, 80c., €1.85 (International)

(b) *AMIEL (with comma in face value)*
Fixed values: 31.10.08 31, 47 (National), 55, 57, 67, 80c., €1.85 (International)

(c) *SMD (Multipost and Distribution System)*
Fixed values: 31.10.08 31, 47 (National), 55, 57, 67, 80c., €1.85 (International)

(d) *e-post*
Fixed values: 31.10.08 31, 47 (National), 55, 57, 67, 80c., €1.85 (International)

Labels overprinted "Correio Azul" were at the national and international rate.

E **16** Recycling Emblem

(Des E. Aires)

2009 (15 Apr). Recycling. Design as Type E **16**. Multicoloured. Simulated perforations (right-hand side).

(a) *AMIEL (Automatic Electronic Printing Machine) (with dot in face value)*
Fixed values: 15.4.09 32, 47 (National), 54, 57, 68, 80c., €1.85 (International)

(b) *AMIEL (with comma in face value)*
Fixed values: 15.4.09 32, 47 (National), 54, 57, 68, 80c., €1.85 (International)

(c) *SMD (Multipost and Distribution System)*
Fixed values: 15.4.09 32, 47 (National), 54, 57, 68, 80c., €1.85 (International)

(d) *e-post*
Fixed values: 15.4.09 32, 47 (National), 54, 57, 68, 80c., €1.85 (International)

Labels overprinted "Correio Azul" were at the national and international rate.

E **17** Food Groups

(Des J. Machado)

2009 (9 Oct). Campaign for Healthy Eating. Design as Type E **17**. Multicoloured. Simulated perforations (right-hand side).

(a) *AMIEL (Automatic Electronic Printing Machine) (with dot in face value)*
Fixed values: 15.4.09 32, 47 (National), 54, 57, 68, 80c., €1.85 (International)

(b) *AMIEL (with comma in face value)*
Fixed values: 15.4.09 32, 47 (National), 54, 57, 68, 80c., €1.85 (International)

(c) *SMD (Multipost and Distribution System)*
Fixed values: 15.4.09 32, 47 (National), 54, 57, 68, 80c., €1.85 (International)

(d) *e-post*
Fixed values: 15.4.09 32, 47 (National), 54, 57, 68, 80c., €1.85 (International)

Labels overprinted "Correio Azul" were at the national and international rate.

E **18** Emblem

2010 (11 May). European Year for Combating Poverty. Design as Type E **18**. Multicoloured. Simulated perforations (right-hand side).

(a) *AMIEL (Automatic Electronic Printing Machine) (with dot in face value)*
Fixed values: 11.5.10 32, 47 (National), 54, 57, 68, 80c., €1.85 (International)

(b) *AMIEL (with comma in face value)*
Fixed values: 11.5.10 32, 47 (National), 54, 57, 68, 80c., €1.85 (International)

(c) *SMD (Multipost and Distribution System)*
Fixed values: 11.5.10 32, 47 (National), 54, 57, 68, 80c., €1.85 (International)

(d) *e-post*
Fixed values: 11.5.10 32, 47 (National), 54, 57, 68, 80c., €1.85 (International)

Labels overprinted "Correio Azul" were at the national and international rate.

STAMP BOOKLETS

The following checklist covers, in simplified form, booklets isssued by Portugal. It is intended that it should be used in conjunction with the main listings and details of stamps and panes listed there are not repeated.

Prices are for complete booklets

Booklet No.	Date	Contents	Price
SB1	1.4.05	King Carlos (T **39**) 4 panes, No. 343×6	
SB2	1.4.05	King Carlos (T **39**) 4 panes, No. 349×6	
SB3	1.4.05	King Carlos (T **39**) 2 panes, No. 349×6; 2 panes, No. 350×6	
SB4	1.4.05	King Carlos (T **39**) 4 panes, No. 350×6	
SB5	1905	King Carlos (T **39**) 2 panes, No. 349×6; 2 panes, No. 351×6	
SB6	1905	King Carlos (T **39**) 4 panes, No. 351×6	
SB7	1.1.06	King Carlos (T **39**) 4 panes, No. 344×6	
SB8	1.1.06	King Carlos (T **39**) 2 panes, No. 344×6; 2 panes, No. 347×6	
SB9	1.1.06	King Carlos (T **39**) 4 panes, No. 347×6	
SB10	1910	King Manoel II (T **48**) 4 panes, No. 391×6	
SB11	1910	King Manoel II (T **48**) 4 panes, No. 392×6	
SB12	1910	King Manoel II (T **48**) 2 panes, No. 392×6; 2 panes, No. 394×6	
SB13	1910	King Manoel II (T **48**) 4 panes, No. 394×6	
SB14	1910	King Manoel II (T **48**) 2 panes, No. 395×6; 2 panes, No. 396×6	
SB15	1910	King Manoel II (T **48**) 4 panes, No. 395×6	
SB16	1910	King Manoel II (T **48**) optd with T **50** 4 panes, No. 405×6	

91

PORTUGAL

SB17	1910	King Manoel II (T **48**) optd with T **50** 4 panes, No. 406×6	
SB18	1910	King Manoel II (T **48**) optd with T **50** 2 panes, No. 406×6; 2 panes, No. 408×6......	
SB19	1910	King Manoel II (T **48**) optd with T **50** 4 panes, No. 408×6	
SB20	1910	King Manoel II (T **48**) optd with T **50** 4 panes, No. 409×6	
SB21	1910	King Manoel II (T **48**) optd with T **50** 2 panes, No. 409×6; 2 panes, No. 410×6......	
SB22	1935	Prince Henry the Navigator (T **98**) and "All for the Nation" (T **99**) 1 pane. No. 886×4; 1 pane, No. 887×4; 2 panes. No. 888×4	£650
SB23	23.2.83	Naval Uniforms 1 pane. No. 1908ab (105E.)	16·00
SB24	15.2.84	Air Force Uniforms 1 pane, No. 1948ab (142E.)	25·00
SB25	23.1.85	Army Uniforms 1 pane, No. 1979ab (226E.)	18·00
SB26	13.12.85	Architecture 1 pane, No. 2003×10 (200E.)	6·00
SB27	18.2.86	Feira Castle 1 pane, No. 2037a (90E.)	10·00
SB28	18.2.86	Beja Castle 1 pane, No. 2038a (90E.)	10·00
SB29	10.3.86	Architecture 1 pane, No. 2004×10 (225E.)	10·00
SB30	10.4.86	Bragança Castle 1 pane, No. 2040a (90E.)	10·00
SB31	10.4.86	Guimarães Castle 1 pane, No. 2041a (90E.)	10·00
SB32	18.9.86	Belmonte Castle 1 pane, No. 2054a (90E.)	10·00
SB33	18.9.86	Montemor-o-Velho Castle 1 pane, No. 2055a (90E.)	10·00
SB34	16.1.87	Silves Castle 1 pane, No. 2065a (100E.)	10·00
SB35	16.1.87	Évora-Monte Castle 1 pane, No. 2066a (100E.)	10·00
SB36	6.3.87	Architecture 1 pane, No. 2005×10 (250E.)	11·00
SB37	10.4.87	Leiria Castle 1 pane, No. 2073a (100E.)	10·00
SB38	10.4.87	Trancoso Castle 1 pane, No. 2074a (100E.)	10·00
SB39	15.9.87	Marvão Castle 1 pane, No. 2086a (100E.)	10·00
SB40	15.9.87	St. George's Castle 1 pane, No. 2087a (100E.)	10·00
SB41	19.1.88	Fernandina Walls, Oporto 1 pane, No. 2093a (108E.)	10·00
SB42	19.1.88	Almourol Castle 1 pane, No. 2094a (108E.)	10·00
SB43	3.2.88	Bartolomeu Dias's Voyages 1 pane, No. 2083ba (104E.)	11·50
SB44	15.3.88	Palmela Castle 1 pane, No. 2102a (108E.)	9·00
SB45	15.3.88	Vila Nova de Cerveira Castle 1 pane, No. 2103a (108E.)	9·00
SB46	15.3.88	Architecture 1 pane, No. 2006×10 (270E.)	13·50
SB47	1.7.88	Chaves Castle 1 pane, No. 2108a (108E.)	9·00
SB48	1.7.88	Penedono Castle 1 pane, No. 2109a (108E.)	9·00
SB49	15.2.89	Greetings Stamps (T **442**) 1 pane, No. 2129×8 (232E.)	9·50
SB50	15.2.89	Greetings Stamps 1 pane, No. 2130×8 (480E.)	17·00
SB51	14.6.89	Windmills 1 pane, No. 2143ab (276E.)	12·50
SB52	17.11.89	Wild Flowers 1 pane, No. 2155ab (276E.)	12·50
SB53	6.3.90	Portuguese Navigators 1 pane, No. 2176×10 (320E.)	11·00
SB54	6.3.90	Architecture 1 pane, No. 2012×10 (600E.)	22·00
SB55	5.6.90	Greetings Stamps 1 pane, No. 2196ab (240E.)	11·00
SB56	21.9.90	Explorers' Ships 1 pane, No. 2202ab (257E.)	11·00
SB57	6.3.91	Portuguese Navigators 1 pane, No. 2177×10 (350E.)	10·00
SB58	6.3.91	Portuguese Navigators 1 pane, No. 2181×10 (600E.)	19·00
SB59	27.5.91	Explorers' Ships 1 pane, No. 2233ab (300E.)	9·00
SB60	8.7.91	"Royal Treasures" Exhibition 1 pane, No. 2240a (350E.)	17·00
SB61	7.2.92	"Royal Treasures" Exhibition 1 pane, No. 2271a (325E.)	25·00
SB62	6.3.92	Portuguese Navigators 1 pane, No. 2178×10 (380E.)	9·50
SB63	6.3.92	Portuguese Navigators 1 pane, No. 2182×10 (650E.)	19·00
SB64	6.4.93	Portuguese Navigators 1 pane, No. 2179×10 (420E.)	10·00
SB65	6.4.93	Portuguese Navigators 1 pane, 2183×10 (700E.)	19·00
SB66	1.10.93	Trawlers 1 pane, No. 2345a (332E.)	8·25
SB67	29.4.94	Portuguese Navigators 1 pane, No. 2180×10 (450E.)	8·50
SB68	29.4.94	Portuguese Navigators 1 pane, No. 2184×10 (750E.)	16·00
SB69	16.9.94	Trawlers 1 pane, No. 2392ab (360E.)	7·75
SB70	20.4.95	Itinerant Trades 1 pane, No. 2435×10 (450E.)	7·50
SB71	20.4.95	Itinerant Trades 1 pane, No. 2439×10 (750E.)	15·00
SB72	1.9.95	Modern Electric Locomotives 1 pane, No. 2465a (320E.)	7·50
SB73	20.3.96	Itinerant Trades 1 pane, No. 2436a (470E.)	7·50
SB74	20.3.96	Itinerant Trades 1 pane, No. 2440a (780E.)	13·50
SB75	12.4.96	U.N.I.C.E.F. 1 pane, No. 2492a (436E.)	8·50
SB76	20.2.97	"No to Drugs – Yes to Life" (T **556**) 1 pane, No. 2548ab (400E.)	7·50
SB77	12.3.97	19th-century Trades 1 pane, No. 2436ba (490E.)	8·00
SB78	12.3.97	19th-century Trades 1 pane, No. 2440ba (800E.)	16·00
SB79	28.1.98	Military Engineering 1 pane, No. 2603ab (370E.)	8·25
SB80	20.3.98	19th-century Trades 1 pane, No. 2437ab (50E.)	7·75
SB81	20.3.98	19th-century Trades 1 pane, No. 2440ca (85E.)	14·00
SB82	26.2.99	Itinerant Trades. Self-adhesive No. 2687×10 (510E.)	7·50
SB83	25.2.99	Itinerant Trades. Self-adhesive No. 2688×10 (950E.)	14·00
SB84	2.3.00	Birds No. 2766×10 (520E.)	8·75
SB85	2.3.00	Birds No. 2777×10 (1000E.)	16·00
SB86	6.3.01	Birds No. 2837×10 (530E.)	7·50
SB87	6.3.01	Birds No. 2838×10 (1050E.)	15·00
SB88	26.2.02	Birds No. 2921×10 (€2.80)	7·50
SB89	26.2.02	Birds No. 2922×10 (€5.40)	15·00
SB90	4.05	Historic Villages. 12 panes. Nos. 3202 and 3214; Nos. 3203 and 3215; Nos. 3204 and 3216; Nos. 3205 and 3217; Nos. 3206 and 3218; Nos. 3207 and 3219; Nos. 3208 and 3220; Nos. 3209 and 3221; Nos. 3210 and 3222; Nos. 3211 and 3223; Nos. 3212 and 3224; Nos. 3213 and 3225 (€10.44)	26·00
SB91	7.2.06	Greetings Stamps. No. 3314a	6·00

DESIGN INDEX

This index provides in a condensed form a key to designs and subjects of portrait and pictorial stamps of Portugal. In order to save space, portrait stamps are listed under surname only, views under the name of the town or area and works of art under the name of the artist. In cases of difficulty part of the inscription has been used to identify the stamp. When the same design or subject appears on more than one stamp in a set, only the first appearance is indexed.

A. SUBSIDIARY GROUPS

Newspaper ... N177
Postage Due ... D386, D392, D418, D484, D578, D662, D663, D741, D865, D912, D1312, D2305, D2445, D2907
Charity Tax ... C455, C484, C485, C486, C594, C662, C666, C669, C741
Parcel Post ... P578, P891
Official ... O900, O1069

B. POSTAGE STAMPS

"046-72" (painting) ... 2148
A Peregrinacão (The Pilgrimage) ... 1803
Abolition of death penalty ... 1332
Abutre do Egipto ... 2836
Academy of Sciences ... 1818
Acinonyx jubatus ... 1945
"Acrobats" (painting) ... 2111, **MS**2113
Admission of Portugal and Spain to the E.E.C. ... 2035
"Adoration of the Magi" ... 1939, 3172
Adoration of the Shepherds" ... 1783
"Adoration of the Three Wise Men" (painting) ... 2030, 2477
"Adoration of the Virgin" ... 1315
Advocacia ... 3006, **MS**3010
Afonso, J. ... 2478
Afonso, N. ... 2149, **MS**2151, **MS**2152
Africa heritage ... 3649a
A.G.P.L. ... 1906
Agricultural Science Congress ... 959
"Agriculture" ... 1838
Aguas Livres aqueduct, Lisbon ... 1442
Aguia imperial ... 2354
Aguia real ... 2761, 2766
Air ... 891
Air Force ... 1279, 1948, 2952, **MS**2958
Airplanes ... 578, 1170, 1237, 1279, 1370, 1489, 1509, 1539, **MS**1542, 1692, 1743, 1772, 1896, **MS**1900, 1948, 2130, 2485, 2703, **MS**2705, 2719, **MS**2768, 2808, **MS**2809, 2952, **MS**2958, **MS**2970
A-Jet ... 2954
Ajuda observatory ... 2938
Ajuda Palace ... 2153, 2238, 2270
Aladores (trawler) ... 2394
Alcaide ... 2822
Alcañices ... 2578
Alcobaça Monastery 2972, **MS**2980
Alentejo ... 2571
Alentejo reaper ... 941, **MS**941*a*
Alfabetizacao ... 1613, **MS**1617
Alfonso I ... 2515
Alfonso II ... 2744
Alfonsine Collection ... 2515
Algarve ... 1007, **MS**1009*a*, 1810, 2572, 2744
Aljubarrota ... 1995
Alluvial soil ... 1706
Almeida ... 735
Almeida-Garrett ... 2701, **MS**2702
Almourol Castle ... 993, 1456, 2094
Alter (horse) ... 2046
Alto Douro ... 2975, **MS**2980
"Aluenda-Tordesillas" (painting) ... 2166, **MS**2169, **MS**2210
Alvares ... 1025, **MS**1028*a*
Alves ... 2509, **MS**2513, **MS**2514
America ... 2930, 3048
American Society of Travel Agents World Congress, Lisbon ... 2410
Amerigo ... 2662
"Ameripex 86" ... 2046
Amolador ... 2438, 2687
Ampulheta ... 2318
A.N.A.C.E.D. ... 2753
Anchieta ... 2567
Anchor ... 1065
Anchor with dove ... 1164
Andador de almas ... 2434
Andorinha daurica ... 3106
Andorinha.do.mar.anã ... 2915, 2920
Angel and gateway ... 1265
"Angels around Baby Jesus, Tree and Kings" (painting) ... 2089, **MS**2092
Angola ... 2414
Animals in Lisbon zoo ... 1796, **MS**1800
Anniversaries ... 1974, 1995, 2022, 2051, 2057, 2126, 2191, 2243, 2288
Anniversary of Independence 1933
Anniversary of Republic ... 1188
Anniversary of Revolution ... 1564, 2366
Ano Santo ... 1035, 1567
"ANO. SANTO 1951" ... 1049
Anti-alcoholic Society ... 1643
Anti-illiteracy Campaign ... 1613, **MS**1617
Anti-smoking Campaign ... 1820
"Antithesis of Calm" (painting) ... 2131, **MS**2134
Apocalypse ... 1570
"Apollo"–"Soyuz" space link ... 1581
Aqueduct ... **MS**2610
Aquila chrysaetus ... 1799/**MS**1800
Arab artefacts ... 2840
Archangel Gabriel ... 383, 2481/**MS**2484
Archeological Park Côa Valley ... **MS**2683
Archery ... 2114
Arches ... 1551
Architecture ... 1998, 2075/**MS**2076, 2245, **MS**2768, 3365, 3452, 3520
"Architecture and Engineering" ... 1020
Arcos de Valdevez ... 2882
Armed Forces Movement ... 1515
Armeria pseudameria ... 2155
Armour ... 2868, **MS**2869
Arms ... 1162, 1178, 1191, 1354, 1375, 1431, 1464, 1484, 1549, **MS**2359, 2517, **MS**2523, 2549, 2578, 2579, **MS**2585
Arms of Vasco da Gama ... 1375
Arrival at Calicut ... 379
Arrival of Expedition ... 2244
Arsenopyrite ... 1426
Art ... 2377/**MS**2378
Art of the Period of Discoveries ... 2473/**MS**2479
Artillery corporal ... 1981
Asgard II ... 2660
Assassination ... 1933
Association of Volunteer Firemen of Lisbon ... 2329
Astrolabe ... 1917, **MS**1922, 2269, 2285/**MS**2287, 2934
Astronaut and spaceships ... 1583
Astronomy ... 2933, **MS**2941
Athletes ... 3559
Athlete with Olympic torch ... 1610
"Australia 99" ... 2697, **MS**2699
Automobile Club ... 1098, 3020
Automobile Museum ... 2257/**MS**2261, 2275/**MS**2279
Aveiro ... 1162, 2079, 2517, **MS**2523
Aveiro (lighthouse) ... 2079
Aveiro River and pulpit from Santa Cruz Monastery, Coimbra ... 1809
Aveiro woman ... 937, **MS**941*a*
"Avejão Lirico" (painting) ... 2123, **MS**2124, **MS**2125
Axe and saws ... 1696
Azeiteiro ... 2432
Azevedo ... 2729, **MS**2731
Azinhoso ... 2878
Azores ... 1009, **MS**1009*a*, 2574
Azorina vidalli ... **MS**2951
Azulejos ... 2841

B.M.X. Cycling ... **MS**2560
Back-staff ... 2321
Badge ... 1388, 1519
Balloon ... 1937
Balustrade ... 1465
Bank Borges and Irmao Agency ... 2075/**MS**2076
Bank emblem ... 1243, 1625
Bank of Portugal ... 997/**MS**997*a*
Banknote ... 2541
Barata ... 2752
Barca ... 2202
Barca da Xávega (Algarve) ... 1677, **MS**1679
Barco da Nazaré ... 1675, **MS**1679
Barco do Mar ... 1674, **MS**1679
Barco Poviero ... 1673, **MS**1679
Barinel ... 2204
Barketta ... 1182, 2202
Barn owl ... 1796, **MS**1800
Barrel and plate ... 2221
Barros ... 2511, **MS**2513, **MS**2514
Bartók ... **MS**2768
Basketball ... **MS**2299, 2961
Batera de Buarcos ... 1678, **MS**1679
Batista ... 2337
Battle of Aljubarrota ... 678, 698
Battle of Atoleiros ... 783
Battle of Montijo ... 730, **MS**2416
Battle of Roliça ... 782
Beach volleyball ... **MS**2807
Beckett ... **MS**2768
Beira Alta ... 2528
Beira Baixa ... 2569
Beira Litoral ... 2529
Beires ... 2703, **MS**2705
Beja ... 1549, 2518, **MS**2523
Beja Castle ... 2038
Belém Monastery, Lisbon ... 1715 **MS**1716
Belém Palace ... 3694
Belém Palace Museum ... 3158
Belém Tower, Lisbon ... 1447
Bell ... 1598, 1877
Bellis azorica ... 2949
Belmonte ... 1714, **MS**1716
Belmonte Castle ... 2054
Benfica's double victory ... 1219
Bento de Goes Commemoration ... 1335
Benz motor cycle ... 2042
Berado Museum ... 3489
Berlenga (lighthouse) ... 2078
Berlenga National Reserve ... 2024, **MS**2028
Beryllium ... 1427
Bicycles ... 2778, **MS**2784
Biombo Namban ... 1921, **MS**1922
Birds ... 1440, 1618, 1620, 1631, 1730, 1799, **MS**1800, 1887, 2024, **MS**2028, 2127, 2228, 2293, 2354, 2374, **MS**2378, 2387/**MS**2391, 2418, **MS**2421, 2761, **MS**2768, 2832, 2914, 2988, 3105, 3578, 3643, 3701
Birth Centenary of Manuel du Bocage ... 1309
Black soil ... 1707
Blesbok ... 1946
Blind person reading Braille ... 1635
Boat prow ... 1841/**MS**1842
Boats ... 1673/**MS**1679, 1906
"Body parts" (painting) ... **MS**2323
Boleeiro ... 2440, 2688
Bom Pastor (trawler) ... 2393
Bombarda ... 2820
Bomtempo ... 1544
Bonifacio ... 1486
Books ... 1112, 2488
Books, bookcases and entrance to Postal Library ... 1740/**MS**1741
Boquilobo Marsh National Reserve ... 2026
Borges ... **MS**2768
Botelho ... 2122, **MS**2124, **MS**2125
Bottle inside human body ... 1643
Bow ... 2238
Boxing ... 2503
Boy sitting in cage ... 1762
Boy with spinning top ... 2136/**MS**2137
Braga ... 1776, 2519, **MS**2523
Braga Cathedral ... 1808, 2126
Bragança ... 2520, **MS**2523, 2880
Bragança Castle ... 995, 2040
Branco ... 631, 2200
"Brasiliana 79" ... 1766
"Brasiliana 83" ... 1928/**MS**1932
Brazil–Portugal Consultation and Friendship Treaty ... 2358
Brazilian Independence ... 1485
Bread ... 3684
Breguet Bre XIV A2 ... 2721, **MS**2725
Bridges ... 1071, 1294, 1443, 1717, 1870, 1958/**MS**1959, 2247, 2616, **MS**2617, 2732, **MS**2734, **MS**2970, 3377, 3628
Broken body and bottle ... 1644
Brotero ... 965/**MS**968*a*
Brussels International Exhibition ... 1148
Bufo real ... 2355, 2916, 2922, 2924
Building ... 1572
Building and stars ... 3497
Building site ... 1699
Bullfighting ... 2300/**MS**2304
Bus ... 1517, 2141
Butterfly ... 2294

C-130 Hercules ... 2955
Cabazeiro ... 2442
Cabete ... 3709
Cable cross-section ... 1401
Cable railway ... 2138
Cabral ... 973/**MS**976*a*, 1353, 1489, 2174
Cabrilho ... 1365, 2180
Cadet and College banner ... 1116
Caimão ... 2833, 2838
Calçada R. dos Santos kiosk ... 1985
Calcidisus leptoporus ... **MS**2601
Caldas da Rainha ... 1996
Calicut ... 379
Calipers, globe and banner ... 2059
Calouste Gulbenkian Foundation ... 3358
Calvet ... 2150, **MS**2151, **MS**2152
Camel ... 2101
Cameras ... 1695
Camoens ... 600, 1493
Camões ... 600, 1801
Camões Day ... 1658, 1759/**MS**1760
Camping and Caravanning Federation Rally ... 1574
Campo Pequeno Bull Ring, Lisbon ... 2300/**MS**2304
Caniçada dam and "Lady of the Milk" ... 1808
Canis lupus signatus . 1798, **MS**1800
Cannon ... 2867, **MS**2869
Cão ... 976/**MS**976*a*, 2051, 2188
Cape Girao, Madeira ... 1458
Cape Mondego (lighthouse) ... 2077
Cape St. Vincent (lighthouse) .. 2080
"Capex '87" ... 2077
Car ... 3020
Caricaturists ... 3248
Car on hand ... 2379
Caraca ... 2826
Caramulo Automobile Museum ... 2257, **MS**2261
Caramulo Shepherdess ... 1002, **MS**1009*a*
Caravanning ... 1576
Caravela Pescareza ... 2203
Caravels ... 942, 1179, 1811, **MS**1815, 1849, 1918, **MS**1922, 2127, 2205, 2233, 2499, **MS**2500, 2897
Carcharias taurus ... 3081
Cargaleiro ... 3418
Carmona ... 1385
Carnation ... 2706, **MS**2708, 3118
Carneiro ... 2215
Carpenters tools ... 1694
Cars ... 3020
Carts ... 1671, 1766
Carvalho ... 1547, 3333
Carved capital ... 1919, **MS**1922

PORTUGAL *Design Index*

Carving of man in frame 2414
Cassegrain telescope 2939
Castel Branco . 1429, 2521, **MS**2523
Castelo de vide 3052
Castle, Vila da Feira 1449
Castles 989/**MS**996*a*, 1397, 1714, **MS**1716, 2037, 2040, 2054, 2065, 2073, 2086, 2093, 2102, 2108, 2127, 2561, **MS**2563, 3468
Castro 2645
Catamarans 3463
Caudron G-3 ....2723, **MS**2725
Cavalo marinho 2619
Cavalry officer 1980
Cave painting **MS**2683
Centenaries 912
Centenary of Medical and Surgical Colleges 897
Centenary of Porto to Lisbon Telephone Lines ...3135
Ceramic plate 3635
Ceramics 3657
Ceratotherium simum 1947
Cerebral angiograph 1560
Ceres 463, 484, 536, 702, 742, 805, 813
Chagas 1778
Chain 1413
Chalcopyrite 1428
Chalice 2413
Chameleon 2229
Chanterenne 2475
Chapel of the Apparitions 1318
Chapim de poupa 3109
Charts 2586, **MS**2590
Chasco.ruitvo 2992
Chaves 1717
Chaves Castle 2108
Cheetah 1945
Chemical plant 1702
Child and computer 1660, **MS**1664
Child and written text 1512
Child eating 1756, **MS**1758
"Child Jesus the Good Shepherd" (carving) 2412
Child jumping 1508
Child playing recorder 1661, **MS**1664
Child running 1506
Child sitting in cage 1762
Child's drawing 1514, 3524
"Children dancing around sunburst" (painting) 2090, **MS**2092
"Children following Star" 1683
Children in car 1710
Children of different races 1757, 2493
Children playing ball 1754, **MS**1758
Children reading book 1764
Children with ball 1211
Children with book 1209
Children's games and toys 2136, **MS**2137
Children's paintings 1680, 2089/**MS**2092, 2846, 2753, 3625, 3716
Children's party 3309
Chinese Junk 2896
Chinese painting 1921/**MS**1922
"Christ on the way to Calvary" (painting) 2478
Christian Civilisation Congress 1286
Christian symbol 1392
Christmas... 1552, 1680, 1782, 1859, 1939, 2029, 2089/**MS**2092, **MS**2417, 2481/**MS**2484, 2753, 3172, 3719
Cigarette contaminating lungs 1820
Cinema 2507, **MS**2513, **MS**2514, **MS**2768
Circus 2943, **MS**2944
Civil engineering 2577
Cladonema radiatum 2614, **MS**2629
Clerigos Tower, Oporto 1446
Clock **MS**2220, 2271
Clothes 1687
Clown 2943
Coach 1057
Coa Valley **MS**2683
Coach and horses 1224
Coastline 3263
Cod fishing 2795, **MS**2801
Coelho 1258
Coffee cup 3703
Coffee pot 2225
Cofrezinho Andalusino 2844
Cogwheels 1312
Coimbra 1073, 1265, 2119, 2473, 2522, **MS**2523
Coimbra Cathedral 890
Coimbra University 1073, 1445, 1484
Coimbra woman 933, **MS**941*a*
Coin 2843, 2898
Coins and bee 2405
Colonial exhibition 878
Colonists 1053
Colonization of Terceira 1053
Colonnade 1356
"Coloquios dos Simples" 1240
Coloured balls 2618
Columbus 2291/**MS**2292
Combatentes 1519
Comic strip 3160
Common dolphin 1929, **MS**1932
"Communications" 1470, 3280
Community of Portuguese Speaking Countries **MS**3357
Compass 1658, 2286/**MS**2287
Computer scale 1497
Condado Portvcalense 2524
Conductors hands 3259
Conquest of space 2760
Consolidation of Democratic Institutions ...1632
Constituent Assembly 2794
Constitucao de 1976 1632
Constitution 2852
Consumer products 1600
Container truck 1473
Contemporary Art 2322/**MS**2323
Contemporary Design 3063
Convent of Lóisos, Évora 2408
Convent sweets 2738, 2785
Cork Production 3535
Cork tree 3535
Coronation 2463/**MS**2464
Corte-Real 2499, **MS**2500
Cortesão 1790
Corticl.de.barriga.branca 2917
Costa, A. 1775
Costa de Prata 1809
Costa, L. 2167, **MS**2169
Costa, V. 2168, **MS**2169
Costa verde 1808
Costumes 932/**MS**941*a*, 1002/ **MS**1009*a*
Cotovia montesina 3108
Council of Europe 1641, 2709
Courtyard 3533
Coutinho 1303, 1370, 1489
Covilhã 1395, 2101
Crane and docks 1726, 2290
Crate 1954
Creoula 2664
Crib figures 1859
Cristo Rei Sanctuary 3659
Cross 1118
Cross of Avis 904
Cross-staff 2283/**MS**2287
Crown 2242
Crustacean 2599, **MS**2629
Cruza bico comum 3105
Cuco.rabilongo 2919, 2921, 2923
Cultural Heritage 3240
Cunhal 3293
Curie 2644
Cycling 1720

d'Orta 1240
Da Costa Mota 1418
Da Gama 385, 442, 972/**MS**976*a*, 1374, 1794/**MS**1795, 2178, 2536, 2592
Da Gama and Camoens and *São Gabriel* (flagship) 382
Da Gama Commemoration 378
Dakar Rally **MS**3536
Da Motta 1368
Dams 3445
Da Nova 2182
Da Regras 729, 1026, **MS**1028*a*
Da Serra 1304
Da Silva, A. 1134
Da Silva, H. 2494/**MS**2495
Dacosta 2131, **MS**2134
Daf truck **MS**2400
Daimler motor car 2043
Damaliscus albifrons 1946
Dancer and tapestry 1840, **MS**1842
Darwin 3643
De Almeida 1420, 1744
De Barras 2491
De Beires 2703
De Castro 1787, 2175, 2645
De Deus 2490
De Dios 1039
De Goes 1335
De Gois 1524, 2925
De Gusmão 1937
de Havilland DH.82A Tiger Moth 2719, **MS**2725
De Lisboa 2179
De Magelhães (Magellan) 974/ **MS**976*a*, 2183
De Matos 1789, 2700
De Melo **MS**3157
De Pombal 1901, 2712
De Queirós 2184
De Queiroz 2480, 2802
De Quental 2243
De Silves 989, **MS**996*a*, 2186
De Sousa 1485, 2171
De Souza-Cardoso 2081, 2110, **MS**2113
De Vasconcelos 1306
Death anniversaries 2200
Death of Camoens 620
Death of Gonçalves 1522
Debussy **MS**2768
Declaration of Human Rights 1733/ **MS**1735
"Decree Founding National Bank" 997/**MS**997*a*
Defence of Faria Castle 1522
Delphinus delphis 1929, **MS**1932
Departure from Lisbon 2537
Departure of fleet 378
Design 3063
Desterrado 1527
Diadem 2270
Diario de Noticias (newspaper) 1258
Dias 971/**MS**976*a*, 2083, 2099, 2189
"Diffusion of Hertzian Radio Waves" 1533
Dinar de ouro 2843
Dinghy 1875
Dinghy racing 2805
Dinophysis acuta **MS**2615
Discoveries 2367/**MS**2368
Discovery of America 2291/ **MS**2292
Discovery of Brazil 2770
Discovery of Radium 2644
Discovery of Tubercle Bacillus 1891
Dish 2164, 2224, 2264
Disney 2887, **MS**2888
Distillation plant and pipelines 1381
District Arms...2517, **MS**2523, 2579, **MS**2585, 2648, **MS**2654
Diving 2806
Do Douro (bastonet player) 1008, **MS**1009*a*
Doces Conventuais 2738, 2785
Doctor examining patient 1781
Dogs 1832
Dolmen of Carrazeda 1453
Dom Luis I 2153
"Dom Sebastiao" (painting) 2206, **MS**2209, **MS**2210
"Domestic Scene with Green Dog" (painting) 2207, **MS**2209, **MS**2210
Domingues .. 1028, **MS**1028*a*, 2730, **MS**2731
Domus Municipalis, Braganza 1448
Don Fernando II e Gloria (frigate) 2546
"Don João IV" 684, 694, 697
"Don Manuel" (sculpture) 2475
"Don't Drink and Drive" 1895
Donkey 1554
Door-to-door delivery 1752/**MS**1753
"Doorway to Peace" 1166
Dos Mártires 2201
Dos Reis 1527, 2236, 2510, **MS**2513, **MS**2514
Dos Santos 1421, 1792
Douro Litoral 2527
Dove 1164, 1234, 1317, 1488, 1539, **MS**1542, 1555, 1564, 1569, 1578, 1755, **MS**1758, 2366
Dove and emblem 1566
Dove and hands 1564
Dove and olive branch 1049
Dressmaking and clothes 1687
Driver in car 1711
Drowning missionaries 1435
Drugs Awareness 2548
Drummer boy **MS**2147
Du Bocage 1309
Ducal Palace, Guimaraes 1457
Ducks 1631
Dunes 3342
Duke of Bragança 1263
Duke of Bragança and open book 1818

E.F.T.A. 1329
"E.X.D." 3035
Earthquake 3306
East Timor 2542
Eanes 969/**MS**976*a*, 1974, 2177
Eighth Centenary of Tomar 1196
Elections to European Parliament 2135
Electric telegraph system 1131
Electric tram-car 2139, 2423
Elephant 2607
Eloy 2121, **MS**2124, **MS**2125
Embarkation at Rastello 380
Embassy of King Manuel to Pope Leo X ... 1879, **MS**1880
Emblem .. 985/**MS**988*a*, 1065, 1148, 1184, 1186, 1219, 1221, 1243, 1268, 1273, 1289, 1362, 1391, 1483, 1748/**MS**1750, 1785, 1907, 1912, 2369
Embroidery 1350
Emigrant at railway station 1742
Emigrants at airport 1743
Encontro de culturas 2714, **MS**2757
"Encounter with Adamastor" ...1495
Endangered Birds of Prey 2354
Energy conservation 1816
Engineer in chemical protection suit 1982
Enhydra lutris 3080
Environmental Protection 3269
Episcopal garden, Castelo Branco 1459
Epsilon **MS**2958
Escada 2322/**MS**2323
Espanca 2364
Estoril 1473
Estrela I (trawler) 2348
Estrela Mountains National Park 2025
Estremadura 2530
Eudyptes chrysolophus **MS**3083
Euphorbia azorica 2947
Euro (currency) 2696, 2898, 3641
Euro 2008 3565
Europa 1184, 1193, 1213, 1234, 1249, 1276, 1298, 1312, 1337, 1356, 1378, 1413, 1470, 1499, 1527, 1570, 1601, 1653/ **MS**1655, 1714/**MS**1716, 1751/ **MS**1753, 1793/**MS**1795, 1840/ **MS**1842, 1879/**MS**1880, 1923/ **MS**1924, 1958/**MS**1959, 1991/ **MS**1992, 2044/**MS**2045, 2075/ **MS**2076, 2104/**MS**2105, 2136/ **MS**2137, 2193/**MS**2194, 2231/ **MS**2232, 2291/**MS**2292, 2322/ **MS**2323, 2367/**MS**2368, 2452, 2494/**MS**2495, 2554/**MS**2555, 2642/**MS**2643, 2710/**MS**2711, 2775/**MS**2776, 2853/**MS**2854, 2943/**MS**2944, 3003/**MS**3005, 3132/**MS**3134, 3229/**MS**3230, 3331/**MS**3332, 3450/**MS**3451, 3557/**MS**3558, 3655/**MS**3656
"Europalia 91 Portugal" Festival, Belgium, ...**MS**2237
Europe in space 2231/**MS**2232

PORTUGAL *Design Index*

European Architectural Heritage Year 1587
European bee-eater 2914
European City of Culture 2860
European Court of Auditors 3421
European Cup 1219
European Economic Community 1867/**MS**1868
European Environment Year 2070
European Football Championship, England 2496, **MS**2498
European Football Championship, Portugal 3014, **MS**3072, 3073, 3084, 3089, 3110, 3119, **MS**3147
European Forum 2877
European Free Trade Association 1329, 1989
European Judo Championship 3544
European Ministers of Transport Conference 1925
European Nature Conservation Year 2418, **MS**2421
European Rheumatological Congress 1326
European Single Market 2313
European Tourism Year 2228/**MS**2230
European Union 2696, 2769, 3129, **MS**3131
European Year of Disabled 2993
European Year of Health, Hygiene and Safety in the Workplace 2314
European Year of Intercultural Dialogue 3635
"Europex 86" **MS**2056
"Europex 88" 2106
"Eutelsat II" Satellite 2231/**MS**2232
Evangelization by Portuguese Missionaries 2411
Events 1954
Évora 1292, **MS**2107, 2579, **MS**2585, 3050
Évora University 1175
Évora-Monte Castle 2066
Examining child's eyes 1633
Exercising 1651
Exhibition hall 1622, **MS**1624
Exhibition of public works 1020
"ExperimentaDesign 2003" 3035
"EXPO 2000" 2792, **MS**2793
"Expo XVII" 1916, **MS**1922
"Expo 70" 1391
"Expo '92" 2282
"Expo'98" 2597, **MS**2601, 2611, **MS**2615, 2621, **MS**2627, **MS**2628, **MS**2629, 2630
Export promotion 1907

F-16 Fighting Falcon 2952
Face and hands holding hammer and chisel 1763
Faces 2886
Falcão peregrino 2356, 2387, **MS**2391
Falconry 2387/**MS**2391
Family group 1780, 3539
Famous Women 2494/**MS**2495
Farmer and soldier 1561
Farmer and tractor 1662, **MS**1664
Faro 2580, **MS**2585, 3012, 3259
Fashion **MS**2768, **MS**3171
Father Manuel da Nobrega 1118
Fatima 1049, 1315
Fatima Apparitions 1315, 2289
Fatima Church 1316
Feira 991, **MS**996*a*
Feira Castle 991, 2037
Felicidades 2129
Felicitações 2196
Fencing 1965, 2254, **MS**2807, 2964,
Fernandes 1096
Fernandina Castle 2093
Fernando 1263
"Fernando Pessoa" 1571
Fiat G-91 2957
Fight against noise 1745
Figueira da Foz City 1869
Figure of man seated on barrel 2266
Figure of woman 2267
Fire cart 2459/**MS**2462
Fire engines 1855, 2460/**MS**2462
Fire Service in Portugal 2458/**MS**2462
Firework display 1347
First Adhesive Postage Stamps Centenary 920/**MS**928
First congress of agricultural science 959
First flight from Lisbon to Rio de Janeiro 1489
First National Traffic Congress, Lisbon 1260
First Portuguese Contacts with Japan 2280, 2342
First Portuguese Landing in Senegal 2415
First Portuguese Postage Stamps 1102, 3011, **MS**3047
First sea chart 1997
Fish 4480
Fish (mosaic) 2120
Fish-woman of Lisbon 935 **MS**941*a*
Fish-woman of Nazaré 932, **MS**941a
Fisheries Congress 1047
Fisherman 1047, 2795, **MS**2801, 3285
Fishermen's Day 2791
Fishes 1047, 1441, 1630, 1725, 2044/**MS**2045, 2120, 2791, 2795, **MS**2801, 2840, 2853, **MS**2854
Fishing boats 1673/**MS**1679, 1689, 2068, 2203, 3285
Flags 1188, 1329, 1520, 1759/**MS**1760, 1867/**MS**1868, 1957, 1989, 2035 **MS**2056, 2135, 2696, 2769, 3089, 3129/**MS**3131, **MS**3357
"Flaming Sun" 1378
Flamingo comun 2763
Flautist and dancers 1661, **MS**1664
Fleet from Atlantic 2538
"Flight into Egypt" 1861
Flowers 1249, 1352, 1621, 2071, 2155, 2710, **MS**2711, 2945, **MS**2951, 3000, **MS**3002
Food 2525, 2569, 3229, 3662
Football 1219, 1476, 1722, 1876, 2296, 2371, 2496/**MS**2498, 2965, **MS**2967, 3014, **MS**3019, **MS**3072, 3084, **MS**3088, 3110, 3119, 3302, **MS**3338, 3339, 3565
Football Clubs 3302
Football mascot 3073
Football stadiums **MS**3072, 3119
"For the Child" 1506
Ford Model "T" **MS**2279
Forests 1646
Formosa Lagoon National Reserve 2027
Formula 1 Grand Prix in Portugal 3583
Fort St. Catherina 1869
Fossil fuel 1637
Fountain 2069, 3048
Fourth centenary of São Paulo 1118
Franciscan Order 3652
Francisco 2289
Franco 1416
Fratercula artica 3082
Frechas 2885
Freedom from Hunger 1221
Freire 2587, **MS**2590
French Alliance 1905
French Revolution **MS**2147
Fróis 2564

Galemys pyrenaicus 2550
Galleão 2236
Galleon 1813, **MS**1815, 2236, 2544
Gallick clock and tricolour 1905
Gameiro 1419
Ganso patola 2764, 2767
Garcia 1779
Gargoyle 2223
Garrano (horse) 2048
Garrett 1142, 2701
Gateway 1197, 1452
Gateway, Castel Branco 1429
Gentil 2747
Geo-thermic sources 1638
Germano 3 (trawler) 2347
Gershwin **MS**2768
Giraldo the "Fearless" 1292
Girao **MS**2851
Glass production 2655, 3054, **MS**3058
Glider 1169, 1580
Globe 1488, 1503, 1586, 1785, 1955, 2735, **MS**2737, 2926, **MS**2929, 2968, **MS**3504
Globe and dove 1488, 2039
Globe and flags **MS**2683
GNR 1198
Gold box 2272
Gold ornaments 1602
Golden eagle 1799/**MS**1800
Golf 2966
Gomes, D. 2185
Gomes, E. 2187
Gomes, T. 1791
Gonsalves 1522, 2476, **MS**2479
Gouveia 784
Gramophone **MS**2088
Grande Oriente Luistano 2942
Grapes 900, **MS**3379
Graph and computer tapes 1496
Graphic poem 2316
Graphs 1498
Greetings stamps 2129, 2196, **MS**2854, 2855, 3309
Group CUF 3589
Gualdim Paes 780
Guarda 2581, **MS**2585, 3053
Guardas em Portugal 2889, **MS**2895
Guardsman and houses 2058
Guimarães 992, **MS**996*a*, 2208, **MS**2209, **MS**2210, 2974, **MS**2980
Guimarães Castle 727, 992, 2041
Guimarães Palace 2214
Guitar 2506
Guitarist 3649a
Gulbenkian 1271
Gymnast 2959
Gymnastics 1481, 1966

Halley's Comet **MS**2050
Hammer, anvil and bellows 1700
Hand 1589
Hand holding bouquet out of car window 2197
Hand holding flower 1956
Hand, sea, shell, moon and rainbow 2072
Hand, sun and trees 2070
Hand with cigarette 1820
Hand with cross 1568
Hand with letters 1537, **MS**1542
Hand writing on postcard 2057
Hand writing with quill pen 2489
Handball 2962
Hands 1340
Hands and letter 1031
Hands, flower and map of Europe 2071
Hang-gliding **MS**2560
Harris 3231
Harvester and jug 1404
Harvesting corn 1579, 1608/**MS**1609
Harvesting grapes 1403
Head and computer punch card 1822
"Head of Youth" 1963/**MS**1964
Headless statue of Angel 1029, 2332
Health awareness 2685
Healthy figure pushing away hand with cigarette 1821
Heart and cardiogram trace 1469
Heart and pendulum 1467
Heart in spiral 1468
Helmet 1916/**MS**1922, 2329
Henry of Burgundy 2524
Hen with chicks **MS**2851
Herculano 1669
High jump 2830, **MS**2831
Highway 2248
Hiking 1574
Hilario 2506
Hilt of sabre 2241
Historical building being protected from development 1589
Historic villages 3190, **MS**3247
History of Art Congress 1029
History of Communications in Portugal 2249/**MS**2252
Holanda 2333
Holding child's hand 2492
Holy Houses of Misericordia 2608
Holy Year 1035, 1567
"Homage to Magritte" (painting) 2208/**MS**2209, **MS**2210
Home Delivery Postal Service 2531
Homem-Reinéis 2586, **MS**2590
"Honeycomb" 1213
Horse and rider 3669
Horsebreeder of Ribatejo 940, **MS**941*a*
Horse-drawn tram-car 1516
Horse-drawn wagon 2396
Horse-rider 2906
Horses 1850, 2034, 2046
Horses and tree 1439
Hour glass 1920, **MS**1922
Houses 1998
Houses and punch-card 1823
Houses on stilts, Tocha 2067
Human rights **MS**2647, **MS**2768
Humpback whale 1931/**MS**1932
Hurdles **MS**2831
Hurdling **MS**1969, 2297
Hydro-electric power 1636
Hypsypops rubicundus 3079

IAF Congress, Lisbon 1580
ILO emblem 1362
Iberian-American Summit **MS**2683
Iberian Lynx 2095
Inauguration of Lisnave shipyard, Lisbon 1322
Inauguration of Salazar bridge, Lisbon 1294
Independence 671, 692, 726
Independence Monument, Lisbon 686, 696, 699
Indepex 97 **MS**2601
India 2412
India 89 stamp exhibition 2127
Indoor Athletics Championship 2827
Industrial Association 2618
Industrial complex 1700
Industrial Progress 1599
Industrial safety equipment 2314
"Industry" 1839
Infante Dom Henrique 1178
Infantry Grenadier 1979
Infertility Awareness Campaign 3539
Information Technology **MS**3588
Inhabitants of Beja 1550
In-line skating 2558
Inoculating child 1210
Inscribed tablet 1718
Institute of Public Credit 2549
Institute of Tropical Medicine 1154
International Economis Association Congress 2968
International Astronautical Federation Congress 1580
International Bureau of Education 1764
International Congress of Tropical Medicine 1154
International Economics Association Congress 2968
International Labour Organisation 1362
International Lawyer's Congress 3006
International Lisbon Fair 1954
International Olympic Committee 2361
International Paediatrics Congress 1209
International Peace Year 2039
International Polar Year 3578
International Quiet Sun Years 1252

PORTUGAL *Design Index*

International Railways Congress, Lisbon.................. 2339/**MS**2341
International Rheumatism Year..1650
International Road Transport Union Congress..................1473
International Scout Conference...........................1203
International Telecommunications Union.....................................1268
International Women's Year...................... 1590/**MS**1594
International Year of Planet Earth..........................3540
International Year of the Child............ 1754/ **MS**1758
International Year of the Deserts and Desertification....................3342
International Year of the Family.............................2369
International Year of the Ocean.............................2619
International Youth Year............1990
"Internment" (painting)............2121, **MS**2124, **MS**2125
"Interphil 1976"...........................1603
Introduction of post code........1729
Iron ore...1667
"Isabella of Portugal and Philip the Good"..........**MS**2237
ISAF World Sailing Championship....................3463
Ismaili Community......................3533
Italia 85.....................................**MS**2028
Itinerant Trades.... 2425/2443, 2687
Ivens..2607

Jacaranda.......................................3513
Jacinta...2289
Jacinto Dunes National Reserve.........**MS**2028
Jazz...3677
Jerónimos Monastery... 1805, 2973, **MS**2980
Jewels...2240
Jewish Heritage...........................3140
João IV..3075
João XXI..1656
João, Master..................................2474
John Paul II....................................2777
Jorge..................................1305, 2746
Joyce...**MS**2768
Judo.....................................2116, 3544
Jug.......................................2162, 2262
Junkers Ju 52/3m......2724, **MS**2725
Junqueiro.......................................1045
Juvalex '98..............................**MS**2647
Juventude.......................................2930

Kafka...**MS**2768
Kama!..2320
Kennel Club of Portugal............1832
Key...1337
Killer whale................. 1930, **MS**1932
King Afonso Henriques...916, 919, **MS**919*a*
King Afonso. 1671, 702, 1122, 3675
King Afonso II...............................1124
King Afonso III..............................1126
King Afonso IV..............................1128
King Afonso V................................2515
King Carlos............................239, 342
King Carlos I of Portugal..........2486
King Diniz.......................................1127
King Fernando................ 1130, 1606, **MS**1609, 2373
King João................ 11021, **MS**1028*a*
King João II. 1849, 2101, 2291, 2373
King João IV..................................3075
King Joseph.................................11359
King Luis..... 24, 35, 52, 69, 134, 178, 194, 207, 2282937
King Luis II..24
King Manoel. 12249, 2463/**MS**2464
King Manuel I in shipyard.........2536, **MS**2540
King Manoel II.......................390, 404
King Pedro....................................11129
King Pedro I of Brazil.................1975
King Pedro IV.................................1975
King Pedro V... 5, 10, 16, 1189, 2936
King Sancho I................................1123
King Sancho II...............................1125
Kitchen equipment.....................1685
Knight on horse.... 1079, 1995, 2367
Knights...1398
Knot...2358
Koch..1891
Kruzenshtern.................................2663

Labourer...959
Lagarto de cabeça azul........2420, **MS**2421
Lamp...3657
Landscape......................................1348
Lanhas....... 2148, **MS**2151, **MS**2152
Lantern on pedestal...................1466
Lantern Tower, Évora Cathedral..................1806
Lápide funerária...........................2842
Lavadeira.....................................2425a
Leiria..990, **MS**996a, 2582, **MS**2585
Leiria Castle.........................990, 2073
Lemos...1307
Letter............................ 1536, **MS**1542
Letters..3387
"Liberty"..1632
Library...2085
Light emission..............................1530
Lightbulbs......................................1816
Lighthouses...........1869, 2077, 3568
Lima..1736
Lima bridge....................................1443
Limonium multiflorum................2158
Linaria lamarckii............................2157
Liner...1156
Linhares..2881
Lion's...2877
Lisbon.................. 961, **MS**964*a*, 994, **MS**996*a*, 1010, 1154, 1186, 1189, 1260, 1286, 1294, 1322, 1326, 1442, 1496, 1580, 1584, 1715/**MS**1716, 1796, **MS**1800, 1805, 1811, **MS**1815, 1818, 1845, 1883, **MS**1884, 1906, 1944, 1954, 1960, **MS**1964, 1986, **MS**2056, 2122, **MS**2124, **MS**2125, 2138, **MS**2142, 2153, 2411, 2562, **MS**2563, 2583, **MS**2585
Lisbon Castle.................994, **MS**996*a*
Lisbon Cathedral......855, 871, 1883/ **MS**1884
Lisbon, European Capital of Culture................. 2374 **MS**2378
Lisbon fish-woman.....935, **MS**941*a*
Lisbon Geographical Society..2817
"Lisbon Houses" (painting).......2122, **MS**2124, **MS**2125
Lisbon kiosks................................1985
Lisbon sail......................................1873
Lisbon to Coimbra Coach Service.....................2681
Lisbon University............1189, 2192
Lisbon Zoo......1796/**MS**1800, 1944, 2870, **MS**2876
Lisnave shipyard.............1322, 1906
Litoral...1408
Lizard...................................1621, 2420
Lobo..1546
Locomotives... 1136, 1541/**MS**1542, 1671, 1742, 1851, 2216, 2339/ **MS**2341, 2401, 2402, 2465, 2732, **MS**2734, **MS**2768, **MS**2970
Loligo vulgaris............2597, **MS**2629
Lopes..............1027, **MS**1028a, 1417
Lophius piscatorius....2612, **MS**2629
Lorry....................................1725, 2129
Loud hailer.....................................1747
Lubrapex 1968...............................1346
Lubrapex 1976.......... 1622/**MS**1624
Lubrapex 80..................1811 **MS**1815
Lubrapex 82................ 1896, **MS**1900
Lubrapex 84................ 1960, **MS**1964
Lubrapex 86................ 2060/**MS**2064
Lubrapex 88..............................**MS**2107
Lubrapex 90..............................**MS**2210
Lubrapex 97..............................**MS**2575
Lúcia...2289
Luis I..2153
Lungs...1892
Lusiadas..................................615, 835
Lusiad (poem)............600, 835, 1493
Lusitano (horse)...........................2047
Lusitanian Horse..........................3669
Lute and score..............................1526
Lynx....................................1619, 2095
Lynx pardina..................................2095
Lysimachia nemorum azorica...2948

M.F.A. P.O.V.O.................................1561
Macao...2413
Macao retrospective............**MS**2758
Machado..............................1777, 2821
Madeira..............................1346, 2573
Madeira Airport.........2808, **MS**2809
Madeira museums....3030, **MS**3034
Madeira shepherdess...938, **MS**941
Madonna and Child.998, **MS**1001a, 1140, 2759
Mafra National Park....................3527
Mafra Palace..................................2213
Maia field labourer.. 726, 1006, **MS**1009*a*
Mail coach.......1224, 2104/**MS**2105, 2591, 2682
Mail coach office..................**MS**2194
Mail sorting....................................1698
Mail van.......1536, 2398, 2399, 2681
Male and Female figures...........2685
Malga Mourisca............................2840
Malhoa..3226
Malpique timbrel player.................1003, **MS**1009*a*
Man and his habitat....................1438
Man greeting child at railway station....................1744
Man on horse..........726, 1292, 1570, 1729, 1751, **MS**1753, 1850, 2034, 2300, 2315, 2906
Man with beard............................1045
Man with bouquet crossing street.....................2198
Man with fish................................1047
Man with musket.........................2342
Mann..**MS**2768
Manned flight..............................1937
Manual and looms.......................1690
Manuel..2052
Manuel..12536
Map............. 1183, 1323, 1376, 1490, 1509, 1641, 2036, 2071, 2100, 2106, 2365, 2371
Maple leaf......................................1610
Marble...1666
Marconi........................ 1533, **MS**2768
Maria Arminda (trawler)............2392
Maria Pia bridge...........................1672
Mariana and Joao da Cruz..........653
Marine mammals...... 1928, **MS**1932
Marine sergeant and cruiser *Adamastor*.............1910
Marinha Grande...........................2655
Marques..2646
Marquis de Pombaline...............1482
Marrequinho.................................2765
Marshal Carmona Bridge..........1071
Marshland......................................1629
Martins..2363
Martyrdom of Brazil Missionaries.........................1435
Marvels of Portugal.....................3468
Masks.......................3177, 3319, 3349
Missionaries..................................1435
Marvão Castle...............................2086
Masonic Grand Lodge................2942
"Maternal Love"............................1340
May Day..1838
Medals.....................1521, 1559, 2404
Mediaeval knight............1079, 1231
Medical and surgical colleges...897
Medical Anniversaries................2745
Medical equipment and operating theatre..............1684
Medicine.................... 897, 2745, 3059
Medieval knight...........................1079
Mediterranean monk seal..........1928, **MS**1932
Mediterranean soil......................1704
Meeting of cultures......................2714
Megaptera novaeangliae..... 1931/**MS**1932
Melro.azul...........................2990, 2992b
Men with axes..............................2458
Mentally handicapped..............1761
Mercedes mail van......................2398
Mergulhao de crista....................2762
Merryweather fire engine.........2460
Metalwork......................................3589
Meteorological service..............1432
Midshipman and frigate *João Belo*................1911
Midshipman and frigate *Vasco de Gama*....................1908
Military Aeronautics.......2719, **MS**2725
Military College..............1116, 2981, **MS**2987
Military Engineering...................2603
Military Museum.......2867, **MS**2869
Military Order of Aviz................1231
Millenary of Aveiro......................1162
Millet...**MS**2368
Minho..2525
Ministry of Communications...1509
Ministry of Public Works............1071, 2969
Mirando do Douro Cathedral..1807
Misericord House, Viana do Castelo................1450
Misericórdia...................................2608
Missionaries...................................2343
Moço de fretes...........................2440*b*
Modern means of communications....**MS**2252
Monachus monachus.........1928, **MS**1932
Monastery interior, Alcobaca..1444
Monastery, Leca do Balio..........1455
Monastery of D. João I........672, 692
Moniz.................................1302, 1558, 1923/**MS**1924, 2748
Monks..2126
Monnet..2106
Monogram of Christ...................1286
Monsanto flautist...1004, **MS**1009a
Montanhas.....................................1807
Montemor-o-Velho Castle........2055
Montepio General Savings Bank........................2404
Montgolfier...................................1938
Monument of Discoveries, Belém...........914, 918, **MS**919*a*
Monument to Camoens.............630
Morse equipment..... 1738, **MS**1741
Mosaic..3344
Mother, baby and dove........... 1755, **MS**1758
Mother, child and Teacher........3560
Mothers' Day.................................1140
Motor car...........................2042, 2424
Motor cyclist.............. 1709, **MS**3536
Motor tricycle...............................2042
Motor-coach..................................1475
Motorcycle........................3021, 3499
Motto..1181
Mountain village and "Jesus with Top-hat"..........1807
Mountains.................. 1654/**MS**1655
Mounted knight........2367, **MS**2368
Mounted postal courier...................961/**MS**964*a*
Mozambique..................................2411
Mozart............................. 2327, 3341*a*
Mug...2226
Mulher de capote.........................2436
Muse of History.............................381
Museum Facade...........................3158
Museums.......................................3030
Music.............................2374, **MS**2378
Musicians.......................................1543
Musschia aurea............................1352
Mutual Assurance........................2576

NATO......1065, 1164, 1748/**MS**1750
Natal.................. *see* under Christmas
National Anthem..........................2191
National Assembly Building.............2707, **MS**2708
National Census..........................1822
National Coach Museum...................1057, 3233
National Fine Arts Society.......2849, **MS**2851
National Flag...............3522/**MS**3523
National Geographical Society..................................1584
National Guard............... 1198, 2889, **MS**2895
National Laboratory of Civil Engineering...........2577
National Library...........................2488
National Merchant Navy Congress....................1156

PORTUGAL *Design Index*

National Overseas Bank 1243
National Parks
and Reserves ... 2024/ **MS**2028
National Philatelic Exhibition....881, 961/**MS**964*a*, 1186
National Press 1359
National Production
Campaign 1599
National Railways 3389
National Republican
Guard..........................1198, 2058
National Revolution........1055, 1289
National Traffic Congress..........1260
National Trust Fund Bank..........1625
National Writers Society............1595
Native Indians...........2770, **MS**2774
"Nativity".......................................1860
Nativity (painting).......................2029
Natural energy.............................1636
Natural resources........... 1646, 1665, 1704, 1725
Nature conservation...................1438
Nau 1812, **MS**1815, 2204, 2234
Nautical instruments.....1697, 2283/ **MS**2287, 2318
Naval School.................985/**MS**988*a*
Navy 3289
Nazare fish-woman.....932, **MS**941*a*
Necklace 2274
Negreiros 1571, 2111, **MS**2113, 2316
Nemésio...2825
New civil law code........................1319
"No to drugs–yes to life"............2548
Noctiluca miliaris.................**MS**2615
Nocturlabe....................................2319
Nonio (navigational instrument)
and diagram 1724
Notibó.de.nuca.vermelha.........2918
Nunes...............1723, 2926, **MS**2929
Nurse in hospital
ward....................1590, **MS**1594

O.S.C.E. Summit meeting...**MS**2543
Obidos Castle...............................2407
Ocean life.........2597, **MS**2601, 2611, **MS**2615, 2621, **MS**2628, **MS**2629
Oceanarium,
Lisbon.................3077, **MS**3083
Oceanographic expeditions....2486
Oil grove 3618
Olhão woman..............936, **MS**941a
Olive oil production...................3618
Olymphilex 92 ....**MS**2299
Olymphilex '96.....................**MS**2505
Olympic flame 1612
Olympic Games.............. 1254, 1476, 1610, 1965/**MS**1969, 2114/ **MS**2118, 2253, 2295/**MS**2299, 2501, **MS**2505, 2803, **MS**2807
Olympic Games, Athens...........3151
Olympic Games, Atlanta 2501
Olympic Games, Sydney 2802
Olympic rings...................1254, 2361
Oporto........................ 1673, **MS**1679, 2653, **MS**2654
Oporto Industrial Association.2618
Oporto University.......................2245
Oporto's public
transport system 1516
Orchids 3000, **MS**3002
Orcinus orca 1930, **MS**1932
Order of engineers......................2059
Organisation of Mothers
for National Education.....1340
Organized tourism......................2067
Otis tarda......................2418, **MS**2421
Our Lady of Fatima......................1035
Ourém.. 996
Overshot
bucket mill.........2062, **MS**2064
Ox-drawn carriage 3426

P-3P..2956
Paddle steamer
with sails........... 1814/**MS**1815
Padeira...2440*d*
Padre Cruz....................................1173
Page of children's primer..........1513
Painter 2850
"Painting" (Da Costa) 2167, **MS**2169, **MS**2210
"Painting" (Costa, V.).2168/**MS**2169, **MS**2210
Paintings.................... 2110, **MS**2113, 2121/**MS**2124, **MS**2125, 2131/ **MS**2134, 2148/**MS**2151, **MS**2152, 2166/**MS**2169, 2206/ **MS**2209, **MS**2210, **MS**2768, 3639, 3650
Pais................................2703, **MS**2705
Palaces................................2153, 2211
Palmela Castle..............................2102
Pandion haliaetus......2419, **MS**2421
"Panel of
St. Vincent" 1960, **MS**1964
Panthera tigris 1944
Papa figos......................................3107
Papal visit 1881/**MS**1884, 2777
Parabens 2855, **MS**2854
Paragliding....................................2559
Paralympic Games, Athens 3153
Paris Postal Conference.............1224
Parker..**MS**2768
Parks and reserves....2024, **MS**2028
Part of a Viola (painting)...........2110, **MS**2113
Passenger in train........................1925
Peace and Freedom....................2452
Peasant cart and lorry................1701
Pedestrian on zebra crossing..1708
Pedro.............................2123/**MS**2124, **MS**2125, 2726
Pedro da Coasta 392
Pedro IV...1487
Pegoes Aquaduct........................3420
Peixeanjo lirios..............................2620
Peixeira..2428
Pen and flag..................................3425
Pen-nib 3280
Pen-nib and post codes 1732
Pen-nib as plough blade...........1595
Pena Palace...................................2211
Peneda-Gerês
National Park 2710, **MS**2711
Penedono Castle..........................2109
Peneireio cinzento 2835
People..2993
People and globe 1586
Peoples Education Plan.............1112
Perdigão..2516
Perdiz-do-mar...............................2834
Pereira.......................859, 2172, 2728, **MS**2731, 3505, 3654
Perestrelo......................................2176
Permanent
education.......... 1660/**MS**1664
Permanent steam
mill 2063/**MS**2064
Pessoa.............. 1571, 2023, **MS**2768
Personalities 3506, 3547, 3639
Pestana................................1301, 2745
Peto.verde 2988
Pharmaceutical ceramics..........3594
Pharmacist's jar 1240
Pharmacy and medicine...........3059
Phila Nippon 91 ....**MS**2261
Philakorea 2002.....................**MS**2967
Philexfrance 82............................1887
Philexfrance 89......................**MS**2147
Philexfrance 99..........2726, **MS**2731
Philippa de Vilhena
arms her sons..............679, 695
Photography and
cinema 2375, **MS**2378
Phyllopteryx taeniolatus............3077
Piano 1368
Pigeon with letter........................1730
Pillories..2878
Pilot and airplane 1948
Pilumnus.....................2611, **MS**2629
Pinheiro........................ 2206, **MS**2209, **MS**2210, **MS**2268
Pinhel's status as a city..............1464
Pinto 1793, **MS**1795, 1803
Pires, D...2473
Planices 1806
Plant-breeding station...............1388
Planting tree.................................1577
Plants and animals......................3513
Plate.................. 2159, **MS**2227, 2263
Plough and farmers repelling
hunters 1607, **MS**1609
Plough and tractor......................1691
Pneumatic drill 1746
Pole vault.....................2828, **MS**2831
Pole vaulting 1968
Political figure **MS**2268
Pomar...........................2132, **MS**2134
Pombaline University
reforms 1482
Pombo.das.rochas........ 2989, 2992a
Pope John Paul II.......1881/**MS**1884, 2777
Pope John XXI...............................1656
Pope Pius XII 1051
Portalegre.................... 2584, **MS**2585
Port of Lisbon Administration.1906
Port wine industry.......................1403
Portable post boxes and
letter balance ... 1737, **MS**1741
Porto.........................2860, 3012, 3049
Porto de Lisboa kiosk.................1987
Porto, European city
of culture...........2860, **MS**2866
Porto oil refinery..........................1381
Portraits......................1021/**MS**1028*a*
Portucale 77 ....1618, 1673/**MS**1679
Portugal–England submarine
telegraph cable..................1399
Portugal–India
Sea Route......2536, 2592, 2665
Portugal–Macao Flight..............2703
Portugal, M. 1548
Portugal '98"...2665, **MS**2680, 2536, **MS**2540, 2592, **MS**2596
"Portugal's Guardian Angel"
(sculpture) 2473
Portuguese Aero Club................1169
Portuguese Airforce 2952
Portuguese Armed
Forces Movement.............1555
Portuguese Artists.......................3510
Portuguese
centenaries...........912/**MS**919*a*
Portuguese Constituent
Assembly..............................1572
Portuguese Emigrants..............1742
Portuguese Faience.2159/**MS**2165, 2221/**MS**2227, 2262/**MS**2268
Portuguese Galleon....................2544
Portuguese in
Australia 2697, **MS**2699
Portuguese in Ceylon.................3394
Portuguese Kings 1122
Portuguese laurel
cherry and blue tit.............1620
Portuguese Legion....................... 904
Portuguese navigators 969/ **MS**976*a*, 2170
Portuguese paper currency.....2082
Portuguese Pavillion 2282
Portuguese Philatelic
Federation 3148
Portuguese Presidency of
European Community......2269
Portuguese Productivity
Conference..........................1496
Portuguese Progress
and Citizens'
Guidance Campaign.........1561
Portuguese Revolution.............1564
Portuguese Road Safety Year..2379
Portuguese Royal Library.........2085
Portuguese World
Exhibition....912, 917, **MS**919*a*
Post bag 2349
Post boxes................... 2349/**MS**2353
Post Museum 1737/**MS**1741
Post Office
buildings........... 2193/**MS**2194
Post Office Emblem 2315
Post rider 1729, 2034
Post van..2129
Post-boy and
mail van............. 1536, **MS**1542
Postal messenger delivering
letter.................... 1751, **MS**1753
"Postal Services"...........................1511
Postal transport......... 2396/**MS**2400
Postbox 1511
Posthom...1499
Postman..2531
Postman and mail van 2251
Potters wheel 1694*a*
Pottery.............2159, **MS**2165, 2221, **MS**2227, 2262, **MS**2268
Pousadas (hotels)
in historic buildings 2406
Pregnant woman.........................1761
Pres. Carmona..... 877, 977/**MS**984*a*
President Medici of Brazil 1502
Presidency of European
Union.........................2769, 3497
Primary state school
education.............................1512
Prince Albert I of Monaco.........2487
Prince Fernando......1023, **MS**1028*a*
Prince Henry.....314, 318, 885, 1024, **MS**1028*a*, 1178, 2365
Prince Henry the Navigator 314
Prince John proclaimed
King of Portugal 1934
Princess St. Joan...........................1100
Principe da Beira (nau)...............2545
Printing press...............................1693
Printing press and
stamps 1739, **MS**1741
Proclamation of St. Mary
of Castile as Patron
Saint of Portugal 998
Profiles...1990
Propeller 891
Protection of
species 1796/**MS**1800
Proust..**MS**2768
Provisional mail rules.................2751
Public transport 3185, 3425*a*
Public works 2969, **MS**2970
Pyrenean Desman.......................2550
Pyrite..1665

Quadrant 2284/**MS**2287, 2936
Quadrante de dois arcos...........2321
Queen Leonora.............................1158
Queen Leonor and hospital.....1996
Queen Maria II 1, 1102
Queen Philippa........1022, **MS**1028*a*
Queiroz..2802
Queluz Palace 2154

R. Artilharia I 1988
Racing car.....................................3022
Radar.................................1697, 1727
"Radio Waves Across Space"....1534
"Radio Waves for
Navigation"..........................1535
Radium 2644
Railway bridge
over river Douro 1671
Railway Congress
(Lisbon).............2339, **MS**2341
Railways 1136, 1851
Rainbow......1555, 1838, 1955, 3625
Rain clouds....................................3322
Ram and weaving frame...........1396
Raptors 3701
Reaper of Alentejo 941/**MS**941*a*
Recapture of Lisbon
from the Moors...................1010
Reconquest of Évora 1292
Records and compact
disc player.......................**MS**2088
Red Cross.......................................1273
Red deer.....................................**MS**2230
Red fox......................... 1797, **MS**1800
Regio 2823
Regional Costumes.....................3404
Rêgo.......... 2207, **MS**2209, **MS**2210
Reinel 1997
Reliquary of Queen Leonor......2474
Republican ideas 3609
Republican personalities......... 1774, 1787
Revolution, 25 April........2706, 3118
Revolutionaries 1055
Rheumatism victim....................1650
Ribatejo..2570
Ribatejo horse-breeder..............940, **MS**941*a*
Ribeiro 740, 2022, 2053, 2512, **MS**2513, **MS**2514, 2588, **MS**2590
Ricardo do Espirito Santo
Silva Foundation 3023
Rights of People in
East Timor 2542
Rights of the Child:
Right to Education............3560
Rio de Janeiro 2085
River boats 1824
River ferry...............................**MS**2142
Road safety 1708
Road Transport
Union Congress.................1473
Road victim...................................1713
Rocha beach and
ornamental chimney........1810
Rock formation............................1705

PORTUGAL *Design Index*

Rocket....1580
Rocks....1425
Rodrigues....2824
Roller hockey....1067, 1874, 2298, 2963
Roman Heritage....3344
Roman mosaics....2119
Roman senators....1319
Roman temple, Évora....1454
Roman tower....1714, **MS**1716
Rose....2661
Rossini....2324
Rossio Railway Station Centenary, Lisbon....2216, **MS**2220
Rotary International....1785, 3231
Royal All Saints Hospital, Lisbon....2288
Royal Family....3537
"Royal Treasures" Exhibition Ajuda Palace....2238, 2270
Rua de Artilharia Um kiosk....1988
Rugby ball....**MS**3509
Rugby World Cup, France..**MS**3509
Running....1477, 1719, 1967, 2295, **MS**2299, 2504, 2803, 2827, **MS**2831, 3553

SA300 Puma helicopter....2953
S. Jorge da Mina Castle....2127
Sagres....1183, 2659
Sailing....2256
Sailing Ships....2544, 2659, 2896
Sailing packet and Modern liner....1538, **MS**1542
Sailor using astrolabe....2128
Saint and invalid....1039
St. Anthony....327, 342, 853, 856, 874
St. Anthony ascending into Heaven....333
St. Anthony from picture in Academy of Fine Arts, Paris....337
"St. Anthony holding Baby Jesus" (statue)....**MS**2457
"St. Anthony holding Child Jesus" (painting)....2454
"St. Anthony holding Child Jesus" (statue)....2456
St. Anthony of Lisbon....1845
St. Anthony of Padua....853, 2454/**MS**2457
"St. Anthony" (painting)....2476
St. Anthony preaching to the fishes....328
St. Elizabeth....1150
St. Elizabeth and St. Teotonio Commemoration....1150
St. Francis....3652
St. Francis of Assisi....1865
St. Francis Xavier....1075
St. Gabriel Commemoration....1201
St. George's Castle....2087
St. Isabel Rainha....1150
"St. James" (panel)....1961, **MS**1964
St. João de Brito....1016
St. John of God....2422
St. Marcos de Tavira....3051
St. Martin of Dume....1094
St. Philips Fort, Setubal....2406
St. Teotonio....1151
St. Vincent....1960, **MS**1964
St. Vincent de Paul....1227
St. Vincent (Gonçalves)....**MS**2479
"St. Vincent" (polyptych)....**MS**2479
St. Zenon....1216
Salazar....1422
Salazar Barrage....1074
Salazar Bridge....1294
Saloio vine-grower....934, **MS**941*a*
Saluting the flag....1759/**MS**1760
Sameiro Sanctuary....1882, **MS**1884
Sameiro Shrine....1246
San Carlos National Theatre, Lisbon....2324/**MS**2328
San Diego, California....1365
Sand clock....2318
Santa and Hearts....3719
"Santa Claus flying on dove" (painting)....2091/**MS**2092
Santa Cruz Cathedral....857, 875
Santa Justa lift....2140
Santa Marinha Monastery, Guimarães....2409
Santana....2508, **MS**2513, **MS**2514
Santarém....780, 1397, 2561, **MS**2563, 2651, **MS**2654
Santarém Fortress....2561
Santo Tirso post office....2193/**MS**2194
Santolina impressa....2156
Santos, J. C....2749
Santos, R....2750
Sao Gabriel (flagship)....384
Sao Paulo....1118
Saramago....**MS**2686
Sash....2240
Satellite....1434, 1510, 1532, 1686, 2231, **MS**2232, **MS**2768
Satellite Communications Station Network....1530
Saturn....2939
"Saved from the Sea"....1494
Scabiosa nitens....2945
Sceptre....2239, 2273
Schoenberg....**MS**2768
School Correspondance....3387, 3524, 3625, 3716
Scientists....1301
Score and singers....2191
Scout badge and tents....1203
Sculptors....1416
Sculptures....2332/**MS**2338, 2380/**MS**2386, 2466/**MS**2472, **MS**2768
Scyllarus arctus....2598, **MS**2629
Sea battle....1804
Seaman and steam corvette Estefania....1909
Seasonal mill....2060, **MS**2064
Second National Merchant Navy Congress....1156
Section of ship's hull....1323
Século XVI....1057
Seixas....1545
Selar o futuro....2846
Selo....3011
Senecio malvifolius....**MS**2951
Sequeira....1963/**MS**1964
Sérgio....1788
Sernancelhe....2884
Serpent symbol....1326
Serralves Foundation....3295
Serrano....1308
Servicemen....1520
Servicemen's League....1519
"Sesmarias" (uncultivated land) law....1606, **MS**1609
Setubal....1191, 2648, **MS**2654
Seven Cities Lake, São Miguel, Azores....1461
Sextant....1371, 1819, 2817
Shad (fish)....2044/**MS**2045
Sheep....1396
Sheep grazing....1628
Shepherdess of Madeira....938, **MS**941*a*
Shield and propeller....891
Ship and colonists....1053
Ship laying cable....1399
Ships....314, 378, 942, 1243, 1298, 1355, 1377, 1399, 1435, 1538, **MS**1542, 1689, 1703, 1873, 1908, 2083, 2099, 2202, 2233, 2544, 2537, 2659, 2682, 2896, 2927, **MS**2929, **MS**2768, **MS**2970, 3289
Shipyard....1322, 1703, 1870
Shooting....2255
Shot put....2829, **MS**2831
Show jumping....1478, 2253, 2502, 2804
Shrine of Fatima....1881, **MS**1884
Siberian tiger....1944
Silva....2507, **MS**2513, **MS**2514, 3023, **MS**3029
Silver coin....2082
Silves Castle....989, 2065
"Sim" (painting)....2150, **MS**2151, **MS**2152
Simao de Botelho....661
"Simumis" (painting)....2133/**MS**2134
Sintra....**MS**2601
Sir Rowland Hill....920/**MS**928
Sisao....2832, 2837
Sixth European Rheumatological Congress, Lisbon....1326
Sixth International Congress of Tropical Medicine....1154
Skateboarding....2557
Snoopy....2810, **MS**2816
Soajo....2879
Solar eclipse....3277
Solar energy....1640
Soldier....1116, 2603, 2981, **MS**2987
Solea senegalensis....2600, **MS**2629
Sorraia (horse)....2049
Sorting letters....1731
Southern plains....1653, **MS**1655
Spaceman....2760
Space pioneers....1582
Space shuttle....**MS**2768
SPAD VII-CI....2722, **MS**2725
Spanish–Portuguese–American Congress of Economic Geology....1425
Sparus aurata....2613, **MS**2629
"Speaking at Sea"....1614, **MS**1617
"Speaking at Work"..1616/**MS**1617
"Speaking in the Country"....1613, **MS**1617
"Speaking in Town"..1615, **MS**1617
Speeding car....1817
Spergularia azorica....2950
Spheniscus magellanicus....3078
Spinner of Vaina do Castelo....939, **MS**941*a*
Spiral waves....1531
"Spirals" (painting)....2149, **MS**2151, **MS**2152
Spoons....1601
Sport for all....1719
Sporting events....1873, 3553, 3559
Sports....1719, 2556, **MS**2560, 2803, 2959, **MS**2967
"Sprig"....1276
SS Germano 3 (trawler)....2347
Stadium....1072
Stained glass window....1939, **MS**3058
Stamp being hand-cancelled....1604
Stamp Day....1216
Stamp designing....1603
Stamp printing....1605
Stamp World London 90....**MS**2195
Stampin the Future....2846
Stamping letter....**MS**2195
Stamps....1739, **MS**1741, 2996, **MS**3047
Star....1395, 2313, 2769, 2775, **MS**2776
"Star over Bethlehem"....1681
State Postal Service....2591
Statue....1029, 1527, 2849
Statue of Brotero....966
Statue of King João IV....913, 915, **MS**919*a*
Statue of St. Vincent....1805
Statuette of Missionary....2411
"Still Life with Viola" (painting)....2112/**MS**2113
Storming of Santarem....781
Stravinsky....**MS**2768
Street with Chairs under Trees....2196
Students and atomic construction....1663/**MS**1664
Students and teacher....2192
Stylized building plan....1588
Stylized map....2360
Subway train....3185
Sueste (trawler)....2395
Sun and globe....1252
Sun behind prison bars and bottle....1645
Supermarine Spitfire V6 fighter....2720, **MS**2725
"Supersonic Flight"....1237
Surfing....2556
Surrealism....2726, **MS**2731
Surrender of the Keys of Lisbon....1010
Survey instruments....1703*a*
Surveying the land....1584
Surveying the sea....1585
Swimming....1479, 1721
Swimming and boating....1575
Symbol of medicine....897
Symbolic arch....1587
Symbolic figure....1733/**MS**1735
Symbolic initials....1393
Symbolical of Prince Henry's studies....323

Taartaranhão-azulado....2357
Tabellaria sp....**MS**2601
Talha de cereâmica....2845
TAP Air Portugal....1237, 1772, 2485
Taxi roof....1474
"Teacher and children"....1515
Teaching a deaf child....1765
Technical education....2971
Teixeira....1069, 2173
"Telecommunications"....1201, 1510
Telegraph key and masts....1686
Telegraph poles....1131
Telephone..1510, 1597, 1877, 3135
Telephone centenary....1597, 1877
Telescope....2933
Television camera....3375
Temple of Diana....882
Tennis....2117
Tenth Anniv of North Atlantic Treaty Organization....1164
Tenth International Paediatrics Congress....1209
Teresa de Albuquerque....646
Termination of Holy Year....1049
"The Adoration"....1680
"The Annunciation"....1552
"The Exile"....1527
"The Flight into Egypt"..1554, 1783, 1940
"The Hand of God"....1567
"The Holy Family"....1682, 1782
"The Horseman of the Apocalypse"....1570
"The Nativity"....1553
"The Stamp Show 2000"....2778, **MS**2784
The Twentieth Century....2760, **MS**2768, 3819
Theatre....**MS**2768
Theatre and dance....2376, **MS**2378
Third Anniv of North Atlantic Treaty Organization....1065
Tile....2841
Tiles....1782, 1830/**MS**1831, 1843/**MS**1844, 1847/**MS**1848, 1862/**MS**1863, **MS**1864, 1871/**MS**1872, 1885/**MS**1886, 1893/**MS**1894, 1902/**MS**1903, **MS**1904, 1914/**MS**1915, 1926/**MS**1927, 1935/**MS**1936, 1941/**MS**1942, **MS**1943, 1952/**MS**1953, 1970**MS**1971, 1972/**MS**1973, 1976**MS**1977, **MS**1978, 1983/**MS**1984, 1993/ **MS**1994, 2020/**MS**2021, 2031/ **MS**2032, **MS**2033, 3397
Title page....1525
Tivoli kiosk....1986
Tobacco box....2272
Todi....1543
Tomar....1196
Tomb of Camoens....625
Tombstones....1332
Tontinegra.carrasqueira....2991, 2992c
Tools....1699
Torre do Tombo....2246
Tourism....3263
Towards a National Health Service....1780
Town....2330/**MS**2331
Town Hall, Sintra....1460
Town square and monument..1430
Trade Secretariat....1110
Traders carrying goods..2280, 2344
Trades....2687
Traditional dishes....2525, 2569
Traffic....1745
Traffic signals....1260
Train....2732, 3389
Tram-car....1518
Trams and Motor Cars in Portugal....2423
Trancoso Castle....2074
Transco-Atlantic Flight....578
Transport....1701, 1745, 2138/**MS**2142
Transport and Communications....2104/**MS**2105

Transport and weather map....1509
Trás-os-Montes..............................2526
Travelling post office 2397
Trawlers...... 1689, 1725, 1870, 2317,
                                  2345, 2392
Treaty of Alcanices 2578
Treaty of Tordesillas 2373
Trees 1646
Tristao 2181
Truck.................................. **MS**2400
Trumpeter 3677
Tudo Pela Nacao 887
Tyto alba................... 1796, **MS**1800

UEFA Under-21 Football
  Championship **MS**3338
UIT emblem 1268
UNESCO **MS**2575, **MS**2601
Uniformed academician,
  Academy and sextant.......1819
Unifor **MS**1908, 1948, 1979
Union of European
  Football Associations
  (UEFA)..............................**MS**3150
Union of Portuguese-speaking
  capital cities...... 2330/**MS**2331
United Nations 1577, 2886, 3273
United Nations
  Children's Fund 2492
United Nations Conference
  on Environment and
  Development 2293
United Nations
  Organization..... 2449/**MS**2451
United Nations Year of
  Dialogue among
  Civilizations..........................2886
University seal..............................1175
"Unskilled Mason's Lunch"
  (painting) 2132, **MS**2134
UPU...............1031, 1536, **MS**1542,
                              2735, **MS**2737
Uranium 1668

Vasco..2477
Vasco da Gama Aquarium 2619
Vasco da Gama
  Bridge................... 2616, **MS**2617
Vasco da Gama Regatta 2659
Vasconcellos..................................2819
Vase 2161, 2222, 3594
Vassoureiro 2427
Velho 975/**MS**976*a*
Vendedor de louça...................2437a
Vendedor de patos 2440c
Vendedora de queijades...........2447
Verde 1146
Verdi 2325
Vespeira.............2133/**MS**2134, 2727
Viagents no Atlantico Sul 2128
Viana 2112/**MS**2113
Viana do Castelo 2650, **MS**2654
Viana do Castelo
  spinner......................939, **MS**941a
*Viburnum tinus
  subcordatum* 2946
Vicente.............................. 898, 1282
"Victory over Disease"...............1343
Vieira 1349, 2568
"View from window"
  (painting) 2322
"View of Lisbon"
  (painting) 1962, **MS**1964
View of road................................1712
Vigo 2348
VIII Cimeira
  Ibero-Americana **MS**2683
Vila Nova de Cerveira Castle 2103
Vila Palace.....................................2212
Vila Real............. 2648, **MS**2654, 3048
Villa de rua 2883
Vine-grower of Saloio 934, **MS**941a
Vineyard..3599
Vineyard, Girao 1346
Violin 2265
"Virgin and Child"......................1859
Virgin of Fatima 1317
Viseu................. 2652, **MS**2654, 3011
Visit of Pres. Medici
  of Brazil.................................1502
Visitors with gifts 2281
Viticulture....................................3165
Volkswagon mail van 2399
Von Stephan..................................2735
Vulpes vulpes.............. 1797, **MS**1800

WHO 1343
WWF 2095, 2550
Wagner..2326
Walking race................................2960
Walt Disney cartoon
  characters **MS**2888
Water...3322
Water conservation...................1628
Water mills 2060, **MS**2064
Water resources......... 2853, **MS**2854
Weather balloon 1433
Weather equipment 1432
Weather satellite 1434
Weavers looms 1690
Weighing baby 1212
Weightlifting 2115
Welder 1634
Western European Union 2360
Wheat..1955
Wheel and star............................1395
White dress **MS**3171
White rhino 1947
Wild animals 1944
Wild carnation and lizard........1621
Wild flowers 2155
Windmills........ 1407, 2143, **MS**2768
Window **MS**2107
Window, Tomar Convent..........1451
Wind-power.................................1639
Wine and Raisin Congress 900
Wine glass and stop sign 1895
Wine-bottle and casks 1406
Wine-glass and barge................1405
Wine regions 3599
"Winter" (mosaic) 2119
With love......................................2130
Wolf 1798, **MS**1800,
                               2710, **MS**2711
Wolframite 1425
Women (of the Republic)..........3709
Woman factory
  worker................. 1593/**MS**1594
Woman farm worker1591, **MS**1594
Woman from
  Coimbra.............933, **MS**941*a*
Woman holding adufe
  (tambourine) 1991/**MS**1992
Woman of Algarve .1007, **MS**1009a
Woman of Aveiro 937, **MS**941a
Woman of Avintes..1005, **MS**1009a
Woman of Olhão........936, **MS**941*a*
Woman of the
  Azores 1009/**MS**1009*a*
Woman office
  worker................. 1592, **MS**1594
Woman on donkey.....................2425
Woman posting letter...............2250
Woman sewing............................1350
Woman with bouquet
  behind pillar box................2199
Women's dress............................3404
Women's relay 1611
Woodland scene 3540
World Communications Year...1912
World Congress du A.S.T.A. 2410
World Congress of Rehabilitation
  International.......................1956
World Congress on
  Economics 2968
World Cup Football
  Championship 1876, 2371,
                                        3339
World Food Day 1955
World Health Day 1633
World Health Organization 1343
World Heart Month...................1467
World Heritage Sites........... **MS**2107,
  MS2602, 2972, **MS**2980
World Indoor Athletics
  Championship . 2827, **MS**2831
World Refugee Year 1166
World Roller Hockey
  Championship 1067
World Tourism
  Conference, Manila 1805
Wrestling 2501
Writers anniversaries.................2490
Writing desk and computer.....1688

Xavier..3328

Yachting........................1480, **MS**2118
Yachts...1875
Year of the child 1754, **MS**1758
Year of the ocean 1990

Zamora Conference............. **MS**2359
Zarco 970/**MS**976a, 1351, 2170,
Zeiss projector............................2940
Zoo animals 2870, **MS**2876
Zoost fire engine No. 1 2461

Angola

1870. 1000 Reis = 1 Milreis
1913. 100 Centavos = 1 Escudo
1932. 100 Centavos = 1 Angolar
1954. 100 Centavos = 1 Escudo

The Portuguese conquest of Angola was a gradual process from 1576 onwards, intensified in the 19th century. The present boundaries were fixed by treaties in the years 1886 to 1927. Angola was declared in 1935 to be an integral part of Portugal and on 11 June 1951 to be an overseas province.

PRINTERS. All the stamps of Angola were printed at the Mint, Lisbon, *unless otherwise stated.*

REPRINTS. Reprints of some of the following issues were made in 1885 and 1905 as indicated in the footnotes. These can generally be distinguished as follows:—
 1885 reprints are on stout very white paper, usually ungummed but sometimes with white gum having yellowish spots. They are perf 13½ with large clean-cut holes producing sharp pointed teeth.
 1905 reprints are on creamy white paper of ordinary quality with shiny white gum, all perf 13½.

1    Plate 1    Plate 2

Both plates were used for the 50r. blue perf 12½ of 1881. Two plates were also employed for the 10, 20, 25 and 40r. values which differ in the figures of value. These are indicated but not illustrated as no stamps of the same colour, shade and perforation exist in both plates.

(Des and eng A. F. Gerard. Typo)

1870 (1 July). Thick paper. P 12½.

1	1	5r. black	£100	85·00
2		10r. pale orange-yellow (Pl. 1)	£140	£110
3		20r. bistre (Pl. 1)	£140	£110
4		25r. red (Pl. 1)	70·00	65·00
		a. Rose (Pl. 1)	70·00	65·00
5		50r. green (Pl. 1)	£100	85·00
6		100r. lilac	£140	80·00
1/6 *Set of 6*			£600	£475

1875–77. Medium paper varying in substance.

(a) P 12½

7	1	5r. black	3·50	2·10
		a. Grey-black	3·50	2·10
8		10r. orange-yellow (Pl. 1)	25·00	19·00
		a. Pale orange (Pl. 1)	25·00	19·00
9		20r. bistre (Pl. 1)	2·75	2·30
		a. Pale bistre (Pl. 1)	2·75	2·30
10		25r. crimson (Pl. 1)	14·00	9·50
		a. Pale rose (Pl. 1)	14·00	9·50
		b. Vertically laid paper	£110	75·00
11		40r. deep blue (Pl. 1) (1.1.77)	£225	£170
		a. Pale blue (Pl. 1)	£225	£170
12		50r. green (Pl. 1)	65·00	17·00
		a. Pale green (Pl. 1)	65·00	17·00
13		100r. grey-lilac	12·50	5·75
		a. Dull purple	14·00	6·50
14		200r. red-orange (1.1.77)	8·00	4·75
		a. Orange	8·00	4·75
		b. Pale orange	8·00	4·75
15		300r. chocolate (1.1.77)	25·00	15·00
		a. Pale brown	25·00	15·00
7/15 *Set of 9 (cheapest)*			£350	£225

(b) P 13½

16	1	5r. black	10·50	5·75
		a. Grey-black	10·50	5·75
17		10r. orange-yellow (Pl. 1)	25·00	15·00
		a. Pale yellow (Pl. 2)	25·00	15·00
18		20r. bistre (Pl. 1)	£550	£450
19		25r. crimson (Pl. 1)	28·00	23·00
		a. Pale rose (Pl. 1)	34·00	30·00
19*b*		40r. deep blue (Pl. 2)	£275	£190
20		50r. pale green (Pl. 1)	£225	£130
21		100r. slate-lilac	6·25	3·75
		a. Dull purple	6·25	3·75
22		200r. red-orange	5·25	2·30
		a. Orange	5·25	2·30
		b. Pale orange	5·25	2·30
23		300r. chocolate	6·25	3·75
		a. Pale brown	6·25	3·75
16/23 *Set of 9 (cheapest)*			£1000	£750

(c) P 14

24	1	25r. crimson	£650	£425

 The stamps of 1875–77 were at first on *thin hard* paper, varying in substance, later printings on *thicker soft* paper in paler shades.
 All values were reprinted perf 13½ in 1885 and 1905, the 10, 20, 25, 40 and 50r. being Plate 2.
 In addition the 5, 10, 25, 40, 100 and 300r. all Plate 1 were reprinted in 1885 on the same paper but perf 12½ and with or without gum.

1881–85. Colours changed. Medium paper varying in substance.

(a) P 12½

25	1	10r. green (Pl. 1) (1883)	48·00	27·00
26		20r. rosine (Pl. 2) (1885)	23·00	16·00
27		25r. dull purple (Pl. 2) (1885)	16·00	5·75
28		40r. yellow-buff (Pl. 1) (1882)	15·00	5·25
		a. Pale yellow (Pl. 1)	15·00	5·25
29		50r. pale blue (Pl. 1)	50·00	10·50
		a. Deep blue (Pl. 1)	50·00	10·50
30		50r. deep blue (Pl. 2)	50·00	10·50

(b) P 13½

31	1	10r. green (Pl. 1)	9·75	5·50
32		25r. dull purple (Pl. 2)	16·00	8·00
33		40r. yellow-buff (Pl. 1)	46·00	7·00
34		50r. pale blue (Pl. 1)	£100	16·00

 In the first printing of the 20r. rosine a cliché of the 40r. (No. 2 in the 2nd row) was inserted; this was found out before issue and the stamp was cancelled in indelible pencil, and is occasionally met with in this form. Sheets with the error were never issued.
 Lithographed stamps perf 12½ are fraudulent.
 All values were reprinted perf 13½ in 1885 and 1905, Plate 2. In addition the 40r. Plate 1 was reprinted imperforate in 1885 and perf 13½, without gum in 1905.

2 King Luis   N **3**   **3** King Carlos

(Des and eng F. A. de Campos. Head embossed, rest typo)

1886 (1 June). Chalk-surfaced paper.

(a) P 12½

35	2	5r. black	20·00	8·00
36		10r. green	20·00	8·00
37		20r. rosine	29·00	16·00
38		25r. claret	21·00	5·75
39		25r. bright mauve	20·00	5·25
40		40r. chocolate	24·00	9·25
41		50r. blue	30·00	5·75
		a. Pale blue	30·00	5·75
42		100r. yellow-brown	46·00	12·50
43		200r. lavender	55·00	17·00
44		300r. orange	55·00	21·00
35/44 *Set of 10*			£300	£100

(b) P 13½

45	2	5r. black	21·00	16·00
46		10r. green	26·00	17·00
47		20r. rosine	22·00	17·00
48		50r. blue	15·00	3·00

 Stamps doubly printed or doubly embossed are met with in this issue and in the corresponding issues of other Portuguese Colonies.
 The 5, 10 and 20r. were reprinted in 1905.

(Des and eng E. C. Azedo Gneco. Typo)

1893 (3 July). NEWSPAPER.

N49	N **3**	2½r. brown (p 11½)	4·00	2·10
N50		2½r. brown (p 12½)	4·00	2·10
N51		2½r. brown (p 13½)	3·50	2·10
N49/51 *Set of 3*			11·00	5·75

 Stamps of this type in this and other Colonies could be, and often were, used for franking ordinary correspondence.

(Des and eng M. D. Neto. Typo)

1894. Chalk-surfaced paper or enamel-surfaced paper (E).

(a) P 11½

49	3	5r. pale orange (5 July)	4·00	1·60
50		5r. pale orange (E)	5·75	2·75
		a. Pale yellow	5·75	2·75

100

51		10r. rosy mauve (25 Sept)	5·25	2·75
52		10r. rosy mauve (E)	4·00	3·00
53		15r. red-brown (25 Sept)	7·00	2·75
54		20r. lavender (5 July)	8·00	3·50
55		25r. green (5 July)	5·25	2·50
56		25r. green (E)	5·75	4·50
57		50r. pale blue (15 May)	7·00	3·25
58		75r. rose (25 Sept)	34·00	22·00
59		75r. rose (E)	17·00	12·50
60		100r. brown/*buff*	£200	£160
61		150r. carmine/*rose* (25 Sept)	29·00	18·00
49/61 Set of 9 (one of each value)			£250	£190

(b) P 12½

62	3	10r. rosy mauve	5·25	3·25
63		15r. red-brown	7·00	2·75
64		25r. green (E)	7·00	2·75
65		50r. pale blue	7·00	3·25
66		50r. pale blue (E)	7·50	3·50
67		75r. rose	14·00	11·50
68		80r. pale green (25 Sept)	20·00	10·50
69		100r. brown/*buff*	20·00	10·50
70		150r. carmine/*rose*	25·00	18·00
71		200r. blue/*blue* (25 Sept)	26·00	18·00
72		300r. blue/*pale brown* (25 Sept)	26·00	18·00
62/72 Set of 10 (one of each value)			£140	90·00

(c) P 13½

73	3	5r. pale orange (E)	4·00	3·00
74		25r. green (E)	5·75	2·50
75		50r. pale blue (E)	23·00	17·00
76		75r. carmine (E)	17·00	11·50
77		200r. blue/*blue*	32·00	17·00
78		300r. blue/*pale brown*	32·00	17·00
73/78 Set of 6			£100	60·00

(4)   5

1894 (Aug). Newspaper stamp, Type N **3**, handstamped with T **4**, in dark blue for use on ordinary mail.

79	N **3**	25r. on 2½r. brown (p 11½)	£110	90·00
		a. Perf 12½	£100	80·00
		b. Perf 13½	80·00	70·00

Stamps exist with the handstamp inverted and double.

(Des and eng E. Mouchon. Typo)

1898 (1 Aug)–**1901**. Name and value in black, on 500r. in carmine. P 11½.

80	**5**	2½r. pale grey	70	55
81		5r. orange-red	70	55
82		10r. green	70	55
83		15r. chocolate	4·00	2·10
84		20r. deep lilac	80	70
85		25r. blue-green	2·10	80
86		50r. blue	3·75	1·10
87		75r. rose	12·50	8·00
88		80r. mauve	11·50	4·00
89		100r. blue/*blue*	2·50	1·60
90		150r. brown/*buff*	12·50	7·50
91		200r. purple/*pink*	7·00	2·30
92		300r. blue/*pink*	8·00	7·00
93		500r. black/*azure* (1901)	8·00	7·00
94		700r. mauve/*yellow* (1901)	39·00	25·00
80/94 Set of 15			£100	60·00

Sets may be made showing early, fine printings, and later, coarse printings. There are many shades.
See also Nos. 142/9.

(6)   (7)

The perforation is given in brackets after each value. (E) denotes enamel-surfaced paper.

1902. Surch as T **6**.

95	**2**	65r. on 40r. (12½)	14·00	8·50
96		65r. on 300r. (12½)	14·00	8·50
97	**3**	65r. on 5r. (11½)	11·50	8·50
98		65r. on 5r. (E) (11½)	11·50	8·50
99		65r. on 10r. (E) (11½)	15·00	8·50
100		65r. on 10r. (12½)	15·00	8·50
101		65r. on 20r. (E) (11½)	15·00	9·25
102		65r. on 20r. (11½)	13·50	8·50
103		65r. on 25r. (11½)	13·50	8·00
104		65r. on 25r. (E) (12½)	14·00	10·50
105		65r. on 25r. (E) (13½)	8·00	7·00
106	**2**	115r. on 10r. (12½)	11·50	8·00
107		115r. on 10r. (13½)	75·00	46·00
108		115r. on 20r. (12½)	11·50	8·00
109	**3**	115r. on 80r. (12½)	20·00	11·50
110		115r. on 100r. (11½)	£275	£225
111		115r. on 100r. (12½)	16·00	10·50
112		115r. on 100r. (13½)	80·00	50·00
113		115r. on 150r. (11½)	21·00	12·50
114		115r. on 150r. (12½)	29·00	16·00
115		115r. on 150r. (13½)	24·00	20·00
116	**2**	130r. on 50r. blue (12½)	16·00	6·25
117		130r. on 50r. pale blue (12½)	16·00	6·25
118		130r. on 100r. (12½)	10·50	6·25
119	**3**	130r. on 15r. (11½)	11·50	6·25
120		130r. on 15r. (12½)	9·25	6·25
121		130r. on 75r. (11½)	80·00	70·00
122		130r. on 75r. (E) (11½)	10·50	9·75
123		130r. on 75r. (E) (13½)	70·00	65·00
124		130r. on 75r. (12½)	11·50	10·50
125		130r. on 300r. (12½)	23·00	20·00
126		130r. on 300r. (13½)	29·00	18·00
127	**2**	400r. on 5r. (12½) (R.)	23·00	17·00
128		400r. on 20r. (12½)	£110	70·00
129		400r. on 20r. (13½)	£225	£150
130		400r. on 25r. claret (12½)	28·00	14·00
130a		400r. on 25r. bright mauve (12½)	28·00	14·00
131	**3**	400r. on 50r. (E) (12½)	10·50	7·00
132		400r. on 50r. (12½)	12·50	8·00
133		400r. on 200r. (12½)	11·50	9·75
134		400r. on 200r. (13½)	£400	£225
135	N **3**	400r. on 2½r. (11½)	5·75	4·00
136		400r. on 2½r. (12½)	2·30	2·00
137		400r. on 2½r. (13½)	2·50	2·30

The 130/50, 400/5, 400/20 and 400/25r. values were reprinted in 1905.

1902. Optd with T **7**.

138	**5**	15r. chocolate	2·75	1·80
139		25r. blue-green	2·30	1·00
140		50r. blue	4·75	2·30
141		75r. rose	8·00	6·25
138/141 Set of 4			16·00	10·00

1903. Colours changed and new values. Name and value in black. P 11½.

142	**5**	15r. deep green	2·00	1·80
143		25r. carmine	90	55
144		50r. brown	9·75	5·75
145		65r. dull blue	10·50	7·00
146		75r. dull purple	4·00	2·50
147		115r. orange-brown/*pink*	16·00	9·75
148		130r. purple-brown/*straw*	16·00	9·75
149		400r. dull blue/*straw*	7·00	4·50
142/149 Set of 8			60·00	37·00

D **8**   (8)   (8a)

(Des and eng J. S. de Carvalho e Silva. Typo)

1904. POSTAGE DUE. Name and value in black. P 11½.

D150	D **8**	5r. yellow-green	45	45
D151		10r. slate	45	45
D152		20r. red-brown	1·00	70
D153		30r. orange	1·00	70
D154		50r. grey-brown	1·30	1·00
D155		60r. pale brown	11·00	7·50
D156		100r. mauve	4·50	3·50
D157		130r. blue	4·50	3·50
D158		200r. carmine	14·00	9·25
D159		500r. deep lilac	11·50	7·50
D150/159 Set of 10			45·00	31·00

See also Nos. D343/52.

ANGOLA

1905. Surch with T **8**.
150	5	50r. on 65r. dull blue	7·00	3·75

1911. Optd with T **8a**, in red or green (G.).
151	5	2½r. pale grey	55	45
152		5r. orange-red	55	45
153		10r. green	55	45
154		15r. dull green	80	70
155		20r. deep lilac	85	75
156		25r. carmine (G.)	85	75
157		50r. brown	3·25	2·00
158		75r. dull purple	6·25	3·75
159		100r. blue/*blue*	6·25	4·25
160		115r. orange-brown/*pink*	4·00	2·30
161		130r. purple-brown/*straw*	4·00	2·30
162		200r. purple/*pink*	4·75	3·00
163		400r. dull blue/*straw*	4·50	2·00
164		500r. black/*azure*	4·50	2·30
165		700r. mauve/*yellow*	4·50	2·50
151/165	Set of 15		41·00	25·00

1911. POSTAGE DUE Optd with T **8a**, in red or green (G.).
D166	D **8**	5r. yellow-green	35	30
D167		10r. slate	35	30
D168		20r. red-brown	35	30
D169		30r. orange	55	45
D170		50r. grey-brown	55	45
D171		60r. pale brown	1·50	1·10
D172		100r. mauve	1·50	1·10
D173		130r. blue	1·70	1·30
D174		200r. carmine (G.)	2·20	1·30
D175		500r. deep lilac	2·30	2·20
D166/175	Set of 10		10·00	8·00

9 King Manoel II   (**9a**)   (**9b**)

(Des and eng D. A. do Rego. Typo)

1912. Optd with T **8a** as shown in T **9**, in red or green (G.). P 11½.
166	**9**	2½r. lilac	70	45
167		5r. black	70	45
168		10r. grey-green	70	45
169		20r. rose-red (G.)	70	45
170		25r. chocolate	70	45
171		50r. blue	1·80	1·40
172		75r. yellow-brown	2·10	1·80
173		100r. brown/*green*	4·00	2·30
174		200r. deep green/*salmon*	4·00	2·30
175		300r. black/*azure*	4·00	2·30
166/175	Set of 10		17·00	11·00

1912 (June). Provisionals issued at Luanda.

*(a) No. 154 surch as T **9a***
176	**5**	2½ on 15r. dull green	5·75	3·25
177		5 on 15r. dull green	6·25	3·25
178		10 on 15r. dull green	4·75	3·25
176/178	Set of 3		15·00	8·75

These stamps are each known with surcharge double; inverted; and double and inverted. These are believed to have been deliberately produced.

*(b) Optd with T **9b**, in violet, and surch with T **9a**, in black*
179	**5**	25 on 75r. rose (No. 141)	90·00	65·00
180		25 on 75r. dull purple (No. 146)	6·25	5·75
		a. "REUPBLICA"	£110	80·00
		b. "REPUBLICA" omitted	£110	80·00

No. 180a occurs on the first stamp in the sheet.

REPUBLICA
ANGOLA
1 C.
(**9c**)   **10** Ceres

1913. New Currency. Vasco da Gama issues surch as T **9c**.

(i) Portuguese Colonies (General Issues)
181		¼c. on 2½r. blue-green	1·30	90
		a. Name and value inverted		
182		½c. on 5r. vermilion	1·30	90
183		1c. on 10r. dull purple	1·30	90
184		2½c. on 25r. yellow-green	1·30	90
185		5c. on 50r. deep blue	1·30	90
186		7½c. on 75r. chocolate	7·50	6·25
187		10c. on 100r. bistre-brown	2·75	1·80
188		15c. on 150r. ochre	2·75	2·30
181/188	Set of 8		18·00	13·50

(ii) Macao
189		¼c. on ½a. blue-green	2·75	2·20
190		½c. on 1a. vermilion	2·75	2·20
191		1c. on 2a. dull purple	2·75	2·20
192		2½c. on 4a. yellow-green	2·30	1·60
193		5c. on 8a. deep blue	2·30	1·60
194		7½c. on 12a. chocolate	9·25	5·75
195		10c. on 16a. bistre-brown	3·50	2·50
196		15c. on 24a. ochre	4·25	2·50
189/196	Set of 8		27·00	18·00

(iii) Timor
197		¼c. on ½a. blue-green	2·75	2·20
198		½c. on 1a. vermilion	2·75	2·20
199		1c. on 2a. dull purple	2·75	2·20
200		2½c. on 4a. yellow-green	2·30	1·60
201		5c. on 8a. deep blue	2·30	1·60
202		7½c. on 12a. chocolate	9·25	5·75
203		10c. on 16a. bistre-brown	3·50	2·50
204		15c. on 24a. ochre	4·25	2·50
197/204	Set of 8		27·00	18·00

(Des C. Fernandes. Eng J. S. de Carvalho e Silva. Typo)

1914. Name and value in black. Chalk-surfaced paper. P 15×14.
205	**10**	¼c. brown-olive	2·30	1·00
206		½c. black	2·30	1·00
207		1c. deep green	2·30	1·00
208		1½c. chocolate	4·50	2·75
209		2c. carmine	8·00	3·75
210		2½c. violet	1·60	70
211		5c. blue	3·50	1·80
212		7½c. yellow-brown	4·50	2·75
213		8c. slate	4·50	2·75
214		10c. brown-red	4·50	2·75
215		15c. claret	7·00	3·00
216		20c. yellow-green	3·50	1·80
217		30c. chocolate/*green*	2·75	2·50
218		40c. brown/*rose*	2·75	2·50
219		50c. orange/*salmon*	11·50	8·00
220		1E. deep green/*azure*	8·50	5·25
205/220	Set of 16		65·00	39·00

See also Nos. 276/329.

1914 (1 Oct). Optd locally with T **9b**.

(a) Stamps of 1898 to 1903
221	**5**	10r. green (R.)	7·00	5·75
222		15r. deep green (R.)	6·25	5·75
223		20r. deep lilac (G.)	2·50	2·00
224		75r. dull purple (R.)	2·50	1·30
225		100r. blue/*blue* (R.)	4·00	3·75
226		200r. purple/*pink* (G.)	2·75	1·80
227		400r. dull blue/*straw* (R.)	48·00	48·00
228		500r. black/*azure* (R.)	6·25	5·75
229		700r. mauve/*yellow* (G.)	32·00	25·00
221/229	Set of 9		£100	90·00

The 130r. (No. 148) with this overprint in red was not regularly issued (*Price* £140 *un*).

(b) Provisional stamps of 1902 and 1905. No gum (Nos. 236/51)
232	**5**	50r. blue (No. 140) (R.)	2·50	2·10
233		50r. on 65r. dull blue (R.)	5·50	3·75
234		75r. rose (No. 141) (G.)	5·75	4·25
235	**2**	115r. on 10r. (12½) (R.)	17·00	17·00
236		115r. on 10r. (13½) (R.)	17·00	17·00
237	**3**	115r. on 80r. (12½) (R.)	£225	£225
238		115r. on 100r. (11½) (R.)	£300	£300
239		115r. on 100r. (12½) (R.)	£275	£250
240		115r. on 100r. (13½) (R.)	£900	£900
241		115r. on 150r. (11½) (G.)	£250	£225
242		115r. on 150r. (12½) (G.)	£275	£225
243		115r. on 150r. (13½) (G.)	£850	£850
244	**2**	115r. on 200r. (12½) (R.)	25·00	25·00
245		130r. on 50r. blue (12½) (R.)	32·00	32·00
246		130r. on 50r. pale blue (12½) (R.)	32·00	32·00
247	**3**	130r. on 75r. (11½) (G.)	9·50	8·75
248		130r. on 75r. (E) (11½) (G.)	4·75	4·25
249		130r. on 75r. (12½) (G.)	10·00	8·25
250		130r. on 300r. (12½) (R.)	18·00	17·00
251		130r. on 300r. (13½) (R.)	11·50	9·50
252	N **3**	400r. on 2½r. (11½) (R.)	5·75	4·50
253		400r. on 2½r. (12½) (R.)	1·10	85
254		400r. on 2½r. (13½) (R.)	1·10	85

1915. Provisionals of 1902 optd at Lisbon with T **8a**, in red. No gum (Nos. 271/2).

255	**2**	115r. on 10r. (12½)	3·00	2·50
256		115r. on 10r. (13½)	2·40	2·30
257	**3**	115r. on 80r. (12½)	3·00	2·50
258		115r. on 80r. (E) (11½)	2·00	1·90
260		115r. on 100r. (11½)	£120	£110
261		115r. on 100r. (12½)	2·50	2·30
262		115r. on 100r. (13½)	19·00	16·00
263		115r. on 150r. (11½)	1·90	1·90
264		115r. on 150r. (12½)	4·50	3·75
265		115r. on 150r. (13½)	3·25	2·50
266	**2**	115r. on 200r. (12½)	2·75	2·30
267	**3**	130r. on 15r. (11½)	2·00	1·90
268		130r. on 15r. (12½)	9·50	8·25
269		130r. on 75r. (11½)	3·75	2·30
270		130r. on 75r. (E) (11½)	3·50	3·00
271		130r. on 75r. (E) (13½)	6·00	5·00
272		130r. on 75r. (12½)	3·75	2·30
273	**2**	130r. on 100r. (12½)	2·30	1·90
274	**3**	130r. on 300r. (12½)	2·30	2·30
275		130r. on 300r. (13½)	4·50	3·00

1915–26. Name and value in black.

(a) Unsurfaced wove paper (thick, medium or thin). P 15×14 (1915-21)

276	**10**	¼c. brown-olive	40	35
		a. Thick carton paper	1·30	1·10
277		½c. black	40	35
		a. Thick carton paper	1·30	1·10
278		1c. green	40	35
		a. Deep green	40	35
		b. Pale yellow-green (1918)	40	35
279		1½c. chocolate	40	35
		a. Thick carton paper	1·30	1·10
280		2c. carmine	40	35
281		2½c. deep violet	40	35
		a. Pale violet (1918)	45	40
282		3c. orange (1921)	37·00	29·00
283		4c. dull claret (1921)	40	35
284		5c. deep blue	1·70	1·40
		a. Pale blue (1918)	40	35
285		6c. mauve (1921)	40	35
286		7c. cobalt (1921)	40	35
287		7½c. yellow-brown (1920)	50	40
288		8c. slate	45	40
289		10c. brown-red (1918)	40	35
290		12c. olive-brown (1921)	1·70	1·00
291		15c. plum (1920)	40	35
		a. Dull rose (1921)	40	35
292		20c. yellow-green (1918)	7·00	5·75
293		30c. deep grey-green (1921)	1·00	70
294		80c. carmine (1921)	2·10	1·00
		a. Bright rosine	2·10	1·00
295		2E. deep purple (1921)	4·00	3·50
276/295 Set of 20			55·00	41·00

(b) Unsurfaced paper. P 12×11½ (1921-26)

296	**10**	¼c. brown-olive (1924)	40	35
297		½c. black	40	35
298		1c. green (1924)	40	35
		a. Deep green	40	35
		b. Pale yellow-green	40	35
299		1½c. chocolate (1924)	40	35
300		2c. rose-scarlet (1924)	40	35
		a. Carmine-red	40	35
301		2c. drab (1925)	70	55
302		2½c. mauve (1924)	40	35
303		3c. orange	35	30
304		4c. dull claret	35	30
		a. Pink	35	30
305		4½c. drab	35	30
306		5c. deep blue (1924)	3·00	2·00
		a. Pale blue	40	35
307		6c. mauve	35	30
308		7c. cobalt	35	30
309		7½c. yellow-brown (1924)	45	40
310		8c. slate (1924)	45	40
311		10c. brown-red (1924)	40	35
312		12c. olive-brown	70	55
313		12c. blue-green (1925)	70	55
314		15c. dull rose (1924)	40	35
315		20c. yellow-green (1924)	2·00	1·70
316		24c. cobalt (1925)	1·70	1·40
317		25c. chocolate (1925)	1·70	1·40
318		30c. deep grey-green	70	55
		a. Dull blue-green	70	55
319		40c. turquoise	1·40	70
320		50c. purple (1925)	1·40	70
321		60c. deep blue	1·70	1·00
322		60c. carmine (1926)	£100	60·00
322*a*		80c. bright rosine	2·10	1·00
323		1E. carmine-pink	2·10	1·00
296/323 Set of 29			£110	70·00

(c) Glazed paper. P 12×11½ (1921-25)

324	**10**	1E. carmine-pink	2·10	1·00
325		1E. deep blue (1925)	3·50	2·10
326		2E. deep purple	2·75	1·40
327		5E. pale yellow-brown (1925)	18·00	15·00
328		10E. pink (1925)	38·00	31·00
329		20E. pale green (1925)	£110	80·00
324/329 Set of 6			£160	£120

(11) ½ C.   (12) 1 cent   (13) $00,5

1919–21. Various stamps surch locally and with old values cancelled with two bars. No gum (Nos. 338/9, 342).

*(a) Surch as T **11** (1919)*

330	**5**	½c. on 75r. dull purple (No. 158)	3·25	2·50
331	**9**	½c. on 75r. yellow-brown	1·60	1·30
332	**5**	½c. on 75r. dull purple (No. 224)	1·80	1·60
333		2½c. on 100r. blue/*blue* (No. 159)	3·25	2·50
334	**9**	2½c. on 100r. brown/*green*	3·00	2·30
335	**5**	2½c. on 100r. blue/*blue* (No. 225)	2·30	1·70

*(b) Surch as T **12** or **13** (1921)*

336	**9**	1c. on 50r. brown	2·00	1·80
337	**5**	4c. on 130r. purple-brown/*straw* (No. 161)	2·50	1·80
338		4c. on 130r. purple-brown/*straw**	7·50	6·25
339	**10**	$04 on 15c. claret	2·50	1·80
340		$04 on 10c. dull rose (No. 314)	25·00	
341	**9**	$00.5 on 75r. yellow-brown	1·80	1·60
342	**10**	$00.5 on 7½c. yellow-brown	2·50	2·10

*No. 338. also overprinted with Type **9b** in red, was not issued without the surcharge (see note after No. 229).

1921. POSTAGE DUE. Name and value ("centavos") in black. P 11½.

D343	D **8**	½c. pale yellow-green	40	35
D344		1c. slate	40	35
D345		2c. deep red-brown	40	35
D346		3c. pale orange	40	35
D347		5c. grey-brown	40	35
D348		6c. pale brown	40	35
D349		10c. mauve	55	45
D350		13c. blue	1·00	90
D351		20c. carmine	1·00	90
D352		50c. lilac-grey	1·00	90
D343/352 Set of 10			5·25	4·75

Sets may be made on soft, smooth paper and thin coarse paper, the shades differing in the latter particularly in the 3c., which is yellow.

CHARITY TAX STAMPS. Stamps bearing C numbers were for compulsory use on internal letters on certain days of the year as an additional postal tax for public charities. Other values in some of the types were for use on telegrams or for fiscal purposes.

1925 (8 May). CHARITY TAX. Marquis de Pombal issue of Portugal, inscr "ANGOLA".

C343	C **73**	15c. dull violet	1·10	90
C344	C **74**	15c. dull violet	1·10	90
C345	C **75**	15c. dull violet	1·10	90
C343/345 Set of 3			3·00	2·40

Nos. C343/5 were in use from 8th to 13th May 1925 and from 5th to 15th May in 1926 and 1929. The Postage Due stamps, Nos. D353/5, were used in default.

1925 (8 May). POSTAGE DUE. As Nos. C343/5 optd "MULTA".

D353	C **73**	30c. dull violet	1·10	90
D354	C **74**	30c. dull violet	1·10	90
D355	C **75**	30c. dull violet	1·10	90
D353/355 Set of 3			3·00	2·40

(14) 40 C.   C 15   (16) 50 C.

1925 (July). Provisionals of 1902 surch with T **14**.

343	**3**	40c. on 400r. on 200r. (12½)	1·00	1·00
344		40c. on 400r. on 200r. (13½)	1·00	1·00
345	N **3**	40c. on 400r. on 2½r. (12½)	1·50	1·10
346		40c. on 400r. on 2½r. (13½)	6·25	5·00

ANGOLA

(Litho Imprensa Nacional de Luanda)
1929 (1 June). CHARITY TAX. P 10½×11.
| C347 | C 15 | 50c. blue | 7·00 | 2·00 |

In use from 1 to 30 June and from 8 December to 8 January in 1929 and 1930.

1931. Surch as T **16**. P 12×11½.
347	10	50c. on 60c. carmine	2·30	2·00
348		70c. on 80c. rosine	4·50	3·50
349		70c. on 1E. deep blue	4·25	3·50
350		1E.40 on 2E. deep purple	2·75	2·10
347/350 Set of 4			12·50	10·00

22 Vasco da Gama   **24** "Fomento" (Symbolising Progress)   **27** Airplane over Globe

17 Ceres   **18**

(Des C. Fernandes. Eng A. Fragoso. Typo)
1932–46. New Currency. W **18**. P 12×11½.
351	17	1c. brown	35	25
352		5c. sepia	35	35
353		10c. mauve	35	35
354		15c. black	35	35
355		20c. grey	35	35
356		30c. blue-green	35	35
357		35c. emerald (1946)	9·25	4·25
358		40c. vermilion	45	25
359		45c. turquoise-blue	1·70	1·40
360		50c. cinnamon	35	25
361		60c. olive-green	1·10	35
362		70c. red-brown	1·10	35
363		80c. emerald	70	25
364		85c. carmine	5·75	2·50
365		1a. claret	1·10	35
366		1a.40 blue	11·50	3·50
367		1a.75 blue (1946)	20·00	5·25
368		2a. mauve	5·75	55
369		5a. yellow-green	11·50	1·80
370		10a. bistre-brown	23·00	5·75
371		20a. orange	55·00	5·75
351/371 Set of 21			£140	31·00

Three examples of No. 369 with "5 A." omitted are known on same piece (with other stamps) postmarked from Lubito in 1938.

(Des A. R. Garcia. Recess Bradbury, Wilkinson)
1938 (26 July). Various centres. Name and value in black. P 13½×13.

(a) POSTAGE
383	22	1c. grey-olive	25	25
384		5c. orange-brown	35	35
385		10c. carmine	45	45
386		15c. brown-purple	45	45
387		20c. slate	45	35
388	A	30c. bright purple	55	45
389		35c. emerald-green	1·10	80
390		40c. brown	35	25
391		50c. magenta	55	25
392	24	60c. grey-black	1·10	35
393		70c. slate-violet	1·10	35
394		80c. orange	1·10	35
395		1a. scarlet	1·10	35
396	B	1a.75 blue	2·30	1·00
397		2a. lake	3·50	1·10
398		5a. olive-green	16·00	1·10
399	C	10a. ultramarine	32·00	1·30
400		20a. red-brown	44·00	4·00
383/400 Set of 18			95·00	12·00

Designs:—A, Mousinho de Albuquerque; B, Prince Henry the Navigator; C, Afonso de Albuquerque.

(b) AIR
401	27	10c. scarlet	45	40
402		20c. bright violet	45	40
403		50c. orange	45	40
404		1a. bright blue	45	40
405		2a. brown-lake	1·00	45
406		3a. blue-green	1·80	70
407		5a. red-brown	7·00	1·00
408		9a. carmine	8·00	2·00
409		10a. magenta	11·00	2·75
401/409 Set of 9			28·00	7·75

CORREIOS

= = ≡ 5 = =

10 C.   **0,15 Cent.**

(19)   (20)   (21)

1934. Surch locally as T **19**.
372	17	10c. on 45c. turquoise-blue	3·75	2·75
373		20c. on 85c. carmine	3·75	2·75
374		30c. on 1a.40 blue	3·75	2·75
375		70c. on 2a. mauve	6·25	2·75
376		80c. on 5a. yellow-green	9·75	2·75

For similarly surcharged stamps see Nos. 413/18.

1935. Surch locally as T **20** for ordinary mail. No gum. P 11½.
377	D 8	5c. on 6c. pale brown	2·50	1·60
378		30c. on 50c. lilac-grey	2·50	1·60
379		40c. on 50c. lilac-grey	2·50	1·60
		a. Surch inverted	23·00	
377/378 Set of 2			6·00	4·00

1938. Surch locally as T **21**.
380	17	5c. on 80c. emerald	1·00	55
381		10c. on 80c. emerald	1·80	90
382		15c. on 80c. emerald	2·50	90
380/382 Set of 3			4·50	2·00

28 Portuguese Colonial Column   **C 29**

(Recess Bradbury, Wilkinson)
1938 (29 July). President's Colonial Tour. P 12½.
410	28	80c. blue-green	3·50	2·20
411		1a.75 blue	23·00	6·25
412		20a. red-brown	70·00	40·00

(Litho Imprensa Nacional de Luanda)
1939 (1 Jan). CHARITY TAX. No gum. P 11.
| C413 | C 29 | 50c. blue-green | 4·00 | 35 |
| C414 | | 1a. scarlet | 9·25 | 2·50 |

A 1a.50 value also exists but was only used for fiscal purposes.

1942. T **17** surch with new value and bars, as T **19**, but distance between surch and bars increased to 8 mm.
413	17	10c. on 45c. turquoise-blue	2·00	1·30
414		15c. on 45c. turquoise-blue	2·00	1·30
415		20c. on 85c. carmine	2·00	1·30
416		35c. on 85c. carmine	2·00	1·30
417		50c. on 1a.40 blue	2·00	1·30
418		60c. on 1a. claret	11·00	8·50
413/418 Set of 6			19·00	13·50

ANGOLA

(30) 31 Arms of Angola

1945–46. Surch locally with new value and bars, as T **30**, or smaller surch on T **17**, with bars above and "CENTAVOS" below the figure.

419	17	5c. on 80c. emerald	1·00	55
420	24	5c. on 80c. orange	1·00	55
421		50c. on 1a. scarlet	1·00	55
422		– 50c. on 1a.75 blue (No. 396)	1·00	55
423		– 50c. on 1a.75 blue (No. 396) (R.)	1·00	55
419/423 Set of 5			4·50	2·50

(Typo Imprensa Nacional de Luanda)

1947 (6 Aug). AIR. No gum. Rough perf 11.

423a	31	1a. red-brown	11·50	7·00
423b		2a. yellow-green	12·50	8·00
423c		3a. orange	12·50	8·00
423d		3a.50 orange	23·00	8·00
423e		5a. olive-green	£110	29·00
423f		6a. rose	£110	23·00
423g		9a. red	£350	£225
423h		10a. green	£225	£100
423i		20a. blue	£375	£110
423j		50a. black	£500	£275
423k		100a. yellow	£800	£700
423a/k Set of 11			£2250	£1300

32 S. Miguel Fortress, Luanda

(Des A. de Sousa. Litho Litografia Maia, Oporto)

1948 (May). Tercentenary of Restoration of Angola. As T **32** (inscr "Tricentenario da Restauracao de Angola 1648–1948"). P 14.

424		5c. violet	35	25
425		10c. chocolate	90	35
426		30c. turquoise-green	35	25
427		50c. purple	35	25
428		1a. carmine	90	25
429		1a.75 blue	1·60	25
430		2a. emerald-green	1·60	25
431		5a. black	3·75	70
432		10a. magenta	12·50	90
433		20a. greenish blue	28·00	5·75
424/433 Set of 10			45·00	8·25
MS433a 162×225 mm. Nos. 424/33 (sold at 42a.50)			£140	£140

Designs: Horiz—10c. Our Lady of Nazareth Hermitage, Luanda; 1a. Surrender of Luanda; 5a. Inscribed rocks at Yelala; 20a. Massangano Fortress. Vert (*portraits*)—30c. Don John IV; 50c. Salvador Correia de Sa Benevides; 1a.75, Dioga Cao, 2a. Manuel Cerveira Pereira; 10a. Paulo Dias de Novais.

33 Our Lady of Fatima

PORTEADO
10
Centavos
(D **34**)

(Des A. Negreiros. Litho Litografia Nacional, Oporto)

1948 (Dec). Honouring the Statue of Our Lady of Fatima. P 14.

434	33	50c. carmine	2·75	1·70
435		3a. ultramarine	11·00	3·50
436		6a. orange	34·00	8·50
437		9a. claret	90·00	11·00
434/437 Set of 4			£120	22·00

1949 (Feb). POSTAGE DUE. Optd as Type D **34**.

D438	17	10c. on 20c. grey	45	40
D439		20c. on 30c. blue-green	55	50
D440		30c. on 50c. cinnamon	1·00	90
D441		40c. on 1a. claret	1·30	1·10
D442		50c. on 2a. mauve	2·00	1·80
D443		1a. on 5a. yellow-green	3·00	2·75
D438/443 Set of 6			7·50	6·75

35 River Chiumbe   36 Pedras Negras

(Des M. Jorge (20c., 40c., 15a.), A. de Sousa (others). Die eng Rosa (20c., 15a.), Fragoso (50c., 3a.50), Americo (2a.50) and Norte (50a.). Typo)

1949 (Feb). Designs as T **35**/**6**. P 13½.

438		20c. grey-blue	80	25
439		40c. blackish brown	80	25
440		50c. brown-lake	80	25
441		2a.50 bright blue	4·00	50
442		3a.50 slate	4·00	2·30
443		15a. deep green	29·00	2·30
444		50a. emerald-green	£160	9·25
438/444 Set of 7			£180	13·50

Designs: Horiz—50c. View of Luanda; 2a.50, View of Bandeira; 3a.50, View of Mocamedes; 50a. Braganza Falls. 33×28 mm. 15a. River Cubal.

37 Boeing 377 Stratocruiser, Douglas DC-3 and Globe

38 *Tentativa Feliz* (19th-century sailing ship)

39 Letter and Globe

(Photo Courvoisier)

1949 (Feb). AIR. P 11½.

445	37	1a. brown-orange	80	25
446		2a. red-brown	1·70	25
447		3a. magenta	2·30	25
448		6a. grey-green	4·25	90
449		9a. purple	6·25	2·20
445/449 Set of 5			14·00	3·50

Although intended for air mail use, the above issue was valid for all classes of mail.

(Des Malheiro. Litho Litografia Maia, Oporto)

1949 (Aug). Centenary of Founding of Mocamedes. P 14.

450	38	1a. brown-purple	9·25	1·00
451		4a. blue-green	28·00	2·75

(Des A. Negreiros. Litho Litografia Maia, Oporto)

1949 (Oct). 75th Anniv of Universal Postal Union. P 14.

| 452 | 39 | 4a. blue-green | 14·00 | 3·50 |

40 Reproduction of T **1**

41 Bells and Dove

42 Angel holding Candelabra

1950 (2 Apr). Philatelic Exhibition and 80th Anniv of First Angolan Stamp. Litho. P 11½×12.

453	40	50c. yellow-green	1·70	55
454		1a. carmine-red	1·70	90
455		4a. black	6·25	2·10
453/455 Set of 3			8·75	3·25
MS455a 120×79 mm. Nos. 453/5 (sold at 6a.50)			34·00	29·00

ANGOLA

(Des J. Araujo. Litho Litografia de Portugal, Lisbon)
1950 (May). Holy Year. P 13½.

456	41	1a. violet	1·60	35
457	42	4a. black	6·25	1·10

43 Dark Chanting Goshawk   **44** Our Lady of Fatima   D **45**

(Photo Courvoisier)

1951 (23 Jan–27 May). Birds as T **43**. Birds, etc. in natural colours. Colours of backgrounds and inscriptions given below. P 11½.

458	5c. grey-blue and black	55	20
459	10c. greenish blue and brown (27.3)	55	20
460	15c. rose and black (22.3)	90	20
461	20c. yellow and brown	1·00	45
462	50c. slate-blue and black (22.3)	1·00	20
463	1a. grey-violet and black	1·00	20
464	1a.50 stone and black (27.3)	1·50	20
465	2a. buff and black	4·00	20
466	2a.50 blue-grey and black	2·20	20
467	3a. lemon and black (27.3)	1·50	20
468	3a.50 grey and black (22.3)	2·20	20
469	4a. brown and black (22.3)	2·50	20
470	4a.50 lilac and black	2·50	20
471	5a. green and blue	8·00	70
472	6a. blue and black (27.3)	10·50	1·70
473	7a. orange and black (22.3)	11·50	2·30
474	10a. mauve and black (27.3)	46·00	2·75
475	12a.50 grey-green and black	14·50	4·00
476	15a. yellow-green and black (27.1)	13·00	4·00
477	20a. flesh and black (22.3)	£100	9·75
478	25a. pink and black (27.3)	48·00	8·00
479	30a. salmon and black (27.3)	48·00	8·50
480	40a. orange-yellow and black	65·00	12·50
481	50a. turquoise and blue-green (27.3)	£140	30·00
458/481 Set of 24		£475	80·00

Birds: Horiz—10c. Racquet-tailed roller; 15c. Bateleur; 20c. European bee eater; 2a.50, African skimmer; 3a. Shikra; 4a.50, Magpie; 12a.50, White-crowned shrike; 30a. Sulphur-breasted bush shrike. Vert—50c. Giant kingfisher; 1a. Anchieto's barbet; 1a.50, African open-bill stork; 2a. Southern ground hornbill; 3a.50, Denham's bustard; 4a. African golden oriole; 5a. Red-shouldered glossy starling; 6a. Sharp-tailed glossy starling; 7a. Fan-tailed whydah; 10a. Half-collared kingfisher; 15a. White-winged starling; 20a. Southern yellow-billed hornbill; 25a. Violet starling; 40a. Secretary bird; 50a. Peach-faced lovebird.

(Litho Litografia Nacional, Oporto)

1951 (Oct). Termination of Holy Year. P 14.

482	44	4a. orange and pale orange	4·50	1·50

To each of these stamps is attached a label of the same size inscribed with a Papal declaration which differs for each over-seas province.

(Litho Litografia Nacional, Oporto)

1952. POSTAGE DUE. Numerals in red, name in black. P 14.

D483	D **45**	10c. red-brown and olive	35	30
D484		30c. yellow-green and light blue	35	30
D485		50c. brown and pale brown	35	30
D486		1a. deep blue, green and orange	65	55
D487		2a. red-brown and vermilion	80	75
D488		5a. brown and light blue	80	75
D483/488 Set of 6			3·00	2·75

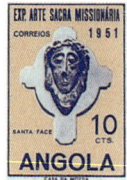

45 Laboratory   **46** The Sacred Face

(Des A. de Sousa. Litho.)

1952 (June). First Tropical Medicine Congress, Lisbon. P 13½.

483	**45**	1a. grey and ultramarine	1·30	45

1952 (Oct). Missionary Art Exhibition. Litho. P 13½.

484	**46**	10c. deep blue and flesh	20	20
485		50c. deep green and stone	1·00	25
486		2a. purple and flesh	3·75	70
484/486 Set of 3			4·50	1·00

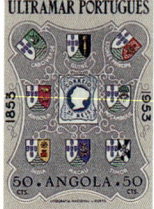

47 Leopard   **48** Stamp of 1853 and Colonial Arms

(Litho Litografia Maia, Oporto)

1953 (15 Aug). Angolan Fauna. T **47** and similar multicoloured designs. P 13.

487	5c. Type **47**	25	25
488	10c. Sable antelope (vert)	25	25
489	20c. African elephant (vert)	25	25
490	30c. Eland (vert)	25	25
491	40c. Crocodile	25	25
492	50c. Impala (vert)	25	25
493	1a. Mountain zebra (vert)	35	25
494	1a.50 Sitatunga (vert)	35	25
495	2a. Black rhinoceros	35	25
496	2a.30 Gemsbok (vert)	35	25
497	2a.50 Lion (vert)	45	25
498	3a. African buffalo	55	25
499	3a.50 Springbok (vert)	55	25
500	4a. Blue wildebeest (vert)	20·00	25
501	5a. Hartebeest (vert)	90	25
502	7a. Warthog (vert)	1·40	25
503	10a. Waterbuck (vert)	2·75	25
504	12a.50 Hippopotamus (vert)	7·50	1·50
505	15a. Greater kudu (vert)	9·25	1·50
506	20a. Giraffe (vert)	11·50	90
487/506 Set of 20		50·00	7·25

(Litho Litografia Nacional, Oporto)

1953 (Nov). Portuguese Stamp Centenary. P 13.

507	**48**	50c. multicoloured	1·30	55

Currency Reversion to Escudos

49 Father M. de Nobrega and Sao Paulo   **50** Route of President's Tour

1954. Fourth Centenary of Sao Paulo. Litho. P 13½.

508	**49**	1E. multicoloured	80	35

1954 (27 May). Presidential Visit. Litho. P 13.

509	**50**	35c. multicoloured	15	15
510		4E.50 multicoloured	1·70	80

51 Map of Angola   C **52** Old Man   **52** Colonel A. de Paiva

(Des J. de Moura. Litho)

1955 (Aug). Map multicoloured; Angola territory in colour given below. P 13½.

511	**51**	5c. white	20	20
512		20c. salmon	20	20
513		50c. pale blue	20	20
514		1E. orange-yellow	20	20

ANGOLA

515	2E.30 greenish yellow		1·30	45
516	4E. pale blue		2·50	25
517	10E. apple-green		3·00	25
518	20E. white		4·25	1·80
511/518	Set of 8		10·50	3·25

(Litho Empresa Grafica de Angola, Luanda)

1955. CHARITY TAX. Type C **52** and similar vert designs. Heads in deep brown. Face value in upright figures. Size 19½×26½ mm. Imprint "FOTO.LITO—E. G. A.—LUANDA" at foot of design. P 13.

C519	50c. ochre-brown		35	35
C520	1E. orange-red (Boy)		80	35
C521	1E.50 apple-green (Girl)		80	35
C522	2E.50 greenish blue (Old woman)		1·00	55
C519/522	Set of 4		2·75	1·40

See also Nos. C544, C630/2 and C646/8.

1956 (9 Oct). Birth Centenary of De Paiva. Litho. P 13½×12½.

519	**52**	1E. black, blue and yellow-orange	45	35

53 Quela Chief

54 Father J. M. Antunes

(Des Neves and Sousa. Photo Courvoisier)

1957 (1 Jan). Native types as T **53**. Multicoloured. P 11½.

520	5c. Type **53**		20	20
521	10c. Andulo flute player		20	20
522	15c. Dernbos man and woman		20	20
523	20c. Quissama dancer (male)		20	20
524	30c. Quibala family		20	20
525	40c. Bocolo dancer (female)		20	20
526	50c. Quissama woman		20	20
527	80c. Cuanhama woman		45	45
528	1E.50 Luanda widow		2·75	45
529	2E.50 Bocolo dancer (male)		3·50	25
530	4E. Muquixe man		1·40	25
531	10E. Cabinda chief		3·00	55
520/531	Set of 12		11·50	3·00

(Des J. de Moura. Litho)

1957 (4 Jan). Birth Centenary of Father Antunes. P 13½.

532	**54**	1E. deep brown, black, pale salmon and turquoise-green	90	45

(C **55**)   (C **56**)

1957. CHARITY TAX. No. C519 surch as Type C **55**.

C533	10c. on 50c. ochre-brown (R.)	35	35
C534	30c. on 50c. ochre-brown	35	35

1958. CHARITY TAX. No. C519 with smaller surch, Type C **56**.

C535	10c. on 50c. ochre-brown	35	35

55 Exhibition Emblem, Globe and Arms

56 *Securidaca longipedunculata*

(Des J. de Moura. Litho)

1958 (July). Brussels International Exhibition. P 12×11½.

533	**55**	1E.50 multicoloured	80	70

(Des J. de Moura. Litho)

1958 (5 Sept). Sixth International Congress of Tropical Medicine. P 13½.

534	**56**	2E.50 multicoloured	3·50	1·00

57 Native Doctor and Patient

C **58** Mother and Child

1958 (10 Oct). 75th Anniv of Maria Pia Hospital, Luanda. Various vert designs as T **57**. P 11½×12.

535	1E. red-brown, black and pale blue	55	35
536	1E.50 multicoloured	1·40	70
537	2E.50 multicoloured	2·50	1·30
535/537	Set of 3	4·00	2·10

Designs:—1E.50, 17th-century doctor and patient; 2E.50, Present-day doctor, orderly and patients.

(Litho Empresa Grafica de Angola, Luanda)

1959. CHARITY TAX. Type C **58** and similar vert design. P 13.

C538	10c. black and orange	35	35
C539	30c. black and slate (Boy and girl)	35	35

58 Welwitschia (plant)

59 Old Map of West Africa

(Des Neves and Sousa. Litho Litografia de Portugal, Oporto)

1959 (3 Sept). Centenary of Discovery of Welwitschia. T **58** and similar horiz designs. P 14×14½.

538	1E.50 multicoloured	1·10	55
539	2E.50 multicoloured	1·70	70
540	5E. multicoloured	2·75	70
541	10E. multicoloured	6·25	2·30
538/541	Set of 4	10·50	3·75

Designs:—2E.50, 5E., 10E. Various types of welwitschia (*Welwitschia mirabilis*).

(Des J. de Moura. Litho)

1960 (29 June). Fifth Centenary of Death of Prince Henry the Navigator. P 13½×13.

542	**59**	2E.50 multicoloured	70	35

60 "Agriculture" (distribution of seeds)

61

(Des Neves and Sousa. Litho Litografia Maia, Oporto)

1960 (1 Oct). Tenth Anniv of African Technical Co-operation Commission. P 14½.

543	**60**	2E.50 multicoloured	80	35

1961 (Nov). CHARITY TAX. No. C520 redrawn with value in italics.

C544	1E. orange-red	35	35

1961 (30 Nov). Angolan Women. T **61** and similar vert portraits. Litho. Portraits multicoloured; background colours below. P 13×13½.

544	10c. light yellow-green	10	10
545	15c. light blue	10	10
546	30c. yellow	10	10
547	40c. green	10	10
548	60c. orange-brown	10	10
549	1E.50 light greenish blue	15	10
550	2E. lilac	1·30	10
551	2E.50 greenish yellow	1·30	10
552	3E. pink	4·50	35
553	4E. light olive-green	2·30	35

ANGOLA

554	5E. light blue		1·50	35
555	7E.50 light yellow		2·10	1·00
556	10E. buff		1·50	80
557	15E. pale brown		2·30	1·00
558	25E. pale rose		3·25	1·50
559	50E. light grey		5·75	3·25
544/559 Set of 16			24·00	8·50

 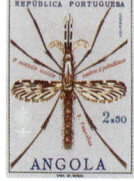

62 Weightlifting   **63** *Anopheles funestus* (mosquito)

(Des J. de Moura. Photo Litografia Nacional, Oporto)

1962 (3 Mar). Sports. T **62** and similar diamond-shaped designs. Multicoloured. P 13.

560	50c. Flying		20	20
561	1E. Rowing		1·40	25
562	1E.50 Water polo		90	35
563	2E.50 Putting the shot		1·10	35
564	4E.50 High jumping		90	70
565	15E. Type **62**		2·30	1·70
560/565 Set of 6			6·00	3·25

(Des J. de Moura. Litho)

1962 (Apr). Malaria Eradication. P 13½.
566	**63**	2E.50 multicoloured	2·10	90

64 Gen. Norton de Matos (statue)   C **65** Yellow, White and Black Men

(Litho Litografia Maia, Oporto)

1962 (8 Aug). 50th Anniv of Nova Lisboa. P 14½.
567	**64**	2E.50 multicoloured	70	35

(Litho Empresa Grafica de Angola, Luanda)

1962. CHARITY TAX. Provincial Settlement Committee. No gum. P 10½.
C568	C **65**	50c. multicoloured	35	35
		a. Perf 11½	35	35
C569		1E. multicoloured	55	25

The tax was used to promote Portuguese settlement in Angola and to improve living standards of immigrants. Higher values were for fiscal use.

65 *Nomadacris Septemfasciata* (Locust)   **66** Arms of St. Paul of the Assumption, Luanda

(Des J. de Moura. Litho Litografia Maia, Oporto)

1963 (17 June). 15th Anniv of International Locust Eradication Service. P 14½.
568	**65**	2E.50 multicoloured	2·10	55

(Des J. de Moura. Litho)

1963 (15 Aug). Angolan Civic Arms (1st series). T **66** and similar diamond-shaped designs. Multicoloured. P 13½.

569	5c. Type **66**		20	20
570	10c. Massangano		20	20
571	30c. Muxima		20	20
572	50c. Carmona		20	20
573	1E. Salazar		80	20
574	1E.50 Malanje		1·50	20
575	2E. Henry of Carvalho		80	20
576	2E.50 Mocamedes		4·50	70
577	3E. Novo Redondo		1·10	20
578	3E.50 St. Salvador (Congo)		1·30	20
579	5E. Luso		1·10	35
580	7E.50 St. Philip (Benguela)		1·50	1·30
581	10E. Lobito		1·80	1·10
582	12E.50 Gabela		2·10	1·80
583	15E. Sa da Bendeira		2·10	1·80
584	17E.50 Silva Porto		3·50	3·00
585	20E. Nova Lisboa		3·50	2·50
586	22E.50 Cabinda		3·50	3·00
587	30E. Serpa Pinto		4·25	4·00
569/587 Set of 19			31·00	19·00

See also Nos. 589/610.

67 Rear-Admiral A. Tomas   **68** Arms of Sanza-Pombo   **69** Map of Africa and Boeing 707 and Lockheed L.1409G Super Constellation Airliners

1963 (16 Sept). Presidential Visit. Litho. P 13½.
588	**67**	2E.50 multicoloured	70	25

(Des J. de Moura. Litho)

1963 (5 Oct). Angolan Civic Arms (2nd series). T **68** and similar vert designs. Multicoloured. P 13½.

589	15c. Type **68**		25	20
590	20c. St. Antonio do Zaire		25	20
591	25c. Ambriz		25	20
592	40c. Ambrizete		25	20
593	60c. Catete		25	20
594	70c. Quibaxe		25	20
595	1E. Maquela do Zombo		25	20
596	1E.20 Bembe		25	20
597	1E.50 Caxito		80	20
598	1E.80 Dondo		80	70
599	2E.50 Damba		3·00	25
600	4E. Cuimba		70	25
601	6E.50 Negage		70	45
602	7E. Quitexe		1·00	70
603	8E. Mucaba		1·00	80
604	9E. 31 de Janeiro		1·50	1·30
605	11E. Novo Caipemba		1·70	1·50
606	14E. Songo		2·00	1·70
607	17E. Quimbele		2·10	2·00
608	25E. Noqui		2·50	2·00
609	35E. Santa Cruz		3·75	3·00
610	50E. General Freire		4·75	2·50
589/610 Set of 22			25·00	17·00

(Des J. de Moura. Litho Litografia Maia, Oporto)

1963 (5 Oct). Tenth Anniv of T.A.P. Airline. P 14½.
611	**69**	1E. multicoloured	1·40	45

70 Bandeira Cathedral   **71** Dr. A. T. de Sousa

ANGOLA

(Litho Litografia Nacional, Oporto)

1963 (1 Nov). Angolan Churches. T **70** and similar multicoloured designs. P 14½×14 (vert) or 14×14½ (horiz).

612	10c. Type **70**	10	10
613	20c. Landana	10	10
614	30c. Luanda (Cathedral)	10	10
615	40c. Gabela	10	10
616	50c. St. Martin, Bay of Tigers (Chapel)	10	10
617	1E. Melange (Cathedral) (horiz)	25	20
618	1E.50 St. Peter, Chibia	25	20
619	2E. Benguela (horiz)	35	20
620	2E.50 Jesus, Luanda	35	20
621	3E. Camabatela (horiz)	45	20
622	3E.50 Cabinda Mission	55	20
623	4E. Vila Folgares (horiz)	70	30
624	4E.50 Arrabida Lobito (horiz)	90	35
625	5E. Cabinda	90	45
626	7E.50 Cacuso, Malange (horiz)	1·50	80
627	10E. Lubanga Mission	2·00	80
628	12E.50 Hula Mission (horiz)	2·30	1·30
629	15E. Island Cape, Luanda (horiz)	2·50	1·40
612/629 Set of 18		12·00	6·50

1964 (Mar)–**65**. CHARITY TAX. As Nos. C519/21 but redrawn, size 20×27 mm and without imprint. Typo. P 11½.

C630	50c. brown-orange	35	30
C631	1E. orange-red (1965)	35	30
C632	1E.50 yellow-green (1965)	35	30
C630/632 Set of 3		90	80

See also Nos. C646/8.

1964 (16 May). Centenary of National Overseas Bank. Litho. P 13½.
| 630 | **71** | 2E.50 multicoloured | 90 | 45 |

72 Arms and Palace of Commerce, Luanda

73 I.T.U. Emblem and St. Gabriel

1964 (13 Apr). Centenary of Luanda Commercial Association. Litho. P 12.
| 631 | **72** | 1E. multicoloured | 45 | 25 |

(Litho Litografia Nacional, Oporto)

1965 (17 May). Centenary of International Telecommunications Union. P 14½.
| 632 | **73** | 2E.50 multicoloured | 1·40 | 70 |

74 Boeing 707 over Petroleum Refinery

C **75** "Full Employment"

75 Fokker F.27 Friendship CR-LEO over Luanda Airport

(Des I. Saslkovits (1E.50), C. Rocha (3E., 4E.50, 5E., 8E.). Litho)

1965 (17 July). AIR. T **74** and similar designs. Multicoloured. P 11½×12 (1E.50) or 12×11½ (others).

633	1E.50 Type **74**	1·40	20
634	2E.50 Cambambe Dam	1·40	20
635	3E. Salazar Dam	2·00	20
636	4E. Capt. Trofilo Duarte Dam	2·00	25
637	4E.50 Creveiro Lopes Dam	1·40	25
638	5E. Cuango Dam	1·40	35
639	6E. Quanta Bridge	2·20	45
	a. Ultramarine ("ANGOLA" and inscr omitted)		
640	7E. Capt. Trofilo Duarte Railway Bridge	3·25	45
641	8E.50 Dr. Oliveira Salazar Bridge	4·00	1·30
642	12E.50 Capt. Silva Carvalho Railway Bridge	4·25	1·70
633/642 Set of 10		21·00	4·75

Nos. 634/42 are horiz and each design includes a Boeing 707 airliner overhead.

(Des V. Santos. Litho Institute Nacional de Assistencia)

1965 (1 Sept). CHARITY TAX. Provincial Settlement Committee. P 13.
C643	C **75**	50c. multicoloured	55	35
C644		1E. multicoloured	55	35
C645		2E. multicoloured	55	35
C643/645 Set of 3			1·50	90

(Litho Imprensa Nacional de Angola, Luanda)

1965. CHARITY TAX. As Nos. C630/2 but size 19×26 mm and with "INA" at foot. P 13.
C646	50c. brown-orange	35	25
C647	1E. orange-red	35	25
C648	1E.50 yellow-green	55	35
C646/648 Set of 3		1·10	75

(Litho Maia, Oporto)

1965 (1 Dec). 25th Anniv of Direccao dos Transportes Aereos (Angolan airline). P 13.
| 643 | **75** | 2E.50 multicoloured | 1·40 | 35 |

76 Arquebusier, 1539

77 St. Paul's Hospital, Luanda, and Sarmento Rodrigues Commercial and Industrial School

(Des A. Cutileiro. Litho Litografia Maia, Oporto)

1966 (25 Feb). Portuguese Military Uniforms. Various vert designs as T **76**. Multicoloured. P 14.

644	50c. Type **76**	10	10
645	1E. Arquebusier, 1640	15	15
646	1E.50 Infantry officer, 1777	20	15
647	2E. Infantry standard-bearer, 1777	35	15
648	2E.50 Infantryman, 1777	40	15
649	3E. Cavalry officer, 1783	45	15
650	4E. Trooper, 1783	70	25
651	4E.50 Infantry officer, 1807	80	35
652	5E. Infantryman, 1807	90	35
653	6E. Cavalry officer, 1807	1·30	70
654	8E. Trooper, 1807	1·70	1·50
655	9E. Infantryman, 1873	2·10	1·70
644/655 Set of 12		8·25	5·25

(Des A. Cutileiro. Litho)

1966 (28 May). 40th Anniv of National Revolution. P 12×11½.
| 656 | **77** | 1E. multicoloured | 45 | 25 |

78 Emblem of Brotherhood

79 Mendes Barata and *Don Carlos I* (cruiser)

1966 (15 Aug). Centenary of Brotherhood of the Holy Spirit. Litho. P 13½.
| 657 | **78** | 1E. multicoloured | 45 | 25 |

(Des A. Cutileiro. Litho Litografia Nacional, Oporto)

1967 (31 Jan). Centenary of Military Naval Association. T **79** and similar horiz design. Multicoloured. P 13.
| 658 | 1E. Type **79** | 1·00 | 45 |
| 659 | 2E.50 Augusto de Castilho and *Mindelo* (sail/steam corvette) | 1·40 | 80 |

109

ANGOLA

 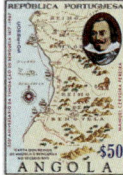

80 Basilica of Fatima
81 17th-century Map and M. C. Pereira (founder)

(Des J. de Moura. Litho)

1967 (13 May). 50th Anniv of Fatima Apparitions. P 12½×13.
660	80	50c. multicoloured	45	25
		a. Black ("ANGOLA" and other inscr) omitted		

1967 (15 Aug). 350th Anniv of Benguela. Litho. P 12½×13.
661	81	50c. multicoloured	45	25

82 Town Hall, Uige-Carmona
83 "The Three Orders"

1967 (12 Oct). 50th Anniv of Uige-Carmona. Litho. P 12.
662	82	1E. multicoloured	25	20

(Des J. de Moura. Litho Litografia Nacional, Oporto)

1967 (31 Oct). Portuguese Civil and Military Orders. T **83** and similar vert designs. Multicoloured. P 14.
663	50c. Type **83**	20	20
664	1E. "Tower and Sword"	20	20
665	1E.50 "Avis"	20	20
666	2E. "Christ"	20	20
667	2E.50 "St. James of the Sword"	20	20
668	3E. "Empire"	35	20
669	4E. "Prince Henry"	45	40
670	5E. "Benemerencia"	70	45
671	10E. "Public Instruction"	1·30	55
672	20E. "Agricultural and Industrial Merit"	2·75	1·50
663/672	Set of 10	6·00	3·75

84 Belmonte Castle
85 Francisco Inocencio de Souza Coutinho

(Des J. de Moura. Litho Litografia Maia, Oporto)

1968 (22 Apr). 500th Birth Anniv of Pedro Cabral (explorer). T **84** and similar multicoloured designs. P 14.
673	50c. Our Lady of Hope (vert)	20	20
674	1E. Type **84**	55	20
675	1E.50 St. Jeronimo's hermitage (vert)	70	20
676	2E.50 Cabral's fleet (vert)	1·30	45
673/676	Set of 4	2·50	95

(Des J. de Moura. Litho Litografia Maia, Oporto)

1969 (7 Jan). Bicentenary of Novo Redondo (Angolan city). P 14.
677	85	2E. multicoloured	45	15

86 *Loge* (Portuguese gunboat) and Admiral Coutinho
87 Compass

(Des J. de Moura. Litho Litografia Nacional, Oporto)

1969 (17 Feb). Birth Centenary of Admiral Gago Coutinho. P 14.
678	86	2E.50 multicoloured	1·00	35

(Des J. de Moura. Litho Litografia Nacional, Oporto)

1969 (29 Aug). 500th Birth Anniv of Vasco da Gama (explorer). P 14.
679	87	1E. multicoloured	45	20

88 L. A. Rebello da Silva
89 Gate of Jeronimos

(Des J. de Moura. Litho Litografia Maia, Oporto)

1969 (25 Sept). Centenary of Overseas Administrative Reforms. P 14.
680	88	1E.50 multicoloured	25	20

(Des J. de Moura. Litho Litografia Nacional, Oporto)

1969 (1 Dec). 500th Birth Anniv of King Manuel I. P 14.
681	89	3E. multicoloured	45	20

90 *Angolasaurus bocagei*
91 Marshal Carmona

(Des J. de Moura. Litho Litografia Maia, Oporto)

1970 (30 Oct). Fossils and Minerals. Diamond-shaped designs as T **90**. Multicoloured. P 13½.
682	50c. Type **90**	55	25
683	1E. Ferro-meteorite	55	25
684	1E.50 Dioptase	90	55
685	2E. *Gondwanidium validum*	90	55
686	2E.50 Diamonds	90	55
687	3E. Estromatolitos	90	55
688	3E.50 *Procarcharodon megalodon*	1·50	90
689	4E. *Microceratodus angolensis teix*	1·50	90
690	4E.50 Muscovite (mica)	1·50	90
691	5E. Barytes	1·50	90
692	6E. *Nostoceras helicinum*	2·75	1·30
693	10E. *Rotula orbiculus angolensis*	3·00	1·80
682/693	Set of 12	15·00	8·50

(Des J. de Moura. Litho Litografia Nacional, Oporto)

1970 (15 Nov). Birth Centenary of Marshal Carmona. P 14.
694	91	2E.50 multicoloured	45	20

92 Cotton-picking
93 *Infante Dom Henrique* and *Principe Perfeito* (mail steamers) and 1870 5r. Stamp

ANGOLA / Portuguese Congo

1970 (20 Nov). Centenary of Malanje Municipality. Litho. P 13½×13.

| 695 | 92 | 2E.50 multicoloured | 55 | 35 |

(Des J. de Moura. Litho Litografia Maia, Oporto)

1970 (1 Dec). Stamp Centenary. T **93** and similar horiz designs. Multicoloured. P 13½.

(a) POSTAGE

| 696 | | 1E.50 Type **93** | 55 | 35 |
| 697 | | 4E.50 Beyer-Garratt steam locomotive and 25r. stamp of 1870 | 3·00 | 3·00 |

(b) Air. Inscr "CORREIO AEREO"

698		2E.50 Fokker F.27 CR-LEO Friendship and Boeing 707 mail planes and 10r. stamp of 1870	2·10	90
696/698	Set of 3		5·00	3·75
MS699	150×105 mm. Nos. 696/8 (sold at 15E.)		14·00	14·00

94 Map and Emblems
C **95** Planting Tree
96 Galleon at Mouth of Congo

(Des J. de Moura. Litho)

1971 (22 Aug). Fifth Regional Soil and Foundation Engineering Conference, Luanda. P 13.

| 700 | 94 | 2E.50 multicoloured | 45 | 20 |

(Litho Imprensa Nacional de Angola, Luanda)

1972 (1 Jan). CHARITY TAX. Provincial Settlement Committee. Type C **95** and similar vert designs. P 13.

C701		50c. red and drab	35	35
C702		1E. black and green	35	35
C703		2E. black and brown	35	35
C701/703	Set of 3		95	95

Designs:—1E. Agricultural workers; 2E. Corncobs and flowers.

(Des A. Cutileiro. Litho Litografia Maia, Oporto)

1972 (25 May). 400th Anniv of Camoens' *The Lusiads* (epic poem). P 13.

| 704 | 96 | 1E. multicoloured | 70 | 25 |

97 Sailing Yachts
98 Seaplane *Santa Cruz* near Fernando de Noronha

(Des A. Cutileiro. Litho Litografia Nacional, Oporto)

1972 (20 Jun). Olympic Games, Munich. P 14×13½.

| 705 | 97 | 50c. multicoloured | 70 | 25 |

(Des A. Cutileiro. Litho Litografia Maia, Oporto)

1972 (20 Sept). 50th Anniversary of First Flight, Lisbon–Rio de Janeiro. P 13½.

| 706 | 98 | 1E. multicoloured | 35 | 20 |

99 W.M.O. Emblem **100** Dish Aerials

(Litho Litografia Maia, Oporto)

1973 (15 Dec). Centenary of World Meteorological Organization. P 13.

| 707 | 99 | 1E. multicoloured | 45 | 20 |

(Litho Litografia Maia, Oporto)

1974 (25 June). Inauguration of Satellite Communications Station Network. P 13½.

| 708 | 100 | 2E. multicoloured | 45 | 20 |

101 Doris Harp (*Harpa doris*)   (**102**)

(Des A. Cutileiro. Litho.

1974 (25 Oct). Sea Shells. T **101** and similar horiz designs. Multicoloured. P 12×12½.

709		25c. Type **101**	10	10
710		30c. West African murex (*Murex melanamathos*)	10	10
711		50c. Scaly-ridged venus (*Venus foliaceo lamellosa*)	10	10
712		70c. Filose latirus (*Lathyrus filosus*)	20	10
713		1E. Cymbium cisium (*Cymbium fragile*)	20	10
714		1E.50 West African helmet (*Cassis tessellata*)	20	10
715		2E. Rat cowrie (*Cypraea stercoraria*)	20	10
716		2E.50 Butterfly cone (*Conus prometheus*)	30	10
717		3E. Bubonian conch (*Strombus latus*)	40	20
718		3E.50 *Tympanotonus fuscatus*	45	20
719		4E. Great ribbed cockle (*Cardium costatum*)	45	20
720		5E. Lightning moon (*Natica fulminea cruentata*)	55	20
721		6E. Lion's paw scallop (*Lyropecten nodosa*)	70	30
722		7E. Giant tun (*Tonna galea*)	85	30
723		10E. Rugose donax (*Donax rugosus*)	1·10	45
724		25E. Smith's distorsio (wrongly inscr "Cymatium trigonum")	3·50	1·30
725		30E. *Olivancillaria acuminata*	3·50	1·50
726		35E. Giant hairy melongena (*Semifusus morio*)	3·75	2·00
727		40E. Wavy-leaved turrid (*Clavatula lineata*)	5·25	2·10
728		50E. American sundial (*Solarium granulatum*)	6·50	2·50
709/728	Set of 20		26·00	11·00

1974 (21 Dec). Youth Philately. No. 511 locally optd with T **102** in blue.

| 729 | 51 | 5c. multicoloured | 25 | 80 |

The Portuguese declared the country independent on 11 November 1975. Subsequent issues are listed in Part 12 (*Africa since Independence A-E*) of this catalogue.

PORTUGUESE CONGO

The area known as Portuguese Congo, now called Cabinda, was the part of Angola north of the River Congo. It had its own stamps from 1894 until 1920.

1894. 1000 Reis = 1 Milreis
1913. 100 Centavos = 1 Escudo

PRINTERS. All stamps of Portuguese Congo were printed at the Mint, Lisbon, *unless otherwise stated*.

1 King Carlos   N **2**   **2**

(Des and eng M. D. Neto. Typo)

1894 (5 Aug). Chalk-surfaced paper or enamel-surfaced paper (E).

(a) P 11½

1	1	15r. red-brown	9·00	5·50
2		20r. lilac	9·00	5·50
3		25r. green	5·75	1·30
4		50r. pale blue	24·00	11·50
5		75r. rose	9·00	5·50
6		80r. pale green	11·50	8·00
7		100r. brown/yellow	10·00	6·75

(b) P 12½

8	1	5r. pale orange	1·70	1·60
9		10r. rosy mauve	2·50	1·70
10		15r. red-brown	4·25	3·50
11		20r. lilac	4·25	3·50

ANGOLA / Portuguese Congo

12	20r. lilac (E)	4·25	3·50
13	25r. green	2·75	1·00
14	25r. green (E)	6·75	1·30
15	75r. rose (E)	36·00	22·00
16	80r. pale green (E)	£110	70·00
17	150r. carmine/*rose*	19·00	16·00
18	200r. blue/*blue*	19·00	16·00
19	300r. blue/*pale brown*	24·00	20·00
8/19 Set of 10 (one of each value)		£200	£140

(c) P 13½

20	1	5r. pale orange	30·00	17·00
21		10r. rosy mauve	30·00	17·00
22		50r. pale blue (E)	4·75	3·00
23		100r. brown/*buff*	60·00	34·00

(Des and eng E. C. Azedo Gneco. Typo)

1894 (5 Aug). NEWSPAPER.

N24	N 2	2½r. brown (perf 13½)	1·90	1·50
N25		2½r. brown (perf 12½)	1·90	1·50

(Des and eng E. Mouchon. Typo)

1898 (1 Aug)–**1901**. Name and value in black or carmine (500r.). P 11½.

24	2	2½r. pale grey	55	45
25		5r. orange-red	55	45
26		10r. green	75	45
27		15r. chocolate	2·10	1·80
28		20r. deep lilac	1·40	95
29		25r. blue-green	2·00	1·30
30		50r. blue	2·30	1·80
31		75r. rose	5·75	3·25
32		80r. mauve	4·25	3·50
33		100r. blue/*blue*	3·50	2·50
34		150r. purple-brown/*straw*	5·75	4·00
35		200r. purple/*flesh*	7·00	4·25
36		300r. blue/*pink*	8·50	4·75
		a. Error. On straw		
37		500r. black/*azure* (1901)	21·00	15·00
38		700r. mauve/*yellow* (1901)	36·00	27·00
24/38 Set of 15			90·00	65·00

See also Nos. 66/73.

1902. Surch as T **6** of Angola.

39	1	65r. on 15r. (11½)	29·00	16·00
40		65r. on 15r. (12½)	6·50	5·00
41		65r. on 20r. (12½)	6·50	5·00
42		65r. on 20r. (E) (12½)	23·00	19·00
43		65r. on 25r. (11½)	29·00	22·00
44		65r. on 25r. (12½)	6·50	5·00
45		65r. on 25r. (E) (12½)	13·50	11·00
46		65r. on 300r. (12½)	8·25	7·75
47		115r. on 10r. (12½)	6·50	4·75
48		115r. on 50r. (11½)	6·25	4·75
49		115r. on 50r. (13½)	6·50	5·00
50	N 2	115r. on 2½r. (12½)	6·50	5·00
51		115r. on 2½r. (13½)	6·50	5·00
		a. Surch inverted	43·00	39·00
52	1	130r. on 5r. (12½)	6·50	4·75
		a. Surch inverted	60·00	55·00
53		130r. on 5r. (13½)	6·50	5·25
54		130r. on 75r. (11½)	6·50	5·00
55		130r. on 75r. (E) (12½)	11·50	9·75
56		130r. on 100r. (11½)	35·00	22·00
57		130r. on 100r. (13½)	6·50	5·25
58		400r. on 80r. (11½)	2·75	2·20
59		400r. on 80r. (E) (12½)	8·75	6·00
60		400r. on 150r. (12½)	4·00	3·25
61		400r. on 200r. (12½)	4·00	3·25

1902. Optd with T **7** of Angola.

62	2	15r. chocolate	3·00	2·10
63		25r. blue-green	3·00	2·10
64		50r. blue	3·00	2·10
65		75r. rose	7·00	5·00

No. 64 is said to exist with a double overprint of T **7**, the second impression being at the top of the stamp, but it was not put on sale in this condition.

1903. Colours changed. Name and value in black. P 11½.

66	2	15r. deep green	1·30	25
67		25r. carmine	1·30	25
68		50r. brown	3·75	2·75
69		65r. dull blue	11·50	9·75
70		75r. dull purple	4·50	4·00
71		115r. orange-brown/*pink*	10·50	8·25
72		130r. purple-brown/*straw*	14·00	12·00
73		400r. dull blue/*cream*	13·50	11·50
66/73 Set of 8			55·00	44·00

1905. Surch with T **8** of Angola.

| 74 | 2 | 50r. on 65r. dull blue | 7·00 | 4·50 |

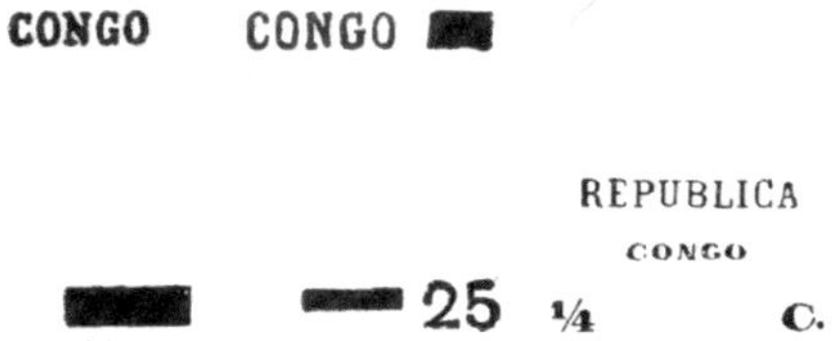

CONGO   CONGO ▬

REPUBLICA

CONGO

▬   ▬ 25 ¼   C.

(3)   (4)   (5)

1911. Stamps of Angola, T **5**, with local opt "REPUBLICA" in red.

(a) Optd with T 3, in black

75	2½r. pale grey	2·20	1·40
	a. "CONGO" and bar as T **4**	4·00	3·00
76	5r. orange-red	3·00	2·20
	a. "REPUBLICA" inverted	12·00	11·00
77	10r. green	3·00	2·20
	a. "REPUBLICA" inverted	12·00	11·00
78	15r. deep green	3·00	2·20
	a. "REPUBLICA" inverted	12·00	11·00

(b) Surch with T 4, in black

79	25r. on 200r. purple/*pink*	3·25	2·30
	a. "REPUBLICA" inverted	12·00	11·00
	b. "CONGO" double	12·00	11·00

1911. Optd with T **8a** of Angola, in red or green (G.).

80	2	2½r. pale grey	45	30
81		5r. orange	65	45
82		10r. green	65	45
83		15r. deep green	65	45
84		20r. deep lilac	65	45
85		25r. carmine (G.)	65	45
86		50r. brown	75	45
87		75r. dull purple	1·30	85
88		100r. blue/*blue*	1·50	85
89		115r. orange-brown/*pink*	2·20	1·40
90		130r. purple-brown/*straw*	2·20	1·40
91		200r. purple/*flesh*	4·00	2·30
92		400r. dull blue/*cream*	7·50	5·75
93		500r. black/*azure*	7·50	6·00
94		700r. mauve/*yellow*	10·50	6·75
80/94 Set of 15			37·00	25·00

1913. New Currency. Vasco da Gama issues surch as T **5**.

(i) Portuguese Colonies (General Issues)

95	¼c. on 2½r. blue-green	1·80	1·50
96	½c. on 5r. vermilion	1·80	1·50
97	1c. on 10r. dull purple	1·80	1·50
98	2½c. on 25r. yellow-green	1·80	1·50
99	5c. on 50r. deep blue	2·20	2·10
100	7½c. on 75r. chocolate	3·75	3·50
101	10c. on 100r. bistre-brown	2·75	2·10
	a. Surch inverted	24·00	24·00
102	15c. on 150r. ochre	2·00	2·10
95/102 Set of 8		16·00	14·00

(ii) Macao

103	¼c. on ½a. blue-green	2·40	2·30
104	½c. on 1a. vermilion	2·40	2·30
105	1c. on 2a. dull purple	2·40	2·30
106	2½c. on 4a. yellow-green	2·40	2·30
107	5c. on 8a. deep blue	2·40	2·30
108	7½c. on 12a. chocolate	4·75	3·25
109	10c. on 16a. bistre-brown	3·00	2·30
110	15c. on 24a. ochre	3·00	2·30
103/110 Set of 8		20·00	17·00

(iii) Timor

111	¼c. on ½a. blue-green	2·40	2·30
112	¼c. on 1a. vermilion	2·40	2·30
113	1c. on 2a. dull purple	2·40	2·30
114	2½c. on 4a. yellow-green	2·40	2·30
115	5c. on 8a. deep blue	2·40	2·30
	a. Surch double	24·00	24·00
116	7½c. on 12a. chocolate	4·75	3·25
117	10c. on 16a. bistre-brown	3·00	2·30
118	15c. on 25a. ochre	3·00	2·30
111/118 Set of 8		20·00	17·00

6 Ceres

(7)

112

(Des C. Fernandes. Eng J. S. de Carvalho e Silva. Typo)
1914–20. Name and value in black. P 15×14.

(a) Chalk-surfaced paper (1914)

119	6	¼c. brown-olive	75	70
120		½c. black	1·10	70
121		1c. deep green	3·75	2·75
122		1½c. chocolate	2·40	1·50
123		2c. carmine	2·40	2·00
124		2½c. violet	75	70
125		5c. blue	1·10	1·10
126		7½c. yellow-brown	2·20	1·50
127		8c. slate	2·30	2·00
128		10c. brown-red	2·30	2·00
129		15c. claret	2·40	2·00
130		20c. yellow-green	2·40	2·00
131		30c. chocolate/*green*	4·75	3·25
132		40c. brown/*rose*	4·75	3·50
133		50c. orange/*salmon*	5·75	3·50
134		1E. deep green/*azure*	7·25	5·25
119/134	Set of 16		42·00	31·00

(b) Unsurfaced paper (1920)

135	6	¼c. brown-olive	85	75
136		2c. carmine	85	75

1914–1918. Optd locally with T **7**. With or without gum (Nos. 141, 144), no gum (138).

137	2	50r. blue (No. 64) (R.)	1·40	1·10
138		50r. brown (G.)	1·40	1·10
139		50r. on 65r. dull blue (No. 74) (R.)	1·90	1·70
140		75r. rose (No. 65) (G.)	2·20	2·00
141		75r. dull purple (G.)	5·50	3·50
142		100r. blue/*blue* (R.)	1·40	1·30
143		200r. purple/*flesh* (G.)	6·75	5·75
144		400r. dull blue/*cream* (R.) (1918)	£110	85·00
145		500r. black/*azure* (R.)	90·00	75·00

1915. Provisionals of 1902-05 optd with T **8a** of Angola, in red (reading down on Nos. 149/50).

146	2	15r. chocolate (No. 62)	1·60	1·10
147		50r. blue (No. 64)	1·60	1·10
148		50r. on 65r. blue (No. 74)	1·60	1·10
149	N 2	115r. on 2½r. (12½)	1·10	55
150		115r. on 2½r. (13½)	1·10	55
151	1	115r. on 10r. (12½)	1·00	75
152		115r. on 10r. (13½)	33·00	31·00
153		115r. on 50r. (11½)	2·50	1·60
154		115r. on 50r. (E) (13½)	2·50	1·60
155		130r. on 5r. (12½)	2·50	1·60
156		130r. on 5r. (13½)	1·60	1·10
		a. Surch and opt inverted	49·00	46·00
157		130r. on 75r. (11½)	2·50	1·90
158		130r. on 75r. (E) (12½)	2·50	1·90
159		130r. on 100r. (11½)	1·20	75
160		130r. on 100r. (13½)	1·20	75

From 1920 the stamps of Angola were again used in Portuguese Congo.

Azores

1868. 1000 Reis = 1 Milreis
1912. 100 Centavos = 1 Escudo
2002. 100 Cents = 1 Euro

The Azores are a group of nine islands in the Atlantic Ocean, over 1000 miles west of Lisbon. They were discovered by Diogo de Sevilla in 1427–31, and later became a province of Portugal. They were divided into the districts of Angra, Horta and Ponta Delgada.

From 1853 to 1868 the stamps of Portugal were used in the Azores, with cancellations of the numbers "48", "49" or "50" amid bars, for the three districts respectively.

PRINTERS. All the stamps of the Azores were printed or overprinted at the Mint, Lisbon, *unless otherwise stated*.

Stamps of Portugal overprinted

AÇORES   AÇORES
(**1**)   (**2**) ("ÇO" closer and "S" wider)

1868–70. King Luis (curved label) type optd with T **1**.

(a) Imperf (1.1.68)

1	14	5r. black	£4250	£2500
2		10r. yellow	£18000	£12000
3		20r. bistre	£250	£200
4		50r. green	£250	£200
5		80r. orange	£275	£225
6		100r. dull purple	£275	£225

All values were reprinted with opt T **2** in 1885 and in 1905.

(b) P 12½ (1868–70)

7	14	5r. black (1) (C.)	85·00	85·00
8		5r. black (2) (C.)	85·00	85·00
9		10r. yellow	£110	85·00
		a. Orange-yellow	£110	85·00
		b. Opt inverted	£140	£140
10		20r. bistre (1869)	85·00	75·00
11		25r. pale rose	85·00	13·00
		a. Deep rose	85·00	13·00
		b. Opt inverted	£140	£140
12		50r. pale green	£250	£225
		a. Green	£250	£225
13		80r. orange	£250	£225
14		100r. deep lilac (1) (1869)	£250	£225
15		100r. pale mauve (2)	£250	£225
16		120r. blue	£225	£140
		a. Deep blue	£225	£140
17		240r. pale dull lilac (1870)	£750	£475

The 25r. with small overprint, previously listed, was prepared for use but not issued. Overprints measuring 12×3 mm on other stamps are now known to have been applied privately.

All values were reprinted with opt T **2** in 1885 and 1905.

1871–73. King Luis (straight label) type optd with T **1**. P 12½.

18	15	5r. black (C.)	26·00	15·00
		a. Opt inverted	£130	£130
19		10r. yellow	37·00	31·00
		a. Opt inverted	65·00	65·00
20		20r. bistre	70·00	50·00
		a. Olive-bistre	42·00	34·00
21		25r. rose	23·00	7·00
22		50r. pale green	£140	46·00
		a. Green	£140	46·00
23		80r. orange	£150	£100
		a. Chalk-surfaced paper	£325	
24		100r. pale mauve	£150	£110
25		120r. blue	£200	£170
		a. Opt inverted	£550	£550
26		240r. pale dull lilac	£1100	£800

1875–76. King Luis (straight label) type optd with T **2**.

(a) P 12½

27	15	5r. black (C.)	16·00	10·50
		a. Opt inverted	60·00	50·00
28		10r. yellow	36·00	31·00
		a. Orange-yellow	36·00	31·00
29		15r. fawn (1)	21·00	19·00
30		15r. fawn (2)	32·00	23·00
31		20r. bistre	36·00	21·00
		a. Yellow-bistre	42·00	34·00

113

AZORES

		b. *Olive-bistre*............		42·00	34·00
32		25r. rose............		21·00	5·00
33		50r. pale green............		£110	40·00
		a. *Green*............		£110	50·00
34		80r. orange (1)............		£130	80·00
		a. *Orange-buff*............		£140	80·00
35		100r. pale mauve............		£110	60·00
		a. *Grey-lilac*............		£110	70·00
36		120r. blue............		£200	£130
37		150r. pale blue............		£225	£160
		a. *Dull blue*............		£225	£160
		b. *Bright blue*............		£225	£160

(b) P 13½

38	15	5r. black (C.)............		16·00	10·50
39		10r. yellow............		65·00	40·00
		a. *Orange-yellow*............		50·00	39·00
40		15r. fawn (1)............		65·00	40·00
		a. Opt inverted............		£160	95·00
41		15r. fawn (2)............		75·00	50·00
42		20r. yellow-bistre............		65·00	40·00
		a. *Olive-bistre*............		75·00	50·00
43		25r. rose............		21·00	7·00
		a. Opt inverted............		90·00	90·00
		b. Opt double............		90·00	90·00
44		50r. pale green............		£120	85·00
		a. *Green*............		£140	90·00
45		80r. orange (1)............		£170	£100
46		80r. orange-buff (2)............		£170	£100
47		100r. pale mauve............		£140	70·00
		a. *Grey-lilac*............		£140	70·00
48		120r. blue............		£225	£130
49		150r. blue............		£225	£190
50		300r. lilac............		£110	70·00

(c) P 14

51	15	25r. rose............		£200	90·00
52		100r. pale mauve............		£225	£160

In 1885 all values were reprinted with opt T **2**, perf 13½ and the 5, 10, 15, 50 and 120r. also perf 12½. In 1905 all values were reprinted with T **2** perf 13½.

1876 (1 July). NEWSPAPER. "Jornaes" type optd with T **2**. Unsurfaced paper.

(a) P 12½

N53	N 17	2½r. olive-green............		15·00	5·75
		a. *Grey-green*............		15·00	5·75
		b. Opt inverted............		£110	55·00

(b) P 13½

N54	N 17	2½r. olive-green............		15·00	5·75
		a. *Grey-green*............		15·00	5·75

No. N54 was reprinted in 1885 and 1905.

1879–80. King Luis (straight label) type, colours changed, optd with T **2**.

(a) P 12½

53	15	10r. blue-green (8.79)............		£200	£170
		a. *Yellow-green*............		£140	£100
54		50r. blue (7.79)............		£190	£100

(b) P 13½

55	15	10r. yellow-green............		£140	£100
		a. Opt double............		£150	£150
56		50r. blue............		£190	£100
		a. *Deep blue*............		£190	£100
57		150r. yellow (1880)............		£275	£200

All values were reprinted in 1885 perf 13½ and the 10 and 50r. also perf 12½. All values were again reprinted in 1905 perf 13½.

1880–81. King Luis types of 1880–81 optd with T **2**.

A. Unsurfaced paper

(a) P 12½

58	16	5r. black (1) (C.) (3.81)............		29·00	12·50
59		5r. black (2) (C.)............		29·00	12·50
60	17	25r. bluish grey (1.80)............		£170	50·00
61	17a	25r. grey (5.80)............		65·00	10·00
		a. *Purple-grey*............		65·00	10·00
		b. *Purple-brown*............		65·00	10·00
62	18	50r. blue (3.81)............		£200	50·00

(b) P 13½

63	16	5r. black (1) (C.)............		29·00	12·50
64		5r. black (2) (C.)............		29·00	12·50
65	17	25r. bluish grey............		£170	46·00
66	17a	25r. grey............		65·00	60·00
		a. *Purple-grey*............		65·00	60·00
		b. *Purple-brown*............		65·00	60·00
67	18	50r. blue............		£200	55·00

B. Chalk-surfaced paper. P 12½

68	16	5r. black (2) (C.)............		£170	£100

All four stamps were reprinted in 1885 and 1905.

1882 (Feb). King Luis type of 1882 optd with T **2**.

A. Unsurfaced paper

(a) P 12½

69	20	25r. brown............		60·00	8·50
		a. *Pale brown*............		60·00	8·50
		b. *Purple-brown*............		60·00	8·50

(b) P 13½

70	20	25r. brown............		60·00	8·50
		a. *Pale brown*............		60·00	8·50
		b. *Purple-brown*............		60·00	8·50

B. Chalk-surfaced paper

(a) P 12½

71	20	25r. brown............		60·00	8·50
		a. *Purple-brown*............		60·00	8·50

(b) P 13½

72	20	25r. brown............		60·00	8·50
		a. *Purple-brown*............		60·00	8·50

AÇORES

(3)

1882–85. King Luis (straight label) type optd with T **3**.

A. Unsurfaced paper

(a) P 12½

73	15	10r. yellow-green (12.82)............		£100	80·00
74		15r. fawn (1) (1.83)............		80·00	60·00
75		15r. fawn (2)............		80·00	60·00
76		20r. bistre (1.83)............		£130	90·00
		a. Opt inverted............		£225	£225
77		50r. blue (date?)............		£1000	£850
78		80r. orange (1) (1.84)............		£140	£120
		a. *Orange-buff*............		£140	£120
79		80r. orange-buff (2)............		£140	£120
80		100r. pale mauve (1.83)............		£140	£100
81		150r. blue (7.83)............		£1100	£900
82		150r. yellow (3.84)............		£140	£120
83		300r. lilac (7.83)............		£140	£120
84		1000r. black (R.) (7.85)............		£170	£140
		a. Opt inverted............		£275	£275
		b. Opt double............		£275	£275

(b) P 13½

85	15	10r. yellow-green............		£110	95·00
86		15r. fawn (2)............		85·00	70·00
		a. Opt inverted............		£150	£150
87		20r. bistre............		£170	95·00
		a. Opt inverted............		£180	£180
88		50r. blue............		£1200	£1000
89		80r. orange-buff (1)............		£200	£160
90		100r. grey-lilac............		£170	£130
91		150r. blue............		£1000	£900
92		150r. yellow............		£130	95·00
93		300r. lilac............		£130	95·00
94		1000r. black (R.)............		£170	£140
		a. Carmine opt............		£170	£140

B. Chalk-surfaced paper

(a) P 12½

95	15	10r. yellow-green............		£140	£120
96		15r. fawn (1)............		£100	85·00
		a. Opt inverted............		£180	£180
		b. Opt double............		£180	£180
97		15r. fawn (2)............		£100	85·00
		a. *Red-brown*............		£100	85·00
98		20r. pale bistre............		£100	85·00
		a. Opt inverted............		£180	£180
99		20r. deep carmine (1) (1.85)............		£170	£130
		a. Opt double............		£225	£170
		b. *Rosine*............		£170	£130
100		20r. rosine (2)............		£170	£130
101		80r. orange-buff (1)............		90·00	70·00
		a. Opt double............		£350	£350
		b. *Orange-yellow*............		90·00	70·00
102		80r. orange-buff (2)............		90·00	70·00
		a. *Orange-yellow*............		90·00	70·00
103		100r. mauve-pink............		70·00	60·00
		a. Opt double............		—	£160
104		150r. yellow............		70·00	60·00
105		300r. mauve............		£100	85·00

(b) P 13½

106	15	10r. yellow-green............		£140	£110
		a. Opt inverted............		£325	£325
107		15r. fawn (2)............		£110	80·00
		a. *Red-brown*............		£110	80·00
108		20r. pale bistre............		£130	£100
109		20r. rosine (1)............		£170	£140

AZORES

110		20r. rosine (2)	£170	£140
		a. Printed on unsurfaced side	£700	£400
111		80r. orange (1)	£110	80·00
		a. Orange-buff	£110	80·00
112		80r. orange (2)	£110	80·00
113		150r. yellow	£130	£100
114		300r. purple	£130	£100

In 1885 the 10r. to 300r. with both colours of the 20r. and 150r. were reprinted perf 13½ and the 10, 15 and 150r. blue also perf 12½. In 1900 the 150r. blue was reprinted perf 11½. In 1905 the 10r. to 1000r., including both colours of the 150r. but excluding the 20r. carmine, were reprinted perf 13½.

1882 (Sept). King Luis type of 1880 optd with T **3**, in carmine.
A. Unsurfaced paper

115	**16**	5r. grey-black (2) (p. 12½)	32·00	15·00
116		5r. grey-black (2) (p. 13½)	32·00	15·00

B. Chalk-surfaced paper

117	**16**	5r. grey-black (2) (p. 12½)	80·00	55·00
		a. Opt inverted	£130	£130

Reprinted in 1885 perf 12½, in 1900 perf 11½ and in 1905 perf 13½.

1882–87. King Luis types of 1882–87 optd with T **3**.
A. Unsurfaced paper
(a) P 12½

118	**20**	25r. brown	30·00	5·00
		a. Pale brown	30·00	5·00
		b. Purple-brown	30·00	5·00
119	**21**	50r. pale blue (6.82)	48·00	5·00
		a. Deep blue	48·00	5·00

(b) P 13½

120	**20**	25r. brown	30·00	5·00
		a. Pale brown	30·00	5·00
		b. Purple-brown	30·00	5·00
121	**21**	50r. pale blue	48·00	5·00
		a. Deep blue	48·00	5·00

(c) P 11½

122	**19**	5r. grey-black (1.1.87)	28·00	6·50
		a. Opt double (C. & Bk.)	£120	£120
123	**20**	25r. purple-brown	29·00	5·00

B. Chalk-surfaced paper
(a) P 12½

124	**19**	5r. drab	21·00	5·00
		a. Grey	21·00	5·00
125	**22**	10r. green (7.84)	34·00	15·00
126	**20**	25r. brown	34·00	5·00
		a. Pale brown	34·00	5·00
		b. Purple-brown	34·00	5·00
127	**21**	50r. blue	42·00	15·00
128	**23**	500r. black (C.) (7.85)	£200	£180
129		500r. magenta (1.7.87)	£170	£110

(b) P 13½

130	**19**	5r. drab	37·00	12·50
		a. Grey	37·00	12·50
		aa. Opt inverted	90·00	90·00
		b. Pearl-grey	37·00	12·50
131		5r. drab (C.)	48·00	46·00
132	**22**	10r. green	34·00	16·00
133	**20**	25r. brown	34·00	5·00
		a. Pale brown	34·00	5·00
		b. Purple-brown	34·00	5·00
134	**21**	50r. blue	42·00	15·00
135	**23**	500r. magenta	£300	£250

(c) P 11

136	**19**	5r. black	17·00	6·25
		a. Grey	17·00	3·25
137		5r. black (C.)	42·00	26·00
		a. Grey	42·00	26·00
		aa. Opt inverted	80·00	80·00
		ab. Opt double	80·00	80·00
138	**22**	10r. green	38·00	15·00
		a. Opt inverted	55·00	55·00
139	**24**	20r. rosine (1.7.87)	38·00	20·00
		a. Opt inverted	£100	£100
		b. Opt double	£110	£110
140	**20**	25r. purple-brown	30·00	5·00
141	**25**	25r. magenta (1.8.87)	38·00	3·25
		a. Opt double	80·00	80·00
		b. Rosy mauve	38·00	3·25
		ba. Opt inverted	80·00	80·00
		bb. Opt double, one inverted	80·00	80·00
142	**21**	50r. blue	30·00	5·00
		a. Opt double	65·00	65·00
		b. Pale blue	30·00	5·00

Reprints: in 1885–93, 5r. (black opt), 10r., 25r. brown, 50r. and 500r. black, perf 13½; in 1900, 5r. (carmine opt) 20r. and 25r. magenta, perf 11½; in 1905, 5r. (black and carmine opt), 10r., 20r., 25r. brown and magenta, 50r. and 500r. black and magenta, perf 13½.

1882–94. NEWSPAPER. Optd with T **3**.
A. Unsurfaced paper
(a) P 12½

N143	N **16**	2r. black (7.85)	7·00	3·25
		a. Opt inverted	23·00	23·00
		b. Opt double, one inverted	45·00	45·00
N144		2r. black (C.)	21·00	17·00
N145	N **17**	2½r. grey-green (12.82)	6·50	1·90
		a. Olive-green	6·50	1·90
		aa. Opt inverted	17·00	17·00
		ab. Opt double (R. & Bk.)	36·00	£350
		b. Olive-ochre	6·50	1·90

(b) P 13½

N146	N **16**	2r. black	7·00	3·25
		a. Opt inverted	40·00	
		b. Opt double, one inverted	75·00	
N147		2r. black (C.)	21·00	17·00
N148	N **17**	2½r. grey-green	6·50	1·90
		a. Opt double	23·00	23·00
		b. Olive-green	6·50	1·90
		c. Olive-ochre	6·50	1·90

(c) P 11½

N149	N **17**	2½r. olive-green	32·00	6·25

B. Chalk-surfaced paper. P 11½ (1887)

N150	N **17**	2½r. olive-ochre	6·50	1·90
		a. Yellow-brown	6·50	1·90
		aa. Opt double	15·00	15·00
		b. Olive-green	6·50	1·90
		ba. Opt inverted	15·00	15·00

C. Enamel-surfaced paper. P 11½ (1894)

N151	N **17**	2½r. yellow	6·50	1·90

The 2r. with black and carmine opts were reprinted in 1885 and 1905 perf 13½; the 2½r. was reprinted in 1885 perf 13½ and 12½ and again in 1905 perf 13½.

From 1892 to 1905, separate issues of stamps were made for each of the three administrative districts of the Azores (see end of country). Nos. 143/D185 were issued for use throughout the three districts.

AÇORES   AÇORES   AÇORES
(**4**)   (**5**)   (D **6**)

1894 (4 Mar). Prince Henry the Navigator issue optd with T **4**.

143	**32**	5r. orange	3·75	3·25
		a. Opt inverted	60·00	60·00
		b. Opt double, one inverted	70·00	70·00
144		10r. rosy lake	3·75	3·25
145		15r. brown	4·75	4·25
146		20r. lilac	5·00	4·50
147	**33**	25r. green	5·50	4·75
		a. Opt inverted	90·00	90·00
		b. Opt double	90·00	90·00
		c. Opt double, one inverted	90·00	90·00
148		50r. blue	13·50	7·25
		a. Aniline blue	25·00	9·50
149		75r. carmine-rose	25·00	10·00
		a. Aniline carmine	36·00	16·00
150		80r. pale green	29·00	11·00
151		100r. brown/buff	29·00	8·75
152	**34**	150r. rose-red	39·00	20·00
153		300r. blue/bright buff	45·00	32·00
154		500r. deep purple/bluish	85·00	48·00
155		1000r. black/straw	£180	90·00
		a. Opt inverted	£325	
		b. Opt triple	£325	
143/155	Set of 13		£425	£225

1895 (13 June). St. Anthony issue optd with T **5** (vert down on 2½r.).

156	**35**	2½r. black (R.)	3·25	1·30
157	**36**	5r. orange	10·50	3·25
158		10r. mauve	10·50	4·75
159		15r. brown	16·00	7·25
160		20r. grey-lilac	18·00	10·50
161		25r. purple and green	11·00	3·25
162	**37**	50r. brown and blue	37·00	16·00
163		75r. brown and rosine	55·00	45·00
164		80r. brown and pale green	60·00	50·00
165		100r. black and chocolate	60·00	46·00
166	**38**	150r. rosine and bistre	£130	£110
167		200r. blue and bistre	£130	£110
168		300r. slate and bistre	£160	£120
169		500r. brown and green	£225	£160
170		1000r. deep lilac and green	£375	£275
156/170	Set of 15		£1200	£850

1898 (1 Apr). Vasco da Gama stamps of Portuguese Africa (General Issues) but inscr "AÇORES". P 14 to 15.

171		2½r. blue-green	3·75	1·40
172		5r. vermilion	3·75	1·70
173		10r. dull purple	7·50	3·25

115

AZORES

174	25r. yellow-green	7·50	3·25
175	50r. deep blue	11·00	10·00
176	75r. chocolate	23·00	15·00
177	100r. bistre-brown	29·00	16·00
178	150r. ochre	46·00	32·00
171/178 Set of 8		£120	75·00

1904. POSTAGE DUE. 1904 issue optd with Type D **6**.

D179	D **49**	5r. brown	1·40	1·20
D180		10r. orange	1·50	1·20
D181		20r. dull mauve	2·50	1·40
D182		30r. green	2·50	1·90
D183		40r. deep lilac	4·25	2·50
D184		50r. carmine	7·25	4·75
D185		100r. blue	9·00	8·75
D179/185 Set of 7			26·00	20·00

Sets may be made on white and on toned paper (except 20r., white only).

By an order of 19 July 1905, general issues for the Azores were resumed.

6 King Carlos

7 King Manoel

(Des and eng E. Mouchon. Typo)

1906. Surch as in T **6** (A=Angra, H=Horta, PD=Ponta Delgada and value). P 11½.

179	**6**	2½r. pale grey (R.)	45	40
		a. Name, letters and numerals inverted	25·00	25·00
180		5r. orange	45	40
		a. Name, letters and numerals inverted	25·00	25·00
181		10r. green (R.)	45	40
182		20r. deep lilac (R.)	75	55
183		25r. carmine	75	40
184		50r. ultramarine	6·75	5·00
185		75r. brown/*yellow* (R.)	2·30	1·40
186		100r. blue/*pale blue*	2·30	1·40
187		200r. purple/*pink*	2·40	1·40
188		300r. blue/*pink*	7·25	6·00
189		500r. black/*azure* (R.)	17·00	15·00
179/189 Set of 11			37·00	29·00

(Head eng D. A. do Rego. Frame des and eng J. S. de Carvalho e Silva. Typo)

1910 (1 Apr). P 14×15.

190	**7**	2½r. lilac	50	40
191		5r. black	50	40
192		10r. grey-green	50	40
193		15r. pale purple-brown	1·00	70
194		20r. rose-carmine	1·40	1·10
		a. Chalk-surfaced paper	29·00	23·00
195		25r. chocolate	50	50
		a. Perf 11½	3·25	1·70
196		50r. blue	3·25	1·70
197		75r. yellow-brown	3·25	1·70
198		80r. French grey	3·25	1·70
199		100r. brown/*green* (*chalk-surfaced*)	5·25	4·00
200		200r. deep green/*salmon* (*chalk-surfaced*)	5·25	4·00
201		300r. black/*azure* (*chalk-surfaced*)	3·25	3·00
202		500r. chocolate and olive	10·50	11·00
203		1000r. black and blue	24·00	20·00
190/203 Set of 14			55·00	46·00

1910 (Dec). Optd with T **50** of Portugal in red or green (G.).

204	**7**	2½r. lilac	40	35
		b. Chalk-surfaced paper	40	35
205		5r. black	40	35
206		10r. grey-green	45	35
		b. Chalk-surfaced paper	45	35
207		15r. pale purple-brown	2·00	1·40
208		20r. rose-carmine (G.)	2·00	1·40
		b. Chalk-surfaced paper	2·00	1·40
209		25r. chocolate	40	30
		a. Chalk-surfaced paper	40	30
		b. Perf 11½	75·00	65·00
210		50r. blue	1·40	1·30
		a. Chalk-surfaced paper	1·40	1·30
211		75r. yellow-brown	1·50	1·00
212		80r. French grey	1·50	1·00
213		100r. brown/*green*	1·40	1·10
214		200r. deep green/*salmon*	1·40	1·10
215		300r. black/*azure*	4·00	2·50
216		500r. chocolate and olive	4·75	3·50
217		1000r. black and blue	12·00	7·00
204/217 Set of 14 (*cheapest*)			30·00	20·00

Double and inverted overprints and red overprint on the 20r. were privately applied.

1911 (Mar). POSTAGE DUE. Nos. D179/85 optd with T **50** of Portugal in red or green (G.).

D218	D **49**	5r. brown	80	70
D219		10r. orange	80	70
D220		20r. dull mauve	1·00	90
D221		30r. green	1·00	90
D222		40r. deep lilac	1·60	1·20
D223		50r. carmine (G.)	8·50	8·00
D224		100r. blue	3·00	3·00
D218/224 Set of 7			15·00	14·00

Note after No. D185 also applies here.

CHARITY TAX STAMPS. The notes after No. 454 of Portugal also apply to Charity Tax stamps of the Azores.

1911 (4 Oct). CHARITY TAX. No. 206 optd "ASSISTENCIA" (Type C **56** of Portugal).

C218	**7**	10r. grey-green (R.)	1·50	1·20
		a. Chalk-surfaced paper	1·50	1·20

REPUBLICA REPUBLICA

AÇORES
REIS **15** REIS   R^S **500** R^s AÇORES
(8)   (9)   (10)

1911–12.

(*a*) Vasco da Gama stamps (Nos. 171 etc.), surch as T **8** or optd only

218	2½r. blue-green (11.11)	70	50
219	15r. on 5r. vermilion (4.12)	70	50
220	25r. yellow-green (11.11)	70	50
221	50r. deep blue (12.11)	2·40	1·60
222	75r. chocolate (2.12)	2·00	1·90
223	80r. on 150r. ochre (2.12)	2·10	2·00
224	100r. bistre-brown (2.12)	2·40	2·10
	a. Opt double	28·00	28·00
225	1000r. on 10r. dull purple (2.12)	22·00	16·00
218/225 Set of 8		30·00	23·00

(*b*) Postage Due stamps of Portugal surch as T **9** or optd only. Unsurfaced paper (229, 231) or chalk-surfaced paper (others)

226	D **48**	5r. black (12.11)	1·40	1·20
227		10r. magenta (12.11)	3·00	1·20
228		20r. orange (11.11)	5·75	4·00
229		200r. brown/*buff* (2.12)	25·00	22·00
230		300r. on 50r. slate (2.12)	24·00	21·00
231		500r. on 100r. carmine/*rose* (2.12)	24·00	20·00
		a. Surch triple	55·00	55·00

Nos. 226/8 on unsurfaced paper were issued irregularly.

1912 (Dec)–21. New Currency. Ceres type with imprint below design optd with T **10**. Chalk-surfaced paper.

(*a*) P 15×14 (1912-19)

232	**56**	¼c. olive-brown	3·25	1·40
233		½c. black (R.)	3·25	1·40
234		1c. deep green (2.13)	3·25	1·40
235		1½c. brown (3.13)	4·50	3·00
236		2c. carmine (2.13)	6·75	3·00
237		2½c. violet (2.13)	5·25	1·20
238		5c. blue (*shades*) (1.13)	5·25	1·20
239		7½c. yellow-brown (2.13)	13·50	7·75
240		8c. slate (3.13)	13·50	7·75
241		10c. chestnut (3.13)	14·00	8·25
242		15c. brown/*purple* (7.13)	19·00	8·25
243		20c. chocolate/*green* (3.13)	13·50	7·75
		a. Pale brown/*green*	13·50	7·75
244		30c. brown/*rose* (3.13)	85·00	65·00
245		30c. brown/*yellow* (11.4.19)	2·50	2·50
246		50c. orange/*salmon* (3.13)	7·00	3·00
247		50c. orange/*yellow* (1918?)	7·00	3·00
248		1E. green/*azure* (*shades*) (3.13)	7·75	6·50

(*b*) P 12×11½

249	**56**	14c. indigo/*yellow* (2.21)	2·50	2·50
232/249 Set of 18			£200	£120

The ¼c. and 2½c. are found on glazed non-chalky paper.

AZORES

1913 (4 Oct). CHARITY TAX. No. 234 optd "ASSISTENCIA" diag (Type C **56** of Portugal).
| C250 | **56** | 1c. deep green (H.) | 5·25 | 4·00 |

1915 (4 Oct). CHARITY TAX. For the Poor. Type C **58** of Portugal optd with T **10**.
| C251 | C **58** | 1c. rose-red | 70 | 35 |
| | | a. Thick carton paper | 70 | 35 |

The 2c. value (for use on telegrams) is known bisected and used for 1c.

1917–30. Ceres type with imprint below design optd with T **10**.

(a) Unsurfaced wove paper (thick, medium or thin). P 15×14 (1917–21)

250	**56**	¼c. olive-brown	60	45
		a. Opt inverted	13·50	
		b. Thick carton paper	3·75	3·50
251		½c. black (R.)	60	45
		a. Thick carton paper	2·50	1·90
252		1c. green	1·20	85
		a. Opt inverted	25·00	
253		1c. brown (*shades*) (19.8.18)	60	60
		a. Opt inverted	60	60
254		1½c. brown	1·20	85
		a. Opt inverted	16·00	
255		1½c. green (19.8.18)	60	60
256		2c. carmine	85	70
		a. Opt inverted	16·00	
257		2c. yellow-orange (2.10.19)	60	60
		a. Thick carton paper	14·50	13·50
		b. Orange-yellow	60	60
258		2½c. lilac (*shades*)	85	70
259		3c. carmine (*shades*) (19.8.18)	60	60
260		3½c. pale yellow-green (19.8.18)	60	60
261		4c. yellow-green (*shades*) (19.10.19)	60	60
262		5c. deep blue	85	70
263		5c. yellow-brown (4.21)	80	70
264		6c. claret (10.20)	60	60
265		7½c. yellow-brown	7·25	4·00
266		7½c. deep blue (1.3.19)	2·00	1·80
267		8c. slate (*shades*)	85	70
268		10c. chestnut	7·25	3·00
269		15c. purple-brown	90	70
270		30c. grey-brown (6.21)	2·30	1·90
271		60c. blue (6.21)	2·00	1·60
250/271		*Set of 22*	30·00	21·00

(b) Unsurfaced paper. P 12×11½ (1918–26)

272	**56**	¼c. olive-brown	60	60
		a. Thick carton paper	2·50	1·90
273		½c. black (R.)	60	60
274		1c. brown	60	60
275		1½c. green	1·00	80
276		2c. yellow-orange (2.10.19)	60	60
		a. Opt inverted	27·00	
		b. Thick carton paper	14·50	13·50
277		3c. carmine	1·00	70
278		3c. blue (10.26)	45	35
279		4c. yellow-green (1919)	60	60
		a. Opt inverted	23·00	
280		5c. olive-brown (1921)	60	60
281		6c. claret (10.20)	65	60
		a. Thick carton paper	1·30	1·00
282		6c. chocolate (1.25)	65	55
282*a*		7½c. deep blue (1.3.19)	95·00	75·00
283		8c. blue-green (6.24)	85	60
284		8c. salmon (12.25)	1·10	1·00
285		10c. brown-red	60	60
286		12c. slate-blue (10.20)	3·00	1·90
287		12c. deep blue-green (7.22)	1·00	80
		a. Opt inverted	23·00	
288		13½c. grey-blue (2.21)	3·00	1·90
289		15c. jet-black (R.) (2.24)	60	60
290		16c. ultramarine (10.26)	1·00	95
291		20c. chocolate (2.21)	1·00	80
		a. Thick carton paper	7·50	6·50
292		20c. deep blue-green (6.24)	1·30	1·00
293		20c. drab (1.25)	85	70
294		24c. greenish blue (6.21)	1·00	65
295		25c. rose-pink (1.24)	75	60
296		30c. grey-brown (6.21)	2·10	1·80
297		32c. deep blue-green (10.26)	3·00	2·50
298		36c. red (6.21)	90	70
299		40c. blue (10.23)	1·10	70
		a. "CORREIC" for "CORREIO"	75·00	75·00
300		40c. sepia (11.25)	2·00	1·10
		a. "CORREIC" for "CORREIO"	75·00	75·00
301		48c. carmine-pink (10.26)	5·25	3·50
302		50c. yellow (4.23)	2·00	1·60
303		60c. blue (6.21)	2·00	1·60
304		64c. cobalt (10.26)	5·25	2·40
305		75c. dull rose (6.24)	5·50	4·25
306		80c. dull claret (6.21)	2·75	2·20
307		80c. lilac (1.25)	3·00	2·10
308		90c. cobalt (6.21)	2·75	2·00
309		96c. dull carmine (10.26)	8·25	3·75
310		1E. lilac (4.21)	2·75	2·20
311		1E.10 yellow-brown (6.21)	3·00	2·20
312		1E.20 apple-green (3.22)	3·50	2·20
313		2E. deep grey-green (3.22)	11·50	7·00

(c) Glazed paper. P 12×11½ (1924–30)

314	**56**	1E. slate-purple (11.24)	4·00	3·50
315		1E.20 yellow-buff (11.24)	9·00	6·50
316		1E.50 slate-purple (6.24)	10·50	7·00
317		1E.50 pale lilac (4.25)	9·25	7·25
318		1E.60 blue (1.25)	9·25	7·75
319		2E.40 sage-green (3.30)	80·00	50·00
320		3E. pink (3.28)	90·00	55·00
321		3E.20 bronze-green (6.21)	10·50	10·50
322		5E. turquoise-green (12.25)	20·00	11·00
323		10E. rose (12.25)	55·00	30·00
324		20E. turquoise-blue (4.26)	£130	90·00
314/324		*Set of 11*	£375	£250

See also Nos. 394/415.

1918 (Aug). POSTAGE DUE. 1915 issue optd with Type D **6**.
D325	D **49**	½c. brown	85	80
		a. Opt inverted	2·00	2·00
		b. Opt double	2·00	2·00
		c. Chalk-surfaced paper	1·00	85
D326		1c. orange	85	80
		a. Opt inverted	2·30	2·30
		b. Opt double	2·30	2·30
		c. Chalk-surfaced paper	1·00	85
D327		2c. maroon	85	80
		a. Opt inverted	2·75	2·75
		b. Opt double	2·75	2·75
		c. Chalk-surfaced paper	1·80	85
D328		3c. green	85	80
		a. Opt inverted	2·75	2·75
		b. Opt double	2·75	2·75
		c. Chalk-surfaced paper	2·00	85
D329		4c. lilac	85	80
		a. Opt inverted	4·25	4·25
		b. Opt double	4·25	4·25
		c. Chalk-surfaced paper	2·00	85
D330		5c. red	85	80
		a. Opt inverted	5·00	5·00
		b. Opt double	5·00	5·00
D331		10c. slate-blue	85	80
		a. Chalk-surfaced paper	1·80	1·70
D325/331		*Set of 7*	5·25	5·00

The 2c. non-chalky paper exists unsurfaced or with enamel surface.

1921–23. PARCEL POST. Stamps of 1920–22 optd with Type D **6**.
P325	P **59**	1c. pale chocolate (3.23)	60	50
		a. Opt inverted	1·80	1·80
		b. Opt double	1·80	1·80
P326		2c. orange (3.22)	60	50
		a. Opt inverted	2·30	2·30
		b. Opt double	2·30	2·30
P327		5c. pale brown (3.22)	60	50
		a. Opt inverted	2·75	2·75
		b. Opt double	2·75	2·75
P328		10c. red-brown (3.22)	80	50
		a. Opt inverted	2·75	2·75
		b. Opt double	2·75	2·75
P329		20c. lavender-blue (3.22)	80	50
		a. Opt inverted	3·50	3·50
		b. Opt double	3·50	3·50
P330		40c. deep carmine (3.22)	80	50
		a. Opt inverted	3·75	3·75
P331		50c. black (R.) (6.23)	1·60	1·10
P332		60c. blue (R.) (3.22)	1·60	1·10
P333		70c. brown (9.21)	3·00	2·50
P334		80c. pale blue (9.21)	3·00	2·50
		a. Opt inverted	6·00	6·00
P335		90c. violet (3.22)	3·00	2·50
P336		1E. pale green (3.22)	3·00	2·50

Glazed paper

P337		2E. pale lilac (3.23)	4·75	3·75
P338		3E. olive (3.23)	8·50	4·00
P339		4E. bright ultramarine (12.22)	10·00	4·00
P340		5E. grey-lilac (12.22)	10·50	8·00
P341		10E. deep brown (12.22)	43·00	24·00
P325/341		*Set of 17*	85·00	55·00

Parcel post stamps for the Azores were, by decree, allowed to be used as postage stamps.

1922–24. POSTAGE DUE. Stamps of 1921–23 optd with Type D **6**.
D332	D **49**	½c. grey-green (6.23)	40	40
		a. Opt inverted	1·80	1·80
		b. Opt double	1·80	1·80
D333		1c. grey-green (6.23)	65	50

117

AZORES

D334	2c. grey-green (7.24)		65	50
D335	3c. grey-green (11.24)		1·00	50
D336	8c. grey-green (2.24)		1·00	50
D337	10c. grey-green (6.24)		1·00	50
	a. Opt inverted		2·75	2·75
D338	12c. grey-green (3.22)		1·00	50
D339	16c. grey-green (3.22)		1·10	50
D340	20c. grey-green (4.22)		1·10	50
D341	24c. grey-green (3.22)		1·10	50
D342	32c. grey-green (3.22)		1·10	50
D343	36c. grey-green (3.22)		1·10	70
D344	40c. grey-green (2.24)		1·10	70
D345	48c. grey-green (2.24)		1·10	70
D346	50c. grey-green (7.24)		1·10	70
D347	60c. grey-green (4.22)		1·20	75
D348	72c. grey-green (4.22)		1·20	75
D349	80c. grey-green (2.24)		5·50	4·50
D350	1E.20 grey-green (4.22)		6·25	5·00
D332/350 Set of 19			26·00	17·00

Sets may be made in pale or deep grey-green.

1924 (24 Dec). CHARITY TAX. No. C251 surch "15 ctvs" (Type C **61** of Portugal).
C325	C **58**	15c. on 1c. rose-red	1·20	95

AÇORES   AÇORES   AÇÔRES
(11)   (C 11)   (12)

1925 (26 Mar). C. C. Branco Centenary issue optd with T **11**.
325	65	2c. orange	25	25
326		3c. green	25	25
327		4c. blue (R.)	25	25
328		5c. scarlet	25	25
329	A	10c. light blue	25	25
330		16c. red-orange	40	30
331	67	25c. carmine	40	30
332	A	32c. green	60	55
333	67	40c. black and green (R.)	60	55
334	A	48c. brown-lake	1·30	1·30
335	B	50c. blue-green	1·30	1·10
336		64c. chestnut	1·30	1·10
337		75c. slate (R.)	1·30	1·10
338	67	80c. brown	1·30	1·10
339	B	96c. carmine	1·50	1·30
340	C	1E.50 deep blue/*blue*	1·50	1·30
341	67	1E.60 deep blue (R.)	1·70	1·50
342	C	2E. green/*green* (R.)	2·75	2·40
343		2E.40 scarlet/*orange*	3·75	2·50
344		3E.20 black/*green*	6·50	5·75
325/344 Set of 20			25·00	21·00

1925 (8 Apr). CHARITY TAX. Portuguese Army in Flanders, 1484 and 1918, type optd with Type C **11**.
C345	C **71**	10c. carmine	1·20	1·20
C346		10c. green	1·20	1·20
C347		10c. ultramarine	1·20	1·20
C348		10c. brown	1·20	1·20

Nos. C345/8 were in use on 8 and 9 April 1925 and on 10 and 11 November 1925.

1925 (8 Apr). POSTAGE DUE. Portuguese Army in Flanders type optd with Type C **11**.
D351	D **72**	20c. yellow-brown	1·20	1·00

1925 (8 May). CHARITY TAX. Marquis de Pombal issue inscr "AÇORES".
C349	C **73**	20c. green	1·20	1·20
C350	C **74**	20c. green	1·20	1·20
C351	C **75**	20c. green	1·20	1·20
C349/351 Set of 3			3·25	3·25

Nos. C349/51 were in use from 8 to 13 May 1925 and from 5 to 15 May of 1926 to 1929.

1925 (8 May). POSTAGE DUE. As Nos. C349/51 optd "MULTA".
D352	C **73**	40c. green	1·20	1·20
D353	C **74**	40c. green	1·20	1·20
D354	C **75**	40c. green	1·20	1·20
D352/354 Set of 3			3·25	3·25

1926 (13 Aug). First Independence Issue. As T **76/7** (dated 1926) optd with T **12**, in red. Centres in black.
345		2c. orange-red	45	35
346		3c. blue	45	35
347		4c. green	45	35
348		5c. sepia	45	35
349		6c. brown-orange	45	35
350		15c. myrtle-green	80	75
351		20c. violet	80	75
352		25c. scarlet	80	75
353		32c. deep green	80	75
354		40c. brown	80	75

355		50c. olive-bistre	1·80	1·70
356		75c. red-brown	1·90	1·80
357		1E. deep violet	2·40	2·30
358		4E.50 olive-green	9·50	9·50
345/358 Set of 14			20·00	19·00

1927 (29 Nov). Second Independence issue. As T **80** (dated 1927) optd with T **12**, in red. Centres in black.
359		2c. light brown	35	35
360		3c. blue	35	35
361		4c. orange	35	35
362		5c. sepia	35	35
363		6c. chestnut	35	35
364		15c. agate	45	35
365		25c. slate	1·70	1·70
366		32c. myrtle green	1·70	1·70
367		40c. green	95	95
368		96c. vermilion	4·25	4·00
369		1E.60 deep turquoise-blue	4·50	4·25
370		4E.50 ochre	11·50	11·50
359/370 Set of 12			24·00	24·00

1928 (27 Nov). Third Independence issue. As T **84** (dated 1928) optd with T **12**, in red. Centres in black.
371		2c. light blue	45	35
372		3c. green	45	35
373		4c. lake	45	35
374		5c. olive	45	35
375		6c. red-brown	45	35
376		15c. slate	85	80
377		16c. purple	95	95
378		25c. bright ultramarine	95	95
379		32c. green	1·00	1·00
380		40c. sepia	1·00	1·00
381		50c. vermilion	2·20	2·10
382		80c. grey	2·20	2·10
383		96c. scarlet	4·25	4·00
384		1E. mauve	4·25	4·00
385		1E.60 indigo	4·25	4·00
386		4E.50 yellow	11·00	10·50
371/386 Set of 16			32·00	30·00

40 C.
(13)

1929–30. Ceres type of 1917–30 surch as T **13**. P 12×11½.
387	56	4c. on 25c. rose-pink (2.30)	95	95
388		4c. on 60c. blue (7.29)	1·90	1·80
		a. Perf 15×14	6·50	6·50
389		10c. on 25c. rose-pink (9.29)	1·90	1·80
390		12c. on 25c. rose-pink (9.29)	1·90	1·80
391		15c. on 25c. rose-pink (8.29)	1·90	1·80
392		20c. on 25c. rose-pink (9.29)	3·25	3·00
393		40c. on 1E.10 yellow-brown (7.29)	6·25	6·00
387/393 Set of 7			16·00	15·00

1929–30. Ceres type without imprint below design optd with T **10**. P 14.
394	79	4c. orange (3.30)	1·20	90
395		5c. grey-brown (1.30)	4·00	3·50
396		10c. vermilion (3.30)	1·90	1·40
397		15c. black (R.) (1.30)	1·90	1·40
398		40c. emerald-green (11.29)	1·80	1·10
399		80c. violet (3.29)	20·00	15·00
400		1E.60 deep blue (3.30)	5·25	2·20
394/400 Set of 7			32·00	23·00

1930–31. Ceres type with imprint below design (Lisbon re-issue), optd with T **10**. P 12×11½.
401	56	4c. orange (10.30)	75	60
402		5c. sepia (7.31)	5·00	4·25
403		6c. brown-red (4.31)	50	35
404		15c. black (R.) (5.30)	1·20	90
405		16c. blue (12.31)	3·50	2·40
406		32c. deep blue-green (5.30)	3·50	2·40
407		40c. green (1.31)	1·90	95
408		48c. rosine (12.31)	4·50	3·75
409		50c. buff (9.30)	6·00	4·50
410		50c. brown-red (1.31)	6·00	4·50
411		64c. dull lake (12.31)	6·00	4·50
412		75c. carmine (1.31)	6·00	4·50
413		80c. myrtle (4.31)	6·00	3·75
414		1E. lake (8.30)	55·00	36·00
415		1E.25 indigo (10.30)	3·50	3·00
401/415 Set of 15			£100	70·00

AZORES

From 1931 the stamps of Portugal were used in the Azores. From 1980 stamps inscribed for the islands were again issued; unlike the earlier issues these were also sold and were valid for postage in mainland Portugal as well as the Azores.

14 10r. Stamp, 1868   **15** Map of the Azores

(Des P.O. Art Dept. Litho)

1980 (2 Jan). 112th Anniv of First Azores Stamps. T **14** and similar vert design. P 11½×12.

416	6E.50 black, yellow & orange-red	45	25
417	19E.50 black, dull purple & new bl	1·50	1·00
MS418	140×115 mm. Nos. 416/17 (sold at 30E.)	6·75	6·75

Design:—19E.50, 100r. stamp, 1868.

No. **MS**418 overprinted for "CAPEX '87" Stamp Exhibition was a private production.

(Des J. Cândido. Litho)

1980 (17 Sept). World Tourism Conference, Manila, Philippines. T **15** and similar horiz designs. Multicoloured. One phosphor band (Nos. 419/23). P 12×11½.

419	50c. Type **15**	20	15
420	1E. Church	30	20
421	5E. Windmill	75	40
422	6E.50 Traditional costume	95	45
423	8E. Coastal scene	1·40	65
424	30E. Coastal village	2·75	1·10
419/424	Set of 6	5·75	2·75

16 St. Peter's Cavalcade, São Miguel Island   **17** Bulls attacking Spanish Soldiers

(Des J. Cândido. Litho)

1981 (11 May). Europa. Folklore. One phosphor band. P 12.

425	**16**	22E. multicoloured	1·90	95
MS426		140×116 mm. No. 425×2	8·50	8·50

(Des L. de Freitas. Litho)

1981 (24 July). 400th Anniv of Battle of Salga. T **17** and similar horiz design. Multicoloured. One phosphor band. P 12×11½.

427	8E.50 Type **17**	80	10
428	33E.50 Friar Don Pedro leading attack	3·00	1·40

18 *Myosotis azorica*   **19** Embarkation of the Heroes of Mindelo

(Des J. Cândido. Litho)

1981 (21 Sept)–**83**. Regional Flowers. T **18** and similar vert designs. Multicoloured. One phosphor band (Nos. 429/38). P 12½×12.

429	4E. Type **18** (29.1.82)	20	10
	a. Booklet pane. Nos. 429, 432, 435, and 437 (29.1.82)	15·00	
430	7E. *Tolpis azorica*	45	30
	a. Booklet pane. Nos. 430/1, 434 and 439	16·00	
431	8E.50 *Ranunculus azoricus*	60	30
432	10E. *Lactuca watsoniana* (29.1.82)	85	30
433	12E.50 *Hypericum foliosum* (16.6.83)	40	10
	a. Booklet pane. Nos. 433, 436, 438 and 440 (16.6.83)	16·00	
434	20E. *Platanthera micranta*	1·00	70
435	27E. *Vicia dennesiana* (29.1.82)	1·90	1·20
436	30E. *Rubus hochstetterorum* (16.6.83)	1·20	50
437	33E.50 *Azorina vidalii* (29.1.82)	2·10	1·40
438	37E.50 *Vaccinium cylindraceum* (16.6.83)	1·70	1·00
439	50E. *Laurus azorica*	2·75	1·50
440	100E. *Juniperus brevifolia* (16.6.83)	3·50	1·60
429/440	Set of 12	15·00	8·00

Nos. 441/4 are vacant.

(Des J. P. Roque. Litho)

1982 (3 May). Europa. One phosphor band. P 12.

445	**19**	33E.50 multicoloured	2·75	1·40
MS446		140×113 mm. No. 445×3	21·00	21·00

20 Chapel of the Holy Ghost   **21** Geothermal Power Station, Pico Vermelho, São Miguel

(Des J. Cândido. Litho)

1982 (24 Nov). Regional Architecture. T **20** and similar vert design. Multicoloured. One phosphor band. P 12½×12.

447	27E. Type **20**	2·00	1·20
448	33E.50 Chapel of the Holy Ghost (different)	2·75	1·60

(Des J. Tinoco. Litho Litografia Maia, Oporto)

1983 (5 May). Europa. One phosphor band. P 12½.

449	**21**	37E.50 multicoloured	2·75	1·10
MS450		114×140 mm. No. 449×3	23·00	23·00

22 Flag of Azores   **23** Two "Holy Ghost" Jesters, São Miguel

(Des A. Leitão. Litho)

1983 (16 June). Flag. One phosphor band. P 12.

451	**22**	12E.50 multicoloured	1·10	20

(Des T. de Mello. Litho Litografia Maia, Oporto)

1984 (8 Mar). Traditional Costumes. T **23** and similar vert design. One phosphor band. P 13½.

452	16E. Type **23**	85	20
453	51E. Two women wearing Terceira cloak	3·00	2·10

(Des J. Larrivière and J. Cândido. Litho)

1984 (2 May). Europa. As T **398** of Portugal but additionally inscr "AÇORES". Two phosphor bands. P 12.

454	51E. multicoloured	4·00	1·90
MS455	114×139 mm. No. 454×3	20·00	20·00

24 *Megabombus ruderatus*   **25** Drummer

119

AZORES

(Des A. Contente. Litho)
1984 (3 Sept). Insects (1st series). T **24** and similar horiz designs. Multicoloured. One phosphor band. P 12.
456	16E. Type **24**...	50	10
	a. Imperf×p 12. Booklets...................	1·20	1·20
	ab. Booklet pane. Nos. 456a/9a.........	13·50	
457	35E. Large white (butterfly) (*Pieris brassicae*)	1·50	1·00
	a. Imperf×p 12. Booklets...................	3·25	3·25
458	40E. *Chrysomela banksi* (leaf beetle).........	2·20	1·00
	a. Imperf×p 12. Booklets...................	3·75	3·75
459	51E. *Phlogophora interrupta* (moth)............	2·50	1·60
	a. Imperf×p 12. Booklets...................	4·75	4·75
456/459	Set of 4	6·00	3·25

See also Nos. 460/3.

(Des A. Contente. Litho)
1985 (13 Feb). Insects (2nd series). Horiz designs as T **24**. Multicoloured. One phosphor band. P 12.
460	20E. *Polyspilla polyspilla* (leaf beetle)........	55	10
	a. Imperf×p 12. Booklets...................	1·30	1·30
	ab. Booklet pane. Nos. 460a/3a.........	13·50	
461	40E. *Sphaerophoria nigra* (hover fly)..........	1·60	85
	a. Imperf×p 12. Booklets...................	3·25	3·25
462	46E. Clouded yellow (butterfly) (*Colias croceus*)..	2·30	1·20
	a. Imperf×p 12. Booklets...................	3·75	3·75
463	60E. Southern grayling (butterfly) (*Hipparchia azorina*).................................	2·50	1·40
	a. Imperf×p 12. Booklets...................	4·75	4·75
460/463	Set of 4	6·25	3·25

(Des J. Tinoco. Litho)
1985 (6 May). Europa. One phosphor band. P 12.
464	**25** 60E. multicoloured...................................	4·00	1·70
MS465	140×114 mm. No. 464×3......................................	25·00	25·00

26 Jeque

27 Northern Bullfinch

(Des A. Alves. Litho)
1985 (19 June). Traditional Boats. T **26** and similar horiz design. Multicoloured. One phosphor band. P 12×12½.
466	40E. Type **26**...	2·10	1·20
467	60E. Bote...	2·75	1·50

(Des J. P. Roque. Litho)
1986 (5 May). Europa. One phosphor band. P 12.
468	**27** 68E.50 multicoloured............................	4·75	1·90
MS469	140×114 mm. No. 468×3.......................................	21·00	21·00

28 Alto das Covas Fountain, Terceira

29 Ox Cart, Santa Maria

(Des J. Cândido. Litho)
1986 (18 Sept). Regional Architecture. Drinking Fountains. T **28** and similar vert designs. Multicoloured. One phosphor band (Nos. 470/2). P 12.
470	22E.50 Type **28**...	90	20
	a. Imperf×p 12. Booklets...................	1·30	1·30
	ab. Booklet pane. Nos. 470a/3a.........	18·00	
471	52E.50 Fajã de Baixo, São Miguel............	2·75	1·40
	a. Imperf×p 12. Booklets...................	4·25	4·25
472	68E.50 Portoes de S. Pedro, Terceira.......	4·00	1·80
	a. Imperf×p 12. Booklets...................	5·00	5·00
473	100E. Água d'Alto, São Miguel..................	5·50	1·60
	a. Imperf×p 12. Booklets...................	6·50	6·50
470/473	Set of 4	12·00	4·50

(Des A. Cardoso. Litho)
1986 (7 Nov). Traditional Carts. T **29** and similar horiz design. Multicoloured. One phosphor band. P 12.
474	25E. Type **29**...	90	10
475	75E. Ram cart, São Miguel.........................	4·00	2·30

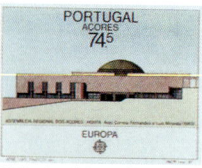
30 Regional Assembly Building (Correia Fernandes and Luis Miranda)

31 Santa Cruz, Graciosa

(Des J. Tinoco. Litho)
1987 (5 May). Europa. Architecture. Two phosphor bands. P 12.
476	**30** 74E.50, multicoloured............................	4·25	1·90
MS477	140×114 mm. No. 476×4.......................................	25·00	25·00

(Des F. Jorge and V. Mestre. Litho)
1987 (1 July). Windows and Balconies. T **31** and similar horiz designs. Multicoloured. One phosphor band. P 12.
478	51E. Type **31**...	2·50	1·40
479	74E.50 Ribeira Grande, São Miguel..........	3·00	1·40

32 A. C. Read's Curtiss NC-4 Flying Boat, 1919

33 19th-century Mule-drawn Omnibus

(Des L. Duran and C. Leitão. Litho)
1987 (9 Oct). Historic Airplane Landings in the Azores. T **32** and similar horiz designs. Multicoloured. Two phosphor bands. P 12.
480	25E. Type **32**...	75	10
	a. Imperf×p 12. Booklets...................	1·10	1·10
	ab. Booklet pane. Nos. 480a/3a.........	17·00	
481	57E. F. Christiansen's Dornier Do-X flying boat...	2·75	1·90
	a. Imperf×p 12. Booklets...................	3·25	3·25
482	74E.50 Italo Balbo's Savoia Marchetti S-55X flying boat...	4·00	1·70
	a. Imperf×p 12. Booklets...................	5·25	5·25
483	125E. Charles Lindbergh's Lockheed 8 Sirius seaplane *Tingmissartoq*, 1933........	4·50	2·40
	a. Imperf×p 12. Booklets...................	6·00	6·00
480/483	Set of 4	11·00	5·50

(Des L. Duran and C. Leitão. Litho)
1988 (21 Apr). Europa, Transport and Communications. Two phosphor bands. P 12.
484	**33** 80E. multicoloured...................................	5·00	1·50
MS485	140×112 mm. As No. 484×4 but with cream background	25·00	25·00

34 Wood Pigeon (*Columba palumbus*)

35 Azores Arms

(Des J. Projecto. Litho)
1988 (18 Oct). Nature Protection. Birds (1st series). T **34** and similar vert designs. Multicoloured. Two phosphor bands. P 12.
486	27E. Type **34**...	90	30
	a. Imperf×p 13½. Booklets.................	1·60	1·60
	ab. Booklet pane. Nos. 486a/9a.........	18·00	
487	60E. Eurasian woodcock (*Scolopax rusticola*)	2·75	1·40
	a. Imperf×p 13½. Booklets.................	4·25	4·25

AZORES

488	80E. Roseate tern (*Sterna dougallii*)	3·00	1·60
	a. Imperf×p 13½. Booklets	5·00	5·00
489	100E. Common buzzard (*Buteo buteo*)	3·75	1·60
	a. Imperf×p 13½. Booklets	5·75	5·75
486/489	Set of 4	9·25	4·50

See also Nos. 492/5 and 500/3.

(Des L. Cândido. Litho)

1988 (18 Nov). Coats of Arms. T **35** and similar horiz design. Multicoloured. Two phosphor bands. P 12.
490	55E. Type **35**	2·30	1·20
491	80E. Bettencourt family arms	3·00	1·60

(Des J. Projecto. Litho)

1989 (20 Jan). Nature Protection (2nd series). Goldcrest (*Regulus regulus azoricus*). Vert designs as T **34**. Multicoloured. Two phosphor bands. P 12.
492	30E. Goldcrest perched on branch	1·30	40
	a. Strip or block of 4. Nos. 492/5	5·50	
493	30E. Pair	1·30	40
494	30E. Goldcrest on nest	1·30	40
495	30E. Goldcrest with outspread wings	1·30	40
492/495	Set of 4	4·75	1·40

Nos. 492/5 were printed together in *se-tenant* blocks and horizontal and vertical strips of four within sheets of 16 stamps, the horizontal strips forming a composite design.

36 Boy in Boat **37** Pioneers

(Des A. Pimentel. Litho)

1989 (26 Apr). Europa. Children's Games and Toys. T **36** and similar horiz design. Multicoloured. Two phosphor bands. P 12.
496	80E. Type **36**	3·75	1·60
MS497	139×112 mm. 80E. ×2, Type **36**; 80E.×2, Boy with toy boat	25·00	25·00

(Des C. A. Santos. Litho)

1989 (20 Sept). 550th Anniv of Portuguese Settlement in Azores. T **37** and similar horiz design. Multicoloured. Two phosphor bands. P 12.
498	29E. Type **37**	85	30
499	87E. Settler breaking land	3·50	1·90

(Des J. Projecto. Litho)

1990 (14 Feb). Nature Protection (3rd series). Northern Bullfinch (*Pyrrhula murina*). Vert designs as T **34**. Multicoloured. Two phosphor bands. P 12.
500	32E. Two bullfinches	1·70	55
	a. Strip or block of 4. Nos. 500/3	7·00	
501	32E. Bullfinch on branch	1·70	55
502	32E. Bullfinch landing on twig	1·70	55
503	32E. Bullfinch on nest	1·70	55
500/503	Set of 4	6·00	2·00

Nos. 500/3 were issued together in *se-tenant* blocks and horizontal and vertical strips of four within sheets of 16 stamps, the horizontal strips forming a composite design.

38 Vasco da Gama Post Office **39** Cart Maker

(Des C. Leitão. Litho)

1990 (11 Apr). Europa. Post Office Buildings. T **38** and similar horiz design. Multicoloured. Two phosphor bands. P 12.
504	80E. Type **38**	3·00	1·50
MS505	139×111 mm. 80E.×2, Type **38**; 80E.×2, Maia Post Office	23·00	23·00

(Des E. Pinto. Litho)

1990 (11 July)–**92**. Traditional Occupations. T **39** and similar horiz designs. Multicoloured. Two phosphor bands. P 12.
506	5E. Type **39**	20	15
	a. Imperf×p 13½. Booklets	30	30
	ab. Booklet pane. Nos. 506a, 508a, 511a and 515a	11·00	
507	10E. Viol maker (12.6.92)	20	15
	a. Imperf×p 13½. Booklets	35	25
	ab. Booklet pane. Nos. 507a, 510a, 514a and 517a	7·50	
508	32E. Potter	80	40
	a. Imperf×p 13½. Booklets	1·30	1·30
509	35E. Making roof tiles (2.8.91)	75	30
	a. Imperf×p 13½. Booklets	85	85
	ab. Booklet pane. Nos. 509a, 512a, 513a and 516a	8·75	
510	38E. Carpenter (12.6.92)	75	35
	a. Imperf×p 13½. Booklets	95	95
511	60E. Tinsmith	2·30	1·20
	a. Imperf×p 13½. Booklets	3·75	3·75
512	65E. Laying pavement mosaics (2.8.91)	1·80	1·10
	a. Imperf×p 13½. Booklets	2·00	2·00
513	70E. Quarrying (2.8.91)	2·00	1·20
	a. Imperf×p 13½. Booklets	2·30	2·30
514	85E. Basket maker (12.6.92)	1·90	1·10
	a. Imperf×p 13½. Booklets	2·75	2·75
515	100E. Cooper	3·25	1·80
	a. Imperf×p 13½. Booklets	5·00	5·00
516	110E. Shaping stones (2.8.91)	3·00	1·40
	a. Imperf×p 13½. Booklets	3·25	3·25
517	120E. Boat builders (12.6.92)	2·50	1·20
	a. Imperf×p 13½. Booklets	3·25	3·25
506/517	Set of 12	18·00	9·25

Nos. 518/19 are vacant.

40 "Hermes" Spaceplane **41** *Helena* (schooner)

(Des P. Vidigal. Litho)

1991 (11 Apr). Europa. Europe in Space. T **40** and similar horiz design. Multicoloured. Two phosphor bands. P 12.
520	80E. Type **40**	5·25	4·00
MS521	140×112 mm. 80E.×2, Type **40**; 80E.×2, "Sänger" spaceplane	20·00	20·00

(Des L. Duran. Litho)

1991 (15 Nov). Inter-Island Transport. T **41** and similar horiz designs. Multicoloured. Two phosphor bands. P 12.
522	35E. Type **41**	75	25
523	60E. Beech Model 18 airplane, 1947	1·50	85
524	80E. *Cruzeiro do Canal* (ferry), 1987	2·30	1·40
525	110E. British Aerospace ATP airliner, 1991	2·75	1·60
522/525	Set of 4	6·50	3·75

42 *Santa Maria* off Azores **43** *Insulano* (steamer, 1868)

(Des L. de Freitas. Litho)

1992 (22 May). Europa. 500th Anniv of Discovery of America by Columbus. Two phosphor bands. P 12.
526	**42** 85E. multicoloured	2·40	1·10

(Des J. Tinoco. Litho)

1992 (7 Oct). The Empresa Insulana de Navegaçao Shipping Fleet. T **43** and similar horiz designs. Multicoloured. Two phosphor bands. P 12.
527	38E. Type **43**	75	30
528	65E. *Carvalho Araújo* (freighter, 1930)	1·50	1·00
529	85E. *Funchal* (ferry, 1961)	1·90	1·20
530	120E. *Terceirense* (freighter, 1948)	2·50	1·40
527/530	Set of 4	6·00	3·50

44 Ox-mill

45 "Two Sirens at the Entrance of a Grotto"

(Des C. Leitão. Litho)
1993 (5 May). Traditional Grinders. T **44** and similar horiz design. Multicoloured. P 12.
531	42E. Type **44**	75	35
532	130E. Hand-mill	3·00	1·80

(Des C. Leitão. Litho)
1993 (5 May). Europa. Contemporary Art. T **45** and similar vert design showing paintings by António Dacosta. Multicoloured. P 12.
533	90E. Type **45**	2·75	1·20
MS534	140×112 mm. 90E.×2, Type **45**; 90E.×2, "Açoriana III"	15·00	15·00

46 Main Entrance, Praia da Vitória Church, Terceira

47 Floral Decoration, Our Lady of Sorrows, Caloura, São Miguel

(Des C. Pinto and Ana Bela Silva. Litho)
1993 (3 Nov). Doorways. T **46** and similar vert designs. Multicoloured. P 12.
535	42E. Type **46**	75	35
536	70E. South door, Praia da Vitória Church	1·40	85
537	90E. Main door, Ponta Delgada Church, São Miguel	1·80	1·10
538	130E. South door, Ponta Delgada Church	2·75	1·40
535/538	Set of 4	6·00	3·25

(Des Ana Bela Silva. Litho)
1994 (28 Mar). Tiles. T **47** and similar horiz designs. Multicoloured. P 12.
539	40E. Type **47**	60	35
	a. Imperf×p 11½. Booklets	80	70
	ab. Booklet pane. Nos. 539a/42a	8·00	
540	70E. Decoration of crosses, Our Lady of Sorrows, Caloura, São Miguel	1·40	80
	a. Imperf×p 11½. Booklets	1·70	1·70
541	100E. "Adoration of the Wise Men", Our Lady of Hope Monastery, Ponta Delgada, São Miguel	1·80	1·10
	a. Imperf×p 11½. Booklets	2·20	2·20
542	150E. "St. Brás" (altar frontal), Our Lady of Anjos, Santa Maria	2·75	1·70
	a. Imperf×p 11½. Booklets	3·00	3·00
539/542	Set of 4	6·00	3·50

48 Monkey and Explorer with Model Caravel

49 Doorway, St. Barbara's Church, Cedros, Faial

(Des L. F. de Abreu. Litho)
1994 (5 May). Europa. Discoveries. T **48** and similar horiz design. Multicoloured. P 12.
543	100E. Type **48**	2·20	1·10
MS544	140×112 mm. 100E.×2, Type **48**; 100E.×2, Armadillo and explorer with model caravel	12·50	12·50

(Des C. Pinto. Litho)
1994 (16 Sept). Manoeline Architecture. T **49** and similar vert design. Multicoloured. P 12.
545	45E. Type **49**	65	35
546	140E. Window, Ribeira Grande, São Miguel	2·40	1·60

50 Aristides Moreira da Motta

51 Santana Palace, Ponta Delgada

(Des J. Tinoco. Litho)
1995 (2 Mar). Centenary of Decree decentralizing Government of the Azores and Madeira Islands. T **50** and similar horiz design showing pro-autonomy activists. Multicoloured. P 12.
547	42E. Type **50**	65	35
548	130E. Gil Mont'Alverne de Sequeira	2·20	1·40

(Des V. Santos. Litho)
1995 (1 Sept). Architecture of São Miguel. T **51** and similar vert designs. Multicoloured. P 12.
549	45E. Type **51**	65	35
	a. Imperf×p 11½. Booklets	85	85
	ab. Booklet pane. Nos. 549a/52a	6·75	
550	80E. Chapel of Our Lady of the Victories, Furnas	1·30	75
	a. Imperf×p 11½. Booklets	1·60	1·60
551	95E. Hospital, Ponta Delgada	1·50	80
	a. Imperf×p 11½. Booklets	1·80	1·80
552	135E. Ernesto do Canto's villa, Furnas	1·80	1·10
	a. Imperf×p 11½. Booklets	2·20	2·20
549/552	Set of 4	4·75	2·75

52 Contendas Lighthouse, Terceira

(Des V. Santos. Litho)
1996 (3 May). Lighthouses. T **52** and similar horiz designs. Multicoloured. P 12.
553	47E. Type **52**	60	35
554	78E. Molhe Lighthouse, São Miguel	1·30	85
555	98E. Arnel Lighthouse, São Miguel	1·50	1·00
556	140E. Santa Clara Lighthouse, São Miguel	2·10	1·30
553/556	Set of 4	5·00	3·25
MS557	110×140 mm. 200E. Ponta da Barca Lighthouse, Graciosa	3·00	3·00

53 Natália Correia (poet)

54 Bird eating Grapes (St. Peter's Church, Ponta Delgada)

(Des L. Duran. Litho)
1996 (3 May). Europa. Famous Women. P 12.
558	**53** 98E. multicoloured	1·70	85
MS559	140×112 mm. No. 558×3	5·75	5·75

AZORES

(Des A. Santos. Litho Litografia Maia, Oporto)

1997 (16 Apr). Gilded Wooden Altarpieces. T **54** and similar horiz designs. Multicoloured. P 12.

560	49E. Type **54**	65	35
	a. Imperf × p 12. Booklets	80	80
	ab. Booklet pane. Nos. 560a/3a	6·50	
561	80E. Cherub (St. Peter of Alcantara Convent, São Roque)	1·20	55
	a. Imperf × p 12. Booklets	1·30	1·30
562	100E. Cherub with wings (All Saints Church, Jesuit College, Ponta Delgada)	1·40	90
	a. Imperf × p 12. Booklets	1·70	1·70
563	140E. Caryatid (St. Joseph's Church, Ponta Delgada)	2·00	1·20
	a. Imperf × p 12. Booklets	2·40	2·40
560/563 Set of 4		4·75	2·75

55 Island of the Seven Cities

56 Emperor and Empress and Young Bulls (Festival of the Holy Spirit)

(Des Nélia Caixinha. Litho Litografia Maia, Oporta)

1997 (5 May). Europa. Tales and Legends. P 12.

564	**55** 100E. multicoloured	1·70	85
MS565	140×106 mm. No. 564 × 3	5·50	5·50

(Des L. de Abreu. Litho Litografia Maia, Oporto)

1998 (21 May). Europa. National Festivals. P 12.

566	**56** 100E. multicoloured	1·60	85
MS567	140×109 mm. No. 566 ×3	4·75	4·75

57 Spotted Dolphin (*Stenella frontalis*)

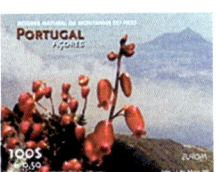
58 Mt. Pico Nature Reserve

(Des P. Salgado and A. Santos. Litho)

1998 (4 Aug). Expo '98 World's Fair, Lisbon. Marine Life. T **57** and similar horiz design. Multicoloured. P 12.

568	50E. Type **57**	65	35
	a. Imperf×p 11½. Booklets	80	80
	ab. Booklet pane. Nos. 568a and 569a plus label	3·25	
569	140E. Sperm whale (*Physeter macrocephalus*) (79×30 *mm*)	1·90	1·20
	a. Imperf × p 11½. Booklets	2·20	2·20

(Des J. Sarmento and P. Oliveira. Litho Litografia Maia, Oporto)

1999 (5 May). Europa. Parks and Gardens. P 12.

570	**58** 100E. multicoloured	1·40	85
MS571	154×109 mm. No. 570×3	4·75	4·75

59 "Emigrants" (Domingos Rebelo)

60 "Building Europe"

(Des C. Leitão. Litho Litografia Maia, Oporto)

1999 (3 Sept). Paintings. T **59** and similar multicoloured designs. P 12.

572	51E. Type **59**	65	35
	a. Imperf×p 12. Booklets	80	80
	ab. Booklet pane. Nos. 572a/5a	6·25	
573	95E. "Portrait of Vitorino Nemésio" (António Dacosta) (*vert*)	1·30	85
	a. P 12×imperf. Booklets	1·50	1·50
574	100E. "Cattle loose on the Alto das Covas" (Zé van der Hagen Bretão)	1·30	85
	a. Imperf×p 12. Booklets	1·60	1·60
575	140E. "Vila Franca Island" (Duarte Maia)	1·70	1·20
	a. Imperf×p 12. Booklets	2·00	2·00
572/575 Set of 4		4·50	3·00

(Des J.-P. Cousin. Litho)

2000 (9 May). Europa. P 12.

576	**60** 100E. multicoloured	1·70	95
MS577	154×108 mm. No. 576×3	5·25	5·25

61 Fishermen retrieving Mail Raft

62 Coast Line

(Des C. Possolo. Litho Litografia Maia, Oporto)

2000 (9 Oct). History of Mail Delivery in the Azores. T **61** and similar multicoloured design. P 12.

578	85E. Type **61**	1·30	80
579	140E. Zeppelin airship dropping mail sacks	2·10	1·40

(Des J. Machado. Litho)

2001 (9 May). Europa. Water Resources. P 12.

580	**62** 105E. multicoloured	1·70	95
MS581	140×110 mm. No. 580 × 3	5·25	5·25

63 Arch and Town

(Des A. Santos. Litho)

2001 (4 June). UNESCO World Heritage Site, Angra do Heroísmo. T **63** and similar horiz designs. Multicoloured. P 12.

582	53E. Type **63**	70	35
583	85E. Monument and town	1·30	85
584	140E. Balcony and view over town	2·00	1·30
582/584 Set of 3		3·50	2·30
MS585	140×112 mm. 350E. Map of town	5·00	5·00

New Currency. 100 Cents = 1 Euro

64 Clown

65 Faial Island, Azores

(Des E. Aires. Litho Litografia Maia, Oporto)

2002 (9 May). Europa. Circus. P 12.

586	**64** 54c. multicoloured	1·70	90
MS587	140×110 mm. No. 586 × 3. P 12½	5·00	5·00

(Des Myriam Voz and T. Martin. Litho)

2002 (12 July). Windmills. T **65** and similar vert design. Multicoloured. P 12.

588	43c. Type **65**	1·10	70
589	54c. Onze-Lieve-Vrouw-Lombeek, Roosdaal	1·50	85

Stamps of a similar design were issued by Belgium.

AZORES

66 Birds (Sebāstiao Rodrigues)   **67** Pineapple Groves

(Des J. Brandāo. Litho)

2003 (5 May). Europa. Poster Art. P 12×12½.

590	**66**	55c. multicoloured	1·80	95
MS591	140×113 mm. No. 590 × 2		3·25	3·25

(Des J. Brandāo. Litho)

2003 (6 June). São Miguel Island. T **67** and similar horiz design. Multicoloured. P 12.

592	30c. Type **67**	80	30
593	43c. Vineyards and grapes	1·10	70
594	55c. Date growing	1·40	90
595	70c. Coffee growing	1·80	1·20
592/595 Set of 4		4·50	2·75
MS596 140×112 mm. €1 Dancers and ceramic figure; €2 Fruit and ceramic bird (Espirito Santos festival)		8·00	8·00

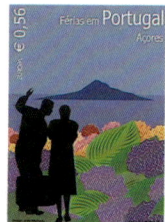

68 Figures, Flowers and Island   **69** Blue Marlin (*Makaira nigricans*)

(Des J. Machado. Litho Enschedé)

2004 (10 May). Europa. Holidays. P 13½×14.

597	**68**	56c. multicoloured	1·60	90
MS598 141×112 mm. No. 597×2			3·25	3·25

(Des V. Marques. Litho Cartor)

2004 (28 June). Endangered Species. Atlantic Marlin. T **69** and similar horiz designs. Multicoloured. P 13×13½.

599	30c. Type **69**	80	55
	a. Strip of 4. Nos. 599/602	3·50	
600	30c. Fin, body and tail	80	55
601	30c. White marlin (*Tetrapturus albidus*)	80	55
602	30c. Back and tail	80	55
599/602 Set of 4		3·00	2·00

Nos. 599/602 were issued in horizontal *se-tenant* strips of four stamps within the sheet, the strip forming a composite design.

70 Torresmos (marinated pork)   **71** Cow

(Des A. Santos. Litho Enschedé)

2005 (5 May). Europa. Gastronomy. T **70** and similar horiz design. Multicoloured. P 14×13½.

603	57c. Type **70**	1·60	90
	a. Booklet pane. No. 603 (2005)	1·70	
MS604 125×95 mm. 57c.×2, Polvo guisado (octopus)×2		4·25	4·25
	a. Booklet pane. No. MS604 (2005)	4·50	

(Des A. Santos. Litho Enschedé)

2005 (13 May). Tourism. T **71** and similar horiz designs. Multicoloured. P 14×13½.

605	30c. Type **71**	70	50
	a. Booklet pane. Nos. 605/6 (2005)	1·50	
606	30c. Arched window and lake	70	50
607	45c. Decorated house	1·10	75
	a. Booklet pane. Nos. 607/8 (2005)	2·30	
608	45c. Windmill	1·10	75
609	57c. Whale's tail	1·40	90
	a. Booklet pane. Nos. 609/10 (2005)	3·50	
610	74c. Pineapple and hot spring	1·80	1·30
605/610 Set of 6		6·00	4·25
MS611 125×95 mm. 30c. Santo Cristo dos Milagres (statue); €1.55 Bird		4·50	4·50
	a. Booklet pane. No. MS611 (2005)	4·75	

Nos. 603a, MS604a, 605a, 607a, 609a and MS611a were issued in booklets of six panes interleaved with five pages of text.

72 Figures standing on Head (Joao Dinis)   **73** Crabs, Lucky Strike

2006 (9 May). Europa. Integration. Winning Entries in ANACED (association for art and creativity by and for people with disabilities) Painting Competition. T **72** and similar horiz designs. Multicoloured. P 12½.

612	60c. Type **72**	1·50	85
	a. Booklet pane. No. 612	1·60	
MS613 125×95 mm. 60c.×2, One legged figure; Figure with irregular outlines		3·00	3·00
	a. Booklet pane. No. MS613	3·25	

(Des V. Marques. Litho Cartor)

2006 (22 July). Hydrothermal Springs. T **73** and similar horiz designs. Multicoloured. P 12.

614	20c. Type **73**	45	30
	a. Booklet pane. Nos. 614/15	1·30	
615	30c. Fish, Lucky Strike	70	45
616	75c. Plumes, Rainbow	1·70	1·10
	a. Booklet pane. Nos. 616/17	6·50	
617	€2 Fish tower, Rainbow	4·50	3·00
614/617 Set of 4		6·50	4·25
MS618 125×95 mm. €2 No. 617		4·75	4·75
	a. Booklet pane. No. MS618a	5·00	

74 Mountain   **75** Scarf

(Des E. Aires. Litho Cartor)

2006 (14 Sept). Wine from Pico Island. T **74** and similar horiz designs. Multicoloured. P 12.

619	30c. Type **74**	70	45
	a. Booklet pane. Nos. 619/20	2·10	
620	60c. Terraces	1·30	85
621	75c. Harvesting	1·70	1·10
	a. Booklet pane. Nos. 621/2	4·25	
622	€1 Wine barrel	2·20	1·50
619/622 Set of 4		5·25	3·50
MS623 125×95 mm. 45c. Young vines; 60c. Harvesting; 75c. Winery; €1 Barrels		6·50	6·50
	a. Booklet pane. No. MS623a	6·75	

Nos. 612a, MS613a, 614a, 616a, MS618a, 619a, 621a and MS623a were issued in booklets consisting of eight panes interleaved with five pages of text.

AZORES

(Des Hulton-Deutsch and Corbis. Litho Cartor)

2007 (9 May). Europa. Centenary of Scouting. T **75** and similar horiz designs. Multicoloured. P 12½×13½.
624	61c. Type **75**	1·40	85
	a. Booklet pane. No. 624	1·50	
MS625	125×95 mm. 61c.×2, Reef knot; Scouts in camp	3·00	3·00
	a. Booklet pane. No. **MS**625	3·25	

The stamps of No. **MS**625 form a composite design.

76 Sao Miguel   77 Capelinhos Volcano

(Des José Brandão and Paulo Falardo. Litho Cartor)

2007 (25 May). Windmills. T **76** and similar horiz designs. Multicoloured. P 12½×13½.
626	30c. Type **76**	65	45
	a. Booklet pane. Nos. 626/9 627	4·75	
627	45c. Sao Jorge	95	65
628	61c. Corvo	1·30	85
629	75c. Blue windmill, Sao Jorge	1·70	1·10
626/629	Set of 4	4·25	2·75
MS630	125×95 mm. 45c. Sao Miguel (different); €2 Red windmill, Sao Jorge	5·50	5·50
	a. Booklet pane. No. **MS**630	5·75	

(Des Francisco Galamba. Litho Cartor)

2007 (27 Sept). 50th Anniv of Eruption of Capelinhos Volcano, Faial Island. T **77** and similar horiz design. Multicoloured. P 12½×13.
631	30c. Type **77**	65	45
	a. Booklet pane. Nos. 631/632	2·50	
632	75c. Erupting volcano and lighthouse	1·70	1·10
MS633	125×95 mm. €2.45 Island showing lighthouse (80×30 mm)	5·75	5·75
	a. Booklet pane. No. **MS**633	6·00	

The stamp and margin of No. **MS**633 form a composite design.

Nos. 624a, **MS**625a, 626a, **MS**630a, 631a and **MS**633a were issued in booklets consisting of panes interleaved with pages of text.

78 Envelope as Boat   79 Cock Bird

(Des Luiz Duran. Litho Cartor)

2008 (9 May). Europa. The Letter. T **78** and similar horiz design. Multicoloured. P 12 (irregular indentation on each vert side).
634	61c. Type **78**	1·50	85
	a. Booklet pane. No. 634	1·60	
MS635	125×95 mm. 61c.×2, Windmill and envelopes; As Type **78**	3·00	3·00
	a. Booklet pane. No. **MS**635	3·25	

The indentation in the vertical perforations forms the shape of a cross when viewed across the sheet.
The stamps of **MS**635 each form a composite design.

(Des Jose Projecto. Litho Cartor)

2008 (23 May). Azores Bullfinch (*Pyrrhula murina*). T **79** and similar horiz design. Multicoloured. P 12 (irregular indentation on each vert side).
636	30c. Type **79**	75	45
	a. Booklet pane. Nos. 636/7	2·40	
637	61c. Female	1·50	85
638	75c. Male facing right	1·80	1·00
	a. Booklet pane. Nos. 638/9	4·50	
639	€1 Male facing left	2·50	1·40
636/639	Set of 4	6·00	3·25
MS640	Two sheets, each 125×95 mm	14·00	14·00
	(a) €2.45 Head of male eating seed		
	a. Booklet pane. No. **MS**640a	6·50	
	(b) €2.95 Head of male with open beak		
	a. Booklet pane. No. **MS**640b	7·00	

The indentation in the vertical perforations forms the shape of a cross when viewed across the sheet.
The stamps and margins of No. **MS**640a/b form a composite design.

80 Ponta do Arnel   81 Woodcock (Lagoa Comprida)

(Des A. Santos and H. Soares. Litho Cartor)

2008 (19 June). Lighthouse. P 12 (irregular indentation on each horiz side).
641	**80** 61c. multicoloured	1·50	85
	a. Booklet pane. No. 641	1·60	

The indentation in the vertical perforations forms the shape of a cross when viewed across the sheet.

Nos. 634a, **MS**635a, 636a, 638a, **MS**640a, **MS**640b, and 641a were issued in booklets consisting of panes interleaved with pages of text.

(Des Nuno Farinha. Litho Cartor)

2009 (22 Apr). Biodiversity. Lakes. T **81** and similar horiz designs. Multicoloured. P 12 (irregular indentation on each vert side).
642	32c. Type **81**	95	45
643	68c. Brown butterfly (Lagoa do Caldeirão)..	2·10	1·00
644	80c. Dragonfly (Lagoa do Capitão)	2·40	1·20
645	€2 Azores juniper (Lagoinha)	6·00	3·00
642/645	Set of 4	10·50	5·00
MS646	125×95 mm. €2.50 Tessellate moray (80×30 mm)	7·50	7·50
MS647	125×95 mm. €2.50 Tufted duck, teal and capped heron (80×30 mm)	7·50	7·50

The indentations in the vertical perforations form the shape of a cross when viewed across the sheet.

82 European Space Agency Satellite Tracking Station, Santa Maria Island, Azores   83 Milho (maize bread)

(Des Elizabete Fonseca. Litho Cartor)

2009 (8 May). Europa. Astronomy. T **82** and similar horiz design. Multicoloured. P 12 (irregular indentation on each vert side).
648	68c. Type **82**	2·10	1·00
MS649	125×95 mm. 68c.×2, Ribeira Grande Astronomical Observatory, Sao Miguel Island, Azores; As Type **82**	4·25	4·25

The stamps and margins of No. **MS**649 form a composite design.
The indentations in the vertical perforations form the shape of a cross when viewed across the sheet.

(Des Elizbete Fonseca and Atelier Acácio Santos. Litho Cartor)

2009 (28 July). Bread. Sheet 125×95 mm. P 12 (irregular indentation on each vert side).
MS650	**83** €2 multicoloured	6·00	6·00

84 Girl   85 *Dardanus callidus*

(Litho Cartor)

2010 (7 May). Europa. Children's Books. T **84** and similar vert design showing illustrations by Teresa Lima. Multicoloured. P 12 (irregular indentation on each horiz side).
651	68c. Type **84**	2·10	1·00
MS652	125×96 mm. 68c.×2, King on horseback; As Type **84**	4·25	4·25

125

AZORES / Angra / Horta

(Des R. Rodigues. Litho Cartor)

2010 (1 July). Invertebrates. T **85** and similar horiz designs. P 13 (irregular indentation on each vert side).

653	32c.	Type **85**	95	45
654	68c.	*Alicia mirabilis*	2·10	1·00
655	80c.	*Orphidiaster orphidianus*	2·40	1·20
653/655	Set of 3		5·00	2·25
MS656	125×95 mm. €2 *Grapsus adscencionis*		6·00	6·00
MS657	125×95 mm. €2 *Sphaerechinus granularis*		6·00	6·00

STAMP BOOKLETS

The following checklist covers, in simplified form, booklets issued for the Azores. It is intended that it should be used in conjunction with the main listing and details of stamps and panes listed there are not repeated.

There was at least one early booklet for the Azores, containing examples of No. 196. Full details are not available but No. SB1 has been left for this booklet.

Prices are for complete booklets

Booklet No.	Date	Contents and Cover Price	Price
SB2	29.1.81	Regional Flowers 1 pane, No. 430a (85E.50)	17·00
SB3	29.1.82	Regional Flowers 1 pane, No. 429a (74E.50)	16·00
SB4	16.6.83	Regional Flowers 1 pane, No. 433a (180E.)	17·00
SB5	3.9.84	Insects (1st series) 1 pane, No. 456ab (142E.)	14·00
SB6	13.2.85	Insects (2nd series) 1 pane, No. 460ab (166E.)	14·00
SB7	19.9.86	Regional Architecture 1 pane, No. 470ab (243E.50)	19·00
SB8	9.10.87	Historic Airplane Landings 1 pane, No. 480ab (281E.50)	18·00
SB9	18.10.88	Nature Protection. Birds 1 pane, No. 486ab (267E.)	19·00
SB10	11.7.90	Traditional Occupations 1 pane, No. 506ab (197E.)	11·50
SB11	2.8.91	Traditional Occupations 1 pane, No. 509ab (280E.)	9·00
SB12	12.6.92	Traditional Occupations 1 pane, No. 507ab (253E.)	7·75
SB13	28.3.94	Tiles 1 pane, No. 539ab (360E.)	8·25
SB14	1.9.95	Architecture of São Miguel 1 pane, No. 549ab (355E.)	7·00
SB15	16.4.97	Gilded Wooden Altarpieces 1 pane, No. 560ab (369E.)	6·75
SB16	4.8.98	"Expo '98". Marine Life 1 pane, No. 568ab (190E.)	3·50
SB17	3.9.99	Paintings 1 pane, No. 572ab (386E.)	6·50
SB18	2005	Tourism. Stamps of 2005 6 panes. Nos. 603a, **MS**604a, 605a, 607a, 609a and **MS**611a. (€6.37)	19·00
SB19	2006	Stamps of 2006 8 panes. Nos. 612a, **MS**613a, 614a, 616a, **MS**618a, 619a, 621a and **MS**623a	32·00
SB20	2007	Stamps of 2007 6 panes. Nos. 624a, **MS**625a, 626a, **MS**630a, 631a and **MS**633a	25·00
SB21	2008	Stamps of 2008 7 panes. Nos. 634a, **MS**635a, 636a, 638a, **MS**640a, **MS**640b and 641a	28·00

From 1892 to 1905 separate issues were made for each of the three administrative districts of the Azores.

ANGRA

1   2

(Head eng M. D. Neto, frame eng J. S. de Carvalho e Silva. Typo)

1892–93. Chalk-surfaced paper or enamel-surfaced paper (E).

(a) P 11½

1	1	5r. yellow (1.7.92)	15·00	8·00
2		25r. deep green (1.6.92)	7·75	1·70
		a. Green	7·75	1·70

(b) P 12½

3	1	5r. orange-yellow	4·75	2·50
4		5r. orange-yellow (E)	7·00	2·75

5		10r. rosy mauve (1.7.92)	4·75	2·50
6		15r. red-brown (1.10.92)	5·50	3·75
7		20r. lavender	5·50	3·75
8		25r. deep green	7·50	1·70
9		50r. pale blue (1.7.92)	11·00	5·75
10		75r. rose (15.12.92)	13·00	7·50
11		80r. pale green (1.8.92)	15·00	14·00
12		100r. brown/*yellow* (1.4.93)	£225	£180
13		150r. carmine/*rose* (1.8.93)	75·00	60·00
14		200r. blue/*blue* (1.8.93)	75·00	60·00
15		300r. blue/*pale brown* (1.8.93)	75·00	60·00
3, 5/15 *Set of 12*			£475	£350

(c) P 13½

16	1	5r. orange-yellow	4·25	2·50
17		5r. orange-yellow (E)	7·75	4·00
18		10r. rosy mauve	5·50	3·75
19		15r. red-brown	5·50	4·00
20		20r. lavender	5·50	4·00
21		25r. green (E)	12·00	7·50
22		50r. pale blue	15·00	8·75
23		50r. pale blue (E)		49·00
24		100r. brown/*yellow*	55·00	20·00
25		150r. carmine/*rose*	85·00	75·00
26		200r. blue/*blue*	85·00	75·00
27		300r. blue/*pale brown*	85·00	75·00
16, 18/22, 24/27 *Set of 10*			£325	£250

Stamps of this type were issued for three districts of the Azores (Angra, Horta and Ponta Delgada) and for Funchal (Madeira). First printings were in sheets of 24 each containing 12 stamps of Angra and Horta or 12 of Funchal and Ponta Delgada. Later printings were in sheets of 28 containing stamps of one district only.

The 50, 150, 200 and 300r. were reprinted perf 11½ in 1900 and all values were reprinted in 1905.

(Des and eng E. Mouchon. Typo)

1897 (1 Jan). Name and value in black or carmine (500r.).

(a) P 11½

28	2	2½r. pale grey	1·00	65
29		5r. orange-red	1·00	65
		a. Bisected (on cover) (used March and Dec 1897)		40·00
30		10r. yellow-green	1·00	65
31		15r. chocolate	13·00	8·50
32		20r. deep lilac	2·50	1·90
33		25r. blue-green	4·25	1·70
34		50r. blue	7·75	2·40
35		75r. rose	4·75	2·30
36		80r. mauve	2·10	1·70
37		100r. blue/*blue*	3·75	2·40
38		150r. purple-brown/*straw*	3·75	2·40
39		200r. purple/*pink*	7·75	6·75
40		300r. blue/*pink*	11·50	8·75
41		500r. black/*azure*	24·00	19·00
28/41 *Set of 14*			80·00	55·00

(b) P 12½

42	2	500r. black/*azure*	32·00	24·00

1898 (1 July)–**1905**. Colours changed and new values. Name and value in black or carmine (75r.). P 11½.

43	2	15r. deep green (1.1.99)	1·30	80
44		25r. carmine (1.1.99)	90	80
45		50r. ultramarine (6.05)	19·00	15·00
46		65r. steel-blue	1·80	80
47		75r. brown/*yellow* (6.05)	19·00	15·00
48		115r. brown-red/*pink*	3·75	2·75
49		130r. sepia/*cream*	3·75	4·25
50		180r. slate/*pale pink*	4·75	4·25
43/50 *Set of 8*			49·00	38·00

HORTA

1   2

(Head eng M. D. Neto, frame eng J. S. de Carvalho e Silva. Typo)

1892. Chalk-surfaced paper or enamel-surfaced paper (E).

(a) P 11½

1	1	5r. orange-yellow (1.7.92)	34·00	26·00
2		25r. deep green (1.6.92)	7·00	1·80
		a. Green	7·00	1·80
3		25r. green (E)	15·00	6·50

AZORES / Horta / Ponta Delgada / British Post Office on São Miguel

(b) P 12½

4	1	5r. orange-yellow		3·75	2·75
5		10r. rosy mauve (1.7.92)		3·75	3·50
6		15r. red-brown (1.10.92)		3·75	3·50
7		20r. lavender (1.10.92)		4·50	4·25
8		50r. pale blue (1.7.92)		11·00	5·00
		a. Ultramarine		11·00	5·00
9		75r. rose (15.12.92)		13·50	7·50
10		80r. pale green (1.8.92)		16·00	14·50
11		100r. brown/yellow (1.4.92)		£225	£180
12		150r. carmine/rose (1.8.93)		80·00	65·00
13		200r. blue/blue (1.8.93)		80·00	65·00
14		300r. blue/pale brown (1.8.93)		80·00	65·00
4/14 Set of 11				£275	£225

(c) P 13½

15	1	5r. orange-yellow		3·75	2·50
16		5r. orange-yellow (E)		8·75	3·50
17		10r. rosy mauve		4·50	3·50
18		15r. red-brown		6·00	5·25
19		20r. lavender		6·75	5·25
20		25r. green (E)		8·75	6·50
21		50r. blue		16·00	8·25
22		75r. carmine (E)		12·50	8·00
23		100r. brown/yellow		70·00	60·00
24		150r. carmine/rose		80·00	65·00
25		200r. blue/blue		80·00	65·00
26		300r. blue/pale brown		80·00	65·00
15/26 Set of 11 (one of each value)				£325	£275

For sheet arrangement see footnote after Angra No. 27.
The 5, 50, 150, 200 and 300r. were reprinted perf 11½ in 1900 and all values perf 13½ in 1905.

1894 (Aug). Bisected diagonally.

27	1	Half of 5r.			26·00

The above was officially authorised.

(Des and eng E. Mouchon. Typo)

1897 (1 Jan)–**1901**. Name and value in black or carmine (500r.). P 11½.

28	2	2½r. grey		80	40
29		5r. orange-red		80	40
30		10r. pale green		80	40
31		15r. chocolate		11·00	8·00
32		20r. deep lilac		2·10	1·70
33		25r. blue-green		3·75	1·80
34		50r. blue		4·25	1·80
35		75r. rose		4·00	1·80
36		80r. mauve		2·20	1·40
37		100r. blue/blue		4·00	1·40
38		150r. purple-brown/straw		2·75	1·40
39		200r. purple/flesh		8·00	6·75
40		300r. pink		14·00	10·50
41		500r. black/azure (1901)		19·00	17·00
28/41 Set of 14				70·00	49·00

1898 (1 July)–**1905**. Colours changed and new values. Name and value in black or carmine (75r.). P 11½.

42	2	15r. deep green (1.1.99)		2·10	1·60
43		25r. carmine (1.1.99)		2·10	1·00
44		50r. ultramarine (6.05)		18·00	14·00
45		65r. steel-blue		1·50	1·10
46		75r. brown/yellow (6.05)		17·00	15·00
47		115r. orange-brown/pink		2·75	2·10
		a. Error. On cream		12·00	7·75
48		130r. sepia/cream		2·75	2·10
49		180r. slate/pale pink		2·75	2·10
42/49 Set of 8				44·00	35·00

PONTA DELGADA

(b) P 12½

6	1	5r. orange-yellow		3·75	2·50
		a. Bisected (2½r.) for newspapers			26·00
7		10r. rosy mauve (1.7.92)		3·75	2·50
8		15r. red-brown (1.10.92)		5·00	3·50
9		20r. lavender (1.10.92)		5·00	3·50
10		25r. green		11·00	2·50
11		25r. green (E)		13·50	7·25
12		50r. pale blue		11·00	5·25
13		75r. rose (15.12.92)		12·00	8·25
14		80r. pale green (1.8.92)		15·00	14·50
15		100r. brown/yellow (1.4.93)		15·00	8·75
16		200r. blue/blue (1.8.93)		85·00	70·00
17		300r. blue/pale brown		85·00	70·00
6/17 Set of 12				£250	£180

(c) P 13½

18	1	5r. orange-yellow		3·75	2·50
19		5r. yellow (E)		3·75	1·20
20		10r. rosy mauve		5·00	3·50
21		15r. red-brown		5·00	3·50
22		20r. lavender		8·00	3·25
23		25r. green (E)		11·00	1·70
24		50r. pale blue		9·00	8·75
25		75r. rose		10·50	8·75
26		80r. pale green		21·00	12·00
27		100r. brown/yellow		21·00	12·00
28		150r. carmine/rose (1.8.93)		85·00	49·00
18/28 Set of 10 (one of each value)				£160	95·00

For sheet arrangement see footnote after Angra No. 27.
The 5, 20, 100, 150, 200 and 300r. were reprinted perf 11½ in 1900 and all values were reprinted perf 13½ in 1905.

(Des and eng E. Mouchon. Typo)

1897 (1 Jan)–**1901**. Name and value in black or red (500r.).

(a) P 11½

29	2	2½r. pale grey		80	50
30		5r. orange-red		80	50
31		10r. pale green		80	50
32		15r. chocolate		11·00	9·75
33		20r. deep lilac		2·75	1·80
34		25r. blue-green		4·00	1·80
35		50r. blue		4·00	1·80
36		75r. rose		8·75	1·80
37		80r. mauve		2·30	1·80
38		100r. blue/blue		5·25	1·80
39		150r. purple-brown/straw		2·75	2·20
40		200r. purple/flesh		9·50	8·50
41		300r. pink		9·50	8·50
42		500r. black/azure (1901)		20·00	16·00
29/42 Set of 14				75·00	50·00

(b) P 12½

43	2	300r. blue/pink		55·00	46·00
44		500r. black/azure		28·00	20·00

1898 (1 July)–**1905**. New values and colours changed. Name and value in black or red (75r.). P 11½.

45	2	15r. deep green (1.1.99)		2·75	1·70
46		25r. carmine (1.1.99)		2·30	60
47		50r. ultramarine (6.05)		22·00	17·00
48		65r. steel-blue		1·70	75
49		75r. brown/yellow (6.05)		18·00	9·75
50		115r. orange-brown/pink		4·50	2·00
51		130r. sepia/cream		2·75	2·00
52		180r. slate/pale pink		2·75	2·00
45/52 Set of 8				50·00	32·00

BRITISH POST OFFICE ON SÃO MIGUEL

A British Postal Agency existed at Ponta Delgada, the chief port of the island, to operate with the services of the Royal Mail Steam Packet Company.

> **CROWNED-CIRCLE HANDSTAMPS.** Under regulations circulated in December 1841, letters and packets forwarded through offices abroad to the United Kingdom or any of its territories were to be sent unpaid, the postage being collected on delivery. Where this was not possible, for example from a British colony to a foreign country or between two foreign ports, then a crowned-circle handstamp was to be applied with the postage, paid in advance, noted alongside in manuscript.
> The dates quoted are those on which the handstamp appears in the G.P.O. Record Books, but it seems to have been normal for the handstamps to be sent to the office concerned immediately following this registration.

Crowned-circle Handstamp. As Type CC **1b** of British Post Offices in Cuba but inscr "PAID AT ST. MICHAELS".

CC1	In black (27.5.1842)	

1 **2**

(Head eng M. D. Neto; frame eng J. S. de Carvalho e Silva. Typo)

1892–93. Chalk-surfaced paper or enamel-surfaced paper (E).

(a) P 11½

1	1	5r. yellow (1.7.92)		13·50	8·75
2		5r. yellow (E)		7·00	2·30
3		25r. green (1.6.92)		11·00	2·50
4		25r. green (E)		19·00	5·25
5		50r. pale blue (1.7.92)		17·00	4·00

Cape Verde Islands

1877. 1000 Reis = 1 Milreis
1913. 100 Centavos = 1 Escudo

The ten islands of the Cape Verde Archipelago, off the west coast of Africa, were discovered in 1456 or 1460 and became part of the Portuguese royal dominions in 1495. On 11 June 1951 they became a Portuguese Overseas Province and on 6 September 1961 their inhabitants were given full Portuguese citizenship.

PRINTERS. All the stamps of Cape Verde Islands were printed at the Mint, Lisbon, *unless otherwise stated.*

REPRINTS. Reprints of some of the following issues were made in 1885 and 1905 as indicated in the footnotes. These can generally be distinguished as follows:—
1885 reprints are on stout very white paper, usually ungummed but sometimes with white gum having yellowish spots. They are perf 13½ with large clean-cut holes producing sharp pointed teeth.
1905 reprints are on creamy white paper of ordinary quality with shiny white gum, all perf 13½.

1   **2** King Luis   N **3**

(Des and eng A. F. Gerard. Typo)

1877 (1 Jan).

(a) P 12½

1	1	5r. black		3·50	2·30
2		10r. pale orange		20·00	11·00
		a. *Yellow*		20·00	11·00
3		20r. deep bistre		2·40	1·60
		a. *Pale bistre*		2·40	1·60
4		25r. deep rose		2·40	1·60
		a. *Pale rose*		2·40	1·60
5		40r. blue		95·00	60·00
		a. "MOÇAMBIQUE" (in pair)		£2000	£2000
6		50r. green		£150	85·00
		a. *Yellow-green*		£150	85·00
7		100r. grey-lilac		8·75	3·50
		a. *Lilac*		8·75	3·50
		b. *Dull purple*		8·75	3·50
8		200r. deep orange		5·25	4·00
		a. *Orange*		5·25	4·00
9		300r. chocolate		6·25	5·25
		a. *Lake-brown*		6·25	5·25
		b. *Pale brown*		6·25	5·25

(b) P 13½

10	1	5r. black		3·50	2·30
11		10r. yellow		23·00	16·00
12		20r. pale bistre		1·90	1·60
13		25r. pale rose		8·25	6·50
14		40r. blue		95·00	60·00
		a. "MOÇAMBIQUE" (in pair)		£2500	£2500
15		50r. yellow-green		£300	£140
16		100r. slate-lilac		9·75	4·50
17		200r. orange		14·00	9·00

See note below No. 22.
All values were reprinted perf 13½ in 1885 and 1905 and the 40r. was also reprinted imperforate in 1885. No. 14a also exists in the 1885 reprint.

1881–85. Colours changed.

A. P 12½

18A	1	10r. yellow-green (*shades*)		3·00	2·30
19A		20r. rosine (1885)		5·75	4·00
20A		25r. deep lilac (1885)		4·25	3·25
21A		40r. orange-yellow		2·40	1·80
		a. "MOÇAMBIQUE" (in pair)		£150	£130
22A		50r. blue		7·25	4·75
		a. *Deep blue*		7·25	4·75

B. P 13½

18B	1	10r. yellow-green (*shades*)		3·00	2·30
19B		20r. rosine (1885)		55·00	49·00
21B		40r. orange-yellow		4·25	4·25
		a. "MOÇAMBIQUE" (in pair)		£200	£180
22B		50r. blue		8·25	6·25
		a. *Deep blue*		8·25	6·25

Nos. 5a, 14a and 21a with inscription "MOÇAMBIQUE" occur on the second stamp, fifth row. To identify them as the errors, they must be *se-tenant* with normal stamp.
All values were reprinted in 1885 and 1905.

(Des and eng F. A. de Campos. Typo and embossed)

1886. Chalk-surfaced paper.

(a) P 12½

23	2	5r. black		7·25	3·25
24		10r. green		7·25	3·25
25		20r. rosine		9·75	5·00
26		25r. bright mauve		8·75	5·75
		a. *Reddish violet*		8·75	5·75
		b. *Claret*		8·75	5·75
27		40r. chocolate		8·75	3·50
28		50r. blue		8·75	3·50
		a. *Pale blue*		8·75	3·50
29		100r. yellow-brown		8·75	5·00
30		200r. lavender		19·00	11·00
31		300r. red-orange		22·00	4·50
		a. *Orange*		22·00	4·50
23/31	*Set of 9*			90·00	40·00

(b) P 13½

33	2	5r. black		4·75	3·25
34		10r. green		4·75	3·25
35		20r. rosine		8·75	5·50
36		40r. chocolate		11·50	6·75

The 25, 50 and 100r. were reprinted in 1905.

(Des and eng E. C. Azedo Gneco. Typo)

1893 (3 June). NEWSPAPER.

N37	N **3**	2½r. brown (*perf 11½*)		1·70	80
N38		2½r. brown (*perf 12½*)		3·25	1·60
N39		2½r. brown (*perf 13½*)		7·75	3·25

3 King Carlos   **4** King Carlos   D **5**

(Des and eng M. D. Neto. Typo)

1894–95. Chalk-surfaced paper, or enamel-surfaced paper (E).

(a) P 11½

37	3	5r. pale orange (5.9.94)		1·70	1·40
38		10r. rosy mauve (5.9.94)		1·70	1·40
39		15r. red-brown (5.9.94)		4·00	2·75
40		20r. lilac (5.9.94)		4·00	2·75
41		25r. green		3·50	2·30
42		50r. pale blue		3·50	2·30
43		80r. pale green (E) (6.5.95)		34·00	27·00
44		100r. brown/*buff* (6.5.95)		9·75	5·50
45		150r. carmine/*rose* (6.5.95)		75·00	60·00
46		300r. blue/*bright buff* (6.5.95)		39·00	18·00
37/46	*Set of 10*			£160	£110

(b) P 12½

47	3	15r. red-brown		£160	£120
48		25r. green		3·75	2·75
49		50r. pale blue			
50		50r. pale blue (E)			
51		75r. carmine (6.5.95)		12·00	6·25
52		100r. brown/*buff*		£140	55·00
53		150r. carmine/*rose*		£550	£475
54		200r. blue/*blue*		£160	£120

(c) P 13½

55	3	50r. pale blue (E)		14·00	4·50
56		75r. carmine		60·00	45·00
57		80r. pale green (E)		48·00	36·00
58		150r. carmine/*rose*		34·00	29·00
59		200r. blue/*blue*		34·00	29·00

(Des and eng E. Mouchon. Typo)

1898 (1 July)–**1901.** Name and numerals in black; on 500r. in carmine. P 11½.

60	4	2½r. pale grey		40	35
61		5r. orange-yellow		55	35
		a. *Orange-red*		55	35
62		10r. green		55	35
63		15r. chocolate		5·75	2·10

CAPE VERDE ISLANDS

64		20r. deep lilac	1·70	95
65		25r. blue-green	3·50	1·30
		a. Perf 12½	£325	£190
66		50r. blue	3·50	1·60
67		75r. carmine	9·00	3·50
68		80r. mauve	9·00	3·50
69		100r. blue/*blue*	3·50	1·90
70		150r. purple-brown/*straw*	9·00	5·25
71		200r. purple/*flesh*	4·25	3·00
72		300r. blue/*pink*	10·50	5·25
73		500r. black/*azure* (1901)	10·50	5·25
74		700r. mauve/*yellow* (1901)	30·00	19·00
60/74 Set of 15			90·00	48·00

See also Nos. 111/18.

1902 (1 Dec). Surch as T **6** of Angola.

75	2	65r. on 5r. (12½)	5·75	4·00
76		65r. on 200r. (12½)	5·75	4·00
77		65r. on 300r. (12½)	5·75	4·00
78	3	65r. on 10r. (11½)	7·25	4·00
79		65r. on 20r. (11½)	7·25	4·00
80		65r. on 100r. (11½)	9·25	5·50
81		65r. on 100r. (12½)	29·00	25·00
82	2	115r. on 10r. (12½)	5·75	4·00
83		115r. on 20r. (12½)	5·75	4·00
84		115r. on 20r. (13½)	48·00	36·00
85	3	115r. on 5r. (11½)	4·25	3·25
86		115r. on 25r. (11½)	60·00	45·00
87		115r. on 25r. (12½)	3·00	2·30
88		115r. on 150r. (11½)	8·75	6·75
89		115r. on 150r. (13½)	39·00	22·00
90	2	130r. on 50r. blue (12½)	5·75	4·00
91		130r. on 50r. pale blue (12½)	5·75	4·00
92		130r. on 100r. (12½)	5·75	4·00
93	3	130r. on 75r. (12½)	4·25	3·25
94		130r. on 75r. (13½)	£250	£225
95		130r. on 80r. (E) (11½)	4·00	3·25
96		130r. on 80r. (E) (13½)	3·50	2·20
97		130r. on 200r. (13½)	3·75	2·75
98	2	400r. on 25r. (12½)	3·00	2·75
99		400r. on 40r. (12½)	5·75	4·00
100		400r. on 40r. (13½)	48·00	36·00
101	3	400r. on 50r. (11½)	5·75	3·25
102		400r. on 50r. (E) (13½)	£325	£325
103		400r. on 300r. (11½)	2·75	1·80
104	N 3	400r. on 2½r. (11½)	2·20	1·60
105		400r. on 2½r. (12½)	£250	£225
106		400r. on 2½r. (13½)	1·70	1·60

The 65/5, 400/25, 400/40 and 400/50r. were reprinted in 1905. Type **2**, 115r. on 10r., perf 13½, exists as a reprint only.

1902 (1 Dec)–**03**. Optd with T **7** of Angola.

107	4	15r. chocolate	1·90	1·30
108		25r. blue-green (11½)	1·90	1·30
109		50r. blue (1.1.03)	1·90	1·30
110		75r. carmine (1.1.03)	3·75	2·75
107/110 Set of 4			8·50	6·00

1903 (1 Jan–Oct). Colours changed. Name and value in black. P 11½.

111	4	15r. dull green (15.1)	2·20	1·50
112		25r. carmine (15.10)	1·20	45
113		50r. brown (15.6)	4·50	3·00
114		65r. dull blue	29·00	18·00
115		75r. dull purple (15.6)	4·00	2·75
116		115r. orange-brown/*pink*	18·00	12·00
117		130r. sepia/*cream*	19·00	12·00
118		400r. dull blue/*straw*	20·00	12·50
111/118 Set of 8			90·00	55·00

(Des and eng J. S. de Carvalho e Silva. Typo)

1904 (1 Aug). POSTAGE DUE. Name and value in black. P 11½.

D119	D 5	5r. yellow-green	65	40
D120		10r. slate	65	40
D121		20r. brown	80	50
D122		30r. orange	2·00	50
D123		50r. deep brown	80	45
D124		60r. pale red-brown	15·00	5·25
D125		100r. mauve	3·00	1·60
D126		130r. blue	3·00	1·60
D127		200r. carmine	2·75	2·40
D128		500r. deep lilac	8·00	4·00
D119/128 Set of 10			33·00	15·00

See also Nos. D252/61.

1905 (1 July). Surch with T **8** of Angola.

119	4	50r. on 65r. dull blue	4·75	3·75

1911 (20 Aug). Optd with T **8a** of Angola, in red or green (G).

120	4	2½r. pale grey	35	30
121		5r. orange-red	35	30
122		10r. green	1·20	95
123		15r. dull green	1·00	50
124		20r. deep lilac	1·70	95
125		25r. carmine (G.)	1·00	50
126		50r. brown	10·50	7·25
127		75r. dull purple	1·60	95
128		100r. blue/*blue*	1·60	95
129		115r. orange-brown/*pink*	1·60	95
		a. Orange-brown/*buff*	18·00	18·00
130		130r. sepia/*cream*	1·60	95
131		200r. purple/*flesh*	8·00	4·75
132		400r. dull blue/*straw*	4·00	1·40
133		500r. black/*azure*	4·00	1·40
134		700r. mauve/*yellow*	4·00	1·40
120/134 Set of 15			38·00	21·00

1911. POSTAGE DUE. Optd with T **8a** of Angola, in red or green (G.).

D135	D 5	5r. yellow-green	45	35
		a. Chalk-surfaced paper	45	35
D136		10r. slate	45	35
D137		20r. brown	55	35
D138		30r. orange	55	35
D139		50r. deep brown	1·00	60
D140		60r. pale red-brown	1·00	60
D141		100r. mauve	1·00	60
D142		130r. blue	1·20	95
D143		200r. carmine (G.)	3·25	2·20
D144		500r. deep lilac	4·00	3·50
D135/144 Set of 10			12·00	8·75

5 King Manoel II   (**6**)

(Des and eng D. A. do Rego. Typo)

1912. Optd with T **8a** of Angola as shown in T **5**, in red or green (G.).

(a) P 11½

135	5	2½r. lilac	25	25
136		5r. black	25	25
137		10r. grey-green	50	45
138		20r. rose-red (G.)	3·00	1·60
139		25c. chocolate (13 Feb)	50	25
140		50r. indigo-blue (13 Feb)	5·75	4·00
141		75r. yellow-brown	1·30	1·20
142		100r. brown/*green*	1·30	1·20
143		200r. deep green/*salmon*	2·10	1·20
144		300r. black/*azure*	2·10	1·20

(b) P 14×15

145	5	400r. blue and black	4·50	3·50
146		500r. chocolate and olive	4·50	3·50
135/146 Set of 12			23·00	17·00

1913 (13 Feb). New Currency. Vasco da Gama issues surch as T **6**.

(i) Portuguese Colonies and Overseas Territories (General Issues)

147	1	¼c. on 2½r. blue-green	1·60	80
148	2	½c. on 5r. vermilion	1·60	80
149	3	1c. on 10r. dull purple	1·60	80
150	4	2½c. on 25r. yellow-green	1·60	80
151	5	5c. on 50r. deep blue	2·20	1·80
152	6	7½c. on 75r. chocolate	4·50	3·50
153	7	10c. on 100r. bistre-brown	2·20	2·20
154	8	15c. on 150r. ochre	3·00	3·00
147/154 Set of 8			16·00	12·50

(ii) Macao

155		¼c. on ½a. blue-green	1·60	1·00
156		½c. on 1a. vermilion	1·60	1·00
157		1c. on 2a. dull purple	1·60	1·00
158		2½c. on 4a. yellow-green	1·60	1·00
159		5c. on 8a. deep blue	8·50	7·50
160		7½c. on 12a. chocolate	6·75	3·00
161		10c. on 16a. bistre-brown	2·75	2·00
162		15c. on 24a. ochre	7·25	4·00
155/162 Set of 8			28·00	18·00

(iii) Timor

163		¼c. on ½a. blue-green	1·60	1·00
164		½c. on 1a. vermilion	1·60	1·00
165		1c. on 2a. dull purple	1·60	1·00
166		2½c. on 4a. yellow-green	1·60	1·00
167		5c. on 8a. deep blue	8·75	7·00
168		7½c. on 12a. chocolate	6·75	3·75
169		10c. on 16a. bistre-brown	2·75	2·20
170		15c. on 24a. ochre	5·50	3·00
163/170 Set of 8			27·00	18·00

129

CAPE VERDE ISLANDS

(7)

8 Ceres

1913 (3 Nov)–**14**. Nos. 110 and 95/6 optd locally with T **7**.
171	4	75r. carmine (G.) (14.1.14)	6·75	4·75
		a. Opt double (G. + R.)	90·00	70·00
172	3	130r. on 80r. (E) (11½) (R.) (3.11.13)	6·25	4·75
173		130r. on 80r. (E) (13½) (R.)	6·25	4·75
171/173		*Set of* 3	18·00	12·00

The 115r. on 150r. and 130r. on 200r. were never issued.

(Des C. Fernandes. eng J. S. de Carvalho e Silva. Typo)

1914 (1 Sept)–**16**. Name and value in black. Chalk-surfaced paper or enamel-surfaced paper (E). P 15×14.
174	8	¼c. brown-olive	95	70
175		¼c. brown-olive (E) (1916)	55	40
176		½c. black	95	70
177		1c. deep green	95	70
178		1½c. chocolate	95	70
179		2c. carmine	1·60	85
180		2½c. violet	75	65
181		5c. deep blue	1·30	1·00
182		5c. deep blue (E) (1916)	1·10	95
183		7½c. yellow-brown	1·60	85
184		8c. slate	1·60	95
185		10c. brown-red	2·50	1·40
186		15c. claret	10·50	6·25
187		20c. yellow-green	2·50	1·10
188		30c. chocolate/*green*	5·75	3·75
189		40c. brown/*rose*	3·25	2·75
190		50c. orange/*salmon*	4·00	2·75
191		1E. deep green/*azure*	4·00	3·00
174/191		*Set of* 16 (*one of each value*)	38·00	25·00

See also Nos. 209/51.

1915. Provisionals of 1902 optd at Lisbon with T **8**a of Angola, in red.
192	3	115r. on 5r. (11½)	1·70	95
		a. Surch and opt inverted	55·00	50·00
193	2	115r. on 10r. (12½)	3·00	1·90
194		115r. on 10r. (13½)	£180	£180
195		115r. on 20r. (12½)	3·25	2·10
196		115r. on 20r. (13½)	45·00	41·00
197	3	115r. on 25r. (11½)	85·00	60·00
198		115r. on 25r. (12½)	3·00	1·90
199		115r. on 150r. (11½)	1·30	60
200		115r. on 150r. (13½)	1·00	95
201	2	130r. on 50r. (12½)	3·00	1·60
202	3	130r. on 75r. (12½)	3·00	1·20
203		130r. on 75r. (13½)	3·00	1·20
204		130r. on 80r. (E) (11½)	3·00	1·20
205		130r. on 80r. (E) (13½)	2·40	1·20
206	2	130r. on 100r. (12½)	2·00	1·20
207	3	130r. on 200r. (12½)	£180	£150
208		130r. on 200r. (13½)	2·00	1·20

1920–26. Name and value in black.

(a) Unsurfaced paper (thick, medium or thin). P 15×14 (1920-22)
209	8	¼c. brown-olive	35	30
210		½c. black	35	30
211		1c. deep blue-green	6·00	4·50
		a. Pale yellow-green (1921)	35	30
212		1½c. chocolate	45	30
213		2c. carmine	45	40
214		2½c. mauve	35	30
215		3c. orange (1922)	30	25
216		4c. carmine (1922)	30	25
217		12c. blue-green (1922)	1·10	90
218		15c. dull rose (1921)	3·00	2·40

(b) Unsurfaced paper. P 12×11½ (1921–26)
219	8	¼c. brown-olive	35	30
220		½c. black	35	30
221		1c. yellow-green	35	30
222		1½c. chocolate	35	30
223		2c. carmine	35	30
224		2c. drab (1926)	40	30
225		2½c. mauve	35	30
226		3c. orange (1922)	3·00	2·75
227		4c. carmine (1922)	40	40
228		4½c. drab (1922)	40	40
229		5c. pale dull blue	45	40
230		6c. mauve (1922)	40	40
231		7c. pale blue (1922)	40	40
232		7½c. yellow-brown	40	40
233		8c. slate	75	55
234		10c. brown-red	40	40
235		12c. blue-green (1922)	70	65
236		15c. dull rose	40	40
237		20c. yellow-green	40	40
238		24c. ultramarine (1926)	1·20	95
239		25c. chocolate (1926)	1·20	95
240		30c. deep grey-green (1922)	55	50
241		40c. turquoise (1922)	55	50
242		50c. mauve (1926)	1·00	80
243		60c. deep blue (1922)	1·40	1·00
244		60c. carmine (1926)	1·60	95
245		80c. bright rosine (1922)	5·00	1·40

(c) Glazed paper. P 12×11½ (1922–26)
246	8	1E. carmine-pink	5·75	3·00
247		1E. blue (1926)	6·25	3·75
248		2E. deep purple	5·75	3·00
249		5E. buff (1926)	10·50	7·25
250		10E. pink (1926)	24·00	14·50
251		20E. emerald-green (1926)	65·00	49·00
219/251		*Set of* 33	£130	85·00

1921. POSTAGE DUE. Value in centavos. P 11½.
D252	D **5**	½c. pale yellow-green	40	30
D253		1c. slate	40	30
D254		2c. deep red-brown	40	30
D255		3c. pale orange	40	30
D256		5c. grey-brown	40	30
D257		6c. pale brown	40	30
D258		10c. mauve	40	30
D259		13c. blue	80	70
D260		20c. carmine	90	80
D261		50c. lilac-grey	2·50	1·80
D252/261		*Set of* 10	6·25	4·75

Sets may be made on soft smooth paper and thin coarse paper, the shades differing in the latter, particularly in the 3c., which is yellow.

6 c.

2 C.

REPUBLICA

(9)

(10)

1921 (3 Feb).

(a) Nos. 153/4 surch locally as T **9**
252		2c. on 15c. on 150r. ochre	2·75	1·90
253		4c. on 10c. on 100r. bistre-brown	3·25	3·00
		a. Error. Surch on No. 161	£250	£250

(b) No. 69 surch locally with T **10**
| 254 | 4 | 6c. on 100r. blue/*blue* | 3·25 | 2·50 |

CABO VERDE

CORREIOS

½ c.

(12)

1921 (3 Feb). Type C **1** of Portuguese Colonies and Overseas Territories (General issues) surch locally as T **12**, or optd only.

A. P 15×14
255A	C **1**	¼c. on 1c. green	60	40
256A		½c. on 1c. green	75	55
257A		1c. green	70	50

B. P 12×11½
255B	C **1**	¼c. on 1c. green	1·20	1·00
256B		½c. on 1c. green	1·20	1·00
257B		1c. green	1·10	95

Nos. 255/7B also exist on enamel-surfaced paper (same prices).

$04

$04

(13)

Smaller dollar sign

CAPE VERDE ISLANDS

1922 (Apr). Surch locally with T **13**, the bars cancelling previous surch.

(a) Nos. 172/3

258	**3**	4c. on 130r. on 80r. (E) (11½)		1·50	1·30
		a. Smaller dollar sign		13·00	12·50
259		4c. on 130r. on 80r. (13½)		2·30	1·70
		a. Smaller dollar sign		25·00	23·00

(b) Nos. 202/5 and 207/8

260	**3**	4c. on 130r. on 75r. (12½)		1·10	85
		a. Smaller dollar sign		10·50	9·50
261		4c. on 130r. on 75r. (13½)		4·00	3·25
		a. Smaller dollar sign		24·00	23·00
262		4c. on 130r. on 80r. (E) (11½)		1·10	85
		a. Smaller dollar sign		9·50	8·50
263		4c. on 130r. on 80r. (E) (13½)		2·30	1·70
		a. Smaller dollar sign		25·00	23·00
264		4c. on 130r. on 200r. (12½)		22·00	17·00
		a. Smaller dollar sign		65·00	60·00
265		4c. on 130r. on 200r. (13½)		1·10	90
		a. Smaller dollar sign		6·50	6·25

The smaller dollar sign occurs on position 20 of the sheet of 28.

CHARITY TAX STAMPS. The notes after Nos. D352 and C345 of Angola also apply to Charity Tax stamps of Cape Verde Islands.

1925 (8 May). CHARITY TAX. Marquis de Pombal issue of Portugal inscr "CABO VERDE".

C266	C **73**	15c. violet	1·40	1·40
C267	C **74**	15c. violet	1·40	1·40
C268	C **75**	15c. violet	1·40	1·40
C266/268 Set of 3			3·75	3·75

1925 (8 May). POSTAGE DUE. As Nos. C266/8 optd "MULTA".

D266	C **73**	30c. dull violet	90	85
D267	C **74**	30c. dull violet	90	85
D268	C **75**	30c. dull violet	90	85
D266/268 Set of 3			2·50	2·40

1925 (17 June). Provisionals of 1902 surch as T **14** of Angola.

266	N **3**	40c. on 400r. on 2½r. (11½)	1·10	90
267		40c. on 400r. on 2½r. (13½)	1·10	90
268	**3**	40c. on 400r. on 300r. (11½)	1·10	90
266/268 Set of 3			3·00	2·50

1931 (Nov). No. 245 surch as T **16** of Angola.

269	**8**	70c. on 80c. bright rosine	29·00	11·50

1934 (1 May). Ceres type of Angola inscr "CABO VERDE". W **18** of Angola (Maltese Crosses). P 12×11½.

270	**17**	1c. brown	20	15
271		5c. sepia	20	15
272		10c. mauve	20	15
273		15c. black	30	25
274		20c. grey	30	25
275		30c. blue-green	30	25
276		40c. vermilion	30	25
277		45c. turquoise	2·20	95
278		50c. cinnamon	1·00	65
279		60c. olive-green	1·00	65
280		70c. red-brown	1·00	65
281		80c. emerald	1·00	65
282		85c. carmine	4·50	3·00
283		1E. claret	3·00	50
284		1E.40 blue	4·00	3·75
285		2E. mauve	5·25	3·00
286		5E. yellow-green	23·00	5·75
287		10E. bistre-brown	36·00	21·00
288		20E. orange	70·00	28·00
270/288 Set of 19			£140	65·00

1938. As Nos. 383/409 of Angola (Vasco da Gama types), inscr "CABO VERDE". Name and value in black. P 13½×13.

(a) POSTAGE

289	**22**	1c. grey-olive	25	20
290		5c. orange-brown	25	20
291		10c. carmine	25	20
292		15c. brown-purple	1·10	95
293		20c. slate	50	30
294	A	30c. bright purple	50	30
295		35c. emerald-green	50	30
296		40c. brown	50	30
297		50c. magenta	50	30
298	**24**	60c. grey-black	50	30
299		70c. slate-violet	50	30
300		80c. orange	50	30
301		1E. scarlet	80	30
302	B	1E.75 blue	2·10	80
303		2E. blue-green	4·00	2·30
304		5E. olive-green	9·25	2·30
305	C	10E. ultramarine	14·50	3·00
306		20E. red-brown	49·00	6·00
289/306 Set of 18			75·00	17·00

(b) AIR

307	**27**	10c. scarlet	85	70
308		20c. bright violet	85	70
309		50c. orange	85	70
310		1E. bright blue	85	70
311		2E. brown-lake	2·00	1·10
312		3E. blue-green	2·75	1·90
313		5E. red-brown	8·00	2·75
314		9E. carmine	13·00	4·75
315		10E. magenta	14·50	6·25
307/315 Set of 9			39·00	18·00

14 Route of President's Tour   (**15**)   C **16** St. Isabel

(Des Zimbarra. Litho.)

1939 (23 June). Pres. Carmona's Second Colonial Tour. P 11½×12.

316	**14**	80c. violet/*mauve*	6·25	4·25
317		1E.75 blue/*pale blue*	50·00	38·00
318		20E. chocolate/*cream*	£110	34·00
316/318 Set of 3			£150	70·00

1948. Nos. 276 and 294 surch locally as T **15**.

319	A	10c. on 30c. bright purple	2·50	1·40
		a. Surch inverted	8·25	7·75
320	**17**	25c. on 40c. vermilion	2·50	1·40

(Des A. de Sousa. Litho Litografia Nacional, Oporto)

1948. CHARITY TAX. P 11–11½.

C321	C **16**	50c. deep bluish green	4·75	3·00
C322		1E. brown-red	9·25	3·75

See also Nos. C369/70.

16 Machado Point, São Vicente   **17** Ribeira Brava, São Nicolau

(Des M. Jorge (5c., 20E.), A. de Sousa (others). Litho Litografia Nacional, Oporto)

1948 (1 Oct). As T **16/17** (views). P 14.

321		5c. brown-purple and bistre	50	40
322		10c. blackish green and pale green	50	40
323		50c. magenta and lilac	1·00	40
324		1E. reddish purple	3·75	1·70
325		1E.75 ultramarine and turquoise	4·50	2·40
326		2E. purple-brown and ochre	10·50	3·00
327		5E. olive-green and lemon	21·00	5·75
328		10E. scarlet and orange	34·00	19·00
329		20E. dull violet and buff	85·00	36·00
321/329 Set of 9			£140	60·00

Designs: Vert—10c. Town of Ribeira Grande. Horiz—1E. Porto Grande, São Vicente; 1E.75, Mindelo; 2E. João de Evora beach, São Vicente; 5E. Mindelo, São Vicente; 10E. Volcano, Fogo; 20E. Paul.

1948 (Oct). Honouring the Statue of Our Lady of Fatima. As T **33** of Angola.

330		50c. deep blue	13·00	8·50

1949 (Oct). 75th Anniv of Universal Postal Union. As T **39** of Angola.

331		1E. bright magenta	10·50	5·00

1950 (May). Holy Year. As T **41/2** of Angola.

332		1E. red-brown	1·20	65
333		2E. greenish blue	4·75	2·75

131

CAPE VERDE ISLANDS

(18)   (19)

1951 (21 May). Surch as T **18**.

334	A	10c. on 35c. emerald-green	65	55
335	**24**	20c. on 70c. slate-violet	85	65
336		40c. on 70c. slate-violet	1·00	65
337		50c. on 80c. orange	1·00	65
338	B	1E. on 1E.75 blue	1·10	65
339	C	2E. on 10E. ultramarine	5·25	2·10
		a. error. 1E. on 10E.	£130	80·00

1951 (Oct). Termination of Holy Year. As T **44** of Angola.
340   2E. deep violet and mauve.................. 1·50   1·00

To each of these stamps is attached a label of the same size inscribed with a Papal declaration which differs for each overseas province.

1952 (25 Jan). No. 302 surch locally as T **19**.

341	10c. on 1E.75 blue	1·30	1·20
342	20c. on 1E.75 blue	1·30	1·20
343	50c. on 1E.75 blue	6·25	6·00
344	1E. on 1E.75 blue	75	20
345	1E.50 on 1E.75 blue	75	20

DATES OF ISSUE. The dates given refer to the dates when the stamps were placed on sale in Cape Verde Is. In a number of instances they were released at different times in Lisbon, usually earlier.

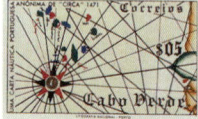

20 Map, c. 1471   **21** V. Dias and G. de Cintra

(Des R. Preto Pacheco. Litho Litografia Nacional, Oporto)

1952 (24 Feb). Portuguese Navigators. T **20/21** and similar horiz designs. Multicoloured. P 14.

346	5c. Type **20**	20	20
	a. Green (islands etc) omitted		
347	10c. Type **21**	20	20
348	30c. D. Afonso and A. Fernandes	20	20
349	50c. Lançarote and S. da Costa	20	20
350	1E. D. Gomes and A. da Nola	20	20
351	2E. Prince Fernando and Prince Henry the Navigator	1·40	20
352	3E. A. Gonçalves and D. Dias	12·00	1·90
353	5E. A. Gonçalves Baldaia & J. Fernandes	4·00	95
354	10E. D. Eanes da Grã and A. de Freitas	8·00	2·30
355	20E. Map, 1502	14·50	2·75
346/355	Set of 10	37·00	8·25

1952. POSTAGE DUE. As Type D **45** of Angola, inscr "CABO VERDE".

D356	10c. brown and olive-grey	30	30
D357	30c. black, blue and mauve	30	30
D358	50c. slate-blue, green and yellow	30	30
D359	1E. deep blue and pale blue	30	30
D360	2E. red-brown and yellow-orange	40	40
D361	5E. olive-green and olive-grey	1·20	1·20
D356/361	Set of 6	2·50	2·50

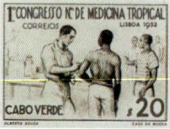

22 Doctor giving Injection   **23** Façade of Monastery

(Des A. de Sousa. Litho.)

1952 (June). First Tropical Medicine Congress, Lisbon. P 13½.
356   **22**   20c. black and grey-green.................. 75   55

1953 (Jan). Missionary Art Exhibition. Litho. P 13½.

357	**23**	10c. brown and yellow-olive	20	20
358		50c. violet and salmon	95	45
359		1E. deep green and orange	2·30	1·40
357/359	Set of 3		3·00	1·80

1953 (Oct). Portuguese Stamp Centenary. As T **48** of Angola.
360   50c. multicoloured.................. 1·90   1·30

1954. Fourth Centenary of São Paulo. As T **49** of Angola.
361   1E. stone, dull yellowish green and black... 85   65

24 Arms of Cape Verde Islands and Portuguese Guinea   **25** Arms of Praia

(Des J. de Moura. Litho.)

1955 (15 May). Presidential Visit. P 13½.

362	**24**	1E. multicoloured	55	40
363		1E.60 multicoloured	75	70

1958 (14 June). Centenary of City of Praia. Litho. P 11½×12.

364	**25**	1E. multicoloured/*pale yellow*	65	55
365		2E.50 multicoloured/*pale salmon*	1·30	1·10

1958 (July). Brussels International Exhibition. As T **55** of Angola.
366   2E. multicoloured.................. 95   45

1958 (5 Sept). Sixth International Congress of Tropical Medicine. As T **56** of Angola. Multicoloured.
367   3E. *Aloe vera* (plant).................. 5·75   2·75

1959. CHARITY TAX. No. C322, surch.
C368   C **16**   50c. on 1E. brown-red.................. 1·60   1·40

1959. CHARITY TAX. Colours changed. P 14.

C369	C **16**	50c. cerise	2·40	1·40
C370		1E. blue	2·40	1·40

26 Prince Henry the Navigator   **27** Antonio da Nola

(Des J. de Moura. Litho.)

1960 (25 June). Fifth Centenary of Death of Prince Henry the Navigator. P 13×13½.
368   **26**   2E. multicoloured.................. 55   30

(Des J. de Moura. Litho Litografia Nacional, Oporto)

1960 (30 Sept). Fifth Centenary of Colonisation of Cape Verde Islands. T **27** and similar vert design. Multicoloured. P 14½.

369	1E. Type **27**	95	55
370	2E.50 Diogo Gomes	2·30	1·20

28 "Education"   **29** Arms of Praia

(Des Neves and Sousa. Litho Litografia Maia, Oporto)

1960 (Oct). Tenth Anniv of African Technical Co-operation Commission. P 14½.
371   **28**   2E.50 multicoloured.................. 1·40   85

132

CAPE VERDE ISLANDS

(Des J. de Moura. Photo)

1961 (July). Urban Arms. Various vert designs as T **29**. Arms multicoloured; inscriptions red and green, background colours given. P 13½.

372	5c. orange-buff	30	20
373	15c. light blue (Nova Sintra)	30	20
374	20c. light yellow (Ribeira Brava)	30	20
375	30c. lilac (Assomada)	30	20
376	1E. light green (Maio)	75	20
377	2E. pale greenish yellow (Mindelo)	75	20
378	2E.50 pink (Santa Maria)	1·10	20
379	3E. light brown (Pombas)	1·80	65
380	5E. cobalt (Sal-Rei)	1·80	65
381	7E.50 pale yellow-olive (Tarrafal)	1·90	1·10
382	15E. pale reddish lilac (Maria Pia)	2·75	1·10
383	30E. pale yellow (San Felipe)	7·25	3·00
372/383	Set of 12	17·00	7·00

1962 (18 Jan). Sports. Diamond-shaped designs as T **62** of Angola. Multicoloured. P 13.

384	50c. Throwing the javelin	40	30
385	1E. Discus thrower	1·10	40
386	1E.50 Batsman (cricket)	75	45
387	2E.50 Boxing	1·10	55
388	4E.50 Hurdler	1·90	1·30
389	12E.50 Golfers	3·50	2·75
384/389	Set of 6	7·75	5·25

1962. Malaria Eradication. Multicoloured design as T **63** of Angola.

390	2E.50 *Anopheles pretoriensis*	1·50	1·20

1963 (8 Oct). Tenth Anniv of T.A.P. Airline. As T **69** of Angola.

391	2E.50 multicoloured	1·10	85

1964 (16 May). Centenary of National Overseas Bank. As T **71** of Angola but with portrait of J. da S. M. Leal.

392	1E.50 multicoloured	1·10	95

1965 (17 May). I.T.U. Centenary. As T **73** of Angola.

393	2E.50 multicoloured	2·30	1·70

30 Militia Regiment Drummer, 1806   **31** St. Isabel   C **32**

(Des A. Cutileiro. Litho Litografia Nacional, Oporto)

1965 (1 Dec). Portuguese Military Uniforms. T **30** and similar vert designs. Multicoloured. P 13½.

394	50c. Type **30**	40	30
395	1E. Militiaman, 1806	55	30
396	1E.50 Infantry grenadiers officer, 1833	70	45
397	2E.50 Infantry grenadier, 1833	1·40	45
398	3E. Cavalry officer, 1834	2·75	65
399	4E. Infantry grenadier, 1835	1·30	65
400	5E. Artillery officer, 1848	1·40	65
401	10E. Infantry drum-major, 1856	3·25	2·10
394/401	Set of 8	10·50	5·00

1966 (28 May). 40th Anniv of National Revolution. As T **77** of Angola but design shows local buildings. Multicoloured.

402	1E. Dr. A. Moreira's Academy and Public Assistance Building	65	55

1967 (31 Jan). Centenary of Military Naval Association. Horiz designs as T **79** of Angola. Multicoloured.

403	1E. F. da Costa and gunboat *Mandovy*	85	65
404	1E.50 C. Araujo and minesweeper *Augusto Castilho*	1·30	1·00

1967 (13 May). 50th Anniv of the Fatima Apparitions. Vert design as T **80** of Angola. Multicoloured.

405	1E. Image of Virgin Mary	40	30

(Des A. de Sousa. Litho Litografia Nacional, Oporto)

1967–72. CHARITY TAX. P 14½.

C406	C **31**	30c. multicoloured	40	40
C407		50c. mult (bright purple panel)	85	85
C408		50c. mult (red panel) (1972)	65	65
C409		1E. multicoloured (brown panel)	95	95
C410		1E. mult (purple panel) (1972)	95	95
C406/410	*Set of 5*		3·50	3·50

Nos. C408 and C410 are in different colour combinations from the 1967 issue, the most noticeable difference being the "ASSISTENCIA" panel at the foot of the design.

(Background litho. Opt typo by José Santos, Cape Verde)

1968–71. CHARITY TAX. Pharmaceutical Tax stamps surch as in Type C **32**. P 12.

C411	C **32**	50c. on 1c. black, yellow-orange and pale blue-green (1969)	15·00	15·00
		a. Blue surch (1970)	1·50	1·10
		b. Green surch (1971)		
C412		50c. on 2c. black, yellow-orange and pale blue-green (1969)	15·00	15·00
		a. Surch inverted	39·00	37·00
		b. Blue surch (1970)	2·10	1·30
		c. Green surch (1971)	70	40
C413		50c. on 3c. black, yellow-orange & pale blue-green (G.) (1971)	1·20	65
C414		50c. on 5c. black, yellow-orange & pale blue-grn (G.) (1971)	1·20	65
C415		50c. on 10c. black, yellow-orange & pale blue-grn (G.) (1971)	1·40	1·10
C416		1E. on 1c. black, yellow-orange and pale blue-green	3·00	2·20
C417		1E. on 2c. black, yellow-orange and pale blue-green	2·20	2·20
		a. Blue surch (1970)	2·10	1·90
		b. Green surch (1971)	2·10	1·70
C411/417	*Set of 7 (cheapest)*		11·00	7·75

33 President Tomás   **34** Port of São Vicente

1968 (9 Feb). Visit of President Tomás of Portugal Litho. P 13½.

406	**33**	1E. multicoloured	40	30

(Des J. de Moura (No. 408))

1968 (22 Apr). 500th Birth Anniv of Pedro Cabral (explorer). Multicoloured designs as T **84** of Angola.

407	1E. Cantino's map, 1502	95	85
408	1E.50 Pedro Alvares Cabral (vert)	1·50	95
	a. Red ("CORREIOS" and value) omitted		

(Des J. de Moura. Litho)

1968 (15 Oct). "Produce of Cape Verde Islands". T **34** and similar multicoloured designs. P 14.

409	50c. Type **34**	30	20
410	1E. "Purgueira" (*Jatrophus curcus*)	45	25
411	1E.50 Groundnuts	45	25
412	2E.50 Castor-oil plant	45	25
413	3E.50 "Inhame" (*Dioscorea alata*)	45	25
414	4E. Date palm	45	25
415	4E.50 "Goiabeira" (*Psidium guajava*)	75	30
416	5E. Tamarind	1·10	40
417	10E. Manioc	1·50	75
418	30E. "Girl of Cape Verde"	3·50	2·75
409/418	*Set of 10*	8·50	5·00

The 1E. to 30E. values are vertical. Nos. 410/17 show agricultural produce.

1969 (17 Feb). Birth Centenary of Admiral Gago Coutinho. Multicoloured design as T **86** of Angola.

419	30c. Fairey IIID seaplane *Lusitania* and map of Lisbon-Rio flight (vert)	30	20

1969 (29 Aug). 500th Birth Anniv of Vasco do Gama (explorer). Vert design as T **87** of Angola. Multicoloured.

420	1E.50 Vasco da Gama	40	30

1969 (25 Sept). Centenary of Overseas Administrative Reforms. As T **88** of Angola.

421	2E. multicoloured	40	30

1969 (1 Dec). 500th Birth Anniv of King Manoel I. Vert design as T **89** of Angola. Multicoloured.

422	3E. Manoel I	55	40

1970 (15 Nov). Birth Centenary of Marshal Carmona. Vert design as T **91** of Angola. Multicoloured.
423 2E.50 Half-length portrait 55 40

35 Desalination Installation

(Des J. de Moura. Litho)

1971 (1 Dec). Inauguration of Desalination Plant, Mindelo. P 13.
424 **35** 4E. multicoloured .... 1·30 1·00

1972 (25 May). 400th Anniv of Camoens' "Lusiad" (epic poem). Vert design as T **96** of Angola. Multicoloured.
425 5E. Galleons at Cape Verde 65 30

1972 (20 June). Olympic Games, Munich. Horiz design as T **97** of Angola. Multicoloured.
426 4E. Basketball and boxing 65 30

1972 (20 Sept). 50th Anniv of First Flight Lisbon–Rio de Janeiro. Horiz design as T **98** of Angola. Multicoloured.
427 3E.50 Fairey IIID seaplane *Lusitania* near São Vicente 65 30

1973 (15 Dec). Centenary of World Meteorological Organization. As T **99** of Angola. Multicoloured.
428 2E.50 multicoloured 65 30

The Cape Verde Islands became independent on 5 July 1975. Subsequent issues are listed in Part 12 (*Africa since Independence A–E*) of this catalogue.

BRITISH POST OFFICE AT ST. VINCENT

The British Packet Agency at St. Vincent opened in 1851 as part of the revised service to South America. The agency was closed by 1860.

CROWNED-CIRCLE HANDSTAMPS. Under regulations circulated in December 1841, letters and packets forwarded through offices abroad to the United Kingdom or any of its territories were to be sent unpaid, the postage being collected on delivery. Where this was not possible, for example from a British colony to a foreign country or between two foreign ports, then a crowned-circle handstamp was to be applied with the postage, paid in advance, noted alongside in manuscript.
The dates quoted are those on which the handstamp appears in the G.P.O. Record Books, but it seems to have been normal for the handstamps to be sent to the office concerned immediately following this registration.

CC **4**

Crowned-circle Handstamp.
CC1   CC **4**   In black (6.1.1851) *Price on cover*
Although recorded in the GPO Proof, no example of No. CC1 is known on cover.

Macao

1884. 1000 Reis = 1 Milreis
1894. 78 Avos = 1 Rupee
1913. 100 Avos = 1 Pataca

Macao consists of a peninsula to the west of Hong Kong and the small islands of Taipa and Colôane, and has a total area of about six square miles. It became a Portuguese trading post in 1557 and then a centre of Jesuit missionary activity. A governor was appointed in 1680. A rental was paid to China until 1849, but Portuguese sovereignty was not recognised by China until 1887. On 11 June 1951 Macao became a Portuguese overseas province. On 17 February 1976 a statute was published giving the territory administrative and economic autonomy while remaining subject to Portuguese constitutional laws.
From *circa* 1854 to 29 February 1884 the Macao postal service worked in conjunction with that of Hong Kong and stamps of Hong Kong were used in Macao, being cancelled on arrival in Hong Kong.

PRINTERS. All the stamps of Macao were printed at the Mint, Lisbon, unless otherwise stated.

REPRINTS. Reprints of some of the following issues were made in 1885 and 1905 as indicated in the footnotes. These can generally be distinguished as follows:
1885 reprints are on stout, very white paper, usually un-gummed but sometimes with white gum having yellowish spots. They are perf 13½ with large clean-cut holes producing sharp, pointed teeth.
1905 reprints are on creamy white paper of ordinary quality with shiny white gum, all perf 13½.

King Luis
11 November 1861–19 October 1889

1

(2) T **2**
normally has acute accent on "e"

(Des and eng A. F. Gerard, Typo)

1884 (1 Mar).

(a) P 12½

1	1	5r. black	21·00	14·00
2		10r. pale orange	40·00	21·00
3		20r. bistre	48·00	34·00
4		25r. rose-red	23·00	9·75
		a. Rose	23·00	9·75
5		40r. deep blue	£225	£100
		a. Blue	£225	£100
6		50r. green	£375	£225
7		100r. grey lilac	70·00	28·00
		a. Dull purple	70·00	28·00
8		200r. red-orange	85·00	65·00
9		300r. lake-brown	70·00	28·00
		a. Yellow-brown	70·00	28·00
1/9 *Set of* 9			£850	£475

(b) P 13½

10	1	5r. black	21·00	14·00
11		10r. orange-buff	40·00	21·00
12		20r. bistre	55·00	29·00
13		25r. rose	22·00	8·50
		a. Carmine-rose	22·00	8·50
14		40r. deep blue	£225	75·00
		a. Blue	£225	75·00
15		50r. green	£250	85·00
16		100r. grey-lilac	55·00	28·00
		a. Dull purple	55·00	28·00
17		200r. orange	65·00	28·00
		a. Red-orange	65·00	28·00
18		300r. yellow-brown	£180	£160
10/18 *Set of* 9			£800	£400

All values were reprinted in 1895 and 1905.

MACAO

1884 (1 Mar). Handstamped locally with T **2**. No gum.

(a) P 12½

19	1	80r. on 100r. grey-lilac	£110	65·00
		a. Without accent	£130	75·00

(b) P 13½

20	1	80r. on 100r. grey lilac	£120	65·00
		a. Without accent	£130	75·00

1885. New value and colours changed.

(a) P 12½

21	1	10r. green	28·00	14·00
22		25r. deep lilac	40·00	21·00
23		40r. buff	50·00	24·00
24		50r. blue	55·00	30·00
25		80r. grey (Jan)	90·00	48·00

(b) P 13½

26	1	10r. green	£100	80·00
27		20r. rosine	50·00	28·00
28		25r. deep lilac	£200	£130
29		40r. buff	£160	£110
30		50r. blue	£160	£110
31		80r. grey	90·00	48·00

All values were reprinted in 1895 and 1905.

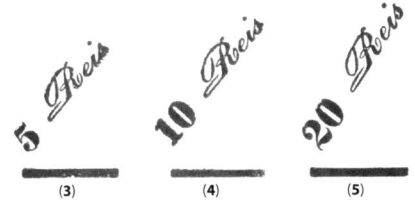

(3)   (4)   (5)

1885 (Jan–17 June). Surch locally as T **3/5**. No gum.

(a) P 12½

32	1	5r. on 25r. rose	26·00	14·00
		a. "Réis" with accent	34·00	16·00
		b. Thin bar	29·00	17·00
		c. Thin bar and "Réis" with accent	44·00	28·00
		d. Thin bar. Surch inverted	£425	£275
33		10r. on 25r. rose (B.)	49·00	23·00
34		10r. on 50r. green (B)	£350	£250
35		20r. on 50r. green	49·00	16·00
		a. Surch double	—	£325
36		40r. on 50r. green (R.) (17.6)	£250	£140

(b) P 13½

37	1	5r. on 25r. rose (*thin bar*)	£150	£100
		a. Surch inverted	£275	£200
38		10r. on 50r. green (B.)	£225	£180
39		20r. on 50r. green	85·00	65·00
40		40r. on 50r. green (R.) (17.6)	£250	£120

(6)   (7)   (8)

1885 (30 Sept). Surch locally as T **6**. No gum. P 12½.

41	1	5 on 25r. rose	39·00	26·00
42		10 on 50r. green	50·00	26·00
		a. Perf 13½	39·00	26·00

Stamps from the top row of the sheet may be found without bar, owing to misplacement of the surcharge. Nos. 42/42a also exist with thinner bar.

1887 (13 Apr). Surch locally as T **7**. P 13½.

43	1	5r. on 80r. grey	39·00	14·00
		a. Surch as T **8**	£100	75·00
		b. Perf 12½	£110	70·00
44		10r. on 80r. grey	70·00	28·00
		a. Surch as T **8**	£120	£110
45		20r. on 80r. grey	£100	40·00
		a. Surch as T **8** (with accent)	£130	£100
		ab. T **8** without accent	£140	£110
		b. Perf 12½		48·00

1887 (11 Aug). Surch as T **7**. No gum.

(a) P 12½

46	1	5r. on 100r. grey-lilac	£110	60·00
47		10r. on 200r. orange	£225	£110

(b) P 13½

48	1	5r. on 100r. grey-lilac	£150	£100
49		10r. on 200r. orange	£225	£110
		a. Surch as T **8** (no accent)	£300	£140

CORREIO   CORREIO

5   **10**

REIS   REIS

9   (10)   (11)

1887 (20 Oct). Fiscal stamps, T **9**, surch as T **10** or **11** (10r.), in red. Stamps are green, value deep brown, background buff lines. No gum. P 12½.

50		5r. on 10r. green and deep brown	£110	£110
		a. Imperf vert (horiz pair)	£450	
51		5r. on 20r. green and deep brown	£110	£110
52		5r. on 60r. green and deep brown	£110	£110
53		10r. on 10r. green and deep brown	£110	£110
54		10r. on 60r. green and deep brown	£140	£130
55		40r. on 20r. green and deep brown	£160	£140

Unused or used prices for stamps with upper and lower labels removed—5r. £10.50; 10r. £10.50; 40r. £23.

12

(Des and eng F. A. de Campos. Typo and embossed)

1888 (Jan). Chalk-surfaced paper.

(a) P 12½

56	12	5r. black	20·00	8·00
57		10r. green	22·00	8·00
58		20r. rosine	36·00	14·00
		a. Double impression	£250	£180
59		25r. bright mauve	39·00	14·00
		a. Violet	39·00	14·00
60		40r. chocolate	39·00	17·00
61		50r. blue	48·00	16·00
62		80r. grey	75·00	29·00
63		100r. yellow-brown	70·00	28·00
64		200r. lavender	£150	50·00
65		300r. orange	£140	50·00
56/65		Set of 10	£575	£200

(b) P 13½

66	12	10r. green	75·00	42·00
67		40r. chocolate	70·00	30·00
68		50r. blue	65·00	29·00
		a. Double impression	£120	£120
69		80r. grey	65·00	25·00
70		100r. yellow-brown	55·00	25·00
71		200r. lavender	£130	40·00
72		300r. orange	£140	40·00
		a. Double impression	£250	
66/72		Set of 7	£550	£200

The 5, 10 (both perfs), 80 (p 13½), 200 (p 13½) and 300r. (p 12½) were issued with gum, the 40r., p 13½, without; all other values came with or without gum.

King Carlos
19 October 1889–1 February 1908

2½   **JORNAES**

JORNAES

■   ■   **2½**   **2½**

(N **13**)   (N **14**)

135

MACAO

1892 (18 Aug)–**93**. NEWSPAPER. T **12** surch locally. No gum.

(a) P 12½

N73	N **13**	2½r. on 10r. green (25.4.93)	11·50	9·25
		a. Fraction bar omitted	11·00	4·00
N74	N **14**	2½r. on 40r. chocolate	11·00	4·00
		a. Surch inverted	70·00	70·00
N75		2½r. on 80r. grey	14·00	8·00
		a. Surch inverted	70·00	70·00

(b) P 13½

N76	N **13**	2½r. on 10r. green (25.4.93)	11·50	11·50
		a. Fraction bar omitted		
N77	N **14**	2½r. on 40r. chocolate	11·00	5·75
		a. Surch inverted	85·00	70·00
N78		2½r. on 80r. grey	70·00	40·00

30 **30**
(15) N **16**

1892 (Sept). Surch with T **15**, in red. No gum.

73	**12**	30 on 200r. lavender (p. 12½)	65·00	29·00
		a. Surch inverted	£325	£160
74		30 on 200r. lavender (p. 13½)	65·00	31·00

(Des and eng E. A. Azedo Gneco. Typo)

1893 (30 June). NEWSPAPER. No gum (No. N79).

N79	N **16**	2½r. brown (p. 11½)	9·25	5·75
N80		2½r. brown (p. 12½)	8·00	5·25
N81		2½r. brown (p. 13½)	8·50	5·25

Stamps of this type could be, and often were, used for franking ordinary correspondence.

½ avo   1 avo
PROVISORIO   PROVISORIO
仙半   仙壹
(N **17**)   (**18**)

1894 (1 Nov). NEWSPAPER. New Currency. No. N79 surch locally with Type N **17**.

N82	N **16**	½a. on 2½r. brown (p. 11½)	7·00	4·50
		a. Surch double	70·00	70·00

1894 (1 Nov). New Currency. Surch locally as T **18**. No gum.

(a) P 12½

75	**12**	1a. on 5r. black (R.)	12·50	7·00
		a. Stamp printed on unsurfaced side of paper	80·00	75·00
		b. Shorter figure "1" and "avo" in wider letters	12·00	5·75
		c. Surch double	£170	£130
		d. Surch inverted	80·00	70·00
76		3a. on 20r. rosine (G.)	14·00	7·00
		a. Surch inverted	80·00	70·00
77		4a. on 25r. violet	23·00	12·00
		a. Surch inverted	80·00	70·00
78		6a. on 40r. chocolate	23·00	11·00
79		8a. on 50r. blue (R.)	50·00	21·00
		a. Surch double	£140	£110
		b. Surch inverted	£180	£170
80		13a. on 80r. grey	28·00	14·00
		a. Surch double	£275	£170
81		16a. on 100r. yellow-brown	46·00	18·00
		a. Surch double	£275	£170
82		31a. on 200r. lavender	70·00	42·00
		a. Surch inverted	£170	£170
83		47a. on 300r. pale orange (G.)	80·00	40·00
		a. Surch double	£170	£110
		b. Orange (G.)	85·00	46·00

(b) P 13½

85		6a. on 40r. chocolate	23·00	15·00
86		8a. on 50r. blue (R.)	75·00	55·00
87		16a. on 100r. yellow-brown	£130	£130
88		31a. on 200r. lavender	65·00	41·00

The 2a. on 10r. green was a clandestine production.

1894 (1 Nov). Nos. 73/4, further surch as T **18** with bars cancelling original surch.

89	**12**	5a. on 30 on 200r. (p. 12½)	£200	£100
90		5a. on 30 on 200r. (p. 13½)	£200	£100

19   19a Arrival at Calicut

(Des and eng M. D. Neto. Typo)

1894 (15 Nov). Chalk-surfaced paper or enamel-surfaced paper (E). No gum (20 to 300r.), with or without gum (15r.).

(a) P 11½

91	**19**	5r. orange-yellow	14·00	5·25
92		10r. rosy mauve	14·00	5·25
93		15r. red-brown	21·00	7·50
94		20r. lilac	28·00	8·00
95		25r. green	55·00	16·00
96		50r. pale blue	55·00	20·00
97		75r. rose	75·00	46·00
98		80r. pale green	48·00	31·00
99		100r. brown/buff	47·00	25·00
100		150r. carmine/rose	47·00	25·00
101		200r. blue/blue	70·00	34·00
102		300r. blue/pale brown	£100	46·00
91/102	*Set of 12*		£500	£250

(b) P 13½

103	**19**	50r. pale blue (†)	£550	£450

(Des R. Gameiro (½a.), M. P. de Faria Luna (1a.), S. Correira Belém (2a.), J. Vaz (4, 12, 24a.), J. J. G. Coelho (8a.), J. R. Cristino de Silva (16a.). Recess Waterlow)

1898 (1 Apr). 400th Anniv of Vasco da Gama's Discovery of Route to India, T **19a** and similar designs, inscr "1498 1898". P 14 to 15.

104		½a. blue-green	7·00	4·25
105		1a. vermilion	8·00	5·75
106		2a. dull purple	14·00	5·75
107		4a. yellow-green	18·00	7·00
108		8a. deep blue	30·00	16·00
109		12a. chocolate	40·00	24·00
110		16a. bistre-brown	46·00	23·00
111		24a. ochre	50·00	34·00
104/111	*Set of 8*		£190	£110

Designs: Horiz—½a. Departure of fleet; 2a. Embarkation at Rastello; 16a. Flagship *São Gabriel*; 24a. Vasco da Gama. Vert—4a. Muse of History; 8a. Flagship *São Gabriel* and portraits of Da Gama and Camoens; 12a. Archangel Gabriel, patron saint of the expedition.

20   PROVISORIO
20   (21)

(Des and eng E. Mouchon. Typo)

1898 (1 July)–**1900**. Name and value in black, on 78a. in carmine.

(a) P 11½

112	**20**	½a. grey	3·25	1·10
		a. Name and value inverted	£100	90·00
113		1a. orange-yellow*	3·25	1·10
		a. Name and value inverted	£170	£160
114		2a. pale yellow-green*	4·50	1·40
		a. Green*	4·50	1·40
		b. Name and value inverted	£140	£110
115		2½a. brown (*no gum*)	9·25	4·25
116		3a. slate-lilac (*no gum*)	9·25	4·25
117		4a. blue-green (*no gum*)	12·50	8·00
118		5a. brown (*no gum*) (1.12.00)	11·00	6·25
119		8a. blue	13·00	6·25
120		10a. dull blue (*no gum*) (1.12.00)	11·50	6·50
121		12a. rose	17·00	10·50
122		13a. mauve	20·00	10·50
123		15a. pale olive-green (*no gum*) (1.12.00)	£110	29·00
124		16a. blue/blue*	21·00	10·50
125		20a. sepia/cream (*no gum*) (1.12.00)	46·00	15·00
126		24a. purple-brown/straw*	25·00	12·00
127		31a. purple	34·00	16·00
128		47a. blue/pink	48·00	20·00
129		78a. black/azure (*no gum*) (1.12.00)	75·00	28·00
112/129	*Set of 18*		£425	£170

(b) P 12½

130	**20**	½a. grey*	21·00	10·50
131		1a. orange-yellow (*no gum*)	21·00	10·50

*These values were issued both with and without gum. See also Nos. 173/83.

136

MACAO

1900 (1 Jan). Surch as T **21**.
132	**20**	5 on 13a. mauve	16·00	5·25
133		10 on 16a. blue/*blue*	20·00	8·00
134		15 on 24a. purple-brown/*straw*	26·00	10·50
135		20 on 31a. purple	36·00	15·00
132/135 *Set of 4*			90·00	35·00

(22) (23)

1902 (1 Nov). Surch as T **22**.
136	**1**	6a. on 10r. dull yellow (11½)	30·00	12·50
		a. Surch double	£130	70·00
137		6a. on 10r. green (11½)	20·00	8·00
138	**12**	6a. on 5r. black (12½) (R.)	9·25	5·25
		a. Surch inverted	£120	70·00
139		6a. on 10r. green (12½)	8·00	5·25
140		6a. on 40r. chocolate (12½)	9·25	5·25
		a. Surch double	£120	55·00
141		6a. on 40r. chocolate (13½)	30·00	14·00
142	**19**	6a. on 5r. yellow (11½)	8·00	4·50
		a. Surch inverted	£140	75·00
143		6a. on 10r. rosy mauve (11½)	23·00	8·50
144		6a. on 15r. red-brown (11½)	21·00	8·00
145		6a. on 25r. green (11½)	9·25	4·50
146		6a. on 80r. pale green (11½)	9·25	4·50
147		6a. on 100r. brown/*buff* (11½)	20·00	12·50
148		6a. on 100r. brown/*buff* (13½)	15·00	6·00
149		6a. on 200r. blue/*blue* (11½)	10·50	4·50
		a. Bisected vert (2a.) on cover (7.10)	—	75·00
150	N **16**	18a. on 2½r. brown (11½)	40·00	16·00
151		18a. on 2½r. brown (12½)	10·50	7·00
152		18a. on 2½r. brown (13½)	26·00	12·50
153	**12**	18a. on 20r. rosine (12½)	21·00	7·50
		a. Surch inverted	£150	
154		18a. on 25r. bright mauve (12½)	£200	75·00
		a. Violet	£170	48·00
155		18a. on 80r. grey (12½)	£200	90·00
		a. Surch double	£250	£180
156		18a. on 100r. yellow-brown (12½)	48·00	30·00
157		18a. on 100r. yellow-brown (13½)	90·00	50·00
158		18a. on 200r. lavender (12½)	£170	80·00
159		18a. on 200r. lavender (13½)	£180	75·00
160		18a. on 300r. orange (12½)	42·00	21·00
161		18a. on 300r. orange (13½)	55·00	32·00
162	**19**	18a. on 20r. lilac (11½)	25·00	10·50
163		18a. on 50r. pale blue (11½)	25·00	10·50
164		18a. on 50r. pale blue (13½)	70·00	30·00
165		18a. on 75r. rose (11½)	25·00	10·50
166		18a. on 150r. carmine/*rose* (11½)	25·00	10·50
167		18a. on 300r. blue/*pale brown* (11½)	25·00	10·50

All stamps in Type **12** were issued without gum except for No. 159. The other designs were issued with or without gum as for the original issues.

The 6a./10r. T **1** and the 6a./5r., 6a./40r., 18a./25r., 18a./80r., 18a./100r., 18a./200r. and 18a./300r. T **12** were reprinted perf 13½ in 1905.

1902 (1–12 Nov). Optd with T **23**. With or without gum (2, 8, 12a.), no gum (others).
168	**20**	2a. pale green	15·00	6·25
169		4a. blue-green	40·00	14·00
170		8a. blue (12 Nov)	21·00	11·50
171		10a. dull blue	22·00	12·50
172		12a. rose (12 Nov)	80·00	30·00
168/172 *Set of 5*			£160	65·00

The 4a. was reprinted in 1905.

1903 (1 Jan–Oct). Colours changed. Name and value in black. With or without gum (2, 3, 5a.), no gum (others). P 11½.
173	**20**	2a. grey-green	5·50	3·00
174		3a. slate	5·50	3·00
		a. Bisected diag (1a.) (on cover) (7.10)	—	85·00
175		4a. carmine	5·50	3·00
176		5a. fawn	8·50	5·00
177		6a. red-brown	11·00	5·00
		a. Bisected diag (2a.) (on cover) (7.10)		£100
178		8a. grey-green	13·50	7·50
179		12a. dull purple	60·00	28·00
180		13a. deep lilac	25·00	15·00
181		18a. orange-brown/*pink*	43·00	22·00
182		31a. purple/*pink*	43·00	22·00
183		47a. dull blue/*straw*	60·00	31·00
173/183 *Set of 11*			£250	£130

D **24**  (25) (26)

(Des and eng J. S. de Carvalho e Silva. Typo)

1904 (July). POSTAGE DUE. Name and value in black. No gum (12a. to 1p.), with or without gum (others). P 11½.
D184	D **24**	½a. blue-green	1·80	1·40
		a. Name and value inverted	£100	60·00
D185		1a. yellow-green	2·50	1·40
D186		2a. slate	3·00	1·40
D187		4a. brown	3·75	1·70
D188		5a. orange	5·00	2·75
D189		8a. deep brown	5·75	3·00
D190		12a. pale red-brown	8·50	4·25
D191		20a. blue	16·00	7·50
D192		40a. carmine	30·00	11·00
D193		50a. brown	37·00	16·00
D194		1p. deep lilac	75·00	25·00
D184/194 *Set of 11*			£170	70·00

1905. No. 179 surch with T **25**.
| 184 | **20** | 10a. on 12a. dull purple | 37·00 | 18·00 |

King Manoel II
1 February 1908–5 October 1910

PORTUGUESE REPUBLIC
5 October 1910

1910 (Oct). Nos. D184/6 with words "PORTEADO" and "RECEBER" cancelled by bars as T **26**, in black.
185	D **24**	½a. blue-green (15 Oct)	16·00	9·50
		a. Opt inverted	49·00	31·00
		b. Bars omitted (pair with normal).		
186		1a. blue-green (17 Oct)	20·00	9·50
		a. Opt inverted	49·00	31·00
187		2a. slate (18 Oct)	34·00	11·00
		a. Opt inverted	75·00	37·00
185/187 *Set of 3*			65·00	27·00

These thick bars are made by joining two thin bars; they sometimes show solidly black and sometimes with a white line between, due to the two bars not exactly joining.

(27) 30

1911 (2 Apr). Optd with T **27**, in red or green (G.). With or without gum (4a.), no gum (8 to 78a.).
188	**20**	½a. grey (11½)	3·75	1·40
189		1a. orange (11½)	3·00	1·00
190		2a. grey-green	3·00	1·00
191		3a. slate	5·00	1·50
192		4a. carmine (G.)	7·50	2·30
		a. Error. 4a. fawn	49·00	41·00
193		5a. fawn	7·50	3·50
194		6a. red-brown	7·50	3·50
195		8a. grey-brown	7·50	3·50
196		10a. dull blue	7·50	3·50
197		13a. grey-lilac	12·50	4·25
198		16a. blue/*blue*	12·50	5·75
199		18a. orange-brown/*pink*	20·00	7·50
200		20a. sepia/*cream*	20·00	7·50
201		31a. purple/*pink*	25·00	8·00
202		47a. dull blue/*straw*	37·00	13·50
203		78a. black/*azure*	49·00	20·00
188/203 *Set of 16*			£200	80·00

See also Nos. 241/51.

1911. POSTAGE DUE. Optd with T **27**, in red or green (G.). With or without gum (8, 40a.), no gum (20, 50a., 1p.).
D204	D **24**	½a. blue-green	1·70	60
D205		1a. yellow-green	2·50	1·00
D206		2a. slate	3·75	1·80
D207		4a. brown	5·00	1·80
D208		5a. orange	6·25	2·50
D209		8a. deep brown	6·75	2·75

D210 12a. pale red-brown 10·50 3·50
D211 20a. blue 14·00 4·50
D212 40a. carmine (G.) 21·00 6·25
D213 50a. orange 27·00 10·50
D214 1p. deep lilac 44·00 18·00
D204/214 *Set of* 11 £130 48·00
See also Nos. D281/91.

1911 (15 July). Fiscal stamp surch "POSTAL 1 AVO" and bar as in T **30**, in red. With or without gum. P 12.
204 **30** 1a. on 5r. brown, yellow and black 27·00 11·00
a. Surch inverted 75·00 49·00
b. Numeral "1" missing 85·00 60·00
No. 204b occurred on the 1st and 6th stamps of the 2nd row but was soon corrected.

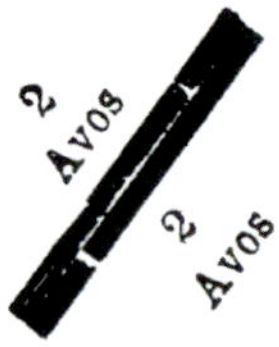

(**31**)

32

1911 (19 July). Nos. 175, 120 and 171 surch as T **31** and bisected diagonally along bar.
205 **20** 2a. on half of 4a. carmine (175) (2.8) 75·00 55·00
a. Surch inverted £250 £140
b. "2" omitted £100 90·00
206 5a. on half of 10a. dull blue (120) (R.) £600 £375
a. Surch inverted £550 £325
b. Surch in black £750 £400
207 5a. on half of 10a. dull blue (171) (R.) £160 £110
a. Surch inverted £275 £170
205/207 *Set of* 3 £750 £475
Entire stamps with these surcharges are sometimes found. Normally they were bisected by the Government before being placed on sale.

(Typo National Printing Works, Macao)

1911 (8 Aug). Label as T **32** (each numbered separately). No gum. P 11½.

(a) Wove paper
208 **32** 1a. black/*white* £600 £500
209 2a. black/*white* £650 £550

(b) Laid paper
210 **32** 1a. black/*white* £600 £500
a. Error. "Corrieo" £2750 £2500
211 2a. black/*white* £650 £550
a. Error. "Corrieo" £2750 £2500
The "Corrieo" error occurs on position 9 of the sheet of 100.
The signature "JM" is that of José Maria d'Almeida.

2 (**34**)   REPUBLICA (**35**)   1 Avo (**36**)

Lisbon overprint, T **27**:—24½ mm long. Shorter letters. Final "A" has flattened top.
Local overprint, T **35**:—23 mm long. Tall letters. Final "A" has pointed top.

1913 (Oct). Provisionals of 1902 surch with T **34** in black and optd with T **35**.
212 **19** 2a. on 18a. on 20r. (11½) (R.) 13·50 5·50
213 2a. on 18a. on 50r. (11½) (R.) 13·50 5·50
214 2a. on 18a. on 50r. (13½) (R.) 15·00 7·50
215 2a. on 18a. on 75r. (11½) (G.) 13·50 5·50
216 2a. on 18a. on 150r. (11½) (G.) 13·50 5·50

1913 (Oct). Provisionals of 1902 optd locally with T **35** in red or green (G.). No gum.
217 **1** 6a. on 10r. (11½) 55·00 11·00
218 **12** 6a. on 5r. (12½) (G.) 18·00 10·00
219 6a. on 10r. (12½) 27·00 16·00
220 6a. on 40r. (12½) 13·50 6·75
221 6a. on 40r. (13½) 75·00 37·00
222 **19** 6a. on 10r. (11½) 15·00 6·75
223 6a. on 10r. (11½) (G.) 43·00 27·00
224 6a. on 15r. (11½) 15·00 6·25
225 6a. on 25r. (11½) 16·00 8·50
226 6a. on 80r. (11½) 16·00 7·50
227 6a. on 100r. (11½) 34·00 12·50
228 6a. on 100r. (13½) 32·00 9·75
229 **12** 18a. on 20r. (12½) (G.) 21·00 9·75
230 18a. on 100r. (12½) £110 50·00
231 18a. on 100r. (13½) £120 85·00
232 18a. on 300r. (12½) 43·00 11·00
233 18a. on 300r. (13½) 47·00 22·00
234 **19** 18a. on 20r. (11½) 43·00 23·00
235 18a. on 50r. (11½) 22·00 7·50
236 18a. on 50r. (13½) 23·00 8·50
237 18a. on 75r. (11½) (G.) 22·00 7·50
238 18a. on 150r. (11½) (G.) 22·00 7·50
239 18a. on 300r. (11½) 43·00 17·00

*No. 184 optd with T **35**, in red*
240 **20** 10a. on 12a. dull purple 32·00 8·50
See also Nos. 281/300.

1913 (Oct). Optd locally with T **35** in red or in green (G.). No gum.
241 **20** 4a. carmine (G.) £300 £110
242 5a. fawn 75·00 21·00
243 6a. red-brown £120 60·00
244 8a. grey brown £850 £375
245 13a. mauve (122) £200 70·00
246 13a. grey lilac (180) £100 37·00
247 16a. blue/*blue* 60·00 22·00
248 18a. orange-brown/*pink* 60·00 22·00
249 20a. sepia-brown/*cream* 75·00 31·00
250 31a. purple/*pink* 75·00 31·00
251 47a. dull blue/*straw* £100 43·00
241/251 *Set of* 11 £1800 £750
The 10a. dull blue also exists with the local overprint. It is believed only one sheet of 28 was overprinted (*Price* £28000 *un.*).

1913 (Oct). Surch locally as T **36**.

*(a) Stamps of 1911 with opt T **27***
252 **20** ½a. on 5a. fawn (193) 21·00 5·50
253 4a. on 8a. grey-brown (195) 44·00 9·25

*(b) Stamps of 1913 with opt T **35***
254 **20** 1a. on 13a. mauve (245) £150 55·00
255 1a. on 13a. grey-lilac (246) 22·00 8·50
a. Without "REPUBLICA"
b. Error. On No. 197

REPUBLICA

REPUBLICA (**37**)   10 A (**38**)

1913 (Oct–Nov). Stamps of 1898 (Vasco da Gama) optd or surch with T **37** or **38**.
256 ½a. blue-green 6·25 2·75
257 1a. vermilion 8·50 2·75
258 2a. dull purple 8·50 2·75
a. Opt double, one inverted £110
259 4a. yellow-green 18·00 7·50
260 8a. deep blue 23·00 8·00
261 10a. on 12a. chocolate 43·00 22·00
262 16a. bistre-brown 37·00 18·00
263 24a. ochre 38·00 16·00
256/263 *Set of* 8 £160 70·00

39 Ceres   ½ AVO (**40**)   2 (**41**)   2 avos (**42**)

(Des C. Fernandes. Eng J. S. de Carvalho e Silva. Typo)

1913 (17 Nov)–**15**. Name and value in black.

(a) Chalk-surfaced paper. P 15×14
264 **39** ½a. brown-olive 2·75 1·40
265 1a. black 2·75 1·60
266 2a. green 2·75 1·60
267 4a. carmine 6·75 2·75
268 5a. chocolate 7·50 4·25
269 6a. violet 7·50 4·25
270 8a. pale brown (1915) 7·50 4·25
271 10a. blue 9·75 4·25
272 12a. yellow-brown 11·00 4·25
273 16a. slate 20·00 15·00
274 20a. brown-red 21·00 11·00
275 40a. plum 21·00 11·00
276 58a. chocolate/*green* 33·00 21·00
277 76a. brown/*rose* 36·00 22·00
278 1p. orange/*salmon* 60·00 28·00
279 3p. deep green/*azure* £160 85·00
264/279 *Set of* 16 £375 £200
The ½, 1 and 2a. exist on glazed paper.

MACAO

(b) Enamel-surfaced paper. P 12×11½ (1915)

| 280 | 39 | 2a. green | 9·75 | 6·25 |

See also Nos. 305/28.

1914. POSTAGE DUE. Optd locally with T **35**, in red or green (G.) With or without gum (4, 8a.), no gum (12, 40, 50a., 1p.).

D281	D 24	½a. blue-green	£1400	£600
D282		1a. yellow-green	6·25	2·75
D283		2a. slate	6·75	3·00
D284		4a. brown	8·50	3·25
D285		5a. orange	9·75	5·25
D286		8a. deep brown	11·00	6·25
D287		12a. pale red-brown	15·00	6·25
D288		20a. blue	20·00	9·75
D289		40a. carmine (G)	31·00	12·50
		a. Opt double, in red and green	£110	55·00
D290		50a. orange	41·00	13·50
D291		1p. deep lilac	60·00	21·00
D281/291 Set of 11			£1500	£550

1915. Provisionals of 1902 to 1905 optd with T **27**, in red (reading downwards on 2½r.). With or without gum (No. 287), with gum (281/2, 284, 286, 293/4), no gum (others).

281	**20**	8a. blue (170)	21·00	11·00
282		10a. dull blue (171)	21·00	11·00
283		10a. on 12a. (184)	22·00	11·50
284	**19**	6a. on 5r. (11½)	15·00	6·25
285	**12**	6a. on 10r. (12½)	49·00	31·00
286	**19**	6a. on 10r. (11½)	15·00	7·50
287		6a. on 15r. (11½)	12·50	6·25
288		6a. on 25r. (11½)	13·50	7·50
289		6a. on 80r. (11½)	13·50	7·50
290		6a. on 100r. (11½)	13·50	7·50
291		6a. on 100r. (13½)	13·50	7·50
292		6a. on 200r. (11½)	18·00	10·50
293	N **16**	18a. on 2½r. (12½)	21·00	10·50
294		18a. on 2½r. (13½)	25·00	12·50
295	**19**	18a. on 20r. (11½)	21·00	10·50
296		18a. on 50r. (11½)	22·00	11·50
297		18a. on 50r. (13½)	22·00	11·50
298		18a. on 75r. (11½)	23·00	11·50
299		18a. on 150r. (11½)	31·00	15·00
300		18a. on 300r. (11½)	49·00	18·00

1919. No gum.

(a) Surch locally with T **40**

| 301 | **39** | ½a. on 5a. chocolate | £100 | 43·00 |

(b) Nos. 288/9 surch locally with T **41**, and bars over old value

| 302 | **19** | 2 on 6a. on 25r. | £600 | £250 |
| 303 | | 2 on 6a. on 80r. | £375 | £180 |

(c) No. 194 surch locally with T **42**

| 304 | **20** | 2a. on 6a. red-brown | £275 | £120 |

Nos. 301/4 are generally found cut with scissors at one side. Uncut specimens were only sold in complete sets.

CHARITY TAX STAMPS. Stamps bearing C numbers were for compulsory use on internal letters on certain days of the year as an additional postal tax for public charities. Other values in some of the types were for use on telegrams or for fiscal purposes.

43

1919 (11 Aug). CHARITY TAX. Fiscal stamps optd "TAXA DE GUERRA". P 15×14.

| C305 | **43** | 2a. green | 9·75 | 6·25 |
| C306 | | 11a. green | 37·00 | 18·00 |

Nos. C305/6 were for use in Timor as well as Macao. The similar 9a. value was for use on receipts and telegrams.

1919–24.

(a) Unsurfaced paper. P 15×14 (1919)

305	**39**	½a. brown-olive	8·50	4·25
306		1a. black	8·50	4·25
307		2a. deep green	22·00	11·00
308		4a. carmine	60·00	22·00

(b) Unsurfaced paper. P 12×11½ (1922-24)

309	**39**	½a. brown-olive	4·25	1·80
310		1a. black	6·25	2·50
311		1½a. yellow-green (1924)	4·00	1·80
312		2a. pale green	9·25	5·50
313		3a. orange (1924)	12·50	4·00
314		4a. carmine	31·00	8·00
315		4a. lemon (1924)	16·00	6·25
316		6a. slate-lilac (1924)	37·00	31·00
317		8a. red-brown	27·00	8·50
318		10a. pale blue	49·00	10·50
319		12a. yellow-brown	47·00	9·75
320		14a. mauve (1924)	42·00	22·00
321		16a. slate	37·00	27·00
322		24a. deep green (1924)	37·00	25·00
323		32a. chestnut (1924)	43·00	32·00
324		56a. dull rose (1924)	60·00	34·00
325		72a. brown (1924)	80·00	37·00
326		1p. orange (1924)	£100	70·00

(c) Glazed paper. P 12×11½ (1924)

327	**39**	3p. turquoise	£425	£180
328		5p. bright carmine	£250	£150
309/328 Set of 20			£1200	£600

44 Pombal Monument

45 Planning the Reconstruction of Lisbon

46 Marquis de Pombal

MULTA
(D **47**)

(Des H. Fleury. Eng J. A. C. Harrison. Recess Waterlow)

1925 (3 Nov). Marquis de Pombal Commemoration. P 12½.

(a) CHARITY TAX

C329	**44**	2a. orange-red	5·00	2·20
C330	**45**	2a. orange-red	5·00	2·20
C331	**46**	2a. orange-red	6·25	3·00

(b) POSTAGE DUE. Optd with Type D **47**

D329	**44**	4a. orange-red	5·00	3·00
D330	**45**	4a. orange-red	5·00	3·00
D331	**46**	4a. orange-red	5·00	3·00
C329/D331 Set of 6			28·00	15·00

Nos. C329/31 were in use from 3 to 13 November 1925 and from 5 to 15 May in 1926 and 1929. Nos. D329/31 were used in default.

C **48** Our Lady of Charity (altarpiece, Macao Cathedral)

(**49**)

(Des J. N. Castela. Litho plates made in Hong Kong. Ptd in Macao)

1930 (25 Dec). CHARITY TAX. No gum. P 11.

C332	C **48**	5a. purple-brown and buff	60·00	34·00
		a. Imperf vert (horiz pair)	£400	
		b. Imperf between (horiz pair)	£375	

For compulsory use from 25 Dec 1930 to 7 Jan 1931 and also during Easter 1931.

For similar stamps in this design, see Nos. C410/20, C468/72 and C486/9.

1931–33. Surch as T **49**.

(a) Chalk-surfaced paper. P 15×14

| 329 | **39** | 5a. on 6a. violet | 11·00 | 6·25 |

139

MACAO

(b) Unsurfaced paper. P 12×11½

330	**39**	1a. on 24a. deep green	8·00	4·00
331		2a. on 32a. chestnut	8·00	4·00
332		4a. on 12a. yellow-brown	8·00	4·25
333		5a. on 6a. slate-lilac	£100	55·00
334		7a. on 8a. red-brown (1931)	11·00	6·75
335		12a. on 14a. mauve (1931)	11·00	6·75
336		15a. on 16a. slate	11·00	6·75
337		20a. on 56a. dull rose	90·00	50·00
330/337 Set of 8			£225	£120

50 "Portugal" and Galeasse (with imprint below design)

51 Maltese Cross

(Die eng A. Fragoso. Typo)

1934 (1 Feb). W **51**. P 11½×12.

338	**50**	½a. brown	1·40	60
339		1a. sepia	1·40	60
340		2a. blue-green	2·20	75
341		3a. mauve	2·20	75
342		4a. black	2·50	90
343		5a. grey	2·50	90
344		6a. cinnamon	3·00	90
345		7a. carmine	3·75	1·40
346		8a. turquoise-blue	3·75	1·40
347		10a. vermilion	5·50	2·10
348		12a. blue	5·50	2·10
349		14a. olive-green	5·50	2·10
350		15a. claret	5·50	2·10
351		20a. orange	6·25	2·10
352		30a. yellow-green	13·50	4·00
353		40a. violet	13·50	4·00
354		50a. bistre-brown	23·00	8·00
355		1p. grey-blue	60·00	20·00
356		2p. red-brown	80·00	26·00
357		3p. emerald	£225	60·00
358		5p. mauve	£275	80·00
338/358 Set of 21			£675	£200

For stamps lithographed and without imprint below design, see Nos. 402/9.

(52) Avião (Greek characters) / **(53)** Avião 5 avos

1936 (25 July–1 Sept). AIR. T **50** optd or surch.

359	**52**	2a. blue-green (25.7)	5·25	2·00
360		3a. mauve	6·75	2·75
361	**53**	5a. on 6a. cinnamon (25.7)	8·00	3·25
362	**52**	7a. carmine	8·00	3·25
363		8a. turquoise-blue	11·00	7·50
364		15a. claret	37·00	17·00
359/364 Set of 6			70·00	32·00

The Greek characters were included in these overprints in order to make forgery difficult.

54 Vasco da Gama   **55** Mousinho de Albuquerque   **56** Airplane over Globe

(Des A. R. Garcia. Recess Bradbury Wilkinson)

1938 (1 Aug). Name and value in black. P 13½×13.

(a) POSTAGE. T **54/5** *and similar designs*

365	**54**	1a. grey-olive	2·30	1·20
366		2a. orange-brown	2·50	1·40
367		3a. slate-violet	2·50	1·40
368		4a. emerald green	2·50	1·40
369	**55**	5a. carmine	2·50	1·40
370		6a. slate	3·75	2·20
371		8a. bright purple	4·00	2·50
372	–	10a. magenta	5·00	3·00
373		12a. scarlet	5·25	3·25
374		15a. orange	6·75	4·25
375		20a. blue	8·00	4·25
376		40a. grey black	20·00	9·25
377		50a. brown	23·00	10·50
378		1p. lake	70·00	26·00
379	–	2p. olive-green	£100	39·00
380	–	3p. ultramarine	£140	49·00
381	–	5p. red-brown	£250	60·00
365/381 Set of 17			£600	£200

Designs:—10, 12, 15a. Henry the Navigator; 20, 40, 50a. Dam; 1, 2, 3, 5p. Afonso de Albuquerque.

(b) AIR

382	**56**	1a. scarlet	1·40	60
383		2a. bright violet	2·50	1·40
384		3a. orange	5·25	2·00
385		5a. bright blue	6·75	4·00
386		10a. brown-lake	8·00	5·25
387		20a. blue-green	16·00	9·25
388		50a. red-brown	25·00	13·50
389		70a. carmine	41·00	17·00
390		1p. magenta	70·00	25·00
382/390 Set of 9			£160	70·00

(57) 5 avos   **(58)** 5 avos

1940–42. Surch with new values.

(a) Local surch as T **57** *(1.10.40)*

391	**50**	1a. on 6a. cinnamon	7·50	5·00
392		5a. on 7a. carmine	£150	90·00
393		5a. on 8a. turquoise-blue	22·00	12·50

(b) Lisbon surch as T **58** *(22.2.41–1942)*

394	**50**	2a. on 6a. cinnamon (27.11 42)	4·00	3·00
395		3a. on 6a. cinnamon (27.11.42)	4·00	3·00
396		5a. on 7a. carmine	12·50	8·50
397		5a. on 8a. turquoise-blue	16·00	9·75
398		8a. on 30a. yellow-green (27.11.42)	12·50	6·25
399		8a. on 40a. violet (27.11.42)	13·50	7·00
400		8a. on 50a. bistre-brown (27.11.42)	13·50	8·25
394/400 Set of 7			70·00	41·00

3 avos **(59)**    D **60**

1941 (1 Oct). No. 370 surch locally with T **59**.

401	**55**	3a. on 6a. slate	80·00	47·00

(Litho Sin Chun & Co Ltd, Macao)

1942 (1 Nov). T **50** redrawn without imprint below design. No gum. P 12.

402		1a. sepia	3·00	2·50
403		2a. blue-green	3·00	2·50
404		3a. mauve	15·00	7·50
		a. Perf 11	22·00	8·00
405		6a. cinnamon	34·00	12·50
		a. Perf 11	44·00	16·00
		b. Perf 10×9½	50·00	25·00
406		10a. vermilion	18·00	8·00
407		20a. orange	13·50	8·00
		a. Perf 11	50·00	20·00
		b. Perf 10×9½		
408		30a. yellow-green	21·00	8·50
409		40a. violet	37·00	11·00
402/409 Set of 8 (*cheapest*)			£130	55·00

The 10a. and 20a. were issued on thin transparent and thick opaque papers.

1945–47. CHARITY TAX. As Type C **48** but values in Arabic and Chinese numerals left and right, at bottom of design. No *gum*.

(a) Litho Hong Kong. P 11½ (1945)

C410	C **48**	5a. brown and yellow	£100	55·00
C411		10a. green and pale green	49·00	31·00
C412		15a. orange and pale orange	49·00	31·00
C413		20a. vermilion and pale salmon	90·00	49·00
C414		50a. lilac and buff	£225	£120
		a. Imperf between (horiz pair)	£425	
		b. Imperf between (vert pair)	£425	
C410/414 Set of 5			£450	£250

MACAO

(b) Litho Macao. P 12 (1947)

C415	C **48**	5a. deep brown and yellow	20·00	16·00
C416		5a. blue and pale blue	55·00	37·00
C417		10a. green and pale green	37·00	25·00
C418		15a. orange and pale orange	37·00	25·00
C419		20a. vermilion and pale salmon	55·00	31·00
C420		50a. lilac and buff (*p.* 10)	70·00	43·00
		a. Imperf horiz (vert pair)	£275	
C415/420 *Set of 6*			£250	£160

(Des and die eng M. Norte. Typo)

1947. POSTAGE DUE. P 11½×12.

D410	D **60**	1a. black and reddish purple	6·25	2·10
D411		2a. black and dull violet	6·25	2·50
D412		4a. black and indigo	6·25	3·75
D413		5a. black and brown	7·75	5·00
D414		8a. black and reddish purple	11·00	6·25
D415		12a. black and chestnut	16·00	6·25
D416		20a. black and yellow-green	18·00	11·50
D417		40a. black and carmine	25·00	12·50
D418		50a. black and yellow	43·00	15·00
D419		1p. black and light blue	75·00	18·00
D410/419 *Set of 10*			£200	75·00

61 Mountain Fort **62** Our Lady of Fatima

(Des A. de Sousa. Litho Litografia Nacional, Oporto, Portugal)

1948 (20 Dec)**–50.** T **61** and similar designs. P 11.

410		1a. brown and orange	7·50	60
411		2a. claret	7·50	60
412		3a. blackish purple	10·50	2·00
413		8a. carmine	8·00	2·50
414		10a. bright purple	12·50	2·50
415		20a. deep blue	31·00	6·25
416		30a. slate	50·00	9·75
417		50a. yellow-brown and buff	85·00	11·00
418		1p. green	£180	25·00
419		1p. ultramarine (1950)	£225	
420		2p. scarlet	£200	25·00
421		3p. grey-green	£200	25·00
422		5p. blue-violet	£300	25·00
410/422 *Set of 13*			£1200	
410/422 *Set of 12* (excl 419)				£120

Designs: Horiz—1a. Macao house; 3a. Part of Macao; 8a. Praia Grande Bay; 10a. Leal Senado Square; 20a. São Jerome Hill; 30a. Street scene, Macao; 50a. Relief of goddess Ma (allegory); 5p. Road through woods. Vert—1p. Cerco Gateway; 2p. Barra Pagoda, Ma-Cok-Miu; 3p. Post Office. See also Nos. 427/34.

(Des A. Negreiros. Litografia Nacional, Oporto, Portugal)

1949 (1 Feb). Honouring the Statue of Our Lady of Fatima. P 14.

423	**62**	8a. scarlet	70·00	22·00

(D **63**) **64** Globe and Letter **65** Bells and Dove

1949 (1 Mar). POSTAGE DUE. Nos. 342, etc surch locally as Type D **63**, in red.

D424	**50**	1a. on 4a. black	4·25	2·30
D425		2a. on 6a. cinnamon	4·25	2·30
D426		4a. on 8a. turquoise-blue	4·25	2·30
D427		5a. on 10a. vermilion	5·00	2·50
D428		8a. on 12a. blue	8·00	4·00
D429		12a. on 30a. yellow-green	11·50	5·00
D430		20a. on 40a. violet	16·00	8·00
D424/430 *Set of 7*			48·00	24·00

(Des A. Negreiros. Litho Litografia Nacional, Oporto)

1949 (24 Dec). 75th Anniv of Universal Postal Union. P 14.

424	**64**	32a. purple	£150	37·00

(Des J. Araujo. Litho Litografia de Portugal, Lisbon)

1950 (26 July). Holy Year. T **65** and similar vert design. P 13½.

425		32a. violet-black	42·00	11·50
426		50a. carmine	43·00	12·50

Design:—50a. Angel holding candelabra.

DATES OF ISSUE. The dates given refer to the dates when stamps were placed on sale in Macao. In a number of instances they were released at different times in Lisbon, usually earlier.

1950 (17 Jan)**–51.** As Nos. 410, etc but colours changed. P 14.

427		1a. violet and pink	5·00	1·50
428		2a. yellow-brown and yellow	5·00	1·80
429		3a. red-orange	12·50	2·50
430		8a. blue-grey	16·00	2·50
431		10a. red-brown and orange	22·00	6·25
432		30a. light blue	25·00	6·75
433		50a. olive-green and yellow-green	60·00	8·50
434		1p. red-brown (1950)	£180	31·00
427/434 *Set of 8*			£300	55·00

66 Arms and Dragon **67** F. Mendes Pinto **68** Junk

(Litho Sin Chun Printing Co, Macao)

1950 (10 Nov–26 Dec). No gum. P 12.

435	**66**	1a. yellow/*cream* (26.12)	4·25	1·80
436		2a. green/*pale green* (26.12)	4·25	1·80
437		10a. maroon/*pale green* (10.11)	15·00	3·75
438		10a. magenta/*pale green* (26.12)	12·50	3·75
435/438 *Set of 4*			32·00	10·00

In the 1a. and 2a. stamps the centre background is plain, in the 10a. lined.

1951 (6 June). POSTAGE DUE. Nos. 435/6 and 438 optd "PORTEADO" as in Type D **63** or surch as Type D **63** (No. D441).

D439	**66**	1a. yellow/*cream*	2·50	1·70
D440		2a. green/*pale green* (R.)	2·50	1·70
D441		7a. on 10a. magenta/*pale green*	3·00	1·80
D439/441 *Set of 3*			7·25	4·75

1951 (1 Nov). Various portraits as T **67**. Litho. P 11½.

439	**67**	1a. indigo and slate-blue	1·20	90
440	–	2a. sepia and olive	2·50	90
441	–	3a. deep green and pale green	4·00	1·60
442	–	6a. violet and blue	5·25	1·80
443	–	10a. red-brown and orange	12·50	2·20
444	**67**	20a. claret and pale claret	22·00	5·00
445	–	30a. purple-brown and pale green	33·00	6·25
446	–	50a. red-orange and orange	85·00	17·00
439/446 *Set of 8*			£150	32·00

Portraits:—2a., 10a. St. Francis Xavier; 3a., 50a. J. Alvares; 6a., 30a. L. de Camoens.

1951 (1 Nov). T **68** and similar designs. Litho. P 11.

447		1p. ultramarine and greenish blue	49·00	4·00
448		3p. black and violet-blue	£180	31·00
449		5p. orange-brown and orange	£250	34·00
447/449 *Set of 3*			£425	60·00

Designs: Horiz—1p. Sampan. Vert—3p. Junk.

69 Our Lady of Fatima D **70** **71** St. Raphael Hospital

(Litho Litografia Nacional, Oporto, Portugal)

1951 (3 Dec). Termination of Holy Year. P 14.

450	**69**	60a. magenta and pink	75·00	13·50

No. 450 was issued *se-tenant* with a stamp-size label bearing a papal declaration.

MACAO

(Litho Litografia Nacional, Oporto, Portugal)
1952 (15 Mar). POSTAGE DUE. P 14.
D451	D 70	1a. multicoloured	1·00	75
D452		3a. multicoloured	1·30	85
D453		5a. multicoloured	1·80	85
D454		10a. multicoloured	2·50	1·70
D455		30a. multicoloured	6·25	2·50
D456		1p. multicoloured	12·50	5·00
D451/456 Set of 6			23·00	10·50

(Des A. de Sousa. Litho)
1952 (16 June). First Tropical Medicine Congress, Lisbon. P 13½.
451	71	6a. bright lilac and black	15·00	5·50

72 St. Francis Xavier Statue

73 The Virgin

74 Honeysuckle

(Litho Litografia Nacional, Oporto)
1952 (28 Nov). 400th Death Anniv of St. Francis Xavier. T **72** and similar vert designs inscr "1552 1952". P 14.
452		3a. black/cream	7·50	1·50
453		16a. deep brown/buff	23·00	5·00
454		40a. black/blue	34·00	7·50
452/454 Set of 3			60·00	12·50

Designs:—16a. Miraculous Arm of St. Francis; 40a. Tomb of St. Francis.

1953 (28 Apr). Missionary Art Exhibition. Litho. P 13½.
455	73	8a. brown and drab	6·25	1·80
456		10a. indigo and pale brown	25·00	6·25
457		50a. deep green and drab	33·00	8·50
455/457 Set of 3			60·00	15·00

(Photo Courvoisier)
1953 (22 Sept). Indigenous Flowers. T **74** and similar vert designs. P 11.
458		1a. yellow, green and vermilion	1·20	45
459		3a. reddish pur, dp blue-grn & pale yellow	1·20	45
460		5a. rose-red, yellow-green & reddish brown	1·20	45
461		10a. multicoloured	1·20	45
462		16a. yellow, green and yellow-brown	2·50	60
463		30a. rose, sepia and deep green	5·00	1·20
464		39a. multicoloured	6·25	1·60
465		1p. yellow, green and purple	11·00	2·10
466		3p. scarlet, sepia and grey	25·00	3·75
467		5p. yellow, green and carmine-red	43·00	8·00
458/467 Set of 10			90·00	17·00

Flowers:—3a. Myosotis; 5a. Dragon claw; 10a. Nunflower; 16a. Narcissus; 30a. Peach blossom, 39a. Lotus blossom; 1p. Chrysanthemum; 3p. Plum blossom; 5p. Tangerine blossom.

1953–58. CHARITY TAX. As Nos. C415/20 but colours changed and new values. Litho in Macao. No Imprint. No gum. P 11½–12 (1a., 2a.) or 10½–11 (others).
C468	C 48	1a. olive-green and green (1958)	1·60	85
		a. Imperf (pair)	12·50	
C469		2a. purple and grey (1958)	2·50	1·20
		a. Imperf (pair)	12·50	
		b. Imperf vert (horiz pair)	12·50	
C470		10a. blue and pale green (1956)	5·50	2·50
		a. Perf 11½×10½	11·00	
C471		20a. chocolate and yellow	12·50	8·50
C472		50a. carmine and rose	25·00	13·50
		a. Imperf between (horiz pair)	42·00	24·00
C468/472 Set of 5			60·00	20·00

75 Portuguese Stamp of 1853 and Arms of Portuguese Overseas Provinces

76 Father M. de Nobrega and View of São Paulo

(Litho Litografia Maia, Oporto, Portugal)
1954 (9 Mar). Portuguese Stamp Centenary. P 13.
468	75	10a. multicoloured	16·00	3·75

1954 (4 Aug). Fourth Centenary of São Paulo. Litho. P 13½.
469	76	39a. multicoloured	21·00	5·25

77 Map of Macao

78 Exhibition Emblem and Atomic Emblems

(Des J. de Moura. Litho Enschedé)
1956 (10 May). P 13×14.
470	77	1a. multicoloured	1·20	60
471		3a. multicoloured	2·50	85
472		5a. multicoloured	3·75	1·20
473		10a. multicoloured	6·25	1·50
474		30a. multicoloured	9·25	1·80
475		40a. multicoloured	12·50	2·50
476		90a. multicoloured	31·00	4·25
477		1p.50 multicoloured	37·00	5·75
470/477 Set of 8			95·00	17·00

(Des J. de Moura. Litho Litografia Nacional, Oporto, Portugal)
1958 (8 Nov). Brussels International Exhibition. P 14×14½.
478	78	70a. multicoloured	7·50	3·00

79 Cinnamomum camphora

80 Globe girdled by Signs of the Zodiac

(Des J. de Moura. Litho)
1958 (15 Nov). Sixth International Congress of Tropical Medicine. P 13½.
479	79	20a. multicoloured	11·00	5·00

(Des J. de Mouru. Litho)
1960 (25 June). Fifth Death Centenary of Prince Henry the Navigator. P 13×13½.
480	80	2p. multicoloured	15·00	5·00

81 Boeing 707 Airliner over Ermida da Penha

82 Hockey

(Des J. de Moura. Litho Litografia Nacional, Oporto, Portugal)
1960 (11 Dec). AIR. T **81** and similar horiz designs. Multicoloured. P 14½.
481		50a. Praia Grande Bay	4·25	85
482		76a. Type **81**	9·25	2·50
483		3p. Macao	21·00	3·75
484		5p. Mong Ha	27·00	3·75
485		10p. Shore of Praia Grande Bay	43·00	4·25
481/485 Set of 5			95·00	13·50

MACAO

(Litho Imprensa Nacional, Macao)

1961–66. CHARITY TAX. As Nos. C468/71 but redrawn with imprint "LITO. IMP. NAC.–MACAU" at foot. Glazed paper. No gum. P 11.

C486	C **48**	1a. olive-green and pale green...........	2·10	1·80
C487		2a. purple and grey...........................	2·10	1·80
C488		10a. blue and green (1962)................	2·10	1·80
C489		20a. chocolate and yellow (1966).......	2·50	2·10
C486/489 *Set of 4*			8·00	6·75

Nos. C486/9 also differ from Nos. C468/71 in having an accent over the "E" of "ASSISTÊNCIA".

(Des J. de Moura. Photo Litografia Nacional, Oporto, Portugal)

1962 (9 Feb). Sports T **82** and similar diamond-shaped designs. Multicoloured. P 13.

486		10a. Type **82**....................................	3·75	85
487		16a. Wrestling..................................	5·00	2·75
488		20a. Table tennis..............................	7·50	2·30
489		50a. Motor cycle racing....................	6·75	3·50
490		1p.20 Relay running..........................	27·00	6·00
491		2p.50 Badminton..............................	55·00	11·00
486/491 *Set of 6*			95·00	24·00

83 *Anopheles hyrcanus* (mosquito)

84 Bank Building

(Des J. de Moura. Litho)

1962 (7 Apr). Malaria Eradication. P 13½.
492 **83** 40a. multicoloured .... 8·50 3·00

1964 (16 May). Centenary of National Overseas Bank. Litho. P 13½.
493 **84** 20a. multicoloured .... 15·00 3·75

85 I.T.U. Emblem and St. Gabriel

86 Infante Dom Henrique Academy and Visconde de São Januario Hospital

(Litho Litografia Nacional, Oporto, Portugal)

1965 (17 May). Centenary of International Telecommunications Union. P 14½.
494 **85** 10a. multicoloured .... 7·50 2·75

(Des A. Cutileiro. Litho.)

1966 (28 May). 40th Anniv of Portuguese National Revolution. P 12×11½.
495 **86** 10a. multicoloured .... 7·50 2·75

87 Drummer, 1548

88 O. E. Carmo and *Vega* (fast patrol boat)

(Des A. Cutileiro. Litho)

1966 (8 Aug). Portuguese Military Uniforms. T **87** and similar vert designs. Multicoloured. P 13×13½.

496		10a. Type **87**....................................	3·00	60
497		15a. Soldier, 1548............................	5·50	1·20
498		20a. Arquebusier, 1649....................	6·25	1·20
499		40a. Infantry officer, 1783...............	8·50	1·40
500		50a. Infantryman, 1783....................	11·00	2·50
501		60a. Infantryman, 1902....................	25·00	3·00
502		1p. Infantryman, 1903......................	31·00	5·00
503		3p. Infantryman, 1904......................	49·00	9·75
496/503 *Set of 8*			£130	22·00

(Des A. Cutileiro. Litho Litografia Nacional, Oporto, Portugal)

1967 (31 Jan). Centenary of Military Naval Association. T **88** and similar horiz design. Multicoloured. P 13.
504 **88** 10a. Type **88**.................................... 5·00 1·30
505   20a. Silva Junior and *Dom Fernando* (sail frigate)................................... 9·75 2·50

89 Arms of Pope Paul VI, and "Golden Rose"

90 Cabral Monument, Lisbon

(Des J. de Moura. Litho.)

1967 (13 May). 50th Anniv of Fatima Apparitions. P 12½×13.
506 **89** 50a. multicoloured .... 11·00 2·50

(Des J. de Moura. Litho Litografia Nacional, Oporto, Portugal)

1968 (22 Apr). 500th Birth Anniv of Pedro Cabral (explorer). T **90** and similar vert design. Multicoloured. P 14.
507 **90** 20a. Type **90**.................................... 8·50 1·80
508   70a. Cabral statue, Belmonte........... 10·50 3·25

91 Admiral Gago Coutinho with Sextant

92 Church and Convent of Our Lady of the Reliquary, Vidigueira

(Des J. de Moura. Litho Litografia Nacional, Oporto, Portugal)

1969 (17 Feb). Birth Centenary of Admiral Gaga Coutinho. P 14.
509 **91** 20a. multicoloured .... 5·50 2·00

(Des J. de Moura. Litho Litografia Nacional, Oporto, Portugal)

1969 (29 Aug). 500th Birth Anniv of Vasco da Gama (explorer). P 14.
510 **92** 1p. multicoloured .... 16·00 2·50

93 L. A. Rebello da Silva

94 Bishop D. Belchior Carneiro

(Des J. de Moura. Litho Litografia Mala, Oporto, Portugal)

1969 (25 Sept). Centenary of Overseas Administrative Reforms. P 14.
511 **93** 90a. multicoloured .... 9·75 1·60

MACAO

1969 (16 Oct). 400th Anniv of Misericordia Monastery, Macao. Litho. P 13.

| 512 | 94 | 50a. multicoloured | 6·25 | 1·40 |

95 Façade of Mother Church, Golega

96 Marshal Carmona

(Des J. de Moura. Litho Litografia National, Oporto, Portugal)
1969 (1 Dec). 500th Birth Anniv of King Manoel I. P 14.

| 513 | 95 | 30a. multicoloured | 9·75 | 1·50 |

(Des J. de Moura. Litho)
1970 (15 Nov). Birth Centenary of Marshal Carmona. P 14.

| 514 | 96 | 5a. multicoloured | 2·50 | 1·40 |

97 Dragon Mask

(Des J. de Moura. Litho)
1971 (30 Sept). Chinese Carnival Masks. T **97** and similar horiz design. Multicoloured. P 13.

515		5a. Type **97**	2·00	60
		a. Blue ("MACAU") omitted	£275	
		b. Black ("REPÚBLICA PORTUGUE SA") omitted	£275	
		c. Blue ("MACAU") double		£250
516		10a. Lion mask	3·75	1·20

98 Portuguese Traders at the Chinese Imperial Court

99 Hockey

(Des A. Cutileiro. Litho Litografia Maia, Oporto, Portugal)
1972 (25 May). 400th Anniv of Camoens' *The Lusiads* (epic poem). P 13.

| 517 | 98 | 20a. multicoloured | 17·00 | 6·25 |

(Des A. Cutileiro. Litho Litografia Nacional, Oporto, Portugal)
1972 (20 June). Olympic Games, Munich. P 13½×13½.

| 518 | 99 | 50a. multicoloured | 5·50 | 1·40 |

100 Fairey IIID Seaplane *Santa Cruz* arriving at Rio de Janeiro

101 Lyre Emblem and Theatre Façade

(Des A. Cutileiro. Litho Litografia Maia, Oporto, Portugal)
1972 (20 Sept). 50th Anniv of First Flight from Lisbon to Rio de Janeiro. P 13.

| 519 | 100 | 5p. multicoloured | 31·00 | 9·75 |

(Des J. de Moura. Litho)
1972 (25 Dec). Centenary of Pedro V Theatre, Macao. P 13.

| 520 | 101 | 2p. multicoloured | 16·00 | 3·75 |

102 W.M.O. Emblem

103 Visconde de São Januario

(Litho Litografia Maia, Oporto, Portugal)
1973 (15 Dec). Centenary of World Meteorological Organization. P 13.

| 521 | 102 | 20a. multicoloured | 9·75 | 2·50 |

(Des A Cutileiro. Litho Litografia Maia, Oporto, Portugal)
1974 (25 Jan). Centenary of Visconde de São Januario Hospital. T **103** and similar vert design. Multicoloured. P 13.

| 522 | | 15a. Type **103** | 1·40 | 60 |
| 523 | | 60a. Hospital buildings of 1874 and 1974 | 6·25 | 1·40 |

104 Chinnery (self-portrait)

105 Macao–Taipa Bridge

(Litho Litografia Nacional, Oporto, Portugal)
1974 (Sept). Birth Bicentenary of George Chinnery (artist). P 14.

| 524 | 104 | 30a. multicoloured | 6·25 | 2·20 |

(Litho Litografia Nacional, Oporto, Portugal)
1974 (Oct). Inauguration of Macao–Taipa Bridge. T **105** and similar horiz design. Multicoloured. P 14×13½.

| 525 | | 20a. Type **105** | 2·50 | 1·00 |
| 526 | | 2p.20 View of Bridge from below | 22·00 | 3·00 |

106 Man waving Banner

107 Pou Chai Pagoda

1975. First Anniv of Portuguese Revolution. Litho. P 12.

| 527 | 106 | 10a. multicoloured | 4·00 | 3·50 |
| 528 | | 1p. multicoloured | 20·00 | 7·50 |

1976 (30 Jan). Pagodas. T **107** and similar square design. Multicoloured. Litho. P 13½.

| 529 | | 10p. Type **107** | 21·00 | 7·50 |
| 530 | | 20p. Tin Hau Pagoda | 41·00 | 9·75 |

A 1p. stamp depicting Macao Cathedral and commemorating the fourth centenary of Macao Diocese was prepared for issue in 1976 but was not placed on sale in Macao. Some copies were however sold from Lisbon.

MACAO

108 Symbolic Figure

(Des A. Marcelino. Litho)

1977 (Mar). Legislative Assembly. P 13½.
531	**108**	5a. new blue, deep slate-blue and black	12·50	6·25
532		2p. orange-brown and black	£180	12·50
533		5p. olive-yellow, olive-green and black	60·00	15·00
531/533 Set of 3			£225	30·00

(C **109**)   (**110**)

1978–79. CHARITY TAX. Higher values (used fiscally) as Nos. C468/72 surch with Type C **109** for postage. No gum. P 11×10½ (C534), 10½×12 (C535) or 12 (C536).
C534	C **48**	20a. on 1p. dull yellow-green and	3·75	2·00
		a. Imperf between (vert pair)		
C535		20a. on 3p. black and brown-rose	3·50	1·50
C536		20a. on 5p. brown and dull lemon		

1979 (20 June)–80. Nos. 462, 464, 469, 523, 482 and 526 surch as T **110** or with similar types.
536		10a. on 16a. yellow, green & yellow-brown (6.8.79)	9·75	5·50
537		30a. on 39a. multicoloured (No. 464) (6.8.79)	10·50	5·50
538		30a. on 39a. multicoloured (No. 469)	50·00	25·00
539		30a. on 60a. multicoloured (1980)	7·50	6·25
540		70a. on 76a. multicoloured (3.8.79)	39·00	9·75
541		2p. on 2p.20 multicoloured (29.9.79)	11·00	8·00
536/541 Set of 6			£110	55·00

On Nos. 536 and 538 the new value is printed on top of the old.

 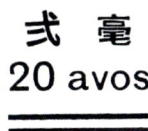

111 Camões and Macao Harbour   (C **112**)

(Des Kam Cheongleng. Litho Litografia Maia, Oporto, Portugal)

1981 (10 June). 400th Death Anniv (1980) of Camoes (Portuguese poet). P 13½.
542	**111**	10a. multicoloured	1·50	1·20
543		30a. multicoloured	2·75	2·50
544		1p. multicoloured	6·75	3·75
545		3p. multicoloured	9·75	5·00
542/545 Set of 4			19·00	11·00

10a., 30a. and 1p. stamps with design as Type **111** but additionally inscr "PORTUGAL" were prepared but not issued.

1981 (26 July). CHARITY TAX. No. C487 surch with Type C **112**.
C546	C **48**	20a. on 2a. purple and grey	3·00	2·50

113 Buddha and Macao Cathedral   (C **114**)

(Des A. da Conceição. Litho)

1981 (7 Sept). Transcultural Psychiatry Symposium. P 13½.
547	**113**	15a. multicoloured	60	50
548		40a. multicoloured	1·00	55
549		50a. multicoloured	1·20	60
550		60a. multicoloured	2·00	75
551		1p. multicoloured	3·75	1·00
552		2p.20 multicoloured	9·75	2·00
547/552 Set of 6			16·00	4·75

1981 (16 Nov). CHARITY TAX. No. C418 surch with Type C **114**.
C553	C **48**	10a. on 15a. orange and pale orange	3·00	2·50
		a. Surch inverted		

115 Health Services Building   **116** Heng-Ho (Moon goddess)

(Des A. da Conceição. Litho Litografia Nacional, Oporto (10, 80a., 1p.50, 2p.50, 7p.50), Litografia Maia. Oporto (20, 60, 90a., 3,15p.), The Mint, Lisbon (others))

1982 (10 June)–**84**. Buildings. T **115** and similar horiz designs. P 12×12½ (30, 40a., 1, 2, 10p.), 13 (10, 80a., 1p.50, 2p.50, 7p.50) or 13½ (others).
554		10a. grey, deep ultramarine and yellow (12.5.83)	50	35
555		20a. grey-black, bright emerald and light blue-green (18.5.84)	60	35
556		30a. deep green, greenish grey and stone	60	35
557		40a. yellow, bright yellow-green and yellow-green	75	35
558		60a. yellow-orange, chocolate and pale grey-brown (18.5.84)	60	35
559		80a. pink, brown-olive and pale grey brown (12.5.83)	1·50	50
560		90a. light purple, grey-blue and rose carmine (18.5.84)	85	60
561		1p. multicoloured	1·60	60
562		1p.50 yellow, red-brown and greenish grey (12.5.83)	5·00	2·00
563		2p. brown-purple, ultramarine and cobalt	3·00	1·40
564		2p.50 dull ultramarine, pale rose and slate-blue (12.5.83)	2·75	1·80
565		3p. yellow, deep bluish green and yellow olive (18.5.84)	2·50	1·00
566		7p.50 rose-lilac, ultramarine and scarlet (12.5.83)	7·50	3·00
567		10p. olive-grey, pale lilac and pale mauve	11·00	5·00
568		15p. orange-yellow, deep brown and vermilion (18.5.84)	11·00	6·25
554/568 Set of 15			45·00	22·00

Designs:—10a. Social Welfare Institute; 20a. Holy House of Mercy; 40a. Guia lighthouse; 60a. St. Lawrence's Church; 80a. St. Joseph's Seminary, 90a. Pedro V Theatre; 1p. Cerco city gate; 1p.50, St. Domenico's Church; 2p. Luis de Camões Museum; 2p.50, Ruins of St. Paul's Church; 3p. Palace of St. Sancha (Governor's residence); 7p.50, Senate House; 10p. Schools Welfare Service building; 15p. Barracks of the Moors (headquarters of Port Captaincy and Maritime Police).

(Des A. da Conceição. Litho)

1982 (1 Oct). Autumn Festival. T **116** and similar horiz designs. Multicoloured. P 12.
569		40a. Type **116**	2·50	1·20
570		1p. Decorated gourds	7·50	2·50
571		2p. Paper lantern	9·75	5·00
572		5p. Warrior riding lion	20·00	7·50
569/572 Set of 4			36·00	14·50

117 Aerial View of Macao, Taipa and Colôane Islands   **118** "Switchboard Operators" (Lou Sok Man)

(Des J. P. Roque, Litho Litografia Maia, Oporto, Portugal)

1982 (1 Dec). Macao's Geographical Situation. T **117** and similar vert design. Multicoloured. P 13.
573		50a. Type **117**	12·50	2·00
574		3p. Map of South China	25·00	8·50

145

MACAO

(Litho Litografia Nacional, Oporto, Portugal)
1983 (16 Feb). World Communications Year. T **118** and similar horiz designs showing children's drawings. Multicoloured. P 13½.
575	60a. Type **118**	2·30	1·10
576	3p. Postman and pillar box (Lai Sok Pek)	5·25	3·50
577	6p. Globe with methods of communications (Los Chak Keong)	9·75	4·50
575/577 Set of 3		16·00	8·25

119 *Asclepias curassavica*

120 Galleon and Map of Macao (left)

(Des Ng Wai Kin. Litho Litografia Maia, Oporto, Portugal)
1983 (14 July). Medicinal Plants. T **119** and similar horiz designs. Multicoloured. P 13.
578	20a. Type **119**	1·10	80
579	40a. *Acanthus ilicifolius*	2·30	80
580	60a. *Melastoma sanguineum*	3·50	1·00
581	70a. Indian lotus (*Nelumbo nucifera*)	4·50	1·40
582	1p.50 *Bombax malabaricum*	5·75	2·30
583	2p.50 *Hibiscus mutabilis*	10·50	5·25
578/583 Set of 6		25·00	10·50
MS584 143×90 mm. Nos. 578/83 (sold at 6p.50)		£170	£140

(Des A. Magalhães. Litho Litografia Nacional, Oporto, Portugal)
1983 (15 Nov). 16th Century Portuguese Discoveries. T **120** and similar vert design. Multicoloured. P 13½×14.
585	4p. Type **120**	8·00	4·50
	a. Horiz pair. Nos. 585/6	17·00	9·25
586	4p. Galleon. astrolabe and map of Macao (right)	8·00	4·50

Nos. 585/6 were printed together in *se-tenant* pairs within the sheet, each pair forming a composite design.

121 Rat

122 Detail of First Macao Stamp, 1884

(Des J. Cândido. Litho Litografia Maia, Oporto, Portugal)
1984 (25 Jan). New Year. Year of the Rat. P 13½.
587	**121** 60a. multicoloured	8·00	5·75
	a. Imperf×p 13½. Booklets	8·00	5·75
	ab. Booklet pane. No. 587a×5	41·00	

See also No. **MS**917.

(Des J. Rocha. Litho Litografia Maia, Oporto, Portugal)
1984 (1 Mar). Centenary of Macao Stamps. P 12½.
588	**122** 40a. black and orange-red	2·30	55
589	3p. black and grey-brown	4·50	1·80
590	5p. black and dull red-brown	10·50	3·75
588/590 Set of 3		16·00	5·50
MS591 116×139 mm. Nos. 588/90		55·00	55·00

123 Jay (*Garrulus glandarius*)

124 Hok Lou T'eng

(Des L. Barros. Litho Litografia Maia, Oporto, Portugal)
1984 (21 Sept). Ausipex 84 International Stamp Exhibition, Melbourne. Birds. T **123** and similar horiz designs. Multicoloured. P 13½.
592	30a. White-throated kingfisher (*Halcyon smyrnensis*) and River kingfisher (*Alcedo atthis*)	1·70	70
593	40a. Type **123**	1·70	70
594	50a. Japanese white-eye (*Zosterops japonica*)	2·30	70
595	70a. Hoopoe (*Upupa epops*)	4·50	4·00
596	2p.50 Pekin robin (*Leiothrix lutea*)	10·50	2·30
597	6p. Mallard (*Anas platyrhynchos*)	11·50	4·00
592/597 Set of 6		29·00	8·25

(Des Ng Wai Kin. Litho Litografia Maia, Oporto, Portugal)
1984 (22 Oct). Philakorea 84 International Stamp Exhibition, Seoul. Local Fishing Boats. T **124** and similar horiz designs. Multicoloured. P 13.
598	20a. Type **124**	1·10	55
599	60a. Tai T'ong	2·30	1·10
600	2p. Tai Mei Chai	5·75	1·80
601	5p. Ch'at Pong T'o	11·50	4·00
598/601 Set of 4		19·00	7·25

125 Ox and Moon

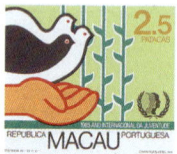
126 Open Hand and Stylized Doves

(Des J. Cândido. Litho Litografia Maia, Oporto, Portugal)
1985 (13 Feb). New Year. Year of the Ox. P 13½.
602	**125** 1p. multicoloured	10·50	3·50
	a. Imperf×p 13½. Booklets	7·00	4·00
	ab. Booklet pane. No. 602a×5	36·00	

See also No. **MS**917.

(Des Chan Yuen Peng. Litho Litografia Maia, Oporto, Portugal)
1985 (19 Apr). International Youth Year. T **126** and similar horiz design. Multicoloured. P 13½.
603	2p.50 Type **126**	6·25	80
604	3p. Open hands and plants	8·50	2·75

127 Pres. Eanes

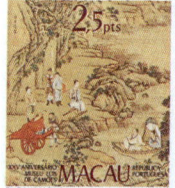
128 Riverside Scene

(Des J. Cândido. Litho Litografia Maia, Oporto, Portugal)
1985 (27 May). Visit of Pres. Ramalho Eanes of Portugal. P 13½.
605	**127** 1p.50 multicoloured	5·25	2·30

(Des A. da Conceição. Litho Litografia Maia, Oporto, Portugal)
1985 (27 June). 25th Anniv of Luís de Camões Museum. T **128** and similar vert designs showing paintings by Cheng Chi Yun. Multicoloured. P 13½.
606	2p.50 Type **128**	8·50	2·30
	a. Strip of 4. Nos. 606/9	35·00	
607	2p.50 Man on seat and boy filling jar from river	8·50	2·30
608	2p.50 Playing harp in summerhouse	8·50	2·30
609	2p.50 Three men by river	8·50	2·30
606/609 Set of 4		31·00	8·25

Nos. 606/9 were issued together in *se-tenant* strips of four stamps within the sheet.

MACAO

129 Euploea midamus   **130** Tou (sailing barge)

(Des J. Rocha. Litho Litografia Maia, Oporto, Portugal)

1985 (27 Sept). World Tourism Day. Butterflies. T **129** and similar vert designs. Multicoloured. P 13½.

610	30a. Type **129**	2·30	55
611	50a. Hebomoia glaucippe	2·30	55
612	70a. Lethe confusa	3·75	70
613	2p. Heliophorus epicles	4·75	1·10
614	4p. Euthalia phemius	9·75	1·80
615	7p.50 Troides helena	12·50	4·75
610/615 Set of 6		32·00	8·50
MS616 95×120 mm. Nos. 610/15		£160	£110

(Des Ng Wai Kin. Litho Litografia Nacional, Oporto, Portugal)

1985 (25 Oct). Italia '85 International Stamp Exhibition, Rome. Cargo Boats. T **130** and similar horiz designs. Multicoloured. P 14.

617	50a. Type **130**	1·10	35
618	70a. Veng Seng Lei (motor junk)	3·50	45
619	1p. Tong Heng Long No. 2 (motor junk)	5·75	1·10
620	6p. Fong Vong San (container ship)	9·25	5·25
617/620 Set of 4		18·00	6·50

131 Tiger and Moon   **132** View of Macao

(Des J. Cândido. Litho Litografia Maia, Oporto, Portugal)

1986 (3 Feb). New Year. Year of the Tiger. P 13½.

621	**131** 1p.50 multicoloured	8·50	1·40
	a. Imperf×p 13½. Booklets	7·00	2·30
	ab. Booklet pane. No. 621a×5	31·00	

See also No. **MS**917.

(Des A. da Conceição. Litho Litografia Maia, Oporto, Portugal)

1986 (10 Apr). Macao, "the Past is still Present". P 13½.
622	**132** 2p.20 multicoloured	7·00	2·75

133 Suo-na   **134** Flying Albatros (Hydrofoil)

(Des J. Rocha. Litho Litografia Maia, Oporto, Portugal)

1986 (22 May). Ameripex '86 International Stamp Exhibition, Chicago. Musical Instruments. T **133** and similar vert designs. Multicoloured. P 13½.

623	20a. Type **133**	4·00	1·40
624	50a. Sheng (pipes)	5·00	1·60
625	60a. Er-hu (bowed instrument)	7·00	2·00
626	70a. Ruan (string instrument)	8·25	2·20
627	5p. Cheng (harp)	26·00	3·50
628	8p. Pi-pa (lute)	30·00	5·75
623/628 Set of 6		70·00	15·00
MS629 119×111 mm. Nos. 623/8		£200	£140

(Des Ng Wai Kin. Litho Litografia Maia, Oporto, Portugal)

1988 (28 Aug). Stockholmia 86 International Stamp Exhibition. Passenger Ferries. T **134** and similar horiz designs. Multicoloured. P 13.

630	10a. Type **134**	55	55
631	40a. Tejo (hovercraft)	5·25	1·10
632	3p. Tercera (jetfoil)	5·75	1·80
633	7p.50 Cheung Kong (high speed ferry)	11·50	3·75
630/633 Set of 4		21·00	6·50

135 Taipa Fortress   **136** Sun Yat-sen

(Des L. Duran. Litho Litografia Maia, Oporto, Portugal)

1966 (3 Oct). Tenth Anniv of Security Forces. Fortresses. T **135** and similar vert designs. Multicoloured. P 12½.

634	2p. Type **135**	11·50	5·75
	a. Horiz strip of 4. Nos. 634/7	75·00	
635	2p. St. Paul on the Mount	11·50	5·75
636	2p. St. Francis	11·50	5·75
637	2p. Guia	11·50	5·75
634/637 Set of 4		41·00	21·00

Nos. 634/7 were issued together in se-tenant strips and blocks of four stamps within the sheet, each horizontal row forming a composite design.

(Des Ng Wai Kin. Litho Litografia Maia, Oporto, Portugal)

1986 (12 Nov). 120th Birth Anniv of Dr. Sun Yat-sen. T **136** and similar vert design. Multicoloured. P 12½.

638	70a. Type **136**	5·75	2·75
MS639 95×70 mm. 1p.30. Dr. Sun Yat-sen (different)		70·00	50·00

137 Hare and Moon   **138** Wá Tó (physician)

(Des J. Cândido. Litho Litografia Maia, Oporto, Portugal)

1987 (21 Jan). New Year. Year of the Hare. P 13½.

640	**137** 1p.50 multicoloured	8·00	1·70
	a. Imperf×p 13½. Booklets	7·75	3·25
	ab. Booklet pane. No. 640a×5	40·00	

See also No. **MS**917.

(Des A. da Conceição, jun. Litho Litographia Maia, Oporto, Portugal)

1987 (10 Apr). Shek Wan Ceramics. T **138** and similar square designs. Multicoloured. P 13½.

641	2p.20 Type **138**	9·25	4·50
	a. Strip of 4. Nos 641/4	38·00	
642	2p.20 Choi San, God of Fortune	9·25	4·50
643	2p.20 Yi, Sun God	9·25	4·50
644	2p.20 Chung Kuei, Keeper of Demons	9·25	4·50
641/644 Set of 4		33·00	16·00

Nos. 641/4 were issued together in se-tenant strips of four stamps within the sheet.

139 Boats   **140** Circular Fan

147

MACAO

(Des Ng Wai Kin. Litho Litografia Maia, Oporto, Portugal)

1987 (29 May). Dragon Boat Festival. T **139** and similar horiz design. Multicoloured. P 13½.
645	50a. Type **139**	4·50	1·10
646	5p. Dragon boat prow	10·50	3·75

(Des H. Estorninho. Litho Litografia Maia. Oporto, Portugal)

1987 (29 July). Fans. T **140** and similar vert designs. Multi-coloured. P 12½.
647	30a. Type **140**	5·75	1·80
648	70a. Folding fan with tree design	11·50	2·75
649	1p. Square-shaped fan with peacock design	29·00	3·75
650	6p. Heart-shaped fan with painting of woman and tree	32·00	9·75
647/650	Set of 4	70·00	16·00
MS651	113×139 mm. Nos. 647/50	£275	£140

141 Fantan

142 Goods Hand-cart

(Des L. Duran. Litho Litografia Maia, Oporto, Portugal)

1987 (30 Sept). Casino Games. T **141** and similar vert designs. Multicoloured. P 13½.
652	20a. Type **141**	9·25	4·25
653	40a. Cussec	10·50	4·75
654	4p. Baccarat	14·00	5·25
655	7p. Roulette	17·00	5·75
652/655	Set of 4	46·00	18·00

(Des Ng Wai Kin. Litho Litografia Maia, Oporto, Portugal)

1987 (18 Nov). Traditional Vehicles. T **142** and similar horiz designs. Multicoloured. P 13½.
656	10a. Type **142**	1·10	1·10
657	70a. Open sedan chair	3·50	1·70
658	90a. Rickshaw	6·25	2·30
659	10p. Cycle rickshaw	17·00	4·00
656/659	Set of 4	25·00	8·25
MS660	90×65 mm. 7p.50, Covered sedan chair	55·00	29·00

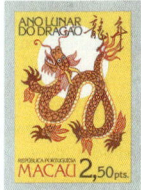

143 Dragon and Moon

144 West European Hedgehog (*Erinaceus europaeus*)

(Des J. Cândido. Litho Litografia Maia, Oporto, Portugal)

1988 (10 Feb). New Year. Year of the Dragon. P 13½.
661	**143** 2p.50 multicoloured	8·00	4·50
	a. Imperf×p 13½. Booklets	7·50	5·75
	ab. Booklet pane. No. 661a×5	39·00	

See also No. **MS**917.

(Des L. Barros. Litho Litografia Maia, Oporto, Portugal)

1988 (14 Apr). Protected Mammals. T **144** and similar horiz designs. Multicoloured. P 12½×12.
662	3p. Type **144** (wrongly inscr "Erinacens")	8·00	2·30
	a. Strip or block of 4. Nos. 662/5	33·00	
663	3p. Eurasian badger (*Meles meles*)	8·00	2·30
664	3p. European otter (*Lutra lutra*)	8·00	2·30
665	3p. Chinese pangolin (*Manis pentadactyla*)	8·00	2·30
662/665	Set of 4	29·00	8·25

Nos. 662/5 were issued together in *se-tenant* strips and blocks of four stamps within the sheet.

145 Breastfeeding   **146** Bicycles

(Des Ung Wai Meng. Litho Litografia Maia, Oporto, Portugal)

1988 (1 June). 40th Anniv of World Health Organization. T **145** and similar horiz designs. Multicoloured. P 13½.
666	60a. Type **145**	3·50	90
667	80a. Vaccinating child	4·50	1·10
668	2p.40 Donating blood	9·25	3·50
666/668	Set of 3	16·00	5·00

(Des Ng Wai Kin. Litho Litografia Maia, Oporto, Portugal)

1988 (15 July). Transport. T **146** and similar horiz designs. Multicoloured. P 13½.
669	20a. Type **146**	1·10	55
670	50a. Lambretta and Vespa	2·30	1·10
671	3p.30 Rover tourer (1907)	7·00	1·70
672	5p. Renault delivery truck (1912)	9·25	6·25
669/672	Set of 4	18·00	6·25
MS673	68×57 mm. 7p.50, Packard touring sedan	70·00	34·00

 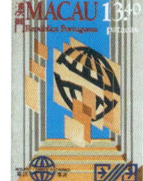

147 Hurdling   **148** Intelpost (electronic mail)

(Des L. Duran. Litho Litografia Maia, Oporto, Portugal)

1988 (19 Sept). Olympic Games, Seoul. T **147** and similar horiz designs. Multicoloured. P 13½.
674	40a. Type **147**	1·60	55
675	60a. Basketball	2·40	75
676	1p. Football	4·00	1·70
677	8p. Table tennis	8·00	3·50
674/677	Set of 4	14·50	5·75
MS678	112×140 mm. Nos. 673/6; 5p. Taek-wondo	55·00	40·00

(Des J. M. Cardoso. Litho Litografia Nacional, Oporto, Portugal)

1988 (10 Oct). New Postal Services. T **148** and similar vert design. Multicoloured. P 14.
679	13p. Type **148**	9·25	2·75
680	40p. Express Mail Service (EMS)	12·00	8·00

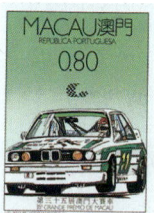 

149 B.M.W. 3 series Saloon Racing Car   **150** Snake and Moon

(Des V. Marreiros. Litho Litografia Maia, Oporto, Portugal)

1988 (24 Nov). 35th Macao Grand Prix. T **149** and similar vert designs. Multicoloured. P 12½.
681	80a. Type **149**	1·70	55
682	2p.80 Racing motorcycle	5·75	1·40
683	7p. Formula 3 racing car	12·50	4·00
681/683	Set of 3	18·00	5·25
MS684	115×139 mm. Nos. 681/3	75·00	46·00

(Des J. Cândido. Litho Litografia Maia, Oporto, Portugal)

1989 (20 Jan). New Year. Year of the Snake. P 13½.
685	**150** 3p. multicoloured	9·75	2·75
	a. Imperf×p 13½. Booklets	8·50	3·00
	ab. Booklet pane. No. 685a×5	44·00	

See also No. **MS**917.

MACAO

151 Water Carrier   **152** White Building

(Des E. Cervantes. Litho Litografia Maia, Oporto, Portugal)

1989 (1 Mar). Traditional Occupations (1st series). T **151** and similar vert designs. Multicoloured. P 12×12½.
686	50a. Type **151**	1·10	35
687	1p. Tan-kyá (boat) woman	2·30	55
688	4p. Tin-tin man (pedlar)	3·50	1·90
689	5p. Tao-fu-fá (soya bean cheese) vendor	5·75	2·50
686/689 Set of 4		11·50	4·75

See also Nos. 714/17 and 743/6.

(Litho Litografia Maia, Oporto, Portugal)

1989 (10 Apr). Paintings by George Vitalievich Smirnoff in Luís Camões Museum. T **152** and similar horiz designs. Multicoloured. P 12½×12.
690	2p. Type **152**	2·75	1·10
	a. Strip or block of 4. Nos. 690/3	11·50	
691	2p. Building with railings	2·75	1·10
692	2p. Street scene	2·75	1·10
693	2p. White thatched cottage	2·75	1·10
690/693 Set of 4		10·00	4·00

Nos. 690/3 were issued together in *se-tenant* strips and blocks of four stamps within the sheet.

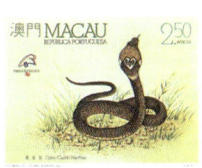 

153 Common Cobra (*Naja naja*)   **154** Talú

(Des L. Barros. Litho Litografia Maia, Oporto, Portugal)

1989 (7 July). Philexfrance '89 International Stamp Exhibition, Paris. Snakes of Macao. T **153** and similar horiz designs. Multicoloured. P 12½×12.
694	2p.50 Type **153**	3·50	1·50
	a. Strip or block of 4. Nos. 694/7	14·50	
695	2p.50 Banded krait (*Bungarus fasciatus*)	3·50	1·50
696	2p.50 Bamboo pit viper (*Trimeresurus albolabris*)	3·50	1·50
697	2p.50 Rat snake (*Elaphe radiata*)	3·50	1·50
694/697 Set of 4		12·50	5·50

Nos. 694/7 were issued together in *se-tenant* strips and blocks of four stamps within the sheet.

(Des V. Marreiros. Litho Litografia Maia, Oporto, Portugal)

1989 (31 July). Traditional Games. T **154** and similar vert designs. Multicoloured. P 13½.
698	10a. Type **154**	1·10	70
699	60a. Triol (marbles)	2·75	85
700	3p.30 Chiquia (shuttlecock)	5·75	1·90
701	5p. Chinese chequers	7·00	2·75
698/701 Set of 4		15·00	5·50

155 Piaggio P-136L Flying Boat   **156** Malacca

(Des Ng Wai Kin. Litho Litografia Maia, Oporto, Portugal)

1989 (9 Oct). Aircraft. T **155** and similar square designs. Multicoloured. P 13½.
702	50a. Type **155**	80	45
703	70a. Martin M-130 flying boat	1·40	55
704	2p.80 Fairey IIID seaplane	1·80	1·10
705	4p. Hawker Osprey seaplane	3·50	1·80
702/705 Set of 4		6·75	3·50
MS706 105×82 mm. 7p.50, de Havilland DH.80A Puss Moth CR-GAA		34·00	17·00

(Des L. Duran. Litho Litografia Maia, Oporto, Portugal)

1989 (17 Nov). World Stamp Expo '89 International Stamp Exhibition, Washington D.C. Portuguese Presence in the Far East. T **156** and similar vert designs. Multicoloured. P 12½.
707	40a. Type **156**	55	35
708	70a. Thailand	1·10	45
709	90a. India	1·70	70
710	2p.50 Japan	3·50	90
711	7p.50 China	5·75	2·50
707/711 Set of 4		11·50	4·50
MS712 144×130 mm. Nos. 707/11; 3p. Macao		46·00	29·00

157 Horse and Moon   **158** Penny Black and Sir Rowland Hill (postal reformer)

(Des J. Cândido. Litho Litografia Maia, Oporto, Portugal)

1990 (19 Jan). New Year. Year of the Horse. P 13½.
713	**157** 4p. multicoloured	5·25	1·80
	a. Imperf×p 13½. Booklets	5·50	2·00
	ab. Booklet pane. No. 713a×5	29·00	

See also No. **MS**917.

(Des E. Cervantes. Litho Litografia Maia, Oporto, Portugal)

1990 (1 Mar). Traditional Occupations (2nd series). Vert designs as T **151**. Multicoloured. P 12×12½.
714	30a. Long-chau singer	1·30	80
715	70a. Cobbler	2·50	1·30
716	1p.50 Travelling penman	3·75	1·70
717	7p.50 Fisherman with wide nets	11·00	3·50
714/717 Set of 4		17·00	6·50

(Des L. Duran. Litho)

1990 (3 May). 150th Anniv of the Penny Black. Sheet 91×130 mm. P 12.
MS718 **158** 10p. multicoloured		29·00	17·00

159 Long-finned Grouper (*Epinephelus megachir*)   **160** Porcelain

(Des L. Barros. Litho Litografia Maia, Oporto, Portugal)

1990 (8 June). Fish. T **159** and similar horiz designs. Multicoloured. P 12½×12.
719	2p.40 Type **159**	2·50	1·30
	a. Strip or block of 4. Nos. 719/22	10·50	
720	2p.40 Malabar blood snapper (*Lutianus malabaricus*)	2·50	1·30
721	2p.40 Spotted snakehead (*Ophiocephalus maculatus*)	2·50	1·30
722	2p.40 Paradise fish (*Macropodus opercularis*)	2·50	1·30
719/722 Set of 4		9·00	4·75

Nos. 719/22 were issued together in *se-tenant* strips and blocks of four stamps within the sheet.

MACAO

(Des Chan leng Hin. Litho Litografia Maia, Oporto, Portugal)

1990 (24 Aug). New Zealand 1990 International Stamp Exhibition, Auckland. Industrial Diversification. T **160** and similar horiz designs. Multicoloured. P 12½.

723	3p. Type **160**	2·75	1·40
	a. Strip or block of 4. Nos. 723/6	11·50	
724	3p. Furniture	2·75	1·40
725	3p. Toys	2·75	1·40
726	3p. Artificial flowers	2·75	1·40
723/726 Set of 4		10·00	5·00
MS727 131×95 mm. Nos. 723/6		39·00	17·00

Nos. 723/6 were issued together in *se-tenant* strips and blocks of four stamps within the sheet.

161 Cycling   **162** Rose by Lazaro Luís

(Des Ng Wai Kin. Litho Litografia Nacional, Oporto, Portugal)

1990 (22 Sept). 11th Asian Games, Peking. T **161** and similar horiz designs. Multicoloured. P 13½.

728	80a. Type **161**	1·10	35
729	1p. Swimming	1·40	55
730	3p. Judo	4·00	1·40
731	4p.20 Shooting	6·25	2·30
728/731 Set of 4		11·50	4·25
MS732 95×140 mm. Nos. 728/31; 6p. Athlete with bamboo pole		40·00	34·00

(Des L. Duran. Litho Litografia Maia, Oporto, Portugal)

1990 (9 Oct). Compass Roses. T **162** and similar vert designs showing roses from ancient charts by cartographer named. Multicoloured. P 13½.

733	50a. Type **162**	1·30	55
734	1p. Diogo Homem	2·40	70
735	3p.50 Diogo Homem (different)	4·25	1·70
736	6p.50 Fernão Vaz Dourado	8·50	2·30
733/736 Set of 4		15·00	4·75
MS737 107×100 mm. 5p. Luiz Teixeira (29×39 mm)		47·00	29·00

163 Cricket Fight   **164** Goat and Moon

(Des Kwok Se. Litho Litografia Nacional, Oporto, Portugal)

1990 (15 Nov). Betting on Animals. T **163** and similar horiz designs. Multicoloured. P 14.

738	20a. Type **163**	1·10	45
739	80a. Hwamei fight	2·75	90
740	1p. Greyhound racing	3·50	1·40
741	10p. Horse racing	10·00	2·50
738/741 Set of 4		16·00	4·75

(Des J. Cândido. Litho Litografia Maia, Oporto, Portugal)

1991 (8 Feb). New Year. Year of the Goat. P 13½.

742	**164** 4p.50 multicoloured	5·25	1·30
	a. Imperf×13½. Booklets	5·25	1·70
	ab. Booklet pane. No. 742a×5	27·00	

See also No. **MS**917.

(Des E. Cervantes. Litho Litografia Nacional, Oporto, Portugal)

1991 (1 Mar). Traditional Occupations (3rd series). Vert designs as T **151**. Multicoloured. P 14.

743	80a. Knife-grinder	1·10	55
744	1p.70 Flour-puppets vendor	2·30	70
745	3p.50 Street barber	5·25	1·40
746	4p.20 Fortune-teller	7·50	2·50
743/746 Set of 4		14·50	4·75

165 True Harp (*Harpa harpa*)   **166** Character and Backcloth

(Des L. Barros. Litho Litografia Nacional, Oporto, Portugal)

1991 (18 Apr). Sea Shells. T **165** and similar horiz designs. Multicoloured. P 14.

747	3p. Type **165**	3·50	1·70
	a. Strip or block of 4. Nos. 747/50	14·50	
748	3p. Oil-lamp tun (*Tonna zonata*)	3·50	1·70
749	3p. Bramble murex (*Murex tribulus*) (wrongly inscr "pecten")	3·50	1·70
750	3p. Rose-branch murex (wrongly inscr "Chicoreus rosarius")	3·50	1·70
747/750 Set of 4		12·50	6·00

Nos. 747/50 were issued together in *se-tenant* strips and blocks of four stamps within the sheet.

(Des No Wai Kin. Litho Litografia Nacional, Oporto, Portugal)

1991 (5 June). Chinese Opera. T **166** and similar vert designs showing different backcloths and costumes. Multicoloured. P 13½.

751	60a. multicoloured	1·80	45
752	80a. multicoloured	2·75	55
753	1p. multicoloured	4·50	1·10
754	10p. multicoloured	13·00	2·75
751/754 Set of 4		20·00	4·25

 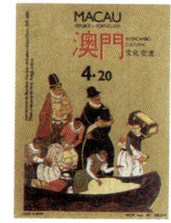

167 *Delonix regia* and Lou Lim loc Garden   **168** Portuguese Traders unloading Boats

(Des Chan leng Hin. Litho Litografia Nacional, Oporto, Portugal)

1991 (9 Oct). Flowers and Gardens (1st series). T **167** and similar horiz designs Multicoloured. P 13½.

755	1p.70 Type **167**	1·80	70
756	3p. *Ipomoea cairica* and São Francisco Garden	2·75	1·40
757	3p.50 *Jasminum mesyi* and Sun Yat Son Park	4·50	2·00
758	4p.20 *Bauhinia variegata* and Seac Pai Van Park	5·50	2·75
755/758 Set of 4		13·00	6·25
MS759 95×137 mm. Nos. 755/8		55·00	29·00

See also Nos. 815/**MS**819.

(Des L. Duran. Litho)

1991 (16 Nov). Cultural Exchange. Nambam Paintings attr. Kano Domi. T **168** and similar vert design. Multicoloured. P 12.

760	4p.20 Type **168**	2·75	1·40
761	4p.20 Portuguese traders displaying goods to buyers	2·75	1·40
MS762 107×74 mm. Nos. 760/1		37·00	23·00

169 Firework Display   **170** Concertina Door

150

MACAO

(Des Ng Wai Kin. Litho Litografia Nacional, Oporto, Portugal)
1991 (29 Nov). Christmas. T **169** and similar square designs. Multicoloured. P 14½.
763	1p.70 Type **169**		1·40	55
764	3p. Father Christmas		2·10	80
765	3p.50 Man dancing		3·50	1·30
766	4p.20 January 1st celebrations		7·00	2·30
763/766 Set of 4			12·50	4·50

(Des Wong Vai Kin. Litho Litografia Nacional, Oporto, Portugal)
1992 (1 Mar). Doors and Windows. T **170** and similar horiz designs. Multicoloured. P 14.
767	1p.70 Type **170**		1·40	80
768	3p. Window with four shutters		2·75	1·50
769	3p.50 Window with two shutters		4·00	2·10
770	4p.20 Louvred door		5·75	2·75
767/770 Set of 4			12·50	6·50

171 Monkey and Moon   **172** T'it Kuai Lei

(Des J. Cândido. Litho Litografia Maia, Oporto, Portugal)
1992 (23 Mar). New Year. Year of the Monkey. P 13½.
771	**171**	4p.50 multicoloured	5·00	2·50
		a. Imperf×p 13½. Booklets	5·00	2·50
		ab. Booklet pane. No. 771a×5	26·00	

See also No. **MS**917.

(Des Lio Man Cheong. Litho Litografia Nacional, Oporto, Portugal)
1992 (3 Apr). Gods of Chinese Mythology (1st series). T **172** and similar horiz designs. Multicoloured. P 14.
772	3p.50 (1) Type **172**		8·00	3·50
	a. Strip or block of 4. Nos. 772/5		33·00	
773	3p.50 (2) Chong Lei Kun		8·00	3·50
774	3p.50 (3) Cheong Kuo Lou on donkey		8·00	3·50
775	3p.50 (4) Lôi Tong Pan		8·00	3·50
772/775 Set of 4			29·00	12·50

The numbers in brackets refer to the final figure in the bottom right-hand corner of the stamp. The issue number is "S 60".
Nos. 772/5 were issued together in *se-tenant* strips and blocks of four stamps within the sheet.
See also Nos. 796/9.

173 Lion Dance   **174** High Jumping

(Des Ng Wai Kin. Litho Litografia Nacional, Oporto, Portugal)
1992 (22 May). World Columbian Stamp Expo '92, Chicago. Chinese Dances. T **173** and similar horiz designs. Multicoloured. P 14.
776	1p. Type **173**		1·10	70
777	2p.70 Lion dance (different)		2·20	80
778	6p. Dragon dance		4·25	1·70
776/778 Set of 3			6·75	3·00

(Des Chan Ieng Hin. Litho Litografia Nacional, Oporto, Portugal)
1992 (1 July). Olympic Games, Barcelona. T **174** and similar vert designs. Multicoloured. P 13.
779	80a. Type **174**		75	45
780	4p.20 Badminton		1·40	90
781	4p.70 Roller hockey		2·20	1·10
782	5p. Sailing		2·75	1·60
779/782 Set of 4			6·50	3·75
MS783 137×95 mm. Nos. 779/82			21·00	11·50

175 Na Chá Temple   **176** Tung Sin Tong Services

(Des Lio Man Cheong. Litho Litografia Nacional, Oporto, Portugal)
1992 (9 Oct). Temples (1st series). T **175** and similar horiz designs. Multicoloured. P 14.
784	1p. Type **175**		1·10	70
785	1p.50 Kun Iam		1·60	80
786	1p.70 Hong Kon		2·30	1·50
787	6p.50 A Má		4·25	2·50
784/787 Set of 4			8·25	5·00

See also Nos. 792/5 and 894/8.

(Des Ng Wai Kin. Litho)
1992 (1 Nov). Centenary of Tung Sin Tong (medical and educational charity). P 12.
788	**176**	1p. multicoloured	2·10	55

177 Rooster and Dragon   **178** Red Junglefowl   **179** Children carrying Banners

(Des L. Duran. Litho Litografia Nacional, Oporto, Portugal)
1992 (27 Nov). Portuguese–Chinese Friendship. P 14.
789	**177**	10p. multicoloured	3·75	2·30
MS790 109×74 mm. **177** 10p. multicoloured. P 13½			17·00	14·00

(Des J. Cândido. Litho Litografia Maia, Oporto, Portugal)
1993 (18 Jan). New Year. Year of the Cock. P 13½.
791	**178**	5p. multicoloured	3·75	1·30
		a. Imperf×p 13½. Booklets	3·75	1·70
		ab. Booklet pane. No. 791a×5	20·00	

See also No. **MS**917.

(Des Lio Man Cheong. Litho Litografia Nacional, Oporto, Portugal)
1993 (1 Mar). Temples (2nd series). Horiz designs as T **175**. Multicoloured. P 14.
792	50a. T'am Kong		55	35
793	2p. T'in Hau		1·10	45
794	3p.50 Lin Fong		1·70	90
795	8p. Pau Kong		2·50	2·10
792/795 Set of 4			5·25	3·50

(Des Lio Man Cheong. Litho Litografia Nacional, Oporto, Portugal)
1993 (1 Apr). Gods of Chinese Mythology (2nd series). Horiz designs as T **172**. Multicoloured. P 14.
796	3p.50 (1) Lam Ch'oi Wo flying on crane		3·25	2·30
	a. Strip or block of 4. Nos. 796/9		13·50	
797	3p.50 (2) Ho Sin Ku (goddess) on peach blossom		3·25	2·30
798	3p.50 (3) Hon Seong Chi crossing sea on basket of flowers		3·25	2·30
799	3p.50 (4) Ch'ou Kuok K'ao crossing river on plank		3·25	2·30
796/799 Set of 4			11·50	8·25

The numbers in brackets refer to the final figure in the bottom right-hand corner of the stamp. The issue number is "S 68".
Nos. 796/9 were issued together in *se-tenant* strips and blocks of four stamps within the sheet.

(Des Ng Wai Kin. Litho Litografia Nacional, Oporto, Portugal)
1993 (19 May). Chinese Wedding. T **179** and similar multicoloured designs. P 14.
800	3p. Type **179**		1·70	85
	a. Strip of 4. Nos. 800/3		7·00	
801	3p. Bride		1·70	85

MACAO

802	3p. Bridegroom		1·70	85
803	3p. Wedding guests		1·70	85
800/803	Set of 4		6·00	3·00
MS804	124×106 mm. 8p. Bride and groom (50×40 mm). P 14½		16·00	12·50

Nos. 800/3 were issued together in *se-tenant* strips of four stamps within the sheet, each strip forming a composite design.

180 Bird perched on Hand   **181** Eurasian Scops Owl (*Asio otus*)

(Des L. Duran. Litho Litografia Nacional, Oporto, Portugal)
1993 (5 June). Environmental Protection. P 14.
| 805 | **180** | 1p. multicoloured | 1·80 | 55 |

(Des Lio Man Cheong. Litho Litografia Nacional, Oporto, Portugal)
1993 (27 June). Birds of Prey. T **181** and similar vert. designs. Multicoloured. P 14.
806	3p. Type **181**	1·40	80
	a. Strip or block of 4. Nos. 806/9	5·75	
807	3p. Barn owl (*Tyco alba*)	1·40	80
808	3p. Peregrine falcon (*Falco peregrinus*)	1·40	80
809	3p. Golden eagle (*Aquila obrysaetos*)	1·40	80
806/809	Set of 4	5·00	3·00
MS810	107×128 mm. Nos. 806/9	23·00	11·50

Nos. 806/9 were issued together in *se-tenant* strips and blocks of four stamps within the sheet.

182 Town Hall   **183** Portuguese Missionaries

(Des J. Cardoso. Litho Litografia Nacional, Oporto, Portugal)
1993 (30 July). Union of Portuguese-speaking Capital Cities. P 13½.
| 811 | **182** | 1p.50 brt turq-grn, dp ultramarine and brown-red | 1·10 | 70 |

(Des C. Leitão. Litho)
1993 (22 Sept). 450th Anniv of First Portuguese Visit to Japan. T **183** and similar horiz. designs. Multicoloured. P 12.
812	50a. Japanese man with musket	70	35
813	3p. Type **183**	1·40	80
814	3p.50 Traders carrying goods	2·20	1·10
812/814	Set of 3	3·75	2·00

184 *Spathodea campanulata* and Luís de Camões Garden   **185** Caravel

(Des Chan Ieng Hin. Litho Litografia Nacional, Oporto, Portugal)
1993 (9 Oct). Flowers and Gardens (2nd series). T **184** and similar square designs. Multicoloured. P 14½.
815	1p. Type **184**	70	35
816	2p. *Tithonia diversifolia* and Montanha Russa Garden	1·30	55
817	3p. *Rhodomyrtus tomentosa* and Cais Garden	1·40	80
818	8p. *Passiflora foetida* and Flora Garden	2·40	2·30
815/818	Set of 4	5·25	3·50
MS819	90×120 mm. Nos. 815/18	21·00	14·00

(Des L. Duran. Litho Litografia Nacional, Oporto, Portugal)
1993 (5 Nov). Sixteenth-century Sailing Ships. T **185** and similar horiz. designs. Multicoloured. P 14.
820	1p. Type **185**	50	25
821	2p. Caravel (different)	1·10	55
822	3p.50 Nau	1·40	90
823	4p.50 Galleon	1·70	1·40
820/823	Set of 4	4·25	2·75
MS824	160×105 mm. Nos. 820/3	14·00	8·00

186 Nissan Skyline GT-R Coupe Racing Car   **187** Chow-chow and Moon

(Des Ng Wai Kin. Litho Litografia Nacional, Oporto, Portugal)
1993 (16 Nov). 40th Anniv of Macao Grand Prix. T **186** and similar horiz. designs. Multicoloured. P 13½.
825	1p.50 Type **186**	70	70
826	2p. Racing motorcycle	1·30	80
827	4p.50 Racing car	2·40	2·00
825/827	Set of 3	4·00	3·25

(Des J. Cândido. Litho Litografia Maia, Oporto, Portugal)
1994 (3 Feb). New Year. Year of the Dog. P 13½.
828	**187**	5p. multicoloured	3·50	1·40
		a. Imperf×p 13½. Booklets	3·75	1·70
		ab. Booklet pane. No. 828a×5	20·00	

See also No. **MS**917.

188 Map and Prince Henry

(Des L. Duran and C. Leitão. Litho)
1994 (4 Mar). 600th Birth Anniv of Prince Henry the Navigator. P 12.
| 829 | **188** | 3p. multicoloured | 2·75 | 1·60 |

189 Lakeside Hut   **190** Lai Sis Exchange

(Litho Litografia Nacional, Oporto, Portugal)
1994 (21 Mar). Birth Bicentenary of George Chinnery (artist). T **189** and similar horiz. designs. Multicoloured. P 14.
830	3p.50 Type **189**	1·40	1·10
	a. Strip or block of 4. Nos. 830/3	5·75	
831	3p.50 Fisherman on sea wall	1·40	1·10
832	3p.50 Harbour	1·40	1·10
833	3p.50 S. Tiago Fortress	1·40	1·10
830/833	Set of 4	5·00	4·00
MS834	138×87 mm. Nos. 830/3	17·00	10·50

Nos. 830/3 were issued together in *se-tenant* strips and blocks of four stamps within the sheet.

(Des Ng Wai Kin. Litho Litografia Nacional, Oporto, Portugal)
1994 (6 Apr). Spring Festival of Lunar New Year T **190** and similar horiz. designs. Multicoloured. P 14.
835	1p. Type **190**	55	35
836	2p. Flower and tangerine tree decorations	1·40	55
837	3p.50 Preparing family meal	1·50	90
838	4p.50 Paper decorations bearing good wishes	2·20	1·40
835/838	Set of 4	5·00	3·00

MACAO

191 "Longevity"   **192** Footballer   **193** Rice Shop

(Des Poon Kam Ling. Litho)

1994 (9 May). Legends and Myths (1st series). Chinese Gods. T **191** and similar vert designs. Multicoloured. P 12.

839	3p. Type **191**	2·75	1·70
	a. Horiz strip of 3. Nos. 839/41	8·50	
840	3p. "Prosperity"	2·75	1·70
841	3p. "Happiness"	2·75	1·70
839/841	Set of 3	7·50	4·50
MS842	138×90 mm. Nos. 839/41	17·00	11·50

Nos. 839/41 were issued together in horizontal *se-tenant* strips of three stamps within the sheet.

See also Nos. 884/**MS**888 and 930/**MS**933.

(Des Chan In Hong. Litho)

1994 (1 June). World Cup Football Championship, U.S.A. T **192** and similar vert designs. Multicoloured. P 12.

843	2p. Type **192**	70	45
844	3p. Tackling	1·30	80
845	3p.50 Heading ball	1·40	90
846	4p.50 Goalkeeper saving goal	1·80	1·50
843/846	Set of 4	4·75	3·25
MS847	138×90 mm. Nos. 843/6	17·00	10·50

(Des Ng Wai Kin. Litho)

1994 (27 June). Traditional Chinese Shops. T **193** and similar vert designs. Multicoloured. P 12.

848	1p. Type **193**	80	35
849	1p.50 Medicinal tea shop	90	45
850	2p. Salt-fish shop	1·70	70
851	3p.50 Pharmacy	2·75	90
848/851	Set of 4	5·50	2·20

194 Astrolabe   **195** Fencing

(Des Marta Carvalho. Litho)

1994 (13 Sept). Nautical Instruments. T **194** and similar vert designs. Multicoloured. P 12.

852	3p. Type **194**	1·00	70
853	3p.50 Quadrant	1·40	90
854	4p.50 Sextant	2·10	1·30
852/854	Set of 3	4·00	2·50

(Des Lio Man Cheong. Litho)

1994 (30 Sept). 12th Asian Games, Hiroshima, Japan. T **195** and similar horiz designs. Multicoloured. P 12.

855	1p. Type **195**	70	45
856	2p. Gymnastics	90	55
857	3p. Water-polo	1·70	80
858	3p.50 Pole vaulting	2·00	1·40
855/858	Set of 4	4·75	3·00

196 Nobre de Carvalho Bridge   **197** Carp

(Des Lio Man Cheong. Litho)

1994 (8 Oct). Bridges. T **196** and similar horiz design. Multi coloured. P 12.

859	1p. Type **196**	1·10	25
860	8p. Friendship Bridge	3·50	2·10

(Des Poon Kam Ling. Litho)

1994 (7 Nov). Good Luck Signs. T **197** and similar vert designs. Multicoloured. P 12.

861	3p. Type **197**	1·70	1·40
862	3p.50 Peaches	2·30	1·50
863	4p.50 Water lily	3·25	2·30
861/863	Set of 3	6·50	4·75

198 Angel's Head (stained glass window, Macao Cathedral)   **199** Pig and Moon

(Des V. Marreiros. Litho)

1994 (30 Nov). Religious Art. T **198** and similar horiz designs. Multicoloured. P 12.

864	50a. Type **198**	35	30
865	1p. Holy Ghost (stained glass window, Macao Cathedral)	45	40
866	1p.50 Silver sacrarium	80	45
867	2p. Silver salver	1·10	55
868	3p. "Flight into Egypt" (ivory statuette)	1·80	80
869	3p. Gold and silver cup	2·30	1·00
864/869	Set of 6	6·00	3·25

(Des J. Cândido. Litho Litografia Maia, Oporto, Portugal)

1995 (25 Jan). New Year Year of the Pig. P 13½.

870	**199** 5p.50 multicoloured	3·50	1·40
	a. Imperf×p 13½. Booklets	3·75	2·10
	ab. Booklet pane. No. 870a×5	20·00	

See also No. **MS**917.

200 "Lou Lim Iok Garden"    **201** Magnifying Glass over Goods

(Des Cheong Veng San. Litho)

1995 (1 Mar). Paintings of Macao by Lio Man Cheong. T **200** and similar horiz designs. Multicoloured. Litho. P 12.

871	50a. Type **200**	40	35
872	1p. "Guia Fortress and Lighthouse"	50	45
873	1p.50 "Barra Temple"	70	55
874	2p. "Avenida da Praia, Taipa"	90	70
875	2p.50 "Kun Iam Temple"	1·40	1·10
876	3p. "St. Paul's Seminary"	2·10	1·40
877	3p.50 "Penha Hill"	2·75	1·50
878	4p. "Gates of Understanding Monument"	2·75	2·10
871/878	Set of 8	10·50	7·25

(Des Cheong Veng San. Litho)

1995 (15 Mar). World Consumer Day. P 12.

879	**201** 1p. multicoloured	1·40	45

202 Pangolin   **203** Kun Sai Iam

153

MACAO

(Des W. Oliver. Litho)

1995 (10 Apr). Protection of Chinese ("Asian") Pangolin (*Manis pentadactyla*). T **202** and similar vert designs. Multicoloured. P 12.
880	1p.50 In fork of tree..................................	1·70	70
	a. Strip or block of 4. Nos. 880/3.............	7·00	
881	1p.50 Hanging from tree by tail.....................	1·70	70
882	1p.50 On leafy branch..................................	1·70	70
883	1p.50 Type **202**.......................................	1·70	70
880/883 *Set of 4*		6·00	2·50

Nos. 880/3 were issued together in *se-tenant* strips and blocks of four stamps within the sheet.

(Des Poon Kam Ling. Litho)

1995 (5 May). Legends and Myths (2nd series). Kun Sai lam (Buddhist god). T **203** and similar vert designs. Multicoloured. P 12.
884	3p. Type **203**......................................	3·25	1·40
	a. Strip or block of 4. Nos. 884/7.............	13·50	
885	3p. Holding baby..................................	3·25	1·40
886	3p. Sitting behind water lily.......................	3·25	1·40
887	3p. With water lily and dragon-fish.............	3·25	1·40
884/887 *Set of 4*		11·50	5·00
MS888 138×90 mm. 8p. Kun Sai lam (*different*).....		23·00	14·00

Nos. 884/7 were issued together in *se-tenant* strips and blocks of four stamps within the sheet.

204/207 Senado Square (illustration reduced)

(Des Ng Wai Kin. Litho)

1995 (24 June). Senado Square. P 12.
889	**204**	2p. multicoloured...........................	1·70	80
		a. Horiz strip of 4. Nos. 889/92........	7·00	
890	**205**	2p. multicoloured...........................	1·70	80
891	**206**	2p. multicoloured...........................	1·70	80
892	**207**	2p. multicoloured...........................	1·70	80
889/892 *Set of 4*			6·00	3·00
MS893 138×90 mm. 8p. multicoloured (Leal Senado building and Post Office clock tower) (*horiz*).......			16·00	8·50

Nos. 889/92 were issued together in horizontal *se-tenant* strips of four stamps within the sheet, each strip forming the composite design illustrated.

(Des Lio Man Cheong. Litho)

1995 (17 July). Temples (3rd series). Horiz designs as T **175**. Multicoloured. P 12.
894	50a. Kuan Tâi..	40	15
895	1p. Pâk Tai...	55	25
896	1p.50 Lin K'ai..	80	35
897	3p. Sek Kam Tóng.................................	1·50	70
898	3p.50 Fôk Talk......................................	1·80	80
894/898 *Set of 5*		4·50	2·00

208 Pekin Robin (*Leiothrix lutea*)   209 Pipa

(Des Lio Man Cheong. Litho)

1995 (1 Sept). Singapore 95 International Stamp Exhibition. Birds. T **208** and similar horiz designs. Multicoloured. P 12.
899	2p.50 Type **208**.................................	2·30	1·00
	a. Strip or block of 4. Nos. 899/902.....	9·50	
900	2p.50 Japanese white-eye (*Zosterops japonica*)....	2·30	1·00
901	2p.50 Islauel canary (*Serinus canarius canarius*)....	2·30	1·00
902	2p.50 Melodious laughing thrush (*Gurrulax canonus*)....	2·30	1·00
899/902 *Set of 4*		8·25	3·50
MS903 137×90 mm. 10p. Magpie robin (*Copsychus saularis*).....		21·00	9·75

Nos. 899/902 were issued together in *se-tenant* strips and blocks of four stamps within the sheet.

(Des Ng Wai Meng. Litho)

1995 (9 Oct). International Music Festival. Musical Instruments. T **209** and similar multicoloured designs. P 12.
904	1p. Type **209**......................................	1·70	45
	a. Block of 6. Nos. 904/9.....................	10·50	
905	1p. Erhu (string instrument).....................	1·70	45
906	1p. Gongo (hand-held drum)..................	1·70	45
907	1p. Sheng (string instrument)..................	1·70	45
908	1p. Xiao (flute).....................................	1·70	45
909	1p. Tamper (drum)................................	1·70	45
904/909 *Set of 6*		9·25	2·40
MS910 137×90 mm. 8p. Two players with instruments (40×29 mm).......		14·00	5·75

Nos. 905/9 were issued together in *se-tenant* blocks of six within sheetlets of 12 stamps.

210 Anniversary Emblem, World Map and U.N. Headquarters, New York   211 Terminal Building

(Des Wong Leung Chung. Litho)

1995 (24 Oct). 50th Anniv of United Nations Organization. P 12.
911	**210**	4p.50 multicoloured....................... 2·50	1·40

(Des Chan leng Hin. Litho)

1995 (8 Dec). Inauguration of Macao International Airport. T **211** and similar horiz designs. Multicoloured. P 12.
912	1p. Type **211**.....................................	45	35
913	1p.50 Terminal (*different*).....................	90	45
914	2p. Loading airplane and cargo building.....	1·50	70
915	3p. Control tower..................................	2·10	1·00
912/915 *Set of 4*		4·50	2·30
MS916 137×90 mm. 8p. Airplane taking off.............		17·00	8·00

(Des J. Cândido. Litho Litografia Maia, Oporto, Portugal)

1995 (15 Dec). Lunar Cycle. Sheet 180×216 mm containing previous New Year designs. P 13½.
MS917 12×1p.50, As Nos. 791, 828, 870, 587, 771, 602, 742, 621, 713, 685, 661 and 640........	23·00	10·50

212 Rat   213 Cage

(Des Lio Man Cheong. Litho)

1996 (12 Feb). New Year Year of the Rat. P 12.
918	**212**	5p. multicoloured.......................... 5·75	3·50
MS919 137×90 mm. **212** 10p. multicoloured.................		14·00	8·00

(Des Lio Man Cheong. Litho)

1996 (1 Mar). Traditional Chinese Cages. T **213** and similar vert designs showing different cages. P 12.
920	1p. multicoloured...............................	45	30
921	1p.50 multicoloured............................	70	45
922	3p. multicoloured................................	1·30	80
923	4p.50 multicoloured............................	2·10	1·10
920/923 *Set of 4*		4·00	2·40
MS924 137×90 mm. 10p. multicoloured....................		16·00	8·00

214 Street   215 Ton Tei (God of Earth)

MACAO

1996 (1 Apr). Paintings of Macao by Herculano Estominho. T **214** and similar multicoloured designs. Litho. P 12.

925	50a. Fishing boats (horiz)	45	25
926	1p.50 Town square	90	35
927	3p. Type **214**	1·50	70
928	5p. Townscape (horiz)	2·75	1·40
925/928	Set of 4	5·00	2·40
MS929	137×90 mm. 10p. Colonnaded entrance	11·50	5·25

(Des Poon Kam Ling. Litho)

1996 (30 Apr). Legends and Myths (3rd series). T **215** and similar vert designs. Multicoloured. P 12.

930	3p.50 Type **215**	1·80	1·30
	a. Horiz strip of 3. Nos. 930/2	5·75	
931	3p.50 Choi San (God of Fortune)	1·80	1·30
932	3p.50 Chou Kuan (God of the Kitchen)	1·80	1·30
MS933	137×89 mm. Nos. 930/2	15·00	7·75

Nos. 930/2 were issued together in horizontal *se-tenant* strips of three stamps within the sheet.

216 Customers   **217** Get Well Soon

(Des Ng Wai Kin. Litho)

1996 (17 May). Traditional Chinese Tea Houses. T **216** and similar horiz designs. Multicoloured. P 12.

934	2p. Type **216**	2·10	85
	a. Block of 4. Nos. 934/7	8·75	
935	2p. Waiter with tray of steamed stuffed bread	2·10	85
936	2p. Newspaper vendor	2·10	85
937	2p. Waiter pouring tea at table	2·10	85
934/937	Set of 4	7·50	3·00
MS938	138×90 mm. 8p. Jar and food snacks	16·00	8·00

Nos. 934/7 were issued together in *se-tenant* blocks of four stamps within the sheet, each block forming a composite design.

(Des Ung Vai Meng. Litho)

1996 (14 June). Greetings Stamps. T **217** and similar horiz designs. Multicoloured. P 12.

939	50a. Type **217**	45	25
940	1p.50 Congratulations on new baby	1·00	45
941	3p. Happy birthday	1·40	80
942	4p. Wedding congratulations	2·10	1·10
939/942	Set of 4	4·50	2·30

218 Swimming

(Des Wong Leung Chung. Litho)

1996 (19 July). Olympic Games, Atlanta, U.S.A. T **218** and similar horiz designs. Multicoloured. P 12.

943	2p. Type **218**	55	45
944	3p. Football	90	70
945	3p.50 Gymnastics	1·40	90
946	4p.50 Wind-surfing	1·70	1·10
943/946	Set of 4	4·00	2·75
MS947	137×90 mm. 10p. Boxing	9·25	4·00

219 Crane (civil, 1st rank)   **220** Trawler with Multiple Nets

(Des Loi Chio Teng. Litho)

1996 (18 Sept). Civil and Military Insignia of the Mandarins (1st Series). T **219** and similar horiz designs. Multicoloured. P 12.

948	2p.50 Type **219**	2·10	80
	a. Block or strip of 4. Nos. 948/51	8·75	
949	2p.50 Lion (military, 2nd rank)	2·10	80
950	2p.50 Golden pheasant (civil, 2nd rank)	2·10	80
951	2p.50 Leopard (military, 3rd rank)	2·10	80
948/951	Set of 4	7·50	3·00

Nos. 948/51 were issued together in *se-tenant* blocks and strips of four stamps within the sheet.
See also Nos. 1061/**MS**1065.

(Des Loi Chio Teng. Litho)

1996 (9 Oct). Nautical Sciences: Fishing Nets. T **220** and similar vert designs. P 12.

952	3p. Type **220**	2·20	90
	a. Block or strip of 4. Nos. 952/5	9·00	
953	3p. Modern trawler with net from stern	2·20	90
954	3p. Two sailing junks with common net	2·20	90
955	3p. Junk with two square nets at sides	2·20	90
952/955	Set of 4	8·00	3·25

Nos. 952/5 were issued together in *se-tenant* blocks or strips of four stamps within the sheet, each horizontal strip forming a composite design.

221 National Flag and Statue

(Des A. Conceição, jnr. Litho)

1996 (15 Oct). 20th Anniv of Legislative Assembly. P 12×12½.

956	**221**	2p.80 multicoloured	1·40	70
MS957	138×90 mm. **221** 8p. multicoloured		12·50	5·25

222 Dragonfly   **223** Doll

(Des Chan Ieng Hin. Litho)

1996 (21 Oct). Paper Kites. T **222** and similar horiz designs. Multicoloured. P 12.

958	3p.50 Type **222**	2·30	90
	a. Block or strip of 4. Nos. 958/61	9·50	
959	3p.50 Butterfly	2·30	90
960	3p.50 Owl	2·30	90
961	3p.50 Swallow	2·30	90
958/961	Set of 4	8·25	3·25
MS962	138×90 mm. 8p. Chinese dragon (50×37 mm). P 12½	15·00	7·00

Nos. 958/61 were issued together in *se-tenant* blocks and strips of four stamps within the sheet.

(Des V. Marreiros. Litho)

1996 (13 Nov). Traditional Chinese Toys. T **223** and similar vert designs. Multicoloured. P 12.

963	50a. Type **223**	70	40
964	1p. Fish	1·50	75
965	3p. Painted doll	3·75	1·40
966	4p.50 Dragon	4·50	2·00
963/966	Set of 4	9·50	4·00

224 Ox   **225** Colourful and Gold Twos

MACAO

(Des Lio Man Cheong. Litho)

1997 (23 Jan). New Year. Year of the Ox. P 12.
967	**224**	5p.50 multicoloured	4·00	2·75
MS968	137×89 mm.	**224** 10p. multicoloured	11·50	7·00

(Des Ng Wai Kin. Litho)

1997 (12 Feb). Lucky Numbers. T **225** and similar horiz designs. Multicoloured. P 12.
969	2p. Type **225**	1·00	50
970	2p.80 Eights	1·40	70
971	3p. Threes	1·50	75
972	3p.90 Nines	1·80	1·00
969/972 Set of 4		5·25	2·75
MS973 137×90 mm. 9p. Numbers around doorway of café		7·00	6·50

No. **MS**973 also commemorates "Hong Kong '97" International Stamp Exhibition.

226 "Sail Boats"   **227** Elderly Woman

1997 (1 Mar). Paintings of Macao by Kwok Se. T **226** and similar vert designs. Multicoloured. Litho. P 12.
974	2p. Type **226**	1·30	55
975	3p. "Fortress on the Hill"	1·70	80
976	3p.50 "Asilum"	2·10	1·00
977	4p.50 "Portas do Cerco"	2·75	1·40
974/977 Set of 4		7·00	3·50
MS978 138×90 mm. 8p. "Rua de São Paulo" (detail)		9·75	8·50

(Des Lio Man Cheong. Litho)

1997 (26 Mar). Tan-Ka (boat) People. T **227** and similar vert designs. Multicoloured. P 12.
979	1p. Type **227**	55	35
	a. Block of 4. Nos. 979/82	5·50	
980	1p.50 Elderly woman holding tiller	70	45
981	2p.50 Woman with child on back	1·40	70
982	5p.50 Man mending fishing nets	2·50	1·50
979/982 Set of 4		4·75	2·75

Nos. 979/82 were issued together in *se-tenant* blocks of four stamps within the sheet.

228 Entrance to Temple   **229** Dragon Dancers

(Des Ng Wai Kin. Litho)

1997 (29 Apr). A-Má Temple. T **228** and similar vert designs. Multicoloured. P 12.
983	3p.50 Type **228**	1·00	80
	a. Horiz strip of 4. Nos. 983/6	4·25	
984	3p.50 Wall and terraces of Temple	1·00	80
985	3p.50 View of incense smoke through gateway	1·00	80
986	3p.50 Incense smoke emanating from pagoda	1·00	80
983/986 Set of 4		3·50	3·00
MS987 138×90 mm. 8p. Ship (representative of land reclamation in front of temple)		6·25	6·25

(Des Lio Man Cheong. Litho)

1997 (14 May). Drunken Dragon Festival. T **229** and similar multicoloured designs. P 12.
988	2p. Type **229**	55	45
	a. Horiz strip of 3. Nos. 988/90	3·50	
989	3p. Dragon dancer	90	70
990	5p. Dancer holding "tail" of dragon	1·70	1·40
988/990 Set of 3		2·75	2·30
MS991 137×90 mm. 9p. Dancer with dragon's head (horiz)		5·75	5·75

230 Fróis with Japanese Man   **231** Wat Lot

(Des C. Leitão and L. Duran (992), Posts and Telecommunications, Macao (993). Litho Litografia Maia, Oporto, Portugal)

1997 (9 June). 400th Death Anniv of Father Luís Fróis (author of *The History of Japan*). T **230** and similar multicoloured design. P 12.
992	2p.50 Type **230**	85	70
993	2p.50 Father Fróis and church (vert)	85	70

(Des Poon Kam Ling. Litho)

1997 (18 June). Legends and Myths (4th series). Door Gods. T **231** and similar vert designs. Multicoloured. P 12.
994	2p.50 Type **231**	90	55
	a. Strip or block of 4. Nos. 994/7	3·75	
995	2p.50 San Su	90	55
996	2p.50 Chon Keng	90	55
997	2p.50 Wat Chi Kong	90	55
994/997 Set of 4		3·25	2·00
MS998 138×90 mm. 10p. Chon Keng and Wat Chi Kong on doors (39×39 mm)		5·25	5·25

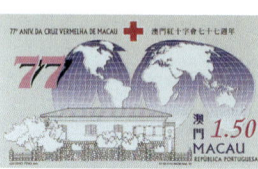

232 Globe and First Aid and Family Health School

(Des Loi Chio Teng. Litho)

1997 (12 July). 77th Anniv of Macao Red Cross. P 12½.
999	**232** 1p.50 multicoloured	55	55

No. 999 was issued with *se-tenant* half stamp-size label listing the society's precepts.

233 Balconies

(Des Ung Vai Meng. Litho)

1997 (30 July). Balconies. T **233** and similar designs showing various balcony styles. P 12.
1000	50a. multicoloured	25	25
	a. Block of 6. Nos. 1000/5	3·75	
1001	1p. multicoloured	30	25
1002	1p.50 multicoloured	45	35
1003	2p. multicoloured	65	45
1004	2p.50 multicoloured	80	70
1005	3p. multicoloured	1·10	80
1000/1005 Set of 6		3·25	2·50
MS1006 138×90 mm. 8p. multicoloured (29×39 mm)		2·75	2·75

Nos. 1000/5 were issued together in blocks of six stamps within the sheet.

234 Plant Leaf Fan   **235** Wood

(Des Poon Kam Ling. Litho)

1997 (24 Sept). Fans. T **234** and similar vert designs. Multicoloured. P 12.
1007	50a. Type **234**	25	25
	a. Horiz strip of 4. Nos. 1007/10	3·25	
1008	1p. Paper fan	30	25
1009	3p.50 Silk fan	1·10	90
1010	4p. Feather fan	1·40	1·10
1007/1010	Set of 4	2·75	2·30
MS1011	138×90 mm. 9p. Woman holding sandalwood fan	5·75	5·25

(Des V. Marreiros. Litho)

1997 (9 Oct). Feng Shui. The Five Elements. T **235** and similar vert designs. Multicoloured. P 12.
1012	50a. Type **235**	35	25
	a. Horiz strip of 5. Nos. 1012/16	3·25	
1013	1p. Fire	45	30
1014	1p.50 Earth	55	35
1015	2p. Metal	70	45
1016	2p.50 Water	1·00	70
1012/1016	Set of 5	2·75	1·80
MS1017	138×90 mm. 10p. Centre of geomancer's chart	6·00	5·50

Nos. 1012/16 were issued in horizontal *se-tenant* strips of five stamps within the sheet.

236 Kung Fu

237 Tiger

(Des V. Marreiros. Litho)

1997 (19 Nov). Martial Arts. T **236** and similar vert designs. Multicoloured. P 12.
1018	1p.50 Type **236**	55	35
	a. Horiz strip of 3. Nos. 1018/20	3·50	
1019	3p.50 Judo	1·10	80
1020	4p. Karate	1·70	1·10
1018/1020	Set of 3	3·00	2·00

Nos. 1018/20 were issued in horizontal *se-tenant* strips of three stamps within the sheet.

(Des Lio Man Cheong. Litho)

1998 (18 Jan). New Year. Year of the Tiger. P 12.
1021	**237** 5p.50 multicoloured	2·10	1·70
MS1022	138×90 mm. **237** 10p. multicoloured	3·75	3·75

No. **MS**1022 also exists overprinted "Amizade Luso-Chinesa Festival de Macau Pequim -05.1998" in English and Chinese in gold on the margin, for sale at this exhibition.

238 Soup Stall

239 Beco da Sè

(Des Lio Man Cheong. Litho)

1998 (13 Feb). Street Traders. T **238** and similar horiz designs. Multicoloured. P 12.
1023	1p. Type **238**	30	25
	a. Block of 6. Nos. 1023/8	4·75	
1024	1p.50 Snack stall	45	35
1025	2p. Clothes stall	65	45
1026	2p.50 Balloon stall	80	65
1027	3p. Flower stall	1·00	80
1028	3p.50 Fruit stall	1·30	1·00
1023/1028	Set of 6	4·00	3·25
MS1029	138×90 mm. 6p. Fruit stall (different)	2·50	2·50

Nos. 1023/8 were issued together in *se-tenant* blocks of six stamps within the sheet.

No. **MS**1029 also exists overprinted "Amizade Luso-Chinesa Festival de Macau Pequim -05.1998" in English and Chinese in gold on the margin, for sale at this exhibition.

(Des Ung Vai Meng. Litho)

1998 (1 Mar). Gateways. T **239** and similar horiz designs. Multicoloured.
1030	50a. Type **239**	25	25
1031	1p. Pátio da Ilusão	40	35
1032	3p.50 Travessa das galinhas	1·40	1·30
1033	4p. Beco das Felicidades	1·80	1·60
1030/1033	Set of 4	3·50	3·25
MS1034	138×90 mm. 9p. St. Joseph's Seminary	4·00	4·00

No. **MS**1034 also exists overprinted "Amizade Luso-Chinesa Festival de Macau Jiangsu Nanjing -07.1998" in English and Chinese in gold on the margin, for sale at this exhibition.

240 Woman and Child

241 São Gabriel (flagship)

(Des Poon Kam Ling. Litho)

1998 (23 Apr). Legends and Myths (5th series). Gods of Ma Chou. T **240** and similar vert designs. Multicoloured. P 12.
1035	4p. Type **240**	1·60	1·00
	a. Strip of 4. Nos. 1035/8	6·75	
1036	4p. Woman and man's face in smoke	1·60	1·00
1037	4p. Woman with children playing instruments	1·60	1·00
1038	4p. Goddess and sailing barges	1·60	1·00
1035/1038	Set of 4	5·75	3·50
MS1039	138×90 mm. 10p. Head of goddess	4·00	4·00

Nos. 1035/8 were issued together in *se-tenant* strips of four stamps within the sheet.

No. **MS**1039 also exists overprinted "Amizade Luso-Chinesa Festival de Macau Jiangsu Nanjing -07.1998" in English and Chinese in gold on the margin, for sale at this exhibition.

(Des V. Marreiros. Litho)

1998 (20 May–Sept). 500th Anniv of Vasco da Gama's Voyage to India via Cape of Good Hope. T **241** and similar horiz designs. Multicoloured. P 12.

(a) Wrongly dated "1598 1998"
1040	1p. Type **241**	65	35
	a. Strip of 3. Nos. 1040/2	3·00	
1041	1p.50 Vasco da Gama	90	45
1042	2p. São Gabriel and map of India	1·20	70
1040/1042	Set of 3	2·50	1·40
MS1043	138×90 mm. 8p. Compass rose	5·75	5·75

(a) Correctly dated "1498 1998"
1044	1p. Type **241**	50	25
	a. Strip of 3. Nos. 1044/6	2·50	
1045	1p.50 As No. 1041	80	35
1046	2p. As No. 1042	1·10	55
1044/1046	Set of 3	2·20	1·00
MS1047	138×90 mm. 8p. As No. **MS**1043	3·50	3·50

Nos. 1040/2 and 1044/6 respectively were issued together in *se-tenant* strips of three stamps within their sheets.

No. **MS**1047 also exists overprinted "Amizade Luso-Chinesa Festival de Macau-Hebei-Shijiazhuang -11.1198" in English and Chinese in gold on the margin, for sale at this exhibition.

242 Mermaid and Caravel

243 Players

(Des Wilson Lam Chi Ian. Litho)

1998 (22 May). International Year of the Ocean. T **242** and similar horiz design. Multicoloured. P 12.
1048	2p.50 Type **242**	90	70
	a. Pair. Nos. 1048/9	2·10	1·60
1049	3p. Whale and oil-rig	1·10	80
MS1050	138×90 mm. 9p. Caravel and whale	3·50	3·50

Nos. 1048/1 were issued together in *se-tenant* pairs within the sheet.

No. **MS**1050 also exists overprinted "Amizade Luso-Chinesa Festival de Macau-Shanxi Xian -10.1998" in English and Chinese in gold on the margin, for sale at this exhibition.

MACAO

(Des Loi Chio Teng. Litho)

1998 (10 June). World Cup Football Championship, France. T **243** and similar horiz designs. Multicoloured. P 12.

1051	3p. Type **243**	1·10	90
1052	3p.50 Players competing for ball	1·30	1·10
1053	4p. Player kicking ball clean while being tackled	1·60	1·40
1054	4p.50 Player beating another to ball	2·00	1·70
1051/1054 Set of 4		5·50	4·50
MS1055 138×90 mm. 9p. Players and ball		4·50	4·00

No. **MS**1055 also exists overprinted "Amizade Luso-Chinesa Festival de Macau-Shanxi Xian -10.1998" in English and Chinese in gold on the margin, for sale at this exhibition.

244 Lio Seak Chong Mask

245 Smiling Buddha

(Des Ng Wai Kin. Litho)

1998 (28 July). Chinese Opera Masks. T **244** and similar horiz designs. Multicoloured. P 12.

1056	1p.50 Type **244**	50	35
	a. Horiz strip of 4. Nos. 1056/9	4·00	
1057	2p. Wat Chi Kong	65	45
1058	3p. Kam Chin Pao	90	70
1059	5p. Lei Kwai	1·60	1·30
1056/1059 Set of 4		3·25	2·50
MS1060 138×90 mm. 8p. Opera mask		3·50	2·75

Nos. 1056/9 were issued together in horizontal se-tenant strips of four stamps within the sheet.

No. **MS**1060 also exists overprinted "Amizade Luso-Chinesa Festival de Macau-Shanxi Xian -10.1998" in English and Chinese in gold in the margin, for sale at this exhibition.

(Des Loi Choi Teng. Litho)

1998 (9 Sept). Civil and Military Insignia of the Mandarins (2nd series). Horiz designs as T **219**. Multicoloured. P 12.

1061	50a. Lion (military, 2nd rank)	25	10
	a. Block or strip of 4. Nos. 1061/4	1·90	
1062	1p. Bear (military, 5th rank)	40	25
1063	1p.50 Golden pheasant (civil, 2nd rank)	50	35
1064	2p. Silver pheasant (civil, 5th rank)	65	45
1061/1064 Set of 4		1·60	1·00
MS1065 138×90 mm. 9p. Crane (civil, 1st rank)		4·00	3·75

Nos. 1061/4 were issued together in se-tenant blocks and strips of four stamps within the sheet.

No. **MS**1065 also exists overprinted "Amizade Luso-Chinesa Festival de Macau-Tianjin -12.1998" in English and Chinese in gold in the margin, for sale at this exhibition.

(Des Ng Wai Kin. Litho)

1998 (9 Oct). Kun Iam Temple. T **245** and similar horiz designs. Multicoloured. P 12.

1066	3p.50 Type **245**	1·10	80
	a. Block of 4. Nos. 1066/9	4·75	
1067	3p.50 Pavilion and temple gardens	1·10	80
1068	3p.50 Temple gateway	1·10	80
1069	3p.50 Pagoda, stream and gardens	1·10	80
1066/1069 Set of 4		4·00	3·00
MS1070 138×90 mm. 10p. Temple		4·00	3·75

Nos. 1066/9 were issued together in se-tenant blocks of four stamps within the sheet, forming a composite design.

No. **MS**1070 also exists overprinted "Amizade Luso-Chinesa Festival de Macau-Tianjin -12.1998" in English and Chinese in gold in the margin, for sale at this exhibition.

246 Carriage in Street

247 Dragon

1998 (11 Nov). Paintings of Macao by Didier Rafael Bayle. T **246** and similar multicoloured designs. Litho. P 12.

1071	2p. Type **246**	80	70
1072	3p. Street (horiz)	1·20	1·00
1073	3p.50 Building (horiz)	1·30	1·10
1074	4p.50 Kiosk in square	2·00	1·70
1071/1074 Set of 4		4·75	4·00
MS1075 138×90 mm. 8p. Balcony (horiz)		3·25	3·00

No. **MS**1075 also exists overprinted "Amizade Luso-Chinesa Festival de Macau-Fujian" in English and Chinese in gold on the margin, for sale at this exhibition.

1998 (8 Dec). Tiles by Eduardo Nery (from panel at Departure Lounge of Macao Airport). T **247** and similar horiz designs. Multicoloured. P 12.

1076	1p. Type **247**	40	25
	a. Block or strip of 4. Nos. 1076/9	3·75	
1077	1p.50 Galleon	50	40
1078	2p.50 Junk	80	55
1079	5p.50 Phoenix	1·70	1·40
1076/1079 Set of 4		3·00	2·30
MS1080 138×90 mm. 10p. Guia Lighthouse		4·00	3·75

Nos. 1076/9 were issued together in se-tenant blocks and strips of four stamps within the sheet.

No. **MS**1080 also exists overprinted "Amizade Luso-Chinesa Festival de Macau-Fujian" in English and Chinese in gold on the margin, for sale at this exhibition.

248 Rabbit

249 Jia Bao Yu

(Des Lio Man Cheong. Litho)

1999 (8 Feb). New Year. Year of the Rabbit. P 12.

1081	**248** 5p.50 multicoloured	2·10	1·80
MS1082 138×90 mm. **248** 10p. multicoloured		4·25	4·00

No. **MS**1082 also exists overprinted "Amizade Luso-Chinesa Transferência da Soberania de MACAU 1999 Guangxi Nanning 04/1999" in English and Chinese in gold on the margin, for sale at this exhibition.

(Des Poon Kam Ling. Litho)

1999 (1 Mar). Literature. Characters from *A Dream of Red Mansions* by Cao Xue Qin. T **249** and similar vert designs. Multicoloured. P 12.

1083	2p. Type **249**	65	50
	a. Block of 6. Nos. 1083/8	4·25	
1084	2p. Lin Dai Yu holding pole and cherry blossom	65	50
1085	2p. Bao Chai holding fan	65	50
1086	2p. Wang Xi Feng sitting in chair	65	50
1087	2p. You San Jie holding sword	65	50
1088	2p. Qing Wen sewing "peacock" cloak	65	50
1083/1088 Set of 6		3·50	2·75
MS1089 138×90 mm. 8p. Jia Bao Yu and Lin Dai Yu		3·25	3·25

Nos. 1083/8 were issued together in se-tenant blocks of six stamps within the sheet.

No. **MS**1089 also exists overprinted "Amizade Luso-Chinesa Transferência da Soberania de MACAU 1999 Guangxi Nanning 04/1999" in English and Chinese in gold on the margin, for sale at this exhibition.

250 Sailing Ships

251 de Havilland D.H.9 Biplane

MACAO

(Des Ung Vai Meng. Litho)

1999 (19 Mar). Australia '99 International Stamp Exhibition, Melbourne. Oceans and Maritime Heritage. T **250** and similar multicoloured designs. P 12.

1090	1p.50 Type **250**	50	45
	a. Horiz pair. Nos. 1090/1	1·50	1·40
1091	2p.50 Marine life	90	80

MS1092 138×90 mm. 6p. Head of whale (vert) .... 2·40 2·20

Nos. 1090/1 were issued together in horizontal *se-tenant* pairs within sheets of eight stamps.

No. **MS**1092 also exists overprinted "Amizade Luso-Chinesa Transferência da Soberania de MACAU 1999 Sichuan Chengdu 05/1999" in English and Chinese in gold on the margin, for sale at this exhibition.

(Des L. Duran and A. Santos. Litho)

1999 (19 Apr). 75th Anniv of Sarmento de Beires and Brito Pais's Portugal–Macao Flight. T **251** and similar horiz design. P 12.

1093	3p. Breguet 16 Bn2 Patria	1·60	1·40
1094	3p. Type **251**	1·60	1·40

MS1095 137×104 mm. Nos. 1093/4 .... 3·25 3·00

No. **MS**1095 also exists overprinted "Amizade Luso-Chinesa Transferência da Soberania de MACAU 1999 Sichuan Chengdu 05/1999" in English and Chinese in gold on the margin, for sale at this exhibition.

252 Carrying Containers on Yoke

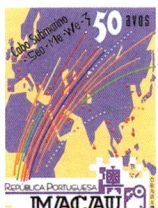

253 "Sea-Me-We-3" Undersea Fibre Optic Cable

(Des Lio Mang Cheong. Litho)

1999 (28 Apr). The Water Carrier. T **252** and similar vert designs. Multicoloured. P 12.

1096	1p. Type **252**	40	25
	a. Strip of 4. Nos. 1096/9	2·75	
1097	1p.50 Filling containers from pump	50	35
1098	2p. Lowering bucket down well	65	45
1099	2p.50 Filling containers from tap	1·00	70
1096/1099	Set of 4	2·30	1·60

MS1100 138×90 mm. 7p. Woman with containers on yoke climbing steps .... 3·00 2·75

Nos. 1096/9 were issued together in *se-tenant* strips of four stamps within the sheet.

No. **MS**1100 also exists overprinted "Amizade Luso-Chinesa Transferência da Soberania de MACAU 1999 China Shanghai 07/1999" in English and Chinese in gold on the margin, for sale at this exhibition.

(Des Ng Wai Kin. Litho and hologram (8p.), litho (others))

1999 (17 May). Telecommunications Services. T **253** and similar multicoloured designs. P 12.

1101	50a. Type **253**	20	10
	a. Horiz strip of 5. Nos. 1101/5	4·75	
1102	1p. Dish aerial at Satellite Earth Station	35	30
1103	3p.50 Analogue mobile phone	1·10	90
1104	4p. Televisions	1·30	1·10
1105	4p.50 Internet and e-mail	1·60	1·40
1101/1105	Set of 5	4·00	3·50

MS1106 138×90 mm. 8p. Emblem and computer mouse (horiz) .... 3·25 3·25

Nos. 1101/5 were issued together in horizontal *se-tenant* strips of five stamps within the sheet.

254 Macao Cultural Centre

255 Health Department

(Des Lei Vai Han. Litho)

1999 (2 June). Modern Buildings. T **254** and similar multicoloured designs. P 12.

1107	1p. Type **254**	35	25
1108	1p.50 Museum of Macao	40	35
1109	2p. Macao Maritime Museum	80	70
1110	2p.50 Ferry terminal	1·10	90
1111	3p. Macao University	1·20	1·00
1112	3p.50 Public Administration building (vert)	1·30	1·10
1113	4p.50 Macao World Trade Centre (vert)	1·70	1·50
1114	5p. Coloane kart-racing track (vert)	1·80	1·60
1115	8p. Bank of China (vert)	2·50	2·30
1116	12p. National Overseas Bank (vert)	4·00	3·50
1107/1116	Set of 10	13·50	12·00

(Des V. Marreiros. Litho)

1999 (24 June). Classified Buildings in Tap Seac District. T **255** and similar vert designs. Multicoloured. P 12.

1117	1p.50 Type **255**	50	45
	a. Horiz strip of 4. Nos. 1117/20	2·10	
1118	1p.50 Central Library (face value in salmon)	50	45
1119	1p.50 Centre of Modern Art of the Orient Foundation (face value in yellow)	50	45
1120	1p.50 Portuguese Institute of the Orient (face value in light blue)	50	45
1117/1120	Set of 4	1·80	1·60

MS1121 138×90 mm. 10p. I.P.O.R. building .... 4·00 3·75

Nos. 1117/20 were issued together in horizontal *se-tenant* strips of four stamps within the sheet, each strip forming a composite design.

No. **MS**1121 also exists overprinted "Amizade Luso-Chinesa Transferência da Soberania de MACAU 1999 Guangdong Cantão 08/1999" in English and Chinese in gold on the margin, for sale at this exhibition.

256 Teapot and Plate of Food

257 "Portuguese Sailor and Chinese Woman" (Lagoa Henriques), Company of Jesus Square

(Des Aser But. Litho)

1999 (21 Aug). Dim Sum. T **256** and similar vert designs. Multicoloured. P 12.

1122	2p.50 Type **256**	80	70
	a. Horiz strip of 4. Nos. 1122/5	3·50	
1123	2p.50 Plates of food, chopsticks and left half of bowls	80	70
1124	2p.50 Plates of food, glass, cups and right half of bowls	80	70
1125	2p.50 Plates of food and large teapot	80	70
1122/1125	Set of 4	3·00	2·50

MS1126 138×90 mm. 9p. Plates of food .... 3·50 3·00

Nos. 1122/5 were issued together in horizontal *se-tenant* strips of four stamps, each strip forming a composite design.

No. **MS**1126 is also inscribed for "China 1999" International Stamp Exhibition, Peking.

No. **MS**1126 also exists overprinted "Amizade Luso-Chinesa Transferência da Soberania de MACAU 1999 Guangdong Cantão 08/1999" in English and Chinese in gold on the margin, for sale at this exhibition.

(Des Wong Ho Sang. Litho)

1999 (9 Oct). Contemporary Sculptures (1st series). T **257** and similar multicoloured designs. P 12.

1127	1p. Type **257**	40	35
1128	1p.50 "The Gate of Understanding" (Charters de Almeida), Praia Grande Bay (vert)	50	45
1129	2p.50 "Statue of the Goddess Kun Iam" (Cristina Leiria), Macao Cultural Centre (vert)	1·10	90
1130	3p.50 "Taipa Viewing Point" (Dorita Castel-Branco), Nobre de Carvalho Bridge, Taipa	1·30	1·10
1127/1130	Set of 4	3·00	2·50

MS1131 138×90 mm. 10p. "The Pearl" (José Rodrigues), Amizade roundabout .... 4·00 3·75

See also Nos. 1186/**MS**1190.

No. **MS**1131 also exists overprinted "Amizade Luso-Chinesa Transferência da Soberania de MACAU 1999 Zhejiang Hangzhou 11/1999" in English and Chinese in gold on the margin, for sale at this exhibition.

MACAO / British Post Office in Macao

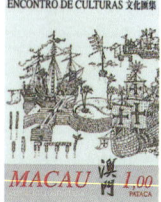

258 Chinese and Portuguese Ships, Christ's Cross and Yin Yang

259 Globe

(Des C. Marreiros. Litho)

1999 (19 Nov). Portuguese–Chinese Cultural Mix. T **258** and similar vert designs. Multicoloured. P 12½.

1132	1p. Type **258**	35	30
	a. Horiz strip of 4. Nos. 1132/5	3·00	
1133	1p.50 Ah Mah Temple and Portuguese and Macanese architecture	50	45
1134	2p. Bridge, steps and Chinese architecture	70	65
1135	3p. Macanese architecture and Portuguese terrace	1·10	90
1132/1135	Set of 4	2·40	2·10
MS1136	138×90 mm. 10p. Enlargement of right-hand part of design in No. 1135	4·00	3·75

Nos. 1132/5 were issued together in horizontal *se-tenant* strips of four stamps within the sheet, each strip forming a composite design.

No. **MS**1136 also exists overprinted "Amizade Luso-Chinesa Transferência da Soberania de MACAU 1999 Zhejiang Hangzhou 11/1999" in English and Chinese in gold on the margin, for sale at this exhibition.

(Des C. Marreiros. Litho)

1999 (19 Dec). Macao Retrospective. T **259** and similar horiz designs. Multicoloured. P 12½.

1137	1p. Type **259**	40	35
	a. Strip or block of 4. Nos. 1137/40	3·50	
1138	1p.50 Roof terrace	65	55
1139	2p. Portuguese and Chinese people	90	80
1140	3p.50 Modern Macao	1·40	1·30
1137/1140	Set of 4	3·00	2·75
MS1141	138×90 mm. 9p. City coat of arms	3·50	3·00

Nos. 1137/40 were issued together in strips and blocks of four stamps within the sheet.

No. **MS**1141 also exists overprinted "Amizade Luso-Chinsea Transferência da Soberania de MACAU 1999 Macau 12/1999" in English and Chinese in gold on the margin, for sale at this exhibition.

Macao became a Special Administrative Region of the People's Republic of China on 20 December, 1999 when all previous stamp issues were withdrawn and invalidated. Issues of Macao after this date are listed in Part 17 (*China*) of this catalogue.

MACHINE LABELS

On 19 October 1993 fifteen Klussendorf machines came into use. These machines dispensed labels in the designs listed below, with the value overprinted at the time of purchase. Labels were available in values from 5a. to 999o.5, in 5a. steps.

A **1** Head Post Office

(Des Ng Wai Kim. Photo Enscedé)

1993 (19 Oct). Design as Type A **1**. Cream, orange-brown and black.
Fixed values: 19.10.93 1, 1.5, 3.5, 4.5p

A **2** Lotus Flower Bridge

(Des Lei Vai Han. Litho The Mint, Lisbon)

1999 (2 June). Design as Type A **2**. Multicoloured.
Fixed values: 2.6.99 1, 1.5, 3.5, 4.5p

STAMP BOOKLETS

The following checklist covers, in simplified form, booklets issued by Macao. It is intended that it should be used in conjunction with the main listing and details of stamps and panes listed there are not repeated.

Prices are for complete booklets

Booklet No.	Date	Contents and Cover Price	Price
SB1	25.1.84	New Year. Year of the Rat (T**121**) 1 pane, No. 587ab (3p.)	42·00
SB2	13.2.85	New Year. Year of the Ox (T **125**) 1 pane, No. 602ab (5p.)	37·00
SB3	3.2.86	New Year. Year of the Tiger (T**131**) 1 pane, No. 621ab (7p.50)	32·00
SB4	21.1.87	New Year. Year of the Hare (T **137**) 1 pane, No. 640ab (7p.50)	41·00
SB5	10.2.88	New Year. Year of the Dragon (T**143**) 1 pane, No. 661ab (12p.50)	40·00
SB6	20.1.89	New Year. Year of the Snake (T **150**) 1 pane, No. 685ab (15p.)	45·00
SB7	19.1.90	New Year. Year of the Horse (T **157**) 1 pane, No. 713ab (20p.)	30·00
SB8	8.2.91	New Year. Year of the Goat (T **164**) 1 pane, No. 742ab (22p.50)	28·00
SB9	23.3.92	New Year. Year of the Monkey (T **171**) 1 pane, No. 771ab (22p.50)	27·00
SB10	18.1.93	New Year. Year of the Cock (T **178**) 1 pane, No. 791ab (25p.)	21·00
SB11	3.2.94	New Year. Year of the Dog (T **187**) 1 pane, No. 828ab (25p.)	21·00
SB12	25.1.95	New Year. Year of the Pig (T **199**) 1 pane, No. 870ab (27p.50)	21·00

BRITISH POST OFFICE IN MACAO

A British Consular Post Office opened in 1841. It had been preceded by the Macao Boat Office, possibly a private venture, which operated in the 1830s. The office ceased when the Consulate closed on 30 September 1845, but was back in operation by 1854. The Agency continued to function, in conjunction with the Hong Kong Post Office, until 28 February 1884 when Portugal joined the U.P.U.

CROWNED-CIRCLE HANDSTAMPS Under regulations circulated in December 1841, letters and packets forwarded through offices abroad to the United Kingdom or any of its territories were to be sent unpaid, the postage being collected on delivery. Where this was not possible, for example from a British colony to a foreign country or between two foreign ports, then a crowned-circle handstamp was to be applied with the postage, paid in advance, noted alongside in manuscript.

The dates quoted are those on which the handstamp appears in the G.P.O. Record Books, but it seems to have been normal for the handstamps to be sent to the office concerned immediately following this registration.

CC **2a**   CC **2b**

Crowned-circle Handstamps.
CC1   – "PAID AT MACAO"
      (crowned oval 20 mm wide).
      In red (1844) .... *Price on cover* £32500
CC2   CC **2a** (1881) ....

No. CC2 with the crown removed was used by the Portuguese post office in Macao as a cancellation until 1890.

A locally-cut mark, Type CC **2b**, is known on covers between 1870 and 1877. It was probably used by the Portuguese postmaster to send letters via the British Post Office (*Price on cover* £10000).

Madeira

1868. 1000 Reis = 1 Milreis
1912. 100 Centavos = 1 Escudo
2002. 100 Cents = 1 Euro

The islands of Madeira and Porto Santo, in the Atlantic Ocean 550 miles west of Casablanca, were first explored in 1418–20 by two of Henry the Navigator's captains, Zarco and Teixeira. They have always been administered as part of Portugal.

PRINTERS. All stamps of Madeira and Funchal were printed at the Mint, Lisbon.

A. MADEIRA

From 1853 to 1868 the stamps of Portugal were used in Madeira, with the cancellation of the number "51" amid bars. The following stamps, Nos. E1/12, were used only in Madeira. They were probably stamps with experimental perforations, sent to Madeira to be used up.

Experimental Perforations

1868. Stamps of Portugal, unsurcharged.

(i) T 13. Percé en croix 11
| E1 | 100r. dull lilac | | |

(ii) T 14
(a) Percé en croix 11
E2	5r. black (1)		
E3	10r. yellow		
E4	20r. bistre		
E5	25r. rose		
E6	80r. orange		
E7	100r. dull purple		
E8	120r. deep blue		

(b) Percé en croix 13½
E9	20r. bistre		
E10	25r. rose		
E11	120r. deep blue		

(c) Rouletted 8
| E12 | 5r. black (1) | | |

From 1868 to 1881 stamps of Portugal, overprinted "MADEIRA" as follows, were used.

MADEIRA (1) **MADEIRA** (2) **MADEIRA** (3)

The difference between the overprints T **1** and **2** is not so much in the measurement as in the formation of the letters. In T **2** the letters are wider, particularly the "M" and "D".

1868 (1 Jan). Optd with T **1** (14¾×3 mm).

(a) Imperf
1	14	20r. bistre	£275	£200
2		50r. green	£275	£200
3		80r. orange	£300	£200
4		100r. dull lilac	£300	£200

(b) Percé en croix 10
5	14	20r. bistre		
6		50r. green		
7		80r. orange		
8		100r. dull lilac		
		a. Percé en croix 13½		

All values were reprinted with opt T **2** in 1885 and with opt T **3** in 1905.
Nos. 5/8a were also probably stamps with experimental perforations, overprinted for Madeira.

1868–70. Optd with T **1**. P 12½.
9	14	5r. black (1) (Vm.)	80·00	55·00
10		5r. black (1) (C.)	80·00	55·00
11		5r. black (2) (Vm.)	80·00	55·00
12		5r. black (2) (C.)	80·00	55·00
13		10r. orange-yellow	£130	£110
14		20r. bistre (1869)	£200	£160
15		25r. rose	85·00	16·00
		a. Opt inverted		
		b. Carmine	85·00	16·00
16		50r. green	£250	£200
		a. Opt inverted		
17		80r. orange	£250	£200
18		100r. deep lilac (1) (1869)	£250	£200
19		100r. pale mauve (2)	£250	£200
		a. Opt inverted		
20		120r. blue	£170	£110
		a. Deep blue	£170	£110
21		240r. reddish lilac (1870)	£700	£600

All values were reprinted with opt T **3** in 1885 and 1905. The 5r. with opt T **3** in black is an 1885 reprint.

1871–76.

*A. Optd with T **1** P 12½ (1871–74)*
22	15	5r. black (C.) (1871)	18·00	11·50
		a. Opt inverted		
23		10r. orange-yellow (12.71)	49·00	33·00
24		20r. bistre (1.72)	55·00	33·00
25		25r. rose (1871)	18·00	7·00
		a. Opt inverted		
		b. Pale rose	18·00	7·00
		c. Carmine	18·00	7·00
26		50r. green (7.72)	£100	55·00
		a. Opt inverted		
		b. Deep green	£100	55·00
27		80r. orange (1) (7.72)	£150	£110
28		100r. pale mauve (7.72)	£140	55·00
29		120r. blue (2.74)	£170	£110

*B. Optd with T **2***
(a) P 12½ (1874)
30	15	5r. black (C.)	12·00	8·50
31		10r. orange-yellow	45·00	38·00
32		15r. fawn	31·00	17·00
33		20r. olive-bistre	45·00	38·00
34		25r. rose	16·00	6·00
35		50r. green	£100	55·00
36		80r. orange (1)	£110	95·00
37		100r. pale mauve	£130	75·00
38		120r. blue	£170	£110
		a. Pale blue	£170	£110
39		240r. pale dull lilac	£1000	£700

(b) P 13½
40	15	10r. orange-yellow	55·00	43·00
41		20r. olive-bistre	55·00	43·00
42		50r. pale green	£100	55·00
		a. Green	£100	55·00
43		80r. orange (1)	£170	£110

(c) P 14
| 44 | 15 | 5r. black (C.) | £120 | 75·00 |
| 45 | | 100r. pale mauve | £200 | £110 |

*C. Optd with T **3***
(a) P 12½ (1876)
46	15	5r. black (C.)	17·00	11·50
		a. Opt double		
47		10r. orange-yellow	40·00	29·00
		a. Yellow	40·00	29·00
48		15r. fawn (1) (2.76)	28·00	16·00
49		20r. yellow-bistre	44·00	29·00
		a. Pale bistre	44·00	29·00
		b. Olive-bistre	44·00	29·00
50		25r. rose	21·00	6·00
		a. Opt inverted	45·00	43·00
		b. Opt double		
		c. Pale rose	21·00	6·00
51		50r. green	90·00	39·00
		a. Deep green	90·00	39·00
52		80r. orange (1)	£130	95·00
		a. Orange-yellow	£130	95·00
53		100r. pale mauve	£120	70·00
54		120r. blue	£160	£110
55		150r. blue (2.76)	£250	£200
56		240r. pale dull lilac	£1000	£700

(b) P 13½
57	15	5r. black (C.)	16·00	8·50
58		10r. yellow	42·00	13·50
59		15r. fawn (1)	70·00	47·00
60		15r. fawn (2)	70·00	47·00
61		20r. bistre	60·00	32·00
62		25r. rose	16·00	6·00
		a. Pale rose	16·00	6·00
63		50r. green	£100	45·00
		a. Deep green	£100	45·00
64		80r. orange (1)	£150	£110
65		100r. pale mauve	£150	80·00
66		150r. blue	£275	£225
67		300r. lilac (2.76)	£110	95·00

All values were reprinted with opt T **3**, perf 13½ in 1885 and 1905. Also all except the 20 and 300r. were reprinted in 1885 perf 12½.

1876 (1 July). NEWSPAPER. Optd with T **3**.

(a) P 12½
| N68 | N **17** | 2½r. olive-green | 12·00 | 6·00 |
| | | a. Opt inverted | | |

MADEIRA / Madeira / Funchal / Madeira

		(b) P 13½		
N69	N 17	2½r. olive-green	12·00	6·00

This was reprinted perf 13½, and 12½ in 1885 and again perf 13½ in 1905.

1879 (Nov)–**80**. Optd with T **3**.

		(a) P 12½		
70	15	10r. blue-green	£200	£160
		a. Yellow-green	£100	75·00
		b. Pale yellow-green	£100	75·00
71		50r. pale blue	£170	90·00
		a. Blue	£170	90·00
		b. Deep dull blue	£170	90·00

		(b) P 13½		
72	15	10r. blue-green	2·50	£190
		a. Yellow-green	95·00	75·00
		b. Pale yellow-green	95·00	75·00
73		50r. pale blue	£200	75·00
		a. Blue	£200	75·00
74		150r. yellow (5.80)	£400	£350

Specimens are known on chalk-surfaced paper but they were never issued.

All three values were reprinted pert 13½ and 12½ in 1885 and again perf 13½ in 1905.

1880. Optd with T **3**.

		(a) P 12½		
75	16	5r. black (1) (C.) (Aug)	40·00	28·00
76		5r. black (2) (C.)	40·00	28·00
77	17	25r. bluish grey (Jan)	40·00	28·00
		a. Opt inverted	75·00	70·00
78	17a	25r. grey (May)	40·00	15·00
		a. Purple-grey	40·00	15·00
		b. Purple-brown	40·00	15·00

		(b) P 13½		
79	16	5r. black (1) (C.)	37·00	28·00
80	17	25r. bluish grey	49·00	35·00
81	17a	25r. grey	55·00	35·00
		a. Purple-grey	55·00	35·00
		b. Purple-brown	55·00	35·00

Both 25 r. were reprinted in 1885 and 1905 and the 5r. in 1885 only.

From 1881 to 1892 unoverprinted stamps of Portugal were again used in Madeira.

B. FUNCHAL

The administrative title of Madeira was changed to the District of Funchal, the chief town in Madeira. From 1892 to 1905 the stamps used in Madeira were inscribed "FUNCHAL".

4   5

(Head eng M. D. Neto, frame eng J. S. de Carvalho e Silva.Typo)

1892–93. Chalk-surfaced paper or enamel-surfaced paper (E).

		(a) P 11		
82	4	5r. orange-yellow (1.7.92)	3·25	2·00
83		25r. deep green (1.6.92)	7·00	1·90
		a. Green	7·00	1·90
84		50r. pale blue (1.7.92)	7·00	3·75

		(b) P 12½		
85	4	5r. orange-yellow	4·50	2·50
86		10r. rosy mauve (1.7.92)	3·75	2·50
87		15r. red-brown (1.10.92)	5·00	4·50
88		15r. red-brown (E)	22·00	17·00
89		20r. lavender (1.10.92)	5·50	3·75
90		25r. green	9·25	2·30
91		50r. blue	11·00	9·50
		a. Pale blue	11·00	9·50
92		75r. rose (15.12.92)	11·00	9·25
93		80r. pale green (1 .8.92)	21·00	16·00
94		80r. pale green (E)	25·00	18·00
95		100r. brown/buff (1.4.93)	13·50	6·75
96		200r. blue (1.8.93)	90·00	65·00
97		300r. blue/pale brown (1.8.93)	95·00	80·00
85/97 Set of 11 (one of each value)			£250	£180

		(c) P 13½		
98	4	5r. orange-yellow	4·50	2·50
99		10r. rosy mauve	5·00	3·75
100		15r. red-brown	7·00	3·75
101		20r. lavender	13·00	10·50

102		50r. pale blue	13·50	9·25
103		50r. pale blue (E)	19·00	12·50
104		75r. rose	13·50	9·25
105		80r. pale green	25·00	20·00
106		100r. brown/buff	13·50	9·00
107		150r. carmine/rose (1.8.93)	80·00	45·00
98/107 Set of 9			£160	£100

Stamps of this type were also issued for the Azores districts of Angra, Horta and Ponta Delgada. First printings were in sheets of 24 each containing 12 stamps of Angra and Horta or 12 of Funchal and Ponta Delgada. Later printings were in sheets of 28 containing stamps of one district only.

The 5, 80, 150, 200 and 300r. were reprinted perf 11½ in 1900 and all values perf 13½ in 1905.

1893–96. Bisected diagonally.

108	4	Half of 5r. (Jan. 1893)	—	27·00
109		Half of 100r. (Nov. 1896)	—	55·00

The above bisections were officially authorised.

(Des and eng E. Mouchon. Typo)

1897 (1 Jan). Name and value in black or carmine (500r.).

		(a) P 11½		
110	5	2½r. pale grey	75	50
111		5r. orange-red	75	50
112		10r. green	75	50
113		15r. chocolate	8·75	6·75
114		20r. deep lilac	2·10	1·20
115		25r. blue-green	4·25	1·20
116		50r. blue	8·75	6·75
117		75r. rose	2·20	1·60
118		80r. mauve	2·20	2·00
119		100r. blue/blue	2·20	2·00
120		150r. purple-brown/straw	4·25	2·10
121		200r. purple/flesh	4·50	3·50
122		300r. blue/pink	4·50	3·50
123		500r. black/azure	4·75	4·00
110/123 Set of 14			46·00	32·00

		(b) P 12½		
124	5	50r. blue	22·00	13·00
125		500r. black/azure	18·00	13·00

1898 (1 July)–**1905**. Colours changed and new values. Name and value in black or carmine (75r.). P 11½.

126	5	15r. deep green (1.1.99)	5·00	3·75
127		25r. carmine (1.1.99)	2·10	95
128		50r. ultramarine (6.05)	2·10	1·50
129		65r. steel-blue	1·80	1·50
130		75r. brown/yellow (6.05)	2·75	1·70
131		115r. brown-red/pink	3·50	2·30
		a. Error. On cream		
132		130r. sepia/cream	3·50	2·30
133		180r. slate/pale pink	3·50	2·30
126/133 Set of 8			22·00	15·00

C. MADEIRA

From 1905 onwards the stamps of Portugal have again been in normal use in Madeira, though certain special issues from 1898 to 1928 and again from 1980 have been inscribed "MADEIRA" for use there. Stamps issued from 1980 were also sold and valid for postage in mainland Portugal.

1898 (1 Apr). Vasco da Gama Commemorative issue. As Nos. 378/85 of Portugal but inscr "MADEIRA". P 14 to 15.

134	40	2½r. blue-green	3·75	1·90
135	41	5r. vermilion	3·75	1·90
136	42	10r. dull purple	4·75	2·20
137	43	25r. yellow-green	4·50	2·00
138	44	50r. deep blue	13·50	5·00
139	45	75r. chocolate	17·00	11·50
140	46	100r. bistre-brown	18·00	11·50
141	47	150r. ochre	26·00	19·00
134/141 Set of 8			70·00	43·00

For Nos. 134/141 with "REPUBLICA" overprint, see Nos. 455/62 of Portugal.

CHARITY TAX STAMPS. The notes after No. 454 of Portugal also apply to the following.

1925 (8 May). CHARITY TAX. Marquis de Pombal issue of Portugal inscr "MADEIRA".

C142	C 73	15c. grey	2·50	2·10
C143	C 74	15c. grey	2·50	2·10
C144	C 75	15c. grey	2·50	2·10
C142/144 Set of 3			5·75	4·75

Nos. C142/4 were in use from 8 to 13 May 1925 and from 5 to 15 May of 1926 to 1929. From 4 January 1934 to 1 October 1945 they were also used on ordinary correspondence.

1925 (8 May). POSTAGE DUE. As Nos. C142/4 optd "MULTA".
D145	C **73**	30c. grey	2·00	1·90
D146	C **74**	30c. grey	2·00	1·90
D147	C **75**	30c. grey	2·00	1·90
D145/147	Set of 3		4·75	4·50

6 Ceres

7 20r. Stamp, 1868

(Recess, values typo Perkins, Bacon & Co)

1928 (1 May). Funchal Museum Fund. Value in black. P 13½.
148	6	3c. violet	95	80
149		4c. orange-yellow	95	80
150		5c. light blue	95	80
151		6c. brown	1·30	1·10
152		10c. vermilion	1·30	1·10
153		15c. green	1·30	1·10
154		16c. chocolate	1·30	1·10
155		25c. claret	1·40	1·20
156		32c. blue-green	1·40	1·20
157		40c. yellow-brown	1·40	1·20
158		50c. slate	1·40	1·20
		a. Value omitted	34·00	
159		64c. greenish blue	1·40	1·20
160		80c. sepia	1·40	1·20
161		96c. rose-carmine	5·50	5·25
162		1E. grey-black	1·10	1·10
163		1E.20 rose	1·10	1·10
164		1E.60 blue	1·10	1·10
165		2E.40 violet	1·70	1·60
166		3E.36 olive-green	2·40	2·10
167		4E.50 lake	2·40	2·10
168		7E. indigo	8·50	8·50
148/168	Set of 21		33·00	30·00

These stamps were issued for obligatory use, on specified dates in 1928 and 1929, instead of the stamps of Portugal, normally in use.

(Des P.O. Art Dept. Litho)

1980 (2 Jan). 112th Anniv of First Overprinted Madeira Stamps. T **7** and similar vert design. P 11½×12.
169		6E.50 black, olive-bistre & bluish grn	45	25
170		19E.50 black, dull purple & verm	1·50	1·00
MS171	140×115 mm. Nos. 169/70 (sold at 30E.)		6·75	6·75

Design: 19E.50, 100r. stamp, 1868.

No. MS171 overprinted for "CAPEX '87" Stamp Exhibition was a private production.

8 Ox Sledge

9 O Bailinho (folk dance)

(Des L. F. de Abreu. Litho)

1980 (17 Sept). World Tourism Conference, Manila, Philippines. T **8** and similar horiz designs. One phosphor band (Nos. 172/6). P 12.
172		50c. Type **8**	20	15
173		1E. Wine and grapes	30	20
174		5E. Map of Madeira	75	40
175		6E.50 Basketwork	95	45
176		8E. Orchid	1·40	65
177		30E. Local fishing boat	2·75	1·10
172/177	Set of 6		5·75	2·75

(Des L. F. de Abreu. Litho)

1981 (11 May). Europa. One phosphor band. P 12.
178	**9**	22E. multicoloured	1·90	95
MS179	141×115 mm. No. 178×2		8·50	8·50

10 Caravel approaching Madeira

11 Dactylorhiza foliosa

(Des T. de Mello. Litho)

1981 (1 July). 560th Anniv (1980) of Discovery of Madeira. T **10** and similar horiz design. Multicoloured. One phosphor band. P 12.
180		8E.50 Type **10**	70	45
181		33E.50 Prince Henry the Navigator and map of Atlantic Ocean	2·75	1·00

(Des L. F. de Abreu. Litho)

1981 (6 Oct)–**83**. Regional Flowers. T **11** and similar vert designs. Multicoloured. One phosphor band (Nos. 182/91). P 12½×12.
182		7E. Type **11**	50	30
		a. Booklet pane. Nos. 182/3, 187 and 192	16·00	
183		8E.50 Geranium maderense	55	30
184		9E. Goodyera macrophylla (31.8.82)	50	10
		a. Booklet pane. Nos. 184/5, 188 and 190 (31.8.82)	16·00	
185		10E. Armeria maderensis (31.8.82)	65	25
186		12E.50 Matthiola maderensis (19.10.83)	45	20
		a. Booklet pane. Nos. 186, 189, 191 and 193 (19.10.83)	16·00	
187		20E. Isoplexis sceptrum	1·10	70
188		27E. Viola paradoxa (31.8.82)	1·90	1·20
189		30E. Erica maderensis (19.10.83)	1·20	75
190		33E.50 Scilla maderensis (31.8.82)	2·00	1·40
191		37E.50 Cirsium latifolium (19.10.83)	1·70	1·00
192		50E. Echium candicans	2·75	1·50
193		100E. Clethra arborea (19.10.83)	3·50	1·60
182/193	Set of 12		15·00	8·50

Nos. 194/8 are vacant.

12 First Sugar Mill

13 Dancer holding Dolls on Staff

(Des J. P. Roque. Litho)

1982 (3 May). Europa. One phosphor band. P 12×11½.
199	**12**	33E.50 multicoloured	3·25	1·50
MS200	139×115 mm. No. 199×3		17·00	17·00

(Des T. de Mello. Litho)

1982 (15 Dec). O Brinco Dancing Dolls. T **13** and similar vert design. Multicoloured. One phosphor band. P 13½.
201		27E. Type **13**	2·20	1·30
202		33E.50 Dancers	3·50	1·80

14 Los Levadas Irrigation Channels

15 Flag of Madeira

(Des J. Tinoco. Litho Litografia Maia, Oporto)

1983 (5 May). Europa. One phosphor band. P 12½.
203	**14**	37E.50 multicoloured	3·25	1·30
MS204	114×140 mm. No. 203×3		21·00	21·00

(Des A. Leitão. Litho)

1983 (1 July). Flag. One phosphor band. P 12×11½.
205	**15**	12E.50 multicoloured	1·30	45

MADEIRA / Madeira

(Des J. Larrivière and J. Cândido. Litho)

1984 (2 May). Europa. As T **398** of Portugal but additionally inscr "MADEIRA". Two phosphor bands. P 12.

206	51E. multicoloured	4·50	2·20
MS207	113×140 mm. No. 206×3	19·00	19·00

16 MG-A Coupe   **17** Basket Sledge

(Des A. Magalhães. Litho)

1984 (3 Aug). 25th Anniv of Madeira Rally. T **16** and similar vert design. Multicoloured. Two phosphor bands. P 12.

208	16E. Type **16**	90	45
209	51E. Lancia Rallye 037 coupe (1982) (*different*)	3·25	1·60

The phosphor bands are at right angles along the left and top of the stamp.

(Des A. Magalhães. Litho)

1984 (22 Nov). Transport (1st series). T **17** and similar horiz designs. Multicoloured. One phosphor band. P 12.

210	16E. Type **17**	80	45
	a. Imperf×p 12. Booklets	1·30	1·30
	ab. Booklet pane. Nos. 210a/13a	18·00	
211	35E. Hammock	1·70	1·10
	a. Imperf×p 12. Booklets	3·75	3·75
212	40E. Borracheiros (wine carriers)	2·40	1·10
	a. Imperf×p 12. Booklets	5·75	5·75
213	51E. Local sailing boat	3·00	1·70
	a. Imperf×p 12. Booklets	6·50	6·50
210/213	Set of 4	7·00	4·00

See also Nos. 218/21.

18 Braguinha Player   **19** Black Scabbardfish (*Aphanopus carbo*)

(Des J. Tinoco. Litho)

1985 (6 May). Europa. One phosphor band. P 12.

214	**18**	60E. multicoloured	4·50	1·90
MS215	140×115 mm. No. 214×3		23·00	23·00

(Des A. da Conceição. Litho)

1985 (5 July). Fishes (1st series). T **19** and similar horiz design. Multicoloured. One phosphor band. P 12.

216	40E. Type **19**	2·40	1·30
217	60E. Opah (*Lampris guttatus*)	3·25	1·90

See also Nos. 222/3 and 250/3.

(Des A. Magalhães. Litho)

1985 (11 Sept). Transport (2nd series). Horiz designs as T **17**. Multicoloured. One phosphor band. P 12.

218	20E. Ox sledge	80	45
	a. Imperf×p 12. Booklets	2·00	1·90
	ab. Booklet pane. Nos. 218a/21a	22·00	
219	40E. Mountain railway	1·90	1·10
	a. Imperf×p 12. Booklets	4·75	4·75
220	46E. Fishing boat and basket used by pesquitos (itinerant fish sellers)	2·50	1·80
	a. Imperf×p 12. Booklets	6·50	6·50
221	60E. Coastal ferry	3·00	1·50
	a. Imperf×p 12. Booklets	7·50	7·50
218/221	Set of 4	7·50	4·25

(Des A. da Conceição. Litho)

1986 (7 Jan). Fishes (2nd series). Horiz designs as T **19**. Multicoloured. One phosphor band. P 12.

222	20E. Big-eye tuna (*Thunnus obesus*)	1·10	45
223	75E. Alfonsino (*Beryx decadactylus*)	5·25	2·10

20 Cory's Shearwater and Tanker   **21** São Lourenço Fort, Funchal

(Des J. P. Roque. Litho)

1986 (5 May). Europa. One phosphor band. P 12.

224	**20**	68E.50 multicoloured	5·25	2·10
MS225	140×114 mm. No. 224×3		21·00	21·00

(Des Maluda. Litho)

1986 (1 July). Fortresses. T **21** and similar horiz designs. Multicoloured. Two phosphor bands. P 12.

226	22E.50 Type **21**	1·10	55
	a. Imperf×p 12. Booklets	1·40	1·40
	ab. Booklet pane. Nos. 226a/9a	22·00	
227	52E.50 São João do Pico Fort, Funchal	3·25	1·60
	a. Imperf×p 12. Booklets	4·25	4·25
228	68E.50 São Tiago Fort, Funchal	4·25	2·10
	a. Imperf×p 12. Booklets	6·50	6·50
229	100E. Nossa Senhora do Amparo Fort, Machico	5·25	1·80
	a. Imperf×p 12. Booklets	8·50	8·50
226/229	Set of 4	12·50	5·50

22 Firecrest (*Regulus ingnicapillus madeirensis*)   **23** Social Services Centre, Funchal (Raul Chorão Ramalho)

(Des J. Projecto. Litho)

1987 (6 Mar). Birds (1st series). T **22** and similar vert designs. Multicoloured. Two phosphor bands. P 12.

230	25E. Type **22**	1·10	45
	a. Imperf×p 12. Booklets	1·40	1·40
	ab. Booklet pane. Nos. 230a/3a	20·00	
231	57E. Trocaz pigeon (*Columba trocaz*)	3·25	1·80
	a. Imperf×p 12. Booklets	4·00	4·00
232	74E.50 Barn owl (*Tyto alba schmitzi*)	4·25	2·40
	a. Imperf×p 12. Booklets	5·25	5·25
233	125E. Soft-plumaged petrel (*Pterodroma madeira*)	5·25	2·75
	a. Imperf×p 12. Booklets	8·00	8·00
230/233	Set of 4	12·50	6·75

See also Nos. 240/3.

(Des J. Tinoco. Litho)

1987 (5 May). Europa. Architecture. Two phosphor bands. P 12.

234	**23**	74E.50 multicoloured	4·75	2·10
MS235	140×113 mm. No. 234×4		21·00	21·00

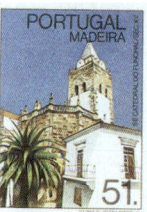

24 Funchal Cathedral   **25** *Maria Cristina* (mail boat)

(Des A. Pimentel. Litho Litografia Maia, Oporto)

1987 (1 July). Historic Buildings. T **24** and similar vert design. Multicoloured. Two phosphor bands. P 12.

236	51E. Type **24**	3·00	1·50
237	74E.50 Old Town Hall, Santa Cruz	3·50	1·50

MADEIRA / Madeira

(Des L. Duran and C. Leitão. Litho)

1988 (21 Apr). Europa. Transport and Communications. Two phosphor bands. P 12.

238	25	80E. multicoloured	5·75	2·10
MS239	139×112 mm. As No. 238×4 but with cream background		21·00	21·00

(Des J. Projecto. Litho)

1988 (15 June). Birds (2nd series). Horiz designs as T **22**. Multicoloured. Two phosphor bands. P 12.

240	27E. European robin (*Erithacus rubecula microrhyncus*)	1·10	30
	a. Imperf×p 12½. Booklets	1·40	1·40
	ab. Booklet pane. Nos. 240a/3a	17·00	
241	60E. Streaked rock sparrow (*Petronia petronia madeirensis*)	2·75	1·70
	a. Imperf×p 12½. Booklets	4·25	4·25
242	80E. Chaffinch (*Fringilla coelebs maderensis*)	3·75	1·80
	a. Imperf×p 12½. Booklets	4·75	4·75
243	100E. Northern sparrow hawk (*Accipiter nisus granti*)	4·25	1·80
	a. Imperf×p 12½. Booklets	5·25	5·25
240/243 Set of 4		10·50	5·00

26 Columbus and Funchal House

27 Child flying Kite

(Des R. Carita. Litho)

1988 (1 July). Christopher Columbus's Houses in Madeira. T **26** and similar multicoloured design. Two phosphor bands. P 12.

244	55E. Type **26**	3·00	1·30
245	80E. Columbus and Porto Santo house (horiz)	3·25	1·70

(Des A. Pimentel. Litho)

1989 (26 Apr). Europa. Children's Games and Toys. T **27** and similar horiz design. Multicoloured. Two phosphor bands. P 12.

246	80E. Type **27**	5·25	2·75
MS247	139×112 mm 80E.×2, Type **27**; 80E.×2, Child flying kite (*different*)	21·00	21·00

28 Church of St. John the Evangelist

29 Spiny Hatchetfish (*Argyropelecus aculeatus*)

(Des C. Leitão. Litho)

1989 (28 July). "Brasiliana 89" Stamp Exhibition, Rio de Janeiro. Madeiran Churches. T **28** and similar vert design. Multicoloured. Two phosphor bands. P 12.

248	29E. Type **28**	85	45
249	87E. St. Clara's Church and Convent	3·75	2·10

(Des J. Projecto. Litho)

1989 (20 Sept). Fishes (3rd series). T **29** and similar horiz designs. Multicoloured. Two phosphor bands. P 12.

250	29E. Type **29**	85	20
	a. Imperf×p 13½. Booklets	1·20	1·10
	ab. Booklet pane. Nos. 250a/3a	12·50	
251	60E. Dog wrasse (*Pseudolepidaplois scrota*)	2·50	1·50
	a. Imperf×p 13½. Booklets	2·75	2·75
252	87E. Rainbow wrasse (*Coris julis*)	3·75	2·00
	a. Imperf×p 13½. Booklets	4·25	4·25
253	100E. Madeiran scorpion fish (*Scorpaena maderensis*)	4·00	2·75
	a. Imperf×p 13½. Booklets	4·75	4·75
250/253 Set of 4		10·00	5·75

30 Zarco Post Office

31 Bananas

(Des C. Leitão. Litho)

1990 (11 Apr). Europa. Post Office Buildings. T **30** and similar horiz design. Multicoloured. Two phosphor bands. P 12.

254	80E. Type **30**	2·50	1·70
MS255	139×111 mm. 80E.×2, Type **30**; 80E.×2, Porto da Cruz Post Office	18·00	18·00

(Des J. Projecto. Litho)

1990 (5 June)–**92**. Sub-tropical Fruits. T **31** and similar vert designs. Multicoloured. Two phosphor bands. P 12.

256	5E. Type **31**	25	15
	a. Imperf×p 13½. Booklets	35	25
	ab. Booklet pane. Nos. 256a, 258a, 261a and 265a	10·50	
257	10E. Thorn apple (21.2.92)	25	15
	a. Imperf×p 13½. Booklets	35	25
	ab. Booklet pane. Nos. 257a, 260a, 264a and 267a	8·75	
258	32E. Avocado	90	50
	a. Imperf×p 13½. Booklets	1·60	1·50
259	35E. Mangoes (7.6.91)	90	50
	a. Imperf×p 13½. Booklets	1·00	95
	ab. Booklet pane. Nos. 259a, 262a, 263a and 266a	10·50	
260	38E. Tomatoes (21.2.92)	1·00	50
	a. Imperf×p 13½. Booklets	1·10	1·00
261	60E. Sugar apple	2·30	1·40
	a. Imperf×p 13½. Booklets	3·50	3·25
262	65E. Surinam cherries (7.6.91)	2·20	1·30
	a. Imperf×p 13½. Booklets	2·50	2·40
263	70E. Brazilian guavas (7.6.91)	2·40	1·40
	a. Imperf×p 13½. Booklets	2·75	2·50
264	85E. Delicious fruits (21.2.92)	2·75	1·60
	a. Imperf×p 13½. Booklets	3·00	3·00
265	100E. Passion fruit	3·50	2·10
	a. Imperf×p 13½. Booklets	4·50	4·25
266	110E. Papayas (7.6.91)	3·50	2·10
	a. Imperf×p 13½. Booklets	3·75	3·50
267	125E. Guava (21.2.92)	3·50	2·10
	a. Imperf×p 13½. Booklets	4·00	3·75
256/267 Set of 12		21·00	12·50

Nos. 268/9 are vacant.

32 Tunny Boat

33 Trocaz Pigeon

(Des A. Magalhães. Litho)

1990 (24 Aug). Boats. T **32** and similar horiz designs. Multicoloured. Two phosphor bands. P 12.

270	32E. Type **32**	70	25
271	60E. Desert Islands boat	1·70	1·00
272	70E. Maneiro (fishing boat)	2·00	1·40
273	95E. Chavelha (fishing boat)	3·00	2·00
270/273 Set of 4		6·75	4·25

(Des J. Projecto. Litho)

1991 (23 Jan). The Trocaz Pigeon (*Columba tocaz*). T **33** and similar vert designs. Multicoloured. Two phosphor bands. P 12.

274	35E. Type **33**	1·60	55
	a. Strip or block of 4. Nos. 274/7	6·75	
275	35E. Two pigeons	1·60	55

MADEIRA / Madeira

276	35E. Pigeon on nest	1·60	55
277	35E. Pigeon alighting on twig	1·60	55
274/277 Set of 4		5·75	2·00

Nos. 274/7 were issued in *se-tenant* strips and blocks of four stamps within the sheet, each horizontal strip forming a composite design.

34 European Remote Sensing ("ERS1") Satellite   **35** Columbus and Funchal House

(Des P. Vidagal. Litho)

1991 (11 Apr). Europa. Europe in Space. T **34** and similar horiz design. Multicoloured. Two phosphor bands. P 12.

278	80E. Type 34	3·25	2·10
MS279	140 × 112 mm 80E.×2, Type **34**; 80E.×2, "Spot" satellite	18·00	18·00

(Des L. de Freitas. Litho)

1992 (22 May). Europa. 500th Anniv of Discovery of America by Columbus. Two phosphor bands. P 12.

| 280 | **35** | 85E. multicoloured | 3·25 | 1·30 |

36 Gavião (ferry)   **37** "Shadow thrown by Christa Maar"

(Des J. Tinoco. Litho)

1992 (18 Sept). Inter-island Ships. T **36** and similar vert designs. Multicoloured. Two phosphor bands. P 12.

281	38E. Type 36	85	35
282	65E. *Independência* (catamaran ferry)	1·70	1·20
283	85E. *Madeirense* (car ferry)	2·10	1·40
284	120E. *Funchalense* (freighter)	3·00	1·60
281/284 Set of 4		7·00	4·00

(Des C. Leitão. Litho)

1993 (5 May). Europa. Contemporary Art. T **37** and similar vert design showing paintings by Lourdes Castro. Multicoloured. P 12.

285	90E. Type 37	3·00	1·40
MS286	140×112 mm 90E.×2, Type **37**; 90E.×2, "Shadow thrown by Dahlia"	13·00	13·00

38 Seals Swimming   **39** Window of St. Francis's Convent, Funchal

(Des J. Projecto. Litho)

1993 (30 June). Mediterranean Monk Seal (*Monachus monachus*). T **38** and similar horiz designs. Multicoloured. P 12.

287	42E. Type 38	1·40	70
	a. Strip or block of 4. Nos. 287/90	5·75	
288	42E. Seal basking	1·40	70
289	42E. Two adult seals on rocks	1·40	70
290	42E. Mother suckling young	1·40	70
287/290 Set of 4		5·00	2·50

Nos. 287/90 were issued together in *se-tenant* strips and blocks of four stamps within the sheet, each horizontal strip forming a composite design.

(Des Ana Bela Silva. Litho)

1993 (30 July). Regional Architecture. T **39** and similar vert design. Multicoloured. P 12.

291	42E. Type 39	85	55
292	130E. Window of Mercy, Old Hospital, Funchal	3·00	1·90

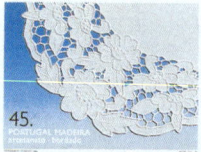

40 Native of Cape of Good Hope and Explorer with Model Caravel   **41** Embroidery

(Des L. F. de Abreu. Litho)

1994 (5 May). Europa. Discoveries. T **40** and similar horiz design Multicoloured. P 12.

293	100E. Type 40	2·10	1·60
MS294	140×112 mm. 100E.×2, Type **40**; 100E.×2, Palm tree and explorer with model caravel	10·50	10·50

(Des F. Coelho. Litho)

1994 (5 May). Traditional Crafts (1st series). T **41** and similar horiz designs. Multicoloured. P 12.

295	45E. Type 41	75	35
	a. Imperf×p 11½. Booklets	85	85
	ab. Booklet pane. Nos. 295a/8a	8·25	
296	75E. Tapestry	1·50	95
	a. Imperf×p 11½. Booklets	1·80	1·80
297	100E. Boots	2·00	1·30
	a. Imperf×p 11½. Booklets	2·10	2·10
298	140E. Wicker chair back	3·00	1·90
	a. Imperf×p 11½. Booklets	3·25	3·25
295/298 Set of 4		6·50	4·00

See also Nos. 301/4.

42 Funchal   **43** Bread Dough Figures

(Des J. Guedes. Litho)

1994 (1 July). District Arms. T **42** and similar vert design. Multicoloured. P 12.

299	45E. Type 42	75	35
300	140E. Porto Santo	2·75	1·60

(Des F. Coelho. Litho)

1995 (30 June). Traditional Crafts (2nd series). T **43** and similar vert designs. Multicoloured. P 12.

301	45E. Type 43	85	50
	a. Imperf×p 11½. Booklets	85	85
	ab. Booklet pane. Nos. 301a/4a	7·25	
302	80E. Inlaid wooden box	1·50	85
	a. Imperf×p 11½. Booklets	1·70	1·70
303	95E. Bamboo cage	1·70	1·20
	a. Imperf×p 11½. Booklets	1·90	1·90
304	135E. Woollen bonnet	2·30	1·50
	a. Imperf×p 11½. Booklets	2·50	2·50
301/304 Set of 4		5·75	3·75

44 Guiomar Vilhena (entrepreneur)   **45** "Adoration of the Magi"

MADEIRA / Madeira

(Des L. Duran. Litho)

1996 (3 May). Europa. Famous Women. P 12.

305	44	98E. multicoloured	2·10	1·10
MS306	140×112 mm. No. 305×3		6·50	6·50

(Des J. Tinoco. Litho)

1996 (1 July). Religious Paintings by Flemish Artists. T **45** and similar multicoloured designs. P 12.

307	47E. Type **45**	80	35
	a. P 12 × imperf. Booklets	90	90
	ab. Booklet pane. Nos. 307a/10a	7·25	
308	78E. "St. Mary Magdalene"	1·40	95
	a. P 12 × imperf. Booklets	1·60	1·60
309	98E. "The Annunciation" (*horiz*)	1·70	1·20
	a. Imperf × p 12. Booklets	1·90	1·90
310	140E. "Saints Peter, Paul and Andrew" (*horiz*)	2·10	1·50
	a. Imperf × p 12. Booklets	2·50	2·50
307/310	Set of 4	5·50	3·50

46 *Eumichtis albostigmata* (moth)   **47** Robert Achim and Anne of Arfet (Legend of Machico)

(Des J. Projecto. Litho)

1997 (12 Feb). Butterflies and Moths (1st series). T **46** and similar horiz designs. Multicoloured. P 12.

311	49E. Type **46**	75	35
	a. Imperf×p 11½. Booklets	80	80
	ab. Booklet pane. Nos. 311a/14a	7·25	
312	80E. *Menophra maderae* (moth)	1·30	65
	a. Imperf×p 11½. Booklets	1·50	1·50
313	100E. Painted lady (*Vanessa indica*)	1·50	1·20
	a. Imperf×p 11½. Booklets	1·70	1·70
314	140E. Large white (*Pieris brassicae*)	2·75	2·50
	a. Imperf×p 11½. Booklets	3·00	3·00
311/314	Set of 4	5·75	4·25

See also Nos. 319/322.

(Des Celeste Maia. Litho Litografia Maia, Oporto)

1997 (5 May). Europa. Tales and Legends. P 12.

315	47	100E. multicoloured	2·10	1·10
MS316	140×106 mm. No. 315 × 3		6·50	6·50

48 New Year's Eve Fireworks Display, Funchal   **49** *Gonepteryx Cleopatra*

(Des L. de Abreu. Litho Litografia Maia, Oporto)

1998 (21 May). Europa. National Festivals. P 12.

317	48	100E. multicoloured	1·90	95
MS318	140×109 mm. No. 317 × 3		6·25	6·25

(Des J. Projecto. Litho Litografia Maia, Oporto)

1998 (6 Sept). Butterflies and Moths (2nd series). T **49** and similar horiz designs. Multicoloured. P 12.

319	50E. Type **49**	75	35
	a. Imperf × p 12. Booklets	85	85
	ab. Booklet. Nos. 319a/22a	4·00	
320	85E. *Xanthorhoe rupicola*	1·10	75
	a. Imperf × p 12. Booklets	1·30	1·30
321	100E. *Noctua teixeirai*	1·50	95
	a. Imperf × p 12. Booklets	1·70	1·70
322	140E. *Xenochlorodes nubigena*	2·10	1·50
	a. Imperf × p 12. Booklets	2·50	2·50
319/322	Set of 4	5·00	3·25

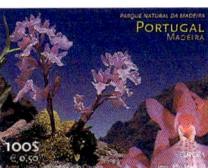 

50 Madeira Island Nature Park   **51** Medieval Floor Tile

(Des J. Sarmento and P. Oliveira. Litho Litografia Maia, Oporto)

1999 (5 May). Europa. Parks and Gardens. P 12.

323	50	100E. multicoloured	1·50	95
MS324	153×108 mm. No. 323 × 3		5·25	5·25

(Des J. Brandão. Litho)

1999 (1 July). Tiles from Frederico de Freitas Collection, Funchal. T **51** and similar horiz designs. Multicoloured. P 12.

325	51E. Type **51**	75	35
326	80E. English art-nouveau tile (19–20th century)	1·20	85
327	95E. Persian tile (14th century)	1·50	95
328	100E. Spanish Moor tile (13th century)	1·60	1·10
329	140E. Dutch Delft tile (18th century)	2·10	1·50
330	210E. Syrian tile (13–14th century)	3·00	2·10
325/330	Set of 6	9·25	6·25
MS331	123×117 mm. Nos. 325/30	10·50	10·50

52 "Building Europe"   **53** Mountain Orchid

(Des J.-P. Cousin. Litho)

2000 (9 May). Europa. P 12.

332	52	100E. multicoloured	2·75	2·10
MS333	154×108 mm. No. 332 × 3		8·50	8·50

(Des C. Pinto. Litho Litografia Maia, Oporto)

2000 (4 July). Plants of Laurissilva Forest. T **53** and similar horiz designs. Multicoloured. P 12.

334	52E. Type **53**	70	35
335	85E. White orchid	1·20	80
336	100E. Leafy plant	1·40	90
337	100E. Laurel	1·40	90
338	140E. Barbusano	2·10	1·50
339	350E. Visco	4·75	3·75
334/339	Set of 6	10·50	7·50
MS340	140×112 mm. Nos. 334/9	11·50	11·50

54 Marine Life   **55** Musicians

(Des J. Machado. Litho)

2001 (9 May). Europa. Water Resources. P 12.

341	54	105E. multicoloured	3·25	2·10
MS342	140×110 mm. No. 341 × 3		7·50	7·50

(Des V. Santos. Litho)

2001 (19 July). Traditions of Madeira. T **55** and similar horiz designs. Multicoloured. P 12.

343	53E. Type **55**	70	55
344	85E. Couple carrying produce	1·20	95
345	105E. Couple selling goods	1·60	1·20
343/345	Set of 3	3·25	2·40
MS346	140×112 mm. 350E. Man carrying birds	5·00	5·00

167

MADEIRA / Madeira

New Currency. 100 Cents = 1 Euro

56 Clown   **57** Doves

(Des E. Aires. Litho Litografia Maia, Oporto)

2002 (9 May). Europa. Circus. P 12.

347	**56**	54c. multicoloured	3·00	2·75
MS348	140×110 mm. No. 347 × 3. P 12½		8·50	8·50

(Des J. Projecto. Litho Litografia Maia, Oporto)

2002 (30 Aug). The Turtle Dove (*Streptopelia turtur*). T **57** and similar vert designs. Multicoloured. P 12.

349		28c. Type **57**	1·00	65
		a. Strip or block of 4. Nos. 349/52	4·25	
350		28c. Perching dove	1·00	65
351		28c. Dove with raised wings	1·00	65
352		28c. Dove with chicks	1·00	65
349/352	Set of 4		3·50	2·30

Nos. 349/52 were issued together in *se-tenant* strips or blocks of four stamps within the sheet.

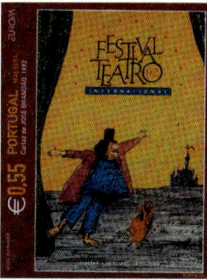 

58 1992 Theatre Festival Poster (José Brandão)   **59** Bird of Paradise Flower, Figure and Yachts

(Des J. Brandão. Litho)

2003 (5 May). Europa. Poster Art. P 12×12½.

353	**58**	55c. multicoloured	2·50	1·80
MS354	140×113 mm. No. 353 × 2		4·75	4·75

(Des J. Machado. Litho Enschedé)

2004 (10 May). Europa. Holidays. P 13½×14.

355	**59**	56c. multicoloured	2·50	1·80
MS356	141×112 mm. No. 355×2		4·75	4·75

60 Selvagens White-faced Storm-Petrel (*Pelagodroma marina hypoleuca*)   **61** Espetada em Pau de Louro (skewered meat)

(Des P. Delgado. Litho Cartor)

2004 (24 May). Selvagens Islands. T **60** and similar horiz designs. Multicoloured. P 13×13½.

357		30c. Type **60**	1·00	70
358		45c. *Monathes lowei* (plant) and beetle	1·60	1·10
359		72c. *Tarentola bischoffi*	2·75	1·80
357/359	Set of 3		4·75	3·25
MS360	140×112 mm. Nos. 357/9		5·75	5·75

No. **MS**360 has the stamps arranged so as to make a composite design with a description of the islands below.

(Des A. Santos. Litho Enschedé)

2005 (5 May). Europa. Gastronomy. T **61** and similar horiz design. Multicoloured. P 14×13½.

361		57c. Type **61**	2·10	1·30
		a. Booklet pane. Nos. 361 (2005)	2·20	
MS362	125×95 mm. 57c.×2, Filete de espada (fish)×2		5·50	5·50
		a. Booklet pane. No. **MS**362 (2005)	5·75	

62 Coastline   **63** *Euphorbia pulcherrima*

(Des A. Santos. Litho Enschedé)

2005 (1 July). Tourism. T **62** and similar horiz designs. Multicoloured. P 14×13½.

363		30c. Type **62**	85	65
		a. Booklet pane. Nos. 363/4 (2005)	1·80	
364		30c. Chaffinch	85	65
365		45c. Hikers	1·30	1·00
		a. Booklet pane. Nos. 365/7 (2005)	2·75	
366		45c. Windmill	1·30	1·00
367		57c. Horse riders and scuba divers	1·50	1·20
		a. Booklet pane. Nos. 367/8 (2005)	3·75	
368		74c. Flowers and fireworks	2·10	1·70
363/368	Set of 6		7·00	5·50
MS369	125×96 mm. 30c. Girl carrying basket; €1.55 Lace and tower		5·25	5·25
		a. Booklet pane. No. **MS**369 (2005)	5·50	

Nos. 361a, **MS**362a, 363a, 365a, 367a and **MS**369a, were issued in booklets consisting six panes interleaved with five pages of text.

(Des A. Santos. Litho Enschedé)

2006 (7 Mar). Flowers. T **63** and similar horiz designs. Multicoloured. P 12½×12.

370		30c. Type **63**	85	65
		a. Booklet pane. Nos. 370/1	2·50	
371		45c. *Aloe arborescens*	1·30	1·00
372		57c. *Senna didymobotrya*	1·50	1·20
		a. Booklet pane. Nos. 372/3	3·75	
373		74c. *Anthurium andraeanum*	2·10	1·70
374		€1 *Strelitzia reginae*	2·75	2·20
		a. Booklet pane. Nos. 374/5	8·50	
375		€2 *Hydrangea macrophylla*	5·50	4·50
370/375	Set of 6		12·50	10·00
MS376	Two sheets, each 124×95 mm		10·00	10·00

(a) 45c.×4, *Rosa*; *Leucospermum nutans*; *Paphiopedilum insigne*; *Hippeastrum vittatum*

    a. Booklet pane. No. **MS**376a .... 5·50

(b) 45c.×4, *Bougainvillea*; *Cymbidium*; *Hibiscus rosa-sinesis*; *Erythrina crista-galli*

    a. Booklet pane. No. **MS**376b .... 5·50

64 Figures (Ana Soares)   **65** Terraces

2006 (9 May). Europa. Integration. Winning Entries in ANACED (association for art and creativity by and for people with disabilities) Painting Competition. T **64** and similar horiz designs. Multicoloured. P 12½.

377		60c. Type **64**	1·70	1·30
		a. Booklet pane. No. 377	1·80	
MS378	125×95 mm. 60c.×2, Swimming pool (Pedro Fonseca); Blind figure with dog (Andre Gaspar)		3·25	2·75
		a. Booklet pane. No. **MS**378	3·50	

(Des E. Aires. Litho Cartor)

2006 (1 July). Madeira Wine. T **65** and similar horiz designs. Multicoloured. P 13.

379		30c. Type **65**	85	65
		a. Booklet pane. Nos. 379/80	2·50	
380		52c. Workers and baskets of grapes	1·30	1·00

MADEIRA / Madeira

381	60c. Barrels in cellar	1·70	1·30
	a. Booklet pane. Nos. 381/2	4·00	
382	75c. Barrels and glass of wine	2·10	1·70
379/382 Set of 4		5·25	4·25
MS383	125×95 mm. 45c. Vines; 60c. Worker amongst vines; 75c. Bottles; €1 Barrels	7·75	7·75
	a. Booklet pane. No. **MS**383	8·00	

Nos. 370a, 372a, 374a, **MS**376a, **MS**376b, 377a, **MS**378a and 379a, 381a and **MS**383a, were issued in booklets consisting of ten panes interleaved with five pages of text.

66 *Monachus monachus* (Mediterranean monk seal) 67 Scarf

(Des José Brandão and Paulo Falardo. Litho Cartor)

2007 (17 Apr). Marine Fauna. T **66** and similar horiz designs. Multicoloured. P 12½×13½.

384	30c. Type **66**	85	65
	a. Booklet pane. Nos. 384/7	6·25	
385	45c. *Caretta caretta* (loggerhead sea turtle)..	1·30	1·00
386	61c. *Calonectris diomedea borealis* (Cory's shearwater)	1·70	1·30
387	75c. *Aphanopus carbo* (black scabbard fish)..	2·10	1·70
384/387 Set of 4		5·25	4·25
MS388	126×95 mm 61c.×4, *Telmatactis cricoides* (sea anemone); *Charonia lampas*; *Patella aspera* (limpet); *Sparisoma cretense* (parrotfish)	7·00	7·00
	a. Booklet pane. No. **MS**388	7·25	

(Des Hulton-Deutsch and Corbis. Litho Cartor)

2007 (9 May). Europa. Centenary of Scouting. T **67** and similar horiz designs. Multicoloured. P 12½×13½.

389	61c. Type **67**	1·70	1·30
	a. Booklet pane. No. 389	1·80	
MS390	125×95 mm. 61c.×2, Reef knot; Scouts in camp	3·25	2·75
	a. Booklet pane. No. **MS**390	3·50	

The stamps of No. **MS**390 form a composite design.

68 Water-powered Mill   69 Early City

(Des Helder Soaores and Atelier Acácio Santos. Litho)

2007 (1 July). Sugar Cane Mills. T **68** and similar horiz designs. Multicoloured. P 13½×13 (**MS**393) or 12½×13½ (others).

391	30c. Type **68**	85	65
	a. Booklet pane. Nos. 391/2	3·25	
392	75c. Cattle and crushing	2·10	1·70
MS393	125×95 mm. €2.45 Ox driven mill (60×40 mm)	7·00	7·00
	a. Booklet pane. No. **MS**393	7·25	

Nos. 384a, 388a, 389a, **MS**390a, 391a and **MS**393a were issued in booklets consisting of panes interleaved with pages of text.

(Des Sofia Martins. Litho Cartor)

2008 (15 Apr). 500th Anniv of Funchal City. T **69** and similar horiz design. Multicoloured. P 12 (irregular indentation on each vert side).

394	30c. Type **69**	90	70
	a. Booklet pane. Nos. 394/5	3·00	
395	61c. Early map of city and environs	1·80	1·40
396	75c. Arms	2·20	1·70
	a. Booklet pane. No. 396/7	5·50	
397	€1 Ship and city from the sea	3·00	2·30
394/397 Set of 4		7·00	5·50
MS398	125×95 mm.	13·50	13·00
	(a) €2.45 King Manuel I of Portugal		
	a. Booklet pane. No. **MS**398a	7·00	
	(b) €2.45 Ships and harbour		
	a. Booklet pane. No. **MS**398b	7·00	

The indentation in the vertical perforations forms the shape of a cross when viewed across the sheet.

The stamps and margins of Nos. **MS**398a/b, each form a composite design.

70 Envelope, Fireworks and Woman   71 Ponta do Pargo

(Des Luiz Duran Litho Cartor)

2008 (9 May). Europa. The Letter. T **70** and similar horiz design. Multicoloured. P 12 (irregular indentation on each vert side).

399	61c. Type **785**	1·80	1·40
	a. Booklet pane. No. 399	1·90	
MS400	125×95 mm. 61c.×2, Horses and envelopes; As Type **70**	3·50	3·50
	a. Booklet pane. No. **MS**400	3·75	

The indentation in the vertical perforations forms the shape of a cross when viewed across the sheet.

The stamps of No. **MS**400 form a composite design.

(Des A. Santos and H. Soares. Litho Cartor)

2008 (19 June). Lighthouse. P 12 (irregular indentation on each horiz side).

401	**71** 61c. multicoloured	1·80	1·40
	a. Booklet pane. No. 401	1·90	

The indentation in the vertical perforations forms the shape of a cross when viewed across the sheet.

Nos. 394a, 396a, **MS**398a, **MS**398b, 399a, **MS**400a and 401a were issued in booklets consisting of panes interleaved with pages of text.

72 *Annona cherimola*   73 Constellation *Canes venatici* (spiral galaxy)

(Des A. Santos and H. Soares. Litho Cartor)

2009 (27 Apr). Fruit. T **72** and similar horiz designs. Multicoloured. P 12 (irregular indentation on each horiz side).

402	32c. Type **72**	1·10	85
403	68c. *Eugenia uniflora*	2·20	1·70
404	80c. *Persea americana*	2·50	2·00
405	€2 *Psidium guajava*	6·25	5·00
402/405 Set of 4		11·00	8·50
MS406	125×95 mm. €2.50 *Passiflora edulis* (80×31 mm)	7·75	7·75
MS407	125×95 mm. €2.50 *Musa* Dwarf Cavendish (80×31 mm)	7·75	7·75

The indentation in the vertical perforations forms the shape of a cross when viewed across the sheet.

(Des Elizabete Fonseca. Litho Cartor)

2009 (8 May). Europa. Astronomy. T **73** and similar horiz design. Multicoloured. P 12 (irregular indentation on each vert side).

408	68c. Type **73**	2·20	1·70
MS409	125×95 mm. 68c.×2, Telescope (built by University of Madeira student); As Type **73**	4·25	4·25

The stamps and margins of No. **MS**409 form a composite design.

The indentations in the vertical perforations form the shape of a cross when viewed across the sheet.

74 Bolo do Caco (rolls)   75 *Musschia aurea*

(Des Elizbete Fonseca and Atelier Acácio Santos. Litho Cartor)

2009 (28 July). Bread. Sheet 125×95 mm. P 12 (irregular indentation on each vert side.

MS410	**74** multicoloured	6·25	6·25

169

(Des Atelier Acácio Santos. Litho Cartor)

2010 (30 Apr). 50th Anniv of Botanic Gardens, Rui Veira. T **75** and similar horiz designs showing plants and views of the gardens (single stamps). Multicoloured. P 12 (irregular indentation on each vert side).

411	32c. Type **75**	1·10	0·85
412	68c. Geranium maderense	2·20	1·70
413	80c. Ranunculus cortusifolius	2·50	2·00
414	€2 Convolvulus massonii	6·25	5·00
411/414	Set of 4	11·00	8·50
MS415	125×96 mm. €2 Topiary garden (80×30 mm)...	6·25	5·00
MS416	125×96 mm. €2 Building, laboratory, climber and seeds (80×30 mm)	6·25	5·00

76 Girl

(Litho Cartor)

2010 (7 May). Europa. Children's Books. T **76** and similar vert design showing illustrations by Antonio Modesto. Multicoloured. P 12 (irregular indentation on each horiz side).

417	68c. Type **76**	2·20	1·70
MS418	125×96 mm. 68c.×2, Man seated wearing hat (Father); As Type **76**	4·25	4·25

STAMP BOOKLETS

The following checklist covers, in simplified form, booklets issued for Madeira. It is intended that it should be used in conjunction with the main listing and details of stamps and panes listed there are not repeated.

Prices are for complete booklets

Booklet No.	Date	Contents and Cover Price	Price
SB1	6.10.81	Regional Flowers 1 pane, No. 182a (85E.50)	17·00
SB2	31.8.82	Regional Flowers 1 pane, No. 184a (79E.50)	17·00
SB3	19.10.83	Regional Flowers 1 pane, No. 186a (180E.)	17·00
SB4	22.11.84	Transport (1st series) 1 pane, No. 210ab (142E.)	19·00
SB5	11.9.85	Transport (2nd series) 1 pane, No. 218ab (166E.)	23·00
SB6	1.7.86	Fortresses 1 pane, No. 226ab (243E.50)	23·00
SB7	6.3.87	Birds (1st series) 1 pane, No. 230ab (281E.50)	21·00
SB8	15.6.88	Birds (2nd series) 1 pane, No. 240ab (267E.)	18·00
SB9	20.9.89	Fishes 1 pane, No. 250ab (276E.)	13·00
SB10	5.6.90	Sub-tropical Fruits 1 pane, No. 256ab (197E.)	11·00
SB11	7.6.91	Sub-tropical Fruits 1 pane, No. 259ab (280E.)	11·00
SB12	21.2.92	Sub-tropical Fruits 1 pane, No. 257ab (258E.)	9·00
SB13	5.5.94	Traditional Crafts 1 pane, No. 295ab (360E.)	8·50
SB14	30.6.95	Traditional Crafts 1 pane, No. 301ab (355E.)	7·50
SB15	1.7.96	Religious Paintings 1 pane, No. 307ab (363E.)	7·50
SB16	12.2.97	Butterflies and Moths 1 pane, No. 311ab (369E.)	7·50
SB17	6.9.98	Butterflies and Moths 1 pane, No. 319ab (375E.)	6·75
SB18	2005	Tourism. Stamps of 2005 6 panes. Nos. 361a, **MS**362a, 363a, 365a, 367a and **MS**369a (€6.37)	23·00
SB19	2006	Stamps of 2006 10 panes. Nos. 370a, 372a, 374a, **MS**376aa, **MS**376ba, 377a, **MS**378a and 379a, 381a and **MS**383a	46·00
SB20	2007	Stamps of 2007 6 panes. Nos. 384a, 388a, 389a, **MS**390a, 391a and **MS**393a	23·00
SB21	2008	Stamps of 2008 7 panes. Nos. 394a, 396a, **MS**398a, **MS**398b, 399a, **MS**400a and 401a	31·00

BRITISH POST OFFICE IN MADEIRA

The British Packet Agency in Madeira was opened in 1767 and was of increased importance from 1808 following the exile of the Portuguese royal family to Brazil. The South American packets ceased to call in 1858. It appears to have closed sometime around 1860.

CROWNED-CIRCLE HANDSTAMPS. Under regulations circulated in December 1841, letters and packets forwarded through offices abroad to the United Kingdom or any of its territories were to be sent unpaid, the postage being collected on delivery. Where this was not possible, for example from a British colony to a foreign country or between two foreign ports, then a crowned-circle handstamp was to be applied with the postage, paid in advance, noted alongside in manuscript.

The dates quoted are those on which the handstamp appears in the G.P.O. Record Books, but it seems to have been normal for the handstamps to be sent to the office concerned immediately following this registration.

Crowned-circle Handstamp. As Type CC1b of British Post Offices in Cuba but inscr "PAID AT MADEIRA".

CC1	In red (28.2.1842)	Price on cover £17500

Mozambique

1876. 1000 Reis = 1 Milreis
1913. 100 Centavos = 1 Escudo

The first European to sight Mozambique was the Portuguese Pedro de Covilhã, who in 1487 came south along the east coast of Africa, reaching the mouth of the Zambesi by land and sea from Cairn. In 1498 Vasco da Gama, on his voyage to India, sailed along the Mozambique coast from the south. During the 16th and 17th centuries the Portuguese established many trading posts in east Africa. In 1698 to 1730 Arabs from Oman compelled them to abandon many of the northern posts, but those in Mozambique were held. The failure to find gold, conflict with the natives and official corruption later led to the collapse of the colony, but Mozambique was reoccupied by the Portuguese in the 19th century. Attempts in 1886–90 to join Mozambique with Angola by a band of Portuguese territory across Africa were opposed by the British government, who in 1889 gave Cecil Rhodes a charter for the British South Africa Company. The borders of Mozambique were fixed by an agreement on 11 June 1891.

Issues made for the districts of Inhambane, Kionga, Lourenço Marques, Quelimane, Tete and Zambezia, and by the two chartered companies, the Mozambique Company and the Nyassa Company, are listed at the end of Mozambique.

Mozambique became an Overseas Province of Portugal on 11 June 1951 and its inhabitants received Portuguese citizenship on 6 September 1961.

PRINTERS. All the stamps of Mozambique and its districts and chartered companies were printed at the Mint, Lisbon, *unless otherwise stated.*

REPRINTS. Reprints of certain issues of Mozambique and its districts and chartered companies were made in 1885 and 1905 as indicated in footnotes in the text. They can generally be distinguished as follows:

1885 reprints are on stout very white paper, usually un-gummed but sometimes with white gum which has yellowish spots. They are perforated 13½ with large, clean-cut holes producing sharp, pointed teeth.

1905 reprints are on creamy paper of ordinary quality with shiny white gum, all perforated 13½.

King Luis
11 November 1861–19 October 1889

     1   **2**

(Des and eng A. F. Gerard. Typo)

1876 (July).

(a) P 12½

1	1	5r. black	2·30	1·40
2		10r. pale orange	13·00	7·00
		a. Orange-buff	13·00	7·00
3		20r. deep bistre	2·20	1·20
		a. Pale bistre	2·20	1·20
4		25r. crimson	1·20	85
		a. Rose	1·20	85
5		40r. blue	30·00	16·00
6		50r. green	£325	£160
7		100r. grey-lilac	2·20	1·30
		a. Dull purple	2·20	1·30
		b. Dull lilac	2·20	1·30
8		200r. deep orange	8·50	6·75
9		300r. lake-brown	5·25	3·25
		a. Yellow-brown	5·25	3·25
1/9	*Set of 9 (cheapest)*		£350	£180

(b) P 13½

10	1	5r. black	4·00	3·50
11		10r. yellow	13·00	6·50
12		20r. pale bistre	5·25	2·75
13		25r. rose	14·00	3·50
		a. Carmine-rose	14·00	3·50
14		40r. blue	40·00	18·00
15		50r. green	£1300	£950

16		100r. grey-lilac	1·40	1·30
		a. Dull purple	1·40	1·30
		b. Dull lilac	1·40	1·30
17		200r. deep orange	7·00	3·00
		a. Orange-buff	7·00	3·00
18		300r. chocolate	5·25	3·50
		a. Lake-brown	5·25	3·50
		b. Yellow-brown	5·25	3·50
10/18	*Set of 9 (cheapest)*		£1300	£900

For 40r. *se-tenant* with stamps inscr "CABO VERDE", see Nos. 5a, 14a and 21a of Cape Verde Islands.

All values were reprinted in 1885 and 1905.

1881–85. Colours changed.

(a) P 13½

19	1	10r. green (8.81)	1·90	1·30
20		20r. rosine (1885)	£1600	£950
21		25r. lilac (1885)	6·25	2·50
22		40r. yellow-buff (7.81)	5·50	5·00
23		50r. blue (8.81)	1·40	1·20

(b) P 12½

24	1	10r. green	1·30	1·20
25		20r. rosine		
26		40r. yellow-buff	4·50	4·25
27		50r. deep blue	1·40	1·20
		a. Blue		1·20

The 20r. rosine, though prepared for use, was never issued in the Colony. Specimens obtained in Lisbon and sent out were allowed to do postal duty.

See note below No. 18 *re* 40r.

All values were reprinted in 1885 and 1905.

(Des and eng F. A. de Campos. Typo and embossed)

1886. Chalk-surfaced paper or enamel-surfaced paper (E).

(a) P 12½

30	2	5r. black	2·20	1·40
31		5r. black (E)	4·50	2·75
32		10r. green	2·20	1·40
34		20r. rosine	2·20	1·40
35		20r. rosine (E)	23·00	21·00
36		25r. dull lilac	38·00	3·75
		a. Bright mauve	38·00	3·75
		b. Dull purple	38·00	3·75
37		40r. chocolate	3·25	2·10
38		50r. pale blue	3·75	1·40
		a. Deep blue	3·75	1·40
39		50r. deep blue (E)	8·75	5·75
40		100r. yellow-brown	3·75	1·40
41		100r. yellow-brown (E)	12·00	8·00
42		200r. slate-violet	7·00	4·25
43		300r. orange	9·00	5·75
30/43	*Set of 9 (one of each value)*		65·00	21·00

(b) P 13½

44	2	5r. black	6·25	4·25
45		10r. green	8·25	5·00
46		20r. rosine	17·00	8·50
47		25r. dull lilac	44·00	12·00
48		25r. dull lilac (E)	20·00	9·25
49		40r. chocolate (E)	20·00	9·25
50		50r. pale blue	14·50	4·50
51		200r. slate-violet	40·00	24·00
52		200r. slate-violet (E)	30·00	21·00
44/52	*Set of 7 (one of each value)*		£100	55·00

The 5, 25, 40, 50, 100 and 300r. were reprinted in 1905.

King Carlos
19 October 1889–1 February 1908

JORNAES   **JORNAES**

2½   2½   2½ REIS
(N 3)   (N 4)

1893 (Jan). NEWSPAPER. T **2** surch locally as Types N **3** or N **4**. No gum. P 12½.

N53	N 3	2½r. on 40r. chocolate	80·00	38·00
		a. Surch double	£120	90·00
N54	N 4	2½r. on 40r. chocolate	£325	£190
		a. Surch double	£425	£250
		b. Surch inverted	£425	£250
N55		5r. on 40r. chocolate	£275	£160
		a. Surch inverted	£350	£225
		b. Surch double	£350	£225
		c. Surch double, both inverted	£425	£325

N56		5r. on 40r. chocolate (B.)	£275	£160
		a. Surch inverted	£425	£250
		b. Surch double	£425	£250
		c. Surch double, one inverted	£425	£250
		d. Surch double, both inverted	£425	£250
		e. Surch double (B.+R.)	£500	£300
N57		5r. on 40r. chocolate (R.)	£190	£100
		a. Surch inverted	£300	£190

PROVISORIO

5 5

(3)

N 5

4

A. "PROVISORIO" 19 mm. long, figures 4½ mm. high.
B. "PROVISORIO" 19½ mm. long, figures 5 mm. high.
C. As B, but with both types of figures.

1893 (Jan). No. 37 surch locally with T **3**. No gum.

53	**2**	5 on 40r. chocolate (A)	£300	£160
		a. "PROVISORIO" double	£425	£250
		b. Surch double	£425	£250
		c. Figures double	£425	£250
		d. Surch inverted	£425	£250
		e. Surch double, both inverted	£450	£275
54		5 on 40r. chocolate (B)	£350	£250
55		5 on 40r. chocolate (C)	£350	£250

(Des and eng E. C. Azedo Gneco. Typo)

1893 (28 June). NEWSPAPER.

N58	**N 5**	2½r. brown (perf 11½)	1·10	80
N59		2½r. brown (perf 13½)	1·10	80

This was reprinted in 1905.

Stamps of this type could be, and often were, used for franking ordinary correspondence.

(Des and eng M. D. Neto. Typo)

1894 (13 Nov–15 Dec). Chalk-surfaced paper or enamel-surfaced paper (E).

(a) P 11½

56	**4**	5r. pale orange	1·00	80
		a. Printed on unsurfaced side of paper	25·00	19·00
57		10r. rosy mauve	1·00	80
58		15r. red-brown	1·50	1·00
59		20r. lilac	1·50	1·30
60		50r. pale blue (15 Dec)	6·50	1·80
61		80r. pale green (15 Dec)	6·50	3·00
62		100r. brown/*buff* (15 Dec)	3·25	2·50
63		150r. carmine/*rose* (15 Dec)	£950	£950
64		200r. blue/*blue* (15 Dec)	7·00	5·75

(b) P 12½

65	**4**	25r. green (15 Dec)	1·00	60
66		50r. pale blue (E) (15 Dec)	9·25	2·30
67		75r. rose (15 Dec)	3·00	2·30
68		150r. carmine/*rose* (15 Dec)	23·00	8·25
69		300r. blue/*pale brown* (15 Dec)	11·50	6·50

(c) P 13½

70	**4**	50r. pale blue (E) (15 Dec)	30·00	7·00
56/62, 64, 68		*Set of 9*	46·00	23·00

The 25, 80, 100 and 150r. were reprinted in 1905.

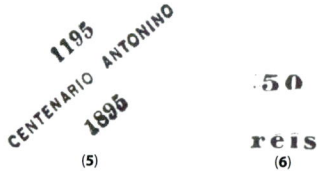

1195 CENTENARIO ANTONINO 1895

(5)

50 reis

(6)

1895 (1 July). 700th Birth Anniv of St. Anthony. Optd locally with T **5**. Chalk-surfaced paper. No gum.

(a) P 12½

71	**2**	5r. black (Vm.)	14·00	10·50
72		10r. green	19·00	13·00
73		20r. rosine	22·00	14·00
74		25r. purple	22·00	14·00
		a. Opt double	£130	£130
75		40r. chocolate	23·00	18·00
76		50r. blue	23·00	18·00
77		100r. yellow-brown	23·00	18·00
		a. Opt double, one inverted		
78		200r. slate-lilac	45·00	32·00
79		300r. orange	55·00	35·00

(b) P 13½

80	**2**	50r. blue	£120	£110
81		200r. slate-lilac	£120	£110

1897 (2 Jan). No. 69 surch locally with T **6**. With or without gum.

82	**4**	50r. on 300r. blue/*pale brown*	£425	£275

MOÇAMBIQUE 2 ½ RÉIS

(7)

MOÇAMBIQUE 2½ RÉIS

(8)

1898. T **2** surch locally. No gum. P 12½.

83	**7**	2½r. on 20r. rosine	75·00	75·00
		a. Surch inverted	£170	£140
84	**8**	2½r. on 20r. rosine	38·00	31·00
85	**7**	5r. on 40r. chocolate	50·00	38·00
		a. Surch inverted	£170	£150

10

D 11

11

(Des and eng E. Mouchon. Typo)

1898 (1 Aug)–**1901**. Name and value in black, on 500r. in carmine. P 11½.

86	**10**	2½r. grey	65	30
87		5r. orange-red	65	35
88		10r. green	65	35
89		15r. chocolate	6·25	3·75
90		20r. deep lilac	1·70	90
91		25r. blue-green	1·80	90
92		50r. blue	2·10	1·10
93		75r. rose	8·00	3·75
94		80r. mauve	8·00	3·75
95		100r. blue/*blue*	4·25	2·75
96		150r. purple-brown/*straw*	4·25	4·50
97		200r. purple/*flesh*	4·00	2·75
98		300r. blue/*pink*	8·75	4·50
99		500r. black/*azure* (1901)	18·00	9·50
100		700r. mauve/*yellow* (1901)	30·00	13·50
86/100		*Set of 15*	90·00	47·00

See also Nos. 138/45.

1902. Surch as T **22** of Macao.

101	**4**	65r. on 10r. (11½)	4·50	4·25
102		65r. on 15r. (11½)	4·50	4·25
103	**2**	65r. on 20r. (12½)	8·75	7·50
104		65r. on 20r. (E) (12½)	7·00	3·50
		a. Surch double	23·00	21·00
105		65r. on 20r. (E) (13½)	6·00	3·25
106	**4**	65r. on 20r. (11½)	4·50	4·25
107	**2**	65r. on 40r. (12½)	8·75	7·50
108		65r. on 40r. (E) (13½)	7·00	3·50
109		65r. on 200r. (12½)	7·50	4·25
110		65r. on 200r. (E) (13½)	6·00	3·25
111	**N 5**	115r. on 2½r. (13½)	4·50	4·25
112	**2**	115r. on 5r. (12½) (R.)	5·25	3·75
113		115r. on 5r. (E) (12½) (R.)	2·50	2·10
114	**4**	115r. on 5r. (11½)	4·50	4·25
115		115r. on 25r. (12½)	4·50	4·25
116	**2**	115r. on 50r. (12½)	30·00	17·00
117		115r. on 50r. (E) (12½)	2·75	2·10
118		115r. on 50r. (E) (13½)	1·90	1·20
119		130r. on 25r. (13½)	5·25	3·25
120		130r. on 25r. (E) (13½)	3·50	2·10
121	**4**	130r. on 75r. (12½)	4·50	4·25
122		130r. on 100r. (11½)	10·00	9·25
123		130r. on 150r. (12½)	4·50	4·25
124		130r. on 200r. (11½)	9·00	8·50
125	**2**	130r. on 300r. (12½)	5·25	3·00
126		130r. on 300r. (E) (13½)	4·00	2·50
127		400r. on 10r. (12½)	14·00	14·00
128		400r. on 10r. (E) (12½)	7·50	6·50
129	**4**	400r. on 50r. (11½)	2·75	2·10
130		400r. on 80r. (11½)	2·75	1·80
131	**2**	400r. on 100r. (12½)	95·00	55·00
132		400r. on 100r. (E) (12½)	60·00	42·00
133	**4**	400r. on 300r. (12½)	2·75	2·10

MOZAMBIQUE

1902. Optd with T **23** of Macao.
134	**10**	15r. chocolate	3·50	1·80
135		25r. blue-green	3·50	1·80
136		50r. blue	7·00	4·00
137		75r. rose	10·00	5·25

1903. Colours changed. Name and value in black. P 11½.
138	**10**	15r. deep green	2·20	1·70
139		25r. carmine	2·20	1·70
140		50r. brown	4·50	3·25
141		65r. dull blue	14·00	10·50
142		75r. dull purple	4·50	3·25
143		115r. orange-brown/*pink*	14·00	8·00
144		130r. purple-brown/*straw*	14·00	8·50
145		400r. dull blue/*cream*	20·00	16·00
138/145 Set of 8			70·00	48·00

(Des and eng J. S. de Carvalho e Silva. Typo)

1904. POSTAGE DUE. Name and value in black. P 11½.
D146	**D 11**	5r. yellow-green	55	50
D147		10r. slate	55	50
D148		20r. brown	65	65
D149		30r. orange	1·40	95
D150		50r. deep brown	1·40	95
D151		60r. pale red-brown	5·00	3·25
D152		100r. mauve	5·00	3·25
D153		130r. blue	3·00	2·30
D154		200r. carmine	4·25	2·30
D155		500r. deep violet	5·50	2·75
D146/155 Set of 10			25·00	16·00

1905. No. 141 surch as T **25** of Macao.
146	**10**	50r. on 65r. dull blue	5·75	4·75

King Manoel II
1 February 1908–5 October 1910

PORTUGUESE REPUBLIC
5 October 1910

1911. Optd with T **27** of Macao, in red or green (G.).
147	**10**	2½r. grey	55	35
148		5r. orange	55	35
149		10r. green	1·80	1·10
150		15r. deep green	45	30
151		20r. deep lilac	1·80	45
152		25r. carmine (G.)	35	30
		a. Error. On 25r. deep lilac (R.)	55·00	55·00
153		50r. brown	65	45
154		75r. dull purple	1·20	1·10
155		100r. blue/*blue*	1·20	1·10
156		115r. orange-brown/*pink*	1·80	1·10
157		130r. purple-brown/*straw*	1·80	1·10
158		200r. purple/*pink*	3·75	1·80
159		400r. dull blue/*straw*	3·75	1·80
160		500r. black/*azure*	3·75	2·30
161		700r. mauve/*yellow*	3·75	2·30
147/161 Set of 15			24·00	14·50

1911. POSTAGE DUE. Optd with T **27** of Macao, in red or green (G.).
D162	**D 11**	5r. yellow-green	50	45
		a. Chalk-surfaced paper	50	45
D163		10r. slate	80	45
		a. Chalk-surfaced paper	80	45
D164		20r. brown	80	45
D165		30r. orange	80	45
D166		50r. deep brown	90	55
D167		60r. pale red-brown	1·20	65
D168		100r. mauve	1·70	90
D169		130r. blue	1·80	1·20
D170		200r. carmine (G.)	2·30	2·00
D171		500r. deep lilac	3·25	2·40
D162/171 Set of 10 (*cheapest*)			12·50	8·50

(Des and eng D. A. do Rego. Typo)

1912. Unissued stamps with portrait of King Manoel II optd with T **27** of Macao, in red or green (G.).

(a) P 11½
162	**11**	2½r. lilac	50	30
163		5r. black	50	35
164		10r. grey-green	50	35
165		20r. rose-red (G.)	1·30	90
166		25r. chocolate	50	35
167		50r. blue	1·10	65
168		75r. yellow-brown	1·10	65
169		100r. brown/*green*	1·10	65
170		200r. deep green/*salmon*	3·25	1·50
171		300r. black/*blue*	2·00	1·50
162/171 Set of 10			10·50	6·50

(b) P 14×15
172	**11**	500r. chocolate and olive	6·50	3·25

(12) REPUBLICA MOÇAMBIQUE ¼ C.

13 Ceres

(14) REPUBLICA MOÇAMBIQUE

1913. New Currency. Vasco da Gama issues surch as T **12**.

(i) Portuguese Colonies (General Issues)
173		¼c. on 2½r. blue-green	1·70	1·20
174		½c. on 5r. vermilion	1·70	1·20
175		1c. on 10r. dull purple	1·70	1·20
		a. Surch double	60·00	60·00
176		2½c. on 25r. yellow-green	1·70	1·20
177		5c. on 50r. deep blue	1·80	1·30
178		7½c. on 75r. chocolate	3·00	2·20
179		10c. on 100r. bistre-brown	2·20	1·70
180		15c. on 150r. ochre	2·20	1·90
173/180 Set of 8			14·50	10·50

(ii) Macao
181		¼c. on ½a. blue-green	2·30	1·90
182		½c. on 1a. vermilion	2·30	1·90
183		1c. on 2a. dull purple	2·30	1·90
184		2½c. on 4a. yellow-green	2·30	1·90
185		5c. on 8a. deep blue	6·50	4·50
186		7½c. on 12a. chocolate	3·50	3·25
187		10c. on 16a. bistre-brown	2·50	1·90
188		15c. on 24a. ochre	2·50	1·90
181/188 Set of 8			22·00	17·00

(iii) Timor
189		¼c. on ½a. blue-green	2·50	2·00
190		½c. on 1a. vermilion	2·50	2·00
191		1c. on 2a. dull purple	2·50	2·00
192		2½c. on 4a. yellow-green	2·50	2·00
193		5c. on 8a. deep blue	3·75	2·75
194		7½c. on 12a. chocolate	3·75	2·75
195		10c. on 16a. bistre-brown	2·30	1·50
196		15c. on 24a. ochre	2·30	1·50
189/196 Set of 8			20·00	15·00

(Des C. Fernandes. Eng J. S. de Carvalho e Silva. Typo)

1914. Name and value in black. Chalk-surfaced paper. P 15×14.
197	**13**	¼c. brown-olive	45	30
198		½c. black	45	30
199		1c. deep green	45	30
200		1½c. chocolate	45	30
201		2c. carmine	50	30
202		2½c. violet	50	30
203		5c. blue	50	30
204		7½c. yellow-brown	1·80	95
205		8c. slate	1·80	95
206		10c. brown-red	1·80	95
207		15c. claret	3·75	1·70
208		20c. yellow-green	1·80	1·20
209		30c. chocolate/*green*	3·50	2·20
210		40c. brown/*rose*	3·75	2·30
211		50c. deep green/*salmon*	6·50	4·75
212		1E. deep green/*azure*	42·00	11·00
197/212 Set of 16			65·00	25·00

See also Nos. 249/305.

1915–20. Provisionals of 1902 optd locally with T **14**, in red.
213	**10**	75r. rose (No. 137)	3·25	1·80
214	**N 5**	115r. on 2½r. (13½)	1·40	1·20
215	**2**	115r. on 5r. (13½)	75·00	60·00
216		115r. on 5r. (E) (12½)	75·00	60·00
217	**4**	115r. on 5r. (11½)	2·20	1·80
218		115r. on 25r. (12½)	2·20	1·80
219		130r. on 75r. (12½)	2·20	1·80
220		130r. on 100r. (11½)	2·20	1·80
221		130r. on 150r. (12½)	2·20	1·80
222		130r. on 200r. (11½)	2·20	1·80
223		400r. on 50r. (11½) (1920)	2·75	2·10
224		400r. on 80r. (12½) (1920)	2·75	2·10
225		400r. on 300r. (12½) (1920)	2·75	2·10
213/225 Set of 13			£160	£130

1915. Provisionals of 1902 and 1905 optd with T **27** of Macao, in red (reading down on 2½r.).
226	**10**	50r. blue (No. 136)	1·40	1·20
227		50r. on 65r. dull blue	1·40	1·20
228	**N 5**	115r. on 2½r. (13½)	1·40	1·20
229	**4**	115r. on 5r. (12½)	1·40	1·20
230		115r. on 25r. (12½)	1·40	1·20
231		130r. on 75r. (12½)	1·40	1·20
232		130r. on 150r. (12½)	1·40	1·20
233		130r. on 200r. (11½)	1·40	1·20
226/233 Set of 8			10·00	8·75

MOZAMBIQUE

CHARITY TAX STAMPS. The notes after No. 304 of Macao apply also to the Charity Tax stamps of Mozambique.

C **15** Arms of Portugal and Mozambique and Allegorical Figures

C **16** Prow of Galley of Discoveries and Symbols of Declaration of War

(Des J. C. P. Ferreira da Costa. Litho Hortor Ltd., Johannesburg)

1916 (8 July). CHARITY TAX. War Tax Fund. Frame at top and bottom shaded with vertical lines. Roul.

C234	C **15**	1c. green	1·80	85
		a. Imperf	1·80	85
C235	C **16**	5c. carmine	1·80	85
		a. Imperf	1·10	1·10
		ab. Do. Paper with fine grey horiz lines	19·00	5·00

For compulsory use on all mail during 1916 and 1917. Type C **16** was for use on parcels and telegrams.
See also Nos. C246/8.

1916. POSTAGE DUE. Optd locally with T **14**, in red. With or without gum.

D234	D **11**	5r. yellow-green	6·25	5·25
D235		10r. slate	9·00	4·75
D236		20r. brown	£130	75·00
D237		30r. orange	27·00	18·00
D238		50r. deep brown	£110	90·00
D239		60r. pale red-brown	90·00	65·00
D240		100r. mauve	£130	£110
D241		130r. blue	4·00	3·50
D242		200r. carmine	4·00	3·50
D243		500r. deep lilac	9·00	5·75
D234/243 Set of 10			£475	£350

1917. Optd locally with T **14**, in red.

234	**10**	2½r. grey	37·00	23·00
235		15r. deep green	37·00	23·00
236		20r. deep lilac	37·00	23·00
237		50r. brown	30·00	18·00
238		75r. dull purple	95·00	70·00
239		100r. blue/*blue*	7·50	4·75
240		115r. orange-brown/*pink*	7·50	4·75
241		130r. purple-brown/*straw*	7·50	4·75
242		200r. purple/*flesh*	7·50	4·75
243		400r. dull blue/*cream*	9·00	4·75
244		500r. black/*azure*	10·00	8·75
245		700r. mauve/*yellow*	14·50	8·75
234/245 Set of 12			£275	£180

1917. POSTAGE DUE. Value in "CENTAVOS". P 11½.

D246	D **11**	½c. yellow-green	65	60
D247		1c. slate	65	60
D248		2c. red-brown	65	60
D249		3c. orange	65	60
D250		5c. deep brown	65	60
D251		6c. pale red-brown	65	60
D252		10c. mauve	65	60
D253		13c. blue	1·20	95
D254		20c. carmine	1·20	95
D255		50c. deep lilac	1·20	95
D246/255 Set of 10			7·25	6·25

Sets may be made on soft smooth paper and on thin coarse paper, the shades differing in the latter, particularly the 3c., which is yellow.

(Litho Argus Ptg and Publishing Co., Johannesburg)

1918. CHARITY TAX. Background of frame solid.

(a) P 11 (Feb)

C246	C **15**	1c. deep green	1·80	1·10
		a. "PEPUBLICA"	10·50	10·50
		b. Imperf (pair)	7·50	7·50
		ba. Do. "PEPUBLICA" (pair)	35·00	35·00
C247	C **16**	5c. carmine	2·20	1·50

(b) P 12 (1 Oct)

C248	C **16**	5c. vermilion	2·10	1·30
		a. "1910" for "1916"	10·50	10·50
		b. "PETRIA"	10·50	10·50
		c. "PEPUBLICA"	10·50	10·50
		d. "TELFGRAFO"	10·50	10·50
		e. Imperf (pair)	12·00	12·00
		ea. Do. "1910" (pair)	65·00	65·00
		eb. Do. "PETRIA" (pair)	60·00	50·00
		ec. Do. "PEPUBLICA" (pair)	60·00	50·00
		ed. Do. "TELFGRAFO" (pair)	60·00	50·00
		f. Imperf between (vert pair)		

Nos. C246a and ba occur on position 47 of the sheet of 100.
There were two settings of No. C248; in one the varieties b, c and d occur 8, 7 and 7 times, in the other 9, 9 and 8 times. The "1910" error occurs on position 26 of the second setting.

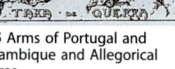

(15)   (D **16**)

1918. Charity Tax stamps surch with T **15** for regular use, at "Government Gazette" Printing Works, Lourenço Marques.

(i) Frame shaded. Roul

246	C **16**	2½c. on 5c. carmine	3·50	1·40

(ii) Frame solid. Perf

247	C **16**	2½c. on 5c. carmine (p 11)	3·50	1·40
248		2½c. on 5c. vermilion (p 12)	1·40	1·20
		a. "1910" for "1916"	13·00	13·00
		b. "PETRIA"	13·00	13·00
		c. "PEPUBLICA"	13·00	13·00
		d. "TELFGRAFO"	13·00	13·00

1918–21. POSTAGE DUE. Charity Tax stamps optd with Type D **16**, at Govt Printing Works, Lourenço Marques.

(a) Frame shaded. Roul (1918)

D256	C **15**	1c. green	2·10	1·60
D257	C **16**	5c. deep carmine	2·10	1·60

(b) Frame solid. P 11 (1921)

D258	C **15**	1c. green	2·10	1·60
		a. "PEPUBLICA"	10·50	9·50
D256/258 Set of 3			5·75	4·25

1919–26. Name and value in black.

(a) Unsurfaced paper (thick, medium or thin). P 15×14 (1919–22)

249	**13**	¼c. brown-olive	35	25
		a. Name and value double	27·00	
		b. Name and value treble	27·00	
		c. Carton paper	10·00	
250		½c. black	35	25
251		1c. deep green	35	25
252		1½c. chocolate (1920)	35	25
253		2c. carmine (1920)	35	25
254		2½c. violet (1920)	35	25
255		3c. orange (1921)	35	25
256		4c. pink (1921)	35	25
257		4½c. drab (1921)	35	25
258		5c. deep blue	35	25
259		7c. pale blue (1921)	35	25
260		7½c. yellow-brown	35	25
261		8c. slate	70	65
262		10c. red-brown (1920)	14·50	9·75
263		30c. deep grey-green (1922)	95	70
264		1E. carmine-pink (1922)	1·90	1·20
249/264 Set of 16			20·00	14·00

(b) Unsurfaced paper. P 12×11½ (1920–26)

265	**13**	¼c. brown-olive (1922)	35	25
266		½c. black	25	25
267		1c. deep green	60	25
		a. Name and value double	27·00	
268		1½c. chocolate	35	25
269		2c. carmine	35	25
270		2c. drab (1926)	35	35
271		2½c. violet	35	35
272		3c. orange (1921)	35	35
273		4c. pink (1921)	35	35
		a. Value omitted	25·00	
		b. Name and value double	27·00	
		c. Carmine-pink	35	35
274		4½c. drab (1921)	35	35
275		6c. mauve (1921)	35	35
276		7c. pale blue (1921)	35	35
277		7½c. yellow-brown (1922)	35	25
278		8c. slate (1922)	35	25
279		10c. brown-red (1922)	35	25
280		12c. pale brown (1921)	35	35
281		12c. blue-green (1922)	35	35
282		15c. dull purple	35	25
283		15c. claret (1922)	35	25
284		20c. yellow-green (1922)	70	65
285		24c. light blue (1926)	45	35
286		25c. chocolate (1926)	55	45
287		30c. deep grey-green (1922)	50	35
288		40c. turquoise (1922)	1·20	45

174

MOZAMBIQUE

289		50c. mauve (1926)	65	45
290		60c. deep blue (1922)	1·30	70
291		60c. carmine-pink (1926)	1·90	1·20
292		80c. bright rosine (1922)	2·00	1·50
293		80c. pink (1922)	1·60	70
294		1E. carmine-pink (1922)	3·25	1·20
265/294	Set of 30		19·00	12·00

(c) Chalk-surfaced paper. P 15×14 (1921)

295	13	30c. lavender/rose	2·20	1·80

(d) Chalk-surfaced paper. P 12×11½ (1921)

296	13	40c. grey-brown/rose	3·25	2·10
297		60c. chestnut/rose	2·30	1·80
298		80c. chocolate/azure	2·00	1·50
299		1E. deep green/azure	4·25	2·50
300		2E. bright mauve/rose	3·00	1·50

(e) Thick glazed paper. P 12×11½ (1922–26)

301	13	1E. blue (1926)	1·90	1·40
302		2E. purple	1·60	90
303		5E. buff (1926)	10·50	6·50
304		10E. pink (1926)	15·00	7·50
305		20E. emerald (1926)	48·00	21·00
301/305	Set of 5		70·00	34·00

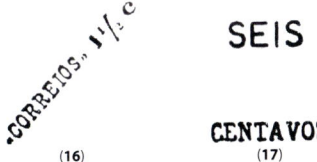

(16)　　SEIS CENTAVOS (17)

1920. Charity Tax stamps (solid background) surch for regular use at Govt Printing Works, Lourenço Marques.

(a) As T 16 (Aug)

306	C 15	1c. on 1c. deep green (p 11)	1·30	1·00
		a. "PEPUBLICA"	9·50	7·50
		b. Rouletted (C234)	21·00	16·00
307	C 16	1½c. on 5c. vermilion (p 12)	1·30	1·00
		a. "1910" for "1916"	9·50	9·50
		b. "PETRIA"	9·50	9·50
		c. "PEPUBLICA"	9·50	9·50
		d. "TELFGRAFO"	9·50	9·50
		e. Rouletted (C235)	27·00	21·00

(b) With T 17, in green (Oct)

308	C 16	6c. on 5c. vermilion (p 12)	1·40	1·20
		a. "1910" for "1916"	9·50	9·50
		b. "PETRIA"	9·50	9·50
		c. "PEPUBLICA"	9·50	9·50
		d. "TELFGRAFO"	9·50	9·50
		e. Imperf (pair)	23·00	23·00
		f. Surch inverted	48·00	48·00

C 18 "Charity"　　　(18)

(Des A. Possacos. Litho National Printing Works, Lourenço Marques)

1920 (1 Dec). CHARITY TAX. 280th Anniv of Restoration of Portugal. Wounded Soldiers and Social Assistance Funds. Type C **18** and similar horiz designs. P 11½.

C309	C 18	¼c. olive	3·00	3·00
C310	–	½c. black	3·00	3·00
C311	–	1c. yellow-brown	3·00	3·00
C312	–	2c. lilac-brown	3·00	3·00
C313	–	3c. lilac	3·25	3·25
C314	–	4c. pale green	3·25	3·25
C315	–	5c. turquoise-green	3·50	3·25
C316	–	6c. turquoise-blue	3·50	3·25
C317	–	7½c. purple-brown	3·50	3·25
C318	–	8c. olive-yellow	3·50	3·25
C319	–	10c. lilac	3·50	3·25
C320	–	12c. pink	3·50	3·25
C321	–	18c. carmine	3·50	3·25
C322	–	24c. purple-brown	4·50	3·75
C323	–	30c. olive	4·50	3·75
C324	–	40c. vermilion	4·50	3·75
C325	–	50c. yellow	4·50	3·75
C326	–	1E. ultramarine	4·50	3·75
C309/326	Set of 18		60·00	55·00

Designs:—5c. to 12c. Wounded soldier and nurse, 18c. to 1E. Family scene.
　In use only on 1 December.

1921. Surch locally as T **18**. With or without gum. P 15×14.

(a) Unsurfaced paper

309	13	10c. on ½c. black (R.)	2·75	1·70
310		30c. on 1½c. chocolate (B.)	2·75	1·70
		a. Surch double	37·00	37·00

(b) Chalk-surfaced paper

311	13	60c. on 2½c. violet (G.)	4·00	2·20

10 C.　　2$00　　PORTEADO
　(19)　　　　(D 20)

1922 (Jan).
*(a) T **8** of Lourenço Marques surch locally as T **18**. Unsurfaced paper or enamel-surfaced paper (E). P 15×14*

312		10c. on ½c. black (R.)	2·75	1·80
313		10c. on ½c. black (E) (R.)	2·75	1·80
314		30c. on 1½c. chocolate (B.)	2·75	1·80

*(b) Charity Tax stamp surch locally with T **19**. Solid frame. P 12*

315	C 16	2$00 on 5c. vermilion (G.)	2·30	1·10
		a. "1910" for "1916"	10·50	9·50
		b. "PETRIA"	7·50	5·25
		c. "PEPUBLICA"	9·50	7·50
		d. "TELFGRAFO"	5·25	4·75

1922. POSTAGE DUE. Surch locally as Type D **20**.

*(a) T **8** of Lourenço Marques. Unsurfaced paper or enamel-surfaced paper (E). P 15×14*

D316		5c. on ½c. black (E) (R.)	1·90	1·40
D317		10c. on 1½c. chocolate (R.)	1·90	1·40

(b) Stamps of Mozambique

(i) Unsurfaced paper. P 15×14

D318	13	6c. on 1c. deep green (R.)	1·90	1·40

(ii) Chalk-surfaced paper. P 15×14

D319	13	20c. on 2½c. violet (R.)	1·90	1·40
		a. Surch inverted	9·50	9·50

(iii) Unsurfaced paper. P 12×11½

D320	13	50c. on 4c. pink (G.)	1·90	1·40
		a. Surch inverted	10·50	10·50

Porteado 50 c.　50 C.　Vasco da Gama 1924
　(20)　(D 21)　(21)

1923 (Apr). No. 273 surch locally with T **20**.

316	13	50c. on 4c. pink	2·20	1·10

1924. POSTAGE DUE. Surch locally as Type D **21**. Unsurfaced paper.

D321	13	20c. on 30c. deep grey-green (p 12×11½)	1·30	90
D322		20c. on 30c. deep grey-green (p 15×14)	29·00	27·00
D323		50c. on 60c. deep bllue (p 12×11½) (R.)	1·90	1·50

1924 (23 Dec). Fourth Centenary of Death of Vasco da Gama. No. 293 optd with T **21**, in green.

317	13	80c. pink	2·20	1·10
		a. Carmine-pink	2·20	1·10

República　　50
40 C.　　　　CENTAVOS
　(21a)　C **22** Society's Emblem　(C 23)

1925. Provisionals of 1902 surch with T **21a**.

318	4	40c. on 400r. on 50r. (11½)	1·50	85
319		40c. on 400r. on 80r. (11½)	1·50	85
		a. "a" of "Republica" omitted	21·00	17·00
		b. "a" of "Republica" inserted by hand	21·00	16·00

175

MOZAMBIQUE

1925 (8 May). Marquis de Pombal Commemoration.
*(a) CHARITY TAX. As T **44/6** of Macao*

C327	**44**	15c. brown	65	45
C328	**45**	15c. brown	65	55
C329	**46**	15c. brown	65	45
C327/329 Set of 3			1·50	1·25

*(b) POSTAGE DUE. Optd with Type D **47** of Macao*

D327	**44**	30c. brown	50	50
D328	**45**	30c. brown	30	30
D329	**46**	30c. brown	50	50
C327/D329 Set of 6			3·00	2·75

Nos. C327/9 were in use from 8 to 13 May 1925 and from 5 to 15 May in 1926 and 1929. Nos. D327/9 were used in default.

(Des A. Possacos. Typo Giesecke and Devrient, Leipzig)

1925 (23 Nov). CHARITY TAX. Surch in Lourenço Marques with Type C **23**. P 11½.

C330	C **22**	50c. yellow and slate	1·90	1·50

In use on 23 and 24 November.

This and the three following issues were for compulsory use on specified dates for the benefit of the local Red Cross Society (Sociedade Humanitaria Cruz de Oriente). Stamps without surcharge were for use without charge on the mail of the Society posted to inland addresses.

CORREIOS

$40
(C **24**)

The width between the lines of this surcharge varies from 19½ mm to 21 mm (Nos. C331/6) and 15½ mm to 21 mm (Nos. C337/46).

1926 (1 June). CHARITY TAX. Surch locally as Type C **24**.

C331	C **22**	40c. yellow and slate	3·50	2·50
C332		50c. yellow and slate (R.)	3·50	2·50
C333		60c. yellow and slate (V.)	3·50	2·50
C334		80c. yellow and slate (Br.)	3·50	2·50
C335		1E. yellow and slate (B.)	3·50	2·50
C336		2E. yellow and slate (G.)	3·75	3·50
C331/336 Set of 6			19·00	14·50

In use on 1 June.

1927 (14 Nov). CHARITY TAX. Surch locally as Type C **24**.

C337	C **22**	5c. yellow and red	2·10	2·00
C338		10c. yellow and emerald	2·10	2·00
C339		20c. yellow and grey	2·50	2·30
C340		30c. yellow and light blue	2·50	2·30
C341		40c. yellow and violet	2·50	2·30
C342		50c. yellow and carmine	3·00	2·75
C343		60c. yellow and brown	3·00	2·75
C344		80c. yellow and blue	3·00	2·75
C345		1E. yellow and olive-green	3·00	2·75
C346		2E. yellow and yellow-brown	3·75	3·25
C337/346 Set of 10			25·00	23·00

In use on 14 November.

C **25**

CORREIOS

50   C.   CORREIOS
(C **26**)   (**22**)

(Des A. Possacos. Litho R & R)

1928 (8 Sept). CHARITY TAX. Surch locally as Type C **26**. P 11½.

C347	C **25**	5c. yellow and green	4·25	4·00
C348		10c. yellow and deep blue	4·25	4·00
C349		20c. yellow and grey-black	4·25	4·00
C350		30c. yellow and brown-carmine	4·25	4·00
C351		40c. yellow and claret	4·25	4·00
C352		50c. yellow and vermilion	4·25	4·00
C353		60c. yellow and red-brown	4·25	4·00
C354		80c. yellow and chocolate	4·25	4·00
C355		1E. yellow and grey	4·25	4·00
C356		2E. yellow and red	4·25	4·00
C347/356 Set of 10			38·00	36·00

In use on 8 September.

1929 (Jan). No. D255 optd with T **22** in black and with bars obliterating "A RECEBER" in red.

320	D **11**	50c. deep lilac	1·90	1·50

  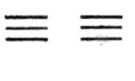

C **27**   **23** Mousinho de Albuquerque   (**24**)

(Des A. Possacos. Photo Govt Ptg Wks, Berlin. Value typo National Ptg Wks, Lourenço Marques)

1929–39. CHARITY TAX. Value in black. Chalky paper. P 14.

C357	C **27**	40c. claret and ultramarine (1929)	4·75	4·25
C358		40c. violet and carmine (1930)	4·75	4·25
C359		40c. violet and olive-green (1932)	4·75	4·25
C360		40c. carmine and yellow-brown (1933)	4·75	4·25
C361		(No value) carmine and green (1934)	4·75	4·25
C362		40c. blue and orange (1935)	7·00	6·50
C363		40c. blue and brown (1936)	4·75	4·25
C364		40c. claret and green (1937)	4·75	4·25
C365		40c. black and yellow (1938)	7·00	6·50
C366		40c. black and brown (1939)	7·00	6·50
C357/366 Set of 10			49·00	44·00

No. C357 was in use from 28 to 31 July 1929 and the others from the 23 to 31 December in their year of issue.

There are two styles of figures used in the value tablets. All have the closed "4" of Type C **27**, with the exception of Nos. C357/8, in which the "4" is open; and No. C361, which has blank value tablets.

(Photo Govt Printing Works, Berlin. Value and name of battle typo National Printing Works, Lourenço Marques)

1930–31. Albuquerque's Victories Commemoration. Vignette in grey. P 14½×14.

321	**23**	50c. lake and red (Macontene)	10·50	10·50
322		50c. orange and red (Mujenga)	10·50	10·50
323		50c. magenta and brown (Coolela)	10·50	10·50
324		50c. grey-green and blue-green (Chaimite)	10·50	10·50
325		50c. deep blue and indigo (Ibrahimo)	10·50	10·50
326		50c. ultramarine and black (Mucutomuno)	10·50	10·50
327		50c. violet and lilac (Naguema)	10·50	10·50
321/327 Set of 7			65·00	65·00

The above were for compulsory use throughout Mozambique in place of ordinary postage stamps on certain days in 1930 and 1931. They are not listed as Charity Tax stamps as the revenue was not applied to any charitable fund.

1931. Surch as T **24**. P 12×11½.

328	**13**	70c. on 2E. purple	1·30	70
329		1E.40 on 2E. purple	1·60	70

25 "Portugal and Camoens" "The Lusiads"   (**26**)   **26a** Route of President's Tour

MOZAMBIQUE

(Des P. Guedes. Die eng A. Fragoso. Typo)

1933 (13 July)–**47**. W **51** of Macao. Value in black or red (1c., 15c. and 1E.40). P 14.

330	25	1c. yellow-brown	20	15
331		5c. sepia	25	20
332		10c. purple	25	20
333		15c. black	25	20
334		20c. greenish grey	25	20
335		30c. grey-green	25	20
336		35c. yellowish green (1947)	9·75	3·75
337		40c. vermilion	25	20
338		45c. greenish blue	45	35
339		50c. brown	45	20
340		60c. olive-green	65	30
341		70c. orange-brown	65	30
342		80c. light green	65	30
343		85c. carmine	1·70	1·00
344		1E. claret	1·20	30
345		1E.40 deep blue	13·50	3·50
346		1E.75 blue (1947)	8·75	3·25
347		2E. reddish lilac	3·00	1·30
348		5E. yellow-green	4·75	1·30
349		10E. olive-sepia	11·00	2·75
350		20E. orange	55·00	7·25
330/350 Set of 21			£100	24·00

1938 (Aug). As Nos. 365/90 of Macao. Name and value in black. P 13½×13.

(a) POSTAGE

351	54	1c. grey-olive	25	25
352		5c. orange-brown	25	25
353		10c. carmine	25	25
354		15c. brown-purple	25	25
355		20c. slate	25	25
356	55	30c. bright purple	25	25
357		35c. emerald-green	50	25
358		40c. brown	50	25
359		50c. magenta	50	25
360	–	60c. grey-black	50	25
361	–	70c. slate-violet	50	25
362	–	80c. orange	50	25
363		1E. scarlet	1·10	50
364	–	1E.75 blue	4·00	85
365		2E. lake	4·00	1·00
366		5E. olive-green	7·50	1·50
367		10E. ultramarine	16·00	2·10
368		20E. red-brown	37·00	4·25
351/368 Set of 18			65·00	12·00

Designs:—60c. to 1E. Dam; 1E.75 to 5E. Henry the Navigator; 10, 20E. Afonso de Albuquerque.

(b) AIR

369	56	10c. scarlet	65	60
370		20c. bright violet	65	60
371		50c. orange	75	65
372		1E. bright blue	75	65
373		2E. brown-lake	1·30	65
374		3E. blue-green	2·75	65
375		5E. red-brown	4·50	95
376		9E. carmine	8·25	1·70
377		10E. magenta	14·00	3·25
369/377 Set of 9			30·00	8·75

1938 (16 June). Surch locally with T **26**.

378	25	40c. on 45c. light blue	6·50	4·25

(Des Zimbarra. Litho)

1939 (17 July). President Carmona's Second Colonial Tour. P 11½×12.

379	26a	80c. violet/*mauve*	4·75	3·25
380		1E.75 blue/*pale blue*	16·00	6·75
381		3E. green/*yellow-green*	28·00	10·50
382		20E. chocolate/*cream*	£140	60·00
379/382 Set of 4			£170	70·00

C **28** "Charity"   C **29** Pelican

1942 (1 Dec). CHARITY TAX. Litho. P 11½.

C383	C **28**	50c. rose and black	14·50	3·75

(Des J. Ayres. Litho (value typo) National Printing Works, Lourenço Marques)

1943–**51**. CHARITY TAX. Inscr "*Colonia de Moçambique*". Value in black.

(a) P 11½

C384	C **29**	50c. vermilion (1943)	11·50	2·20
		a. "50" larger	16·00	10·50
C385		50c. blue (1947)	10·50	2·20
C386		50c. violet (1947)	10·50	2·20
C387		50c. red-brown	10·50	2·20
C388		50c. yellow-brown	10·50	2·20
C389		50c. ultramarine (1949)	10·50	2·20
C390		50c. rose-carmine (1950)	11·50	2·20

(b) P 14

C391	C **29**	50c. rose-carmine (1950)	9·75	1·30
C392		50c. violet (1950)	9·75	2·20
C393		50c. green (1951)	9·75	2·20
C384/393 Set of 10			95·00	20·00

See also Nos. C468/70 and C512/15.

27 New Cathedral, Lourenço Marques   (**28**)

(Des A. de Sousa. Litho Litografia Nacional, Oporto. Perforated at the Mint, except No. 386a)

1944 (Nov)–**46**. 400th Anniv of Lourenço Marques. T **27** (inscr "IV. Centenário DE LOURENÇO MARQUES") and similar designs. P 11½ (No. 383), 11½×12 (384) or 12×11½ (others).

383	**27**	50c. purple-brown	2·20	80
384		50c. green	2·20	80
385	–	1E.75 ultramarine	9·75	2·75
386	–	20E. black	25·00	2·75
		a. Perf 11 (9.46)	27·00	2·75
383/386 Set of 4 (*cheapest*)			35·00	6·50

Designs: Horiz—1E.75, Railway Station; 20E. Town Hall, Lourenço Marques. See also No. 405.

1946. Nos. 354, 364 and 375 surch locally as T **28**.

(a) POSTAGE

387		10c. on 15c. brown-purple (15.6)	1·30	75
388		60c. on 1E.75 blue (R.) (2.3)	2·20	85

(b) AIR

389		3E. on 5E. red-brown (2.11)	18·00	17·00

(**29**)

1946 (2 Nov). No. 386a surch locally with T **29**. P 11.

390		2E. on 20E. black (R)	3·50	1·30

30 Lockheed L.18 Lodestar   **31** Antonio Enes

(Des A. Possacos. Designs litho; values typo Govt Printing Works, Lourenço Marques)

1946 (2 Nov). AIR. Values in black. P 11½.

391	**30**	1E.20 carmine	3·25	1·70
392		1E.60 greenish blue	3·25	1·80
393		1E.70 bright purple	6·00	2·50
394		2E.90 brown	9·50	5·00
395		3E. green	10·50	5·00
391/395 Set of 5			29·00	14·50

177

MOZAMBIQUE

1946 (20 May). AIR. As T **30** but optd "Taxe percue" at left with values at right in black or carmine (C.).

397	30	50c. black (C.)	1·50	95
398		1E. pink	1·50	95
399		3E. green	2·75	1·10
400		4E.50 yellow-green	4·50	2·00
401		5E. brown-lake	6·50	2·20
402		10E. ultramarine	18·00	5·75
403		20E. violet	47·00	16·00
404		50E. orange	95·00	40·00
397/404 Set of 8			£160	60·00

1948. As T **27**, but without "IV. Centenario DE LOURENÇO MARQUES". P 11½.

405		4E.50 scarlet	4·25	1·10

(Des A. de Sousa. Litho Litografia Maia, Oporto)

1948 (4 Oct). Birth Centenary of Antonio Enes. P 14.

406	31	50c. black and cream	1·60	75
407		5E. purple and cream	3·75	2·30

32 Zumbo River **33** Lourenço Marques

(Des M. Jorge (2E.50, 10E., 15E., 20E.), A. de Sousa (others). Die eng Rosa (5c., 30c.), Santos (10c., 1E.20), Norte (20c., 40c.), "G.A." (60c., 1E.75, 3E., 3E.50), A. Fragoso (50c., 80c., 1E., 2E.50, 5E., 10E.) and Americo (1E.50, 2E., 15E., 20E.). Typo)

1948–49. T **32/3** and similar designs. P 13½.

408	–	5c. brown (1948)	45	25
409	–	10c. purple	45	25
410	32	20c. purple-brown	45	25
411	–	30c. reddish purple	45	25
412	32	40c. grey-green	55	25
413	33	50c. slate-grey	55	25
414	–	60c. claret	55	25
415	33	80c. grey-violet	55	25
416	–	1E. carmine	85	45
417	–	1E.20 bluish grey	95	45
418	–	1E.50 deep violet (1948)	1·30	50
419	–	1E.75 blue	1·90	65
420	–	2E. yellow-brown (1948)	1·70	50
421	–	2E.50 grey-blue	5·75	45
422	–	3E. olive-green	2·75	45
423	–	3E.50 olive (1948)	3·75	45
424	–	5E. blue-green (1948)	3·75	45
425	–	10E. chocolate	9·00	60
426	–	15E. scarlet	22·00	3·25
427	–	20E. orange	43·00	5·25
408/427 Set of 20			90·00	14·00

Designs. Vert—5c., 30c. Gogogo Peak; 60c., 3E.50, Nhanhangare Waterfall. Horiz—10c., 1E.20, Zambesi Bridge; 1E., 5E. Gathering coconuts; 1E.50, 2E. River Pungué at Beira; 1E.75, 3E. Polana beach, Lourenço Marques; 2E.50, 10E. Bird's eye view of Lourenço Marques; 15E., 20E. Malema river.

The dollar sign is in reverse on No. 423.

1948 (Oct). Honouring the Statue of Our Lady of Fatima. As T **62** of Macao.

428		50c. light blue	3·75	1·70
429		1E.20 magenta	8·25	3·50
430		4E.50 yellow-green	32·00	10·50
431		20E. brown	60·00	16·00
428/431 Set of 4			95·00	29·00

35 Boeing 377 Stratocruiser, Douglas DC-3, other Aircraft and Globe

36 Clown Triggerfish (*Ballistoides conspicillum*)

(Photo Courvoisier)

1949 (Mar). AIR. P 11½.

432	35	50c. sepia	75	30
433		1E.20 violet	1·50	70
434		4E.50 deep blue	3·50	1·10
435		5E. green	6·00	1·40
436		20E. brown	17·00	7·00
432/436 Set of 5			26·00	9·50

1914 (18 Oct). 75th Anniv of Universal Postal Union. As T **64** of Macao.

437		4E.50 blue	4·50	1·80

1950 (May). Holy Year. As Nos. 425/6 of Macao.

438		1E.50 red-orange	1·20	65
439		3E. blue	1·70	95

> **DATES OF ISSUE.** The dates given for Nos. 440/624 refer to the dates when the stamps were placed on sale in Mozambique. In a number of instances they were released at different times in Lisbon, usually earlier.

(Litho Litografia Nacional, Oporto, Portugal)

1951. Fishes. T **36** and similar multicoloured designs. P 14½×14 (1, 6, 8E.) or 14×14½ (others).

440		5c. Type 36	35	15
441		10c. Thread-finned butterflyfish (*Chaetodon auriga*)	20	15
442		15c. Racoon butterflyfish (*Chaetodon inula*)	90	45
443		20c. Lionfish (*Pterois volitans*)	30	15
444		30c. Pearl puffer (*Canthigaster margaritatus*)	25	15
445		40c. Golden filefish (*Stephanolepis auratus*)	20	15
446		50c. Spot-checked Surgeonfish (*Teuthis nigrofuscus*)	20	15
447		1E. Pennant coralfish (*Heniochus acuminatus*) (vert)	30	15
448		1E.50 Seagrass wrasse (*Novaculichthys macrolepidotus*)	30	15
449		2E. Sombre Sweetlips (*Gaterin schotaf*)	30	15
450		2E.50 Blue-striped Snapper (*Lutianus kasmira*)	1·00	20
451		3E. Convict tang (*Acauthurus triostegus*)	1·00	20
452		3E.50 Starry triggerfish (*Abalistes stellaris*)	1·20	15
453		4E. Cornetfish (*Fistularia petimba*)	1·80	35
454		4E.50 Vagabond butterflyfish (*Chaetodon vagabundus*)	2·75	35
455		5E. Sail-backed mailcheek (*Amblyapistus binotata*)	2·75	15
456		6E. Dusky batfish (*Platax pinnatus*) (vert)	2·75	15
457		8E. Moorish idol (*Zanclus canescens*) (vert)	4·50	60
458		9E. Triangulate boxfish (*Tetrosomus concatenatus*)	4·50	45
459		10E. Eastern flying gurnard (*Dactyloptena orientalis*)	11·00	2·30
460		15E. Red-toothed triggerfish (*Odonus niger*)	65·00	19·00
461		20E. Picasso triggerfish (*Rhinecanthus aculeatus*)	34·00	7·00
462		30E. Long-horned cowfish (*Lactoria cornutus*)	41·00	9·50
463		50E. Spotted cowfish (*Lactoria fornasina*)	50·00	18·00
440/463 Set of 24			£200	55·00

1951 (Oct). Termination of Holy Year. As T **69** of Macao.

464		3E. carmine and salmon	2·75	1·50

No. 464 was issued *se-tenant* with a stamp-size label bearing a papal declaration.

37 Victor Cordon (colonist)

39 Liner and Lockheed Constellation Airliner

1951 (Oct). Birth Centenary of Cordon. Litho. P 11½.

465	37	1E. brown and orange-brown	2·75	65
466		5E. black and slate-blue	14·00	1·70

1952 (19 June). First Tropical Medicine Congress, Lisbon. Horiz design as T **71** of Macao.

467		3E. orange and deep blue	1·80	75

Design:—3E. Miguel Bombarda Hospital.

1952. POSTAGE DUE. As Type D **70** of Macao.

D468		10c. multicoloured	20	20
D469		30c. multicoloured	20	20
D470		50c. multicoloured	30	25
D471		1E. multicoloured	35	30
D472		2E. multicoloured	35	30
D473		5E. multicoloured	1·00	65
D468/473 Set of 6			2·20	1·70

MOZAMBIQUE

1952–56. CHARITY TAX. Inscr "Provincia de Moçambique". Value in black. No imprint at foot. P 14.
C468	C **29**	50c. orange (1952)	1·40	95
C469		50c. olive-green (1955)	1·40	95
C470		50c. red-brown (1956)	1·40	95
C468/470 Set of 3			3·75	2·50

(Des Sousa and Araujo. Litho)

1952 (15 Sept). Fourth African Tourist Congress. P 13½.
468	**39**	1E.50 multicoloured	1·00	70

40 Missionary

41 *Papilio demodocus*

42 Stamps

1953 (Jan). Missionary Art Exhibition. Litho. P 13½.
469	**40**	10c. lake and lilac (5 Jan)	20	15
470		1E. brown-lake and pale yellow-green	1·10	30
471		5E. brown-black and pale blue	2·75	90
469/471 Set of 3			3·75	1·20

(Photo J. Enschedé & Sons)

1953 (28 May). As T **41** (butterflies and moths in natural colours). Colours given are those of the backgrounds and inscriptions. P 13½×14.
472	10c. slate-blue and black	15	15
473	15c. buff and black	15	15
474	20c. pale green and brown	15	15
475	30c. pale purple and brown	15	15
476	40c. pale brown and brown	15	15
477	50c. slate and black	15	15
478	80c. light blue and brown	20	15
479	1E. turquoise-green and brown	20	15
480	1E.50 yellow-bistre and black	25	15
481	2E. pale chestnut and brown	6·50	60
482	2E.30 blue and black	5·25	60
483	2E.50 pale yellow-green and black	11·50	60
484	3E. pale claret and blue	2·10	20
485	4E. pale blue and black	75	15
486	4E.50 yellow-orange and green	95	15
487	5E. pale blue-green and black	95	15
488	6E. lilac and black	1·10	30
489	7E.50 pale sepia and brown	6·50	60
490	10E. pink and black	10·50	1·90
491	20E. grey-green and black	18·00	1·90
472/491 Set of 20		60·00	7·75

Designs:—15c. *Amphicalia thelwalli*; 20c. *Euxanthe wakefieldi*; 30c. *Axiocerses harpax*; 40c. *Colotis euippe* (*Teracolus omphale*); 50c. *Papilio dardanus*; 80c. *Bunaeopsis hersilia* (*Nudaurelia hersilia*); 1E. *Argema mimosae* (*Aigenia mimosae*); 1E.50, *Graphium antheus* (*Papilio antheus*); 2E. *Athletes ethra* (*Athletes ethica*); 2E.30, *Danais chrysippus*; 2E.50, *Papilio phorcas*; 3E. *Arniocera ericata*; 4E. *Pseudaphelia apollinaris* (*Pseudaphelia pollinaris*); 4E.50, *Egybolis vaillantina*; 5E. *Hebena lateritia* (*Metarctia lateritia*); 6E. *Heraclia mozambica* (*Xanthospilopteryx mozambica*); 7E.50, *Chiromachla leuconoe* (*Nyctemera leuconoe*); 10E. *Charaxes protoclea* (*Charaxes azota*); 20E. *Aegocera fervida*.

(Litho Litografia Maia, Oporto)

1953 (23 July). Philatelic Exhibition, Lourenço Marques. P 14.
492	**42**	1E. multicoloured	1·50	55
493		3E. multicoloured	5·75	1·40

1953 (Oct). Portuguese Stamp Centenary. As T **75** of Macao.
494	50c. multicoloured	1·20	75

1954 (2 July). Fourth Centenary of São Paulo. As T **76** of Macao.
495	3E.50 multicoloured	60	30

43 Map of Mozambique

44 Arms of Beira

45 Mousinho de Albuquerque

(Des J. de Moura. Litho)

1954 (15 Oct). Map multicoloured; Mozambique territory in colour given below. P 13½.
496	**43**	10c. lilac	20	15
497		20c. greenish yellow	20	15
498		50c. pale violet-blue	20	15
499		1E. orange-yellow	25	15
500		2E.30 white	85	65
501		4E. salmon	95	50
502		10E. pale green	2·50	30
503		20E. pale brown	4·25	65
496/503 Set of 8			8·50	2·40

1954 (1 Dec). First Philatelic Exhibition, Manica and Sofala. Litho. Network background colour in italics. P 13½.
504	**44**	1E.50 red, gold, silver, green and deep blue/*blue*	60	30
505		3E.50 red, gold, silver, green and orange-brown/*salmon*	1·40	60

1956 (1 Feb). Birth Centenary of M. de Albuquerque. T **45** and another design inscr "1855 1955". Litho. P 11½×12.
506		1E. black-brown and grey	85	50
507		2E.50 black, blue, buff and deep blue	1·70	85

Design: Vert—2E.50, Equestrian statue of Albuquerque.

46 Arms and Inhabitants

47 Freighters in Beira Harbour

(47a)

1956 (4 Aug). Visit of President of Portugal. P 14½.
508	**46**	1E. multicoloured	60	20
509		2E.50 multicoloured	1·20	60

(Des J. de Moura. Litho Litografia Nacional, Oporto)

1957 (15 Aug). 50th Anniv of Beira. P 14½.
510	**47**	2E.50 multicoloured	1·20	60

1957. CHARITY TAX. No. C470 surch locally with T **47a**.
C511	C **29**	30c. on 50c. red-brown	1·00	55

1958–64. CHARITY TAX. Inscr "Provincia de Moçambique". Value in black. P 14.

(a) No imprint at foot
C512	C **29**	30c. lemon (1958)	1·30	95
C513		50c. salmon (1958)	1·30	95

(b) Imprint: "IMPRENSA NACIONAL DE MOÇAMBIQUE"
C514	C **29**	30c. lemon (1964)	1·30	95
C515		50c. salmon (1963)	1·30	95

1958 (14 Sept). Sixth International Congress of Tropical Medicine. Diamond-shaped design as T **79** of Macao. Multicoloured.
511	1E.50 *Strophanthus grandiflorus*	3·25	1·40

1958 (8 Oct). Brussels International Exhibition. As T **78** of Macao.
512	3E.50 multicoloured	50	30

48 Caravel

49 "Arts and Crafts"

(Des J. de Moura. Litho)

1960 (25 June). Fifth Death Centenary of Prince Henry the Navigator. P 13×13½.
513	**48**	5E. multicoloured	1·00	30

(Des Neves and Sousa. Litho Litografia Maia, Oporto)

1960 (21 Nov). Tenth Anniv of African Technical Co-operation Commission. P 14½.
514	**49**	3E. multicoloured	80	50

179

MOZAMBIQUE

50 Arms of Lourenço Marques

51 Fokker F.27 Friendship and de Havilland D.H.89 Dragon Rapide over Route Map

54 Arms of Mozambique and Statue of Vasco da Gama

55 Nef, 1430

(Des J. de Moura. Litho)

1961 (30 Jan). As T **50**. Arms multicoloured; "MOÇAMBIQUE" etc, blue; values, red; background colours below. P 13½.

515	5c. light salmon	20	15
516	15c. light blue-green	20	15
517	20c. pale violet	20	15
518	30c. cream	20	15
519	50c. light grey-blue	20	15
520	1E. light yellow-olive	35	15
521	1E.50 light blue	35	15
522	2E. pale lilac	65	15
523	2E.50 light turquoise-blue	2·00	20
524	3E. light orange-brown	75	20
525	4E. yellow-buff	75	20
526	4E.50 pale grey-green	75	20
527	5E. light turquoise-green	75	20
528	7E.50 light pink	1·60	55
529	10E. light yellow-green	2·40	60
530	20E. light cinnamon	5·25	95
531	50E. light grey	10·50	2·20
515/531	Set of 17	24·00	5·75

Arms (inscr)—15c. Chibuto; 20c. Nampula; 30c. Inhambane; 50c. Mozambique (city); 1E. Matola; 1E.50, Quelimane; 2E. Mocuba; 2E.50, Antonio Enes; 3E. Cabral; 4E. Manica; 4E.50, Pery; 5E. St. Tiago de Tete; 7E.50, Porto Amelia; 10E. Chinde; 20E. João Belo; 50E. Beira.

1962 (10 Feb). Sports. Diamond-shaped designs as T **82** of Macao. Multicoloured. P 13½.

532	50c. Water-skiing	20	15
533	1E. Wrestling	1·30	30
534	1E.50 Gymnastics	60	25
535	2E.50 Hockey	50	25
536	4E.50 Netball	1·40	65
537	15E. Outboard speedboat racing	2·75	1·50
532/537	Set of 6	6·00	2·75

1962 (5 Apr). Malaria Eradication. Vert design as T **83** of Macao. Multicoloured.

| 538 | 2E.50 *Anopheles funestus* (mosquito) | 1·90 | 55 |

(Litho Litografia Nacional, Oporto)

1962 (15 Oct). 25th Anniv of D.E.T.A. (Mozambique Airline). P 14½.

| 539 | **51** | 3E. multicoloured | 95 | 30 |

52 Lourenço Marques in 1887 and 1962

53 Oil Refinery, Sonarep

(Des J. de Moura. Litho Litografia de Portugal, Oporto)

1962 (1 Nov). 75th Anniv of Lourenço Marques. P 13.

| 540 | **52** | 1E. multicoloured | 65 | 30 |

(Des A. Rabanal (1E.50). J. de Moura (others). Litho)

1963 (5 Mar). AIR. Horiz designs as T **53** showing aircraft in flight. Multicoloured. P 13.

541	1E.50 Type **53**	85	30
542	2E. Salazar Academy	75	20
543	3E.50 Aerial view of Lourenço Marques Port	75	20
544	4E.50 Salazar Barrage	75	20
545	5E. Trigo de Morais Bridge and Dam	75	20
546	20E. Marcelo Caetano Bridge and Dam	2·75	95
541/546	Set of 6	6·00	1·80

(Litho Litografia Maia. Oporto)

1963 (25 Apr). Bicentenary of City of Mozambique. P 14½.

| 547 | **54** | 3E. multicoloured | 65 | 30 |

1963 (21 Oct). Tenth Anniv of T.A.P. Airline. As T **69** of Angola.

| 548 | 2E.50 multicoloured | 60 | 25 |

(Des A. Cutileiro. Litho Litografia Maia, Oporto)

1963 (1 Dec). Evolution of Sailing Ships. Various designs as T **55**. Multicoloured. P 14½.

549	10c. Type **55**	20	15
550	20c. Caravel, 1436 (vert)	20	15
551	30c. Lateen-rigged caravel, 1460 (vert)	20	15
552	50c. Vasco da Gama's *São Gabriel*, 1947 (vert)	20	15
553	1E. Don Manuel's nau, 1498 (vert)	60	15
554	1E.50 Galleon, 1530 (vert)	60	15
555	2E. Nau *Flor de la Mar*, 1511 (vert)	60	15
556	2E.50 Caravel *Redonda*, 1519	60	15
557	3E.50 Nau, 1520 (vert)	75	20
558	4E. Portuguese Indies galley, 1521	85	25
559	4E.50 Galleon *Santa Tereza*, 1639 (vert)	85	25
560	5E. Nao *N. Senhora de Conçeiçao*, 1716 (vert)	17·00	45
561	6E. Warship *N. Senhora de Bom Sucesso*, 1764	1·20	45
562	7E.50 Bomb launch, 1788	1·60	55
563	8E. Naval brigantine *Lebre*, 1793	1·60	55
564	10E. Corvette *Andorinha*, 1799	1·60	55
565	12E.50 Naval schooner *Maria Teresa*, 1820	1·80	95
566	15E. Warship *Vasco da Gama*, 1841	2·50	95
567	20E. Sail frigate *Don Fernando II e Gloria*, 1843 (vert)	3·25	1·20
568	30E. Cadet ship *Sagres I*, 1924 (vert)	5·50	2·10
549/568	Set of 20	38·00	8·75

C **56** Women and Children

56 Pres. Tomas

(Des A. Possacos. Litho Imprensa National de Moçambique)

1963–73. CHARITY TAX. P 14.

C569	C **56**	30c. black, light green and red (1973)	55	35
C570		50c. black, yell-bistre and rose-red	55	35
C571		50c. black, pink and red (1965)	55	35
C572		50c. blk, yell-green and red (29.6.67)	55	35
C573		50c. black, light blue and red (1969)	55	35
C574		50c. black, buff and red (1970)	55	35
C575		50c. black, pale grey and red (1972)	55	35
C576		50c. black, greenish yellow and red (1974)	45	20
C577		1E. black, pale grey and red (1973)	1·50	70
C578		1E. black, pale buff and red (1973)	45	25
C578a		1E. black, pale mauve and vermilion (1974)	45	25

1964 (16 May). Centenary of National Overseas Bank. Horiz design as T **84** of Macao. Multicoloured.

| 569 | 1E.50 Bank building, Lourenço Marques | 60 | 20 |

(Des L. Almeida. Litho)

1964 (23 July). Presidential Visit. P 13½×12½.

| 570 | **56** | 2E.50 bistre, black, red, ultram and grey | 60 | 20 |

MOZAMBIQUE

57 State Barge of João V, 1728

C **58** Telegraph Poles and Map

1964 (18 Dec). Portuguese Marine, 18th and 19th Centuries. T **57** and similar designs. Multicoloured. P 14½.
571	15c. Type **57**	20	15
572	35c. State barge of José I, 1753	20	15
573	1E. Barge of Alfandega, 1768	55	20
574	1E.50 Oarsman of 1780 (vert)	65	25
575	2E.50 *Pinto de Fonseca* (state barge), 1780	35	15
576	5E. State barge of Carlota Joaquina, 1790	65	30
577	9E. Don Miguel's state barge, 1831	1·60	95
571/577	Set of 7	3·75	1·90

(Des Marinho. Litho Imprensa Nacional de Moçambique)

1965 (1 Apr). CHARITY TAX. Mozambique Telecommunications Improvement. Type C **58** and similar design inscr "TELECOMUNICAÇOES". Ordinary or chalky paper. P 14½.
C579	30c. black, pink and reddish violet	25	20
C580	50c. black, yellow-brown and blue	25	20
C581	1E. black, yellow-orange & bronze-grn.	35	30
C579/581	Set of 3	75	65

Design: Vert (19½×36 mm)—50c., 1E. Telegraph linesman.
A 2E.50 in Type C **58** was also issued for compulsory use on telegrams.

1965 (17 May). I.T.U. Centenary. As T **85** of Macao.
| 578 | 1E. multicoloured | 60 | 30 |

1966 (28 May). 40th Anniv of Portuguese National Revolution. Horiz design as T **86** of Macao. Multicoloured.
| 579 | 1E. Railway station, Beira and Antonio Enes Academy | 55 | 30 |

58 Arquebusier, 1560

59 Luis de Camoens (poet)

(Des A. Cutileiro. Litho Litografia Nacional, Oporto)

1967 (12 Jan). Portuguese Military Uniforms. T **58** and similar vert designs. Multicoloured. P 14½.
580	20c. Type **58**	20	15
581	30c. Arquebusier, 1640	20	15
582	40c. Infantryman, 1777	20	15
583	50c. Infantry officer, 1777	20	15
584	80c. Drummer, 1777	60	25
585	1E. Infantry sergeant, 1777	60	20
586	2E. Infantry major, 1784	65	20
587	2E.50 Colonial officer, 1788	70	25
588	3E. Infantryman, 1789	70	25
589	5E. Colonial bugler, 1801	1·40	45
590	10E. Colonial officer, 1807	1·50	65
591	15E. Infantryman, 1817	2·75	1·70
580/591	Set of 12	8·75	4·00

1967 (31 Jan). Centenary of Military Naval Association. Horiz designs as T **88** of Macao. Multicoloured.
| 592 | 3E. A. Coutinho and *Tete* (paddle-gunboat) | 45 | 20 |
| 593 | 10E. J. Roby and *Granada* (paddle-gunboat) | 1·40 | 65 |

1967 (13 May). 50th Anniv of the Fatima Apparitions. Vert design as T **89** of Macao. Multicoloured.
| 594 | 50c. "Golden Crown" | 30 | 20 |
| | a. Red (face value) omitted | 55·00 | |

1968 (22 Apr). 500th Birth Anniv of Pedro Cabral (explorer). Multicoloured designs as T **90** of Macao.
595	1E. Erecting the Cross at Porto Seguro (horiz)	20	15
596	1E.50 First mission service in Brazil (horiz)	50	15
597	3E. Church of Grace, Santarem	95	50
595/597	Set of 3	1·50	70

1969 (17 Feb). Birth Centenary of Admiral Gage Coutinho. Horiz design as T **91** of Macao. Multicoloured.
| 598 | 70c. Admiral Gago Coutinho Airport, Lourenço Marques | 35 | 20 |

(Des J. de Moura. Litho)

1969 (10 June). 400th Anniv of Camoens' visit to Mozambique. T **59** and similar multicoloured designs. P 12½×13 (vert) or 13×12½ (horiz).
599	15c. Type **59**	20	15
600	50c. Nau of 1553 (horiz)	25	15
601	1E.50 Map of Mozambique, 1554	35	20
602	2E.50 Chapel of Our Lady of Baluarte (horiz)	50	25
603	5E. Part of the "Lusiad" (poem)	70	55
599/603	Set of 5	1·80	1·20

1969 (29 Aug). 500th Birth Anniv of Vasco da Gama (explorer). Horiz design as T **92** of Macao. Multicoloured.
| 604 | 1E. Map of Da Gama's voyage to India | 30 | 20 |

1969 (25 Sept). Centenary of Overseas Administrative Reforms. As T **93** of Macao.
| 605 | 1E.50 multicoloured | 35 | 20 |

1969 (1 Dec). 500th Birth Anniv of King Manoel I. Horiz design as T **95** of Macao. Multicoloured.
| 606 | 80c. Illuminated arms | 30 | 20 |

1970 (15 Nov). Birth Centenary of Marshal Carmona. Vert design as T **96** of Macao. Multicoloured.
| 607 | 5E. Portrait in ceremonial dress | 55 | 30 |

60 Fossilized Fern

61 Racing Dinghies

(Des J. de Moura. Litho Litografia Maia, Oporto)

1971 (15 Jan). Rocks, Minerals and Fossils. T **60** and similar diamond-shaped designs. Multicoloured. P 13.
608	15c. Type **60**	30	15
609	50c. *Lytodiscoides conduciensis* (fossilised snail)	30	15
610	1E. Stibnite	45	20
611	1E.50 Pink beryl	65	20
612	2E. Endothiodon and fossil skeleton	75	20
613	3E. Tantalocolumbite	1·20	20
614	3E.50 Verdelite	1·60	30
615	4E. Zircon	2·10	45
616	10E. Petrified tree-stump	3·75	1·20
608/616	Set of 9	10·00	2·75

1972 (25 May). 400th Anniv of Camoens' "The Lusiads" (epic poem). Vert design as T **98** of Macao. Multicoloured.
| 617 | 4E. Mozambique Island in 16th century | 60 | 30 |

1972 (20 June). Olympic Games, Munich. Horiz design as T **99** of Macao. Multicoloured.
| 618 | 3E. Hurdling and swimming | 45 | 30 |

1972 (20 Sept). 50th Anniv of First Flight Lisbon–Rio de Janeiro. Horiz design as T **100** of Macao. Multicoloured.
| 619 | 1E. Fairey IIID seaplane *Santa Cruz* at Recife | 30 | 20 |

(Des A. Cutileiro. Litho)

1973 (21 Aug). World Championships for "Vauriens" Class Yachts, Lourenço Marques. T **61** and similar horiz designs, showing yacht races. P 12×11½.
620	1E. multicoloured	20	15
621	1E.50 multicoloured	30	15
622	3E. multicoloured	60	30
620/622	Set of 3	1·00	55

(Des A. Cutileiro. Litho)

181

1973 (15 Dec). Centenary of World Meteorological Organization. As T **102** of Macao.
623   2E. multicoloured 50   30

62 Dish Aerials

63 Bird with "Flag" Wings

(Des A. Cutileiro. Litho Litografia Maia, Oporto)

1974 (25 June). Inauguration of Satellite Communications Station Network. P 13.
624   **62**   50c. multicoloured 30   20

(Des R. Couto. Litho)

1975 (Jan). Implementation of Lusaka Agreement. P 14.
625   **63**   1E. multicoloured 20   15
626   1E.50 multicoloured 25   15
627   2E. multicoloured 30   20
628   3E.50 multicoloured 55   45
629   6E. multicoloured .... 1·20   50
625/629 Set of 5 .... 2·30   1·30
MS630 150×75 mm. Nos. 625/9 .... 7·00   7·00

The 1E., 1E.50 and 3E.50 values have been seen with carmine (face values) omitted. There is no evidence that these were ever sold in Mozambique post offices.

On 7 September 1974 an agreement was signed in Lusaka, Zambia between Portugal and the Frente da Libertação de Moçambique (FRELIMO) that Mozambique should become independent.

The People's Republic of Mozambique was proclaimed on 25 June 1975. Subsequent issues are listed in Part 13 (*Africa since Independence F-M*) of this catalogue.

INHAMBANE

This district, in the south of Mozambique, overprinted the 1895 St. Anthony commemorative issue and had its own stamps from 1903 to 1920, since when the stamps of Mozambique have again been used.

CENTENARIO
DE
S. ANTONIO
—
Inhambane
MDCCCXCV
(**1**)   **2**

1895 (1 July). 700th Birth Anniv of St. Anthony. No gum.
*(i) T **2** of Mozambique optd locally with T **1***
(a) P 12½
1   5r. black .... 55·00   40·00
     a. Opt inverted .... —   90·00
2   10r. green .... 55·00   40·00
3   20r. rosine .... 80·00   60·00
4   25r. dull purple £130   £100
5   40r. chocolate .... 80·00   40·00
     a. Opt inverted .... —   90·00
6   50r. blue .... 80·00   40·00
7   100r. yellow-brown £225   £200
8   200r. slate-violet .... £110   90·00
9   300r. orange .... £110   90·00

There is some doubt as to whether the 25r. and 100r. were authorised.

(b) P 13½
10   10r. green £225   £120
     a. Opt inverted .... £190   90·00
11   50r. blue £190   £180
     a. Opt inverted .... 90·00   80·00

*(ii) T **4** of Mozambique optd locally with T **1***
(a) P 11½
12   50r. pale blue .... 80·00   60·00
13   80r. pale green .... 85·00   70·00
     a. Opt inverted .... £100   90·00
14   100r. brown/*yellow* £300   £275
     a. Opt inverted .... —   90·00

(b) P 12½
15   50r. pale blue (E) £160   £120
16   75r. rose £130   £100
     a. Opt inverted .... £100   90·00
17   150r. carmine/*rose* £130   £100

(Des and eng E. Mouchon. Typo)

1903 (1 Jan). Name and value in black (on 500r. in carmine). P 11½.
18   **2**   2½r. grey 70   65
19   5r. orange 75   65
20   10r. pale green 80   75
21   15r. deep green .... 2·10   1·50
22   20r. deep lilac .... 2·10   1·50
23   25r. carmine .... 2·10   1·50
24   50r. chocolate .... 5·00   2·10
25   65r. dull blue .... 23·00   16·00
26   75r. dull purple .... 3·25   2·10
27   100r. blue/*azure* .... 3·25   2·10
28   115r. orange-brown/*pink* ..... 8·50   7·50
        a. Error. On straw .... 11·50   11·50
29   130r. purple-brown/*straw* ..... 8·50   7·50
30   200r. purple/*pink* .... 8·50   7·50
31   400r. blue/*yellow* .... 14·00   11·50
32   500r. black/*azure* .... 25·00   17·00
33   700r. slate/*yellow* .... 32·00   23·00
18/33 Set of 16 .... £130   95·00

1905. No. 25 surch as T **25** of Macao.
34   **2**   50r. on 65r. dull blue .... 7·25   5·50

1911. Optd with T **27** of Macao, in red or green (G.).
35   **2**   2½r. grey 55   50
36   5r. orange 55   50
37   10r. pale green 65   50
38   15r. deep green 65   50
39   20r. deep lilac .... 1·20   90
40   25r. carmine (G.) .... 1·20   90
41   50r. chocolate 65   50
42   75r. dull purple 90   65
43   100r. blue/*blue* 90   65
44   115r. orange-brown/*pink* ..... 1·20   90
        a. Error. On straw .... 1·60   1·10
45   130r. purple-brown/*straw* ..... 2·75   2·10
46   200r. purple/*pink* .... 1·80   1·20
47   400r. dull blue/*straw* .... 2·75   2·10
48   500r. black/*azure*................... 3·00   2·10
49   700r. slate/*yellow* .... 3·50   2·75
35/49 Set of 15 .... 20·00   15·00

REPUBLICA
INHAMBANE
¼   C.
(3)   REPUBLICA
               (4)

1913. New Currency. Vasco da Gama issues surch as T **3**.
(i) Africa (General Issues)
50   ¼c. on 2½r. blue-green .... 1·80   1·40
51   ½c. on 5r. vermilion .... 1·80   1·40
52   1c. on 10r. dull purple .... 1·80   1·40
53   2½c. on 25r. yellow-green .... 1·80   1·40
     a. Error. On No. 220 of Azores .... 55·00   48·00
54   5c. on 50r. deep blue .... 2·10   1·40
55   7½c. on 75r. chocolate .... 3·25   2·75
56   10c. on 100r. bistre-brown .... 3·25   2·75
57   15c. on 150r. ochre .... 3·25   3·00
     a. Surch inverted .... 27·00   16·00
50/57 Set of 8 .... 17·00   14·00

(ii) Macao
58   ¼c. on ½a. blue-green .... 2·30   1·90
59   ½c. on 1a. vermilion .... 2·30   1·90
60   1c. on 2a. dull purple .... 2·30   1·90
     a. Surch inverted .... 32·00   29·00
61   2½c. on 4a. yellow-green .... 2·30   1·90
62   5c. on 8a. deep blue .... 2·30   1·90
63   7½c. on 12a. chocolate .... 4·00   3·25
64   10c. on 16a. bistre-brown .... 3·25   2·10
65   15c. on 24a. ochre .... 3·25   2·10
58/65 Set of 8 .... 20·00   15·00

(iii) Timor
66   ¼c. on ½a. blue-green .... 2·30   1·90
     a. Surch inverted .... 32·00   29·00
67   ½c. on 1a. vermilion .... 2·30   1·90
68   1c. on 2a. dull purple .... 2·30   1·90
69   2½c. on 4a. yellow-green .... 2·30   1·90
70   5c. on 8a. deep blue .... 2·30   1·90
71   7½c. on 12a. chocolate .... 4·00   3·25
72   10c. on 16a. bistre-brown .... 3·25   2·10
73   15c. on 24a. ochre .... 3·25   2·10
66/73 Set of 8 .... 20·00   15·00

MOZAMBIQUE / Inhambane / Kionga / Lourenço Marques

1914. No. 34 optd locally with T **4**.
| 74 | **2** | 50r. on 65r. dull blue (R.) | 4·25 | 2·20 |

5 Ceres

(Des C. Fernandes. Eng J. S. de Carvalho e Silva. Typo)

1914–15. Name and value in black. Chalk-surfaced paper. P 15×14.

75	**5**	¼c. brown-olive	1·20	75
76		½c. black	5·25	2·50
		a. Unsurfaced paper (1915)	3·50	2·50
77		1c. deep green	1·30	75
78		1½c. chocolate	1·30	75
79		2c. carmine	1·30	75
80		2½c. violet	60	55
81		5c. blue	80	75
82		7½c. yellow-brown	2·20	1·60
83		8c. slate	2·20	1·60
84		10c. brown-red	2·20	1·80
85		15c. claret	2·75	2·10
86		20c. yellow-green	2·75	2·10
87		30c. chocolate/*green*	3·75	2·30
88		40c. brown/*rose*	3·75	2·30
89		50c. orange/*salmon*	7·00	4·75
90		1E. deep green/*azure*	7·00	4·75
75/90 Set of 16			39·00	27·00

1915. No. 34 optd with T **27** of Macao.
| 91 | **2** | 50r. on 65r. dull blue (R.) | 9·50 | 8·00 |

1917. Optd locally with T **4**, in red.
92	**2**	2½r. grey	12·50	9·75
93		5r. orange	12·50	9·75
94		15r. deep green	1·90	1·30
95		20r. deep lilac	1·90	1·30
96		50r. chocolate	1·20	1·30
97		75r. dull purple	2·10	1·30
98		100r. blue/*azure*	2·20	1·30
99		115r. orange-brown/*pink*	2·30	1·60
100		130r. purple-brown/*straw*	2·30	1·40
101		200r. purple/*pink*	2·30	1·40
102		400r. dull blue/*straw*	3·00	2·10
103		500r. black/*azure*	3·00	2·20
104		700r. slate/*yellow*	14·50	7·00
92/104 Set of 13			55·00	37·00

KIONGA

This small area of German East Africa, south of the R. Rovuma, was occupied by Portuguese troops after Germany declared war on Portugal on 9 March 1916. By the Treaty of Versailles in 1919 it was awarded to Portugal and incorporated in Mozambique.

KIONGA
(1)

1916 (29 May). No. 177 of Lourenço Marques surch as T **1**, in red.
1	**4**	½c. on 100r. blue/*blue*	17·00	13·50
2		1c. on 100r. blue/*blue*	17·00	13·50
3		2½c. on 100r. blue/*blue*	17·00	13·50
4		5c. on 100r. blue/*blue*	17·00	13·50

Sets may be made in deep blue and pale blue.

LOURENÇO MARQUES

The seaport and capital of Mozambique, Lourenço Marques (renamed Maputo in 1975), used the stamps of Mozambique until 1893 and again from 1920.

L. MARQUES

CENTENARIO
DE
S. ANTONIO

MDCCCXCV

N **1**　　　**1**　　　(2)

(Des and eng E. C. Azedo Gneco. Typo)

1893 (28 July). NEWSPAPER.
| N1 | N **1** | 2½r. brown (p 11½) | 65 | 60 |
| N2 | | 2½r. brown (p 12½) | 32·00 | 30·00 |

Stamps of this type could be, and often were, used for franking ordinary correspondence.

(Des and eng M. D. Neto. Typo)

1895 (28 May). Chalk-surfaced paper or enamel-surfaced paper (E).

(a) P 11½
1	**1**	5r. orange-yellow	60	55
2		10r. rosy mauve	60	55
3		15r. red-brown	1·40	1·00
4		20r. lilac	1·40	95
5		25r. green	5·00	1·70
6		75r. rose	2·50	1·70
7		100r. brown/*yellow*	3·25	1·70
8		200r. blue/*blue*	5·50	3·50
9		300r. blue/*pale brown*	5·75	3·75
1/9 Set of 9			23·00	14·00

The 50r. value was prepared but not issued.

(b) P 12½
10	**1**	25r. green	1·10	55
11		25r. green (E)	3·75	2·30
12		50r. pale blue (E)	2·75	2·10
13		75r. rose	3·00	2·10
14		80r. pale green (E)	7·25	4·75
15		100r. brown/*yellow*	7·25	4·75
16		150r. carmine/*rose*	5·75	4·75
10/16 Set of 6 (cheapest)			28·00	19·00

(c) P 13½
| 17 | **1** | 50r. pale blue (E) | 25·00 | 11·50 |
| 18 | | 75r. rose | 2·50 | 1·70 |

1895 (1 July). 700th Death Anniv of St. Anthony. No gum.

(i) T **2** of Mozambique optd locally with T **2**
(a) P 12½
19		5r. black	25·00	21·00
20		10r. green	28·00	21·00
21		20r. rosine	31·00	23·00
22		25r. purple	38·00	23·00
23		40r. chocolate	38·00	23·00
24		50r. blue	75·00	60·00
25		100r. yellow-brown	£120	£110
26		200r. slate-violet	50·00	41·00
27		300r. orange	80·00	70·00
19/27 Set of 9			£425	£350

(b) P 13½
| 27a | | 50r. blue | 25·00 | 23·00 |

(ii) T **4** of Mozambique optd locally with T **2**
(a) P 11½
28		5r. orange	25·00	14·50
		a. Opt double	55·00	55·00
29		10r. rosy mauve	38·00	23·00
		a. Opt double	55·00	55·00
30		50r. blue	65·00	47·00
31		50r. blue (E)		
32		80r. pale green	£100	80·00
33		100r. brown/*yellow*	£190	£190

(b) P 12½
34		50r. pale blue (E)	£275	£275
35		75r. rose	75·00	60·00
35a		150r. carmine/*rose*	65·00	46·00

1895 (1 July). NEWSPAPER. 700th Death Anniv of St. Anthony. Type N **5** of Mozambique optd locally with T **2**.
| N36 | | 2½r. brown (p 11½) | 9·50 | 6·50 |
| N37 | | 2½r. brown (p 13½) | 9·50 | 6·50 |

183

MOZAMBIQUE / Lourenço Marques

50 réis
(3)   4

1897 (2 Jan). No. 9 surch locally with T **3**. With or without gum.

| 36 | 1 | 50r. on 300r. blue/*pale brown* | £275 | £250 |

(Des and eng E. Mouchon. Typo)

1898 (1 Aug)–**1901**. Name and value in black, on 500r. in carmine.

(a) P 11

37	4	2½r. grey	50	50
38		5r. orange-red	50	50
		a. Orange-yellow	50	50
39		10r. green	50	50
40		15r. chocolate	1·80	1·30
41		20r. deep lilac	1·10	65
42		25r. blue-green	1·10	65
43		50r. blue	1·80	1·30
44		75r. rose	3·50	2·10
45		80r. mauve	3·00	2·00
46		100r. blue/*blue*	2·30	1·30
47		150r. purple-brown/*straw*	3·50	2·10
48		200r. purple/*pink*	5·25	2·75
49		300r. blue/*pink*	3·75	2·75
50		500r. black/*azure* (1901)	7·50	4·00
51		700r. mauve/*yellow* (1901)	32·00	14·00
37/51	Set of 15		60·00	33·00

(b) P 12½

| 52 | 4 | 25r. blue-green | £180 | £150 |

(c) P 13½

| 53 | 4 | 25r. blue-green | 55·00 | 13·00 |
| 54 | | 100r. blue/*blue* | 28·00 | 7·50 |

Correio de Lourenço Marques

50 réis   **50 Réis**
(5)   (6)

1899 (Feb). Fiscal stamps of Mozambique (see Macao T **9**) divided in half horizontally, and each half surch locally as T **5**. Toned paper. Imperf.

(a) Double stamp, unused
(b) Single stamp, unused
(c) Single stamp, used

		(a)	(b)	(c)
55	5r. on half of 10r. green and brown	12·50	5·00	3·50
56	25r. on half of 10r. green and brown	12·50	5·00	3·50
57	50r. on half of 30r. green and brown	12·50	5·00	3·50
	a. Surch inverted	19·00	—	—
	b. Surch inverted (top half), omitted (bottom half)	21·00	—	—
58	50r. on half of 800r. grn & grey-brown	38·00	12·50	9·25

Apart from the difference in the brown colour, the lower half of the 800r. can be distinguished from that of the 30r., the former having a *white network* on vertical lines under the word "REIS".

1899 (June). No. 44 surch locally with T **6**. With or without gum.

| 59 | 4 | 50r. on 75r. rose | 8·00 | 5·00 |

1902. Surch as T **22** of Macao.

60	N **1**	65r. on 2½r. (11½)	3·75	3·25
		a. Surch inverted	21·00	19·00
61		65r. on 2½r. (12½)	4·25	3·50
62	1	65r. on 5r. (11½)	3·75	3·00
63		65r. on 15r. (11½)	3·75	3·00
64		65r. on 20r. (11½)	3·75	3·00
65		65r. on 20r. (12½)	95·00	85·00
66		115r. on 10r. (11½)	3·75	3·00
		a. Surch inverted	21·00	19·00
67		115r. on 200r. (11½)	3·75	3·00
68		115r. on 300r. (11½)	3·75	3·00
69		130r. on 25r. (11½)	38·00	32·00
70		130r. on 25r. (11½)	3·50	3·25
71		130r. on 25r. (E) (12½)	31·00	28·00
72		130r. on 80r. (E) (12½)	3·75	3·25
73		130r. on 150r. (12½)	3·75	3·25
74		400r. on 50r. (E) (12½)	12·50	5·50
75		400r. on 75r. (11½)	10·00	5·50
76		400r. on 75r. (12½)	10·00	5·50
77		400r. on 75r. (13½)	9·50	7·00
78		400r. on 100r. (12½)	7·00	4·75

The 130/25, 400/50 and 400/75r. were reprinted perf 13½ in 1905.

1902. Optd with T **23** of Macao.

79	4	15r. chocolate	2·20	1·70
80		25r. blue-green	2·20	1·20
81		50r. blue	3·25	1·80
82		75r. rose	4·25	2·75
79/82	Set of 4		10·50	6·75

1903. Colours changed. Name and value in black. P 11½.

83	4	15r. deep green	1·20	80
84		25r. carmine	85	50
85		50r. brown	1·50	1·20
86		65r. dull blue	6·00	4·75
87		75r. dull purple	2·20	1·70
88		115r. orange-brown/*pink*	7·00	6·25
89		130r. purple-brown/*straw*	7·00	6·25
90		400r. dull blue/*straw*	7·75	6·75
83/90	Set of 8		30·00	25·00

1905 (Mar). No. 86 surch as T **25** of Macao.

| 91 | 4 | 50r. on 65r. dull blue | 4·50 | 3·75 |

1911. Optd with T **27** of Macao, in red or green (G.).

92	4	2½r. grey	50	35
		a. Opt inverted	6·50	6·50
93		5r. orange	50	35
94		10r. green	80	65
95		15r. deep green	80	65
96		20r. deep lilac	80	65
97		25r. carmine (G.)	1·50	90
98		50r. brown	1·30	90
99		75r. dull purple	2·10	90
100		100r. blue/*blue*	1·30	90
101		115r. orange-brown/*pink*	15·00	6·25
		a. On straw		
102		130r. purple-brown/*straw*	1·50	90
103		200r. purple/*pink*	1·50	90
104		400r. dull blue/*straw*	2·50	2·00
105		500r. black/*azure*	2·50	2·00
106		700r. mauve/*yellow*	3·25	2·00
92/106	Set of 15		32·00	18·00

The 2½, 5, 25 and 100r. have a variety "F" for "E" in "MARQUES" (4th stamp, 1st row).

REPUBLICA
LOURENÇO MARQUES

¼   C.
(7)   8 Ceres

1913. New Currency. Vasco da Gama issues surch as T **7**.

(i) Portuguese Colonies (General Issues)

107	¼c. on 2½r. blue-green	2·20	1·80
108	½c. on 5r. vermilion	2·20	1·80
109	1c. on 10r. dull purple	2·20	1·80
110	2½c. on 25r. yellow-green	2·20	1·80
111	5c. on 50r. deep blue	2·20	1·80
112	7½c. on 75r. chocolate	5·75	4·25
113	10c. on 100r. bistre-brown	3·25	1·80
114	15c. on 150r. ochre	3·25	1·80
107/114	Set of 8	21·00	15·00

(ii) Macao

115	¼c. on ½a. blue-green	1·70	1·30
116	½c. on 1a. vermilion	1·70	1·30
117	1c. on 2a. dull purple	1·70	1·30
118	2½c. on 4a. yellow-green	1·70	1·30
119	5c. on 8a. deep blue	1·70	1·30
120	7½c. on 12a. chocolate	3·25	2·30
121	10c. on 16a. bistre-brown	2·30	1·20
	a. Surch inverted	32·00	29·00
122	15c. on 24a. ochre	2·30	1·90
115/122	Set of 8	14·50	10·50

(iii) Timor

123	¼c. on ½a. blue-green	1·70	1·30
124	½c. on 1a. vermilion	1·70	1·30
125	1c. on 2a. dull purple	1·70	1·30
126	2½c. on 4a. yellow-green	1·70	1·30
127	5c. on 8a. deep blue	1·70	1·30
128	7½c. on 12a. chocolate	3·25	2·30
129	10c. on 16a. bistre-brown	2·30	1·20
130	15c. on 24a. ochre	2·30	1·90
123/130	Set of 8	14·50	10·50

MOZAMBIQUE / Lourenço Marques / Mozambique Company

(Des C. Fernandes. Eng J. S. de Carvalho e Silva. Typo)

1914–18. Name and value in black. P 15×14.

(a) Chalk surfaced paper (1914)

131	8	¼c. brown-olive	65	50
132		½c. black	65	50
133		1c. deep green	60	45
134		1½c. chocolate	1·10	90
135		2c. carmine	1·80	95
136		2½c. violet	1·80	95
137		5c. blue	1·40	95
138		7½c. yellow-brown	2·10	1·60
139		8c. slate	2·10	1·60
140		10c. brown-red	2·00	1·20
141		15c. claret	1·90	1·40
142		20c. yellow-green	2·20	1·80
143		30c. chocolate/*green*	2·00	1·70
144		40c. brown/*rose*	7·50	5·75
145		50c. orange/*salmon*	3·50	2·75
146		1E. deep green/*azure*	3·50	2·75
131/146 *Set of 16*			31·00	23·00

The 1c. and 2½c. also exist on glazed paper.

(b) Unsurfaced paper (1915–18)

147	8	¼c. brown-olive	45	35
148		½c. black	45	35
149		1c. green	45	35
150		1½c. chocolate	50	45
151		2c. carmine	50	45
152		2½c. violet	50	45
153		5c. blue	1·10	95
154		7½c. yellow-brown (1918)	1·10	95
155		8c. slate (1918)	1·10	95
156		10c. brown-red (1918)	31·00	23·00
157		15c. claret (1918)	1·90	1·80
147/157 *Set of 11*			35·00	27·00

The ½c. and 1½c. surcharged 5c. and 10c. respectively and "PORTEADO" were issued in 1922 to serve as Postage Due stamps in Mozambique and are listed there.

(9) 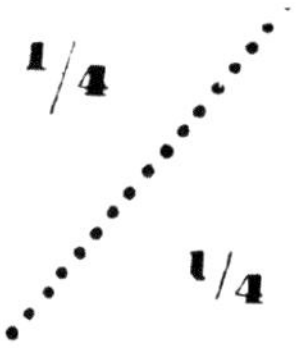 (10)

1914. Provisionals of 1902 optd locally with T **9**, in red.

158	1	115r. on 10r. (11½)	2·00	1·80
159		115r. on 200r. (11½)	2·00	1·80
160		115r. on 300r. (11½)	2·00	1·80
161		130r. on 25r. (11½)	2·00	1·80
162		130r. on 25r. (12½)	2·00	1·80
163		130r. on 25r. (E) (12½)	19·00	14·00
164		130r. on 80r. (12½)	2·00	1·80
165		130r. on 150r. (12½)	2·00	1·80

1915. Provisionals of 1902 optd with T **27** of Macao, in red.

166	1	115r. on 10r. (11½)	1·20	95
167		115r. on 200r. (11½)	1·40	95
168		115r. on 150r. (11½)	1·40	95
169		130r. on 150r. (12½)	1·40	95

1915 (Jan). Nos. 93 and 132 perforated diagonally and each half surch locally as in T **10**, in red.

170	4	¼ on half of 5r. orange	4·25	3·25
171	8	¼ on half of ½c. black	4·25	3·25

Prices of Nos. 170/1 are for whole stamps.
No. 170 exists with the variety "F" for "E" in "MARQUES".

(11) (12) (13)

1915 (July). Nos. 83 and 95 surch locally with T **11**.

172	4	2c. on 15r. deep green (83)	1·90	1·40
173		2c. on 15r. deep green (95)	1·90	1·40

1917. Optd locally with T **9**, in red.

174	4	15r. deep green	1·40	1·20
175		50r. brown	3·00	2·30
176		75r. dull purple	3·00	2·30
177		100r. blue/*blue*	2·10	1·80
178		115r. orange-brown/*pink*	2·10	1·80
179		130r. brown/*yellow*	11·50	8·50
180		200r. purple/*pink*	3·00	2·30
181		400r. dull blue/*straw*	6·25	4·50
182		500r. black/*blue*	4·25	3·50
183		700r. mauve/*yellow*	8·00	4·50
174/183 *Set of 10*			40·00	29·00

1917. Provisionals of 1902 optd locally with T **9**, in red.

184	1	400r. on 50r. (E) (12½)	2·20	1·70
185		400r. on 75r. (11½)	3·50	2·75
186		400r. on 75r. (12½)	3·75	2·75
187		400r. on 75r. (13½)	3·75	2·75

1918. Red Cross Fund. Stamps of 1914 optd with T **12**, in red, or surch as T **13**, in black, in addition. Unsurfaced paper (¼ to 5c., 40c.) or chalk-surfaced paper (others).

188	8	¼c. brown-olive	3·75	3·50
189		½c. black	3·75	3·50
190		1c. deep green	3·75	3·50
191		2½c. violet	3·75	3·50
192		5c. blue	8·75	7·75
		a. Chalk-surfaced paper	3·75	3·50
193		10c. brown-red	4·50	4·00
194		20c. on 1½c. chocolate	4·50	4·00
195		30c. chocolate/*green*	5·00	4·75
196		40c. on 2c. carmine	5·00	4·75
197		50c. on 7½c. yellow-brown	5·00	4·75
198		70c. on 8c. slate	5·00	4·75
199		1E. on 15c. claret	5·00	4·75
188/199 *Set of 12 (cheapest)*			47·00	44·00

The 1c. and 2½c. also exist on glazed paper.
The unsurfaced paper examples show a distinct diamond pattern when held to the light. All overprints on the unsurfaced paper not showing this pattern are forgeries.

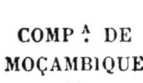

(14) (15) (16)

1920–21.

*(a) No. 158 surch with T **14**, in green*

200	1	¼c. on 115r. on 10r. (2.21)	1·40	95

*(b) No. 152 surch as T **15** or with T **16***

201	15	1c. on 2½c. violet (2.21)	1·10	65
202		1½c. on 2½c. violet (2.21)	1·10	65
203	16	4c. on 2½c. violet (R.) (8.20)	1·10	65

Nos. 200/3 were valid for use throughout Mozambique. No. 202 also exists on glazed paper.

MOZAMBIQUE COMPANY

The Mozambique Company was granted a charter by Portugal on 30 July 1891 to administer the territory of Manica and Sofala, between the Zambesi and Save Rivers, for fifty years. By decree of 8 August 1892, the Company was authorised to issue its own stamps. After the expiry of the charter the administration of the company's territory was taken over by Mozambique in January 1942 and ceased to have its own stamps.

COMP.ᴬ DE MOÇAMBIQUE
(1) 2 (a) (b)

1892–93. T **2** of Mozambique optd with T **1**. Chalk-surfaced paper.

(a) P 12½

1		5r. black (R.)	1·40	1·10
		a. Opt omitted (in pair with normal)	48·00	48·00
2		10r. green	1·40	1·10
3		20r. rosine	1·80	1·10
4		25r. bright mauve	1·40	1·10
		a. Opt double	10·50	
5		40r. chocolate	1·40	1·10
		a. Opt double	21·00	19·00
		b. Opt omitted (in pair with normal)	48·00	48·00
6		50r. pale blue	1·90	1·30
		a. Deep blue	1·90	1·30
7		100r. yellow-brown	1·90	1·30
8		200r. slate-violet	2·30	1·80
9		300r. orange-red	3·25	1·90
		a. Pale orange	3·25	1·90

185

MOZAMBIQUE / Mozambique Company

(b) P 13½

10	5r. black (R.)		1·30	75
11	10r. green		2·10	95
12	20r. rosine		70·00	55·00
13	25r. bright mauve (1893)		1·30	75
14	50r. pale blue		17·00	5·75
	a. Deep blue		17·00	5·75

To meet a philatelic demand most of the above as well as the 200r. and 300r. perf 12½ and 13½ were reprinted in 1894 on *enamel-surfaced* paper, a paper which had not been used until after the original issue had become obsolete. The remainder of these reprints was used for the 1902 provisional surcharges of Mozambique.

In addition the 5r. to 40r. were reprinted in 1905 on chalk-surfaced paper, and the 40, 50, 200 and 300r. on enamel-surfaced paper.

1894 (1 July). NEWSPAPER. Mozambique Type **N 5** optd with T **1**.

N15	2½r. brown (perf 11½)	1·40	1·10
	a. Opt inverted	10·50	9·50
N16	2½r. brown (perf 12½)	3·00	1·90

This was reprinted in 1905 perf 13½ on enamel-surfaced paper.

Two types of figure "1" for 10, 15, 100 and 150r. The 1000r. is Type (a).

(Des and eng J. S. de Carvalho e Silva. Typo)

1895–1902. Chalk-surfaced paper, or enamel-surfaced paper (E). Numerals of value in black or carmine (500r., 1000r.).

(a) With or without gum. P 11½ (1902)

15	2	2½r. olive-yellow (E)	55	50
16		5r. orange	55	50
17		5r. orange (E)	55	50
18		10r. rosy mauve (b)	70	65
19		15r. lake brown (E) (a)	70	65
20		20r. lavender	60	50
		a. Value omitted	18·00	17·00
21		20r. grey-lilac (E)	70	65
22		25r. bluish green	60	50
23		25r. bluish green (E)	70	65
24		50r. blue (E)	70	65
25		75r. carmine (E)	80	50
26		80r. pale green (E)	1·30	1·00
27		100r. brown/buff (a)	2·20	1·30
28		150r. brown-orange/rose (a)	2·30	1·60
29		200r. blue/*blue*	2·30	1·60
30		300r. blue/*pale brown*	2·30	1·60
31		500r. black (E)	1·30	1·00
32		1000r. bright mauve (E)	1·60	1·20
15/32	Set of 15 (one of each value)		17·00	12·50

(b) No gum (50r., 80 to 1000r.). with or without gum (others).
P 12½ (1895–1902)

33	2	2½r. olive-yellow (E)	55	50
34		5r. orange (1902)	45	35
35		5r. orange (E)	55	50
36		10r. rosy mauve (b) (1902)	80	55
37		10r. rosy mauve (E) (a)	70	65
38		10r. rosy mauve (E) (b)	5·25	4·75
39		15r. lake-brown (b) (1902)	80	55
40		15r. lake-brown (E) (a)	70	65
41		15r. lake-brown (E) (b)	5·25	4·75
42		20r. lavender (1902)	80	55
43		20r. lavender (E)	70	65
44		25r. bluish green (1902)	80	55
45		25r. bluish green (E)	70	65
46		50r. blue (1902)	80	55
47		50r. blue (E)	70	65
48		75r. carmine (1902)	80	55
49		75r. carmine (E)	1·10	65
50		80r. pale green (1902)	80	55
51		80r. pale green (E)	1·80	1·30
52		100r. brown/buff (a) (1902)	2·20	1·30
53		100r. brown/buff (b) (1902)	6·50	5·75
54		150r. brown-orange/*rose* (a) (1902)	2·20	1·30
54a		150r. brown-orange/*rose* (b)	6·50	5·75
55		200r. blue/*blue* (1902)	1·80	1·60
56		300r. blue/*pale brown* (1902)	2·10	1·60
57		500r. black (1902)	2·10	1·60
58		500r. black (E)	1·80	1·30
59		1000r. bright mauve (1902)	2·30	1·60
60		1000r. bright mauve (E)	2·10	1·60
33/60	Set of 15 (one of each value)		16·00	12·50

(c) With or without gum (25r.), no gum (others).
P 13½. (1895–1902)

61	2	5r. orange (E)	1·80	95
62		10r. rosy mauve (E) (a)	70	65
63		10r. rosy mauve (E) (b)	5·25	4·75
64		15r. lake-brown (E) (a)	70	65
65		20r. lavender (E)	70	65
66		25r. bluish green (1902)	1·80	95
67		25r. bluish green (E)	2·75	1·30
68		50r. blue (E)	1·10	95
69		75r. carmine (E)	1·10	95
70		100r. brown/buff (E) (1902)	2·75	1·90
71		100r. brown/*buff* (b) (1902)	6·50	5·75
72		150r. brown-orange/*rose* (a) (1902)	2·75	1·90
73		200r. blue/*blue* (1902)	3·50	2·50
74		300r. blue/*pale brown* (1902)	3·50	2·50
75		500r. black (E)	2·10	1·60
76		1000r. bright mauve (E)	2·10	1·60
61/76	Set of 13 (one of each value)		22·00	16·00

There are numerous shades in this issue.

PROVISORIO

25

(3)

PROVISORIO

(4)

1895 (30 Apr). No. 50 surch with T **3**.

77	2	25 on 80r. pale green (R.)	38·00	29·00
		a. Black surch	55·00	48·00

1895 (25 May). Nos. 6 and 14 locally optd with T **4**, in red. With or without gum.

78	50r. blue (p 12½)	7·50	6·50
79	50r. blue (p 13½)	7·50	6·50

1498

Centenario
da India

1898

(5)

25

PROVISORIO

(6)

1898 (16 May). Vasco da Gama Commemoration. Optd with T **5** in the colour of the stamp but in a deeper shade or in black (Bk.).

(a) With or without gum (2½, 10, 15, 20r.),
no gum (others). P 12½

80	2	2½r. olive-yellow (E)	2·20	1·80
		a. Opt double	27·00	27·00
		b. Do. in green and olive-yellow	49·00	49·00
		c. Opt in red	10·50	10·50
81		5r. orange (E)	3·00	2·10
		a. Opt double	29·00	29·00
		b. Opt inverted	37·00	37·00
82		10r. rosy mauve (b)	3·00	2·00
83		10r. rosy mauve (E) (a)	3·00	2·10
		a. Opt double	21·00	
		b. Opt inverted	50·00	50·00
84		15r. lake-brown (b)	3·75	3·25
		a. Opt in red	14·00	14·00
85		15r. lake-brown (E) (a)	5·25	3·50
86		20r. lavender	5·25	3·50
87		25r. bluish green (E)	5·75	3·50
		a. Opt inverted	43·00	43·00
88		50r. blue (E) (Bk.)	25·00	17·00
89		75r. carmine	10·00	6·50
		a. Opt inverted	55·00	55·00
90		75r. carmine (E)	19·00	13·00
91		80r. pale green	7·00	5·00
92		100r. brown/*buff* (b)	7·50	5·75
93		150r. brown-orange/*rose* (b)	7·50	5·75
		a. Opt double	43·00	43·00
94		200r. blue/*blue* (Bk.)	11·50	7·50
95		300r. blue/*pale brown* (Bk.)	14·00	9·25
		a. Opt in green		
80/95	Set of 13 (one of each value)		95·00	65·00

(b) No gum. P 13½

96	2	15r. lake-brown (E) (a)	10·50	5·50
97		20r. lavender (E)	5·25	4·25
98		25r. bluish green (E)	10·50	5·00
99		50r. blue (E) (Bk.)	3·75	3·25
		a. Opt double	32·00	32·00
		b. Opt inverted	19·00	19·00
100		75r. carmine (E)	10·50	7·00
101		100r. brown/*buff* (a)	7·50	6·50
102		150r. brown-orange/*rose* (a)	7·50	6·50
		a. Opt inverted	39·00	39·00
103		200r. blue/*blue* (Bk.)	10·00	7·00
104		300r. blue/*pale brown* (Bk.)	14·00	9·25
		a. Opt inverted	37·00	37·00
96/104	Set of 9		70·00	49·00

MOZAMBIQUE / Mozambique Company

1899 (20 Feb). No. 49 surch with T **6**. No gum.
| 105 | 2 | 25 on 75r. carmine (E) | 6·00 | 5·00 |

1900 (8 June). Surch. P 12½.
*(a) With T **7**, in carmine. With or without gum*
| 106 | 2 | 25r. on 5r. orange (E) | 4·75 | 2·75 |

*(b) P 11½ down centre and surch with T **8**, in bright mauve. No gum*
| 107 | 2 | 50r. on half of 20r. lavender | 2·20 | 1·80 |
| 108 | 2 | 50r. on half of 20r. lavender (E) | 2·20 | 1·80 |

1902–04. New values. P 11½.
(a) Enamel-surfaced paper (2.12.02)
| 109 | 2 | 65r. deep blue (E) | 1·10 | 85 |

(b) Chalk-surfaced paper (17.10 04)
110	2	115r. rose/rose	3·00	2·30
111		130r. green/rose	3·00	2·30
112		400r. black/blue	3·00	2·30
113		700r. violet/buff	9·00	7·00

1906. POSTAGE DUE. Figures of value in black. Typo. P 11½.
D114	D **9**	5r. green	85	75
D115		10r. slate	85	75
D116		20r. pale brown	85	75
D117		30r. dull orange	1·60	1·10
D118		50r. grey-brown	1·60	1·10
D119		60r. pale red-brown	24·00	9·50
D120		100r. mauve	3·25	2·75
D121		130r. blue	32·00	10·50
D122		200r. carmine	10·50	4·25
D123		500r. deep lilac	16·00	5·25
D114/123 Set of 10			80·00	32·00

1907 (1 Apr). Colours changed. Chalk-surfaced paper. P 11½.
114	2	2½r. grey	1·90	1·10
115		10r. pale green	1·40	1·10
		a. Value inverted at top of stamp	21·00	21·00
116		15r. deep green	1·90	1·10
117		25r. carmine	1·90	1·10
		a. Value omitted	19·00	16·00
118		50r. brown	1·90	1·40
		a. Value omitted	19·00	16·00
119		75r. rosy mauve	3·75	2·10
120		100r. blue/blue	3·75	2·75
		a. Value misplaced	18·00	
121		115r. brown/rose	5·00	3·50
122		130r. brown/straw	5·25	3·50
123		200r. lilac/rose	5·25	3·50
124		400r. blue/straw	7·00	5·75
125		500r. black/blue	7·00	5·75
		a. Error. Mauve/straw		
126		700r. mauve/straw	7·00	6·50
114/126 Set of 13			48·00	35·00

1911 (Feb). Optd at Beira with T **9**.
(a) P 11½
127	2	2½r. grey (R.)	90	70
128		5r. orange (G.)	1·80	90
129		10r. pale green (R.)	1·30	1·10
		a. Opt inverted	13·00	
130		10r. pale green (E) (R.)	1·30	1·20
131		15r. deep green (R.)	1·80	1·20
		a. Opt inverted	13·00	
132		20r. lavender (G.)	3·50	2·75
133		20r. lavender (E) (G.)	1·30	85
134		25r. carmine (G.)	1·80	1·30
135		50r. brown (G.)	1·80	1·30
136		75r. rosy mauve (G.)	2·20	1·30
137		100r. blue/blue (R.)	2·20	1·30
138		115r. brown/rose (G.)	3·25	1·80
		a. Opt inverted	13·00	
139		130r. brown/straw (G.)	3·25	1·80
140		200r. lilac/rose (G.)	3·25	1·80
141		400r. blue/straw (R.)	3·25	1·80
142		500r. black/blue (R.)	4·50	3·25
143		700r. mauve/straw (G.)	4·50	3·25
		a. Surch double (R.+G.)		
127/143 Set of 15 (one of each value)			33·00	21·00

(b) P 13½
| 144 | | 2 20r. lavender (E) (G.) | 1·30 | 85 |

All values except 2½, 10 and 25r. exist with a second type of T **9** which inclines more steeply.

1911 (Feb). Optd in Lisbon with T **27** of Macao, in red or green (G.).
(a) P 11½
145	2	2½r. grey	70	65
146		5r. orange	70	65
147		5r. orange (E)	70	65
148		10r. pale green	70	65
149		10r. pale green (E)	70	65
150		15r. deep green	45	35
151		20r. lavender	70	65
152		20r. grey-lilac (E)	70	65
153		25r. carmine (G.)	70	65
		a. Value inverted at top of stamp	28·00	
154		25r. carmine (E) (G.)	70	65
155		50r. brown	70	65
156		75r. rosy mauve	70	65
		a. Value omitted	16·00	
157		100r. blue/blue (a)	70	65
158		100r. blue/blue (b)	3·25	3·25
159		115r. brown/rose	1·40	95
160		130r. brown/straw	1·40	95
		a. Opt double	31·00	
161		200r. lilac/rose	1·40	95
162		400r. blue/straw	1·40	95
163		500r. black/blue	1·40	95
164		700r. mauve/straw	2·10	1·30
145/164 Set of 15 (one of each value)			13·50	10·50

(b) P 12½
| 165 | 2 | 5r. yellow-orange (E) | 1·40 | 1·30 |

The 2½, 5, 10 and 50r. also exist on glazed paper, perf 11½.

1911. POSTAGE DUE. Optd in Lisbon with T **27** of Macao, in red or green (G.).
D166	D **9**	5r. green	50	50
D167		10r. slate	55	55
D168		20r. pale brown	55	55
D169		30r. dull orange	55	55
D170		50r. grey-brown	55	55
D171		60r. pale red-brown	1·10	80
D172		100r. mauve	1·10	80
D173		130r. blue	2·30	2·10
D174		200r. carmine (G.)	3·00	2·30
D175		500r. deep lilac	3·25	3·00
D166/175 Set of 10			12·00	10·50

1916 (25 Oct). New Currency. Stamps optd as Nos. 145/64 surch in addition as T **10**.
166	2	¼c. on 2½r. grey	45	35
167		¼c. on 2½r. grey (E)	60	55
168		½c. on 5r. orange	45	35
		a. Surch double	13·00	
169		½c. on 5r. orange (E)	1·40	95
170		1c. on 10r. pale green	70	55
171		1c. on 10r. pale green (E)	60	55
172		1½c. on 15r. deep green (a)	70	55
		a. Surch double	18·00	
173		1½c. on 15r. deep green (E) (a)	60	55
174		1½c. on 15r. deep green (E) (b)	4·25	3·75
175		2c. on 20r. lavender	70	55
		a. Surch double	18·00	
176		2c. on 20r. grey-lilac (E)	60	55
177		2½c. on 25r. carmine	1·10	55
178		2½c. on 25r. carmine (E)	60	55
		a. "REPUBLICA" omitted	13·00	
179		5c. on 50r. brown	70	65
180		5c. on 50r. brown (E)	60	55
181		7½c. on 75r. rosy mauve	1·10	80
182		10c. on 100r. blue/blue	1·10	60
183		11½c. on 115r. brown/rose	2·50	1·20
		a. Surch inverted	32·00	29·00
184		13c. on 130r. brown/straw	2·50	1·20
		a. Surch double	35·00	
185		20c. on 200r. lilac/rose	2·75	1·10
186		40c. on 400r. blue/straw	2·75	1·10
187		50c. on 500r. black/blue (R.)	3·00	1·40
188		90c. on 700r. mauve/straw	3·00	1·70

The ½c., 1c. and 5c. also exist on glazed paper. The 1c., 2c. and 5c. exist with wider spacing between the figures and "c" of surcharge.

187

MOZAMBIQUE / Mozambique Company

1916. POSTAGE DUE. Value in "CENTAVOS". P 11½.
D189	D 9	½c. green	50	50
D190		1c. slate	50	50
D191		2c. pale brown	50	50
D192		3c. dull orange	50	50
D193		5c. grey-brown	50	50
D194		6c. pale red-brown	75	75
D195		10c. mauve	1·20	1·20
D196		13c. blue	2·30	2·30
D197		20c. carmine	2·30	2·30
D198		50c. deep lilac	3·75	3·75
D189/198 Set of 10			11·50	11·50

1917 (31 July). Red Cross Fund. Nos. 145, etc, optd locally with T **11**, in red. Chalk-surfaced paper.
189	2	2½r. grey	10·00	8·00
		a. Opt double	£110	£110
190		10r. pale green	10·00	8·00
191		20r. lavender	12·00	10·00
192		50r. brown	40·00	32·00
193		75r. rosy mauve	90·00	85·00
194		100r. blue/*blue*	£100	£100
195		700r. mauve/*straw*	£250	£250
189/195 Set of 7			£450	£450

(12) 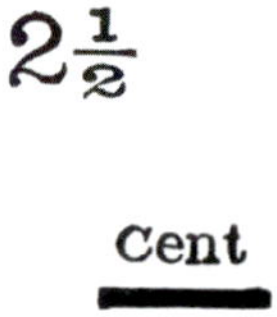   (13)

1918 (20 Nov). Nos. 162/4 surch locally as T **12** or **13** (2½c.).
196	2	½c. on 700r. mauve/*straw*	3·25	2·50
197		2½c. on 500r. black/*blue* (B.)	3·25	2·50
198		5c. on 400r. blue/*straw*	3·25	2·50

14 Native Village
15 Ivory 
16 Law Court 
17 Mozambique Co.'s Arms 

(Recess Waterlow & Sons)

1918 (16 Dec)–**24**. T **14/17** and similar designs.
A. P 14 (16.12.18–21)
199A		¼c. green and brown	55	35
		a. Perf 15		
200A		½c. black	55	35
		a. Perf 15		
201A		1c. black and deep green	55	35
		a. Perf 15		
202A		1½c. green and black	55	35
		a. Perf 15		
203A		2c. black and lake	55	35
		a. Perf 15		
204A		2½c. black and lilac	55	35
		a. Perf 15		
205A		4c. brown and green (1921)	55	35
		a. Perf 15		
206A		5c. black and blue	55	55
207A		6c. blue and claret (1921)	55	35
208A		7½c. green and orange	1·40	70
		a. Perf 15		
209A		8c. black and deep lilac	1·40	95
210A		10c. black and scarlet	1·40	95
211A		15c. black and lake	2·10	95
212A		20c. black and green	1·40	55
		a. Perf 15		
213A		30c. black and brown	1·40	95
		a. Perf 15		
214A		40c. black and bright green	1·40	95
		a. Perf 15		
215A		50c. black and orange	1·40	95
		a. Perf 15		
216A		1E. black and deep blue-green	2·75	2·10
199A/216A Set of 18			18·00	11·00

B. P 12½ (1924)
199B		¼c. green and brown	3·25	2·10
200B		½c. black	55	35
201B		1c. black and deep green	55	35
202B		1½c. green and black	55	35
203B		2c. black and lake	55	35
204B		2½c. black and lilac	55	35
205B		4c. brown and green (1921)	55	35
206B		5c. black and blue	1·40	55
208B		7½c. green and orange	1·40	95
209B		8c. black and deep lilac	1·40	95
210B		10c. black and scarlet	1·40	95
211B		15c. black and lake	1·10	95
212B		20c. black and green	1·80	55
213B		30c. black and brown	1·80	95
214B		40c. black and bright green	1·80	95
215B		50c. black and orange	2·75	95
216B		1E. black and deep blue-green	2·75	2·10
199B/216B Set of 17			22·00	12·50

Designs: Horiz—1c. Maize; 2c. Sugar factory; 5c. Beira; 40c. Mangrove swamp. Vert—1½c. India-rubber; 2½c. River Buzi; 4c. Tobacco bushes; 6c. Coffee bushes; 7½c. Orange tree; 8c. Cotton plants; 10c. Sisal plantation; 15c. Steam train; 30c. Coconut palm; 50c. Cattle breeding.
There are numerous shades in this issue.
See also Nos. 226/50.

D **32**   (32) Um e meio Centavo

(Recess Waterlow & Sons)
1919 (1 Nov)–**24**. POSTAGE DUE.
A. P 14 or 15
D217A	D **32**	½c. green	35	35
D218A		1c. slate	35	35
D219A		2c. brown-lake	35	35
D220A		3c. orange	35	35
D221A		5c. sepia	35	35
D222A		6c. pale brown	55	55
D223A		10c. dull claret	1·10	1·10
D224A		13c. blue	1·60	1·60
D225A		20c. carmine	1·60	1·60
D226A		50c. grey	2·50	2·50
D217A/226A Set of 10			8·25	8·25

B. P 12½ (1924)
D217B	D **32**	½c. green	35	35
D218B		1c. slate	35	35
D219B		2c. brown-lake	35	35
D220B		3c. orange	35	35
D221B		5c. sepia	35	35
D222B		6c. pale brown	55	55
D223B		10c. dull claret	1·10	1·10
D224B		13c. blue	1·60	1·60
D225B		20c. carmine	1·60	1·60
D226B		50c. grey	2·50	2·50
D217B/226B Set of 10			8·25	8·25

1920. Stamps of 1918 surch as T **32** (4c. with figure). P 14.
217		½c. on 30c. black and brown (Bk.)	6·50	5·75
218		½c. on 1E. black and deep blue-green (R.)	6·50	5·75
219		1½c. on 2½c. black and lilac (B.)	4·75	2·75
		a. Perf 15		
220		1½c. on 5c. black and blue (V.)	4·75	2·75
221		2c. on 2½c. black and lilac (R.)	4·75	2·75
222		4c. on 20c. black and green (V.)	5·25	4·00

223	4c. on 40c. black and bright green (V.)		5·25	4·00
224	6c. on 8c. black and deep lilac (R.)		6·75	4·00
	a. Perf 15			
225	6c. on 50c. black and orange (Bk.)		6·75	4·00
	a. Perf 15			
217/225	Set of 9		46·00	32·00

The surcharge on No. 219 is sideways (reading down) between two bars.

(Recess Waterlow)

1923–24. Types of 1918–24. New values.

A. P 14 (1923)

226A	3c. black and ochre		55	35
227A	4½c. black and grey		55	35
228A	7c. black and bright blue		55	35
229A	12c. black and brown		1·90	1·40
230A	60c. brown and carmine		2·20	1·50
231A	80c. brown and bright blue		2·20	1·50
232A	2E. violet and carmine		3·25	2·50
226A/232A	Set of 7		10·00	7·25

B. P 12½ (1924)

226B	3c. black and ochre		55	35
227B	4½c. black and grey		55	35
228B	7c. black and bright blue		55	35
229B	12c. black and brown		1·90	1·40
230B	60c. brown and carmine		2·20	1·50
231B	80c. brown and bright blue		2·20	1·50
232B	2E. violet and carmine		3·25	2·50
226B/232B	Set of 7		10·00	7·25

Designs: Horiz—3c. Maize; 4½c. Type **14**; 2E. Beira. Vert—7c. Steam train; 12c. Cotton plant; 60c. Cattle breeding; 80c. Sisal plantation.

(Recess Waterlow)

1925–31. Types of 1918–24. Colours changed. P 12½.

233	¼c. black and olive		45	35
234	1c. black and yellow-green		45	35
235	2c. black and drab		45	45
236	3c. black and orange		55	50
237	4c. black and carmine		55	50
238	6c. black and mauve		65	50
239	8c. black and slate-purple		1·30	1·00
240	10c. black and brown-red		1·40	95
241	12c. black and blue-green		1·10	75
242	15c. black and pale rose-red		1·10	95
243	20c. black and yellow-green		1·80	55
244	30c. black and grey-green		1·30	1·10
245	30c. black and emerald (1931)		1·50	1·30
246	40c. black and greenish blue		1·70	1·30
247	50c. black and mauve		2·10	1·70
248	80c. black and carmine		2·10	1·70
249	1E. black and blue		2·10	1·70
250	2E. black and pale lilac		3·75	2·20
233/250	Set of 18		22·00	16·00

33   **36** Tea

(Recess Bradbury. Wilkinson & Co)

1925–31. New designs. P 12.

251	24c. black and blue		2·75	2·00
252	25c. blue and brown		2·75	2·00
253	85c. black and scarlet (1931)		2·10	1·50
254	1E.40 black and blue (1931)		2·10	1·50
255	5E. blue and yellow-brown		3·25	1·30
256	10E. black and rose-carmine		5·75	1·70
257	20E. black and green		7·00	2·50
251/257	Set of 7		23·00	11·50

Designs: Vert—24, 85c. Type **33**; 25c., 1E.40, Beira; 5E. Tapping rubber. Horiz—20E. River Zambesi.

38 Ivory   **39** Gold mining

(Litho De La Rue)

1931. New designs. P 14.

258	**38**	45c. pale blue	4·25	2·40
259	**39**	70c. chestnut	2·10	1·50

CHARITY TAX STAMPS. The notes after No. 304 of Macao also apply to Charity Tax stamps of Mozambique Company.

Assistência ═══
═══ Publica

2 Ctvos. 2

(C **40**)   C **41** "Charity"

1932. CHARITY TAX. No. 236 surch locally with Type C **40**.
C260   2c. on 3c. black and orange   2·50   1·80
In use until 27 April 1934 and again from 27 December 1940 to 16 December 1941.

1934 (27 Apr). CHARITY TAX. Litho. P 11.
C261   C **41**   2c. black and magenta   2·75   1·80
In use until 6 June 1940.

40 Zambesi Bridge

(Recess Waterlow)

1935 (1 Aug). Opening of Zambesi Bridge. P 12½.
260   **40**   1E. black and blue   6·50   3·25

41 Armstrong-Whitworth A.W.15 Atalanta Airliner over Beira   **42** Armstrong-Whitworth A.W.15 Atalanta Airliner over Beira

(Recess Waterlow)

1935 (5 Oct). Inauguration of Blantyre–Beira–Salisbury Air Route. P 12½.

261	**41**	5c. black and blue	1·30	85
		a. Tête-bêche (pair)	3·00	1·90
262		10c. black and orange-red	1·30	85
		a. Tête-bêche (pair)	3·00	1·90
		ab. Imperf between (pair)	50·00	
263		15c. black and brown-red	1·30	85
		a. Tête-bêche (pair)	3·00	1·90
		ab. Imperf between (pair)	50·00	
264		20c. black and yellowish green	1·30	85
		a. Tête-bêche (pair)	3·00	1·90
		ab. Imperf between (pair)	50·00	
265		30c. black and myrtle green	1·30	85
		a. Tête-bêche (pair)	3·00	1·90
266		40c. black and deep turquoise-blue	1·70	1·10
		a. Tête-bêche (pair)	3·75	2·40
267		45c. black and new blue	1·70	1·10
		a. Tête-bêche (pair)	3·75	2·40
		ab. Imperf between (pair)	50·00	
268		50c. black and purple	1·70	1·10
		a. Tête-bêche (pair)	3·75	2·40
		ab. Imperf between (pair)	50·00	
269		60c. brown and carmine	2·75	1·70
		a. Tête-bêche (pair)	6·00	4·00
270		80c. black and carmine-red	2·75	1·70
		a. Tête-bêche (pair)	6·00	4·00
261/270	Set of 10		15·00	9·75

Nos. 261/70 were each issued in *tête-bêche* pairs within their sheets.

MOZAMBIQUE / Mozambique Company

(Recess Waterlow)
1935 (1 Nov). AIR. P 12½.

271	42	5c. black and blue	35	30
272		10c. black and orange-red	35	30
273		15c. black and brown-red	35	30
274		20c. black and yellowish green	35	30
275		30c. black and myrtle green	35	30
276		40c. black and deep turquoise-blue	35	30
277		45c. black and new blue	35	30
278		50c. black and purple	35	30
279		60c. brown and carmine	35	30
280		80c. black and carmine-red	35	30
281		1E. black and blue	35	30
282		2E. black and reddish lilac	85	75
283		5E. blue and orange-brown	1·40	1·20
284		10E. black and carmine	1·90	1·40
285		20E. black and emerald	3·75	1·80
271/285 Set of 15			10·50	7·50

43 Coastal Dhow   **44** Leopard

45 Crocodile

46 Palms at Beira   **47** Arms

(Des J. Webb (1c. to 50c., 85c., 1E. and frames of all values except 1E.40, 5E., 10E. and 20E.). Recess Waterlow)
1937 (16 May). As T **43/47**. P 12½.

286	1c. reddish lilac and bright green	35	30
287	5c. yellowish green and dull ultramarine	35	30
288	10c. dull ultramarine and vermilion	35	30
289	15c. black and carmine-red	45	30
290	20c. dull ultramarine and yellowish green	45	30
291	30c. indigo and myrtle green	45	30
	a. Tête-bêche (pair)	1·00	70
292	40c. black and deep turquoise-blue	45	30
	a. Tête-bêche (pair)	1·00	70
293	45c. brown and new blue	45	30
	a. Tête-bêche (pair)	1·00	70
	ab. Imperf between (pair)	90·00	
294	50c. emerald and deep reddish violet	45	30
	a. Tête-bêche (pair)	1·00	70
295	60c. deep blue and carmine	45	30
296	70c. green and orange-brown	45	30
297	80c. green and carmine	55	45
298	85c. black and brown-red	65	50
	a. Tête-bche (pair)	1·50	1·20
299	1E. black and blue	65	50
	a. Tête-bêche (pair)	1·50	1·20
300	1E.40 green and deep blue	1·30	50
301	2E. brown and reddish lilac	2·10	60
	a. Tête-bêche (pair)	4·75	3·00
302	5E. blue and orange-brown	1·30	60
303	10E. black and carmine	2·10	1·00
304	20E. maroon and emerald	3·25	1·90
286/304 Set of 19		15·00	8·50

Designs: 21×29 mm—1c. Giraffe; 20c. Common zebra; 70c. Native woman. 23×31 mm—10E. An old Portuguese gate at Sena. 29×21 mm—5c. Native huts; 15c. S. Caetano fortress at Sofala; 80c. Hippopotami. 37×22 mm—5E. Railway bridge over River Zambesi. Triangular—30c. Python; 40c. White rhinoceros; 45c. Lion; 85c. Vasco da Gama's flagship *São Gabriel*; 1E. Native in dugout canoe; 2E. Greater kudu.

The triangular stamps were issued in *tête-bêche* pairs within their sheets.

28-VII-1939
Visita Presidencial
(**48**)   **49** King Afonso Henriques

1939 (28 Aug). Pres. Carmona's Colonial Tour. Stamps of 1937 optd with T **48**, at Beira.

305	30c. indigo and myrtle green (R.)	1·90	1·50
	a. Tête-bêche (pair)	4·25	3·50
	b. Inverted "e"	10·50	9·50
306	40c. black and deep turquoise-blue (R.)	1·90	1·50
	a. Tête-bêche (pair)	4·25	3·50
	b. Inverted "e"	10·50	9·50
	c. Opt in black		
307	45c. brown and new blue	1·90	1·50
	a. Tête-bêche (pair)	4·25	3·50
	b. Inverted "e"	10·50	9·50
308	50c. emerald and deep reddish violet (R.)	1·90	1·50
	a. Tête-bêche (pair)	4·25	3·50
	b. Inverted "e"	10·50	9·50
309	85c. black and brown-red	1·90	1·50
	a. Tête-bêche (pair)	4·25	3·50
	b. Inverted "e"	10·50	9·50
	c. Opt double	21·00	19·00
310	1E. black and blue (R.)	3·50	1·80
	a. Tete-beche (pair)	10·50	9·50
311	2E. brown and reddish lilac	4·25	3·25
	a. Tête-bêche (pair)	9·00	8·00
	b. Inverted "e"	10·50	9·50
305/311 Set of 7		16·00	11·50

The inverted "e" is the first "e" in "Presidential". This occurs on position 12 of the setting of 50, which was applied twice to the sheet of 100 with the sheet rotated 180° before making the second strike. The error was corrected for part of the printing.

(Die eng A. Fragoso. Typo)
1940 (16 Feb). 800th Anniv of Portuguese Independence. P 12.
312	**49**	1E.75 light blue and blue	3·25	1·50

C 50   **51** "Don John IV" after Alberto de Souza   (**C 52**)

1940 (6 June). CHARITY TAX. Litho. P 11.
C313	C **50**	2c. ultramarine and black	16·00	10·50

(Des A. de Sousa. Recess Waterlow)
1940 (10 Oct). Third Centenary of Restoration of Independence. P 12½.

313	51	40c. black and grey-blue	85	65
314		50c. blue-green and violet	85	65
315		60c. blue and carmine	85	65
316		70c. blue-green and orange-brown	85	65
317		80c. green and carmine	85	65
318		1E. black and blue	85	65
313/318 Set of 6			4·50	3·50

1941 (16 Dec). CHARITY TAX. Litho. P 11.
C319	C **52**	2c. vermilion and black	16·00	10·50

MOZAMBIQUE / Nyassa Company

NYASSA COMPANY

In 1894 the Nyassa Company was granted a charter by Portugal to develop the area north of the River Lurio in Mozambique. By decree of 22 November 1894 it was authorised to issue its own stamps. As development was relatively slow the Portuguese government took over administration of the area on 27 October 1929 and stamps of Mozambique again came into use there.

NYASSA
(1)

1898. Mozambique T **4** and N **5** optd with T **1**. Wove paper (2½r.); chalk-surfaced paper (others) or enamel-surfaced paper (E). P 11½.

1	2½r. brown (p. 13½)	3·75	3·50
2	5r. pale orange	3·75	3·50
3	10r. rosy mauve	3·75	3·50
4	15r. red-brown	3·75	3·50
5	20r. lilac	3·75	3·50
6	25r. green (p. 12½)	3·75	3·50
7	50r. pale blue	3·75	3·50
	a. Opt inverted	27·00	27·00
7b	50r. pale blue (E) (p. 12½)	11·50	7·00
8	75r. rose (p. 12½)	4·50	4·25
9	80r. pale green	4·50	4·25
10	100r. brown/*buff*	4·50	4·25
11	150r. carmine/*rose* (p. 12½)	14·00	13·00
12	200r. blue/*blue*	8·25	7·50
13	300r. blue/*pale brown* (p. 12½)	8·25	7·50
1/13	Set of 13	65·00	60·00

The 2½, 5, 25, 80, 100, 150 and 300r. were reprinted in 1905. See notes at beginning of Mozambique.

1898. Mozambique T **10** optd with T **1**.

14	2½r. grey	2·50	2·50
15	5r. orange-red	2·50	2·50
16	10r. green	2·50	2·50
17	15r. chocolate	3·50	2·75
18	20r. deep lilac	3·50	2·75
19	25r. blue-green	3·50	2·75
20	50r. blue	3·50	2·75
21	75r. rose	3·75	3·50
22	80r. mauve	4·50	2·50
23	100r. blue/*blue*	4·50	2·50
24	150r. purple-brown/*straw*	4·50	2·50
25	200r. purple/*flesh*	4·75	2·75
26	300r. blue/*pink*	6·25	2·75
14/26	Set of 13	45·00	32·00

2 Giraffe

3 Dromedaries

(Des Sir Robt. Edgcumbe. Eng H. Bourne. Recess Waterlow & Sons)

1901 (1 Aug). Frame in black. P 13½ to 15.

27	**2**	2½r. chocolate	2·30	1·20
		a. Centre inverted	95·00	95·00
28		5r. deep violet	2·30	1·20
		a. Centre inverted	95·00	95·00
29		10r. green	2·30	1·20
		a. Centre inverted	95·00	95·00
30		15r. yellow-brown	2·30	1·20
		a. Centre inverted	95·00	95·00
31		20r. vermilion	2·30	1·50
		a. Centre inverted	95·00	95·00
32		25r. orange	2·30	1·50
		a. Centre inverted	95·00	95·00
33		50r. blue	2·30	1·50
		a. Centre inverted	95·00	95·00
34	**3**	75r. carmine	2·75	1·90
		a. Centre inverted	95·00	95·00
35		80r. mauve	2·75	1·90
		a. Centre inverted	95·00	95·00
36		100r. bistre	2·75	1·90
		a. Imperf between (horiz pair)	—	12·00
		b. Centre inverted	95·00	95·00
37		150r. orange-brown	3·25	2·20
		a. Centre inverted	95·00	95·00
38		200r. blue-green	3·25	2·20
		a. Centre inverted	95·00	95·00
39		300r. green	3·25	2·20
		a. Centre inverted	95·00	95·00
27/39	Set of 13		31·00	19·00

Most supplies of Nos. 27 to 39 (including the inverted centres), Nos. 40 to 44, and Nos. 53 to 64, offered at low prices, are reprints.

65 REIS PROVISORIO
(4) (5)

1903.

A. Surch or optd in London
*(a) Surch as T **4***

40	**3**	65r. on 80r. mauve and black	2·10	1·60
41		115r. on 150r. orange-brown and black	2·10	1·60
42		130r. on 300r. green and black	2·10	1·60

*(b) Optd with T **5***

43	**2**	15r. yellow-brown and black	2·10	1·60
44		25r. orange and black	2·10	1·60

See note after No. 39 *re* reprints.

65 reis PROVISORIO. 5 REIS
(6) (7) (8)

B. Surch or optd locally
*(a) Surch as T **6***

45	**3**	65r. on 80r. mauve and black	65·00	55·00
46		115r. on 150r. orange-brown and black	65·00	55·00
47		130r. on 300r. green and black	65·00	55·00
		a. Surch double		

*(b) Optd with T **7***

48	**2**	15r. yellow-brown and black	£275	£200
49		25r. orange and black	£275	£200

Collectors are warned against dangerous forgeries.

1910. Optd with T **5** and surch as T **8**.

50	**2**	5r. on 2½r. chocolate and black	2·20	1·80
51	**3**	50r. on 100r. bistre and black	2·20	1·80
		a. "50 REIS" omitted	£275	

9 Dromedaries

12 Vasco da Gama's Flagship *São Gabriel*

REPUBLICA

REPUBLICA

5C

(13) (14)

(Des Sir Robt. Edgcumbe. Recess Waterlow)

1911 (1 Mar). Optd with T **13**, in red. P 13½ to 15.

53	**9**	2½r. violet and black	2·10	1·30
54		5r. black	2·10	1·30
55		10r. olive-green and black	2·10	1·30
56	A	20r. carmine and black	2·10	1·30
		a. Opt omitted	28·00	
57		25r. purple-brown and black	2·10	1·30
58		50r. blue and black	2·10	1·30
59	B	75r. brown and black	2·10	1·30
60		100r. brown and black/*green*	2·10	1·30
61		200r. green and black/*salmon*	2·30	2·10
62	**12**	300r. black/*blue*	5·00	3·50
63		400r. brown and black	5·75	4·00
64		500r. violet and olive	7·50	6·25
53/64	Set of 12		34·00	24·00

Designs: Horiz—A. Common zebra. Vert—B. Giraffe.
See note after No. 39 *re* reprints. Stamps without overprint exist but were not issued thus.

1918. New Currency.

*(a) Stamps of 1901 surch locally as T **14***

65	**2**	¼c. on 2½r. chocolate and black	£275	£200
66		½c. on 5r. deep violet and black	£275	£200
67		1c. on 10r. green and black	£275	£200
68		1½c. on 15r. yellow-brown and black	4·50	2·30
69		2c. on 20r. vermilion and black	2·75	2·10
70		3½c. on 25r. orange and black	2·75	2·10
71		5c. on 50r. blue and black	2·75	2·10
72	**3**	7½c. on 75r. carmine and black	2·75	2·10
73		8c. on 80r. mauve and black	2·75	2·10
74		10c. on 100r. bistre and black	2·75	2·10
75		15c. on 150r. orange-brown and black	4·50	4·25
76		20c. on 200r. blue-green and black	4·25	4·25
77		30c. on 300r. green and black	6·75	5·00

MOZAMBIQUE / Nyassa Company

(b) Provisionals of 1903 with London opt or surch, further surch locally as T **14** *(Nos. 80/2 with bar obliterating previous surch)*

78	**2**	1½c. on 15r. (No. 43)	8·50	6·50
79		3½c. on 25r. (No. 44)	3·25	2·10
80	**3**	40c. on 65r. on 80r. (No. 40)	38·00	35·00
81		50c. on 115r. on 150r. (No. 41)	5·50	4·25
82		1E. on 130r. on 300r. (No. 42)	5·50	4·25

3
Centavos
(15)

Lisbon	¼	*Centavo*	2	2½
London	¼	*Centavo*	2	2½

(½, 1, 1½c.)

Lisbon	3	*Centavos*	7½	12
London	3	*Centavos*	7½	12

(5c.)

Lisbon	*Centavos*	20	
London	*Centavos*	20	

(10c.)

1921. Stamps of 1911 (Nos. 53, etc), surch as T **15**.

A. Lisbon surcharges

83A	**9**	¼c. on 2½r.	3·25	3·25
85A		½c. on 5r. (R.)	3·25	3·25
86A		1c. on 10r.	3·25	3·25
87A	**12**	1½c. on 300r. (R.)	3·25	3·25
88A	A	2c. on 20r.	3·25	3·25
89A		2½c. on 25r.	3·25	3·25
90A	**12**	3c. on 400r.	3·25	3·25
		a. "REPUBLICA" omitted (pair with normal)	3·25	3·25
91A	A	5c. on 50r.	3·25	3·25
92A	B	7½c. on 75r.	3·25	3·25
93A		10c. on 100r.	3·25	3·25
94A	**12**	12c. on 500r.	3·25	3·25
95A	B	20c. on 200r.	3·25	3·25

B. London surcharges

83B	**9**	¼c. on 2½r.	4·25	4·00
85B		½c. on 5r. (R.)	4·25	4·00
86B		1c. on 10r.	4·25	4·00
87B	**12**	1½c. on 300r. (R.)	4·25	4·00
88B	A	2c. on 20r.	4·25	4·00
89B		2½c. on 25r.	4·25	4·00
90B	**12**	3c. on 400r.	4·25	4·00
		a. "REPUBLICA" omitted (pair with normal)	4·25	4·00
91B	A	5c. on 50r.	4·25	4·00
92B	B	7½c. on 75r.	4·25	4·00
93B		10c. on 100r.	4·25	4·00
94B	**12**	12c. on 500r.	4·25	4·00
95B	B	20c. on 200r.	4·25	4·00

16 Giraffe    **17** Vasco da Gama

19 Common Zebra    **20** Native Dhow

(Recess Waterlow)

1921–23.

(a) P 14 or 15

96	**16**	¼c. deep claret	1·90	1·40
97		½c. deep slate-blue	1·90	1·40
98		1c. black and green	1·90	1·40
99		1½c. dull orange and black	1·90	1·40
100	**17**	2c. black and scarlet	1·90	1·40
101		2½c. deep olive and black	1·90	1·40
102		4c. orange-red and black	1·90	1·40
103		5c. black and blue	1·90	1·40
104		6c. violet and black	1·90	1·40
105	–	7½c. sepia and black	1·90	1·40
		a. Imperf between (pair)	43·00	
106	–	8c. olive and black	1·90	1·40
107	–	10c. reddish brown and black	1·90	1·40
108	–	15c. carmine and black	1·90	1·40
109	–	20c. light blue and black	1·90	1·40
110	**19**	30c. yellow-brown and black	1·90	1·40
111		40c. deep violet-blue and black	1·90	1·40
112		50c. green and black	1·90	1·40
113		1E. reddish brown and black	1·90	1·40
114	**20**	2E. black and chestnut (30.1.23)	6·25	5·00
115		5E. chestnut and ultramarine (30.1.23)	5·75	4·50
96/115 *Set of 20*			42·00	31·00

(b) P 12½

116	**16**	1c. black and green	1·50	1·20
117		1½c. dull orange and black	1·50	1·20
118	**17**	2c. black and scarlet	1·50	1·20
119		2½c. deep olive and black	1·50	1·20
120		4c. orange-red and black	1·50	1·20
121		5c. black and blue	1·50	1·20
122		6c. violet and black	1·50	1·20
123	–	7½c. sepia and black	1·50	1·20
124	–	8c. olive and black	1·50	1·20
125	–	10c. reddish brown and black	1·50	1·20
126	–	15c. carmine and black	1·50	1·20
127	–	20c. light blue and black	1·50	1·20
128	**19**	30c. yellow-brown and black	1·50	1·20
129		40c. deep violet-blue and black	1·50	1·20
130		50c. green and black	1·50	1·20
131		1E. reddish brown and black	1·50	1·20
116/131 *Set of 16*			22·00	17·00

Designs: Vert—7½ to 20c. Vasco da Gama's flagship *São Gabriel*.

D **21** São Gabriel   **NYASSA** (C **22**)

(Recess Waterlow & Sons)

1924. POSTAGE DUE. Type D **21** and similar designs. P 14.

D132	½c. green	4·50	3·50
D133	1c. deep violet-blue	4·50	3·50
D134	2c. scarlet	4·50	3·50
D135	3c. orange-red	4·50	3·50
D136	5c. deep brown	4·50	3·50
D137	6c. chestnut	4·50	3·50
D138	10c. deep claret	4·50	3·50
D139	20c. carmine-red	4·50	3·50
D140	50c. slate-purple	4·50	3·50
D132/140 *Set of 9*		36·00	28·00

Designs:—½, 1c. Giraffe; 2, 3c. Common zebra; 5 to 10c. Type D **21**; 20, 50c. Vasco da Gama.

1925 (8 May). Marquis de Pombal Commemoration.

(a) CHARITY TAX. Nos. C327/9 of Mozambique optd with Type C **22**, *in red*

C141	15c. brown	12·50	10·00
C142	15c. brown	12·50	10·00
C143	15c. brown	12·50	10·00

(b) POSTAGE DUE. Nos. D327/9 of Mozambique optd with Type C **22**, *in red*

D144	30c. brown	15·00	15·00
D145	30c. brown	15·00	15·00
D146	30c. brown	15·00	15·00
C144/D146 *Set of 6*		75·00	70·00

Charity Tax stamps were for compulsory use on internal letters on certain days of the year as an additional postal tax for public charities. Nos. C141/3 were in use from 8 to 13 May 1925 and from 5 to 15 May in 1926 and 1929. Nos. D144/6 were used in default.

QUELIMANE

Until 1893 the district of Quelimane, to the north-east of the Lower Zambesi, used the stamps of Mozambique. By decree of 27 April 1893, Quelimane was joined with Tete to form the district of Zambezia and used the stamps of that district until, by decree of 31 May 1913, it was provided with its own stamps. From 1920 the stamps of Mozambique have again been in use there.

(1)   2 Ceres

1913. Vasco da Gama issues surch as T **1**.

(i) Portuguese Colonies (General Issues)

1		¼c. on 2½r. blue-green	2·75	2·00
2		½c. on 5r. vermilion	2·75	2·00
3		1c. on 10r. dull purple	2·75	2·00
4		2½c. on 25r. yellow-green	2·75	2·00
5		5c. on 50r. deep blue	2·75	2·00
6		7½c. on 75r. chocolate	4·75	2·75
7		10c. on 100r. bistre-brown	3·00	1·50
8		15c. on 150r. ochre	3·00	1·50
1/8 Set of 8			22·00	14·00

(ii) Macao

9		¼c. on ½a. blue-green	2·75	2·00
10		½c. on 1a. vermilion	2·75	2·00
11		1c. on 2a. dull purple	2·75	2·00
12		2½c. on 4a. yellow-green	2·75	2·00
13		5c. on 8a. deep blue	2·75	2·00
14		7½c. on 12a. chocolate	4·75	2·75
15		10c. on 16a. bistre-brown	3·00	1·50
	a.	Surch inverted	32·00	32·00
16		15c. on 24a. ochre	3·00	1·50
9/16 Set of 8			22·00	14·00

(iii) Timor

17		¼c. on ½a. blue-green	2·75	2·00
18		½c. on 1a. vermilion	2·75	2·00
19		1c. on 2a. dull purple	2·75	2·00
20		2½c. on 4a. yellow-green	2·75	2·00
21		5c. on 8a. deep blue	2·75	2·00
22		7½c. on 12a. chocolate	4·75	2·75
23		10c. on 16a. bistre-brown	3·00	1·50
24		15c. on 24a. ochre	3·00	1·50
17/24 Set of 8			22·00	14·00

(Des C. Fernandes. Eng J. S. de Carvalho e Silva. Typo)

1914–16. Name and value in black. P 15×14.

(a) Chalk-surfaced paper (1914)

25	2	¼c. brown-olive	1·20	1·10
26		½c. black	2·30	1·50
27		1c. deep green	2·30	1·50
28		1½c. chocolate	3·00	1·90
29		2c. carmine	3·00	2·30
30		2½c. violet	1·20	85
31		5c. deep blue	2·10	1·60
32		7½c. yellow-brown	2·50	1·90
33		8c. slate	2·50	1·90
34		10c. brown-red	2·50	1·90
35		15c. claret	3·50	3·00
36		20c. yellow-green	3·50	3·00
37		30c. chocolate/*green*	5·25	4·00
38		40c. brown/*rose*	5·75	4·00
39		50c. orange/*salmon*	5·75	4·00
40		1E. deep green/*azure*	6·50	4·50
25/40 Set of 16			48·00	35·00

(b) Unsurfaced paper (1916)

41	2	¼c. brown-olive	2·10	1·60
42		1c. deep green	2·10	1·60
43		7½c. yellow-brown	2·10	1·60
44		10c. brown-red	2·10	1·60
45		20c. yellow-green	2·10	1·60

TETE

The postal history of the district of Tete, on the Middle Zambesi, between Rhodesia and Malawi, has been exactly similar to that of Quelimane.

(1)   2 Ceres

1913. Vasco da Gama issues surch as T **1**.

(i) Portuguese Colonies (General Issues)

1		¼c. on 2½r. blue-green	3·00	2·20
2		½c. on 5r. vermilion	3·00	2·20
3		1c. on 10r. dull purple	3·00	2·20
4		2½c. on 25r. yellow-green	3·00	2·20
5		5c. on 50r. deep blue	3·00	2·20
6		7½c. on 75r. chocolate	4·25	2·50
7		10c. on 100r. bistre-brown	3·00	2·50
8		15c. on 150r. ochre	3·00	2·50
1/8 Set of 8			23·00	17·00

(ii) Macao

9		¼c. on ½a. blue-green	3·00	2·20
10		½c. on 1a. vermilion	3·00	2·20
11		1c. on 2a. dull purple	3·00	2·20
12		2½c. on 4a. yellow-green	3·00	2·20
13		5c. on 8a. deep blue	3·00	2·20
14		7½c. on 12a. chocolate	4·25	2·50
15		10c. on 16a. bistre-brown	3·00	2·20
16		15c. on 24a. ochre	3·00	2·20
9/16 Set of 8			23·00	17·00

(iii) Timor

17		¼c. on ½a. blue-green	3·00	2·20
18		½c. on 1a. vermilion	3·00	2·20
19		1c. on 2a. dull purple	3·00	2·20
	a.	Surch inverted	32·00	32·00
20		2½c. on 4a. yellow-green	3·00	2·20
21		5c. on 8a. deep blue	3·00	2·20
22		7½c. on 12a. chocolate	4·25	2·50
23		10c. on 16a. bistre-brown	3·00	2·20
24		15c. on 24a. ochre	3·00	2·20
17/24 Set of 8			23·00	17·00

(Des C. Fernandes. Eng J. S. de Carvalho e Silva. Typo)

1914. Name and value in black. Chalk-surfaced paper. P 15×14.

25	2	¼c. brown-olive	1·80	1·20
26		½c. black	1·80	1·20
27		1c. deep green	1·80	1·20
28		1½c. chocolate	1·80	1·20
29		2c. carmine	1·80	1·20
30		2½c. violet	1·80	1·20
31		5c. deep blue	1·80	1·20
32		7½c. yellow-brown	2·75	2·50
33		8c. slate	2·75	2·50
34		10c. brown-red	3·50	2·50
35		15c. claret	4·25	4·00
36		20c. yellow-green	4·25	4·00
37		30c. chocolate/*green*	4·25	4·00
38		40c. brown/*rose*	5·00	4·25
39		50c. orange/*salmon*	5·50	4·50
40		1E. deep green/*azure*	6·50	5·50
25/40 Set of 16			46·00	38·00

ZAMBEZIA

Until 1893 the district of Zambezia, north-east of Quelimane, used the stamps of Mozambique. After Quelimane and Tete had been incorporated in it, Zambezia was provided with its own stamps by decree of 8 May 1893. It continued to use its own stamps after 1913, when Quelimane and Tete were provided with their own issues, until 1920, when the stamps of Mozambique again came into use.

N 1   1   2

(Des and eng E. C. Azedo Gneco. Typo)

1893 (28 July). NEWSPAPER. P 12½.

N1	N **1**	2½r. brown	75	70

MOZAMBIQUE / Zambezia

(Des and eng M. D. Neto. Typo)
1894 (Nov). Chalk-surfaced paper.

(a) P 11½

1	1	5r. pale orange	60	50
2		10r. rosy mauve	95	85
3		15r. red-brown	1·80	1·30
4		20r. lilac	1·80	1·30
6		50r. blue	3·00	2·30
7		75r. rose	£130	95·00
8		100r. brown/*buff*	4·50	3·50
9		200r. blue/*blue*	£1300	£1100
10		300r. blue/*pale brown*	65·00	35·00

(b) P 12

11	1	15r. red-brown	£170	£120
12		25r. green	3·25	2·30
13		50r. pale blue	3·25	2·30
14		75r. rose	7·50	6·50
15		80r. pale green	6·00	5·00
16		150r. carmine/*rose*	7·50	5·50
17		200r. blue/*blue*	7·50	5·50
18		300r. blue/*pale brown*	11·50	8·50
11/18 Set of 8			£190	£140

(c) P 13½

19	1	200r. blue/*blue*	65·00	47·00

The 25r. to 300r. were issued in Dec 1894.

(Des and eng E. Mouchon. Typo)
1898–1901. Name and value in black; on the 500r. in carmine. P 11½.

20	2	2½r. pale grey	75	65
21		5r. orange-red	75	65
22		10r. green	1·20	65
23		15r. chocolate	2·10	1·50
24		20r. deep lilac	2·10	1·50
25		25r. blue-green	2·10	1·50
26		50r. blue	2·10	1·50
27		75r. rose	15·00	8·00
28		80r. mauve	8·75	4·75
29		100r. blue/*blue*	3·25	2·50
30		150r. purple-brown/*straw*	9·25	5·50
31		200r. purple/*flesh*	9·75	5·25
32		300r. blue/*pink*	10·50	5·25
33		500r. black/*azure* (1901)	18·00	9·75
34		700r. mauve/*yellow* (1901)	22·00	12·50
20/34 Set of 15			95·00	55·00

1902.

*(a) Surch as T **22** of Macao*

35	1	65r. on 10r. (11½)	14·00	10·50
36		65r. on 15r. (11½)	14·00	10·50
37		65r. on 20r. (11½)	14·00	10·50
38		65r. on 300r. (11½)	14·00	10·50
39		65r. on 300r. (12½)	14·00	10·50
40		115r. on 5r. (11½)	14·00	10·50
41		115r. on 25r. (11½)	14·00	10·50
42		115r. on 80r. (12½)	14·00	10·50
43		130r. on 75r. (11½)	10·50	7·00
44		130r. on 75r. (12½)	10·50	7·00
45		130r. on 150r. (12½)	8·25	7·50
46	N 1	130r. on 2½r. (12½)	14·00	10·50
47	1	400r. on 25r. (11½)	3·25	3·00
48		400r. on 50r. (12½)	3·00	2·75
49		400r. on 100r. (11½)	3·25	3·00
50		400r. on 200r. (12½)	2·75	2·75

*(b) Optd with T **23** of Macao*

51	2	15r. chocolate	3·00	1·90
52		25r. blue-green	3·00	1·90
53		50r. blue	3·00	1·90
54		75r. rose	8·75	4·50

1903. Colours changed. Name and value in black. P 11½.

55	2	15r. deep green	2·30	2·00
56		25r. carmine	2·00	1·20
57		50r. brown	4·00	3·50
58		65r. dull blue	12·50	10·00
59		75r. dull purple	5·50	3·50
60		115r. orange-brown/*pink*	14·00	9·00
61		130r. purple-brown/*straw*	14·00	9·00
62		400r. dull blue/*cream*	18·00	13·50
55/62 Set of 8			65·00	47·00

Type I. Figures same height
Type II. Taller "5"

1905. No. 58 surch as T **25** of Macao.

63	2	50r. on 5r. dull blue (I)	9·00	5·00
		a. Type II	£160	£160

1911. Optd with T **27** of Macao, in red or green (G.).

64	2	2½r. pale grey	55	35
65		5r. orange-red	55	35
66		10r. green	60	50
67		15r. deep green	60	50
68		20r. deep lilac	80	55
69		25r. carmine (G.)	2·30	1·40
70		50r. brown	60	55
71		75r. dull purple	1·80	1·20
72		100r. blue/*blue*	1·80	1·20
73		115r. orange-brown/*pink*	1·80	1·20
74		130r. purple-brown/*straw*	1·80	1·20
75		200r. purple/*pink*	1·80	1·20
76		400r. dull blue/*cream*	3·25	1·70
77		500r. black/*azure*	3·25	1·70
78		700r. mauve/*yellow*	3·25	2·50
64/78 Set of 15			22·00	14·50

1914. Provisionals of 1902–5 optd locally with T **3** in red or in green (G.).

79	2	50r. blue (53)	2·20	1·80
80		50r. on 65r. (I) (63)	£1600	£1600
81		75r. rose (54)	2·20	1·80
82	1	115r. on 5r. (11½)	2·10	1·60
83		115r. on 25r. (12½)	2·10	1·60
84		115r. on 80r. (12½)	2·10	1·60
85	N 1	130r. on 2½r. (12½) (G.)	2·10	1·60
86		130r. on 2½r. (12½)	21·00	16·00
87	1	130r. on 75r. (11½)	2·10	1·60
88		130r. on 75r. (12½)	7·00	6·50
89		130r. on 150r. (12½)	2·10	1·60
90		400r. on 25r. (11½)	3·25	2·50
91		400r. on 50r. (12½)	16·00	16·00
92		400r. on 100r. (11½)	3·75	3·00
93		400r. on 200r. (12½)	3·75	3·00

1915. Provisional of 1902–5 optd with T **27** of Macao, in red (reading down on 130r. on 2½r.).

94	2	50r. blue (No. 53)	1·10	85
95		50r. on 65r. (I) (No. 63)	4·50	2·75
96	1	115r. on 5r. (11½)	1·10	80
97		115r. on 25r. (12½)	1·10	80
98		115r. on 80r. (12½)	1·10	80
99	N 1	130r. on 2½r. (12½)	1·10	80
100	1	130r. on 75r. (11½)	1·10	80
101		130r. on 75r. (12½)	6·75	4·50
102		130r. on 150r. (12½)	1·10	85

1917. Optd locally with T **3**, in red.

103	2	2½r. pale grey	1·80	1·30
104		5r. orange-red	9·00	6·25
105		10r. green	9·00	6·25
106		15r. deep green	9·00	6·25
107		20r. deep lilac	9·00	6·25
108		25r. blue-green	18·00	14·50
109		100r. blue/*blue*	4·50	4·25
110		115r. orange-brown/*pink*	4·50	4·25
111		130r. purple-brown/*straw*	4·50	4·25
112		200r. purple/*flesh*	4·50	4·25
113		400r. dull blue/*cream*	4·50	4·25
114		500r. black/*azure*	6·00	5·50
115		700r. mauve/*yellow*	14·00	8·00
103/115 Set of 13			90·00	70·00

50 (I)   50 (II)   REPUBLICA (3)

Portuguese Colonies and Overseas Territories

GENERAL ISSUES

1898. 1000 Reis = 1 Milreis
1919. 100 Centavos = 1 Escudo

By a law of 11 June 1951 the status of Portuguese overseas possessions was changed from that of "colonies" to that of "overseas provinces". On 6 September 1961 all inhabitants of overseas provinces received Portuguese citizenship.

A. AFRICAN COLONIES

The following were for use in Angola, Cape Verde Islands, Mozambique, Portuguese Guinea and St. Thomas and Prince Islands.

1 Departure of Fleet

(Des R. Gameiro (2½r.), M. P. de Faria Luna (5r.), S. Correira Belem (10r.), J. Vaz (25r., 75r., 150r.), J. J. G. Coelho (50r.), J. R. Cristiano de Silva (100r.). Recess Waterlow)

1898 (1 Apr). 400th Anniv of Vasco da Gama's Discovery of Route to India. T **1** and similar designs. P 12½ to 16.

1	2½r. blue-green	1·20	1·00
2	5r. vermilion	1·20	1·00
3	10r. dull purple	1·20	1·00
4	25r. yellow-green	1·20	1·00
5	50r. deep blue	1·20	1·00
6	75r. chocolate	10·50	9·00
7	100r. bistre-brown	10·50	7·00
8	150r. ochre	15·00	7·00
1/8 Set of 8		38·00	25·00

Designs: Horiz—5r. Arrival at Calicut; 10r. Embarkation at Rastello; 100r. Flagship *São Gabriel*; 150r. Vasco da Game. Vert—25r. Muse of History; 50r. Flagship *São Gabriel* and portraits of Da Gama and Camoens; 75r. Archangel Gabriel, patron saint of the expedition.

C **1**

1919. CHARITY TAX. Fiscal stamp optd "TAXA DE GUERRA" as in Type C **1**. Value in black. Wove paper or enamel-surfaced paper (E). Typo.

(a) P 15×14

C1	C **1**	1c. green	1·40	1·40
		a. Value omitted	11·50	
C2		5c. green (R.)	1·40	1·40

(b) P 12×11½

C3	C **1**	1c. green	1·40	1·40
C4		1c. green (E)	1·40	1·40
C5		5c. green (R.)	1·40	1·40

The 4c. with this overprint was for use on receipts and telegrams. Nos. C1/5 were not used in Mozambique.

D **1**

(Des M. Norte. Typo Mint, Lisbon)

1945. POSTAGE DUE. Numerals of value in black. P 11½×12.

D1	D **1**	0$10 claret	55	55
D2		0$20 purple	55	55
D3		0$30 blue	55	55
D4		0$40 chocolate	55	55
D5		0$50 lilac	55	55
D6		1$00 orange-brown	2·50	2·50
D7		2$00 yellow-green	4·25	4·25
D8		3$00 carmine	7·00	7·00
D9		5$00 orange-yellow	10·50	10·50
D1/9 Set of 9			24·00	24·00

The use of these stamps ceased on 31 August 1958.

B. GENERAL ISSUES

(Litho Litografia Nacional, Oporto)

1951. Holy Year. Miniature sheet 171×122 mm containing one stamp from each of the eight provinces as T **33** of Angola and also No. 575 (T **56**) of Portuguese India. P 14.

MS1 Angola 435; Cape Verde Is. 330; Macao 423; Mozambique 428; Portuguese Guinea 317; Portuguese India 570, 575; St. Thomas 411; Timor 318 (sold at 11E.) £325

(Des J. Araujo. Litho Litografia de Portugal, Oporto)

1951. Holy Year. Miniature sheet 112×145 mm comprising the following. Imperf.

MS2 Angola 456; Cape Verde Is. 333; Macao 426; Mozambique 439; Portuguese Guinea 319; Portuguese India 580; St. Thomas 414; Timor 322 (sold at 17E.) .... 75·00

Portuguese Guinea

1881. 1000 Reis = 1 Milreis
1913. 100 Centavos = 1 Escudo

The territory now known as Guinea-Bissau was discovered by Nuno Tristão in 1446. In the 16th century it was an early source of slaves for the American markets. It became a dependency of the Cape Verde Islands and used the stamps of those islands from 1877 to 1880. By a decree of 18 March 1879 it became a separate colony, Portuguese Guinea, the boundaries of which were fixed by a convention with France in 1886.

PRINTERS. All the stamps of Portuguese Guinea were printed at the Mint, Lisbon, *unless otherwise stated*.

REPRINTS. Reprints of some of the following issues were made in 1885 and 1905 as indicated in the footnotes. These can generally be distinguished as follows:—
1885 reprints are on stout very white paper, usually un-gummed but sometimes with white gum having yellowish spots. They are perf 13½ with large clean-cut holes producing sharp pointed teeth.
1905 reprints are on creamy white paper of ordinary quality with shiny white gum, all perf 13½.

King Luis
11 November 1861–19 October 1889

Type **1** of Cape Verde Islands

GUINÉ (1)   GUINÉ (2)

1881. Type **1** of Cape Verde Islands optd locally with T **1**. No gum. P 12½.

1	5r. black	£1800	£1400
2	10r. orange-yellow	£2750	£1500
3	20r. deep bistre	£900	£450
4	25r. deep rose	£2750	£1500
5	40r. blue	£2250	£1500
	a. Error. "MOÇAMBIQUE"	£32000	£30000
6	50r. green	£2750	£1500
7	100r. grey-lilac	£425	£325
8	200r. deep orange	£1100	£900
10	300r. chocolate	£1100	£900

The "MOCAMBIQUE" errors (which occur on No. 18 in the sheet) do not have to be in pairs for identification, as in Cape Verde Is, as the overprint is sufficient.
The "E" of "GUINE" exists with or without accent.

1881–84. Type **1** of Cape Verde Islands optd with T **2**.

(a) P 12½

11	5r. black (C.)	7·50	5·00
12	20r. bistre	5·50	4·25
13	25r. deep rose	4·50	3·25
	a. Pale rose	4·50	3·25
	b. Crimson	4·50	3·25
14	40r. blue	£1400	£950
	a. Error. "MOÇAMBIQUE"	£2500	£2000
15	50r. green	£1100	£750
	a. Opt double	—	£850
	b. Pale yellow-green	£1100	£750
16	100r. slate-lilac	15·00	11·50
	a. Pale purple	15·00	11·50
17	200r. deep orange	22·00	15·00
	a. Brown-orange	22·00	15·00
18	300r. lake-brown	26·00	20·00

(b) P 13½

19	5r. black (C.)	7·50	5·75
20	10r. yellow	£300	£300
21	20r. bistre	6·25	4·25
22	25r. rose	£130	60·00
23	40r. blue	£325	£225
	a. Error. "MOÇAMBIQUE"	£2250	£1700
24	50r. green	£325	£225
25	100r. slate-lilac	17·00	10·50

All values were reprinted in 1885 and 1905.
See note below No. 34.

1885. Type **1** of Cape Verde Islands in new colours optd with T **2**.

(a) P 12½

26	10r. yellow-green	11·50	9·50
27	20r. rosine	13·00	9·50
28	25r. deep lilac	5·75	3·50
29	40r. yellow-buff	3·50	3·00
	a. Error. "MOÇAMBIQUE"	90·00	70·00
30	50r. deep blue	10·50	5·00
	a. Opt double		
	b. Blue	10·50	5·00

(b) P 13½

31	10r. green	13·00	8·75
	a. Grey-green	13·00	8·75
32	20r. rosine	13·00	9·50
33	40r. yellow-buff	7·50	5·75
	a. Error. "MOÇAMBIQUE"	£120	£110
34	50r. deep blue	20·00	7·50
	a. Opt in blackish red	—	£110
	b. Blue	20·00	7·50

Varieties of the overprint may be found with acute accent, grave accent, or no accent over the letter "E" of "GUINE".
All values were reprinted in 1885 and 1905.

3   N 4   5

(Des and eng E. C. Azedo Gneco. Typo)

1886.

(a) P 12½

35	3	5r. black	11·50	10·50
36		10r. green	14·00	7·50
37		20r. rosine	20·00	7·50
38		25r. purple	20·00	11·50
		a. Pale rose	20·00	11·50
39		40r. brown	£160	£125
40		50r. blue	33·00	11·50
41		80r. grey	£160	£120
42		100r. bistre-brown	70·00	42·00
43		200r. lilac	70·00	42·00
44		300r. orange	90·00	65·00
35/44	Set of 10		£600	£400

(b) P 13½

45	3	10r. green	16·00	13·00
46		40r. chocolate	16·00	11·50
47		80r. grey	30·00	21·00
48		100r. bistre-brown	30·00	21·00
49		300r. orange	£400	£400

All values except the 20r. were reprinted in 1905.

King Carlos
19 October 1889–1 February 1908

(Des and eng E. C. Azedo Gneco. Typo)

1893 (19 July). NEWSPAPER.

N50	N **4**	2½r. brown (perf 12½)	2·40	1·50
N51		2½r. brown (perf 13½)	2·40	1·50

Stamps of this type could be, and often were, used for franking ordinary correspondence.

(Des and eng M. D. Neto. Typo)

1893 (22 Oct)–**94.** Chalk-surfaced paper or enamel-surfaced paper (E).

(a) P 11½

50	5	5r. orange-yellow (8.7.94)	3·50	2·10
51		10r. rosy mauve (8.7.94)	3·50	2·10
52		15r. red-brown	4·50	3·00
53		20r. lavender (8.7.94)	4·50	3·00
54		25r. green (8.7.94)	4·50	3·00
55		50r. pale blue (8.7.94)	8·00	4·25
56		50r. pale blue (E) (date?)	£170	£130
57		75r. rose	21·00	13·50
58		80r. pale green (8.7.94)	21·00	13·50
59		100r. brown/*buff* (8.7.94)	21·00	13·50
60		150r. carmine/*rose*	21·00	13·50
61		200r. blue/*blue* (8.7.94)	36·00	28·00
62		300r. pale brown (8.7.94)	34·00	28·00
50/55, 57/62	Set of 12		£160	£110

(b) P 12½

63	5	5r. orange-yellow	3·25	2·10
64		50r. pale blue (E)	31·00	23·00

PORTUGESE GUINEA

6   (7)   (8)

D 9   (10)   (11)

(Des and eng E. Mouchon. Typo)

1898 (1 July)–**1901**. Name and value in black; on 500r. in carmine.

(a) P 11½

65	6	2½r. grey	70	55
66		5r. orange-red	70	55
67		10r. green	70	55
68		15r. chocolate	5·75	4·25
69		20r. deep lilac	2·75	1·80
70		25r. blue-green	3·25	2·10
71		50r. blue	4·25	2·20
72		75r. rose	23·00	16·00
73		80r. mauve	5·75	3·50
74		100r. blue/*blue*	5·25	3·50
75		150r. purple-brown/*straw*	17·00	7·25
76		200r. purple/*flesh*	17·00	7·25
77		300r. blue/*pink*	15·00	8·75
78		500r. black/*azure* (1901)	23·00	13·50
79		700r. mauve/*yellow* (1901)	33·00	23·00
65/79 Set of 15			£140	85·00

(b) P 12½

| 80 | 6 | 100r. blue/*blue* | £300 | £130 |

See also Nos. 114/21.

1902 (20 Oct). Surch as T **7**. The perforation is given in brackets after each value.

81	3	65r. on 10r. (12½)	12·50	7·00
		a. Surch inverted	65·00	60·00
82		65r. on 20r. (12½)	12·50	7·00
83		65r. on 25r. (12½)	12·50	7·00
84	5	65r. on 10r. (11½)	10·50	5·50
85		65r. on 15r. (11½)	10·50	5·50
86		65r. on 20r. (11½)	10·50	5·50
87		65r. on 50r. (11½)	6·00	4·75
88		65r. on 50r. (E) (12½)	5·50	4·75
89	3	115r. on 40r. (12½)	11·00	6·75
90		115r. on 40r. (13½)	25·00	11·50
91		115r. on 50r. (12½)	11·00	6·75
92		115r. on 300r. (12½)	14·00	8·75
93	5	115r. on 5r. (11½)	10·00	5·25
		a. Surch inverted	65·00	60·00
94		115r. on 5r. (12½)	£100	95·00
95		115r. on 25r. (11½)	11·50	5·75
96	N 4	115r. on 2½r. (11½)	10·00	5·75
		a. Surch inverted	65·00	60·00
97		115r. on 2½r. (13½)	7·50	5·25
		a. Surch inverted	65·00	60·00
98	3	130r. on 80r. (12½)	14·00	10·00
99		130r. on 80r. (13½)	25·00	11·50
100		130r. on 100r. (12½)	14·50	10·00
101		130r. on 100r. (13½)	38·00	29·00
102	5	130r. on 150r. (11½)	11·50	5·75
103		130r. on 200r. (12½)	12·50	6·75
104		130r. on 300r. (11½)	12·50	7·25
105	3	400r. on 5r. (12½)	65·00	60·00
106		400r. on 200r. (12½)	24·00	13·50
107	5	400r. on 75r. (11½)	8·25	7·25
108		400r. on 80r. (11½)	5·50	3·25
109		400r. on 100r. (11½)	7·00	3·25

No. 105 was reprinted in 1905.

1902 (20 Oct). Optd with T **8**.

110	6	15r. chocolate	4·50	3·00
111		25r. blue-green	4·50	3·00
112		50r. blue	5·50	3·25
113		75r. rose	11·00	9·00
110/113 Set of 4			23·00	16·00

1903. Colours changed. Name and value in black. No gum. P 11½.

114	6	15r. dull green	3·50	1·80
115		25r. carmine	1·80	1·10
116		50r. brown	4·50	3·50
117		65r. dull blue	14·50	11·00
118		75r. dull purple	6·25	5·50
119		115r. orange-brown/*pink*	16·00	11·50
		a. Error. On straw	16·00	11·50
120		130r. purple-brown/*straw*	17·00	11·50
121		400r. dull blue/*straw*	18·00	12·00
114/121 Set of 8			75·00	50·00

(Des and eng J. S. de Carvalho e Silva. Typo)

1904. POSTAGE DUE. Name and value in black. With or without gum (10, 20r.), no gum (others). P 11½.

D122	D 9	5r. yellow-green	1·60	90
D123		10r. slate	1·60	90
D124		20r. red-brown	1·60	90
D125		30r. orange	2·50	2·10
D126		50r. grey-brown	2·50	2·10
D127		60r. pale brown	7·00	5·25
D128		100r. mauve	7·00	5·25
D129		130r. blue	7·00	5·25
D130		200r. carmine	11·00	10·00
D131		500r. deep lilac	26·00	10·00
D122/131 Set of 10			60·00	38·00

See also Nos. D244/53.

1905. No. 117 surch with T **10**. No gum.

| 122 | 6 | 50r. on 65r. dull blue | 8·75 | 5·75 |

King Manoel II
1 February 1908–5 October 1910

PORTUGUESE REPUBLIC
5 October 1910

1911. Optd in Lisbon with T **11**, in red or green (25r.). With or without gum (5, 15, 20, 100r.), no gum (50, 75, 115, 130, 400r.).

123	6	2½r. grey	90	65
124		5r. orange-red	1·10	65
125		10r. green	1·20	65
126		15r. dull green	1·20	95
		a. Opt double	16·00	16·00
127		20r. deep lilac	1·20	95
128		25r. carmine	1·20	95
129		50r. brown	1·20	95
130		75r. dull purple	1·20	95
131		100r. blue/*blue*	3·00	1·10
132		115r. orange-brown/*pink*	3·00	1·30
133		130r. purple-brown/*straw*	3·00	1·30
134		200r. purple/*flesh*	13·00	5·25
135		400r. dull blue/*straw*	4·25	3·25
136		500r. black/*azure*	4·25	3·25
137		700r. mauve/*yellow*	6·75	5·00
123/137 Set of 15			42·00	24·00

1911. POSTAGE DUE. Optd in Lisbon with T **11**, in red or green (200r.). With or without gum (5, 30r.), no gum (50 to 500r.).

D138	D 9	5r. yellow-green	35	25
		a. Opt inverted	16·00	
D139		10r. slate	45	35
D140		20r. brown	70	45
D141		30r. orange	70	45
D142		50r. deep brown	90	45
D143		60r. pale red-brown	2·10	1·60
D144		100r. mauve	4·25	3·25
D145		130r. blue	4·25	3·25
D146		200r. carmine	4·25	3·25
D147		500r. deep lilac	3·25	2·50
D138/147 Set of 10			19·00	14·00

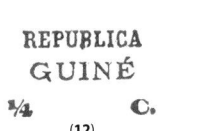 

(12)   (13)

1913. New Currency. Vasco da Gama issues surch as T **12**.

(a) Nos. 1/8 of Portuguese Colonies and Overseas Territories

138		¼c. on 2½r. blue-green	3·00	2·50
139		½c. on 5r. vermilion	3·00	2·50
140		1c. on 10r. dull purple	3·00	2·50
141		2½c. on 25r. yellow-green	3·00	2·50
142		5c. on 50r. deep blue	3·00	2·50
143		7½c. on 75r. chocolate	6·50	5·00
144		10c. on 100r. bistre-brown	3·00	2·00
145		15c. on 150r. ochre	8·00	6·75
138/145 Set of 8			29·00	24·00

197

PORTUGESE GUINEA

(b) Nos. 104/11 of Macao

146	¼c. on ½a. blue-green		3·25	2·50
147	½c. on 1a. vermilion		3·25	2·50
148	1c. on 2a. dull purple		3·25	2·50
149	2½c. on 4a. yellow-green		3·25	2·50
150	5c. on 8a. deep blue		3·25	2·50
151	7½c. on 12a. chocolate		5·75	4·00
152	10c. on 16a. bistre-brown		5·00	4·00
	a. Surch inverted		29·00	
153	15c. on 24a. ochre		6·25	4·25
146/153 Set of 8			30·00	22·00

(c) Nos. 58/65 of Timor

154	¼c. on ½a. blue-green		3·25	2·50
155	½c. on 1a. vermilion		3·25	2·50
156	1c. on 2a. dull purple		3·25	2·50
157	2½c. on 4a. yellow-green		3·25	2·50
158	5c. on 8a. deep blue		3·25	2·50
159	7½c. on 12a. chocolate		5·75	4·00
160	10c. on 16a. bistre-brown		5·00	4·00
161	15c. on 24a. ochre		6·25	4·25
154/161 Set of 8			30·00	22·00

1913. Stamps of 1898-1903 optd locally with T **13**, in red. No gum.

162	6	15r. chocolate (110)	25·00	16·00
163		15r. dull green (114)	25·00	16·00
164		75r. rose (113)	25·00	16·00
165		75r. dull purple (118)	25·00	16·00
166		100r. blue/*blue* (74)	12·50	10·00
167		200r. purple/*flesh* (76)	65·00	48·00
162/167 Set of 6			£160	£110

14 Ceres   **(15)**

(Des C. Fernandes. Eng J. S. de Carvalho e Silva. Typo)

1914 (20 Aug). Name and value in black. Chalk-surfaced paper. P 15×14.

168	**14**	¼c. brown-olive	90	65
169		½c. black	90	65
170		1c. green	2·10	1·10
171		1½c. chocolate	1·30	80
172		2c. carmine	1·40	75
173		2½c. violet	2·20	55
174		5c. blue	1·40	75
175		7½c. yellow-brown	2·10	1·30
176		8c. slate	1·40	1·20
177		10c. brown-red	1·80	1·30
178		15c. claret	16·00	9·25
179		20c. yellow-green	2·75	1·90
180		30c. chocolate/*green*	10·00	6·50
181		40c. brows/*rose*	6·50	1·30
182		50c. orange/*salmon*	6·50	1·30
183		1E. deep green/*azure*	8·75	4·25
168/183 Set of 16			60·00	30·00

The 2c. in orange red is a colour-changeling. See also Nos. 204/40.

1915. Provisionals of 1902 to 1905 optd with T **11**, in red (reading downwards on 2½r.).

184	6	15r. chocolate (110)	2·00	1·80
185		50r. blue (112)	2·00	1·80
186		50r. on 65r. (122)	2·00	1·80
187	N **4**	115r. on 2½r. (12½)	3·25	1·90
		a. Surch and opt inverted	75·00	70·00
188		115r. on 2½r. (13½)	£225	£200
189	5	115r. on 5r. (11½)	9·00	7·00
190		115r. on 5r. (12½)	2·20	1·40
191		115r. on 25r. (11½)	2·00	1·80
192	3	115r. on 40r. (12½)	1·90	1·80
193		115r. on 40r. (13½)	11·50	7·00
194		115r. on 50r. (12½)	1·90	1·80
195		130r. on 80r. (12½)	75·00	41·00
196		130r. on 80r. (13½)	6·00	3·75
197		130r. on 100r. (12½)	5·00	4·25
198		130r. on 100r. (13½)	15·00	10·50
199	5	130r. on 150r. (11½)	2·00	1·80
200		130r. on 200r. (11½)	2·00	1·80
201		130r. on 300r. (11½)	2·00	1·80

1919. Nos. 121 and 79 optd locally with T **15**. No gum.

202	6	400r. dull blue/*straw*	50·00	35·00
203		700r. mauve/*yellow*	31·00	23·00

1919. POSTAGE DUE. Optd locally with T **15**. No gum.

D204	D **9**	10r. slate	8·00	7·50
D205		20r. brown	9·00	8·50
D206		30r. orange	7·50	4·25
D207		50r. deep brown	3·75	2·75
D208		100r. mauve	3·75	3·25
D209		130r. blue	45·00	34·00
D210		200r. carmine	5·75	5·00
D211		500r. deep lilac	36·00	29·00
D204/211 Set of 8			£110	85·00

The 60r. was also overprinted but there were so few that it was not used.

1919–26.

(a) Unsurfaced paper (thick, medium or thin). P 15×14 (1919–20)

204	**14**	¼c. brown-olive	1·40	95
205		½c. black (1920)	55	50
206		1c. green	4·00	3·75
207		2c. carmine	1·40	1·00

(b) Unsurfaced paper. P 12×11½ (1921–26)

208	**14**	¼c. brown-olive	11·00	6·00
209		½c. black	55	50
210		1c. yellow-green (1922)	55	50
211		1½c. chocolate	55	50
212		2c. deep carmine	55	50
213		2c. drab (1925)	55	50
214		2½c. mauve	55	50
215		3c. orange (1922)	55	50
216		4c. carmine (1922)	55	50
217		4½c. drab (1922)	55	50
218		5c. pale dull blue (1922)	55	50
219		6c. mauve (1922)	55	50
220		7c. pale blue (1922)	75	45
221		7½c. yellow-brown	55	50
222		8c. slate	55	50
223		10c. brown-red	55	50
224		12c. blue-green (1922)	1·30	75
225		15c. dull rose (1922)	55	50
226		20c. yellow-green	60	55
227		24c. ultramarine (1925)	3·25	2·20
228		25c. chocolate (1925)	3·75	2·75
229		30c. deep grey-green (1922)	1·60	75
230		40c. turquoise (1922)	1·60	85
231		50c. mauve (1925)	3·75	2·00
232		60c. deep blue (1922)	2·75	2·30
233		60c. carmine (1926)	3·75	1·60
234		80c. bright rosine (1922)	4·25	2·75
235		1E. deep blue (1926)	5·75	3·25

(c) Glazed paper (1922–25)

236	**14**	1E. pink	5·50	2·40
237		2E. purple	5·50	3·00
238		5E. bistre (1925)	32·00	16·00
239		10E. pink (1925)	46·00	17·00
240		20E. pale emerald-green (1925)	£130	65·00
208/240 Set of 33			£250	£120

CHARITY TAX STAMPS. Stamps bearing C numbers were for compulsory use on internal letters on certain days of the year as an additional postal tax for public charities. Other values in some of the types were for use on telegrams or for fiscal purposes.

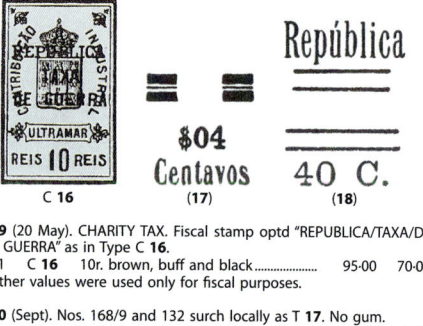

C **16**   (**17**)   (**18**)

1919 (20 May). CHARITY TAX. Fiscal stamp optd "REPUBLICA/TAXA/DE GUERRA" as in Type C **16**.

C241	C **16**	10r. brown, buff and black	95·00	70·00

Other values were used only for fiscal purposes.

1920 (Sept). Nos. 168/9 and 132 surch locally as T **17**. No gum.

241	**14**	4c. on ¼c. brown-olive	7·50	5·00
242		6c. on ½c. black	7·50	5·00
243	6	12c. on 115r. orange-brown/*pink*	19·00	11·50

PORTUGESE GUINEA

1921. POSTAGE DUE. Value in centavos. P 11½.

D244	D **9**	½c. pale yellow-green	50	45
D245		1c. slate	50	45
D246		2c. deep red-brown	50	45
D247		3c. pale orange	50	45
D248		5c. grey-brown	50	45
D249		6c. pale brown	1·30	1·20
D250		10c. mauve	1·30	1·20
D251		13c. blue	1·30	1·20
D252		20c. carmine	1·30	1·20
D253		50c. lilac-grey	1·30	1·20
D244/253 *Set of 10*			8·00	7·50

All values exist on smooth soft and on thin coarse paper.

1925. Nos. 107/9 surch as T **18**.

244	**5**	40c. on 400r. on 75r.	1·90	1·50
		a. "a" of "Republica" omitted	55·00	48·00
		b. "a" of "Republica" inserted by hand	16·00	14·00
245		40c. on 400r. on 80r.	1·90	1·50
246		40c. on 400r. on 100r.	1·90	1·50
244/246 *Set of 3*			5·00	4·00

C **19** Pombal Monument   C **20** Planning the Reconstruction of Lisbon

C **21** Marquis de Pombal   **MULTA** (D **22**)

(Des H. Fleury. Eng J. A. C. Harrison. Recess Waterlow)

1925. Marquis de Pombal Commemoration. P 12½.

(a) CHARITY TAX

C247	C **19**	15c. black and scarlet	1·20	95
C248	C **20**	15c. black and scarlet	1·20	95
C249	C **21**	15c. black and scarlet	1·20	95

*(b) POSTAGE DUE. Optd with Type D **22***

D254	C **19**	30c. black and scarlet	1·20	1·10
D255	C **20**	30c. black and scarlet	1·20	1·10
D256	C **21**	30c. black and scarlet	1·20	1·10
C247/D256 *Set of 6*			6·50	5·50

Nos. C247/9 were in use from 8 to 13 May 1925 and from 5 to 15 May in 1926 and 1929. Nos. D254/6 were used in default.

(23)   **24** Ceres   **25** Maltese Cross

1931–33. Surch as T **23**. P 12×11½.

247	**14**	50c. on 60c. carmine	4·00	3·00
248		70c. on 80c. bright rosine	4·25	4·00
249		1E.40 on 2E. slate-purple	9·75	7·00
250		1E.40 on 2E. purple (*glazed*)	9·75	7·00
247/250 *Set of 4*			25·00	19·00

No. 249 was not issued without surcharge.

(Des C. Fernandes. Die eng A. Fragoso. Typo)

1933. W **25**. P 12×11½.

251	**24**	1c. brown	30	25
252		5c. sepia	30	25
253		10c. mauve	30	25
254		15c. black	65	55
255		20c. grey	65	55
256		30c. blue-green	65	55
257		40c. vermilion	1·50	65
258		45c. turquoise	1·50	65
259		50c. cinnamon	1·50	65
260		60c. olive-green	1·50	95
261		70c. red-brown	1·50	95
262		80c. emerald	2·75	1·10
		a. Value omitted	43·00	43·00
263		85c. carmine	4·75	2·20
264		1E. claret	2·30	1·50
265		1E.40 blue	8·00	5·00
266		2E. mauve	4·50	2·50
267		5E. yellow-green	15·00	9·00
268		10E. bistre-brown	27·00	12·00
269		20E. orange	85·00	41·00
251/269 *Set of 19*			£140	70·00

C **26**

(Des R. L. Rodrigues. Typo Imprensa Nacional de Guiné)

1934 (1 Apr). CHARITY TAX. No gum. P 11½.

C270	C **26**	50c. claret and yellow-green	17·00	9·75

No. C270 was in use from 1 to 30 April and from 15 December to 15 January of 1934 to 1937.

27 Vasco da Gama   **28** Mousinho de Albuquerque   **29** Airplane over Globe

(Des A. R. Garcia. Recess Bradbury, Wilkinson)

1938. Name and value in black. P 13½×13.

*(a) POSTAGE. T **27/8** and similar vert designs*

270	**27**	1c. grey-olive	25	25
271		5c. orange-brown	25	25
272		10c. carmine	35	30
273		15c. brown-purple	35	30
274		20c. slate	85	35
275	**28**	30c. bright purple	85	60
276		35c. emerald-green	85	65
277		40c. brown	85	65
278		50c. magenta	85	65
279	–	60c. grey-black	85	65
280	–	70c. slate-violet	85	65
281	–	80c. orange	1·50	75
282	–	1E. scarlet	2·10	75
283	–	1E.75 blue	2·75	1·60
284	–	2E. lake	6·75	2·40
285	–	5E. olive-green	9·75	4·75
286	–	10E. ultramarine	13·50	6·00
287	–	20E. red-brown	46·00	9·50
270/287 *Set of 18*			80·00	28·00

Designs:—60c. to 1E. Dam; 1E.75 to 5E. Prince Henry the Navigator; 10E., 20E. Afonso de Albuquerque.

(b) AIR

288	**29**	10c. scarlet	1·50	1·10
289		20c. bright violet	1·50	1·10
290		50c. orange	1·50	1·10
291		1E. bright blue	1·50	1·10
292		2E. brown-lake	13·00	6·50
293		3E. blue-green	4·25	2·10
294		5E. red-brown	9·00	2·75
295		9E. carmine	13·00	7·00
296		10E. magenta	23·00	7·75
288/296 *Set of 9*			60·00	27·00

PORTUGESE GUINEA

 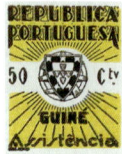

C **29a** Arms   C **30** Arms

(Des L. Seixas. Typo Imprensa Nacional de Guiné)

1938–39. CHARITY TAX. No gum. P 11½.
C297	C **29a**	50c. yellow	16·00	8·00
C298		50c. olive-brown and emerald-green ('39)	16·00	8·00

1942 (1 Apr)–**67**. CHARITY TAX. No gum. P 11.
C299	C **30**	30c. black and ochre-brown (7.59)	30	30
C300		50c. black and olive-yellow	4·00	2·20
		a. Black and yellow	2·30	1·30
C301		50c. brown and yellow (1961)	6·50	4·00
C302		2E.50 black and lt blue (1.12.67)	55	55
C303		5E. black and deep green (1.12.67)	85	85
C304		10E. black and deep blue (1.12.67)	1·70	1·70
C299/304 Set of 6			12·50	8·75

Nos. C302/4 were used at several small post offices as ordinary postage stamps during a temporary shortage.

31 Cacheu Castle   **32** Native Huts

(Des A. de Sousa. Litho Litografia Nacional, Oporto)

1946 (12 Jan)–**47**. 500th Anniv of Discovery of Portuguese Guinea. T **31** and similar designs. P 11.
297		30c. black and grey	1·50	1·10
298		50c. green and light green	75	75
299		50c. purple and claret	75	75
300		1E.75 blue and light blue	5·00	1·90
301		3E.50 carmine and rose	8·00	3·00
302		5E. brown and chocolate	23·00	9·75
303		20E. violet and mauve	41·00	16·00
297/303 Set of 7			70·00	30·00
MS303a 175×221 mm. Nos. 297/303 (sold at 40E.) (2.1.47)			£130	£130

Designs: Vertical portraits—50c. Nuno Tristão; 1E.75, President Grant; 3E.50, Teixeira Pinto; 5E. Honorio Barreto. Horiz—20E. Church at Bissau.

(Photo Courvoisier)

1948 (Apr). T **32** and similar vert designs. P 11½.
304		5c. chocolate	25	20
305		10c. purple (Crowned crane)	4·75	2·75
306		20c. magenta (Youth)	1·20	80
307		35c. light green (Woman)	1·50	80
308		50c. brown-red (Musician)	75	25
309		70c. dull blue (Man)	1·20	75
310		80c. blackish green (Girl)	1·80	75
311		1E. carmine (Drummer)	1·80	75
312		1E.75 ultramarine (Bushbuck)	21·00	9·00
313		2E. light blue (Drummer)	23·00	2·75
314		3E.50 red-brown (Youth)	5·00	2·50
315		5E. grey-blue (Woman)	8·25	4·75
316		20E. violet (Girl)	38·00	12·00
304/316 Set of 13			£100	34·00
MS316a 176×158 mm. Nos. 304/16 (sold at 40E.)			£160	£160

33 Our Lady of Fatima   **34** Letter and Globe

(Des A. Negreiros. Litho Litografia Nacional, Oporto, Portugal)

1948 (Oct). Honouring the Statue of Our Lady of Fatima. P 14.
317	**33**	50c. olive-green	7·25	6·25

(Des A. Negreiros. Litho Litografia Maia, Oporto, Portugal)

1949 (Oct). 75th Anniv of Universal Postal Union. P 14.
318	**34**	2E. orange	9·00	4·25

35 Bells and Dove   **36** Our Lady of Fatima

(Des J. Araujo. Litho Litografia de Portugal, Lisbon)

1950 (May). Holy Year. T **35** and similar vert design. P 13½.
319		1E. claret	3·50	2·10
320		3E. blue-green	5·50	3·00

Design:—3E. Angel holding candelabra.

(Litho Litografia Nacional, Oporto, Portugal)

1951 (Oct). Termination of Holy Year. P 14.
321	**36**	1E. brown and buff	1·70	90

No. 321 was issued *se-tenant* with a stamp-size label bearing a papal declaration.

 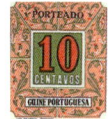

37 Doctor examining Patient   D **38**

(Des A. de Sousa. Litho)

1952 (June). First Tropical Medicine Congress, Lisbon. P 13½.
322	**37**	50c. chocolate and purple	70	70

(Litho Litografia Nacional, Oporto, Portugal)

1952. POSTAGE DUE. P 14.
D323	D **38**	10c. multicoloured	25	25
D324		30c. multicoloured	25	25
D325		50c. multicoloured	25	25
D326		1E. multicoloured	25	25
D327		2E. multicoloured	35	35
D328		5E. multicoloured	90	90
D323/328 Set of 6			2·00	2·00

39 Exhibition Entrance   **40** *Analeptes trifasciata*

1953 (Jan). Missionary Art Exhibition. Litho. P 13½.
323	**39**	10c. brown-lake and yellow-olive	20	20
324		50c. deep blue and ochre	1·60	60
325		3E. greenish black and salmon	3·75	1·80
323/325 Set of 3			5·00	2·30

PORTUGUESE GUINEA

(Photo Courvoisier)

1953. Bugs and Beetles. T **40** and similar vert designs. Multicoloured. P 11½.

326	5c. Type **40**	20	15
327	10c. *Callidea panaethiopica*	20	20
328	30c. *Craspedophorus brevicollis*	20	15
329	50c. *Anthia nimrod*	30	15
330	70c. *Platypria luctuosa*	75	35
331	1E. *Acanthophorus maculatus*	70	20
332	2E. *Cordylomera nitidipennis*	1·60	30
333	3E. *Lycus latissimus*	3·50	55
334	5E. *Cicindela bruneti*	3·75	1·40
335	10E. *Colliuris dimidiata*	9·25	4·25
326/335	Set of 10	18·00	7·00

41 Portuguese Stamp of 1853 and Arms of Portuguese Overseas Provinces

42 Father M. de Nobrega and View of São Paulo

(Litho Litografia Nacional, Oporto, Portugal)

1953 (Oct). Portuguese Stamp Centenary. P 13.
336	**41**	50c. multicoloured	1·60	1·30

1954. Fourth Centenary of São Paulo. Litho. P 13½.
337	**42**	1E. multicoloured	55	30

43 Arms of Cape Verde Islands and Portuguese Guinea

44 Exhibition Emblem, Globe and Arms

(Des J. de Moura. Litho)

1955 (14 Apr). Presidential Visit. P 13½.
338	**43**	1E. multicoloured	55	30
339		2E.50 multicoloured	95	65

(Des J. de Moura. Litho)

1958 (July). Brussels International Exhibition. P 12×11½.
340	**44**	2E.50 olive-green	1·10	75

45 *Maytenus senegalensis*

46 Statue of Barreto at Bissau

(Des J. de Moura. Litho)

1958 (5 Sept). Sixth International Congress of Tropical Medicine. P 13½.
341	**45**	5E. multicoloured	4·75	2·10

1959 (29 Apr). Death Centenary of Honorio Barreto (statesman). Litho. P 13½.
342	**46**	2E.50 multicoloured	55	45

47 Astrolabe

48 "Medical Service"

(Des J. de Moura. Litho)

1960 (25 June). Fifth Death Centenary of Prince Henry the Navigator. P 13×13½.
343	**47**	2E.50 multicoloured	60	50

1960 (Oct). Tenth Anniv of African Technical Co-operation Commission. P 14½.
344	**48**	1E.50 multicoloured	55	45

49 Motor Racing

50 *Anopheles gambiae*

(Des J. de Moura. Litho Litografia Nacional, Oporto, Portugal)

1962 (18 Jan). Sports T **49** and similar diamond-shaped designs. Multicoloured. P 13.
345	50c. Type **49**	60	15
346	1E. Tennis	95	45
347	1E.50 Putting the shot	70	45
348	2E.50 Wrestling	85	50
349	3E.50 Shooting	95	50
350	15E. Volleyball	2·50	1·30
345/350	Set of 6	6·00	3·00

(Des J. de Moura. Litho)

1962. Malaria Eradication. P 13½.
351	**50**	2E.50 multicoloured	95	60

51 Common Spitting Cobra (*Naja nigricollis*)

52 Map of Africa and Boeing 707 and Lockheed L.1049G Super Constellation Airliners

(Litho Litografia Nacional, Oporto, Portugal)

1963 (17 Jan). Snakes. T **51** and similar multicoloured designs. P 13½.
352	20c. Type **51**	25	20
353	35c. African rock python (*Python sebae*)	25	20
354	70c. Boomslang (*Dispholidus typus*)	85	50
355	80c. West African mamba (*Dendroaspis viridis*)	80	35
356	1E.50 Smythe's watersnake (*Grayia smythii*)	80	25
357	2E. Common night adder (*Causus rhombeatus*) (horiz)	35	20
358	2E.50 Green swampsnake (*Philothamnus irregularis*)	3·25	50

201

PORTUGESE GUINEA

359		3E.50 Brown house snake (*Boaedon lineatus*) .	60	30
360		4E. Spotted wolfsnake (*Lycophidium semicinctum*)	75	30
361		5E. Common puff adder (*Bitis lachesis*)	90	50
362		15E. Striped beauty snake (*Psammophis elegans*)	2·20	1·50
363		20E. African egg-eating snake (*Dasypeltis scaber*) (horiz)	3·00	2·30
352/363		Set of 12	12·50	6·50

(Des J. de Moura. Litho Litografia Maia, Oporto, Portugal)

1963 (8 Oct). Tenth Anniv of Transportes Aéreos Portugueses. (Airline). P 14½.

364	52	2E.50 multicoloured	1·10	55

53 J. de A. Corvo

54 I.T.U. Emblem and St. Gabriel

1964 (16 May). Centenary of National Overseas Bank. Litho. P 13½.

365	53	2E.50 multicoloured	1·20	65

(Litho Litografia Nacional, Oporto, Portugal)

1965 (17 May). Centenary of International Telecommunications Union. P 14½.

366	54	2E.50 multicoloured	2·75	1·10

55 Soldier, 1548

56 B. C. Lopes School and Bissau Hospital

(Des A. Cutileiro. Litho)

1966 (5 Jan). Portuguese Military Uniforms. T **55** and similar vert designs. Multicoloured. P 13½.

367		25c. Type **55**	25	15
368		40c. Arquebusier, 1578	35	15
369		60c. Arquebusier, 1640	50	20
370		1E. Grenadier, 1721	60	20
371		2E.50 Captain of Fusiliers, 1740	1·10	20
372		4E.50 Infantryman, 1740	2·50	45
373		7E.50 Sergeant-major, 1762	5·00	2·10
374		10E. Engineer's officer, 1806	5·00	2·10
367/374		Set of 8	14·00	5·00

(Des A. Cutileiro. Litho)

1966 (28 May). 40th Anniv of Portuguese National Revolution. P 12×11½.

375	56	2E.50 multicoloured	90	65

57 O. Muzanty and *Republica* (cruiser)

58 Chapel of the Apparitions and Monument of the Holy Spirit

(Des A. Cutileiro. Litho Litografia Nacional, Oporto, Portugal)

1967 (31 Jan). Centenary of Military Naval Association. T **57** and similar horiz design. Multicoloured. P 13.

376		50c. Type **57**	45	25
377		1E. A. de Cerqueira and *Guadiana* (destroyer)	1·40	60

(Des J. de Moura. Litho)

1967 (13 May). 50th Anniv of Fatima Apparitions. P 12½×13.

378	58	50c. multicoloured	30	15

C **59**

C **60**

C **61** Carved Statuette of Woman

(Typo National Ptg Wks, Portuguese Guinea)

1967. CHARITY TAX. National Defence. No gum. P 11×11½.

C379	C **59**	50c. rosine, pale rose and black	20	20
C380		1E. rosine, emerald and black	35	35
C381		5E. rosine, pale grey and black	1·10	1·10
C382		10E. rosine light grey-blue and black	3·25	3·25
C379/382		Set of 4	4·50	4·50

A 50E. in the same design was for fiscal use only.

(Typo National Ptg Wks, Portuguese Guinea)

1967. CHARITY TAX. National Defence. No gum. P 11×11½.

C383	C **60**	50c. vermilion, pale rose and black	1·30	1·30
C384		1E. vermilion, pale green and black	1·60	1·10
C385		5E. vermilion, pale grey and black	3·25	2·10
C386		10E. vermilion, light grey-blue and black	5·25	4·25
C383/386		Set of 4	10·50	7·75

1967–68. CHARITY TAX. Guinean Artifacts from Bissau Museum. Type C **61** and similar multicoloured designs. Litho. P 13½.

C387		50c. Type C **61** (12.67)	45	25
C388		1E. "Tree of life" (carving) (horiz) (3.68)	45	25
C389		2E. Cow-headed statuette (3.68)	45	25
		a. Error. Inscr "TOCADOR DE BOMBOLON"	16·00	
C390		2E.50 "The Magistrate" (statuette) (3.68)	65	45
C391		5E. "Kneeling Servant" (statuette) (3.68)	85	55
C392		10E. Stylized pelican (carving) (3.68)	1·60	1·30
C387/392		Set of 6	4·00	2·75
MSC393		149×199 mm. Nos. C387/92. Imperf. No gum (sold at 25E.)	16·00	16·00

Nos. C387/92 were for use on all inland mail from 15 March to 15 April, 15 December to 15 January and all the year on parcels.

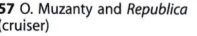

(C **62**)

63 President Tomás

64 Cabral's Arms

1968. CHARITY TAX. No. C389a surch as Type C **62**.

C394		50c. on 2E. multicoloured	45	45
C395		1E. on 2E. multicoloured	45	45

1968 (2 Feb). Visit of President Tomás of Portugal. Litho. P 13½.

396	63	1E. multicoloured	35	20

(Des J. de Moura. Litho Litografia Maia, Oporto, Portugal)

1968 (22 Apr). 500th Birth Anniv of Pedro Cabral (explorer). P 14.

397	64	2E.50 multicoloured	85	30

C **65** Hands grasping Sword

66 Admiral Coutinho's Astrolabe

67 Arms of Vasco da Gama

202

PORTUGESE GUINEA

(Des R. Graça. Litho Litografia de Portugal, Lisbon)
1968. CHARITY TAX. National Defence. P 13½.

C398	C 65	50c. multicoloured	45	45
C399		1E. multicoloured	45	45
C400		2E. multicoloured	35	35
C401		2E.50 multicoloured	45	45
C402		3E. multicoloured	45	45
C403		4E. multicoloured	55	45
C404		5E. multicoloured	65	55
C405		8E. multicoloured	1·10	1·10
C406		9E. multicoloured	1·30	1·30
C407		10E. multicoloured	1·10	1·10
C408		15E. multicoloured	1·60	1·60
C398/408 Set of 11			7·75	7·50

30, 50 and 100E. stamps in the same design were for fiscal purposes.

(Des J. de Moura. Litho Litografia Nacional, Oporto, Portugal)
1969 (17 Feb). Birth Centenary of Admiral Gago Coutinho. P 14.
409 66 1E. multicoloured 45 20

(Des J. de Moura. Litho Litografia Nacional, Oporto, Portugal)
1969 (29 Aug). 500th Birth Anniv of Vasco da Gama (explorer). P 14.
410 67 2E.50 multicoloured 50 15

68 L. A. Rebello da Silva   **69** Arms of King Manoel I   **70** Ulysses Grant and Square, Bolama

(Des J. de Moura. Litho Litografia Maia, Oporto, Portugal)
1969 (25 Sept). Centenary of Overseas Administrative Reforms. P 14.
411 68 50c. multicoloured 35 15

(Des J. de Moura. Litho Litografia Nacional, Oporto, Portugal)
1969 (1 Dec). 500th Birth Anniv of King Manoel I. P 14.
412 69 2E. multicoloured 50 15

(Des J. de Moura. Litho)
1970 (25 Oct). Centenary of Arbitral Judgement on Sovereignty of Bolama. P 13½×13.
413 70 2E.50 multicoloured 60 30

71 Marshal Carmona   C **72** Mother and Children

(Des J. de Moura. Litho Litografia Nacional, Oporto, Portugal)
1970 (15 Nov). Birth Centenary of Marshal Carmona. P 14.
414 71 1E.50 multicoloured 50 20

(Des A. Trigo. Litho Litografia de Portugal, Lisbon)
1971 (June). CHARITY TAX. P 13.

C415	C 72	50c. multicoloured	30	25
C416		1E. multicoloured	30	25
C417		2E. multicoloured	30	25
C418		3E. multicoloured	30	25
C419		4E. multicoloured	30	25
C420		5E. multicoloured	55	30
C421		10E. multicoloured	1·10	65
C415/421 Set of 7			2·75	2·00

Higher values were intended for fiscal use.

73 Camoens   **74** Weightlifting and Hammer-throwing

(Des A. Cutileiro. Litho Litografia Maia, Oporto)
1972 (25 May). 400th Anniv of Camoens' "The Lusiads" (epic poem). P 13.
422 73 50c. multicoloured 55 30

(Des A. Cutileiro. Litho Litografia Nacional, Oporto)
1972 (20 June). Olympic Games, Munich. P 14×13½.
423 74 2E.50 multicoloured 75 20

75 Fairey IIID Seaplane *Lusitania* taking-off from Lisbon   **76** W.M.O. Emblem

(Des A. Cutileiro. Litho Litografia Maia, Oporto)
1972 (20 Sept). 50th Anniv of First Flight from Lisbon to Rio de Janeiro. P 13½.
424 75 1E. multicoloured 30 20

(Des A. Cutileiro. Litho Litografia Maia, Oporto)
1973 (15 Dec). Centenary of World Meteorological Organization. P 13.
425 76 2E. multicoloured 50 30

An armed rebellion against colonial rule was launched in January 1963 by the PAIGC (Partido Africano da Independência da Guiné e do Cabo Verde) under Amilcar Cabral. On 24 September 1973 a "Republic of Guinea-Bissau" was formed by the rebels, who claimed to be in control of two-thirds of the country. In the following year the new revolutionary government in metropolitan Portugal followed up the *de facto* ceasefire which had come about by recognising the independence of Guinea-Bissau on 10 September 1974 and withdrawing its troops on 15 October 1974. Stamps of Guinea-Bissau are listed in Part 13 (*Africa since Independence F-M*) of this catalogue.

Portuguese India

1871. 1000 Reis = 1 Milreis
1882. 12 Reis (singular Real) = 1 Tanga
      16 Tangas = 1 Rupia
1959. 100 Centavos = 1 Escudo

Portuguese India consisted of three territories on the Arabian Sea, namely Goa, Damão and Diu. Goa, with an area of 1268 square miles, was founded in 1510 by Afonso de Albuquerque in territory seized from the ruler of Bijapur. In 1542–52 St. Francis Xavier, "the apostle of the Indies", converted the inhabitants to Catholicism. In 1842 New Goa (Pangim) was built to replace Old Goa as the capital. Damão, with an area of 86 square miles, was acquired in 1558. It consisted of a coastal area and the detached inland area of Nagar-Aveli. Diu is a town established in 1535 on an island with an area of 20 square miles, south of the Kathiawar peninsula.

PRINTERS. All the stamps of Portuguese India were printed at the Mint, Lisbon, *unless otherwise stated*.

REPRINTS. Reprints of some of the following issues were made in 1885 and 1905 as indicated in the footnotes. These can generally be distinguished as follows:
1885 reprints are on stout very white paper, usually ungummed but sometimes with white gum having yellowish spots. When perforated they are perf 13½ with large clean-cut holes producing sharp pointed teeth.
1905 reprints are on creamy white paper of ordinary quality with shiny white gum, all perf 13½.

King Luis
11 November 1861–19 October 1889

1 (Die I)   **2 (Die II)**

Die I. "REIS" in thin Roman capitals; "S" and "R" of "SERVIÇO" smaller, and "E" larger than the other letters; 33 lines in background; side ornaments of 4 dashes.
Die II. "REIS" in sans-serif capitals; all letters of "SERVIÇO" in same size; 44 lines in background; side ornaments of 5 dots.

(Des J. A. Castel-Branco. Eng Gohindozo, Goa)

1871 (1 Oct). Die I. Large figures of value.

(a) Thin hard yellowish paper. P 14 to 18

1	1	10r. black	£750	£450
2		20r. carmine-red	£2000	£500
3		40r. Prussian blue	£700	£500
4		100r. yellow-green	£750	£550
5		200r. ochre-yellow	£1500	8·00

(b) Stout paper, white or yellowish. P 13 to 16

6	1	10r. black	£2500	£550
7		20r. carmine-red	£2500	£650
8		20r. orange-vermilion	£2750	£650
9		200r. ochre-yellow		£1500
10		300r. deep claret		£2750

The stamps of this and similar types were handprinted one by one, as were also the figures of value. The perforation was done with toothed strips of ivory and is very irregular.

1871–73. Die II. Large figures of value. P 12½ to 14½.

(a) Stout wove paper, white or yellowish (12.71)

11	2	10r. black	£450	£160
12		20r. vermilion	£350	£140
		a. "20" omitted	—	£1600
13		40r. ultramarine	£120	90·00
		a. Dull blue	£150	90·00
		aa. Tête-bêche (pair)	£10000	
		b. Indigo	£150	90·00
14		100r. deep green	£100	60·00
		a. Yellow-green	£120	90·00
15		200r. yellow	£450	£350
16		300r. claret	£450	£350
17		600r. claret	£300	£225
		a. Double figures	£1200	
18		900r. claret	£350	£225
		a. Double figures	£25000	£14500

(b) Laid paper (4.72)

19	2	10r. black	65·00	50·00
		a. Tête-bêche (pair)		
20		20r. vermilion	55·00	46·00
21		40r. blue	£120	90·00
		a. Tête-bêche (pair)		
		b. Double figures		
22		100r. green	£100	65·00
		a. Deep green	£110	75·00
23		200r. yellow	£300	£250

(c) Thin hard paper (1.73)

24	2	20r. vermilion	£350	£225

3 (Die I) Large Figures   **4 (Die I) Small Figures**   **6 (Die II) Small Figures**

In T **4** the "A" of "INDIA" is always without trace of the horizontal line.

1873–75. Reissue of both dies on thin soft wove paper, slightly bluish. Lines of background thicker owing to wear. P 12½ to 14½.

A. Die I (worn)
(a) Large figures of value (7.73)

25	3	10r. black	20·00	11·00
		a. Double figures	£700	£250
		b. "1" inverted	£100	90·00
26		20r. vermilion	25·00	16·00
		a. Double figures	£700	£350
27		300r. deep purple	£200	£140
		a. Double figures	£850	
28		600r. deep purple	£250	£160
		a. Double figures	£1000	
		b. Figures inverted	£1000	
29		900r. deep purple	£250	£160
		a. Double figures	£1200	

(b) Small figures of value (end 1874)

30	4	10r. black	55·00	41·00
31		20r. vermilion	£950	£550
		a. Double figures	—	£800

B. Die II
Small figures of value (2.75)

32	6	10r. black	65·00	37·00
33		15r. rose	20·00	13·50
		a. Pink	20·00	13·50
		b. Value omitted	£2000	
34		20r. vermilion	£120	70·00
		a. Figures sideways (reading upwards)	£1500	
		b. "O" omitted	£1500	

7 (Die III)   **8 (Die IV)**   **9 (Die IV)**

Die III. Background of 41 lines above, and 43 lines below "REIS"; letters of inscription recut; "SERVIÇO" has "V" barred like an inverted "A".

1876 (Mar). Die III, first recut. Small figures of value. Thin bluish paper. P 12½ to 13½.

35	7	10r. black	9·00	6·75
		a. Double figures	£900	
36		15r. rose	£750	£500
		a. "15" omitted	£2500	
		b. Pink	£750	£500
37		20r. vermilion	40·00	27·00
38		40r. blue	£180	£140
		a. Pale blue	£180	£140
39		100r. green	£275	£250
		a. Yellow-green	£275	£250
40		200r. yellow	£1200	£1100
41		300r. deep purple	£800	£650
42		600r. deep purple	£900	£800
43		900r. deep purple	£1100	£1000

A stamp in deep purple is known with value omitted.

Die IV. Background of 33 lines as before, but redrawn; letters of inscription larger; "V" of "SERVIÇO" barred; "REIS" in thick roman capitals; side ornaments of 5 dots.

1876 (May). Die IV. Small figures of value. Thin bluish paper. P 12½ to 13½.
44	**8**	10r. black	35·00	23·00
45		20r. vermilion	27·00	18·00

1877 (1 June). Die IV, with star added above, and bar below the value. Small figures of value. Thin bluish paper. P 12½ to 13½.
46	**9**	10r. black	47·00	37·00

10 (Die III)   **11** (Die V)   **12**

1877. Die III, background of 41 lines; star added above, and bar below the value. Small figures of value. Thin bluish paper. P 12½ to 13½.
47	**10**	10r. black	75·00	60·00

Die V. Background of 41 lines above, and 38 lines below "REIS", with white oval round it; star and bar as before.

1877. Die V. Small figures of value. Thin bluish paper. P 12½ to 13½.
48	**11**	10r. black	48·00	41·00
49		15r. rose	50·00	45·00
50		20r. vermilion	14·50	13·50
51		40r. ultramarine	29·00	26·00
		a. Dull blue	29·00	26·00
52		100r. green	£120	95·00
53		200r. yellow	£120	£120
54		300r. deep purple	£170	£140
55		600r. deep purple	£170	£140
56		900r. deep purple	£170	£140

(Des and eng A. F. Gerard. Typo)

1877 (15 July). "REIS" with serifs.

(a) P 12½
57	**12**	5r. black	8·75	6·00
58		10r. yellow-buff	14·50	12·50
		a. Orange-buff	14·50	12·50
59		20r. deep bistre	14·50	12·50
		a. Pale bistre	14·50	12·50
60		25r. rose	18·00	13·00
61		40r. deep blue	£225	£200
62		50r. yellow-green	44·00	29·00
		a. Blue-green	44·00	29·00
63		100r. grey-lilac	20·00	18·00
64		200r. orange	39·00	29·00

(b) P 13½
65	**12**	5r. black	8·75	6·00
66		10r. yellow-buff	18·00	14·50
		a. Orange-buff	18·00	14·50
67		20r. deep bistre	12·50	9·25
		a. Pale bistre	12·50	9·25
68		25r. rose	14·50	12·50
69		40r. deep blue	25·00	14·50
		a. Blue	25·00	14·50
70		50r. yellow-green	44·00	29·00
		a. Blue-green	44·00	29·00
		b. Deep green	44·00	29·00
71		100r. grey-lilac	20·00	18·00
72		200r. orange	39·00	29·00
73		300r. lake-brown	42·00	39·00
		a. Yellow-brown	42·00	39·00

All values were reprinted in 1885 and 1905.

1880 (Sept)–**81**. Colours changed.

(a) P 12½
74	**12**	10r. yellow-green	29·00	24·00
		a. Blue-green	29·00	24·00
75		25r. slate-grey	£130	95·00
76		25r. dull purple (4.81)	65·00	44·00
77		50r. blue (1.81)	65·00	44·00

(b) P 13½
78	**12**	10r. yellow-green	18·00	14·50
		a. Blue-green	18·00	14·50
79		25r. slate-grey	65·00	47·00
80		25r. dull purple	47·00	35·00
81		40r. yellow (2.81)	55·00	44·00
82		50r. deep blue	29·00	27·00

The 10, 25 dull purple, 40 and 50r. were reprinted in 1885 and 1905. The 10r. in rose and in *slate-grey* are from the 1885 reprints.

$1\tfrac{1}{2}$ 5 $4\tfrac{1}{2}$ 6   1 T
(13)   (14)   (15)   (16)    (17)

1881. Stamps of early types surch locally with T **13** or **14**.
82a	**1**	1½ on 10r. black (1)	—	£1400
83		1½ on 20r. carmine-red (2)	£600	£550
84		1½ on 20r. orange-vermilion (8)	—	£425
85	**2**	1½ on 20r. vermilion (12)	—	£325
86		1½ on 20r. vermilion (20)	—	£250
87	**3**	1½ on 20r. vermilion (26)	£275	£250
88	**6**	1½ on 20r. vermilion (34)	£180	£150
		a. Surch inverted	—	£425
89	**7**	1½ on 20r. vermilion (37)	£120	£110
90	**8**	1½ on 20r. vermilion (45)	£120	£110
91	**11**	1½ on 20r. vermilion (50)	£275	£200
92	**2**	5 on 10r. black (19) (R.)	£325	£325
93	**3**	5 on 10r. black (25) (R.)	£325	£325
94	**4**	5 on 10r. black (30) (R.)	£1800	
95	**6**	5 on 10r. black (32) (R.)	£110	85·00
96	**7**	5 on 10r. black (35) (R.)	12·50	9·75
		a. "5" omitted (in pair with normal)	£550	
97	**8**	5 on 10r. black (44) (R.)	14·50	14·50
		a. Surch double	24·00	
98	**9**	5 on 10r. black (46) (R.)	70·00	44·00
99	**10**	5 on 10r. black (47) (R.)	90·00	70·00
100	**11**	5 on 10r. black (48) (R.)	90·00	60·00
101	**6**	5 on 15r. rose (33)	2·75	2·75
		a. Surch inverted	36·00	
		b. Surch double	36·00	36·00
102	**7**	5 on 15r. rose (36)	£275	£275
103	**1**	5 on 20r. carmine-red (7)	—	£1000
104	**2**	5 on 20r. vermilion (20)	—	£1200
105	**3**	5 on 20r. vermilion (26)	—	£550
105a	**4**	5 on 20r. vermilion (31)	—	£700
106	**7**	5 on 20r. vermilion (37)	4·00	4·00
		a. Surch inverted	32·00	
		b. Surch double	27·00	
107	**8**	5 on 20r. vermilion (45)	4·00	4·00
		a. Surch inverted	27·00	
		b. Surch double	30·00	30·00
108	**11**	5 on 20r. vermilion (50)	4·00	4·00

There are two types of Type **14** for the 5 on 15r., and three types for the 5 on 20r.

1881 (17 May). Crown type surch locally as T **13** and **15/17**.

(a) P 12½
109	**12**	1½ on 5r. black	2·50	1·60
110		1½ on 10r. green	2·50	2·10
111		1½ on 20r. bistre	28·00	21·00
		a. Surch inverted	50·00	
		b. Pair, one without surch	—	36·00
112		1½ on 25r. slate-grey	95·00	75·00
113		1½ on 100r. grey-lilac	£120	95·00
114		4½ on 5r. black (B.)	13·00	13·00
		a. Surch inverted	70·00	41·00
115		4½ on 10r. green	£275	£275
116		4½ on 20r. bistre	5·75	5·25
		a. Surch inverted	27·00	
117		4½ on 25r. dull purple	26·00	21·00
118		4½ on 100r. grey-lilac	£190	£190
119		6 on 10r. yellow-buff	£100	95·00
		a. Orange-buff	£100	95·00
		b. Surch inverted	—	£140
120		6 on 10r. green	21·00	16·00
121		6 on 20r. bistre	29·00	21·00
122		6 on 25r. slate-grey	85·00	60·00
123		6 on 25r. dull purple	7·00	4·50
124		6 on 40r. blue	£225	£190
125		6 on 40r. yellow	£225	£190
126		6 on 50r. green	£120	95·00
127		6 on 50r. blue	£110	95·00
128		1T. on 10r. green	£225	£200
129		1T. on 20r. bistre	90·00	70·00
130		1T. on 25r. slate-grey	95·00	70·00
131		1T. on 25r. dull purple	26·00	19·00
132		1T. on 40r. blue	32·00	26·00
133		1T. on 40r. yellow	£110	85·00
134		1T. on 50r. blue	48·00	32·00
136		1T. on 100r. grey-lilac	38·00	24·00
137		1T. on 200r. orange	70·00	60·00
138		2T. on 25r. slate-grey	75·00	60·00
139		2T. on 25r. dull purple	26·00	17·00
140		2T. on 40r. blue	£120	80·00
141		2T. on 40r. yellow	60·00	48·00
142		2T. on 50r. blue-green	45·00	36·00
		a. Yellow-green	45·00	36·00
		b. Surch inverted	£150	
143		2T. on 50r. blue	£150	£130

144		2T. on 100r. grey-lilac	21·00	17·00
145		2T. on 200r. orange	80·00	60·00
146		4T. on 10r. green	35·00	26·00
		a. Surch inverted	£160	
147		4T. on 50r. green	35·00	23·00
148		4T. on 200r. orange	85·00	60·00
149		8T. on 20r. bistre	90·00	70·00
150		8T. on 25r. rose	£400	£375
151		8T. on 40r. blue	80·00	65·00
152		8T. on 100r. grey-lilac	70·00	60·00
153		8T. on 200r. orange	70·00	60·00
		(b) P 13½		
154	12	1½ on 5r. black	6·50	5·25
155		1½ on 10r. green	6·50	5·25
156		1½ on 20r. bistre	28·00	21·00
		a. Surch double		
157		1½ on 25r. slate-grey	65·00	50·00
158		1½ on 100r. grey-lilac	£100	90·00
159		4½ on 5r. black (B.)	13·00	13·00
160		4½ on 10r. green	£275	£275
161		4½ on 20r. bistre	8·00	6·50
162		4½ on 25r. dull purple	26·00	21·00
163		4½ on 100r. grey-lilac	£190	£190
164		6 on 10r. yellow-buff	95·00	70·00
		a. Surch inverted	—	£140
165		6 on 10r. green	26·00	19·00
166		6 on 20r. bistre	65·00	38·00
167		6 on 25r. slate-grey	65·00	38·00
168		6 on 25r. dull purple	5·00	3·75
169		6 on 40r. blue	£130	95·00
170		6 on 40r. yellow	14·50	80·00
171		6 on 50r. green	90·00	80·00
172		6 on 50r. blue	£120	90·00
173		1T. on 10r. green	£225	£225
174		1T. on 20r. bistre	£100	85·00
175		1T. on 25r. slate-grey	60·00	48·00
176		1T. on 25r. dull purple	26·00	19·00
177		1T. on 40r. blue	80·00	75·00
178		1T. on 50r. green	£100	90·00
179		1T. on 50r. blue	90·00	75·00
180		1T. on 100r. grey-lilac	90·00	75·00
181		1T. on 200r. orange	85·00	70·00
182		2T. on 25r. slate-grey	65·00	50·00
183		2T. on 25r. dull purple	45·00	37·00
184		2T. on 40r. blue	60·00	50·00
185		2T. on 40r. yellow	60·00	48·00
186		2T. on 50r. green	32·00	19·00
187		2T. on 50r. blue	£160	£130
188		2T. on 200r. orange	70·00	50·00
189		2T. on 300r. yellow-brown	65·00	60·00
190		4T. on 10r. green	19·00	16·00
191		4T. on 50r. green	19·00	16·00
192		4T. on 200r. orange	85·00	60·00
193		8T. on 20r. bistre	80·00	60·00
194		8T. on 25r. rose	£375	£325
195		8T. on 40r. blue	90·00	85·00
196		8T. on 100r. grey-lilac	70·00	60·00
197		8T. on 200r. orange	60·00	50·00
198		8T. on 300r. yellow-brown	70·00	55·00

With additional surch in black

(a) P 12½

199	12	1½ on 4½ on 5r. black	£120	£100
200		1½ on 6 on 10r. green	£170	£150
200*a*		1½ on 1T. on 20r. bistre	—	£150
201		2 on 4T. on 50r. green	£425	£350
202		6 on 1T. on 10r. green	£160	
		(b) P 13½		
202*a*	12	1½ on 4½ on 5r. black	—	£180
203		2 on 4T. on 50r. green	£500	£425

All the surcharges of 1881 are type-set, and there are several different settings of most values. There is a variety of surcharge in Nos. 138 and 182, in which the "T" is considerably smaller than in the normal type, while Nos. 131 and 176 show a variety in which the figure "1" is much thicker.

Nos. 109/203 were mostly issued without gum.

(I)

(II)

Two types of orb at top of Crown

1882 (1 Jan). New Currency. As T **12** but with value in sans-serif capitals.

A. P 12½

(a) Type I. Plain cross

204A(I)	12	1½r. black	1·20	1·10
205A(I)		4½r. olive-green	1·40	70
206A(I)		6r. green	1·60	1·30
207A(I)		1t. rose	1·60	95
208A(I)		2t. blue	1·60	95
209A(I)		4t. dull purple	5·75	3·75
210A(I)		8t. orange	5·75	5·00
		(b) Type II. Pearl in cross		
204A(II)	12	1½r. black	1·60	1·30
205A(II)		4½r. olive-green	1·60	1·30
206A(II)		6r. green	1·60	1·30
207A(II)		1t. rose	19·00	16·00

B. P 13½

(a) Type I. Plain cross

204B(I)	12	1½r. black	1·60	1·10
205B(I)		4½r. olive-green	1·60	1·10
206B(I)		6r. green	1·60	1·10
207B(I)		1t. rose	1·60	1·30
208B(I)		2t. blue	1·60	1·30
209B(I)		4t. dull purple	32·00	27·00
210B(I)		8t. orange	8·00	5·75
		(b) Type II. Pearl in cross		
204B(II)	12	1½r. black	1·60	1·10
205B(II)		4½r. olive-green	16·00	14·50
206B(II)		6r. green	16·00	14·50
207B(II)		1t. rose	19·00	16·00
208B(II)		2t. blue	16·00	14·50
209B(II)		4t. dull purple	32·00	27·00
210B(II)		8t. orange	32·00	27·00

There were three printings of these stamps. (1) has "REIS" in thick letters with "E" accented. (2) has "REIS" in thin letters with "E" accented. (3) has "REIS" without accent. In printings (1) and (2) varieties occur in which the accent over "E" is circumflex instead of acute. Printing (3) was in two types, one with plain cross, and the other with pearl in cross on the orb at the top of the crown (see illustrations I and II), which we list separately.

All values in Type II were reprinted in 1885 and 1905.

1883 (May). Stamps of early types handstamped with types nearly identical with T **13**, **15** and **16**.

211	2	1½ on 10r. black (11)	£500	£475
212	3	1½ on 10r. black (25)	—	£475
213	7	1½ on 10r. black (35)	—	£475
214	8	1½ on 10r. black (44)	—	£475
215	11	1½ on 10r. black (48)		£500
216	1	4½ on 40r. Prussian blue (3)	£2250	£750
217	2	4½ on 40r. ultramarine (13)	50·00	50·00
		a. 4½ on 40r. indigo (13*b*)		£375
218		4½ on 40r. blue (21)	50·00	50·00
219	7	4½ on 40r. blue (38)	50·00	50·00
220	1	4½ on 100r. yellow-green (4)	£2250	£750
221	2	4½ on 100r. deep green (14)	50·00	50·00
222		4½ on 100r. green (22)	50·00	50·00
223	7	4½ on 100r. green (39)	38·00	32·00
224	6	6 on 20r. vermilion (34)		
225	1	6 on 100r. yellow-green (4)	—	£750
226	2	6 on 100r. deep green (14)	—	£350
227		6 on 100r. green (22)	—	£250
228	7	6 on 100r. green (39)	£475	£450
229	1	6 on 200r. ochre-yellow (5)	—	£750
230	2	6 on 200r. yellow (15)	—	£750
231		6 on 200r. yellow (23)	—	£225
232	7	6 on 200r. yellow (40)	—	£600
233	11	6 on 200r. yellow (53)	£650	£650

There are two varieties of type in the surcharges of Nos. 219 and 221, differing from each other in the shape of the small figure "2" of the fraction.

(**18**)

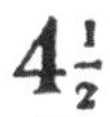

(**19**)

INDIA PORTUGUEZA
1½ REIS 1½

20

1883. Handstamped with T **18** and **19**.

(a) P 12½

234	12	1½ on 5r. black	2·50	1·60
235		1½ on 10r. green	2·50	2·10
		(b) P 13½		
236	12	1½ on 5r. black	6·50	5·25
237		1½ on 10r. green	6·50	5·25
238		42 on 100r. grey-lilac	£140	£140

1883 (Sept). Reissue of old types with the new currency. Thin bluish paper. Imperf.

A. Die IV, with Star and Bar

239	9	1½r. black	£120	32·00
		a. Value omitted	£800	£650
		b. Value double	£800	£800

PORTUGUESE INDIA

240		6r. green		£110	65·00
		a. "6" omitted		£800	£650
		b. Value double			£650
	B. Die V, with white oval round background, and Star and Bar				
241	11	1½r. black		2·50	1·80
		a. Tête-bêche (pair)		£5000	
		b. Double figures		£900	£700
242		4½r. olive-green		25·00	20·00
		a. Value omitted		£700	£600
243		6r. green		20·00	15·00
		a. Tête-bêche (pair)		£2500	
		b. Value omitted		£900	£800
		c. *Deep green*		20·00	15·00

(Des and eng F. A. de Campos. Head embossed, rest typo)

1886 (23 Apr). Chalk-surfaced paper.

(a) P 12½

244	20	1½r. black		3·75	2·00
245		4½r. olive-green		4·50	2·20
		a. *Bistre*		5·00	2·75
246		6r. blue-green		5·00	2·75
247		1t. rosine		7·75	4·50
248		2t. blue		14·50	7·00
249		4t. lavender		14·50	7·00
250		8t. orange		14·50	7·00

(b) P 13½

251	20	1½r. black		£1000	£550
252		4½r. olive-green		60·00	25·00
		a. *Bistre*		60·00	25·00
253		6r. blue-green		60·00	25·00
254		1t. rosine		17·00	10·00
255		2t. blue		16·00	10·50
256		4t. lavender		16·00	7·00
257		8t. orange		13·00	7·00

The 2t. and 4t. values were reprinted in 1905.

King Carlos
19 October 1889–1 February 1908

21   21a Arrival at Calicut

(Des and eng M. D. Neto. Typo)

1895 (Apr)–**96**. Enamel-surfaced paper only.

(a) P 11½

258	21	1½r. black		2·50	1·20
259		4½r. pale orange		1·90	1·20
260		1t. pale blue		2·50	1·80
261		2t. carmine		2·50	1·20
262		4t. dull blue		3·25	1·80

(b) P 12½

263	21	1½r. black		2·30	1·00
264		4½r. pale orange		1·90	1·00
265		6r. green		5·75	2·30
266		9r. lilac (3.96)		8·00	6·00
267		1t. pale blue		8·00	3·50
268		2t. carmine		20·00	13·00
269		4t. blue		6·75	4·75
270		8t. lilac (4.96)		5·75	3·50

(c) P 13½

271	21	1½r. black		1·90	1·00
272		4½r. pale orange		13·00	2·40
273		6r. green		1·90	1·00
274		9r. lilac		7·75	5·50

The 9r. was reprinted in 1905.

(Des R. Gameiro (1½r.), M. P. de Faria Luna (4½r.), S. Correia Belem (6r.), J. Vaz (9r., 2t., 8t.), J. J. G. Coelho (1t.), J. R. Cristiano de Silva (4t.). Recess Waterlow)

1898 (1 May). 400th Anniv of Vasco da Gama's Discovery of Route to India. T **21**a and similar designs. P 14 to 15.

275	1½r. blue-green		1·60	70
276	4½r. vermilion		1·60	70
277	6r. deep purple		1·60	1·00
278	9r. yellow-green		2·30	1·00
279	1t. deep blue		3·25	2·30
280	2t. chocolate		3·75	2·30
281	4t. bistre-brown		3·75	3·00
282	8t. ochre		8·00	4·75
275/282 *Set of 8*			23·00	14·00

Designs: Horiz—1½r. Departure of fleet; 4½r. Fleet; 6r. Embarkation at Rastello; 4t. Flagship *São Gabriel*; 8t. Vasco da Gama. Vert—9r. Muse of History; 1t. Flagship *São Gabriel* and portraits of Da Gama and Camoens; 2t. Archangel Gabriel, patron saint of the expedition.

22 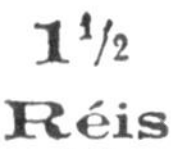   (23)    (24)

(Des and eng E. Mouchon. Typo)

1898 (1 Aug)–**1900**. Value in black; in carmine on the 1 rupee.

(a) P 11½

283	22	1½r. orange-red		55	35
		a. *Orange*		55	35
284		4½r. pale green		1·60	1·00
285		6r. chocolate		1·60	1·00
286		9r. deep lilac		1·60	1·00
		a. *Grey-lilac*		1·60	1·00
287		1t. blue-green		1·60	70
288		2t. blue		1·90	70
289		4t. blue/*blue*		3·75	1·80
		a. Error. On yellow			
290		8t. purple/*flesh*		3·75	2·00
291		12t. blue/*pink* (1900)		5·75	3·50
292		1rp. black/*blue* (1900)		11·50	5·00
293		2rp. mauve/*yellow* (1900)		16·00	9·75
283/293 *Set of 11*				45·00	24·00

(b) P 13½

294	22	2t. blue		38·00	11·00

See also Nos. 323/36.

1900. Surch locally with T **23**.

(a) P 11½

295	22	1½r. on 2t. blue		3·25	1·80
		a. Surch inverted		70·00	70·00
		b. Figures of fraction on same line		29·00	21·00

(b) P 13½

296	22	1½r. on 2t. blue		85·00	70·00

1902.

*(a) Surch as T **24** (currency in real, reis or tangas)*

297	20	1r. on 2t. (12½)		1·60	90
298		1r. on 2t. (13½)		1·10	70
299	21	1r. on 6r. (12½)		95	60
300	20	2r. on 4½r. (12½)		75	60
		a. Surch inverted		9·00	8·50
		b. Surch double		9·00	8·50
301	21	2r. on 8t. (12½)		95	60
302	20	2½r. on 6r. (12½)		95	60
303	21	2½r. on 9r. (12½)		95	60
304	20	3r. on 1t. (12½)		75	60
		a. Printed on reverse of paper		6·50	6·00
305	21	3r. on 4½r. (12½)		2·10	1·50
		a. Surch inverted		27·00	25·00
306		3r. on 1t. (11½)		1·90	1·80
307	20	2½r. on 1½r. (12½) (C.)		2·50	2·00
308		2½r. on 4t. (12½)		21·00	14·50
309		2½r. on 4t. (13½)		2·50	1·80
310	21	2½r. on 1½r. (11½) (C.)		2·50	1·80
311		2½r. on 1½r. (12½) (C.)		5·25	3·50
312		2½r. on 1½r. (13½) (C.)		3·25	1·80
313	20	5t. on 8t. (12½)		38·00	24·00
314		5t. on 8t. (13½)		1·60	1·00
315	21	5t. on 2t. (11½)		2·50	1·80
316		5t. on 2t. (12½)		£250	£180
317		5t. on 4t. (11½)		2·50	1·80
318		5t. on 4t. (12½)		£250	£180

*(b) Optd with T **13** of St. Thomas and Prince Is*

319	22	6r. chocolate		2·75	1·80
320		1t. blue-green		2·75	1·80
321		2t. blue (11½)		2·75	1·80
322		2t. blue (13½)		£900	£5500

The 1r./2t., 1r./6r., 2½r./9r., 3r./4½r., 3r./1t. (T **21**), 2½t./4t. and 5t./4t. were reprinted in 1905.

1903. Colours changed and new values. Value in black. P 11½.

323	22	1r. pale grey		55	45
324		1½r. slate		70	35
325		2r. orange		55	35
326		2½r. chestnut		70	35
327		3r. dull blue		70	35
328		6r. green		70	35
		a. *Deep green*		70	35
329		1t. carmine		80	35
330		2t. brown		3·25	1·50
331		2½t. dull blue		11·50	6·00
332		5t. purple-brown/*straw*		3·75	2·20
333		8t. purple/*pink*		7·50	3·50
334		12t. green/*pink*		7·50	3·50

207

PORTUGUESE INDIA

335	1rp. dull blue/*straw*	16·00	15·00
336	2rp. grey-black/*straw*	31·00	31·00
323/336	Set of 14	75·00	60·00

D 25 (26) (27)

(Des and eng J. S. de Carvalho e Silva. Typo)

1904. POSTAGE DUE. Name and value in black. P 11½.

D337	D 25	2r. blue-green	55	55
D338		3r. yellow-green	55	50
D339		4r. orange	55	50
D340		5r. slate	55	50
D341		6r. grey	55	50
D342		9r. brown	80	75
D343		1t. orange-red	80	75
D344		2t. deep brown	1·50	90
D345		5t. blue	4·00	3·25
D346		10t. carmine	4·00	3·75
D347		1rp. deep lilac	18·00	8·50
D337/347	Set of 11		29·00	18·00

1905. No. 331 surch with T **26**.

337	22	2t. on 2½t. dull blue	3·50	3·00

King Manoel II
1 February 1908–5 October 1910

PORTUGUESE REPUBLIC
5 October 1910

1911. Optd with T **27**, in red or green (G.).

338	22	1r. pale grey	45	30
339		1½r. slate	45	30
340		2r. orange	45	30
341		2½r. chestnut	70	30
342		3r. dull blue	70	30
343		4½r. pale green	70	30
344		6r. green	55	30
		a. Deep green	55	30
345		9r. deep lilac	70	30
346		1t. carmine (G.)	1·00	30
347		2t. brown	1·10	30
348		4t. blue/*blue*	2·10	1·70
349		5t. purple-brown/*straw*	2·50	1·70
350		8t. purple/*pink*	7·50	4·25
351		12t. green/*pink*	8·25	4·25
352		1rp. dull blue/*straw*	11·50	10·00
353		2rp. grey-black/*straw*	16·00	10·50
338/353	Set of 16		49·00	32·00

See also Nos. 397/405.

1911. POSTAGE DUE. Optd with T **27**, in red or green (G.).

D354	D 25	2r. blue-green	35	25
D355		3r. yellow-green	35	25
D356		4r. orange	35	25
D357		5r. slate	35	25
D358		6r. grey	45	25
D359		9r. brown	60	25
D360		1t. orange-red	60	25
D361		2t. deep brown	1·00	55
D362		5t. blue	2·20	1·80
D363		10t. carmine (G.)	6·50	4·00
D364		1rp. deep lilac	6·50	4·00
D354/364	Set of 11		17·00	11·00

See also Nos. D423/33.

The following issue abounds in errors and minor varieties. There were several different issues, during different months, and some of the varieties were issued in exceedingly limited quantities. There are many errors in addition to those listed, but in view of the fact that most of them were of purely speculative origin we do not propose to add to the list.

PRICES. The prices quoted for this issue are for the entire stamp, showing both halves.

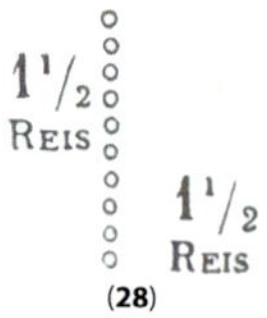

(28)

1911–13. Various stamps divided by vertical perforation, and each half surch locally with new value as T **28**.

(a) On 1898–1900 issue. No gum (Nos. 356/9d)

354	22	1½r. on 4½r. pale green (1913)	23·00	11·00
355		1½r. on 9r. deep lilac (8.12)	95	70
		a. "1" in first fraction thick	95	70
		b. "1" in second fraction thick	95	70
		c. "1" in both fractions thick	95	70
		d. Small "2" in fraction	1·90	1·80
		e. Surch inverted	9·00	9·00
356		1½r. on 4t. blue/*blue* (8.12)	95	70
		a. "1" in first fraction thick	95	70
		b. "1" in second fraction thick	95	70
		c. "1" in both fractions thick	95	70
		d. Surch double	1·90	1·80
		e. Surch inverted	7·25	7·25
357		2r. on 4t. blue/*blue* (8.12)	1·60	70
		a. Italic "S" in "REIS"	4·50	4·50
		b. Surch double	11·50	11·50
358		6r. on 4½r. pale green (8.12)	1·30	1·00
		a. Italic "S" in "REIS"	3·50	3·50
		b. Smaller figure "6"	5·25	3·50
		c. Surch inverted	8·00	4·50
		d. No dividing perf		
359		6r. on 9r. deep lilac (8.12)	1·30	1·00
		a. Smaller figure "6"	5·25	3·50
		b. Italic "S"	4·00	4·00
		c. Surch inverted	2·50	2·40
359d		6r. on 9r. grey-lilac (7.11)	1·30	1·00
		e. Smaller figure "6"	5·75	5·00
		f. Italic "S"	2·30	2·30

On the normal stamps the "1" in the fraction has a short curved serif at the top; in the varieties with thick number the whole figure "1" and the "1" in the fraction are identical in shape.

(b) On 1902 Provisional issue. The two surcharges set on a level except in Nos. 364/5. No gum (10.12)

360	21	1r. on 5t. on 2t. (11½)	11·50	9·50
361		1r. on 5t. on 4t. (11½)	9·50	7·00
362	20	1r. on 5t. on 8t. (12½)	£110	£110
363		1r. on 5t. on 8t. (13½)	4·25	3·00
364		2r. on 2½r. on 6r. (12½)	3·75	3·50
		a. Surch inverted	6·25	6·25
365	21	2r. on 2½r. on 9r. (12½)	27·00	21·00
366		3r. on 5t. on 2t. (11½)	11·50	7·00
367		3r. on 5t. on 4t. (11½)	11·50	7·00
		a. No dividing perf	45·00	
368		3r. on 5t. on 4t. (12½)	70·00	55·00
369	20	3r. on 5t. on 8t. (12½)	21·00	17·00
370		3r. on 5t. on 8t. (13½)	3·25	2·20
		a. Surch inverted	35·00	35·00
		b. Surch double		
		c. No dividing perf	35·00	

(c) On 1903 Don Carlos issue

371	22	1r. on 2r. orange (7.11)	65	60
372		1r. on 1t. carmine (8.11)	65	60
373		1r. on 5t. purple-brown/*straw* (10.12)	48·00	27·00
374		1½r. on 2½r. chestnut (7.11)	1·10	90
		a. "1" in first fraction thick	1·10	90
		b. "1" in second fraction thick	1·10	90
		c. "1" in both fractions thick	1·10	90
		d. Fraction figures on a level	26·00	24·00
		e. Surch inverted	26·00	24·00
		f. Only one half surch		
		g. No dividing perf		
375		2r. on 2½r. chestnut (7.11)	95	70
		a. Surch inverted	5·50	5·50
376		3r. on 2½r. chestnut (7.11)	95	70
		a. Surch inverted	6·25	6·25
377		3r. on 2t. brown (8.11)	1·10	90
		a. Italic "S" in "REIS"	3·50	3·50

As last, but the two surcharges set on a level

378	22	1r. on 5t. purple-brown/*straw* (10.12)	4·25	3·50
		a. Surch inverted	41·00	
379		6r. on 8t. purple/*pink* (10.12)	3·25	2·75
		a. Italic "S" in "REIS"	4·50	3·50
		b. Smaller figure "6"	9·00	7·25

Nos. 371/9 were mostly issued without gum. See note below No. 359d.

(d) On 1911 "REPUBLICA" issue

380	22	1r. on 1r. grey (7.12)	60	55
		a. Surch inverted	4·50	4·50
381		1r. on 2r. orange (11.11)	60	55
382		1r. on 1t. carmine (10.12)	60	55
		a. Surch inverted	7·25	7·25
		b. Surch inverted, and no dividing perf		
383		1r. on 5t. brown/*straw* (10.12)	60	55
384		1½r. on 4½r. pale green (1913)	95	55
385		3r. on 2t. brown (10.12)	17·00	13·50

386		6r. on 9r. grey-lilac (7.12)	95	55
		a. Smaller figure "6"	4·50	3·50
		b. No dividing perf.	3·50	3·50
		c. Inverted "S" in "REIS"	4·50	3·50

As No. 381, but diagonally slit instead of perforated, and old value cancelled with two black bars

387	22	1r. on 2r. orange (5.11)	1·30	90

As No. 387, but perforated diagonally

388	22	1r. on 2r. orange (5.11)	1·30	90

REPUBLICA (29)   REPÚBLICA (30)

1913. Vasco da Gama issue (1898) optd with T **29**.

389	1½r. blue-green	60	40
390	4½r. vermilion	60	40
391	6r. deep purple	70	55
392	9r. yellow-green	80	55
393	1t. deep blue	1·50	55
394	2t. chocolate	2·10	2·20
395	4t. chestnut	1·80	55
396	8t. ochre	3·00	1·30
389/396	*Set of 8*	10·00	5·75

1914–15. Various stamps optd at Government Press, Goa, with T **30**.

(a) Don Carlos. No gum (Nos. 397/8, 401/5)

397	22	2r. orange (R.)	12·50	9·00
398		2½r. chestnut (R.)	1·80	1·40
		a. Opt double, both inverted	5·50	
399		4½r. pale green (R.)	4·50	3·50
		a. Opt double	7·25	7·25
		b. Opt inverted	7·25	7·25
400		9r. grey-lilac (R.)	5·50	5·00
		a. Opt double	8·00	
		b. Opt inverted	8·00	
401		4t. blue/*blue* (R.)	22·00	16·00
402		12t. green/*pink* (R.)	9·00	7·25
403		1rp. dull blue/*straw* (R.)	18·00	11·00
404		2rp. mauve/*yellow* (R.)	22·00	16·00
405		2rp. grey-black/*straw* (R.)	22·00	16·00
397/405	*Set of 9*	£110	75·00

(b) Provisionals of 1902

406	21	2r. on 8t. (12½) (R.)	13·50	9·00
407	20	2½r. on 6r. (12½) (R.)	1·80	1·40
		a. Opt inverted	6·25	6·25
408	21	5t. on 2t. (11½) (G.)	9·00	7·25
409		5t. on 4t. (11½) (G.)	20·00	13·50
410		5t. on 4t. (11½) (G.)	9·00	5·50
411		5t. on 4t. (12½) (G.)	9·00	6·25
412	20	5t. on 8t. (12½) (G.)	27·00	22·00
413		5t. on 8t. (13½) (R.)	14·50	13·50
414		5t. on 8t. (13½) (G.)	14·50	13·50

(c) Nos. 320/1

415	22	1t. blue-green (R.)	22·00	12·50
416		2t. blue (11½) (R.)	18·00	11·00

(d) Provisionals of 1911–13

417	22	1r. on 2r. (No. 371) (R.)	11·50	9·00
418		1½r. on 4½r. (No. 354) (R.)	11·50	9·00
419		3r. on 2t. (No. 377) (R.)	9·00	6·25
420		6r. on 4½r. (No. 358) (R.)	8·00	6·25
		a. Small figure "6"	13·50	9·00
421		6r. on 9r. (No. 359d) (R.)	11·00	7·25
		a. Small figure "6"	13·50	11·00
422		6r. on 8t. (No. 379) (R.)	11·00	9·00
		a. Small figure "6"	13·50	11·00

See also Nos. 458/60.

1914. POSTAGE DUE. Optd at Government Press, Goa, with T **30**, in red.

D423	D **25**	2r. blue-green	55	35
D424		3r. yellow-green	55	35
D425		4r. orange	55	35
D426		5r. slate	55	35
D427		6r. grey	55	35
D428		9r. brown	55	35
D429		1t. orange-red	55	35
D430		2t. deep brown	4·00	2·30
D431		5t. blue	4·25	2·75
D432		10t. carmine	7·50	3·25
D433		1rp. deep lilac	12·00	6·25
D423/433	*Set of 11*	28·00	15·00

1½ RÉIS (31)   1½ RÉIS (32)    33 Ceres

1914. Surch locally as T **31**.

(a) "REPUBLICA" stamps of 1911

423	22	1½r. on 4½r. pale green	75	70
424		1½r. on 9r. deep lilac	75	70
425		1½r. on 12t. green/*pink*	1·30	1·20
426		3r. on 1t. carmine	85	70
427		3r. on 2t. brown	7·25	6·25
428		3r. on 8t. purple/*pink*	9·00	7·25
429		3r. on 1rp. dull blue/*straw*	1·20	75
430		3r. on 2rp. grey-black/*straw*	1·40	1·10

(b) Nos. 402 and 405

431	22	1½r. on 12t. green/*pink*	5·50	4·00
432		3r. on 2rp. grey-black/*straw*	14·50	12·50

1914. Vasco da Gama stamps of 1913 surch locally as T **32**.

433		1½r. on 4½r. vermilion	75	60
		a. Error. "1½"	9·50	9·00
		b. "1" in fraction inverted	13·00	12·00
434		1½r. on 9r. yellow-green	75	60
		a. Surch inverted	6·25	
		b. Surch double	6·25	
435		3r. on 1t. deep blue	75	60
		a. Surch inverted	6·25	
		b. Surch double	6·25	
436		3r. on 2t. chocolate	3·75	3·25
437		3r. on 4t. chestnut	75	60
		a. *Bistre-brown*	50	40
438		3r. on 8t. ochre	3·50	1·80
		a. Surch inverted	13·50	
433/438	*Set of 6*	9·25	6·75

Numerous errors exist in the issues Nos. 389 to 438, and the list might be extended almost indefinitely.

(Des C. Fernandes. Eng J. S. de Carvalho e Silva. Typo)

1914 (12 Mar). Name and value in black. Chalk-surfaced paper. P 15×14.

439	**33**	1r. brown-olive	70	60
440		1½r. yellow-green	70	60
441		2r. black	1·00	65
442		2½r. deep grey-green	1·00	65
443		3r. grey-lilac	1·20	65
444		4½r. brown-red	1·20	65
445		5r. deep green	1·20	65
446		6r. pale brown	1·20	65
447		9r. cobalt-blue	1·30	70
448		10r. carmine	1·60	90
449		1t. violet	2·50	90
450		2t. deep blue	2·75	1·20
451		3t. yellow-brown	3·75	1·50
452		4t. slate	2·75	1·80
453		8t. claret	7·75	6·50
454		12t. chocolate/*green*	7·00	5·50
455		1rp. brown/*rose*	32·00	18·00
456		2rp. orange/*salmon*	19·00	15·00
457		3rp. deep green/*azure*	22·00	15·00
439/457	*Set of 19*	£100	65·00

The 1, 2, 2½, 3, 4½, 5, 6 and 10r., and the 1 and 3t., exist on glazed paper.

1915. Provisionals of 1902–5 optd with T **27**, in red.

458	22	2t. blue (11½) (321)	1·80	1·70
459		2t. on 2½t. dull blue (337)	2·30	1·70
460	20	5t. on 8t. (13½) (314)	2·75	2·00
458/460	*Set of 3*		

1915–23.

(a) Unsurfaced paper. P 15×14 (1915–19)

461	**33**	1r. brown-olive	1·60	1·50
462		1½r. pale green	1·60	1·50
463		2r. black (1919)	1·60	1·50
464		2½r. olive-green (1919)	1·60	1·50
465		3r. grey-lilac (1916)	1·60	1·50
466		4½r. brown-red (1919)	1·60	1·50
467		6r. chocolate (1916)	1·60	1·50
468		1t. violet (1916)	1·60	1·50
469		2t. deep blue (1916)	1·60	1·50
461/469	*Set of 9*	13·00	12·00

(b) Unsurfaced paper. P 12×11½ (1921–23)

470	**33**	1r. brown-olive	1·60	1·50
471		1½r. pale-green	1·60	1·50
472		2r. black	2·10	2·00

PORTUGUESE INDIA

473		3r. grey-lilac (1922)	1·60	1·50
474		4r. blue (1922)	2·00	1·40
475		4½r. brown-red	6·50	6·00
476		5r. deep green	18·00	16·00
477		6r. chocolate	1·30	1·20
478		9r. cobalt blue	3·75	3·00
479		10r. carmine	4·25	3·50
480		1t. violet	5·75	4·25
481		1½t. olive-green (1922)	2·00	90
482		2t. deep blue	5·75	4·25
483		2½t. turquoise (1922)	2·00	90
484		3t. 4r. yellow-brown (1923)	7·00	3·25
485		4t. slate	5·75	4·25
486		8t. brown-red (1922)	9·50	7·00
	(c) Glazed paper. P 12×11½ (1922)			
487	33	1rp. grey-brown	26·00	20·00
488		2rp. yellow	27·00	20·00
489		3rp. emerald	41·00	33·00
490		5rp. bright carmine	47·00	37·00
470/490 *Set of 21*			£200	£150

CHARITY TAX STAMPS. Stamps bearing C numbers were for compulsory use on internal letters on certain days of the year as an additional postal tax for public charities. Other values in some of the types were for use on telegrams or for fiscal purposes.

1919 (15 Apr). CHARITY TAX. Fiscal stamp as Type C **1** of Portuguese Colonies and Overseas Territories optd "TAXA DE GUERRA". P 15×14.
C491	Rps. 0:00:05, 48, green	3·50	2·75
C492	Rps. 0:02:03, 43, green (R.)	7·50	4·75

Another value, Rps. 0:01:09, 94 was for fiscal use.

1922 (June). Surch locally "1½ REAL", as T **31**, in red. P 15×14.
(a) Chalk surfaced paper
491	33	1½r. on 2r. black	1·00	70

(b) Unsurfaced paper
492	33	1½r. on 2r. black	1·50	1·40

Also exists on glazed paper.

 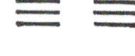

34 Vasco da Gama and Flagship *São Gabriel* 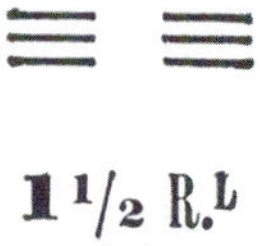   (**35**)

(Des P. Ramos. Litho in Goa)

1925 (30 Jan). 400th Death Anniv of Vasco da Gama. No gum. P 11½.
493	34	6r. brown	7·00	4·25
494		1t. magenta	9·50	4·25

1925 (8 May). Marquis de Pombal Commemoration.
(a) CHARITY TAX. As Nos. C323/5 of St. Thomas and Prince Islands
C495	27	6r. rose	70	65
C496	28	6r. rose	70	65
C497	29	6r. rose	70	65

(b) POSTAGE DUE. As Nos. D323/5 of St. Thomas and Prince Islands (optd with T 30)
D495	27	1t. rose	55	55
D496	28	1t. rose	55	55
D497	29	1t. rose	55	55
C495/D497 *Set of 6*			3·50	3·25

Nos. C495/7 were in use from 8 to 13 May 1925 and from 5 to 15 May in 1926 and 1929. Nos. D495/7 were used in default.

1931–32. Surch as T **35**.
(a) Chalk-surfaced paper. P 15×14
495	33	1½r. on 8t. claret (1932)	5·75	3·25

(b) Unsurfaced paper. P 12×11½
496	33	1½r. on 8t. dull claret (1932)	4·00	2·75
497		2½r. on 3t.4r. yellow-brown	70·00	60·00

No. 496 was not issued without surcharge.

36 The Signature of Francis   **37** St. Francis Xavier

38 Bom Jesus Church, Goa   **39** St. Francis's Tomb

(Typo Security Printing Press, Nasik, India)

1931 (3 Dec). St. Francis Xavier Exhibition. T **36/9** (and similar types). P 14.
498	–	1r. blue-green	1·10	1·00
499	36	2r. purple-brown	1·20	1·00
500	–	6r. purple	2·30	1·10
501	37	1½t. yellow-brown	8·00	5·50
502	38	2t. blue	13·50	7·75
503	39	2½t. rosine	19·00	8·00
498/503 *Set of 6*			41·00	22·00

Designs: Vert—1r. Monument to St. Francis; 6r. St. Francis in surplice and cassock.

40 "Portugal" and Galeasse    (**41**)

(Eng A. Fragoso. Typo)

1933. W **33** of St. Thomas and Prince Islands. P 11½×12.
504	40	1r. bistre-brown	30	25
505		2r. sepia	30	25
506		4r. mauve	30	25
507		6r. blue-green	30	25
508		8r. black	65	50
509		1t. grey	65	50
510		1½t. carmine	65	50
511		2t. brown	65	50
512		2½t. blue	2·00	80
513		3t. turquoise	2·40	80
514		5t. vermilion	3·50	80
515		1rp. olive-green	8·50	3·25
516		2rp. carmine	17·00	8·50
517		3rp. orange	23·00	13·00
518		5rp. yellow-green	48·00	31·00
504/518 *Set of 15*			95·00	55·00

1938 (1 Sept). As Nos. 344/70 of St. Thomas and Prince Islands, inscr "ESTADO DA INDIA".
(a) POSTAGE
519	34	1r. grey-olive	30	25
520		2r. orange-brown	30	25
521		3r. slate-violet	30	25
522		6r. emerald-green	30	25
523	35	10r. carmine	65	40
524		1t. magenta	65	40
525		1½t. scarlet	65	40
526	–	2t. orange	65	40
527	–	2½t. blue	65	40
528	–	3t. slate	1·40	50
529	–	5t. bright purple	2·50	65
530	–	1rp. lake	6·50	1·30
531	–	2rp. olive-green	10·00	3·75
532	–	3rp. ultramarine	19·00	8·75
533	–	5rp. red-brown	38·00	10·50
519/533 *Set of 15*			75·00	26·00

Designs:—2 to 3t. Prince Henry the Navigator; 5t. to 2rp. Dam; 5rp. Afonso de Albuquerque.

(b) AIR
534	36	1t. scarlet	2·00	95
535		2½t. bright violet	2·00	95
536		3½t. orange	2·00	95
537		4½t. bright blue	2·00	95
538		7t. brown-lake	2·40	95
539		7½t. blue-green	2·75	95
540		9t. red-brown	9·25	2·75
541		11t. magenta	10·00	2·75
534/541 *Set of 8*			29·00	10·00

PORTUGUESE INDIA

1942. Surch with T **41**, in Lisbon.
542	**40**	1t. on 1½r. carmine	3·75	3·00
543		1t. on 1rp. olive-green	3·75	3·00
544		1t. on 2rp. claret	3·75	3·00
545		1t. on 5rp. yellow-green	3·75	3·00
542/545 Set of 4			13·50	11·00

(42) (43) (44)

1942 (Jan)–**45**. Surch locally with T **42/4**.
546	**40**	1r. on 5t. vermilion (B.) (1945)	1·30	1·00
547		3r. on 1½t. carmine	1·30	1·10
548		1t. on 2t. brown	3·25	2·50
546/548 Set of 3			5·00	4·00

(D 45) (46) D 47

1943. POSTAGE DUE. Optd locally with Type D **45** and surch as T **44**.
D549	**40**	3r. on 2½t. blue (R.)	65	55
D550		6r. on 3t. turquoise (R.)	1·50	85
D551		1t. on 5t. vermilion	2·75	2·30
D549/551 Set of 3			4·00	3·00

1944–46. Surch locally as T **46**.
549	**40**	1r. on 8r. black (R.) (1946)	1·30	1·00
550		2r. on 8r. black (R.)	1·30	1·00
551		3r. on 2t. brown (1946)	1·30	1·10
552		3r. on 3rp. orange (B.) (1945)	3·25	2·50
553		6r. on 2½t. blue (R.) (1945)	3·25	2·50
554		6r. on 3t. turquoise (1946)	3·25	2·50
549/554 Set of 6			12·50	9·50

(Des and eng M. Norte. Typo)

1945. POSTAGE DUE. P 11½×12.
D555	D **47**	2r. black and carmine	1·20	1·10
D556		3r. black and blue	1·20	1·10
D557		4r. black and yellow	1·20	1·10
D558		6r. black and green	1·20	1·10
D559		1t. black and brown	1·50	1·30
D560		2t. black and chocolate	1·50	1·30
D555/560 Set of 6			7·00	6·25

48 St. Francis Xavier
49 Viceregal Archway
50 D. João de Castro 

(Des A. de Sousa, all except 2 and 9 reis. Litho Litografia Nacional. Oporto)

1946. T **48** and similar vert portrait designs and T **49**. P 11–11½.
555		1r. black and grey	75	40
556		2r. claret and rose	75	40
557		6r. bistre and buff	75	40
558		7r. violet and mauve	3·25	1·30
559		9r. chocolate and buff	3·25	1·30
560		1t. green and pale green	3·25	1·30
561		3½t. blue and pale blue	3·50	1·80
562		1rp. maroon and bistre	8·00	2·20
555/562 Set of 8			21·00	8·25
MS563 169×280 mm. Nos. 555/62 (sold at 1½rp.)			47·00	42·00

Portraits:—2r. Luis de Camoens; 6r. Garcia de Orta, 7r. Beato João Brito; 1t. Afonso de Albuquerque; 3½t. Vasco da Gama; 1rp. D. Francisco de Almeida.

(Des A. de Sousa. Litho Litografia Nacional, Oporto)

1948. As T **50** (vert historical portraits). P 11½.
564		3r. blue and pale blue	1·80	90
565		1t. green and yellow-green	2·00	1·10
566		1½t. purple and mauve	3·00	2·10
567		2½t. vermilion and salmon	4·00	2·50
568		7½t. maroon and red-brown	6·00	3·50
564/568 Set of 5			15·00	9·00
MS569 108×149 mm. Nos. 564/8 (sold at 1rp.). P 14½			49·00	44·00

Designs:—1t. St. Francis Xavier; 1½t. P. José Vaz; 2½t. D. Luis de Ataide; 7½t. Duarte Pacheco Pereira.

51 Our Lady of Fatima
C **52** Mother and Child
53 Our Lady of Fatima

1948 (Oct). Honouring the Statue of Our Lady of Fatima. P 14.
570	**51**	1t. blue-green	6·00	4·75

For No. 570 in miniature sheet see No. **MS**1 of Portuguese Colonies and Overseas Territories.

(Des J. Franco. Litho Public Assistance, Goa)

1948 (1 Nov)–**56**. CHARITY TAX. Inscr "ASSISTENCIA PUBLICA". P 11.
C571	C **52**	6r. yellow-green	5·50	3·25
C572		6r. pale yellow (1953)	3·75	2·50
C573		1t. carmine	5·50	3·25
C574		1t. red-orange (1953)	3·75	2·50
C575		1t. deep blue-green (1956)	6·00	3·50
C571/575 Set of 5			22·00	13·50

See also No. C607.

(Litho Litografia Nacional, Oporto)

1949. Honouring the Statue of Our Lady of Fatima. P 14.
571	**53**	1r. light blue and greenish blue	1·50	1·10
572		3r. yellow, orange and lemon	1·50	1·10
573		9r. carmine and magenta	2·20	1·30
574		2t. green and pale green	8·00	2·20
575		9t. scarlet and vermilion	7·00	3·25
576		2rp. brown and maroon	13·50	4·25
577		5rp. black and olive-green	26·00	11·00
578		8rp. blue and violet	55·00	19·00
571/578 Set of 8			£100	39·00

54 Globe and Letter
55 Bells and Dove

1949 (Oct). 75th Anniv of Universal Postal Union. P 14.
579	**54**	2½t. scarlet	7·25	3·00

1950 (May). Holy Year (1st issue). T **55** and similar vert design. P 13½.
580		1r. bistre	1·70	65
581		2t. bronze green	2·20	1·00

Design:—2t. Angel holding candelabra.
For No. 580 in miniature sheet see No. **MS**2 of Portuguese Colonies and Overseas Territories.
See also Nos. 588/95.

(56) (D 57)

PORTUGUESE INDIA

1950–51. Nos. 523 and 527 surch locally as T **56**.

582	1 real on 10r. carmine		65	55
583	1 real on 2½t. blue (1951)		65	55
584	2 reis on 10r. carmine		65	55
585	3 réis on 2½t. blue (R.) (1951)		65	55
	a. "ê" for "é"		2·40	2·30
586	6 réis on 2½t. blue (R.) (1951)		65	55
	a. "ê" for "é"		2·40	2·30
587	1 tanga on 2½t. blue (R.) (1951)		65	55
582/587 Set of 6			3·50	3·00

No. 585a occurs in positions 8, 12, 65, 81 to 87 and 91 to 100; No. 586a in positions 2 to 12, 16 to 21 and 83.

1951 (1 Jan). POSTAGE DUE. Nos. 558 and 562 surch locally as Type D **57**.

D588	2r. on 7r. violet and mauve (R.)	70	65
D589	3r. on 7r. violet and mauve (R.)	70	65
D590	1t. on 1rp. maroon and bistre	70	65
D591	2t. on 1rp. maroon and bistre	70	65
D588/591 Set of 4			

1951 (Feb). Holy Year (2nd issue). As Nos. 580/1. P 13½.

588	**55**	1r. carmine	65	40
589	–	2r. light green	65	40
590	–	3r. purple-brown	65	40
591	**55**	6r. grey	65	40
592	–	9r. pale magenta	1·70	1·10
593	**55**	1t. violet-blue	1·70	1·10
594	–	2t. yellow	1·70	1·10
595	**55**	4t. chocolate	1·70	1·10
588/595 Set of 8			8·50	5·50

58 Our Lady of Fatima

59 Father José Vaz

(C **60**)

1951 (Oct). Termination of Holy Year. P 14.

596	**58**	1rp. deep ultramarine and pale grey	2·40	1·70

No. 596 was issued se-tenant with a stamp-size label bearing a papal declaration.

(Litho Litografia de Portugal, Lisbon)

1951. Tercentenary of Birth of Father José Vaz. T **59** and similar vert designs inscr "1651–1951". P 14.

597	**59**	1r. blue-grey and slate	25	15
598	–	2r. orange and chestnut	25	15
599	**59**	3r. grey and black	85	40
600	–	1t. ultramarine and indigo	40	35
601	**59**	2t. claret and maroon	40	35
602	–	3r. grey-green and black	70	40
603	**59**	9t. blue-violet and deep blue	70	40
604	–	10t. reddish violet and mauve	1·80	95
605	–	12t. grey-brown and black	3·25	1·30
597/605 Set of 9			7·75	4·00

Designs:—2r., 1r., 3t., 10t. Ruins of Sancoale Church; 12t. Veneravel Altar.

1951. CHARITY TAX. Surch locally with Type C **60**.

C606	C **52**	1t. on 6r. carmine	5·25	2·75

(Litho Costa and Valerio, Lisbon)

1952. CHARITY TAX. Inscr "PROVEDORIA DE ASSISTENCIA PUBLICA". P 12½.

C607	C **52**	1t. olive-grey	6·50	3·50

D **60**

60 Goa Medical School

(Litho Litografia Nacional, Oporto, Portugal)

1952 (15 Mar). POSTAGE DUE. P 14.

D606	D **60**	2r. multicoloured	30	20
D607		3r. multicoloured	30	20
D608		6r. multicoloured	40	20
D609		1t. multicoloured	45	35
D610		2t. multicoloured	1·10	75
D611		10t. multicoloured	4·00	3·50
D606/611 Set of 6			6·00	4·75

(Des A. de Sousa. Litho The Mint, Lisbon)

1952 (June). First Tropical Medicine Congress, Lisbon. P 13½.

606	**60**	4½t. turquoise and black	7·00	3·00

61 St. Francis Xavier Statue

62 St. Francis Xavier

(Litho Litografia Nacional, Oporto, Portugal)

1952 (25 Oct). Fourth Death Centenary of St. Francis Xavier. T **61** and similar vert designs, and T **62**. P 14.

607	6r. multicoloured (T **61**)	45	35
608	2t. multicoloured (Miraculous Arm of St. Francis)	3·00	75
609	5t. bronze green, silver and light magenta (Tomb of St. Francis)	6·00	1·70
607/609 Set of 3		8·50	2·50
MS610 76×65 mm. 4t. bronze-green, silver and ochre (as No. 609 but smaller); 8t. slate (T **62**)		24·00	21·00
MS611 90×100 mm. 9t. sepia and yellow-brown (T **62**)		24·00	21·00

63 Stamp of 1871

64 The Virgin

(Litho Litografia Nacional, Oporto)

1952 (4 Dec). Philatelic Exhibition, Goa. P 13½.

612	**63**	3t. black	19·00	16·00
		a. Vert strip. Nos. 612/13 plus label	39·00	33·00
613	**62**	5t. black and lilac	19·00	16·00

Nos. 612/13 were issued together in sheets comprising two rows of stamps (one row of each value), tête-bêche, separated by a row of square grey labels, showing arms of Goa, arranged sideways.

1953 (Jan). Missionary Art Exhibition. Litho. P 13½.

614	**64**	6r. black and azure	30	20
615		1t. yellow-brown and buff	1·30	1·00
616		3t. slate-lilac and olive-yellow	4·00	2·00
614/616 Set of 3			5·00	3·00

(C **65**)

66 Dr. Gama Pinto

67 Academy Buildings

1953. CHARITY TAX. No. C573 optd with Type C **65**.

C617	C **52**	1t. carmine	15·00	7·75

1953 (Oct). Portuguese Stamp Centenary. As No. 426 of St. Thomas and Prince Islands.

617	1t. multicoloured	1·80	1·20

1954 (10 Apr). Birth Centenary of Dr. Gama Pinto. Litho. P 12.

618	**66**	3r. sage-green and grey	40	20
619		2t. slate-black and indigo	90	50

1954 (2 Oct). Fourth Centenary of São Paulo. As No. 429 of St. Thomas and Prince Islands.

620	2t. multicoloured	1·00	55

(Des J. de Moura. Litho)

1955 (26 Feb). Centenary of Afonso de Albuquerque National Academy. P 13½.

621	**67**	9t. black, red, green and blue	2·50	75

212

PORTUGUESE INDIA

68 Mgr. Daigado

C **69** Mother and Child

C **70** Mother and Child

1955 (15 Nov). Centenary of Birth of Mgr. Dalgado. Litho. P 13½.
622	**68**	1r. magenta, blk, grey, pale grn and red	50	20
623		1t. mag, blk, flesh, pale grn and dp maroon	90	35

1956. CHARITY TAX. Surch as in Type C **69** Litho. P 11.
C624	C **69**	1t. on 4t. pale blue	19·00	12·00

1956–58. CHARITY TAX. Litho. P 13.
C625	C **70**	1t. black, pale green and red	1·30	65
C626		1t. deep blue, salmon and green (1958)	1·10	65

71 M. A. de Sousa

72 F. de Almeida

73 Map of Baçaim

(Litho Litografia Nacional, Oporto (Nos. 624/9); The Mint, Lisbon (630/5); Litografia Maia, Oporto (636/41))

1956 (24 Mar). 450th Anniv of Portuguese Settlements in India. Multicoloured designs.

*(a) Famous Men. Various vert portraits as T **71**. P 14½*
624		6r. M. A. de Sousa	45	35
625		1½t. F. N. Xavier	45	35
626		4t. A. V. Lourenço	45	40
627		8t. Father José Vaz	1·10	55
628		9t. M. G. de Herédia	1·10	55
629		2rp. A. C. Pacheco	4·50	2·75
624/629		Set of 6	7·25	4·50

*(b) Viceroys. Various vert portraits as T **72**. P 11½×12*
630		3r. F. de Almeida	45	35
631		9r. A. de Albuquerque	45	35
632		1t. Vasco da Gama	65	45
633		3t. N. da Cunha	95	45
634		10t. J. de Castro	1·30	45
635		3rp. C. de Bragança	6·25	3·00
630/635		Set of 6	9·00	4·50

*(c) Settlements. Various vert views as T **73**. P 13*
636		2t. Baçaim	5·25	3·00
637		2½t. Mombaim	2·40	1·70
638		3½t. Damão	2·40	1·70
639		5t. Diu	1·10	75
640		12t. Cochim	1·80	85
641		1rp. Goa	4·25	2·50
636/641		Set of 6	11·00	10·00

74 Map of Damão, Dadrá and Nagar Aveli Districts

(74a)

75 Arms of Vasco da Gama

(Litho The Mint, Lisbon)

1957 (Aug). P 11½×12.
642	**74**	3r. multicoloured	25	20
643		6r. multicoloured	25	20
644		3t. multicoloured	40	30
645		6t. multicoloured	40	30
646		11t. multicoloured	1·30	55
647		2rp. multicoloured	2·20	1·20
648		3rp. multicoloured	3·25	2·50
649		5rp. multicoloured	5·25	3·25
642/649		Set of 8	12·00	7·75

1957. CHARITY TAX. No. C625 surch with T **74a**.
C650	C **70**	6r. on 1t. black, pale green and red (R.)	1·80	95

(Des J. de Moura. Litho)

1958 (3 Apr). Heraldic Arms of Famous Men. Various multicoloured designs as T **75**. P 13½.
650		2r. Vasco da Gama	40	30
651		6r. Lopo Soares de Albergaria	40	30
652		9r. D. Francisco de Almeida	40	30
653		1t. Garcia de Noronha	45	35
654		4t. Afonso de Albuquerque	45	40
655		5t. D. João de Castro	90	40
656		11t. D. Luis de Ataide	1·50	1·20
657		1rp. Nuno do Cunha	2·30	1·30
650/657		Set of 8	6·00	4·00

Stamps in similar values and design to the above were prepared for release on 28 February 1957, but were never placed on sale in Goa.

1958 (5 Sept). Sixth International Congress of Tropical Medicine Diamond-shaped design similar to No. 431 of St. Thomas and Prince Islands. Multicoloured.
658		5t. *Holarrhena antidysenterica*	1·50	1·00

1958 (15 Dec). Brussels International Exhibition As T **78** of Macao.
659		1rp. multicoloured	1·00	85

$40

(76) (77)

1959. New Currency. Various issues surch as Types **76** or **77**.

*(a) Surch with small figures as T **76** (1.1.59)*
660		5c. on 2r. (No. 650)	45	40
661		10c. on 3r. (No. 642)	45	40
662		15c. on 6r. (No. 651)	45	40
663		20c. on 9r. (No. 652)	45	40
664		30c. on 1t. (No. 653)	45	40
665		40c. on 2t. (No. 636)	45	40
666		40c. on 2½t. (No. 637)	1·00	75
667		40c. on 3½t. (No. 638)	45	40
668		50c. on 3t. (No. 644)	45	40
669		80c. on 3t. (No. 633)	1·70	75
670		80c. on 10t. (No. 634)	1·00	75
671		80c. on 3rp. (No. 635)	1·70	75
672		1E. on 4t. (No. 654)	45	40
673		1E.50 on 6t. (No. 655)	75	40
674		2E. on 6t. (No. 645)	45	40
675		2E.50 on 11t. (No. 646)	1·00	40
676		4E. on 11t. (No. 656)	1·30	75
677		4E.50 on 1rp. (No. 657)	1·80	1·10
678		5E. on 2rp. (No. 647)	1·70	75
679		10E. on 3rp. (No. 648)	2·50	1·90
680		30E. on 5rp. (No. 649)	7·50	1·90
660/680		Set of 21	24·00	13·00

*(b) Surch with large figures as T **77** (5.59)*
681		40c. on 1½t. (No. 566)	45	40
682		40c. on 1½t. (No. 625)	45	40
683		40c. on 2t. (No. 620)	45	40
684		80c. on 3t. (No. 616)	45	40
685		80c. on 3½t. (No. 561)	45	40
686		80c. on 5t. (No. 658)	1·80	55
687		80c. on 1rp. (No. 659)	3·50	1·90
681/687		Set of 7	6·50	4·00

1959 (Jan). CHARITY TAX. No. C626 surch as T **77** but with four bars.
C688	C **70**	20c. on 1t. deep blue, salmon and green	85	65
C689		40c. on 1t. deep blue, salmon and green	85	65

213

1959 (Jan). POSTAGE DUE. Nos. D606/8, D610/11 surch as T **76** (5c.) or T **77** (others).

D688	D **60**	5c. on 2r. multicoloured	40	30
D689		10c. on 3r. multicoloured	40	30
D690		15c. on 6r. multicoloured	55	45
D691		60c. on 2t. multicoloured	1·70	1·40
D692		60c. on 10t. multicoloured	5·00	4·00
D688/692 Set of 5			6·75	5·75

On No. D692 the surcharge has three thick bars cancelling the old value, on Nos. D688/91 there are four thinner bars.

78 Coin of Manoel I   **79** Prince Henry's Arms   C **80** Arms and People

(Litho The Mint, Lisbon)

1959 (1 Dec). Portuguese Indian Coins. T **78** and similar vert designs showing both sides of coins of various rulers. Multicoloured. P 13½.

688	5c. Type **78**	25	20
689	10c. João III	25	20
690	15c. Sebastião	25	20
691	30c. Filipe I	45	40
692	40c. Filipe II	45	40
693	50c. Filipe III	55	20
694	60c. João IV	55	20
695	80c. Afonso VI	55	20
696	1E. Pedro II	55	20
697	1E.50 João V	55	20
698	2E. José I	85	50
699	2E.50 Maria I	90	40
700	3E. Prince Regent João	90	50
701	4E. Pedro IV	90	55
702	4E.40 Miguel	1·20	75
703	5E. Maria II	1·20	75
704	10E. Pedro V	1·80	1·60
705	20E. Luis	4·00	3·25
706	30E. Carlos	6·00	4·00
707	50E. Portuguese Republic	9·50	5·25
688/707 Set of 20		28·00	18·00

(Des J. de Moura. Litho The Mint, Lisbon)

1960 (25 June). Fifth Death Centenary of Prince Henry the Navigator. P 13×13½.

708	**79**	3E. multicoloured	2·40	1·00

(Litho The Mint, Lisbon)

1960. CHARITY TAX. P 13.

C709	C **80**	20c. brown and red	85	65

Indian troops invaded and occupied Portuguese India on 17 December 1961 and the territories were incorporated in India. The sale of Portuguese Indian stamps ceased on 28 December 1961 but their use continued until 7 January 1962.

A set of six sports stamps similar to Nos. 434/9 of St. Thomas and Prince Islands was ready for issue when the invasion took place but was not put on sale in Portuguese India.

Nos. 688/707 and 708 exist overprinted "INDIA" and surcharged in Indian currency. These were not issued.

BRITISH INDIA POST OFFICE AT DAMÃO

A British post office was open in Damão by 1823 and unoverprinted Indian stamps were used there until November 1883, some with "13" and "3/B-19" numeral cancellations.

No other British post offices were opened in Portuguese India, but from 1854 Indian stamps were sold by the local post offices. Between 1871 and 1877 mail intended for, or passing through, British India required combined franking of India and Portuguese India issues. After 1877 the two postal administrations accepted the validity of each other's stamps.

St. Thomas & Prince Islands

1870. 1000 Reis = 1 Milreis
1913. 100 Centavos = 1 Escudo

The island São Tome (330 square miles) and Principe (42 square miles), in the Gulf of Guinea, were uninhabited when discovered by the Portuguese explorers Joao Gomes and Pedro Escobar in 1471. The first inhabitants, in 1493, were Portuguese criminals and young Jews taken from their parents to be baptised. In the 16th century the islands were prosperous with 80 sugar mills and a population of 50,000, but great damage was done by French and Dutch attacks during the wars of the next two centuries, and prosperity did not return until cocoa plantations were started after 1890. On 11 June 1951 the islands became an Overseas Province of Portugal.

King Luis
11 November 1861–19 October 1889

REPRINTS. Reprints of some of the following issues were made in 1885 and 1905 as indicated in the footnotes. These can generally be distinguished as follows:—

1885 reprints are on stout very white paper, usually ungummed but sometimes with white gum having yellowish spots. They are generally perf 13½ with large clean-cut holes producing sharp pointed teeth. Some also exist perf 12½ and these are indicated in the footnotes.

1905 reprints are on creamy white paper of ordinary quality with shiny white gum, all perf 13½.

1

(Des and eng A. F. Gerard. Typo The Mint, Lisbon)

1870. Thick paper. P 12½.

1	**1**	5r. black	40·00	23·00
2		10r. orange	40·00	27·00
		a. Pale orange	40·00	27·00
3		20r. deep bistre	30·00	23·00
		a. Olive-bistre	30·00	23·00
4		25r. red	23·00	13·50
		a. Rose	23·00	13·50
5		50r. green	44·00	27·00
		a. Yellow-green	44·00	27·00
6		100r. bright lilac	47·00	27·00
		a. Dull purple	47·00	27·00

Nos. 1/5 are all Plate 1.

Pl. 1   Pl. 2   Pl. 1   Pl. 2

Pl. 1   Pl. 2   Pl. 1   Pl. 2

The different types of the 20r. and 25r. respectively only occur in different colours.

1875–77. Paper varying in substance. Two plates of each value up to and including the 50r.

(a) P 12½

7	**1**	5r. black (Pl. 1)	4·50	3·00
8		5r. black (Pl. 2)	4·50	3·00
9		10r. orange (Pl. 1)	38·00	23·00
		a. Orange-buff	38·00	23·00
10		20r. deep bistre	8·25	4·25
		a. Olive-bistre	8·25	4·25
11		25r. crimson	5·50	2·30
		a. Rose	5·50	2·30
		b. Pale rose	5·50	2·30
12		40r. deep blue (Pl. 1)	9·50	6·50
		a. Blue	9·50	6·50
13		50r. deep green (P1.1)	41·00	23·00
		a. Green (1877)	41·00	23·00
14		100r. dull purple	16·00	14·50
15		200r. red-orange (1.1.77)	20·00	16·00
16		300r. chocolate (1.1.77)	20·00	16·00
7/16 Set of 9 *(cheapest)*			£150	£100

(b) P 13½

17	1	5r. black (Pl. 1)	4·50	3·00
18		10r. pale orange (Pl. 1)	31·00	16·00
19		10r. pale orange (Pl. 2)	31·00	16·00
20		20r. deep bistre	6·75	4·25
		a. Bistre	6·75	4·25
21		25r. crimson	3·50	2·10
		a. Rose	3·50	2·10
		b. Pale rose	3·50	2·10
22		40r. blue (Pl. 1)	10·00	7·50
23		40r. deep blue (Pl. 2)	10·00	7·50
24		50r. deep green (Pl. 1)	31·00	23·00
25		50r. green (Pl. 2)	31·00	23·00
26		100r. dull purple	16·00	8·75
		a. Lilac-grey	16·00	8·75
		b. Slate-lilac	16·00	8·75
27		300r. chocolate (1877)	18·00	10·50
17/27 *Set of 8 (cheapest)*			£110	70·00

The issues of 1875–85, like those of Angola of the same period, were first on thin hard paper, varying a little in thickness. The later printings were on *thicker soft* paper.

The 5, 10, 40 and 50r. all Plate 2 as well as the remaining values were reprinted in 1885 and 1905. Some values in the 1885 reprints are known perf 12½.

1881–85. Colours changed.

(a) P 12½

28	1	10r. grey-green (Pl. 1)	14·00	8·50
29		10r. grey-green (Pl. 2)	14·00	8·50
30		20r. rosine (1885)	7·00	5·00
31		25r. dull lilac (1885)	5·75	3·50
32		40r. yellow-buff (Pl. 1)	10·00	8·50
33		50r. pale blue (Pl. 1)	4·50	3·50
		a. Deep blue	4·50	3·50
34		50r. deep blue (Pl. 2)	4·50	3·50
		a. Indigo	4·50	3·50

(b) P 13½

35	1	10r. deep green (Pl. 1)	19·00	10·50
		a. Grey-green	19·00	10·50
36		40r. yellow-buff (Pl. 1)	12·50	9·25
37		50r. pale blue (Pl. 1)	4·50	3·25
		a. Deep blue	4·50	3·25

The 10, 40 and 50r. all Plate 2 and the 20 and 25r. were reprinted in 1885 and 1905.

2

(Des and eng F. A. de Campos. Head embossed, frame typo The Mint, Lisbon)

1887 (29 June–19 July). Chalk-surfaced paper.

(a) P 12½

38	2	5r. black (29.6)	8·25	6·50
39		20r. rosine	£160	£130
40		50r. blue	11·50	5·00
		a. Pale blue	11·50	5·00

(b) P 13½

41	2	5r. black (29.6)	14·00	4·25
42		10r. green (29.6)	14·00	4·75
43		20r. rosine	16·00	5·00
		a. Printed on unsurfaced side	80·00	80·00
44		25r. bright mauve	9·00	3·50
		a. Doubly embossed		
45		40r. chocolate (29.6)	9·00	5·00
46		50r. blue	11·50	4·75
		a. Pale blue	11·00	4·75
47		100r. yellow-brown (29.6)	9·00	4·75
		a. Bisected (50r.) (Aug. 1888)	—	29·00
48		200r. lavender (29.6)	31·00	17·00
49		300r. orange (29.6)	23·00	17·00

The 5, 10, 40, 100, 200 and 300r. were reprinted in 1905.

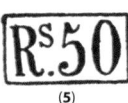

5 réis (**3**)

5 cinco réis (**4**)

Rs.50 (**5**)

1889–91. T **2** surch locally. No gum. P 13½.

50	3	5r. on 10r. blue-green (8.89)	65·00	55·00
51	4	5r. on 20r. rosine (25.12.89)	65·00	55·00
52	5	50r. on 40r. chocolate (25.6.91)	£250	£200

There are two minor varieties of the figures in T **3**, and T **3** and **4** exist without the accent.

Stamps with surcharge inverted or double, or with "5" inverted and other varieties were not officially issued.

2½RS. (N **6**)

2 ½ rs. (N **7**)

N **8**

1892 (2 Oct). NEWSPAPER. No gum. P 13½. Surch locally.

(a) With Type N **6**

N53	2	2½r. on 5r. black (G.)	80·00	65·00
N54		2½r. on 10r. green	£100	95·00
		a. Green surch	£110	£110
N55		2½r. on 20r. rosine	£160	£130
		a. Green surch	£190	£160

(b) With Type N **7**

N56	2	2½r. on 5r. black (G.)	£200	£140
N57		2½r. on 10r. green	£160	£130
		a. Green surch	£190	£160
N58		2½r. on 20r. rosine	£200	£160
		a. Green surch	£275	£200
		b. Surch double (Bk.+G.)	£375	£300

Other errors exist but were not officially issued.

(Des and eng E. C. Azedo Gneco. Typo The Mint, Lisbon)

1893 (1 Oct). NEWSPAPER. Unsurfaced paper.

N59	N 8	2½r. brown (p. 11½)	1·40	1·30
N60		2½r. brown (p. 13½)	1·40	1·30

Stamps of this type could be, and often were, used for franking ordinary correspondence.

King Carlos
19 October 1889–1 February 1908

9

10

PROVISORIO

(N **11**)

(Des and eng M. D. Neto. Typo The Mint, Lisbon)

1895 (30 Mar–20 Apr). Chalk-surfaced paper or enamel-surfaced paper (E).

(a) P 11½

53	9	15r. red-brown (E) (20.4)	3·50	2·10
54		20r. lilac (E)	3·50	2·30
55		75r. rose (E) (20.4)	9·00	6·50
56		100r. brown/*buff* (20.4)	8·75	6·50
57		150r. carmine/*rose* (20.4)	11·50	8·50
58		200r. blue/*blue* (20.4)	16·00	13·00
59		300r. blue/*pale brown* (20.4)	18·00	14·50
53/59 *Set of 7*			65·00	48·00

(b) P 12½

60	9	5r. yellow (E)	1·80	1·70
61		10r. rosy mauve (E)	2·20	1·40
62		25r. green (E)	3·50	1·40
63		50r. pale blue (E)	3·50	1·40
64		80r. pale green (E) (20.4)	20·00	16·00

(c) P 13½

65	9	50r. pale blue (E)	4·00	2·50

(Des and eng E. Mouchon. Typo The Mint, Lisbon)

1898 (1 Aug)–**1901**. Name and value in black, on 500r. in carmine. P 11½.

66	10	2½r. pale grey	50	35
		a. Error. Green	55·00	55·00
67		5r. orange-red	70	35
68		10r. green	70	50
69		15r. chocolate	2·10	1·70
70		20r. deep lilac	1·30	75
71		25r. blue-green	80	50
72		50r. blue	1·20	75
73		75r. rose	21·00	11·50
74		80r. mauve	10·50	10·00
75		100r. blue/*blue*	3·50	3·25
76		150r. purple-brown/*straw*	4·25	3·00
77		200r. purple/*flesh*	8·00	5·75

78		300r. blue/*pink*	11·50	6·25
79		500r. black/*azure* (1901)	12·50	9·00
80		700r. mauve/*yellow* (1901)	25·00	19·00
66/80 *Set of* 15			95·00	65·00

See also Nos. 113/20.

1899 (23 Jan). NEWSPAPER. Optd locally with Type N **11**, in blue. No gum.

N81	N **8**	2½r. brown (p. 11½)	75·00	35·00
		a. Opt inverted	£110	75·00
N82		2½r. brown (p. 13½)	75·00	35·00
		a. Opt inverted	£110	75·00

(12)  (13)

1902. Surch as T **12**.

81	**2**	65r. on 20r. (12½)	16·00	7·00
82		65r. on 20r. (13½)	48·00	25·00
83		65r. on 25r. (13½)	10·00	6·50
84		65r. on 100r. (13½)	10·00	6·50
85	**9**	65r. on 5r. (E) (12½)	8·00	5·00
86		65r. on 10r. (E) (12½)	8·00	5·00
87		65r. on 15r. (E) (11½)	8·00	5·00
88		65r. on 20r. (E) (11½)	8·00	5·00
89	**1**	115r. on 50r. green (11½)	20·00	6·50
90	**2**	115r. on 10r. (13½)	10·00	6·50
91		115r. on 300r. (13½)	10·00	6·50
92	**9**	115r. on 25r. (E) (12½)	8·00	5·00
93		115r. on 150r. (11½)	8·00	5·00
94		115r. on 200r. (11½)	8·00	5·00
95	**2**	130r. on 5r. (12½) (R.)	10·00	6·50
96		130r. on 5r. (13½) (R.)	75·00	60·00
97		130r. on 200r. (13½)	12·50	6·50
98	**9**	130r. on 75r. (E) (11½)	8·00	5·00
99		130r. on 100r. (11½)	8·00	5·00
100		130r. on 300r. (11½)	8·00	5·00
101	**1**	400r. on 10r. yellow (11½)	95·00	70·00
102	**2**	400r. on 40r. (13½)	18·00	13·00
103		400r. on 50r. (12½)	8·00	5·00
104		400r. on 50r. (13½)	£850	£650
105	**9**	400r. on 50r. (E) (12½)	2·20	2·10
106		400r. on 50r. (E) (13½)	3·50	3·00
107		400r. on 80r. (E) (12½)	4·50	3·50
108	N **8**	400r. on 2½r. (11½)	2·20	2·10

The 65/100, 115/50, 400/10, 400/40 and 400/50r. (T **2**) were reprinted in 1905.

1903. Optd with T **13**.

109	**10**	15r. chocolate	4·00	1·80
110		25r. blue-green	4·00	1·80
111		50r. blue	4·50	1·80
112		75r. rose	10·00	7·50
109/112 *Set of* 4			20·00	11·50

1903. Colours changed. Name and value in black. P 11½.

113	**10**	15r. deep green	2·20	1·30
114		25r. carmine	2·20	1·10
115		50r. brown	9·00	5·75
116		65r. dull blue	17·00	10·50
117		75r. dull purple	4·75	2·10
118		115r. orange-brown/*pink*	16·00	11·50
119		130r. purple-brown/*straw*	16·00	11·50
120		400r. dull blue/*cream*	23·00	13·00
113/120 *Set of* 8			80·00	50·00

D **14**  (15)  (16)

(Des and eng J. S. de Carvalho e Silva. Typo The Mint, Lisbon)

1904. POSTAGE DUE. Name and value in black. P 11½.

D121	D **14**	5r. yellow-green	1·20	1·10
D122		10r. slate	1·70	1·40
D123		20r. brown	1·70	1·40
D124		30r. orange	1·70	1·40
D125		50r. deep brown	3·00	2·10
D126		60r. pale red-brown	4·25	2·75
D127		100r. mauve	7·00	4·25
D128		130r. blue	7·00	4·25
D129		200r. carmine	7·25	5·50
D130		500r. deep lilac	13·50	10·50
D121/130 *Set of* 10			43·00	31·00

See also Nos. D313/22.

1905. Surch with T **15**.

121	**10**	50r. on 65r. dull blue	7·00	4·25

King Manoel II
1 February 1908–5 October 1910

PORTUGUESE REPUBLIC
5 October 1910

1911. Optd with T **16**, in red or green (G.).

122	**10**	2½r. pale grey	50	35
		a. Double impression of stamp	60·00	27·00
123		5r. orange	50	45
124		10r. green	50	45
125		15r. deep green	50	45
126		20r. deep lilac	50	45
127		25r. carmine (G.)	50	45
128		50r. brown	50	45
129		75r. dull purple	50	45
130		100r. blue/*blue*	1·20	90
131		115r. orange-brown/*pink*	2·30	1·50
132		130r. purple-brown/*straw*	2·30	1·50
133		200r. purple/*flesh*	12·00	7·25
134		400r. dull blue/*cream*	3·25	1·30
135		500r. black/*azure*	3·25	1·30
136		700r. mauve/*yellow*	3·25	1·30
122/136 *Set of* 15			28·00	17·00

See also Nos. 146a/58, 172/84 and 263/9.

1911. POSTAGE DUE. Optd with T **16**, in red or green (G.).

D137	D **14**	5r. yellow-green	50	45
D138		10r. slate	50	45
D139		20r. brown	50	45
D140		30r. orange	50	45
D141		50r. deep brown	60	55
D142		60r. pale red-brown	1·70	1·20
D143		100r. mauve	1·70	1·20
D144		130r. blue	1·70	1·20
D145		200r. carmine (G.)	1·30	1·20
D146		500r. deep lilac	3·50	2·50
D137/146 *Set of* 10			11·00	8·75

See also Nos. D203/12.

17  (18)

(Des and eng D. A. do Rego. Typo The Mint, Lisbon)

1912. Optd with T **16** as shown in T **17**, in red or green (G.). P 11½×12.

137	**17**	2½r. pale grey	50	45
		a. Opt double	6·50	5·75
138		5r. black	50	45
139		10r. grey-green	50	45
140		20r. rose-red (G.)	2·10	1·20
141		25r. chocolate	1·20	75
142		50r. blue	1·20	75
143		75r. yellow-brown	1·20	80
144		100r. brown/*green*	2·10	1·10
145		200r. deep green/*salmon*	3·25	3·00
146		300r. black/*azure*	5·00	2·00
137/146 *Set of* 10			16·00	9·75

1913. Optd locally with T **18**.

(a) Stamps of 1898–1903. No gum (Nos. 153/5)

146a	**10**	2½r. pale grey	1·90	1·50
		ab. Opt inverted	7·25	
147		5r. orange-red	2·20	1·70
148		15r. deep green	65·00	50·00
149		20r. deep lilac	2·20	1·70
150		25r. carmine	8·75	4·50
151		75r. dull purple	3·25	3·25
152		100r. blue/*blue*	12·00	10·50
153		115r. orange-brown/*pink*	14·00	9·50
154		130r. purple-brown/*straw*	14·00	10·50
155		200r. purple/*flesh*	34·00	20·00
156		400r. dull blue/*cream*	16·00	10·50
157		500r. black/*azure*	55·00	40·00
158		700r. mauve/*yellow*	80·00	65·00
146a/158 *Set of* 13			£275	£200

ST. THOMAS & PRINCE ISLANDS

(b) Provisionals of 1902–5

159	10	15r. chocolate (109)	3·75	3·25
160		50r. blue (111)	3·75	3·25
161		50r. on 65r. (121)	20·00	14·50
162	2	115r. on 10r. (13½)	5·50	3·50
163	9	115r. on 25r. (E) (12½)	3·75	3·00
164	1	115r. on 50r. (11½)	£225	£180
165	9	115r. on 150r. (11½)	80·00	80·00
166		115r. on 200r. (11½)	3·75	3·00
167		130r. on 75r. (E) (11½)	3·75	3·00
168	2	400r. on 50r. (12½)	£150	£100
169	9	400r. on 50r. (E) (12½)	7·00	4·50
170		400r. on 50r. (E) (13½)	8·75	7·00
171		400r. on 80r. (E) (12½)	8·75	4·50

The 400r. on 10r. yellow (No. 101) exists with this overprint but is not believed to have been officially issued.

1913. POSTAGE DUE. Optd locally with T **18**. No gum.

D172	D **14**	5r. yellow-green	7·50	5·75
D173		10r. slate	9·75	5·75
D174		20r. brown	7·50	5·75
D175		30r. orange	7·50	5·75
D176		50r. deep brown	7·50	6·50
D177		60r. pale red-brown	7·50	6·50
D178		100r. mauve	7·50	6·50
D179		130r. blue	31·00	16·00
D180		200r. carmine	60·00	55·00
D181		500r. deep lilac	70·00	44·00
D172/181 Set of 10			£190	£140

(19) 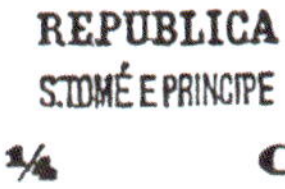 (20)

1913. Optd locally with T **19**.

(a) Stamps of 1898–1903

172	10	2½r. pale grey	1·50	1·50
173		5r. orange-red	50·00	38·00
174		15r. deep green	3·00	3·00
175		20r. deep lilac	£130	80·00
176		25r. carmine	60·00	47·00
177		75r. dull purple	3·00	3·00
178		100r. blue/*blue*	4·50	3·50
179		115r. orange-brown/*pink*	13·00	8·50
180		130r. purple-brown/*straw*	13·00	10·00
181		200r. purple/*flesh*	4·50	3·50
182		400r. dull blue/*cream*	14·50	10·00
183		500r. black/*azure*	12·50	10·00
184		700r. mauve/*yellow*	16·00	14·00
172/184 Set of 13			£300	£200

(b) Provisionals of 1902–5

185	10	15r. chocolate (109)	3·75	1·30
186		50r. blue (111)	3·75	1·30
187		50r. on 65r. (121)	4·25	2·75
188	2	115r. on 10r. (13½)	4·50	3·75
		a. Opt inverted		
189	9	115r. on 25r. (E) (12½)	3·75	2·50
190	1	115r. on 50r. (11½)	£325	£250
		a. Opt inverted		
191	9	115r. on 150r. (11½)	4·75	4·25
192		115r. on 200r. (11½)	4·75	4·25
193	2	115r. on 300r. (13½)	£275	£200
194		130r. on 5r. (12½)	£275	£200
195	9	130r. on 75r. (E) (11½)	4·75	4·25
196		130r. on 100r. (11½)	£550	£400
197	N **8**	400r. on 2½r. (11½)	4·75	4·25
198	2	400r. on 50r. (12½)	£130	£110
199		400r. on 50r. (13½)	£130	£110
200	9	400r. on 50r. (E) (12½)	4·75	4·25
201		400r. on 50r. (E) (13½)	29·00	23·00
202		400r. on 80r. (E) (12½)	5·00	3·50

Nos. 172/202 were mostly issued without gum.
See also Nos. 243/54.

1913. POSTAGE DUE. Optd locally with T **19**. No gum.

D203	D **14**	5r. yellow-green	5·75	4·50
D204		10r. slate	5·75	4·50
D205		20r. brown	5·75	4·50
D206		30r. orange	5·75	4·50
D207		50r. deep brown	5·75	4·50
D208		60r. pale red-brown	7·50	5·75
D209		100r. mauve	7·50	5·75
D210		130r. blue	7·50	5·75
D211		200r. carmine	13·00	9·00
D212		500r. deep lilac	28·00	23·00
D203/212 Set of 10			85·00	65·00

1913. New Currency. Vasco da Gama issues surch as T **20**.

(i) Nos. 1/8 of Portuguese Colonies and Overseas Territories

203	¼c. on 2½r. blue-green	2·10	1·40
204	½c. on 5r. vermilion	2·10	1·40
205	1c. on 10r. dull purple	2·10	1·40
206	2½c. on 25r. yellow-green	2·10	1·40
207	5c. on 50r. deep blue	2·10	1·40
208	7½c. on 75r. chocolate	4·00	3·50
	a. Surch double	32·00	
209	10c. on 10r. bistre-brown	2·10	1·40
210	15c. on 150r. ochre	2·30	1·70
203/210 Set of 8		17·00	12·00

(ii) Nos. 104/11 of Macao

211	¼c. on ½a. blue-green	3·00	2·00
212	½c. on 1a. vermilion	3·00	2·00
213	1c. on 2a. dull purple	3·00	2·00
214	2½c. on 4a. yellow-green	3·00	2·00
215	5c. on 8a. deep blue	3·25	2·75
216	7½c. on 12a. chocolate	5·50	4·25
217	10c. on 16a. bistre-brown	3·25	2·20
218	15c. on 24a. ochre	3·25	2·20
211/218 Set of 8		25·00	17·00

(iii) Nos. 58/65 of Timor

219	¼c. on ½a. blue-green	3·00	2·00
220	½c. on 1a. vermilion	3·00	2·00
221	1c. on 2a. dull purple	3·00	2·00
	a. Surch double, one "1" and "C" spaced, the other "1" and "C" closer	25·00	
222	2½c. on 4a. yellow-green	3·00	2·00
223	5c. vdeep blue	3·25	2·75
224	7½c. on 12a. chocolate	5·50	4·25
225	10c. on 16a. bistre-brown	3·25	2·20
226	15c. on 24a. ochre	3·25	2·20
219/226 Set of 8		25·00	17·00

21 Ceres  (22)  (23)

(Des C. Fernandes. Eng J. S. de Carvalho e Silva.
Typo The Mint, Lisbon)

1914 (11 Apr). Name and value in black. Chalk-surfaced paper. P 15×14.

227	21	¼c. brown-olive	70	65
228		½c. black	70	65
229		1c. deep green	1·10	65
230		1½c. chocolate	1·10	65
231		2c. carmine	70	65
232		2½c. violet	70	65
233		5c. deep blue	70	65
234		7½c. yellow-brown	1·90	1·50
235		8c. slate	1·90	1·50
236		10c. brown-red	1·90	1·50
237		15c. claret	3·25	1·30
238		20c. olive-green	2·30	1·40
239		30c. chocolate/*green*	3·75	1·90
240		40c. brown/*rose*	3·75	1·90
241		50c. orange/*salmon*	9·25	6·00
242		1E. deep green/*azure*	9·25	4·75
227/242 Set of 16			39·00	24·00

See also Nos. 276/312.

1915. Provisionals of 1902–5 optd with T **16**, in red.

243	10	50r. blue (111)	1·50	1·10
244		50r. on 65r. (121)	1·50	1·10
245	2	115r. on 10r. (13½)	4·50	3·25
246	9	115r. on 25r. (E) (12½)	1·40	70
247		115r. on 150r. (11½)	1·40	70
248		115r. on 200r. (11½)	1·40	70
249	2	115r. on 300r. (13½)	4·50	3·25
250		130r. on 5r. (12½)	9·50	5·00
251	9	130r. on 75r. (E) (11½)	1·40	70
252		130r. on 100r. (11½)	2·50	2·30
253	2	130r. on 200r. (13½)	3·00	2·10
254	9	130r. on 300r. (11½)	2·20	1·30

1919 (Mar).

(a) No. 109 optd locally "REPUBLICA" diag. upwards in blue and new value in black

255	10	2½c. on 15r. chocolate	1·50	1·10

(b) No. 122 surch locally

256	10	½c. on 2½r. pale grey	7·25	5·75
257		1c. on 2½r. pale grey	5·00	3·25
258		2½c. on 2½r. pale grey	2·00	1·40

217

ST. THOMAS & PRINCE ISLANDS

(c) No. 227 surch locally

259	**21**	½c. on ¼c. brown-olive	4·50	3·50
260		2c. on ¼c. brown-olive	4·50	3·50
261		2½c. on ¼c. brown-olive	15·00	11·00

1919 (Dec). No. 232 surch locally with T **22**. No gum.

262	**21**	4c. on 2½c. violet	2·00	1·40

1920 (18 May). Optd locally with T **23**.

(a) Stamps of 1893–1903

263	**10**	75r. dull purple (G.)	1·40	80
264		100r. blue/*blue* (R.)	1·40	80
265		115r. orange-brown/*pink* (G.)	3·50	2·10
266		130r. purple-brown/*straw* (G.)	35·00	28·00
267		200r. purple/*flesh* (G.)	3·50	2·10
268		500r. black/*azure* (G.)	2·50	2·10
269		700r. mauve/*yellow* (G.)	3·50	2·30
263/269 *Set of 7*			46·00	34·00

(b) Provisionals of 1902–5

270	**10**	50r. blue (111) (R.)	2·50	2·10
271		50r. on 65r. (121) (R.)	16·00	8·25
272		75r. rose (112) (G.)	15·00	10·00
273	**9**	115r. on 25r. (E) (12½) (R.)	2·20	1·40
274		115r. on 200r. (11½) (R.)	2·50	2·10
275		130r. on 75r. (E) (11½) (G.)	3·25	2·10

Nos. 263/75 were mostly issued without gum.

1920 (18 May). POSTAGE DUE. Optd locally with T **23**. No gum.

D276	D **14**	50r. deep brown (G.)	41·00	30·00

1920–26.

(a) Unsurfaced paper. P 15×14 (1920)

276	**21**	¼c. brown-olive	45	35
277		1½c. chocolate	2·75	2·50
278		7½c. yellow-brown	3·50	3·25
279		10c. red-brown	3·50	3·25

(b) Unsurfaced paper. P 12×11½ (1922–26)

280	**21**	¼c. brown-olive	45	35
		a. Olive	45	35
281		½c. black	45	35
282		1c. yellow-green	45	35
283		1½c. chocolate	2·75	2·50
284		2c. carmine	45	35
285		2c. drab (1926)	45	35
286		2½c. violet	45	35
287		3c. orange	45	35
288		4c. dull claret	45	35
289		4½c. drab	45	35
290		5c. pale dull blue	70	65
291		6c. mauve	45	35
292		7c. pale blue	45	35
293		7½c. yellow-brown	70	50
294		8c. slate	70	50
295		10c. red-brown	70	50
296		12c. blue-green	85	65
297		15c. dull rose	85	65
298		20c. yellow-green	85	65
299		24c. light blue (1926)	1·70	1·30
300		25c. chocolate (1926)	1·70	1·30
301		30c. deep grey-green	1·30	85
302		40c. turquoise	1·30	85
303		50c. mauve (1926)	1·30	95
304		60c. deep blue	1·30	85
305		60c. carmine-pink (1926)	2·75	1·30
306		80c. bright rosine	3·00	1·00

(c) Glazed paper. P 12×11½ (1922–26)

307	**21**	1E. pink	4·25	2·10
308		1E. blue (1926)	2·30	1·50
309		2E. purple	4·50	2·30
310		5E. buff (1926)	26·00	7·00
311		10E. pink (1926)	41·00	15·00
312		20E. emerald (1926)	£130	55·00
280/312 *Set of 33*			£200	90·00

1921. POSTAGE DUE. As Type D **14**, but name spelt "S. TOMÉ", etc, and value in centavos.

D313		½c. yellow-green	65	55
		a. "S. THOMÉ"	16·00	15·00
D314		1c. slate	65	55
		a. "S. THOMÉ"	16·00	15·00
D315		2c. brown	65	55
		a. "S. THOMÉ"	16·00	15·00
D316		3c. orange	65	55
		a. "S. THOMÉ"	16·00	15·00
D317		5c. deep brown	65	55
		a. "S. THOMÉ"	16·00	15·00
D318		6c. pale red-brown	70	60
		a. "S. THOMÉ"	16·00	15·00
D319		10c. mauve	70	60
		a. "S. THOMÉ"	16·00	15·00
D320		13c. blue	70	60
		a. "S. THOMÉ"	16·00	15·00
D321		20c. carmine	70	60
		a. "S. THOMÉ"	16·00	15·00
D322		50c. deep lilac	1·80	1·40
		a. "S. THOMÉ"	16·00	15·00
D313/322 *Set of 10*			7·00	6·00

One stamp on each sheet has the error "S. THOMÉ".
Sets may be made on coarser paper, without the error "S. THOMÉ", the shades differing in some values, particularly in the 3c., which is yellow.

(24) DEZ CENTAVOS

(25) República 40 C.

1923 (18 May). Surch with T **24**.

(a) Provisionals of 1915

313	**9**	10c. on 115r. on 25r. (B.)	95	70
314		10c. on 115r. on 150r. (B.)	95	70
315		10c. on 115r. on 150r. (Bk.)	95	70
316		10c. on 115r. on 200r. (R.)	95	70
317		10c. on 130r. on 75r. (B.)	95	70
318		10c. on 130r. on 100r. (B.)	95	70
319		10c. on 130r. on 300r. (R.)	95	70

(b) Provisional of 1920

320	**9**	10c. on 115r. on 25r. (B.)	80·00	75·00

1925. Nos. 108 and 107 surch as T **25**.

321	N **8**	40c. on 400r. on 2½r.	1·90	90
322	**9**	40c. on 400r. on 80r.	1·90	90

CHARITY TAX STAMPS. Stamps bearing C numbers were for compulsory use on internal letters on certain days of the year as an additional postal tax for public charities. Other values in some of the types were for use on telegrams or for fiscal purposes.

27 Pombal Monument

28 Planning the Reconstruction of Lisbon

29 Marquis de Pombal

MULTA (30)

(Des H. Fleury. Eng J. A. C. Harrison. Recess Waterlow)

1925 (8 May). Marquis de Pombal Commemoration. P 12½.

(a) CHARITY TAX

C323	**27**	15c. black and orange	85	45
C324	**28**	15c. black and orange	85	45
C325	**29**	15c. black and orange	85	45

*(b) POSTAGE DUE. Optd with T **30***

D323	**27**	30c. black and orange	85	45
D324	**28**	30c. black and orange	85	45
D325	**29**	30c. black and orange	85	45
C323/D325 *Set of 6*			4·50	2·40

Nos. C323/5 were in use from 8 to 13 May 1925 and from 5 to 15 May in 1926 and 1929. Nos. D323/5 were used in default.

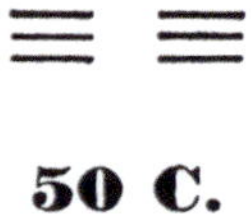

(31) 50 C.

32 Ceres

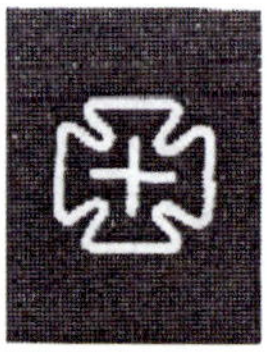

33 Maltese Cross

1931. Surch as T **31**. P 12×11½.

323	**21**	70c. on 1E. pink	4·00	2·00
324		1E.40 on 2E. purple	4·75	2·40

ST. THOMAS & PRINCE ISLANDS

(Des C. Fernandes. Die eng A. Fragoso. Typo The Mint, Lisbon)
1934. W **33**. P 12×11½.

325	**32**	1c. brown	25	20
326		5c. sepia	45	30
327		10c. mauve	45	30
328		15c. black	45	30
329		20c. grey	45	30
330		30c. blue-green	45	30
331		40c. vermilion	45	30
332		45c. turquoise	80	75
333		50c. cinnamon	65	60
334		60c. olive-green	1·00	60
335		70c. red-brown	1·00	60
336		80c. emerald	1·00	60
337		85c. carmine	5·00	2·00
338		1E. claret	1·50	70
339		1E.40 blue	4·00	2·00
340		2E. mauve	4·00	2·00
341		5E. yellow-green	9·00	6·00
342		10E. bistre-brown	25·00	13·50
343		20E. orange	£100	55·00
325/343 Set of 19			£140	80·00

34 Vasco da Gama   **35** Mousinho de Albuquerque   **36** Airplane over Globe

(Des A. R. Garcia. Recess Bradbury Wilkinson)
1938 (Aug). Inscr "S. TOMÉ". Name and value in black. P 13½×13.

(a) POSTAGE. T **34/5** *and similar vert designs*

344	**34**	1c. grey-olive	35	30
345		5c. orange-brown	35	30
346		10c. carmine	35	30
347		15c. brown-purple	35	30
348		20c. slate	35	30
349	**35**	30c. bright purple	35	30
350		35c. emerald-green	65	45
351		40c. brown	65	45
352		50c. magenta	65	45
353	–	60c. grey-black	65	45
354	–	70c. slate-violet	65	45
355	–	80c. orange	65	45
356	–	1E. scarlet	1·30	80
357	–	1E.75 blue	2·20	1·20
358	–	2E. lake	29·00	8·25
359	–	5E. olive-green	29·00	9·25
360	–	10E. ultramarine	34·00	10·00
361	–	20E. red-brown	55·00	4·00
344/361 Set of 18			£140	34·00

Designs:—60c. to 1E. Dam; 1E.75 to 5E. Prince Henry the Navigator; 10E., 20E. Afonso de Albuquerque.

(b) AIR

362	**36**	10c. scarlet	£130	95·00
363		20c. bright violet	65·00	46·00
364		50c. orange	3·75	3·50
365		1E. bright blue	12·00	3·50
366		2E. brown-lake	9·50	6·50
367		3E. blue-green	12·00	8·25
368		5E. red-brown	20·00	16·00
369		9E. carmine	22·00	16·00
370		10E. magenta	22·00	16·00
362/370 Set of 9			2·75	£190

See also Nos. 374/400.

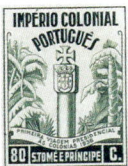

37 Portuguese Colonial Column

(Recess Bradbury Wilkinson)
1938. Portuguese President's Colonial Tour. P 12½.

371	**37**	80c. blue-green	3·75	2·10
372		1E.75 blue	13·00	7·00
373		20E. red-brown	80·00	41·00
371/373 Set of 3			85·00	45·00

1939. As Nos. 344/70 but inscr "S. TOMÉ e PRINCIPE".

(a) POSTAGE

374	**34**	1c. grey-olive	35	30
375		5c. orange-brown	35	30
376		10c. carmine	35	30
377		15c. brown-purple	35	30
378		20c. slate	35	30
379	**35**	30c. bright purple	35	30
380		35c. emerald-green	35	30
381		40c. brown	45	30
382		50c. magenta	45	45
383	–	60c. grey-black	95	60
384	–	70c. slate-violet	1·10	60
385	–	80c. orange	1·10	60
386	–	1E. scarlet	1·30	85
387	–	1E.75 blue	2·20	1·20
388	–	2E. lake	3·75	2·00
389	–	5E. olive-green	8·25	5·00
390	–	10E. ultramarine	23·00	8·25
391	–	20E. red-brown	30·00	10·00
374/391 Set of 18			70·00	29·00

(b) AIR

392	**36**	10c. scarlet	70	60
393		20c. bright violet	70	60
394		50c. orange	70	60
395		1E. bright blue	70	60
396		2E. brown-lake	1·70	95
397		3E. blue-green	2·20	1·40
398		5E. red-brown	6·50	3·50
399		9E. carmine	12·50	7·00
400		10E. magenta	13·00	7·25
392/400 Set of 9			35·00	20·00

(37a)

 (38)   (39)

1946. CHARITY TAX. Fiscal stamps as T **37a** surch as T **38** or T **39**. No gum.

(a) P 15×14

C401		50c. on 1E. green	25·00	23·00
C402		50c. on 4E. carmine	30·00	30·00
C403		1E. on 4E. carmine	30·00	30·00
C404		1E. on 5E. carmine	30·00	30·00
C405		1E. on 6E. green	25·00	23·00
C406		1E. on 7E. green	25·00	23·00

(b) P 12×11½

C407		1E. on 6E. green	25·00	23·00
C408		1E. on 7E. green	32·00	23·00
C409		1E. on 10E. carmine	25·00	30·00
C410		1E.50 on 7E. green	29·00	23·00
C411		1E.50 on 8E. green	29·00	27·00
C412		2E.50 on 7E. green	29·00	27·00
C413		2E.50 on 9E. green	29·00	27·00
C414		2E.50 on 10E. green	25·00	23·00

In each sheet of 100 there are 52 stamps with surcharge Type **38** (of which 2 are without the accent), and 48 in Type **39** (of which 14 are without accent). Prices for stamps with the accent are worth more.

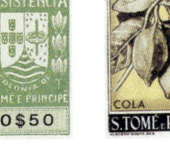 

40 Arms   **41** Cola Nuts   **42** Our Lady of Fatima

ST. THOMAS & PRINCE ISLANDS

1948–58. CHARITY TAX. Value in black. Typo. P 12×11½.
C415	**40**	50c. green	1·30	1·10
C416		1E. carmine-rose	3·25	2·40
C417		1E. green (1958)	1·40	1·00
C418		1E.50 brown	4·00	3·00
C415/418	Set of 4		9·00	6·75

Higher values were for fiscal use only.

(Des A. de Sousa. Litho Litografia Nacional, Oporto, Portugal)

1948 (1 Oct). Fruits. T **41** and similar vert designs. P 14.
401	5c. black and yellow	85	30
402	10c. blackish brown and salmon	1·10	75
403	30c. slate and grey	5·75	3·00
404	50c. brown and yellow	6·50	4·75
405	1E. scarlet and rose	7·25	4·75
406	1E.75 blue and grey	13·00	8·25
407	2E. black and apple-green	11·50	4·75
408	5E. brown and magenta	38·00	18·00
409	10E. black and pale magenta	40·00	19·00
410	20E. black and grey	80·00	60·00
401/410	Set of 10	£180	£110
MS410*a*	149×136 mm. Nos. 401/10 (sold at 42E.50)	£225	£250

Designs:—10c. Bread-fruit; 30c. Custard-apple; 50c. Cocoa beans; 1E. Coffee; 1E.75, Dendem; 2E. Abacate; 5E. Pineapple; 10E. Mango; 20E. Coconuts.

(Des A. Negreiros. Litho Litografia Nacional, Oporto, Portugal)

1948 (Oct). Honouring the Statue of Our Lady of Fatima. P 14.
411	**42**	50c. violet	10·50	7·75

For No. 411 in miniature sheet see No. **MS**1 of Portuguese Colonies and Overseas Territories.

43 Letter and Globe   **44** Bells and Dove

(Des A. Negreiros. Litho Litografia Maia, Oporto, Portugal)

1949 (Oct). 75th Anniv of Universal Postal Union. P 14.
412	**43**	3E.50 black	11·00	7·75

(Des A. Araujo. Litho Litografia de Portugal, Lisbon)

1950 (May). Holy Year. T **44** and similar vert design. P 13½.
413		2E.50 light blue	4·00	2·50
414		4E. orange	8·25	6·00

Design:—Angel holding candelabra.

For No. 414 in miniature sheet see No. **MS**2 of Portuguese Colonies and Overseas Territories.

45 Our Lady of Fatima   **46** Doctor examining Patients

(Litho Litografia Nacional, Oporto, Portugal)

1951 (Oct). Termination of Holy Year. P 14.
415	**45**	4E. indigo and grey-blue	3·75	3·25

No. 415 was issued *se-tenant* with a stamp-size label bearing a papal declaration.

(Des A. de Sousa. Litho The Mint, Lisbon)

1952 (5 May). First Tropical Medicine Congress, Lisbon. P 13½.
416	**46**	10c. blue and chocolate	50	35

D **47**   **48** J. de Santarem

(Litho Litografia Nacional, Oporto, Portugal)

1952. POSTAGE DUE. P 14.
D417	D **47**	10c. multicoloured	25	20
D418		30c. multicoloured	25	20
D419		50c. multicoloured	25	20
D420		1E. multicoloured	30	25
D421		2E. multicoloured	35	35
D422		5E. multicoloured	65	45
D417/422	Set of 6		1·80	1·50

(Des A. de Sousa. Litho Litografia Maia, Oporto, Portugal)

1952 (27 Aug). Portuguese Navigators. T **48** and similar vert designs. Multicoloured. P 14½.
417	10c. Type **48**	20	15
418	30c. P. Escobar	20	15
419	50c. F. de Po	35	20
420	1E. A. Esteves	45	30
421	2E. L. Goncalves	1·10	50
422	3E.50 M. Fernandes	1·10	50
417/422	Set of 6	3·00	1·60

49 Cloisters of Monastery   **50** Portuguese Stamp of 1853 and Arms of Portuguese Overseas Provinces

(Litho The Mint, Lisbon)

1953 (28 May). Missionary Art Exhibition. P 13½.
423	**49**	10c. brown and grey-green	15	10
424		50c. orange-brown and orange	95	75
425		3E. indigo and grey-blue	3·25	1·80
423/425	Set of 3		4·00	2·40

(Litho Litografia Nacional, Oporto, Portugal)

1953 (3 Nov). Portuguese Stamp Centenary. P 13.
426	**50**	50c. multicoloured	1·60	90

51 Route of President's Tour   **52** Father M. de Nobrega and View of São Paulo

(Litho The Mint, Lisbon)

1954 (22 May). Presidential Visit. P 13½.
427	**51**	15c. multicoloured	20	15
428		5E. multicoloured	1·70	1·10

(Litho The Mint, Lisbon)

1954 (20 Aug). Fourth Centenary of São Paulo. P 13½.
429	**52**	2E.50 multicoloured	85	55

53 Exhibition Emblem, Globe and Arms   **54** *Cassia occidentalis*

ST. THOMAS & PRINCE ISLANDS

(Des J. de Moura. Litho The Mint, Lisbon)
1958 (15 July). Brussels International Exhibition. P 12×11½.
430   **53**   2E.50 multicoloured .... 1·10   65

(Des J. de Moura. Litho The Mint, Lisbon)
1958 (5 Sept). Sixth International Congress of Tropical Medicine. P 13½.
431   **54**   5E. multicoloured .... 3·75   2·30

55 Points of Compass   **56** "Religion"

(Des J. de Moura. Litho The Mint, Lisbon)
1960 (25 June). 500th Death Anniv of Prince Henry the Navigator. P 13×13½.
432   **55**   10E. multicoloured .... 1·60   85

(Des Neves and Sousa. Litho Litografia Maia, Oporto, Portugal)
1960 (Oct). Tenth Anniv of African Technical Co-operation Commission. P 14½.
433   **56**   1E.50 multicoloured 70   45

57 Fishing   **58** *Anopheles gambiae*

(Des J. de Moura. Litho Litografia Nacional, Oporto, Portugal)
1962 (21 Feb). Sports. T **57** and similar diamond-shaped designs. Multicoloured. P 13.
434   50c. Type **57** 20   15
     a. "$50 CORREIOS" omitted................ 80·00
435   1E. Gymnastics 85   20
436   1E.50 Handball 90   35
437   2E. Sailing .... 1·10   55
438   2E.50 Running .... 1·40   1·10
439   20E. Skin-diving .... 4·00   2·10
434/439   Set of 6 .... 7·50   4·00

(Des J. de Moura. Litho The Mint, Lisbon)
1962 (24 Mar). Malaria Eradication. P 13½.
440   **58**   2E.50 multicoloured .... 2·10   1·10

 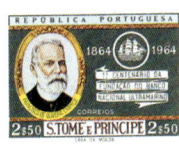

59 Map of Africa and Boeing 707 and Lockheed L.1049G Super Constellation Airliners   **60** F. de Oliveira Chamico

(Des J. de Moura. Litho Litografia Maia, Oporto, Portugal)
1963 (5 Oct). Tenth Anniv of Transportes Aereos Portugueses (airline). P 14½.
441   **59**   1E.50 multicoloured 95   65

(Litho The Mint, Lisbon)
1964 (16 May). Centenary of National Overseas Bank. P 13½.
442   **60**   2E.50 multicoloured .... 1·00   80

61 I.T.U. Emblem and St. Gabriel   **62** Infantry Officer, 1788

(Litho Litografia Nacional, Oporto, Portugal)
1965 (17 May). Centenary of International Telecommunications Union. P 14½.
443   **61**   2E.50 multicoloured .... 2·10   1·40

(Des A. Cutileiro. Litho The Mint, Lisbon)
1965 (30 Aug). Portuguese Military Uniforms. T **62** and similar vert designs. Multicoloured. P 13½.
444   20c. Type **62** 25   20
445   35c. Infantry sergeant, 1788 25   20
446   40c. Infantry corporal, 1788 25   20
447   1E. Infantryman, 1788 .... 2·00   80
448   2E.50 Artillery officer, 1806 .... 2·00   85
449   5E. Light Infantryman, 1811 .... 3·00   1·90
450   7E.50 Infantry sapper, 1833 .... 4·75   2·50
451   10E. Lancers officer, 1834 .... 5·75   3·75
444/451   Set of 8 .... 16·00   9·25

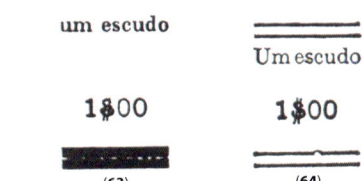

(63)   (64)

1965. CHARITY TAX.
             (a) Surch with T **63**
C452   **40**   1E. on 5E. yellow .... 1·80   1·30
             (b) Surch "Um escudo" only as in T **64**
C453   **40**   1E. on 1E. green .... 2·30   2·20
             (c) As No. C417 but inscr "UM ESCUDO", surch "1$00"
C454   **40**   1E. on 1E. green .... 1·80   1·50
             (d) Surch with T **63**
C455   **40**   1E. on 5E. yellow .... 4·00   3·25
In No. C455 the bars at top obliterate a previous surcharge "Cinco escudos".

65 Arts and Crafts School and Anti-Tuberculosis Clinic   **66** C. Rodrigues and *Vasco da Gama* (steam corvette)

(Des A. Cutileiro. Litho The Mint, Lisbon)
1966 (28 May). 40th Anniv of Portuguese National Revolution. P 12×11½.
452   **65**   2E.50 multicoloured .... 1·10   65

(Des A. Cutileiro. Litho Litografia Nacional, Oporto, Portugal)
1967 (31 Jan). Centenary of Military Naval Association. T **66** and similar horiz design. Multicoloured. P 13.
453   1E.50 Type **66** .... 1·70   65
454   2E.50 A. Kopke, microscope and insect *Glossina palpalis*........................... 2·50   1·10

ST. THOMAS & PRINCE ISLANDS

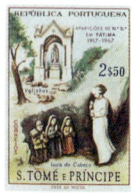 

67 Apparition appearing to Children and Valinhos Monument

68 Medal of the Jeronimos Monastery

(Des J. de Moura. Litho The Mint, Lisbon)
1967 (13 May). 50th Anniv of Fatima Apparitions. P 12½×13.
455   67   2E.50 multicoloured 45   30

(Des J. de Moura. Litho Litografia Maia, Oporto, Portugal)
1968 (22 Apr). 500th Birth Anniv of Pedro Cabral (explorer). P 14.
456   68   1E.50 multicoloured 90   60

69 Island Route-map and Monument

70 Vasco da Gama's Fleet and Fireship

(Des J. de Moura. Litho Litografia Nacional, Oporto, Portugal)
1969 (17 Feb). Birth Centenary of Admiral Gago Coutinho. P 14.
457   69   2E. multicoloured 65   30

(Des J. de Moura. Litho Litografia Nacional, Oporto, Portugal)
1969 (29 Aug). 500th Birth Anniv of Vasco da Gama (explorer). P 14.
458   70   2E.50 multicoloured 85   55

71 L. A. Rebelloda Silva

72 Manoel Gate, Guarda See

(Des J. de Moura. Litho Litografia Nacional, Oporto, Portugal)
1969 (25 Sept). Centenary of Overseas Administrative Reforms. P 14.
459   71   2E.50 multicoloured 55   45

(Des J. de Moura. Litho Litografia Nacional, Oporto, Portugal)
1969 (1 Dec). 500th Birth Anniv of King Manoel I. P 14.
460   72   4E. multicoloured 65   55

73 Pero Escobar and João de Santarem

74 President A. Tomás

(Des J. de Moura. Litho Litografia Maia, Oporto, Portugal)
1970 (25 Feb). 500th Anniv of Discovery of St. Thomas and Prince Islands. P 14.
461   73   2E.50 multicoloured 55   45

(Litho The Mint, Lisbon)
1970 (23 July). Visit of President of Portugal. P 12½.
462   74   2E.50 multicoloured 60   25

75 Marshal Carmona

76 Stamps on Coffee Plant

(Des J. de Moura. Litho Litografia Nacional, Oporto, Portugal)
1970 (15 Nov). Birth Centenary of Marshal Carmona. P 14.
463   75   5E. multicoloured 85   55

(Des J. de Moura. Litho The Mint, Lisbon)
1970 (1 Dec). Stamp Centenary. T **76** and similar multicoloured designs. P 13½.
464   1E. Type **76**... 30   15
465   1E.50 Head Post Office, St. Thomas (horiz).... 65   20
466   2E.50 Se Cathedral, St. Thomas..................... 85   35
464/466 Set of 3 .... 1·60   65

77 "Descent from the Cross" and Caravel at St. Thomas

78 Running and Throwing the Javelin

(Des A. Cutileiro. Litho Litografia Maia, Oporto, Portugal)
1972 (25 May). 400th Anniv of Camoens' "*The Lusiads*" (epic poem). P 13.
467   77   20E. multicoloured .... 2·75   1·10

(Des A. Cutileiro. Litho Litogratia Nacional, Oporto, Portugal)
1972 (20 June). Olympic Games, Munich. P 14×13½.
468   78   1E.50 multicoloured 45   25

79 Fairey IIID Seaplane *Lusitania* and *Gladiolus* (cruiser) off Rock of San Pedro

80 WMO Emblem

(Des A. Cutileiro. Litho Litografia Maia, Oporto, Portugal)
1972 (20 Sept). 50th Anniv of First Flight from Lisbon to Rio de Janeiro. P 13½.
469   79   2E.50 multicoloured 55   30

(Des A. Cutileiro. Litho Litografia Maia, Oporto, Portugal)
1973 (15 Dec). Centenary of World Meteorological Organization. P 13.
470   80   5E. multicoloured 85   65

Following an agreement signed in Algiers on 26 November 1974, the St. Thomas and Prince Islands became an independent republic on 12 July 1975. Subsequent issues are listed in Part 14 (*Africa since independence N-Z*) of this catalogue.

Timor

1885. 1000 Reis = 1 Milreis
1894. 100 Avos = 1 Pataca
1960. 100 Centavos = 1 Escudo

The island of Timor is one of the Lesser Sunda islands in the south of the Indonesian archipelago. Portuguese merchants began trading there in about 1520 and took the island under their administration in 1586. The Dutch established themselves in Kupang in 1613 and the Portuguese moved to the north and east. Treaties ratified in 1860 and 1908 established boundaries whereby the eastern half of the island, the enclave of Ocussi Ambeno further west along the north coast, and the islands of Cambing and Jako were administered by Portugal, and the rest of the main island was made part of the Dutch East Indies. Portuguese Timor was administered from Macao until 1896, when it became a separate colony, with Dili as capital. On 11 June 1951 it became an Overseas Province of Portugal and its inhabitants received Portuguese citizenship on 6 September 1961.

The Dutch retained the western part of Timor until 1949, when it became part of Indonesia.

PRINTERS. All the stamps of Portuguese Timor were printed at the Mint, Lisbon, Portugal *unless otherwise stated.*

REPRINTS. Reprints of the following issues were made in 1885 and 1905 as indicated in the footnotes. These can generally be distinguished as follows:—
1885 reprints are on stout very white paper, usually ungummed but sometimes with white gum having yellowish spots. They are perf 13½ with large clean-cut holes producing sharp pointed teeth.
1905 reprints are on creamy white paper of ordinary quality with shiny white gum, all perf 13½.

King Luis
11 November 1861–19 October 1889

TIMOR
(1)   2

1885. Stamps of Macao optd with T **1**.

(a) P 12½

1	5r. black (R.)	2·40	2·10
2	10r. deep green	6·75	4·75
	a. Grey-green	6·75	4·75
	b. On Mozambique stamp	15·00	15·00
	c. On Portuguese India stamp	£100	£100
3	20r. rosine	11·00	6·25
4	25r. dull lilac	2·20	1·30
5	40r. yellow	5·25	4·00
6	50r. deep blue	2·40	1·70
7	80r. grey	6·75	4·00
8	100r. dull purple	2·40	2·10
9	200r. orange	8·75	4·75
10	300r. yellow-brown	5·25	4·00
1/10	*Set of 10*	48·00	31·00

(b) P 13½

11	5r. black (R.)	3·00	2·30
12	10r. deep green	6·00	4·75
	a. Grey-green	6·00	4·75
13	20r. rosine	8·75	3·00
14	25r. dull lilac	24·00	16·00
15	40r. yellow	17·00	13·50
16	50r. deep blue	17·00	13·50
	a. Pale blue	17·00	13·50
17	80r. grey	6·75	4·75
18	100r. lilac-grey	13·50	4·75
	a. Dull purple	13·50	4·75
19	200r. orange	5·00	4·00
20	300r. yellow-brown	5·00	4·00
11/20	*Set of 10*	95·00	65·00

Nos. 2b/c were of an experimental nature and were not intended for issue.
Varieties of the above with *double* and *inverted* overprints are only printer's waste.
The 20r. bistre, 25r. rose and 50r. green were prepared for use but were not issued.
All values were reprinted in 1885 and 1905.

(Des and eng F. A. de Campos. Head embossed, rest typo)

1887. Chalk-surfaced paper. P 12½.

21	**2**	5r. black	3·75	2·30
22		10r. green	4·25	3·00
		a. Double impression	50·00	50·00
		b. Deep green	4·25	3·00
23		20r. rosine	6·00	3·00
24		25r. bright mauve	7·75	3·75
25		40r. chocolate	13·50	5·50
26		50r. blue	13·50	5·50
27		80r. grey	15·00	6·25
28		100r. yellow-brown	17·00	7·75
29		200r. lavender	35·00	16·00
30		300r. red-orange	40·00	20·00
		a. Orange	40·00	20·00
21/30a	*Set of 10*		£140	65·00

The 5, 25, 50 and 100r. were issued both with and without gum.
The 5, 50, 100 and 200r. were reprinted in 1905.

King Carlos
19 October 1889–1 February 1908

JORNAES **TIMOR**

TIMOR

2½   2½   30   30

(N 3)   (4)   N 5

1892 (Aug). NEWSPAPER. As T **2** but inscr "MACAU", surch with Type N **3**. No gum.

(a) P 12½

N31		2½ on 20r. rosine	2·75	1·90
		a. "TIMOR" inverted	21·00	18·00
N32		2½ on 40r. chocolate	2·75	1·90
		a. "TIMOR" inverted	21·00	18·00
N33		2½ on 80r. grey	2·75	1·90
		a. "TIMOR" inverted	21·00	18·00

(b) P 13½

N34		2½ on 40r. chocolate	8·25	6·25
		a. "TIMOR" inverted	21·00	18·00
N35		2½ on 80r. grey	15·00	13·00

1892 (Sept). As T **2** but inscr "MACAU", surch with T **4**. No gum.

31	30 on 300r. orange (p. 12½)	10·00	4·00
32	30 on 300r. orange (p. 13½)	6·75	5·00

(Des and eng E. C. Azedo Gneco. Typo)

1893 (25 Oct). NEWSPAPER. P 11½.

N36	N **5**	2½r. brown (*no gum*)	1·30	1·00
		a. Perf 12½	4·50	2·75
		b. Perf 13½	1·30	1·00

Stamps of this type could be, and often were, used for franking ordinary correspondence.

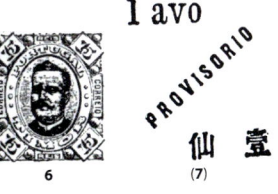

1 avo   5 avos
PROVISORIO   PROVISORIO
仙壹   仙伍

6   (7)   (8)

(Des and eng M. D. Neto. Typo)

1894 (15 Nov).

(a) Chalk-surfaced paper. With or without gum (5, 10, 15r.), no gum (others). P 11½

33	**6**	5r. pale orange	2·40	1·30
34		10r. rosy mauve	2·40	1·30
35		15r. red-brown	3·50	1·30
36		20r. lilac	3·50	1·30
37		25r. green	3·75	2·10
38		50r. pale blue	5·50	4·00
39		75r. rose	7·25	5·50
40		80r. pale green	7·25	5·50
41		100r. brown/*buff*	5·75	4·75
42		150r. carmine/*rose*	24·00	11·50
43		200r. blue/*blue*	24·00	12·50
44		300r. blue/*pale brown*	29·00	13·50
33/44	*Set of 12*		£110	60·00

223

TIMOR

(b) Enamel-surfaced paper. P 13½

45	6	50r. pale blue	£160	£150

1894. New Currency. No gum.

(a) Surch as T 7. P 12½

46	2	1a. on 5r. black (R.)	2·50	1·50
47		2a. on 10r. green	2·75	2·30
48		3a. on 20r. rosine (G.)	4·00	2·30
49		4a. on 25r. bright purple	4·00	2·30
50		6a. on 40r. chocolate	6·75	3·00
51		8a. on 50r. blue (R.)	8·25	4·50
52		13a. on 80r. grey	15·00	14·50
53		16a. on 100r. yellow-brown	15·00	14·50
54		31a. on 200r. lavender	41·00	31·00
55		47a. on 300r. orange (G.)	46·00	36·00
46/55 Set of 10			£130	£100

Nos. 46/9 and 51 exist with broken "y" for "v" in "avo" or "avos".

(b) Nos. 31/2 further surch with T 8

56		5a. on 30 on 300r. (p. 12½)	9·00	5·50
57		5a. on 30 on 300r. (p. 13½)	9·00	5·50
		a. "avos" omitted	26·00	26·00

(N **9**) 10

1894. NEWSPAPER. Surch with Type N **9**.

N58	N **5**	½a. on 2½r. brown (p. 11½)	90	80
N59		½a. on 2½r. brown (p. 12½)	1·00	1·00

1898 (1 Apr). 400th Anniv of Vasco da Gama's Discovery of Route to India. As Nos. 1/8 of Portuguese Colonies and Overseas Territories. P 14 to 15.

58		1a. blue-green	2·75	2·00
59		1a. vermilion	2·75	2·00
60		2a. dull purple	2·75	2·00
61		4a. yellow-green	2·75	2·00
62		8a. deep blue	4·25	2·50
63		12a. chocolate	5·75	3·50
64		16a. bistre-brown	5·75	4·25
65		24a. ochre	8·75	6·00
58/65 Set of 8			32·00	22·00

(Des and eng E. Mouchon. Typo)

1898 (1 July)–**1900**. Name and value in black, on the 78a. in carmine. With or without gum (Nos. 68, 78), no gum (66/7, 70/4, 79, 83).

(a) P 12½

66	10	½a. pale grey	4·25	3·50
67		1a. orange-red	4·25	3·50

(b) P 11½

68	10	½a. pale grey	75	65
69		1a. orange-red	75	65
70		2a. green	75	65
71		2½a. chocolate	2·20	1·60
72		3a. deep lilac	2·20	1·60
73		4a. blue-green	2·20	1·60
74		8a. blue	2·20	1·60
75		10a. blue (1899)	2·20	1·60
76		12a. rose	6·00	5·25
77		13a. mauve	6·00	5·25
78		16a. deep blue/*blue*	6·00	5·25
79		20a. brown/*straw* (1899)	6·00	5·25
80		24a. brown/*buff*	6·00	5·25
81		31a. purple/*flesh*	6·00	5·25
82		47a. blue/*pink*	11·50	8·25
83		78a. black/*azure* (1900)	16·00	10·50
68/83 Set of 16			70·00	55·00

See also Nos. 112/23.

PROVISORIO
(11)

(12)

D 13

1899. Surch as T **11**.

84	10	10 on 16a. blue/*blue*	4·25	3·75
85		20 on 31a. purple/*flesh*	4·25	3·75

1902. Surch as T **12**.

86	2	5a. on 25r. (12½)	3·75	2·10
87		5a. on 200r. (12½)	5·75	3·50
88	6	5a. on 5r. (11½)	2·20	1·60
		a. Surch inverted	26·00	26·00
89		5a. on 25r. (11½)	2·20	1·60
90		5a. on 50r. (11½)	2·40	2·10
91		5a. on 50r. (E) (13½)	2·40	2·10
92	2	6a. on 10r. (12½)	£250	£190
93		6a. on 300r. (12½)	5·50	5·00
94	6	6a. on 20r. (11½)	2·40	2·10
95	N **5**	6a. on 2½r. (11½)	1·40	1·25
		a. Surch inverted	26·00	26·00
96		6a. on 2½r. (12½)	£250	£250
97		6a. on 2½r. (13½)	1·40	1·20
98	2	9a. on 40r. (12½)	6·75	5·00
99		9a. on 100r. (12½)	6·75	5·00
100	6	9a. on 15r. (11½)	2·40	2·10
101		9a. on 75r. (11½)	2·40	2·10
102	2	15a. on 20r. (12½)	6·75	5·00
103		15a. on 50r. (12½)	£200	£170
104	6	15a. on 10r. (11½)	4·00	3·00
105		15a. on 100r. (11½)	4·00	3·00
106		15a. on 300r. (11½)	4·00	3·00
107	2	22a. on 80r. (12½)	13·50	10·00
108	6	22a. on 80r. (11½)	6·75	5·50
109		22a. on 200r. (11½)	6·75	5·50

The 5/25, 5/200, 6/10, 6/300, 9/40, 9/100, 15/50 and 22/200 values, all T **2**, were reprinted in 1905.

PROVISORIO
(13a)

1902. Optd with T **13a**.

110	10	3a. deep lilac	3·00	2·10
111		12a. rose	7·25	5·50

1903 (1 Jan). Colours changed. Name and value in black. No gum. P 11½.

112	10	3a. deep green	3·50	2·00
113		5a. carmine	2·75	2·00
114		6a. pale yellow-brown	2·75	2·00
115		9a. red-brown	2·75	2·00
116		10a. grey-brown	2·75	2·00
117		12a. dull blue	15·00	12·50
118		13a. dull purple	4·00	2·30
119		15a. grey-lilac	6·75	4·00
120		22a. orange-brown/*pink*	6·75	5·00
121		31a. sepia/*cream*	6·75	5·00
122		47a. purple/*pink*	7·00	5·00
123		78a. dull blue/*straw*	15·00	10·50
112/123 Set of 12			70·00	49·00

(Des and eng J. S. de Carvalho e Silva. Typo)

1904. POSTAGE DUE. Name and value in black. With or without gum (1, 2a.). no gum (others). P 11½.

D124	D **13**	1a. yellow-green	75	65
D125		2a. slate	75	65
D126		5a. brown	1·70	1·30
D127		6a. orange	1·70	1·30
D128		10a. deep brown	2·20	1·30
D129		15a. pale red-brown	3·75	3·00
D130		24a. blue	10·50	6·25
D131		40a. carmine	11·00	6·50
D132		50a. orange	14·50	7·00
D133		1p. deep lilac	31·00	17·00
D124/133 Set of 10			70·00	40·00

10 AVOS
(14)

Republica
(15)

1905. Surch with T **14**.

124	10	10a. on 12a. dull blue	4·25	3·50

TIMOR

King Manoel II
1 February 1908–5 October 1910

PORTUGUESE REPUBLIC
5 October 1910

(15a)

1911. Optd with T **15a**, in red or green (G.). P 11½.

125	10	½a. grey	75	60
126		1a. orange-red	75	60
		a. Perf 12½	4·25	4·00
127		2a. green	75	60
128		3a. deep green	75	60
129		5a. carmine (G.)	1·40	75
130		6a. pale yellow-brown	1·40	75
131		9a. red-brown	1·40	75
132		10a. grey-brown	2·20	1·70
133		13a. dull purple	2·20	1·70
134		15a. grey-lilac	2·20	1·70
135		22a. orange-brown/*pink*	2·20	1·70
136		31a. sepia/*cream*	2·20	1·70
137		47a. purple/*pink*	4·50	3·50
138		78a. dull blue/*straw*	6·25	4·75
125/138 Set of 14 (cheapest)			26·00	19·00

1911. POSTAGE DUE. Optd with T **15a**, in red or green (G.).

D139	D 13	1a. yellow-green	40	35
D140		2a. slate	40	35
D141		5a. brown	65	60
D142		6a. orange	95	75
D143		10a. deep brown	1·50	1·00
D144		15a. pale red-brown	1·90	1·20
D145		24a. blue	3·25	2·30
D146		40a. carmine (G.)	4·25	3·00
D147		50a. orange	5·75	3·25
D148		1p. deep lilac	14·50	8·50
D139/148 Set of 10			30·00	19·00

1913. Various stamps of 1902–5 optd locally.

*(a) With T **15**, in red*

139	10	3a. deep green	5·75	4·00
		a. Opt inverted	26·00	
140	6	5a. on 5r. (11½)	2·20	1·90
141		5a. on 25r. (11½)	2·20	1·90
142		5a. on 50r. (11½)	5·00	4·00
143		5a. on 50r. (E) (13½)	5·00	4·00
144	N 5	6a. on 2½r. (11½)	4·50	2·50
145		6a. on 2½r. (13½)	4·50	2·50
146	6	6a. on 20r. (11½)	2·50	1·90
147		9a. on 15r. (11½)	2·50	1·90
148	10	10a. on 12a. (14)	2·50	1·90
149	6	15a. on 100r. (11½)	3·00	2·75
150		22a. on 80r. (11½)	5·75	3·25
151		22a. on 200r. (11½)	5·75	3·25

(16)  (17)  (18)

*(b) With T **16***

152	10	5a. carmine (G.)	3·00	2·75
153	6	9a. on 75r. (11½) (G.)	3·00	2·75
154		15a. on 10r. (11½) (G.)	3·00	2·75
155		15a. on 300r. (11½) (R.)	4·50	4·00
		a. "REPBLICAU" (pos. 11)	26·00	23·00
		b. "REUBPLICA" (pos. 12)	26·00	23·00

*(c) With T **17**, in red*

156	10	6a. pale yellow-brown	2·50	1·90
157		9a. red-brown	2·50	1·90
158		10a. grey-brown	2·50	1·90
159		13a. mauve	2·50	1·90
160		13a. dull purple	2·50	1·90
161		15a. grey-lilac	3·50	2·75
162		22a. orange-brown/*pink*	4·50	2·75
163		31a. purple/*flesh*	4·50	3·25
164		31a. sepia/*cream*	4·50	3·25

165		47a. blue/*pink*	7·00	5·50
166		47a. purple/*pink*	7·00	5·50
167		78a. dull blue/*straw*	9·00	7·75

*(d) With T **18**, in red*

168	10	78a. black/*azure*	9·00	5·75

1913. POSTAGE DUE. Optd locally with T **17**, in red or green (G.).

D169	D 13	1a. yellow-green	13·50	9·75
D170		2a. slate	13·50	9·75
D171		5a. brown	6·00	3·75
D172		6a. orange	6·00	3·75
D173		10a. deep brown	6·00	4·75
D174		15a. pale red-brown	6·00	4·75
D175		24a. blue	7·25	4·75
D176		40a. carmine (G.)	7·25	4·75
D177		50a. orange	14·50	7·00
D178		1p. deep lilac	14·50	7·00
D169/178 Set of 10			85·00	55·00

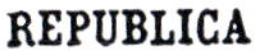

REPUBLICA **10** A.
(19) (20)  **21** Ceres

1913. Stamps of Vasco da Gama Issue optd or surch in Lisbon with T **19** or **20**.

169		½a. blue-green	85	65
170		1a. vermilion	85	65
171		2a. dull purple	95	75
172		4a. yellow-green	95	75
173		8a. deep blue	2·00	1·30
174		10a. on 12a. chocolate	3·50	2·75
175		16a. bistre-brown	2·50	2·00
176		24a. ochre	4·00	3·25
169/176 Set of 8			14·00	11·00

(Des C. Fernandes. Eng J. S. de Carvalho a Silva. Typo)

1914. Name and value in black. Chalk-surfaced paper. P 15×14.

177	21	½a. brown-olive	75	55
178		1a. black	75	55
179		2a. deep green	75	55
180		3a. chocolate	1·40	1·00
181		4a. carmine	1·40	1·00
182		6a. violet	1·70	1·00
183		10a. deep blue	1·70	1·00
184		12a. yellow-brown	2·50	1·70
185		16a. slate	2·50	1·70
186		20a. brown-red	24·00	6·75
187		40a. claret	13·50	6·75
188		58a. chocolate/*green*	13·50	6·25
189		76a. brown/*rose*	13·50	10·00
190		1p. orange/*salmon*	22·00	15·00
191		3p. deep green/*azure*	50·00	26·00
177/191 Set of 15			£130	70·00

See also Nos. 209/27.

1915. Provisionals of 1902–5 optd with T **15a**, in red (reading down on 2½r.).

192	10	3a. deep lilac (110)	1·10	80
193		10a. on 12a. (124)	1·10	80
194	6	5a. on 5r. (11½)	1·10	75
195		5a. on 25r. (11½)	1·10	75
196		5a. on 50r. (11½)	1·10	75
197		5a. on 50r. (E) (13½)	1·80	1·50
198	N 5	6a. on 2½r. (11½)	1·10	75
199		6a. on 2½r. (12½)	1·80	1·30
200		6a. on 2½r. (13½)	1·10	75
201	6	6a. on 20r. (11½)	1·10	75
202		9a. on 15r. (11½)	1·10	75
203		9a. on 75r. (11½)	1·30	75
204		15a. on 10r. (11½)	1·30	75
205		15a. on 100r. (11½)	1·40	75
206		15a. on 300r. (11½)	1·40	75
207		22a. on 80r. (11½)	3·75	2·30
208		22a. on 200r. (11½)	5·75	4·00

1919–23. Name and value in black.

(a) Unsurfaced paper. P 15×14 (1919)

209	21	1a. black	1·80	1·30
210		2a. deep green	1·80	1·30

(b) Unsurfaced paper. P 12×11½ (1922–23)

211	21	½a. brown-olive	1·40	1·30
212		1a. black	1·40	1·30
213		1½a. yellow-green (1923)	1·20	1·10

TIMOR

214	2a. deep green	1·40	1·30
215	4a. carmine	3·75	2·75
216	7a. yellow-green (1923)	2·00	1·20
217	7½a. pale blue (1923)	2·00	1·20
218	9a. pale dull blue (1923)	2·00	1·20
219	11a. drab (1923)	3·00	2·50
220	12a. yellow-brown	3·75	2·75
221	15a. mauve (1923)	10·00	5·75
222	18a. deep blue (1923)	10·00	5·75
223	19a. deep grey-green (1923)	10·00	5·75
224	36a. turquoise (1923)	10·00	5·75
225	54a. chocolate (1923)	10·00	5·75
226	72a. bright rosine (1923)	20·00	11·50

(c) Glazed paper. P 12×11½ (1923)

227	21	5p. bright carmine	80·00	37·00
211/227 Set of 17			£150	85·00

CHARITY TAX STAMPS. Stamps bearing C numbers were for compulsory use on internal letters on certain days of the year as an additional postal tax for public charities. Other values in some of the designs were for use on telegrams or for fiscal purposes.

```
2 AVOS           ½ Avo
TAXA      2
DE            P. P. n.º 68
GUERRA   TAXA DE GUERRA   19-3-1920
(C 22)         (C 23)        (24)
```

1919 (1 July). CHARITY TAX. No. 177 surch locally with Type C **22**. With or without gum.

C228	21	2a. on ½a. brown-olive (R.)	8·50	3·75
		a. Surch inverted	£110	£100

A similar 9a. surcharge was only for fiscal use.

1919. CHARITY TAX. Nos. 196/7 surch locally with Type C **23** in red, with bars obliterating "5" of previous surcharge in black.

C229	6	2 on 5a. on 50r. (11½)		
C230		2 on 5a. on 50r. (E) (13½)	75·00	60·00

A similar 9a. value was only for fiscal use.

1920 (Mar). Nos. 196/7 surch locally with T **24**.

228	6	½a. on 5a. on 50r. (11½)	21·00	19·00
229		½a. on 5a. on 50r. (E) (13½)	26·00	25·00

1925 (8 May). Marquis de Pombal Commemoration. P 12½.

(a) CHARITY TAX

C231	2a. carmine-lake	70	50
C232	2a. carmine-lake	70	50
C233	2a. carmine-lake	70	50

Designs:—C231; Pombal Monument; C232; Planning the reconstruction of Lisbon; C233 Marquis de Pombal.

(b) POSTAGE DUE. Optd with "MULTA" Islands

D231	4a. carmine-lake	70	55
D232	4a. carmine-lake	70	55
D233	4a. carmine-lake	70	55
C231/D233 Set of 6		3·75	2·75

Nos. C231/3 were in use from 8 to 13 May 1925 and from 5 to 15 May in 1926 and 1929. Nos. D231/3 were used in default.

```
    ≡ ≡
    50 C.
     (24a)
```

1931. Nos. 226 and 221 surch as T **24a**.

230	21	6a. on 72a. rosine	2·00	1·50
231		12a. on 15a. mauve	2·00	1·50

```
    7 avos
   Instrução
D. L. n.º 7 de 3-2-1934   Assistência
       ≡                  D. L. n.º 72
     (C 25)                  (C 26)
```

1934–35. CHARITY TAX for Education. Fiscal stamps with values in black, optd or surch locally as Type C **25**. With or without gum. P 12×11½.

C234	2a. green (R.)	4·75	3·25
	a. Inverted "5" for "ç"	15·00	10·00
C235	5a. green (R.)	7·25	3·75
	a. Inverted "5" for "ç"	15·00	10·00
C236	7a. on ½a. rose ('35)	7·75	4·50
	a. Inverted "5" for "ç"	15·00	10·00
C234/236 Set of 3		18·00	10·50

The above were in use in Nov and Dec 1934, Jan, Nov and Dec 1935, and Jan 1936.

1935 (8 July). As T **50** of Macao. W **51** of Macao.

232	½a. brown	45	30
233	1a. sepia	45	30
234	2a. blue-green	45	30
235	3a. mauve	45	30
236	4a. black	80	50
237	5a. grey	80	50
238	6a. cinnamon	80	50
239	7a. carmine	80	50
240	8a. turquoise	1·30	70
241	10a. vermilion	1·30	70
242	12a. blue	1·30	70
243	14a. olive-green	1·30	70
244	15a. claret	1·30	70
245	20a. orange	1·30	70
246	30a. yellow-green	1·60	70
247	40a. violet	5·25	2·50
248	50a. bistre-brown	5·25	2·50
249	1p. grey-blue	12·50	7·50
250	2p. red-brown	32·00	11·00
251	3p. emerald	46·00	15·00
252	5p. mauve	60·00	31·00
232/252 Set of 21		£160	70·00

1936 (1 Nov)–**37**. CHARITY TAX. Fiscal stamps with values in black, optd locally with Type C **26**. With or without gum. P 12×11½.

C253	10a. rose	5·00	3·50
C254	10a. grey-green (1.11.37)	3·75	3·25

1938 (1 Oct). Name and value in black. P 13½×13.

(a) POSTAGE

253	1a. grey-olive	45	40
254	2a. orange-brown	45	40
255	3a. slate-violet	45	40
256	4a. emerald-green	45	40
257	5a. carmine	55	45
258	6a. slate	55	45
259	8a. bright purple	55	45
260	10a. magenta	55	45
261	12a. scarlet	80	55
262	15a. orange	1·30	90
263	20a. blue	1·30	90
264	40a. grey-black	2·00	1·20
265	50a. brown	3·00	1·80
266	1p. lake	10·00	5·75
267	2p. olive-green	27·00	6·75
268	3p. ultramarine	30·00	14·50
269	5p. red-brown	60·00	30·00
253/269 Set of 17		£130	60·00

Designs:—1a. to 4a. Vasco de Gama; 5a. to 8a. Mousinho de Albuquerque; 10 to 15a. Prince Henry the Navigator; 20 to 50a. Dam; 1 to 5p. Afonso de Albuquerque.

(b) AIR

270	1a. scarlet	1·10	1·00
271	2a. bright violet	1·20	80
272	3a. orange	1·20	80
273	5a. bright blue	1·30	1·10
274	10a. brown-lake	1·60	1·30
275	20a. blue-green	4·00	1·80
276	50a. red-brown	8·00	5·50
277	70a. carmine	9·50	7·00
278	1p. magenta	19·00	10·00
270/278 Set of 9		42·00	26·00

Designs:—1a. to 1p. Airplane over Globe.

The whole of Timor was occupied by the Japanese in the Second World War, though Japan was not at war with Portugal. From November 1942 to December 1945 there were no postal facilities for the civilian population. A shortage of stamps after liberation was met by overprinting stamps of Mozambique.

```
      TIMOR
        8
      AVOS
```

(27)

TIMOR

* LIBERTAÇÃO *
(28)

C 29

1946 (7 Sept). 1938 issue of Mozambique surch as T **27**.

(a) POSTAGE. Nos. 354/64 surcharged

279	1a. on 15c. brown-purple	7·25	5·25
280	4a. on 35c. emerald-green	7·25	5·25
281	8a. on 50c. magenta	7·25	5·25
282	10a. on 70c. slate-violet	7·25	5·25
283	12a. on 1E. scarlet	7·25	5·25
284	20a. on 1E.75 blue	7·25	5·25

(b) AIR. Nos. 371/7 surcharged

285	8a. on 50c. orange	7·75	5·75
286	12a. on 1E. bright blue	7·75	5·75
287	40a. on 3E. blue-green	7·75	5·75
288	50a. on 5E. red-brown	7·75	5·75
289	1p. on 10E. magenta	7·75	5·75
279/289	Set of 11	75·00	55·00

1947 (15 Mar). Liberation. Nos. 253, etc., optd with T **28**.

(a) POSTAGE

290	1a. grey-olive	21·00	11·50
291	2a. orange-brown	45·00	24·00
292	3a. slate-violet	19·00	7·25
293	4a. emerald-green	19·00	7·25
294	5a. carmine	8·25	2·75
295	8a. bright purple	2·10	90
296	10a. magenta	7·75	3·25
297	12a. scarlet	7·75	3·25
298	15a. orange	7·75	3·25
299	20a. blue	£100	50·00
	a. Opt inverted	£250	£250
300	40a. grey-black	22·00	13·50
290/300	Set of 11	£225	£110

(b) AIR

301	1a. scarlet	32·00	8·00
302	2a. bright violet	32·00	8·00
303	3a. orange	32·00	8·00
304	5a. bright blue	32·00	8·00
305	10a. brown-lake	7·50	2·75
306	20a. blue-green	7·50	2·75
307	50a. red-brown	7·50	2·75
308	70a. carmine	19·00	8·00
309	1p. magenta	13·50	2·75
301/309	Set of 9	£160	46·00

1948. CHARITY TAX. Typo locally. No gum. P 11½.

C310	C **29**	10a. deep blue	3·75	1·90
C311		20a. green	4·75	3·25

The 20a. has a different emblem.

30 Girl with Gong   31 Pottery-making   32

(Des A. de Sousa. Litho Litografia Maia, Oporto)

1948 (Sept). As T **30**. P 14.

310	1a. red-brown and turquoise	1·30	60
311	3a. red-brown and grey	2·75	1·20
312	4a. myrtle green and magenta	3·75	2·75
313	8a. greenish slate and vermilion	2·10	70
314	10a. blue-green and orange-brown	2·10	70
315	20a. ultramarine and light blue	2·10	1·20
316	1p. ultramarine and orange	39·00	9·00
317	3p. red-brown and violet	42·00	15·00
310/317	Set of 8	85·00	28·00
MS317a	130×99 mm. Nos. 310/17 (sold at 5p.)	£150	£120

Designs:—1a. Native woman; 4a. Girl with baskets; 8a. Chief of Aleixo de Ainaro; 10a. Timor chief; 20a. Warrior and horse; 1, 3p. Tribal chieftains.

1948 (Oct). Honouring the Statue of Our Lady of Fatima. P 14.

318	8a. grey (Statue of Our Lady of Fatima)	12·50	11·50

For No. 318 in miniature sheet see No. **MS**1 of Portuguese Colonies and Overseas Territories (Part 9, *Portugal and Spain*).

1949 (Oct). 75th Anniv of Universal Postal Union. As T **64** of Macao. P 14.

319	16a. yellow-brown (Globe)	30·00	16·00

(Litho Litografia Nacional, Oporto)

1950 (Apr). T **31** and similar type. P 14.

320	20a. blue	1·40	1·30
321	50a. brown (Young girl)	4·25	1·70

1950 (May). Holy Year. P 13½.

322	40a. green (Bells and dove)	3·00	1·90
323	70a. sepia (Angel)	4·75	2·75

For No. 322 in miniature sheet see No. **MS**2 of Portuguese Colonies and Overseas Territories (Part 9, *Portugal and Spain*).

(Des V. P. da C. Sequeira. Litho Litografia Nacional, Oporto)

1950 (Oct). T **32** and similar floral designs. P 14.

324	1a. carmine, green and grey	1·00	60
325	3a. yellow, green and olive-brown	4·50	3·25
326	10a. rose, green and blue	5·25	3·50
327	16a. red, orange, green and brown	10·00	4·75
328	20a. yellow, green and blue-green	4·50	3·25
329	30a. yellow, green and deep blue	5·25	3·50
330	70a. red, yellow, green and purple	6·75	4·00
331	1p. carmine, yellow and green	11·50	7·00
332	2p. yellow, green and crimson	17·00	12·00
333	5p. pink, green and black	27·00	22·00
324/333	Set of 10	85·00	60·00

Flowers:—1a. *Belamcanda chinensis*; 3a. *Caesalpinia pulcherrima*; 10a. *Calotropis gigantea*; 16a. *Delonix regia*; 20a. *Plumeria rubra*; 30a. *Allamanda cathartica*; 70a. *Haemanthus multiflorus*, 1p. *Bauhinia*; 2p. *Eurycles amboiniensis*; 5p. *Crinum longiflorum*.

1951 (Oct). Termination of Holy Year. P 14.

334	86a. greenish blue and turquoise (Our Lady of Fatima)	3·25	2·50

No. 334 was issued *se-tenant* with a stamp-size label bearing a papal declaration.

1952 (June). First Tropical Medicine Congress, Lisbon. P 13½.

335	10a. brown and blackish green	1·70	1·30

Design:—Nurse weighing baby.

1952. POSTAGE DUE. P 14.

D336	1a. multicoloured	25	20
D337	3a. multicoloured	25	20
D338	5a. multicoloured	25	20
D339	10a. multicoloured	30	20
D340	30a. multicoloured	30	20
D341	1p. multicoloured	1·30	75
D336/341	Set of 6	2·40	1·60

33 St. Francis Xavier Statue

34 Statue of The Virgin (Litho Litografia Nacional, Oporto, Portugal)

1952 (25 Oct). 400th Death Anniv of St. Francis Xavier. T **33** and similar vert designs. P 14.

336	1a. black and grey	35	20
337	16a. sepia and buff	1·60	75
338	1p. lake and bluish grey	6·00	2·50
336/338	Set of 3	7·25	3·00

Designs:—16a. Miraculous arm of St. Francis; 1p. Tomb of St. Francis.

1953 (Jan). Missionary Art Exhibition. Litho P 13½.

339	**34**	3a. reddish brown and grey-brown	35	20
340		16a. red-brown and stone	1·50	95
341		50a. deep ultramarine and grey-brown	3·00	2·20
339/341		Set of 3	4·25	3·00

1954. Portuguese Stamp Centenary. Multicoloured. P 13.

342	10a. Arms of Portuguese Overseas Provinces	2·10	1·70

227

TIMOR

1954. Fourth Centenary of São Paulo. Multicoloured. P 13½.
343   16a. Father M. de Nabrega .... 1·50 1·00

35 Map of Timor   (**36**)

(Des J. Moura. Litho Enschedé)

1956 (21 May). P 14×13.
344	**35**	1a. multicoloured	30	15
345		3a. multicoloured	30	15
346		8a. multicoloured	65	45
347		24a. multicoloured	70	45
348		32a. multicoloured	85	50
349		40a. multicoloured	1·30	65
350		1p. multicoloured	4·00	85
351		3p. multicoloured	10·00	5·00
344/351 Set of 8			16·00	7·50

1958 (5 Sept). Sixth International Congress of Tropical Medicine. Diamond-shaped design. Multicoloured. P 13½.
352   32a. *Calophyllum inophyllum* .... 5·25 3·75

1958 (Sept). Brussels International Exhibition. As T **78** of Macao. Multicoloured. P 12×11½.
353   40a. Exhibition emblem .... 1·00 55

1960 (1 Jan). New Currency. Nos. 344/51 surch as T **36**.
354	**35**	5c. on 1a. multicoloured	30	15
355		10c. on 3a. multicoloured	30	15
356		20c. on 8a. multicoloured	30	15
357		30c. on 24a. multicoloured	30	15
358		50c. on 32a. multicoloured	30	15
359		1E. on 40a. multicoloured	40	35
360		2E. on 40a. multicoloured	65	40
361		5E. on 1p. multicoloured	1·30	90
362		10E. on 3p. multicoloured	4·25	2·00
363		15E. on 3p. multicoloured	4·25	2·75
354/363 Set of 10			11·00	6·50

(C **37**)   **38** Elephant Jar

1960–66. CHARITY TAX. New Currency. Sans-serif lettering. Typo locally. No gum.

(a) P 11½ (1960)
C364	**37**	70c. indigo	1·40	1·30
C365		1E.30 green	2·75	2·50

(b) P 10½ (1966)
C366	**37**	70c. deep blue	1·40	1·30
C367		1E.30 emerald	2·75	2·50

In No. C364 "PORTUGUESA" is 17 mm wide and in No. C366 it is 18 mm; No. C365 has "1$30" 8 mm wide and in No. C367 it is 7 mm. There are other differences also.
See also Nos. C398/400.

1960 (25 June). Fifth Death Centenary of Prince Henry the Navigator. Multicoloured. P 13½×13.
364   4E.50 Prince Henry's motto (horiz) .... 1·00 60

1961 (28 Apr). Timor Art. T **38** and similar multicoloured designs. Litho. P 11½×12 (vert) or 12×11½ (horiz).
365		5c. Type **38**	30	15
366		10c. House on stilts	30	15
		a. Blue (inscription) inverted	26·00	
367		20c. Idol	40	25
368		30c. Rosary	60	45
369		50c. Model of outrigger canoe (horiz)	80	50
370		1E. Casket	1·00	50
371		2E.50 Archer	1·10	50
372		4E.50 Elephant	1·50	50
373		5E. Native climbing palm tree	2·10	50
374		10E. Statuette of woman	5·00	1·50
375		20E. Model of cockfight (horiz)	12·50	3·75
376		50E. House, bird and cat	14·50	4·50
365/376 Set of 12			36·00	12·00

1962 (22 Mar). Sports. Multicoloured. P 13.
377		50c. Game shooting	40	15
378		1E. Horse-riding	1·40	45
379		1E.50 Swimming	1·30	60
380		2E. Athletes	1·50	70
381		2E.50 Football	1·80	95
382		15E. Big-game hunting	3·50	2·20
377/382 Set of 6			9·00	4·50

1962. Malaria Eradication. Multicoloured. P 13½.
383   2E.50 *Anopheles sundaicus* .... 1·80 1·00

1964 (16 May). Centenary of National Overseas Bank. Multicoloured. P 13½.
384   2E.50 M. P. Chagas .... 1·20 1·00

1965 (17 May). I.T.U. Centenary. P 14½.
385   1E.50 multicoloured .... 1·80 1·10

1966 (28 May). 40th Anniv of Portuguese National Revolution. Multicoloured. P 12½×11½.
386   4E.50 Dr. V. Machado's College and Health Centre, Dili .... 1·50 1·00

1967 (31 Jan). Centenary of Military Naval Association. P 13.
387		10c. Gago Coutinho and gunboat *Patria*	40	30
388		4E.50 Sacadura Cabral and Fairey IIID seaplane *Lusitania*	2·75	1·50

39 Sepoy Officer, 1792   **40** Pictorial Map of 1834, and Arms

(Des A. Cutileiro. Litho)

1967 (12 Feb). Portuguese Military Uniforms. T **39** and similar vert designs. Multicoloured. P 13×13½.
389		35c. Type **39**	25	20
390		1E. Infantry Officer, 1815	2·30	60
391		1E.50 Infantryman, 1879	40	35
392		2E. Infantryman, 1890	40	35
393		2E.50 Infantry officer, 1903	60	35
394		3E. Sapper, 1918	1·00	55
395		4E.50 Commando, 1964	1·70	55
396		10E. Parachutist, 1964	2·40	1·30
389/396 Set of 8			8·25	3·75

1967 (13 May). 50th Anniv of the Fatima Apparitions. Multicoloured.
397   3E. Virgin of the Pilgrims 80 40

1967. CHARITY TAX. Designs similar to Type C **37**. No gum. P 10½.

(a) Serifed lettering
C398   70c. deep blue .... 10·50 7·25

(b) Sans-serif lettering. Whole design smaller ("PORTUGUESA" 12 mm long)
C399		70c. violet-blue	1·40	1·30
C400		1E.30 emerald	2·75	2·50

1968 (22 Apr). 500th Birth Anniv of Pedro Cabral (explorer). Multicoloured. P 14.
398   4E.50 Lopo Homen-Reineis' map, 1519 (horiz) .... 1·50 80

1969 (17 Feb). Birth Centenary of Admiral Gago Coutinho. Multicoloured. P 14.
399   4E.50 Frigate *Almirante Gago Coutinho* (horiz) ..... 1·80 1·20

(Des J. de Moura. Litho Litografia Nacional, Oporto)

1969 (25 July). Bicentenary of Dili (Capital of Timor). P 14.
400   **40**   1E. multicoloured 70 50

1969 (29 Aug). 500th Birth Anniv of Vasco da Gama (explorer). Multicoloured. P 14.
401   5E. Convert Medallion............ 70   50

1969 (25 Sept). Centenary of Overseas Administrative Reforms. P 14.
402   5E. multicoloured................ 80   50

1969 (1 Dec). 500th Birth Anniv of King Manoel I. Multicoloured. P 14.
403   4E. Emblem of Manoel I, Jeronimos Monastery........ 60   40

41 Map, Sir Ross Smith and Arms of Britain, Timor and Australia

C **42** Woman and Star

(Des J. de Moura. Litho Litografia Nacional, Oporto)

1969 (9 Dec). 50th Anniv of First England–Australia Flight. P 14.
404   **41**   2E. multicoloured........ 90   70

1969–70. CHARITY TAX. Litho. P 13.
C405   C **42**   30c. deep blue and light blue (1970)........ 55   50
C406   50c. reddish purple & lt yell-orange........ 55   50
C407   1E. yellow-brown and pale yellow........ 55   50
C405/407 Set of 3 .... 1·50   1·40

D. L. n.° 776

$30

(C **43**)

1970. CHARITY TAX. Nos. C399/400 surch as Type C **43**, in red.
C408   30c. on 70c. violet-blue........ 13·50   13·00
C409   30c. on 1E.30 emerald........ 13·50   13·00
C410   50c. on 70c. violet-blue........ 31·00   28·00
C411   50c. on 1E.30 emerald........ 13·50   13·00
C412   1E. on 70c. violet-blue........ 18·00   15·00
C413   1E. on 1E.30 emerald........ 13·50   13·00

1970 (15 Nov). Birth Centenary of Marshal Carmona. Multicoloured. P 14.
414   1E.50 Portrait in civilian dress........ 50   30

1972 (25 May). 400th Anniv of Camoens' "*The Lusiads*" (epic poem). Multicoloured. P 13.
415   1E. Missionaries, natives and galleon........ 60   40

1972 (20 June). Olympic Games, Munich. Multicoloured. P 14×13½.
416   4E.50 Football........ 80   50

1972 (20 Sept). 50th Anniv of 1st Flight from Lisbon to Rio de Janeiro. Multicoloured. P 13½.
417   1E. Aviators Gago Coutinho and Sacadura Cabral in Fairey IIID seaplane........ 80   70

1973 (15 Dec). Centenary of World Meterological Organization. P 13.
418   20E. multicoloured........ 2·75   2·10

In August 1975 a coup d'etat was staged by the right-wing UDT (Democratic Union of Timor). In the ensuing civil war Fretilin (the Front for the Independence of East Timor) soon gained the upper hand and occupied the capital, Dili. By 8 September they claimed total control of the colony and on 27 November 1975 declared the independence of the People's Democratic Republic of East Timor.

Following disputes over border clashes, Indonesian troops, backed by local pro-Indonesian factions, invaded East Timor on 7 December 1975 and quickly gained complete control, despite a U.N. resolution of 11 December calling on them to withdraw. On 17 July 1976 East Timor was declared a province of Indonesia.

EAST TIMOR

UNITED NATIONS TRANSITIONAL ADMINISTRATION IN EAST TIMOR

100 cents = 1 dollar

Following negotiations between Portugal and Indonesia a referendum was conducted on 30 August 1999 with the majority voting for independence for East Timor.

On the 20 September 1999 the first United Nations peace keeping troops arrived in East Timor and the Indonesian troops began to withdraw.

By October the United Nations had established the International Force for East Timor (I.N.T.E.R.F.E.T.).

On the 19 October 1999 the Indonesian Consultative Assembly confirmed the establishment and on the 25 October 1999 the United Nations voted to replace I.N.T.E.R.F.E.T. with a force to help with the establishment of a United Nations Transitional Administration of East Timor (U.N.T.A.E.T.).

The East Timor National Council (E.T.N.C.), which was formed to help with policy recommendations, held its first meeting on 11 December 1999.

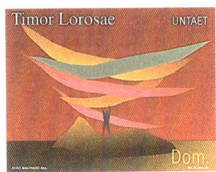

1 Man with Arms Raised

(Des J. Machado. Litho The Mint, Lisbon, Portugal)
2000 (29 Apr). P 12.
                    (a) Inscr "Dom."
1   1   (21c.) multicoloured........ 70   70
                    (b) Inscr "Int."
2   1   ($1.05.) multicoloured........ 3·50   3·50

No. 1 was for use on Domestic mail and No. 2 was for use on International mail.

A passion for philately

Advising in selling through auctions
and in valuations of collections

We auction your collection

Request for our catalogue

Hileras, 9 • 28013 Madrid • 915 480 799
Fax: 915 416 070 • info@iberphil.com • www.iberphil.com

The Ultimate Stamp Magazine

- Monthly colour catalogue supplement
- Written by stamp collectors for stamp collectors
- Philatelic news from around the world

- The UK's biggest selling stamp magazine
- Consistently 150 pages per issue

FREE SAMPLE
For your FREE sample, contact us by:

Telephone: 01425 472 363
Email: subscriptions@stanleygibbons.co.uk
Post: Stanley Gibbons Limited, 7 Parkside, Christchurch Road, Ringwood, Hampshire, BH24 3SH

For more information, please visit **www.gibbonsstampmonthly.com**

Spain

1850. 8½ (later 8) Cuartos = 1 Real
1866. 80 Cuartos = 100 Céntimos de Escudo = 1 Escudo
1867. 1000 Milésimas = 100 Céntimos de Escudo = 80 Cuartos = 1 Escudo
1872. 100 Céntimos = 1 Peseta
2002. 100 Cents = 1 Euro

Queen Isabella II
29 Sept 1833—30 Sept 1868

PRINTERS. All the stamps of Spain, except some of the issues of the National State from 1936 to 1939, were printed at the Government Printing Works, Madrid, unless otherwise stated.

1   2   3

Stamps of T **1** to **8** are inscribed "FRANCO" for the cuarto values and the 1r., and "CERTIFICADO", "CERTIFo" or "CERTDo" for the higher values.

(Dies eng B. Coromina. Litho)
1850 (1 Jan). Imperf.
(a) Thick paper

1	**1**	6c. black (Pl. I)	£550	21·00
2		6c. black (Pl. II)	£475	18·00
3	**2**	12c. pale lilac	£2750	£325
		a. Lilac	£3250	£325
4		5r. dull red	£2750	£325
5		6r. blue	£3750	£900
		a. Deep blue	£4000	£1200
6		10r. blue-green	£5000	£2500

(b) Thin paper

7	**1**	6c. black (Pl. II)	£550	25·00
8	**2**	12c. pale lilac	£3500	£300

The 6c. Plate II can be identified by the "T" and "O" of "CUARTOS" which are joined. However, one stamp in Plate I has "TO" joined and one on Plate II has it unjoined. An additional test is the presence on Plate II of two minute white dots, one below each corner of the square in the top left corner.

(Dies eng B. Coromina. Typo)
1851 (1 Jan). Imperf.
(a) Thin paper

9	**3**	6c. black	£300	3·50
10		12c. pale lilac	£4750	£200
		a. Deep lilac	£5000	£225
11		2r. red	£22000	£13000
12		5r. rose	£2750	£300
		a. Error. Chocolate-brown	£14000	
		b. Deep rose	£3500	£375
13		6r. blue	£4250	£1200
		a. Error. 2r. blue		
		b. Deep blue	£5000	£1500
14		10r. green	£3250	£550
		a. Deep green	£3250	£600

(b) Thick paper

15	**3**	6c. black	£500	14·00

No. 12a comes from a small consignment of sheets printed in this colour, most of which were withdrawn and destroyed.

No. 13a was caused by the insertion of a 2r. cliché in the plate of 6r. Only three examples are known, two singles (one of which is in the Tapling collection) and one in pair *se-tenant* with 6r.

4   5   6 Arms of Madrid

(Dies eng B. Coromina. Typo)
1852 (1 Jan). Imperf.
(a) Thick paper

16	**4**	6c. dull rose	£425	3·00
		a. Brown-rose	£475	5·00
		b. No stop after "CORREOS"	£650	35·00
17		12c. dull purple	£2250	£160
		a. Brown-purple	£2750	£275
		b. Grey-lilac	£3250	£275
18		2r. pale red	£18000	£6000
19		5r. blue-green	£2500	£140
		a. Yellow-green	£3000	£140
20		6r. pale blue	£3750	£550
		a. Greenish blue	£3750	£550

(b) Thin paper

21	**4**	6c. dull rose	£450	3·50
		a. Rose-red	£500	3·75
		b. No stop after "CORREOS"	£550	21·00

Nos. 16b and 21b occurred at least six times in every sheet.

(Dies eng J. P. Varela. Typo)
1853 (1 Jan). Imperf.
(a) Thin paper

22	**5**	6c. rose	£550	2·75
		a. Carmine	£425	1·90
23		12c. reddish purple	£2250	£130
		a. Deep purple	£3000	£200
24		2r. vermilion	£13000	£2250
25		5r. green	£2500	£130
		a. Yellow-green	£2750	£150
26		6r. blue	£3500	£475
		a. Deep blue	£3750	£500

(b) Bluish paper

27	**5**	6c. carmine	£850	11·50

(c) Thick paper

28	**5**	6c. carmine	£750	12·50
29		12c. deep purple	£3000	£500

(Dies eng Bartolomé Coromina. Typo)
1853 (10 Apr–15 Oct). Local Issue for Madrid. Imperf.

30	**6**	1c. bronze (15.10)	£2750	£600
31		3c. bronze	£17000	£8500

Both these stamps have been reprinted on very white paper, without gum. The colour of the reprints is dull grey-bronze, instead of brown-bronze. A 2 cuartos value was prepared for use in 1854, but never issued.

BARRED CANCELLATIONS. Stamps of issues from 1854 onwards cancelled with three horizontal bars are remainders, worth much less than postally used stamps. Stamps on which they exist are marked with *.

7   8   O 9

Arms of Castile and Leon

(Dies eng J. P. Varela. Typo)
1854 (1 Jan–Nov). Imperf.
(a) Thin paper

32	**7**	2c. green (Nov)	£2250	£550
33		4c. carmine (Nov)	£450	2·50
34	**8**	6c. carmine*	£375	1·80
		a. Deep carmine	£400	3·00
35	**7**	1r. indigo (Nov)*	£3750	£375
36	**8**	2r. orange-vermilion*	£1700	£120
		a. Vermilion*	£2250	£200
37		5r. green*	£1700	£110
		a. Deep green	£1700	£130
38		6r. blue*	£2750	£350
		a. Deep blue*	£3000	£400

(b) Thick bluish paper

39	**7**	2c. green	£14000	£2250
40		4c. rose*	£425	6·00
41	**8**	6c. carmine	£1600	£190
42	**7**	1r. pale blue*	£27500	£8500
43	**8**	2r. vermilion*	£5000	£600

231

SPAIN

(c) Thick white paper

44	**7**	4c. rose	£500	16·00
45	**8**	6c. carmine*	£700	19·00

The 2 to 6r. are inscribed "CERT Do" (instead of "FRANCO") at the foot. The 2c. is undated.

The 2 cuartos, *green*, on *bluish* paper watermarked with T **10**, was prepared for use in 1855, but not issued. The 2c., Nos. 32 and 39 have "CORREOS" only, at top.

(Dies eng J. P. Varela. Typo)

1854 (1 July). OFFICIAL. Black impression. Imperf.

O46	O **9**	½o. on *orange*	2·75	1·90
		a. On *orange-yellow*	2·75	1·90
O47		1o. on *rose*	4·75	4·75
O48		4o. on *green*	11·50	9·50
O49		1l. on *blue*	70·00	65·00

The face values of this and the 1855 Official issue, Nos. O50/7, are expressed in onzas (ounces) and libra (pound). This is not a currency, but refers to the maximum weight for which each value could prepay postage.

  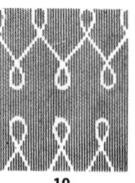

O **10**   9   10

(Dies eng J. P. Varela. Typo)

1855 (1 Jan). OFFICIAL. Black impression. Imperf.

(a) Thin paper

O50	O **10**	½o. on *yellow*	2·50	2·50
		a. On *straw*	2·75	1·90
O51		1o. on *pale rose*	2·75	1·90
O52		4o. on *green*	5·50	5·00
		a. On *yellow-green*	5·75	3·75
O53		1l. on *grey-blue*	18·00	25·00
		a. On *lavender*	24·00	19·00

(b) Thicker paper

O54	O **10**	½o. on *yellow*	2·40	1·60
		a. On *straw*	2·75	1·90
O55		1o. on *flesh*	5·75	3·25
		a. On *pale rose*	2·75	1·90
		b. On *rose*	3·75	2·40
O56		4o. on *green*	5·75	3·75
		a. On *yellow-green*	5·75	3·75
		b. On *blue-green*	7·00	4·25
O57		1l. on *grey-blue*	21·00	19·00
		a. On *lavender*	24·00	19·00

Postal forgeries of this and contemporary regular issues exist and used examples are not uncommon.

See note below No. O49.

For similar design but litho and without full points after "OFICIAL" and "ONZA" or "LIBRA", see Cuba Nos. O12/15.

(Dies eng J. P. Varela. Typo)

1855 (1 Apr). Bluish paper. W **10**. Imperf.

46	**9**	2c. yellow-green*	£3000	£150
47		4c. carmine*	£275	2·40
		a. Rose	£300	95
		b. Brownish red	£300	95
48		1r. blue*	£1100	14·00
		a. Error. 2r. blue	£16000	£3000
		b. Dull blue	£1200	16·00
		c. Greenish blue*	£1200	16·00
49		2r. deep purple*	£850	16·00
		a. Dull purple*	£850	20·00

No. 48a resulted from a cliché of the 2r. being included in the 1r. plate. It is known *se-tenant* with No. 48.

The 4c., 1r. and 2r. of this and the two following issues are found with defective lettering due to flaws in the plate.

11   Die II

Die III

Three Dies of 4c.

I. No special characteristics.
II. Distinct row of regular dots at base of bust; small break at middle of left frame.
III. Thick line of bust merges with dots. No frame break at left but major frame break at upper right.

In addition Die II has faint pairs of white dots inserted above and below the four groups of frame ornaments which are more pronounced in Die III.

1856 (1 Jan). White paper. W **11**. Imperf.

50	**9**	2c. yellow-green*	£3250	£225
		a. Green	£2500	£160
51		4c. rose-red*	9·50	2·40
		a. Carmine-red	12·50	2·75
52		1r. greenish blue*	£3750	£225
		a. Blue-green	£3750	£225
53		2r. deep purple*	£550	27·00
		a. Dull purple	£600	35·00

1856 (11 Apr)–**59**. No wmk. Imperf.

(a) Thin white paper

54	**9**	2c. bluish green*	£600	45·00
		a. Yellow-green*	£550	47·00
55		4c. rose-red*	4·75	45
		a. Pale rose-red	4·75	45
56		1r. blue*	22·00	26·00
		a. Deep blue*	30·00	28·00
		b. Greenish blue*	30·00	28·00
57		2r. dull purple*	75·00	27·00

(b) Thick white paper

58	**9**	2c. yellow-green*	£650	55·00
		a. Green	£700	55·00
59		4c. rose-red*	9·25	1·00
		a. Pale rose-red	9·25	1·00
60		4c. carmine-lake (Die II) (10.59)	70·00	10·00
60a		4c. carmine-lake (Die III)	8·00	20·00
61		1r. blue*	20·00	25·00
		a. Deep blue*	25·00	35·00
		b. Greenish blue*	25·00	30·00
62		2r. deep purple	85·00	25·00
		a. Dull purple*	80·00	30·00

No. 59 exists unofficially perforated 9½ from Valencia in 1858.

A 12c. orange in the same series was prepared in 1859, but not issued, although it exists with remainder cancellation.
(Price £100 *un*).

12   13

*(T **12/13** dies eng J. P. Varela. Typo)*

1860 (1 Feb)–**61**. Tinted paper. Imperf.

63	**12**	2c. green/*greenish*	£375	22·00
		a. Yellow-green/*greenish*	£300	25·00
64		4c. pale orange/*greenish*	44·00	80
		a. Deep orange/*greenish*	45·00	1·25
65		12c. carmine/*buff*	£375	14·00
66		19c. brown/*brown* (14.9.61)	£3000	£1600
67		1r. pale blue/*greenish*	£350	12·50
		a. Deep blue/*greenish*	£250	50
68		2r. lilac/*lilac*	£400	1·00
		a. Deep lilac/*lilac*	£450	15·00

The 4c. exists unofficially perforated 9½ (Valencia) or 15½ (Barcelona).

SPAIN

16

17

18 (T 14 modified)

(Dies eng J. P. Varela. Typo)

1866 (1 Jan). Currency changed. White paper. P 14.

92	16	2c. rose*	£300	34·00
		a. Deep rose	£350	35·00
93		4c. blue*	48·00	95
		a. Pale blue	37·00	65
94		12c. red-orange	£250	19·00
		a. Orange	£275	13·50
		b. Orange-yellow	£250	19·00
95		19c. brown*	£1200	£475
96	17	10c. de e. green*	£325	30·00
		a. Deep green	£325	45·00
97		20c. de e. lilac*	£225	22·00

Imperforate examples of the 2, 4, 12 and 19c. with fewer than 65 horizontal lines in the centre shading are known forgeries.

1866 (1 Aug). Typo. White paper. P 14.

98	18	20c. de e. lilac*	£1200	80·00

19   20   21

1862 (16 July–1 Aug). Tinted or white paper. Imperf.

69	13	2c. deep blue/pale yellow (1.8)	39·00	15·00
		a. Blue/yellow	35·00	9·50
		b. Deep blue/yellow	40·00	15·00
70		4c. brown/brown*	5·75	65
		a. Chocolate/brown	8·00	2·50
		b. Brown/white	19·00	4·75
71		12c. pale blue/pale rose (1.8)*	49·00	9·25
		a. Deep blue/pale rose	60·00	18·00
72		19c. carmine/lilac (1.8)	£200	£275
		a. Carmine/white	£275	£190
73		1r. brown/straw (1.8)*	65·00	22·00
		a. Brown/yellow	75·00	25·00
		b. Brown/bright yellow	75·00	25·00
74		2r. pale green/pale rose (1.8)	41·00	14·00
		a. Green/pale rose	41·00	14·00
		b. Deep green/pale rose*	41·00	14·00

No. 70 is known perf 9½ or 12, No. 70a perf 15 and No. 70b perf 12½. These are experiments carried out by the Govt Ptg Works. They were not officially issued, but No. 70a perf 15 is known used and on cover.

14

15

(Dies eng J. P. Varela. Typo)

1864 (1 Jan–1 Mar). Tinted or white paper. Imperf.

75	14	2c. blue/lilac (1.3)	60·00	21·00
		a. Deep blue/lilac	70·00	30·00
		b. Blue/white	60·00	28·00
76		4c. rose-red/pale red	2·50	80
		a. Carmine/pale red	20·00	2·50
		b. Orange-red/pale red	2·50	1·00
		c. Rose/white	19·00	9·50
77		12c. green/pale rose (1.3)	49·00	15·00
		a. Yellow-green/pale rose	42·00	12·00
78		19c. lilac/lilac (1.3)	£225	£225
		a. Deep lilac/lilac	£250	£250
79		1r. brown/green (1.3)*	£200	95·00
80		2r. blue/pale rose (1.3)*	49·00	15·00
		a. Deep blue/pale rose	60·00	14·00
		b. Blue/white	65·00	24·00

The 4c. is known unofficially perforated 12½ (Barcelona) or 13 (Murcia). The 2c. perf 14 is an experiment from the Govt Ptg Wks, but was not issued.

(Des E. Jover and B. Coromina. Litho)

1865 (1 Jan–1 June). White paper.

(a) Imperf

81	15	2c. rose	£275	33·00
		a. Carmine	£375	41·00
82		12c. rose and blue*	£450	22·00
		a. Frame inverted	£9500	£1200
		b. Rose and deep blue	£550	32·00
83		19c. rose and brown*	£1600	£850
84		1r. yellow green*	£450	75·00
		a. Deep yellow-green	£600	95·00
85		2r. pale mauve*	£450	37·00
		a. Mauve*	£550	45·00
		b. Dull rose	£1300	£275
		c. Rose-red	£500	60·00
		d. Pale orange-red*	£650	£120
		e. Orange-yellow	£500	75·00
		f. Salmon	£950	£180

(b) P 14

86	15	2c. rose (1.6)*	£500	£140
		a. Carmine	£850	£150
87		4c. pale blue*	40·00	95
		a. Blue	45·00	2·50
		b. Bright blue	55·00	2·50
88		12c. rose and blue (1.6)*	£650	65·00
		a. Frame inverted	£17000	£2200
		b. Rose and deep blue	£750	70·00
89		19c. rose and brown (1.6)	£4000	£2750
90		1r. yellow-green (1.6)*	£1900	£550
91		2r. lilac (1.6)*	£1300	£275
		a. Purple	£1300	£275
		b. Dull orange*	£1500	£350
		c. Orange-yellow	£1300	£275

The 4c. exists imperf. (*Price* £2000 un). The only known used copies come from Salamanca.

22   23

(Dies eng E. Jover and B. Coromina. Typo)

1867 (1 Jan). T **19/23** (and similar type for 20c. de e.). White paper. P 14.

99	19	2c. deep brown	£475	49·00
		a. Pale brown	£425	42·00
100	20	4c. blue	26·00	1·10
		a. Deep blue	34·00	2·25
101	21	12c. orange	£325	11·50
		a. Pale orange	£225	8·25
102	22	19c. pale rose*	£1500	£450
		a. "UA" in "CUARTOS" retouched	£2700	£700
103	23	10c. de e. green*	£275	25·00
		a. Deep green	£300	30·00
104	–	20c. de e. lilac*	£130	11·00
		a. Slate-lilac	£150	25·00

A 4 cuartos value in black was prepared, but not issued.
For 12c. red-orange and 19c. brown, see Nos. 149/50.

24

25

26

(Dies eng E. Jover. Typo)

1867 (1 July–1 Nov). Currency changed. P 14.

105	24	5m. green (1.11)*	48·00	19·00
		a. Deep green	55·00	30·00
		b. Bluish green	55·00	30·00
106	25	10m. brown	48·00	19·00
		a. Tête-bêche (pair)	£15000	
		b. Chestnut	35·00	20·00
		c. Deep brown	45·00	25·00
107	26	25m. rose and blue	£275	27·00
		a. Frame inverted	—	£16000
		b. Rose and deep blue	£250	35·00
108		50m. pale brown*	22·00	80
		a. Deep brown	22·00	2·50

For 25m. blue, see No. 145.

233

SPAIN

PROVISIONAL GOVERNMENT
6 Oct 1868–15 June 1869

After the revolution in Madrid in September 1868 the following overprinted issues were made by order of the Provisional Revolutionary Assembly.

All have been extensively forged. Stamps are also known with inscription applied in pen and ink.

(27) (28)

(29) (30) (31)

(32) (34)

1868. Stamps of 1867 optd.

(a) For all Spain with T 27, diagonally upwards, in black. Optd at Govt Printing Works, Madrid

109	24	5m. green	19·00	5·75
110	25	10m. brown	14·00	4·75
111	26	25m. rose and blue	38·00	14·00
112		50m. brown	7·50	4·75
113	23	10c. de e. green	28·00	14·00
114	–	20c. de e. lilac	24·00	9·50
115	21	12c. orange	38·00	9·50
116	22	19c. pale rose	£375	£140

(b) For Andalusia with T 28, in blue. Optd at Cadiz

117	24	5m. green	21·00	6·50
118	25	10m. brown	14·00	4·75
119	26	25m. rose and blue	42·00	14·00
120		50m. brown	8·50	4·75
121	23	10c. de e. green	42·00	14·00
122	–	20c. de e. lilac	28·00	17·00
123	19	2c. brown	80·00	38·00
124	20	4c. blue	38·00	19·00
125	21	12c. orange	42·00	11·50
126	22	19c. pale rose	£475	£225

(c) For Villa de Orotava (Canary Is.) with T 29, in blue

127	26	50m. brown	—	£275

(d) For Llanes (Oroviedo) as T 30, in black

128	26	50m. brown	£190	£120
129	–	20c. de e. lilac	£190	£120

(e) For Teruel with T 31, in black

130	26	25m. rose and blue	£140	85·00
131		50m. brown	95·00	42·00
132	–	20c. de e. lilac	£130	85·00
133	21	12c. orange	£140	95·00

(f) For Salamanca with T 32, in blue

134	25	10m. brown	95·00	65·00
135	26	50m. brown	£130	80·00
136	22	19c. pale rose		
137	–	20c. de e. lilac	£130	75·00

(g) For Valderrobles with "H.P.N." in blue with serifs on letters

138	26	50m. brown	—	£275

(h) For Valladolid with T 34, in black

139	26	25m. rose and blue	50·00	14·00
140		50m. brown	19·00	9·50
141	23	10c. de e. green	42·00	24·00
142	–	20c. de e. lilac	38·00	19·00
143	21	12c. orange	50·00	19·00
144	22	19c. pale rose	£550	£275

There is a second and rarer type of T 34 with larger letters, especially "POR LA".

35 F 36

(Dies eng E. Jover and B. Coromina. Typo)

1868 (1 Jan)–**69**. Colours changed and new values. P 14.

145	26	25m. blue*	£300	17·00
		a. Pale blue	£200	17·00
146	35	50m. deep purple*	30·00	1·25
		a. Purple	25·00	1·00
147	21	100m. brown*	£600	80·00
		a. Red-brown	£650	£110
148	22	200m. green*	£200	13·50
		a. Deep green	£225	30·00
		b. Yellow-green	£225	30·00
149	21	12c. red-orange	£950	43·00
150	22	19c. brown (12.68)	£2500	£600
		a. "UA" in "CUARTOS" re-touched	£2250	£700

Nos. 145/*a* differ slightly from T **26** in the shape of the numerals and the space between "25" and "MILS" is greater.

1868–69. Nos. 145/50 overprinted.

(a) For all Spain with T 27, diagonally upwards, in black

151	26	25m. blue	38·00	11·50
152	35	50m. purple	7·50	3·75
153	21	100m. brown	75·00	28·00
154	22	200m. green	26·00	9·50
155	21	12c. red-orange	£140	28·00
156	22	19c. brown	£750	£190

(b) For Andalusia with T 28, in blue

157	26	25m. blue	42·00	14·00
158	35	50m. purple	9·50	3·75
159	21	100m. brown	70·00	33·00
160	22	200m. green	26·00	11·50
161	21	12c. red-orange	£190	47·00
162	22	19c. brown	£850	£325

(c) For Teruel with T 31, in black

163	35	50m. purple	95·00	47·00
164	21	100m. brown	£190	£100
165	22	200m. green	£110	47·00

(d) For Salamanca with T 32, in blue

166	22	19c. brown		

(e) For Valladolid with T 34, in black

167	26	25m. blue	50·00	16·00
168	35	50m. purple	19·00	9·50
169	21	100m. brown	85·00	38·00
170	22	200m. green	42·00	16·00
171		19c. brown	£950	£275

1869 (1 Jan). FRANK. Litho. White paper. Imperf.

F172	F 36	(–) Blue	65·00	60·00
		a. Tête-bêche (pair)	£190	£190

This stamp was allowed to be used by Señor Castell for franking a work—*Cartilla Postal de España*—which he had written, and which was considered of public utility.

There were two printings of No. F172, both in sheets of 28 stamps. In the first printing eleven stamps were inverted, giving horizontal and vertical tête-bêche pairs; in the second printing all positions were normal.

REGENCY
15 June 1869–30 Dec 1870
Regent, Marshal Francisco Serrano (Duke de la Torre)

> **PUNCHED HOLE CANCELLATIONS.** Postage stamps issued between 1870 and 1900 were also used for the payment of Telegraph fees. Copies so used were cancelled by means of a punched hole and are worth much less than postally used stamps. Values on which this cancellation occurs are marked.

36

234

SPAIN

(Dies eng E. Jover. Typo)
1870 (1 Jan–1 June). P 14.

172	**36**	1m. purple-brown/*flesh* (1.6)	8·50	8·25
		a. *Purple-brown/rose*	7·00	5·75
		b. *Purple-brown/buff*	9·50	8·00
173		2m. black/*flesh* (1.6)	11·00	10·00
		a. *Black/buff*	11·50	8·50
174		4m. cinnamon (1.6)	22·00	17·00
175		10m. pale rose	23·00	8·00
		a. *Rose-red**	28·00	10·00
176		25m. grey-lilac	75·00	8·75
		a. *Mauve*	85·00	9·75
		b. *Bright mauve*	£110	9·50
177		50m. pale ultramarine*	45·00	5·00
		a. *Ultramarine*	13·50	45
		b. *Blue**	£140	7·00
178		100m. pale red-brown*○	39·00	8·25
		a. *Deep red-brown*	43·00	9·25
		b. *Brown*	40·00	8·00
179		200m. pale brown*○	45·00	8·75
		a. *Deep brown*	33·00	7·50
180		400m. pale green*○	£350	33·00
		a. *Green*	£350	33·00
		b. *Myrtle-green*	£400	40·00
181		12c. pale brown-red	£275	8·50
		a. *Brown-red*	£350	11·00
182		19c. yellow-green	£450	£275
183		1e.600m. grey-lilac*○	£1600	£1000
		a. *Deep lilac*	£1800	£1200
184		2e. pale blue*○	£1800	£750
		a. *Blue*	£1400	£550

A stamp in pale brown-red as No. 181, but with a face value of 12c. de peseta, was prepared in 1872, but not issued.

King Amadeo (Duke of Aosta)
30 Dec 1870—12 Feb 1873

   37   38   38a

(Note differences in Crowns)

(Dies eng L. Plañol. Typo)
1872 (1 Oct)–**76**. Currency changed. Value in centimos de peseta. Imperf.

185	**37**	¼c. ultramarine*	2·50	2·50
		a. Double print (*complete stamp*)	£200	£200
186	**38**	¼c. green (1.7.73)*○	2·10	1·60
		a. *Blue-green*	2·50	2·00
		b. *Yellow-green*	2·40	1·40
		c. *Myrtle-green*	2·50	1·75
187	**38a**	¼c. pale green (1876)	25	15
		a. *Blue-green*	90	90
		b. *Yellow-green*	30	10
		c. *Myrtle-green*	95	95

Prices quoted are for quarter stamps as illustrated. Prices for complete stamps are:—No. 185, £95 *un.*, £90 *us.*; No. 186, £44 *un.*, £23 *us.*; No. 187, 65p. *un.*, 30p. *us.*

Tête-bêche errors (complete stamps)

      I   II   III

188	**37**	44c. ultramarine (I)	£1900	£1900
189	**38a**	44c. green (I) (1885)	£1000	£475
190		44c. green (II) (1904)	£180	£180
191		44c. green (III) (1910)	£200	£200

   39   40   41

   I   II

Two types of T **40**:—
I. Righthand value tablet complete.
II. Righthand value tablet broken at top.

(Dies eng E. Jover. Typo)
1872 (1 Oct)–**73**. P 14.

192	**39**	2c. lilac	26·00	19·00
		a. *Grey-lilac*	26·00	19·00
		b. *Bright mauve*	33·00	24·00
193		5c. green	£190	90·00
		a. Imperf (*pair*)	£450	
194	**40**	5c. rose (II) (1.1.73)	26·00	8·25
		a. *Deep rose* (II)	35·00	12·50
195		6c. pale blue (I)	£140	55·00
		a. Imperf (*pair*)	£450	
		b. *Blue* (I)	£180	70·00
196		10c. deep lilac (I)	£375	£325
197		10c. ultramarine (I) (1.1.73)*○	7·25	45
198		10c. ultramarine (II) (1873)	19·00	2·40
199		12c. grey-lilac (I)*○	17·00	2·20
		a. *Lilac* (I)	22·00	3·25
200		20c. deep lilac (II) (1.1.73)*	£160	85·00
201		25c. yellow-brown (I)*○	60·00	10·00
		a. *Brown* (I)	75·00	15·00
202		40c. pale brown (I)*○	85·00	11·00
		a. *Chestnut* (I)	65·00	8·00
203		50c. green (1)*○	£110	10·00
		a. *Deep green* (I)	95·00	9·50
204	**41**	1p. lilac*○	£110	55·00
205		4p. chestnut*○	£650	£600
206		10p. blue-green○	£2500	£2500

FIRST REPUBLIC
12 Feb 1873–31 Dec 1874

For stamps issued in 1873–75 under the authority of Don Carlos, see Carlist issues at the end of the Spanish list.

42 Allegorical Figure of Peace   W **42**   **43** Allegorical Figure of Justice

(Dies eng E. Juliá. Typo)
1873 (1 July). P 14.

207	**42**	2c. pale orange	14·00	5·75
		a. *Orange*	17·00	8·00
		b. *Deep orange*	25·00	12·00
208		5c. dull rose*	43·00	8·00
209		10c. green*	9·00	45
		a. Tête-bêche (*pair*)	—	£25000
		b. *Deep green*	12·00	1·00
210		20c. black○	£120	38·00
211		25c. brown*○	42·00	8·00
		a. *Deep brown*	55·00	12·00
212		40c. brown-purple*○	45·00	8·00
213		50c. ultramarine*○	17·00	8·00
		a. *Bright ultramarine*	15·00	7·50
214		1p. grey-lilac*○	70·00	60·00
		a. *Lilac*	60·00	42·00
215		4p. chestnut*○	£750	£600
216		10p. brown-purple*○	£2500	£2500

> **WAR TAX STAMPS.** These and all later War Tax issues were used to collect a fee in addition to the normal postal rate.
> They also had fiscal use, but our used prices are for *postally used* stamps.

(Dies eng E. Jover. Typo)
1874 (1 Jan). WAR TAX. 2nd Carlist War (1873/6) and Cuban War (1868/78). P 14.

W217	W **42**	5c. deep black	12·50	1·30
		a. Imperf (*pair*)	18·00	
W218		10c. deep pale blue	16·00	2·50
		a. *Deep blue*	14·00	2·40
		b. Imperf (*pair*)	35·00	

Nos. W217/8 also exist overprinted "Adm. Econr. Tarragona Hab. pr 1875" for use in that city during 1875.

235

SPAIN

(Dies eng E. Jover. Typo)

1874 (1 July). P 14.

217	**43**	2c. lemon-yellow*°		27·00	11·50
218		5c. bright mauve*°		42·00	9·00
		a. Mauve		42·00	9·00
219		10c. pale ultramarine*°		17·00	45
		a. Bright ultramarine		19·00	65
220		20c. deep green*°		£200	60·00
221		25c. chestnut*°		42·00	9·00
		a. Purple-brown		50·00	12·00
		b. Error. 25c. lilac-rose*		£350	
222		40c. bright mauve*°		£475	11·00
		a. Dull mauve		£475	11·00
		b. Error. 40c. brown*		£400	
223		50c. orange-yellow*°		£150	11·00
		a. Orange		£160	12·00
224		1p. yellow-green*°		£110	55·00
		a. Deep yellow-green		95·00	47·00
		b. Emerald-green		£120	75·00
225		4p. rose*°		£850	£600
		a. Carmine		£850	£500
226		10p. black*°		£3500	£2500

The 1p. exists in black, but is only known with the telegraph "punched hole" cancellation.
The 25c. brown is known on very thick paper watermarked figures and with control figures in blue on back, similar to the 1875 issue. The 2, 5, 10, 20 and 50c., together with the 1, 4 and 10p. are also known on very thick paper without watermark.

44   W **45**

(Dies eng L. Plañol. Typo)

1874 (1 Oct). P 14.

227	**44**	10c. pale brown		27·00	85
		a. Brown*		26·00	1·40
		b. Chestnut-brown		24·00	75
		c. Imperf (pair)		£175	

Three types of this stamp can be identified by the differences in the figures of value.

King Alfonso XII
31 Dec 1874–25 Nov 1885
(House of Bourbon restored)

(Dies eng L. Plañol. Typo)

1875 (1 Jan). WAR TAX. 2nd Carlist War (1873/6) and Cuban War (1868/78). P 14.

W228	W **45**	5c. de p. pale yellow-green		7·25	95
		a. Deep green		5·75	95
		b. Pale blue-green		5·75	95
		c. Deep blue-green		5·75	95
		d. Tête-bêche (pair)		£9500	£40000
W229		10c. de p. dull mauve		17·00	4·25
		a. Deep lilac		14·00	3·50
		b. Tête-bêche (pair)		£15000	£9000

Both values exist on paper watermarked figures and with blue control as 1875 postage issue.

45

(Dies eng J. G. Morago. Typo)

1875 (1 Aug). P 14.

228	**45**	2c. brown°		22·00	11·00
		a. Red-brown		30·00	18·00
229		5c. lilac°		80·00	13·00
		a. Dull purple		95·00	14·00
230		10c. pale blue°		9·00	45
		a. Deep blue		25·00	12·00
231		20c. orange-brown°		£325	£160
232		25c. rose*°		70·00	8·25
		a. Carmine-rose		75·00	12·50
233		40c. brown*°		£130	43·00
		a. Deep brown		£150	50·00
		b. Chocolate		£150	50·00
234		50c. lavender°		£200	38·00
		a. Dull mauve		£225	80·00
235		1p. grey-black*°		£225	95·00
		a. Black		£225	£110
236		4p. blue-green°		£550	£550
		a. Deep green		£700	£575
237		10p. ultramarine°		£1800	£1900

On the back of each stamp of this issue there is a rectangular frame enclosing a dotted background in the centre of which is an uncoloured rectangle containing a number, all in blue. The numbers range from 1 to 100—the number of stamps on the pane.

46   **47**   W **48**

Plate 1. Thick line of shading beneath triangular ornament on the left side of "COMUNICACIONES"; background between the inner square frame and outer frame, over the numerals in the right lower corner, roughly cut.
Plate 2. No line of shading; background between frames redrawn.

(Dies eng A. Wion. Recess Bradbury, Wilkinson & Co)

1876–77. W **47**. P 14.

(a) Plate 1 (1 June 1876)

238	**46**	5c. yellow-brown°		13·50	3·75
		a. Bistre		13·50	3·75
239		10c. dull blue°		3·75	45
240		20c. olive-green°		23·00	17·00
241		25c. brown°		8·75	5·50
242		40c. sepia°		90·00	£100
243		50c. yellow-green°		17·00	7·00
		a. Green		19·00	9·00
244		1p. blue°		23·00	10·50
245		4p. plum°		65·00	75·00
		a. Claret		75·00	90·00
246		10p. vermilion°		£150	£160

(b) Plate 2 (1877)

247	**46**	5c. bistre°		15·00	6·75
248		10c. dull blue°		4·25	1·20
		a. Bright blue		4·25	1·20
249		25c. brown°		9·50	6·75
250		50c. bluish green°		15·50	8·75
251		1p. blue°		35·00	15·00
252		10p. vermilion°		£200	£175

In Plate 2 the figures in the 5c., 25c. and 50c. are slightly larger and more sharply engraved; the 1p. has thick numerals in pl. 1 and thinner in pl. 2, other irregular lines of shading may also be found in pl. 2; these are very prominent in the 1p., each stamp on the sheet differing in this respect.
All values except the 20c. and 40c. exist imperf from Plate 1.

(Dies eng E. Juliá. Typo)

1876 (1 June). WAR TAX. 2nd Carlist War (1873/6) and Cuban War (1868/78). P 14.

W253	W **48**	5c. de p. pale green		5·50	85
		a. Deep green		12·50	7·75
		b. Blue		30·00	30·00
W254		10c. de p. pale blue		5·50	85
		a. Deep blue		7·50	9·25
		b. Se-tenant pair of 5c. and 10c. blue		£1200	
W255		25c. de p. black		42·00	15·00
W256		1p. grey-lilac		£500	£110
W257		5p. rose		£800	£325

No. W254b was caused by the inclusion of a 5c. de p. cliché in a plate of the 10c. de p. No. W253b comes from complete sheets of the 5c. printed in blue.

W **49**   W **50**   **48**

(Types W**49**/**50** and **48** dies eng E. Juliá. Typo)

1877 (1 Sept). WAR TAX. Cuban War (1868/78). P 14.

W258	W **49**	15c. de p. claret		25·00	80
W259		50c. de p. pale yellow		£850	£120
		a. Orange-yellow		£650	95·00

War Tax stamps of 5, 10, 15, 25, 50c.; 1p. and 5p. face values, as Type W **50**, were prepared in 1879, but were not put into use.

(Die eng E. Jover)

1878 (1 July). P 14.

253	48	2c. dull mauve	42·00	13·00
254		5c. yellow	47·00	11·50
		a. Dull orange	60·00	15·00
255		10c. brown	8·50	50
		a. Deep brown	10·50	65
256		20c. black	£200	£150
257		25c. bistre-olive°	25·00	2·75
		a. Deep bistre-olive	35·00	3·25
258		40c. red-brown	£190	£170
259		50c. blue-green*°	£110	11·00
		a. Deep blue-green	£125	12·50
260		1p. pale grey*°	85·00	22·00
		a. Grey	95·00	25·00
261		4p. dull violet*°	£250	£150
		a. Deep violet	£275	£175
262		10p. deep blue*°	£450	£450
		a. Pale blue	£375	£375

A 2c. black exists, both perf and imperf, but was not issued.

49   F 50   50

(T **49**/**50** dies eng E. Jover. Typo)

1879 (1 May). P 14.

263	49	2c. grey-black*°	9·25	4·25
		a. Black	12·50	7·25
264		5c. pale blue-green*°	13·50	1·10
		a. Blue-green	22·50	1·50
265		10c. pale rose*°	12·50	45
		a. Rose	18·00	1·50
		b. Carmine-rose	18·00	1·50
266		20c. brown*°	£130	17·00
267		25c. grey*°	17·00	45
		a. Lavender	22·00	1·75
268		40c. bistre-brown*°	31·00	5·50
269		50c. lemon*°	£130	5·50
		a. Pale yellow	£130	5·50
		b. Orange	£100	4·50
270		1p. pale rosine*°	£150	2·20
		a. Deep rosine	£160	4·25
271		4p. lilac-grey*°	£800	42·00
272		10p. olive-bistre*°	£2000	£275

1881 (July). FRANK. Litho. Coloured paper. Imperf.

F273	F **50**	(–) Black/buff	47·00	21·00

This stamp was allowed to be used by Senor A. F. Duro for franking a work—*Reseña Historicó-Descriptiva de los Sellos de Correos de España*—which he had written, and which was also considered of public utility. The stamp has been reprinted on various coloured papers.

1882 (1 Jan). P 14.

273	**50**	15c. flesh*	10·50	20
		a. Rosy orange	29·00	60
		b. Yellow	65·00	1·50
274		30c. mauve*°	£375	6·00
275		75c. lavender*°	£325	6·00

King Alfonso XIII
17 May, 1886–14 April, 1931

51   O 52   W 52

(Dies eng E. Jover. Typo)

1889 (1 Oct). P 14.

276	**51**	2c. sage green	5·50	45
		a. Deep blue-green	7·00	1·50
277		5c. blue	9·25	20
		a. Ultramarine	12·00	1·75
278		10c. orange-brown	16·00	20
		a. Chestnut	19·00	20
279		15c. reddish brown	4·00	20
		a. Double print	£170	£150
		b. Deep reddish brown	5·25	30

280		20c. yellowish green°	42·00	4·00
281		25c. Prussian blue	16·00	20
		a. Indigo	22·00	20
		b. Slate-blue	22·00	20
282		30c. olive-slate	65·00	3·75
283		40c. brown°	65·00	2·50
		a. Deep brown	75·00	4·25
284		50c. rose-carmine	65·00	1·50
		a. Brown-lake	80·00	3·00
285		75c. orange	£225	4·00
		a. Reddish orange	£250	6·00
286		1p. deep dull purple	49·00	40
287		4p. aniline rose-red°	£700	46·00
288		10p. red°	£1100	£120

No. 279a is known used from Carlet (Valencia).
A 1p. value in a similar colour to the 50c. exists, postmarked from Pamplona in 1894.
The 15c. *yellow* of this type was for official use. See No. O289.
See also Nos. 289/91.

1895–98. OFFICIAL. For use by members of the Chamber of Deputies. Typo. P 14.

O289	**51**	15c. yellow	11·00	4·25
O290	O **52**	(–) Deep rose (24.4.96)	8·25	17·00
O291		(–) Blue (1898)	27·00	8·50

1897 (1 July). WAR TAX. Cuban War of Independence (1895/8). Inscr "1897 – 1898" (15c.) or "1897 A 1898" (others). Typo. P 14.

W289	W **52**	5c. deep bluish green	4·50	1·90
W290		10c. deep bluish green	4·50	1·90
W291		15c. deep bluish green	£550	£325
W292		20c. deep bluish green	10·00	3·25

Higher values to 10p. were for fiscal use.

1898 (1 July). WAR TAX. Cuban War of Independence (1895/8) and Spanish-American War (1898). Inscr "1898–99". Typo. P 14.

W293	W **52**	5c. black	3·50	1·90
W294		10c. black	3·50	1·90
W295		15c. black	65·00	19·00
W296		20c. black	5·25	3·25

Higher values to 40p. were for fiscal use.

W **53**   **52**   E **53**

(Dies eng B. Mauro. Typo)

1898 (1 July). WAR TAX. Cuban War of Independence (1895/8) and Spanish-American War (1898). P 14.

W297	W **53**	5c. black	10·50	80

1899. Colours changed. P 14.

289	**51**	2c. brownish black	33·00	6·50
290		5c. deep bluish green	£110	1·20
291		10c. orange-red	£325	4·00
289/291 Set of 3			£450	10·50

A 20c. orange in this type is a proof.

> **CONTROL FIGURES ON BACK.** From this point until 1932 stamps normally have control figures printed on the back, usually in blue. Each sheet has a different number and every stamp in the sheet has the same number. Errors are known with different numbers on the same sheet.
> The 1901 issue had six-figure numbers without prefix letter but from 1904 the prefix letter "A" was introduced and later other prefix letters were used.
> In the 1901 issue stamps bearing "000,000" are "Specimen" stamps; later "Specimen" stamps have "A,000,000" or are overprinted "MUESTRA".

(Eng B. Maura. Recess)

1901 (1 Jan)–05. With blue control figures on back. P 14.

292	**52**	2c. bistre-brown	5·00	20
		a. Yellow-brown	3·75	30
293		5c. deep green	8·00	20
		a. Imperf (pair)	30·00	30·00
		b. Green/greenish	6·50	30
294		10c. rose-red	10·50	25
		a. Imperf (pair)	30·00	30·00
295		15c. blue-black	19·00	25
		a. Imperf (pair)	£140	£140
296		15c. mauve (Mar 1902)	12·50	25
		a. Imperf (pair)	£110	£110
		b. Green control figures (1902)	16·00	45
297		15c. bright violet (June 1905)	7·00	25
		a. Imperf (pair)	25·00	25·00

SPAIN

298	20c. olive-black		43·00	2·50
299	25c. blue		6·50	25
	a. Imperf (pair)		19·00	19·00
	b. Ultramarine		5·75	60
	c. Error. Green		£3750	
300	30c. bluish green		43·00	50
	a. Imperf (pair)		£275	£275
301	40c. olive-bistre		£150	4·75
	a. Imperf (pair)		£550	£550
302	40c. rose (Apr 1905)		£325	5·00
303	50c. slate-blue		43·00	60
	a. Imperf (pair)		£300	£300
	b. Greenish blue		38·00	45
	c. Error. Light green		£1600	£1100
304	1p. claret		39·00	60
	a. Imperf (pair)		£140	£140
305	4p. plum		£325	22·00
306	10p. orange		£300	85·00

The 15c. red-brown, 30c. blue and 1p. olive, blue or plum were prepared, but not issued.

(Des B. Maura. Typo (No. E307) or litho (No. E308))

1905-25. EXPRESS LETTER. P 14.

E307	E **53**	20c. red	55·00	1·60
E308		20c. rose (1925)	42·00	1·10

Numbered on back similar to issues of 1900, etc.

54 Don Quixote setting out   **64**

(Dies eng B. Maura. Typo)

1905 (1 May). Tercentenary of Publication of Cervantes' "Don Quixote". T **54** and similar horiz scenes. Control numbers on back. P 14.

307		5c. deep green	1·30	1·20
308		10c. scarlet	3·00	2·00
309		15c. violet	3·00	2·00
310		25c. indigo	10·00	3·75
311		30c. blue-green	50·00	10·50
312		40c. aniline carmine	£110	36·00
313		50c. slate	24·00	8·00
314		1p. brownish lake	£350	£100
315		4p. plum	£180	£100
316		10p. orange	£225	£190
307/316 Set of 10			£950	£450

Designs:—10c. Quixote attacking the windmill; 15c. Meeting with country girls; 25c. Sancho Panza tossed in a blanket; 30c. Don Quixote knighted by the innkeeper; 40c. Tilting at the flock of sheep; 50c. Don Quixote on the wooden horse; 1p. Adventure with the lions; 4p. Don Quixote in the bullock-cart; 10p. The enchanted lady.

The issue was made in Madrid only, and was available for postage *within Spain* from 1st to 15th May, 1905.

A set of six stamps in a common horiz design, showing the King and Queen, was issued on 1 Oct 1907 for the Madrid Exhibition. This issue only had postal validity within the Exhibition ground. The originals were recess printed, perf 11½; stamps with other perforation measurements or printed by different process are reprints. (*Price for originals £50 per set un, £47 used.*)

(Eng B. Maura. Recess)

1909-22.

(a) P 14 (line). Figures in blue on back

317	64	2c. sepia	14·00	7·00
318		5c. deep green	14·00	9·50
319		10c. carmine	21·00	11·50
320		15c. violet	24·00	11·50
321		20c. bronze-green	£190	11·50
322		25c. blue	25·00	11·50
323		30c. blue-green	55·00	11·50
324		40c. rose	50·00	11·50
325		50c. greenish blue	42·00	19·00
326		1p. claret	85·00	24·00
327		4p. plum	£110	95·00
328		10p. orange	£300	£120

(b) P 13×12½, 13 or 13½×13, all comb
(i) Figures in blue on back

329	64	2c. sepia	80	55
330		5c. deep green	2·00	20
331		10c. carmine	2·50	20
332		15c. violet	12·50	20
		a. Imperf (pair)	25·00	25·00
333		15c. yellow (1917)	38·00	1·20
334		20c. bronze-green	65·00	75
335		20c. bright violet (1921)	49·00	20
336		25c. blue	4·75	20
337		30c. blue-green	12·50	20
338		40c. rose	18·00	95
		a. Salmon (1917)	£120	5·50
339		50c. greenish blue	17·00	45
		a. Blue	17·00	45
340		1p. claret (1912)	41·00	35
		a. Rose-red (1917)	42·00	30
341		4p. plum	£110	13·50
342		10p. orange	£140	25·00
329/342 Set of 14 (cheapest)			£450	41·00

(ii) Figures in red or orange on back

343	64	15c. yellow (1917)	6·00	20
		a. Orange	4·75	20

(iii) Without figures on back

344	64	2c. sepia (1917)	65	65
345		2c. bistre (1922)	65	65

The 5c. exists in carmine, the 15c. in blue and 4p. in carmine. It is not known if these were issued, but the 4p. carmine is only known with the perforated initials "B.H.A.".

See also Nos. 359/60a.

Bisected and used for half value

346	64	½ of 2c. sepia	—	9·00
347		½ of 5c. deep green	—	10·00
348		½ of 10c. carmine	—	9·00
349		½ of 15c. yellow	—	10·00
350		½ of 20c. bronze green	—	8·50
351		½ of 30c. blue-green	—	25·00
352		½ of 40c. rose	—	25·00

When the authorities increased the postage rates but failed to provide adequate supplies of stamps in the new denominations, authorisation was given in May 1920 to use bisected stamps. Prices quoted are for bisects on piece; on cover they are worth more.

O **65** Chamber of Deputies   O **67** Cervantes (from painting by J. de Jauregui)

O **66** National Library   O **68** Statue of Cervantes by A. Solá

(Eng E. Vaquer (Type O **67**). Recess Bradbury, Wilkinson)

1916 (22 Apr). OFFICIAL. Cervantes' Death Centenary. P 12.

(a) For use by Members of Chamber of Deputies

O353	O **65**	(—) Black and violet	1·70	1·30
O354	O **66**	(—) Black and green	1·70	1·30
O355	O **67**	(—) Black and violet	1·70	1·30
O356	O **68**	(—) Black and carmine	1·70	1·30

(b) For use by Members of the Senate

O357	O **65**	(—) Black and green	1·70	1·30
O358	O **66**	(—) Black and carmine	1·70	1·30
O359	O **67**	(—) Black and brown	1·70	1·30
O360	O **68**	(—) Black and brown	1·70	1·30
O353/360 Set of 8			12·00	9·50

Reprints of these stamps exist.

(65)   66   67 G.P.O., Madrid

SPAIN

1920 (4 Apr). AIR. Optd with T **65**.

353	64	5c. deep green (R.)	1·70	1·10
		a. Imperf (pair)	£130	£130
		b. Opt double	75·00	55·00
		c. Opt inverted	£125	£125
354		10c. carmine	2·75	1·60
		a. Imperf (pair)	£130	£130
		b. Opt double	85·00	65·00
355		25c. blue (R.)	4·25	3·00
		a. Opt inverted	£120	£120
		b. Opt double	75·00	55·00
356		50c. greenish blue (R.)	18·00	9·00
		a. Imperf (pair)	95·00	95·00
357		1p. claret	65·00	37·00
		a. Imperf (pair)	£375	£375
353/357 Set of 5			90·00	50·00

No. 337 with this overprint was prepared, but not issued.

(Dies eng J. Espinós Gisbert. Typo)

1920 (July). Imperf.

| 358 | **66** | 1c. green (shades) | 40 | 15 |

No. 358 also exists perf 11 unofficially.

1920–22.

(a) Figures on back in blue

(b) No figures on back. Litho. P 12½–14 and compounds

359	64	2c. bistre (b)	14·50	20
360		20c. lilac (a)	65·00	20
		a. Bright violet	60·00	20

1920 (16 Oct). Seventh Universal Postal Union Congress, Madrid. Typo. Portrait and building in black. Numbers on back in blue, except on 1c. and 2c.

A. P 13½ (comb)

361	67	1c. blue-green	60	25
362		2c. brown	60	20
363		5c. green	2·30	1·20
364		10c. red	2·30	1·10
365		15c. yellow	3·25	1·70
366		20c. violet	5·00	1·80
367		25c. blue	5·50	3·50
368		30c. deep green	18·00	6·75
369		40c. carmine	65·00	9·50
370		50c. ultramarine	80·00	26·00
371		1p. rose	80·00	21·00
372		4p. purple-brown	£225	£110
373		10p. orange	£500	£225
361/373A Set of 13			£900	£360

B. P 14 (line)

361	67	1c. blue-green	95	20
362		2c. brown	—	—
363		5c. green	2·75	85
364		10c. red	—	—
365		15c. yellow	4·75	2·10
366		20c. violet	9·50	2·50
367		25c. blue	8·50	3·00
368		30c. deep green	19·00	4·75
369		40c. carmine	£110	11·50
370		50c. ultramarine	—	—
371		1p. rose	—	—
372		4p. purple-brown	—	—
373		10p. orange	£1100	£375

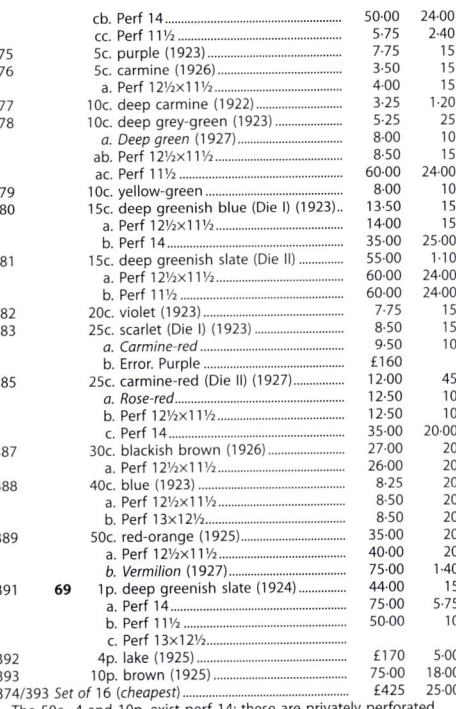

68  69

Die I Die II Die I Die II Die I Die II

2c. In Die I the "2" is more angular than in Die II.
15c. The "5" is narrower in Die I than in Die II.
25c. The vertical stroke of the "5" is shorter in Die I than in Die II.

(Eng E. Vaquer. Recess)

1922–29. Figures in blue on back, except 2c. P 13½×13.

374	**68**	2c. yellow-green (Die I) (1924)	1·30	15
		a. Deep olive	2·75	45
		b. Error. Red-orange (1929)	£190	£130
374c		2c. deep yellow-green (Die II)	1·70	15
		ca. Perf 12½×11½	1·20	20
		cb. Perf 14	50·00	24·00
		cc. Perf 11½	5·75	2·40
375		5c. purple (1923)	7·75	15
376		5c. carmine (1926)	3·50	15
		a. Perf 12½×11½	4·00	15
377		10c. deep carmine (1922)	3·25	1·20
378		10c. deep grey-green (1923)	5·25	25
		a. Deep green (1927)	8·00	10
		ab. Perf 12½×11½	8·50	15
		ac. Perf 11½	60·00	24·00
379		10c. yellow-green	8·00	10
380		15c. deep greenish blue (Die I) (1923)	13·50	15
		a. Perf 12½×11½	14·00	15
		b. Perf 14	35·00	25·00
381		15c. deep greenish slate (Die II)	55·00	1·10
		a. Perf 12½×11½	60·00	24·00
		b. Perf 11½	60·00	24·00
382		20c. violet (1923)	7·75	15
383		25c. scarlet (Die I) (1923)	8·50	15
		a. Carmine-red	9·50	10
		b. Error. Purple	£160	
385		25c. carmine-red (Die II) (1927)	12·00	45
		a. Rose-red	12·50	10
		b. Perf 12½×11½	12·50	10
		c. Perf 14	35·00	20·00
387		30c. blackish brown (1926)	27·00	20
		a. Perf 12½×11½	26·00	20
388		40c. blue (1923)	8·25	20
		a. Perf 12½×11½	8·50	20
		b. Perf 13×12½	8·50	20
389		50c. red-orange (1925)	35·00	20
		a. Perf 12½×11½	40·00	20
		b. Vermilion (1927)	75·00	1·40
391	**69**	1p. deep greenish slate (1924)	44·00	15
		a. Perf 14	75·00	5·75
		b. Perf 11½	50·00	10
		c. Perf 13×12½		
392		4p. lake (1925)	£170	5·00
393		10p. brown (1925)	75·00	18·00
374/393 Set of 16 (cheapest)			£425	25·00

The 50c., 4 and 10p. exist perf 14; these are privately perforated.
The 5c. vermilion, 25c. blue (Dies I & II), 25c. violet (Die I) in T **68** and the 4p. brown and 10p. reddish purple, as T **69**, were prepared, but not issued.

70 Princesses Maria Cristina and Beatriz

71 King Alfonso XIII

75 CASA-built Dornier Do-J Wal Flying Boat *Plus Ultra*

E **77** The Spanish Royal Family

76 Route Map and Gallarza and Loriga's Breguet 19A2 Biplane

(Recess Waterlow)

1926 (15 Sept). Red Cross. P 12½.

*(a) POSTAGE. T **70**, **71** and similar types*

394	**70**	1c. black	3·25	2·40
395	–	2c. ultramarine	3·25	2·40
396	–	5c. purple	8·00	5·25
397	–	10c. myrtle	6·50	4·75
398	**70**	15c. indigo	2·50	2·00

239

SPAIN

399	–	20c. violet	3·50	2·75
		a. Error. Purple	£800	
400	71	25c. red	1·10	50
401	70	30c. blue-green	70·00	48·00
402	–	40c. indigo	43·00	29·00
403	–	50c. vermilion	42·00	28·00
404	–	1p. deep greenish slate	2·50	1·70
405	–	4p. carmine	3·50	2·75
406	71	10p. brown	3·50	2·75
394/406 Set of 13			£170	£120

(b) AIR. Trans-Atlantic and Madrid–Manila flights

407	75	5c. violet and black	4·00	2·20
408	–	10c. black and ultramarine	5·00	2·50
409	76	15c. deep ultramarine and vermilion	70	45
410	–	20c. red and myrtle	70	45
411	75	25c. black and red	70	45
412	76	30c. sepia and ultramarine	70	45
413	–	40c. myrtle and brown	70	45
414	75	50c. black and vermilion	70	45
415	–	1p. myrtle and black	4·75	3·25
416	76	4p. carmine and yellow	£170	£120
407/416 Set of 10			£170	£110

(c) EXPRESS LETTER

E417	E 77	20c. dull purple and purple	15·00	9·00

Designs (Postage): Vert—2c., 10c. Queen Victoria Eugénie as nurse; 5c., 40c., 4p. Queen Victoria Eugénie; 10c., 20c., 1p. Prince of the Asturias.

Nos 394/406 were printed in different colours for use, with overprints, in Cape Juby, Spanish Guinea and Spanish Sahara. No. 399a is one of these printings with the overprint omitted.

(77) 17-V-1902 A XIII
(78) 17-V-1927 A XIII ALFONSO XIII
(79) 75 CTS. 75 ALFONSO XIII 17-V-1902 17-V-1927
(80) 17-V-1902 17-V-1927 A XIII A XIII
(81) 17 MAYO 17 1902 1927 ALFONSO XIII

1927 (17 May). 25th Anniv of Coronation. Red Cross stamps variously optd "ALFONSO XIII 17 V 1902/1927" or surch also, as T **77/81** or similar types.

(a) POSTAGE. Nos. 394/406, optd

417	70	1c. black (R.)	8·75	6·50
418	–	2c. ultramarine (B.)	16·00	13·00
419	–	5c. purple (R.)	4·75	3·50
		a. Opt double	45·00	
		b. Opt triple	50·00	
420	–	10c. myrtle (B.)	£110	80·00
421	70	15c. indigo (R.)	3·00	2·50
422	–	20c. violet (B.)	5·50	4·25
423	71	25c. red (B.)	95	80
424	70	30c. blue-green (B.)	1·50	1·20
425	–	40c. indigo (R.)	1·40	1·10
426	–	50c. vermilion (B.)	1·40	1·10
427	–	1p. slate (R.)	3·25	2·20
428	–	4p. carmine (B.)	17·00	13·00
429	71	10p. brown (G.)	65·00	50·00
417/429 Set of 13			£200	£160

(b) Types as last, surch

430	–	3c. on 2c. (G.)	16·00	13·00
431	–	4c. on 2c. (G.)	15·00	12·00
432	71	10c. on 25c.	80	55
433	–	25c. on 25c. (B.)	80	55
434	–	55c. on 2c. (R.)	1·30	1·20
435	–	55c. on 10c.	85·00	65·00
		a. Surch triple	£110	
436	–	55c. on 20c.	85·00	65·00
437	70	75c. on 15c. (R.)	1·20	80
438	–	75c. on 30c. (R.)	£300	£225
		a. Surch double, one inverted	£325	£250
439	–	80c. on 5c. (R.)	80·00	60·00
		a. Surch inverted	£150	£150
		b. Error. 80c. on 2c. (R.)	£175	£175
440	–	2p. on 40c. (R.)	1·50	1·10
		a. Surch inverted	45·00	45·00
		b. Surch double	25·00	25·00
		c. Black surch		
441	–	2p. on 1p. (R.)	1·50	1·10
442	–	5p. on 50c. (G.)	3·25	2·10
		a. "1627" for "1927"	25·00	25·00
		b. Surch inverted	40·00	40·00
443	–	5p. on 4p.	5·00	3·25
		a. Surch inverted	35·00	35·00
444	71	10p. on 10p. (G.)	36·00	25·00
430/444 Set of 15			£575	£425

(c) AIR. T **75** *optd with T* **80** *and T* **76** *optd with T* **81**

445	75	5c. violet and black (R.)	3·50	1·90
		a. Opt inverted	55·00	55·00
446	–	10c. black and ultramarine (R.)	7·75	3·75
		a. Opt inverted	55·00	55·00
447	76	15c. dp ultramarine and vermilion (Br.)	70	45
		a. Opt double	35·00	
		b. Error. Red opt	£125	£125
448	–	20c. red and myrtle (B.)	70	45
		a. Opt inverted	35·00	35·00
		b. Error. Red opt	65·00	65·00
449	75	25c. black and red (B.)	70	45
450	76	30c. sepia and ultramarine (R.)	70	45
		a. Opt double	35·00	35·00
		b. Error. Blue opt	65·00	65·00
451	–	40c. myrtle and brown (Br.)	70	45
		a. Opt inverted	35·00	35·00
		b. Opt double (Br. and B.)	95·00	95·00
452	75	50c. black and vermilion (B.)	70	45
		a. Opt double, one inverted	65·00	65·00
453	–	1p. myrtle and black (R.)	4·75	4·25
		a. Opt inverted	95·00	95·00
454	76	4p. carmine and yellow (B.)	£200	£140
		a. Opt inverted	£225	£225
445/454 Set of 10			£200	£140

(d) AIR. T **75** *optd with T* **80** *and surch also*

455	75	75c. on 5c. (R.)	8·50	6·75
		a. Surch inverted	55·00	55·00
456	–	75c. on 10c. (R.)	46·00	29·00
		a. Surch inverted	65·00	65·00
457	–	75c. on 25c. (B.)	85·00	60·00
		a. Surch double	£110	
458	–	75c. on 50c. (B.)	33·00	25·00

(e) EXPRESS LETTER. Type E **77**, *optd*

E459	E 77	20c. dull purple and purple (V.)	14·50	8·25

(f) Nos. 24/5 of Spanish Post Offices in Tangier opid, No. 25 surch also

460	–	1p. on 10p. violet (Br.)	£200	£200
461	–	4p. bistre (G.)	80·00	80·00

(g) Nos. 122/3 of Spanish Morocco surch

462	–	55c. on 4p. bistre (B.)	40·00	40·00
463	–	80c. on 10p. violet (Br.)	40·00	40·00

(h) Stamps of Cape Juby, surch

464	–	5p. on 4p. bistre (R.) (No. 34)	£100	£100
		a. Surch double, one inverted	£425	
465	–	10p. on 10p. violet (R.) (No. 35)	80·00	80·00

(i) Stamps of Spanish Guinea, surch

466	–	1p. on 10p. violet (B.) (No. 232)	40·00	40·00
		a. Surch double, one inverted	£250	
467	–	2p. on 4p. bistre (R.) (No. 231)	40·00	40·00

(j) Stamps of Spanish Sahara, surch

468	–	80c. on 10p. violet (R.) (No. 24)	6·00	60·00
469	–	2p. on 4p. bistre (R.) (No. 23)	40·00	40·00

82 Pope Pius XI and King Alfonso XIII

SPAIN

(Recess Waterlow)
1928 (23 Dec). Rome Catacombs Restoration Fund. P 12½.
(a) Issued at Santiago

470	82	2c. black and violet	55	30
471		2c. black and claret	60	50
472		3c. violet and blue-black	55	30
473		3c. violet and blue	60	50
474		5c. violet and sage-green	1·10	80
475		10c. black and yellow-green	1·80	1·50
476		15c. violet and blue-green	8·00	5·75
477		25c. violet and lake	8·00	5·75
478		40c. black and ultramarine	55	30
479		55c. violet and sepia	55	30
480		80c. black and red	55	30
481		1p. violet and grey	55	30
482		2p. black and brown	9·50	7·25
483		3p. violet and pink	9·50	7·25
484		4p. black and maroon	9·50	7·25
485		5p. violet and black	9·50	7·25
470/485 Set of 16			55·00	40·00

(b) Issued at Toledo

486	82	2c. carmine and blue-black	55	30
487		2c. carmine and ultramarine	60	50
488		3c. ultramarine and bistre	55	30
489		3c. ultramarine and sage-green	60	50
490		5c. ultramarine and purple	1·10	80
491		10c. ultramarine and yellow-green	1·80	1·50
492		15c. ultramarine and slate-blue	8·00	5·75
493		25c. ultramarine and red-brown	8·00	5·75
494		40c. carmine and ultramarine	55	30
495		55c. carmine and sepia	55	30
496		80c. carmine and black	55	30
497		1p. carmine and chrome-yellow	55	30
498		2p. ultramarine and grey	9·50	7·25
499		3p. ultramarine and violet	9·50	7·25
500		4p. carmine and maroon	9·50	7·25
501		5p. ultramarine and orange-yellow	9·50	7·25
486/501 Set of 16			55·00	40·00

83 A Spanish Caravel. Seville in background

84 Miniature of Exhibition Poster

87 *Spirit of St. Louis* over Coast

E **88** Gazelle

1929 (15 Feb). Seville and Barcelona Exhibitions. Inscr "EXPOSICION GENERAL ESPAÑOLA". Recess.
A. P 11 (comb)
(a) POSTAGE

502	83	1c. turquoise-green	2·50	2·10
		b. Perf 14 (line)	3·75	3·75
503	84	2c. yellow-green	40	25
504	–	5c. carmine-lake	65	45
505	–	10c. green	70	45
		b. Perf 14 (line)	47·00	47·00
506	83	15c. turquoise-blue	2·30	2·10
		b. Perf 14 (line)	40·00	40·00
507	84	20c. violet	80	55
		b. Perf 14 (line)	47·00	47·00
508	83	25c. carmine	80	45
		b. Perf 14 (line)	1·40	20
509	–	30c. blackish brown	7·50	5·00
		b. Perf 14 (line)	47·00	47·00
510	–	40c. blue	12·50	9·25
		b. Perf 14 (line)	70·00	70·00
511	84	50c. red-orange	7·50	5·00
		b. Perf 14 (line)	47·00	47·00
512	–	1p. greenish slate	17·00	10·00
		b. Perf 14 (line)	47·00	47·00
513	–	4p. claret	46·00	37·00
		b. Perf 14 (line)	47·00	47·00
514	–	10p. brown	£110	80·00
		b. Perf 14 (line)	£120	£110
502/514 Set of 13			£185	£140

Designs: Vert—5, 30c., 1p. View of exhibition. Horiz—10, 40c., 4, 10p. Alfonso XIII and Barcelona.

(b) AIR

515	87	5c. brown	8·50	6·00
516		10c. carmine	9·00	6·50
517		25c. blue	17·00	13·50
518		50c. violet	13·00	9·00
519		1p. yellow-green	65·00	46·00
520		4p. black	44·00	32·00
515/520 Set of 6			£140	£100

(c) EXPRESS LETTER

E521	E 88	20c. red-brown	28·00	19·00
		b. Perf 14 (line)	47·00	47·00

All these stamps are numbered in *blue* at back with the exception of Nos. 502/3.

E **89**

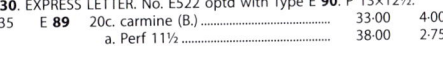
(**88**)   URGENCIA (E **90**)

(Des C. Delhom. Recess)
1929–32. EXPRESS LETTER. P 13×12½.

E522	E **89**	20c. carmine	28·00	4·00
		a. Perf 11½ (1932)	£190	5·75

1929 (10 June). Meeting of Council of the League of Nations at Madrid. Stamps of 1920, 1922-27 and No. E522 optd with T **88**.

(a) POSTAGE

521	66	1c. green (R.)	90	75
522	68	2c. deep yellow-green (R.)	90	75
523		5c. carmine (B.)	90	75
524		10c. deep green (R.)	90	75
525		15c. deep greenish blue (Die I) (R.)	90	75
526		20c. violet (R.)	90	75
527		25c. rose-red (Die II) (B.)	90	75
528		30c. blackish brown (R.)	4·00	3·50
529		40c. blue (R.)	4·00	3·50
530		50c. red-orange (B.)	4·00	3·50
531	69	1p. deep greenish slate (R.)	19·00	17·00
532		4p. lake (B.)	19·00	17·00
533		10p. brown (B.)	70·00	60·00
521/533 Set of 13			£110	£100

(b) EXPRESS LETTER

E534	E **89**	20c. carmine (B.)	20·00	19·00

1930. EXPRESS LETTER. No. E522 optd with Type E **90**. P 13×12½.

E535	E **89**	20c. carmine (B.)	33·00	4·00
		a. Perf 11½	38·00	2·75

89 Norte Railway Class 4601 Hanomag Steam Locomotive, 1924

90 Stinson Junior over Congress Emblem

E **91** Electric Locomotive

241

SPAIN

1930 (10 May). Eleventh International Railway Congress, Madrid. Inscr as in T **89**. Blue figures at back except on 1c. and 2c. Litho. P 14.

*(a) POSTAGE. T **89** and similar type (peseta values)*

534		1c. blue-green	1·20	80
535		2c. yellow-green	1·20	80
536		5c. claret	1·20	80
537		10c. green	1·20	80
538		15c. greenish blue	1·20	80
539		20c. violet	1·20	80
540		25c. rosine	1·20	75
541		30c. grey-brown	3·50	2·75
542		40c. blue	3·50	2·50
543		50c. orange	10·50	5·75
544		1p. slate	10·50	6·25
545		4p. carmine	£200	£120
546		10p. brown	£800	£600
534/546 Set of 13			£925	£675

Design: Vert—1 to 10p. Class 1301 steam locomotive, 1914.

*(b) AIR. T **90***

547		5c. brown	10·00	7·75
548		10c. carmine	10·00	7·75
549		25c. blue	10·00	7·75
550		50c. violet	29·00	19·00
551		1p. green	60·00	41·00
552		4p. black	65·00	43·00
547/552 Set of 6			£160	£115

(c) EXPRESS LETTER

E553	E **91**	20c. red	95·00	75·00

91 Francisco Goya (after Lopez)   **92** Francisco Goya (after Lopez)

93 "The Naked Maja"   **95** Asmodeus and Cleofas

94 "Flight"

URGENTE (E **96**)   URGENTE (E **97**)

(Eng J. L. Sánchez Toda. Nos. 553/8 litho, remainder recess Waterlow)

1930 (15 June). Death Centenary of Goya (painter). P 12½.

(a) POSTAGE

553	**91**	1c. orange-yellow	20	15
554		2c. bistre-brown	20	15
555	**92**	2c. olive-green	20	15
556	**91**	5c. bright mauve	20	15
557	**92**	5c. slate-violet	20	15
558	**91**	10c. green	25	15
559		15c. blue	25	15
560		20c. claret	25	15
561		25c. vermilion	25	15
562	**92**	25c. carmine-red	35	35
		a. Perf 14 (Madrid ptg.)	9·50	9·50
563	**91**	30c. red-brown	7·00	5·75
564		40c. deep blue	7·00	5·75
565		50c. orange-vermilion	7·00	5·75
566		1p. black	8·25	7·75
567	**93**	1p. purple	1·10	1·10
568		4p. grey-black	80	75
569		10p. red-brown	17·00	17·00
553/569 Set of 17			55·00	50·00

*(b) EXPRESS LETTER. Optd with Type E **96***

E570	**91**	20c. bright mauve	50	25

*(c) AIR. T **94/5** and similar types*

570	**94**	5c. orange-yellow and vermilion	20	20
571	**95**	5c. blue-green and olive	20	20
572		10c. green and blue-green	20	20
573	**94**	15c. orange-vermilion and black	55	40
574	**95**	20c. carmine and ultramarine	20	20
575	**94**	25c. scarlet and claret	25	25
576	–	30c. violet and bistre-brown	40	40
577	**95**	40c. light blue and ultramarine	75	60
578	–	50c. deep green and vermilion	75	60
579	–	1p. violet and plum	1·90	1·20
580	–	4p. black and claret	2·50	2·30
581	–	4p. greenish blue and grey-blue	3·75	3·00
582	–	10p. bistre-brown and sepia	16·00	13·00
570/582 Set of 13			25·00	20·00

*(d) AIR EXPRESS. Optd with Type E **97***

E583	**95**	20c. brown and grey-blue	40	40

Designs: (AIR)—Goya Fantasy Etchings. Vert—1p., 4p. (581) and 10p. Woman and dwarfs in flight. Inscr "VOLAVERUNT". Horiz—30c., 50c. and 4p. (580), Weird flying methods. Inscr "MANERA DE VOLAR".

97 King Alfonso XIII   Die I   Die II

(Des E. Vaquer. Recess)

1930–**31**. With blue figures on back (except 2c.). P 11½ or 12×11½.

583	**97**	2c. brown	15	15
584		5c. grey-brown	1·20	15
585		10c. yellow-green	6·25	15
586		15c. blue-green	28·00	15
587		20c. bright violet	12·00	90
588		25c. carmine	1·20	15
589		30c. deep lake	31·00	2·20
590		40c. deep blue (I)	55·00	1·50
591		40c. deep blue (II) (1931)	36·00	1·00
592		50c. orange	41·00	2·50
583/592 Set of 10			£190	8·00

98 Santa Maria   **99** Santa Maria

100 Santa Maria, Pinta and Nina

SPAIN

101 The Departure from Palos

102 Arrival in America

URGENTE
(E **103**)

103 Monastery of La Rabida

104 Martin Pinzon

105 Vincent Pinzon

106 Columbus

107 Monastery of La Rabida

108 Columbus

109 Columbus and the brothers Pinzon

(Des J. L. Sanchez Toda, A. Gisbert and D. Puebla. Eng C. Delhom and J. L. Sanchez Toda. Litho (T **98/9**, **103**, **107**), recess (others). Waterlow)

1930 (29 Sept). Columbus Issue. P 12½.

(a) POSTAGE

593	**98**	1c. greyish brown	55	20
594		2c. bronze-green	55	20
595	**99**	2c. bronze-green	55	20
596	**98**	5c. claret	55	20
597	**99**	5c. claret	55	20
598		10c. blue-green	1·60	1·00
599	**98**	15c. ultramarine	1·60	1·00
600	**99**	20c. violet	2·20	1·50
601	**100**	25c. scarlet	2·20	1·50
602	**101**	30c. brown, blue and sepia	12·00	8·00
603	**100**	40c. ultramarine	11·00	7·50
604	**101**	50c. violet, blue and purple	13·50	11·00
605	**100**	1p. black	13·50	11·00
606	**102**	4p. black and deep blue	14·50	12·00
607		10p. brown and purple	60·00	55·00
593/607 Set of 15			£120	£100

*(b) EXPRESS LETTER. Optd with Type E **103***

E608	**99**	20c. purple	3·50	2·50

T **100** was issued with *se-tenant* triangular labels in two different ornamental designs.

(c) AIR (for Europe and Africa)

608	**103**	5c. red	25	15
609		5c. bistre-brown	25	15
610		10c. blue-green	40	30
611		15c. violet	40	30
612		20c. ultramarine	40	30
613	**104**	25c. carmine	40	30
614	**105**	purple-brown	2·75	2·40
615	**104**	40c. slate-blue	2·75	2·40
616	**105**	50c. orange	2·75	2·40
617	**104**	1p. deep violet	2·75	2·40
618	**106**	4p. olive-green	2·75	2·40
619		10p. brown	18·00	16·00
608/619 Set of 12			30·00	26·00

(d) AIR (for America and Philippine Is.)

620	**107**	5c. vermilion	25	15
621		10c. green	25	15
622	**108**	25c. scarlet	30	25
623		50c. slate	3·25	2·75
624		1p. red-brown	3·25	2·75
625	**109**	4p. blue	3·25	2·75
626		10p. purple	19·00	14·50
620/626 Set of 7			26·00	21·00

110 Arms of Bolivia and Paraguay

111 Pavilion and Map of C. America

112 Cuba Pavilion

E **113** Seville Exhibition

113 Sidar and Douglas 0-2-M Biplane

114 Breguet 19GR *Jesus del Gran Poder* over *Santa Maria*

243

SPAIN

(Photo or recess (No. 642) Miralles, Aurioles, Gómez Ptg Wks, Madrid)

1930 (10 Oct). Spanish–American Exhibition. Various perfs, 10 to 14 and compound.

(a) POSTAGE. T 110/12 and similar types
(i) Photo

627	1c. blue-green	30	15
628	2c. yellow-brown	30	15
629	5c. sepia	30	15
630	10c. deep green	65	40
631	15c. indigo	65	40
632	20c. violet	65	40
633	25c. carmine	65	40
634	25c. carmine	65	40
635	30c. purple	3·50	2·30
636	40c. slate-blue	1·80	1·30
637	40c. slate-blue	1·80	1·30
638	50c. orange	3·50	2·50
639	1p. ultramarine	5·00	3·50
640	4p. purple	65·00	46·00
641	10p. chocolate	4·25	3·00
627/641	Set of 15	80·00	55·00

(ii) Recess

642	10p. orange-brown	£120	70·00

Designs (Exhibition pavilions, etc.): Vert—5c. Venezuela; 10c. Colombia; 4p. Portugal; 10p. King Alfonso and Queen Victoria, maps of S. America and Spain, and the Giralda, Seville. Horiz—15c. Dominican Republic; 20c. Uruguay; 25c. (No. 633), Argentina; 25c. (No 634), Chile; 30c. Brazil; 40c. (No. 636), Mexico; 40c. (No. 637), Cuba; 50c. Peru; 1p. U.S.A.

No. 641 measures 26½×37½ mm., No. 642 is smaller, 25½×37 mm.

(b) EXPRESS LETTER

E643	E **113**	20c. orange	1·90	1·70

(c) AIR. T 113/14 and similar designs

643	5c. grey-black	1·80	95
644	10c. olive-green	1·80	95
645	25c. bright ultramarine	1·80	95
646	50c. grey-blue	3·25	2·00
647	50c. black	3·25	2·00
648	1p. crimson	7·25	4·75
649	1p. brown-purple	£160	85·00
650	1p. green	6·25	4·75
651	4p. slate-blue	21·00	10·00
643/651	Set of 9	£190	£100

Designs: Horiz—5c. Alberto Santos Dumont and Wright Flyer I over Rio de Janeiro; 10c. Teodoro Fels and Douglas O-2-M biplane; 25c. Dagoberto Godoy and Nieuport 17 biplane; 50c. Admiral Gago Coutinha, Sacadura Cabral and Fairey IIID seaplane; 1p. (650) Charles Lindbergh and *Spirit of St. Louis*. Vert—1p. (648/9) Jimenez, Iglesias and Breguet 19GR *Jesus del Gran Poder*.

A part of the 1p. green printing was produced in two operations, the oval portrait being added after the remainder of the design had been printed.

Nos. 627/651 have been privately reprinted.

115

1930 (31 Dec). Litho. P 11½.

652	**115**	5c. black	10·50	15

This stamp was originally issued for Postage Due purposes connected with a Personal Delivery charge. The experiment was later abandoned and No. 652 was released for ordinary inland postal use.

SECOND REPUBLIC
14 April, 1931–1 April, 1939

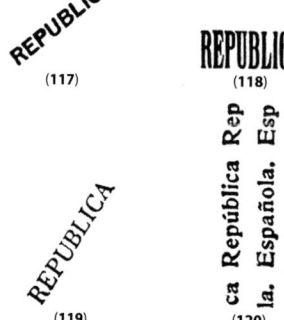

1931. Contemporary types optd.

*(a) Madrid opt, T **117** (14 April)*
(i) POSTAGE. Imperf

653	66	1c. green	10	10
		a. Opt in red	6·00	6·00

P 11½

654	97	2c. brown (G.)	30	30
655		5c. grey-brown (R.)	30	30
656		10c. yellow-green	55	55
657		15c. blue-green (R.)	1·60	1·60
658		20c. bright violet (R.)	1·60	1·60
659		25c. carmine (G.)	1·90	1·90

(ii) EXPRESS LETTER. P 11½

E660	E **89**	20c. carmine (No. E535a) (G.)	4·25	4·25

*(b) First Catalan opt, T **118** (15 April)*
(i) POSTAGE

660	66	1c. green	20	20
		a. "REPUBLIGA"	80	80
		b. Accent over "U"	80	80
661	97	2c. brown	40	40
		a. "REPUBLIGA"	1·50	1·50
		b. Accent over "U"	1·50	1·50
662		5c. grey-brown	20	20
		a. "REPUBLIGA"	1·75	1·75
		b. Accent over "U"	1·75	1·75
663		10c. yellow-green	1·50	1·50
		a. "REPUBLIGA"	5·00	5·00
		b. Accent over "U"	5·00	5·00
664		15c. blue-green (R.)	65	65
		a. "REPUBLIGA"	6·00	6·00
		b. Accent over "U"	6·00	6·00
665		20c. bright violet (R.)	1·20	1·20
		a. "REPUBLIGA"	6·00	6·00
		b. Accent over "U"	6·00	6·00
666		25c. carmine	65	65
		a. "REPUBLIGA"	8·00	8·00
		b. Accent over "U"	8·00	8·00
667		30c. deep lake	5·25	5·25
		a. "REPUBLIGA"	55·00	55·00
		b. Accent over "U"	55·00	55·00
668		40c. deep blue (II) (R.)	1·60	1·60
		a. "REPUBLIGA"	9·00	9·00
		b. Accent over "U"	9·00	9·00
669		50c. orange	1·60	1·60
		a. "REPUBLIGA"	7·50	7·50
		b. Accent over "U"	7·50	7·50
670	69	1p. deep greenish slate (R.)	9·50	9·50
		a. "REPUBLIGA"	45·00	45·00
		b. Accent over "U"	45·00	45·00

No. 652 optd

671	115	5c. black (R.)	1·90	1·90
		a. "REPUBLIGA"	10·00	10·00
		b. Accent over "U"	10·00	10·00

(ii) EXPRESS LETTER

E672	E **89**	20c. carmine (No. E522a)	4·75	4·75
		a. "REPUBLIGA"	35·00	
		b. Accent over "U"	30·00	

The, "REPUBLIGA" variety occurs on position 49 and "REPUBLICA" on position 1 in the setting of 50.

*(c) Second Catalan opt, T **119** (29 April)*
(i) POSTAGE. Imperf

672	66	1c. green	30	30

P 11½

673	97	2c. brown	30	30
674		5c. grey-brown (R.)	30	30
675		10c. yellow-green	30	30
676		15c. blue-green (R.)	1·60	1·60
677		20c. bright violet (R.)	45	45
678		25c. carmine	45	45
679		30c. deep lake	7·00	7·00
680		40c. deep blue (II) (R.)	1·60	1·60
681		50c. orange	6·25	6·25

No. 652 optd

682	115	5c. black (R.)	4·25	4·25

(ii) AIR. Nos. 353/6 optd

683	64	5c. green (R.)	11·50	11·50
684		10c. carmine	11·50	11·50
685		25c. blue (R.)	16·00	16·00
686		50c. greenish-blue (R.)	33·00	33·00

Many double and inverted overprints exist on these provisionals.

Nos. 653/686 were withdrawn during April and May by direction of the central Government. Similar overprints of a more local nature were produced by the towns of Almeria, Tolosa and Valencia.

Following the withdrawal of the provisionals, unoverprinted stamps were used until Nos. 687, etc. were issued.

1931. Continuously optd as T **120**.

(a) POSTAGE

687	97	2c. brown (B.) July	15	15
688		5c. grey-brown (R.) (Sept)	45	15
689		10c. yellow-green (R.) (Sept)	65	15
690		15c. blue-green (R.) (Sept)	6·25	20
691		20c. bright violet (R.) (Sept)	2·20	1·40
692		25c. carmine (B.) (27 May)	60	15
		a. Opt reading down	9·50	6·00
		b. Double opt, both reading down	55·00	45·00
693		30c. deep lake (B.) (July)	10·00	1·60
694		40c. deep blue (II) (R.) (Aug)	8·25	80
695		50c. orange (B.) (Aug)	16·00	95
696	69	1p. deep greenish slate (R.) (Sept)	£100	1·20

(b) EXPRESS LETTER

E697	E 89	20c. carm (No. E522a) (B.) (Sept)	19·00	3·00

This overprint was applied eighteen times in continuous succession, upon each vertical row of ten stamps, so that stamps show varying portions of the overprint.

121 The Fountain of the Lions   **122** Cordoba Cathedral

123 The Royal Palace and San Francisco el Grande   **124** G.P.O., and Cibeles Fountain

125 The Calle de Alcalá

Oficial.   OFICIAL
(O **126**)   (O **127**)

(Eng C. Delhom, J. L. Sánchez Toda and Mr. Harrison. Recess. Waterlow)

1931 (10 Oct). Third Pan-American Postal Union Congress.

(a) POSTAGE. T **121**, **122** *and similar types. P* 12½

697	121	5c. maroon	25	15
698	122	10c. blue-green	75	55
699	–	15c. violet	75	55
700	122	25c. scarlet	75	55
701	–	30c. bronze-green	75	55
702	121	40c. indigo	2·00	1·30
703	122	50c. scarlet-vermilion	2·00	1·30
704	–	1p. black	4·00	2·75
705	–	4p. purple	21·00	14·50
706	–	10p. chocolate	65·00	46·00
697/706 Set of 10			90·00	60·00

(b) OFFICIAL. Nos. 697/706 in different shades and optd with Type O **126**

O707	121	5c. brown-purple (R.)	40	30
O708	122	10c. green (R.)	40	30
O709	–	15c. bright violet (R.)	25	25
O710	122	25c. carmine (B.)	40	30
O711	–	30c. olive (B.)	40	30
O712	121	40c. ultramarine (R.)	95	65
O713	122	50c. orange (R.)	95	65
O714	–	1p. slate (R.)	95	65
O715	–	4p. magenta (B.)	17·00	15·00
O716	–	10p. brown (R.)	43·00	34·00
O707/716 Set of 10			60·00	50·00

Designs: Horiz—15c., 1p. Alcántara Bridge, Toledo; 30c. Medallion portrait of Dr. F. García y Santos; 4p., 10p. Revolutionists hoisting the Republican flag, 14 April, 1931.

(c) AIR. P 12

707	123	5c. maroon	20	15
708		10c. deep green	20	15
709		25c. scarlet	20	15
710	124	50c. blue	60	60
711		1p. violet	1·10	90
712	125	4p. black	14·50	12·50
707/712 Set of 6			15·00	13·00

(d) OFFICIAL. AIR. Nos. 707/712 in different shades optd with Type O **127**

O717	123	5c. red-brown (R.)	20	15
O718		10c. green (R.)	20	15
O719		25c. carmine (B.)	20	15
O720	124	50c. light blue (R.)	20	15
O721		1p. lilac (R.)	20	15
O722	125	4p. grey (R.)	7·75	5·75
O717/722 Set of 6			8·00	6·00

125a Montserrat Arms   **125b** Airplane over Montserrat   E **126**

(Eng L. Sesé, J. L. Sánchez Toda, C. Delhom and P. Pascual. Recess)

1931 (9 Dec). 900th Anniv of Montserrat Monastery. Inscr "1031–1881–1931". Blue figures on back except 1c. and 2c.

A. P 11½
B. P 14

(a) POSTAGE. T **125a** *and similar vert designs*

		A	B
713	1c. blue-green	2·20	1·90
714	2c. chestnut	1·20	85
715	5c. sepia	1·50	1·00
716	10c. yellow-green	1·50	1·00
717	15c. blue-green	2·10	1·30
718	20c. purple	4·50	3·25
719	25c. claret	6·00	4·50
720	30c. carmine	70·00	50·00
721	40c. blue	40·00	22·00
722	50c. orange	95·00	60·00
723	1p. indigo	95·00	60·00
724	4p. magenta	£850	£550
725	10p. brown	£700	£475
713/725 Set of 13 (cheapest)		£1700	£1100

Designs:—1c. to 10c. T **125a**; 15c., 50c. Monks planning the monastery; 20c., 30c. The "Black Virgin" (full length); 25c., 1p., 10p. The "Black Virgin" (profile); 40c., 4p. Montserrat Monastery.

(b) AIR

726	125b	5c. sepia	70	60
727		10c. yellow-green	3·75	3·50
728		25c. claret	14·00	13·00
729		50c. orange	49·00	43·00
730		1p. slate-blue	33·00	29·00

(c) EXPRESS LETTER

E731	E **126**	20c. scarlet	38·00	33·00

Same prices for unused or used except the 1c. and 10p. perf 14, which were issued but not used for postal purposes.

126 Blasco Ibáñez   **127** Pi y Margall   **128** Joaquin Costa

129 Mariana Pineda   **130** Nicolás Salmerón   **131** Concepción Arenal

245

SPAIN

132 Ruiz Zorilla **133** Pablo Iglesias **134** Ramón y Cajal

135 Azcárate **136** Jovellanos **137** Pablo Iglesias

138 Emilio Castelar **139** Pablo Iglesias **140** Velázquez

141 F. Salvoechea **142** Cuenca

(Eng C. Delhom, P. Pascual and J. L. Sánchez Toda. Recess)

1931–38.

A. P 11½
I. With blue control figures on back

731A	127	5c. sepia (1932)	5·25	40
732A	128	10c. yellow-green (1932)	13·00	40
733A	130	15c. blue-green	15·00	20
734A	133	25c. deep lake (1932)	47·00	1·10
735A		30c. carmine	14·00	35
736A	138	40c. deep ultramarine (1932)	£110	8·25
737A	130	50c. orange (1932)	£140	16·00

II. Without control figures

738A	126	2c. red-brown (1932)	20	15
739A	127	5c. sepia (1933)	9·25	15
740A	126	5c. chocolate (4.34)	15	15
741A	128	10c. yellow-green (1932)	8·75	15
742A	129	10c. green (3.35)	20	15
743A		10c. blue-green (10.2.38)	20	20
744A	130	15c. blue-green (1932)	1·30	15
745A	131	15c. blue-green (12.34)	40	15
746A		15c. yellow-green (14.5.37)	1·70	10
747A		15c. greenish black (1938)	40	10
748A	127	20c. violet (1932)	50	15
749A	133	25c. deep lake (1932)	80·00	15
750A	132	25c. deep lake (1933)	1·00	15
751A	133	30c. carmine (1932)	3·50	15
752A	134	30c. sepia (11.34)	16·00	2·40
753A	135	30c. carmine (with imprint) (1.35)	17·00	30
754A		30c. carmine (no imprint) (1935)	10·00	60
755A	136	30c. carmine (4.35)	15	15
756A	137	30c. scarlet (19.7.36)	20	10
757A	139	30c. scarlet (10.2.37)	3·50	45
758A	138	40c. deep ultramarine (1932)	20	15
759A		40c. scarlet (14.5.37)	3·25	45
760A	139	45c. carmine (14.5.37)	30	10
761A	130	50c. orange (1932)	65·00	1·10
		c. Perf 10 (1938)	95·00	1·10
762A		50c. deep ultramarine (4.35)	2·75	1·10
763A	140	50c. slate-blue (15.8.36)	20	10
764A	138	60c. yellow-green (1932)	20	15
765A	141	60c. blue (25.5.37)	1·90	1·20
766A		60c. orange (1.38)	17·00	11·50
767A	142	1p. black (1932)	30	20
		c. Perf 10 (1938)	20	15
768A	–	4p. magenta (1932)	1·50	1·70
		c. Perf 10 (1938)	95	30
769A	–	10p. brown (1932)	4·25	4·75
		c. Perf 10 (1938)	1·10	1·10

B. P 14
I. With blue control figures on back

731B	127	5c. sepia (1932)	65·00	
733B	130	15c. blue-green	65·00	
734B	133	25c. deep lake (1932)	65·00	
735B		30c. carmine	65·00	

II. Without control figures

739B	127	5c. sepia (1933)	10·50	9·50
741B	128	10c. yellow-green (1932)	11·50	9·50
744B	130	15c. blue-green (1932)	11·50	11·50
748B	127	20c. violet (1932)	9·50	9·50
750B	132	25c. deep lake (1933)	—	—
751B	133	30c. carmine (1932)	9·50	9·50
752B	134	30c. sepia (11.34)	28·00	28·00
753B	135	30c. carmine (with imprint) (1.35)	18·00	
754B		30c. carmine (no imprint) (1935)	—	—
755B	136	30c. carmine (4.35)	2·25	—
756B	137	30c. scarlet (19.7.36)	16·00	—
757B	139	30c. scarlet (10.2.37)	16·00	—
758B	138	40c. deep ultramarine (1932)	—	—
759B		40c. scarlet (14.5.37)	15·00	—
760B	139	45c. carmine (14.5.37)	12·00	—
762B		50c. deep ultramarine (4.35)	—	—
763B	140	50c. slate-blue (15.8.36)	—	—
764B	138	60c. yellow-green (1932)	14·00	14·00
765B	141	60c. blue (25.5.37)	14·00	
766B		60c. orange (1.38)	25·00	—
767B	142	1p. black (1932)	9·50	7·50
		c. Perf 10 (1938)		
768B	–	4p. magenta (1932)	11·50	9·50
		c. Perf 10 (1938)		

Pictorial designs as T **142**—4p. Castle of Segovia; 10p. Sun Gate, Toledo.

Other values exist with the imprint missing, but these are the result of faulty printing.

143   **144**

1933–38. Typo. Without control figures.

I. Imperf

770	143	1c. blue-green (1933)	20	20

II. A. P 11½

771A	143	2c. chestnut (1935)	55	10
772A	144	2c. chestnut (1936)	†	†
773A	143	5c. brown (1938)	†	†
		a. Granite paper	20	20
774A		10c. yellow-green (1938)	†	†
		a. Granite paper	20	20
775A		15c. blue-green (1938)	20	20
		a. Granite paper	20	20
776A		20c. violet (1938)	2·00	2·00
		a. Granite paper	1·50	1·50
777A		25c. magenta (1938)	20	20
		a. Granite paper	20	20
778A		30c. carmine (1938)	†	†
		a. Granite paper	1·50	1·50

D. P 13½×13

771D	143	2c. chestnut (1935)	20	20
772D	144	2c. chestnut (1936)	20	20
773D	143	5c. brown (1938)	20	20
		a. Granite paper	20	20
774D		10c. yellow-green (1938)	20	20
775D		15c. blue-green (1938)	20	20
		a. Granite paper	40	40
776D		20c. violet (1938)	20	20
		a. Granite paper	20	20
777D		25c. magenta (1938)	20	20
778D		30c. carmine (1938)	20	20
		a. Granite paper	20	20

A 45c. value as T **143** was prepared in red and in green during March, 1939, but was not issued.

E **145**   **145** Cierva C.30A Autogyro over Seville

1934. EXPRESS LETTER. Recess. P 10.
E779 E **145** 20c. red.. 30 20

No. 779 Sky unshaded

No. 780/b Sky shaded

(Des J. L.Sánchez Toda. Recess)

1935 (June)–**38**. P 11½.
779 **145** 2p. dull blue.. 40·00 7·75
780   2p. blue (*redrawn*) (1938).................... 30 20
           a. Perf 10. *Dull blue*............................ 3·25 1·90
           b. Perf 14. *Dull blue*............................ 1·90 1·40

146 Lope de Vega's Book-plate

147 Lope de Vega, after Tristan

148 Scene from *Peribáñez*

1935 (1 Aug). Tercentenary of Death of Lope de Vega (author). Recess. P 11½.
781 **146** 15c. deep blue-green........................... 12·00 30
782 **147** 30c. carmine.. 5·25 25
           b. Perf 14.. 9·50 9·50
783   50c. deep blue...................................... 29·00 3·50
           b. Perf 14.. 55·00 47·00
784 **148** 1p. black.. 47·00 2·30
           b. Perf 14.. 75·00 47·00

149 Old-time Map of the Amazon

150 M. Moya

151 House of Nazareth and Rotary Press

E **152** Newspaper Boy

152 Pyrenean Eagle and Newspapers

153 Airplane over Press Association Building

154 Don Quixote on the Wooden Horse

1935 (12 Oct). Iglesias Amazon Expedition. Recess. P 11½.
785 **149** 30c. carmine.. 4·75 1·20
           a. Perf 14.. 50·00 24·00

(Des J. L. Sánchez Toda (portraits), J. F. Cano (T **151**), M. Bertuchi (Type E **152**), F. Cano (T **152**) and M. Bertuchi (remainder). Photo Waterlow)

1936 (14 Feb–11 Mar). 40th Anniv of Madrid Press Association. P 12½.
   (a) POSTAGE. As T **150**/1
         (i) As T **150** *(22×27 mm.)*
786   1c. scarlet... 15 15
787   2c. red-brown................................... 15 15
788   5c. sepia... 15 15
789   10c. emerald-green.......................... 15 15
         (ii) As T **150** *(24×30 mm.)*
790   15c. turquoise-green....................... 20 15
791   20c. bright violet............................. 20 15
792   25c. bright magenta........................ 20 15
793   30c. scarlet... 15 15
         (iii) As T **150** *(26×31½ mm.)*
794   40c. orange.. 70 25
795   50c. blue.. 40 15
796   60c. olive... 90 30
797   1p. grey-black.................................... 90 30
         (iv) T **151**
798   2p. turquoise-blue............................ 12·50 4·50
799   4p. bright claret................................ 12·50 7·50
800   10p. brown-lake................................. 29·00 18·00
786/800 Set of 15.. 55·00 30·00
Portraits:—1c., 15c., 40c. M. Moya; 2c., 20c., 50c. T. Luca de Tena; 5c., 25c., 60c. J. Francos Rodriguez; 10c., 30c., 1p. A. Lerroux.
   (b) EXPRESS LETTER
E801 E **152** 20c. rose-carmine.............................. 40 35
   (c) AIR. T **152**/4 *and similar design* (11 Mar)
801 **152** 1c. carmine... 15 15
802 **153** 2c. brown.. 15 15
803 **152** 5c. sepia... 15 15
804 **153** 10c. green.. 15 15
805 —   15c. greenish blue............................... 35 15
806 **152** 20c. bright violet................................. 35 15
807 **153** 25c. bright magenta............................ 35 15
808 —   30c. vermilion...................................... 15 15
809 **152** 40c. orange... 75 35
810 —   50c. turquoise-blue............................. 50 35
811 **153** 60c. olive.. 1·20 35
812 —   1p. brown-black.................................. 1·20 35
813 **154** 2p. bright blue.................................... 7·50 4·25
814   4p. bright claret.................................. 8·25 6·75
815   10p. brown-lake.................................... 25·00 16·00
801/815 Set of 15.. 40·00 25·00
   Design: As T **153**—15c., 30c., 50c., 1p. Cierva C.30A Autogyro over House of Nazareth.

155 Gregorio Fernández

156

CORREO AEREO
(157)

SPAIN

(Eng J. L. Sánchez Toda. Recess)

1936 (10 Mar). Third Centenary of Birth of G. Fernández (sculptor). P 11½.
816	**155**	30c. carmine	2·20	1·00
		a. Perf 14	11·50	8·50

1936 (3 Apr). First National Philatelic Exhibition, Madrid. Recess. Imperf.

(a) POSTAGE
817	**156**	10c. black-brown	65·00	55·00
818		15c. green	65·00	55·00

*(b) AIR. Optd with T **157** diagonally upwards*
819	**156**	10c. scarlet (G.)	£225	£190
820		15c. blue (R.)	£225	£190

An entrance fee of 5p. entitled visitors to buy one set of Air or Postage stamps (not both) on first day of Exhibition and a maximum of 4 Air or 15 Postage sets per person on second day.

On 17 July 1936 Civil War began with a rising by a junta of Army commanders, supported by sections of the country opposed to the policies of the Popular Front Republican Government. Nos. 821 to 861j were issued by the Republican Government based in Madrid, Valencia and Barcelona.

During the war various fiscal stamps did duty as postal issues. This was allowed by the postal authorities, especially where no other stamps were available, but was not specifically authorised. The local War Tax and other charity labels were rarely accepted by the postal authorities for the payment of postage.

(158)   159   (160)

1936 (1 Aug). Manila–Madrid Flight of Arnaiz and Calvo. Optd with T **158**.
821	**137**	30c. scarlet (p 11½)	8·50	6·25
		a. Perf 14	55·00	

1937 (May). Fiscal tax stamp of Asturias and León surch in blue. P 11.
822	**159**	25c. on 5c. red	16·00	8·00
823		45c. on 5c. red	8·50	4·75
824		60c. on 5c. red	45	95
825		1p. on 5c. red	45	65

These surcharges were authorized when the provinces of Asturias and León were cut off by General Franco from the rest of Republican Spain. Other similar surcharges exist but probably had no real postal use.

1938 (15 Jan–1 June). Surch with T **160**. P 13½ (827, 829), P 10 (828), P 11 (830), P 11½ (832), P 13½×13 (831) or imperf (826).
826	**143**	45c. on 1c. blue-green (R.) (1 June)	6·00	3·75
827		45c. on 1c. blue-green (R.) (1 June)	65	30
828		45c. on 1c. blue-green (R.) (1 June)	75	60
829		45c. on 2c. chestnut (B.)	24·00	20·00
830		45c. on 2c. chestnut (B.)	47·00	45·00
831	**144**	45c. on 2c. chest (B.)	20	15
832	**126**	45c. on 2c. red-brown (B.)	36·00	16·00

160a Republican Symbol

14 ABRIL 1938
VII Aniversario
de la República
45 cts.
(161)

CORREO AÉREO
14 Abril 1938
VII Aniversario
de la República
2'50 pts.
(162)

1938. Litho. P 11½.
833	**160a**	40c. rose (Apr)	15	15
		b. Perf 14 (Apr)	40	20
834		45c. carmine (Apr)	15	15
		b. Perf 14 (Apr)	40	20
835		50c. blue (Sept)	15	15
		b. Perf 14 (Sept)	40	20
836		60c. blue (Oct)	80	40
		b. Perf 14 (Oct)	1·70	1·10

1938 (Apr). Seventh Anniv of Republic. Nos. 308/9 surch with T **161/2**.

(a) POSTAGE (13 Apr)
| 837 | **161** | 45c. on 15c. violet | 19·00 | 18·00 |

(b) AIR (14 Apr)
| 838 | **162** | 2.50p. on 10c. scarlet | £140 | £130 |

W **163**   F **163**

1938. WAR TAX. Litho. P 13½.
W839	W **163**	10c. red	95	1·40
W840		20c. blue	95	95
W841		60c. rose	3·25	3·75
W842		1p. ultramarine	95	1·10
W843		2p. grey-green	95	1·10
W844		10p. blue	4·75	5·75

Nos W842/3 have coloured figures of value on white backgrounds.

(Litho Oliva de Vilanova, Barcelona)

1938. FRANK. For use by the Agencia Filatélica Oficial (AFO), Barcelona. P 16.
F839	F **163**	(–) Blue	—	4·75
F840		(–) Lilac	—	4·75
F841		(–) Green	—	4·75
F842		(–) Brown	—	4·75
F843		(–) Black	—	4·75

Nos. F839/43 unused are remainders.

163 Defence of Madrid   AEREO + 5 Pts. (164)

(Des G. López. Litho Rieusset, Barcelona)

1938 (15 Apr). Defence of Madrid Relief Fund. P 11½.

(a) POSTAGE
839	**163**	45c.+2p. dull blue and light blue	95	85
		a. Blue and blue-green	14·00	9·50
MS840	120×105 mm. No. 839		40·00	48·00
		a. No. 839a	£425	£325

*(b) AIR. Surch with T **164***
841	**163**	45c.+2p.+5p. dull blue and light blue	£550	£425
MS842	120×105 mm. No. 841		£7500	£9500

Beware of forged surcharges.
The blue-green shade was from the first printing, most of which was destroyed in an air-raid. New plates were made for the second printing.

(165)

Fiesta del Trabajo
1 MAYO
1938
1 Peseta
(166)

1938 (1 May). Labour Day. No. 309 (Don Quixote) surch.
843	**165**	45c. on 15c. violet	4·25	4·25
844	**166**	1p. on 15c. violet	7·75	7·25

Three other surcharges, 1p.25 on 15c., 5p. on 10c. and 10p. on 25c., on the Quixote issue were prepared by the Republic in 1939, but were not issued.

248

SPAIN

167 Statue of Liberty and Flags (**168**)

(Litho Rieusset, Barcelona)

1938 (1 June). 150th Anniv of U.S. Constitution. P 11½.

(a) POSTAGE

845	**167**	1p. multicoloured	29·00	26·00
MS846	120×105 mm. No. 845		45·00	41·00

*(b) AIR. Surch with T **168***

847	**167**	1p.+5p. multicoloured	£450	£375
MS848	120×105 mm. No. 847		£1700	£1700

Beware of forged surcharges.
There were two printings of Nos. 845 and 847. They can be identified by the shade *behind* the figure of value. On stamps from the first printing it is grey and on the second printing lilac.

(Eng Camilo Delhom. Recess)

1938 (1 June). Red Cross. P 10.

(a) POSTAGE

849	**169**	45c.+5p. red	85	65

*(b) AIR. Surch with T **170***

850	**169**	45c.+5p.+3p. red	17·00	13·00

172 Steelworks

1938 (Aug). AIR. No. 719 surch as T **171**.

851		50c. on 25c. claret	50·00	44·00
852		1p. on 25c. claret (G.)	1·90	1·40
853		1.25p. on 25c. claret (R.)	1·90	1·40
854		1.50p. on 25c. claret (B.)	2·00	1·50
855		2p. on 25c. claret (R., Bk.)	55·00	44·00
851/855	Set of 5		£100	85·00

On No. 855 the figures of value are in red and the rest of the surcharge in black.

(Photo Oliva de Vilanova, Barcelona)

1938 (9 Aug). Workers of Sagunto. P 16.

856	**172**	45c. black	20	15
857	–	1p.25 deep greenish blue	20	15

Design: Vert—1p.25, Blast furnace and air raid victims.

173 Isaac Peral   **174** Troops on the Alert

(Photo Oliva de Vilanova, Barcelona)

1938 (11 Aug). Submarine Service. T **173** and similar horiz views of submarine. P 16.

857a	**173**	1p. blue	6·75	6·75
857b	–	2p. red-brown	12·50	12·50
857c	–	4p. reddish orange	14·50	14·50
857d	–	6p. indigo	43·00	29·00
857e	–	10p. claret	55·00	50·00
857f	**173**	15p. myrtle-green	£550	£500
857a/857f	Set of 6		£600	£550

Designs:—2, 6p. *Narciso Monturiol*; 4, 10p. *B-2*.

Miniature sheet
Size 150×118 mm. Recess and photo. P 10½

MS857g   4p. black and carmine; 6p. black and ultramarine; 15p. black and myrtle-green........ £650   £550

The above were issued for use on a submarine service between Barcelona and Port Mahon, Minorca. The submarine C4 made one mail-carrying trip with 400 covers but the stamps were also valid on ordinary mail.

(Photo Oliva de Vilanova, Barcelona)

1938 (1 Sept). In honour of 43rd Division. T **174** and similar design.

A. P 11½×11 or 11×11½ (No. 859)

858		25c. deep green	20·00	13·00
		b. Imperf	17·00	13·00
859	–	45c. red-brown	20·00	13·00
		b. Imperf	17·00	13·00

Design: Vert—45c. Two soldiers on guard.

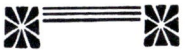

SEGUNDO ANIVERSARIO DE LA

7 NOV. 1938

HEROICA DEFENSA DE MADRID

(**175**)

1938 (7 Nov). Second Anniv of Defence of Madrid. No. 839 optd singly with T **175** or across blocks of four with similar type.

860	**163**	45c.+2p. dull blue and light blue (T **175**)	4·25	4·75
		a. Block of four with larger opt	22·00	27·00

The sheets of 50 (5×10) had the first four vertical rows overprinted across blocks of four with a larger overprint in two lines, and the right vertical row overprinted on each stamp with Type **175**. The latter therefore only exists as singles, in vertical strips or *se-tenant* with No. 860a.

(**176**)   **176a** Man and Woman in Firing Position

(Surch typo Oliva de Vilanova, Barcelona)

1938 (10 Nov). No. 719 surch with T **176**.

861		2p.50 on 25c. claret (p 11½)	30	30
		a. Perf 14	7·50	7·50

Stamps with further overprint "Correo Aereo 1939" are bogus.

(Eng Camilo Delhom. Recess)

1938 (25 Nov). In honour of the Militia. T **176a** and similar designs. P 10.

861b	**176a**	5c. sepia	4·75	4·25
861c	–	10c. deep purple	4·75	4·25
861d	–	25c. deep bluish green	4·75	4·25
861e	–	45c. rose-red	4·75	4·25
861f	–	60c. deep blue	10·00	7·25
861g	–	1p.20 black	£200	£160
861h	–	2p. yellow-orange	60·00	47·00
861i	–	5p. red-brown	£375	£300
861j	–	10p. myrtle-green	65·00	55·00
861b/861j	Set of 9		£650	£500

249

SPAIN

Designs: Horiz—45c. to 1p.20, Militia with machine gun. Vert—2p. to 10p. Grenade-thrower.

Although only on sale at the Philatelic Agency against foreign currency, the above were used on mail to stamp dealers and philatelic publishers abroad.

The Civil War ended on 1 April 1939 in the defeat of the Republican Government.

JUNTA OF NATIONAL DEFENCE, 1936

Nos. 862 to 947 were for use throughout the areas controlled by the Nationalists. Other authorised issues of a more localised nature are listed at the end of Spain. The arms stamp inscribed "ESPANA Julio 1936" is listed among the Regionals and Local Civil War issues under Granada.

During the war the Nationalist authorities permitted the use of fiscal stamps for postage and this usage was regularised for internal postage by decree of 9 November 1936. The concession ended on 31 July 1937. The use of local War Tax issues for postage was forbidden by another decree of 25 September 1937.

177 Seville Cathedral

178 Xavier Castle, Navarre

I II

The imprints on Nos. 865 and 866 measure 12 mm. and 8 mm. respectively.

(Des J. L. Sánchez Toda. Litho M. Portabella, Zaragoza)

1936 (Sept). Designs as T **177/8** inscr "ESPANA CORREOS. JUNTA DE DEFENSA NACIONAL". P 11½.

862	–	5c. grey-brown	95	80
863	–	15c. blue-green (*shades*)	95	80
864	177	25c. rose-carmine	95	80
865	178	30c. carmine (I)	95	80
866		30c. carmine (II)	1·10	1·00
867		1p. black	8·25	5·25
862/867 Set of 6			12·00	8·75

Designs: Vert—5c. Burgos Cathedral. Horiz—15c. Zaragoza Cathedral; 1p. Alcántara Bridge and Alcazar, Toledo.

Forgeries exist.

NATIONAL STATE, 1 October 1936

179 **180** Cordoba Cathedral

(Des J. L. Sánchez Toda. Litho M. Portabella, Zaragoza)

1936–37. As T **179/80**. Inscr "ESPANA CORREOS". Imperf (1c.) or P 11½ (others).

868	179	1c. pale green	8·25	6·25
869		2c. chestnut	95	70
870	–	10c. green	95	70
871	–	50c. blue	24·00	13·50
872	180	60c. yellow-green	1·60	90
873		4p. lilac, red and yellow (19.10.37)	95·00	41·00
874		10p. brown (19.10.37)	85·00	41·00
868/874 Set of 7			£195	95·00

Designs (as T **180**): Horiz—10c. Salamanca University; 50c. Court of the Lions, Granada; 10p. Troops disembarking at Algeciras. Vert—4p. National flag at Malaga.

Forgeries exist.

181 **182** **183** "El Cid"

184 Isabella the Catholic   A. Short figs   B. Tall figs

C. Gothic "5"   D. Normal "5"

Two types of 2c.:—
 E. "ESTADO ESPANOL" 19 mm. long.
 F. "ESTADO ESPANOL" 18 mm. long.

Imprints: I. "Hija de B. Fournier, Burgos" length 10 mm., No. 877.
 II. "Hija de B. Fournier, Burgos" length 14½ mm., Nos. 878, 883.
 III. "Fournier, Burgos" length 6 mm., No. 884.

(Des Blas Pérez Irujo. Litho)

1937–50. P 11.

A. Printed by B. Fournier, Burgos

(a) With imprint (1937–39)

875	181	1c. green (imperf)	20	15
		a. "CENTIMO" for "CÉNTIMO"	30	15
876	182	2c. red-brown (E)	20	15
877	183	5c. olive-brown (I)	35	15
878		5c. sepia (II) (12.38)	70	25
879		10c. yellow-green	20	15
880	184	15c. black (3.37)	35	20
881		20c. violet (3.37)	75	20
882		25c. lake (20.4.37)	65	20
883		30c. rose-lake (II)	1·00	20
		a. Imprint at left instead of right	£400	£250
884		30c. rose-lake (III)	37·00	3·75
885		40c. orange (27.4.37)	3·75	20
886		50c. deep blue	3·75	20
887		60c. yellow (20.4.37)	65	20
888		1p. blue (6.4.37)	29·00	75
889		4p. magenta (11.5.37)	35·00	7·25
890	183	10p. blue (A) (11.5.37)	£120	49·00
891		10p. blue (B)	70·00	20·00
875/891 Set of 17			£200	55·00

(b) Without imprint (1939)

892	181	1c. green (imperf)	80	30
893	182	2c. chocolate (E) (*shades*)	80	30
894	183	5c. sepia	6·00	40
895		10c. carmine (*shades*) (22.2.39)	20	15
		a. Pair, one with imprint, one without	75·00	45·00
896		15c. yellow-green (C)	25	15
897	184	70c. blue	1·20	20
892/897 Set of 6			9·00	1·50

B. Printed at State Printing Works, Madrid without imprint

(a) P 11½ (rough) (1939–48)

898	182	2c. chocolate (E) (*shades*)	20	10
898a		2c. chocolate (F) (1948)	20	10
899	183	5c. sepia	40	20
900		10c. carmine (*shades*)	45	20
		a. Brown red (*shades*)	50	10
901		15c. yellow-green (D)	1·90	10

(b) P 13½×13 (1949–50)

902	183	5c. sepia	25	15
		a. Brown	25	15
903		10c. carmine	20	15
904		15c. yellow-green (D)	1·50	15

A 1c. imperf value as No. 892 was also printed in Madrid, but this is very difficult to distinguish from the Burgos issue.

SPAIN

E **185** Pegasus

(Des Blas Perez Irujo. Litho B. Fournier, Burgos)
1937–**38**. EXPRESS LETTER. P 11.
(a) With imprint
E905 E **185** 20c. reddish brown .... 11·50 6·00
(b) Without imprint (1938)
E906 E **185** 20c. chocolate .... 2·40 50

185 St. James of Compostela
186 Santiago Cathedral

187 Portico de la Gloria

Two types of 30c. I. "1937" without dots.
II. Dot before and after "1937".

(Des Blas Pérez Irujo. Litho Fournier, Vitoria)
1937 (1 Aug). Holy Year of Compostela. P 11–11½.
905 **185** 15c. reddish brown .... 3·50 80
906 **186** 30c. rose-carmine (I) .... 12·00 70
907 30c. rose-carmine (II) .... 45·00 7·00
908 **187** 1p. red-orange and blue .... 41·00 4·25
  a. Centre inverted £475 £225

188 Alcazar, Toledo (before Siege)

(Photo Orell Füssli, Zurich)
1937 (16 Aug). First Anniv of National Uprising. Miniature sheets (140×110 mm). T **188** and similar design. Control figures on back. P 11½.
MS909 **188** 2p. (+2p.) orange .... 42·00 30·00
MS910 Imperf £600 £500
MS911 – 2p. (+2p.) blue-green .... 42·00 30·00
MS912 – Imperf £600 £500
Design:—No. MS911/12, Alcazar in ruins.

189

189a Covadonga Monastery
190 Ferdinand the Catholic

(Litho M. Roel, Vigo)
1937 (23 Dec). Anti-Tuberculosis Fund. Cross in red. P 11½.
913 **189** 10c. blue and black .... 15·00 6·00

(Photo Orell Füssli, Zurich)
1938 (10 Feb). Historic Monuments. Sheet 140×100 mm, comprising T **189a** and similar designs. Control figures and selling price on back. P 12×12½.
MS914 20c. violet, 30c. red, 50c. blue, 1p. grey-green (sold at 4p.) .... 75·00 65·00
MS915 Imperf £130 £100
Designs: Horiz—30c. Cathedral, Palma de Mallorca; 50c. Alcazar, Segovia. Vert—1p. Leon Cathedral.

Imprints:—I. "Lit. Fournier Vitoria". II. "Fournier Vitoria".

(Des J. L. Sánchez Toda. Litho Fournier, Vitoria)
1938 (Feb). P 11 or 11½×11.
916 **190** 15c. blue-green (I) .... 4·00 15
917 15c. blue-green (II) .... 4·00 15
  a. Perf 10×10½
918 20c. bright violet (II) .... 17·00 2·50
919 25c. lake (II) .... 1·20 15
920 30c. scarlet (I) .... 15·00 15
921 30c. scarlet (II) .... 11·50 15
  a. Perf 10
916/921 Set of 6 .... 45·00 3·00

(**191**)

191a Soldier with Flag

192

1938 (17 May). AIR. Unissued values with imprint "FOURNIER, VITORIA" optd with T **191**. P 10½×11 or 10.
922 **190** 50c. grey-blue (R.) .... 1·70 80
923 1p. blue (R.) .... 4·75 80

(Photo Orell Füssli, Zurich)
1938 (1 July). Honouring Army and Navy. Sheet 175×132 mm, comprising designs as T **191a** (various frames). Control figures and selling price on back. P 13½.
MS924 2c. violet (Type **191a**); 3c. blue (b); 3c. blue (c); 5c. sepia (a); 5c. sepia (Type **191a**); 10c. green (b); 10c. green (c); 30c. orange (b); 30c. orange (c); Two of each stamp (sold at 4p.) .... 50·00 48·00
MS925 Imperf £250 £190
Designs: (a) Cruiser *Almirante Cervera*: (b) Trenches near Teruel; (c) General Franco's Moorish bodyguard.

(Litho Fournier, Vitoria)
1938 (17 July). Second Anniv of National Uprising. P 10.
926 **192** 15c. green and pale green .... 7·25 5·50
927 25c. carmine and pink .... 7·25 5·50
928 30c. blue and pale blue .... 3·75 3·00
929 1p. brown and yellow £160 £110
926/929 Set of 4 .... £160 £110

193 Isabella the Catholic

193a Don Juan of Austria

194

(Des J. L. Sánchez Toda. Litho Fournier, Vitoria)
1938–**39**. P 10.
930 **193** 20c. bright violet (1939) .... 2·75 20
931 25c. lake .... 14·50 80
932 30c. scarlet 40 20
933 40c. mauve 40 15
934 50c. slate-blue (1939) .... 55·00 3·25
935 1p. bright blue .... 19·00 1·30
930/935 Set of 6 .... 85·00 5·25

251

SPAIN

(Recess Enschedé)

1938 (18 Dec). Battle of Lepanto. Sheets (each 90×75 mm.). T **193a** and another design. Control figures on back.

(a) P 13½ (30c.) or 12½ (50c.)

MS936	**193a**	30c. carmine	24·00
MS937	–	50c. deep blue	24·00

(b) Imperf

MS938	**193a**	30c. grey-violet	£500
MS939	–	50c. grey-green	£500

Design (36½×23 mm.):—50c. Naval Battle of Lepanto.

(Litho M. Roel, Vigo)

1938 (23 Dec). Anti-Tuberculosis Fund. Cross in red. P 11.

940	**194**	10c. pale blue and black	9·25	2·40

195 Juan de la Cierva and Cierva C.30A Autogyro **196** General Franco

(Des J. L. Sánchez Toda. Litho B. Fournier, Burgos)

1939 (Jan–Mar). AIR. P 11.

941	**195**	20c. orange (4.3)	80	40
942		25c. carmine-red (5.2)	55	15
943		35c. magenta (5.2)	80	40
944		50c. purple-brown (14.1)	1·20	25
945		1p. bright blue (14.1)	1·20	25
946		2p. green (4.3)	5·25	2·10
947		4p. slate-blue (4.3)	8·25	3·50
941/947	*Set of 7*		16·00	6·50

For later printings and new 10p., all perf 10, see Nos. 1010/17.

Issues for the Whole of Spain

On 1 April 1939 the Civil War ended in victory for the Nationalists.

(Des J. L. Sánchez Toda. Litho Fournier, Vitoria)

1939–40. With imprint "SANCHEZ TODA" at foot. P 10.

948	**196**	20c. violet	50	20
949		25c. claret	50	20
950		30c. carmine	40	20
951		40c. blue-green	40	20
952		45c. scarlet (1940)	3·25	2·50
953		50c. slate	40	20
954		60c. orange	4·75	4·00
955		70c. blue	50	20
956		1Pts. black	19·00	60
957		2Pts. sepia	28·00	1·60
958		4Pts. dull purple	£170	19·00
959		10Pts. brown	80·00	45·00
948/959	*Set of 12*		£275	65·00

I II III

Three types of 40c.:—
 I. "CTS" does not touch bottom frame-line. Ragged edge to value tablet.
 II. "CTS" on bottom frame-line.
 III. As Type I, but edges of value tablet have outer frame-line.

I II I II

Two types of 25c.:—
 I. Shading fine and regular; value centred.
 II. Shading irregular; value to left and figures not square.

Two types of 60c.:—
 I. No frame to value tablet.
 II. Frame of white and coloured lines round tablet.

(Litho State Printing Works, Madrid)

1939–48. Without imprint. P 9½×10½.

960	**196**	5c. purple-brown (1940)	50	20
		a. Perf 10	14·00	2·40
961		10c. brown-red	2·50	20
		a. Perf 10	28·00	3·25
962		15c. emerald-green	70	20
963		20c. bright violet	60	15
		a. *Deep violet*	60	15
		b. *Lilac*	95	15
964		25c. claret (I)	60	15
964a		25c. maroon (II) (1943)	3·50	2·00
965		30c. blue	60	15
		a. *Light blue*	1·50	60
966		40c. greenish slate (I) (1940)	60	15
967		40c. greenish slate (II) (1941)	95	20
968		40c. greenish slate (III) (1945)	1·20	20
969		45c. ultramarine (1941)	80	20
		a. Perf 10 (10.48)	14·00	2·40
970		50c. slate (1940)	60	15
		a. Perf 11½ (1947)	35·00	7·50
971		60c. orange (I) (1940)	85	30
972		60c. orange (II) (1948)	20	10
973		70c. dull blue (1940)	1·20	20
		a. *Deep blue*	2·50	40
974		1PTA. black (1940)	8·50	15
975		1PTS. grey (1943)	90·00	95
976		2PTAS. sepia (1940)	11·50	30
977		4PTAS. rose (1940)	42·00	30
		a. *Carmine*	42·00	30
		b. Perf 10	£120	4·75
978		10PTS. brown (1940)	£250	4·75
		a. Perf 10	£325	21·00
979		10PTAS. brown (1945)	25·00	40
960/979	*Set of 15 (one of each value)*		£425	9·50

No. 973 can be found with part or complete "SANCHEZ TODA" imprint. It is thought that a plate of the 70c. value was transferred to Madrid from Burgos and was then used, after an attempt had been made to erase the imprints.

There are numerous shades in this issue. We only list the most prominent.

For similar stamps, perf 13, see Nos. 1114/26.

For the 10c., imperf, purple-brown, see No. 981.

197 "Spain" and Wreath of Peace   E **198** Pegasus

(Des R. Velasco. Eng J. L. Sánchez Toda. Litho B. Fournier, Burgos)

1939 (15 July). Homage to the Army. P 11.

980	**197**	10c. blue	35	15

(Des J. L. Sánchez Toda. Litho Fournier, Burgos)

1939. EXPRESS LETTER. With imprint. P 11.

E981	E **198**	25c. carmine-red	7·00	90

For this design without imprint, see No. E1022.

1939 (22 Dec). Anti-Tuberculosis Fund. Without imprint. Imperf.

981	**196**	10c. purple-brown	35	15

198 Ruins of Belchite   E **199**

(Des J. L. Sánchez Toda. Litho I. G. Rieusset, Barcelona)

1940 (1 Feb)–**46**. 19th Cent of Apparition of Virgin of El Pilar at Zaragoza and Zaragoza Cathedral Restoration Fund. Various designs inscr as in T **198**. P 11, 11½ and compound.

(a) POSTAGE

982	10c.+5c. brown and blue	20	15
983	15c.+10c. olive-green and lilac	20	15
984	20c.+10c. blue and violet	20	15
985	25c.+10c. brown and carmine-red	20	15
986	40c.+10c. claret and green	20	15
	a. Without imprint in lower corners (1.1.46)	2·75	20

SPAIN

987		45c.+15c. carmine and ultramarine..	40	30
988		70c.+20c. black and brown...............	40	30
989		80c.+25c. violet and carmine-red......	50	40
990		1p.+30c. brown-violet and black	50	40
991		1p.40+40c. black and brown-violet...	60·00	48·00
992		1p.50+50c. purple and blue	70	60
993		2p.50+50c. blue and purple	70	60
994		4p.+1p. slate and lilac.........................	21·00	16·00
995		10p.+4p. chestnut and blue................	£300	£225
982/995 Set of 14...			£350	£275

(b) AIR

996		25c.+5c. slate and purple...................	30	30
997		50c.+5c. violet and carmine	30	30
998		65c.+15c. blue and violet....................	30	30
999		70c.+15c. violet and slate...................	30	30
1000		90c.+20c. red and brown....................	30	30
1001		1p.20+30c. purple and violet	30	30
1002		1p.40+40c. brown and blue...............	70	35
1003		2p.+50c. violet and purple	1·10	70
1004		4p.+1p. purple and green	16·00	11·00
1005		10p.+4p. blue and brown...................	£400	£300

(c) EXPRESS LETTER

E1006	E **199**	25c.+5c. rose-red and buff................	40	30
996/E1006 Set of 11...			£375	£275

Designs: Postage (Horiz)—10c., 70c. Ruins of Belchite; 15c., 80c. Procession of the Rosary; 20c., 1p.50, El Pilar; 25c., 1p. Mother Rafols praying; 45c., 1p.40, The oath of the besieged; 40c., 2p.50, Sanctuary of the Virgin; 4p. Miracle of Calanda; 10p. The Virgin appears to St. James. Air (Vert)—25c., 70c. Prayer during bombardment; 50c., 1p.40, Caravel and Image of the Virgin; 65c., 90c. The Assumption; 1p.20, 2p. Coronation of the Virgin; 4p. Goya painting; 10p. Bombing of Zaragoza Cathedral.

Nos. 994/5 measure 46×34 mm and Nos. 1004/5 34×46 mm.

No. 986a was issued for use as a 50c. postage stamp, without charity premium.

199 General Franco   **200** Knight and Cross of Lorraine   **201** General Franco

(Des J. L. Sánchez Toda. Litho)

1940 (22 Dec). Anti-Tuberculosis Fund. Cross in red. P 10.

(a) POSTAGE

1006	**199**	10c. violet	25	20
1007		20c.+5c. green.....................	1·20	80
1008		40c.+10c. blue......................	1·90	50

(b) AIR. Inscr "CORREO AEREO"

1009	**199**	10c. bright pink.....................	1·80	1·10
1006/1009 Set of 4			4·75	2·50

1941–50. AIR. Redrawn. Litho. P 10.

1010	**195**	20c. orange	25	15
1011		25c. carmine-red (6.45).......	25	15
1012		35c. pale magenta (11.46)....	2·40	65
1013		50c. purple-brown................	55	15
1014		1p. ultramarine	2·00	15
1015		2p. green (4.47).....................	2·40	20
1016		4p. slate-blue (4.47)..............	8·25	30
1017		10p. bright violet (4.7.50).....	6·50	80
1010/1017 Set of 8			20·00	2·25

Apart from the perforation, the above stamps differ from Nos. 941/7 in the shading, which is heavier, particularly on the face of the portrait, giving a coarser appearance to this issue.

Stamps of this issue overprinted "EXPOSICION NACIONAL DE FILATELIA 1948 SAN SEBASTIAN" in continuous parallel lines over the entire sheet were produced without official sanction.

1941 (22 Dec). Anti-Tuberculosis Fund. Cross in red. Litho. P 10.

(a) POSTAGE

1018	**200**	10c. black...............................	35	20
1019		20c.+5c. violet......................	90	40
1020		40c.+10c. slate......................	90	40

(b) AIR. Inscr "CORREO AEREO"

1021	**200**	10c. blue................................	65	30
1018/1021 Set of 4			2·50	1·20

1942. EXPRESS LETTER. As No. E981 but without imprint. P 10.

E1022	E **198**	25c. carmine-red (shades).....	35	20

(Des C. Delhom)

1942 (June)–**49**.

1022	**201**	40c. chestnut (p 12½×13)....	45	20
1023		75c. blue (p 9½×10½) (5.9.46).....	5·25	70
		a. Perf 10.............................	22·00	3·25
1024		90c. green (p 9½×10½) (7.4.47)...	3·25	50
		a. Perf 12½×13 (5.49).........	40	20
1025		1p.35 violet (p 10) (5.9.46)..	1·20	75
		a. Perf 9½×10½ (23.10.48)..	80	35
		b. Perf 12½×13 (1949)........	45	20
1022/1025 Set of 4 (cheapest)................................			5·75	1·20

 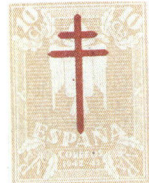

202 St. John of the Cross   **203** Arms and Lorraine Cross

(Des C. Delhom. Litho)

1942 (24 Nov). 400th Birth Anniv of St. John of the Cross. P 9½×10½.

1026	**202**	20c. violet..............................	1·00	20
1027		40c. red-orange....................	2·40	40
1028		75c. ultramarine	2·50	2·10

1942 (23 Dec). Anti-Tuberculosis Fund. T **203** and similar design. Cross in red. Litho. P 10.

(a) POSTAGE

1029	**203**	10c. salmon..........................	20	20
1030		20c.+5c. brown....................	2·10	1·90
1031		40c.+10c. green....................	1·70	50

(b) AIR. Inscr "CORREO AEREO"

1032	–	10c. salmon..........................	1·40	65
1029/1032 Set of 4			4·75	2·75

Design: Horiz—No. 1032, Two doves and Lorraine Cross.

204 St. James of Compostela   **205** St. James of Compostela

1943 (Oct)–**44**. Holy Year. As T **204/5** inscr "ANO SANTO 1943" (except No. 1033, inscr "ANO SANTO"). Litho. P 10½×9½ (Nos. 1035, 1037) or 9½×10½ (others).

1033	**204**	20c. blue................................	30	20
1034	–	20c. rose-red (2.44)..............	30	20
1035	–	20c. lilac (5.44).....................	30	20
1036	–	40c. chocolate.....................	85	20
1037	**205**	40c. grey-green (12.43).......	70	20
1038	–	40c. chocolate (3.44)...........	85	20
1039	–	75c. blue................................	4·00	2·30
1040	–	75c. blue (4.44).....................	4·50	2·50
1041	–	75c. blue (7.44).....................	65·00	47·00
1033/1041 Set of 9			75·00	50·00

Designs: Vert—Nos. 1034, 1040, Details of pillars, Santiago Cathedral; 1036, St. James of Compostela enthroned; 1038, Portal of Santiago Cathedral; 1039, Censer; 1041, Santiago Cathedral. Horiz—No. 1035, Tomb of St. James of Compostela.

206   **207** Tenth Century Tower   **208** Arms of Soria

1943 (22 Dec). Anti-Tuberculosis Fund. T **206** (and similar type inscr "1943–1944"). Litho. P 10 or 11½.

(a) POSTAGE

1042	**206**	10c. violet and red................	45	30
1043		20c.+5c. green and red	6·00	1·90
1044		40c.+10c. blue and red........	3·75	1·30

253

SPAIN

		(b) AIR. Inscr "CORREO AEREO"		
1045	—	10c. violet and red	1·80	1·30
1042/1045 Set of 4			11·00	4·25

Design:—No. 1045, Cross of Lorraine and outline of bird.

1944. Millenary of Castile. T **207** and various Arms designs as T **208** inscr "MILENARIO DE CASTILLA". Litho. P 9½×10½.

1046	207	20c. deep lilac (July)	40	25
1047	208	20c. lilac (Mar)	30	25
1048	—	20c. lilac (Sept)	30	25
1049	—	40c. chocolate (Apr)	5·00	80
1050	—	40c. chocolate (June)	5·00	80
1051	—	40c. chocolate (Aug)	3·75	85
1052	—	75c. blue (May)	5·25	4·50
1053	—	75c. blue (Dec)	4·50	4·50
1054	—	75c. blue (Dec)	6·25	5·00
1046/1054 Set of 9			30·00	15·00

Arms: No. 1048, Avila (*Shield at left*); 1049, Castile (*Arms in centre*); 1050, Segovia (*Shield at left*); 1051, Burgos (*Shield at right*); 1052, Avila (*Shield at left*); 1053, Fernán González, founder of Castile (*Helmet, bow and arrows at left*); 1054, Santander (*Shield at right*).

209 "Dr. Thebussem"
(M. P. de Figueroa, author and postal historian)

210

(Eng G. M. Orbe. Recess)

1944 (12 Oct). AIR. Stamp Day. P 10.
| 1055 | 209 | 5p. bright ultramarine | 27·00 | 20·00 |

This stamp was available for postal use only on the day of issue.

1944 (22 Dec). Anti-Tuberculosis Fund. T **210** (and another, inscr "1944 1945"). Litho. Cross in carmine.

(a) POSTAGE. P 9½×10½
1056	210	10c. orange	20	15
1057	—	20c.+5c. greenish black	40	40
1058	—	40c.+10c. violet	90	70
1059	—	80c.+10c. blue	15·00	13·00

(b) AIR. Inscr "CORRESPONDENCIA AEREA". P 10
| 1060 | — | 25c. orange (Hospital) (horiz) | 7·00 | 5·75 |
| 1056/1060 Set of 5 | | | 21·00 | 18·00 |

211 Quevedo

212 Conde de San Luis, Mail Vehicle of 1850 and Airplane

(Des and eng J. L. Sánchez Toda. Recess)

1945 (8 Sept). Death Tercentenary of Francisco de Quevedo (author). P 10.
| 1061 | 211 | 40c. dull brown | 1·20 | 80 |

(Des C. Delhom. Recess)

1945 (12 Oct). AIR. Stamp Day. P 10.
| 1062 | 212 | 10p. bright green | 35·00 | 21·00 |

This stamp was available for postal use only on the day of issue.

213 Carlos de Haya González

214 J. García Morato and Fiat

(Eng J. L. Sánchez Toda (4p.) and C. Delhom (10p.). Recess)

1945 (27 Nov–14 Dec). AIR. Civil War Air Aces. P 10.
| 1063 | 213 | 4p. scarlet (14 Dec) | 18·00 | 9·50 |
| 1064 | 214 | 10p. purple | 48·00 | 9·75 |

215 St. George and Dragon

216 Lorraine Cross and Eagle

1945 (22 Dec). Anti-Tuberculosis Fund. Litho. Cross typo in carmine.

(a) POSTAGE. P 9½×10½
1065	215	10c. red-orange	25	15
1066	—	20c.+5c. green	40	35
1067	—	40c.+10c. violet	70	20
1068	—	80c.+10c. blue	17·00	11·50

(b) AIR. P 10
| 1069 | 216 | 25c. vermilion | 2·75 | 1·70 |
| 1065/1069 Set of 5 | | | 19·00 | 12·50 |

217 E. A. de Nebrija (compiler of first Spanish grammar)

218 Salamanca University and Signature of F. F. de Vitoria (founder of International Law)

219 Statue of Fray Bartolomé de las Casas and native Indian

(Eng A. Sánchez Toda. Recess)

1946 (12 Oct). Day of the Race and Stamp Day.

(a) POSTAGE. P 9½×10½
| 1070 | 217 | 50c. lake | 85 | 25 |
| 1071 | 218 | 75c. blue | 1·00 | 70 |

(b) AIR. P 11½×11
| 1072 | 219 | 5p.50 green | 5·50 | 3·50 |

220 Self-portrait of Goya

221 Woman and Child

222 B. J. Feijoo y Montenegro

(Eng A. Sánchez Toda. Recess)

1946 (26 Oct). Birth Bicentenary of Goya (painter). P 9½×10½.
1073	220	25c. brown-lake	20	15
1074	—	50c. green	25	15
1075	—	75c. blue	1·20	85
		a. Deep blue	2·75	1·60

1946 (22 Dec). Anti-Tuberculosis Fund. T **221** (and another, inscr "1946 1947"). Litho. Cross in red or carmine (25c.).

(a) POSTAGE. P 9½×10½
| 1076 | 221 | 5c. violet | 30 | 15 |
| 1077 | — | 10c. grey-green | 30 | 15 |

(b) AIR. inscr "CORREO AEREO". P 10
| 1078 | — | 25c. red-orange (Eagle) (horiz) | 55 | 25 |

(Eng C. Delhom Recess)

1947 (1 June). P 9½×10½.
| 1079 | 222 | 50c. green | 1·40 | 70 |

223 Don Quixote in Library

224 Don Quixote

225 Don Quixote on Wooden Horse (after Gustav Doré)

SPAIN

(Des G. M. Orbe (50c.), C. Velamazán (75c.),
J. L. Sánchez Toda (5p.50). Recess)

1947 (9 Oct). Stamp Day and 400th Birth Anniv of Cervantes.

(a) POSTAGE. P 9½×10½
1080	223	50c. deep brown	50	20
1081	224	75c. indigo	1·10	50

(b) AIR. P 10½×9½
| 1082 | 225 | 5p.50 violet | 10·00 | 6·25 |

226 Manuel de Falla (composer) **227** Ignacio Zuloaga (painter) **228** Lorraine Cross

(Eng C. Velamazán. Recess)

1947 (1 Dec). AIR. With control figures on back. P 9½×10½.
1083	226	25p. brown-purple	75·00	27·00
1084	227	50p. scarlet	£275	60·00

1947 (22 Dec). Anti-Tuberculosis Fund. T **228** and similar types inscr "1947 1948". Litho. Cross in red.

(a) POSTAGE. P 9½×10½
1085	228	5c. chocolate	25	15
1086	–	10c. violet-blue	25	20

(b) AIR. Inscr "CORREO AERO". P 11½
| 1087 | – | 25c. magenta | 55 | 25 |

Designs: Vert—10c. Deckchair in garden. Horiz—25c. Sanatorium.

229 General Franco **230** Hernando Cortés **231** M. Alemán (writer)

1948–54. Photo. P 12½×13.
1088	229	5c. brown (12.48)	25	20
		a. Brown-olive (1954)	20	20
1089		15c. yellow-green (20.5.48)	25	20
1090		50c. yell-brn (shades) (23.10.48)	4·50	20
1091		80c. brownish lake (6.8.54)	6·50	20
1088/1091	Set of 4		10·75	90

1948 (15 June). Recess. P 12½×13 (35c.), 9½×10½ (70c.).
1092	230	35c. black	25	20
1093	231	70c. deep purple	4·25	2·50

232 Gen. Franco and Castillo de la Mota **233** Ferdinand III of Castile **234** Admiral Ramon de Bonifaz

1948–54. Litho. P 12½×13.
1094	232	25c. vermilion (11.48)	30	20
1095		30c. bronze green (20.10.54)	40	15
1096		35c. blue-green (11.48)	30	20
1097		40c. red-brown (11.48)	1·70	20
1098		45c. rose-carmine (2.3.49)	1·20	20
1099		45c. red (1950)	1·20	20
1100		50c. purple (6.9.48)	2·40	20
1101		70c. violet (1949)	3·50	20
1102		75c. deep blue (11.48)	3·25	20
1103		1p. rose-carmine (12.48)	9·75	20
1094/1103	Set of 10		22·00	1·70

1948 (20 Sept). 700th Anniv of Institution of Castilian Navy. Photo. P 12½×13.
1104	233	25c. reddish violet	55	20
1105	234	30c. red	35	20

235 Marquis of Salamanca **236** Diesel Train and Lockheed Constellation Airliner **238** Aesculapius

1948 (9 Oct). Stamp Day and Spanish Railway Centenary. T **235**/6 and similar design inscr "1848 1948". Photo. P 12½×13 (50c.), 13×12½ (others).

(a) POSTAGE
1106	235	50c. brown	90	20
1107	–	5p. blue-green	3·75	20

(b) AIR
| 1108 | 236 | 2p. carmine | 4·25 | 2·20 |

Design: as T **236**—5p. Garganta de Pancorbo Viaduct.

1948 (22 Dec). Anti-Tuberculosis Fund. T **238** and another, inscr "1948 1949" Photo. Cross in red. P 12½×13.

(a) POSTAGE
1109	238	5c. yellow-brown	25	15
1110		10c. green	25	20
1111		50c.+10c. red-brown	1·70	1·00

(b) AIR Inscr "CORREO AÉREO"
| 1112 | – | 25c. ultramarine | 70 | 40 |
| 1109/1112 | Set of 4 | | 2·60 | 1·60 |

Design: Vert—25c. Lockheed Constellation airliner over sanatorium.

 (partial)

239 "El Cid" **240** Globe and Buildings

1949 (1 Feb). War Victims Relief. Litho. P 10½×9½.
| 1113 | 239 | 5c. violet | 40 | 25 |

(Litho State Printing Works, Madrid)

1949–1953. Without imprint. P 13.
1114	196	20c. bright violet (6.49)	25	15
1115		25c. dull purple (II) (6.49)	30	15
1116		30c. light blue (10.49)	35	15
		a. Deep blue ('53)	40	15
1117		35c. turquoise-blue (11.51)	55	20
1118		40c. grey-olive ('50)	50	15
1119		45c. ultramarine (12.51)	25	15
1120		50c. slate	45	15
		a. Indigo (2.52)	9·00	20
1121		60c. orange ('50)	25	15
1122		70c. dull blue ('53)	34·00	15
1123		1PTA. black (11.51)	17·00	15
1124		2PTAS. sepia (5.50)	7·00	15
1125		4PTAS. carmine-red (6.49)	16·00	20
1126		10PTAS. sepia (1.53)	3·75	60
1114/1126	Set of 13		75·00	2·40

1949 (9 Oct). 75th Anniv of Founding of Universal Postal Union. Photo. P 12½×13.

(a) POSTAGE
1127	240	50c. red-brown	1·40	25
1128		75c. ultramarine	1·00	50

(b) AIR
| 1129 | 240 | 4p. blackish olive | 75 | 45 |

  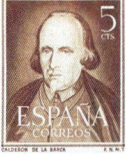

241 Galleon **242** San Juan de Dios and a Leper **243** Calderón de la Barca (dramatist)

255

SPAIN

1949 (22 Dec). Anti-Tuberculosis Fund. T **241** (and another, inscr "1949 1950"). Photo. Cross recess, in red. P 12½×13.

(a) POSTAGE

1130	**241**	5c. violet	15	15
1131		10c. green	15	15
1132		50c.+10c. yellow-brown	1·00	40

(b) AIR. Inscr "CORREO AÉREO"

| 1133 | – | 25c. red-brown (Bell) | 30 | 25 |
| 1130/1133 *Set of 4* | | | 1·50 | 85 |

1950 (8 Mar). 400th Death Anniv of San Juan de Dios. Recess. P 13.

| 1134 | **242** | 1p. violet | 23·00 | 7·00 |

1950–53. Portraits as T **243**. Photo. P 12½×13.

1135		5c. brown (1.8.51)	25	20
1136		10c. claret (15.9.51)	25	25
1137		15c. deep bluish green (2.2.53)	50	20
1138		20c. violet (1.9.50)	1·10	20
1139		2p. bright blue (8.7.52)	35·00	35
1140		4p.50 purple-brown (8.7.52)	1·70	1·40
1135/1140 *Set of 6*			35·00	2·50

Portraits:—10c. Lope de Vega (author); 15c. Tirso de Molina (poet); 20c. Ruiz de Alarcón (author); 2p. Dr. Ramón y Cajal (physician); 4p.50. Dr. Ferrán y Clua (bacteriologist).

 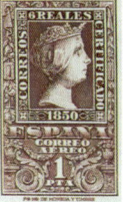

244 Queen Isabella II   **245** Queen Isabella II

VISITA
DEL
CAUDILLO
A CANARIAS
OCTUBRE 1950
SOBRETASA:
DIEZ CTS
(245a)

1950 (12 Oct). Stamp Centenary. Recess. Imperf.

(a) POSTAGE

1141	**244**	50c. violet	16·00	8·25
1142		75c. ultramarine	16·00	8·25
1143		10p. blackish green	£170	£120
1144		15p. vermilion	£170	£120

(b) AIR

1145	**245**	1p. purple	16·00	8·25
1146		2p.50 orange-brown	16·00	8·25
1147		20p. deep blue	£170	£120
1148		25p. green	£170	£120
1141/1148 *Set of 8*			£675	£225

1950 (23 Oct). General Franco's Canary Island Visit.

*(a) POSTAGE. Nos. 1100 and 1103 surch with T **245a**, in blue*

A. "CAUDILLO" 16½ mm long

| 1149A | **232** | 10c. on 50c. | £200 | £150 |
| 1150A | | 10c. on 1p. | £200 | £150 |

B. "CAUDILLO" 15 mm long

| 1149B | **232** | 10c. on 50c. | £100 | 60·00 |
| 1150B | | 10c. on 1p. | £100 | 60·00 |

(b) AIR. No. 1083 surch "Correspondencia/por avion/ VISITA DEL/ CAUDILLO/A CANARIAS/OCTUBRE 1950/ Sobretasa/DIEZ CTS"

| 1151 | **226** | 10c. on 25p. brown-purple | £750 | £350 |
| | | a. Without control figures | £4500 | £1800 |

246 Candle and Conifer   **247** Map   **248** Isabella the Catholic

1950 (22 Dec). Anti-Tuberculosis Fund. T **246** and another, inscr "1950 1951" Photo. Cross recess, in red. P 12½×13.

(a) POSTAGE

1152	**246**	5c. violet	20	20
1153		10c. green	20	20
1154		50c.+10c. yellow-brown	3·00	1·40

(b) AIR. Inscr "CORREO AERÉO"

| 1155 | – | 25c. blue (Dove and flowers) | 90 | 40 |
| 1152/1155 *Set of 4* | | | 3·75 | 2·00 |

1951 (16 Apr). AIR. Sixth Conference of Spanish-American Postal Union. Photo. P 12½×13.

| 1156 | **247** | 1p. blue | 9·50 | 3·50 |

1951 (22 Apr). Fifth Centenary of Birth of Isabella. Photo. P 12½×13.

1157	**248**	50c. brown	1·40	50
1158		75c. blue	1·80	45
1159		90c. maroon	70	25
1160		1p.50 orange	19·00	10·00
1161		2p.80 olive-green	43·00	28·00
1157/1161 *Set of 5*			60·00	35·00

248a St. Antonio Claret   **249** Children on Beach

1951 (9 Sept). Stamp Day. Recess. P 12½×13.

| 1162 | **248a** | 50c. indigo | 6·50 | 4·25 |

1951 (1 Oct). Anti-Tuberculosis Fund. T **249** and similar vert design. Photo. Cross recess in red. P 12½×13.

(a) POSTAGE

| 1163 | **249** | 5c. claret | 20 | 15 |
| 1164 | | 10c. green | 90 | 20 |

(b) AIR

| 1165 | | 25c. yellow-brown (Nurse and child) | 1·20 | 20 |

250 Isabella the Catholic   **251** Ferdinand the Catholic

1951 (12 Oct). AIR. Stamp Day and Fifth Centenary of Birth of Isabella. Recess. P 13.

1166	**250**	60c. green	10·00	55
1167		90c. orange-yellow	1·30	70
1168		1p.30 claret	13·50	6·25
1169		1p.90 blackish brown	10·00	7·75
1170		2p.30 deep blue	6·00	4·00
1166/1170 *Set of 5*			36·00	17·00

1952 (10 May). Fifth Centenary of Birth of Ferdinand the Catholic. Photo. P 12½×13.

1171	**251**	50c. green	1·10	25
1172		75c. indigo	10·50	2·00
1173		90c. brown-lake	75	25
1174		1p.50 orange	20·00	10·50
1175		2p.80 brown	32·00	22·00
1171/1175 *Set of 5*			60·00	35·00

252 St. Maria Micaela   **252a** St. Francis Xavier

1952 (26 May). 35th International Eucharistic Congress, Barcelona. T **252** and similar vert design. Photo. P 13.

(a) POSTAGE

| 1176 | **252** | 90c. brown-lake | 35 | 20 |

(b) AIR

| 1177 | – | 1p. slate-green | 5·50 | 60 |

Design: 1p. "The Eucharist" (Tiepolo).

1952 (3 July). AIR. 400th Death Anniv of St. Francis Xavier. P 13.
1178 252a 2p. deep blue.. 85·00 30·00

253 Ferdinand the Catholic

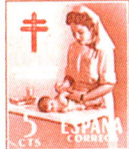
254 Nurse and Baby

1952 (12 Oct). AIR. Stamp Day and Fifth Centenary of Birth of Ferdinand Recess. P 13.
1179	253	60c. grey-green	25	20
1180		90c. orange	25	20
1181		1p.30 claret	1·10	1·10
1182		1p.90 blackish brown	4·00	2·75
1183		2p.30 deep blue	19·00	12·00
1179/1183		Set of 5	22·00	14·50

1953. Anti-Tuberculosis Fund. T **254** and similar vert design. Photo. Cross recess in red. P 12½×13.
(a) POSTAGE
1184	254	5c. brownish lake (5 Nov)	90	15
1185		10c. deep blue-green (1 Oct)	2·30	20

(b) AIR
| 1186 | | 25c. brown (Girl and angel) (5 Nov) | 8·75 | 6·75 |

255 J. Sorolla (painter)

256 Bas Relief

257 Fray Luis de Leon

1953 (9 Oct). AIR. Recess. P 13×12½.
1187 255 50p. blackish violet.................. £850 31·00

1953 (12 Oct). Stamp Day and Seventh Centenary of Salamanca University. T **256/7** and horiz design as T **257** inscr "UNIVDAD DE SALAMANCA". Photo. P 13 (50c.), 13×12½ (90c.) or 12½×13 (2p.).
1188	256	50c. claret	55	25
1189	257	90c. blackish green	3·25	3·00
1190	—	2p. deep bistre-brown	24·00	6·25

Design:—2p. Salamanca University.

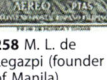
258 M. L. de Legazpi (founder of Manila)

259 "St. Mary Magdalene"

260 St. James of Compostela

1953 (5 Nov). AIR. Signing of Filipino-Spanish Postal Convention. Recess. P 13×12½.
1191 258 25p. greenish black......................... £190 45·00

1954 (10 Jan). Third Centenary of Death of Ribera (painter). Photo. P 12½×13.
1192 259 1p.25 carmine-lake 35 20

1954 (1 Mar). Holy Year. T **260** and similar vert design inscr "AÑO SANTO COMPOSTELANO". Photo. P 12½×13.
1193		50c. deep brown	65	25
1194		3p. deep blue (Santiago Cathedral)	80·00	5·75

261 "Purity" (after Cano)

262 M. Menendez Pelayo (historian)

263 Gen. Franco

1954. Marian Year. T **261** and similar vert designs inscr "ANO MARIANO". Photo. P 12½×13.
1195		10c. carmine-lake (19.7)	35	15
1196		15c. bronze green (16.12)	35	15
1197		25c. reddish violet (28.9)	35	15
1198		30c. light brown (19.7)	35	15
1199		50c. brown-olive (16.9)	1·20	15
1200		60c. black (23.12)	35	15
1201		80c. slate-green (6.10)	4·75	15
1202		1p. blackish violet (9.11)	4·75	15
1203		2p. red-brown (24.12)	1·40	20
1204		3p. blue (16.9)	2·00	1·30
1195/1204		Set of 10	14·00	2·50

Designs:—15c. Virgin of Begona, Bilbao; 25c. Virgin of the Abandoned, Valencia Cathedral; 30c. The "Black Virgin" of Montserrat; 50c. El Pilar Virgin, Zaragoza; 60c. Covadonga Virgin; 80c. Virgin of the Kings, Seville Cathedral; 1p. Almudena Virgin, Madrid; 2p. Virgin of Africa; 3p. Guadalupe Virgin.

1954 (12 Oct). Stamp Day. Photo. P 12½×13.
1205 262 80c. grey-green .... 10·50 20

1955 (14 Feb)–**75**. Photo. P 13.
(i) Imprint "F.N.M.T."
1206	263	10c. brownish lake	15	15
1207		15c. ochre (15.3.55)	15	15
1208		20c. blackish green (3.5.55)	15	15
1209		25c. blackish violet (18.2.55)	15	15
1210		30c. bistre-brown	15	15
1211		40c. reddish purple (3.5.55)	15	15
1212		50c. olive-brown (28.2.55)	15	15
1213		60c. dull purple (15.3.55)	20	15
1214		70c. bronze-green (15.3.55)	20	15
1215		80c. deep turquoise-green	20	15
1216		1p. orange-red (28.2.55)	15	15
1217		1p.40 magenta (24.4.56)	25	20
1218		1p.50 turquoise-green (24.4.56)	25	20
1219		1p.80 bright green (24.4.56)	25	20
1220		2p. red (28.2.55)	23·00	1·00
1221		2p. bright mauve (24.4.56)	25	20
1222		3p. Prussian blue	20	15
1222a		4p. carmine-red (15.7.75)	15	15
1223		5p. red-brown (15.3.55)	25	15
1224		6p. grey-black (3.5.55)	25	15
1224a		7p. bright blue (4.12.74)	20	15
1225		8p. bright violet (24.4.56)	25	20
1226		10p. yellow-green (3.5.55)	25	15
1226a		12p. blue-green (4.12.74)	20	15
1226b		20p. deep carmine (4.12.74)	20	15
1206/1226b		Set of 25	25·00	4·50

(ii) Imprint "F.N.M.T.—B" (27.5.60)
1227	263	1p. orange-red	90	55
1228		5p. red-brown	2·10	1·10

Nos. 1227/8 were printed at the International Philatelic Exhibition, Barcelona.
The 1p.50, 2p. (1221), 3, 4 and 6p. were also issued in coils, with every fifth stamp numbered on the reverse.

264 Torres Quevedo (engineer and inventor)

265 St. Ignatius of Loyola

(Des A. Sánchez-Toda. Recess)

1955 (6 Sept)–**56**. AIR. T **264** and similar vert portrait. P 13×12½.
1229	—	25p. greenish black (10.1.56)	34·00	90
1230	264	50p. blackish violet	13·00	2·20

Portrait:—25p. Fortuny (painter).

SPAIN

1955 (12 Oct). Stamp Day and Fourth Centenary of Death of St. Ignatius of Loyola. T **265** and similar design. Photo. P 13×12½ (vert) or 12½×13 (horiz).

1231	**265**	25c. slate-lilac	20	20
1232	–	60c. ochre	1·00	45
1233	**265**	80c. deep turquoise-green	4·50	45

Design: Horiz—60c. St. Ignatius and Loyola Castle.

266 Lockheed L.1049 Super Constellation and Caravel

267 "Telecommunications"

(Des F. J. Ontiveros. Photo)

1955 (1 Nov)–**56**. AIR. P 12½×13.

1234	**266**	20c. blackish green (3.3.56)	20	20
1235		25c. blackish violet	15	15
1236		50c. olive-brown (3.3.56)	20	20
1237		1p. orange-red	15	15
1238		1p.10 emerald (3.3.56)	35	20
1239		1p.40 rose-magenta	20	15
1240		3p. blue (3.3.56)	35	20
1241		4p.80 lemon	20	15
1242		5p. red-brown	2·00	15
1243		7p. deep mauve (3.3.56)	1·00	20
1244		10p. yellow-green (3.3.56)	90	35
1234/1244	Set of 11		5·00	1·90

(Des F. Jesús. Photo)

1955 (8 Dec). Centenary of Telegraphs in Spain. P 13×12½.

1245	**267**	15c. brown-ochre	55	25
1246		80c. blackish blue-green	13·00	25
1247		3p. blue	23·00	1·40
1245/1247	Set of 3		35·00	1·70

268 St. Vincent Ferrer (after C. Vilar)

269 "The Holy Family" (after El Greco)

1955 (20 Dec). Fifth Centenary of Canonisation of St. Vincent Ferrer. Photo. P 13.

| 1248 | **268** | 15c. ochre | 60 | 25 |

1955 (24 Dec). Christmas. Photo. P 13×12½.

| 1249 | **269** | 80c. blackish green | 7·00 | 70 |

E **270** "Speed"

E **271** Centaur

(Des J. A. Gámez (Type E **270**), T. Miciano (Type E **271**). Photo)

1956 (12 Feb)–**66**. EXPRESS LETTER. P 13×12½ (vert) or 12½×13 (horiz).

E1250	E **270**	2p. scarlet	20	15
E1251		3p. carmine-red (25.5.65)	20	15
E1252	E **271**	4p. reddish purple and black	20	15
E1253	E **270**	5p. orange-red (20.12.66)	15	15
E1254	E **271**	6p.50 brown-red and deep slate-violet (20.12.66)	20	15
E1250/1254	Set of 5		85	70

270

271 *Ciudad de Toledo* (cargo liner)

(Des C. Sáenz de Tejada. Photo)

1956 (17 July). Twentieth Anniv of Civil War. Photo. P 13×12.

1250	**270**	15c. bistre-brown and bistre	20	20
1251		50c. deep olive and yellow-green	90	50
1252		80c. blackish green and magenta	9·25	25
1253		3p. deep blue and ultramarine	13·00	2·50
1250/1253	Set of 4		21·00	3·00

1956 (3 Aug). First Floating Exhibition of National Products. Photo. P 12½×13.

| 1254 | **271** | 3p. blue | 6·50 | 2·75 |

272 The "Black Virgin"

273 Archangel Gabriel

(Des T. Miciano. Photo)

1956 (11 Sept). 75th Anniv of "Black Virgin" of Montserrat. T **272** and similar vert design. P 13×12½.

1255	**272**	15c. yellow-brown	35	20
1256	–	60c. blackish purple	40	25
1257	**272**	80c. deep blue-green	45	45

Design:—60c. Montserrat Monastery.

1956 (12 Oct). Stamp Day. Recess. P 13×12½.

| 1258 | **273** | 80c. deep dull green | 70 | 40 |

274 "Statistics"

275 Hermitage and Monument

(Des F. Jesús. Photo)

1956 (3 Nov). Centenary of Statistics in Spain. P 12½×13.

1259	**274**	15c. brown-ochre	45	30
1260		80c. green	5·50	65
1261		1p. orange-red	5·50	65
1259/1261	Set of 3		10·25	1·40

258

(Des T. Miciano. Photo)

1956 (4 Dec). Twentieth Anniv of General Franco's Assumption of Office as Head of the State. P 12½×13.
| 1262 | **275** | 80c. deep bluish green | 6·50 | 40 |

276 Refugee Children

277 Apparition of the Sacred Heart

278 "The Great Captain"

(Des F. Jesús Photo)

1956 (17 Dec). Hungarian Children's Relief. P 13×12½.
1263	**276**	10c. brownish lake	20	20
1264	–	15c. brown-ochre	20	20
1265	–	50c. deep olive-brown	55	20
1266	–	80c. blackish blue-green	5·00	25
1267	–	1p. orange-red	5·00	25
1268	–	3p. blue	19·00	2·75
1263/1268	Set of 6		27·00	3·50

(Des T. Miciano. Photo)

1957 (12 Oct). Stamp Day and Centenary of Feast of the Sacred Heart. P 13×12½.
1269	**277**	15c. olive brown	20	15
1270	–	60c. slate-purple	25	20
1271	–	80c. deep bluish green	25	20
1269/1271	Set of 3		65	50

(Eng A. Sánchez Toda. Recess)

1958 (28 Feb). Fifth Centenary of Birth of Gonzalves de Cordoba. P 13×12½.
| 1272 | **278** | 1p.80 light green | 20 | 15 |

279 Francisco Goya (painter), after López

280 Exhibition Emblem

1958 (24 Mar). Stamp Day and Goya Commemoration. T **279** and similar designs. Photo. Frames in gold: centre colours given below. P 13.
1273	15c. brown-ochre	20	15
1274	40c. reddish purple	20	15
1275	50c. brown-olive	20	15
1276	60c. slate-purple	20	15
1277	70c. bronze-green	20	15
1278	80c. blackish green	20	15
1279	1p. deep orange-red	20	15
1280	1p.80 emerald	20	15
1281	2p. bright purple	45	25
1282	3p. blue	1·10	50
1273/1282	Set of 10	2·75	1·75

Goya paintings: Horiz—15c. "The Sunshade"; 3p. "The Drinker". Vert—40c. "The Bookseller's Wife"; 50c. "The Count of Fernán-Nuñez"; 60c. "The Crockery Vendor"; 70c. "Doña Isabel Cobos de Porcel"; 80c. T **279**; 1p. "The Carnival Doll"; 1p.80 "Marianito Goya"; 2p. "The Vintage".

(Des T. Miciano. Photo)

1958 (7 June). Brussels International Exhibition. P 13×12½.
| 1283 | **280** | 80c. drab, rose-red and chocolate | 20 | 15 |
| 1284 | – | 3p. blue, rose-red and blue-black | 95 | 90 |

1958 (25 June). Philatelic Exhibition, Madrid. Sheets (each 49×83 mm) comprising Nos. 1283/4 in new colours. Imperf.
| MS1285 | 80c. green, red and chocolate (sold at 2p.) | 37·00 | 27·00 |
| MS1286 | 3p. violet, orange and black-brown (sold at 5p.) | 37·00 | 27·00 |

281 Emperor Charles V (after Strigell)

(Des T. Miciano. Photo)

1958 (30 July). Fourth Centenary of Death of Emperor Charles V. Portraits of the Emperor as T **281**. P 13.
1287	**281**	15c. brown and light ochre	15	15
1288	–	50c. blackish olive and dull green	15	15
1289	–	70c. deep green, black and olive-grey	20	15
1290	–	80c. deep greenish bl, and light brown	20	15
1291	**281**	1p. vermilion and buff	25	15
1292	–	1p.80 bluish green and dull green	20	15
1293	–	2p. purple and brownish grey	65	50
1294	–	3p. deep bright blue and light brown	1·70	1·30
1287/1294	Set of 8		3·00	2·50

Portraits:—Charles V: 50c., 1p.80, At the Battle of Muhlberg (after Titian); 70c., 2p. (after Leoni); 80c., 3p. (after Titian).

282 American-built Diesel Locomotive and Talgo II Articulated Train and Esconal

(Des T. Miciano. Photo)

1958 (29 Sept). 17th International Railway Congress, Madrid. As T **282** Inscr "XVII CONGRESO INTERNACIONAL DE FERROCARRILES-MADRID-1958". P 13×12½ (60c., 2p.) or 12½×13 (others).
1295	**282**	15c. yellow-brown	15	15
1296	–	60c. plum	15	15
1297	–	80c. deep bluish green	20	15
1298	**282**	1p. red-orange	60	20
1299	–	2p. bright purple	60	25
1300	–	3p. blue	2·75	1·20
1295/1300	Set of 6		4·00	2·30

Designs: Vert—60c., 2p. Class 1600 ALCO. diesel-electric train on viaduct, Despenaperros Gorge. Horiz—80c., 3p. Class 242F steam locomotive and Castillo de la Mota.

1959 (24 Mar). Stamp Day and Velázquez Commemoration. Designs as T **279**. Frames in gold; centre colours given below. Photo. P 13.
1301	15c. sepia	20	20
1302	40c. reddish purple	20	20
1303	50c. olive	20	20
1304	60c. black-brown	20	20
1305	70c. green	20	20
1306	80c. blackish green	20	20
1307	1p. chestnut	20	20
1308	1p.80 bright emerald	20	20
1309	2p. bright purple	50	30
1310	3p. blue	1·00	50
1301/1310	Set of 10	2·75	2·20

Velazquez paintings: Horiz—15c. "The Drunkards". Vert—40c. "The Spinners" (detail); 50c. "The Surrender of Breda"; 60c. "Las Meninas"; 70c. "Balthasar Don Carlos"; 80c. Self-portrait; 1p. "The Coronation of the Virgin"; 1p.80, "Aesop"; 2p. "The Forge of Vulcan"; 3p. "Menippus".

284 The Holy Cross of the Valley of the Fallen

285 Mazarin and Luis de Haro (after tapestry by Lebrun)

SPAIN

(Des T. Miciano. Photo)

1959 (1 Apr). Completion of Monastery of the Holy Cross of the Valley of the Fallen. P 13.
1311 **284** 80c. green and blackish brown.............. 20 15

1959 (24 Oct). 300th Anniv of the Treaty of the Pyrenees. Photo. P 13×12½.
1312 **285** 1p. red-brown and gold..................... 20 20

286 Monastery from Courtyard

(Eng P. P. Escribano. Recess)

1959 (16 Nov). 50th Anniv of Entry of Franciscan Community into Guadalupe Monastery. Horiz designs as T **286**. P 12½×13.
1313   15c. brown.. 25 15
1314   80c. slate-green...................................... 30 15
1315   1p. red.. 30 20
1313/1315 Set of 3.. 75 45

Designs:—80c. Exterior view of monastery; 1p. Entrance doors of church.

287 "The Holy Family" (after Goya)   **288** Pass with Muleta

1959 (10 Dec). Christmas. Photo. P 13×12½.
1316 **287** 1p. chestnut... 35 15

(Eng G. M. Orbe (1320), A. Sánchez Toda (1322, 1326/7, 1329, 1331/2), J. L. Sánchez Toda (others). Recess)

1960 (29 Feb). Bullfighting Commemoration. As T **288**. P 12½×13 (horiz) or 13×12½ (vert).

(a) POSTAGE
1317   15c. bistre-brown and ochre.................. 20 20
1318   20c. violet and violet-blue..................... 20 20
1319   25c. black.. 20 20
1320   30c. sepia and bistre............................. 20 20
1321   50c. sepia and deep violet.................... 20 20
1322   70c. deep bluish green and bistre-brown 20 20
1323   80c. deep emerald and blue-green....... 20 20
1324   1p. chocolate and vermilion.................. 25 20
1325   1p.40 claret and bistre-brown............... 20 20
1326   1p.50 green and turquoise-blue............ 20 20
1327   1p.80 blue-green and green................. 20 20
1328   5p. brown-lake and bistre-brown.......... 70 55

(b) AIR. Inscr "CORREO AEREO"
1329   25c. deep dull purple and brown-purple...... 20 20
1330   50c. light blue and turquoise-blue......... 20 20
1331   1p. brown-red and vermilion.................. 25 20
1332   5p. reddish violet and bright purple....... 65 45
1317/1332 Set of 16.. 3·75 3·50

Designs: Horiz—No. 1317, Fighting bull; 1318, Rounding-up bull; 1327, Placing darts from horseback; 1330, Pass with cape; 1332, Bull-ring. Vert—1319, Corralling bulls at Pamplona; 1320, Bull entering ring; 1321, As 1330 (different pass); 1322, Banderillero placing darts; 1323/6, Various passes with muleta; 1328, Old-time bull-fighter; 1329, Village bull-ring; 1331, Dedicating the bull.

1960 (24 Mar). Stamp Day and Murillo Commemoration. Paintings as T **279**. Photo. Frames gold; centre colours below. P 13.
1333   25c. slate-violet..................................... 15 15
1334   40c. purple... 15 15
1335   50c. deep olive...................................... 15 15
1336   70c. deep green..................................... 15 15
1337   80c. deep bluish green.......................... 15 15
1338   1p. chocolate... 20 15
1339   1p.50 turquoise-blue............................. 20 15
1340   2p.50 crimson.. 20 15
1341   3p. rose.. 1·90 80
1342   5p. brown... 45 25
1333/1342 Set of 10.. 3·25 1·80

Murillo paintings: Vert—25c. "The Good Shepherd"; 40c. "Rebecca and Eliezer"; 50c. "The Virgin of the Rosary"; 70c. "The Immaculate Conception"; 80c. "Children with Shells"; 1p. Self-portrait; 2p.50, "The Dice Game"; 3p. "Children Eating"; 5p. "Children with Coins". Horiz—1p.50, "The Holy Family with Bird".

289 "Christ of Lepanto"   **290** Pelota Player

1960 (27 Mar). International Philatelic Congress and Exhibition, Barcelona. T **289**/**90** and similar design inscr "CIF". Photo.

(a) POSTAGE. P 13×12½
1343 **289** 70c. lake and green............................... 1·80 1·50
1344 –   80c. black and sage-green................... 1·80 1·50
1345 **289** 1p. purple and vermilion........................ 1·80 1·50
1346 –   2p.50 deep slate-violet and red dish violet ..... 1·80 1·50
1347 **289** 5p. sepia and yellow-bistre.................... 1·80 1·50
1348 –   10p. sepia and ochre.............................. 1·80 1·50

(b) AIR. P 12½×13
1349 **290** 1p. black and deep vermilion................ 5·00 3·25
1350   5p. carmine and chocolate................... 5·00 3·25
1351   6p. carmine and black-purple............... 5·00 3·25
1352   10p. carmine and green........................ 5·00 3·25
1343/1352 Set of 10.. 28·00 20·00

Design: Vert—Nos. 1344, 1346, 1348, Church of the Holy Family, Barcelona.

291 St. John of Ribera   **291a** Conference Emblem

1960 (16 Aug). Canonization of St. John of Ribera. Photo. P 13.
1353 **291** 1p. brown-orange.................................. 20 15
1354   2p.50 magenta....................................... 25 20

(Des P. Rahikainen. Photo)

1960 (19 Sept). Europa. First Anniv of European Postal and Telecommunications Conference. P 12½×13.
1355 **291a** 1p. drab and blackish green................ 65 35
1356   5p. red and brown................................. 1·20 1·10

292 St. Vincent de Paul   **293** Menéndez de Aviles   **294** Running

1960 (27 Sept). 300th Death Anniv of St. Vincent de Paul. Photo. P 13.
1357 **292** 25c. deep violet..................................... 20 15
1358   1p. brown-orange.................................. 25 15

SPAIN

1960 (12 Oct). 400th Anniv of Discovery and Colonization of Florida. T **293** and similar vert portraits inscr: "IV CENTENARIO DE FLORIDA". Photo. P 13×12½.

1359	293	25c. violet-blue and light blue	20	15
1360	–	70c. bronze-green and salmon	20	15
1361	–	80c. deep green and stone	20	15
1362	–	1p. orange-brown and yellow	20	15
1363	293	2p. crimson and pink	40	20
1364	–	2p.50 magenta and olive	60	25
1365	–	3p. deep blue and dull green	4·00	85
1366	–	5p. sepia and bistre	2·75	1·40
1359/1366		Set of 8	7·75	3·00

Portraits:—70c., 2p.50, Hernando de Solo; 80c., 3p. Ponce de León; 1p., 5p. Cabeza de Vaca.

(Des T. Miciano. Photo)

1960 (31 Oct). Sports. As T **294**. P 12½×13 (horiz) or 13×12½ (vert).

(a) POSTAGE

1367		25c. brown and deep violet-blue	15	15
1368		40c. orange and reddish violet	15	15
1369		70c. carmine-red and emerald	35	20
1370		80c. carmine-red and green	25	15
1371		1p. blue-green and vermilion	80	15
1372		1p.50 sepia & deep turquoise-green	35	20
1373		2p. emerald and bright purple	2·00	15
1374		2p.50 green and magenta	40	20
1375		3p. orange-red and ultramarine	90	40
1376		5p. blue and chestnut	75	70

(b) AIR. Inscr "CORREO AEREO"

1377		1p.25 red and chocolate	20	20
1378		1p.50 red-brown and red-violet	35	25
1379		6p. rose and blackish violet	1·10	85
1380		10p. red, and deep yellow-olive	1·70	1·10
1367/1380		Set of 14	9·25	4·50

Designs: Horiz—40c., 2p. Cycling; 70c., 2p.50, Football; 1p., 5p. Hockey; 1p.25, 6p. Horse-jumping. Vert—25c., 1p.50 (postage), T **294**; 80c., 3p. Gymnastics; 1p.50 (air), 10p. Pelota.

295 Albéniz   **296** Cloisters

1960 (7 Nov). Birth Centenary of Isaac Albéniz (composer). Photo. P 13.

1381	295	25c. deep slate-violet	15	15
1382		1p. bright chestnut	25	15

(Eng D. Carande Boto. Recess)

1960 (21 Nov). Samos Monastery. T **296** and similar designs. P 12½×13 (80c.) or 13×12½ (others).

1383		80c. blue-green and turquoise-blue	20	15
1384		1p. lake and orange-brown	1·30	20
1385		5p. olive-brown and yellow-brown	1·50	1·10
1383/1385		Set of 3	2·75	1·30

Designs: Vert—1p. Fountain; 5p. Portico and façade.

297 "The Nativity"   **298** "The Flight to Egypt"
(Velázquez)   (after Bayeu)

1960 (1 Dec). Christmas. Photo. P 13×12½.

| 1386 | 297 | 1p. bright chestnut | 40 | 15 |

1961 (23 Jan). World Refugee Year. Photo. P 12½×13.

1387	298	1p. brown-red	25	20
1388		5p. chocolate	55	35

299 L. F. Moratin   **301** Velázquez   **302** "Stamp" and
(after Goya)   (Prado Memorial)   "Postmark"

1961 (13 Feb). Birth Bicentenary of Moratin (poet and dramatist). Photo. P 13.

1389	299	1p. brown-red	20	15
1390		1p.50 deep turquoise-green	20	15

1961 (24 Mar). Stamp Day and El Greco Commemoration. As T **279** and similar vert designs. Photo. Frames gold; centre colours below. P 13.

1391		25c. slate-purple	20	15
1392		40c. purple	20	15
1393		70c. green	25	20
1394		80c. deep bluish green	25	15
1395		1p. purple-brown	2·75	15
1396		1p.50 turquoise-blue	25	15
1397		2p.50 carmine-lake	45	25
1398		3p. blue	2·10	1·20
1399		5p. sepia	4·50	2·50
1400		10p. bright violet	90	50
1391/1400		Set of 10	10·50	4·75

Greco paintings:—25c. "St. Peter"; 40c. Madonna (detail, "The Holy Family" ("Madonna of the Good Milk")); 70c. Detail of "The Agony in the Garden"; 80c. "Man with Hand on Breast"; 1p. Self-portrait; 1p.50, "The Baptism of Christ"; 2p.50, "The Holy Trinity"; 3p. "Burial of the Count of Orgaz"; 5p. "The Spoliation"; 10p. "The Martyrdom of St. Maurice".

1961 (17 Apr). 300th Death Anniv of Velázquez. T **301** and similar designs. Recess. P 13.

1401		80c. blackish green and indigo	1·40	20
1402		1p. chocolate and Venetian red	6·75	20
1403		2p.50 violet and violet-blue	1·00	55
1404		10p. green and light green	9·25	2·10
1401/1404		Set of 4	17·00	2·50

Velazquez paintings: Vert—1p. "The Duke of Olivares"; 2p.50, "Princess Margarita". Horiz—10p. Part of "The Spinners".

Sheets (each 71×86 mm). Colours changed. Imperf (28 April)

MS1405	80c. slate and red-brown	8·50	8·75
MS1406	1p. violet and blue	8·50	8·75
MS1407	2p.50 blue and green	8·50	8·75
MS1408	10p. greenish blue and slate	8·50	8·75

Sold at 1p,10, 1p.40, 3p.50 and 14p. respectively.

1961 (6 May). World Stamp Day. Photo. P 13×12½.

1409	302	25c. grey-black and red	20	15
1410		1p. orange-red and maroon	1·20	20
1411		10p. olive-green and maroon	1·30	65
1409/1411		Set of 3	2·50	90

303 Vázquez   **304** Gen. Franco
de Mella

1961 (8 June). Birth Centenary of Juan Vázquez de Mella (politician and writer). Photo. P 13.

1412	303	1p. brown-red	45	20
1413		2p.30 bright purple	20	20

(Des F. Jesús and G. Perez Baylo (70c., 1, 2p.), S. Algora (2p.50, 3, 8p.), E. Marin (5p.), J. L. Sánchez Toda and E. Marin (10p.), G. Perez Baylo (others). Photo)

1961 (10 July). 25th Anniv of National Uprising. T **304** and similar designs inscr "XXV ANNIVERSARIO ALZAMIENTO NACIONAL". P 13.

1414		70c. multicoloured	15	15
1415		80c. multicoloured	15	15
1416		1p. multicoloured	20	15

261

SPAIN

1417	1p.50 multicoloured		15	15
1418	2p. multicoloured		15	15
1419	2p.30 multicoloured		25	15
1420	2p.50 multicoloured		25	15
1421	3p. multicoloured		30	25
1422	5p. multicoloured		2·40	1·60
1423	6p. multicoloured		1·80	1·80
1424	8p. multicoloured		95	75
1425	10p. multicoloured		80	65
1414/1425 Set of 12			7·50	5·50

Designs: Vert—70c. Angel and flag; 80c. Straits of Gibraltar; 1p. Knight and Alcazar, Toledo; 1p.50, Victory Arch; 2p. Knight crossing River Ebro; 2p.30, Soldier, flag and troops; 2p.50, Shipbuilding; 3p. Steelworks; 6p. Irrigation (woman beside dam); 8p. Mine. Horiz—5p. Map of Spain showing electric power stations.

305 "Portico de la Gloria" (Cathedral of Santiago de Compostela) **306** L. de Góngora (after Velázquez)

(Des S. Algora Photo)

1961 (24 July). Council of Europe's Romanesque Art Exhibition. T **305** and similar vert designs inscr "EXPOSICION ARTE ROMANICO" etc. P 13.

1426	25c. blackish violet and gold		15	15
1427	1p. red-brown and gold		25	15
1428	2p. purple and gold		60	20
1429	3p. brown-red, black, turquoise and gold		60	65
1426/1429 Set of 4			1·50	1·10

Designs:—1p. Courtyard of Dominican Monastery, Santo Domingo de Silos; 2p. Madonna of Irache; 3p. "Christos Pantocrator" (from Tahull church fresco).

(Des E. Marin. Photo)

1961 (10 Aug). 400th Both Anniv of De Góngora (poet). P 13.

1430	**306**	25c. blackish violet	15	15
1431		1p. brown-red	30	15

307 Doves and C.E.P.T. Emblem **308** Burgos Cathedral

(Des T. Kurpershoek. Photo)

1961 (18 Sept). Europa. P 12½×13.

1432	**307**	1p. vermilion	20	20
1433		5p. deep brown	50	45

(Des E. Marin. Photo)

1961 (1 Oct). 25th Anniv of Gen. Franco as Head of State. P 13.
| 1434 | **308** | 1p. bronze-green and gold | 20 | 20 |

309 S. de Belalcázar **310** Courtyard **311** King Alfonso XII Monument

(Des T. Miciano (25, 70c., 2p., 2p.50). E. Marin (others). Photo)

1961 (12 Oct). Explorers and Colonisers of America (1st series). Vert portrait designs as T **309**. P 13×12½.

1435	25c. slate-violet and light green		15	15
1436	70c. green and buff		15	15
1437	80c. deep green and pink		15	15
1438	1p. deep blue and flesh		45	15
1439	2p. carmine and light blue		3·75	40
1440	2p.50 purple and mauve		95	45
1441	3p. blue and grey		2·30	90
1442	5p. brown and yellow		2·30	1·30
1435/1442 Set of 8			9·00	3·25

Portraits:—70c., 2p.50, B. de Lezo; 80c., 3p. R. de Bastidas; 1p., 5p. N. de Chaves; 2p. T **309**.

See also Nos. 1515/22, 1587/94, 1683/90, 1738/45, 1810/17, 1877/84, 1947/51, 1997/2001 and 2054/58.

(Eng G. M. Orbe (70c.), D. Carande (6p.), A. Manso (others). Recess)

1961 (31 Oct). Escorial. T **310** and similar designs. P 13×12½ (vert) or 12½×13 (horiz).

1443	70c. dull green and turquoise-blue		30	20
1444	80c. slate and bluish green		25	15
1445	1p. brown-red and yellow-brown		60	20
1446	2p.50 purple and violet		40	20
1447	5p. sepia and ochre		1·80	95
1448	6p. reddish violet and indigo		3·00	2·40
1443/1448 Set of 6			5·75	3·75

Designs: Vert—70c. Patio of the Kings; 2p.50, Grand Staircase; 6p. High Altar. Horiz—1p. Monks' Garden; 5p. View of Escorial.

(Des E. Mann. Eng A. Sánchez Toda (1p.), J. L. Sánchez Toda (2p.50, 3p.). Photo (25c., 2, 5p.) or recess (others))

1961 (13 Nov). 400th Anniv of Madrid as Capital of Spain. T **311** and similar designs. P 13.

1449	25c. deep purple and deep grey-green		20	15
1450	1p. brown and yellow-brown		35	15
1451	2p. brown-purple and grey		40	15
1452	2p.50 deep violet and red-purple		25	15
1453	3p. black and slate-blue		80	55
1454	5p. slate-blue and brown		1·70	1·10
1449/1454 Set of 6			3·50	2·20

Designs: Vert—1p. King Philip II (after Pantoja); 5p. Plaza, Madrid. Horiz—2p. Town Hall, Madrid; 2p,50, Fountain of Cybele; 3p. Portals of Alcala Palace.

312 Santa Maria del Naranco Church **313** "The Nativity" (after Ginés) **314** Clerva C.30A Autogyro

(Des E. Marin (25c., 5p.), S. Algora (2p.); photo. Des and eng D. Carande (1p.), A. Manso (2p.50); G. M. Orbe (3p.); recess)

1961 (27 Nov). 1200th Anniv of Oviedo. T **312** and similar vert designs. P 13.

1455	25c. reddish violet and light yellow-green		15	15
1456	1p. brown and yellow-brown		45	15
1457	2p. sepia and reddish purple		1·20	15
1458	2p.50 slate-violet and reddish purple		20	15
1459	3p. black and slate-blue		95	55
1460	5p. olive-brown and green		95	1·10
1455/1460 Set of 6			3·75	2·20

Designs:—1p. Fruela (portrait); 2p. Cross of the Angels; 2p,50, Alfonso II; 3p. Alfonso III; 5p. Apostles of the Holy Hall, Oviedo Cathedral.

(Des E. Marin. Photo)

1961 (1 Dec). Christmas. P 13×12½.
| 1461 | **313** | 1p. plum | 30 | 15 |

(Des S. Algora. Photo)

1961 (11 Dec). 50th Anniv of Spanish Aviation. T **314** and similar designs. P 13.

1462	1p. violet and slate-blue		20	15
1463	2p. green and slate-lilac		40	15
1464	3p. black and olive-lilac		1·40	70
1465	5p. purple and slate		3·75	1·60
1466	10p. olive-brown and light blue		1·50	60
1462/1466 Set of 5			6·50	3·00

Designs: Horiz—2p. CASA-built Dornier Do-J Wal flying boat *Plus Ultra*; 3p. Breguet 19GR airplane *Jesus de Gran Poder* (Madrid–Manila flight). Vert—5p. Avro 504K biplane hunting great bustard; 10p. Madonna of Loreto (patron saint) and North American F-86F Sabre jet fighters.

315 Arms of Alava   316 "Ecstasy of St. Teresar", after Bernini   317 Mercury

318 "St. Benedict"   319 El Cid (R. Diaz de Vivar), after statue by J. Cristobal

(Des E. Carlos Velamazán. Photo)

1962 (15 Jan–10 Dec). Arms of Provincial Capitals as T **315**. Multicoloured. P 13×12½.

1467	5p. Alava	20	20
1468	5p. Albacete (12 Feb)	20	20
1469	5p. Alicante (9 Mar)	25	25
1470	5p. Almeria (16 Apr)	25	25
1471	5p. Avila (21 May)	25	25
1472	5p. Badajoz (11 June)	25	25
1473	5p. Baleares (26 July)	25	20
1474	5p. Barcelona (13 Aug)	25	20
1475	5p. Burgos (2 Sept)	1·00	50
1476	5p. Caceres (31 Oct)	70	45
1477	5p. Cadiz (12 Nov)	75	45
1478	5p. Castellon de la Plana (10 Dec)	4·00	2·75

Set price see after No. 1764.
See also Nos. 1542/53, 1612/23, 1692/1703 and 1756/64.

(Des T. Miciano (1p.), E. Marin (2p.50, 3, 5p.), M. Salamanca (10p.), C. Cano (others). Photo)

1962 (24 Mar). Stamp Day and Zurbaran Commemoration. Paintings as T **279**. Frames gold; centre colours below. P 13.

1479	25c. blackish olive	20	15
1480	40c. maroon	25	20
1481	70c. green	30	20
1482	80c. deep bluish green	25	20
1483	1p. sepia	8·00	35
1484	1p.50 turquoise	80	20
1485	2p.50 carmine-lake	80	30
1486	3p. blue	1·50	1·00
1487	5p. brown	3·50	1·90
1488	10p. bronze-green	3·50	1·70
1479/1488	Set of 10	17·00	5·50

Zurbaran paintings: Horiz—25 c. "Martyr". Vert—40c. "Burial of St. Catalina"; 70c. "St. Casilda"; 80c. "Jesus crowning St. Joseph"; 1p. Self-portrait; 1p.50, "St. Hieronymus"; 2p.50, "Madonna of the Grace"; 3p. "Apotheosis of St. Thomas Aquinas"; 5p. "Madonna as a Child"; 10p. "The Immaculate Madonna".

(Des E. Marin. Photo)

1962 (10 Apr). Fourth Centenary of Teresian Reformation. T **316** and similar vert designs. P 13×12½ (3p.) or 13 (others).

1489	25c. slate-violet	15	15
1490	1p. brown	20	15
1491	3p. bright blue	1·40	60
1489/1491	Set of 3	1·50	80

Designs: As T **316**—25c. St. Joseph's Monastery, Avila. 22×38½ mm—3p. "St. Teresa of Avila" (Velázquez).

(Des F. Jesús. Photo)

1962 (7 May). World Stamp Day. P 13×12½.

1492	317	25c. rose-pink, reddish pur and violet	20	15
1493		1p. yellow, brown and bistre-brown	25	20
1494		10p. olive, green & bluish green	1·90	1·10
1492/1494	Set of 3		2·10	1·30

(Des E Marin. Photo)

1962 (28 May). Rubens Paintings. Designs as T **279**. Frames in gold; centre colours below. P 13×12½ (10p.) or 13 (others).

1495	25c. violet	25	20
1496	1p. red-brown	3·75	25
1497	3p. greenish blue	5·75	2·50
1498	10p. bronze green	7·00	2·40
1495/1498	Set of 4	15·00	4·75

Paintings: As T **279**—25c. Ferdinand of Austria; 1p. Self-portrait; 3p. Philip II. 26×39 mm—10p. Duke of Lerma.

(Des S. Algora Photo)

1962 (9 July). 400th Anniv of Death of Alonso Berruguete (sculptor). Vert designs as T **318**. P 13×12½.

1499	25c. magenta and light slate-blue	20	15
1500	80c. deep green and orange-brown	20	15
1501	1p. red and stone	45	15
1502	2p. magenta and light drab	4·00	15
1503	3p. blue and mauve	1·40	1·20
1504	10p. chocolate and rose-pink	1·90	1·40
1499/1504	Set of 6	7·50	3·00

Designs (sculptures by Berruguete):—80c. "The Apostle"; 1p. "St. Peter"; 2p. "St. Christopher and Child Jesus"; 3p. "Ecce Homo"; 10p. "St. Sebastian".

1962 (30 July). El Cid Campeador Commemoration. T **319** and similar designs. Recess. P 13×12½ (vert) or 12½×13 (horiz).

1505	1p. drab and yellow-green	20	20
1506	2p. black-violet and sepia	1·70	20
1507	3p. bluish green and deep blue	4·75	2·40
1508	10p. olive-green and yellow-green	2·75	1·60
1505/1508	Set of 4	8·50	4·00

Designs: Vert—2p. El Cid (equestrian statue by A. Huntington). Horiz—3p. El Cid's treasure chest; 10p. Oath-taking ceremony at Santa Gadea.

320 Honey Bee and Honeycomb   321 Throwing the Discus

(Des S. Algora. Photo)

1962 (13 Sept). Europa. P 12½×13.

1509	320	1p. brown-red	35	20
1510		5p. deep bluish green	1·30	70

1962 (7 Oct). Second Spanish-American Athletic Games, Madrid. T **321** and similar vert designs. Photo. P 13×12½.

1511	25c. deep violet-blue and pale pink	25	20
1512	80c. deep bluish green and pale yellow	25	20
1513	1p. sepia and salmon-pink	25	20
1514	3p. blue and pale blue	30	25
1511/1514	Set of 4	95	75

Designs:—80c. Running; 1p. Hurdling; 3p. Start of sprint.

1962 (12 Oct). Explorers and Colonisers of America (2nd Series). Vert portrait designs as T **309**. Photo. P 13×12½.

1515	25c. magenta and blue-grey	25	20
1516	70c. green and pale pink	80	20
1517	80c. bluish green and pale yellow	55	20
1518	1p. orange-brown and light grey-grn	1·20	20
1519	2p. carmine-lake and pale blue	3·25	40
1520	2p.50 deep slate-violet and pale brn	75	25
1521	3p. deep blue and pale pink	8·00	1·90
1522	5p. brown and pale greenish yellow	3·75	2·75
1515/1522	Set of 8	17·00	5·50

Portraits:—25c., 2p. A. de Mendoza; 70c., 2p.50, J. de Quesada; 80c., 3p. J. de Garay; 1p., 5p. P. de la Gasca.

SPAIN

322 U.P.A.E. Emblem **323** "The Annunciation" (after Murillo) **324** "The Nativity" (after Pedro de Mena) **327** St. Paul (after El Greco) **328** Poblet Monastery **329** Mail Coach

1962 (20 Oct). 50th Anniv of U.P.A.E. (Postal Union of the Americas and Spain). Recess. P 13.
1523 322 1p. sepia, green and deep green 20 15

1962 (26 Oct). Mysteries of the Rosary. T **323** and similar vert designs. Recess. P 13.

(a) POSTAGE
1524	25c. chocolate and reddish violet..............	15	15
1525	70c. deep bluish green and yellow-green.....	15	15
1526	80c. turquoise-blue and olive	15	15
1527	1p. sepia and yellow-green	5·75	75
1528	1p.50 grey-blue and green	20	15
1529	2p. sepia and violet	1·30	55
1530	2p.50 claret and purple-brown	20	20
1531	3p. black and reddish violet	20	20
1532	5p. carmine-lake and brown	90	85
1533	8p. black and maroon	75	85
1534	10p. yellow-green and deep green	75	45

(b) AIR. Inscr "CORREO AEREO"
1535	25c. violet and deep slate-violet..............	15	15
1536	1p. olive-green and brown-purple	20	20
1537	5p. carmine-lake and maroon..................	65	40
1538	10p. yellow-green and greenish grey........	1·70	1·00
1524/1538	Set of 15	11·00	5·50

Paintings: "Joyful Mysteries"—No. 1524, T **323**; No. 1525, "Visit of Elizabeth" (Correa); No. 1526, "The Birth of Christ" (Murillo); No. 1527, "Christ shown to the Elders" (Campaña); No. 1528, "Jesus lost and found in the Temple" (unknown artist). "Sorrowful Mysteries"—No. 1529, "Prayer on the Mount of Olives" (Giaquinto); No. 1530, "Scourging" (Cana); No. 1531, "The Crown of Thorns" (Tiepolo); No. 1532, "Carrying the Cross" (El Greco); No. 1533, "The Crucifixion" (Murillo). "Glorious Mysteries"—No. 1534, "The Resurrection" (Murillo); No. 1535, "The Ascension" (Bayeu); No. 1536, "The Sending-forth of the Holy Ghost" (El Greco); No. 1537, "The Assumption of the Virgin" (Cerezo); No. 1538, "The Coronation of the Virgin" (El Greco).

1962 (6 Dec). Christmas. Photo. P 13×12½.
1539 324 1p. olive-brown 40 20

325 Campaign Emblem and Swamp   **326** Pope John and Dome of St. Peter's

1962 (21 Dec). Malaria Eradication. Photo. P 12½×13.
1540 325 1p. black, yellow and yellow-green....... 20 15
The shade of the yellow-green background colour varies considerably on stamps within the same sheet.

1962 (29 Dec). Ecumenical Council, Vatican City (1st issue). Recess. P 12½×13.
1541 326 1p. slate-purple and reddish purple 30 20
See also Nos. 1601 and 1755.

(Des E. Carlos Velamanzán. Photo)

1963 (16 Jan–9 Dec). Arms of Provincial Capitals. As T **315**. Multicoloured. Photo. P 13×12½.
1542	5p. Ciudad Real	60	60
1543	5p. Cordoba (18 Feb)............................	5·00	2·20
1544	5p. Coruna (18 Mar)	70	65
1545	5p. Cuenca (22 Apr).............................	75	60
1546	5p. Fernando Poo (27 May)...................	1·10	1·30
1547	5p. Gerona (17 June)	20	20
1548	5p. Gran Canaria (15 July)....................	25	25
1549	5p. Granada (12 Aug)	45	40
1550	5p. Guadalajara (9 Sept).......................	75	40
1551	5p. Guipuzcoa (21 Oct)	20	20
1552	5p. Huelva (18 Nov).............................	20	20
1553	5p. Huesca (9 Dec)..............................	20	20

Set price see after No. 1764.

1963 (25 Jan). 1900th Anniv of Arrival of St Paul in Spain. Recess. P 13.
1554 327 1p. sepia, olive-brown and brown 30 20

1963 (25 Feb). Poblet Monastery. T **328** and similar designs. Recess. P 12½×13 (3p.) or 13×12½ (others).
1555	25c. purple, sepia and green...................	20	20
1556	1p. carmine and red-orange	45	20
1557	3p. grey-blue and violet-blue..................	1·20	35
1558	5p. yellow-ochre and brown...................	2·30	1·80
1555/1558	Set of 4	3·75	2·50

Designs: Vert—1p. Tomb; 5p. Arch. Horiz—3p. Aerial view of monastery.

1963 (24 Mar). Stamp Day and Ribera Commemoration. Paintings as T **279**. Frames gold; centre colours below. Photo. P 13.
1559	25c. bluish violet.................................	20	15
1560	40c. purple...	20	15
1561	70c. green..	45	20
1562	80c. deep bluish green	45	20
1563	1p. brown	55	15
1564	1p.50 deep blue-green..........................	60	20
1565	2p.50 cerise	2·50	20
1566	3p. blue..	4·50	1·10
1567	5p. olive-brown	13·50	3·75
1568	10p. brown-purple	4·50	1·70
1559/1568	Set of 10	25·00	7·00

Ribera paintings: Vert—25c. "Archimedes"; 40c. "Jacob's Flock"; 70c. "Triumph of Bacchus"; 80c. "St. Christopher"; 1p. Self-portrait; 1p.50, "St. Andrew"; 2p.50, "St. John the Baptist"; 3p. "St. Onofrius"; 5p. "St. Peter"; 10p. "The Madonna".

1963 (3 May). Centenary of Paris Postal Conference. Photo. P 13×12½.
1569 329 1p. red, yellow, blue, grey and black ... 20 15

330 Globe   **331** "Give us this day our daily bread"

(Des Sánchez Toda. Photo)

1963 (6 May). World Stamp Day. P 12½×13.
1570	**330** 25c. carmine, blue, black and violet.......	20	15
1571	1p. vermilion, blue-grn, blk and drab..	25	15
1572	10p. purple, yell, blk and yellow-brown	1·20	70
1570/1572	Set of 3	1·50	90

1963 (1 June). Freedom from Hunger. Photo. P 12½×13.
1573 331 1p. black, blue, red, green and gold..... 20 15

332 Pillars and Globes   **333** Civic Seals

1963 (4 June). Spanish Cultural Institutions Congress. T **332** and similar vert designs. Multicoloured. Photo. P 13.
1574	25c. Type **332**...................................	20	15
1575	80c. *Santa Maria, Pinta* and *Nina*.........	50	20
1576	1p. Columbus	50	20
1574/1576	Set of 3	1·10	50

1963 (27 June). 150th Anniv of San Sebastian. T **333** and similar horiz designs. Photo. P 13.

1577	25c. deep ultramarine and grey-green	15	15
1578	80c. red and slate-purple	20	15
1579	1p. olive-green and bistre	20	15
1577/1579	Set of 3	50	40

Designs:—80c. City aflame; 1p. View of San Sebastian, 1836.

  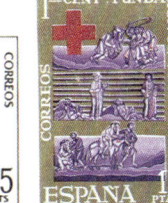

334 "St. Maria of Europe"   **335** Arms of the Order of Mercy   **336** Scenes from Parable of the Good Samaritan

1963 (16 Sept). Europa. Recess. P 13×12½.

1580	**334**	1p. chocolate and yellow-brown	20	20
1581		5p. bistre-brown & deep bluish green	65	60

1963 (24 Sept). 75th Anniv of the Order of Mercy. T **335** and similar vert designs inscr "75 ANIV. CORONACION CANONICA". Photo (25c.) or recess (others). P 13.

1582	25c. carmine, gold and black	20	15
1583	80c. sepia and green	20	15
1584	1p. dull purple and indigo	20	15
1585	1p.50 olive-brown and deep blue	20	15
1586	3p. black and slate-violet	20	20
1582/1586	Set of 5	90	70

Designs:—80c. King Jaime I; 1p. Our Lady of Mercy; 1p.50, St. Pedro Nolasco; 3p. St. Raimundo de Peñafort.

1963 (12 Oct). Explorers and Colonisers of America (3rd Series). Vert portrait designs as T **309**. Photo. P 13×12½.

1587	25c. ultramarine and pale blue	20	15
1588	70c. green and pale salmon	20	15
1589	80c. deep bluish green and pale cream	45	15
1590	1p. deep blue and pale salmon	60	15
1591	2p. carmine and light blue	1·80	15
1592	2p.50 deep violet and flesh	1·40	15
1593	3p. ultramarine and pale pink	2·75	1·60
1594	5p. brown and pale cream	3·75	3·00
1587/1594	Set of 8	10·00	5·00

Portraits:—25c., 2p. Brother J. Serra; 70c., 2p.50, Vasco Núñez de Balboa; 80c., 3p. J. de Gálvez; 1p., 5p. D. García de Paredes.

1963 (28 Oct). Red Cross Centenary. Photo. P 13×12½.

1595	**336**	1p. violet, red and gold	15	15

337 "The Nativity" (after sculpture by Berruguete)   **338** Fr. Raimondo Lulio

1963 (2 Dec). Christmas. Photo. P 13×12½.

1596	**337**	1p. bronze-green	20	15

1963 (5 Dec). Famous Spaniards (1st Series). T **338** and similar vert portraits. Recess. P 13×12½.

(a) POSTAGE

1597	1p. black and slate-violet	25	15
1598	1p.50 reddish violet and sepia	20	15

(b) AIR. Inscr "CORREO AEREO"

1599	25p. purple and reddish purple	1·40	35
1600	50p. black and green	1·80	55
1597/1600	Set of 4	3·50	1·10

Portraits:—1p.50. Cardinal Belluga; 25p. King Recaredo; 50p. Cardinal Cisneros.

See also Nos. 1714/17.

SPAIN

339 Pope Paul and Dome of St. Peter's   **340** Alcazar de Segovia

1963 (30 Dec). Ecumenical Council, Vatican City (2nd issue). Recess. P 12½×13.

1601	**339**	1p. black and deep bluish green	15	15

1964. Tourist Series. Designs as T **340**. Recess. P 13.

1602	40c. chocolate, lt blue & green (14.12)	25	20
1603	50c. sepia and indigo (26.10)	25	20
1604	70c. deep slate-blue and bluish grn (22.6)	25	20
1605	70c. chocolate and lilac (30.11)	20	15
1606	80c. black and blue (27.9)	25	20
1607	1p. deep lilac and bluish violet (8.1)	20	15
1608	1p. carmine and maroon (10.2)	20	15
1609	1p. black and green (16.3)	20	15
1610	1p. rose-carmine and deep reddish purple (shades) (6.4)	20	15
1611	1p.50 choc, bl-grn & Indigo (27.7)	25	20
1602/1611	Set of 10	2·10	1·60

Designs: Horiz—No. 1602, Potes; No. 1601, Crypt of St. Isidore (Leon); No. 1607, T **340**; No. 1608; Lion Court of the Alhambra (Granada); No. 1611, Gerona. Vert—No. 1603, Leon Cathedral; No. 1605, Costa Brava; No. 1606, "Christ of the Lanterns" (Cordoba); No 1609, Drach Caves (Majorca); No. 1610, Mosque (Cordoba).

Further designs in this series are listed individually in the Design Index.

(Des E. Carlos Velamazán. Photo)

1964 (13 Jan–7 Dec). Arms of Provincial Capitals as T **315**. Multicoloured. P 13×12½.

1612	5p. Ifni	20	20
1613	5p. Jaen (3 Feb)	20	20
1614	5p. Leon (9 Mar)	20	15
1615	5p. Lerida (13 Apr)	20	15
1616	5p. Logrono (25 May)	20	15
1617	5p. Lugo (9 June)	20	15
1618	5p. Madrid (18 July)	20	15
1619	5p. Malarga (10 Aug)	20	15
1620	5p. Murcia (14 Sept)	20	15
1621	5p. Navarra (19 Oct)	20	15
1622	5p. Orense (16 Nov)	20	15
1623	5p. Oviedo (7 Dec)	20	15

Set price see after No. 1764.

341 Santa Maria Monastery   **342** "25 Years of Peace"

1964 (24 Feb). Monastery of Santa Maria, Huerta. T **341** and similar designs. Recess. P 12½×13 (5p.) or 13×12½ (others).

1624	1p. bronze-green and green	20	15
1625	2p. sepia, black and turquoise	25	20
1626	5p. slate-blue and slate-violet	1·50	80

Designs: Vert—1p. Great Hall; 2p. Cloisters.

1964 (24 Mar). Stamp Day and Sorolla Commemoration. Paintings as T **279**. Frames gold; centre colours below. Photo. P 13.

1627	25c. violet	15	15
1628	40c. purple	15	15
1629	70c. deep yellow-green	15	15
1630	80c. deep bluish green	15	15
1631	1p. brown	15	15
1632	1p.50 deep greenish blue	15	15
1633	2p.50 magenta	15	15
1634	3p. grey-blue	45	40
1635	5p. chocolate	1·90	1·20
1636	10p. deep green	1·30	35
1627/1636	Set of 10	4·50	2·75

Scrota paintings: Vert—25c. "The Earthen Jar"; 70c. "La Mancha Types"; 80c. "Valencian Fisherwoman"; 1p. Selfportrait; 5p. "Pulling the Boat"; 10p. "Valencian Couple on Horse". Horiz—40c. "Castilian Oxherd"; 1p.50, "The Cattlepen"; 2p.50 "And people say fish is dear" (fish market); 3p. "Children on the Beach".

265

SPAIN

1964 (1 Apr). 25th Anniv of End of Spanish Civil War T **342** and similar designs. Photo. P 13.

1637	25c. gold, light green and black	15	15
1638	30c. salmon-red, light blue and black-green	15	15
1639	40c. black and gold	15	15
1640	50c. multicoloured	15	15
1641	70c. multicoloured	15	15
1642	80c. multicoloured	15	15
1643	1p. multicoloured	30	15
1644	1p.50 olive, brown-red and blue	20	15
1645	2p. multicoloured	20	15
1646	2p.50 multicoloured	20	15
1647	3p. multicoloured	1·10	1·20
1648	5p. red, green and gold	35	35
1649	6p. multicoloured	50	50
1650	10p. multicoloured	60	65
1637/1650 Set of 14		4·00	3·75

Designs: Vert—30c. Athletes ("Sport"); 50c. Apartment houses ("National Housing Plan"); 1p. Graph and symbols ("Economic Development"); 1p. Graph and symbols ("Economic Development"); 1p.50, Rocks and tower ("Construction"); 2p.50, Wheatear and dam ("Irrigation"); 5p. "Tree of Learning" ("Scientific Research"); 10p. Gen. Franco. Horiz—40c. T.V. screen and symbols ("Radio and T.V."); 70c. Wheatears, tractor and landscape ("Agriculture"); 80c. Tree and forests ("Reafforestation"); 2p. Forms of transport ("Transport and Communications"); 3p. Pylon and part of dial ("Electrification"); 6p. Ancient buildings ("Tourism").

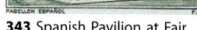
343 Spanish Pavilion at Fair

344 6c. Stamp of 1850 and Globe

1964 (23 Apr). New York World's Fair. T **343** and similar designs. Recess. P 12½×13 (1p.) or 13×12½ (others).

1651	1p. green and deep bluish green	20	15
1652	1p.50 chocolate and carmine	25	15
1653	2p.50 grey-green and grey-blue	25	15
1654	5p. carmine	25	35
1655	50p. deep blue and grey-blue	1·10	40
1651/1655 Set of 5		2·00	1·10

Designs: Vert—1p.50, Bullfighting; 2p.50, Castillo de la Mota; 5p. Spanish dancing; 50p. Pelota.

1964 (6 May). World Stamp Day. Recess. P 13×12½.

1656	**344**	25c. crimson and deep purple	20	15
1657		1p. yellow-green and grey-blue	20	20
1658		10p. red-orange and rose-red	35	30
1656/1658 Set of 3			70	60

345 Macarena Virgin

346 Medieval Ship

347 Europa "Flower"

1964 (30 May). Canonical Coronation of Macarena Virgin. Photo. P 13×12½.

| 1659 | **345** | 1p. deep green and yellow-green | 15 | 15 |

1964 (16 July). Spanish Navy Commemoration. T **346** and similar designs. Recess. P 13.

1660	15c. slate-violet and reddish purple	15	15
1661	25c. bronze-green and yellow-orange	15	15
1662	40c. grey-blue and blue	15	15
1663	50c. green and slate	15	15
1664	70c. violet and indigo	15	15
1665	80c. ultramarine and blue-green	15	15
1666	1p. reddish purple and yellow-brown	15	15
1667	1p.50 sepia and carmine-red	15	15
1668	2p. black and green	1·30	30
1669	2p.50 rose and violet	15	15
1670	3p. indigo and brown	15	15
1671	5p. indigo and green	90	90
1672	6p. violet and turquoise-green	70	70
1673	10p. scarlet and orange	25	25
1660/1673 Set of 14		4·25	3·50

Ships: Vert—25c. Carrack; 1p. Ship of the line *Santissima Trinidad*; 1p.50, Corvette *Atrevida*. Horiz—40c. *Santa Maria*; 50c. Galley; 70c. Galleon; 80c. Xebec; 2p. Steam frigate *Isabel II*; 2p.50, Frigate *Numancia*; 3p. Destroyer *Destructor*; 5p. Isaac Peral's submarine; 6p. Cruiser *Baleares*; 10p. Cadet schooner *Juan Sebastian de Elcano*.

(Des G. Bétemps. Photo)

1964 (14 Sept). Europa. P 13×12½.

1674	**347**	1p. yellow-ochre, red and green	40	30
1675		5p. light blue, bright pur and green	95	90

348 "The Virgin of the Castle" **349** Putting the Shot **350** "Adoration of the Shepherds" (after Zurbarán)

1964 (9 Oct). 700th Anniv of the Reconquest of Jerez. Photo. P 13.

1676	**348**	25c. brown and light yellow-brown	15	15
1677		1p. deep blue and grey	20	15

1964 (10 Oct). Olympic Games, Tokyo and Innsbruck (1p.). T **349** and similar vert designs. Olympic rings in gold Photo. P 13.

1678	25c. indigo and orange-red	15	15
1679	80c. indigo and yellow-green	15	15
1680	1p. deep blue and light blue	15	15
1681	3p. indigo and light yellow-brown	20	20
1682	5p. deep violet-blue & light reddish violet	20	20
1678/1682 Set of 5		80	80

Designs—80c. Long jumping; 1p. Skiing (slalom); 3p. Judo; 5p. Throwing the discus.

1964 (12 Oct). Explorers arid Colonisers of America (4th Series). Vert portrait designs as T **309**. Inscr "1964" at foot. Photo. P 13×12½.

1683	25c. violet and pale lilac	15	15
1684	70c. yellow-olive and light pink	15	15
1685	80c. deep bluish green and pale buff	30	25
1686	1p. deep bluish violet and pale brown	30	15
1687	2p. deep yellow-olive and light blue	30	15
1688	2p.50 maroon and pale turquoise-green	25	15
1689	3p. deep blue and light grey	3·50	1·20
1690	5p. brown and light cream	2·30	1·60
1683/1690 Set of 8		6·50	3·50

Portraits:—25c., 2p. D. de Almagro; 70c., 2p.50, F. de Toledo; 80c., 3p. T. de Mogrovejo; 1p., 5p. F. Pizarro.

1964 (4 Dec). Christmas. Photo. P 13×12½.

| 1691 | **350** | 1p. olive-brown | 25 | 20 |

(Des E. Carlos Velamazán. Photo)

1965 (14 Jan–6 Dec). Arms of Provincial Capitals as T **315**. Multicoloured. P 13×12½.

1692	5p. Palencia	20	15
1693	5p. Pontevedra (9 Feb)	20	15
1694	5p. Rio Muni (8 Mar)	20	15
1695	5p. Sahara (2 Apr)	20	15
1696	5p. Salamanca (20 May)	20	15
1697	5p. Santander (25 June)	20	15
1698	5p. Segovia (12 July)	20	15
1699	5p. Seville (9 Aug)	20	15
1700	5p. Soria (6 Sept)	20	15
1701	5p. Tarragona (4 Oct)	20	15
1702	5p. Tenerife (8 Nov)	20	15
1703	5p. Teruel (6 Dec)	20	15

Set price see after No. 1764.

1965. Tourist Series. Designs as T **340**. Recess. P 13.

1704	25c. black and ultramarine (17.3)	20	15
1705	30c. deep purple-brn and turquoise (15.2)	20	15
1706	50c. purple and crimson (26.7)	20	15
1707	70c. indigo and blue (29.1)	20	15
1708	80c. slate-purple and magenta (31.5)	20	15
1709	1p. brown-purple, rose-red and sepia (12.4)	20	15
1710	2p.50 purple and yellow-brn (29.11)	20	15

1711	2p.50 blackish olive, grey blue and light blue (9.1)		20	15
1712	3p. deep brown-purple and purple (15.9)		20	15
1713	6p. deep violet and slate (25.10)		20	15
1704/1713	Set of 10		1·80	1·40

Designs: Vert—25c. Columbus Monument, Barcelona; 30c. Santa Maria Church, Burgos; 50c. Synagogue, Toledo; 80c. Seville Cathedral; 1p. Cudillero Port; 2p.50 (No. 1710), Burgos Cathedral (interior); 3p. Bridge at Cambados (Pontevedra); 6p. Ceiling, Lonja (Valencia). Horiz—70c. Zamora; 2p.50 (No. 1711), Mogrovejo (Santander).

1965 (25 Feb). Famous Spaniards (2nd series). Vert portraits as T **338**. Recess. P 13×12½.

1714	25c. sepia and deep bluish green		15	15
1715	70c. indigo and light blue		20	20
1716	2p.50 sepia and bronze green		20	20
1717	5p. bronze green and green		35	35
1714/1717	Set of 4		85	85

Portraits:—25c. Donoso Cortes; 70c. King Alfonso X (the Saint); 2p.50, G. M. de Jovellanos; 5p. St. Dominic de Guzman.

1965 (24 Mar). Stamp Day and J. Romero de Torres Commemoration. Paintings as T **279**. Frames gold; centre colours below. Photo. P 13.

1718	25c. purple		20	15
1719	40c. reddish purple		20	15
1720	70c. bronze-green		20	15
1721	80c. deep bluish green		20	15
1722	1p. red-brown		20	15
1723	1p.50 turquoise		20	15
1724	2p.50 magenta		30	20
1725	3p. deep blue		40	35
1726	5p. brown		40	35
1727	10p. bronze-green		75	35
1718/1727	Set of 10		2·75	2·00

Romero de Torres paintings; Vert—25c. "Girl with Jar"; 40c. "The Song"; 70c. "The Virgin of the Lanterns"; 80c. "Girl with Guitar"; 1p. Self-portrait; 1p.50, "Poem of Cordoba"; 2p.50, "Marta and Maria"; 3p. "Poem of Cordoba" (different); 5p. "A Little Charcoal-maker"; 10p. "Long live the Hair!".

The 1p. exists in a greenish colour but its status is uncertain.

351 Bull tossing "Stamps"
352 I.T.U. Emblem and Symbols

1965 (6 May). World Stamp Day. Photo. P 13×12½.

1728	**351**	25c. multicoloured	15	15
1729		1p. multicoloured	15	15
1730		10p. multicoloured	45	40
1728/1730	Set of 3		70	65

1965 (17 May). Centenary of International Telecommunications Union. Photo. P 12½×13.

1731	**352**	1p. red, black and pink	15	15

353 Pilgrim
354 Spanish Knight and Banners
355 St. Benedict (after sculpture by Pereira)

1965 (26 July). Holy Year of Santiago de Compostela. T **353** and similar vert design. Photo. Multicoloured. P 13.

1732		1p. Type **353**	15	15
1733		2p. Pilgrim (profile)	15	15

(Des B. Temple. Photo)

1965 (28 Aug). 400th Anniv of Florida Settlement. P 13×12½.

1734	**354**	3p. black, red and yellow	20	15

1965 (27 Sept). Europa. Recess. P 13×12½.

1735	**355**	1p. deep green and bright green	25	25
1736		5p. bright violet and reddish purple	55	35

356 Sports Palace, Madrid
357 Cloisters

1965 (9 Oct). International Olympic Committee Meeting, Madrid. Photo. P 13.

1737	**356**	1p. olive-brn, gold & light olive-grey	15	15

1965 (12 Oct). Explorers and Colonisers of America (5th Series). Vert portrait designs as T **309**. Inscr "1965" at foot. Photo. P 13×12½.

1738		25c. deep violet and pale green	15	15
1739		70c. bistre-brown and light pink	15	15
1740		80c. deep bluish green and pale cream	15	15
1741		1p. deep bluish violet and pale buff	15	15
1742		2p. olive-brown and pale blue	20	15
1743		2p.50 reddish purple and pale turquoise	20	20
1744		3p. blue and pale grey	1·20	50
1745		5p. brown and pale yellow	1·20	45
1738/1745	Set of 8		3·00	1·70

Portraits:—25c., 2p. Don Fadrique de Toledo; 70c., 2p.50, Padre José de Anchieta; 80c., 3p. Francisco de Orellana; 1p., 5p. St. Luis Beltrán.

1965 (15 Nov). Yuste Monastery. T **357** and similar designs. Recess. P 13×12½ (2p) or 12½×13 (others).

1746		1p. grey-blue and sepia	15	15
1747		2p. sepia and brown	20	15
1748		5p. green and deep blue	25	25
1746/1748	Set of 3		55	50

Designs: Vert—2p. Charles V room. Horiz—5p. Courtyard.

358 Spanish 1r. Stamp of 1865
359 "The Nativity" (after Mayno)

1965 (22 Nov). Centenary of Spanish Perforated Stamps. T **358** and similar vert designs. Recess. P 13×12½.

1749		80c. yellow-green and bronze-green	15	15
1750		1p. rose-brown and purple	15	15
1751		5p. yellow-brown and sepia	15	15
1749/1751	Set of 3		40	40

Designs:—1p. 1865 19c. stamp; 5p. 1865 2r. stamp.

1965 (1 Dec). Christmas. Photo. P 12½×13.

1752	**359**	1p. green and pale blue	15	15

360 Madonna of Antipolo
361 Globe
362 Admiral Alvaro de Bazán

1965 (3 Dec). 400th Anniv of Christianity in the Philippines. T **360** and similar vert design. Photo. P 13×12½.

1753		1p. olive-brown, black & orange-buff	20	15
1754		3p. blue and pale grey	20	20

Design:—3p. Father Urdaneta.

1965 (29 Dec). 21st Ecumenical Council, Vatican City (3rd issue). Photo. P 13×12½.

1755	**361**	1p. multicoloured	15	15

1966. Arms of Provincial Capitals as T **315**. Multicoloured. Photo. P 13×12½.

1756	5p. Toledo (24.1)	20	15
1757	5p. Valencia (15.2)	20	15
1758	5p. Valladolid (17.3)	20	15
1759	5p. Vizcaya (27.4)	20	15
1760	5p. Zamora (28.5)	20	15
1761	5p. Zaragoza (25.6)	20	15
1762	5p. Ceuta (22.7)	20	15
1763	5p. Melilla (8.8)	20	15
1764	10p. Spain (19.9)	25	20

1467/1478, 1542/1553, 1612/1623, 1692/1703,
1756/1764 *Set of 9* ... 17·00 11·00

No. 1764 showing the arms of Spain is larger, 26×38½ mm.

1966 (26 Feb). Celebrities (1st Series). T **362** and similar vert portraits. Recess. P 13×12½.

(a) POSTAGE

1765	25c. black and grey-blue	20	15
1766	2p. violet and reddish purple	25	20

(b) AIR. Inscr "CORREO AEREO"

1767	25p. bronze-green and bright green	1·30	25
1768	50p. grey-blue and light greenish blue	2·00	75

1765/1768 *Set of 4* ... 3·50 1·20

Portraits:—2p. Benito Daza de Valdés (doctor); 25p. Seneca; 50p. St. Damaso.

See also Nos. 1849/52.

363 Exhibition Emblem

364 Luno Church

1966 (4 Mar). Graphic Arts Exhibition, "Graphispack", Barcelona. Photo. P 13.

1769	**363**	1p. emerald, ultramarine and red	15	15

1966 (23 Mar). Stamp Day and J. M. Sert Commemoration. Various paintings as T **279**. Frames in gold; centre colours below. Photo. P 13.

1770	25c. violet	20	15
1771	40c. bright reddish purple	20	15
1772	70c. myrtle-green	20	15
1773	80c. bronze-green	20	15
1774	1p. red-brown	20	15
1775	1p.50 Prussian blue	20	15
1776	2p.50 carmine-red	20	15
1777	3p. blue	20	15
1778	5p. sepia	20	15
1779	10p. slate-green	20	15

1770/1779 *Set of 10* ... 1·80 1·30

J. M. Sert paintings: Vert—25c. "The Magic Ball"; 70c. "Christ Addressing the Disciples"; 80c. "The Balloonists"; 1p. Self-portrait; 1p.50, "Audacity"; 2p.50, "Justice"; 3p. "Jacob's Struggle with the Angel"; 5p. "The Five Parts of the World"; 10p. "St. Peter and St. Paul". Horiz—40c. "Memories of Toledo".

1966 (28 Apr). 600th Anniv of Guernica. T **364** and similar vert designs. Multicoloured. Photo. P 13.

1780	80c. Type **364**	15	15
1781	1p. Arms of Guernica	15	15
1782	3p. "Tree of Guernica"	15	15

1780/1782 *Set of 3* ... 40 40

365 Postmarked 6 cuartos Stamp of 1850

366 Tree and Globe

1966 (6 May). World Stamp Day. T **365** and similar horiz designs showing postmarked stamps on cover. Multicoloured. Photo. P 12½×13.

1783	25c. Type **365**	15	15
1784	1p. 5r. of 1850	15	15
1785	10p. 10r. of 1850	20	20

1783/1785 *Set of 3* ... 45 45

1966. Tourist Series. Designs as T **340**. Recess. P 13.

1786	10c. dp bluish green & grey-grn (16.5)	15	15
1787	15c. bistre-brown and green (16.5)	15	15
1788	40c. brown and yellow-brown (8.9)	15	15
1789	50c. brown-purple and rose-red (8.9)	15	15
1790	80c. dull purple and mauve (8.9)	15	15
1791	1p. turquoise-blue and ultram (16.5)	15	15
1792	1p.50 black and blue (16.5)	15	15
1793	2p. olive-brown and blue (16.5)	15	15
1794	3p. blackish brown and blue (8.9)	15	15
1795	10p. blue and turquoise-blue (8.9)	15	15

1786/1795 *Set of 10* ... 1·40 1·40

Designs: Vert—10c. Bohi waterfalls, Lerida; 40c. Sigena monastery, Huesca; 50c. Santo Domingo Church, Soria; 80c. Golden Tower, Seville; 1p. El Teide, Canaries; 10p. Church of St Gregory, Valladolid. Horiz—15c. Torla, Huesca; 1p.50, Cathedral, Guadalupe; 2p. University, Alcala de Henares; 3p. La Seo Cathedral, Lerida.

1966 (6 June). World Forestry Congress. Photo. P 12½×13.

1796	**366**	1p. deep green, choc and yellow-brown	15	15

367 Crown and Anchor

368 Butron Castle (Vizcaya)

1966 (1 July). Naval Week, Barcelona. Photo. P 13.

1797	**367**	1p. deep blue and pale grey	15	15

1966 (13 Aug). Spanish Castles (1st Series). T **368** and similar designs. Recess. P 13.

1798	10c. sepia and blue	15	15
1799	25c. purple and slate-violet	15	15
1800	40c. blue-green and turquoise-blue	15	15
1801	50c. bright blue and greenish blue	15	15
1802	70c. grey-blue and ultramarine	15	15
1803	80c. deep bluish green and slate-violet	15	15
1804	1p. deep yellow-olive and yellow-brown	15	15
1805	3p. bright purple and rose-red	15	15

1798/1805 *Set of 8* ... 1·00 1·00

Castles: Horiz—10c. Guadamur (Toledo); 25c. Alcazar (Segovia); 40c. La Mota (Medina del Campo); 50c. Olite (Navarra); 70c. Monteagudo (Murcia); 1p. Manzanares (Madrid). Vert—3p. Almansa (Albacete).

See design index below No. 1611.

369 Don Quixote, Dulcinea and Aldonza Lorenzo

371 Horseman in the Sky

370 "Europa and the Bull"

1966 (5 Sept). Fourth World Psychiatric Congress, Madrid. Photo. P 13.

1806	**369**	1p.50 multicoloured	15	15

1966 (26 Sept). Europa. Photo. P 12½×13.

1807	**370**	1p. multicoloured	20	20
1808		5p. multicoloured	40	40

SPAIN

1966 (9 Oct). 17th International Astronautics Federation Congress, Madrid. Photo. P 13×12½.
| 1809 | 371 | 1p.50 brn-red, blk & dp greenish bl | 15 | 15 |

1966 (12 Oct). Explorers and Colonisers of America (6th Series). Vert designs as T **309**. Inscr "1966" at foot. Photo. P 13×12½.
1810	30c. bistre-brown and pale brown	15	15
1811	50c. carmine-red and pale green	15	15
1812	1p. deep bluish violet and pale blue	15	15
1813	1p.20 slate and pale grey	15	15
1814	1p.50 myrtle-green and pale green	15	15
1815	3p. blue	15	15
1816	3p.50 reddish violet and pale lilac	20	20
1817	6p. deep olive-brown and pale buff	20	15
1810/1817 Set of 8		1·20	1·10

Designs:—30c. A. de Mendoza; 50c. Title page of Dominican Fathers' "Christian Doctrine"; 1p. J. A. Manso de Velasco; 1p.20, Coins of Lima Mint (1699); 1p.50, M. de Castro y Padilla; 3p. Oruro Convent; 3p.50, M. de Amat; 6p. Inca postal runner.

372 R. del Valle Inclán

373 Monastery Façade

1966 (7 Nov). Spanish Writers. T **372** and similar vert portraits. Photo. P 13.
1818	1p.50 olive-green and black	15	15
1819	3p. slate-violet and black	15	15
1820	6p. Prussian blue and black	15	15
1818/1820 Set of 3		40	40

Writers: 3p. Carlos Arniches; 6p. J. Benavente y Martinez. See also Nos. 1888/91.

1966 (24 Nov). St. Mary's Carthusian Monastery, Jerez. T **373** and similar designs. Recess. P 13×12½ (1p.) or 12½×13 (others).
1821	1p. slate-blue and turquoise-blue	15	15
1822	2p. yellow-green and green	20	15
1823	5p. plum and purple	20	15
1821/1823 Set of 3		50	40

Designs: Horiz—2p. Cloisters; 5p. Gateway.

374 "The Nativity" (after P. Duque Cornejo)

375 Alava Costume

1966 (5 Dec). Christmas. Photo. P 12½×13.
| 1824 | **374** 1p.50 multicoloured | 15 | 15 |

1967 (14 Jan–11 Dec). Provincial Costumes. T **375** and similar vert designs. Multicoloured. Photo. P 13×12½.
1825	6p. Type **375**	20	15
1826	6p. Albacete (13.2)	15	15
1827	6p. Alicante (9.3)	15	15
1828	6p. Almeria (17.4)	20	15
1829	6p. Avila (22.5)	15	15
1830	6p. Badajoz (12.6)	15	15
1831	6p. Baleares (7.7)	15	15
1832	6p. Barcelona (21.8)	15	15
1833	6p. Burgos (5.9)	20	15
1834	6p. Caceres (16.10)	15	15
1835	6p. Cadiz (6.11)	15	15
1836	6p. Castellon de la Plana (11.12)	15	15
1825/1836 Set of 12		1·60	1·50

See also Nos. 1897/1908, 1956/67, 2007/18 and 2072/6.

376 Archers

377 Cathedral, Palma de Mallorca, and Union Emblem

1967 (27 Mar). Stamp Day. Cave Paintings. T **376** and similar multicoloured designs. Photo. P 13.
1837	40c. Type **376**	15	15
1838	50c. Boar-hunting	15	15
1839	1p. Trees (vert)	15	15
1840	1p.20 Bison	15	10
1841	1p.50 Hands	15	15
1842	2p. Hunter (vert)	15	15
1843	2p.50 Deer (vert)	15	15
1844	3p.50 Hunters	15	15
1845	4p. Chamois-hunters (vert)	15	15
1846	6p. Deer-hunting (vert)	15	15
1837/1846 Set of 10		1·30	1·20

1967 (28 Mar). Interparliamentary Union Congress, Palma de Mallorca. Photo. P 13.
| 1847 | **377** 1p.50 bright blue-green | 20 | 20 |

378 Wilhelm Röntgen (physicist)

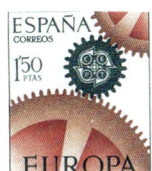

379 Cogwheels

1967 (3 Apr). Radiology Congress, Barcelona. Photo. P 13.
| 1848 | **378** 1p.50 myrtle-green | 20 | 20 |

1967 (6 Apr). Celebrities (2nd series). Vert designs as T **362**. Recess. P 13×12½.
1849	1p.20 reddish violet and purple	15	15
1850	3p.50 dull purple and reddish purple	20	20
1851	4p. sepia and light brown	15	20
1852	25p. grey and greenish blue	25	20
1849/1852 Set of 4		65	65

Portraits:—1p.20, Averroes (physician and philosopher); 3p.50, Acosta (poet); 4p. Maimonides (physician and philosopher); 25p. Andrés Laguna (physician).

(Des O. Bonnevalle. Photo)

1967 (2 May). Europa. P 13.
| 1853 | **379** 1p.50 dp bluish grn, red-brn and red | 20 | 20 |
| 1854 | 6p. bright vio, new bl and brn-purple | 25 | 25 |

380 Fair Building

381 Spanish 5r. Stamp of 1850 with Numeral Postmark

1967 (3 May). 50th Anniv of Valencia International Samples Fair. Photo. P 13.
| 1855 | **380** 1p.50 bronze-green | 15 | 15 |

1967 (6 May). World Stamp Day. T **381** and similar vert designs. Photo. P 13.
1856	40c. orange-brown, blue and black	15	15
1857	1p.50 lake-brown, black & deep grn	15	15
1858	6p. blue, carmine-red and black	15	15
1856/1858 Set of 3		40	40

Designs:—1p.50, Spanish 12c. stamp of 1850 with crowned "M" (Madrid) postmark; 6p. Spanish 6r. stamp of 1850 with "1.R." postmark. See also Nos. 1927/28, 1980/1, 2032, 2091, 2150 and 2185.

SPAIN

382 Sleeping Vagrant and "Guardian Angel"

383 I.T.Y. Emblem

1967 (16 May). National Day for Caritas Welfare Organisation. Photo. P 13.
1859	**382**	1p.50 multicoloured	15	15

1967 (26 July). Tourist Series and International Tourist Year (3p.50). Vert designs as T **340**, and T **383**. Recess. P 13.
1860	10c. black and violet-blue	20 15
1861	1p. black and blue	20 15
1862	1p.50 black and yellow-brown	20 15
1863	2p.50 steel-blue and turquoise-blue	25 15
1864	3p.50 deep ultram & reddish purple	25 20
1865	5p. bronze-green and yellow-green	25 15
1866	6p. purple and mauve	25 15
1860/1866 Set of 7		1·30 1·00

Designs:—10c. Betanzos Church (Corunna); 1p. St. Miguel's Tower (Palencia); 1p.50, Castellers (acrobats); 2p.50, Columbus Monument (Huelva); 5p. "Enchanted City" (Cuenca); 6p. Church of Our Lady, Sanlucar (Cadiz).

1967 (11 Aug). Spanish Castles (2nd Series). Designs as T **368**. Recess. P 13.
1867	50c. brown and bluish grey	20 15
1868	1p. slate-violet and bluish grey	20 15
1869	1p.50 dull green and slate-blue	20 15
1870	2p. light brown and dull orange-red	20 15
1871	2p.50 light brown & turquoise-green	20 15
1872	5p. violet-blue and purple	20 15
1873	6p. sepia and yellow-brown	20 15
1874	10p. slate-green and turquoise-blue	20 15
1867/1874 Set of 8		1·40 1·10

Castles: Horiz—50c. Balsareny (Barcelona); 1p. Jarandilla (Caceres); 1p.50, Almodovar (Cordoba); 2p.50, Peniscola (Castellon); 5p. Coca (Segovia); 6p. Loarre (Huesca); 10p. Belmonte (Cuenca). Vert—2p. Ponferrada (Leon).

384 Globe and Snow Crystal

385 Maps of the Americas, Spain and the Philippines

1967 (30 Aug). 12th International Refrigeration Congress, Madrid. Photo. P 13.
1875	**384**	1p.50 greenish blue	15	15

1967 (10 Oct). Fourth Spanish, Portuguese, American and Philippine Municipalities Congress, Barcelona. Photo. P 13.
1876	**385**	1p.50 bright reddish violet	15	15

1967 (12 Oct). Explorers and Colonisers of America (7th Series). Portraits as T **309** and other designs inscr "1967" at foot. Photo. P 13×12½ (vert) or 12½×13 (horiz).
1877	40c. blackish olive and pale orange	15 15
1878	50c. agate and pale grey	15 15
1879	1p. deep magenta and pale blue	15 15
1880	1p.20 bronze-green and pale cream	15 15
1881	1p.50 deep bluish green & pale flesh	15 15
1882	3p. deep slate-violet and pale buff	20 15
1883	3p.50 blue and pale pink	25 20
1884	6p. chestnut	25 15
1877/1884 Set of 8		1·30 1·10

Designs: Vert—40c. J. Francisco de la Bodega y Quadra, 50c. Map of Nutka coast; 1p. F. A. Mourelle; 1p.50, E. J. Martinez; 3p.50, Cayetano Valdes y Florez. Horiz—1p.20, View of Nutka; 3p. Map of Californian coast; 6p. San Elias, Alaska.

387 Ploughing with Oxen

388 Main Portal, Veruela Monastery

1967 (31 Oct). Bimillenary of Caceres. T **387** and similar designs. Photo. P 12½×13 (3p.50) or 13×12½ (others).
1885	1p.50 multicoloured	15 15
1886	3p.50 multicoloured	15 15
1887	6p. multicoloured	20 20
1885/1887 Set of 3		45 45

Designs: Vert—1p.50, Statue and archway; 6p. Roman coins.

1967 (15 Nov). Anniversaries. Vert portraits as T **372**. Photo. P 13.
1888	1p.20 lake-brown and black	15 15
1889	1p.50 myrtle green and black	15 15
1890	3p.50 reddish violet and black	15 15
1891	6p. grey-blue and black	15 15
1888/1891 Set of 4		55 55

Designs:—1p.20, P. de S. José Bethencourt (founder of Bethlehemite Order, 300th death anniv); 1p.50, Enrique Granados (composer, birth centenary); 3p.50, Ruben Dario (poet, birth centenary); 6p. San Ildefonso, Archbishop of Toledo (after El Greco) (1900th death anniv).

1967 (24 Nov). Veruela Monastery. T **388** and similar designs. Recess. P 13×12½ (1p.50) or 12½×13 (others).
1892	1p.50 blue and ultramarine	15 15
1893	3p.50 deep olive-grey and green	15 15
1894	6p. purple and light brown	20 20
1892/1894 Set of 3		45 45

Designs: Horiz—3p.50, Aerial view of Monastery; 6p. Cloisters.

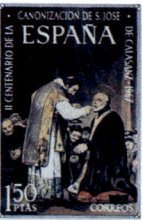

389 "The Canonization of San José de Calasanz" (from painting by Goya)

390 "The Nativity" (Salzillo)

1967 (27 Nov). Bicentenary of Canonization of San José de Calasanz. Photo. P 13×12½.
1895	**389**	1p.50 multicoloured	15	15

1967 (5 Dec). Christmas. Photo. P 13.
1896	**390**	1p.50 multicoloured	15	15

1968 (15 Jan–9 Dec). Provincial Costumes. Vert designs as T **375**. Multi coloured. Photo. P 13×12½.
1897	6p. Ciudad Real	25 20
1898	6p. Cordoba (13.2)	25 20
1899	6p. Coruna (8.3)	25 20
1900	6p. Cuenca (18.4)	20 15
1901	6p. Fernando Poo (20.5)	25 20
1902	6p. Gerona (12.6)	25 20
1903	6p. Las Palmas (Gran Canaria) (8.7)	25 20
1904	6p. Granada (5.8)	20 15
1905	6p. Guadalajara (9.9)	20 15
1906	6p. Guipúzcoa (1.10)	20 15
1907	6p. Huelva (4.11)	25 20
1908	6p. Huesca (9.12)	25 20
1897/1908 Set of 12		2·30 2·00

391 Slalom

392 Beatriz Galindo

1968 (6 Feb). Winter Olympic Games, Grenoble. T **391** and similar designs. Multicoloured. Photo. P 13×12½ (3p.50) or 12½×13 (others).
1909	1p.50 Type **391**	20	20
1910	3p.50 Bobsleighing (vert)	20	20
1911	6p. Ice hockey	20	20
1909/1911	Set of 3	55	55

1968 (25 Mar). Stamp Day and Fortuny Commemoration. Various paintings as T **279**. Photo. Frames gold; centre colours below. P 13.
1912	40c. bright purple	20	15
1913	50c. deep bluish green	20	15
1914	1p. deep brown	20	15
1915	1p.20 reddish violet	20	15
1916	1p.50 emerald	20	15
1917	2p. deep orange-brown	20	15
1918	2p.50 carmine	20	15
1919	3p.50 brown-purple	20	15
1920	4p. olive-brown	20	15
1921	6p. blue	20	15
1912/1921	Set of 10	1·60	1·40

Fortuny paintings: Horiz—40c. "The Vicarage"; 1p.20, "The Print Collector"; 6p. "Queen Christina". Vert—1p. "Idyll"; 1p.50, Self-portrait; 2p. "Old Man Naked to the Sun"; 2p.50, "Typical Calabrian"; 3p.50, "Portrait of Lady"; 4p. "Battle of Tetuán".

1968 (8 Apr). Famous Spanish Women. T **392** and similar horiz designs with background scenes. Recess. P 12½×13.
1922	1p.20 blackish brown & lt bistre-brn	15	15
1923	1p.50 steel-blue and turquoise-green	15	15
1924	3p.50 violet	15	15
1925	6p. black and grey-blue	20	20
1922/1925	Set of 4	60	60

Portraits:—1p.50, Agustina de Aragon; 3p.50, Maria Pacheco; 6p. Rosalia de Castro.

393 Europa "Key"

394 Emperor Galba's Coin (obverse and reverse)

(Des H. Schwarzenbach. Photo)

1968 (29 Apr). Europa. P 12½×13.
| 1926 | **393** | 3p.50 gold, deep brn and new blue | 25 | 25 |

1968 (6 May). World Stamp Day. Vert designs as T **381**, but with stamps and postmarks changed. inscr "1968". Photo. P 13.
| 1927 | 1p.50 black, yellow-brown and black | 15 | 15 |
| 1928 | 3p.50 blue, black and blackish green | 15 | 15 |

Designs:—1p.50, Spanish 6c. stamp of 1850 with Puebla (Galicia) postmark; 3p.50, Spanish 6r. stamp of 1850 with Serena postmark.

1968 (15 June). 1900th Anniv of the Foundation of Leon by VIIth Roman Legion. T **394** and similar designs. Photo. P 12½×13 (3p.50) or 13×12½ (others).
1929	1p. lake-brown and light purple	20	20
1930	1p.50 brown and pale yellow	20	20
1931	3p.50 blue-green and yellow-ochre	20	20
1929/1931	Set of 3	55	55

Designs: Vert—1p. Inscribed tile and town map of Leon. (26×47 mm.)—1p.50, Legionary with standard (statue).

395 Human Rights Emblem

396 Rifle-shooting

1968 (25 June). Human Rights Year. Photo. P 13×12½.
| 1932 | **395** | 3p.50 orange-red, green & light blue | 25 | 20 |

1968 (15 July). Tourist Series. Designs as T **340**. Recess. P 13.
1933	50c. brown and lake-brown	20	15
1934	1p.20 bright green and blackish green	20	15
1935	1p.50 slate-blue and myrtle-green	20	15
1936	2p. dull purple and reddish purple	20	15
1937	3p.50 reddish purple and purple	20	15
1933/1937	Set of 5	90	70

Designs: Vert—50c. Count Benavente's Palace, Baeza; 1p.50, Sepulchre, St. Vincent's Church, Avila; 3p.50, Main portal, Church of Santa Maria, Sanguesa (Navarra). Horiz—1p.20, View of Salamanca; 2p. "The King's Page" (statue), Siguenza Cathedral.

1968 (29 July). Spanish Castles (3rd Series). Designs as T **368**. Recess. P 13.
1938	40c. sepia and grey-blue	20	15
1939	1p.20 purple and brown-purple	20	15
1940	1p.50 black and bistre	20	15
1941	2p.50 bronze-green & yellow-green	20	15
1942	6p. deep turquoise and blue	20	15
1938/1942	Set of 5	90	70

Castles: Horiz—40c. Escalona; 1p.20, Fuensaldaña; 1p.50, Peñafiel; 2p.50, Villasobroso. Vert—6p. Frias.

1968 (24 Sept). Olympic Games, Mexico. T **396** and similar multicoloured designs. Photo. P 13×12½ (6p.) or 12½×13 (others).
1943	1p. Type **396**	25	15
1944	1p.50 Horse-jumping	25	15
1945	3p.50 Cycling	25	20
1946	6p. Dinghy racing (vert)	25	20
1943/1946	Set of 4	90	60

1968 (12 Oct). Explorers and Colonisers of America (8th Series). Portraits as T **309** and similar designs inscr "1968" at foot. Photo. P 12½×13 (6p.) or 13×12½ (others).
1947	40c. greenish blue and pale blue	15	15
1948	1p. bright purple and pale blue	15	15
1949	1p.50 slate-green and pale flesh	15	15
1950	3p.50 blue and pale mauve	30	1·50
1951	6p. light brown and pale yellow	30	25
1947/1951	Set of 5	95	2·00

Designs: Vert—40c. Map of Orinoco missions; 1p. Diego de Losada (founder of Caracas); 1p.50, Arms of the Losadas; 3p.50, Diego de Henares (builder of Caracas). Horiz—6p. Old plan of Santiago de Leon de Caracas.

397 Monastery Building

398 "The Nativity" (Barocci)

1968 (25 Nov). Santa Maria del Parral Monastery. T **397** and similar vert designs. Recess. P 13×12½.
1952	1p.50 reddish lilac and light blue	20	15
1953	3p.50 red-brown and chocolate	25	20
1954	6p. brown and rose	25	20
1952/1954	Set of 3	55	50

Designs:—3p.50, Cloisters; 6p. "Santa Maria del Parral".

1968 (2 Dec). Christmas. Photo. P 13×12½.
| 1955 | **398** | 1p.50 multicoloured | 25 | 20 |

1969 (13 Jan–10 Dec). Provincial Costumes. Vert designs as T **375**. Multicoloured. Photo. P 13×12½.
1956	6p. Ifni	20	15
1957	6p. Jaén (7.2)	20	15
1958	6p. Leon (7.3)	20	15
1959	6p. Lerida (2.4)	20	15
1960	6p. Logroño (20.5)	25	20
1961	6p. Lugo (12.6)	25	20
1962	6p. Madrid (8.7)	25	20
1963	6p. Malaga (8.8)	20	15
1964	6p. Murcia (9.9)	20	15
1965	6p. Navarra (2.10)	20	15
1966	6p. Orense (4.11)	20	15
1967	6p. Oviedo (10.12)	20	15
1956/1967	Set of 12	2·10	1·60

SPAIN

1969 (24 Mar). Stamp Day and Alonso Cano Commemoration Paintings as T **279**. Photo. Frames gold; centre colours below. P 13.

1968	40c. crimson	15	15
1969	50c. green	15	15
1970	1p. deep sepia	15	15
1971	1p.50 blackish green	15	15
1972	2p. red-brown	15	15
1973	2p.50 magenta	15	15
1974	3p. ultramarine	15	15
1975	3p.50 brown-purple	15	15
1976	4p. slate-purple	15	15
1977	6p. deep turquoise-blue	15	15
1968/1977	Set of 10	1·40	1·40

Alonso Cano paintings: Vert—40c. "St. Agnes"; 50c. "St. Joseph"; 1p. "Christ supported by an Angel"; 1p.50, "Alonso Cano" (Velázquez); 2p. "The Holy Family"; 2p,50, "The Circumcision"; 3p. "Jesus and the Samaritan"; 3p.50, "Madonna and Child"; 6p. "The Vision of St. John the Baptist". Horiz—4p. "St. John Capistrano and St. Bernardin".

399 Molecules and Diagram **400** Colonnade

1969 (7 Apr). 6th European Biochemical Congress. Photo. P 13.
1978   **399**   1p.50 multicoloured 20   20

(Des L. Gasbarra and G. Belli. Photo)

1969 (28 Apr). Europa. P 13.
1979   **400**   3p.50 multicoloured 25   25

1969 (6 May). World Stamp Day. Vert designs similar to T **381**. Photo. P 13×12½.
1980	1p.50 black, red and deep green	15	15
1981	3p.50 deep green, red and light blue	15	15

Designs:—1p.50, Spanish 6c. stamp of 1851 with "A 3 1851" postmark; 3p.50, Spanish 10r. stamp of 1851 with "CORVERA" postmark.

401 Spectrum   **402** Red Cross Symbols and Globe

1969 (26 May). 15th International Spectroscopical Conference, Madrid. Photo. P 13.
1982   **401**   1p.50 multicoloured 25   20

1969 (30 May). 50th Anniv of League of Red Cross Societies. Photo. P 13.
1983   **402**   1p.50 multicoloured 25   20

403 Capital, Lugo Cathedral   **404** Franciscan Friar and Child

1969 (4 June). 300th Anniv of the Dedication of Galicia to Jesus Christ. Photo. P 13×12½.
1984   **403**   1p.50 brown, black and green 15   15

1969 (24 June). Spanish Castles (4th Series). Horiz designs as T **368**. Recess. P 13.
1985	1p. slate-purple and blue-green	15	15
1986	1p.50 deep blue and reddish violet	15	15
1987	2p.50 slate-lilac and ultramarine	15	15
1988	3p.50 brown and green	35	25
1989	6p. drab and bluish green	15	15
1985/1989	Set of 5	85	75

Castles:—1p. Turegano; 1p.50, Villalonso; 2p.50, Velez Blanco; 3p.50, Castilnovo; 6p. Torrelobaton.

1969 (16 July). Bicentenary of San Diego, California. Photo. P 13.
1990   **404**   1p.50 multicoloured 25   20

405 Rock of Gibraltar   **406** "Adoration of the Three Kings" (Maino)

1969 (18 July). Aid for Spanish "ex-Gibraltar" Workers. T **405** and similar horiz design. Photo. P 13.
1991	1p.50 turquoise-blue	20	15
1992	2p. bright purple (Aerial view of Rock)	20	15

1969 (23 July). Tourist Series. Designs as T **340**. Recess. P 13.
1993	1p.50 slate-green and turquoise	20	15
1994	3p. turquoise-green and yellow-green	15	15
1995	3p.50 greenish blue and blue-green	20	15
1996	6p. slate-violet and green	20	15
1993/1996	Set of 4	70	55

Designs: Horiz—1p.50, Alcaniz (Teruel). Vert—3p. Murcia Cathedral; 3p.50, "The Lady of Elche" (sculpture); 6p. Church of Our Lady of the Redonda, Logroño.

1969 (12 Oct). Explorers and Colonisers of America (9th Series). Chile. Portraits as T **309** and similar designs inscr "1969" at foot. P 13×12½ (vert) or 12½×13 (horiz).
1997	40c. brown/pale blue	15	15
1998	1p.50 slate-violet/pale flesh	25	15
1999	2p. bronze-green/pale mauve	25	15
2000	3p.50 deep bluish green/pale cream	45	40
2001	6p. blackish brown/pale cream	30	20
1997/2001	Set of 5	1·30	90

Designs: Vert—40c. Convent of Santo Domingo, Santiago de Chile; 2p. Ambrosio O'Higgins; 3p.50, Pedro de Valdivia (founder of Santiago de Chile). Horiz—1p.50, Chilean Mint; 6p. Cal y Canto Bridge.

1969 (3 Nov). Christmas. T **406** and similar vert design. Multicoloured. Photo. P 13.
2002	1p.50 Type **406**	15	15
2003	2p. "The Nativity" (Gerona Cathedral)	15	15

407 Las Huelgas Monastery   **408** Blessed Juan of Avila (after El Greco)

1969 (22 Nov). Las Huelgas Monastery, Burgos. T **407** and similar designs. Recess. P 13×12½ (6p.) or 12½×13 (others).
2004	1p.50 greenish slate & turquoise-grn	25	15
2005	3p.50 blue and bright blue	45	45
2006	6p. blackish olive and yellow-green	25	45
2004/2006	Set of 3	85	1·10

Designs: Horiz—3p.50, Tombs. Vert—6p. Cloisters.

1970 (13 Jan–10 Dec). Provincial Costumes. Vert designs as T **375**. Multicoloured. Photo. P 13×12½.
2007	6p. Palencia	20	15
2008	6p. Pontevedra (7.2)	20	15
2009	6p. Sahara (7.3)	20	15
2010	6p. Salamanca (2.4)	20	15
2011	6p. Santa Cruz de Tenerife (23.5)	20	15
2012	6p. Santander (12.6)	20	15
2013	6p. Segovia (8.7)	20	15
2014	6p. Seville (7.8)	20	15
2015	6p. Soria (9.9)	20	15
2016	6p. Tarragona (2.10)	20	15
2017	6p. Teruel (21.11)	20	15
2018	6p. Toledo (10.12)	20	15
2007/2018	Set of 12	2·10	1·50

SPAIN

1970 (25 Feb). Spanish Celebrities. T **408** and similar vert design. Recess. P 13×12½.
| 2019 | 25p. indigo and reddish lilac | 4·75 | 35 |
| 2020 | 50p. red-brown and brown-orange | 2·10 | 40 |

Designs:—25p. T **408** (400th Death Anniv); 50p. Cardinal Rodrigo Ximenes de Rada, after J. de Borgena (800th Birth Anniv).
See also Nos. 2129/31.

409 "St. Stephen"

410 "Flaming Sun"

1970 (24 Mar). Stamp Day and Luis de Morales Commemoration. T **409** and similar vert paintings. Multicoloured. Photo. P 13.
2021	50c. Type **409**	20	15
2022	1p. "The Annunciation"	20	15
2023	1p.50 "Virgin and Child with St. John"	20	15
2024	2p. "Virgin and Child"	20	15
2025	3p. "The Presentation of the Infant Christ"	20	15
2026	3p.50 "St. Jerome"	20	15
2027	4p. "St. John of Ribera"	20	15
2028	5p. "Ecce Homo"	20	15
2029	6p. "Pietá"	20	20
2030	10p. "St. Francis of Assisi"	20	20
2021/2030	Set of 10	1·80	1·40

(Des L. le Brocquy. Photo)

1970 (4 May). Europa. P 13.
| 2031 | **410** 3p.50 gold and ultramarine | 25 | 25 |

1970 (8 May). World Stamp Day. Vert design similar to T **381**. Photo. P 13×12½.
| 2032 | 2p. deep orange-red, black and green | 15 | 15 |

Design:—2p. Spanish 12c. stamp of 1860 with railway cachet.

411 Fair Building

412 General Primo de Rivera

1970 (27 May). 50th Anniv of Barcelona Fair. Photo. P 13.
| 2033 | **411** 15p. multicoloured | 25 | 15 |

1970 (6 June). Birth Centenary of General Primo de Rivera. Photo. P 13×12½.
| 2034 | **412** 2p. deep olive-green, brn & pale buff | 15 | 15 |

1970 (24 June). Spanish Castles (5th Series). Designs similar to T **368**. Recess. P 13.
2035	1p. black and indigo	45	25
2036	1p.20 violet-blue and turquoise	20	15
2037	3p.50 brown and green	20	15
2038	6p. bluish violet and orange-brown	20	15
2039	10p. deep olive-brown and chestnut	1·00	20
2035/2039	Set of 5	1·90	80

Castles: Horiz—1p. Valencia de Don Juan, 1p.20, Monterrey, 3p.50, Mombeltran; 6p. Sadaba; 10p. Bellver.

1970 (23 July). Tourist Series. Designs as T **340**. Recess. P 13.
2040	50c. slate-lilac and blue	15	15
2041	1p. chestnut and yellow-ochre	20	15
2042	1p.50 grey-green and slate-blue	20	15
2043	2p. steel-blue and indigo	50	15
2044	3p.50 blue and violet	25	20
2045	5p. red-brown and slate-blue	90	20
2040/2045	Set of 6	2·00	90

Designs: Horiz—50c. Alcazaba, Almeria; 1p. Malaga Cathedral; 2p. St. Francis' Convent, Orense. Vert—1p.50, Our Lady of the Assumption, Lequeitio; 3p.50, The Lonja, Zaragoza; 5p. The Portalon, Vitoria.

413 17th-century Tailor

414 Diver on Map

1970 (18 Aug). International Tailoring Congress. Photo. P 13.
| 2046 | **413** 2p. slate-violet, magenta and brown | 15 | 15 |

1970 (25 Aug). 12th European Swimming, Diving and Waterpolo Championships, Barcelona. P 13.
| 2047 | **414** 2p. light drab, ultram and bluish green | 15 | 15 |

415 Concha Espina

416 Survey Map of Southern Spain and North Africa

1970 (21 Sept). Spanish Writers. T **415** and similar vert portraits. Photo. P 13×12½.
2048	50c. blue, bistre-brown and pale buff	15	15
2049	1p. bright reddish violet, myrtle green and pale drab	15	15
2050	1p.50 blue-green, blue and pale drab	15	15
2051	2p. olive-green, green and pale buff	20	15
2052	2p.50 brn-pur, reddish vio and pale ochre	20	15
2053	3p.50 red, brown and pale lilac	20	15
2048/2053	Set of 6	95	80

Writers:—1p. Guillen de Castro, 1p.50, J. R. Jimenez; 2p. G. A. Becquer; 2p.50, Miguel de Unamuno; 3p.50. J. M. Gabriel y Galan.

1970 (12 Oct). Explorers and Colonisers of America (10th Series). Mexico. Portraits as T **309** and similar designs inscr "1970" at foot. P 12½×13 (1p.50) or 13×12½ (others).
2054	40c. bronze-green/pale green	20	15
2055	1p.50 brown/pale blue	20	15
2056	2p. slate-violet/pale cream	70	20
2057	3p.50 deep bluish green/pale green	20	15
2058	6p. turquoise-blue/pale flesh	30	15
2054/2058	Set of 5	1·50	75

Designs: Vert—40c. House in Queretaro; 2p. Vasco de Quiroga; 3p.50, F. Juan de Zumarraga; 6p. Morelia Cathedral. Horiz—1p.50, Cathedral, Mexico City.

1970 (20 Oct). Centenary of Spanish Geographical and Survey Institute. Photo. P 13.
| 2059 | **416** 2p. multicoloured | 20 | 15 |

417 "The Adoration of the Shepherds" (El Greco)

418 U. N. Emblem and New York Headquarters

1970 (30 Oct). Christmas. T **417** and similar vert design. Multicoloured. Photo. P 13.
| 2060 | 1p.50 Type **417** | 15 | 15 |
| 2061 | 2p. "The Adoration of the Shepherds" (Murillo) | 15 | 15 |

1970 (3 Nov). 25th Anniv of United Nations. Photo. P 13.
| 2062 | **418** 8p. multicoloured | 20 | 15 |

SPAIN

419 Ripoll Monastery

420 Pilgrims' Route Map

1970 (12 Nov). Ripoll Monastery. Horiz designs as T **419**. Recess. P 12½×13.

2063	2p. purple and violet	50	20
2064	3p.50 brown-purple and red-orange	20	15
2065	5p. green and slate-green	1·10	20
2063/2065	Set of 3	1·60	50

Designs:—2p. Entrance; 5p. Cloisters.

1971 (4 Jan). Holy Year of Compostela (1st Issue). "St. James in Europe." T **420** and similar designs. Recess. P 13×12½ (vert) or 12½×13 (horiz).

2066	50c. sepia and turquoise-blue	15	15
2067	1p. black and brown	15	15
2068	1p.50 plum and deep bluish green	25	20
2069	2p. blackish brown and deep plum	30	15
2070	3p. grey-blue and violet-blue	25	20
2071	4p. greyish olive	45	20
2066/2071	Set of 6	1·40	90

Designs: Vert—1p. Statue of St. Brigid, Vadstena (Sweden); 1p.50, St. Jacques' Church tower, Paris; 2p. "St. James" (carving from altar, Pistoia, Italy). Horiz—3p. St. David's Cathedral, (Wales); 4p. Carving from Ark of Charlemagne (Aachen, West Germany).

See also Nos. 2105/11 and 2121/8.

1971 (20 Jan–3 May). Provincial Costumes. Vert designs as T **375**. Multicoloured. Photo. P 13×12½.

2072	6p. Valencia	25	20
2073	8p. Valladolid (10.2)	45	20
2074	8p. Vizcaya (9.3)	45	20
2075	8p. Zamora (13.4)	45	20
2076	8p. Zaragoza (3.5)	45	20
2072/2076	Set of 5	1·90	90

1825/1836, 1897/1908, 1956/1967, 2007/2018,
2072/2076 Set of 53 .... 8·00 7·00

1971 (24 Mar). Stamp Day and Ignacio Zuloaga Commemoration. Multicoloured designs similar to T **409**, showing paintings. Photo. P 13.

2077	50c. "My Uncle Daniel"	20	15
2078	1p. "Segovia" (horiz)	20	15
2079	1p.50 "The Duchess of Alba"	20	15
2080	2p. "Ignacio Zuloaga" (self-portrait)	20	15
2081	3p. "Juan Belmonte"	25	15
2082	4p. "The Countess of Noailles"	20	15
2083	5p. "Pablo Uranga"	30	20
2084	8p. "Boatmen's Houses, Lerma" (horiz)	30	25
2077/2084	Set of 8	1·70	1·20

421 Amadeo Vives (composer)

422 Europa Chain

1971 (20 Apr). Spanish Celebrities. T **421** and similar vert portraits. Multicoloured. Photo. P 13.

2085	1p. Type **421**	20	15
2086	2p. St. Teresa of Avila (mystic)	25	20
2087	8p. B. Perez Galdos (writer)	25	20
2088	15p. R. Menendez Pidal (writer)	20	20
2085/2088	Set of 4	85	70

(Des H. Haflidason. Photo.)

1971 (29 Apr). Europa. P 13.

2089	**422**	2p. red-brown, bluish vio and pale blue	70	30
2090		8p. bistre-brown, emer and pale green	45	45

1971 (6 May). World Stamp Day. Vert design similar to T **381**. Photo. P 13×12½.

2091	2p. black, blue and olive-green	20	15

Design:—2p. Spanish 6c. stamp of 1850 with "A.s" postmark.

423 Gymnast on Vaulting-horse

1971 (14 May). 9th European Male Gymnastics Cup Championships, Madrid. T **423** and similar diamond-shaped design. Multicoloured. Photo. P 12½.

2092	1p. Type **423**	20	15
2093	2p. Gymnast on bar	20	15

424 Great Bustard   E **425** Roman Chariot

1971 (24 May). Spanish Fauna (1st series). T **424** and similar multicoloured designs. Photo. P 13.

2094	1p. Type **424**	35	20
2095	2p. Lynx	30	15
2096	3p. Brown bear	30	15
2097	5p. Red-legged partridge (vert)	45	25
2098	8p. Spanish ibex (vert)	65	45
2094/2098	Set of 5	1·85	1·10

See also Nos. 2160/4, 2192/6, 2250/4, 2317/21, 2452/6 and 2579/83.

1971 (1 June). EXPRESS. Type E **425** and similar design. Photo. P 13.

E2099	10p. apple-green, black and red	20	15
E2100	15p. new blue, black and scarlet	20	15

Design: Vert—15 p. Letter encircling Globe.

426 Legionaries in Battle

427 "Children of the World"

1971 (21 June). 50th Anniversary of Spanish Foreign Legion. T **426** and similar diamond-shaped designs. Multicoloured. Photo. P 12½.

2101	1p. Type **426**	20	20
2102	2p. Ceremonial parade	25	20
2103	5p. Memorial service	30	20
2104	8p. Officer and mobile column	30	25
2101/2104	Set of 4	1·00	80

1971 (24 July). Holy Year of Compostela (2nd Issue). Designs similar to T **420**. Recess. P 12½×13 (horiz) or 13×12½ (vert).

2105	50c. plum and deep bluish	20	15
2106	6p. light violet-blue	20	15
2107	7p. purple and dull purple	45	20
2108	7p.50 brown-red and dull purple	20	20

SPAIN

2109	8p. dull purple and green	20	20
2110	9p. reddish violet and green	20	20
2111	10p. brown and green	25	20
2105/2111 Set of 7		1·60	1·20

Designs: Horiz—50c. Pilgrims' route map of northern Spain; 7p.50, Cloisters, Najera Monastery; 9p. Eunate Monastery. Vert—6p. "Pilgrims" (sculpture, Royal Hospital, Burgos); 7p. Gateway. St. Domingo de la Calzada Monastery; 8p. Statue of Christ, Puente de la Reina; 10p. Cross of Roncesvalles.

1971 (20 Sept). 25th Anniv of United Nations Children Fund. Photo. P 13.

| 2112 | 427 | 8p. multicoloured | 25 | 20 |

428 "Battle of Lepanto" (L. Valdés)

429 Hockey Players

1971 (7 Oct). 400th Anniversary of Battle of Lepanto T **428** and similar designs Recess. P 12½×13 (5p.) or 13×12½ (others).

2113	2p. deep bluish green and sepia	45	15
2114	5p. chocolate and blackish brown	90	20
2115	8p. violet-blue and carmine	75	75
2113/2115 Set of 3		1·90	1·00

Designs: Vert—2p. "Don John of Austria" (S. Coello); 8p. Standard of the Holy League.

1971 (15 Oct). World Hockey Cup Championships, Barcelona. Photo. P 13.

| 2116 | 429 | 5p. multicoloured | 65 | 15 |

430 de Havilland DH.9B Biplane over Seville

431 "The Nativity" (detail from altar, Avia)

1971 (25 Oct). 50th Anniv of Spanish Airmail Services. T **430** and similar horiz design. Multicoloured. Photo. P 13.

| 2117 | 2p. Type **430** | 30 | 20 |
| 2118 | 15p. Boeing 747-100 airliner over Madrid | 30 | 20 |

1971 (4 Nov). Christmas. T **431** and similar horiz design Multicoloured. Photo. P 12½×13.

| 2119 | 2p. Type **431** | 20 | 15 |
| 2120 | 8p. "The Birth" (detail from altar, Sagas) | 20 | 15 |

1971 (30 Dec). Holy Year of Compostela (3rd Issue). Designs similar to T **420**. Recess. P 12½×13 (vert) or 12½×13 (horiz).

2121	1p. black and deep bluish green	20	15
2122	1p.50 deep slate-violet and purple	25	25
2123	2p. blue and deep green	90	20
2124	2p.50 violet and claret	15	15
2125	3p. purple and brown-red	50	20
2126	3p.50 bronze-green and salmon	20	15
2127	4p. chocolate and turquoise-blue	20	15
2128	5p. black and green	40	15
2121/2128 Set of 8		2·50	1·30

Designs: Vert—1p. Santiago Cathedral; 2p. Lugo Cathedral; 3p. Astorga Cathedral; 4p. San Tirso, Sahagun. Horiz—1p.50, Pilgrim approaching Santiago de Compostela; 2p.50, Villafranca del Bierzo; 3p.50, San Marcos. Leon; 5p. San Martin, Fromista.

1972 (27 Jan). Spanish Celebrities. Vert portraits similar to T **408**. Recess. P 13×12½.

2129	15p. bronze-green and orange-brown	30	15
2130	25p. blackish green and yellow-green	30	20
2131	50p. purple brown and crimson	55	20
2129/2131 Set of 3		1·00	50

Designs:—15p. Emilia Pardo Bazan (novelist); 25p. José de Espronceda (poet); 50p. Fernan Gonzalez (first king of Castile).

432 Ski Jumping

433 Title-page of *Don Quixote* (1605)

1972 (10 Feb). Winter Olympic Games, Sapporo, Japan. T **432** and similar multicoloured design. Photo. P 13.

| 2132 | 2p. Type **432** | 45 | 20 |
| 2133 | 15p. Figure skating (vert) | 25 | 25 |

1972 (24 Feb). International Book Year. Recess. P 13×12½.

| 2134 | **433** | 2p. brown-lake and brown | 15 | 15 |

1972 (24 Mar). Stamp Day and Solana Commemoration. Multicoloured designs similar to T **409**, showing paintings. Photo. P 13.

2135	1p. "Clowns" (horiz)	20	20
2136	2p. "Solana and Family" (self-portrait)	35	15
2137	3p. "Blind Musician"	45	15
2138	4p. "Return of the Fishermen"	25	15
2139	5p. "Decorating Masks"	1·30	30
2140	7p. "The Bibliophile"	60	20
2141	10p. "Merchant Navy Captain"	60	20
2142	15p. "Pombo Reunion" (horiz)	55	25
2135/2142 Set of 8		4·00	1·50

434 *Abies pinsapo*

435 "Europeans"

1972 (21 Apr). Spanish Flora (1st series). T **434** and similar vert designs. Multicoloured. Photo. P 13.

2143	1p. Type **434**	25	15
2144	2p. Strawberry tree (*Arbutus unedo*)	40	15
2145	3p. Maritime pine (*Pinus pinaster*)	45	15
2146	5p. Holm oak (*Quercus ilex*)	70	25
2147	8p. *Juniperus thurifera*	40	25
2143/2147 Set of 5		2·10	85

See also Nos. 2178/82, 2278/82 and 2299/303.

(Des P. Huovinen (8p.). Photo)

1972 (2 May). Europa. T **435** and similar vert design. Multi coloured. P 13.

| 2148 | 2p. Type **435** | 1·30 | 30 |
| 2149 | 8p. "Communications" | 75 | 45 |

436 Cordoba Pre-stamp Postmark

437 Fencing

1972 (6 May). World Stamp Day. Photo. P 12½×13.

| 2150 | **436** | 2p. carmine, black and light buff | 15 | 15 |

1972 (22 June). Spanish Castles (6th Series). Designs similar to T **368**. Recess. P 13×12½.

2151	1p. brown and turquoise-green	50	40
2152	2p. brown and bronze-green	85	20
2153	3p. red-brown and claret	90	20
2154	5p. blue-green and steel-blue	90	20
2155	10p. reddish violet and slate-blue	2·75	20
2151/2155 Set of 5		5·25	1·10

Castles: Vert—1p. Sajazarra. Horiz—2p. Santa Catalina; 3p. Bar; 5p. San Servando; 10p. Pedraza.

275

1972 (26 Aug). Olympic Games, Munich. T **437** and similar multicoloured designs. Photo. P 13.
2156	1p. Type **437**	25	15
2157	2p. Weightlifting (vert)	30	15
2158	5p. Rowing (vert)	25	20
2159	8p. Pole vaulting (vert)	25	20
2156/2159 Set of 4		1·00	65

438 Chamois

439 Brigadier M. A. de Ustariz

1972 (14 Sept). Spanish Fauna (2nd series). T **438** and similar multicoloured designs. Photo. P 13.
2160	1p. Pyrenean desman	25	20
2161	2p. Type **438**	25	20
2162	3p. Wolf	30	20
2163	5p. Egyptian mongoose (horiz)	70	20
2164	7p. Small-spotted genet (horiz)	65	20
2160/2164 Set of 5		2·00	90

1972 (12 Oct). "Spain in the New World" (1st series). 450th Anniv of Puerto Rico. T **439** and similar multi coloured designs. Photo. P 13.
2165	1p. Type **439**	20	15
2166	2p. View of San Juan, 1870 (horiz)	30	15
2167	5p. View of San Juan, 1625 (horiz)	50	20
2168	8p. Map of Plaza de Bahia, 1792 (horiz)	40	40
2165/2168 Set of 4		1·30	85

See also Nos. 2212/15, 2271/4, 2338/41 and 2430/3.

440 Façade of Monastery

441 Grand Lyceum Theatre

1972 (26 Oct). Monastery of St. Thomas, Avila. T **440** and similar designs. Recess. P 12½×13 (15p.) or 13×12½ (others).
2169	2p. grey-green and turquoise-blue	95	20
2170	8p. reddish purple and blackish brown	80	30
2171	15p. deep violet-blue and purple	45	20
2169/2171 Set of 3		2·00	60

Designs: Vert—8p. Interior of Monastery. Horiz—15p. Cloisters.

1972 (7 Nov). 125th Anniv of Grand Lyceum Theatre, Barcelona. Recess. P 12½×13.
2172	**441**	8p. brown and pale blue	30	20

442 "The Nativity"

443 J. de Herrera and Escorial

1972 (14 Nov). Christmas. Murals in Royal Collegiate Basilica of San Isidoro, Leon. T **442** and similar horiz design. Multicoloured. Photo. P 13.
2173	2p. Type **442**	20	15
2174	8p. "The Annunciation"	20	15

1973 (29 Jan). Spanish Architects. T **443** and similar horiz designs. Recess. P 12½×13.
2175	8p. green and sepia	50	15
2176	10p. indigo and blackish brown	1·80	20

2177	15p. greenish blue and turquoise-green	35	20
2175/2177 Set of 3		2·40	50

Designs:—10p. J. de Villanueva and Prado; 15p. V. Rodriguez and Apollo Fountain, Madrid.

See also Nos. 2295/7.

444 Apollonias canariensis

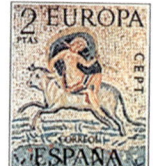
445 Roman Mosaic

1973 (21 Mar). Spanish Flora (2nd series). Canary Islands. T **444** and similar multicoloured designs. Photo. P 13.
2178	1p. Type **444**	20	20
2179	2p. *Myrica faya* (vert)	65	20
2180	4p. *Phoenix canariensis* (vert)	20	20
2181	5p. *Ilex canariensis* (vert)	80	25
2182	15p. *Dracaena draco* (vert)	40	20
2178/2182 Set of 5		2·00	95

1973 (30 Apr). Europa. T **445** and similar design. Photo. P 13×12½ (2p.) or 13 (8p.).
2183	2p. multicoloured	70	25
2184	8p. cobalt and red	65	25

Design: Horiz (37×26 mm)—8p. Europa "Posthorn".

1973 (5 May). World Stamp Day. Vert design similar to T **381**. Photo. P 13×12½.
2185	2p. red, Prussian blue and black	20	15

Design:—2p. Spanish 6r. stamp of 1853 with Madrid postmark.

446 Iznajar Dam

447 Black-bellied Sandgrouse (*Pterocles orientalis*)

1973 (9 June). 11th Congress of International High Dams Commission, Madrid Photo. P 12½×13.
2186	**446**	8p. multicoloured	20	15

1973 (11 June). Tourist Series. Designs similar to T **340**. Recess. P 13.
2187	1p. sepia and blackish olive	25	15
2188	2p. blackish green and green	60	15
2189	3p. chestnut and brown	60	15
2190	5p. slate-violet and deep blue	1·50	20
2191	8p. lake and deep bluish green	70	20
2187/2191 Set of 5		3·50	75

Designs: Horiz—1p. Gateway, Onate University, Guipuzcoa; 2p. Town Square, Lugo; 5p. Columbus' House, Las Palmas; 8p. Windmills, La Mancha. Vert—3p. Llerena Square, Badajoz.

1973 (3 July). Spanish Fauna (3rd series). Birds. T **447** and similar multicoloured designs. Photo. P 13.
2192	1p. Type **447**	30	20
2193	2p. Black stork (*Ciconia nigra*)	40	20
2194	5p. Azure-winged magpie (*Cyanopica cyanus*) (vert)	70	50
2195	7p. Imperial eagle (*Aquila heliaca*)	75	20
2196	15p. Red-crested pochard (*Netta rufina*) (vert)	35	25
2192/2196 Set of 5		2·25	1·20

448 Hermandad Standard-bearer, Castile, 1488

449 Fishes in Net and Trawler

SPAIN

1973 (17 July). Spanish Military Uniforms (1st series). T **448** and similar multicoloured designs. Photo. P 13.

2197	1p. Type **448**	20	20
2198	2p. Mounted knight, Castile, 1493 (horiz)	55	15
2199	3p. Arquebusier, 1534	60	15
2200	7p. Mounted arquebusier, 1560	40	20
2201	8p. Infantry sergeant, 1567	40	20
2197/2201	Set of 5	2·00	85

See also Nos. 2225/9, 2255/9, 2290/4, 2322/6, 2410/14, 2441/5, 2472/6 and 2499/2503.

1973 (12 Sept). World Fishing Fan and Congress, Virgo. Photo. P 13.

| 2202 | **449** | 2p. multicoloured | 15 | 15 |

450 Conference Building

451 Leon Cathedral, Nicaragua

1973 (14 Sept). International Telecommunications Union Conference, Torremolinos. Photo. P 13.

| 2203 | **450** | 8p. multicoloured | 20 | 15 |

1973 (29 Sept). Stamp Day and Vicente Lopez Commemoration. Multicoloured designs similar to T **409**, showing paintings. Photo. P 13.

2204	1p. "Ferdinand VII"	25	15
2205	2p. Self-portrait	25	15
2206	3p. "La Senora de Carvallo"	25	15
2207	4p. "M. de Castelldosrrius"	25	15
2208	5p. "Isabella II"	40	20
2209	7p. "Goya"	25	20
2210	10p. "Maria Amalia of Saxony"	25	20
2211	15p. "Felix Lopez, the Organist"	25	20
2204/2211	Set of 8	2·00	1·30

1973 (12 Oct). "Spain in the New World" (2nd series). Nicaragua. T **451** and similar multicoloured designs, showing buildings. Photo. P 13.

2212	1p. Type **451**	20	15
2213	2p. Subtiava Church	35	20
2214	5p. Colonial-style house (vert)	60	25
2215	8p. Rio San Juan Castle	35	20
2212/2215	Set of 4	1·40	75

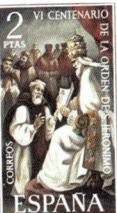

452 Pope Gregory XI receiving St. Jerome's Petition

453 Courtyard

1973 (18 Oct). 600th Anniv of Order of St. Jerome. Photo. P 12½×13.

| 2216 | **452** | 2p. multicoloured | 15 | 15 |

1973 (26 Oct). Monastery of Santo Domingo de Silos, Burgos. T **453** and similar designs. Recess. P 12½×13 (8p.) or 13×12½ (others).

2217	2p. claret and deep brown	55	15
2218	8p. purple and blue	20	15
2219	15p. slate-blue and deep bluish green	25	20
2217/2219	Set of 3	90	45

Designs: Horiz—8p. Cloisters. Vert—15p. "Three Saints" (statue).

454 "The Nativity" (pillar capital, Silos)

455 Map of Spain and the Americas

1973 (6 Nov). Christmas. T **454** and similar multicoloured design. Photo. P 13.

| 2220 | 2p. Type **454** | 20 | 15 |
| 2221 | 8p. "Adoration of the Kings" (bas relief, Butrera) (horiz) | 15 | 15 |

1973 (11 Dec). 500th Anniv of Printing in Spain. T **455** and similar designs. Recess. P 12½×13 (1p.) or 13×12½ (others).

2222	1p. indigo and grey-green	40	15
2223	7p. reddish violet and deep blue	25	20
2224	15p. blackish green and purple	30	25
2222/2224	Set of 3	85	55

Designs: Vert—7p. "Teacher and Pupils" (ancient woodcut, Valencia); 15p. Title-page of *Los Sinodales*.

1974 (5 Jan). Spanish Military Uniforms (2nd series). Vert designs as T **448**. Multicoloured. Photo. P 13.

2225	1p. Mounted arquebusier, 1603	20	15
2226	2p. Arquebusier, 1632	65	20
2227	3p. Mounted cuirassier, 1635	80	20
2228	5p. Mounted drummer, 1677	1·20	35
2229	9p. Musketeers, "Viejos Morados" Regiment, 1694	35	25
2225/2229	Set of 5	3·00	1·00

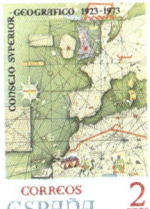

456 14th-century Nautical Chart

457 M. Biada (construction engineer) and Jones and Potts Locomotive *Mataro*, 1848

1974 (26 Jan). 50th Anniv of Spanish Higher Geographical Council. Photo. P 13.

| 2230 | **456** | 2p. multicoloured | 15 | 15 |

1974 (2 Apr). 125th Anniv of Barcelona-Mataro Railway. Photo. P 13×12½.

| 2231 | **457** | 2p. multicoloured | 15 | 15 |

458 Stamp Collector, Album and Magnifier

459 "Woman with Offering"

1974 (4 April). "ESPANA 75" International Stamp Exhibition, Madrid (1st Issue). T **458** and similar designs. Photo. P 13 (2p.) or 12½ (others).

2232	2p. multicoloured	20	20
2233	5p. blue, black and cinnamon	45	35
2234	2p. multicoloured	35	30
2232/2234	Set of 3	90	75

Designs: Diamond-shaped (43×43 mm)—5p. Exhibition emblem; 8p. Globe and arrows.

See also No. **MS**2298.

1974 (29 Apr). Europa. Stone Sculptures. T **459** and similar vert design. Multicoloured Photo. P 13.

| 2235 | 2p. Type **459** | 75 | 20 |
| 2236 | 8p. "Woman from Baza" | 35 | 30 |

460 2r. Stamp of 1854 with Seville Postmark

461 Jaime Balmes (philosopher) and Monastery

SPAIN

1974 (6 May). World Stamp Day. Photo. P 13×12½.
2237 **460** 2p. multicoloured 15 15

1974 (28 May). Spanish Celebrities. T **461** and similar horiz designs. Recess. P 13×12½.
2238 8p. blackish brown and indigo 20 20
2239 10p. deep red-brown and pale claret 65 35
2240 15p. deep blue and purple-brown 25 20
2238/2240 Set of 3 .... 95 70
Designs:—10p. Pedro Poveda (educationalist) and mountain village; 15p. Jorge Juan (cosmographer and mariner) and shipyard.

462 Bramante's "Little Temple", Rome

463 Roman Aqueduct, Segovia

1974 (4 June). Centenary of Spanish Fine Arts Academy. Rome. Photo. P 12½×13.
2241 **462** 5p. multicoloured 20 20

1974 (25 June). Spain as a Province of the Roman Empire. T **463** and similar designs. Recess. P 13×12½ (horiz) or 12½×13 (vert).
2242 1p. black and purple-brown 10 10
2243 2p. brown and yellow-green 35 10
2244 3p. sepia and chestnut 10 10
2245 4p. indigo and green 10 10
2246 5p. dull purple and deep blue 10 10
2247 7p. bright purple and grey-green 10 10
2248 8p. myrtle-green and crimson 20 15
2249 9p. brown-lake and bright purple 20 20
2242/2249 Set of 8 .... 1·20 85
Designs: Horiz—2p. Roman Bridge, Alcantara; 3p. Martial (poet) giving public reading; 5p. Theatre, Merida; 7p. Ossio, 1st Bishop of Cordoba, addressing the Synod. Vert—4p. Triumphal Arch, Bara; 8p. Ruins of Curia, Talavera la Vieja; 9p. Statue of Emperor Trajan.

464 Tortoise

465 Swimmer making Rescue

1974 (3 July). Spanish Fauna (4th series). Reptiles. T **464** and similar horiz designs. Multicoloured. Photo. P 13.
2250 1p. Type **464** 20 15
2251 2p. Chameleon 35 15
2252 5p. Gecko 55 55
2253 7p. Green lizard 45 25
2254 15p. Adder 20 15
2250/2254 Set of 5 .... 1·60 1·10

1974 (17 July). Spanish Military Uniforms (3rd series). Vert designs as T **448**. Multicoloured. Photo. P 13.
2255 1p. Dismounted trooper, Hussars de la Muerte, 1705 .... 15 10
2256 2p. Officer, Royal Regiment of Artillery, 1710 .... 40 10
2257 3p. Drummer and fifer, Granada Regiment, 1734 .... 45 15
2258 7p. Guidon-bearer, Numancia Dragoons, 1737 .... 35 15
2259 8p. Ensign with standard, Zamora Regiment, 1739 .... 15 15
2255/2259 Set of 5 .... 1·30 60

1974 (5 Sept). 18th World Life-saving Championships, Barcelona. Photo. P 13.
2260 **465** 2p. multicoloured 20 15

1974 (29 Sept). Stamp Day and E. Rosales (painter) Commemoration. Multicoloured designs as T **409**. Photo. P 13.
2261 1p. "Tobias and the Angel" 15 10
2262 2p. "Self-portrait" 15 15
2263 3p. "Testament of Isabella the Catholic" (horiz) 15 10
2264 4p. "Nena" 15 15
2265 5p. "Presentation of Don Juan of Austria" (horiz) 15 10
2266 7p. "The First Steps" (horiz) 15 15
2267 10p. "St. John the Evangelist" 30 15
2268 15p. "St. Matthew the Evangelist" 15 15
2261/2268 Set of 8 .... 1·10 85

466 Figure with Letter and Posthorns

467 Sobremonte's House, Cordoba

1974 (9 Oct). Centenary of Universal Postal Union. T **466** and similar vert design. Multicoloured. Photo. P 13.
2269 2p. Type **466** 15 10
2270 8p. UPU monument, Berne 20 15

1974 (12 Oct). "Spain in the New World" (3rd series). Argentina. T **467** and similar multicoloured designs. Photo. P 13.
2271 1p. Type **467** 15 10
2272 2p. Town Hall, Buenos Aires 35 15
2273 5p. Ruins of St. Ignacio de Mini (vert) ... 30 15
2274 10p. "The Gaucho" (Martin Fierro) (vert) . 20 15
2271/2274 Set of 4 .... 1·00 60

468 "Nativity" (detail, Valdavia Church)

469 Teucrium lanigerum

1974. Christmas. Church Fonts. T **468** and similar multicoloured design. Photo. P 13.
2275 2p. Type **468** (4.11) 10 10
2276 3p. "Adoration of the Kings", Valcebro Church (vert) (2.12) 15 10
2277 8p. As No. 2276 (vert) (4.11) 15 10
2275/2277 Set of 3 .... 35 95

1974 (8 Nov). Spanish Flora (3rd series). Wild Flowers. T **469** and similar vert designs. Multicoloured. Photo. P 13.
2278 1p. Type **469** 15 10
2279 2p. Hypericum ericoides 20 10
2280 4p. Thymus longiflorus 15 10
2281 5p. Anthyllis onobrychioides 25 20
2282 8p. Helianthemum paniculatum 15 15
2278/2282 Set of 5 .... 80 60
The 1 and 8p. stamps are wrongly inscribed "Teucriun" and "Helianthemun" respectively.

470 Leyre Monastery

471 Spanish 6c. and 5p. Stamps of 1850 and 1975

278

SPAIN

1974 (10 Dec). Leyre Monastery Commemoration. T **470** and similar designs. Recess. P 13×12½ (8p.) or 12½×13 (others).

2283	2p. deep slate and bronze-green	50	10
2284	8p. carmine-red and chestnut	15	10
2285	15p. bottle-green & deep grey-green	35	10
2283/2285 Set of 3		90	25

Designs: Vert—8p. Pillars and bas-relief. Horiz—15p. Crypt.

1975 (2 Jan). 125th Anniv of Spanish Postage Stamps. T **471** and similar designs. Recess. P 13.

2286	2p. blue-black	35	35
2287	3p. deep brown and deep dull green	45	40
2288	8p. purple and deep violet-blue	1·00	45
2289	10p. deep dull green and deep brown	50	40
2286/2289 Set of 4		2·10	1·40

Designs: Horiz—3p. Mail coach, 1850; 8p. Indies service sailing packet. Vert—10p. St. Mark's Chapel.

1975 (7 Jan). Spanish Military Uniforms (4th series). Vert designs as T **448**. Multicoloured. Photo. P 13.

2290	1p. Toledo regiment, 1750	15	10
2291	2p. Royal Artillery Corps, 1762	35	15
2292	3p. Queen's Regiment of the Line, 1763	1·70	25
2293	5p. Vitoria Regiment of Fusiliers, 1766	50	15
2294	10p. Sagunto Dragoon Regiment, 1775	1·50	20
2290/2294 Set of 5		3·75	75

1975 (25 Feb). Spanish Architects (2nd series). Horiz designs as T **443**. Recess. P 13.

2295	8p. black and deep green	15	15
2296	10p. reddish brown and brown-red	45	10
2297	15p. black and deep brown	20	15
2295/2297 Set of 3		70	35

Designs:—8p. Antonio Gaudi and apartment building, 10p. Antonio Palacios and palace; 15p. Secundino Zuazo and block of flats.

472 Agate Casket   **473** Almonds

1975 (4 Apr). "Espana 75" International Stamp Exhibition, Madrid (2nd issue). Two sheets 124×88 mm or 88×124 mm containing T **472** and similar designs. Recess. P 13.

MS2298 (a) 2p. dp turquoise-blue & blackish brown; 8p. brown & dp turq-bl; 15p. carm & blackish brn; 50p. carm, brn & blackish brn. (b) 3p. bottle green & blackish brown; 10p. bottle green, brown & blackish brown; 12p. ind & blackish brn; 25p. ind, brn & blackish brown .... 14·00 16·00

Designs: Vert—3p. Recesvinto votive crown; 10p. Chalice of Infanta Donna Urraca; 12p. Processional monstrance, St. Domingo de Silos; 25p. Charles V and sword. Horiz—8p. Evangelistary cover; 15p. Sword of Boabdil; 50p. Aliseda earring and bracelet.

1975 (21 Apr). Spanish Flora (4th series). Fruits. T **473** and similar multicoloured designs. Photo. P 13.

2299	1p. Type **473**	10	10
2300	2p. Pomegranates (vert)	25	15
2301	3p. Oranges (vert)	25	10
2302	4p. Chestnuts (vert)	20	10
2303	5p. Apples (vert)	20	15
2299/2303 Set of 5		90	55

474 Woman and pitcher, La Aranya   **475** Early Leon Postmark

1975 (28 Apr). Europa. Primitive cave paintings. T **474** and similar design. Photo. P 13.

2304	3p. brown-red, brown & stone	35	15
2305	12p. mauve black and brown	70	25

Design: Horiz—12p. Horse, Tito Bustillo.

1975 (6 May). World Stamp Day. Photo. P 12½×13.

2306	**475**	3p. greenish blue, buff and black	10	10

476 Emblem and Inscription   **477** Farm Scene

1975 (12 May). 1st General Assembly of World Tourism Organization, Madrid. Photo. P 13.

2307	**476**	3p. royal blue	10	10

1975 (14 May). 25th Anniv of "Feria del Campo". Photo. P 13.

2308	**477**	3p. multicoloured	10	10

478 Heads of Different Races   **479** Virgin of Cabeza Sanctuary and Forces Emblems

1975 (3 June). International Women's Year. Photo. P 13.

2309	**478**	3p. multicoloured	10	10

1975 (18 June). Defence of Virgin of Cabeza Sanctuary during Civil War Commemoration. Photo. P 13.

2310	**479**	3p. multicoloured	10	10

1975 (25 June). Tourist series. Designs as T **340**. Recess. P 13.

2311	1p. blackish lilac and reddish violet	15	10
2312	2p. deep brown and brown	15	10
2313	3p. brownish black and grey-blue	20	10
2314	4p. carmine and salmon	20	10
2315	5p. greenish black and myrtle-green	30	15
2316	7p. indigo and deep ultramarine	35	15
2311/2316 Set of 6		1·20	60

Designs: Horiz—1p. Cervantes' cell, Argamasilla de Alba; 2p. St. Martin's Bridge, Toledo; 3p. St. Peter's Church, Tarrasa. Vert—4p. Alhambra archway, Granada; 5p. Mijas village, Malaga; 7p. St. Mary's Chapel, Tarrasa.

480 Salamander Lizard   **481** Child

1975 (9 July). Spanish Fauna (5th series) Reptiles and Amphibians. T **480** and similar horiz designs. Multicoloured. Photo. P 13.

2317	1p. Type **480**	10	10
2318	2p. Triton lizard	25	10
2319	3p. Tree-frog	25	10
2320	6p. Toad	20	15
2321	7p. Frog	20	15
2317/2321 Set of 5		90	55

1975 (17 July). Spanish Military Uniforms (5th series). Vert designs as T **448**. Multicoloured. Photo. P 13.

2322	1p. Montesa Regiment, 1788	15	10
2323	2p. Asturias Regiment of Fusiliers, 1789	55	20
2324	3p. Infantry of the Line, 1802	15	10
2325	4p. Royal Artillery Corps, 1803	15	15
2326	7p. Royal Engineers Regiment, 1809	15	15
2322/2326 Set of 5		1·00	65

279

1975 (9 Sept). Child Welfare. Photo. P 13.
2327 **481** 3p. multicoloured 10 10

482 Scroll   **483** "Blessing the Birds"

1975 (25 Sept). Latin Notaries' Congress, Barcelona. Photo. P 13.
2328 **482** 3p. multicoloured 10 10

1975 (29 Sept). Stamp Day and Millenary of Gerona Cathedral. Beatitude Miniatures. T **483** and similar multicoloured designs. Photo. P 13.
2329	1p. Type **483**	15	10
2330	2p. "Angel and River of Life" (vert)	15	10
2331	3p. "Angel at Gates of Paradise" (vert)	15	10
2332	4p. "Fox seizing Cockerel"	15	10
2333	6p. "Daniel and the Lions"	15	10
2334	7p. "Blessing the Multitude" (vert)	25	25
2335	10p. "The Four Horsemen of Apocalypse" (vert)	15	15
2336	12p. "Peacock and Snake" (vert)	20	15
2329/2336 Set of 8		1·20	95

484 Industry Emblems   **485** El Cabildo, Montevideo

1975 (7 Oct). Spanish industry. Recess. P 13.
2337 **484** 3p. deep magenta and deep purple.... 10 10

1975 (12 Oct). "Spain in the New World" (4th series). 150th Anniv of Uruguayan Independence. T **485** and similar multicoloured designs. Photo. P 13.
2338	1p. Type **485**	10	10
2339	2p. Ox wagon	20	10
2340	3p. Fortress, St. Teresa	25	10
2341	8p. Cathedral, Montevideo (vert)	20	15
2338/2341 Set of 4		65	40

486 San Juan de la Pena Monastery   **487** "Virgin and Child"

1975 (28 Oct). San Juan de la Pena Monastery Commemoration. T **486** and similar designs. Recess. P 13.
2342	3p. brown and bronze-green	30	10
2343	8p. deep magenta and deep lilac	15	10
2344	10p. crimson and cerise	25	15
2342/2344 Set of 3		65	30

Designs: Horiz—8p. Cloisters. Vert—10p. Pillars.

1975 (4 Nov). Christmas. Navarra Art. T **487** and similar multicoloured design. Photo. P 13.
| 2345 | 3p. Type **487** .... | 15 | 10 |
| 2346 | 12p. "Flight into Egypt" (horiz) .... | 15 | 10 |

King Juan Carlos I
22 November 1975

488 King Juan Carlos I   **489** Virgin of Pontevedra

1975 (29 Dec). Proclamation of King Juan Carlos I. T **488** and similar designs. Multicoloured. Photo. P 13×12½ (Nos. 2347/8) or 12½ (others).
2347	3p. Type **488**	15	10
2348	3p. Queen Sophia	15	10
2349	3p. King Juan Carlos I and Queen Sophia (33×33 mm)	15	10
2350	12p. As No. 2349 (33×33 mm)	15	15
2347/2350 Set of 4		55	40

1976 (2 Jan). Holy Year of Compostela. Recess. P 13.
2351 **489** 3p. brown and vermilion 15 10

490 Mountain Scene and Emblem   **491** Cosme Damian Churruca and San Juan Nepomuceno

1976 (10 Feb). Centenary of Catalunya Excursion Centre. Photo. P 13.
2352 **490** 6p. multicoloured 15 10

1976 (1 Mar). Spanish Navigators. T **491** and similar designs. Recess. P 13.
2353	7p. greenish black and agate	1·50	25
2354	12p. bluish violet	30	20
2355	50p. sepia, brown and grey-olive	55	15
2353/2355 Set of 3		2·10	65

Designs: Vert—12p. Luis de Requesens. Horiz—50p. Juan Sebastian del Cano and *Vitoria*.

492 Alexander Graham Bell and Telephone Equipment   **493** Pedestrian Crossing and Car

1976 (10 Mar). Telephone Centenary. Photo. P 13.
2356 **492** 3p. multicoloured .... 1·10 30

1976 (6 Apr). Road Safety. T **493** and similar multicoloured designs. Photo. P 13.
2357	1p. Type **493**	10	10
2358	3p. Dangerous driving (vert)	30	10
2359	5p. Wearing of seat-belts	20	15
2357/2359 Set of 3		55	30

494 St. George on Horseback   **495** Talavera Pottery

SPAIN

1976 (23 Apr). 700th Anniv of St. George's Guardianship of Alcoy. Photo. P 13.
2360	**494**	3p. multicoloured	15	10

1976 (3 May). Europa. Spanish Handicrafts. T **495** and similar horiz design. Multicoloured. Photo. P 13.
2361	3p. Type **495**	70	15
2362	12p. Camarinas lace-making	80	45

496 Spanish 6r. Stamp of 1851 with Coruna Postmark

497 Coins

1976 (6 May). World Stamp Day. Photo. P 13×12½.
2363	**496**	3p. vermilion, dull blue and black	15	10

1976 (26 May). Bimillenary of Zaragoza. Roman Antiquities. T **497** and similar designs. Recess. P 13.
2364	3p. reddish brown and black	2·10	15
2365	7p. deep violet-blue and black	95	35
2366	25p. bistre-brown and black	55	10
2364/2366	Set of 3	3·25	55

Designs: Horiz—7p. Plan of site and coin. Vert—25p. Mosaic.

498 Rifle, 1757

1976 (29 May). Bicentenary of American Revolution. T **498** and similar horiz designs. Recess. P 13.
2367	1p. deep ultramarine and sepia	15	10
2368	3p. myrtle green and sepia	95	10
2369	5p. myrtle green and sepia	45	15
2370	12p. sepia and myrtle green	45	25
2367/2370	Set of 4	1·80	55

Designs:—3p. Bernardo de Galvez; 5p. Richmond $1 banknote. 1861; 12p. Battle of Pensacola.

499 Customs-house, Cadiz

500 Savings Jar and "Industry"

1976 (9 June). Spanish Customs Buildings. T **499** and similar horiz designs. Recess. P 13.
2371	1p. chocolate and black	15	10
2372	3p. sepia and deep green	65	15
2373	7p. deep rose-lilac and brown-red	1·10	35
2371/2373	Set of 3	1·70	55

Buildings:—3p. Madrid; 7p. Barcelona.

1976 (16 June). Spanish Post Office. T **500** and similar multicoloured designs. Photo. P 13.
2374	1p. Type **500**	10	10
2375	3p. Railway mail-sorting van	35	10
2376	6p. Mounted postman (horiz)	15	15
2377	10p. Automatic letter sorting equipment (horiz)	25	15
2374/2377	Set of 4	75	45

501 King Juan Carlos I, Queen Sophia and Map of the Americas

502 Rowing

1976 (25 June). Royal Visit to America (1st issue). Photo. P 13.
2378	**501**	12p. multicoloured	25	15

See also No. 2434.

1976 (30 June). Tourist Series. Designs as T **340**. Recess. P 13.
2379	1p. sepia and slate-blue	15	10
2380	2p. myrtle-green and slate-blue	70	10
2381	3p. chocolate and brown	50	10
2382	4p. slate-blue and sepia	30	10
2383	7p. sepia and slate-blue	85	40
2384	12p. deep purple and lake	1·30	25
2379/2384	Set of 6	3·50	95

Designs: Horiz—1p. Cloisters, San Marcos, Leon; 2p. Las Canadas, Tenerife; 4p. Cruz de Tejeda, Las Palmas; 7p. Gredos, Avila; 12p. La Arruzafa, Cordoba. Vert—3p. Hospice of Catholic Kings, Santiago de Compostela.

1976 (9 July). Olympic Games. Montreal. T **502** and similar multicoloured designs. Photo. P 13.
2385	1p. Type **502**	15	10
2386	2p. Boxing	45	15
2387	3p. Wrestling (vert)	40	15
2388	12p. Basketball (vert)	25	15
2385/2388	Set of 4	1·10	55

503 King Juan Carlos I

503a King Juan Carlos I

1976 (15 July)–**84**.

(a) Photo. P 13
2389	**503**	10c. orange (8.2.77)	10	10
2390		25c. olive-yellow (6.6.77)	10	10
2391		30c. bright new blue (6.6.77)	10	10
2392		50c. purple (8.2.77)	10	10
2393		1p. bright yellowish green (8.2.77)	10	10
2394		1p.50 rosine	10	10
2395		2p. deep blue	10	10
2396		3p. blue-green	10	10
2397		4p. brt turquoise-green (8.2.77)	10	10
2398		5p. deep carmine-red	10	10
2399		6p. bright blue-green (6.6.77)	10	10
2400		7p. brown-olive	15	10
2401		8p. new blue (6.6.77)	15	10
2402		10p. bright magenta (6.6.77)	15	10
2403		12p. orange-brown	20	10
2403a		13p. dull chocolate (30.1.81)	25	10
2403b		14p. red-orange (26.4.82)	20	10
2404		15p. deep blue-violet (6.6.77)	30	10
2405		16p. sepia (18.2.80)	25	10
2405a		17p. deep slate-blue (27.6.84)	35	10
2406		19p. yellow-orange (18.2.80)	30	10
2407		20p. deep magenta (6.6.77)	30	10
2408		30p. deep grey-green (30.1.81)	40	10
2409		50p. vermilion (21.10.81)	70	10
2409a		60p. brt ultramarine (21.10.81)	80	10
2409b		75p. bright yellow-green (21.10.81)	1·00	25
2409c		85p. grey-black (21.10.81)	1·20	40

(b) Recess. P 13×12½
2409d	**503a**	100p. sepia (21.10.81)	1·40	10
2409e		200p. blackish green (21.10.81)	2·75	10
2409f		500p. deep grey-blue (21.10.81)	6·75	85
2389/2409f	Set of 30		17·00	3·75

The 17p. was issued on phosphorescent paper only, and the 30c., 1p.50 and 12p. on ordinary paper only. The other values were originally issued on ordinary paper but later printings were on phosphorescent paper: 1982–6, 14p.; 1983–10, 50c., 1, 2 to 5, 7, 16, 50p.; 1984–10, 15, 19, 30p.; 1985–8, 75p.; 1986–60p.; 1988–85, 100, 200p.; 1989–13, 500p.

In 1979 the 3, 5 and 8p. were issued in coils, in 1982 the 6 and 14p., in 1983 the 7 and 16p., and in 1984 the 10p. The coils had every fifth stamp numbered on the back.

281

SPAIN

1976 (17 July). Spanish Military Uniforms (6th series). Vert designs as T **448**. Multicoloured. Photo. P 13.
2410	1p. Alcantara Regiment, 1815	15	15
2411	2p. Regiment of the Line, 1821	85	15
2412	3p. Gala Engineers, 1825	30	15
2413	7p. Artillery Regiment, 1828	25	25
2414	25p. Light Infantry Regiment, 1830	30	20
2410/2414 Set of 5		1·70	80

504 Giving Blood   **505** Batitales Mosaic

1976 (7 Sept). Blood Donors Publicity. Recess. P 13.
2415	**504**	3p. carmine-red & brownish blk	20	15

1976 (22 Sept). Bimillenary of Lugo. T **505** and similar vert designs. Recess. P 13.
2416	1p. deep mauve and black	15	15
2417	3p. deep brown and black	20	15
2418	7p. carmine and green	50	25
2416/2418 Set of 3		75	50

Designs:—3p. Old city wall; 7p. Roman coins.

506 Parliament House, Madrid   **507** "The Nativity"

1976 (23 Sept). 63rd International Parliamentary Union Congress, Madrid. Recess. P 13.
2419	**506**	12p. sepia and bronze-green	20	15

1976 (29 Sept*). Stamp Day and L. E. Menendez (painter) Commemoration. Still Lifes. Multicoloured designs as T **409**. Photo. P 13.
2420	1p. "Jug, Cherries, Plums and Cheese"	10	10
2421	2p. "Jar, Melon, Oranges and Savouries"	10	10
2422	3p. "Barrel, Pears and Melon"	10	10
2423	4p. "Pigeons, Basket and Bowl"	15	10
2424	6p. "Fish and Oranges" (horiz)	20	10
2425	7p. "Melon and Bread" (horiz)	25	25
2426	10p. "Jug, Plums and Bread" (horiz)	25	15
2427	12p. "Pomegranates, Apples and Grapes" (horiz)	25	15
2420/2427 Set of 8		1·25	95

*Although first day covers appear with the 29 September postmark, because of a postal strike Nos. 2420/7 were not released until 1 October.

1976 (8 Oct). Christmas. Statuettes. T **507** and similar multicoloured design. Photo. P 13.
2428	3p. Type **507**	80	10
2429	12p. "St. Christopher carrying Holy Child" (vert)	1·50	55

508 Nicoya Church   **509** King Juan Carlos I, Queen Sophia and Map of South America

1976 (12 Oct). "Spain in the New World" (5th series). Costa Rica. T **508** and similar multicoloured designs. Photo. P 13.
2430	1p. Type **508**	15	10
2431	2p. Juan Vazquez de Coronado	25	15
2432	3p. Orosi Mission (horiz)	20	15
2433	12p. Tomas de Acosta	25	20
2430/2433 Set of 4		75	55

1976 (12 Oct). Royal Visit to America (2nd issue). Photo. P 13.
2434	**509**	12p. multicoloured	20	15

510 San Pedro de Alcantara Monastery   **511** Hand releasing Doves

1976 (29 Oct). San Pedro de Alcantara Monastery T **510** and similar designs. Recess. P 13.
2435	3p. deep brown and agate	35	15
2436	7p. blue-black and deep reddish lilac	15	15
2437	20p. agate and deep brown	35	15
2435/2437 Set of 3		75	40

Designs: Vert—7p. High Altar; 20p. S. Pedro de Alcantara.

1976 (23 Nov). Civil War Invalids' Association Commemoration. Photo. P 13.
2438	**511**	3p. multicoloured	20	15

512 Pablo Casals and Cello   **513** King James I and Arms of Aragon

1976 (29 Dec). Birth Centenaries. T **512** and similar vert design. Recess. P 13.
2439	3p. blue-black and deep ultramarine	15	10
2440	5p. greenish black and rose-red	20	10

Design: 5p. Manuel de Falla and "Fire Dance".

1977 (5 Jan). Spanish Military Uniforms (7th series). Vert designs as T **448**. Multicoloured. Photo. P 13.
2441	1p. Calatrava Regiment of Lancers, 1844	15	10
2442	2p. Engineers Regiment, 1850	35	10
2443	3p. Light Infantry Regiment, 1861	20	10
2444	4p. Infantry of the Line, 1861	20	15
2445	20p. Horse Artillery. 1862	25	15
2441/2445 Set of 5		1·00	55

1977 (10 Feb). 700th Death Anniv of King James I. Recess. P 12½.
2446	**513**	4p. deep brown and deep reddish violet	20	15

514 Jacinto Verdaguer (poet)   **515** King Charles III

1977 (22 Feb). Spanish Celebrities. T **514** and similar vert designs. Recess. P 13.
2447	5p. brown-red and deep purple	25	10
2448	7p. bottle green and olive-brown	15	15
2449	12p. deep blue-green and deep ultramarine	20	15
2450	50p. deep brown and deep green	75	15
2447/2450	Set of 4	1·20	50

Designs:—7p. Miguel Servet (theologian and physician) 12p. Pablo Sarasate (violinist); 50p. Francisco Tarrega (guitarist).

1977 (24 Feb). Bicentenary of Economic Society of Friends of the Land. Recess. P 13.
2451	**515**	4p. deep brown and bottle-green	20	15

516 Atlantic Salmon   **517** Skiing

1977 (8 Mar). Spanish Fauna (6th series). Freshwater Fishes. T **516** and similar multicoloured designs. Photo. P 13.
2452	1p. Type **516**	20	10
2453	2p. Brown trout (horiz)	20	10
2454	3p. European eel (horiz)	20	10
2455	4p. Common carp (horiz)	20	10
2456	6p. Barbel (horiz)	20	10
2452/2456	Set of 5	90	55

1977 (24 Mar). World Ski Championships, Granada. Recess. P 12½.
2457	**517**	5p. multicoloured	20	15

518 La Cuadra Tourer, 1902   **519** Doñana

1977 (23 Apr). Vintage Cars. T **518** and similar horiz designs. Multicoloured. Photo. P 13.
2458	2p. Type **518**	10	10
2459	4p. Hispano Suiza tourer, 1916	10	10
2460	5p. Elizade landaulette, 1915	15	15
2461	7p. Abadal landaulette, 1914	15	15
2458/2461	Set of 4	45	45

1977 (2 May). Europa. Landscapes. National Parks. T **519** and similar horiz design. Multicoloured. Photo. P 13.
2462	3p. Type **519**	15	15
2463	12p. Ordesa	25	25

520 Plaza Mayor, Madrid and Stamps   **521** Enrique de Osso (founder)

1977 (7 May). 50th Anniv of Philatelic Bourse on Plaza Mayor, Madrid. Recess and litho. P 13.
2464	**520**	3p. grey-olive, rosine and deep reddish violet	20	15

1977 (7 June). Centenary of Society of St. Theresa of Jesus. Photo. P 13.
2465	**521**	8p. multicoloured	20	15

1977 (24 June). Tourist Series. Designs as T **340**. Recess. P 13.
2466	1p. brown and red-orange	10	10
2467	2p. slate and olive-brown	10	10
2468	3p. deep purple and ultramarine	10	10
2469	4p. deep blue-green and blue	10	10
2470	7p. slate and deep brown	10	10
2471	12p. brown and violet	15	10
2466/2471	Set of 6	60	55

Designs: Horiz—1p. Toledo Gate, Ciudad Real; 2p. Roman Aqueduct, Almunecar; 7p. Ampudia Castle, Palencia; 12p. Bisagra Gate, Toledo. Vert—3p. Jaen Cathedral; 4p. Bridge and Gate, Ronda Gorge, Malaga.

1977 (16 July). Spanish Military Uniforms (8th series). Vert designs as T **448**. Multicoloured. Photo. P 13.
2472	1p. Administration officer, 1875	20	10
2473	2p. Lancer, 1883	20	10
2474	3p. General Staff commander, 1884	20	10
2475	7p. Trumpeter, Divisional Artillery, 1887	20	15
2476	25p. Medical Corps officer, 1895	25	15
2472/2476	Set of 5	90	55

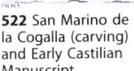

522 San Marino de la Cogalla (carving) and Early Castilian Manuscript   **523** West Indies Sailing Packet and Map of Mail Routes to America

1977 (9 Sept). Millenary of Castilian Language. Recess. P 12½.
2477	**522**	5p. deep brn, grey-grn & deep purple	20	15

1977 (29 Sept). Stamp Day and F. Madrazo (painter) Commemoration. Portraits. Vert designs as T **409**. Multicoloured Photo. P 13.
2478	1p. "The Youth of Florez"	10	10
2479	2p. "Duke of San Miguel"	10	10
2480	3p. "C Coronado"	10	10
2481	4p. "Campoamor"	10	10
2482	6p. "Marquesa de Montelo"	10	10
2483	7p. "Rivadeneyra"	15	10
2484	10p. "Countess of Vilches"	15	10
2485	15p. "Gomez de Avellaneda"	20	10
2478/2485	Set of 8	90	75

1977 (7 Oct). Bicentenary of Mail to the Indies, and Espamer 77 Stamp Exhibition, Barcelona. Recess. P 12½.
2486	**523**	15p. deep green & reddish brn	25	25

No. 2486 was issued in sheets of eight stamps and eight half stamp-size labels bearing the Exhibition emblem.

524 St. Francis's Church   **525** Monastery Building

1977 (12 Oct). Spanish–Guatemalen Relations. Guatemala City Buildings. T **524** and similar horiz designs. Multicoloured. Photo. P 13.
2487	1p. Type **524**	10	10
2488	3p. High-rise flats	10	10
2489	7p. Government Palace	10	10
2490	12p. Monument, Columbus Square	15	15
2487/2490	Set of 4	40	40

SPAIN

1977 (28 Oct). St. Peter's Monastery, Cardeña Commemoration. T **525** and similar horiz designs. Recess. P 13.

2491	3p. slate and blue	10	10
2492	7p. red-brown and brown	15	10
2493	20p. slate and blue-green	25	15
2491/2493 Set of 3		45	30

Designs:—7p. Cloisters; 20p. El Cid (effigy).

526 Adoration of the Kings

1977 (3 Nov). Christmas. Miniatures from Manuscript "Romanico de Huesca". T **526** and similar multicoloured design. Photo. P 13.

2494	5p. Type **526**	15	10
2495	12p. Flight into Egypt (vert)	20	10

527 Rohrbach Ro.VII Roland M-CBBB, 1927, and Douglas DC-10 EC-CPN

528 Crown Prince Felipe

1977 (8 Nov). 50th Anniv of IBERIA (State airline). Photo. P 13.

2496	**527**	12p. multicoloured	20	15

1977 (22 Dec). Felipe de Borbón, Prince of Asturias. Photo. P 13.

2497	**528**	5p. multicoloured	20	15

529 Judo **530** Hilarión Eslava (composer)

1977 (29 Dec). Tenth World Judo Championships. Photo. P 13.

2498	**529**	3p. blk, dull rose & lake-brn	20	15

The championships in Barcelona were cancelled but, as small quantities of No. 2498 were accidentally released for sale in September, the stamp was later issued on the above date.

1978 (5 Jan). Spanish Military Uniforms (9th series). Vert designs as T **448**. Multicoloured. Photo. P 13.

2499	1p. Standard bearer, Royal Infantry Regiment, 1908	10	10
2500	2p. Lieutenant-Colonel, Pavia Hussars, 1909	10	10
2501	3p. Lieutenant, Horse Artillery, 1912	10	10
2502	5p. Engineers Captain, 1921	10	10
2503	12p. Captain-General, 1925	10	10
2499/2503 Set of 5		45	45

1978 (20 Feb). Spanish Celebrities. T **530** and similar horiz designs. Recess. P 13.

2504	5p. black and maroon	10	10
2505	8p. slate-black and deep bluish green	15	10
2506	25p. black and green	30	10
2507	50p. dull purple and sepia	65	20
2504/2507 Set of 4		1·10	45

Designs:—8p. José Clará (sculptor); 25p. Pio Baroja (writer); 50p. Antonio Machado (writer).

531 "The Deposition of Christ" (detail, Juan de Juni)

532 Eidelweiss and Pyrenees

1978 (28 Mar). Anniversaries of Artists. T **531** and similar designs. Recess and photo. P 13.

2508	3p. multicoloured	10	10
	a. Horiz strip of 3 (Nos. 2508/10)	50	
2509	3p. multicoloured	10	10
2510	3p. mauve and reddish violet	10	10
2511	5p. multicoloured	10	10
	a. Horiz strip of 3 (Nos. 2511/13)	50	
2512	5p. multicoloured	10	10
2513	5p. red-brown and black	10	10
2514	8p. multicoloured	10	10
	a. Horiz strip of 3 (Nos. 2514/16)	50	
2515	8p. multicoloured	10	10
2516	8p. flesh and blackish green	10	10
2508/2516 Set of 9		80	80

Designs: As T **531**—No. 2510, Portrait of Juan de Juni (sculptor, 400th death anniv); 2511, Detail of "Rape of the Sabines" (Rubens); 2513, Artist's palette and Rubens's signature; 2514, Detail of "Bacchanal" (Titian); 2516, Artist's palette and Titian's initial. 46×25 mm—2509, Different detail of "Deposition of Christ" and sculptor's tools; 2512, Different detail of "Rape of the Sabines" and portrait of Rubens (400th birth anniv); 2515, Different detail of "Bacchanal" and portrait of Titian (500th birth anniv).

The three designs of each value were printed together *se-tenant* within the sheet, the two details of each work forming a composite design.

1978 (4 Apr). Protection of the Environment. T **532** and similar multicoloured designs. Photo. P 13.

2517	3p. Type **532**	10	10
2518	5p. Brown trout and red-breasted merganser	10	10
2519	7p. Forest (fire prevention)	15	10
2520	12p. Tanker, oil rig and industrial complex (protection of sea)	15	10
2521	20p. Audouin's gull and Mediterranean monk seals (vert)	25	10
2517/2521 Set of 5		70	55

533 Palace of Charles V, Granada

1978 (2 May). Europa. T **533** and similar horiz design. Recess. P 13.

2522	5p. deep green & deep yellow-grn	20	15
2523	12p. brown-lake & deep yellow-grn	30	20

Design:—12p. Exchange building, Seville.

534 Council Emblem and Map of Spain

535 Columbus Hermitage

1978 (5 May). Membership of Council of Europe. Photo. P 12½.

2524	**534**	12p. multicoloured	15	15

1978 (23 June). 500th Anniv of Las Palmas, Gran Canaria. T **535** and similar horiz designs. Multicoloured. Photo. P 13.

2525	3p. 16th-century plan of city	10	10
2526	5p. Type **535**	15	10
2527	12p. View of Las Palmas (16th cent)	15	10
2525/2527	Set of 3	30	25

536 Post Box, Stamp, U.P.U. Emblem and Postal Transport

537 José de San Martin

1978 (27 June). World Stamp Day. Recess. P 13.

| 2528 | **536** | 5p. deep green and blackish olive | 20 | 15 |

1978 (29 Sept). Stamp Day and Picasso Commemoration. Paintings. Multicoloured designs as T **409**. Photo. P 13.

2529	3p. "Portrait of Sra. Canals"	15	10
2530	5p. Self-portrait	15	10
2531	8p. "Portrait of Jaime Sabartes"	15	10
2532	10p. "The End of the Number"	15	10
2533	12p. "Science and Charity" (horiz)	15	10
2534	15p. "Las Meninas" (horiz)	15	10
2535	20p. "The Pigeons"	20	15
2536	25p. "The Painter and Model" (horiz)	25	15
2529/2536	Set of 8	1·20	80

1978 (12 Oct). Latin-American Heroes. T **537** and similar horiz design. Recess. P 13.

| 2537 | 7p. deep brown and scarlet | 10 | 10 |
| 2538 | 12p. reddish violet and scarlet | 15 | 10 |

Design:—12p. Simón Bolivar.

538 Flight into Egypt

539 Aztec Calendar

1978 (3 Nov). Christmas. Capitals from Santa Maria de Nieva. T **538** and similar horiz design. Multicoloured. Photo. P 13.

| 2539 | 5p. Type **538** | 10 | 10 |
| 2540 | 12p. The Annunciation | 15 | 10 |

1978 (17–26 Nov). Royal Visit to Mexico, Peru and Argentina. T **539** and similar horiz designs. Multicoloured. Photo. P 13.

2541	5p. Type **539**	10	10
2542	5p. Macchu Picchu, Peru (22.11)	10	10
2543	5p. Pre-Columbian pots, Argentina (26.11)	10	10
2541/2543	Set of 3	25	25

540 Philip V

541 Miniatures from Bible

1978 (22 Nov). Spanish Kings and Queens of the House of Bourbon. T **540** and similar vert designs. Recess. P 13.

2544	5p. scarlet and deep grey-blue	10	10
2545	5p. bottle green and dull yellow-green	10	10
2546	8p. lake and blue	20	15
2547	10p. black and blue-green	20	15
2548	12p. lake and red-brown	20	15
2549	15p. indigo and grey-green	25	15
2550	20p. indigo and deep olive	25	15
2551	25p. deep reddish violet and blue	30	20
2552	50p. reddish brown and carmine-red	55	25
2553	100p. deep violet and blue	1·40	55
2544/2553	Set of 10	3·25	1·80

Designs:—5p. (2545) Luis I; 8p. Ferdinand VI; 10p. Charles III; 12p. Charles IV; 15p. Ferdinand VII; 20p. Isabel II; 25p. Alfonso XII; 50p. Alfonso XIII; 100p. Juan Carlos I.

1978 (27 Dec). Millenary of Consecration of Third Basilica of Santa Maria de Ripoll. Photo. P 13×12½.

| 2554 | **541** | 5p. multicoloured | 25 | 20 |

542 Flag, First Lines of Constitution and Cortes Building

543 Car in Oil Drop

1978 (29 Dec). New Constitution. Photo. P 13.

| 2555 | **542** | 5p. multicoloured | 25 | 20 |

1979 (24 Jan). Energy Conservation. T **543** and similar vert designs. Multicoloured. Photo. P 13.

2556	5p. Type **543**	15	15
2557	8p. Insulated house and thermometer	20	15
2558	10p. Hand removing electric plug	20	15
2556/2558	Set of 3	55	40

544 St. Jean Baptiste de la Salle (founder)

545 Jorge Manrique (poet)

1979 (14 Feb). Centenary of Brothers of the Christian Schools in Spain. Photo. P 13.

| 2559 | **544** | 5p. olive-brn, new bl & bright mauve | 15 | 15 |

1979 (28 Feb). Spanish Celebrities. T **545** and similar vert designs. Recess. P 13.

2560	5p. reddish brown and bottle green	15	15
2561	8p. blue and carmine-red	15	15
2562	10p. bright violet and lake-brown	15	15
2563	20p. myrtle green and bistre	30	15
2560/2563	Set of 4	65	55

Designs:—8p. Fernán Caballero (novelist); 10p. Francisco Villaespesa (poet); 20p. Gregorio Marañón (writer).

546 Running and Jumping

547 School Library (child's drawing)

1979 (16 Mar). Sport for All. T **546** and similar horiz designs. Photo. P 13.

2564	5p. carmine-rose, dull blue-grn & blk	15	15
2565	8p. dull blue, ochre and black	20	15
2566	10p. brown, turquoise-blue & black	20	15
2564/2566	Set of 3	55	40

Designs:—8p. Football, running, skipping and cycling; 10p. Running.

1979 (27 Apr). International Year of the Child. Photo. P 13.

| 2567 | **547** | 5p. multicoloured | 15 | 15 |

SPAIN

548 Cabinet Messenger and Postillion, 1761

549 Wave Pattern and Television Screen

1979 (30 Apr). Europa. T **548** and similar horiz design. Recess. P 13.
| 2568 | 5p. blackish brn & reddish brn/*pale yellow* | 35 | 20 |
| 2569 | 12p. dp dull green & chestnut/*pale yellow* | 35 | 20 |

Design:—12p. Manuel de Ysasi (postal reformer).

1979 (17 May). World Telecommunications Day. T **549** and similar horiz design. Multicoloured. Photo. P 13.
| 2570 | 5p. Type **549** | 15 | 15 |
| 2571 | 8p. Satellite and Receiving aerial | 15 | 15 |

550 First Bulgarian Stamp and Exhibition Hall

551 Tank, Destroyer *Roger de Lauria* and Dassault Mirage III

1979 (18 May). Philaserdica 79 Stamp Exhibition, Sofia. Photo. P 13.
| 2572 | **550** | 12p. multicoloured | 15 | 10 |

1979 (25 May). Armed Forces Day. Photo. P 13.
| 2573 | **551** | 5p. multicoloured | 10 | 10 |

552 King receiving Messenger

1979 (15 June). Stamp Day. Pale yellow paper. Recess and litho. P 12½.
| 2574 | **552** | 5p. multicoloured | 10 | 10 |

1979 (27 June). Tourist Series. Vert designs as T **340**. Recess. P 13×12½.
2575	5p. deep reddish lilac and royal blue	15	10
2576	8p. blackish brown and deep blue	15	10
2577	10p. deep green and blackish green	15	15
2578	20p. blackish brown and reddish brown	25	15
2575/2578	Set of 4	65	45

Designs:—5p. Daroca Gate, Zaragoza; 8p. Gerona Cathedral; 10p. Interior of Carthusian Monastery Church, Granada; 20p. Portal of Marqués de Dos Aguas Palace, Valencia.

553 Turkey Sponge (*Eusponja officinalis*)

554 Antonio Gutiérrez

1979 (11 July). Spanish Fauna (7th series). Invertebrates. T **553** and similar horiz designs. Multicoloured. Photo. P 13½.
2579	5p. Type **553**	10	10
2580	7p. Crayfish (*Astacus pallipes*)	15	10
2581	8p. Scorpion (*Buthus europaeus*)	15	10
2582	20p. Starfish (*Astropecten sp.*)	20	10
2583	25p. Sea anemone (*Actinia equina*)	25	15
2579/2583	Set of 5	75	50

1979 (24 July). Defence of Tenerife (1797). Recess and litho. P 13.
| 2584 | **554** | 5p. multicoloured | 15 | 10 |

1979 (28 Sept). Stamp Day and Juan de Juanes Commemoration. Multicoloured designs as T **409**. Photo. P 13.
2585	8p. "Immaculate Conception"	15	10
2586	10p. "Holy Family"	15	10
2587	15p. "Ecce Homo"	15	10
2588	20p. "St. Stephen in the Synagogue"	25	10
2589	25p. "The Last Supper"	30	15
2590	50p. "Adoration of the Mystic Lamb" (horiz)	55	20
2585/2590	Set of 6	1·40	70

555 Cathedral and Statue of Virgin and Child, Zaragoza

556 St. Bartholomew's College, Bogotá

1979 (3 Oct). Eighth Mariological Congress, Zaragoza. Photo. P 13.
| 2591 | **555** | 5p. multicoloured | 15 | 10 |

1979 (12 Oct). Latin-American Buildings. T **556** and similar horiz design. Recess. P 13.
| 2592 | 7p. blackish green, deep blue and brown | 15 | 10 |
| 2593 | 12p. indigo, reddish purple and deep brown | 15 | 15 |

Design:—12p. San Marcos University, Lima.

557 Hands and Governor's Palace, Barcelona

558 Autonomy Statute

1979 (27 Oct). Catalonian Autonomy. Grey paper. Recess and litho. P 13.
| 2594 | **557** | 8p. multicoloured | 20 | 15 |

1979 (27 Oct). Basque Autonomy. Grey paper. Recess and litho. P 13.
| 2595 | **558** | 8p. multicoloured | 20 | 15 |

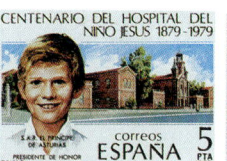
559 Prince of Asturias and Hospital

560 Barcelona Tax Stamp, 1929

1979 (6 Nov). Centenary of Hospital of the Child Jesus, Madrid Photo. P 13.
| 2596 | **559** | 5p. multicoloured | 20 | 15 |

1979 (9 Nov). 50th Anniv of Barcelona Exhibition Tax Stamps. Recess and litho. P 13.
| 2597 | **560** | 5p. multicoloured | 20 | 15 |

561 The Nativity

562 Charles I

SPAIN

1979 (14 Nov). Christmas. Capitals from San Pedro el Viejo, Huesca. T **561** and similar horiz design. Multicoloured. Photo. P 13.
2598		8p. Type **561**	10	10
2599		19p. Flight into Egypt	25	10

1979 (22 Nov). Spanish Kings of the House of Hapsburg. T **562** and similar horiz designs. Recess. P 13.
2600	15p. deep dull green & dp grey-blue		30	10
2601	20p. deep blue and crimson		30	10
2602	25p. bright violet and ochre		35	10
2603	50p. brown and deep green		65	15
2604	100p. crimson and red brown		1·10	35
2600/2604 Set of 5			2·50	70

Designs:—20p. Philip II; 25p. Philip III; 50p. Philip IV; 100p. Charles II.

563 Olive Plantation and Harvester

564 Electric Train

1979 (4 Dec). International Olive Oil Year. Photo. P 13.
2605	**563**	8p. multicoloured	20	15

1980 (20 Feb). Public Transport. T **564** and similar horiz designs. Recess. P 13.
2606	3p. brown-lake and brown		10	10
2607	4p. blue, blue-grey and brown		10	10
2608	5p. deep grey-green and brown		10	10
2606/2608 Set of 3			25	25

Designs:—4p. Bus; 5p. Underground train.

565 Steel Products

566 Federico Garcia Lorca

1980 (12 Mar). Spanish Exports (1st series). T **565** and similar horiz designs. Multicoloured. Photo. P 13.
2609	5p. Type **565**		10	10
2610	8p. Tankers		15	10
2611	13p. Footwear		15	10
2612	19p. Industrial machinery		25	10
2613	25p. Factory, buildings, bridge and symbols of technology		35	20
2609/2613 Set of 5			90	55

See also Nos. 2653/5.

1980 (28 Apr). Europa. Writers. T **566** and similar horiz designs. Recess. P 13.
2614		8p. bright violet and deep green	20	15
2615		19p. deep dull green & reddish brown	25	20

Design:—19p. José Ortega y Gasset.

567 Footballers

568 Armed Forces

1980 (23 May). World Cup Football Championship, Spain (1982) (1st issue). T **567** and similar horiz design. Multicoloured. Photo. P 13.
2616		8p. Type **567**	15	10
2617		19p. Football and flags	25	10

See also Nos. 2640/1, 2668/9 and 2683/**MS**2685.

1980 (24 May). Armed Forces Day. Photo. P 13.
2618	**568**	8p. multicoloured	15	10

569 Bourbon Arms, Ministry of Finance, Madrid

570 Helen Keller

1980 (9 June). Public Finances under the Bourbons. Recess. P 13.
2619	**569**	8p. dp purplish brown and red-brown	15	10

1980 (27 June). Birth Centenary of Helen Keller. Recess. P 13.
2620	**570**	19p. crimson and green	25	10

571 Postal Courier (14th century)

1980 (28 June). Stamp Day. Recess and photo. P 13.
2621	**571**	8p. blackish brown, stone and scarlet	15	10

572 King Alfonso XIII and Count of Maceda at Exhibition

573 Altar of the Virgin, La Palma Cathedral

1980 (1 July). 50th Anniv of First National Stamp Exhibition. Photo. P 13.
2622	**572**	8p. multicoloured	15	10

1980 (12 July). 300th Anniv of Appearance of Holy Virgin at La Palma. Recess. P 13.
2623	**573**	8p. reddish brown and black	15	10

574 Ramón Pérez de Ayala

575 Manuel de Falla, Ruins of Atlantis and Bonampak Musicians

1980 (9 Aug). Birth Centenary of Ramón Pérez de Ayala (writer). Recess. P 13.
2624	**574**	100p. blackish green and sepia	1·30	15

1980 (3 Oct). Espamer '80 International Stamp Exhibition, Madrid. Sheet 150×100 mm, containing T **575** and similar horiz designs. Recess. P 13×12½.
MS2625 25p.×2, 50p., 100p. each reddish brown, deep green and deep dull blue (sold at 250p.) ... 2·30 2·10

Designs:—25p. Type **575**; 25p. Sun Gate, Tiahuanaco and Roman arch, Medinaceli; 50p. Alonso de Ercilla, Garcilaso de la Vega and title pages from *La Araucana* and *Commentarios Reales*; 100p. Virgin of Quito and Virgin of Seafarers.

SPAIN

576 Juan de Garay and Founding of Buenos Aires (after Moreno Carbonero) **577** Tapestry Detail

1980 (24 Oct). 400th Anniv of Buenos Aires. Recess. P 13.
2626 576 19p. new blue, blackish green and Indian red.................... 25 10

1980 (25 Oct). The Creation Tapestry, Gerona. Sheet 132×106 mm, containing T **577** and similar designs showing tapestry details. Photo. P 13½×13.
MS2627 25p.×3 (each 33×26 mm), 50p.×3, multicoloured.................. 2·40 2·30

578 Palace of Congresses, Madrid **579** "Nativity" (mural from Church of Santa María de Cuiña, Oza de los Ríos)

1980 (11 Nov). European Security and Co-operation Conference, Madrid. Photo. P 13.
2628 578 22p. multicoloured.................... 25 15

1980 (12 Nov). Christmas. T **579** and similar horiz design. Multicoloured. Photo. P 13½.
2629   10p. Type 579........................ 15 10
2630   22p. "Adoration of the Kings" (doorway of Church of St. Nicholas of Cines, Oza de los Ríos)................. 25 10

580 Pedro Vives and Farman H.F.III Biplane **581** Games Emblem and Skier

1980 (10 Dec). Aviation Pioneers. T **580** and similar horiz designs. Multicoloured. Photo. P 13½.
2631   5p. Type 580........................ 15 10
2632   10p. Benito Loygorri and Farman H.F.20 type biplane............. 15 10
2633   15p. Alfonso de Orleans Bourbon and Caudron G-3............... 20 10
2634   22p. Alfredo Kindelán Duany and biplane....................... 25 15
2631/2634 Set of 4.................................. 70 40

1981 (4 Mar). Winter University Games. Photo. P 13½.
2635 581 30p. multicoloured............... 30 15

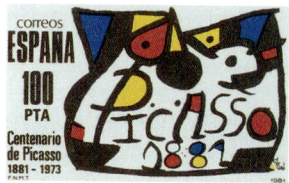

582 "Homage to Picasso" (Joan Miró)

1981 (27 Mar). Birth Centenary of Pablo Picasso (artist) (1st issue). Litho. P 13.
2636 582 100p. multicoloured............... 1·50 20
See also No. MS2657.

583 Newspaper, Camera, Notepaper and Pen **584** Map of Galicia, Arms and National Anthem

1981 (8 Apr). The Press. Photo. P 13½.
2637 583 12p. multicoloured............... 15 10

1981 (28 Apr). Galician Autonomy. Recess and photo. P 13.
2638 584 12p. multicoloured............... 15 10
No. 2638 was accidentally pre-released on 8 April in Catalonia.

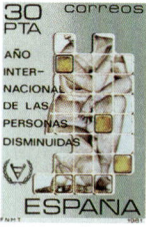 

585 Mosaic forming Human Figure **586** Heading Ball

1981 (29 Apr). International Year of Disabled Persons. Litho. P 13.
2639 585 30p. multicoloured............... 35 10

1981 (2 May). World Cup Football Championship, Spain (1982) (2nd issue). T **586** and similar horiz design. Multicoloured. Photo. P 13.
2640   12p. Type 586...................... 15 10
2641   30p. Kicking ball.................... 30 10

587 La Jota (folk dance) **588** King Juan Carlos reviewing Army

1981 (4 May). Europa. T **587** and similar horiz design. Recess. P 13½.
2642   12p. blackish brown and reddish brown...... 25 15
2643   30p. blackish lilac and deep reddish lilac..... 40 20
Design:—30p. Procession of the Virgin of Rocío.

1981 (29 May). Armed Forces Day. Photo. P 13½.
2644 588 12p. multicoloured............... 15 10

288

SPAIN

589 Gabriel Miró (writer) **590** Messenger (14th century woodcut)

1981 (17 June). Spanish Celebrities. T **589** and similar vert designs. Recess. P 13.
2645	6p. bright violet and deep dull green............	15	15
2646	12p. reddish brown and bright violet............	15	15
2647	30p. deep dull green and reddish brown......	40	15
2645/2647	Set of 3	65	40

Designs:—12p. Francisco de Quevedo (writer); 30p. St. Benedict.

1981 (19 June). Stamp Day. Recess and photo. P 13.
| 2648 | **590** | 12p. flesh, reddish brown and blackish green.. | 15 | 10 |

591 Map of Balearic Islands (from Atlas of Diego Homem, 1563)

1981 (8 July). Spanish Islands. T **591** and similar horiz design. Multicoloured. Photo. P 13.
| 2649 | 7p. Type **591**... | 15 | 10 |
| 2650 | 12p. Map of Canary Islands (from map of Mateo Prunes, 1563)........................ | 15 | 10 |

592 Alfonso XII, Juan Carlos and Arms   **593** King Sancho VI of Navarre with Foundation Charter

1981 (28 July). Centenary of Public Prosecutor's Office. Recess. P 13.
| 2651 | **592** | 50p. reddish brown, blackish green and deep blue .... | 55 | 10 |

1981 (5 Aug). 800th Anniv of Vitoria. Photo. P 13.
| 2652 | **593** | 12p. multicoloured................................. | 15 | 10 |

594 Citrus Fruit   **595** Foodstuffs

1981 (30 Sept). Spanish Exports (2nd series). T **594** and similar horiz designs. Multicoloured. Photo. P 13.
2653	6p. Type **594**	10	10
2654	12p. Wine	15	10
2655	30p. CASA C-212 Aviocar, car and truck......	35	10
2653/2655	Set of 3	60	45

1981 (16 Oct). World Food Day. Photo. P 13½.
| 2656 | **595** | 30p. multicoloured............................. | 35 | 10 |

596 "Guernica"

1981 (25 Oct). Birth Centenary of Pablo Picasso (2nd issue) and Return of "Guernica" to Spain. Sheet 163×105 mm. Photo. P 13.
| MS2657 | **596** | 200p. black, grey and dull turquoise-green .... | 2·40 | 2·40 |

Each sheet is individually numbered in one of two typefaces: "Nº" in sans-serif, "Nº" in fancy serif.

 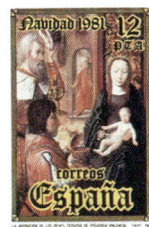

597 Congress Palace, Buenos Aires   **598** "Adoration of the Kings" (from Cervera de Pisuerga)

1981 (13 Nov). Espamer '81 International Stamp Exhibition, Buenos Aires. Recess. P 13.
| 2658 | **597** | 12p. crimson and deep blue..................... | 15 | 10 |

1981 (18 Nov). Christmas. T **598** and similar vert design. Multicoloured. Litho. P 13.
| 2659 | 12p. Type **598** .... | 15 | 10 |
| 2660 | 30p. "Nativity" (from Paredes de Nava) .... | 30 | 10 |

599 Plaza de España, Seville

1981 (26 Nov). AIR. T **599** and similar horiz design. Recess. P 13.
| 2661 | 13p. deep dull green and deep blue............... | 15 | 10 |
| 2662 | 20p. deep blue and deep brown..................... | 25 | 10 |

Design:—20p. Rande Bridge, Ría de Vigo.

600 Telegraph Operator

289

SPAIN

1981 (30 Nov). Postal and Telecommunications Museum, Madrid. T **600** and similar horiz designs. Recess. P 13.

2663	7p. deep grey-green and reddish brown	30	10
2664	12p. reddish brown and bright violet	30	10
MS2665	135×100 mm. Nos. 2663/4; 50p. bright violet and deep grey-green; 100p. deep grey-green and deep brown	2·20	2·20

Designs:—12p. Post wagon; 50p. Emblem of Spanish-American and Philippines Postal Academy; 100p. Cap, pouch, posthorn, books and cancellation.

601 Royal Mint, Seville   **602** Iparraguirre

1981 (4 Dec). Financial Administration by the Bourbons in Spain and the Indies. Recess. P 13.

2666	**601**	12p. sepia and slate	15	10

1981 (16 Dec). Death Centenary of José María Iparraguirre Recess. P 13.

2667	**602**	12p. deep blue and greenish black	15	10

603 Publicity Poster by Joan Miró   **604** Andrés Bello (writer and philosopher)

1982 (24 Feb). World Cup Football Championship, Spain (3rd issue) T **603** and similar vert design. Multicoloured. Photo. P 13.

2668	14p. Type **603**	20	10
2669	33p. World Cup trophy and championship emblem	35	10

1982 (10 Mar). Anniversaries (1981). T **604** and vert designs as T **602**. Recess. P 13.

2670	30p. dp dull green and dull yellowish green	35	10
2671	30p. deep dull green and deep blue	35	15
2672	50p. bright violet and greenish black	65	15
2670/2672	Set of 3	1·20	35

Designs:—No. 2670, Type **604** (birth bicentenary); 2671, Juan Ramón Jiménez (author, birth centenary); 2672, Pedro Calderón (playwright, 300th death anniv).

605 St. James of Compostela (Codex illustration)   **606** Manuel Fernández Caballero

1982 (31 Mar). Holy Year of Compostela. Photo. P 13.

2673	**605**	14p. multicoloured	15	10

1982 (28 Apr). Masters of Operetta (1st series). T **606** and similar vert designs (2674, 2676, 2678) or horiz designs as T **625** (others). Multicoloured. Recess and litho. P 13.

2674	3p. Type **606**	10	10
	a. Horiz pair. Nos. 2674/5	40	
2675	3p. Scene from *Gigantes y Cabezudos* (horiz)	10	10
2676	6p. Amadeo Vives Roig	10	10
	a. Horiz pair. Nos. 2676/7	40	
2677	6p. Scene from *Maruxa* (horiz)	10	10
2678	8p. Tomás Bretón y Hernandez	10	10
	a. Horiz pair. Nos. 2678/9	65	
2679	8p. Scene from *La Verbena de la Paloma* (horiz)	10	10
2674/2679	Set of 6	55	55

The two designs of each value were printed together in *se-tenant* pairs within their sheets.

See also Nos. 2713/18 and 2772/7.

607 Arms, Seals and Signatures (Unification of Spain, 1479)

1982 (3 May). Europa. T **607** and similar horiz design. Multicoloured. Recess. P 13.

2680	14p. Type **607**	25	20
2681	33p. Symbolic ship, Columbus map of "La Spañola" and signature (Discovery of America)	40	30

608 Swords, Arms and Flag   **609** Tackling

1982 (28 May). Armed Forces Day and Centenary of General Military Academy. Photo. P 13×13½.

2682	**608**	14p. multicoloured	15	10

1982 (13 June). World Cup Football Championship, Spain (4th issue). T **609** and similar horiz designs. Multicoloured. Photo. P 13½×13.

2683	14p. Type **609**	25	10
2684	33p. Goal	45	25
MS2685	163×105 mm. 9p. Handshake; 14p. Type **609**; 33p. As No. 2684; 100p. Players with cup	3·00	3·00

No. **MS**2685 was issued in two versions showing a different group of host town arms in the sheet margin.

610 "Sts. Andrew and Francis"   **611** Map of Tenerife and Letter

SPAIN

1982 (7 July). AIR. Paintings by El Greco. T **610** and similar vert design. Multicoloured. Photo. P 13×13½.
| 2686 | | 13p. Type **610** | 15 | 10 |
| 2687 | | 20p. "St. Thomas" | 30 | 15 |

1982 (16 July). Stamp Day. Recess and litho. P 13.
| 2688 | **611** | 14p. multicoloured | 20 | 10 |

612 "Transplants"

613 White Storks and Diesel Locomotive

1982 (28 July). Organ Transplants. Photo. P 13×13½.
| 2689 | **612** | 14p. multicoloured | 20 | 10 |

1982 (27 Sept). 23rd International Railway Congress, Malaga. T **613** and similar horiz designs. Multicoloured. Photo. P 13.
2690		9p. Type **613**	20	10
2691		14p. Steam locomotive *Antigua* (37×26 mm)	30	15
2692		33p. Steam locomotive *Montaña* (wrongly inscr "Santa Fe") (37×26 mm)	45	15
2690/2692 Set of 3			85	35

614 La Fortaleza, San Juan

615 St. Theresa of Avila (sculpture by Gregorio Hernández)

1982 (12 Oct). Espamer '82 International Stamp Exhibition, San Juan, Puerto Rico. Recess. P 13½×13.
| 2693 | **614** | 33p. deep blue and deep lilac | 45 | 15 |

1982 (15 Oct). 400th Death Anniv of St. Theresa of Avila. Recess. P 13½×13.
| 2694 | **615** | 33p. sepia, deep blue and deep bluish green | 45 | 15 |

616 Pope John Paul II

1982 (31 Oct). Papal Visit. Recess. P 13.
| 2695 | **616** | 14p. indigo and chocolate | 20 | 15 |

1982 (5 Nov). Tourist Series. Designs as T **340**. Recess. P 13.
2696		4p. deep blue and blackish green	15	15
2697		6p. blackish green and deep blue	15	15
2698		9p. deep lilac and bright blue	15	15
2699		14p. deep lilac and bright blue	15	15
2700		33p. reddish brown and crimson	35	15
2696/2700 Set of 5			85	70

Designs: Vert—4p. Arab water-wheel, Alcantarilla, 9p. Dying Christ, Seville; 14p. St. Martin's Tower, Teruel; 33p, St. Andrew's Gate, Villalpando. Horiz—6p. Bank of Spain, Madrid.

617 "Adoration of the Kings" (sculpture, Covarrubias Collegiate Church)

618 "The Prophet"

1982 (17 Nov). Christmas. T **617** and similar horiz design. Multicoloured. Photo. P 13½×13.
| 2701 | | 14p. Type **617** | 15 | 10 |
| 2702 | | 33p. "The Flight into Egypt" (painting) | 40 | 15 |

1982 (9 Dec). Birth Centenary of Pablo Gargallo (sculptor). Recess. P 13×13½.
| 2703 | **618** | 14p. deep dull green and deep blue | 15 | 10 |

619 St. John Bosco (founder) and Children

620 Arms of Spain

1982 (16 Dec). Centenary of Salesian Schools in Spain. Photo. P 13.
| 2704 | **619** | 14p. multicoloured | 15 | 10 |

1983 (9 Feb). Photo. P 13.
| 2705 | **620** | 14p. multicoloured | 20 | 10 |

621 Sunrise over Andalusia

622 Arms of Cantabria, Mountains and Monument

1982 (28 Feb). Andalusian Autonomy. Recess and litho. P 13½×13.
| 2706 | **621** | 14p. multicoloured | 25 | 10 |

1983 (15 Mar). Cantabrian Autonomy. Recess and litho. P 13½×13.
| 2707 | **622** | 14p. multicoloured | 25 | 10 |

623 National Police

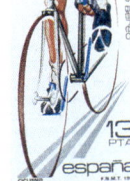

624 Cycling

291

SPAIN

1983 (23 Mar). State Security Forces. T **623** and similar horiz designs. Multicoloured. Photo. P 13½×13.

2708	9p. Type **623**	15	10
2709	14p. Civil Guard	20	15
2710	33p. Superior Police Corps	35	25
2708/2710	Set of 3	65	45

1983 (13 Apr). AIR. Sports. T **624** and similar horiz design. Multicoloured. Photo. P 13½.

| 2711 | 13p. Type **624** | 20 | 10 |
| 2712 | 20p. Bowling | 30 | 10 |

625 Scene from *La Parranda*

1983 (22 Apr). Masters of Operetta (2nd series). T **625** and similar horiz designs (2714, 2716, 2718) or vert designs as T **606** (others). Multicoloured. Recess and litho. P 13.

2713	4p. Francisco Alonso (vert)	10	10
	a. Horiz pair. Nos. 2713/14	40	
2714	4p. Type **625**	10	10
2715	6p. Jacinto Guerrero (vert)	10	10
	a. Horiz pair. Nos. 2715/16	40	
2716	6p. Scene from *La Rosa del Azafrán*	10	10
2717	9p. Jesús Guridi (vert)	15	15
	a. Horiz pair. Nos. 2717/18	40	
2718	9p. Scene from *El Caserío*	15	15
2713/2718	Set of 6	65	65

The two designs of each value were printed together in *se-tenant* pairs within their sheets.

626 Cervantes and Scene from *Don Quixote*

1983 (5 May). Europa. T **626** and similar horiz design. Recess. P 13.

| 2719 | 16p. crimson and blackish green | 30 | 20 |
| 2720 | 38p. sepia and crimson | 60 | 35 |

Design:—38p. Torres Quevedo and Niagara cable-car.

627 Francisco Salzillo (artist) **628** W.C.Y. Emblem

1983 (14 May). Spanish Celebrities. T **627** and similar vert designs. Recess. P 13×13½.

2721	16p. deep purple and blackish green	20	15
2722	38p. blue and purple-brown	50	25
2723	50p. deep turquoise-blue and sepia	65	25
2724	100p. purple-brown and deep purple	1·30	50
2721/2724	Set of 4	2·40	1·00

Designs:—38p. Antonio Soler (composer); 50p. Joaquín Turina (composer); 100p. St. Isidro Labrador (patron saint of Madrid).

1983 (17 May). World Communications Year. Photo. P 13×13½.

| 2725 | **628** | 38p. multicoloured | 45 | 15 |

 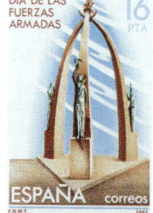

629 Leaves **630** Army Monument, Burgos

1983 (25 May). Riojan Autonomy. Recess and litho. P 13½×13.

| 2726 | **629** | 16p. multicoloured | 25 | 15 |

1983 (26 May). Armed Forces Day. Photo. P 13×13½.

| 2727 | **630** | 16p. multicoloured | 25 | 15 |

631 Burgos Setter **632** Juan-José and Fausto Elhúyar y de Suvisa

1983 (8 June). Spanish Dogs. T **631** and similar horiz designs. Recess and litho. P 13½×13.

2728	10p. lt blue, dp purple-brn & orange-red	20	15
2729	16p. multicoloured	30	15
2730	26p. multicoloured	45	25
2731	38p. multicoloured	65	20
2728/2731	Set of 4	1·40	70

Designs:—16p. Spanish mastiff; 26p. Ibiza spaniel; 38p. Navarrese basset.

1983 (22 June). Anniversaries. T **632** and similar horiz designs. Multicoloured. Photo. P 13½×13.

2732	16p. Type **632** (bicentenary of discovery of wolfram)	25	20
2733	38p. Scout camp (75th anniv of Boy Scout Movement)	60	20
2734	50p. University of Zaragoza (400th anniv)	80	20
2732/2734	Set of 3	1·50	55

633 Arms of Murcia **634** Covadonga Basilica and Victory Cross

1983 (8 July). Murcian Autonomy. Recess and litho. P 13½×13.

| 2735 | **633** | 16p. multicoloured | 25 | 15 |

1983 (8 Sept). Autonomy of Asturias. Recess and litho. P 13½×13.

| 2736 | **634** | 14p. multicoloured | 25 | 15 |

635 National Statistical Institute, Madrid **637** Palace and Arms of Valencia

636 Roman Horse-drawn Mail Cart

SPAIN

1983 (12 Sept). 44th International Institute of Statistics Congress. Photo. P 13½×13.
| 2737 | **635** | 38p. multicoloured | 50 | 20 |

1983 (8 Oct). Stamp Day. Recess and litho. P 13.
| 2738 | **636** | 16p. flesh, sepia and black | 30 | 30 |

No. 2738 was issued with *se-tenant* half stamp-size label bearing "España 84" stamp exhibition emblem.

1983 (10 Oct). Valencian Autonomy. Recess and litho. P 13½×13.
| 2739 | **637** | 16p. multicoloured | 30 | 15 |

638 Seville (illus from *Floods of Guadalquivir* by Francisco Palomo)

1983 (12 Oct). America–Spain. Recess. P 13.
| 2740 | **638** | 38p. bright violet and indigo | 50 | 25 |

639 "Biblical King" and León Cathedral

640 "Nativity" (altarpiece, Tortosa)

1983 (28 Oct). Stained Glass Windows. T **639** and similar vert designs. Multicoloured. Recess and litho. P 12½.
2741		10p. Type **639**	20	15
2742		16p. "Epiphany" and Gerona Cathedral	30	20
2743		38p. "St. James" and Santiago de Compostela Hospital	55	20
2741/2743 Set of 3			90	50

1983 (9 Nov). Tourist Series. Vert designs as T **340**. Recess. P 13.
2744		3p. deep blue and deep dull green	20	15
2745		6p. deep blue	20	15
2746		16p. reddish violet and chestnut	25	15
2747		38p. lake and yellow-brown	45	25
2748		50p. deep brown and orange-vermilion	65	20
2744/2748 Set of 5			1·60	80

Designs:—3p. Church and tower, Llivia, Gerona; 6p. Santa María del Mar, Barcelona; 16p. Ceuta Cathedral; 38p. Bridge gateway, Melilla; 50p. Charity Hospital, Seville.

1983 (23 Nov). Christmas. T **640** and similar vert designs. Multicoloured. Photo. P 13×13½.
| 2749 | | 16p. Type **640** | 25 | 15 |
| 2750 | | 38p. "Adoration of the Kings" (altar-piece, Vich) | 55 | 20 |

641 Indalecio Prieto

642 Worker falling from Scaffolding

1983 (14 Dec). Birth Centenary of Indalecio Prieto (politician). Recess. P 13×13½.
| 2751 | **641** | 16p. purple-brown and black | 25 | 15 |

1984 (25 Jan). Safety at Work. T **642** and similar horiz designs. Multicoloured. Photo. P 13½×13.
2752		7p. Type **642**	10	10
2753		10p. Burning factory and extinguisher	15	10
2754		16p. Electric plug and wiring, cutters, gloved hands and warning sign	20	10
2752/2754 Set of 3			35	30

643 Tree

644 Burgos Cathedral and Coat of Arms

1984 (25 Feb). Extremaduran Autonomy. Recess and litho. P 13×13½.
| 2755 | **643** | 16p. multicoloured | 25 | 10 |

1984 (1 Mar). 1500th Anniv of Burgos City. Recess. P 13½×13.
| 2756 | **644** | 16p. sepia and blue | 20 | 10 |

645 Carnival Dancer, Santa Cruz, Tenerife

646 "Man" (Leonardo da Vinci)

1984 (5–16 May). Festivals. T **645** and similar horiz design. Multicoloured. Photo. P 13½×13.
| 2757 | | 16p. Type **645** | 25 | 10 |
| 2758 | | 16p. Carnival figure and fireworks, Valencia (16.3) | 25 | 10 |

1984 (11 Apr). Man and the Biosphere. Photo. P 13½×13.
| 2759 | **646** | 38p. multicoloured | 45 | 15 |

647 Map and Flag of Aragon and "Justice"

648 King Juan Carlos I

1984 (23 Apr). Autonomy of Aragon. Recess and litho. P 13½×13.
| 2760 | **647** | 16p. multicoloured | 25 | 10 |

(Des M. S. Castrejon. Eng A. M. Fernandez, P. S. Molero, A. S. Gutierrez, J. M. Martin, J. T. de Coca. Recess and litho)

1984 (27 Apr). España 84 International Stamp Exhibition, Madrid. Sheet 146×102 mm containing T **648** and similar vert designs, each maroon. P 13×13½.
MS2761 38p. Type **648**; 38p. Queen Sophia; 38p. Princess Cristina; 38p. Prince of Asturias; 38p. Princess Elena .... 3·50 3·50

649 F.I.P. Emblem

650 Bridge

SPAIN

1984 (3 May). 53rd International Philatelic Federation Congress, Madrid. Recess. P 13×13½.
2762   **649**   38p. scarlet and violet 45   15

(Des J. Larrivière. Recess)
1984 (5 May). Europa. P 13½×13.
2763   **650**   16p. dull vermilion 50   15
2764   38p. deep blue 60   45

651 Monument to the Alcántara Cazadores Regiment, Valladolid (Mariano Benlliure)

652 Arms of Canary Islands

1984 (19 May). Armed Forces Day. Photo. P 13½×13.
2765   **651**   17p. multicoloured 20   10

1984 (29 May). Autonomy of Canary Islands. Recess and litho. P 13×13½.
2766   **652**   16p. multicoloured 25   10

653 Arms of Castilla-La Mancha

654 King Alfonso X, the Wise, of Castile and Leon (700th death anniv)

1984 (31 May). Autonomy of Castilla-La Mancha. Recess and litho. P 13×13½.
2767   **653**   17p. multicoloured 25   10

1984 (20 June). Anniversaries. T **654** and similar horiz design. Recess. P 13½×13.
2768   16p. scarlet, deep blue and black 25   10
2769   38p. deep blue, deep carmine-red and black 50   25
Design:—38p. Ignacio Barraquer (ophthalmologist, birth centenary).

655 "James III confirming Grants"

656 Running before Bulls

1984 (29 June). Autonomy of Balearic Islands. Recess and litho. P 13×13½.
2770   **655**   17p. multicoloured 25   10

1984 (5 July). Pamplona Festival, San Fermín. Photo. P 13½×13.
2771   **656**   17p. multicoloured 25   10

1984 (20 July). Masters of Operetta (3rd series). Horiz designs as T **625** (2772, 2775/6) or vert designs as T **606** (others). Multicoloured. Recess and litho. P 13×12½.
2772   6p. Scene from *El Niño Judío* 15   10
        a. Horiz pair. Nos. 2772/3 40
2773   6p. Pablo Luna 15   10
2774   7p. Ruperto Chapí 15   10
        a. Horiz pair. Nos. 2774/5 40
2775   7p. Scene from *La Revoltosa* 15   10
2776   10p. Scene from *La Reina Mora* 15   10
        a. Horiz pair. Nos. 2776/7 40
2777   10p. José Serrano 15   10
2772/2777 *Set of 6* 80   55
The two designs of each value were printed together in horizontal *se-tenant* pairs within their sheets.

657 Bronze of Swimmer ready to Dive

658 Arms and Map of Navarra

1984 (27 July). Olympic Games, Los Angeles. T **657** and similar multicoloured designs. Phosphorescent paper. Photo. P 13½×13 (vert) or 13½×13 (horiz).
2778   1p. Roman quadriga (horiz) 10   10
2779   2p. Type **657** 10   10
2780   5p. Bronze of two wrestlers (horiz) 10   10
2781   8p. "The Discus-Thrower" (statue, Miron) 15   10
2778/2781 *Set of 4* 40   35

1984 (16 Aug). Autonomy of Navarra. Recess and litho. P 13½×13.
2782   **658**   17p. multicoloured 25   10

659 Cyclist

660 Arms (Levante Building, Salamanca University)

1984 (27 Aug). International Cycling Championships, Barcelona. Photo. P 13×13½.
2783   **659**   17p. multicoloured 20   10

1984 (5 Sept). Autonomy of Castilla y León. Recess and litho. P 13½×13.
2784   **660**   17p. multicoloured 25   10

661 Women gathering Grapes

662 Egeria on Donkey and Map of Middle East

1984 (20 Sept). Vintage Festival, Jerez. Photo. P 13½×13.
2785   **661**   17p. multicoloured 25   10

1984 (26 Sept). 1600th Anniv of Nun Egeria's Visit to Middle East. Photo. P 13.
2786   **662**   40p. multicoloured 45   25

SPAIN

663 Arab Courier

(Des P. Gonzales. Eng P. Molero. Recess and litho)
1984 (5 Oct). Stamp Day. P 13×12½.
2787   663   17p. multicoloured 20   10

664 Father Junipero Serra   665 "Adoration of the Kings" (Miguel Moguer) (Campos altarpiece)

1984 (12 Oct). Death Bicentenary of Father Junipero Serra (missionary). P 13½×13.
2788   664   40p. deep rose-red & dull ultramarine ..   45   20

1984 (21 Nov). Christmas. T 665 and similar multicoloured design. Phosphorescent paper. Photo. P 13½×13 (17p.) or 13×13½ (40p.).
2789   17p. "Nativity" (15th-century retable) (horiz)   20   10
2790   40p. Type 665   55   25

666 Arms, Buildings and Trees   667 Flags and Andean Condor

(Des A. Olagaray. Eng J. Martin. Recess and litho)
1984 (28 Nov). Autonomy of Madrid. P 13½×13.
2791   666   17p. multicoloured   25   10

1985 (16 Jan). 15th Anniv (1984) of Andean Pact. Phosphorescent paper. Photo. P 13.
2792   667   17p. multicoloured   20   10

668 "Virgin of Louvain" (attr. Jan Gossaert)   669 College Porch and Tympanum

1985 (21 Jan). Europalia 85 España Festival. Photo. P 13×13½.
2793   668   40p. multicoloured   55   30

1985 (20 Feb). 500th Anniv of Santa Cruz College, Valladolid University. Recess and litho. P 13×13½.
2794   669   17p. bistre-yell, reddish brn and brown-lake   20   10

670 Flames and "Olymphilex '85"   671 Havana Cathedral

1985 (18 Mar). Olymphilex 85 International Olympic Stamps Exhibition, Lausanne. Phosphorescent paper. Photo. P 13½×13.
2795   670   40p. dull scarlet, lemon and black   55   20

1985 (20 Mar). Espamer '85 International Stamp Exhibition, Havana, Cuba. Recess. P 13½×13.
2796   671   40p. dull ultramarine and brown-purple   55   25

672 Couple in Traditional Dress on Horseback   673 Heads as Holder for Flames

1985 (16 Apr). April Fair, Seville. Phosphorescent paper. Photo. P 13½×13.
2797   672   17p. multicoloured   25   10

1985 (17 Apr). International Youth Year. Recess. P 13½×13.
2798   673   17p. bronze green, black and orange-red   20   10

674 Moors and Christians fighting   675 Don Antonio de Cabezón (organist)

1985 (22 Apr). Festival of Moors and Christians, Alcoy. Phosphorescent paper. Photo. P 13½×13.
2799   674   17p. multicoloured   25   10

1985 (3 May). Europa. T 675 and similar horiz design. Recess. P 13½×13.
2800   18p. scarlet, black and blue/*pale yellow*   30   15
2801   45p. scarlet, black & olive-green/*pale yellow*   85   50
Designs:—45p. Musicians of National Youth Orchestra.

676 Capitanía General Headquarters, La Coruña

1985 (24 May). Armed Forces Day. Phosphorescent paper. Photo. P 13½×13.
2802   676   18p. multicoloured   25   10

295

SPAIN

677 Charles III's Arms, 1785 Decree and *Santíssima Trinidad* (ship of the line)

1985 (28 May). Bicentenary of National Flag. T **677** and similar horiz design. Multicoloured. Recess and litho. P 13.
2803	18p. Type **677**		25	15
	a. Vert pair. Nos. 2803/4		60	
2804	18p. State arms, 1978 constitution and lion (detail from House of Deputies)		25	15

Nos. 2803/4 were printed together in vertical *se-tenant* pairs within the sheet.

678 Sunflower and Bird **679** Monstrance in Decorated Street

1985 (5 June). World Environment Day. Phosphorescent paper. Photo. P 13.
2805	**678**	17p. multicoloured	20	15

1985 (6 June). Corpus Christi Festival, Toledo. Phosphorescent paper. Photo. P 13½×13½.
2806	**679**	18p. multicoloured	25	15

680 King Juan Carlos I **681** Planetary System

1985 (12 June)–92. Phosphorescent paper. Photo. P 14×13½.
2807	**680**	10c. deep slate-blue (16.5.89)	15	10
2808		50c. bright blue-green (16.5.89)	15	10
2809		1p. new blue	15	15
2810		2p. deep grey-green (3.4.86)	10	10
2811		3p. yellow-brown (3.4.86)	10	10
2812		4p. olive-bistre (3.4.86)	15	10
2813		5p. bright purple	2·50	90
2814		6p. bistre-brown (26.1.87)	15	10
2815		7p. bright violet (16.7.85)	15	10
2816		7p. bright yellow-olive (17.1.86)	10	10
2817		8p. deep violet-grey	1·00	50
2818		10p. carmine-lake (3.4.86)	15	10
2819		12p. rosine	15	15
2820		13p. greenish blue (16.5.89)	20	10
2821		15p. bright yellowish green (16.5.89)	20	10
2822		17p. yellow-orange (16.7.85)	25	10
2823		18p. bright turquoise-green	25	15
2824		19p. dull purple-brown (5.9.86)	30	10
		a. Red-brown (booklets) (11.3.87)	25	25
		ab. Booklet pane. No. 2824*a*×6	1·70	1·40
2825		20p. bright magenta (26.1.87)	30	10
2825*a*		25p. olive-green (14.12.90)	30	10
2825*b*		27p. deep magenta (3.3.92)	30	10
2826		30p. dull ultramarine (26.1.87)	45	10
2827		45p. bright emerald	55	15
2828		50p. bright violet-blue (24.4.89)	65	10
2828*a*		55p. blackish brown (14.12.90)	70	10
2829		60p. orange-red (24.4.89)	90	15
2830		75p. deep mauve (24.4.89)	1·00	15
2807/2830 Set of 27			10·00	3·75

The booklet pane has a narrow margin around the block of stamps.

(Des C. Manrique. Litho)

1985 (25 June). Inauguration of Astrophysical Observatories, Canary Islands. P 14.
2831	**681**	45p. multicoloured	55	20

682 Ataulfo Argenta (conductor)

1985 (26 June). European Music Year. T **682** and similar horiz designs. Multicoloured. Recess and litho. P 13×12½.
2832		12p. Type **682**	15	15
2833		17p. Tomas Luis de Victoria (composer)	25	15
2834		45p. Fernando Sor (guitarist and composer)	65	35
2832/2834 Set of 3			95	60

683 Bernal Díaz del Castillo (conquistador) **684** Canoeist

1985 (24 July). Celebrities. T **683** and similar horiz designs. Recess. P 13½×13.
2835		7p. scarlet, black & bronze grn/*pale yellow*	15	10
2836		12p. orange-red, blk & dp ultram/*pale yellow*	20	10
2837		17p. bronze green, scarlet & blk/*pale yellow*	30	15
2838		45p. bronze grn, blk & orge-brn/*pale yellow*	65	25
2835/2838 Set of 4			1·20	55

Design:—12p. Esteban Terradas (mathematician); 17p. Vicente Aleixandre (poet); 45p. León Felipe Camino (poet).

1985 (2 Aug). "Descent down the Sella" Canoe Festival, Asturias. Phosphorescent paper. Photo. P 13½×13.
2839	**684**	17p. multicoloured	25	10

 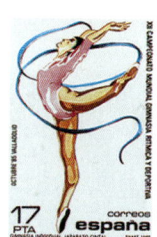

685 Monk returning with Rotulet to Savigni Abbey, 1122 **686** Ribbon Exercise

1985 (27 Sept). Stamp Day. Phosphorescent paper. Recess and litho. P 12½×13.
2840	**685**	17p. multicoloured	25	10

1985 (9 Oct). 12th World Rhythmic Gymnastics Championship, Valladolid. T **686** and similar vert design. Multicoloured. Phosphorescent paper. Photo. P 13×13½.
2841		17p. Type **686**	20	10
2842		45p. Hoop exercise	60	25

SPAIN

687 Prado Museum and "La Alcachofa" Fountain

688 "Virgin and Child" (Escalas Chapel, Seville Cathedral)

1985 (18 Oct). Exfilna '85 National Stamp Exhibition, Madrid. Sheet 120×80 mm. Phosphorescent paper. Recess and litho. P 13×12½.
MS2843 687 17p. multicoloured 70 70

1985 (24 Oct). Stained Glass Windows. T **688** and similar vert designs. Multicoloured. Phosphorescent paper. Recess and litho. P 12½×13.
2844	7p. Type **688**	10	10
2845	12p. Monk (Toledo Cathedral)..........................	15	10
2846	17p. King Enrique II of Castile and Leon (Alcazar of Segovia)................................	25	15
2844/2846	Set of 3	45	30

689 "Nativity" (detail of altarpiece by Ramón de Mur)

690 Subalpine Warbler (*Sylvia cantillans*)

1985 (27 Nov). Christmas. T **689** and similar horiz design. Multicoloured. Photo. P 13½×13.
2847	17p. Type **689**	15	10
2848	45p. "Adoration of the Magi" (embroidered frontal, after Jaume Huguet).............	60	25

1985 (4 Dec). Birds. T **690** and similar vert designs. Multicoloured. Phosphorescent paper. Recess and litho. P 13×13½.
2849	6p. Type **690**	20	10
2850	7p. Rock thrush (*Monticola saxatilis*)	20	10
2851	12p. Spotless starling (*Sturnus unicolor*).........	25	10
2852	17p. Bearded reedling (*Panurus biarmicus*)....	55	15
2849/2852	Set of 4	1·10	40

691 Count of Peñaflorida

692 Royal Palace, Madrid

1985 (11 Dec). Death Bicentenary of Count of Peñaflorida (founder of Economic Society of Friends of the Land). Phosphorescent paper. Recess. P 13½×13.
2853 691 17p. deep blue.................................... 20 10

(Des A. Santos (45p.). Litho)

1986 (7 Jan). Admission of Spain and Portugal to the European Economic Community. T **692** and similar horiz designs. Multicoloured. Litho. P 13½×13.
2854	7p. Type **692**	15	15
	a. Booklet pane. Nos. 2854/7...........................	3·75	2·75
2855	17p. Map and flags of member countries......	15	15
2856	30p. Hall of Columns, Royal Palace................	35	15
2857	45p. Flags of Portugal and Spain uniting with those of other members....................	65	35
2854/2857	Set of 4	1·20	75

PHOSPHORESCENT PAPER. From No. 2858 all stamps are printed on phosphorescent paper unless otherwise stated.

1986 (20 Jan). Tourist Series. Vert designs as T **340**. Recess. P 13×12½.
2858	12p. agate and deep claret................................	15	10
2859	35p. deep brown and blue.................................	45	15

Designs:—12p. Lupiana Monastery, Guadalajara; 35p. Balcony of Europe, Nerja.

693 Merino

694 "Revellers" (detail, F. Hohenleiter)

1986 (27 Jan). Second World Conference on Merinos. Photo. P 13½×13.
2860 693 45p. multicoloured......................... 45 15

1986 (5 Feb). Cadiz Carnival. Photo. P 13½×13.
2861 694 17p. multicoloured......................... 25 10

695 Helmets and Flower

1986 (12 Feb). International Peace Year. Recess and litho. P 13.
2862 695 45p. multicoloured......................... 45 15

696 Organ Pipes

697 "Swearing in of Regent, Queen Maria Cristina" (detail, Joaquin Sorolla y Bastida)

1986 (26 Mar). Religious Music Week, Cuenca. Photo. P 13½×13.
2863 696 17p. multicoloured......................... 25 10

1986 (9 Apr). Centenary of Chambers of Commerce, Industry and Navigation. Recess. P 13½×13.
2864 697 17p. greenish black and bronze green.. 20 10

698 Man with Suitcase

699 Boy and Birds

1986 (22 Apr). Emigration. Photo. P 13×13½.
2865 698 45p. multicoloured......................... 45 15

1986 (5 May). Europa. T **699** and similar horiz design. Multicoloured. Recess and litho. P 13.
2866	17p. Type **699**	30	15
2867	45p. Woman watering young tree....................	65	45

297

SPAIN

700 Our Lady of the Dew

701 Captainía General Building, Tenerife

1986 (14 May). Our Lady of the Dew Festival, Rocío, near Almonte. Photo. P 13½×13.
2868   700   17p. multicoloured 25   10

1986 (16 May). Armed Forces Day. Photo. P 13½×13.
2869   701   17p. multicoloured 20   10

1986 (16 June). Tourist Series. Horiz designs as T **340**. Recess. P 12½×13.
2870   12p. blue-black and blue 15   15
2871   35p. sepia and blue 45   15
Designs:—12p. Ciudad Rodrigo Cathedral, Salamanca; 35p. Calella lighthouse, Barcelona.

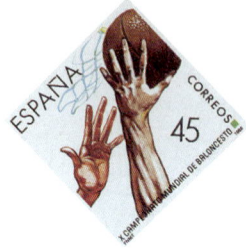
702 Hands and Ball

703 Francisco Loscos (botanist)

1986 (4 July). Tenth World Basketball Championship. Photo. P 12½.
2872   702   45p. multicoloured 45   15

1986 (16 July). Celebrities. T **703** and similar vert designs. Recess. P 13×13½.
2873   7p. bronze green and black 10   10
2874   11p. carmine-red and black 15   10
2875   17p. chocolate and black 20   10
2876   45p. deep claret, red-orange and black.. 70   35
2873/2876 Set of 4 .... 1·00 60
Designs:—11p. Salvador Espriu (writer); 17p. Azorin (José Martinez Ruiz) (writer); 45p. Juan Gris (artist).

704 Apostles awaiting Angels carrying Virgin's Soul

705 Swimmer

1986 (11 Aug). Elche Mystery Play. Photo. P 13×13½.
2877   704   17p. multicoloured 25   10

1906 (13 Aug). Fifth World Swimming, Water Polo, Leap and Synchronous Swimming Championships. Photo. P 13½×13.
2878   705   45p. multicoloured 45   15

706 Pelota Player

1986 (12 Sept). Tenth World Pelota Championship. Photo. P 13½×13.
2879   706   17p. multicoloured 25   10

707 King's Messenger with Letter summoning Nobleman to Court

1986 (27 Sept). Stamp Day. Recess and photo. P 13×12½.
2880   707   17p. multicoloured 20   10

708 Man releasing Dove and Córdoba Mosque

1986 (7 Oct). Exfilna '86 National Stamp Exhibition, Córdoba. Sheet 120×80 mm. Recess and litho. P 13×12½.
MS2881   708   17p. multicoloured 30   30

709 Aristotle

710 Gaspar de Portolá

1986 (15 Oct). 500th Anniv (1992) of Discovery of America by Columbus (1st issue). T **709** and similar horiz designs showing historic figures and properties of discovery of New World. Recess and litho. P 13.
2882   7p. black and mauve 10   10
             a. Booklet pane. Nos. 2882/7 .... 2·50 1·70
2883   12p. black and bright reddish lilac 15   10
2884   17p. black and orange-yellow 20   15
2885   30p. black and bright purple 40   15
2886   35p. black and blue-green 50   15
2887   45p. black and pale orange 65   15
2882/2887 Set of 6 .... 1·80   70
Designs:—2p. Seneca and quote from *Medea*; 17p. St. Isidoro of Seville and quote from *Etymologies*; 30p. Cardinal Pierre d'Ailly and quote from *Imago Mundi*; 35p. Mayan and quote from *Chilam Balam* books; 45p. Conquistador and quote from *Chilam Balam* books.
See also Nos. 2932/7, 2983/8, 3035/40, 3079/82, 3126/9, **MS**3147, 3175/6, **MS**3177 and 3190.

1986 (6 Nov). Death Bicentenary of Gaspar de Portolá (first governor of California). Recess and litho. P 13×13½.
2888   710   22p. deep blue, bright scarlet & black.. 30   10

711 "Holy Family" (detail, Diego de Siloe)

712 Abd-er Rahman II and Córdoba Mosque

SPAIN

1986 (19 Nov). Christmas. Wood Carvings. T **711** and similar multicoloured design. Photo. P 13×13½ (19p.) or 13½×13 (48p.).

2889	19p. Type **711**	25	10
2890	48p. "Nativity" (detail, Toledo Cathedral altarpiece, Felipe de Borgoña) (horiz)	65	15

1986 (3 Dec). Hispanic Islamic Culture. T **712** and similar horiz designs. Recess. P 13½×13.

2891	7p. reddish brown and orange-red	10	10
2892	12p. sepia and dull scarlet	15	10
2893	17p. deep blue and black	20	10
2894	45p. deep olive and black	70	15
2891/2894	Set of 4	1·00	40

Designs:—12p. Ibn Hazm (writer) and burning book; 17p. Al-Zarqali (astronomer) and azophea (astrolabe); 45p. King Alfonso VII of Castile and Leon and scholars of Toledo School of Translators.

713 "The Good Curate"

1986 (11 Dec). Birth Centenary of Alfonso Castelao (artist and writer). Recess and litho. P 13.

2895	**713**	32p. multicoloured	40	15

714 Château de la Muette (headquarters)   **715** Abstract Shapes

1987 (14 Jan). 25th Anniv of Organization for Economic Co-operation and Development. Recess and litho. P 13½×14.

2896	**714**	48p. multicoloured	55	15

1987 (21 Jan). Expo '92 World's Fair, Seville (1st issue). T **715** and similar horiz design. Multicoloured. Photo. P 13½×14.

2897	19p. Type **715**	35	10
2898	48p. Moon surface, Earth and symbol	90	10

See also Nos. 2941/2, 2951/2, 3004/7, 3052/5, 3094/7, 3143 and 3148/**MS**3172.

716 Francisco de Vitoria

1987 (11 Feb). 500th Birth Anniv of Francisco de Vitoria (jurist). Recess. P 13½×14.

2899	**716**	48p. lake-brown	55	15

717 18th-century Warship and Standard Bearer   **718** University

1987 (25 Feb). 450th Anniv of Marine Corps. Photo. P 13½×14.

2900	**717**	19p. multicoloured	25	10

1987 (26 Feb). Centenary of Deusto University. Recess. P 14×13½.

2901	**718**	19p. Indian red, dp grey-green & black	25	10

719 Breastfeeding Baby   **720** Crowd

1987 (4 Mar). U.N.I.C.E.F. Child Survival Campaign. Recess. P 13½×14.

2902	**719**	19p. lake-brown and sepia	25	10

1987 (18 Mar). 175th Anniv of Constitution of Cadiz. T **720** and similar vert designs. Multicoloured. Fluorescent paper. Litho. P 13½.

2903	25p. Type **720**	35	15
	a. Horiz strip of 4. Nos. 2903/6	2·00	
2904	25p. Crowd and herald on steps	35	15
2905	25p. Dignitaries on dais	35	15
2906	25p. Crown and Constitution	35	15
2903/2906	Set of 4	1·30	55

Nos. 2903/6 were printed together in horizontal *se-tenant* strips of four within the sheet, the first three stamps forming a composite design showing "The Promulgation of the Constitution of 1812" by Salvador Viniegra.

721 15th-century Pharmacy Jar, Manises   **722** "Procession at Dawn, Zamora" (Gallego Marquina)

1987 (20 Mar). Ceramics. T **721** and similar vert designs. Multicoloured. Recess and litho. P 12½×13.

2907	7p. Type **721**	10	10
	a. Block. Nos. 2907/12 plus 3 labels	3·00	3·00
2908	14p. 20th-century glazed figure, Sargadelos	15	15
2909	19p. 18th-century vase, Buen Retiro	25	15
2910	32p. 20th-century pot, Salvatierra de los Barros	45	20
2911	40p. 18th-century jar, Talavera	55	20
2912	48p. 18th-19th century jug, Granada	70	20
2907/2912	Set of 6	2·00	80

Nos. 2907/12 were printed together in *se-tenant* blocks of six stamps with a centre vertical row of three different labels.

1987 (13 Apr). Holy Week Festivals. T **722** and similar horiz design. Multicoloured. Photo. P 14×13½ (19p.) or 13½×14 (48p.).

2913	19p. Type **722**	30	10
2914	48p. Gate of Pardon, Seville Cathedral. and "Passion" (statue by Martínez Montañés)	65	15

1987 (21 Apr–June). Tourist Series. Designs as T **340**. Recess. P 13×12½ (48p.) or 12½×13 (others).

2915	14p. bottle green and deep ultramarine (10.6)	20	10
2916	19p. blackish green and bronze green	20	10
2917	40p. purple-brown (10.6)	50	15
2918	48p. black	90	15
2915/2918	Set of 4	1·60	45

Designs: Horiz—14p. Ifach Rock, Calpe, Alicante; 19p. Ruins of Church of Santa Mariña d'Ozo, Pontevedra; 40p. Palace of Soñanes, Vllacarriedo, Santander. Vert—48p. 11th-century monastery of Sant Joan de les Abadesses, Gerona.

SPAIN

723 Bilbao Bank, Madrid (Saenz de Oiza)
724 Horse's Head and Harnessed Pair

1987 (4 May). Europa Architecture. T **723** and similar design. Recess and litho. P 14×13½ (19p.) or 13½×14 (48p.).
2919		19p. multicoloured	60	35
2920		48p. agate, olive-bistre and myrtle green	75	35

Design: Horiz—48p. National Museum of Roman Art, Merida (Rafael Moneo).

1987 (6 May). Jerez Horse Fair. Photo. P 13½×14.
2921	**724**	19p. multicoloured	35	15

725 Carande
726 Numbers on Pen Nib

1987 (29 May). Birth Centenary of Ramón Carande (historian and Honorary Postman). Recess. P 13½×14.
2922	**725**	40p. black and reddish brown	55	20

1987 (1 June). Postal Coding. Litho. P 13½×14.
2923	**726**	19p. multicoloured	25	15

727 Arms and School
728 Batlló House Chimneys (Antonio Gaudí)

1987 (2 July). 75th Anniv of Eibar Armoury School. Litho. P 13½×14.
2924	**727**	20p. multicoloured	25	15

1987 (15 July). Nomination of Barcelona as 1992 Olympic Games Host City. T **728** and similar horiz design. Multicoloured. Photo. P 13½×14.
2925		32p. Type **728**	55	20
2926		65p. Athletes	95	20

729 Festival Poster (Fabri)
730 Monturiol (after Marti Alsina) and Diagrams of Submarine *Ictineo*

1987 (22 July). 25th Pyrenees Folklore Festival. Jaca. Photo. P 14×13½.
2927	**729**	50p. multicoloured	75	15

1987 (7 Sept). Death Centenary of Narcis Monturiol (scientist). Recess. P 13½×14.
2928	**730**	20p. black and brown	25	15

731 Detail from Jaime II of Majorca's Law appointing Couriers

1987 (16 Sept). Stamp Day. Recess and litho. P 13×12½.
2929	**731**	20p. multicoloured	25	15

732 18th-Century Pre-stamp Letter

1987 (2 Oct). Espamer '87 Stamp Exhibition, La Coruña. Maritime Post to America. Sheet 149×83 mm containing T **732** and similar horiz designs. Multicoloured. Recess and litho. P 13.

MS2930 8p. Type **732**; 12p. 19th-century engraving of La Coruña harbour; 20p. 18th-century view of Havana harbour; 50p. 18th-century sailing packets running between La Coruña and Havana (sold at 180p.) .... 4·50 4·25

No. **MS**2930 included an entrance coupon divided from the sheet by a line of rouletting. Price quoted is for the sheet with coupon attached.

733 "Aesculapius" and Olympic Torch Bearer

1987 (24 Oct). Exfilna '87 National Stamp Exhibition, Gerona. Sheet 120×80 mm. Photo. P 13×12½.
MS2931	**733**	20p. multicoloured	60	35

734 Amérigo Vespucci
735 Star and Baubles

1987 (30 Oct). 500th Anniv (1992) of Discovery of America by Columbus (2nd issue). Explorers. T **734** and similar horiz designs. Multicoloured. Recess and litho. P 13.
2932		14p. Type **734**	20	20
		a. Booklet pane. Nos. 2932/7	4·25	
2933		20p. King Ferdinand and Queen Isabella the Catholic and arms on ships	25	20
2934		32p. Juan Pérez and departing ships	40	20
2935		40p. Juan de la Cosa and ships	55	20
2936		50p. Map, ship and Christopher Columbus	65	30
2937		65p. Native on shore, approaching ships and Martín Alonzo and Vicente Yáñez Pinzón	90	30
2932/2937		Set of 6	2·75	1·30

300

SPAIN

1987 (17 Nov). Christmas. T **735** and similar vert design. Multicoloured. Photo. P 14×13½.
2938	20p. Type **735**	35	15
2939	50p. Zambomba and tambourine	75	30

736 Macho (self-sculpture)

737 Queen Sofia

1987 (23 Dec). Birth Centenary of Victorio Macho (sculptor). Recess. P 14×13½.
2940	**736** 50p. agate and black	65	20

1987 (29 Dec). Expo '92 World's Fair, Seville (2nd issue). As Nos. 2897/8 but values changed. Multicoloured. Photo. P 13½×14.
2941	20p. Type **715**	35	15
2942	50p. As No. 2898	75	15

1988 (5 Jan). 50th Birthdays of King Juan Carlos I and Queen Sofia. T **737** and similar vert design, each reddish brown, yellow and bright reddish violet. Photo. P 13×12½.
2943	20p. Type **737**	20	15
	a. Strip. Nos. 2943/4 plus label	70	50
2944	20p. King Juan Carlos	20	15

Nos. 2943/4 were printed together in *se-tenant* pairs with intervening label bearing the anniversary emblem.

738 Campoamor

739 Speed Skating

1988 (12 Feb). Birth Centenary of Clara Campoamor (politician and women's suffrage campaigner). Photo. P 13½×14.
2945	**738** 20p. multicoloured	25	15

1988 (15 Feb). Winter Olympic Games, Calgary. Photo. P 14×13½.
2946	**739** 45p. multicoloured	75	15

740 "Christ tied to the Pillar" (statue) and Valladolid Cathedral

741 Ingredients for and Dish of Paella

1988 (30 Mar). Holy Week Festivals. T **740** and similar vert design. Multicoloured. Photo. P 14×13½.
2947	20p. Type **740**	30	10
2948	50p. Float depicting Christ carrying the Cross, Málaga	65	15

1988 (7 Apr). Tourist Series. T **741** and similar horiz design. Multicoloured. Photo. P 13½×14.
2949	18p. Type **741**	30	10
2950	45p. Covadonga National Park (70th anniv of National Parks)	65	15

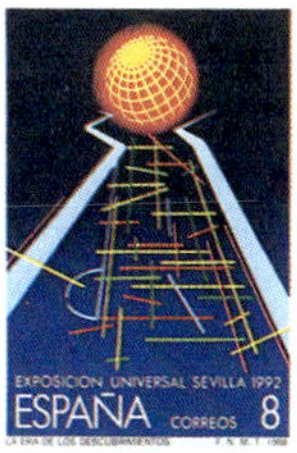

742 Globe and Stylized Roads

743 18th-Century Valencian Chalice

1988 (12 Apr). Expo '92 World's Fair, Seville (3rd issue). T **742** and similar multicoloured design. Photo. P 14×13½ (8p.) or 13½×14 (45p.).
2951	8p. Type **742**	15	10
2952	45p. Compass rose and globe (horiz)	55	10

1988 (13 Apr). Glassware. T **743** and similar vert designs. Multicoloured. Recess and litho. P 12½×13.
2953	20p. Type **743**	25	10
	a. Block. Nos. 2953/8 plus 6 labels	2·10	
2954	20p. 18th-century pitcher, Cadalso de los Vidrios, Madrid	25	10
2955	20p. 18th-century crystal sweet jar, La Granja de San Ildefonso	25	10
2956	20p. 18th-century Andalusian two-handled jug, Castril	25	10
2957	20p. 17th-century Catalan four-spouted jug	25	10
2958	20p. 20th-century bottle, Balearic Islands	25	10
2953/2958	Set of 6	1·40	55

Nos. 2953/8 were printed together in *se-tenant* blocks of six stamps and six half stamp-size labels of different designs.

744 Francis of Taxis (organizer of European postal service, 1505)

745 Pablo Iglesias (first President)

1988 (29 Apr). Stamp Day. Recess. P 12½×13.
2959	**744** 20p. slate-violet and red-brown	25	10

(Des E. A. Moya. Photo)

1988 (1 May). Centenary of General Workers' Union. P 13½×14.
2960	**746** 20p. multicoloured	20	10

746 *La Junta* (first Cuban locomotive), 1837

747 Monnet

1988 (5 May). Europa. Transport and Communications. T **746** and similar horiz design. Recess. P 13.
2961	20p. scarlet and black	30	30
2962	50p. deep dull green and black	95	50

Designs:—50p. Light telegraph, Philippines, 1818.

301

SPAIN

1988 (9 May). Birth Centenary of Jean Monnet (statesman). Recess. P 14×13½.
2963 747 45p. indigo.. 65 30

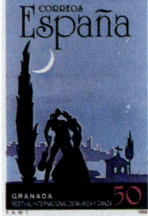

748 Emblem   749 Couple in Granada

1988 (31 May). Centenary of 1888 Universal Exhibition, Barcelona. Photo. P 13½×14.
2964 748 50p. multicoloured.............................. 65 10

1988 (1 June). International Festival of Music and Dance, Granada. Photo. P 14×13½.
2965 749 50p. multicoloured.............................. 65 10

750 Bull   751 "Virgin of Hope"

1988 (14 June). Expo 88 World's Fair, Brisbane. Photo. P 13½×14.
2966 750 50p. multicoloured.............................. 65 10

1988 (18 June). Coronation of "Virgin of Hope", Malaga. Photo. P 14×13½.
2967 751 20p. multicoloured.............................. 25 10

752 Plan of Pamplona Fortress

1988 (25 June). Exfilna 88 National Stamp Exhibition. Pamplona. Sheet 120×81 mm. Photo. P 13×12½.
MS2968 752 20p. multicoloured.............................. 30 25

753 Orreo (agricultural store), Cantabria

1988 (11 July). Tourist Series. T 753 and similar horiz design. Recess. P 13½×14.
2969   18p. blackish green, red-brown and blue 25 10
2970   45p. black, red-brown and brown-ochre 60 15
Design:—45p. Dulzaina (wind instrument), Castilla y León.

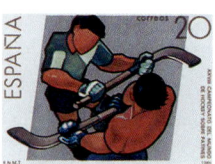

754 Players   755 Congress Emblem

1988 (7 Sept). 28th World Roller Skate Hockey Championship. La Coruña. Photo. P 13½×14.
2971 754 20p. multicoloured.............................. 25 10

1988 (9 Sept). First Spanish Regional Homes and Centres World Congress, Madrid. Photo. P 14×13½.
2972 755 20p. multicoloured.............................. 25 10

756 Olympic Class Dinghy   757 Borrell II, Count of Barcelona

1988 (10 Sept). Olympic Games, Seoul. Photo. P 14×13½.
2973 756 50p. multicoloured.............................. 65 15

1988 (21 Sept). Millenary of Catalonia. Photo. P 12½.
2974 757 20p. multicoloured.............................. 25 10

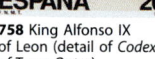

758 King Alfonso IX of Leon (detail of Codex of Toxos Outos)   759 Emblem on Band around Peace Year Stamps

1988 (26 Sept). 800th Anniv of First Leon Parliament. Photo. P 12½×13.
2975 758 20p. multicoloured.............................. 25 10

1988 (27 Sept). 25th Anniv of Spanish Philatelic Associations Federation. Photo. P 13½×14.
2976 759 20p. multicoloured.............................. 25 10

760 Games Emblem   761 Palace of the Generality, Valencia, and Seal of Jaime I

302

1988 (3 Oct). Olympic Games, Barcelona (1992) (1st issue). T **760** and similar horiz designs showing stylized representations of sports. Multicoloured. Photo. P 13½×14.

2977	8p. Type **760**	10	10
2978	20p.+5p. Athletics	35	35
2979	45p.+5p. Badminton	70	70
2980	50p.+5p. Basketball	85	75
2977/2980	Set of 4	1·80	1·70

See also Nos. 3008/11, 3031/3, 3056/8, 3076/8, 3098/3100, 3123/5, 3144/6, 3180/2 and 3183/5.

1988 (7 Oct). 750th Anniv of Re-conquest of Valencia by King Jaime I of Aragon. Photo. P 14×13½.

| 2981 | **761** | 20p. multicoloured | 25 | 10 |

762 Manuel Alonso Martínez (statesman)

763 Hernán Cortés and Quetzalcoatl Serpent

1988 (10 Oct). Centenary of Civil Code. Photo. P 14×13½.

| 2982 | **762** | 20p. multicoloured | 25 | 10 |

1988 (13 Oct). 500th Anniv (1992) of Discovery of America by Columbus (3rd issue). T **763** and similar horiz designs, each carmine-lake, blue and orange-red. Recess. P 13.

2983	10p. Type **763**	20	10
	a. Booklet pane. Nos. 2983/8	3·25	
2984	10p. Vasco Núñez de Balboa and waves	20	10
2985	20p. Francisco Pizarro and guanaco	30	10
2986	20p. Ferdinand Magellan, Juan Sebastián del Cano and globe	30	10
2987	50p. Alvar Núñez Cabeza de Vaca and river	65	15
2988	50p. Andrés de Urdaneta and maritime currents	65	15
2983/2988	Set of 6	2·00	65

Nos. 2983/8 were issued both in separate sheets and together in booklets.

764 Enrique III of Castile and Leon (first Prince of Asturias)

1988 (26 Oct). 600th Anniv of Title of Prince of Asturias. Photo. P 13×12½.

| 2989 | **764** | 20p. multicoloured | 25 | 10 |

765 Snowflakes

766 Córdoba Mosque

1988 (24 Nov). Christmas. T **765** and similar multicoloured design. Photo. P 13½×14 (20p.) or 14×13½ (50p.).

| 2990 | 20p. Type **765** | 30 | 10 |
| 2991 | 50p. Shepherd carrying sheep (vert) | 65 | 25 |

1988 (1 Dec). U.N.E.S.C.O. World Heritage Sites. T **766** and similar designs. Recess. P 12½×13 (vert) or 13×12½ (horiz).

2992	18p. lake-brown	25	10
2993	20p. blue	30	15
2994	45p. brown	65	15
2995	50p. grey-green	80	15
2992/2995	Set of 4	1·80	50

Designs: Vert—20p. Burgos Cathedral. Horiz—45p. San Lorenzo Monastery, El Escorial; 50p. Alhambra, Granada.

767 Representation of Political Parties

1988 (7 Dec). Tenth Anniv of Constitution. Photo. P 13½×14.

| 2996 | **767** | 20p. multicoloured | 30 | 15 |

768 Courtiers in Palace Grounds

1988 (14 Dec). Death Bicentenary of King Charles III. Sheet 100×80 mm. Recess. P 13×12½.

| MS2997 | **768** | 45p. deep green and black | 65 | 35 |

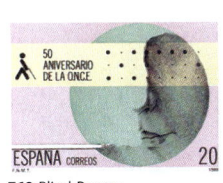
769 Blind Person

770 Luis de Granada

1988 (27 Dec). 50th Anniv of National Organization for the Blind. Photo. P 13½×14.

| 2998 | **769** | 20p. multicoloured | 30 | 15 |

1988 (31 Dec). 400th Death Anniv of Brother Luis de Granada (mystic). Photo. P 14×13½.

| 2999 | **770** | 20p. multicoloured | 30 | 15 |

771 Olympic Rings and Sails (Natalia Barrio Fernández)

772 Abstract

1989 (3 Jan). Children's Stamp Designs. T **771** and similar multicoloured designs. Photo. P 13½×14 (3000) or 14×13½ (3001).

| 3000 | 20p. Type **771** | 30 | 10 |
| 3001 | 20p. Magnifying glass on stamp (José Luis Villegas López) (vert) | 30 | 10 |

SPAIN

1989 (24 Jan). **Bicentenary of French Revolution**. Photo. P 12½×13.
3002   **772**   45p. bright scarlet, blue and black   65   15

773 María de Maeztu   774 London, 1851

1988 (7 Feb). **107th Birth Anniv of María de Maeztu** (educationist). Photo. P 13½×14.
3003   **773**   20p. multicoloured   25   10

1989 (9 Feb). **Expo '92 World's Fair, Seville (4th issue). Great Exhibitions**. T **774** and similar vert designs. Multicoloured. Photo. P 14×13½.
3004   8p.+5p. Type **774**   15   15
3005   8p.+5p. Paris, 1889   15   15
3006   20p.+5p. Brussels, 1958   35   30
3007   20p.+5p. Osaka, 1970   35   30
3004/3007   *Set of 4*   90   80

1989 (7 Mar). **Olympic Games, Barcelona (1992) (2nd issue)**. Horiz designs as T **760**. Photo. P 13½×14.
3008   8p.+5p. Handball   30   15
3009   18p.+5p. Boxing   35   25
3010   20p.+5p. Cycling   35   35
3011   45p.+5p. Show jumping   90   70
3008/3011   *Set of 4* ....   1·70   1·30

775 Uniforms, 1889   776 International Postal Service Treaty, 1601

1988 (11 Mar). **Centenary of Post Office**. Recess and litho. P 13½×14.
3012   **775**   20p. multicoloured   25   10

1989 (4 Apr). **Stamp Day**. Recess. P 12½×13.
3013   **776**   20p. black   25   10

777 Entrance Door   778 Skittles

1989 (22 Apr). **Cordon House, Burgos**. Recess. P 14×13½.
3014   **777**   20p. black   25   10

1989 (5 May). **Europa. Children's Toys**. T **778** and similar vert design. Multicoloured. Photo. P 14×13½.
3015   40p. Type **778**   60   35
3016   50p. Spinning top   85   60

 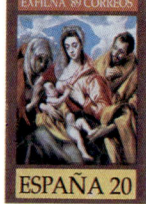

779 European Flag   780 "Holy Family with St. Anne" (El Greco)

1989 (9 May). **Spanish Presidency of European Economic Community**. Photo. P 13½×14.
3017   **779**   45p. multicoloured   65   35

1989 (20 May). **Exfilna 89 National Stamp Exhibition, Toledo**. Sheet 105×78 mm. Recess and litho. P 14×13½.
MS3018   **780**   20p. multicoloured   45   45

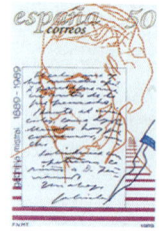  

781 Manuscript and Portrait   782 Flags forming Ballot Box

1989 (1 June). **Birth Centenary of Gabriela Mistral (poet)**. Recess and litho. P 14×13½.
3019   **781**   50p. multicoloured   70   15

1989 (12 June). **European Parliament Elections**. Photo. P 13.
3020   **782**   45p. multicoloured   65   35

783 Catalonia

1989 (20 June). **Lace**. T **783** and similar horiz designs showing typical designs from named region. P 13×12½.
3021   20p. chalky blue and sepia   25   15
    a. Block. Nos. 3021/6 plus 3 labels ......   1·90
3022   20p. chalky blue and sepia   25   15
3023   20p. chalky blue   25   15
3024   20p. chalky blue   25   15
3025   20p. chalky blue and sepia   25   15
3026   20p. chalky blue and sepia   25   15
3021/3026   *Set of 6* ....   1·40   80

Designs:—No. 3022, Andalucia; 3023, Extremadura; 3024, Canary Islands; 3025, Castilla-La Mancha; 3026, Galicia.

Nos. 3021/6 were printed together in *se-tenant* blocks of six stamps with a centre vertical row of three different labels.

784 Pope John Paul II and Youths

304

1989 (19 Aug). Third Papal Visit. Recess. P 13×12½.
3027   784   50p. slate-green, lake-brown and black   65   15

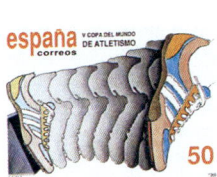
785 Foot leaving Starting Block

786 Chaplin

1989 (1 Sept). World Cup Athletics Championships, Barcelona. Photo. P 13½×14.
3028   785   50p. multicoloured   55   15

1989 (19 Sept). Birth Centenary of Charlie Chaplin (actor). Recess and litho. P 14×13½.
3029   786   50p. multicoloured   65   15

787 1p. Stamp

788 Fr. Andrés Manjón (founder)

1989 (2 Oct). Centenary of First King Alfonso XIII Stamps. Photo. P 14×13½.
3030   787   50p. sepia, brownish grey and red.........   65   15

1989 (3 Oct). Olympic Games, Barcelona (1992) (3rd issue). Horiz designs as T **760**. Photo. P 13½×14.
3031   18p.+5p. Fencing   70   55
3032   20p.+5p. Football   70   60
3033   45p.+5p. Gymnastics ....   1·00   95
3031/3033 Set of 3 ....   2·10   1·90

1989 (13 Oct). Centenary of Ave Maria Schools. Photo. P 14×13½.
3034   788   20p. multicoloured   25   10

789 Maize

790 Inca irrigating Corn (from *New Chronicle* by Waman Puma)

1989 (16 Oct). 500th Anniv (1992) of Discovery of America by Columbus (4th issue). T **789** and similar horiz designs. Multicoloured. Litho. P 13×13½.
3035   8p.+5p. Type **789**   15   15
            a. Booklet pane. Nos. 3035/40 ....   3·50
3036   8p.+5p. Cacao nut   15   15
3037   20p.+5p. Tomato   30   25
3038   20p.+5p. Horse   30   25
3039   50p.+5p. Potato   70   55
3040   50p.+5p. Turkey   70   55
3035/3040 Set of 6 ....   2·10   1·70

1989 (7 Nov). America. Pre-Columbian Life. Recess and litho. P 14×13½.
3041   790   50p. multicoloured   55   10

791 "Navidad 89"   792 Altamira Caves

1989 (29 Nov). Christmas. T **791** and similar multicoloured design. Photo. P 14×13½ (20p.) or 13½×14 (45p.).
3042   20p. Type **791**   25   10
3043   45p. Girl with Christmas present (horiz)   60   15

1989 (5 Dec). World Heritage Sites. T **792** and similar horiz designs. Multicoloured. Recess and litho. P 13×12½.
3044   20p. Type **792**   30   10
3045   20p. Segovia Aqueduct   30   10
3046   20p. Santiago de Compostela   30   10
3047   20p. Guell Park and Palace and Milá House..   30   10
3044/3047 Set of 4 ....   1·10   45

793 San Lorenzo Monastery, El Escorial

1989 (20 Dec). National Heritage. Royal Palaces. Sheet 162×92 mm containing T **793** and similar horiz designs. Multicoloured. Recess and litho. P 13.
MS3048 45p. Type **793**; 45p. Aranjuez; 45p. La Granja de San Ildefonso; 45p. Madrid ....   2·20   2·20

794 Olympic Rings, Compass Rose, Church of Holy Family, Barcelona, and Seville

795 Getxo City Hall and Competitor

(Des D. García Pérez. Photo)

1990 (29 Jan). Children's Stamp Design. Photo. P 14×13½.
3049   794   20p. multicoloured   25   10

1990 (2 Feb). World Cyclo-cross Championship, Getxo. Photo. P 14×13½.
3050   795   20p. multicoloured   25   10

796 Victoria Kent

797 Curro (mascot) flying over Path of Discoveries

1990 (12 Feb). Third Death Anniv of Victoria Kent (prison reformer). Recess. P 14×13½.
3051   796   20p. deep lilac....................................   25   10

1990 (22 Feb). Expo '92 World's Fair, Seville (5th issue). T **797** and similar horiz designs. Multicoloured. Photo. P 13½×14.

3052	8p.+5p. Type **797**	15	15
3053	20p.+5p. Curro and Exhibition buildings	30	30
3054	45p.+5p. Curro and view of Project Cartuja '93	65	65
3055	50p.+5p. Curro crossing bridge in Project Cartuja '93	80	80
3052/3055 Set of 4		1·70	1·70

1990 (7 Mar). Olympic Games, Barcelona (1992) (4th issue). Horiz designs as T **760**. P 13½×14.

3056	18p.+5p. Weightlifting	45	35
3057	20p.+5p. Hockey	45	35
3058	45p.+5p. Judo	90	60
3056/3058 Set of 3		1·60	1·20

798 Rafael Alvarez Sereix (Honorary Postman)

(Des M. Salamanca. Eng J. Heras Vicario. Recess and litho)

1990 (18 Apr). Stamp Day. P 13×12½.

3059	**798**	20p. flesh, sepia and dull blue-green	25	10

799 Vitoria Post Office   **800** "Hispasat" Communications Satellite

(Des M. Salamanca (20p.), M. Plaza Torralba (50p.). Photo)

1990 (4 May). Europa. Post Office Buildings. T **799** and similar multicoloured design. P 13½×14 (20p.) or 14×13½ (50p.).

3060	20p. Type **799**	55	30
3061	50p. Málaga Post Office (vert)	95	55

(Des M. Salamanca. Photo)

1990 (17 May). 125th Anniv of International Telecommunications Union. P 13½×14.

3062	**800**	8p. multicoloured	20	10

801 Door Knocker, Aragón   **802** Infanta's Patio, Zaragoza

(Des M. Escobar. Eng J. M. Mata (3063), J. Terriza (3064), A. Sánchez (3065), A. de Oro (3066), J. González de la Lastra (3067), P. San Pedro (3068). Recess and litho)

1990 (18 May). Wrought Ironwork. T **801** and similar vert designs, each black, olive-grey and carmine-red. P 12½×13.

3063	20p. Type **801**	30	15
	a. Block. Nos. 3063/8 plus 3 labels	2·10	
3064	20p. Door knocker, Andalucia	30	15
3065	20p. Pistol, Catalonia	30	15
3066	20p. Door knocker, Castilla-La Mancha	30	15
3067	20p. Mirror with lock, Galicia	30	15
3068	20p. Basque fireback	30	15
3063/3068 Set of 6		1·60	80

Nos. 3063/8 were printed together in *se-tenant* blocks of six stamps with a central vertical row of three different labels.

(Des P. Sánchez. Eng J. M. Mata. Recess and litho)

1990 (25 May). Exfilna 90 National Stamp Exhibition, Zaragoza. Sheet 105×78 mm. P 14×13½.

MS3069	**802**	20p. chestnut	35	35

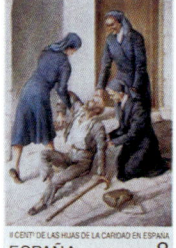 

803 "Charity" (Lopez Alonso)   **804** St. Antolin's Crypt, Palencia Cathedral

(Des J. Suárez (45p.), M. Salamanca (others). Eng A. Sánchez (45p.), J. Terriza (50p.). Litho (8p.), photo (20p.) or recess and litho (others))

1990 (19 June). Anniversaries. T **803** and similar designs. P 12½×13 (vert) or 13×12½ (horiz).

3070	8p. multicoloured	15	10
3071	20p. multicoloured	25	10
3072	45p. dull orange and sepia	60	15
3073	50p. dull vermilion and blue	65	15
3070/3073 Set of 4		1·50	45

Designs: Vert—8p. Type **803** (bicentenary of arrival in Spain of Daughters of Charity); 50p. First page of book (500th anniv of publication of *Tirant lo Blanch* by Joanot Martorell and Martí Joan de Galba. Horiz—20p. Score of *Leilah* and José Padilla (composer, birth centenary (1989)); 45p. Palace of Kings of Navarre (900th anniv of grant of privileges to Estella).

(Des J. Suárez. Eng A. Sánchez. Recess and litho)

1990 (22 June). Filatem '90 Third National Thematic Stamps Exhibition, Palencia. Sheet 105×77 mm. P 13½×13½.

MS3074	**804**	20p. lake-brown	35	35

805 Poster   **806** Caravel and Compass Rose

1990 (27 Aug). 17th International Historical Sciences Congress, Madrid. Litho. P 14×13½.

3075	**805**	50p. multicoloured	70	15

1990 (3 Oct). Olympic Games, Barcelona (1992) (5th issue). Horiz designs as T **760**. Multicoloured. Photo. P 13½×14.

3076	8p.+5p. Wrestling	20	15
3077	18p.+5p. Swimming	35	30
3078	20p.+5p. Baseball	45	35
3076/3078 Set of 3		90	70

(Des Carmen Díez. Photo)

1990 (18 Oct). 500th Anniv of Discovery of America by Columbus (5th issue). T **806** and similar horiz designs. Multicoloured. P 13×13½.

3079	8p.+5p. Type **806**	20	15
	a. Booklet pane. Nos. 3079/82	3·00	
3080	8p.+5p. Caravels	20	15
3081	20p.+5p. Caravel	35	30
3082	20p.+5p. Galleons	35	30
3079/3082 Set of 4		1·00	80

SPAIN

807 Puerto Rican Todys   **808** Sun

(Des M. Escobar. Eng J. González de la Lastra. Recess and litho)

1990 (14 Nov). America. The Natural World. P 14×13½.
3083   **807**   50p. multicoloured 70   15

1990 (22 Nov). Christmas. T **808** and similar multicoloured design showing details of "Cosmic Poem" by José Antonio Sistiaga. Photo. P 14×13½ (25p.) or 13½×14 (45p.).
3084   25p. Type **808** 35   10
3085   45p. Moon (horiz) 65   15

809 "Flemish Soldiers"   **810** Tourism Logo
(after Philips Wouvermans)   (Joan Miró)

(Des M. Salamanca. Eng J. M. Mata, P. Sampedro and A. Sánchez. Recess and litho)

1990 (28 Nov). Tapestries. Sheet 105×151 mm containing T **809** and similar vert designs. Multicoloured. P 13.
MS3086   20p.×4: "Calvary" (Peter Pannemaker, after Jan van Roome and Bernard van Orley); Type **809**; "Wreck of the *Telemach*" (Urbano Leyniers, after Miguel Houasse); "Flower Sellers" (Antonio Moreno and Eusebio de Candano. after Goya) .... 1·40   1·20

(Des M. Escobar. Photo)

1990 (1 Dec). European Tourism Year. P 14×13½.
3087   **810**   45p. multicoloured 65   40

811 Church of St. Miguel   **812** Conductor and Orchestra
de Lillo, Oviedo

(Des J. Suárez. Eng J. Terriza (3088). J. González de la Lastra (3089), A. Sánchez (3090), J. M. Mata (3091). Recess and litho)

1990 (10 Dec). World Heritage Sites. T **811** and similar designs. Multicoloured. P 12½×13 (vert) or 13×12½ (horiz).
3088   20p. Type **811** 25   10
3089   20p. St. Peter's Tower, Teruel 25   10
3090   20p. Bujaco Tower, Cáceres 25   10
3091   20p. St. Vincent's Church, Avila 25   10
3088/3091 *Set of 4* 90   45

(Des M. Salamanca. Photo)

1990 (20 Dec). Spanish National Orchestra. P 13½×14.
3092   **812**   25p. yellow-green, dull blue-grn and black 35   10

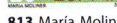

813 María Moliner   **814** La Cartuja (Santa María de la Cuevas Monastery)

(Des P. Sánchez. Photo)

1991 (21 Jan). Tenth Death Anniv of Maria Moliner (philologist). P 14×13½.
3093   **813**   25p. multicoloured 35   10

(Des M. Salamanca and J. Angel. Eng J. M. Mata (15p.), P. Sampedro (25p.), A. Sánchez (45p.), J. González de la Lastra (55p.). Recess and litho)

1991 (12 Feb). Expo '92 World's Fair, Seville (6th issue). T **814** and similar horiz designs showing views of Seville. Multicoloured. P 13½×14.
3094   15p.+5p. Type **814** 25   25
3095   25p.+5p. The Auditorium 45   35
3096   45p.+5p. La Cartuja bridge 65   65
3097   55p.+5p. La Barqueta bridge 80   75
3094/3097 *Set of 4* .... 2·00   1·80

(Des P. Pastor. Litho)

1991 (7 Mar). Olympic Games, Barcelona (1992) (6th series). Horiz designs as T **760**. P 13½×14 (15, 45p.) or 13 (25p.).
3098   15p.+5p. brownish grey, black & carm 35   30
3099   25p.+5p. multicoloured 40   40
3100   45p.+5p. multicoloured 75   65
3098/3100 *Set of 3* .... 1·40   1·20
Designs:—15p. Modern pentathlon; 25p. Canoeing; 45p. Rowing.

815 Olympic Rings   **816** Loja Gate
and Yachts

(Des Ana Perelló Rebasa. Photo)

1991 (12 Apr). Children's Stamp Design. P 14×13½.
3101   **815**   25p. multicoloured 35   10

(Des J. Prieto. Eng A. Sánchez. Recess and litho)

1991 (19 Apr). Granada '92 International Thematic Stamp Exhibition (1st issue) and 500th Anniv of Santa Fe. Sheet 106×78 mm. P 13½×14.
MS3102   **816**   25p. deep reddish purple and gold 40   40
See also No. **MS**3174.

817 Juan de Tassis y   **818** Talavera
Peralta (Chief Courier to   Apothecary Jar
Kings Philip III and IV)

307

SPAIN

(Des and eng J. Heras. Recess)
1991 (26 Apr). Stamp Day. P 12½×13.
3103 **817** 25p. black 35 15

(Des J. de Miguel. Recess and litho)
1991 (3 May). Porcelain and Ceramics. Sheet 106×150 mm containing T **818** and similar vert designs. Multicoloured. P 13.
MS3104 25p. Type **818**; 25p. Buen Retiro figurine; 25p. Pickmann bottle; 25p. La Moncloa plate .... 1·60 1·60

819 Dish Aerials, INTA-NASA Earth Station, Robledo de Chavela

820 Brother Luis Ponce de León (translator and poet, 400th death anniv)

(Des M. Salamanca. Photo)
1991 (28 May). Europa. Europe in Space. T **819** and similar horiz design. Multicoloured. P 13½×14.
3105 25p. Type **819** 55 30
3106 45p. "Olympus I" telecommunications satellite .... 1·10 55

(Des R. Gaya (3107), M. Quetglas (3108), S. Martin (3109), C. Franco (3110). Photo)
1991 (6 June). Anniversaries. T **820** and similar designs. P 13½×14 (3107) or 14×13½ (others).
3107 15p. multicoloured 25 15
3108 15p. yellow-orange, bright scarlet and black 25 15
3109 25p. multicoloured 40 15
3110 25p. multicoloured 40 15
3107/3110 Set of 4 .... 1·20 55
Designs: Horiz—No. 3107, Table and chair (400th death anniv of St. John of the Cross). Vert—No. 3109, Banner and cap (500th birth anniv of St. Ignatius of Loyola (founder of Society of Jesus)); 3110, Abd-er Rahman III, Emir of Córdoba (1100th birth anniv).

821 Apollo Fountain

822 Choir (after mosaic mural, Palau de la Música)

(Des J. Lazkano. Photo)
1991 (29 July). Madrid, European City of Culture (1st issue). T **821** and similar horiz designs. Multicoloured. P 13½×14.
3111 15p.+5p. Type **821** 45 45
3112 25p.+5p. "Don Alvaro de Bazán" (statue, Mariano Benlliure) 50 50
3113 45p.+5p. Bank of Spain 80 80
3114 55p.+5p. Cloisters, St. Isidro Institute 90 90
3111/3114 Set of 4 .... 2·40 2·40
See also Nos. 3195/8.

(Des J. Mariscal. Litho)
1991 (6 Sept). Centenary of Orfeó Catalá (Barcelona choral group). P 14×13½.
3115 **822** 25p. multicoloured 30 10

823 Basque Drug Cupboard

824 Hands holding Net

(Des M. Escobar. Eng A. de Oro (3116, 3118), V. Morán (3117, 3119), A. Sánchez (3120), J. M. Mata (3121). Recess and litho)
1991 (9 Sept). Furniture. T **823** and similar vert designs. Multicoloured. P 12½×13.
3116 25p. Type **823** 30 10
  a. Block. Nos. 3116/21 plus three labels .... 2·20 2·20
3117 25p. Kitchen dresser, Castilla y León 30 10
3118 25p. Chair, Murcia 30 10
3119 25p. Cradle, Andalucia 30 10
3120 25p. Travelling chest, Castilla-La Mancha 30 10
3121 25p. Bridal chest, Catalonia 30 10
3116/3121 Set of 6 .... 1·62 55
Nos. 3116/21 were issued together in se-tenant blocks of six stamps with a central vertical row of three different labels.

(Des P. Sánchez. Litho)
1991 (10 Sept). World Fishing Exhibition, Vigo. P 14×13½.
3122 **824** 55p. multicoloured 85 15

(Des J.-P. Viladecans. Photo)
1991 (3 Oct). Olympic Games, Barcelona (1992) (7th series). Horiz designs as T **760**. P 13½×14.
3123 15p.+5p. Tennis 45 40
3124 25p.+5p. Table tennis 65 60
3125 55p.+5p. Shooting .... 1·30 1·20
3123/3125 Set of 3 ....

825 Garcilaso de la Vega, the Inca (Spanish-Inca poet)

826 Nocturlabe

(Des V. Urosa. Photo)
1991 (15 Oct). 500th Anniv (1992) of Discovery of America by Columbus (6th issue). T **825** and similar horiz designs. Multicoloured. P 13.
3126 15p.+5p. Type **825** 25 25
  a. Booklet pane. Nos. 3126/9 .... 3·75
3127 25p.+5p. Pope Alexander VI 45 40
3128 45p.+5p. Luis de Santángel (banker) 70 70
3129 55p.+5p. Brother Toribio Motolinia (missionary) 90 80
3126/3129 Set of 4 .... 2·00 2·00

(Des M. Escobar. Eng J. M. Mata. Recess and litho)
1991 (4 Nov). America. Voyages of Discovery. P 14×13½.
3130 **826** 55p. orange-brown and brown-purple .. 80 20

827 "Nativity" (from New Chronicle by Guaman Poma de Ayala)

828 "The Meadow of San Isidro" (Francisco Goya)

SPAIN

1991 (22 Nov). Christmas. T **827** and similar vert design. Photo. P 14×13½.
3131	25p. buff and deep chestnut	40	15
3132	45p. multicoloured	80	20

Design:—45p. "Nativity" (16th-century Russian icon).

(Des M. Salamanca. Eng A. de Oro. Recess and litho)

1991 (12 Dec). Exfilna 91 National Stamp Exhibition, Madrid. Sheet 106×78 mm. P 13½×14.
MS3133	**828**	25p. multicoloured	45	45

829 Alcántara Gate, Toledo

830 Gen. Carlos Ibañez de Ibero (cartographer)

(Des J. Prieto. Eng A. de Oro (3134), V. Morán (3135), J. González de la Lastra (3136), J. Heras (3137). Recess)

1991 (16 Dec). World Heritage Sites. T **829** and similar designs. P 12½×13 (vert) or 13×12½ (horiz).
3134	25p. agate and lake-brown	45	15
3135	25p. black and chocolate	45	15
3136	25p. brown and blue	45	15
3137	25p. bluish violet and bottle green	45	15
3134/3137	Set of 4	1·70	55

Designs: Vert—No. 3135, Casa de las Conchas, Salamanca. Horiz—No. 3136, Seville Cathedral; 3137, Aeonio (flower) and Garajonay National Park, Gomera.

(Des M. Garcia. Photo)

1991 (27 Dec). Anniversaries and Events. T **830** and similar vert design. Multicoloured. P 14×13½.
3138	25p. Type **830** (death centenary)	50	15
3139	55p. *Las Palmas* (Antarctic survey ship) (signing of Antarctic Treaty Protocol of Madrid declaring the Antarctic a nature reserve)	95	20

831 Margarita Xirgu

832 "Expo 92, Seville"

(Des P. Sánchez. Photo)

1992 (20 Jan). 23rd Death Anniv of Margarita Xirgu (actress). P 13½×14.
3140	**831**	25p. ochre and deep carmine	35	15

(Des Esther Lucas Rodriguez. Photo)

1992 (14 Feb). Children's Stamp Design. P 13½×14.
3141	**832**	25p. multicoloured	35	15

833 Pedro Rodriguez, Count of Campomanes (administrator and postal consultant)

(Des M. Escobar, Photo)

1992 (21 Feb). Stamp Day. P 13×12½.
3142	**833**	27p. multicoloured	40	15

834 Spanish Pavilion

(Des J. Suárez. Photo)

1992 (28 Feb). Expo '92 World's Fair, Seville (7th issue). P 13½×14.
3143	**834**	27p. brownish grey, black & yell-brown	40	15

(Des X. Armenter. Litho)

1992 (6 Mar). Olympic Games, Barcelona (8th issue). Horiz designs as T **760**. Multicoloured. P 13½×14.
3144	15p.+5p. Archery	50	50
3145	25p.+5p. Yachting	70	70
3146	55p.+5p. Volleyball	1·20	1·10
3144/3146	Set of 3	2·10	2·00

835 Columbus's Fleet

(Des M. Salamanca. Eng J.-L. Sánchez Toda. Recess and litho)

1992 (31 Mar). 500th Anniv of Discovery of America by Columbus (7th issue). Sheet 164×95 mm reproducing 1930 Columbus design. P 14.
MS3147	**835**	17p.+5p. scarlet; 17p.+5p. ultramarine; 17p.+5p. black	1·50	1·50

836 Cable-cars

837 Wheelchair Sports

(Des M. Salamanca and A. Millán. Litho)

1992 (20–21 Apr). Expo '92 World's Fair, Seville (8th issue). T **836** and similar horiz designs. Multicoloured. P 13½×14.
3148	17p. Exhibition World Trade Centre	30	25
	a. Sheetlet. Nos. 3148/59 plus 4 labels	4·75	
3149	17p. Type **836**	30	25
3150	17p. Fourth Avenue	30	25
3151	17p. Barqueta entrance	30	25
3152	17p. Nature Pavilion	30	25
3153	17p. Bioclimatic sphere	30	25
3154	17p. Alamillo bridge	30	25
3155	17p. Press centre	30	25
3156	17p. Pavilion of the 15th Century	30	25
3157	17p. Expo harbour	30	25
3158	17p. Tourist train	30	25
3159	17p. One-day entrance ticket showing bridge	30	25
3160	27p. Santa Maria de las Cuevas Carthusian monastery	50	40
	a. Sheetlet. Nos. 3160/71 plus 4 labels	6·25	
3161	27p. Palisade	50	40
3162	27p. Monorail	50	40
3163	27p. Avenue of Europe	50	40
3164	27p. Pavilion of Discovery	50	40
3165	27p. Auditorium	50	40
3166	27p. First Avenue	50	40
3167	27p. Square of the Future	50	40
3168	27p. Italica entrance	50	40
3169	27p. Last avenue	50	40
3170	27p. Theatre	50	40
3171	27p. Curro (official mascot)	50	40
3148/3171	Set of 24	8·75	7·00
MS3172	105×77 mm. 17p.+5p. View of 16th-century Seville (after A. Sánchez Coello) (21.4)	40	40

309

SPAIN

Stamps of the same value were issued together in *se-tenant* sheetlets of 12 stamps and four central labels showing a composite view of Seville in the 16th century from an engraving by George Braun and Frans Hoegenberg (17p.) or a composite plan of the exhibition compound (27p.).

(Des A. Ráfols Casamada. Photo)

1992 (22 Apr). Paralympic (Physically Handicapped) Games, Barcelona. P 13½×14.
3173 **837** 27p. multicoloured 45 20

838 Arrival in America

(Des M. Salamanca. Eng J.-L. Sánchez Toda and C. Delhom. Recess and litho)

1992 (24 Apr). Granada '92 International Thematic Stamp Exhibition (2nd issue). Sheet 114×105 mm reproducing 1930 Columbus stamps. P 14.
MS3174 **835** 250p. black; **838** 250p. pur-brn............. 7·75 7·75

839 "Preparation before leaving Palos" (R. Espejo)

840 Columbus soliciting Aid of Isabella

(Des J. Suárez. Photo)

1992 (5 May). Europa. 500th Anniv of Discovery of America by Columbus (8th issue). T **839** and similar horiz design. P 13½×14.
3175   17p. multicoloured 65 45
3176   45p. greenish slate and chestnut...................... 70 45
Design:—45p. Map of the Americas, Columbus's fleet and Monastery of Santa María de La Rábida.

(Eng A. Sánchez, J. Heras, J. M. Mata, A. de Oro, V. Morán and J. González de La Lastra. Recess and litho)

1992 (22 May). 500th Anniv of Discovery of America by Columbus (9th issue). Six sheets, each 107×91 mm, containing horiz designs as T **840** reproducing scenes from United States 1893 Columbian Exposition issue. P 14.
MS3177 Six sheets. (a) 60p. reddish brown (Type **840**); (b) 60p. indigo (Columbus sighting land); (c) 60p. purple-brown (Landing of Columbus); (d) 60p. deep reddish violet (Columbus welcomed at Barcelona); (e) 60p. black (Columbus presenting natives); (f) 60p. blue-blk ("America", Columbus and "Liberty").................................. 7·75 7·75

841 "Water and the Environment"

842 "Albertville", Olympic Rings and "Barcelona"

(Des A. Corazón. Photo)

1992 (5 June). World Environment Day. P 14×13½.
3178 **841** 27p. ultramarine and lemon 40 15

(Des M. Salamanca and A. Millán. Photo)

1992 (19 June). Winter Olympic Games, Albertville, and Summer Games, Barcelona. P 13½×14.
3179 **842** 45p. multicoloured 65 20

843 Victorious Athlete   **844** Olympic Stadium

(Des N. Thomas (3180), J. Mariscal (3181), A. Puig (3182). Photo)

1992 (16 July). Olympic Games, Barcelona (9th issue). T **843** and similar multicoloured designs. P 13½×14 (3182) or 14×13½ (others).
3180   17p.+5p. Type **843** 40 40
3181   17p.+5p. Cobi (official mascot) 40 40
3182   17p.+5p. Olympic torch (horiz) 40 40
3180/3182 Set of 3 .... 1·10 1·10

(Des Pilar Villuendas and J. Gómez. Photo)

1992 (25 July). Olympic Games, Barcelona (10th issue). T **844** and similar horiz designs. Multicoloured. P 13½×14.
3183   27p.+5p. Type **844** 40 40
           a. Strip of 3. Nos. 3183/5..................... 1·70
3184   27p.+5p. San Jordi sports arena 40 40
3185   27p.+5p. I.N.E.F. sports university 40 40
3183/3185 Set of 3 .... 1·10 1·10
Nos. 3183/5 were issued together in *se-tenant* strips of three stamps within the sheet.

845 Cobi holding Magnifying Glass and Stamp Album

846 Athletes

(Des J. Mariscal (3186). Photo)

1992 (29 July). Olymphilex 92 International Sports Stamp Exhibition, Barcelona. T **845** and similar vert design. Multicoloured. P 14×13½.
3186   17p.+5p. Type **845** 35 30
3187   17p.+5p. Church of the Holy Family, Barcelona, and exhibition emblem... 35 30

1992 (7 Sept). Paralympic (Mentally Handicapped) Games, Madrid. Photo. P 13½×14.
3188 **846** 27p. ultramarine and brown-red............. 40 20

847 St. Paul's Church   **848** Quarterdeck of *Santa Maria*

(Des J. Suárez. Eng A. Sánchez. Recess and litho)

1992 (9 Oct). Exfilna '92 National Stamp Exhibition, Valladolid. Sheet 105×78 mm. P 14×13½.
MS3189 **847** 27p. reddish brown 45 45

(Des M. Escobar. Eng A. de Oro. Recess and litho)

1992 (15 Oct). America. 500th Anniv of Discovery of America by Columbus (10th issue). P 13½×14.
3190 **848** 60p. reddish brown, cinnamon and yellow-ochre.. 90 35

310

SPAIN

849 Luis Vives (philosopher)   **850** Helmet of Mercury and European Community Emblem

(Des E. Arroyo (17p.). L. Garrido (27p.). Litho)

1992 (29 Oct). Anniversaries. T **849** and similar multicoloured design. P 14×13½ (17p.) or 13½×14 (27p.).
3191		17p. Type **849** (500th birth anniv)	20	15
3192		27p. Pamplona Choir (centenary) (horiz)	45	20

(Des J. Prieto. Photo)

1992 (4 Nov). European Single Market. P 14×13½.
3193	**850**	45p. ultramarine and yellow	70	40

851 "Nativity" (Obdulia Acevedo)   **852** Municipal Museum

(Des M. Escobar. Photo)

1992 (5 Nov). Christmas. P 13½×14.
3194	**851**	27p. multicoloured	35	15

(Des S. Martin. Photo)

1992 (24 Nov). Madrid, European City of Culture (2nd issue). T **852** and similar vert designs. Multicoloured. P 14×13½.
3195		17p.+5p. Type **852**	40	30
3196		17p.+5p. Queen Sofia Art Museum	40	30
3197		17p.+5p. Prado Museum	40	30
3198		17p.+5p. Royal Theatre	40	30
3195/3198		Set of 4	1·40	1·10

853 Huitzilopochtli, Mexican God of War    **854** Bird, Sun, Leaves and Silhouettes

1992 (10 Dec). Codices. Sheet 106×151 mm containing T **853** and similar vert designs. Multicoloured. Recess and litho. P 13.
MS3199		27p. Type **853** (Codex Veitia); 27p. "Mounted Spaniard" (Bishop Baltasar Jaime's *History of the Diocese of El Trujillo del Peru*); 27p. 13th-century miniature from King Alfonso X's *Book of Chess, Dice and Tablings*; 27p. "Of the Months and the Festivals" from Bernardino de Sahagún's *General History of the Matters of New Spain*	1·60	1·60

(Des J. Prieto. Photo)

1993 (4 Jan). Public Services. Protection of the Environment. P 14.
3200	**854**	28p. new blue and myrtle green	40	15

855 María Zambrano   **856** Figures and Blue Cross

1993 (18 Jan). Second Death Anniv of María Zambrano (writer). Photo. P 13½×14.
3201	**855**	45p. multicoloured	70	25

(Des J. Prieto. Photo)

1993 (12 Feb). Public Services. Health and Sanitation. P 14.
3202	**856**	65p. new blue and bright emerald	95	25

857 Segovia   **858** Post-box, Cadiz, 1908

(Des P. Sánchez. Engp. Sampedro. Recess)

1993 (19 Feb). Birth Centenary of Andrés Segovia (guitarist). P 13½×14.
3203	**857**	65p. black and reddish brown	1·00	25

(Des J. Prieto. Eng A. Sánchez. Recess and litho)

1993 (12 Mar). Stamp Day. P 13½×14.
3204	**858**	28p. multicoloured	50	15

859 *Macrolepiota procera* (*Lepiota procera*)   **860** Holy Week Procession

(Des J. Suárez. Photo)

1993 (18 Mar). Fungi (1st series). T **859** and similar horiz designs. Multicoloured. P 13½×14.
3205		17p. Type **859**	40	15
3206		17p. *Amanita caesarea*	40	15
3207		28p. *Lactarius sanguifluus*	55	20
3208		28p. *Russula cyanoxantha*	55	20
3205/3208		Set of 4	1·70	65

See also Nos. 3256/9 and 3312/13.

(Des T. Pérez Bordetas. Recess and litho)

1993 (2 Apr). Exfilna '93 National Stamp Exhibition, Alcañiz. Sheet 105×78 mm. P 14×13½.
MS3209	**860**	100p. multicoloured	1·50	1·50

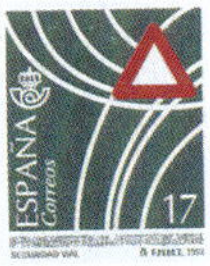

861 Road Safety    E **862** Communications

(Des J. Prieto. Photo)

1993 (20 Apr). Public Services.

(a) POSTAGE. P 14
3210	**861**	17p. deep dull green and bright scarlet	30	15

(b) EXPRESS LETTER. P 14×13½
E3211	E **862**	180p. bright scarlet and bright lemon ..	2·75	65

311

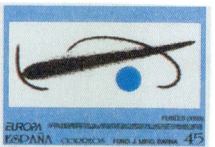 

863 "Fuseés"   **864** "Translation of Body from Palestine to Galicia" (detail of altarpiece, Santiago de Compostela Cathedral)

(Des P. Sánchez. Eng J. González de la Lastra (65p.). Photo (45p.), recess and litho (65p.))

1993 (5 May). Europa. Contemporary Art. Paintings by Joan Miró. T **863** and similar design. P 13½×14 (45p.) or 14×13½ (65p.).
3212	45p. black and new blue	85	35
3213	65p. multicoloured	1·50	55

Design: Vert—65p. "La Bague d'Aurore".

(Des J. Prieto. Photo)

1993 (13 May). St. James's Holy Year (1st issue). T **864** and similar horiz designs. Multicoloured. P 13½×14.
3214	17p. Type **864**	30	20
3215	28p. "Discovery of St. James's tomb by Bishop Teodomiro" (miniature from *Tumbo A* (codex))	40	20
3216	45p. "St. James" (illuminated initial letter from Bull issued by Pope Alexander III declaring Holy Years of St. James)	70	20
3214/3216	Set of 3	1·30	55

See also Nos. 3218/**MS**3219.

865 Letters, Map and Satellite   **866** Bagpipe Player (Isaac Diaz Pardo)

1993 (17 May). World Telecommunications Day. Photo. P 13½×14.
3217	**865**	28p. multicoloured	40	15

(Des J. Prieto. Photo)

1993 (18 May). St. James's Holy Year (2nd issue). T **866** and similar multicoloured design. P 13½×14 (28p.) or 14×13½ (100p.).
3218	28p. Type **866**	40	15
MS3219	106×82 mm. 100p. Pilgrim under the star tree (Eugenio Granell) (vert)	2·00	1·80

867 King Juan Carlos I (photo by Jorge Martín Burguillo)   **868** "Water and the Environment"

1993 (21 May)–**2000**. Photo. P 14×13½.
3220	867	1p. new blue and gold (31.1.94)	20	15
		a. Block. Nos. 3220, 3225, 3230, 3235 plus 2 labels (27.5.94)	2·20	
3221		2p. deep blue-green and gold (19.5.97)	15	15
3222		10p. lake and gold (5.6.95)	20	20
		a. Block. Nos. 3222, 3226, 3231, 3236 plus 2 labels (5.6.95)	2·10	
3222b		15p. bright yellowish green and gold (6.3.98)	20	20
3223		16p. red-brown and gold (19.5.97)	20	15
3224		17p. dull orange and gold	20	15
		a. Block. Nos. 3224, 3229, 3234, 3237 plus 2 labels	2·40	
3225		18p. turquoise and gold (2.94)	30	15
3226		19p. chocolate and gold (3.1.95)	40	20
3226a		20p. bright magenta and gold (20.11.00)	60	25
3227		21p. deep grey-green and gold (27.1.97)	25	15
3229		28p. dull chocolate and gold	35	15
3230		29p. olive-green and gold (31.1.94)	70	20
3231		30p. dull ultramarine and gold (3.1.95)	45	25
3232		32p. dull blue-green and gold (27.1.97)	40	15
3233		35p. red and gold (13.2.98)	40	20
3234		45p. blue-green and gold	65	15
3235		55p. blackish brown and gold (9.5.94)	80	20
3236		60p. Indian red and gold (5.6.95)	90	25
3237		65p. reddish orange and gold	90	15
3238		70p. vermilion and gold (30.1.98)	85	20
3220/3238	Set of 20		8·00	3·50

Nos. 3220/37 were each issued in separate sheets (the 10 and 60p. on 3 July 1995) and also in *se-tenant* sheets containing four of the values in blocks with two different labels.

Nos. 3228 and 3239/40 are vacant.

(Des A. Corazón. Litho)

1993 (4 June). World Environment Day. P 14×13½.
3240	**868**	28p. multicoloured	40	15

869 Count of Barcelona (after Ricardo Macarrón)   **870** Tank Locomotive

1993 (20 June). Juan de Borbón, Count of Barcelona (King Juan Carlos's father) Commemoration. Photo. P 14×13½.
3241	**869**	28p. multicoloured	40	15

1993 (4 July). Centenary of Igualada–Martorell Railway. Recess. P 13½×14.
3242	**870**	45p. yellowish green and black	70	20

871 "The Mint" (lithograph, Pic de Leopold, 1866)   **872** Alejandro Malaspina (navigator)

(Des M. Escobar. Eng J. González de la Lastra. Recess)

1993 (13 Sept). Centenary of National Coin and Stamp Mint. P 13½×14.
3243	**871**	65p. deep blue	95	30

(Des P. Sánchez. Photo)

1993 (20 Sept). Explorers. T **872** and similar multicoloured design. P 13½×14 (45p.) or 14×13½ (65p.).
3244	45p. Type **872**	65	20
3245	65p. José Celestino Mutis (naturalist) (vert)	1·00	40

873 "Road to Santiago"   **874** Black Stork

SPAIN

(Des Alejandro Mayor Gamo. Photo)
1993 (2 Oct). Children's Stamp Design. P 13½×14.
3246 **873** 45p. multicoloured 70   20

(Des M. Escobar and J. Suárez. Eng V. Morán (3247),
J. M. Mata (3248). Recess and litho)
1993 (11 Oct). America. Endangered Animals. T **874** and similar horiz design. P 13½×14.
3247   65p. black and salmon 95   35
3248   65p. black and red 95   35
Design:—No. 3248, Lammergeier.

875 Old and Young Hands   **876** Star and Three Wise Men

1993 (29 Oct). European Year of Senior Citizens and Solidarity between Generations. Photo. P 13½×14.
3249 **875** 45p. multicoloured 70   30

(Des P. Sánchez and J. Suárez. Photo (17p.)
or recess, photo and litho (28p.))
1993 (23 Nov). Christmas. T **876** and similar multicoloured design. P 13½×14 (17p.) or 14×13½ (28p.).
3250   17p. Type **876** 30   15
3251   28p. Holy Family (vert) 45   25

877 Guillén   **878** Santa María de Poblet Monastery, Tarragona

1993 (29 Nov). Birth Centenary of Jorge Guillén (poet). Recess. P 14×13½.
3252 **877** 28p. bottle green 45   20

(Des M. Escobar. Eng A. Sánchez. Recess and litho)
1993 (3 Dec). World Heritage Sites. P 13×12½.
3253 **878** 50p. sepia, dp violet-bl and blackish green 85   30

879 Luis Buñuel and Camera   **880** Cinnabar

(Des M. Salamanca and A. Millán. Photo)
1994 (28 Jan). Spanish Cinema (1st series). T **879** and similar horiz design. Multicoloured. P 13½×14.
3254   29p. Type **879** 55   20
3255   55p. Segundo de Chomón and scene from Goblin House 90   30
See also Nos. 3308/9.

(Des J. Suárez. Photo)
1994 (18 Feb). Fungi (2nd series). Horiz designs as T **859**. Multicoloured. P 13½×14.
3256   18p. *Boletus edulis* 30   15
3257   18p. *Boletus satanas* 30   15
3258   29p. *Amanita phalloides* 60   25
3259   29p. *Lactarius deliciosus* 60   25
3256/3259 Set of 4 .... 1·60   70

(Des J. Suárez. Photo)
1994 (25 Feb). Minerals (1st series). T **880** and similar horiz designs. P 13½×14.
3260   29p. multicoloured 50   20
       a. Block. Nos. 3260/3 plus 2 labels .... 2·30
3261   29p. multicoloured 50   20
3262   29p. multicoloured 50   20
3263   29p. black and slate-blue 50   20
3260/3263 Set of 4 .... 1·80   70
Designs:—No. 3261, Blende (inscr "Esfalerita"); 3262, Pyrites; 3263, Galena.
Nos. 3260/3 were issued together in *se-tenant* blocks of four stamps and two labels within the sheet, the labels forming a composite design of the hall of the Geology and Mining Museum, Madrid.
See also Nos. 3314/16 and 3366/7.

881 Barristers' Mailbox, Barcelona

(Des J. Angel. Eng J. Heras. Recess and litho)
1994 (9 Mar). Stamp Day. P 13½×14.
3264 **881** 29p. reddish brown & pale cinnamon ... 50   20

882 Worker (detail of sculpture),   **883** "Poetry of America"
I.L.O. Building, Geneva

(Des M. Escobar. Photo)
1994 (7 Apr). 75th Anniv of International Labour Office, Geneva. P 13½×14.
3265 **882** 65p. multicoloured .... 1·00   35

(Des P. Sánchez. Photo)
1994 (22 Apr). 90th Birth Anniv of Salvador Dali (painter). T **883** and similar multicoloured designs. P 14×13½ (vert) or 13½×14 (horiz).
3266   18p. Type **883** 30   15
3267   18p. "Portrait of Gala" (horiz) 30   15
3268   29p. "Port Alguer" 45   20
3269   29p. "The Great Masturbator" (horiz) 45   20
3270   55p. "The Bread Basket" 85   30
3271   55p. "Soft Self-portrait" 85   30
3272   65p. "Galatea of the Spheres" .... 1·00   30
3273   65p. "The Enigma without End" (horiz) ...... 1·00   30
3266/3273 Set of 8 .... 4·75   1·70

884 Pla   **885** "Martyrdom of St. Andrew" (Peter Paul Rubens)

(Des M. Escobar. Eng A. Sánchez. Recess)
1994 (23 Apr). 13th Death Anniv of Josep Pla (writer). P 13½×14.
3274 **884** 65p. bottle green and brown-lake .... 1·00   30

(Des J. Angel. Photo)
1994 (29 Apr). 400th Anniv of Carlos de Amberes Foundation (philanthropic organization). P 14×13½.
3275 **885** 55p. multicoloured 90   30

313

SPAIN

886 "Foundation of Santa Cruz de Tenerife" (González Méndez)
887 Severo Ochoa (biochemist)

(Des M. Salamanca and A. Millán. Eng J. Terriza (29p.). Litho (18p.) or recess, photo and litho (29p.))

1994 (3 May). Anniversaries. T **886** and similar multicoloured design. P 14×13½ (18p.) or 13½×14 (29p.).
3276	18p. Type **886** (500th anniv of city)		30	15
3277	29p. Sancho IV's Foundation Charter at Alcalá, 1293 (700th anniv of Complutense University, Madrid) (horiz)		55	20

(Des M. Escobar and P. Sánchez. Eng J. Heras and A. de Oro. Recess and litho)

1994 (5 May). Europa. Discoveries. T **887** and similar horiz design. Multicoloured. P 13½×14.
3278	55p. Type **887** (research into DNA)		1·50	55
3279	65p. Miguel Catalán (spectrochemist) (research into atomic structures)		1·60	55

888 Family of Pascual Duarte
889 Sancho I Ramírez

(Des P. Sánchez. Photo)

1994 (11 May). Spanish Literature. Works of Camilo José Cela. T **888** and similar horiz design. Multicoloured. P 13½×14.
3280	18p. Type **888**		30	15
3281	29p. Walker and horse rider (*Journey to Alcarria*)		55	25

1994 (7 June). 900th Death Anniv of King Sancho I Ramírez of Aragon (3282) and 500th Anniv of Treaty of Tordesillas (defining Portuguese and Spanish spheres of influence) (others). T **889** and similar designs. Recess and litho. P 14×13½ (18p.) or 13½×14 (others).
3282	18p. lake, greenish yellow and blue		25	15
3283	29p. multicoloured		50	20
3284	55p. deep green, dull orange and brown		85	35
3282/3284	Set of 3		1·50	65

Designs: Horiz—29p. Compass rose and arms of Tordesillas, 55p. Treaty House, Tordesillas.

890 St. Anne's Cathedral
891 Giralda (yacht)

1994 (1 July). Exfilna '94 National Stamp Exhibition, Las Palmas, Gran Canaria. Sheet 105×78 mm. Recess and litho. P 13½×14.
MS3285	**890**	100p. multicoloured	1·50	1·50

(Des P. Sánchez. Photo)

1994 (15 July). Ships sailed by Count of Barcelona. T **891** and similar vert design. Multicoloured. P 14×13½.
3286	16p. Type **891**		25	15
3287	29p. *Saltillo* (schooner)		50	20

892 Forum Caryatid and Tablet bearing Roman Name of Mérida
893 Knight of Swords (14th-century Catalan deck)

(Des A. Millán and M. Salamanca. Recess and litho)

1994 (8 Sept). World Heritage Site. Mérida. P 13×12½.
3288	**892**	55p. reddish brown, cinnamon and deep carmine-red	85	30

(Des J. Prieto. Photo)

1994 (20 Sept). Playing Card Museum, Vitoria. T **893** and similar vert designs. Multicoloured. P 14×13½.
3289	18p. Type **893**		25	20
3290	29p. Jack of Clubs (Catalan Tarot deck, 1900)		40	20
3291	55p. King of Cups (Spanish deck by Juan Barbot, 1750)		80	30
3292	65p. "Mars", Jack of Diamonds (English deck by Stopforth, 1828)		1·10	30
3289/3292	Set of 4		2·30	90

894 Globe and Douglas DC-8
895 Civil Guard (150th anniv)

(Des P. Sánchez. Litho)

1994 (11 Oct). America. Postal Transport. P 13½× 14.
3293	**894**	65p. multicoloured	95	30

(Des M. Escobar. Photo)

1994 (17 Oct). Public Services. T **895** and another design. P 14 (18p.) or 13½×14 (29p.).
3294	18p. bright scarlet and royal blue		30	20
3295	29p. multicoloured		50	25

Design: As T **854**—18p. Underground train (75th anniv of Madrid Metro).

896 Map of Member Countries
897 Running

(Des M. Escobar. Photo)

1994 (21 Oct). 40th Anniv of Western European Union. P 13½×14.
3296	**896**	55p. multicoloured	85	30

(Des M. Escobar. Photo)

1994 (27 Oct). Centenary of International Olympic Committee. Spanish Olympic Gold Medal Sports. T **897** and similar horiz designs. Multicoloured. P 13½×14.
3297	29p. Type **897**		40	30
	a. Block. Nos. 3297/3306 plus 10 labels		5·25	
3298	29p. Cycling		40	30
3299	29p. Skiing		40	30
3300	29p. Football		40	30
3301	29p. Show jumping		40	30
3302	29p. Hockey		40	30

3303	29p. Judo		40	30
3304	29p. Swimming		40	30
3305	29p. Archery		40	30
3306	29p. Yachting		40	30
3297/3306 Set of 10			3·75	2·75

Nos. 3297/3306 were issued together in *se-tenant* blocks of ten stamps and ten labels variously showing names of the gold medal winners and the I.O.C. anniversary emblem.

See also Nos. 3332/45 and 3373/81.

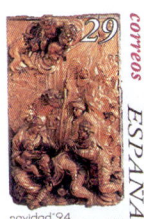 

898 "Adoration of the Kings" (detail of Ripoll altarpiece, Esteve Bover)

899 *Belle Epoque* (dir. Fernando Trueba)

(Des P. Sánchez. Photo)

1994 (18 Nov). Christmas. P 14×13½.
3307	**898**	29p. multicoloured	50	20

(Des J. Suárez. Photo)

1995 (20 Jan). Spanish Cinema (2nd series). T **899** and similar horiz design showing film posters. Multicoloured. P 13½×14.
3308		30p. Type **899**	45	20
3309		60p. *Volver a Empezar* (dir. José Luis Garci)	90	40

900 Logroño

901 Snow Star

(Des J. Palacios and p. Sánchez. Photo)

1995 (25 Jan). 900th Anniv of Logroño Law Code. P 13½×14.
3310	**900**	30p. multicoloured	50	20

(Des M. Plaza. Photo)

1995 (30 Jan). Filatem 95 National Thematic Stamp Exhibition, Granada, and World Alpine Skiing Championships, Sierra Nevada. Sheet 105×78 mm. P 13½×14.
MS3311	**901**	130p. multicoloured	2·00	2·30

902 *Coprinus comatus*

903 19th-century Lion's Head Letter Box

(Des P. Sánchez. Photo)

1995 (9 Feb). Fungi (3rd series). T **902** and similar horiz design. Multicoloured. P 13½×14.
3312		19p. Type **902**	30	15
3313		30p. *Dermocybe cinnamomea*	50	25

(Des M. Plaza. Photo)

1995 (24 Feb). Minerals (2nd series). Horiz designs as T **880**. Multicoloured. P 13½×14.
3314		30p. Aragonite	45	20
		a. Strip of 3. Nos. 3314/16	1·50	
3315		30p. Advanced Mining Engineering Technical School and Mining Museum, Madrid	45	20
3316		30p. Dolomite	45	20
3314/3316 Set of 3			1·20	55

Nos. 3314/16 were issued together in *se-tenant* strips of three stamps within the sheet.

(Des M. Escobar. Eng J. Heras. Recess)

1995 (9 Mar). Stamp Day. P 13½×14.
3317	**903**	30p. reddish brown and bottle green	50	20

904 Goicoechea and Modern Train

905 Globe as Tree on Hand

(Des M. Escobar. Photo)

1995 (17 Mar). Birth Centenary of Alejandro Goicoechea (inventor of TALGO articulated train). P 13½×14.
3318		30p. multicoloured	45	20
3319		60p. violet-blue and dull chocolate	95	35

Design:—60p. Goicoechea and early TALGO train.

(Des M. Escobar. Photo)

1995 (6 Apr). European Nature Conservation Year. P 14×13½.
3320	**905**	60p. multicoloured	1·20	65

906 "*San Juan Nepomuceno*"

907 Angel (from illuminated manuscript)

(Des and eng J. Suárez. Recess and litho)

1995 (7 Apr). Ship Paintings by Alejo Berlinquero de la Marca y Gallego. Two sheets, each 87×164 mm, containing vert designs as T **906**. Multicoloured. P 14×13½.
MS3321 Two sheets. (a) 19p.×4, Type **906**; (b) 30p.×4, "San Telmo"			3·00	3·00

(Des J. Angel. Photo)

1995 (21 Apr). 900th Anniv of Monastery of Liébana. T **907** and similar diamond-shaped design. Multicoloured. P 12½.
3322		30p. Type **907**	45	20
3323		60p. Liébana landscape	90	40

908 Miguel Hernández and part of *El Niño Yuntero*

909 Marti

(Des M. Escobar; eng J. González de la Lastra; recess (19p.). Des M. Salamanca and A. Millán; eng A. Sánchez; recess and litho (30p.))

1995 (27 Apr). Literature. T **908** and similar design. P 13½×14 (19p.) or 14×13½ (30p.).
3324		19p. multicoloured	35	20
3325		30p. dp blue, dp dull green & blackish green	50	20

Design: Vert—30p. Juan Valera and scene from *Juanita la Larga*.

SPAIN

(Des J. Plaza. Photo)
1995 (28 Apr). Death Centenary of José Martí (Cuban poet). P 13½×14.
| 3326 | **909** | 60p. multicoloured | 95 | 35 |

910 Captain Trueno   **911** Chain and Laurel Twig

(Des J. Angel. Photo)
1995 (4 May). Comic Strip Characters. T **910** and similar design. Multicoloured. P 13½×14 (30p) or 14×13 (60p).
| 3327 | 30p. Type **910** | 50 | 20 |
| 3328 | 60p. Carpanta (vert) | 95 | 40 |

(Des A. Millán and M. Salamanca. Photo)
1995 (5 May). Europa, Peace and Freedom. P 13½×14.
| 3329 | **911** | 60p. multicoloured | 1·60 | 85 |

912 Lumière Brothers   **913** Typewriter, Pen and Camera

(Des J. Suárez. Recess)
1995 (12 May). Centenary of Motion Pictures. P 13½×14.
| 3330 | **912** | 19p. blackish brown | 35 | 15 |

(Des M. Escobar. Litho)
1995 (12 May). Centenary of Madrid Press Association. P 13½×14.
| 3331 | **913** | 30p. multicoloured | 50 | 25 |

(Des M. Escobar. Photo)
1995 (2 June). Spanish Olympic Silver Medal Sports. Horiz designs as T **897**. Multicoloured. Dated "1995". P 13½×14.
3332	30p. Type **897**	45	40
	a. Block. Nos. 3332/45 plus 6 labels	6·50	
3333	30p. Basketball	45	40
3334	30p. Boxing	45	40
3335	30p. As No. 3300	45	40
3336	30p. Gymnastics	45	40
3337	30p. As No. 3301	45	40
3338	30p. As No. 3302	45	40
3339	30p. Canoeing	45	40
3340	30p. Polo	45	40
3341	30p. Rowing	45	40
3342	30p. Tennis	45	40
3343	30p. Shooting	45	40
3344	30p. As No. 3306	45	40
3345	30p. Water polo	45	40
3332/3345 Set of 14		5·75	5·00

Nos. 3332/45 were issued together in *se-tenant* blocks of fourteen stamps and six labels showing names of the medal winners.
The block has an overall grey pattern. For 30p. stamps, some in the same design, with an overall brown pattern see Nos. 3373/81.

914 King Juan Carlos I at National Assembly, 1986   **915** Presidency Emblem

(Des M. Salamanca and A. Millán (3346), J. Suárez (3347), M. Plaza (3348). Photo)
1995 (26 June). Anniversaries. T **914** and similar multicoloured designs. P 14×13½ (3347) or 13½×14 (others).
3346	60p. Type **914** (50th anniv of United Nations Organization)	90	40
3347	60p. Anniversary emblem, globes and wheat ears (50th anniv of Food and Agriculture Organization) (vert)	90	40
3348	60p. Emblem and coloured bands (20th anniv of World Tourism Organization)	90	40
3346/3348 Set of 3		1·60	1·10

(Des J. Angel. Photo)
1995 (1 July). Spanish Presidency of the European Union. P 14×13½.
| 3349 | **915** | 60p. scarlet-verm, orge-yell and ultram | 1·20 | 65 |

916 Spotlight on Woman   **917** Cover Illustration of National Atlas of Spain

(Des J. Suárez. Photo)
1995 (4 Sept). Fourth United Nations Conference on Women, Peking. P 14×13½.
| 3350 | **916** | 60p. multicoloured | 95 | 40 |

(Des J. Angel. Photo)
1995 (5 Sept). 17th International Cartography Conference, Barcelona. Sheet 105×78 mm. P 13½×14.
| MS3351 | **917** | 130p. multicoloured | 2·00 | 2·00 |

918 Entrance to Hospital de la Azabachería   **919** Royal Monastery of Santa Maria, Guadalupe

(Des M. Plaza. Photo)
1995 (15 Sept). 500th Anniv of University of Santiago de Compostela. P 13½×14.
| 3352 | **918** | 30p. multicoloured | 50 | 25 |

(Des J. Angel. Eng A. Sánchez; recess (3353). Eng J. González de la Lastra; recess and litho (3354))
1995 (29 Sept). World Heritage Sites. T **919** and similar design. P 12½×13 (3353) or 13×12½ (3354).
| 3353 | 60p. sepia | 90 | 40 |
| 3354 | 60p. multicoloured | 90 | 40 |

Design: Horiz—No. 3354, Route map of Spanish section of road to Santiago de Compostela and statue of pilgrim.

920 "The Peddler" (sculpture, Jaime Pimentel)   **921** Ducks and Lagoon of La Mancha

SPAIN

(Des J. Suárez. Recess and litho)
1995 (6 Oct). Exfilna '95 National Stamp Exhibition, Málaga. Sheet 105×78 mm. P 14×13½.
MS3355 **920** 130p. bottle green .... 2·00 2·00

(Des M. Escobar. Photo)
1995 (11 Oct). America. Environmental Protection. P 13½×14.
3356 **921** 60p. multicoloured 85 40

922 La Cueva de Menga, Málaga (Bronze Age)   **923** Recitation

(Des J. Angel. Photo)
1995 (20 Oct). Archaeology. T **922** and similar horiz design. Multicoloured. P 13½×14.
3357 30p. Type **922** 45 25
3358 30p. La Taula de Torralba, Minorca (c. 700 BC) 45 25

(Des J. Suárez. Photo)
1995 (27 Oct). Art. Sheet 145×95 mm containing vert designs as T **923**, showing details of "The Contemporary Poets" by Antonio Esquivel. Multicoloured. P 14×13½.
MS3359 19, 30, 60, 60p. Composite design of painting .... 2·50 2·75

924 "Adoration of the Kings" (capital, Collegiate Church, San Martín de Elines)   **925** King Juan Carlos

(Des M. Escobar. Photo)
1995 (17 Nov). Christmas. P 13½×14.
3360 **924** 30p. multicoloured 55 20

1995 (24 Nov). 20th Anniv of Accession of King Juan Carlos I. Recess. P 14×13½.
3361 **925** 1000p. slate-violet .... 47·00 8·25

926 Plaza de Armas Railway Station, Seville (venue)

1995 (20 Dec). "Espamer" Spanish-Latin American and "Aviation and Space" Stamp Exhibitions, Seville (1st issue). T **926** and similar multicoloured design. P 13×12½ (3362) or 12½×13 (3363).
3362 60p. Type **926** 95 35
3363 60p. Dr. Lorenzo Galíndez de Carvajal (Master Courier of the Indies and Terra Firma of the Ocean Sea, 1514) 95 35
See also No. **MS**3382.

927 Leaving Mass at Pilar de Zaragoza (first Spanish film, 1896)   **928** Miner's Lamp

(Des M. Escobar and M. Salamanca. Photo)
1996 (30 Jan). Centenary of Motion Pictures. T **927** and similar horiz design. P 13½×14.
3364 30p. chocolate, magenta and black 40 20
3365 60p. multicoloured 65 40
Design:—60p. Bienvenido, Mister Marshall! (poster).

(Des P. Sánchez. Photo)
1996 (7 Feb). Minerals (3rd series). T **928** and similar vert design. Multicoloured. P 14×13½.
3366 30p. Type **928** 60 20
3367 60p. Amber fluorite .... 1·00 40

929 José Mathé Aragua (General Director) and Telegraph Tower   **930** Columbus (statue), "B" and Arch of Triumph

(Des M. Escobar. Eng J. Heras. Recess)
1996 (8 Mar). Stamp Day. 150th Anniv of Madrid–Irún Telegraph Signal Line. P 13½×14.
3368 **929** 60p. bottle green and lake 80 40

(Des P. Sánchez. Photo)
1996 (22 Mar). Tenth Anniv (1995) of Start of Barcelona Urbanisation Programme. P 13½×14.
3369 **930** 30p. multicoloured 35 20

931 Brown Bear with Cubs   **932** Real Phelipe (ship of the line)

(Des M. Escobar. Photo)
1996 (27 Mar). Endangered Species. P 14×13½.
3370 **931** 30p. multicoloured .... 4·00 20

(Des J. Suárez. Recess and litho)
1996 (19 Apr). 18th-century Ships. Two sheets each 87×165 mm, containing vert designs as T **932**. Multicoloured. P 14×13½.
MS3371 Two sheets. (a) 30p.×4, Type **932**; (b) 60p.×4, El Catalán (after Rafael Moleón) .... 5·50 5·50

933 Scales   **934** Map of Seville-Larache Postal Route

317

(Des P. Sánchez. Photo)

1996 (23 Apr). 400th Anniv of Madrid Bar Association. P 13½×14.
3372 **933** 19p. multicoloured 30 20

(Des M. Escobar. Photo)

1996 (26 Apr). Spanish Olympic Bronze Medal Sports. Horiz designs as T **897**. Multicoloured. Dated "1996". P 13½×14.
3373	30p. Type **897**	35	25
	a. Block. Nos. 3373/81 plus 6 labels	3·50	
3374	30p. As No. 3334	35	25
3375	30p. As No. 3299	40	30
3376	30p. As No. 3302	40	30
3377	30p. As No. 3304	40	30
3378	30p. As No. 3339	40	30
3379	30p. As No. 3342	40	30
3380	30p. As No. 3343	40	30
3381	30p. As No. 3306	40	30
3373/3381 Set of 9		3·25	2·30

Nos. 3373/81 were issued together in *se-tenant* blocks of nine stamps and six labels showing names of the medal winners.

(Des J. Suárez. Photo)

1996 (4 May). "Espamer" Spanish–Latin American and "Aviation and Space" Stamp Exhibitions, Seville (2nd issue). Two sheets, each 164×87 mm, containing T **934** and similar horiz designs (sheet a) or single stamp (b). Multicoloured. P 13½×14.
MS3382 Two sheets. (a) 100p. Type **934**; 100p. Cover flown by airship *Graf Zeppelin*, 1930; 100p. Rocket launch, El Arenosillo, Huelva; 100p. Hispano HA200 Saeta jet fighter. (b) 400p. The Royal Family (78×54 mm).................................... 8·25 8·25

935 Carmen Amaya (flamenco dancer)

936 El Jabato (Victor Mora and Francisco Darnis)

(Des P. Sánchez. Photo)

1996 (6 May). Europa. Famous Women. P 14×13½.
3383 **935** 60p. multicoloured .... 1·60 85

(Des J. Suárez. Photo)

1996 (10 May). Comic Strip Characters. T **936** and similar multicoloured design. P 14×13½ (19p.) or 13½×14 (30p.).
3384	19p. Type **936**	30	20
3385	30p. Reporter Tribulete (Guillermo Cifré) (horiz)....................................	50	20

937 "General Don Antonio Ricardos"

938 Magnifying Glass and Stamp Album

(Des P. Sánchez. Photo)

1996 (31 May). 250th Birth Anniv of Francisco de Goya (artist). T **937** and similar multicoloured designs. P 14×13½ (vert) or 13½×14 (horiz).
3386	19p. Type **937**	40	20
3387	30p. "The Milkmaid of Bordeaux"	45	25
3388	60p. "Boys with Mastiffs" (horiz)	1·00	40
3389	130p. "3rd of May 1808 in Madrid" (horiz)........	2·20	85
3386/3389 Set of 4		3·75	1·50

(Des M. Plaza. Photo)

1996 (4 June). 50th Anniv of Philatelic Service. P 13½×14.
3390 **938** 30p. multicoloured 45 25

939 José Monge Cruz (Camarón de la Isla)

940 Lanuza Market, Zaragoza (Félix Navarró Pérez)

(Des M. Escobar (19p.), P. Sánchez (30p.). Photo)

1996 (14 June). Flamenco Artistes. T **939** and similar design. P 14×13½ (19p.) or 13½×14 (30p.).
3391	19p. multicoloured	25	20
3392	30p. deep claret and carmine	40	25

Design: Horiz—30p. Lola Flores.

(Des J. Prieto. Photo)

1996 (5 July). 19th International Architects Congress, Barcelona. Metallic Buildings. P 14.
3393 **940** 30p. multicoloured 45 20

941 Gerardo Diego and Pen (poet, birth centenary)

942 Naveta (tomb) des Tudons, Minorca

(Des A. Tápies (60p.), J. Prieto (19p.), recess and litho (30p.), photo (60p.))

1996 (13 Sept). Anniversaries. T **941** and similar designs. P 14×13½ (60p.) or 13½×14 (others).
3394	19p. violet and vermilion	25	20
3395	30p. multicoloured	40	25
3396	60p. black, rosine and ultramarine..................	85	40
3394/3396 Set of 3		1·40	75

Designs: Horiz—30p. Joaquín Costa and birthplace (politician and historian, 150th birth anniv). Vert—60p. The five senses (50th anniv of United Nations Children's Fund).

1996 (27 Sept). Archaeology. T **942** and similar horiz design. Multicoloured. Photo. P 13½×14.
3397	30p. Type **942**	50	20
3398	30p. Cabezo de Alcalá de Azila, Teruel............	50	20

943 Eduardo Dato Street (after Isidoro Díaz Olano)

944 Salamancan Costumes

(Des J. Prieto. Eng E. Paniagua. Recess)

1996 (11 Oct). Exfilna 96 National Stamp Exhibition, Vitoria. Sheet 105×77 mm. P 14×13½.
3399 **943** 130p. lake .... 1·90 1·90

(Des P. Sánchez. Photo)

1996 (15 Oct). America. Traditional Costumes. P 14.
3400 **944** 60p. multicoloured 80 40

SPAIN

945 Albaicín Quarter, Granada

946 Oviedo Cathedral, Leopoldo Alas and Quotation from "La Regenta"

947 "Nativity" (Fernando Gallego)

(Des M. Escobar and J. Suárez. Eng A. de Oro and J. Heras. Recess)
1996 (25 Oct). World Heritage Sites. T **945** and similar designs. P 13×12½ (30p.) or 12½×13 (others).
3401		19p. deep ultramarine	30	20
3402		50p. deep reddish purple	50	25
3403		60p. deep blue	1·00	40
3401/3403		Set of 3	1·60	75

Designs: Horiz—30p. Tiberíades Square and statue of Maimonides (centre of Cordova). Vert—60p. Deer, Doñana National Park.

(Des M. Escobar. Eng J. Heras and A. de Oro. Recess)
1996 (13 Nov). Literature. T **946** and similar design. P 14×13½ (30p.) or 13½×14 (60p.).
3404		30p. blue and deep reddish purple	35	25
3405		60p. deep blue and deep dull purple	80	45

Design: Horiz—60p. Scene from *Don Juan Tenorio* by José Zorrilla.

(Des P. Sánchez. Photo)
1996 (22 Nov). Christmas. P 14.
3406	**947**	30p. multicoloured	45	20

948 Map

(Des M. Escobar. Photo)
1996 (5 Dec). Autonomous Communities of Spain. Sheet 164×87 mm. P 13½×14.
MS3407	**948**	130p. multicoloured	1·90	1·90

1996 (12 Dec). King Juan Carlos I. As No. 3361. Recess. P 14×13½.
3408	**925**	100p. sepia	2·75	35
3409		200p. blackish green	6·50	70
3410		300p. maroon	13·50	2·40
3411		500p. indigo	24·00	5·25
3408/3411		Set of 4	42·00	8·00

Numbers have been left for possible additions to this series.

949 Genet

950 Exhibition Poster (José Sánchez)

(Des J. Prieto. Photo)
1997 (30 Jan). Endangered Species. P 14×13½.
3416	**949**	32p. multicoloured	40	20

1997 (28 Feb). Juvenia '97 National Youth Stamp Exhibition, El Puerto de Santa Maria. Photo. P 14.
3417	**950**	32p. multicoloured	40	25

951 Stone Post Box, Madrid

952 *The Journey to Nowhere* (dir. Fernando Fernán)

(Des J. Prieto. Recess)
1997 (7 Mar). Stamp Day. P 13½×14.
3418	**951**	65p. indigo and crimson	85	45

(Des J. Plaza. Photo)
1997 (12 Mar). Spanish Cinema (3rd series). T **952** and similar vert design showing posters. Multicoloured. P 14×13½.
3419		21p. Type **952**	25	20
3420		32p. *The South* (dir. Victor Erice)	45	25

953 La Caprichosa and Baño de Diana Waterfalls, Monastery of Piedra Park

954 *Asturias* (frigate)

(Des J. Plaza. Photo)
1997 (22 Mar). World Water Day. P 14.
3421	**953**	65p. multicoloured	80	40

(Des M. Plaza. Recess and litho)
1997 (16 Apr). 19th-century Ships. Two sheets each 87×164 mm containing vert designs as T **954**. Multicoloured. P 14×13½.
MS3422	Two sheets. (a) 21p.×4, Type **954**; (b) 32p.×4, 16-gun brigantine (after Rodríguez and Gasco)		3·75	3·75

955 Vizcaya Bridge

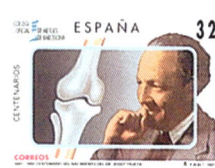
956 Joint and Trueta

(Des P. Sánchez. Photo)
1997 (22 Apr). Anniversaries. Metal Structures. T **955** and similar horiz design. Multicoloured. P 14.
3423		32p. Type **955** (centenary of Engineering School, Bilbao)	40	20
3424		194p. Atocha railway station and AVE locomotive (fifth anniv of AVE high-speed train)	2·50	1·20

(Des P. Sánchez. Photo)
1997 (30 Apr). Birth Centenary of Josep Trueta i Raspall (orthopaedic surgeon). P 13½×14.
3425   956   32p. multicoloured 40   25

957 Prince and Princess, Castle and Forest

958 Lázaro with Blind Beggar

(Des M. Escobar. Photo)
1997 (5 May). Europa. Tales and Legends. P 14×13½.
3426   957   65p. multicoloured .... 1·60   90

(Des R. Seco and J. Suárez, Eng A. de Oro and J. Heras. Recess)
1997 (8 May). Spanish Literature. T 958 and similar design. P 14×13½ (21p.) or 13½×14 (32p.).
3427   21p. black and bronze green 25   15
3428   32p. agate and deep blue 45   25
Designs: Vert—21p. Type 958 (Life of Lázarillo de Tormes and his Fortunes and Setbacks). Horiz—32p. José María Pemán and character El Séneca.

959 Anxel Fole (writer) (after Siro López Lorenzo)

960 The Ulysses Family (Mariano Benejam)

(Des M. Escobar. Photo)
1997 (17 May). Galician Literature Day. P 13½×14.
3429   959   65p. multicoloured 85   40

(Des J. Suárez. Photo)
1997 (30 May). Comic Strip Characters. T 960 and similar horiz design. Multicoloured. P 13½×14.
3430   21p. Type 960 25   15
3431   32p. The Masked Warrior (Manuel Gago) 45   25

961 Manolete (Manuel Rodríguez Sánchez) (matador)

962 "The Annunciation" (from Church of Our Lady of Sorrow, Agreda)

(Des J. Prieto and J. Suárez. Photo)
1997 (5 June). Anniversaries. T 961 and similar horiz design. Multicoloured. P 13½×14.
3432   32p. Type 961 (50th death anniv) 45   25
3433   65p. Charlie Rivel (Josep Andreu i Lasserre)
                     (clown, birth centenary (1996)) 90   40

(Des M. Escobar. Photo)
1997 (13 June). Sixth "The Ages of Man" Exhibition, El Burgo de Osma. Sheet 92×148 mm containing T 962 and similar vert designs. Multicoloured. P 13.
MS3434 21p. Type 962; 32p. El Burgo de Osma Cathedral; 65p. Illustration from Codex, 1086; 140p. Santo Domingo de Silos (17th-century statue) .... 3·75   3·75

963 Championship Poster (Manel Esclusa)

964 Cibeles Fountain, Madrid

(Des J. Suárez. Photo)
1997 (24 June). 30th Men's European Basketball Championship, Barcelona, Girona and Badalona. P 14×13½.
3435   963   65p. multicoloured .... 1·10   40

(Des P. Sánchez. Photo)
1997 (8 July). North Atlantic Co-operation Council Summit, Madrid. P 13×12½.
3436   964   65p. multicoloured .... 1·10   40

965 Grape Harvest Monument (José Esteve Edo)

966 Antonio Cánovas del Castillo (author of 1876 Constitution)

(Des P. Sánchez. Litho)
1997 (11 July). 50th Anniv of Grape Harvest Festival, Requena. P 14×13½.
3437   965   32p. multicoloured 50   20

(Des M. Escobar (21, 32p.), J. Suárez (65p.). Photo)
1997 (24 July). Anniversaries. T 966 and similar multicoloured designs. P 14×13½.
3438   21p. Type 966 (death centenary) 35   15
3439   32p. Roman coin and arrival of "Virgin of
                     the Assumption" (statue) (2000th anniv
                     of Elche) 55   25
3440   65p. Ships attacking city (after
                     contemporary painting) (bicentenary
                     of defence of Tenerife) (horiz) 95   40
3438/3440 Set of 3 .... 1·70   70

967 Blue Ribbon

968 Mariano Benlliure and "Breath of Life"

(Des M. Escobar. Photo)
1997 (30 July). Campaign for Peaceful Co-existence. P 14×13½.
3441   967   32p. new blue and black 40   20

1997 (12 Sept). Spanish Art. T **968** and similar vert design. Photo. P 14×13½.
| 3442 | 32c. multicoloured | 45 | 20 |
| 3443 | 65c. black and stone | 90 | 40 |

Designs:—32p. Type **968** (sculptor, 50th death anniv); 65p."Basque Rower" (photograph by Jose Ortiz Echagüe).

969 Net and Boat

970 City

1997 (17 Sept). Fourth World Fishing Fair, Vigo. Litho. P 14×13.
| 3444 | **969** | 32p. greenish blue, royal blue and gold | 40 | 20 |

1997 (24 Sept). Anniversaries. T **970** and similar designs. Recess (65p.) or photo (others). P 13½×14 (65p.) or 14×13½ (others).
3445	21p. multicoloured	25	15
3446	32p. multicoloured	45	25
3447	65p. slate-violet and bright scarlet	85	40
3445/3447	Set of 3	1·40	70

Designs: Vert—21p. Type **970** (500th anniv of Spanish administration of Melilla); 32p. St. Pascual Baylón (after Vincente Carducho) (centenary of proclamation as World Patron of Eucharistic Congresses). Horiz—65p. Ausias March (after Jacomart) (poet, 600th birth anniv).

971 San Julián de los Prados Church, Oviedo

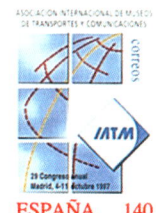
972 Emblem

1997 (26 Sept). World Heritage Sites. T **971** and similar horiz design. Recess. P 13×12½.
| 3448 | 21p. reddish brown, blue and deep green | 40 | 15 |
| 3449 | 32p. sepia, blue and deep green | 65 | 25 |

Design:—32p. Santa Cristina de Lena.

1997 (1 Oct). 29th Annual Congress of International Transport and Communications Museum Association, Madrid. Photo. P 14×13½.
| 3450 | **972** | 140p. multicoloured | 1·80 | 85 |

973 Statue of Don Palayo (José María López)

974 Postman

(Des J. Suárez. Eng J. Heras. Recess and litho)

1997 (4 Oct). Exfilna 97 National Stamp Exhibition, Gijón. Sheet 105×78 mm. P 14×13½.
| MS3451 | **973** | 140p. multicoloured | 2·00 | 2·00 |

1997 (10 Oct). America. Postal Delivery. Photo. P 14×13½.
| 3452 | **974** | 65p. multicoloured | 85 | 40 |

975 Miguel Fleta (tenor)   **976** Town Arms

(Des M. Escobar. Recess)

1997 (11 Oct). Re-opening of Royal Theatre, Madrid. T **975** and similar vert design. P 14×13½.
| 3453 | 21p. chocolate | 25 | 15 |
| 3454 | 32p. sepia | 45 | 25 |

Designs:—21p. Type **975** (birth centenary); 32p. Theatre façade.

(Des J. Plaza. Recess and litho)

1997 (17 Oct). 500th Anniv of San Cristóbal de la Laguna, Tenerife. P 14×13½.
| 3455 | **976** | 32p. multicoloured | 40 | 20 |

977 Emblem   **978** School

(Des J. Suárez. Photo)

1997 (23 Oct). Sixth World Downs Syndrome Congress, Madrid. P 13½×14.
| 3456 | **977** | 65p. ultramarine and chrome yellow | 85 | 40 |

(Des J. Suárez. Eng A. de Oro. Recess)

1997 (14 Nov). 150th Anniv of Córdoba Veterinary School. P 13½×14.
| 3457 | **978** | 21p. myrtle green and blue | 30 | 15 |

979 "Adoration of the Kings" (detail, Pedro Berruguete)   **980** New Gate, Ribadavia

(Des M. Escobar. Photo)

1997 (20 Nov). Christmas. P 14×13½.
| 3458 | **979** | 32p. multicoloured | 40 | 20 |

(Des M. Escobar. Eng J. Heras (3459), A. de Oro (3460), E. Paniagua (3461), P. Sampedro (3462). Recess)

1997 (28 Nov). Jewish Quarters. T **980** and similar horiz designs. P 13½×14.
3459	21p. chocolate and black	25	25
	a. Strip of 4. Nos. 3459/62	2·10	
3460	32p. bright violet and black	45	40
3461	32p. chocolate and black	45	40
3462	65p. bright violet and black	80	70
3459/3462	Set of 4	1·80	1·50

Designs:—No. 3460, Women's Gallery, Córdoba Synagogue; 3461, Façade of 15th-century building, St. Anthony's Quarter, Cáceres; 3462, Street, El Call, Girona.

SPAIN

981 Ball in Net   **982** Emblem

(Des P. Sánchez. Photo)
1997 (5 Dec). Spanish Sporting Success. Zarra's Winning Goal in Spain v England Match, World Cup Football Championship, Brazil, 1950. P 14.
3463   **981**   32p. multicoloured .... 1·30   70

(Des J. Plaza. Photo)
1998 (12 Jan). St. James's Holy Year (1999). P 14.
3464   **982**   35p. bright orange, deep grey and black.. 40   20

983 Lynx   **984** Club Flag and Emblem

(Des M. Escobar. Photo)
1998 (5 Feb). Endangered Species. P 14×13½.
3465   **983**   35p. multicoloured 40   20

(Des P. Sánchez. Photo)
1998 (10 Feb). Centenary of Athletic Bilbao Football Club. P 13½×14.
3466   **984**   35p. multicoloured 40   20

985 Clever and Smart (Francisco Ibáñez)   **986** Gredos Parador

1998 (26 Feb). Comic Strip Characters. T **985** and similar multicoloured design. Photo. P 14×13½ (35p.) or 13½×14 (70p.).
3467   35p. Type **985** 45   20
3468   70p. Zipi and Zape (Josep Escobar) (horiz) ... 90   55

(Des P. Sánchez. Photo)
1998 (12 Mar). 70th Anniv of Paradores (state hotels). P 13½×14.
3469   **986**   35p. multicoloured 40   20

987 St. Philip's Fort and Harbour, Ceuta   **988** 1898 Generation

(Des J. Plaza. Photo)
1998 (19 Mar). Third Anniv of Autonomy of Ceuta and Melilla. T **987** and similar multicoloured design. P 14×13½ (3470) or 13½×14 (3471).
3470   150p. Type **987** .... 1·90   90
3471   150p. Plaza de Menéndez Pelayo, Melilla (horiz).. 1·90   90

(Des M. Escobar. Photo)
1998 (3 Apr). 1898 Generation of Spanish Writers. P 13½×14.
3472   **988**   70p. multicoloured 90   45
The writers depicted are Azorin, Pio Baroja, Miguel de Unamuno, Ramiro de Maeztu, Antonio Machado and Valle Inclán.

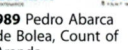

989 Pedro Abarca de Bolea, Count of Aranda   **990** The Celestine (Fernando de Rojas)

(Des J. Suárez. Photo)
1998 (17 Apr). Death Bicentenary of Pedro Abarca de Bolea, Count of Aranda (politician). P 14×13½.
3473   **989**   35p. multicoloured 40   20

(Des P. Sánchez. Recess)
1998 (29 Apr). Spanish Literature. T **990** and similar vert design. P 14×13½.
3474   35p. deep dull green and yellow-green.......... 45   20
3475   70p. deep dull green and red 90   45
Design:—70p. *Fortunata and Jacinta* (Benito Pérez Galdós).

991 Royal Boat   **992** St. John's Bonfires, Alicante

(Des J. Plaza. Litho)
1998 (30 Apr). Ship Paintings by Carlos Broschi from *Royal Celebrations in Reign of Fernando VI*. T **991** and similar horiz design. Multicoloured. P 13½×14.
3476   35p. Type **991** 45   20
3477   70p. Tajo xebec (vessel for court officials) 90   45

(Des P. Sánchez. Photo)
1998 (5 May). Europa. National Festivals. P 14×13½.
3478   **992**   70p. multicoloured .... 1·60   90

993 Jiménez Díaz   **994** Félix Rodríguez de la Fuente (naturalist, 70th anniv)

(Des J. Plaza. Photo)
1998 (18 May). Centenary of Professional Institute of Doctors of Madrid and Birth Centenary of Carlos Jiménez Díaz (physician). P 13½×14.
3479   **993**   35p. black and new blue 40   20

(Des J. Suárez. Photo)
1998 (28 May). Birth Anniversaries. T **994** and similar design. P 13½×14 (35p.) or 14×13½ (70p.).
3480   35p. multicoloured 45   20
3481   70p. orange and brown-red 90   45
Design: Vert—70p.Fofó (Alfonso Aragón) (clown, 75th anniv).

322

SPAIN

995 Felipe II (after Antonio Moro)   996 Lorca

(Des M. Escobar. Photo)
1998 (1 June). 400th Death Anniv of King Felipe II. P 14×13½.
3482 **995**   35p. multicoloured   40   20

(Des J. Suárez. Eng J. Heras. Recess and litho)
1998 (2 June). Birth Centenary of Federico García Lorca (writer). P 14×13½.
3483 **996**   35p. multicoloured   60   20

997 Antonio Manso Fernández and 1978 Queen Isabel II Stamp

998 Spanish and Philippine Flags, Cebú Basilicá (after M. Miguel) and "Holy Child" (statuette)

(Des M. Escobar. Eng J. Heras (35p.), A. de Oro (70p.). Recess and litho)
1998 (5 June). Spanish Engravers. T **997** and similar horiz design. P 13½×14.
3484   35p. reddish brown, blue and deep turquoise-blue................... 50   20
3485   70p. brown-purple, blue and black................. 95   45
Design:—70p. José Luis Sánchez Toda and 1935 Mariana Pineda stamp.

(Des J. Plaza. Photo)
1998 (12 June). Centenary of Philippine Independence. P 13½×14.
3486 **998**   70p. multicoloured   85   45

999 "Foster Brothers" (sculpture, Aniceto Marinas)

1000 "Union of the Oceans"

(Des P. Sánchez. Photo)
1998 (10 July). Spanish Art. P 14×13½.
3487 **999**   35p. multicoloured   40   20

(Des M. Escobar. Photo)
1998 (4 Sept). Expo '98 World's Fair, Lisbon. P 13½×14.
3488 **1000**   70p. multicoloured   85   45

1001 Computer, Computer Disk and Letter

1002 Barcelona Cathedral

(Des P. Sánchez. Litho)
1998 (16 Sept). 20th International Data Protection Conference, Santiago de Compostela. P 13½×14.
3489 **1001**   70p. multicoloured   85   45

(P. Sánchez. Recess and litho)
1998 (18 Sept). Exfilna 98 National Stamp Exhibition, Barcelona. Sheet 106×78 mm. P 14×13½.
MS3490 **1002**   150p. black and new blue ....   2·30   2·30

1003 Fortified City, Cuenca

(Des P. Sánchez. Recess)
1998 (19 Sept). World Heritage Sites. T **1003** and similar horiz design. P 13×12½.
3491   35p. red-brown and indigo   55   20
3492   70p. chocolate and bright scarlet............   1·10   45
Designs:—70p. Silk Exchange, Valencia.

1004 Man writing with Quill

(Des A. Mingote. Litho)
1998 (25 Sept). School Correspondence Programme. Scenes from *Don Quixote* (novel by Cervantes) (1st series). T **1004** and similar horiz designs. Multicoloured. P 13×12½.
3493   20p. Type **1004**.....................................   35   25
         a. Sheetlet of 12. Nos. 3493/3504................   4·25
3494   20p. Man reading book...........................   35   25
3495   20p. Priest dubbing Quixote   35   25
3496   20p. Quixote riding off at dawn (angel blowing trumpet)..............................   35   25
3497   20p. Man beating Quixote with stick.......   35   25
3498   20p. Investigator burning books   35   25
3499   20p. Quixote and Sancho on horseback.......   35   25
3500   20p. Quixote and horse on sail of windmill..   35   25
3501   20p. Quixote watching Sancho fly through air...   35   25
3502   20p. Quixote charging through flock of sheep   35   25
3503   20p. Quixote and galley slaves   35   25
3504   20p. Quixote piercing goat-skins of wine   35   25
3505   20p. Quixote in cage   35   25
         a. Sheetlet of 12. Nos. 3505/16................   4·25
3506   20p. Quixote and Sancho on knees and woman on donkey.................................   35   25
3507   20p. Quixote on foot holding sword to Knight of the Mirrors   35   25
3508   20p. Lion escaping cage...........................   35   25
3509   20p. Quixote attacking birds...................   35   25
3510   20p. Quixote on wooden horse................   35   25
3511   20p. Sancho as governor at meal   35   25
3512   20p. Quixote surprised in bed by Dona Rodríguez..   35   25
3513   20p. Sancho and donkey   35   25
3514   20p. Quixote and Sancho looking over lake.   35   25
3515   20p. Quixote on horse holding sword to Knight of the White Moon......................   35   25
3516   20p. Quixote and Sancho returning home at night..   35   25
3493/3516 Set of 24   7·50   5·50
Nos. 3493/3504 and 3505/16 respectively were issued together in *se-tenant* sheetlets of 12 stamps, each sheetlet with an enlarged right-hand margin showing Don Quixote or Sancho.
See also Nos. 3598/3609, 3677/3700, 3775/3786 and 3882/3893.

SPAIN

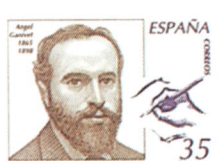 

1005 Angel Ganivet (writer, death centenary)

1006 Ladies' Tower and El Partal Gardens, Alhambra, Granada

(Des P. Sánchez; eng A. de Oro (35p.). Des J. Suárez; eng J. Heras (70p.). Recess)

1998 (9 Oct). Anniversaries. T **1005** and similar design. P 13½×14 (35p.) or 14×13½ (70p.).
3517   35p. red-brown and bright violet 45   20
3518   70p. orange-brown and blue.............................. 85   45
Design: Vert—70p. Giralda Tower, Seville (800th anniv).

(Des P. Sánchez. Eng A. de Oro. Recess)

1998 (8 Oct). Aga Khan 1998 Architecture Award. P 14×13½.
3519   **1006**   35p. red-brown and yellowish green .. 40   20

1007 U.P.U. Emblem

1008 María Guerrero (actress) and Scene from *The Lioness of Castille* by Francisco Villaespesa

(Des J. Sánchez. Litho)

1998 (9 Oct). World Stamp Day. P 13½×14.
3520   **1007**   70p. dull ultramarine and bright green 85   45

(Des M. Escobar. Photo)

1998 (13 Oct). America. Famous Women. P 13½×14.
3521   **1008**   70p. multicoloured 85   45

1009 Steam Locomotive *Mataró* (1848) and Euromed Electric Train (1998)

1010 Antarctic Base

(Des M. Escobar. Eng J. Heras. Recess)

1998 (28 Oct). 150th Anniv of Spanish Railways. P 13½×14.
3522   **1009**   35p. steel-blue and black 40   20

(Des J. Suárez. Photo)

1998 (6 Nov). Tenth Anniv of Juan Carlos I Antarctic Base. P 13½×14.
3523   **1010**   35p. multicoloured 40   20

1011 Altarpiece (detail)

1012 Chestnut Seller

(Des M. Plaza. Photo)

1998 (11 Nov). Restoration of San Salavador's Cathedral, Zaragoza. Details of Altarpiece by Hans of Swabia. Sheet 105×122 mm containing T **1011** and similar vert design. Multicoloured. P 14×13½.
MS3524 35p. Type **1011**; 35p. Adoration of the Wise Men (detail) .... 1·40   1·40

(Des R. Seco (35p.), P. Sánchez (70p.). Photo)

1998 (13 Nov). Christmas. T **1012** and similar vert design. Multicoloured. P 14×13½.
3525   35p. Type **1012**... 45   20
3526   70p. "Wedding of Virgin Mary and Joseph" (detail of capital from Oviedo Cathedral).. 85   45

1013 Juan de Oñate (expedition leader)

1014 House, Hervás

1998 (20 Nov). 400th Anniv of Foundation of Spanish Province of New Mexico. T **1013** and similar horiz design. Multicoloured. Photo. P 13½×14.
3527   35p. Type **1013**... 45   20
3528   70p. Map and arms of New Mexico................. 85   45

(Des M. Escobar. Eng P. Sampedro (3530) or E. Paniagua (others). Recess)

1998 (23 Nov). Jewish Quarters. T **1014** and similar horiz designs. P 13½×14.
3529   35p. reddish purple and deep blue................. 45   25
          a. Strip of 4. Nos. 3529/32 .... 3·25
3530   35p. deep green and deep blue...................... 45   25
3531   70p. reddish purple and deep blue................. 65   40
3532   70p. deep green and deep blue...................... 65   40
3529/3532 *Set of 4* .... 2·00   1·20
Designs:—No. 3530, Bust of Benjamin Tudela (travel writer); 3531, Corpus Christi Church (former synagogue), Segovia; 3532, Santa María la Blanca synagogue, Toledo.
Nos. 3529/32 were issued together in *se-tenant* strips of four stamps within the sheet.

1015 Alaior and Mt. Toro

1016 Bust of Plato and Ancient Greek Amphora

(Des J. Suárez. Photo)

1998 (2 Dec). UNESCO Biosphere Reserve, Minorca. P 13½×14.
3533   **1015**   35p. multicoloured 40   20

(Des P. Sánchez. Photo)

1998 (9 Dec). 30th Anniv of Spanish Olympic Academy. P 13½×14.
3534   **1016**   70p. multicoloured 85   45

1017 Angel Sanz Briz (diplomat)

1018 Mare and Foal

(Des J. Suárez. Photo)

1998 (10 Dec). 50th Anniv of Universal Declaration of Human Rights. T **1017** and similar vert design. Multicoloured. P 14×13½.
3535   35p. Type **1017**... 45   20
3536   70p. Fingerprints forming heart (painting, Javier Valmaseda Calvo)............................... 85   45

SPAIN

(Des F. Pedreo. Photo)

1998 (29 Dec). España 2000 International Stamp Exhibition, Madrid (1st issue). La Cartuja-Hierro del Bocado Horses. T **1018** and similar horiz designs. Multicoloured. P 13½×14.

3537	20p. Type **1018** (emblem bottom right)..........	55	55
	a. Sheetlet of 12. No. 3537/48......................	31·00	
3538	20p. Type **1018** (emblem top left and right)..	55	55
3539	35p. Brown horse (emblem top right).............	90	90
3540	35p. As No. 3538 (emblem bottom left)........	90	90
3541	70p. Horse's head (emblem bottom left and bottom right)..	1·90	1·90
3542	70p. As No. 3541 (emblem bottom left)........	1·90	1·90
3543	100p. Mare and foal (*different*) (emblem top left and top right).................................	3·00	3·00
3544	100p. As No. 3543 (emblem bottom right)......	3·00	3·00
3545	150p. Grey (emblem bottom left)	4·00	4·00
3546	150p. As No. 3545 (emblem bottom right)......	4·00	4·00
3547	185p. Two white horses (emblem top left)......	5·00	5·00
3548	185p. As No. 3547 (emblem bottom left and bottom right)..	5·00	5·00
3537/3548 Set of 12..		30·00	30·00

Nos. 3537/4 were issued together in *se-tenant* sheetlets of 12 stamps.

Two different emblems are each printed twice in orange within the sheet, occurring in each case at the intersection of four stamps so that each stamp carries only part of one or two emblems as described in brackets.

See also Nos. 3612/3623, 3662/3673 and **MS**3701.

1019 Giant Lizard, El Hierro Island

1020 Stone Cross, Perelada, Galicia

(Des M. Plaza. Photo)

1999 (28 Jan). Endangered Species. T **1019** and similar multicoloured designs. P 14×13½ (70p.) or 13×14½ (others).

3549	35p. Type **1019**..	50	20
3550	70p. Osprey (*vert*).......................................	1·00	30
3551	100p. Manx shearwater	1·50	55
3549/3551 Set of 3		3·50	95

(Des J. Suárez. Recess and litho)

1999 (22 Feb). St. James's Holy Year. T **1020** and similar multicoloured designs. P 13½×14 (70p.) or 14×13½ (others).

3552	35p. Type **1020**..	40	20
3553	70p. Figure of St. James on tympanum, St. James's Church, Sangüesa, Navarra (horiz)..	1·00	40
3554	100p. Stone cross and Cizur bridge, Pamplona, Navarra	1·30	55
3555	185p. Jurisdictional stone pillar, Boadilla del Camino, Palencia..................................	2·50	55
3552/3555 Set of 4		4·75	1·50

1021 Poster (Antoni Tápies)

1022 "Alaior" (Aroa Vidal)

1999 (11 Mar). Centenary of Barcelona Football Club. Photo. P 14×13½.

| 3556 | **1021** | 35p. multicoloured............................... | 50 | 20 |

1999 (12 Mar). Juvenia '99 National Youth Stamp Exhibition, Alaior, Minorca. Litho. P 13½×14.

| 3557 | **1022** | 35p. black, orange-vermilion and yellow .... | 50 | 20 |

1023 Police Moped, Helicopter and Men in Protective Suits

1024 Aljafería Palace, Zaragoza

(Des P. Sánchez. Photo)

1999 (26 Mar). 175th Anniv of Spanish Police Force. P 13½×14.

| 3558 | **1023** | 35p. multicoloured......................... | 50 | 20 |

(Des J. Suárez. Recess)

1999 (9 Apr). Exfilna 99 National Stamp Exhibition, Zaragoza. Sheet 106×79 mm. P 14×13½.

| **MS**3559 | **1024** | 185p. deep green and chestnut.......... | 2·75 | 2·75 |

1025 Radio Transmitter and Receiver

1026 Emblem and Athletes

1999 (9 Apr). 50th Anniv of Spanish Amateur Radio Union. Photo. P 14.

| 3560 | **1025** | 70p. multicoloured......................... | 90 | 40 |

(Des F. Rivas. Photo)

1999 (30 Apr). Seventh World Athletics Championship, Seville. P 14×13½.

| 3561 | **1026** | 70p. multicoloured......................... | 90 | 40 |

1027 Monfragüe Nature Park, Cáceres, and Wild Cat

1028 Underground Train

(Des and eng P. Sánchez. Recess and litho)

1999 (5 May). Europa. Parks and Gardens. P 13½×14.

| 3562 | **1027** | 70p. multicoloured......................... | 1·50 | 90 |

(Des Disseny Gràfic)

1999 (7 May). 75th Anniv of Barcelona Metro. P 13½×14.

| 3563 | **1028** | 70p. multicoloured......................... | 90 | 40 |

1029 "King Solomon" (detail of reredos from Becerril de Campos Church)

1030 European Community Flag

(Des P. Sánchez. Photo)

1999 (14 May). "The Ages of Man" Exhibition, Palencia. T **1029** and similar vert design. Multicoloured. P 14×13½.

3564	35p. Type **1029**..	45	20
3565	70p. Detail of choir railing, Palencia Cathedral...	90	40

325

SPAIN

(Des M. Escobar. Photo)
1999 (28 May). The Euro (European single currency). T **1030** and similar horiz designs showing maps of the participating countries and the appropriate exchange rate. Multicoloured. P 13½×14.

3566	166p. Type **1030**	2·75	1·70
	a. Sheetlet of 12. Nos. 3566/77	33·00	
3567	166p. Germany	2·75	1·70
3568	166p. Austria	2·75	1·70
3569	166p. Belgium	2·75	1·70
3570	166p. Spain	2·75	1·70
3571	166p. Finland	2·75	1·70
3572	166p. France	2·75	1·70
3573	166p. Netherlands	2·75	1·70
3574	166p. Republic of Ireland	2·75	1·70
3575	166p. Italy	2·75	1·70
3576	166p. Luxembourg	2·75	1·70
3577	166p. Portugal	2·75	1·70
3566/3577 Set of 12		30·00	18·00

Nos. 3566/77 were issued together in *se-tenant* sheetlets of 12 stamps.

1031 Footballers and Club Badge

1032 Doña Urraca (Jorge (Miguel Bernet Toledano))

(Des P. Sánchez. Photo)
1999 (7 June). Real Club Recreativo (Royal Recreation Club) of Huelva. P 13½×14.
3578 **1031** 35p. multicoloured 50 20

1999 (11 June). Comic Strip Characters. T **1032** and similar vert design. Multicoloured. Photo. P 14×13½.
3579 35p. Type **1032** 45 20
3580 70p. El Coyote (José Mallorquí and Francisco Batet) 90 40

1033 Games Emblem

1034 Attack of Dutch Navy (after De Bry) and Arms of Las Palmas

(Des C. Lopez del Rey. Photo)
1999 (18 June). World University Summer Games and Fifth National Thematic Stamps Exhibition, Palma de Mallorca. Sheet 105×78 mm. P 14×13½.
MS3581 **1033** 185p. multicoloured .... 2·50 2·50

1999 (25 June). 400th Anniv of Defence of Las Palmas, Gran Canaria. Recess and litho. P 13½×14.
3582 **1034** 70p. black and yellow-ochre 90 40

1035 Cangas de Onís Parador (former Monastery of San Pedro de Villanueva)

1036 Old Bridge

(Des P. Sánchez. Photo)
1999 (2 July). Paradores (state hotels). P 14×13½.
3583 **1035** 35p. multicoloured 50 20

(Des P. Sánchez. Photo)
1999 (12 July). 800th Anniv of Granting of Township Rights to Balmaseda. P 14×13½.
3584 **1036** 35p. multicoloured 45 20

1037 Society and Anniversary Emblems

1038 Illuminated Fountain

1999 (12 July). Centenary of Society of Authors and Publishers. Photo. P 14×13½.
3585 **1037** 70p. multicoloured 90 40

(Des Mariscal Studio. Photo)
1999 (12 July). Birth Centenary of Carles Buigas (engineer). P 13½×14.
3586 **1038** 70p. multicoloured 90 40

1039 Queen Isabel II, Geological Map of Spain and Founding Decree

1040 El Cid (after Vela Zanetti)

1999 (12 July). 150th Anniv of Spanish Technical Institute of Geology and Mining. Photo. P 13½×14.
3587 **1039** 150p. multicoloured .... 2·10 90

1999 (16 July). 900th Death Anniv of El Cid (Rodrigo Díaz de Vivar). Photo. P 14×13½.
3588 **1040** 35p. multicoloured 45 35

1041 "Winter"

1042 "The Jester Don Sebastián de Morra"

1999 (10 Sept). Spanish Art. Paintings by Vela Zanetti. T **1041** and similar multicoloured design. Photo. P 13½×14 (70p.) or 14×13½ (150p.).
3589 70p. Type **1041** 85 40
3590 150p. "The Harvest" (vert) .... 1·90 85

1999 (24 Sept). 400th Birth Anniv of Diego de Silva Velázquez (artist). T **1042** and similar vert design. Multicoloured. Photo. P 14×13½.
3591 35p. Type **1042** 45 20
3592 70p. "A Sibyl" 90 40

SPAIN

1043 Emblem, Couple, Man and Baby   **1044** Oix Castle

(Des M. Plaza. Photo)

1999 (30 Sept). International Year of the Elderly. P 13½×14.
3593 **1043** 35p. multicoloured........................ 50 20

(Des P. Sánchez. Recess)

1999 (1 Oct). Catalan Lower Pyrenees Region. P 13½×14.
3594 **1044** 70p. reddish brown and blue................. 90 40

1045 St. Millán of Yuso Monastery, La Rioja   **1046** U.P.U. Monument, Berne

(Des J. Suárez. Recess)

1999 (8 Oct). World Heritage Sites. T **1045** and similar horiz design. P 13×12½.
3595 35p. brown, bottle green and blue................ 60 20
3596 70p. brown, deep green and blue................ 1·30 40
Design:—70p. St. Millán of Suso Monastery, La Rioja.

(Des J. Suárez. Photo)

1999 (9 Oct). Stamp Day. 125th Anniv of Universal Postal Union. P 14.
3597 **1046** 70p. multicoloured........................ 90 40

 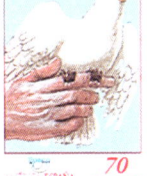

1047 First Spanish Stamp, 1850   **1048** Dove on Hand

(Des F. Sánchez. Photo)

1999 (13 Oct). School Correspondence Programme (2nd series). T **1047** and similar horiz designs showing a stamp at various activities. Multicoloured. P 13.
3598 20p. Type **1047**........................ 25 20
       a. Sheetlet of 12. Nos. 3598/609........ 3·75
3599 20p. Airliner taking off and city........ 25 20
3600 20p. As postman delivering letter........ 25 20
3601 20p. Writing letter..................... 25 20
3602 20p. Reading book....................... 25 20
3603 20p. With bird, butterfly and fish (nature)..... 25 20
3604 20p. With historical buildings (heritage)...... 25 20
3605 20p. Painting portrait.................. 25 20
3606 20p. With football, tennis racquet and sailboard........................ 25 20
3607 20p. With baton, cello and saxophone.... 25 20
3608 20p. Holding magnifying glass over 40c. stamp........................ 25 20
3609 20p. On horseback...................... 25 20
3598/3609 Set of 12................................. 2·75 2·20
Nos. 3598/3609 were issued together in *se-tenant* sheetlets of 12 stamps, each sheetlet with an enlarged right-hand margin showing the stamp character posting a letter.

(Des R. Seco. Photo)

1999 (15 Oct). America. A New Millennium without Arms. P 14×13½.
3610 **1048** 70p. multicoloured........................ 90 40

1049 "The Money Changer and his Wife" (Marinus Reymerswaele)

1999 (18 Oct). International Money Museums Congress, Madrid. Recess. P 13×12½.
3611 **1049** 70p. reddish brown and deep ultramarine........................ 90 40

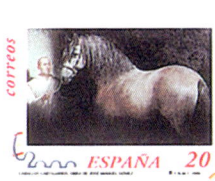 

1050 Horse and Rider   **1051** "The Epiphany" (altarpiece, Toledo Cathedral)

(Des J. Carrero. Photo)

1999 (3 Nov). España 2000 International Stamp Exhibition, Madrid (2nd issue). La Cartuja-Hierro del Bocado Horses. T **1050** and similar horiz designs showing paintings by José Manuel Gómez. Multicoloured. P 13½×14.
3612 20p. Type **1050** (emblem bottom right)........ 85 85
       a. Sheetlet of 12. Nos. 3612/23........ 42·00
3613 20p. Type **1050** (emblem top left)........ 85 85
3614 35p. Exhibition emblem and horses (emblems top left and right)........ 1·30 1·30
3615 35p. As No. 3614 (emblems top left and right but transposed)........ 1·30 1·30
3616 70p. Exhibition emblem (emblems bottom left and right)........ 2·20 2·20
3617 70p. As No. 3616 (emblems bottom left and right but transposed)........ 2·20 2·20
3618 100p. White horses (emblem top right)........ 3·75 3·75
3619 100p. As No. 3618 (emblem bottom left)........ 3·75 3·75
3620 150p. Heads of two white horses (emblem bottom left)........ 5·00 5·00
3621 150p. As No. 3620 (emblem top right)........ 5·00 5·00
3622 185p. Men inspecting horse (emblem top left)........ 6·75 6·75
3623 185p. As No. 3622 (emblem bottom right)........ 6·75 6·75
3612/3623 Set of 12........ 36·00 36·00
Nos. 3612/23 were issued together in *se-tenant* sheetlets of 12 stamps.
Two different emblems are each printed twice in orange within the sheet, occurring in each case at the intersection of four stamps so that each stamp carries only part of one or two emblems as described in brackets.

(Des P. Sánchez. Photo)

1999 (5 Nov). Christmas. T **1051** and similar multicoloured design. P 14×13½ (35p.) or 13½×14 (70p.).
3624 35p. Type **1051**........................ 45 20
3625 70p. "Christmas" (Isabel Guerra) (horiz)........ 90 40

1052 King Juan Carlos and 1850 12c. Stamp   **1053** Apollo (*Parnassius apollo*)

2000 (3 Jan). 150th Anniv of First Spanish Stamp. T **1052** and similar horiz designs. Multicoloured. Recess and litho. P 13½×14.
3626 35p. Type **1052**........................ 45 35
       a. Sheetlet of 12. Nos. 3626/29 and 3631, each×2 and Nos. 3630 and 3632........ 6·00
3627 35p. King Juan Carlos and 6c. stamp........ 45 35
3628 35p. King Juan Carlos and 5r. stamp........ 45 35

327

SPAIN

3629	35p. King Juan Carlos and 6r. stamp	45	35
3630	35p. Anniversary emblem and 6c. stamp	45	35
3631	35p. King Juan Carlos and 10r. stamp	45	35
3632	35p. King Juan Carlos and State arms	45	35

Nos. 3626/32 were issued together in *se-tenant* sheetlets of 12 stamps.

(Des J. Suárez. Photo)

2000 (31 Jan). Endangered Butterflies. T **1053** and similar horiz design. Multicoloured. P 14.
| 3633 | 35p. Type **1053** | 45 | 20 |
| 3634 | 70p. *Agriades zullichi* | 90 | 45 |

1054 Virgin Mary and Baby Jesus (xylographic engraving, Juan Luschner)

1055 "Charles V as Sovereign Master of the Order of the Golden Fleece" (anon)

2000 (4 Feb). 500th Anniv of the Monastery of Santa María of Montserrat Printing House. Photo. P 14.
| 3635 | **1054** 35p. multicoloured | 45 | 20 |

2000 (24 Feb). 500th Birth Anniv of King Charles V, Holy Roman Emperor. T **1055** and similar vert designs. Multicoloured. Photo. P 12½×13.
3636	35p. Type **1055**	45	25
3637	70p. "Charles V" (Corneille da la Haye)	90	45
MS3638	126×91 mm. 150p. "Charles V on Horseback" (40×49 mm). P 13½ × 13	2·10	2·10

1056 The Virgin de al Majestad (12th-century statue), Astorga Cathedral

1057 Sos del Rey Católico, Saragossa

(Des M. Plaza. Photo)

2000 (24 Mar). "The Age of Man" Exhibition, Astorga, León. T **1056** and similar vert design. Multicoloured. P 14.
| 3639 | 70p. Type **1056** | 90 | 45 |
| 3640 | 100p. 12th-century Lignum Crucis and 10th-century Arab perfume bottle | 1·40 | 75 |

(Des J. Plaza. Photo)

2000 (7 Apr). Paradores (state hotels). P 13½×14.
| 3641 | **1057** 35p. multicoloured | 45 | 25 |

1058 Lleida University

1059 Emblem

(Des M. Escobar. Recess)

2000 (12 Apr). University Anniversaries. T **1058** and similar horiz design. P 13½×14.
| 3642 | 35p. orange-brown and deep magenta | 45 | 25 |
| 3643 | 70p. purple-brown and new blue | 90 | 45 |

Designs:—35p. Type **1058** (700th anniv); 70p. Valencia (500th anniv (1999)).

(Des P. Durán. Photo)

2000 (28 Apr). Centenary of Reial Club Deportiu Espanyol Football Club, Barcelona. P 14×13½.
| 3644 | **1059** 35p. multicoloured | 45 | 25 |

1060 Maria de las Mercedes (painting, Ricardo Macarrón)

1061 "Building Europe"

2000 (4 May). Maria de las Mercedes de Borbón y Orleans (mother of King Juan Carlos I) Commemoration. P 14×13½.
| 3645 | **1060** 35p. multicoloured | 45 | 25 |

(Des J.-P. Cousin. Photo)

2000 (9 May). Europa. P 14×13½.
| 3646 | **1061** 70p. multicoloured | 1·60 | 1·20 |

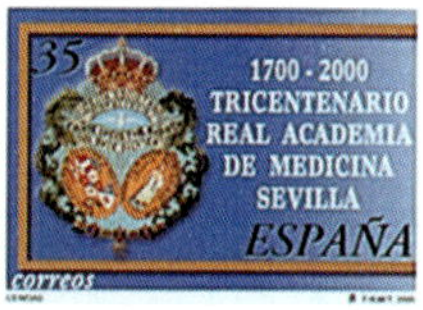

1062 Emblem

1063 Hermenegilda and Leovigilda (Manuel Vázquez Gallego)

(Des M. Plaza (3647, 3649), P. Sánchez (3648) and J. Suárez (3650). Photo)

2000 (25 May). World Mathematics Year (3648) and Science (others). T **1062** and similar multicoloured designs. P 14×13½ (3649) or 13½×14 (others).
3647	35p. Type **1062** (300th anniv of Royal Academy of Medicine, Seville)	45	25
3648	70p. Julio Rey Pastor (mathematician) (painting, Pedro Piug Adam) and mathematical equation	90	45
3649	100p. School of Pharmacy, Granada (150th anniv) (vert)	1·30	75
3650	185p. Prince Felipe Science Museum, Valencia	2·50	1·20
3647/3650	Set of 4	4·75	2·50

2000 (26 May). Comic Strip Characters. T **1063** and similar multicoloured design. Photo. P 13½×14 (3651) or 14×13½ (3652).
| 3651 | 35p. Type **1063** | 45 | 25 |
| 3652 | 70p. Roberto Alcázar and Pedrín (Eduardo Vañó and Juan Bautista Puerto Belda) (vert) | 90 | 45 |

1064 Guggenheim Museum

1065 "Prayer in the Garden" (detail, Francisco Salzillo)

(Des M. Escobar. Photo)

2000 (2 June). 700th Anniv of Bilbao. P 13½×14.

| 3653 | **1064** | 70p. multicoloured | 90 | 45 |

2000 (9 June). Spanish Art. Photo. P 14×13½.

| 3654 | **1065** | 70p. multicoloured | 90 | 45 |

1066 Water Fountain   **1067** Wild Pine (*Pinus silvestris*)

(Des M. Escobar. Eng J. Heras. Recess and photo)

2000 (16 June). EXFILNA 2000 National Philatelic Exhibition, Avilés. Sheet 105×78 mm. P 14×13½.

| MS3655 | **1066** | 185p. red-brown and blue | 2·40 | 2·40 |

(Des P. Sanchez. Photo)

2000 (19 June). Trees (1st series). T **1067** and similar diamond-shaped design. Multicoloured. P 12½.

| 3656 | 70p. Type **1067** | 90 | 45 |
| 3657 | 150p. Holm oak (*Quercus ilex*) | 1·90 | 1·00 |

See also Nos. 3757/3758, 3837/3838, 3994/3995 and 4021.

1068 Fire Walking, San Pedro Manrique, Soria   **1069** Escrivá

(Des J. Suárez. Photo)

2000 (23 June). Festivals (1st series). T **1068** and similar horiz design. Multicoloured. P 13½×14.

| 3658 | 35p. Type **1068** | 45 | 25 |
| 3659 | 70p. Rearing horse, crowd and flag (700th anniv of Chivalry Festival of San Juan, Ciudadela, Menorca) | 90 | 45 |

See also Nos. 3760/3761.

(Des J. Suárez. Eng A. Oro. Recess and litho)

2000 (26 June). 25th Death Anniv of Josemaría Escrivá de Balaguer (founder of Opus Dei (religious organization)). P 13½×14.

| 3660 | **1069** | 70p. black and orange | 90 | 40 |

1070 Detail of Chart

(Des M. Plaza. Photo)

2000 (14 July). 500th Anniv of Chart by Juan de la Cosa (sailor and cartographer) (first chart showing the Americas). Sheet 164×87 mm. P 13½×14.

| MS3661 | **1070** | 150p. multicoloured | 2·30 | 2·30 |

1071 Horse and Emblem

(Des F. Pedrero and M. Plaza. Photo)

2000 (28 July). España 2000 International Stamp Exhibition, Madrid (3rd issue). La Carbija-Hierro de Bocado Horses. T **1071** and similar horiz designs. Multicoloured. P 13½×14.

3662	20p. Type **1071** (emblem bottom right)	1·00	1·00
	a. Sheetlet of 12. Nos. 3662/73	55·00	
3663	20p. Type **1071** (emblems top right)	1·00	1·00
3664	35p. Horse on beach (emblem top right)	1·70	1·70
3665	35p. As No. 3664 (emblem bottom left)	1·70	1·70
3666	70p. Galloping horses and horse's head (emblems bottom left and right)	3·50	3·50
3667	70p. As No. 3666 (emblem top left)	3·50	3·50
3668	100p. Two horses' heads (emblems top left and right)	4·75	4·75
3669	100p. As No. 3668 (emblems bottom right)	4·75	4·75
3670	150p. Horse and horse's head (emblem bottom left)	7·50	7·50
3671	150p. As No. 3670 (emblem bottom right)	7·50	7·50
3672	185p. Horse outside stable (emblem top left)	8·75	8·75
3673	185p. As No. 3672 (emblems bottom left and right)	8·75	8·75
3662/3673	Set of 12	50·00	50·00

Nos. 3662/73 were issued together in *se-tenant* sheetlets of 12 stamps. Two different emblems were each printed twice in orange within the sheet, occurring in each case at the intersection of four stamps so that each stamp carries only part of one or two emblems as described in brackets.

1072 Las Médulas, León

(Des P. Sánchez. Eng A. Oro (3675), J. Heras (3676). Photo (3674), Recess (others))

2000 (21 Sept). UNESCO World Heritage Sites. T **1072** and similar designs. P 12½×13 (3675) or 13×12½ (others).

3674	35p. multicoloured	50	25
3675	70p. blackish brown and new blue (vert)	95	45
3676	150p. brown-red and red-brown	2·10	1·00
3674/3676	Set of 3	3·25	1·70

Designs:—70p. Mount Perdido, Pyrenees; 150p. Catalan Music Palace, Barcelona.

1073 Atapuercan Man wearing Football Scarf

(Des J. Gallego and J. Rey. Photo)

2000 (22 Sept). School Correspondence Programme. Spanish History (3rd series). T **1073** and similar horiz designs. Multicoloured. P 13×12½.

3677	20p. Type **1073**	30	25
	a. Sheetlet of 12. Nos. 3677/88	6·25	
3678	20p. Cave artists, Altamíra	30	25
3679	20p. Phoenician ship	30	25
3680	20p. Question marks in Roman helmets (Tartessos)	30	25
3681	20p. Celtic and Iberian men	30	25
3682	20p. "The Lady of Elche" listening to music	30	25
3683	20p. Elephant on low-loader (Carthage) (first Punic war)	30	25
3684	20p. Romans	30	25
3685	20p. Viriathus (leader) attacking Roman (uprising in northern Spain)	30	25

SPAIN

3686	20p. Roman preparing to kick football into net full of Numanians (fall of the city of Numantia).............................		30	25
3687	20p. Aqueduct of Segova.............................		30	25
3688	20p. Roman facing Vandal, Suevian and Alani (invasion, 409).............................		30	25
3689	20p. Visigoth kings Teodoredo I, Wallia, Sigerico and Ataulfo.............................		30	25
	a. Sheetlet of 12. Nos. 3689/98................		6·25	
3690	20p. King Recaredo I (conversion to Christianity, 589).............................		30	25
3691	20p. Map showing extent of Arab rule (conquest by Arab forces, 711).............................		30	25
3692	20p. Pelayo (Visigoth soldier), Covadonga, 722 (victory over the Moors).............................		30	25
3693	20p. Horseman (discovery of Tomb of the Apostle, 813).............................		30	25
3694	20p. Kings (union of Castille and Navarre)		30	25
3695	20p. Death of El Cid (soldier), 1099.............		30	25
3696	20p. Battle of Las Navas de Tolosa represented by chess game.............................		30	25
3697	20p. Accession of Alfonso (1252).............		30	25
3698	20p. Enrique II and slain Pedro I (foundation of House of Trastamara (Kingdom of Castille and Leon), 1396 ...		30	25
3699	20p. Monk with magnifying glass (The Inquisition, established 1478)................		30	25
3700	20p. Two crowns (unification of Kingdoms of Castile and Aragón, 1479).............		30	25
3677/3700 Set of 24			6·00	5·40

Nos. 3677/88 and 3689/3700 respectively were issued together in *se-tenant* sheetlets of 12 stamps, each sheetlet with an enlarged right-hand margin showing a Celt watering a column or a Crusader chopping down a minaret.

1074 Record and Hand (Julio Iglesias, singer)

1075 Boy putting up Poster

(Des F. Sánchez. Litho)

2000 (6–13 Oct). España 2000 International Stamp Exhibition, Madrid (4th issue) Eleven sheets 105×78 mm containing T **1074** and similar multicoloured designs. P 12 (**MS**3701a/b, e/f) (circular) or 13½×14 (others).

MS3701 Eleven sheets (a) 200p. Type **1074**; (b) 200p. Record and signature (Alejandro Sanz, singer-songwriter); (c) 200p. Film projector (Antonio Banderas, actor) (7 Oct); (d) 200p. Designer's mannequin (Jesús de Pozo, designer and couturier) (8 Oct); (e) 200p. Football (Raúl González Blanco, footballer) (9 Oct); (f) 200p. Cycle wheel (Miguel Induráin, cyclist) (9 Oct); (g) 200p. Hands (Joaquin Cortés, dancer and choreographer) (10 Oct); (h) 200p. Dancing feet (Sara Baras, flamenco dancer) (10 Oct); (i) 200p. Emblem (television) (11 Oct); (j) 200p. Radio and mast (12 Oct); (k) 200p. Newspaper titles (the press) (13 Oct) .... 32·00 32·00

One or two (**MS**3701a/b and **MS**3701e/h) miniature sheets were issued on each day of the exhibition.

(Des R. Seco. Photo)

2000 (19 Oct). America. A.I.D.S. Awareness. P 14×13½.
3702 **1075** 70p. multicoloured 90 45

1076 Portrait and Treble Clef

1077 The Adoration of Jesus (triptych) (Cristiane Hemmerich)

(Des J. Suárez. Photo)

2000 (27 Oct). First Death Anniv of Alfred Kraus (tenor). P 14.
3703 **1076** 70p. multicoloured 90 45

2000 (9 Nov). Christmas. T **1077** and similar square design. Multicoloured. Photo. P 12½.
3704 35p. Type **1077**............................. 45 25
3705 70p. "Birth of Christ" (Conrad von Soest) 90 45

1078 Building Façade

1079 Couple in Orange Grove (Etre Naranjos, Vicente Blasco Ibáñez)

(Des P. Sánchez. Recess)

2000 (10 Nov). Millenary of Santa María la Real Church, Aranda de Duero. P 14×13½.
3706 **1078** 35p. blackish brown 45 25

(Des P. Sánchez (Nos. 3707, 3709). Photo (Nos. 3707/8) or recess (No. 3709))

2000 (17 Nov). Literature. T **1079** and similar horiz designs. P 14×13½.
3707 35p. Type **1079**............................. 50 25
3708 70p. Troubadour with lute, figures and castle (*La Venganza de Don Mendo*, Pedro Muñzo Seca)............................. 90 45
3709 100p. Soldiers (*El Alcalde Zalamea*, Pedro Calaerón de la Barca)............................. 1·40 75
3707/3709 Set of 3 .... 3·50 1·30

1080 "Tribute to Broker" (sculpture) (Francisco López Hernández) and Emblem

1081 Firefighters

(Des J. Suárez. Photo)

2001 (8 Jan). 75th Anniv of Brokers' Schools. P 14×13½.
3710 **1080** 40p. multicoloured 50 20

(Des P. Sánchez. Photo)

2001 (19 Jan). P 14×13½.
3711 **1081** 75p. multicoloured 90 50

 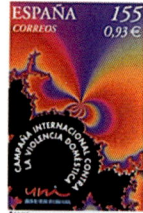

1082 Soldier, Building and Emblem

1083 Emblem

(Des M. Plaza. Photo)

2001 (16 Feb). 150th Anniv of Infantry College, Toledo. P 13½×14.
3712 **1082** 120p. multicoloured .... 1·50 80

(Des M. Escobar. Photo)

2001 (22 Feb). Campaign Against Domestic Violence. P 14×13½.
3713 **1083** 155p. multicoloured .... 1·90 1·00

SPAIN

1084 First Post Box in Spain, Mayorga (1793)

1085 Young Couple and Dinghy

(Eng J. Rincón. Recess)

2001 (2 Mar). Stamp Day. P 13½×14.
3714	**1084**	155p. black	1·90	1·00

(Des P. Sánchez. Photo)

2001 (9 Mar). Juvenia 2001 Youth Stamp Exhibition, Cádiz. P 13½×14.
3715	**1085**	120p. multicoloured	1·50	85

1086 Plasencia Hotel (former monastery of San Vicente Ferrer)

1087 Joaquín Rodrigo (composer, birth centenary)

(Des P. Sánchez. Photo)

2001 (16 Mar). Paradores (state hotels). P 14×13½.
3716	**1086**	40p. multicoloured	50	30

(Des M. Escobar. Recess)

2001 (22 Mar). Personalities. T **1087** and similar horiz design. P 13½.
3717	40p. bluish violet	50	30
3718	75p. red-brown and blue	90	50

Design:—75p. Rafael Alberti (poet and dramatist, first death anniv).

1088 Zuda Castle, Tortosa

1089 Books forming Flower

2001 (20 Apr). Castles. T **1088** and similar designs. Recess. P 14×13½ (40p.) or 13½ (others).
3719	40p. Type **1088**	50	30
3720	75p. Castle of El Cid, Jadraque (horiz)	90	45
3721	155p. San Fernando Castle, Figueres (horiz)	1·90	1·10
3722	260p. Montesquiu Castle (horiz)	3·25	1·90
3719/3722	Set of 4	6·00	3·50

(Des M. Escobar. Photo)

2001 (23 Apr). World Book Day. P 14×13½.
3723	**1089**	40p. multicoloured	50	30

1090 Dornier Do-J Wal Flying Boat, *Plus Ultra* and Map of South America

1091 Decorated Ceiling and Emblem

2001 (26 Apr). 75th Anniv of Spanish Aviation. T **1090** and similar horiz designs. Multicoloured. Photo. P 13½×14.
3724	40p.	Type **1090** (flight from Palos de Fontera, Spain to Buenos Aires, 1926)	50	50
	a.	Sheetlet of 4. Nos. 3724/7	7·00	7·00
3725	75p.	Breguet 19A2 and map of Europe (flight by Gallariza and Loruga from Madrid to Manilla, 1926)	90	90
3726	155p.	Dornier flying boat and map of Africa (flight from Melilla to Santa Isabel, Equatorial Guinea, 1926)	1·90	1·90
3727	260p.	C-295 (transport) (commemorative flight)	3·25	3·25
3724/3727		Set of 4	6·75	6·75

Nos. 3724/7 were issued together in *se-tenant* sheetlets of four stamps, the backgrounds forming the composite design of a map.

2001 (27 Apr). 154th Anniv of Liceu Theatre. Photo. P 14×13½.
3728	**1091**	120p. multicoloured	1·50	80

1092 King Juan Carlos I

1093 Garden

2001 (4 May). Photo. P 13×13½.
3729	**1092**	5p. cerise and silver (28.6.01)	15	15
3730		40p. apple-green and silver	50	20
3731		75p. bluish-violet and silver (28.6.01)	90	35
3732		100p. red-brown and silver (15.6.01)	1·20	40
3729/3732		Set of 4	2·50	1·00

Nos. 3733/3749 are vacant.

2001 (9 May). Europa. Water Resources. Photo. P 14×13½.
3750	**1093**	75p. multicoloured	1·20	1·00

1094 Church Façade (church of San Martiño, Noia)

1095 Peninsula, Marina and Bay

(Des M. Escobar. Eng M. Torralba (Nos. 3751, 3753). Photo (No. 3752) or recess and photo (others))

2001 (17 May). Architecture. T **1094** and similar vert designs. P 14×13½.
3751	40p. brown-olive and turquoise-blue	50	30
3752	75p. multicoloured	90	50
3753	155p. blue and purple-brown	1·90	1·00
3751/3753	Set of 3	3·00	1·60

Designs:—75p. Tui Cathedral, Pontevedra; 155p. Dovecote, Villaconcha, Frechilla.

(Des M. Plaza. Photo)

2001 (26 May). Luarca. P 13½×14.
3754	**1095**	40p. multicoloured	50	30

1096 De Castro (statue, Juan de Bologna) and School of Our Lady of Antigua

1097 Children and Calf (Adios Corderia, Leopodo Alas ("Clarin"))

331

SPAIN

(Des J. Suárez. Photo)

2001 (1 June). 400th Death Anniv of Cardinal Rodrigo de Castro (Supreme Counsellor of The Inquisition). P 13½×14.
3755 **1096** 40p. multicoloured 50 30

(Des J. Suárez. Photo)

2001 (13 June). Literature. P 13½×14.
3756 **1097** 75p. multicoloured 90 50

(Des P. Sanchez. Photo)

2001 (22 June). Trees (2nd series). Diamond-shaped designs as T **1067**. Multicoloured. P 12½.
3757 40p. Olive 50 30
3758 75p. Beech 90 50

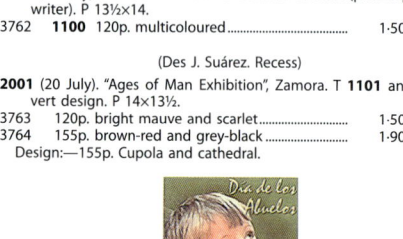

1098 Emblem and Shield

1099 Hooded Dancer being pelted with Tomatoes, Zaragoza

(Des J. Rincón. Photo)

2001 (6 July). 25th Anniv of Copa del Rey Football Championship. P 14.
3759 **1098** 40p. multicoloured 50 30
No. 3759 was issued in sheets of eight stamps and four labels.

(Des J. Suárez. Photo)

2001 (10 July). Festivals (2nd series). T **1099** and similar multicoloured design. P 13½×14 (40p.) or 14×13½ (70p.).
3760 40p. Type **1099** 50 30
3761 70p. Giants, Barcelona (vert) .... 1·50 85

1100 Gracián

1101 Our Lady of Calva (statue), Zamora Cathedral

(Des M. Torralba. Photo)

2001 (13 July). 400th Birth Anniv of Baltasar Gracián (philosopher and writer). P 13½×14.
3762 **1100** 120p. multicoloured .... 1·50 50

(Des J. Suárez. Recess)

2001 (20 July). "Ages of Man Exhibition", Zamora. T **1101** and similar vert design. P 14×13½.
3763 120p. bright mauve and scarlet .... 1·50 85
3764 155p. brown-red and grey-black .... 1·90 1·10
Design:—155p. Cupola and cathedral.

1102 Boy looking up (Grandmothers' Day)

(Des M. Escobar (No. 3765), J. Suárez (No. 3766). Photo)

2001 (26 July). Social Activities. T **1102** and similar multicoloured design. P 14×13½ (40p.) or 13½×14 (75p.).
3765 40p. Type **1102** 50 30
3766 75p. Nun and building (Servants of Jesus for Charity (social relief organization)) .. 90 50

1103 View of City

2001 (5 Sept). Salamanca, European City of Culture, 2002. Photo. P 13.
3767 **1103** 75p. multicoloured .... 1·00 75

1104 Covadonga Basilica

1105 Emblem

(Des P. Sánchez. Photo)

2001 (7 Sept). Centenary of Consecration of Basilica of Covadonga. P 13½×14.
3768 **1104** 40p. multicoloured 50 30

2001 (15 Sept). Formation of State Post and Telegraph Company. Photo. P 13½×14.
3769 **1105** 40p. multicoloured 50 25

1106 View of Vigo

1107 Musicians

(Des P. Sánchez. Eng E. Paniagua. Recess)

2001 (21 Sept). EXFILNA 2001 National Philatelic Exhibition, Vigo. Sheet 105×78 mm containing T **1106**. P 13½×14.
MS3770 **1106** 260p. dull ultramarine and deep ultramarine .... 3·25 3·25

2001 (4 Oct). Birth Millenary of St. Dominic of Silos (Benedictine monk and abbot). Recess and litho. P 14×13½.
3771 **1107** 40p. multicoloured 50 30
MS3772 106×79 mm. No. 3771 .... 6·50 6·50
No. MS3772 was issued with two different margins.

1108 Children encircling Globe

1109 Grasses, Ses Salines Nature Reserve

2001 (9 Oct). United Nations Year of Dialogue among Civilizations. Photo. P 14.
3773 **1108** 120p. multicoloured .... 1·50 85

(Des J. Suárez. Photo)

2001 (15 Oct). America. UNESCO World Heritage Sites. P 14.
3774 **1109** 155p. multicoloured .... 1·90 1·10

332

SPAIN

(Des J. Gallego and J. Rey. Photo)

2001 (19 Oct). School Correspondence Programme. Spanish History (4th series). Horiz designs as T **1073** but with currency inscribed in both euros and pesetas. Multicoloured. P 13×12½.

3775	25p. Christopher Columbus juggling eggs (discovery of America, 1492)		35	30
	a. Sheetlet of 12. Nos. 3775/86		4·50	
3776	25p. Spanish and Portuguese boys each holding balloons showing maps (Treaty of Tordesillas, 1494)		35	30
3777	25p. King Carlos I of Spain (elected Emporor Charles V, 1519)		35	30
3778	25p. Hernán Cortés and Mexican musicians (conquest of Mexico, 1519)		35	30
3779	25p. Juan Sebastián Elcano (first circumnavigation of globe, 1522)		35	30
3780	25p. Inca city and bull on mountain (Francisco Pizarro's conquest of Peru, 1532)		35	30
3781	25p. King Felipe II with globe shaped as map of Spain (accession, 1556)		35	30
3782	25p. King Felipe II drawing plans (commencement of Monastery San Lorenzo de El Escorial, 1563)		35	30
3783	25p. Severed arm attacking Turk (Battle of Lepanto, 1571)		35	30
3784	25p. St. John of the Cross, St. Teresa of Avila and El Greco being drawn up into spacecraft		35	30
3785	25p. Lope de Vega Carpio using his open skull as inkwell (Spanish playwright, died 1593)		35	30
3786	25p. King Felipe III surrounded by buckets collecting water (accession, 1599)		35	30
3775/3786 Set of 12			3·75	3·25

Nos. 3775/86 were issued together in *se-tenant* sheetlets of 12 stamps with an enlarged margin showing Columbus and aboriginal American with black eye.

 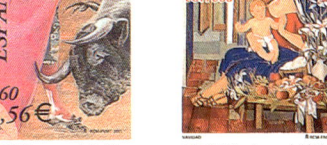

1110 Cape and Bull's Head
1111 "Virgin and Child" (Alfredo Roldán)

(Des M. Plaza. Photo)

2001 (25 Oct). Retirement of Francisco Romero López (Curro Romero) (bullfighter). Sheet 104×78 mm. P 14.

MS3787	**1110**	260p. multicoloured	3·25	3·25

(Des J. Villalba. Photo)

2001 (8 Nov). Christmas. Religious Paintings. T **1111** and similar square design. Multicoloured. P 12½.

3788	40p. Type **1111**		50	30
3789	75p. "The Shepherd's Adoration" (Jusepe de Ribera)		95	50
MS3790 106×133 mm. Nos. 3788/9 together with Nos. 3082/3 of Germany			4·75	4·75

1112 Music Score
1113 Man driving Car

2001 (14 Nov). 125th Birth Anniv of Manuel de Falla (composer). Photo. P 13½×14.

3791	**1112**	75p. multicoloured	90	50

2001 (20 Nov). 75th Birth Anniv of Josep Coll (cartoonist). T **1113** and similar horiz designs. Multicoloured. Photo. P 13½×14.

3792	40p. Type **1113**		50	30
3793	75p. Man and dog		90	50

1114 Cano
1115 Woman and Flowers

(Des M. Escobar. Photo)

2001 (23 Nov). 55th Birth Anniv of Carlos Cano (singer). P 14×13½.

3794	**1114**	40p. black	50	30

(Des D. Seco. Photo)

2001 (27 Nov). International Volunteers' Day. P 14×13½.

3795	**1115**	120p. multicoloured	1·50	85

1116 12th-century Church of San Climent, Taüll (Lleida)

2001 (30 Nov). UNESCO World Heritage Sites. T **1116** and similar horiz designs. Multicoloured. P 13×12½.

3796	40p. Type **1116**		50	40
	a. Sheetlet of 12. Nos. 3796/3807		7·25	
3797	40p. El Misteri d'Elx (religious festival at Elche cathedral)		50	40
3798	40p. Sant Pau Hospital, Barcelona		50	40
3799	40p. Map of St. Cristóbal, La Laguna		50	40
3800	40p. Archeological excavations, Atapuerca		50	40
3801	40p. Protected palm trees, Elche		50	40
3802	40p. La Foncalada (medieval monument), Oviedo		50	40
3803	40p. Roman walls, Lugo		50	40
3804	40p. Cave painting, Cueva de los Caballos, Albocacer, Castellon		50	40
3805	40p. Dalt Villa, Eivissa, Ibiza		50	40
3806	40p. Roman amphitheatre, Tarraco		50	40
3807	40p. Renaissance university building, Alcalá de Henares		50	40
3796/3807 Set of 12			5·50	4·50

Nos. 3796/3807 were issued together in *se-tenant* sheetlets of 12 stamps.

1117 Map and Postal Emblem (Postal Service)
1118 Crown Prince Felipe de Borbon

2001 (11 Dec). 150th Anniv of Ministry of Public Works. T **1117** and similar horiz designs. P 13×12½.

3808	40p. multicoloured	50	50
3809	75p. lilac, black and greenish blue	90	90
3810	120p. greenish blue, green and black	1·50	1·50
3811	155p. multicoloured	1·90	1·90
3812	260p. multicoloured	3·25	3·25
3808/3812 Set of 5		7·25	7·25

Designs: Maps showing—75p. Ports; 120p. Railways; 155p. Airports; 260p. Motorways.

Nos. 3808/12 were issued together in *se-tenant* sheetlets of five stamps and one label with enlarged illustrated margins.

2001 (14 Dec). Silver Jubilee of King Juan Carlos I. Sheet 125×80 mm containing T **1118** and similar multicoloured designs. P 13.

MS3813 40p. Type **1118**; 40p. Infanta Elena; 40p. Arms; 40p. Infanta Cristina; 75p. King Juan Carlos; 75p. Queen Sofia; 260p. Palace (49×28 mm) .... 7·75 7·75

333

SPAIN

New Currency.
100 cents = 1 euro

1119 King Juan Carlos I **1120** Emblem **1123** Emblem **1124** Father Francisco Piquer (founder)

2002 (2 Jan)–**06**. Photo. P 13½×14.

3814	**1119**	1c. black and silver..................	15	15
3815		2c. magenta and silver (2.1.04).........	15	15
3818		5c. new blue and silver................	15	15
3823		10c. deep bluish green and silver.......	20	20
3826		25c. deep claret and silver............	35	20
3827		27c. blue and silver (2.1.04)............	50	20
3827*a*		28c. olive yellow (14.1.05)...........	55	25
3827*aa*		29c. olive-sepia and silver (1.2.06)...	55	20
3827*b*		35c. orange (28.1.05).................	65	25
3827*c*		40c. deep grey blue (28.1.05).........	60	20
3828		50c. slate-green and silver...........	95	25
3829		52c. cinnamon and silver (2.1.04).....	1·00	25
3829*a*		53c. dull purple (14.1.05)............	1·00	25
3829*b*		57c. reddish orange and silver (1.2.06).............................	1·10	25
3830		75c. bright purple and silver..........	1·40	30
3831		77c. dull yellowish green and silver (2.1.04).............................	1·60	30
3831*a*		78c. bright rosine (14.1.05)...........	1·50	30
3832		€1 emerald and silver................	1·90	40
3832*a*		€1.95 brown ochre (14.1.05).........	3·75	80
3833		€2 red and silver.....................	3·75	55
3833*a*		€2.21 olive bistre (28.1.05)..........	4·25	1·20
3833*b*		€2.26 reddish lilac and silver (5.1.06)...	4·00	1·00
3833*c*		€2.33 carmine and silver (13.2.06)...	4·50	1·30
3833*d*		€2.39 bronze-green and silver (13.2.06)............................	4·50	1·50
3814/3833 *Set of 12*			35·00	10·00
MS3834 100×87 mm. No. 3827×4 (25.5.04).............			2·40	2·40

Numbers have been left for additions to this series.

2002 (2 Jan). Spanish Presidency of European Union. Photo. P 13½×14.

3835	**1120**	25c. bright carmine-red, black and orange-yellow..............	55	30
3836		50c. bright carmine-red, orange-yellow and black.............	1·10	50

1121 Sabina   **1122** Orchids

2002 (25 Jan). Trees (3rd series). T **1121** and similar diamond-shaped design. Multicoloured. Photo. P 12½.

3837		50c. Type **1121**.....................	1·00	50
3838		75c. Elm...........................	1·50	85

2002 (20 Feb). Flowers. Booklet stamps. T **1122** and similar vert designs depicting paintings by Eduardo Naranjo. Multicoloured. Litho. Self-adhesive. Die-cut perf 13.

3839		25c. Type **1122**.....................	50	30
3840		25c. Gardenia in vase................	50	30
3841		25c. Hands holding white rose........	50	30
3842		25c. Iris............................	50	30
3843		25c. Two white orchid blooms........	50	30
3844		25c. Pink-tinged rose in vase.........	50	30
3845		25c. Two pink orchid blooms.........	50	30
3846		25c. Three pink orchid blooms on one stem............................	50	30
3839/3846 *Set of 8*			3·50	2·25

Nos. 3839/46 are peeled directly from the booklet cover and cannot therefore be collected as separate panes.

2002 (22 Feb). España 2002 International Youth Stamp Exhibition, Salamanca (1st issue). T **1123** and similar multicoloured design. Photo. P 13½×14 (3847) or 14×13½ (**MS**3848).

3847		50c. Type **1123**.....................	1·00	45
MS3848 80×105 mm. €1.80 Salamanca Cathedral.........			4·25	3·75

See also Nos. 3913/**MS**3922.

2002 (25 Feb). 300th Anniv of Caja Madrid Savings Bank. Litho. P 14×13½.

3849	**1124**	25c. multicoloured...................	50	30

1125 Anniversary Emblem

2002 (25 Feb). Centenary of Real Madrid Football Club. Photo. P 13½×14.

3850	**1125**	75c. greenish yellow and brownish grey.............................	1·50	95

1126 Town Hall Portico, Tarazona   **1127** Alejandro Mon

2002 (26 Feb). PHILAIBERIA '02 Spanish–Portuguese Stamp Exhibition, Tarazona. Sheet 106×80 mm. Photo. P 13½×14.
MS3851 **1126** €2.10 multicoloured................... 4·50 4·50

2002 (27 Feb). Birth Centenary (2001) of Alejandro Mon (politician). Photo. P 14×13½.

3852	**1127**	25c. multicoloured...................	50	30

1128 Stylized Coin   **1129** Canon do Sil, Ribeira Sacra

2002 (28 Feb). "Homage to the Peseta". Litho. P 14×13½.

3853	**1128**	25c. multicoloured...................	50	35

2002 (8 Mar). Nature. T **1129** and similar multicoloured design. Photo. P 14×13½ (3854) or 13½×14 (3855).

3854		75c. Type **1129**.....................	1·50	95
3855		€2.10 Cabo de Gata, Nijer Park, Almeria (horiz)............................	4·25	2·40

SPAIN

1130 Cadets on Parade, 1886   **1131** Emblem

2002 (15 Mar). 75th Anniv of Military Academy, Zaragoza. Photo. P 14×13½.
3856   **1130**   25c. multicoloured 50   30

2002 (22 Mar). Centenary of Real Union Irún Football Club. Photo. P 14×13½.
3857   **1131**   50c. multicoloured .... 1·00   45

1132 Tweezers, Stamp and Magnifying Glass   **1133** Banyeres de Mariola Castle, Alicante

2002 (25 Mar). Stamp Day. Photo. P 13½×14.
3858   **1132**   25c. multicoloured 50   30

2002 (8 Apr). Castles. T **1133** and similar horiz designs. Recess. P 13½×14.
3859   25c. red-brown and greenish blue 50   35
3860   50c. black .... 1·00   55
3861   75c. black .... 1·50   95
3859/3861 Set of 3 .... 2·75   1·90
Designs:—50c. Soutomaior Castle, Pontevedra; 75c. Calatorao Castle, Zaragoza.

1134 View across River   **1135** Luis Cernuda

2002 (8 Apr). Anniversaries. T **1134** and similar horiz design. Multicoloured. Photo. P 13½×14.
3862   75c. Type **1134** (1200th anniv of Tudela) ...... 1·50   95
3863   €1·80 View through pillars (millennium of St. Cugat Monastery) .... 3·75   1·90

2002 (8 May). Birth Anniversaries. T **1135** and similar horiz design. Multicoloured. Photo. P 13½×14.
3864   50c. Type **1135** (poet, centenary) .... 1·00   50
3865   50c. Dr. Federico Rubio and nurses (175th anniv) .... 1·00   50

1136 Clown (Sara Blanco Quintas)   **1137** Soldiers on Horseback

2002 (9 May). Europa. The Circus. Photo. P 13½×14.
3866   **1136**   50c. multicoloured .... 1·20   95

2002 (10 May). Bicentenary of Inclusion of Menorca under Spanish Rule. Photo. P 13½×14.
3867   **1137**   50c. multicoloured .... 1·00   50

1138 Driving

2002 (11 May). World Equestrian Games, Jerez. T **1138** and similar horiz designs. Multicoloured. Photo. P 12½×13.
3868   25c. Type **1138** 50   35
       a. Sheetlet. Nos. 3868/74 plus two labels . 8·00
3869   25c. Hunting 50   35
3870   25c. Dressage 50   35
3871   25c. Reining 50   35
3872   25c. Acrobats 50   35
3973   75c. Racing .... 4·00   1·90
3874   €1·80 Show jumping .... 3·75   1·90
3868/3874 Set of 7 .... 7·00   4·00
Nos. 3868/74 were issued together in *se-tenant* sheetlets of seven stamps and two labels showing the games emblem and mascot.

1139 Maria de las Dolores   **1140** Plaza Mayor, Salamanca

2002 (31 May). 108th Death Anniv of Maria "La Dolores" de las Dolores. Photo. P 13½×14.
3875   **1139**   50c. multicoloured .... 1·00   50

2002 (7 June). EXFILNA 2002 National Stamp Exhibition, Salamanca. European City of Culture. Sheet 155×94 mm containing T **1140** and similar horiz designs. Multicoloured (€1·80) or red-orange and deep blue (others). Litho (€1·80) or recess (others). P 13½×14.
MS3876 25c. Type **1140**; 25c. Centre view of Plaza; 25c. Right side of Plaza; €1·80 Aerial view of Plaza .. 5·50   5·50

1141 Rohrbach R-VIII Aircraft, 1927   **1142** Grapes (Rias Baixas)

2002 (10 June). 75th Anniv of IBERIA Airlines. T **1141** and similar horiz designs. Multicoloured. Photo. P 13½×14.
3877   25c. Type **1141** 50   35
3878   50c. Boeing 747 .... 1·00   55

2002 (27 July). Wine Regions (1st series). Photo. P 14.
3879   **1142**   25c. multicoloured 50   35
See also Nos. 3880/3881.

1143 Grapes and Glass of Red Wine (Rioja)   **1144** Temple Expiatori de la Sagrada Família, Barcelona

335

SPAIN

2002 (20 Sept). Wine Regions (2nd series). T **1143** and similar vert design. Multicoloured. Photo. P 14×13½.
3880	50c. Type **1143**	1·00	45
3881	75c. Grapes, wine bottle and glass of sherry (Manzanilla)	1·50	95

2002 (27 Sept). School Correspondence Programme. Spanish History (5th series). Horiz designs as T **1073** but with currency inscribed in euros. Multicoloured. Photo. P 13×12½.
3882	10c. Man being knighted with pen (Don Quixote by Miguel de Cervantes)	25	20
	a. Sheetlet of 12. Nos. 3882/93	3·00	
3883	10c. Felipe IV and the Count–Duke of Olivares (accession, 1621)	25	20
3884	10c. Quevedo and Góngora pulling on rope of words (literary rivalry)	25	20
3885	10c. Velazquez (artist) sitting at easel	25	20
3886	10c. Carlos II and witch holding apple	25	20
3887	10c. Man rolling out carpet and Felipe V (start of War of the Spanish Succession)	25	20
3888	10c. Fernando VI (accession, 1746)	25	20
3889	10c. Carlos III holding architectural drawings (accession, 1759)	25	20
3890	10c. Bull and toreador (Esquilanche's revolt)	25	20
3891	10c. Book escaping from bird cage	25	20
3892	10c. Carlos IV (accession, 1788) and Napoleon	25	20
3893	10c. Manuel de Godoy (politician) and open door	25	20
3882/3893	Set of 12	2·75	2·10

Nos. 3882/93 were issued together in *se-tenant* sheetlets of 12 stamps with an enlarged margin showing soldiers and horse.

2002 (27 Sept). 150th Birth Anniv of Antoni Gaudi (architect). Litho. P 14×13½.
3894	**1144**	50c. new blue and black	1·00	50

1145 Musicians

1146 Alphabet Jigsaw Puzzle

2002 (30 Sept). Music. Booklet stamps. T **1145** and similar horiz designs depicting paintings by G. Domínguez. Multicoloured. Litho. Self-adhesive. Die-cut perf 13.
3895	25c. Type **1145**	50	30
3896	25c. Vase of flowers and lute	2·50	2·40
3897	25c. Woman holding lute	50	30
3898	25c. Flowers and open book of music	50	30
3899	25c. Vase of flowers, clock and violin	50	30
3900	25c. Man holding lute with woman	50	30
3901	25c. Flowers, violin, compass and sheet music	50	30
3902	25c. Woman wearing blue dress holding lute	50	30
3895/3902	Set of 8	3·50	2·10

Nos. 3895/902 are peeled directly from the booklet cover and cannot therefore be collected as separate panes.

(Des F. J. Paniagua. Photo)

2002 (14 Oct). America. Education and Literacy Campaign. P 13½×14.
3903	**1146**	75c. multicoloured	1·50	95

1147 Cordoba Mosque and Silhouette of Almanzor

1148 Basket

2002 (25 Oct). Death Millenary of Abu Amir Muhammad al-Ma'afiri (Almanzor) (Arab ruler). Photo. P 13½×14.
3904	**1147**	75c. multicoloured	1·50	95

2002 (4 Nov). Dijous Bó Fair, Inca, Mallorca. Photo. P 14×13½.
3905	**1148**	75c. multicoloured	1·50	95

1149 Cupola, Aranjuez

1150 Alcañiz (former Monastery of Calatrava)

2002 (8 Nov). UNESCO World Heritage Sites. T **1149** and similar vert designs. Multicoloured. Photo. P 14×13½.
3906	25c. Type **1149**	50	35
	a. Sheetlet of 7. Nos. 3906/9, 3910×2, 3911, plus 5 labels	16·00	
3907	25c. Santa Maria church, Calatayud, Aragon	50	35
3908	50c. San Martín church, Teruel, Aragon	1·00	55
3909	75c. Santa Maria church, Tobed, Aragon	1·50	1·10
3910	€1.80 Santa Tecla church, Cervera de la Canada, Aragon	3·75	2·00
	a. *Tête-bêche* pair. Nos. 3910×2	8·00	
3911	€2.10 San Pablo church, Zaragoza, Aragon	4·25	2·50
3906/3911	Set of 6	10·00	6·25

Nos. 3906/9, 3910×2 and 3911 were issued together in *se-tenant* sheetlets of seven stamps plus five labels, Nos. 3910×2 as a *tête-bêche* pair forming a composite design.

2002 (15 Nov). Paradores (state hotels). Photo. P 13½×14.
3912	**1150**	25c. multicoloured	50	35

1151 Capitán Alatriste (Arturo Pérez-Reverte)

1152 San Jorge Church, Alicante

2002 (17–24 Nov). España 2002 International Youth Stamp Exhibition, Salamanca (2nd issue). T **1151** and similar multicoloured design. Photo.

(a) Self-adhesive gum Die-cut perf 13
3913	50c. As No. 3847	1·00	55
	a. Sheetlet of 9. Nos. 3913/21	16·00	17·00
3914	75c. Type **1151** (comic strip character)	1·50	95
3915	75c. Television screen and emblem (television)	1·50	95
3916	75c. Hand and record (music)	1·50	95
3917	75c. Radio and music score (radio)	1·50	95
3918	75c. Cyclist, skier and football (sport)	1·50	95
3919	75c. Person holding camera (the press)	1·50	95
3920	75c. Film clapper board (film)	1·50	95
3921	€1.80 Salamanca Cathedral (vert)	3·75	2·30
3913/3921	Set of 9	11·75	7·25

(b) Ordinary gum. P 13½×14
MS3922 Seven sheets 79×106 mm (g) or 106×79 mm (others). (a) 75c. As No. 3920 (18 Nov); (b) 75c. As 3915 (19 Nov); (c) 75c. As 3919 (20 Nov); (d) 75c. As 3917 (21 Nov); (e) 75c. As 3918 (22 Nov); (f) 75c. As 3916 (23 Nov); (g) 75c. As 3914 (24 Nov)	12·50 12·50

A different miniature sheet was issued on each day of the exhibition.

2002 (25 Nov). Recess. P 14×13½.
3923	**1152**	75c. multicoloured	1·50	95

SPAIN

1153 Cruceiro do Hío (crucifix) (Jose Cerviño) Hío, Galicia

1154 Mary (detail, stained glass window) (Carlos Muñoz de Pablos)

2002 (27–29 Nov). Historical Monuments. T **1153** and similar multicoloured design. Recess and litho. P 14×13½ (25c.) or 13½×14 (50c.).
3924   25c. Type **1153** 50   35
3925   50c. Herrería de Compludo (smithy), Leon (horiz) (27.11) .... 1·00   50

2002 (27 Nov). 140th Anniv of St. Mary's Cathedral, Vitoria-Gasteiz. Sheet 106×79 mm. Recess and litho. P 14×13½.
MS3926 **1154**   50c. multicoloured .... 1·00   95

1155 "Adoration of Kings" (alterpiece, Calzadilla de los Barros Church)

1156 Somport Tunnel Entrance

2002 (29 Nov). Christmas. T **1155** and similar vert design. Multicoloured. Photo. P 14×13½.
3927   25c. Type **1155** 50   30
3928   50c. "Maternity" (Goyo Domínguez) .... 1·00   50

2003 (17 Jan). Spain–France Tunnel through Pyrenees. Photo. P 13½×14.
3929   **1156**   51c. multicoloured .... 1·00   50

1157 Costumes from Ansó (Huesca)

1158 Fingerprints forming Flower

2003 (20 Jan). Traditional Costumes. Photo. P 14×13½.
3930   **1157**   76c. multicoloured .... 1·60   95

2003 (21 Jan). 50th World Leprosy Awareness Day. Photo. P 14×13½.
3931   **1158**   26c. multicoloured 55   30

1159 Pedro Campomanes

1160 Benissa Cathedral

2003 (14 Feb). Death Bicentenary of Pedro Rodriguez Campomanes (statesman and writer). Photo. P 14×13½.
3932   **1159**   26c. multicoloured 55   30

2003 (21 Feb). Juvenia 2003 National Youth Stamp Exhibition, Benissa, Alicante. Photo. P 13½×14.
3933   **1160**   51c. multicoloured .... 1·00   50

1161 Práxedes Sagasta   **1162** "ABC"

2003 (11 Mar). Death Centenary of Práxedes Mateo Sagasta (politician). Photo. P 13½×14.
3934   **1161**   26c. purple-brown and dull blue 55   30

2003 (17 Mar). Centenary of "ABC" (newspaper). Photo. P 13½×14.
3935   **1162**   €2.15 multicoloured .... 4·50   2·20

1163 Santiago Ramony Cajal (1906)

1164 Tui Bridge to Valença do Minho (Portugal)

(Des Hannu Järviö. Eng C. Slania. Recess and litho)

2003 (20 Mar). Nobel Prize Winners for Medicine. T **1163** and similar horiz design. Multicoloured. P 13×12½.
3936   51c. Type **1163** .... 1·00   50
     a. Pair. Nos. 3936/7 .... 2·50   1·40
3937   76c. Severo Ochoa (1959) .... 1·50   95
Nos. 3936/7 were issued in *se-tenant* pairs within the sheet. Stamps of the same design were issued by Sweden.

2003 (21 Mar). Bicentenary of School of Civil Engineers, Madrid. T **1164** and similar horiz designs. Photo. P 13½×14.
3938   26c. Type **1164** 55   30
MS3939 106×78 mm. 26c. Type **1164**; 51c. Murcia valley; 76c. Madrid Port.............................. 3·50   3·25

1165 Anniversary Emblem   **1166** "La Hoz de Priego"

(Des Arterisco. Photo)

2003 (26 Mar). Centenary of "La Laverdad" (Catholic newspaper). P 13½×14.
3940   **1165**   26c. multicoloured 55   30

2003 (28 Mar). Paintings. Booklet stamps. T **1166** and similar horiz designs depicting paintings by Chico Montilla. Multicoloured. Litho. Self-adhesive. Die-cut perf 13.
3941   26c. Type **1166** 55   30
3942   26c. "Fields of Gold" 55   30
3943   26c. "Los Tornos Gorge" 55   30
3944   26c. "Armilla Countryside" 55   30
3945   26c. "Nenúfar" 55   30
3946   26c. "What Colour is the Wind?" 55   30
3947   51c. "Pastrana Countryside" .... 1·00   50
3948   76c. "Early Flowers" .... 1·60   90
3941/3948 *Set of 8* .... 5·25   2·75
Nos. 3941/8 are peeled directly from the booklet cover and cannot therefore be collected as separate panes.

337

SPAIN

1167 Ramon Sender and Book Cover
1168 Blackboard and Pupil

2003 (31 Mar). Ramon Jose Sender (writer) Commemoration. Recess and litho. P 13½×14.
| 3949 | **1167** | €2.15 purple-brown, yellow and lake-brown | 4·50 | 1·90 |

2003 (3 Apr). Rural Schools. Photo. P 13½×14.
| 3950 | **1168** | 26c. multicoloured | 55 | 30 |

1169 Pillar Capital, Lion Patio, Alhambra, Granada
1170 Valdecarzana Palace, Avilés, Asturias

2003 (7 Apr). Exfilna 2003 National Stamp Exhibition, Granada. Sheet 79×106 mm. Recess and litho. P 13½×14.
| MS3951 | **1169** | €2.15 reddish brown and deep bluish green | 4·50 | 4·50 |

2003 (11 Apr). Avilés Villa Millenary. Photo. P 13½×14.
| 3952 | **1170** | 51c. multicoloured | 1·00 | 50 |

1171 Anniversary Emblem
1172 Toy Cars (Jiménez Carrero)

2003 (11 Apr). Stamp Day. 25th Anniv of Spanish Philatelic Academy. Photo. P 13½×14.
| 3953 | **1171** | €1.85 multicoloured | 3·75 | 1·30 |

2003 (24 Apr). Europa. Poster Art. Photo. P 13½×14.
| 3954 | **1172** | 76c. multicoloured | 1·80 | 1·30 |

1173 Centenary Emblem
1174 Roman Amphitheatre, Zaragoza

2003 (25 Apr). Centenary of Athletic Club of Madrid. Photo. P 14×13½.
| 3955 | **1173** | 26c. vermilion and bright royal blue | 55 | 30 |

2003 (5 May). Photo. P 13½×14.
| 3956 | **1174** | €1.85 multicoloured | 3·75 | 1·30 |

1175 Map of Europe, Faces and Wheelchair User
1176 San Felipe Castle, Ferrol, Coruña

2003 (8 May). European Year of the Disabled. Photo and thermography. P 13½×14.
| 3957 | **1175** | 76c. multicoloured | 1·60 | 80 |

No. 3957 has "correos" written in Braille across it.

2003 (17 May). Castles. Recess and litho. P 13½×14.
3958		26c. maroon and new blue	55	30
3959		51c. reddish brown and deep bluish green	1·00	55
3960		76c. orange and black	1·50	80
3958/3960	Set of 3		2·75	1·50

Designs:—21c. Type **1176**; 51c. Cuéllar Castle, Segovia; 76c. Montilla Castle, Córdoba (500th Anniv of Battles of Cerinola and Garellano).

1177 Swimmer
1178 Max Aub

2003 (17 May). Barcelona '03 International Swimming Championship. T **1177** and similar vert designs. Multicoloured. Photo. P 14×13½.
3961		26c. Type **1177**	55	30
3962		51c. Diver	1·00	50
MS3963	115×106 mm. 26c. Type **1177**; 51c. No. 3962; 76c. Synchronised swimmers; €1.85 Freestyle swimmer; €2.15 Water polo		12·50	12·50

2003 (2 June). Birth Centenary of Max Aub (writer). Recess. P 14×13½.
| 3964 | **1178** | 76c. black and carmine vermilion | 1·60 | 85 |

1179 Football and Club Emblem
1180 Juan Murillo

2003 (4 June). Centenary of Centre D'Esports Sabadell Football Club. Photo. P 14×13½.
| 3965 | **1179** | 76c. multicoloured | 1·60 | 85 |

2003 (9 June). Birth Bicentenary of Juan Bravo Murillo (politician). P 14×13½.
| 3966 | **1180** | 51c. multicoloured | 1·30 | 75 |

1181 Newspaper Vendor
1182 Dodge Dart Barreiros (1967)

2003 (16 June). 135th Anniv of "Diario de Cadiz" Newspaper. Photo. P 14×13½.
| 3967 | **1181** | 26c. multicoloured | 55 | 30 |

2003 (27 June). Centenary of Royal Automobile Club (RACE). Sheet 106×80 mm containing T **1182** and similar horiz designs. Multicoloured. Photo. P 13½×14.
| MS3968 | 26c. Type **1182**; 51c. Seat 600 (1967–73); 76c. Hispano Suiza 20/30 HP (1907); €1.85 Pegaso Z102 Touring Berlinetta (1953) | | 7·25 | 7·25 |

SPAIN

1183 5c. Chile Stamp of 1853   **1184** "El Diario Montañés"

2003 (1 July). 150th Anniv of First Chilean Stamp. Photo. P 14×13½.
3969   1183   76c. orange-brown and black .... 1·60   85

2003 (4 July). Centenary of "El Diario Montanés" Newspaper. Photo. P 14×13½.
3970   1184   26c. multicoloured 55   30

1185 Santa Catalina Castle   **1186** Front Page

2003 (9 July). Paradores (state hotels). Photo. P 13½×14.
3971   1185   25c. multicoloured .... 1·40   85

2003 (11 July). Centenary of "Diario de Navarra" Newspaper. P 13½×14.
3972   1186   26c. multicoloured 55   30

1187 Doorway   **1188** Stylized Hat and Newspaper

2003 (22 July). 800th Anniv of Seu Vella Old Cathedral, Lleida, Segrià. Recess. P 13½×14.
3973   1187   €1.85 sepia, bright violet and olive-brown .... 3·75   60

2003 (24 July). 120th Anniv of "El Adelanto de Salamanca" Newspaper. P 14×13½.
3974   1188   26c. multicoloured 55   30

1189 Woman attaching Flowers to Hat   **1190** Building Interior, Ferrol

2003 (28 July). Paintings. Booklet stamps. No value expressed. T **1189** and similar vert designs depicting portraits of women and flowers by Alfredo Roldán. Multicoloured. Self-adhesive. Litho. Die-cut perf 13.
3975   A   (26c.) Type **1189** 55   30
3976   A   (26c.) With bouquet 55   30
3977   A   (26c.) Stood behind lilies 55   30
3978   A   (26c.) With raised arms arranging flowers in hair 55   30
3979   A   (26c.) Wearing flowers in hair 55   30
3980   A   (26c.) Woman lying with fruit and flowers 55   30
3981   A   (26c.) Wearing dark dress putting flowers in hair 55   30
3982   A   (26c.) With vase of flowers 55   30
3975/3982 Set of 8 .... 4·00   2·10

2003 (1 Aug). 125th Anniv of "El Correo Gallego" Newspaper. Photo. P 13½×14.
3983   1190   26c. multicoloured 55   30

1191 Masthead   **1192** Reliquary, Chapel of La Vera Cruz

2003 (2 Sept). 125th Anniv of "El Comercio" Newspaper. Photo. P 13½×14.
3984   1191   26c. multicoloured 55   30

2003 (4 Sept). Granting of Perpetual Jubilee to Caravaca de la Cruz. Photo. P 14×13½.
3985   1192   76c. multicoloured .... 1·60   65

1193 49er Dinghy, Map and Statue   **1194** Wine Glass (Penedés)

2003 (9 Sept). ISAF World Sailing Championship, Cadiz. Photo. P 13½×14.
3986   1193   76c. multicoloured .... 1·60   65

2003 (22 Sept–30 Oct). Wine. T **1194** and similar vert designs. Multicoloured. Photo. P 14×13½.
3987   26c. Type **1194** (30.10) 55   30
3988   51c. Angel holding wine dipper (Montilla-Moriles) .... 1·00   55
3989   76c. Grapes and hands holding wine glass (Valdepeñas) .... 1·60   85
3990 $1.85 Bottles (Bierzo) .... 3·75   1·90
3987/3990 Set of 4 .... 6·25   3·25

1195 College Building and Emblem   **1196** Stained Glass Window (detail)

2003 (24 Sept). Bicentenary of Military Engineering College, Madrid. Photo. P 14.
3991   1195   51c. multicoloured .... 4·25   2·10

2003 (26 Sept). 700th Anniv of León Cathedral. Sheet 105×78 mm. Photo. P 14.
MS3992   1196   76c. multicoloured .... 1·60   1·60

339

SPAIN

1197 Society Emblem and Map (*detail*)
1198 *Ficus Macrophylla*

2003 (1 Oct). Centenary of Real Geographic Society. Sheet 105×78 mm. Photo. P 13½×14.
MS3993	**1197**	€1.85 multicoloured...............	4·00	4·00

2003 (3 Oct). Trees (4th issue). T **1198** and similar vert design. Multicoloured. Photo. P 14×13½.
3994	26c. Type **1198**...............	55	30
3995	51c. Pedunculate oak (*Quercus robur*)............	1·00	55

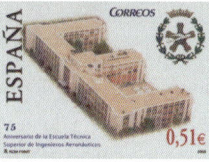

1199 College Building
1200 Type 1-2-0 Engine Madrilena (1851)

2003 (6 Oct). 75th Anniv of Aircraft Engineering Technical College, Madrid. Photo. P 13½×14.
3996	**1199**	51c. multicoloured...............	1·00	55

2003 (14 Oct). America. Railways. Photo. P 13½×14.
3997	**1200**	76c. multicoloured...............	1·60	85

1201 "El Virjo y el Pajaro"
1202 "La Voz de Galicia"

2003 (17 Oct). 93rd Birth Anniv of Luis Seoane (artist). Photo. P 14×13½.
3998	**1201**	€1.85 multicoloured...............	4·00	1·90

2003 (3 Nov). Newspaper Anniversaries. T **1202** and similar horiz designs. Photo. P 13½×14.
3999	26c. bright scarlet and black...............	55	30
4000	26c. bright scarlet, pale orange and black....	55	30
4001	26c. multicoloured...............	55	30
3999/4001	Set of 3...............	1·50	80

Designs:—Type **1202** (120th anniv (2002); "El Correo de Andalucia" (centenary (1999)); "Faro de Vigo" (150th anniv).

1203 Camilo José Cela
1204 Donkey and Child (Los Reyes Magos festival, Alcoy)

2003 (10 Nov). First Death Anniv of Camilo José Cela Trulock (writer (winner of 1989 Nobel Prize for Literature)). Photo. P 14×13½.
4002	**1203**	26c. multicoloured...............	55	30

2003 (10 Nov). Christmas. T **1204** and similar vert design. Multicoloured. Photo. P 14×13½.
4003	26c. Type **1204**...............	55	25
4004	51c. "Christmas" (Raquel Fariñas)............	1·00	55

1205 Exhibition Emblem
1206 Organos de Montoro, Teruel Mountains

2003 (14 Nov). España 2004 International Stamp Exhibition, Valencia. T **1205** and similar horiz design. Multicoloured. Photo. P 13½×14.
4005	76c. Type **1205**...............	1·60	85
MS4006	78×106 mm. €1.85 City of Arts and Sciences Building, Valencia	4·75	4·25

2003 (17 Nov). Photo. P 13½×14.
4007	**1206**	51c. multicoloured...............	1·00	55

1207 Geological Map
1208 Blindfolded Woman

2003 (24 Nov). New National Geological Survey. Sheet 106×79 mm. Photo. P 13½×14.
MS4008	**1207**	26c. multicoloured...............	55	55

2003 (5 Dec). 25th Anniv of Constitution. Ten sheets, each 78×105 mm containing T **1208** and similar multicoloured designs. Photo. P 14×13½ (vert) or 13½×14 (horiz).
MS4009 (a) 26c. Type **1208** (Juan Bautista Nieto) (judicial power); (b) 26c. Dove and doors (J. Carrero) (general courts); (c) 26c. Ship (Araceli Alarcón) (state territorial organization) (*horiz*); (d) 26c. Families (R. Seco) (economy and property) (*horiz*); (e) 26c. King Juan Carlos (*horiz*); (f) 26c. Boy writing (fundamental rights and duties) (*horiz*); (g) 26c. Woman and bird (Goyo Domínguez) (relations between government and courts); (h) 26c. Flower and window (Galicia) (constitutional reform) (*horiz*); (i) 26c. Scales containing child and couple (J. Carrero) (Constitutional Court) (*horiz*); (j) 26c. Seated woman holding Arms (Fesanpe) (government and administration) (*horiz*)............... 6·25 6·25

1209 Control Tower, Four Winds Aerodrome, Madrid and Biplane
1210 Ironwork, Santa Maria de Iguácel, Jaca

2003 (17 Dec). Centenary of Powered Flight. Photo. P 13½×14.
4010	**1209**	76c. reddish brown and blue............	1·60	85

SPAIN

2004 (16 Jan). Romanic Architecture, Aragon. Booklet stamps. No value expressed. T **1210** and similar horiz designs. Multicoloured. Self-adhesive. Litho. Die-cut perf 13.

4011	A	(26c.) Type **1210**	55	30
4012	A	(26c.) Bible (*detail*), Huesca	55	30
4013	A	(26c.) Apostles (fresco)	55	30
4014	A	(26c.) Cloister, San Juan Bautista de Ruesta	55	30
4015	A	(26c.) Jacobean dinars	55	30
4016	A	(26c.) Column capital, La Iglesia de Santiago	55	30
4017	A	(26c.) Sarcophagus of Dona Sancha	55	30
4018	A	(26c.) Crucifix, Jaca Cathedral	55	30
4011/4018 Set of 8			4·00	2·10

1211 Woman Reading whilst Boating **1212** Hand and Damaged Leaf

(Des F. Hurtado. Photo)

2004 (16 Jan). Women and Reading. Two sheets, each 106×79 mm containing T **1211** and similar horiz designs showing women reading. Multicoloured. P 13½×14.
MS4019 (a) 27c. Type **1211**; 52c. With head resting in hand; 77c. Reading newspaper; (b) 27c. Lying facing left; 52c. Lying facing right; 77c. Looking over top of book .... 6·75 6·75

Nos. **MS**4019a/b each contain a stamp size label with inscriptions from "Don Quijote de la Mancha".

(Des J. Carrero. Photo)

2004 (2 Feb). 50th (2003) Anniv of Spanish Cancer Association. P 14.
4020 **1212** 27c. multicoloured 55 30

1213 "La Terrona" (oak tree), Zarza de Montánchez **1214** Stylized Canoe

2004 (6 Feb). Trees (5th series). Photo. P 14.
4021 **1213** 52c. multicoloured .... 1·00 50

2004 (9 Feb). World Rowing Championship, Banyoles. P 14.
4022 **1214** 77c. multicoloured .... 1·60 85

1215 Woman standing on Cliff **1216** Stairs and Arches

2004 (10 Feb). School Correspondence Programme. Trazo y Tiza (graphic novel by Miguelanxo Prado). Sheet 183×145 mm containing T **1215** and similar horiz designs. Multicoloured. Photo. P 14.
MS4023 27c.×4, Type **1215**; Yacht and lighthouse; Seagull, yacht, lighthouse and woman; Lighthouse .... 2·40 2·40

The block of stamps in No. **MS**4023 are enclosed within a border of stamp size labels each showing scenes from the book and inscribed with a month of the year.

2004 (8 Mar). Saint Maria de Carracedo Monastery. Sheet 80×105 mm. P 14.
MS4024 **1216** €1.90 multicoloured .... 4·00 4·00

1217 Emblem **1218** 19th-century Bronze Clock (La Almudaina Palace, Palma De Mallorca)

2004 (18 Mar). 36th Chess Olympiad, Calviá, Mallorca. P 13½.
4025 **1217** 77c. multicoloured .... 1·60 85

2004 (31 Mar). Cultural Heritage. Clocks. Sheet 106×151 mm containing T **1218** and similar vert designs. Each orange-brown, deep ultramarine and gold. Recess and photo. P 13.
MS4026 27c. Type **1218**; 52c. 18th-century bronze (La Granja Palace, Segovia); 77c. 19th-century bronze clock (La Granja Palace, Segovia); €1.90 18th-century bronze clock (El Pardo Palace, Madrid) .... 7·00 7·00

1219 Newspaper Vendor (statue) **1220** Ribbon

2004 (1 Apr). Centenary (2001) of "Diario de Burgos" Newspaper. Photo. P 14×13½.
4027 **1219** 27c. multicoloured 60 35

2004 (2 Apr). European Day (11 March) for Victims of Terrorism. Photo.

(a) Ordinary gum. P 14
4028 **1220** 27c. black 60 35

(b) Booklet stamps. No value expressed. Self-adhesive gum. Die-cut perf 13
4029 **1220** A (27c.) black 60 30

1221 Eggs **1222** Floral Shawl and Shell

2004 (5 Apr). Painted Eggs Festival. P 13½×14.
4030 **1221** 27c. multicoloured 60 35

2004 (7 Apr). Shawls. Sheet 80×105 containing T **1222** and similar vert designs showing details of paintings by Soledad Fernández. Multicoloured. P 14.
MS4031 27c. Type **1222**; 52c. Hands across dark shawl; 77c. Gladioli and part of shawl; €1.90 Shawl draped over chair .... 7·00 7·00

341

SPAIN

1223 Saint Domingo de la Calzada   **1224** Cable Inglés Bridge, Almería

2004 (15 Apr). 150th Anniv of Public Technical Engineering Works. P 14.
4032   **1223**   52c. multicoloured .... 1·00   50

2004 (27 Apr). Centenary of Cable Inglés Bridge, Almería. P 13½×14.
4033   **1224**   52c. multicoloured .... 1·00   50

1225 Historical Buildings (Sagrada Familia, Barcelona, Antoni Gaudí's Church, Fuente de Cibeles, Madrid, Giralda and Torre del Oro, Seville) and Parasols on Beach   **1226** "e" enclosing Figures

2004 (29 Apr). Europa. Holidays. P 14×13½.
4034   **1225**   77c. multicoloured .... 1·80   1·30

2004 (3 May). Enlargement of European Union. P 13½×14.
4035   **1226**   52c. multicoloured .... 1·10   60

1227 "Self Portrait with Neck of Raphael"   **1228** "100" containing Football and FIFA Emblem

2004 (11 May). Birth Centenary of Salvador Dali (artist). P 13½×14.
4036   **1227**   77c. multicoloured .... 1·60   85

2004 (21 May). Centenary of FIFA (Fédération Internationale de Football Association). P 13½×14.
4037   **1228**   77c. multicoloured .... 1·60   85

1229 Bourbon Royal Arms   **1230** Vicente Martín y Soler

2004 (22 May). Wedding of Crown Prince Felipe de Bourbon and Letizia Ortiz. P 13½×14.
4038   **1229**   27c. multicoloured 60   40

2004 (23 May). Espana 2004 International Stamp Exhibition, Madrid (1st issue). 350th Birth Anniv of Vincente Martin y Soler (musician). T **1230** and similar horiz design. P 13½×14.
4039   27c. Type **1230** 60   35
           a. Strip of 3. Nos. 4039/40 plus label .... 1·70   1·60
4040   52c. Saxophone and drum .... 1·10   65
Nos. 4039/40 were issued in horizontal *se-tenant* strips of two stamps and a central stamp size label showing a musician.

1231 Crown Prince Felipe and Princess Letizia   **1232** Entry of the Bulls

2004 (24 May). Espana 2004 International Stamp Exhibition, Madrid (2nd issue). The Royal Family. Sheet 151×86 mm containing T **1231** and similar horiz designs. P 13½×14.
MS4041   27c. multicoloured; 77c. multicoloured; €6 new blue and deep blue................ 14·00   14·00
Designs:—Type **1231**; 77c. Prince Felipe; €6 King Juan Carlos and Queen Sophia.

2004 (26 May). Espana 2004 International Stamp Exhibition, Madrid (3rd issue). Festivals. T **1232** and similar horiz design. P 13½×14.
4042   27c. Type **1232** 60   35
           a. Strip of 3. Nos. 4042/3 plus label .... 2·20   2·10
4043   52c. Lance taurino (bullfighter's cape pass).. 1·60   85
Nos. 4042/3 were issued in horizontal *se-tenant* strips of two stamps and a central stamp size label showing Enrique Ponce (bullfighter).

1233 Tennis Player

2004 (27 May). Espana 2004 International Stamp Exhibition, Madrid (4th issue). Sport. Sheet 232×86 mm containing T **1233** and similar horiz designs. P 13½×14.
MS4044   35c. Type **1233**; 52c. Ricardo Tormo (motorcyclist) and Valencia circuit; €1.90 Golf course................ 5·75   5·75
No. **MS4044** contains three stamp size labels showing Spanish Davis Cup tennis team, a motorcyclist and Severiano Ballesteros (golfer) respectively.

1234 *Bravo Espana* (yacht)   **1235** Newsboy and Masthead

2004 (28 May). Espana 2004 International Stamp Exhibition (5th issue). Valencia. T **1234** and similar horiz design. P 13½×14.
4045   52c. Type **1234**................ 1·00   55
           a. Strip of 3. Nos. 4045/6 plus label .... 2·75   2·40
4046   77c. Architectural heritage .... 1·60   95
Nos. 4045/6 were issued horizontal se-tenant strips of two stamps and a central stamp size label showing buildings and a yacht.

2004 (29 May). 214th Anniv of "Diario de Valencia" Newspaper. P 13½×14.
4047   **1235**   27c. multicoloured 60   35

1236 Pórtico de la Gloria and Nave, Santiago Cathedral   **1237** Lerma (former Ducal palace)

2004 (11 June). Xacobeo 2004 Holy Year (St. James jubilee year). P 13½×14.
4048   **1236**   52c. multicoloured .... 1·00   50

2004 (18 June). Paradores (state hotels). Photo. P 13½×14.
4049   **1237**   52c. multicoloured .... 1·00   50

SPAIN

1238 Granadilla Castle, Caceres   **1239** Danforth Anchor

2004 (1–19 July). Castles. Recess. P 13½×14.
4050	27c. orange-red and brown-red	60	30
4051	52c. red-brown (19.7)	1·10	45
4052	77c. deep blue-green	1·60	1·10
4053	€1.90 black (vert) (19.7)	4·00	1·90
4050/4053	Set of 4	7·00	3·50

Designs:—27c. Type **1238**; 52c. Aguas Mansas, Agoncillo; 77c. Mota, Alcala la Real, Jaen; €1.90 Villafuerte de Esgueva, Valladolid.

2004 (16 July). Salinas Anchor Museum, Castrillón, Asturias. P 14.
4054	**1239**	€1.90 multicoloured	3·75	2·10

1240 Pot with Handles and Lid   **1241** Building Façade

2004 (22 July). Paintings. Booklet stamps. T **1240** and similar vert designs depicting paintings of ceramics by Antonio Miguel Gonzalez. Multicoloured. Self-adhesive. Litho. Die-cut perf 13.
4055	A	(27c.) Type **1240**	60	30
4056	A	(27c.) Tall pot with handles, wide-necked pot and pot containing brushes	60	30
4057	A	(27c.) Pot with central handle, bread and figs	60	30
4058	A	(27c.) Pot with long neck and decorated body	60	30
4059	A	(27c.) Broken bread, onions, tall pot and pentagon	60	30
4060	A	(27c.) Decorated vase	60	30
4061	A	(27c.) Fruit and jug	60	30
4062	A	(27c.) Decorated storage jar	60	30
4055/4062	Set of 8		4·25	2·25

2004 (23 July). Centenary of the Circulo Oscense Building, Huesca. Photo. P 13½×14.
4063	**1241**	52c. multicoloured	1·00	50

1242 Virgin and Celebrating Crowds   **1243** Grapes and Bottle (Ribeiro)

2004 (30 July). White Virgin Festival, Vitoria-Gasteiz. P 14.
4064	**1242**	27c. multicoloured	60	35

2004 (1 Sept). Wine. T **1243** and similar vert designs. Multicoloured. Photo. P 14×13½.
4065	27c. Type **1243**	60	30
4066	52c. Glass and bottle (Malaga)	1·10	50

1244 1854 Philippine Stamp and Postmark   **1245** Mural (detail)

2004 (6 Sept). 150th Anniv of First Philippine Stamp. Photo. P 14.
4067	**1244**	77c. multicoloured	1·60	85

2004 (20 Sept). 109th Anniv of *Heraldo de Aragón* (newspaper). Photo. P 14×13½.
4068	**1245**	27c. multicoloured	60	35

1246 Jorge Juan (sailor and scientist)   **1247** Columbus Monument

2004 (24 Sept). 250th Anniv of Nautical Astronomy. Photo. P 14.
4069	**1246**	€1.90 multicoloured	4·00	1·90

2004 (1 Oct). Exfilna 2004 National Stamp Exhibition, Valladolid. Sheet 78×106 mm. Recess and litho. P 14.
MS4070	**1247**	€1.90 reddish brown and deep bluish green	4·25	4·25

1248 Parc Guell, Barcelona   **1249** Rainbow, Torn Sky and Fire (J. Carrero)

2004 (8 Oct). Urban Architecture. T **1248** and similar vert design. Multicoloured. Photo. P 14.
4071	52c. Type **1248**	1·10	50
4072	77c. Jinmao Tower, Shanghai	1·60	85

Stamps of the same design were issued by China.

2004 (14 Oct). America. Environmental Protection. Photo. P 14.
4073	**1249**	77c. multicoloured	1·60	85

1250 Accelerator   **1251** Cies Archipelago

2004 (19 Oct). 50th Anniv of European Organization for Nuclear Research (CERN). Photo. P 14.
4074	**1250**	€1.90 multicoloured	4·00	1·90

SPAIN

2004 (21 Oct). Nature. T **1251** and similar multicoloured designs. Photo. P 14.

4075	27c. Type **1251**	60	30
4076	52c. Ebro Delta National Park (horiz)	1·10	50
4077	77c. La Palm National Park (horiz)	1·60	85
4075/4077	Set of 3	3·00	1·50

1252 Letter

1253 Observatory

2004 (22 Oct). Stamp Day. 400th Anniv of First Registered Letter. Photo. P 14.

4078	**1252**	77c. multicoloured	1·60	85

2004 (5 Nov). Centenary of Erbe Observatory. Photo. P 14.

4079	**1253**	€1.90 multicoloured	3·75	1·90

1254 Alfonso I (statue) (Jose Bueno)

1255 The Nativity (18th-century)

2004 (12 Nov). 900th Anniv of Coronation of Alfonso I (king of Aragon and Navarre). Photo. P 14.

4080	**1254**	€1.90 multicoloured	3·75	1·90

2004 (17 Nov). Christmas. T **1255** and similar vert design. Multicoloured. Photo. P 14.

4081	27c. Type **1255**	60	30
4082	52c. The Nativity (Juan Manuel Cossio)	1·10	60

1256 Queen Isabel and Castle

1257 Ship leaving Port

2004 (26 Nov). 500th Death Anniv of Queen Isabel the Catholic. Photo. P 14.

4083	**1256**	€2.19 multicoloured	4·50	2·20

2004 (30 Nov). 200th Anniv of Royal Expedition to take Anti-Smallpox Vaccine to America and Asia. Recess. P 14.

4084	**1257**	77c. reddish brown	1·60	85

1258 Santiago el Mayor (stained glass window)

1259 Jugglers at Rest

2004 (3 Dec). Toledo Cathedral. Sheet 105×79 mm. Recess and litho. P 14.

MS4085	**1258**	€1.90 multicoloured	4·25	4·25

2005 (3 Jan). Circus. Self-adhesive Booklet Stamps. T **1259** and similar vert designs depicting paintings by Manola Elices. Multicoloured. Litho. Die-cut perf 13.

4086	A	(28c.) Type **1259**	55	35
4087	A	(28c.) Performing dogs	55	35
4088	A	(28c.) Unicyclist and juggler	55	35
4089	A	(28c.) Balancing act	55	35
4090	A	(28c.) Women with hoops	55	35
4091	A	(28c.) Tightrope walker	55	35
4092	A	(28c.) Two women and man balancing	55	35
4093	A	(28c.) Fire-eating	55	35
4086/4093	Set of 8		4·25	2·50

Nos. 4086/93 were for standard mail within Spain weighing up to 20grams.

1260 Emblem

1261 Ahuehuete Tree, Retiro Park, Madrid

2005 (12 Jan). European Constitution. Photo. P 14.

4094	**1260**	28c. multicoloured	55	35

2005 (17 Jan). Trees. Photo. P 14.

4095	**1261**	78c. multicoloured	1·50	85

1262 Stylized Car and Pedestrians

1263 Seville University

2005 (26 Jan). Civic Responsibility. T **1262** and similar horiz design. Multicoloured. Photo. P 14.

4096	28c. Type **1262** (road safety campaign)	55	35
4097	53c. Stylized blood transfusion (blood donation campaign)	1·00	60

2005 (3 Feb). Anniversaries. T **1263** and similar vert design. Recess (4098) or recess and litho (4099). P 14.

4098	28c. brown and carmine lake	55	35
4099	28c. yellow ochre, lake and bright green	55	35

Designs:—Type **1263** (500th anniv); No. 4099 Frontispiece Royal Pharmacopoeia.

1264 Woman watering Flowers ("Al levantar una lancha")

1265 Belfry, Sant Esteve Church, Tordera

SPAIN

(400th anniv of publication)

2005 (14 Feb). Children's Songs. Paintings by Raquel Fariñas. Sheet 144×124 mm containing T **1264** and similar vert designs. Multicoloured. P 14.
MS4100 28c. Type **1264**; 28c. "Aqui te espero"; 28c. "Estaba la pajara pinta"; 53c. "Cuatro esquinitas"; 53c. "El patio de mi casa"; 53c. "Pero mira como beben"; 78c. "Los pollitos cantan"; 78c. "Para entraer en clase".. 7·75 7·75

2005 (25 Feb). Juvenia 2005 National Youth Stamp Exhibition, Tordera. Photo. P 14.
4101 **1265** 28c. multicoloured..................... 55 35

1266 Emblem   **1267** Footballer

2005 (1 Mar). Centenary of Seville Football Club. Photo. P 14.
4102 **1266** 35c. light carmine 65 40

2005 (1 Mar). Centenary of Real Sporting de Gijón Football Club. Photo. P 14.
4103 **1267** 40c. multicoloured 75 45

1268 Emblem   **1269** Ham, Bread and Wine

2005 (1 Mar). 15th Mediterranean Games, Almería. Photo. P 14.
4104 **1268** 78c. multicoloured .... 1·50 85

2005 (15 Apr). Europa. Gastronomy. Photo. P 14.
4105 **1269** 53c. multicoloured .... 1·10 55

1270 Juan Valera   **1271** Don Quixote and Sancho Panza

2005 (18 Apr). Death Centenary of Juan Valera (writer). Recess. P 14.
4106 **1270** €2.21 chocolate and new blue................ 4·25 2·50

2005 (22 Apr). 400th Anniv of Publication of *El Ingenioso Hidalgo Don Quixote de la Mancha* (novel) by Miguel de Cervantes. Sheet 80×107 mm containing T **1271** and similar vert designs. Each black. Recess. P 14.
MS4107 28c. Type **1271**; 53c. Tilting at windmill; 78c. With sheep; €2.21 In cage............................ 7·25 7·25

1272 Telegraph Machine   **1273** Emblem and "E mc²"

2005 (26 Apr). 150th Anniv of Telegraph System. Photo. P 14.
4108 **1272** 28c. multicoloured 55 35

2005 (28 Apr). International Year of Physics. Self-adhesive. Photo. Die-cut perf 13.
4109 **1273** 28c. multicoloured 55 35

1274 Fan

2005 (9 May). National Heritage. Fans. Sheet 164×92 mm containing T **1274** and similar triangular designs. Multicoloured. Photo. P 14.
MS4110 28c. Type **1274**; 53c. 18th-century Madrid; 78c. Nymphs and cherubs .... 3·25 3·25

1275 "Diario Palentino"   **1276** Oropesa (former palace)

2005 (16 May). Newspaper Anniversaries. T **1275** and similar multicoloured designs. Photo. P 14.
4111 78c. Type **1275** (120th anniv (2001))................ 1·50 85
4112 €1.90 "Ultima Hora" (110th anniv (2003)) (horiz)... 3·75 2·00
4113 €2.21 "Diario de Ibiza" (110th anniv (2003)) (horiz)... 4·25 2·50
4111/4113 Set of 3 .... 8·50 4·75

2005 (13 June). Paradores (state hotels). Recess. P 14.
4114 **1276** €1.95 chocolate....................... 3·75 2·20

1277 Santa Barbara Castle, Alicante   **1278** Alcaudete Castle, Jaen

2005 (20 June). Exfilna 2005 National Stamp Exhibition, Alicante. Sheet 80×107 mm. Recess and litho. P 14.
MS4115 **1277** €2.21 multicoloured .... 4·25 4·25

345

SPAIN

2005 (4 July). Castles. T **1278** and similar horiz designs. Recess. P 13½×14.
4116		78c. black	1·50	85
4117		€1.95 reddish brown and myrtle green	3·75	2·00
4118		€2.21 black	4·25	2·50
4116/4118 Set of 3			8·50	4·75

Designs:—78c. Type **1278**; €1.95 Valderrobres, Teruel; €2.21 Molina de Aragon, Guadalajara.

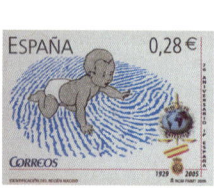 

1279 Baby and Fingerprint   **1280** Postal Delivery

2005 (11 July). 76th Anniv of Spanish Interpol. P 14.
4119	**1279**	28c. multicoloured	55	35

2005 (1 Sept). Stamp Day. Self-adhesive. Litho. Die-cut perf 13.
4120	**1280**	28c. multicoloured	55	35

1281 Our Lady of Asuncion Church, Pont de Suert   **1282** Lunnispark

2005 (7 Sept). P 14.
4121	**1281**	28c. multicoloured	55	35

2005 (16 Sept). For Children. Los Lunnis (children's television programme). Self-adhesive Booklet Stamps. T **1282** and similar vert designs. Multicoloured. Litho. Die-cut perf 13.
4122		28c. Type **1282**	55	35
4123		28c. Lucho	55	35
4124		28c. Lunnispark (green house)	55	35
4125		28c. Lulila	55	35
4126		28c. Lupita	55	35
4127		28c. Lupita in bed	55	35
4128		28c. Lublu	55	35
4129		28c. Lunnispark (orange house)	55	35
4122/4129 Set of 8			4·25	2·50

 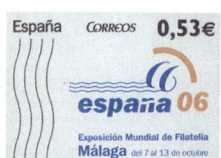

1283 Championship Emblem   **1284** Emblem

2005 (20 Sept). World Cycling Championship, Madrid. P 14.
4130	**1283**	78c. multicoloured	1·50	85

(Des J. Carrero. Photo)

2005 (8 Oct). Espana 2006 International Stamp Exhibition, Malaga. P 14.
4131	**1284**	53c. black, new blue and dull orange	1·00	60

1285 La Granja de San Ildefonso Garden, Segovia   **1286** Salamanca University

2005 (10 Oct). Gardens. T **1285** and similar horiz design. Multicoloured. Photo. P 14.
4132		78c. Type **1285**	1·50	85
		a. Horiz strip. Nos. 4132/3 plus label	6·00	
4133		€2.21 Bagh-e-Shahzadeh, Kerman	4·25	2·50

Nos. 4132/3 were issued in horizontal se-tenant strips of two stamps, separated by a stamp size label showing country flags, within the sheet. Stamps of a similar design were issued by Iran.

2005 (13 Oct). IberoAmerican Summit Conference, Salamanca. Photo. P 14.
4134	**1286**	78c. multicoloured	1·50	85

1287 Hands   **1288** Foundation Emblem and Trophy

(Des J. Carrero. Photo)

2005 (14 Oct). America. Struggle against Poverty. P 13.
4135	**1287**	78c. multicoloured	1·50	85

2005 (20 Oct). 25th Anniv of Prince of Asturias Awards. P 14.
4136	**1288**	28c. multicoloured	55	30

No. 4136 was issued with a se-tenant stamp size label, inscribed for the awards, within sheets of eight stamps and eight labels.

1289 Arms and Town Hall, La Orotava (500th anniv)   **1290** Diver

2005 (20 Oct). Anniversaries. T **1289** and similar multicoloured design. P 14.
4137	**1289**	€2.21 Type **1289**	4·25	2·50
4138		€2.21 Envelope and stamp (150th anniv of Cuba and Puerto Rico post) (horiz)	4·25	2·50

2005 (24 Oct). For the Young. *Al filo de lo Imposible* (On the edge of Impossible (television programme)) Sheet 145×164 mm containing T **1290** and similar vert designs. Multicoloured. Photo. P 14.
MS4139	28c.×6, Type **1290**; Ballooning; Traversing polar ice; White water canoeing; Mountaineering; Rock climbing	3·25	3·25

The stamps of No. **MS**4139 are arranged amongst stamp size labels to construct composite designs of six scenes from the programme. See also No. **MS**4159.

1291 "Adoration of the Kings" (Francisco Ribalta)   **1292** St. Paul (stained glass window)

SPAIN

2005 (31 Oct). Christmas. T **1291** and similar vert design. Multicoloured. P 14.
4140	28c. Type **1291**	60	35
4141	53c. Three kings	1·10	60

2005 (2 Nov). Avila Cathedral. Sheet 78×105 mm. Recess and litho. P 14.
MS4142	**1292** €2.21 multicoloured	4·75	4·75

1293 Barcelona

1294 Juana I of Castille

2005 (3 Nov). Euromediterranean (Euromed) Summit, Barcelona. Photo. P 14.
4143	**1293** 53c. multicoloured	1·00	60

2005 (4 Nov). 500th Anniv of Parliament of Toro. P 14.
4144	**1294** 28c. multicoloured	55	35

1295 Puppets

1296 Dianthus

2006 (2 Jan). Toys. Self-adhesive Booklet Stamps. T **1295** and similar horiz designs. Multicoloured. Litho. Die-cut perf 13½.
4145	A Type **1295**	55	40
4146	A Spinning tops	55	40
4147	A Car	55	40
4148	A Lorry	55	40
4149	A Doll	55	40
4150	A Marbles	55	40
4151	A Horse and cart	55	40
4152	A Motorcycle	55	40
4145/4152	Set of 8	4·25	3·00

Nos. 4145/52 were for use on letters up to 20 grams within Spain.

2006 (20 Jan). Flora and Fauna (1st issue). Self-adhesive. Litho. Die-cut perf 13.
4153	**1296** 28c. multicoloured	55	30

No. 4153 was issued in panes of ten in books of 100 stamps.
See also Nos. 4156, 4160, 4187/8, 4207/8, 4231/2, 4245/6, 4270/1, 4280/1, 4328/9, 4354/5, 4371/2, 4389/90, 4418/19, 4432/3, 4452/3 and 4471/2.

1297 Building Façade

1298 "La Anunciada" Cypress, Villafranca del Bierzo, Léon

2006 (27 Jan). 150th Anniv of National Bank. Recess. P 14.
4154	**1297** 78c. chestnut and black	1·50	1·20

(Des Alexis (4141). Photo)

2006 (31 Jan). Trees (7th series). Photo. P 14.
4155	**1298** 53c. multicoloured	1·00	80

1299 Sparrow

1300 Desert overlaying Green Hills

2006 (1 Feb). Flora and Fauna (2nd issue). Self-adhesive. Litho. Die-cut perf 13.
4156	**1299** A multicoloured	55	45

No. 4156 was issued in panes of ten in books of 100 stamps.

2006 (6 Feb). International Day against Desertification. Photo. P 14.
4157	**1300** 29c. multicoloured	55	45

1301 Women voting

1302 Goldfinch

2006 (8 Mar). 75th Anniv of Votes for Women. P 14.
4158	**1301** 29c. red-brown and blue	55	35

2006 (22 Mar). For the Young. Al filo de lo Imposible (On the edge of Impossible (television programme)) (2nd issue). Sheet 145×164 mm containing vert designs as T **1290**. Multicoloured. Photo. P 14.
MS4159	29c. Cycling; 38c. Traversing sand dunes; 41c. Paragliding; 57c. Sea canoeing; 78c. White water rafting; €2.39 Abseiling waterfall	9·25	7·25

The stamps of No. **MS**4159 are arranged amongst stamp size labels to construct composite designs of six scenes from the programme.

2006 (1 Apr). Flora and Fauna (3rd issue). Self-adhesive Booklet Stamps. T **1302** and similar horiz design. Multicoloured. Litho. Die-cut perf 13.
4160	29c. Type **1302**	55	40
4161	38c. Strelitzia flower	75	60

1303 Stylized Figure and Tap (water conservation campaign)

1304 "Diario de Leon" (centenary)

2006 (4 Apr). Civic Responsibility. T **1303** and similar multicoloured designs. Litho. P 13½.
4162	29c. Type **1303**	55	35
4163	29c. Figure holding balloons ("Say no to Drugs" campaign)	55	35
4164	38c. Workers and factories (centenary of Social Security and Labour Inspectorate) (horiz)	75	45
4165	57c. Legs (Campaign against people trafficking) (horiz)	1·10	65
4162/4165	Set of 4	2·50	1·50

347

SPAIN

2006 (20 Apr). Newspapers' Anniversaries. T **1304** and similar designs. Litho. P 14.

4166	41c. multicoloured	80	45
4167	41c. multicoloured	80	45
4168	41c. multicoloured	80	45
4169	41c. bright scarlet and black	80	45
4170	41c. multicoloured	80	45
4166/4170	Set of 5	4·50	1·75

Designs:—Type **1304**; *Diario de Pontevedra* (115th (2003) anniv) (horiz); *Levante-El Mercantil Valenciano* (135th (2007) anniv) (horiz); *El Norte de Castilla* (150th anniv); *Diario de Avila*.

1305 Christopher Columbus

1306 Santa Maria de los Remedios

(120th (2008) anniv)

2006 (24 Apr). 500th Death Anniv of Christopher Columbus. Sheet 105×78 mm. Litho. P 14.

MS4171 **1305** €2.39 multicoloured .... 4·50 4·50

2006 (27 Apr). Centenary of Coronation of Santa Maria de los Remedios. Litho. P 14.

4172 **1306** €2.33 multicoloured .... 4·50 2·75

1307 City Council Building Facade

2006 (5 May). Exfilna 2006 National Stamp Exhibition. Sheet 106×78 mm. Recess and litho. P 14.

MS4173 **1307** €2.39 multicoloured .... 4·50 4·50

1308 Horseman

2006 (9 May). 500th Anniv of the Tasso Family (postal service suppliers) in Spain. Litho. P 14.

4174 **1308** 29c. multicoloured 55 35

1309 Emblem

2006 (17 May). Science. Internet Day (29c.) and International Mathematicians' Congress, Madrid (57c.). T **1309** and similar multicoloured design. Litho. Self-adhesive Die-cut perf 13½.

4175	29c. Type **1309**	45	35
4176	57c. Emblem and numerals (vert)	1·10	60

1310 Faces and Star

2006 (23 May). Centenary of Socialist Youth Organization. Litho. P 14.

4177 **1310** 78c. multicoloured .... 1·50 80

1311 Posy as Parasol

1313 Casa Batlló, Barcelona

2006 (23 May). Espana 2006 International Stamp Exhibition, Malaga. Sheet 78×105 mm. Litho. P 14.

MS4178 **1311** 78c. multicoloured .... 1·50 1·50

No. 4179 and Type **1312** have been left for "Festivals" issued 5 June 2006, not yet received.

2006 (8 June). Architecture. T **1313** and similar designs. Litho. P 14.

4180	29c. slate-grey	55	35
4181	38c. slate-green	75	50
4182	41c. multicoloured	80	50
4183	57c. light brown	1·10	60
4184	78c. multicoloured	1·50	80
4185	€2.33 multicoloured	4·50	2·50
4180/4185	Set of 6	8·50	4·50

Designs:—29c. Type **1313**; 38c. Vapor Aymerich, Terrassa; 41c. Depósitos del Sol Library, Albacete; 57c. Campos Eliseos Theatre, Bilbao; 78c. Alfredo Kraus auditorium, Las Palmas de Gran Canaria (horiz); €2.33 Bus Station, Casar de Cáceres.

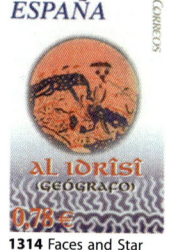
1314 Faces and Star

1315 Walls, Los Millares

(horiz)

2006 (15 June). Abu Abdallah Mohamed Ben Idrisi (Al Idrisi) (geographer and cartographer) Commemoration. Litho. P 14.

4186 **1314** 78c. multicoloured .... 1·50 80

2006 (5 July). Flora and Fauna (4th issues). Self-adhesive. Vert designs as T **1296**. Multicoloured. Litho. Die-cut perf 13.

4187	29c. Greenfinch	55	25
4188	41c. Iris	80	35

Nos. 4187/8 were issued in panes of ten in books of 100 stamps.

2006 (6 July). Archaeology. T **1315** and similar multicoloured designs. Litho. P 14.

4189	29c. Type **1315**	55	35
4190	57c. Fresco, L'Alcudia (horiz)	1·10	60
4191	78c. Guerrer de Moixent (3rd–4th century Iberian statue)	1·50	80
4189/4191	Set of 3	2·75	1·50

SPAIN

1316 Horses and Riders   **1317** Teneguía Volcano erupting and Seismograph (vulcanology)

2006 (6 July). Festivals. Carreras de Caballos de Sanúucar de Barrameda (horse race). Litho. P 14.
4192   **1316**   €2.33 multicoloured........................   4·50   2·75

2006 (13 July). Earth and Universe Sciences. T **1317** and similar horiz design. Multicoloured. Litho. P 14.
4193   29c. Type **1317**...............................   55   35
4194   29c. Magnifier and map (cartography)............   55   35

1318 Anniversary Emblem   **1319** 13th-century Capital, Misericordia Convent, Palma and Shrine of the Book, Jerusalem

2006 (20 July). Anniversaries. T **1318** and similar horiz design. Litho. P 14.
4195   38c. new blue and Prussian blue (700th anniv)...............................   0·75   0·50
4196   38c. multicoloured (centenary)..............   0·75   0·50
Designs: 4195, Type **1318**; 4196, Aqueduct.

(Des Efemerides. Photo)

2006 (1 Sept). 20th Anniv of Spain–Israel Diplomatic Relations. P 14.
4197   **1319**   78c. multicoloured........................   1·50   85

1320 Banos de la Encina Castle, Jaen   **1321** Hand and Braille Numerals

2006 (8 Sept). Castles. T **1320** and similar horiz designs. Recess. P 13½×14.
4198   29c. black...............................   55   35
4199   €2.39 deep brown and blue................   4·50   3·00
Designs:—29c. Type **1320**; €2.39 Torroella de Montgri castle, Girona.

2006 (12 Sept). Europa. Integration. T **1321** and similar vert designs. Photo. P 14.
4200   29c. Type **1321**..............................   55   35
4201   57c. Hands...................................   1·10   60

1322 Puente Internacional de Ayamonte (Illustration reduced. Actual size 80×30 mm)

(Des Atelier Acacio Santos. Litho)

2006 (14 Sept). Bridges. T **1322** and similar horiz design. Multicoloured. P 12.
4202   29c. Type **1322**...............................   55   45
4203   57c. Puente de Alcántara.......................   1·10   85
Stamps of similar design were issued by Portugal.

1323 Grape Treading   **1324** Emblem

2006 (21 Sept). 50th Anniv of Rioja Wine Harvest Festival. P 14.
4204   **1323**   29c. multicoloured........................   55   35

2006 (25 Sept). Centenary of Real Club Deportivo de la Coruna. P 14.
4205   **1324**   57c. ultramarine and Prussian blue.....   1·10   60

1325 Hand, Ball and Hoop   **1326** Swallow

2006 (2 Oct). Spain—2006 World Basketball Champions. Sheet 107×80 mm. P 14.
MS4206   **1325**   29c. multicoloured........................   55   55

2006 (4 Oct). Flora and Fauna (5th issue). Self-adhesive gum. T **1302** and similar vert design. Multicoloured. Litho. Die-cut perf 13.
4207   29c. Type **1326**...............................   55   45
4208   29c. Poinsettia...............................   55   45

1327 "Victorio & Luchino"   **1328** Symbols of Energy Use

2006 (8–13 Oct). España 2006 International Stamp Exhibition, Malaga. Seven sheets, each 105×78 mm containing T **1327** and similar designs. Photo. P 14.
MS4209   (a)   €2.33 orange-red, yellow-orange and black (8 Oct); (b) €2.33 multicoloured (9 Oct); (c) €2.33 multicoloured (10 Oct); (d) €2.33 multicoloured (10 Oct); (e) €2.33 multicoloured (10 Oct); (f) €2.33 multicoloured (12 Oct); (g) €2.33 multicoloured (13 Oct)...........................
Designs: **MS**4209a Type **1327** (fashion); **MS**4209b Hat, "Alfredo Landa" "Concha Velasco" and "Belén Rueda" (cinema) (vert); **MS**4209c Music annotation and "El canto del loco" (music); **MS**4209d Stylized guitarist, "Ana Belén" "Victor Manuel" and "Miguel Rios" (music) (vert); **MS**4209e Hand, "Cristina Hoyos" and "José Mercé" (flamenco); **MS**4209f Ball, "Pau Gasol" and "Rafael Nadal" (sport) (vert); **MS**4209g Pablo Picasso (art).
A different miniature sheet was issued on each day of the exhibition.

2006 (14 Oct). America. Energy Conservation. Photo. P 14.
4210   **1328**   78c. multicoloured........................   1·50   80

1329 Stylized Early and Modern Postmen   **1330** Ramón Rubal

2006 (25 Oct). 250th Anniv of First Postman. Self-adhesive gum. Litho. Die-cut perf 13½.
4211   **1329**   29c. multicoloured........................   55   35

349

SPAIN

2006 (27 Oct). Birth Centenary of Ramón Rubal (politician). Recess. P 14.
| 4212 | **1330** | 57c. black and orange-vermilion | 1·10 | 70 |

1331 "Adoración de los Pastores" (sculpture), Cuenca Cathedral

1332 Construction (stained glass window)

2006 (2 Nov). Christmas. T **1331** and similar multicoloured design. Self-adhesive. Die-cut perf 13½.
| 4213 | 29c. Type **1331** | 55 | 35 |
| 4214 | 57c. "Entrañable Navidad" (painting) (Belén Elorrieta) (vert) | 1·10 | 60 |

2006 (3 Nov). Higher Architecture School of Madrid. Sheet 106×80 mm. Recess and litho. P 14.
| MS4215 | **1332** | €2.39 multicoloured | 4·50 | 4·50 |

1333 Francis Xavier 1334 Symbols of Television

2006 (7 Nov). 500th Birth Anniv of Saint Francis Xavier. Recess and litho. P 14.
| 4216 | **1333** | 29c. multicoloured | 55 | 35 |

2006 (8 Nov). 50th Anniv of Spanish Television. Photo. P 14.
| 4217 | **1334** | 29c. multicoloured | 55 | 35 |

1335 Piles of Newspaper 1336 Pío Baroja

2006 (9 Nov). 125th Anniv of *La Vanguardia* (newspaper). Photo. P 14.
| 4218 | **1335** | 29c. multicoloured | 55 | 35 |

2006 (23 Nov). 50th Death Anniv of Pío Baroja (writer). Photo. P 14.
| 4219 | **1336** | 29c. multicoloured | 55 | 35 |

1337 Arms

1338 Dove and Flag

2006 (23 Nov). 25th Anniv of Arms of Spain. Photo. P 14.
| 4220 | **1337** | 29c. multicoloured | 55 | 35 |

2006 (30 Nov). International Year of Historical Memory. T **1338** and similar horiz design. P 14.
| 4221 | 29c. scarlet-vermilion and lemon | 55 | 35 |
| 4222 | 29c. multicoloured | 55 | 35 |
Designs: 4221, Type **1338**; 4222, Adult and child.

1339 Early Tricycle 1340 Hoopoe

2007 (2 Jan). Toys. Self-adhesive Booklet Stamps. T **1339** and similar horiz designs. Multicoloured. Litho. Die-cut perf 13.
4223	A	(30c.) Type **1339**	55	45
4224	A	(30c.) Bus	55	45
4225	A	(30c.) Train	55	45
4226	A	(30c.) Skittles	55	45
4227	A	(30c.) Wooden pram	55	45
4228	A	(30c.) Aeroplane	55	45
4229	A	(30c.) Printing set	55	45
4230	A	(30c.) Fire truck	55	45
4223/4230 Set of 8			4·25	3·25
Nos. 4223/30 were for standard mail within Spain weighing up to 20grams.

2007 (20 Jan). Flora and Fauna (6th issue). Self-adhesive gum. T **1340** and similar vert design. Multicoloured. Litho. Die-cut perf 13.
| 4231 | 30c. Type **1340** | 55 | 45 |
| 4232 | 39c. Rose | 75 | 60 |

1341 Teacher and Pupils 1342 Masthead

(Des M. Escobar. Litho)

2007 (23 Jan). Teacher Awareness. Self-adhesive gum. Die-cut perf 13.
| 4233 | **1341** | 58c. multicoloured | 1·10 | 85 |

2007 (31 Jan). 140th Anniv (2006) of La Provincias (newspaper). Photo. P 14.
| 4234 | **1342** | 42c. multicoloured | 80 | 65 |

1343 Stylized Table of Elements 1344 Emblem and Courtyard

(Des J. Garcia Martinez (30c.). Litho)

2007 (2 Feb). Science. Self-adhesive gum. T **1343** and similar multicoloured design. Die-cut perf 13½.
| 4235 | 30c. Type **1343** (birth centenary of Dimtri Mendeleyiev (first classification)) | 55 | 45 |
| 4236 | 42c. Astrolabe (425th anniv of Gregorian calendar) (vert) | 80 | 65 |

2007 (5 Feb). Centenary of Institut d'Estudis Catalans (Institute of Catalan Studies). Photo. P 14.
| 4237 | **1344** | 30c. multicoloured | 55 | 45 |

1345 Yacht 1346 Map

SPAIN

2007 (8 Feb). Desafio Espanol 2007 (Spanish entry in 32nd America's Cup Challenge Yacht Race, Valencia). Photo. P 14.

| 4238 | **1345** | 30c. multicoloured | 55 | 45 |

2007 (16 Feb). Earth and Universe Sciences. Self-adhesive gum. T **1346** and similar horiz design. Multicoloured. Die-cut perf 13½.

| 4239 | | 30c. Type **1346** (basic cartography) | 55 | 45 |
| 4240 | | 78c. Radio telescope (Astronomy centre, Yebes) | 1·50 | 1·20 |

See also Nos. 4193/4.

Nos. 4241 and Type **1347** have been left for "Tree" issued on 5 March 2007, not yet received.

1348 Mosaic, Roman Villa, La Olmeda   **1349** Map of Europe

2007 (8 Mar). Archaeology. T **1348** and similar horiz design. Multicoloured. Litho. P 14.

| 4242 | | 30c. Type **1348** | 55 | 45 |
| 4243 | | 30c. Roman baths, Campo Valdés | 55 | 45 |

2007 (23 Mar). 50th Anniv of Treaty of Rome. Photo. P 14.

| 4244 | **1349** | 58c. multicoloured | 1·30 | 85 |

1350 Canary   **1351** "Movida Madrileña"

2007 (2 Apr). Flora and Fauna (7th issue). Self-adhesive gum. T **1350** and similar vert design. Multicoloured. Litho. Die-cut perf 13.

| 4245 | | 30c. Type **1350** | 55 | 45 |
| 4246 | | 42c. Violet | 80 | 65 |

2007 (13 Apr). 25th Anniv of Movida Madrileña (Madrid movement). Sheet 79×106 mm. Litho. P 14.

| MS4247 | **1351** | 30c. multicoloured | 1·10 | 1·10 |

1352 Mallorca Cathedral   **1353** Emblem and Doves

2007 (16 Apr). EXFILNA 2007 National Philatelic Exhibition, Palma. Sheet 79×106 mm. Recess and litho. P 14.

| MS4248 | **1352** | €2.43 steel blue | 4·75 | 4·75 |

2007 (23 Apr). Europa. Centenary of Scouting. Litho. P 14.

| 4249 | **1353** | 58c. multicoloured | 1·10 | 85 |

1354 Chapel of Valleacerón, Almadenejos   **1355** Calahorra

2007 (26 Apr). Architecture. T **1354** and similar designs. Recess (39c., 58c.) or photo (others). P 14.

4250		30c. multicoloured	55	45
4251		39c. deep rose-red	75	60
4252		42c. multicoloured	80	65
4253		58c. multicoloured	1·10	85
4254		78c. slate-black	1·50	1·20
4255		€2.49 multicoloured	4·75	3·50
4250/4255		Set of 6	8·75	6·50

Designs:—30c. Type **1354**; 39c. El Capricho, Comilla; 42c. Santa Caterina market; 58c. Vizcaya Bridge, Las Arenas (*horiz*); 78c. Terminal 4, Barajas Airport, Madrid; €2.49 Casa Lis Museum, Salamanca (*horiz*).

2007 (28 Apr). JUVENIA 2007 Youth Stamp Exhibition, Calahorra. Photo. P 14.

| 4256 | **1355** | 30c. multicoloured | 55 | 45 |

1356 Stylized Figures and Stamp   **1357** Script

2007 (7 May). Stamp Day. Spanish Philatelic Associations. Self-adhesive. Litho. Die-cut perf 13½.

| 4257 | **1356** | 30c. multicoloured | 55 | 45 |

(Des J. I. Chillón)

2007 (9 May). 800th Anniv of Cantar de Mio Cid (epic poem). Self-adhesive. Litho. Die-cut perf 13½.

| 4258 | **1357** | 30c. multicoloured | 55 | 45 |

1358 Court of Auditors Building   **1359** "somos differntes somos iguales"

2007 (12 May). 25th Anniv of Court of Auditors. Photo. P 14.

| 4259 | **1358** | 30c. multicoloured | 55 | 45 |

(we are different we are the same)

2007 (16 May). Civic Values. T **1359** and similar vert designs. Multicoloured. Photo. P 14.

4260		30c. Type **1359**	55	45
4261		39c. Stylized students and open book (we are all classmates, against school violence)	75	60
4262		58c. Stylized couple (organ donation)	1·10	85
4263		78c. Multicoloured figure (sexual equality)	1·50	1·20
4260/4263		Set of 4	3·50	2·75

SPAIN

1360 Tricholoma equestre   **1361** Carmen Conde

2007 (1 June). Fungi. T **1360** and similar vert design. Multicoloured. Photo. P 14.
| 4264 | 30c. Type **1360** | 55 | 45 |
| 4265 | 78c. Amanita muscaria | 1·50 | 1·20 |

(birth centenary)

2007 (4 June). Women Writers. T **1361** and similar horiz design. Recess. P 14.
| 4266 | €2.49 black and carmine vermillion | 4·75 | 3·50 |
| 4267 | €2.49 black and salmon | 4·75 | 3·50 |

Designs: 4266, Type **1361**; 4267, Rosa Chacal (birth centenary (1998)).

1362 Emblem and Colours   **1363** Virgin Mary

(Des M. Mirman. Photo)

2007 (14 June). Centenary of Real Betis Balompié Football Club. P 14.
| 4268 | **1362** | 78c. multicoloured | 1·50 | 1·20 |

(wooden sculpture by Antonio Castillo Lastrucci)

2007 (16 June). Coronation of Maria Santísima de la O, Triana, Seville. Photo. P 14.
| 4269 | **1363** | 30c. multicoloured | 55 | 45 |

1364 Nightingale   **1365** Soldiers and Globe (*Illustration reduced. Actual size 74×28 mm*)

2007 (2 July). Flora and Fauna (8th issue). Self-adhesive gum. T **1364** and similar vert design. Multicoloured. Litho. Die-cut perf 13.
| 4270 | 30c. Type **1364** | 55 | 45 |
| 4271 | 30c. Hyacinth | 55 | 45 |

2007 (4 July). Armed Forces Peace Missions. Photo. P 14.
| 4272 | **1365** | 30c. multicoloured | 55 | 50 |

1366 Expo Emblem and Fluvi   **1367** Dehesa de Saler, L'Albufera Park

(Expo mascot)

2007 (5 July). Zaragoza 2008 International Water and Sustainable Development Exhibition. (1st issue). Self-adhesive gum. Litho. Die-cut perf 13.
| 4273 | **1366** | 58c. multicoloured | 85 | 60 |

2007 (12 July). For the Young. Al filo de lo Imposible (On the edge of Impossible) (television programme) (3rd issue). Sheet 145×164 mm containing vert designs as T **1290**. Multicoloured. Photo. P 14.
MS4274 Antarctic diving; 39c. Traversing mountain approach; 42c. Crossing snowfield with sleds; 58c. On board *Le Sourire*; 78c. Canoeing; €2.43 With dog sled during Iditarod race, Alaska .... 9·50 7·50
The stamps of No. **MS**4274 are arranged amongst stamp size labels to construct composite designs of six scenes from the programme.

2007 (19 July). Parks. T **1367** and similar horiz design. Multicoloured. Litho. P 13.
| 4275 | 30c. Type **1367** | 55 | 45 |
| 4276 | 30c. Waterfall, Las Lagunas de Ruidera | 55 | 45 |

1368 Punta del Hidalgo Lighthouse, Tenerife   **1369** Almenar Castle, Soria

2007 (6 Sept). Lighthouses. Sheet 116×106 mm containing T **1368** and similar vert designs showing lighthouses. Multicoloured. Photo. P 14.
MS4277 Type **1368**; 39c. Cabo Mayor, Cantabria; 42c. Punta Almina, Ceuta; 58c. Melilla; 78c. Cabo de Palos, Murcia; €2.43 Gorliz, Vizcaya .... 9·25 9·25

2007 (8 Sept). Castles. T **1369** and similar horiz designs. Recess. P 13½×14.
| 4278 | €2.49 agate and yellowish green | 4·75 | 3·50 |
| 4279 | €2.49 black and deep yellowish green | 4·75 | 3·50 |

Designs: No. 4278, Type **1369**; No. 4279, Villena Castle, Alicante.

1369a Asclepius (statue) (Ampuria Museum, Spain)   **1370** Dupont's Lark

2007 (28 June). Asclepius (demigod of medicine). Sheet 120×76 mm containing T **1363**a and similar vert design. Multicoloured. P 13.
MS4279a 30c. Type **1363**a; 58c. Asclepius (head) (Greek National Archaeological Museum) .... 4·75 3·50
Stamps of a similar design were issued by Greece.

2007 (1 Oct). Flora and Fauna (9th issue). Self-adhesive gum. T **1370** and similar vert design. Multicoloured. Litho. Die-cut perf 13.
| 4280 | 30c. Type **1370** | 55 | 45 |
| 4281 | 30c. Daisy | 55 | 45 |

1371 Masthead   **1372** "education para todos"

2007 (4 Oct). Centenary (1901) of *El Adelantado de Segovia* (newspaper). Photo. P 14.
| 4282 | **1371** | 78c. multicoloured | 1·50 | 1·20 |

2007 (11 Oct). America. Education for All. Photo. P 14.
| 4283 | **1372** | 78c. multicoloured | 1·50 | 1·20 |

1373 Ivory Chantilly Lace over Taffeta, Empire Line Dress (1948—50)

1374 Adoration of the Kings (sculpture) (Damian Forment)

2007 (18 Oct). Fashion. Cristóbal Balenciaga (designer). Sheet 105×150 mm containing T **1373** and similar vert designs showing his designs. Multicoloured. Photo. P 14.
MS4284 Type **1373**; 42c. Red embroidered jacket and long dress (1960); 58c. Red coat and dress (c. 1960); 78c. Yellow linen button through dress with belt .... 4·25 4·25

2007 (31 Oct). Christmas. T **1374** and similar horiz design. Multicoloured. Self-adhesive gum. Die-cut perf 13½.
| 4285 | 30c. Type **1374** | 55 | 45 |
| 4286 | 58c. Children in envelope | 1·10 | 85 |

1375 *Self Portrait* (Pedro Berruguete)

1376 Foundry worker (stained glass window)

2007 (5 Nov). Art. T **1375** and similar vert design. Multicoloured. P 13.
| 4287 | 39c. Type **1375** | 75 | 60 |
| 4288 | 42c. *Self Portrait* (Mariano Salvador Maella).. | 80 | 65 |

2007 (9 Nov). Operations Courtyard of the Bank of Spain. Sheet 106×80 mm. Recess and litho. P 13.
MS4289 **1376** multicoloured .... 4·75 4·75

1377 King Juan Carlos

1378 Ship

2008 (2 Jan)–10. P 13.
4290	**1377**	1c. black and pale orange	15	15
4291		2c. magenta and pale orange	15	15
4292		5c. new blue and pale orange	15	15
4293		10c. grey-green and pale orange	20	20
4293a		30c. blue and pale orange		
4294		31c. purple-brown and pale orange	60	40
4294a		32c. scarlet and pale orange (14.1.09)	65	40
4294b		34c. blue and pale orange (5.2.10)		
4294c		45c. yellow-olive and pale orange (5.2.10)		
4294d		58c. dull yellow-green and pale orange		
4295		60c. ultramarine and pale orange	1·10	70
4295a		62c. slate and pale orange (14.1.09)	1·20	80
4295b		64c. olive-bistre and pale orange (5.2.10)		
4296		78c. bright carmine and pale orange	1·50	95
4296a		€2.47 yellow-olive and pale orange (14.1.09)	4·75	3·00
4296b		€2.43 Indian red and pale orange		
4296c		€2.49 bright purple and pale orange		
4297		€2.60 deep dull green and pale orange	5·00	3·00
4298		€2.70 ultramarine and pale orange (14.1.09)	5·25	3·50
4299		€2.75 deep purple and pale orange (5.2.10)		

Numbers have been left for additions to this series.

2008 (2 Jan). Toys. Self-adhesive Booklet Stamps. T **1378** and similar horiz designs. Multicoloured. Litho. Die-cut perf 13
4320	A	(31c.) Type **1378**	60	45
4321	A	(31c.) Clown-shaped bean bag catcher...	60	45
4322	A	(31c.) Beach buckets	60	45
4323	A	(31c.) Stage coach	60	45
4324	A	(31c.) Barquillero (rolled wafer container)	60	45
4325	A	(31c.) Diablo	60	45
4326	A	(31c.) Architecture bricks	60	45
4327	A	(31c.) Submarine	60	45
4320/4327 Set of 8			4·25	3·25

Nos. 4320/7 were for use on standard mail within Spain weighing up to 20grams.

 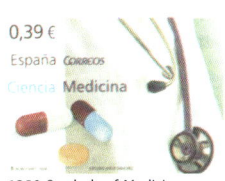

1379 Green Woodpecker

1380 Symbols of Medicine

2008 (10 Jan). Flora and Fauna (10th issue). Self-adhesive gum. T **1379** and similar vert design. Multicoloured. Litho. Die-cut perf 13.
| 4328 | 31c. Type **1379** | 60 | 45 |
| 4329 | 60c. Camellia | 1·10 | 85 |

2008 (17 Jan). Science. Self-adhesive gum. T **1380** and similar vert design. Multicoloured. Litho. Die-cut perf 13.
| 4330 | 39c. Type **1380** | 75 | 60 |
| 4331 | 43c. Symbols of meteorology | 85 | 65 |

1381 Masthead

1382 Globe

2008 (30 Jan). Centenary of *La Voz de Avilés* (newspaper). Photo. P 14.
| 4332 | **1381** | 31c. multicoloured | 60 | 45 |

2008 (4 Feb). Science. Self-adhesive gum. T **1382** and similar horiz design. Multicoloured. Litho. Die-cut perf 13.
| 4333 | 78c. Type **1382** (International Polar Year)...... | 1·50 | 1·20 |
| 4334 | €2.60 Leaves growing from rock (International Year of Planet Earth)......... | 5·00 | 3·75 |

1383 Hand and "016" (help line telephone number)

1384 Black Poplar, Horcajjuelo (Alamo negro de Horajuelo)

SPAIN

2008 (11 Feb). Stop Violence against Women Campaign. Self adhesive. Die-cut perf 13.
4335   **1383**   31c. multicoloured 60   45

2008 (18 Feb). Trees (9th series). Photo. P 14.
4336   **1384**   €2.44 multcoloured .... 4·75   3·50

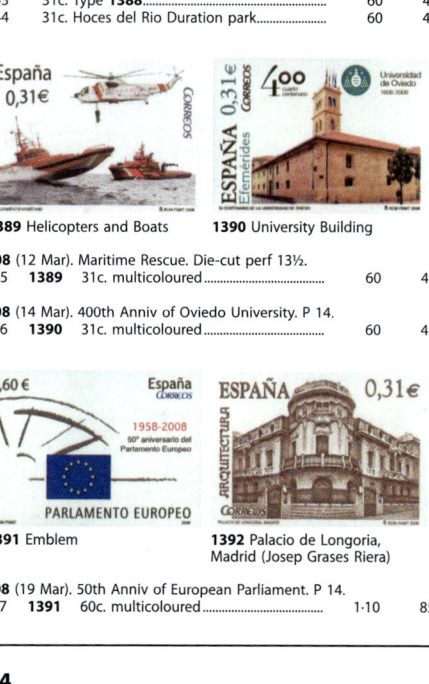

1385 Pabellon Puente and Torre del Agua (bridge pavillion and water tower), Zaragoza

1386 'Contra la explocíon infantil' (fight against child exploitation)

2008 (22 Feb). Zaragoza 2008 International Water and Sustainable Development Exhibition (2nd issue). Self adhesive. Litho. Die-cut perf 13.
4337   **1385**   31c. multicoloured 60   45

2008 (29 Feb). Civic Values. T **1386** and similar vert designs. Multicoloured. Photo. P 14.
4338   31c. Type **1386** 60   45
4339   39c. Two hands (intergenerational solidarity) 75   60
4340   43c. Multicoloured fingers (cultural diversity) 80   65
4338/4340 Set of 3 .... 2·00   1·50

1387 Bicha of Balzote (6th century BC sculpture)

1388 Toledo Mountains

2008 (3 Mar). Archaeology. T **1387** and similar horiz design. Multicoloured. Photo. P 14.
4341   31c. Type **1387** 60   45
4342   31c. Apep I funerary vase ("Vaso cinerario Apofis I") 60   45

2008 (10 Mar). Nature. T **1388** and similar horiz design. Multicoloured. Photo. P 14.
4343   31c. Type **1388** 60   45
4344   31c. Hoces del Rio Duration park 60   45

1389 Helicopters and Boats

1390 University Building

2008 (12 Mar). Maritime Rescue. Die-cut perf 13½.
4345   **1389**   31c. multicoloured 60   45

2008 (14 Mar). 400th Anniv of Oviedo University. P 14.
4346   **1390**   31c. multicoloured 60   45

1391 Emblem

1392 Palacio de Longoria, Madrid (Josep Grases Riera)

2008 (19 Mar). 50th Anniv of European Parliament. P 14.
4347   **1391**   60c. multicoloured .... 1·10   85

2008 (2 Apr). Architecture. T **1392** and other designs. Recess (4348/9) or photo (others). P 14.
4348   31c. deep brown 60   45
4349   31c. reddish brown 60   45
4350   31c. multicoloured 60   45
4351   31c. multicoloured 60   45
4352   31c. multicoloured 60   45
4353   31c. multicoloured 60   45
4348/4353 Set of 6 .... 3·25   2·50
Designs: 4348 Type **1392**; 4349 Casa Vicens, Barcelona (Antoni Gaudí) (vert); 4350 Auditorio de Tenerife (Tenerife Auditorium) (Santiago Calatrava); 4351 Torre Agbar, Barcelona (Agbar Tower) (Jean Nouvel) (vert); 4352 Torrespana (television tower) (28×74 mm); 4353 Torre de Comunicaciones de Montjuic, Barcelona (Montjuic Comunications Tower) (Santiago Calatrava) (28×74 mm).

1393 Kestrel   **1394** Pelota Valencia

2008 (2 Apr). Flora and Fauna (11th issue). Self-adhesive gum. T **1393** and similar vert design. Multicoloured. Litho. Die-cut perf 13.
4354   31c. Type **1393** 60   45
4355   43c. Tulip 85   65

2008 (16 Apr). Traditional Sports. T **1394** and similar multicoloured design. P 14.
4356   43c. Type **1394** 85   65
4357   43c. Pelota Vasca (Basque) (vert) 85   65
Nos. 4356/7 were each printed with a *se-tenant* label at foot (4356) or at left (4357), the stamp and the label forming a composite design.

1395 Envelopes   **1396** Cross of Victory, Oviedo Cathedral

2008 (23 Apr). Europa. The Letter. Sheet 80×105 mm. P 14.
MS4358   **1395**   multicoloured .... 1·10   1·10

2008 (28 Apr). Exfilna 2008 Philatelic Exhibition. Sheet 80×105 mm. P 14.
MS4359   **1396**   multicoloured .... 4·75   4·75

1397 Arms from Maritime Post Royal Decree

1398 "El Progreso" and Tree (painting by Garcia Gesto)

2008 (5 May). Stamp Day. Self-adhesive gum. Die-cut perf 14
4360   **1397**   39c. light brown, blue and black 75   60

2008 (9 May). Centenary of *El Progreso* (newspaper). P 14.
4361   **1398**   31c. multicoloured 60   45

2008 (16–30 May). Traditional Sports. Vert designs as T **1394**. Multicoloured. P 14.
4362	43c. Levantamiento de Piedras (stone lifting)	85	65
4363	43c. Tira con Honda (sling shot) (30.5)	85	65
4364	43c. Lanzamiento de Barra (pitching the bar) (30.5)	85	65
4362/4364	Set of 3	2·25	1·75

Nos. 4362/4, respectively, were each issued with a *se-tenant* stamp size label attached at either right (4363) or left (others), each stamp and label forming a composite design of the sport played.

1399 Joan Oro   **1400** Goya Monument, Zaragoza

2008 (2 June). Personalities. T **1399** and similar designs. Recess. P 14.
4365	31c. black	55	45
4366	31c. black and orange-vermilion	55	45
4367	31c. black and orange-vermilion	55	45
4368	31c. black and orange-vermilion	55	45
4365/4368	Set of 4	2·00	1·50

Designs: 4365, Type **1399** (biochemist); 4366, Maria Lejárraga (Maria Martinez Sierra) (writer) (horiz); 4367, Carmen Martin Gaite (writer) (horiz); 4368, Zenobia Camprubi (writer and translator).

2008 (5 June). Traditional Sports. Skittles. Sheet 144×86 mm containing horiz designs as T **1394**. Multicoloured. P 14.
MS4369	43c.×3 Bolo Leones; Bolo Palma; Cuatreada Bolo Asturiano	2·50	2·50

No. **MS**4369 contains three stamp size labels which, with the respective stamp, form a composite design of the sport played.

2008 (13 June). Zaragoza 2008 International Water and Sustainable Development Exhibition (3rd issue). Sheet 105×80 mm. Recess. P 14.
MS4370	**1400**	deep blue-green	5·00	5·00

1401 European Bee-eater   **1402** Water Plaza

2008 (1 July). Flora and Fauna (12th issue). T **1401** and similar vert design. Multicoloured. Self-adhesive gum. Litho. Die-cut perf 13.
4371	31c. Type **1401**	60	45
4372	60c. Dahlia	1·10	80

2008 (4 July). Zaragoza 2008 International Water and Sustainable Development Exhibition (4th issue). Sheet 106×80 mm containing T **1402** and similar horiz designs. Multicoloured. Photo. P 14.
MS4373	31c. Type **1402**; 78c. Exhibition compound; €2.60 Pabellón-Puente	7·00	7·00

The stamps and margins of No. **MS**4373 form a composite design of the exhibition site.

1403 Long-jumper   **1404** Ball and Foot

2008 (8 July). Olympic Games, Beijing. P 14.
4374	**1403**	31c. multicoloured	60	45

2008 (16 July). Traditional Sports. Horiz design as T **1394**. Multicoloured. P 14.
4375	43c. Regatas de Traineras (rowing boat race)	85	65

No. 4375 was issued with a *se-tenant* stamp size label attached at left, each stamp and label forming a composite design of the sport.

2008 (16 July). Traditional Sports. Horiz design as T **1394**. Multicoloured. P 14.
MS4376	144×115 mm. 43c.×2, Palo Canario (stick fighting); Lucha Leonesa (wrestling)	3·00	2·75

No. **MS**4376 includes six stamp size labels which, with the stamps, form composite designs of the sport.

2008 (24 July). Spain–Euro 2008 Championship Winners. Sheet 106×79 mm. P 14.
MS4377	**1404**	multicoloured	1·90	1·90

1405 The Swing   **1406** Barbaria, Formentera

2008 (29 July). National Heritage. Tapestries. Two sheets containing T **1405** and similar vert design. Multicoloured. P 14.
MS4378	79×106 mm. 60c. Type **1405**	1·10	1·10
MS4379	106×79 mm. €2.60 The Blind Man and the Guitar	5·00	5·00

2008 (2 Sept). Lighthouses. T **1406** and similar vert designs. Multicoloured. P 14.
4380	60c. Type **1406**	1·10	1·10
	a. Sheetlet. Nos. 4380/5		
4381	60c. Irta, Castellón	1·10	1·10
4382	60c. Pechiguera, Lanzarote	1·10	1·10
4383	60c. Silleiro, Pontevedra	1·10	1·10
4384	60c. Torredembarra, Tarragona	1·10	1·10
4385	60c. Punta Orchilla, El Hierro	1·10	1·10
4380/4385	Set of 6	6·00	6·00

Nos. 4380/5 were issued in *se-tenant* sheetlets of six stamps.

1407 Self-Portrait (Antonio Maria Esquivel)   **1408** Emblem

2008 (8 Sept). Spanish Artists. T **1407** and similar vert design. Multicoloured. P 14.
4386	31c. Type **1407**	60	45
4387	43c. Self-Portrait (Darío de Regoyos)	85	65

2008 (19 Sept). Centenary of Royal Spanish Tennis Federation. Litho. P 14.
4388	**1408**	31c. carmine-vermilion and orange-yellow	60	45

1409 Jay   **1410** *Lepista nuda*

SPAIN

2008 (1 Oct). Flora and Fauna (13th issue). T **1409** and similar vert design. Multicoloured. Self-adhesive gum. Litho. Die-cut perf 13.
4389	31c. Type **1409**	60	45
4390	31c. Narcissi	60	45

2008 (9 Oct). Traditional Sports. Horiz design as T **1394**. Multicoloured. P 14.
4391	43c. Castillos humanos (human tower)	85	65

No. 4391 was issued with a *se-tenant* stamp size label attached at left, each stamp and label forming a composite design of the sport.

2008 (10 Oct). Fungi. T **1410** and similar horiz design. Multicoloured. P 14.
4392	31c. Type **1410**	60	45
4393	31c. *Boletus regius*	60	45

1411 Emblem   1412 Maqueda Castle, Toledo

2008 (13 Oct). America. Festivals. 12 October 1492 Festival (National Day). P 14.
4394	**1411** 78c. bright scarlet, chrome yellow and black	1·50	1·10

2008 (16 Oct). Castles. T **1412** and similar horiz designs. Recess. P 14.
4395	€2.60 brown-olive and deep magenta	5·00	3·75
4396	€2.60 black and deep violet	5·00	3·75

Designs: No. 4395, Type **1412**; No. 4396, La Calahorra Castle, Granada.

1413 Evening Dress   1414 Belén del Príncipe (18th–century crib)

2008 (23 Oct). Fashion. Pedro Rodriguez (designer). T **1413** and similar vert designs. Multicoloured. Photo and embossed. P 14.
4397	31c. Type **1413**	60	60
	a. Pair. Nos. 4397/8	1·40	
	b. Sheetlet. Nos. 4397/400	2·50	
4398	31c. Strapless embroidered evening gown	60	60
4399	31c. Multicoloured halter-neck dress	60	60
	a. Pair. Nos. 4399/400	1·40	
4400	31c. Pink evening coat	60	60
4397/4400	Set of 4	2·25	2·25

Nos. 4397/8 and 4399/400 were issued in horizontal *se-tenant* pairs within sheetlet of four stamps with enlarged illustrated margins and gutter.

2008 (27 Oct). Traditional Sports. Horiz design as T **1394**. Multicoloured. P 14.
MS4401 106×115 mm. 43c.×3, Chito (throwing at wooden cylinder); Chave (throwing at post); La calva (throwing at curved piece of wood (morillo)) .... 2·50   2·50

No. **MS**4401 includes three stamp size labels which, with the stamps, form composite designs of the sport.

2008 (3 Nov). Christmas. T **1414** and similar multicoloured design. Self-adhesive gum. Litho. Die-cut perf 13.
4402	31c. Type **1414**	60	45
4403	60c. *Maternidad* (painting, Jiménez Carrero) (vert)	1·10	85

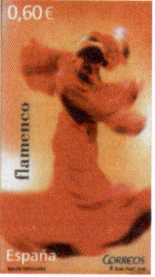 

1415 Flamenco Dancer   1416 *Elocuencia* (eloquence) (stained glass window)

(Des Estudio Jesús Sánchez (60c.) or Conor Walton (78c.). Photo)
2008 (7 Nov). Traditional Dances. Sheet 120×76 mm containing T **1415** and similar vert design. Multicoloured. P 13½.
MS4404 60c. Type **1415**; 78c. Irish dancer .... 2·75   2·75

Stamps of a similar design were issued by Ireland.

2008 (14 Nov). Real Academia Española (Royal Spanish Academy). Sheet 106×80 mm. Recess and litho. P 13.
MS4405 **1416** multicoloured .... 3·75   5·00

1417 National Flag   1418 Fan and Manila Shawl

2008 (14 Nov). Autonomous Communities within Spain. Self-adhesive Booklet Stamps.T **1417** and similar horiz designs showing the community's flag and area outline. Multicoloured. Litho. P 13½.
4406	A Type **1417**	65	50
4407	A Asturias	65	50
4408	A Galicia	65	50
4409	A Cantabria	65	50
4410	A National arms	65	50
4411	A Cataluña	65	50
4412	A Basque Country	65	50
4413	A Andalucia	65	50
4406/4413	Set of 8	4·75	3·75

Nos. 4402/13 were for use on mail within Spain up to 20g. and were issued in booklets of eight stamps.

2009 (2 Jan). Cultural Heritage. Self-adhesive. Litho. Die-cut perf 13½.
4414	**1418** B multicoloured	1·20	90

No. 4414 was for use on mail within Europe up to 20g.

1419 Leaf   1420 Emblems

2009 (12 Jan). Science. T **1419** and similar horiz design. Multicoloured. Self-adhesive. Litho. Die-cut perf 13½.
4415	39c. Type **1419** (Botany)	75	60
4416	€2.60 DNA strand (Genetics)	85	65

2009 (15 Jan). 120th Anniv of *La Rioja* (newspaper). Photo. P 14.
4417	**1420** 32c. multicoloured	65	50

1421 Great Tit   1422 Oceanus, Materno-Villa, Calanque

SPAIN

2009 (20 Jan). Flora and Fauna (14th issue). T **1421** and similar vert design. Multicoloured. Self-adhesive. Litho. Die-cut perf 13½.
4418	32c. Type **1421**	65	50
4419	62c. Hydrangea	1·20	90

2009 (10 Feb). Archaeology. Mosaics, Casa sel Mitreo. T **1422** and similar horiz design. Multicoloured. Photo. P 14.
4420	€2.70 Type **1422**	5·25	4·00
4421	€2.70 Oriens, Casa del Mitreo, Merida	5·25	4·00

1423 'Plantemos para el Planeta' (plant for the planet)

1424 Dam (hydro electricity)

(Des. J. Sánchez. Litho)

2009 (17 Feb). Civic Values. T **1423** and similar horiz designs. Multicoloured. P 14.
4422	32c. Type **1423**	65	50
4423	62c. Key board (reconciliation of work and family life)	1·20	90
4424	78c. "DESCO2ECTA" (climate change awareness campaign)	1·50	1·10
4422/4424 Set of 3		3·00	2·25

2009 (20 Feb). Renewable Energy. T **1424** and similar vert designs. Multicoloured. Photo. P 13×13½.
4425	32c. Type **1424**	65	50
4426	62c. Wind turbines	85	65
4427	62c. Solar energy	1·20	90
4428	78c. Geothermal energy	1·50	1·10
4425/4428 Set of 4		3·75	3·00

1425 Globe enclosing Face

1426 Izki Nature Park, Alava

2009 (2 Mar). Millenium Development Goals. P 13×13½.
4429	**1425**	32c. multicoloured	65	50

2009 (9 Mar). Nature. T **1426** and similar horiz designs. Multicoloured.
4430	43c. Type **1426**	85	65
4431	43c. Canon del Río Lobos Nature Park, Segovia	85	65

1427 Gladioli

1428 Emblem

2009 (1 Apr). Flora and Fauna (15th issue). T **1427** and similar vert design. Multicoloured. Self-adhesive. Litho. Die-cut perf 13½.
4432	32c. Type **1427**	65	50
4433	43c. Capercaillie	85	65

2009 (6 Apr). 60th Anniv of Council of Europe. P 14.
4434	**1428**	62c. multicoloured	1·20	90

1429 Porto Colom, Mallorca

1430 Globe and Space

2009 (15 Apr). Lighthouses. T **1429** and similar vert designs. Multicoloured. P 14.
4435	62c. Type **1429**	1·20	90
	a. Sheetlet. Nos. 4435/40		
4436	62c. La Higuera, Huelva	1·20	90
4437	62c. Igueldo, Guipuzcoa	1·20	90
4438	62c. Arinaga, Gran Canaria	1·20	90
4439	62c. Torre del Hercules, La Coruña	1·20	90
4440	62c. Torrox, Málaga	1·20	90
4435/4440 Set of 6		6·50	5·00

Nos. 4435/40 were issued in *se-tenant* sheetlets of six stamps.

2009 (23 Apr). Europa. Astronomy. Litho. P 14.
4441	**1430**	62c. multicoloured	1·20	90

1431 La Isa

1432 King Alfonso VI of León and Castilla (Alfonso the Brave)

2009 (27 Apr). Popular Dances (1st series). T **1431** and similar multicoloured design. P 13 (horiz) or 14 (vert).
4442	43c. Type **1431**	85	65
MS4443 106×79 mm. 43c. Las Sevillanas (vert)		1·50	1·30

See also Nos. 4446/7, 4449/50, 4460/1, 4467/8 and 4476/MS4477.

2009 (7 May). 900th Death Anniversaries. T **1432** and similar vert design. Multicoloured. P 14.
4444	39c. Type **1432**	75	60
4445	62c. Domingo García (Santo Domingo de La Calzada) (bishop of Ostia)	1·20	90

2009 (14 May). Popular Dances (2nd series). Horiz designs as T **1431**. Multicoloured. P 13.
4446	43c. La Mateixa	85	65
4447	43c. El Bolero	85	65

No. 4447 was issued with a stamp size label, which with the stamp, forms a composite design of a dancer.

1433 Paper Making (stained glass window)

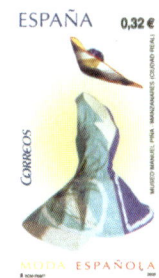
1434 Sleeveless Top and Hat

2009 (29 May). Spanish National Mint (main stairway, Paper Factory). Sheet 80×106 mm. Recess and litho. P 13.
MS4448	**1433**	multicoloured	5·00	5·00

357

SPAIN

2009 (4 June). Popular Dances (3rd series). Multicoloured designs as T **1431**. P 13.
4449	43c. La Rueda (74×28 mm)	85	65
4450	43c. El Aurresku (28×74 mm)	85	65

2009 (15 June). Fashion. Manuel Piña (designer). Sheet 106×150 mm containing T **1434** and similar vert designs. Multicoloured. Photo and embossed. P 13½×13.
MS4451 32c.×4, Type **1434**; Dress and jacket; Multicoloured evening gown; White evening gown   2·50   2·50
The design of the lower right stamp forms part of the margin.

1435 *Graellsia isabelae*   **1436** *El Juego de la pelota a pala* (after Francisco de Goya)

2009 (1 July). Flora and Fauna (16th issue). T **1435** and similar vert design. Multicoloured. Self-adhesive. Litho. Die-cut perf 13½.
4452	32c. Type **1435**	65	50
4453	62c. Geranium	1·20	90

2009 (6 July). National Heritage. Tapestries. Sheet 144×115 mm containing T **1436** and similar horiz design. Multicoloured. Photo with gold- die-stamp. P 14.
MS4454 78c. Type **1436**; €2.70 *Juego de bolos* (after Antonio González Velázquez)   6·50   6·50

1437 Euro Coin   **1438** Wine Bottle and Crashed Car

2009 (10 July). Tenth Anniv of Euro. Sheet 115×105 mm. Recess and litho. P 14.
MS4455 **1437** multicoloured   1·90   1·90

2009 (14 July). Road Safety Campaign. Perils of Drink Driving. P 13×13½.
4456	**1438**	32c. light bright carmine, black and grey	65	17·00

1439 Charles Darwin (naturalist and evolutionary theorist)   **1440** Bi-plane (designed by Gaspar Brunet)

2009 (15 July). Birth Bicentenaries. T **1439** and similar vert designs. Recess and litho (4459) or recess (others). P 14.
4457	32c. black and reddish lilac	60	35
4458	32c. black and carmine-vermilion	60	35
4459	32c. black and carmine	60	35
4457/4459 Set of 3		1·50	90

Designs: Type **1439**; Claudio Moyano Samaniego (politician); Louis Braille (inventor of Braille writing for the blind).
No. 4459 has raised Braille letters on the surface of the stamp.

2009 (22 July). Popular Dances (4th series). Multicoloured designs as T **1431**. P 13.
4460	43c. La Muneira (33×50 mm)	85	65
4461	43c. El Fandango (33×50 mm)	85	65

Nos. 4460/1 each have a stamp size label attached at right, which with the stamp, creates a composite design.

2009 (5 Sept). Centenary of First Spanish Powered Flight by Juan Olivert Serra. P 14.
| 4462 | **1440** | 32c. multicoloured | 65 | 50 |

1441 Footballer and Emblem   **1442** Puente de los Tilos (built by Santiago Pérez-Fadón Martinez and José Emilio Herrero Beneítez), La Palma

2009 (7 Sept). Centenary of Real Sociedad de Futbol. P 14.
| 4463 | **1441** | 32c. multicoloured | 65 | 50 |

2009 (9 Sept). Architecture. T **1442** and similar horiz design. Multicoloured. P 14.
4464	32c. Type **1442**	65	50
4465	32c. Canal de Castilla, Valldolid	65	50

2009 (9 Sept). Architecture. T **1442** and similar horiz design. Multicoloured. P 14.
MS4466 150×105 mm. 32c.×4, Torre de Cristal (César Pelli); Torre Espacio (Pei, Cobb Freed & Partners); Torre Sacyr Vallehermoso (Carlos Rubio Carvajal and Enrique Alvarez-Sala Walter); Torre Torre Caja Madrid (Norman Foster)   2·50   2·50

2009 (14 Sept). Popular Dances (5th series). Multicoloured designs as T **1431**. P 13.
4467	43c. El Candil (33×50 mm)	85	65
4468	43c. Las Seguidillas (33×50 mm)	85	65

Nos. 4467/8 each have a stamp size label attached at right, which with the stamp, creates a composite design.

1443 Javier Castle, Navarra   **1444** *Hyphoraia dejeani*

2009 (21 Sept). Castles. T **1443** and similar horiz design. Recess. P 14.
4469	€2.70 black	5·00	3·75
4470	€2.70 black and orange-brown	5·00	3·75

Designs: No. 4469, Type **1443**; No. 4470, Arevalo Castle, Avila.

2009 (1 Oct). Flora and Fauna (17th issue). T **1444** and similar multicoloured design. Self-adhesive. Litho. Die-cut perf 13½.
4471	32c. Type **1444**	65	65
4472	32c. Pansy (vert)	65	65

1445 *Lisle de la Conference* (engraving by Adam Perelle) (showing Isla de los Faisanes, Bidosa river (neutral territory used in Royal marriages negotiations))   **1446** Spanish Baraja Cards

2009 (6 Oct). EXFILNA 2009, the National Philatelic Exhibition, Irun. Sheet 106×80 mm. P 14.
MS4473 **1445** multicoloured   4·75   4·75

2009 (8 Oct). America. Games. P 14.
4474 **1446** 78c. multicoloured .... 1·50 1·50

1447 Player and Emblem

1448 *Cantharellus cibarius*

(Des F. Paniagua. Recess and Litho)

2009 (14 Oct). Centenary of Royal Spanish Football Federation. P 14.
4475 **1447** 32c. multicoloured 65 65

2009 (15 Oct). Popular Dances (6th series). Multicoloured designs as T **1431**. P 13.
4476   43c. La Sardana 85 85
MS4477 106×80 mm. 43c. La Jota (29×41 mm) 85 85
No. 4476 has a stamp size label attached at left, which with the stamp, creates a composite design.

2009 (16 Oct). Fungi. T **1448** and similar horiz design. Multicoloured. P 14.
4478   32c. Type **1448** 65 65
4479   32c. *Boletus pinophilus* 65 65

1449 *Las Meninas (The Royal Family of Felipe IV)*

2009 (22 Oct). Diego Rodríguez de Silva y Velázquez (artist) Commemoration. Sheet 106×151 mm containing T **1449** and similar horiz design. Multicoloured. P 14.
MS4480 62c. Type **1449**; 78c. *The Infanta Margarita Teresa in a Blue Dress* .... 2·75 2·75
Stamps of the same design were issued by Austria.

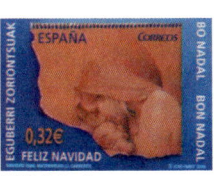
1450 Maternity

1451 Cartoon Airplane over Plaza de Requejo, Mieres

2009 (31 Oct). Christmas. T **1450** and similar multicoloured designs showing paintings by J. Carrero.
(a) *Self-adhesive. Die-cut perf 13½*
4481   32c. Type **1450** 65 65
4482   62c. *The Arrival of the Magi* .... 1·20 1·20
(b) *Miniature sheet. Ordinary gum. P 14*
MS4483 115×105 mm. €2.47×2, The Nativity (detail); Adoration (detail, different) (old wood carving from the Italian school and a painting by J. Carrero) .... 9·50 9·50

2009 (6 Nov). Juvenia 2009–Youth Stamp Exhibition, Mieres. Litho. P 14.
4484 **1451** 39c. multicoloured 75 75

1452 *Mujer con Manton de Manila* (J. Carrero)

1453 Congress Building

2010 (2 Jan). Tourism. Self-adhesive. Litho. Die-cut perf 13½.
4485 **1452** B multicoloured ....

2010 (2 Jan). Autonomous Communities. Booklet stamps. T **1453** and similar horiz designs. Multicoloured. Self-adhesive. Litho. Die-cut perf 13½.
4486   A Type **1453** .... 65 0·50
4487   A La Rioja, map and flag .... 65 0·50
4488   A Castilla la Mancha, map and flag .... 65 0·50
4489   A Valencia, map and flag .... 65 0·50
4490   A Senate building .... 65 0·50
4491   A Canary Islands, map and flag .... 65 0·50
4492   A Murcia, map and flag .... 65 0·50
4493   A Aragon, map and flag .... 65 0·50
4486/4493 Set of 8 .... 4·75 3·75
Nos. 4486/93 were issued in booklets of eight stamps.

1454 *Artimelia latreillei*

1455 Hand holding Paper (recycling)

2010 (20 Jan). Fauna. Moths. T **1454** and similar horiz design. Multicoloured. Self-adhesive. Litho. Die-cut perf 13½.
4494   34c. Type **1454** 65 65
4495   64c. *Zygaena rhadamanthus* .... 1·20 1·20

2010 (11 Feb). Civic Values. T **1455** and similar horiz design. Multicoloured. Litho. P 14.
4496   €1 Type **1455** .... 2·75 2·75
4497   €2 Locked jar (responsible consumerism) .. 5·75 5·75

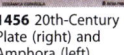
1456 20th-Century Plate (right) and Amphora (left)

1457 "Presidencia de la Unión Europea"

2010 (18 Feb). Spanish Ceramics. T **1456** and similar vert designs. Multicoloured. Litho. P 13½×14.
4498   34c. Type **1456** 65 65
         a. Horiz strip of 4. Nos. 4498/501 .... 2·50
4499   34c. Amphora (right) and 18th-century inkwell (left) 65 65
4500   34c. Inkwell (right) and 18th-century Pitcher (left) 65 65
4501   34c. Pitcher (right) and plate (left) 65 65
4498/4501 Set of 4 .... 2·25 2·25
Nos. 4498/501 were printed, *se-tenant*, in horizontal strips of four stamps within the sheet, each strip forming a composite design.

2010 (22 Feb). Spain's Presidency of European Union. Self-adhesive. Litho. Die-cut perf 13½.
4502 **1457** 34c. multicoloured 65 65
4503   64c. multicoloured .... 1·20 1·20

SPAIN

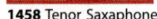
1458 Tenor Saxophone

1459 Hand Print on Page

2010 (24 Feb). Musical Instruments. Self-adhesive. Litho. Die-cut perf 13½.
4504   **1458**   45c. multicoloured 80   80

2010 (1 Mar). Bicentenary of Constituent Assembly. Litho. P 14.
4505   **1459**   34c. multicoloured 65   65

1460 Old Chapter House (Sala Capitular), Plasencia Cathedral

1461 Trophy and Poster for *Celda 211*

2010 (4 Mar). Cathedrals. Sheet 80×106 mm. Litho. P 14.
MS4506   **1460**   chocolate and light blue .... 4·75   4·75

2010 (9 Mar). Spanish Cinema. *Agora* (film)–winner of Premios Goya awarded by Academy of Arts and Cinematographic Sciences of Spain. Litho. P 14×13½.
4507   **1461**   34c. multicoloured 65   65

1462 *Euphydryas aurinia*

1463 Trophy and Film Poster

2010 (1 Apr). Fauna. Butterflies. T **1462** and similar horiz design. Multicoloured. Self-adhesive. Litho. Die-cut perf 13½.
4508   34c. Type **1462** 65   65
4509   64c. *Zerynthia rumina* .... 1·20   1·20

2010 (5 Apr). Spanish Cinema. *Agora* (film)–winner of seven Premios Goyas awarded by Academy of Arts and Cinematographic Sciences of Spain. Litho. P 14×13½.
4510   **1463**   34c. multicoloured 65   65

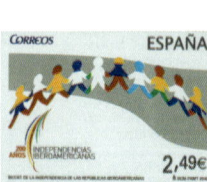
1464 Stylized figures

1465 Trumpet

2010 (7 Apr). Bicentenary of Independence of Latin American Republics. Photo. P 14×13½.
4511   **1464**   €2.49 multicoloured .... 4·50   4·50

2010 (9 Apr). Musical Instruments. Self-adhesive. Litho. Die-cut perf 13½.
4512   **1465**   34c. multicoloured 65   65

1466 Casa de las Torres, Ubeda

2010 (15 Apr). World Heritage. Ubeda and Baeza. T **1466** and similar horiz design. Multicoloured. Litho. P 13.
4513   45c. Type **1466** 80   80
4514   45c. Jabalquinto Palace, Baeza 80   80

1467 Carlos María de Castro and Map of Expansion of Madrid

1468 Anniversary Emblem

2010 (20 Apr). Town Planning. Carlos María de Castro (engineer, architect and town planner) Commemoration. Litho. P 14×13½.
4515   **1467**   34c. multicoloured 65   65

2010 (21 Apr). Centenary of Gran Via, Madrid. Litho. P 13½×14.
4516   **1468**   34c. new blue and yellow........................ 65   65

1469 Stylized Spain and Madrid Pavillions

1470 Club and Anniversary Emblems

2010 (21 Apr). Expo 2010, Shanghai. Sheet 106×80 mm. P 14×13½.
MS4517   **1469**   multicoloured .... 4·50   4·50

2010 (23 Apr). Centenary of Levante U D Football Club. P 14×13½.
4518   **1470**   34c. multicoloured 65   65

1471 Newspapers

1472 Infant with Book

2010 (30 Apr). Centenary of *El Correo* (newspaper). P 13½×14.
4519   **1471**   34c. multicoloured 65   65

(Des J. Carrero)
2010 (6 May). Europa. Children's Books. P 14×13½.
4520   **1472**   64c. multicoloured .... 1·10   1·10

1473 Early Banner of León with Lion Passant (½-size illustration)

SPAIN

(Litho and embossed)

2010 (6 May). 1100th Anniv of Kingdom of Leon. Sheet 120×76 mm. P 13 (with elliptical hole on each horiz side and rouletted at each point).

| MS4521 | 1473 | scarlet and gold | 4·50 | 4·50 |

The stamp of No. **MS**4521 is cut around in the shape of a banner with the points outlined by rouletting.
The top right margin of No. **MS**4521 contains a perforated outline of a lion passant.

1474 Pilgrim and Cathedral of Santiago de Compostela

1475 Sierra de Cazorla, Segura y Las Villas Natural Park

2010 (13 May). Compostelian Jubilee Year (Ano Santo Xacobeo in Galician) (when St James's Day (July 25) falls on a Sunday). Self-adhesive. Litho. Die-cut perf 13.

| 4522 | **1474** | 34c. multicoloured | 65 | 65 |

2010 (20 May). Nature Reserves. T **1475** and similar horiz designs. Multicoloured. P 13½×14.

4523	45c. Type **1475**	1·10	1·10
4524	45c. Garajonay National Park	1·10	1·10
4525	45c. Doñana National Park	1·10	1·10
4523/4525	Set of 3	3·00	3·00

1476 Athlete (Ibero-American Athletics Championship, San Fernando, Cádiz)

1477 Gregorio Marañón and Microscope

2010 (4 June). Sporting Events in 2010. T **1476** and similar vert designs. Multicoloured. P 13½×14.

4526	34c. Type **1476**	65	65
4527	64c. Barni (official mascot) (European Athletics Championships, Barcelona)	1·10	1·10
4528	78c. Championship emblem (World Cup Football Championships, South Africa)	1·25	1·25
4526/4528	Set of 3	2·75	2·75

2010 (11 June). Personalities. T **1477** and similar design. P 14×13½.

| 4529 | 34c. black, deep ultramarine and dull orange | 65 | 65 |
| 4530 | 34c. dull violet and dull orange (vert) | 65 | 65 |

Designs: 4529 Type **1477** (doctor and writer) (50th death anniv); 4530 Julián Gabino Arcas Lacal (Julián Arcas) (guitarist) Commemoration.

1478 '25' and European 'Stars'

1479 Oscar Niemeyer International Cultural Centre, Asturias

2010 (12 June). 25th Anniv of Spain and Portugal's Accession to European Economic Community (EEC). Self-adhesive. Litho. Die-cut perf 13½.

| 4531 | **1478** | 34c. multicoloured | 65 | 65 |

2010 (19 June). FILATEM 2010 Thematic Philatelic Exhibition, Avilés. Sheet 80×106 mm. Litho. P 14×13½.

| MS4532 | **1479** | €2.49 multicoloured | 4·50 | 4·50 |

1480 Horn

1481 José Luis López Vázquez

2010 (1 July). Musical Instruments. Self-adhesive. Litho. Die-cut perf 13½.

| 4533 | **1480** | 64c. multicoloured | 1·10 | 1·10 |

(Des Estudio Jesús Sánchez. Litho)

2010 (6 July). Spanish Cinema. José Luis López Vázquez de la Torre (actor and director) Commemoration. P 13½×14.

| 4534 | **1481** | 45c. multicoloured | 80 | 80 |

1482 Julia Aurelia (Septimia Zenobia) captured by Emperor Aurelian

1483 Cathedral Façade

2010 (12 July). Cultural Heritage. Zenobia and Aurelian (17th-century tapestry). Sheet 115×144 mm. P 13½×14.

| MS4535 | **1482** | 78c. multicoloured | 1·25 | 1·25 |

(Recess and litho)

2010 (15 July). Cathedrals. Segovia Cathedral. Sheet 106×80 mm. P 14.

| MS4536 | **1483** | reddish brown and deep turquoise-blue | 5·00 | 5·00 |

1484 Cantabrian Brown Bear, Picos de Europa National Park

2010 (19 July). Nature Reserves. T **1484** and similar horiz designs. Multicoloured. P 13½×14.

4537	45c. Type **1484**	65	65
4538	45c. Egyptian vulture, Monfragüe National Park	65	65
4539	45c. Ibex, Sierra Nevada National Park	65	65
4537/4539	Set of 3	1·80	1·80

361

SPAIN

MACHINE LABELS

A

FRAMA LABELS. From 15 September 1989 labels, in design A, printed in red on paper with a yellow underprint, were available from automatic machines in Madrid and from April 1990, Barcelona. Values from 1 to 99p., in 1p. steps, could be obtained.

From 1992 automatic machines of various makes were installed. The different designs are grouped according to type of machine. The value in all cases was applied in black.

KLUSSENDORF

All Klussendorf labels are multicoloured and were printed in typography by Enschedé. Every fifth label is numbered on the bakc.

B 1

1992. As Type B **1**. Values available from 1p. to 999p. in 1p. steps.
    (20 Apr). Expo '92 World's Fair, Seville (Type B **1**)
    (24 Apr). Granada '92 International Thematic Stamp Exhibition
    (28 July). Olympic Games, Barcelona
    (25 Nov). Madrid, European City of Culture

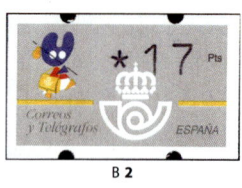

B 2

1993 (16 July). St. Jame's Holy Year. Type B **2**. Values available 13p. and 17p. to 9999p. in 1p. steps.

EPELSA

All Epelsa labels are self-adhesive. Values from 1 to 9999p. in 1p. steps, were available.

1992 (16 June). Similar design to Type B **1** but with "CORREOS ESPANA" at top and no commemorative inscription. Printed in typography by Eduardo Albeniz (Pamplona), Ovelar (Madrid) or the Govt Printing Works. Multicoloured.

C 1

(Type Ovelar, Madrid)

1993. Design as Type C **1**. Values from 1 to 9999p. in 1p. steps.
Fixed values: (8 July) 13, 17p. (Type C **1**)

C 2

1994. Design as Type C **2**. Values from 1 to 9999p. in 1p. steps.
Fixed values: (26 Sept) 13, 18p. (Type C **2**)

1995. Design as Type C **2**. Values from 1 to 9999p. in 1p. steps.
Fixed values: (Feb) 15, 21p. (Hand writing letter)

C 3

1996. Designs as Type C **3**. Litho. Values from 1 to 9999p. in 1p. steps.
Fixed values: (Jan) (Satellite and Globe (wavy edge))
    (May) 19, 30, 60p. (Type C **3**)
    (July) 19, 30, 60p. (Satellite and Globe (straight edge))
    (Oct) 19, 30, 60p. (Cervantes)

C 4

1997. Designs as Type C **4**. Litho. Values from 1 to 9999p. in 1p. steps.
Fixed values: (May) 21, 32, 65p. (Type C **4**)
    (Nov) 21, 32, 65p. (Paint palette)
    (Dec) 21, 32, 65p. (Musical instruments)

D 1

1998. Designs as Type D **1**. Litho. Values 1p. to 999999p. in 1p. steps.
Fixed values: (Apr) 23, 35, 70p. (Type D **1**)
    (July) 23, 35, 70p. (Felix Rodriguez de la Fuente)
    (July) 23, 35, 70p. (CALPE)
    (July) 23, 35, 70p. (Ibn Al-Abbar)
    (July) 23, 35, 70p. (Cartoon character)
    (Oct) 23, 35, 70p. (Federico Garcia Lorca)
    (Nov) 23, 35, 70p. ("Expo '98")
    (Nov) 23, 35, 70p. (Felipe II)
    (Dec) 23, 35, 70p. (Christmas)

D 2

1999. Designs as Type D **2**. Litho. Values 1p. to 999999p. in 1p. steps.
Fixed values:
  (Jan) 25, 35, 70p. (Type D **2**)
  (Feb) 25, 35, 70p. (Road Safety Awareness)
  (Mar) 25, 35, 70p. (Post Emblem)
  (Apr) 25, 35, 70p. (St. Maria de Puerto Santona)
  (May) 25, 35, 70p. (Centenary of Barcelona Real Tennis Club)
  (June) 25, 35, 70p. (Statue of Virgin of Carmen)
  (July) 25, 35, 70p. (Statue, Madonna of Seville)
  (July) 25, 35, 70p. (Tourism, building and horse)
  (Oct) 25, 35, 70p. (Espana 2000 Stamp Exhibition)
  (Nov) 25, 35, 70p. (Statue of Virgin of Bethlehem)

D **3**

2000. Designs as Type D **3**. Litho. Values 1p. to 999999p. in 1p. steps.
Fixed values:
  (Jan) 25, 35, 70p. (Type D **3**)
  (Feb) 25, 35, 70p. (Congress Emblem, Centenary of Social Insurance)
  (Mar) 25, 35, 70p. (Emblem)
  (Apr) 25, 35, 70p. (Sailing Regatta)
  (May) 25, 35, 70p. (Carnival)
  (June) 25, 35, 70p. ("Expo 2000", Hanover)
  (June) 25, 35, 70p. (Virgin of Castroverde)
  (July) 25, 35, 70p. (Virgin of Los Dolores)
  (Sept) 25, 35, 70p. ("HISPASAT 1C" satellite)
  (Oct) 25, 35, 70p. (Santo Toribio de Liebana)
  (Oct) 25, 35, 70p. ("Terra Mitica")
  (Nov) 25, 35, 70p. (European Convention on Human Rights)

D **4**

2001. Designs as Type D **4**. Litho. Values 1p. to 999999p. in 1p. steps.
Fixed values:
  (Feb) 30, 40, 75p. (Type D **4**)
  (Mar) 30, 40, 75p. (Locomotive 141, 1918)
  (Mar) 30, 40, 75p. (Museum Façade)
  (Apr) 30, 40, 75p. (Locomotive 030-2103, 1861)
  (Apr) 30, 40, 75p. (Locomotive 030 2577, 1882)
  (June) 30, 40, 75p. (Tourism, International Museum Congress (ICOM))
  (July) 30, 40, 75p. (Alejandro Mon)
  (July) 30, 40, 75p. (Ford Model T)
  (Aug) 30, 40, 75p. (Hispano Suiza)
  (Sept) 30, 40, 75p. (Peugeot Bebe)
  (Oct) 30, 40, 75p. (Rolls Royce)
  (Oct) 30, 40, 75p. (Hispano Suiza)
  (Nov) 30, 40, 75p. (Humber T)
  (Dec) 20, 25, 50p. (Monet Goyon)

D **5**

2001. Designs as Type D **5**. Litho. Face values in euros. Values 1c. to 9999c.
Fixed values: (Dec) 20, 25, 50c. (Type D **5**)

D **6**

2002. Designs as Type D **6**. Litho. Face values in euros. Values 1c. to 9999c.
Fixed values:
  (Jan) 20, 25, 50c. (Type D **6**)
  (Jan) 20, 35, 70c. (Congress emblem)
  (Feb) 20, 25, 50c. (Motorbike and sidecar)
  (Feb) 20, 25, 50c. (New Hudson)
  (Mar) 20, 25, 50c. (Nimbus)
  (Mar) 20, 25, 50c. (Santa Eulalia)
  (Apr) 20, 25, 50c. (*Isabel* (ship))
  (Apr) 20, 25, 50c. (Postal emblem)
  (June) 20, 25, 50c. (Miguel M. Pinillos)
  (June) 20, 25, 50c. (Tourism)
  (June) 20, 25, 50c. (*Jabeque* (ship))
  (July) 20, 25, 50c. (Postal Architecture, Cadiz)
  (July) 20, 25, 50c. (Postal Architecture, Zaragoza)
  (July) 20, 25, 50c. (Postal Architecture, Logrono)
  (Sept) 20, 25, 50c. (Postal Architecture, Osorno)
  (Sept) 20, 25, 50c. (Postal Architecture, Coruna)
  (Oct) 20, 25, 50c. (Postal Architecture, Ferrol)
  (Oct) 20, 25, 50c. (Postal Architecture, San Sebastián)
  (Nov) 20, 25, 50c. (Postal Architecture, Madrid)
  (Nov) 20, 25, 50c. (Salamanca 2002, European City of Culture)
  (Dec) 20, 25, 50c. ("pinta el teu segell")

D **7**

2003. Designs as Type D **7**. Litho. Face values in euros. Values 1c. to €99.99.
Fixed values:
  (Jan) 26, 51, 76c. (Type D **7**)
  (Feb) 26, 51, 76c. (Sanglas 350/1 motorcycle)
  (June) 26, 51, 76c. (Soriano Puma motorcycle and sidecar)
  (5 June) 26, 51, 76c. (Amilcar, 1927)
 (17 June) 26, 51, 76c. (Summer (painting), Sammer Gallery)
 (17 June) 26, 51, 76c. (Still-life with Tulips (painting), Sammer Gallery)
 (26 June) 26, 51, 76c. (Horse-drawn carriage, 1850)
  (9 July) 26, 51, 76c. (Autumn (painting) Sammer Gallery)
 (25 July) 26, 51, 76c. (Hispano Suiza 20-30 HP, 1910)
 (12 Sept) 26, 51, 76c. (Still-life with Fruit (painting), Sammer Gallery)
 (16 Sept) 26, 51, 76c. (Sill-life (painting), Sammer Gallery)
 (25 Sept) 26, 51, 76c. (DKW with side-car, 1938)
  (Nov) 26, 51, 76c. (Spider horse-drawn carriage, 1705)
  (5 Nov) 26, 51, 76c. (Still-life with Glass Bottles (painting), Sammer Gallery)
 (21 Nov) 26, 51, 76c. (Berliet, 1926)
  (5 Dec) 26, 51, 76c. (Still-life Autumn (painting), Sammer Gallery)
 (15 Dec) 26, 51, 76c. (Donosti car, 1928)
  (Dec) 26, 51, 76c. (Sill-life with Oranges (painting), Sammer Gallery)

D **8**

SPAIN

2004. Designs as Type D **8**. Litho. Face values in euros. Values 1c. to €99.99.
Fixed values:
- (2 Mar) 27, 52, 77c. (Type D **8**)
- (22 Mar) 27, 52, 77c. (Locomotive and tender, 1900-1901)
- (4 Apr) 27, 52, 77c. (Symbol for European Victims of Terrorism)
- (16 Apr) 27, 52, 77c. (Still-life with Fruit and Bottle (painting), Sammer Gallery)
- (20 May) 27, 52, 77c. (Red Still-life (painting), Sammer Gallery)
- (22 May) 27, 52, 77c. (Espana 2004)
- (15 Dec) 27, 52, 77c. (Still-life with Pumpkin (painting), Sammer Gallery)
- (15 Dec) 27, 52, 77c. (Rolls Royce, 1947)
- (25 Nov) 27, 52, 77c. (Pegaso Z-102 SS Spyder, 1955)
- (29 Nov) 27, 52, 77c. (Letter from my Land (painting), Sammer Gallery)

D **9**

2005. Designs as Type D **9**. Litho. Face values in euros. Values 1c. to €99.99.
Fixed values:
- (13 Jan) 28, 53, 78c. (Type D **9**)
- (Feb) 27, 52, 77c. (Postcard (painting), Sammer Gallery)
- (18 Mar) 28, 53, 78c. (Milford horse-drawn carriage, 1900)
- (21 Apr) 28, 53, 78c. (Locomotive, 1887)
- (17 May) 28, 53, 78c. (Africans (painting), Sammer Gallery)
- (17 May) 28, 53, 78c. (Fruits and Sunflowers (paintings), Sammer Gallery)
- (17 May) 28, 53, 78c. (Guitar and Fruits (painting), Sammer Gallery)
- (1 June) 28, 53, 78c. (I Have to Paint It (painting), Sammer Gallery)
- (28 June) 28, 53, 78c. (The Afternoon Grows Endless (painting), Sammer Gallery)
- (28 June) 28, 53, 78c. (Whale Stone (painting), Sammer Gallery)
- (21 July) 28, 53, 78c. (Wildflowers (painting), Sammer Gallery)
- (21 July) 28, 53, 78c. (Morning in the Garden (painting), Sammer Gallery)
- (7 Oct) 28, 53, 78c. (Untitled (painting), Sammer Gallery)
- (7 Oct) 28, 53, 78c. (Adelaide Fantasy (painting), Sammer Gallery)
- (18 Nov) 28, 53, 78c. (Locomotive, series 1000)

D **10**

2006. Designs as Type D **10**. Litho. Face values in euros. Values 1c. to €99.99.
Fixed values:
- (25 Jan) 28, 53, 78c. (Type D **10**)
- (3 Mar) 28, 53, 78c. (painting, "The chocolates and Love at First Sight" by Igor Fomin)
- (11 Dec) 29, 57, 78c. (Fingerprint, 2006 Year of Historical Memory)
- (11 Dec) 28, 57, 78c. (Text, 2006 Year of Historical Memory)

STAMP BOOKLETS

The following checklist covers, in simplified form, booklets issued by Spain. It is intended that it should be used in conjunction with the main listings and details of stamps and panes listed there are not repeated.

An additional premium was charged for Nos. SB1/2 and 5/8.

Prices are for complete booklets

Booklet No.	Date	Contents and Cover Price	Price
SB1	7.1.86	Admission of Spain and Portugal to E.E.C. 1 pane, No. 2854a (105p.)	5·00
SB2	15.10.86	Discovery of America (1st issue) 1 pane, No. 2882a (160p.)	4·00
SB3	11.3.87	Juan Carlos I (T **680**) 1 pane, No. 2824ab (114p.)	3·50
SB4	11.3.87	Juan Carlos I (T **680**) 2 panes, No. 2824ab (228p.)	5·00
SB5	30.10.87	Discovery of America (2nd issue) 1 pane, No. 2932a (235p.)	4·50
SB6	13.10.88	Discovery of America (3rd issue) 1 pane, No. 2983a (174p.)	3·50
SB7	16.10.89	Discovery of America (4th issue) 1 pane, No. 3035a (200p.)	3·75
SB8	18.10.90	Discovery of America (5th issue) 1 pane, No. 3079a (76p.)	3·75
SB9	15.10.91	Discovery of America (6th issue) 1 pane, No. 3126a (160p.)	3·75
SB10	22.2.02	Flowers No. 3839/46 (€2)	4·50
SB11	30.9.02	Music Nos. 3895/902 (€2)	4·50
SB12	28.3.03	Paintings Nos. 3941/8 (€2)	6·25
SB13	28.7.03	Paintings Nos. 3975/82 (€2.08)	4·75
SB14	16.1.04	Romantic Architecture. Self adhesive. (T **1210**) Nos. 4011/4018 (€2.08)	4·75
SB15	2.4.04	European Day (11 March) for Victims of Terrorism. Self Adhesive. Nos. 4029 ×8 (€2.18)	4·75
SB16	22.7.04	Paintings. Self adhesive. Nos. 4055/62	
SB17	3.1.05	Circus. Self adhesive. Nos. 4086/93	4·50
SB18	16.9.05	Los Lunnis. Self adhesive. Nos. 4122/9	4·50
SB19	2.1.06	Toys. Self adhesive. Nos. 4145/52	4·50
SB20	1.4.06	Fauna and Flora. Self adhesive. Nos. 4160×10	5·50
SB21	1.4.06	Fauna and Flora. Self adhesive. Nos. 4161×10	7·25
SB22	2.1.07	Toys. Self adhesive. Nos. 4223/30	4·50
SB23	2.1.08	Toys. Self-adhesive. Nos. 4320/7	4·75
SB24	10.1.08	Flora and Fauna. Self-adhesive. No. 4328×10	5·75
SB25	10.1.08	Flora and Fauna. Self-adhesive. No. 4329×10	11·50
SB26	2.4.08	Flora and Fauna. Self-adhesive. No. 4354×10	5·75
SB27	2.4.08	Flora and Fauna. Self-adhesive. No. 4355×10	8·50
SB28	10.1.08	Flora and Fauna. Self-adhesive. No. 4371×10	5·75
SB29	1.7.08	Flora and Fauna. Self-adhesive. No. 4372×10	11·50
SB30	1.1.08	Flora and Fauna. Self-adhesive. No. 4389×10	5·75
SB31	1.1.08	Flora and Fauna. Self-adhesive. No. 4390×10	5·75
SB32	14.11.09	Autonomous Communities. Self-adhesive. Nos. 4406/13	5·00
SB33	20.1.09	Flora and Fauna. Self-adhesive. No. 4418×10	6·25
SB34	20.1.09	Flora and Fauna. Self-adhesive. No. 4419×10	12·00
SB35	1.4.09	Flora and Fauna. Self-adhesive. No. 4432×10	6·25
SB36	1.4.09	Flora and Fauna. Self-adhesive. No. 4433×10	8·50
SB37	1.7.09	Flora and Fauna. Self-adhesive. No. 4452×10	6·25
SB38	1.7.09	Flora and Fauna. Self-adhesive. No. 4453×10	12·00
SB39	10.10.09	Flora and Fauna. Self-adhesive. No. 4471×10	6·25
SB40	1.10.09	Flora and Fauna. Self-adhesive. No. 4472×10	6·25
SB41	2.1.10	Autonomous Communities. Self-adhesive. No. 4486×93	5·00

FISCAL STAMPS USED FOR POSTAGE

F 1   F 2   F 3

1882–1908. Dated. White paper. P 14.

F1	F 1	10c. 1882, flesh	2·50	2·25
F2	F 2	10c. 1883, lavender	1·75	2·25
F3		10c. 1884, mauve	1·75	2·25
F4		10c. 1885, green	1·75	2·25
F5		10c. 1886, blue	1·75	2·25
F6	F 1	10c. 1887, brown	1·40	1·90
F7	F 3	10c. 1888, blue	1·40	1·90
F8		10c. 1889, green	1·40	1·90
F9		10c. 1890, violet	1·40	1·90
F10		10c. 1891, carmine	1·40	1·90
F11		10c. 1892, olive-grey	1·40	1·90
F12		10c. 1893, blue	1·40	1·90
F13		10c. 1894, vermilion	1·40	1·90
F14		10c. 1895, violet	1·40	1·90
F15		10c. 1896, green	1·40	1·90
F16		10c. 1897, lake	1·40	1·90
F17		10c. 1898, blue	1·40	1·90
F18	–	10c. 1899, blue-green	1·40	1·90
F19	–	10c. 1900, carmine	1·40	1·90
F20	–	10c. 1901, black	1·40	1·90
F21	–	10c. 1902, blue	1·40	1·90
F22	–	10c. 1903, orange	1·40	1·90
F23	–	10c. (—), yellow-brown (1904)	8·75	7·25
F24	–	10c. (—), yellow-brown (1908)	1·25	75

Nos. F18/23 are similar to Type F **3**, but show a different version of the arms. No. F24 is also similar, but is inscr "ESPECIAL MOVIL".

1918. Post Office Savings Bank stamps inscr "CAJA POSTAL DE AHORROS".

(a) P 14

F25	5c. green and sepia	1·40	50
F26	5c. green and red	2·75	1·00
F27	5c. red and grey	2·25	1·00

(b) P 11

F28	5c. carmine and grey	5·00	1·00
F29	5c. red and lilac	2·25	1·00

Many other fiscal stamps can be found used for postage, especially during the Civil War period. These are collectable items on cover, but are too numerous to list.

Other stamps bearing F numbers are Frank stamps and these are included in chronological order in the main list.

POSTAL TAX STAMPS

Stamps in the above designs were on sale at post offices in Barcelona, originally to help defray the costs of various exhibitions but later for general municipal funds. They had no franking value and were not always for compulsory use and so we do not list them. The concession ended in 1945 with the issue of the above type which incorporates the designs used since 1929.

In 1963 a similar concession was introduced in Valencia, the stamps being inscribed "PLAN SUR DE VALENCIA".

Many other charity labels exist but they had no postal validity.

DESIGN INDEX

This index provides in a condensed form a key to the designs of Spanish stamps.

Where the same design, or subject, appears more than once in a set only the first number is given. Scenes and buildings are listed under the town or geographical area in which they are situated. Portraits are listed under surname only; those without surnames (e.g. rulers and some saints) are under forenames. Works of art and inventions are indexed under the artist's, or inventor's, name, where this appears on the stamp. In cases of difficulty part of the inscription has been used to identify the stamp.

A. SUBSIDIARY GROUPS

Express Letter........E307, E521, E522, E534, E535, E553, E570, E583, E608, E643, E660, E672, E697, E779, E801, E905, E981, E1022, E1250, E2099, E3211
Frank........................F172, F273, F839
Official 046, 050, 0289, 0353, 0707, 0717
War Tax . W217, W228, W253, W258, W289, W293, W297, W839

B. POSTAGE STAMPS

ABC (newspaper)..........................3935
Abd al-Rahman II.........................2891
Abd al-Rahman III........................3110
Abu Abdallah Mohamed Ben Idrisi (Al Idrisi)............4186
Abu Amir Muhammad al-Ma'afiri 3904
Accelerator....................................4074
Accession ot European Economic Community (EEC)..............4531
Acosta, J. de..................................1850
Acosta, T. de...................................2433
Actinia...2583
Admission of Spain and Portugal to E.E.C................2854
"Ages of Man" Exhibition.........3564, 3639, 3763
Agriculture........................1641, 3041
ahorre energia!.............................2556
Air post...2117
Aircraft.................... 1462, 2117, 2496, 3293, **MS**3382
Aircraft Engineering College...3996
Airplane and portrait 1063
Airplane and ship 1234
Alarcón 1138
Alaska..1884
Alaya.................................1467, 1825
Albacete.............................1468, 1826
Alboniz 1387
Alberti 3718
Alcala de Henares.........................1793
Alcaniz......................................**MS**3209
Alcantara............................2243, 2435
Alcantarilla 2696
Alcazar........**MS**909, **MS**910, **MS**911, **MS**912
Alcoy 2360, 2799
Aleixandre.......................................2837
Alejandro VI 3127
Aleman..1093
Alfonso I 4080
Alfonso II...1458
Alfonso III..1459
Alfonso VI.......................................4444
Alfonso VII 2894
Alfonso X 1715, 2768
Alfonso XII....... 228, 238, W253, 253, 263, 2551
Alfonso XIII......... 276, 400, 470, 583, 2552, 3030
Alicante 1469, 1827, 2915
Almagro 1683
Almansa 1805
Almeria...................1470, 1828, 2040
Almodovar.....................................1869
Almonte 2868
Almunecar......................................2467
Alonso...2714
Altamira...3044
Alzamiento Nacional......1250, 1414
Al-Zarqali..2893
Amat...1816
Amateur Radio Union 3560
Amaya..3383
Amber...3367
Amberes Foundation 3275
America...... 2740, 2882, 2932, 2983, 3035, 3041, 3083, 3126, 3130, **MS**3147, 3175, **MS**3177, 3190, 3247, 3293, 3356, 3452, 3521, 3610, 3702, 3774, 3903, 4073, 4135, 4210, 4283, 4394, 4474
Amphitheatre 3956
Anchieta..1739
Anchor and crown........................1797
Andalucia 2706, 3064
Angel...1186
A.N.I.C. 2438
Animals 2095, 2160, 2250, 2317, 2860, 2866
Anniversaries........ 3445, 3862, 3864, 4137, 4195
Año Europeo de la Conservacion.......................3320
Año Europeo de la Musica 2832
Año Europeo del Turismo.........3087
Año Internacional de la Mujer...........................2309
Año Internacional de la Paz.....2862
Año Intemacional de las Personas Disminuidas......2639
Año Internacional de los Derechos Humanos 1932
Año Intemacional del Libro.....2134
Año Internacional del Nino......2567
Año Internacional del Turismo..........................1864
Año Jacobeo..................................3214
Año Jubilar Lebaniego..............3322
Año Mariano..................................1195
Año Mundial de las Comunicaciones.................2725
Año Mundial del Refugiado....1387
Año Oleicola Mundial 2605
Año Santo.......................................1033
Año Santo Compostelano....... 1193, 1732, 2066, 2105, 2121, 2351, 2673
Años de Paz 1637
Antarctic Base..............................3523
Antipolo..1753
Anti-Tuberculosis Fund............... 913
Apollo (fountain) 3111
Apples...2303
Aragon................................2760, 3063
Aragon, A. de................................1923
Aragonite.......................................3314
Aragua 3368
Aranjuez.................................**MS**3048
Archaeology......... 3397, 4189, 4242, 4341, 4420
Archery..............................3144, 3305
Architects Congress...................3393
Architecture.......... 3751, 3924, 4180, 4250, 4348, 4464, **MS**4466
Architecture Award....................3519
Arenal..745
Argenta 2832
Argentina...........................2271, 2543
Arglla de Alba 2311
Armed Forces......980, **MS**924, 1419, 2573, 2618, 2644, 2682, 2727, 2765, 2802, 2869
Arms 1467, 1542, 1582, 1612, 1692, 1756, 1781, 1949, 2619, 2680, 2735, 2739, 2782, 2924
Arms (state)........................1764, 2705
Arms (spain)..................................4220
Arniches..1819
Arquelologia..................................3357
Art 3442, 3487, 3589, 3591, 3654, 3941, 4287
Artesania Espanola 3116
Asclepius (statue) **MS**4279a
Asociacion de la Prensa............3331
Astorga...2125
Astronautics congress................1809
Asturias...............................2736, 2989
Asturias (frigate)...................**MS**3422
Athletes...1638
Athletic Bilbao Football Club ..3466
Athletics......2978, 3028, 3561, 3955
Atlas..**MS**3351
Atrevida (ship)..............................1667
Aub 3964
Augusta Emerita 3288
Australia...2966
Autonomous Communities within Spain.............4406/13, 4486/93
Auxilio a las Victimas de la Guera 1113
Averroes...1849
Avia..2119
Aviation..3724
Avila............ 1471, 1489, 1829, 1935, 2169, 2383, 3091
Avila Cathedral **MS**4142
Avila, J. de.....................................2019
Avilés Villa....................................3952
Ayala..2624
Azcárate 753
Azorin 2875
Badajoz........1472, 1830, 1839, 2189
Baby and fingerprint.................4119
Badminton 2979
Baeza...1933
Balaguer...3660
Balboa...2984
Baleares.....................1473, 1831, 2649
Balearas (ship).............................1672
Balears 2770
Ball and foot **MS**4377
Ballot box.......................................3020
Balmaseda.....................................3584
Balmes 2238
Balsareny 1867
Banco de Espana........................3113
Bandera Espanola.......................2803
Banknote 2245
Bará..2245
"Barcelona '92"..................3098, 3123
Barcelona... 1474, 1704, 1832, 2172, 2373, 2745, 2847, 2871, 3183, 3369, 4143
Barcelona, Conde de 3241
Barcelona Exhibition 2597
Barcelona Fair..............................2033
Barcelona Football Club...........3556
Barcelona Metro..........................3563
Barocci 1955
Baroja...................................2506, 4219
Barraquer.......................................2769
Baseball..3078
Basketball............. 2388, 2872, 2980, 3333, **MS**4206
Bastidas..1437
Bayen 1437
Bazzn.....................................1765, 3112
Bear..2096, 3370
Beato..2329
Beatrix.. 394
Becquer...2051
Bee 1509
Beinvenida Mister Marshall! (film) 3365
Belalcazár 1509
Bell 1435
Belle Epoque (film).......................3308
Bello...2670
Belluga...1598
Bellver..2039
Belmonte 1874
Beltran 1741
Benavente 1820
Benissa Cathedral.........................3933
Benito, St..2647
Bernini 1490
Berruguete.........................1499, 1596
Bethencourt 1888
Biada 2231
Biar...2153
Bilbao...3653
Bioquimica......................................1978
Birds............ 2094, 2192, 2518, 2690, 2792, 2849, 2950, 3083, 3247, 3356
Blue cross..3202
Blue ribbon 3441
Bobsleighing 1910
Bogota 2592
Boles...3473
Bolivar..2538
Bonampak...............................**MS**2625
Bonifaz..1105
Book 2134, 2223, 2595
Borbon, J. de..................................3241
Bourbon, F......................................4038
Bourbons 2619, 2666
Bowling 2712
Boxing.......... 2386, 3009, 3334, 3374
Bramante 2241
Bravo Espana (yacht)...................4045
Breastfeeding................................2902
Breton 2678
Bridges 4202
Brigid, St...2067
Brindis...1331
Brokers' School 3710
Brown bear 4537
Bruselas........................ *see* Brussels
Brussels 3006
Buenos Aires.........2272, 2626, 2658
Buigas...3586
Building facade 4154
Bull 2966
Bullfighting...........1317, 1652, 4042
Bumper cars..................................2359
Bunuel 3254
Burgos 1475, 1705, 1710, 1833, 2106, 2756, 2993, 3014
Buses...2607
Butera 2221
Butron...1803
Butterflies..........................3633, 4508
Caballero, Fernan........................2561
Caballero, M. Fdez 2674
Cabeza de Vaca............................1362
Cable Ingles Bridge.....................4033
Cable-cars.....................................3149
Cacao nut 3036
Caceres........1476, 1834, 1885, 3090
Cadiz............1477, 1835, 1866, 2371
Cadiz Carnival 2861
Cajal 752, 3936
Calderon 2672
Calderón de la Barca..................1135
California 1882
Camaras de comercio, industria y navegacion.....2864
Camera 3331
Camino...2838
Campaign Against Domestic Violence............3713
Campana 1527
Campoamor 2945
Campomanes, Conde de 3142
Campomanes, P.R. 3932
Canarias.......1791, 2650, 2766, 2831
Candle and fir branch 1152
Cangrejo de Rio...........................2580
Cano, A. 1530, 1968
Cano, C. 3794
Canoeing 2839, 3099, 3339, 3378
Cantabria 2707, 3360
Cantar de Mio Cid (poem).........4258
Capitan Trueno 3327
Car and pedestrians...................4096
Caracas 1951
Carande 2922
Caravel.. 502
Cardena..2491
Carlomagno..................................2071
Carlos 11287, 2600
Carlos II..2604
Carlos III......................2547, **MS**2997
Carolo IV..2548
Carpanta 3328
Cars...2458
Casals 2439
Casas regionales centros 2972
Caserio, El (operetta) 2718
Castelao 2895
Castelar... 758
Castellers 1862
Castellon..1837
Castellon de la Plana 1478, 1836
Castile 32
Castilla..1046
Castilla y Leon..............................2784
Castilla-La Mancha.........2767, 3066
Castillo, A. 3438
Castillo, B. 2835
Castilnovo 1988
Castles 3719, 3859, 3958, 4050, 4116, 4198, 4278, 4395, 4469

SPAIN *Design Index*

Castro, G. de....2049
Castro, R. de....1925, 3755
Castro y Padilla....1814
Catalán....3279, 3594
Catalonia....2594, 2974, 3065
Cataluña.... *see* Catalonia
Catalunya.... *see* Catalonia
Cathedrals.... **MS**4506, **MS**4536
Cattle....1317
Cavalry....2198, 2225, 2255, 2291, 2322, 2410, 2441, 2472, 2499
Cave paintings....1837, 2304
Cenachero....**MS**3355
Centenary of Powered Flight..4010
Centre D'Esports Sabadell Football Club....3965
Centre Excursionista de Catalunya....2352
Ceramics....2907
Cerezo....1537
CERN....4074
Cernuda....3864
Cervantes....0355, 0356, 2719
Ceuta....1762, 2746
Chair....3118
Chamber of Deputies....0353
Chameleon....2251
Chapí....2774
Chaplin....3029
Chariot....2778
Charles V....3636
Charruca....2353
Chasqui....1817
Chaves....1438
Chess....4025
Chest....3120
Child....2327
Children's Songs....**MS**4100
Chile....1997
Chilean Stamps....3969
Chomon....3255
Christmas...1249, 1316, 1386, 1461, 1539, 1596, 1691, 1752, 1824, 1896, 1955, 2002, 2060, 2119, 2173, 2220, 2275, 2345, 2428, 2494, 2539, 2598, 2629 2659, 2701, 2749, 2789, 2847, 2889, 2938, 2990, 3042, 3084, 3131, 3194, 3250, 3307, 3360, 3406, 3458, 3525, 3624, 3704, 3788, 3927, 4003, 4081, 4140, 4213, 4285, 4402, 4481
Ciencias Historicas....3075
Cierva....941, 1010
Cinabrio....3260
Cine Espanol....3308, 3364
Cinema....3419
CIO....1737
Circulo Oscense Building....4063
Circus....4086
Cisneros....1600
City Council building....**MS**4173
Ciudad Real....1542, 1897, 2466
Civil Guard....2709
Civic Responsibility....4162
Civic Values....4260, 4338, 4422, 4496
Clara....2505
Clocks....**MS**4026
Coach....1569, 2287
Cobi Filatelico....3818
Coca....1872
Codices....**MS**3199
Coins....1813, 1887, 1931, 2364
Colegio de Abogados....3372
Coll....3792
Colon....2936, **MS**3147, **MS**3174, **MS**3177
Columbus....618, **MS**4171
Columbus Monument....**MS**4070
Comic Strip Characters....3467, 3579, 3651
Communications Year....2725
Compostela 93....3218
Compostelian Jubilee Year....4522
Comunicaciones....E3211
Comunidades Europeas....3017
Cones....2143
Consejo de Europa....2524
Consejo Superior Geografico..2230
Constituent Assembley....4505
Constitution....**MS**4009
Constitucion....2903, 2996
Constitucion de los Estados Unidos....2367
Construction....1644
Contruction (stained glass window)....**MS**4215
Cordoba....1543, 1610, 1898, 2384, 2992
Cordoba Cathedral....698, 872
Cordoba Veterinary School....3457
Coronacion Canonica....1582
Correa....1525
Correo de Indias....2486
Correspondence Programme.3493, 3598, 3677, 3775, 3882, **MS**4023
Cortés, D....1714
Cortés, H....1092, 2983
Coruña....1544, 1860, 1899, 2629
Cosa....2935, **MS**3661
Costa....732, 3395
Costa Brava....1605
Costa de Nutka....1878
Costa Rica....2430
Costumes...1825, 1897, 1956, 2007, 2072, 3930
Council of Europe....4434
Court of Auditors....4259
Covadonga....3768
Covadonga Monastery....**MS**914
Covadonga National Park....2950
Cradle....3119
Cristina....394
Cristo, Sto, de Lepanto....1343
Cristo de los Faroles....1606
Cristobal....1505
Cross....1311
Cross of Lorraine.1006, 1018, 1029, 1042, 1056, 1065, 1076, 1085, 1109, 1130, 1152, 1163, 1184
Cross of Victory....**MS**4359
Crucifixion....1343, 1606, 2109, 2913, 2947
Cuban War of Independence....W297
Cudillero....1709
Cuenca....1545, 1865, 1900, 2863
Cuerpo de Abogados del Estado....2651
Cultural Heritage....4414, **MS**4535
Cupboard....3116
Cycling....1368, 1945, 2711, 2783, 3010, 3050, 3298

Dalí....3266, 4036
Dam....1423, 2186, 4425
Damaso, St....1768
Dancing....1654, 2642
Danforth anchor....4054
Dario....1890
Darwin....4457
Data Protection Congress....3489
Daza de Valdes....1766
Dejadles Nacer....2327
Deporte pera Todos....2564
Descubrimiento de America....2882, **MS**3147
Deusto University....2901
Dia de las Fuerzas Armadas....2573, 2618, 2644, 2682, 2727, 2765, 2802, 2869
Dia del Sello.... *see* Stamp Day
Dia Mundial de las Telecomunicaciones....2570
Dia Mundial del Medio Ambiente....2805, 3178, 3240
Dia Mundial del Sello....1409, 1492, 1570, 1656, 1728, 1783, 1856, 1927, 1980, 2032, 2091, 2150, 2185, 2237, 2306, 2363
Dia National de Caridad....1859
Diario de Cadiz (newspaper)....3967
Diario de Navarra (newspaper)....3972
Diario de Valencia (newspaper)....4047
Diaz....3479
Diego....3394
Discus, Throwing the....1511, 1682, 2781
Diseno Infantil....3000, 3049, 3101, 3141, 3246
Dish aerials....819
Diving....2047, 2779
Doctrina Christiana....1811
Dogs....2728
Dolomite....3316
Dolores....3875
Domingo, St., de Guzman....1717
Dominic, St....3771
Don Juan....**MS**936
Don Quixote..307, 813, 1080, 3493, **MS**4107
Donantes de Sangre....2415
Door knocker....3063
Dove....1155
Dove and flag....4221
Downs Syndrome Congress....3456
Drach....1609
Ducks....3356
Dulque-Cornejo....1824
Dulzaina....2970

"ĕ"....3349
E = mc²....4109
Eagle....1069, 1078
Earth and Universe Sciences....4193, 4239
Egeria....2786
Eggs....4030
Eibar....2924
El Adelanto de Salamanca (newspaper)....3974
El Adelantado de Segovia (newspaper)....4282
El Catalan (ship)....**MS**3371
El Cid....877, 1505, 3588
El Comercio (newspaper)....3984
El Correo (newspaper)....4519
El Correo Gallego (newspaper)....3983
El Diario Montanes (newspaper)....3970
El Greco....1249, 1391, 1532, 1554, 2060, 2686
Elche....1995, 2877
Elcano....2355, 2986
Electric Locomotive....E553
Electricity....1647
Elhuyar....2732
El Jabato....3384
El Progreso (newspaper)....4361
Emblem....4094, 4175
Emigration....2865
En la Duda no Adelante....2358
Endangered Species....3549
Engravers....3484
Equestrian Games....3868
Erbe Obervatory....4079
Ercilia and Vega....**MS**2625
Escalona....1938
Escorial....1443, 2994, **MS**3048
Esfalerita....3261
Eslava....2504
Espamer Aviación y Espacer....3362, **MS**3382
Espamer 80....**MS**2625
Espamer 81....2658
Espamer 82....2693
Espamer 84....**MS**2761
Espamer 85....2796
Espamer 87....**MS**2930
Espana Exporta....2609, 2653
ESPANA 75....2232, **MS**2298
Espana 2000....3537, 3612, 3662, **MS**3701
Espana 2002...3847, **MS**3876, 3913
Espana 2004...4005, 4039, **MS**4041, 4042, **MS**4044, 4045
Espana 2006....4131, **MS**4178, **MS**4209
Espina....2048
Espiru....2874
Espronceda....2130
Esquivel....**MS**3359
Estadistica....1259
Estella....3072
Eunate....2110
Euro....3566
Euro coin....**MS**4455
Euro 2008 Championship Winners....**MS**4377
Europa....1355, 1432, 1509, 1580, 1674, 1735, 1807, 1853, 1926, 1979, 2031, 2089, 2148, 2183, 2235, 2304, 2361, 2462, 2522, 2568, 2614, 2642, 2680 2719, 2763, 2800, 2866, 2919, 2961, 3015, 3060, 3105, 3175, 3212, 3278, 3329, 3383, 3426, 3478, 3562, 3646, 3750, 3866, 3954, 4034, 4105, 4200, 4249, **MS**4358, 4441, 4520
Europalia 85....2793
European Basketball Championship....3957
European Constitution....4094
European Day....4028
European Parliament....4348
European Union....3835, 4035
European Year of the Disabled....3435
Evening dress....4397
Exfilna '85....**MS**2843
Exfilna '86....**MS**2881
Exfilna '87....**MS**2931
Exfilna '88....**MS**2968
Exfilna '89....**MS**3018
Exfilna '90....**MS**3069
Exfilna '91....**MS**3133
Exfilna '92....**MS**3189
Exfilna '93....**MS**3209
Exfilna '94....**MS**3285
Exfilna '95....**MS**3355
Exfilna '96....3399
Exfilna '97....**MS**3451
Exfilna '98....**MS**3490
Exfilna '99....**MS**3559
Exfilna 2000....**MS**3655
Exfilna 2001....**MS**3770
Exfilna 2003....**MS**3951
Exfilna 2004....**MS**4070
Exfilna 2005....**MS**4115
Exfilna 2006....**MS**4173
EXFILNA 2007....**MS**4248
Exfilna 2008....**MS**4359
EXFILNA 2009....**MS**4473
Expo Bruselas....1283
Expo 88....2966
Expo '92....2897, 2941, 2951, 3004, 3052, 3094, 3141, 3143, 3148, **MS**3172
Expo '98....3488
EXPO 2010....**MS**4517
Exports....2609, 2653
Exposición Arta Romanico....1426
Exposición de ls Pesca....3122
Expositión Flotante....1254
Exposición Universal....2951, 2964
Extremadura....2755

Fabrica National de Moneda y Timbre....3243
Faces and Stars....4177
Falla....1083, 1151, 2440, 3791
Fans....**MS**4110
F.A.O....2656, 3346
Farmer....2308
Fashion....**MS**4284, 4397, **MS**4451
Federacion Española de Sociedades Filatélicas....2976
Federacion Int de Filatelia....2762
Feijoo....1079
Felipe II....1450, 1497, 2601, 3482
Felipe III....2602
Felipe IV....2603
Felipe V....2544
Felipe de Borbón....2497
Fencing....2156, 3031
Ferdinand the Catholic..1171, 1179
Feria del Campo....2308
Feria Mundial de Nueva York...1651
Fernan Gonzalez....2131
Fernãndez....816
Fernando III....1104
Fernando VI....2546
Fernando VII....2549
Fernando de Austria....1495
Fernando el Catolici.. *see* Ferdinand
Fernando Poo....1546, 1901
Ferrán....1248
Festivals....3658, 3760, 4192
Fierro....2274
Fiesta del S. Corazan de Jesus.1269
F.I.F.A....4037
Figure and tap....4162
Figure skating....2133
Filatem '90....**MS**3074
Filatem 95....**MS**3311
Firefighters....3711
First Spanish Powered Flight...4462
Fishes....2202, 2452, 2518
Fishing Fair....3444
Flag....2555, 2792, 2803, 3020
Flamenco....3391, **MS**4404
Flora and Fauna....4153, 4165, 4160, 4187/8, 4207/8, 4231/2, 4245/6, 4270/1, 4280/1,

SPAIN *Design Index*

4328/9, 4354/5, 4371/2, 4389/90, 4418/19, 4432/3, 4452/3, 4471/2
Florida 1734
Flowers *see* Plants
Fluorita Ambar 3367
Football 1369, 2616, 2640, 2668, 2683, **MS**2685, 3032, 3300, 3335, 4103, 4475
Forestry 1642, 1796
For the Young **MS**4139, **MS**4159, **MS**4274
Fortuny 1229, 1912
Foundry Worker (stained glass window) **MS**4289
France 2068
Franco 948, 981, 1006, 1022, 1088, 1094, 1114, 1149, 1206, 1650
Franco Jefatura Estado 1262, 1434
Frias 1942
Frio 1875
Frogs 2319
Fromista 2128
Fruela 1456
Fuensaldaña 1939
Fuente 3480
Fuero de Logroño 3310
Fundación Carlos de Amberes 3272
Fungi 3205, 3256, 3312, 4392, 4478

Gabriel, Archangel 1258
Gabriel y Galan 2053
Galena 3263
Galicia 1984, 2638, 3067
Galindez de Carvajal 3363
Galindo 1922
Galvez, B. de 2368
Gálvez, J. de 1589
Ganivet 3517
Garay 1517
Garcia, D. 4445
Garcia Lorca 2614
Garcilaso de la Vega 3126
Gardens 4132
Gargallo 2703
Gaudi 2295, 3894
Genet 2164, 3416
Geographical Institute 2059
Geological Survey **MS**4008
Gerona 1547, 1611, 1902, 2003, 2576, 2742, 2744, 2918
Gexto 90 3050
Giaquinto 1529
Gibraltar 1991
Gigantes y Cabezudos (operetta) 2675
Giralda (ship) 3286
Glassware 2953
Globe 1570, 1755, 1875, 3320, 4272, 4333, 4429
Globe and airplane 3293
Globe and tree 1796
Globes and stamps 1656
Gomera 3137
Gongora 1430
Gossaert 2793
Goya 553, 1073, 1273, 1316, **MS**3133, 3386
GPO, Madrid 361
Gracian 3762
Gran Bretana *see* Great Britain
Gran Canaria 1548, 2525
Gran Captain 1272
Granados 1889
Granja de San Ildefonso **MS**3048
Gran Via 4516
Grape Harvest Festival 3437
Grapes 4065
Grape treading 4204
Graph 1643
Graphispack 1769
Great Britain 2070
Greco *see* El Greco
Grenada, L. de 2999
Grenada '92 **MS**3102, **MS**3174
Grenada 1549, 1608, 1904, 2314, 2522, 2577, 2965, 2995
Gris 2876
Guadalajara 1550, 1905, 2858
Guadalupe 1313, 1792, 3353
Guadamur 1798
Guardia Civil 3295
Guatemala 2487
Guell 3047
Guernica 1780
Guerrero 2715
Guillén 3252
Guipuzcoa 1551, 1906, 2187
Guirdi 2717
Gutierrez 2584
Gymnastics 1370, 2092, 2841, 3033, 3336

Handball 3008
Hand 4335
Hand and Braille numerals 4200
Hand holding papers 4496
Hands 3122, 3249, 4135
Havana 2796
Hazm 2892
Helicopters and boats 4345
Henares 1950
Heraldo de Aragon (newspaper) 4068
Herrera 2175
Higher Architecture School of Madrid **MS**4215
Hijas de la Caridad 3070
Hockey 1371, 2116, 2971, 3057, 3302, 3338, 3376
Holy Year 4048
Hombre y la Biosfera 2759
Homenaje al Ejercito 980
Horn 4533
Horreo 2969
Horse jumping 1377, 1944, 3011, 3301, 3337
Horsemen 4174
Horses 2225, 2921, 3038, 3537, 3612, 3662
Hospital del Niño Jesus 2596
Housing 1640
Huelva 1552, 1863, 1907
Huerta 1624
Huesca 1553, 1787, 1908
Huntington 1506
Hurdling 1513

Ibáñez 738
Iberia 2496
Iberia Airlines 3877
Ibero 3138
Ibero-American Summit Conference 4134
Ibex 2098
Ice hockey 1911
Ifni 1612, 1956
Iglesias 734, 2960
Ignacio de Loyola, St. 1231, 3109
Ignacio de Mini 2273
Igualada Martorell 3242
Ildefonso, St. 1891
Imprenta 2222
Independence of Latin America 4511
Indian 1817
Industrializacion Espanola 2337
Infanteria de Marina 2900
Infantry 2197, 2226, 2256, 2290, 2322, 2410, 2441, 2472, 2499
Infantry College, Toledo 3712
Ingreso...en la CE 2854
Institute of Catalan Studies 4237
Instituciones Hispanicas 1574
Instituto Int de Estadistica 2737
Instituto San Isidro 3114
INTA-NASA 3105
International Day against Dersertification 4157
International Money Museums Congress 3611
International Philatelic Federation Congress 2762
International Transport and Communications Museum 3450
International Year of Historical Memory 4221
International Year of Physics 4109
Iparraguirre 2667
Isabel II 2550
Isabel II (ship) 1668
Isabella II 1, 9, 16, 22, 63, 69, 75, 81, 92, 98, 99, 145, 172
Isabella the Catholic 880, 930, 1157, 1166
Italy 2069
Jabato, El 3384
Jaca 2927
Jaen 1613, 1957, 2468
Jaime 11583, 2446, 2981
James, St. 905
Jarandilla 1868
Javier *see* Xavier
Jerez 1676, 1821, 2785
Jeronimo, St. 2216
Jewish Quarters 3459, 3529
Jimenez 2050, 2671
John XXIII, Pope 1541
John Paul II, Pope 2695, 3027
José de Calasanz, St. 1895
Jovellanos 755, 1716
Juan 4069
Juan XXIII *see* John XXIII
Juan Carlos 12347, 2389, 2553, 2807, 2944, 3361, 3408, 3730, **MS**3813, 3814
Juan Carlos I and Sofia 2378, 2434
Juan de Dios, St. 1134
Juan de la Cruz, St. 1026, 3107
Juan de Ribera, St. 1353
Juan, J. 2240
Juana I of Castille 4144
Juan of Austria 2113
Juan Pablo II *see* John Paul
Juan Sebastian Elcano (ship) 1673
Juanes 2585
Judo 1681, 2498, 3058, 3303
July, 25 3180
Juni 2508
"Justice" 217
Juvenia '97 3417
Juvenia '99 3557
Juvenia 2000 3715
Juvenia 2003 3933
Juvenia 2005 4101
JUVENIA 2007 4256
Juvenia 2009 4484
Juventud 2798

Keller 2620
Kent 3051
Kindelan 2634
Kingdom of Leon **MS**4521
King Juan Carlos 4290/4299
Knight 1042, 1065, 1113, 1272, 1416, 1734, 2197
Kraus 3703

La Bodega 1877
La Coruña 1860
La Cruz *see* S. Juan
La Gasca 1518
La Laverdad (newspaper) 3940
La Mancha 2191
La Mota 1800
La Rabida Monastery 620
Labour Day 843
Labrador 2724
Lace 3021
Laguna 1852
Las Casas 1072
Las Huelgas Monastery 2004
Las Palmas 1903, 2190, 2382, **MS**3285, 3582
La Provincias (newspaper) 4234
La Rioja (newspaper) 4417
La Vanguardia (newspaper) 4218
La Voz de Aviles (newspaper) 4332
Leaf 4415
Lebrun 1312
Legazpi 1191
Legion, Spanish 2101
Lengua Castellana 2477
Leon (town) 34, 1603, 1614, 1929, 1958, 2126, 2173, 2379, 2741, 2975
Leon Cathedral **MS**3992
Leon, L. de 1189, 3108
Leon postmark 2306
Lepanto, Battle of 2113
Leprosy Awareness 3931
Lequeitio 2042
Lerida 1615, 1786, 1794, 1959
Lerma 1498
Letter 4078, **MS**4358
Levante U D Football Club 4518
Leyre 2283
Lazo 1436
Library 1080
Liceu Theatre 3728
Life-saving 2260
Lighthouses **MS**4277, 4380, 4435
Lima 1813, 2593
Literatura Española 3280, 3324
Literature 3404, 3427, 3472, 3707, 3774, 3756, **MS**4019
Literature Day 3429
Lizard 2252, 2317, 3549
Lleida University 3642
Loarre 1873
Logrono 1616, 1960, 1996, 3310
London 3004
Londres *see* London
Long jumping 1679, 4374
Lope de Vega 781, 1136
Lopez, F. **MS**3787
Lopez, V. 2204
Lorca 3483
Los Losadas 1949
Losada 1948
Loscos 2873
Los Lunnis (children's TV programme) 4122
Loygorri 2632
Loyola *see* Ignacio
Luarca 3754
Lucha contra el Paludismo 1540
Lugo 1617, 1961, 2123, 2188, 2416
Luis 12545
Lulio 1597
Lumiere 3330
Luna 2773
Lynx 2095, 3465

"M" 3195
Machado 2507
Macho 2940
Madrazo 2478
Madrid 30, 839, 860, 1449, 1618, 1737, 1806, 1962, 2372, 2419, 2697, **MS**2761, 2791, **MS**2843, 2919, **MS**3048, 3195
Madrid Press Association 786
Madrid Savings Bank 3849
Madrid University 3277
Maeztu 3003
Maimonides 1851
Maino 2002
Maize 3035
Malaga 1619, 1963, 2041, 2315, 2469, 2948, 3061, 3357
Malaspina 3244
Mallorca 1847, 2789, 3905
Mallorca Cathedral **MS**4248
Manjón 3034
Manrique 2560
Manso de Velasco 1812
Manx Shearwater 3551
Manzanares 1804
Map of Europe 4244
Maps 1156, 1415, 1876, 1878, 1947, 2059, 2066, 2105, 2222, 2230, 2378, 2434, 2486, 2638, 2649, 2688, 3296, **MS**3382
Marañon 2563
Martial 2244
Marcus, Capilla de 2289
Margal 1731
Maria 394
Maria, Sta., del Alcazar 1676
Maria, Sta., del Parral 1952
Mariologico 2591
Marshal Francisco Serrano 192
Marti 3326
Maritime Rescue 4345
Martinez, E. J. 1881
Martinez, M. A. 2982
Maruxa (operetta) 2677
Masthead 3984
Mayno 1752
Medio Ambiente 3200
Mediterranean Games 4104
Melilla 1763, 2747
Mena 1539
Mendoza, Alonso de 1515
Mendoza, Antonio de 1810
Menendez 2420
Menéndez de Avilés 1359
Menéndez Pidal 2088
Menorca 3358, 3867
Mercado Filatelico 2464
Mercado Unico 3193
Mercury 1492
Merida 2183, 2246, 2920
Merino 2860

SPAIN *Design Index*

Messenger 2648
Metro 3294
Mexico 2054, 2541
Micaela 1176
Mila 3047
Military Academy, Zagreb 3856
Military Engineering College 3991
Millennium Development Goals 4429
Minerals 3260, 3314, 3366
Miner's lamp 3366
Mini 2273
Ministry of Public Works 3808
Mire antes de Cruzar 2357
Miro, G. 2645
Miro, J. 3212
Misterio de Elche 2877
Misterios Smo Rosario 1524
Mistral 3019
Mogrovejo 1685
Molina 1137
Moliner 3093
Mombeltran 2037
Mon 3852
Monastery of St. Thomas 2169
Monastery of Santo Domingo de Silos 2217
Monnet 2693
Monteagudo 1802
Monterrey 2036
Montevideo 2339
Montserrat 1255
Montserrat Monastery 713
Monturiol 2928
Morales 2021
Moratin 1389
Morato 1064
Mosaics 4242, 4420
Mota 1653
Moths 4494
Motolinia 3129
Mourelle 1879
Movida Madrilena (Madrid movement) **MS**4247
Mujer 3350
Murcia 1620, 1964, 1994, 2735
Murillo 1333, 1524, 2061
Murillo, J. 3966
Museo Postal 2663
Mushrooms *see* Fungi
Music 3895
Musical instruments 4504, 4512, 4533
Mutis 3245

Najera 2108
Nativity 3131, 3194
NATO 3436
National Bank 4154
National Flag 4406
National Heritage **MS**4378, **MS**4379
Natural Heritage **MS**4110, **MS**4454
Nature 3854, 4075, 4343, 4430
Nature Reserves 4523, 4537
Nautical Astronomy 4069
Navarra 1621, 1937, 1965, 2782
Navidad *see* Christmas
Nebrija 1070
Nerja 2859
New Mexico 3527
New York 1651
Newspaper and camera 2637
Newspapers 3999, 4027, 4111, 4166
Nicaragua 2212
Niño Judio, El (operetta) 2772
Nobel Prize Winners 3936
Nocturlabio 3130
Nolasco 1585
Notariado Latino 2328
Ntra Sra de Antipolo 1753
Ntra Sra de la Merced 1582
Numancia (ship) 1667
Nuñez de Balboa 1588
Nurse 1184
Nutka 1878
Nuts 2146, 2302

OCDE 2896
Ochoa 3278, 3937
O'Higgins 1999
OIT 3265
Olite 1801
Olymphilex 85 2795
Olymphilex 92 3187
Olympic Games, Beijing 4374
Olympics 1678, 1737, 1909, 1943, 2132, 2156, 2778, 2925, 2946, 2973, 2977, 3008, 3031, 3056, 3076, 3098, 3123, 3144, 3179, 3180, 3183
"Olympus" Satellite 3106
O.N.C.E. 2998
Oranges 2301
Orellana 1740
Orense 1622, 1966, 2043
Orfeo Catala 3115
Orfeo Pamplones 3192
Organización Mundial del Turismo 2307, 3348
Orinoco 1947
Orleans, A. de 2633
Orleans, Maria de las Mercedes de Borbón y 3645
Oro 4365
Orquesta nacional 3092
Ortega y Gasset 2615
Oruro 1815
Osaka 3007
Oscar Niemeyer International Cultural Centre **MS**4532
Osprey 3550
Ossio 2247
Our Lady of Asuncion Church 4121
Oviedo 1455, 1623, 1967, 3088
Oviedo University 4346

Pablo, San *see* Paul
Pablo VI *see* Paul VI
Pacheco 1924
Pacto And ino 2792
Padilla 3071
Paella 2949
Paintings 3941, 3975, 1055
Pais Vasco 3068
Palacios 2296
Palencia 1692, 1861, 2007, 2470, 2659, **MS**3074
Pan-American Postal Congress 697
Panem Nostrum Quotidiánum 1573
Pantocrator de Tahull 1429
Paper making (stained glass window) **MS**4448
Paradores 3469, 3583, 3641, 3716, 3912, 3971, 4049, 4114
Paralimpiada 3188
Paralympics 3173, 3188
Parc Guell 4071
Pardo Bazán 2129
Paredes 1590
Paris 3005
Parks 4275
Parliament of Toro 4144
Parral 1952
Parranda, La (operetta) 2713
Patrimonio Mundial de la Humanidad 3134
Paul, St. 1554
Paul VI, Pope 1601
Pavo 3040
Paz y Liberated 3329
Peace 207
Pedraza 2155
Pelayo 1205
Peligro del Fuego 2753
Pelota 1349, 1378, 1655, 2879
Peñafiel 1940
Peñaflorida, Conde de 2853
Peñiacola 1871
Pensacola, Battle of 2370
Pentathlon 3098
Pérez 2934
Perez Galdos 2087
Personalities 4365, 4529
Peru 2542
Peseta 3853
PHILAIBERIA '02 **MS**3851
Philaserdica 79 2572
Philippine Independence 3486
Philippine stamp 4067
Picasso 2529, 2636, **MS**2657
Pineda 742
Pinzon, M. 613
Pinzón, V. 616, 2937
Piquer 3849
Pirita 3262
Pistol 3065
Pius XI, Pope 470
Pizarro 1686, 2985
Pla 3274
Plants 2143, 2178, 2278, 2299, 2517, 2866, **MS**3311, 3839
Playing cards 3289
Plaza de Toros 1332
Poblet 1555
Pole vaulting 2159
Police 2708, 3558
Polo 3340
Ponce de León 1361
Ponferrada 1870
Pontevedra 1693, 1712, 2008, 2916
Popular dances 4442, 4446/7, 4449/50, 4460/1, 4467/8, 4476/**MS**4477
Porcelana y Ceramica **MS**3104
Portolá 2888
Postal service 2374, 3769
Postcodes 2923
Postmark 2150
Postmen 4211
Potato 3039
Potes 1602
Pottery 2361
Poveda 2239
Pre-Olímpica 2977, 3008, 3031, 3056, 3076
Presidency of European Union 4502
Prevenir las Caidas 2752
Prieto 2751
Prince of Asturias Awards 4136
Principe de Asturias 2989
Pro Infancia Hungara 1263
"Protege..." 2517
Psiquiatria 1806
Puerto Rico 2166, 2693
Puppets 4145

Queen Isabel 4083
Quesada 1516
Quevedo 1061, 2646
Quiroga 2056

Rada 2020
Radiologia 1848
Railway 1107, 1295, 2606, 2690, 2961, 3242, 3294, 3318, 3997
Railway Congress 534
Raimundo de Penafort, St. 1586
Rainbow 4073
Ram 2860
Ramon y Cajal 1139
Raspall 3425
Real Betis Balompie Football Club 4268
Real Club Deportivo de la Coruna 3578
Real Club Recreativo 3578
Real Geographic Society **MS**3993
Real Madrid Football Club 3850
Real Phelipe (ship) **MS**3371
Real Sociedad de Futbol 4463
Real Union Iron Football Club 3857
Recaredo 1599
Red Cross 849, 1595, 1983, 2202
Reial Club Deportiu Espanyol Football Club 3644
Reina Mora, La (operetta) 2776
Renewable Energy 4425
Reporter Tribulete 3385
Requesens 2354
Revoltosa, La (operetta) 2775
Revolución francesa 3002
Reyes Catolicos 2933
Ribera, Jose 1192, 1559
Ribera, Juan *see* Juan
Riesgos de la Electricidad 2754
Rio Muni 1694
Rioja 2726
Rioja Wine Harvest Festival 4204
Ripoll 2063, 2554, 3307
Rivera 2034
Road safety 2357, 4456
Rodrigo 3717
Rodriguez 2177
Romanic Architecture 4011
Rome 2241
Romero de Torres 1718
Roncesvalles 2111
Rosa del Azafran (operetta) 2716
Rosales 2261
Rowing 2158, 2385, 3100, 3341, 4022
Royal Automobile Club **MS**3968
Royal Family E417, **MS**3382
Royal Spanish Academy **MS**4405
Royal Spanish Football Federation 4475
Royal Spanish Tennis Federation 4388
Royal Theatre, Madrid 3453
Rubal 4212
Rubens 1495, 2511
Rubio 3865
Running 1367, 1512, 2566, 3188, 3297
Rural schools 3950

Sadaba 2038
Safety at work 2752
Sagas 2120
Sagasta 3934
Sagunto 856
Sahagun 2127
Saint Maria de Carracedo Monastery **MS**4024
St. Domingo de la Calzada 2107
St. James Holy Year 3464, 3552
St. Mary's Cathedral **MS**3926
Sahara 1695, 2009
Sailing 3986
Sajazarra 2151
Salamanca. 1696, 1934, 2010, 2870, 3135, 3400, 3767
Salamanca, Marqués de 1106
Salamanca University 1188, 4134
Salinas Anchor Museum 4054
Salesianos en Espana 2704
Salle 2559
Salmeren 737
Saltilla 3287
Salvoechea 765
Salzillo 1896, 2721
Samos 1383
San Cristóbel de la Laguna 3455
San Diego 1990
San Fermín 2771
San Jorge 2360
San Jorge Church 3923
San Juan de la Pena Monastery 2342
San Juan Nepomuceno (ship) **MS**3321
San Luis, Conde de 1062
San Martín 2537
San Salvador Cathedral **MS**3524
San Sebastian 1577
San Servando 2154
San Talmo (ship) **MS**3321
Sancho Ramirez 3282
Sanidad 3202
Santa Catalina 2152
Santa Cruz College 2794
Santa Cruz de Tenerife 3276
Santa Fe **MS**3102
Santa Maria (ship) 593, 1662
Santa Maria de Nieva 2539
Santa Maria de los Remedios 4172
Santa Maria la Real Church 3706
Santa Maria of Montserrat Monaster, 3635
Santander 1697, 1711, 1840, 2012, 2917
Santángel 3128
Sant Esteve Church 4101
Santiago 2121, 2381, 2745, 3046, 3354
Santiago Cathedral 906
Santiago de Leon de Caracas 1951
Santiago University 3352
Santissima Trinidad (ship) 1666
Sarasate 2449
"Sastreria" 2046
Satellite 3062
Scales 3372
School of Civil Engineers 3938
Science 1648, 4235, 4330, 4333, 445
Scorpion 2581
Scouting 2733, 4249
Script 4258
Seals (animals) 2521
Seals (documentary) 1577

Securidad Vial 3210
Segovia.... 1607, 1698, 1799, 2013, 2242, 2846, 3045
Segovia, A. 3203
Seguridad y la Cooperacion 2628
Sender 3949
Seneca 1767
Seoane 3998
Serra 1587, 2788
Serrano 2777
Sert 1770
Servet 2448
Servicio Filatélico 3390
Seu Villa Old Cathedral 3973
Seventh Anniv of Republic 837
Sevilla 1699, 1708, 1790, 2014, 2523, 2661, 2666, 2698, 2740, 2748, 2797, 2844, 2914, 3136, 3143, 3362, 3518
Seville Cathedral 864
Seville Football Club 4102
Seville University 4098
Shawls **MS**4031
Shepherd 2991
Ship leaving port 4084
Ships 1130, 1254, 1420, 1575, 1660, 1876, 2288, 2486, 2803, 2900, 3079, 3139, **MS**3147, **MS**3174, 3176, 3286, **MS**3321, **MS**3371
Shooting 1943, 3125, 3343, 3380, 3476
Shot, Putting the 1678
Shrine of the Book 4197
"sierra nevada 95" **MS**3311
Signature and building 1071
Siguenza 1936
Silos 1427, 2217, 2220
Skating 2133, 2946
Ski jumping 2132
Skiing 1680, 1909, 2457, 2635, 3299, **MS**3311, 3375
Snake 2254
Snowflakes 2990
Socialist Youth Movement 4177
Sociedades Economicas de Amigos del Pais 2451
Society of Authors and Publishers 3585
Sofia, Queen 2348, 2943
Solana 2135
Soldier 1250
Soler 2722
Somport Tunnel 3929
Sor 2834
Soria 1700, 1789, 2015
Sorolla 1187, 1627
Soto 1360
Space rocket **MS**3382
Spain-Israel Diplomatic Relations 4197
Spanish-American Exhibition 627
Spanish Artists 4386
Spanish Cancer Association 4020
Spanish Ceramics 4498
Spanish Cinema ...4507, 4510, 4534
Spanish Interpol 4119
Spanish National Mint **MS**4448
Spanish Olympic Academy 3534
Spanish Philatelic Associations 4257
Spanish Television 4217
Spectroscopicum Internationale 1982
Spirit of St. Louis 515
Sponge 2579
Sporting Events in 2010 4526
Stained glass windows 2741, 2844
Stamp Day 1055, 1080, 1205, 1231, 1258, 1492, 1570, 1656, 1718, 2528, 2574, 2621, 2688, 2738, 2787, 2840, 2880, 2929, 2959, 3013, 3059, 3103, 3142, 3204, 3264, 3317, 3368, 3418, 3520, 3714, 3858, 3953, 4078, 4120, 4360
Stamps 1141, 1409, 1656, 1718, 1749, 1783, 1856, 1927, 1980, 2032, 2091, 2185, 2237, 2286, 2363, 2464, 2597, 2622, 2976, 3001, 3030, **MS**3382, 3390, 3626
Starfish 2582
Statue of Liberty 845
Steam Locomotive 534
Stop Violence against Women Campaign 4335
Stylized figures 4511
Submarine Service 857a
Swimming 2047, 2260, 2878, 3077, 3304, 3377, 3961

Table and chair 3107
Table tennis 3124
Tahull 1429
Talavera 2248
Talgo 3318
Tank 2573, 2618
Tapestry **MS**2627, **MS**3086, **MS**4378, **MS**4379, **MS**4454, **MS**4535
Tarrasa 2313
Tarrega 2450
Tarrogona 1701, 2016, 3253
Tassis 2959
Tassis y Peralta 3103
Teacher and pupil 4233
Technical Institute of Geology and mining 3587
Technology Engineering Works 4032
Telecomunicaciones 1731
Telecomunicaciones y Desarrollo Humano 3217
Telegraph 1245, 3368, 4108
Telephone 2356
Templo de la Sa. Familia 1345
Tenerife 1702, 2011, 2380, 2584, 2757, 3276
Tenor saxophone 4504
Tennis 3123, 3342, 3379, **MS**4044
Teresa, St., de Jesus 2465
Teresa, St., of Avila 1490, 2086, 2694
Teresian Reformation 1489
Terradas 2836
Teruel1703, 1993, 2017, 2699, 3089
Teruel Mountains 4007
Thebussem 1055
Tiahuanaco **MS**2625
Tiepolo 1531
Tirant to Blanch (book) 3073
Titian 2514
Tiziano .... *see* Titian
Toledo (town) 1706, 1756, 2018, 2312, 2471, 2806, 2845, 2890, 2894, 3134
Toledo, Fadrique de 1738
Toledo, Francisco de 1684
Toledo Cathedral **MS**4085
Toledo Mountains 4343
Tomato 3037
Tordesillas 3283
Torero Antiguo 1328
Torrelobaton 1989
Torres Quevedo 1230, 2720
Tortoise 2250
Tourism 1649, 2307, 3087, 4485
Town planning 4515
Toys 4145, 4223, 4320
Traditional sports 4356, 4362, **MS**4369, 4375, **MS**4376, 4391, **MS**4401
Trains .... *see* Railway
Trajano 2249
Transport 1645
Trasplante de Organes 2689
Tratado Antartico 3139
Treaty of Rome 4244
Tree and globe 1796
Trees 2143, 2178, 2462, 2519, 3656, 3759, 3837, 3994, 4021, 4095, 4155, 4336
Trulock 4002
Trumpet 4512
Turegano 1985
Turina 2723
Typewriter 3331

UGT 2960
UIT 1731, 2203, 3062
Unamuno 2052
UNESCO 3533
UNICEF 2112, 2902
Uniforms 2197, 2225, 2255, 2290, 2322, 2410, 2441, 2472, 2499, 3012
Union Europea 3349
Union Europea Occidental 3296
Union Interparlamentaria 2419
United Nations 2062, 3346, 3773
Universal Declaration of Human Rights 3535
Universal Postal Union 2269
UPAE 1523
UPU 1127, 3597
Urban Architecture 4071
Urdaneta 1754, 2988
Uruguay 2338
Ustariz 2165

Vaca 2987
Valcobero 2276
Valdavia 2275
Valdes 1883
Valdivia 2000
Valencia de Don Juan 2035
Valencia de., P. 2000
Valencia (town) 1713, 1757, 1855, 2072, 2578, 2739, 2757, 2981
Valencia University 3643
Valera 3325, 1406
Vallodolid ... 1758, 1795, 2073, 2885 2947, **MS**3189
Valladolid University 2794
Valle de los Caidos 1311
Valle Inclán 1818
Vazquez de Coronado 2431
Vazquez de Melia 1412
Vega .... *see* Garcilaso de Vega
Vega .... *see* Lope de Vega
Velazquez 763, 1301, 1386, 1401, **MS**1405, 1491, 3591, **MS**4480
Velez Blanco 1987
Verbena de la Paloma (operetta) 2679
Verdaguer 2447
Veruela 1892
Vespucio 2932
Victoria 2833
Vigo, River 2662
Villaespesa 2562
Villafranca del Bierzo 2124
Villalonso 1986
Villalpando 2700
Villanueva 2176
Villasobroso 1941
Vincente de Paul, St. 1357
Virgin and Crowds 4064
Virgen de Irache 1428
Virgen de la Cabeza 2310
Virgen de la Esperanza 2967
Virgen del Pilar 982
Virgen Macarena 1659
Virgin Mary (wooden carving) 4269
Virgin of La Palma 2623
Virgins **MS**2625
"Visita del Caudillo a Canarias" (opt) 1149
Vitoria 2045, 2652, 3060
Vitoria, F. de 2899
Vives, A. 2085, 2676
Vives, L. 3191
Vives, P. 2631
Vizcaya 1759, 2074
Volleyball 3146
Volunteer's Day 3795
Volver a Empezar 3309

Water polo 3345
Weightlifting 2157, 3056
Wheat 1646
White Virgin Festival 4064
Wine 3879, 3880, 3987, 4065
Wolf 2162
Women's Conference 3350
Women writers 4266
Women voting 4158
World Athletics Championship 3561
World Book Day 3723
World Cup Football Championship, Brazil 3463
World Cycling Championship 4130
World Heritage Sites 3401, 3448, 3491, 3595, 3674, 3796, 3906, 4513
World Mathematics Year 3647
World University Summer Games **MS**3581
World Water Day 3421
Wrestling 2387, 2780, 3076
Xavier 4216
Xavier Castle 865
Xavier, St. 1178
Xirgu 3140
XXV Años de Paz 1637

Yacht 4238
Yachting 1946, 2973, 3145, 3306, 3344, 3381
Year of the Elderly 3593
Ysasi 2569
Yuste 1746

Zambrano 3201
Zamora 1707, 1760, 2075, 2913
Zanetti 3589
Zaragoza 2008 .... 4273, 4337, **MS**4370, **MS**4373
Zaragoza 1761, 2044, 2076, 2364, 2575, **MS**3069
Zaragoza University 2734
Zorilla 750
Zuazo 2297
Zuloaga 1084, 2077
Zumarraga 2057
Zurbaran 1479, 1691

CARLIST ISSUES

2nd Carlist War, 1872–76

The following stamps were issued by the Carlists in those parts of Northern Spain controlled by them in 1872–76.

The Carlist movement began in 1833, when King Ferdinand VII abrogated the Salic Law, which debarred a woman from ascending the throne, in order to assure the succession of his daughter Isabella; his brother, Don Carlos, was deprived of his right of kingship. After Ferdinand died, Don Carlos claimed the throne, and from 1834 to 1839 he unsuccessfully fought the First Carlist War to make good his claim.

The Second Carlist War began in 1872, when another Don Carlos, grandson of the first pretender, claimed the throne as Carlos VII. After King Amadeo's abdication in 1873 was followed by a republic, the Carlists gained firm support in Navarra and Catalonia; but the proclamation of Alfonso XII as king in December 1874 won over many Carlist supporters, and on 28 February 1876 Don Carlos left Spain for the last time.

BISCAY, NAVARRA, GUIPÚZCOA and AVALA

(Basque Region)

100 Céntimos = 1 Real

1   2

(Litho J. Cluzeau, Bayonne)

1873 (1 July). Without "tilde" (~) over "N" of "ESPANA". Imperf.

(a) Thin white paper

1	1	1r. blue	£600
		a. Pale blue	£600

(b) Thick white glazed paper

2	1	1r. blue	£600
		a. Bright blue	£600

1873 (Sept). With "tilde" over "N" of "ESPANA". Thick white glazed paper. Imperf.

3	2	1r. blue	£500	£450
		a. Deep blue	£500	£450

In the early settings with "tilde" over "N" the "tilde" was added by removing the white line above "ESPANA" from each stamp on the stone, leaving a segment above the "N" to represent the "tilde" which in these settings varies considerably but usually appears as a short line rather than a properly curved "tilde". In the last setting (Feb. 1874) the "tilde" is a properly curved one, and is the same on all stamps in the sheet.

This stamp, with and without "tilde", has been reprinted four times. The reprints have the impression more blurred; and the space in the right lower spandrel above "1rl." is either a shapeless blot or contains a different number of horizontal lines from the original, which has 22.

3   4

(Des Sotero Aresse. Litho J. de Parada, Burdeos)

1874 (1 Aug). Imperf.

4	3	1r. deep lilac°	£275	£275

°Exists with punched hole cancellation. See note above No. 172.

(Des Sotero Aresse. Litho J. J. Laborde, Tolosa)

1875 (1 Mar). Imperf.

(a) White paper

5	4	50c. green	9·75	95·00
		a. Yellow-green	9·75	95·00
		b. Error. Brown	£550	
		c. "C" omitted after "50" at right	£100	
		d. Greek border reversed	£400	
6		1r. brown	9·75	95·00
		a. Greek border reversed	£500	

(b) Bluish paper

7	4	50c. green	55·00	
		a. Emerald-green	55·00	
8		1r. brown	55·00	

This issue was first produced with horizontal margins of 2 mm between the stamps. This setting was later altered to give a horizontal margin of 1½ mm. Nos. 5d and 6a come from the narrow setting; and the values on bluish paper only come from the narrow setting.

On the normal 1r. the Greek border is as illustrated; on the normal 50c. the top key faces outwards. In setting up the stones for these two values, one transfer of the wrong value was inserted in each, being the last stamp in the third row in each instance. This was discovered before printing and the lower label was erased and redrawn to give the correct value, but this resulted in a variety in each case, namely 50c. with the Greek border as in 1r. and *vice versa*, Nos. 5d and 6a.

CATALONIA

34 Maravedis Vellon (copper) = 1 Real

5

(Typo Soler y Arqués, Besova)

1874 (15 Apr). Imperf.

9	5	16m. rose	4·75	85·00
		a. Bright rose	4·75	85·00

There are 100 varieties of type of this stamp.

Although inscribed 16 maravedis vellon Nos. 9/a did duty as a ½ real stamp.

VALENCIA

100 Céntimos = 1 Real

6

(Litho F. Carrera)

1874 (1 Sept). Imperf.

10	6	1r. rose	£130	£130
		a. Rose-lake	£130	£130

There are two types of this stamp, arranged in alternate horizontal rows. In one type the scroll containing the words "ESPANA VALENCIA" touches the frame-line, while in the other it is 1½ mm. from it. There are other minor differences.

CIVIL WAR, 1936–39

REGIONAL AND LOCAL ISSUES IN THE NATIONALIST AREAS

We list below stamps which we understand were authorised by local civil governors or military commanders and which were actually put into use. A number of issues were privately produced without authority and must be considered as being merely propaganda labels; others were duly authorised but circumstances intervened to prevent them from being put on sale and used at the time.

A very large number of overprint errors exist and we have not attempted to list them.

In addition in default of any other stamps being available it was common practice to use fiscal stamps either with or without overprints and this was legalised by a decree of 9 November 1936.

Stamps of Spain overprinted

ANTEQUERA

(Province of Malaga)

Antequera
—
"Viva
España"
Julio-1936

(1)

SPAIN / Civil War, 1936–39

1936 (10 Oct). Optd with T **1**.

(a) POSTAGE

1	143	1c. blue-green	10	10
2		2c. chestnut (p 11½)	45	45
3	144	2c. chestnut	10	10
4	126	5c. chocolate	30	30
5	129	10c. green	45	45
6	130	15c. blue-green (R.)	65	65
7	131	15c. blue-green (R.)	95	95
8	127	20c. violet (R.)	65	65
9	132	25c. deep lake	65	65
10	136	30c. carmine	65	65
11	138	40c. deep ultramarine (R.)	95	95
12	130	50c. deep ultramarine (R.)	3·75	3·75
13	138	60c. yellow-green	2·75	2·75
14	142	1p. black (R.)	1·60	1·60
15	–	4p. magenta (768)	30·00	30·00
16	–	10p. brown (769)	42·00	42·00

(b) AIR

17	145	2p. dull blue	£125	£125

(c) EXPRESS LETTER

E18	E **145**	20c. red	95	95
1/E18 Set of 18			£200	£200

Authorised by decree of the Military Commander on 26 Sept 1936. The overprint is known on some of the above stamps in different colours and also on other postage stamps and on the Lope de Vega issue, but it is believed these were not regularly issued.

AVILA

(Province of Avila)

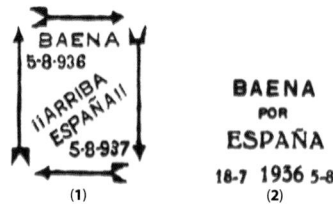

(1)

1937 (24 July). Optd with T **1**.

1	143	1c. pale green	15·00	15·00
2	144	2c. chestnut	12·00	12·00
3	127	20c. violet	12·00	12·00
4	130	50c. orange	35·00	35·00
5	138	60c. yellow-green	35·00	35·00
1/5 Set of 5			£100	£100

Authorised by the President of the Commission of Communications and Public Works on 29 May 1937.

BAENA

(Province of Córdoba)

(1)   (2)

(Applied by D. José Hector)

1937 (July–Aug). Landing of Nationalist Troops in Cadiz on 18 July 1936 and Liberation of Baena on 5 Aug 1936.

*(a) Handstamped with T **1***

1	181	1c. green	1·25	1·25
2	182	2c. red-brown	1·25	1·25
3	183	5c. olive-brown (opt sideways)	2·00	2·00
4		10c. yellow-green (opt sideways)	2·50	2·50
5	184	15c. black	6·00	6·00
6		20c. violet	9·50	9·50
7		25c. lake	8·25	8·25
8		30c. rose-lake (II)	2·50	2·50
9		50c. deep blue	12·00	12·00
10		1p. blue	12·00	12·00
1/10 Set of 10			50·00	50·00

*(b) Optd with T **2***

11	181	1c. green (R.)	60	60
12	143	2c. chestnut (B.)	60	60
13	182	2c. red-brown (Bk.)	60	60
14	184	15c. black (R.)	2·50	2·50
		a. Blue opt	30·00	30·00
15		30c. rose-lake (II) (B.)	2·50	2·50
11/15 Set of 5			6·00	6·00

Authorised by decree of the Civil Governor of Córdoba and the Military Commander of Baena.

Nos. 11/15 exist with tryptych overprints in the sheet comprising Type **2**, and two other types (a) with "VIVA FRANCO" and (b) "VIVA QUEIPO" in place of "POR ESPANA".

BILBAO

¡VIVA ESPAÑA!
BILBAO
19 Junio 1937

¡VIVA ESPAÑA!
BILBAO
19 Junio 1937
—
CORREO
AÉREO

(1)   (2)

1937 (17 July). Liberation of Bilbao on 5 July 1937.

*(a) POSTAGE. Optd as T **1***

1	143	1c. blue-green	55	55
2	144	2c. chestnut	20	20
3	126	5c. chocolate	45	45
4	129	10c. green	45	45
5	131	15c. blue-green	1·00	1·00
6	127	20c. violet	1·00	1·00
7	132	25c. deep lake	1·00	1·00
8	136	30c. carmine	1·00	1·00
9	147	30c. carmine	£150	£150

*(b) AIR. Optd with T **2***

10	155	30c. carmine	2·00	2·00
		a. Blue opt	3·25	3·25
1/10 Set of 10			£140	£140

Authorised by D. Herminio Alvarez.

BURGOS

Republican stamps exist overprinted "VIVA ESPANA Burgos Julio 1936" but we have no evidence that these were authorised. Various fiscal stamps were overprinted "VIVA ESPANA' CORREOS Orden 9 Nvbre, 1936." with authority but some were done unofficially so we have not attempted to list these.

HABILITA
DO PARA
LA CO-
RRESPON-
DENCIA
URGENTE

Habilitado
para la co-
rrespond.ia
urgente

(E 1)   (E 2)

1936 (Oct–Nov). EXPRESS LETTER. No. 652 optd over blocks of four.

*(a) With Type E **1** (Oct)*

E1	115	5c. (×4) black		

*(b) With Type E **2** (Nov)*

E2	115	5c. (×4) black	21·00	21·00

Correspondencia
URGENTE

(E 3)   4

1936 (Oct). EXPRESS LETTER. Pair of No. 742 optd with Type E **3**.

E3	129	10c. (×2) green	3·75	3·75

1936. AIR. Fiscal stamps as in T **4**. Control number on front. P 11½.

4		25c. grey-green and black (B.)	40·00	40·00
		a. Red opt	30·00	30·00
5		1p.50 blue and black (R.)	6·50	6·50
6		3p. rose and black (B.)	6·50	6·50

SPAIN / Civil War, 1936–39

5 (Royal Crown)   E 6

1936 (Dec). AIR. Various fiscal stamps optd as in T **5**.

*(a) Inscr "TIMBRE PARA FACTURAS". Blue control number on back.
P 13½–14 or 11½*

7		15c. blue-green (Royal Crown) (R.)	4·25	4·25
8		25c. blue (Royal Crown) (R.)	35·00	35·00
9		25c. blue (Mural Crown) (R.)	£275	£275

(b) Mural Crown. Inscr "ESPECIAL PARA FACTURAS Y RECIBOS". Black control number on back. P 11½

10		15c. grey-green (R.)	12·00	12·00
11		25c. olive (R.)	95·00	95·00

(c) Inscr "PARA EFECTOS DE COMMERCIO"

(i) Royal Crown. Blue control number on back. P 14

12		1p.20 green	30·00	30·00
13		2p.40 green	30·00	30·00

(ii) Mural Crown. Without control number. P 11½

14		20c. green	15·00	15·00
15		1p.20 green	30·00	30·00

1936 (Dec). EXPRESS LETTER. Fiscal stamps optd as in Type E **6**. P 11½.

(a) Inscr "CLASE 12a". Blue control number on back

E16	E **6**	20c. green	32·00	32·00
		a. Red opt	32·00	32·00

(b) Inscr "CLASE 13a". Without control number

E17	E **6**	20c. green	10·50	10·50
		a. Red opt	10·50	10·50

CORRESPONDENCIA

URGENTE   **URGENTE**
(E **7**)   (E **8**)

1936–37. EXPRESS LETTER.

*(a) Optd with Type E **7***

E18	**127**	20c. violet	15·00	15·00

*(b) Optd with Type E **8***

E19	**127**	20c. violet	20·00	20·00
		a. Red opt	25·00	25·00

(Litho A. Roel, Corunna)

1937 (Mar). AIR. Fiscal stamps (crown and shield over sword type) optd as in T **5**. P 11½.

20		1p.50 blue	12·00	12·00
21		3p. carmine	12·00	12·00

E **9**   E **10**

E **11**   E **12**

1937. EXPRESS LETTER. Fiscal stamps optd in blocks of four as in Types E **9/12**. P 11½.

(a) Without imprint

E22	E **9**	20c. grey-green		
E23	E **10**	20c. grey-green		
E24	E **11**	20c. grey-green		
E25	E **12**	20c. grey-green		
E22/25	Set of 4		35·00	35·00

(b) With imprint. "LIT. e IMP. ROEL"

E26	E **9**	20c. grey-green (R.)		
E27	E **10**	20c. grey-green (R.)		
E28	E **11**	20c. grey-green (R.)		
E29	E **12**	20c. grey-green (R.)		
E26/29	Set of 4		£125	£125

¡VIVA ESPAÑA!
Correo
Aéreo
13

1937. AIR. Republican stamps optd as T **13**.

(a) Opt 15–16 mm high (April)

30	**138**	40c. deep ultramarine (R.)	1·75	1·75
31	**130**	50c. deep ultramarine	2·00	2·00
32	**138**	60c. yellow-green (R.)	2·75	2·75
33	**145**	2p. dull blue (R.)	35·00	35·00
		a. Black opt	55·00	45·00
		b. Blue opt	65·00	60·00
34	**69**	10p. brown	75·00	75·00

(b) Opt 13 mm high (May)

35	**138**	40c. deep ultramarine (R.)	1·75	1·75
36	**130**	50c. deep ultramarine	1·90	1·90
37	**138**	60c. yellow-green (R.)	3·00	3·00
38	**145**	2p. dull blue (R.)	35·00	35·00
		a. Blue opt	65·00	60·00
39	**69**	10p. brown	80·00	80·00

¡VIVA ESPAÑA!   ¡VIVA ESPAÑA!
CORREO   CORREO
AÉREO   AÉREO
(14)   (15)

1937 (May)–**38**. AIR. Republican stamps optd.

*(a) With T **14***

40	**155**	30c. carmine (B.)	2·00	2·00
		a. Black opt	3·25	3·25

*(b) With T **15***

41	**139**	30c. scarlet (B.)	2·00	2·00
		a. Black opt	3·25	2·25

*(c) As T **13***

42	**140**	50c. blue (R.)	1·90	1·90
43	**142**	1p. black	6·50	6·50
44	—	4p. magenta (768)	6·50	6·50
45	—	10p. brown (769) (1.38)	15·00	15·00

These stamps were recovered from the captured Republican steamship "Galdames" and then overprinted.

1937. EXPRESS LETTER. Nationalist issue optd with Type E **7**.

E46	**184**	20c. violet	4·00	4·00
		a. Red opt	9·50	9·50

In 1938 various miniature sheets were overprinted but it is doubtful whether they served any postal purpose.

CADIZ

(Province of Cadiz)

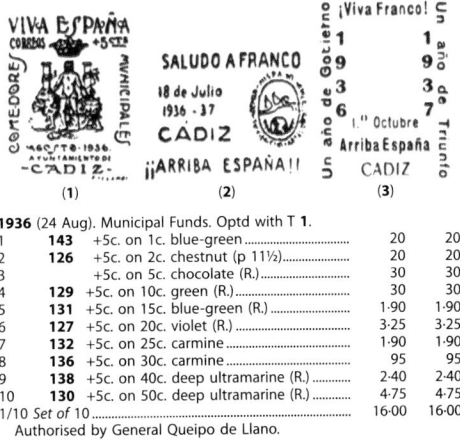

(1)   (2)   (3)

1936 (24 Aug). Municipal Funds. Optd with T **1**.

1	**143**	+5c. on 1c. blue-green	20	20
2	**126**	+5c. on 2c. chestnut (p 11½)	20	20
3		+5c. on 5c. chocolate (R.)	30	30
4	**129**	+5c. on 10c. green (R.)	30	30
5	**131**	+5c. on 15c. blue-green (R.)	1·90	1·90
6	**127**	+5c. on 20c. violet (R.)	3·25	3·25
7	**132**	+5c. on 25c. carmine	1·90	1·90
8	**136**	+5c. on 30c. carmine	95	95
9	**138**	+5c. on 40c. deep ultramarine (R.)	2·40	2·40
10	**130**	+5c. on 50c. deep ultramarine (R.)	4·75	4·75
1/10	Set of 10		16·00	16·00

Authorised by General Queipo de Llano.

373

SPAIN / Civil War, 1936–39

1937 (16 July). Spanish Academy of Arts and Sciences, Cadiz. Variously optd as T **2**.
11	**181**	1c. green	6·50	6·50
12	**182**	2c. red-brown	6·50	6·50
13	**183**	5c. olive-brown	6·50	6·50
14		10c. yellow-green	8·00	8·00
15	**184**	15c. black (Gold)	8·00	8·00
16		30c. rose-lake	6·50	6·50
11/16 Set of 6			37·00	37·00

Authorised by the Technical Junta as published in the Technical Bulletin of Cadiz Province No. 168 of 1937.

1937 (1 Oct). First Anniv of Nationalist Government. Variously optd as T **3**.
17	**181**	1c. green	20	20
		a. Red opt	20	20
18	**182**	2c. red-brown	20	20
		a. Green opt	10	10
19	**183**	5c. olive-brown	1·70	1·70
20		10c. yellow-green (R.)	95	95
21	**184**	15c. black (R.)	95	95
22		20c. violet (R.)	1·10	1·10
23		25c. lake (B.)	65	65
24		30c. rose-lake (B.)	65	65
17/24 Set of 8			6·25	6·25

Authorised by decree of Governor-General of Cadiz.

CANARY ISLANDS

AIR STAMPS

After the airmail service to Seville and Madrid carried out by the Lineas Aereas Postales Españolas Company had been cut off, the Chief Administrator of Las Palmas, with the authorisation of the Junta de Defensa Nacional, organised a provisional airmail service between Las Palmas and Seville, from where it connected with the rest of Europe via Europa-Südamerika Airlines, acting on behalf of the German Lufthansa Company.

Spanish stamps were accordingly surcharged in order to meet the premium required by Lufthansa and each issue was intended to have a currency of about two months pending the restoration of the original service, but the National Government were not able to do this until 5 May 1938; hence the large number of temporary issues.

All these issues contain a large number of errors and we make no attempt to list any of these. Reprints also exist.

```
VIVA ESPAÑA           VIVA ESPAÑA
18 JULIO 1936         18 JULIO 1936
HABILITADO            HABILITADO
AVIÓN                 AVIÓN
                      CANARIAS

Pts. 0'80             80 Cts.
    (1)                  (2)
```

1936 (27 Oct). Surch as T **1**, in blue.
1	143	50c. on 1c. blue-green	33·00	11·50
2		80c. on 2c. chestnut	16·00	4·00
3	126	1p.25 on 5c. chocolate	47·00	16·00

1936 (28 Nov). Surch as T **2** with 2½ mm. space between figure of value and "Cts." or "Pts.". "Pts." after value.
4	143	50c. on 1c. blue-green	5·75	2·75
5		80c. on 2c. chestnut	2·75	1·40
6	126	1.25Pts. on 5c. chocolate (R.)	8·50	3·75

1937 (7 Jan–12 Feb). Surch as T **2** with 1½ mm. space between figure of value and "Cts." or "Pts.". "Pts." before value.
7	143	50c. on 25c. blue-green	14·00	7·50
8		80c. on 2c. chestnut	5·75	3·25
9	126	Pts.1.25 on 5c. chocolate	21·00	13·50

1937 (2 Mar). Surch as T **2** (narrow spacing).
10	143	50c. on 1c. blue-green (R.)	9·50	3·00
11		80c. on 2c. chestnut (G.)	6·50	1·90
12	183	1p.25 on 5c. olive-brown (G.)	6·50	1·90

```
   CANARIAS              VIVA ESPAÑA
      ^                  18 JULIO 1936
   FRANCO                   AVIÓN
 18 JULIO 1936            CANARIAS
   ———
   AVIÓN
   80 Cts.                  +80
     (3)                     (4)
```

1937 (31 Mar). Surch as T **3**, in blue.

(a) 20 mm. between "CANARIAS" and base of value figures
13	143	50c. on 1c. blue-green	16·00	9·00
14		80c. on 2c. chestnut	16·00	9·00

(b) 18 mm. between "CANARIAS" and base of value figures
15	143	50c. on 1c. blue-green	5·75	2·50
16		80c. on 2c. chestnut	5·00	1·50
17	183	1p.25 on 5c. olive-brown	5·00	1·50

1937 (15 Apr). Surch as T **4**, in blue. Plus sign united to value.
18	184	+80c. on 30c. rose-lake	21·00	8·00
19	138	+80c. on 60c. yellow-green	28·00	10·50

1937 (5 May). Surch as T **4**. Plus sign separated from value.
20	132	+50c. on 25c. deep lake (B.)	60·00	15·00
21	184	+80c. on 30c. rose-lake (B.)	25·00	15·00
22	138	+80c. on 60c. yellow-green (B.)	35·00	20·00
23	184	+1p.25 on 30c. rose-lake (B.)	28·00	10·50
24	130	+1p.25 on 50c. deep ultram (R.)	25·00	12·50
25	142	+1p.25 on 1p. black (R.)	70·00	21·00
20/25 Set of 6			£200	85·00

```
 ARRIBA ESPAÑA
18 JULIO 1936              CANARIAS
  CANARIAS
    AVION               CORREO AÉREO
  80 Cts.                 50 Cts.
    (5)                     (6)
```

1937 (25 May). Surch as T **5**, in brownish black.
26	143	50c. on 1c. blue-green	7·50	1·60
27	179	80c. on 2c. chestnut	5·75	1·40
28	183	1p.25 on 5c. olive-brown	5·75	1·40

1937 (1 July). Surch as T **6**.
29	179	50c. on 2c. chestnut	1·70	55
30	144	80c. on 2c. chestnut	£275	£275
31	183	80c. on 5c. olive-brown	2·10	95
32	143	1p.25 on 1c. blue-green (as 770 but perf 11)	2·50	95
33	183	2p.50 on 10c. yellow-green	14·00	4·75
34	184	+80c. on 30c. rose-lake (II)	1·50	1·00
35		+1p.25 on 50c. deep blue (R.)	6·50	3·25
36		+1p.25 on 1p. blue (R.)	10·50	5·50
29/36 Set of 8			£300	£175

(7)

```
  Pts. 1'25
 CORREO AÉREO
  CANARIAS
    (8)
```

1937 (16 July). Tax stamp of Las Palmas (inscr "PRO LAS PALMAS"), surch as T **7**. Wmk Crosses and Circles (as Type M **7** of Wurttemburg). P 14½x13½.
37		50c. on 5c. blue (Br.)	4·75	2·75
38		80c. on 5c. blue (G.)	2·75	1·90
39		1p.25 on 5c. blue (V.)	3·75	1·90

1937 (29 Oct). Surch as T **8**.
40	183	50c. on 5c. olive-brown (G.)	14·00	2·75
41		80c. on 10c. yellow-grn (O.)	4·75	1·90
42	182	1p.25 on 2c. red-brown (G.)	17·00	5·75

```
 CANARIAS              CANARIAS
  80 Cts.             Correo Aéreo
Correo Aéreo            +30 C
   (9)                   (10)
```

1937 (23 Dec). Surch as T **9**.
43	181	50c. on 1c. green (R.) (892)	14·00	3·75
44	182	80c. on 2c. red-brown (B.)	4·75	1·90
45	183	1p.25 on 10c. yellow-green (V.)	14·00	3·75

1937 (27 Dec). Surch as T **10**.
46	**184**	+30c. on 30c. rose-lake	2·75	1·90
47		+2p.30 on 60c. yellow (G.)	33·00	19·00
48		+2p.50 on 50c. deep blue (G.)	33·00	19·00
49		+5p. on 1p. blue (Br.)	38·00	19·00

(11) (12) (13)

1938 (4 Feb). Surch as T **11** or **12** (Nos. 53/54).
50	**182**	50c. on 2c. chocolate (893)	3·75	1·40
51	**183**	80c. on 5c. olive-brown (G.)	2·75	1·10
52		1p.25 on 10c. yellow-green (B.)	3·75	1·40
53	**184**	+80c. on 30c. rose-lake (B.) (II)	3·25	1·10
54		+1p.25 on 50c. deep blue (R.)	4·75	1·40
50/54	Set of 5		18·00	6·50

1938 (14 Feb). Surch as T **13**.
55	**184**	2p.50 on 20c. violet (Br.)	55·00	28·00
56		5p. on 25c. lake (G.)	55·00	28·00
57		10p. on 40c. orange (V.)	55·00	28·00

DURANGO

(Province of Vizcaya)

(1)

1937 (1 May). Liberation of Durango, 28 April 1937. Optd as T **1**.

(a) POSTAGE
1	**143**	1c. green	50	50
2		2c. chestnut (p 11½)	90	90
3	**144**	2c. chestnut	30	30
4	**126**	5c. chocolate (B.)	40	40
5	**129**	10c. green	60	60
6	**131**	15c. blue-green (R.)	70	70
7	**127**	20c. violet (B.)	1·00	1·00
8	**132**	25c. deep lake	90	90
9	**136**	30c. carmine	70	70
10	**138**	40c. deep ultramarine (R.)	1·50	1·50
11	**130**	50c. deep ultramarine (R.)	4·00	4·00
12	**138**	60c. yellow-green	2·25	2·25
13	**142**	1p. black (R.)	2·25	2·25
14	–	4p. magenta (768)	£125	£125
15	–	10p. brown (769)	£125	£125

(b) EXPRESS LETTER
E16	E **145**	20c. red	1·00	1·00
1/E16	Set of 16		£225	£225

Authorised by Burgomaster D. Adolfo Uribasterra.
Some of the above exist overprinted in other colours but it is doubtful whether they were authorised.

GRANADA

1 Arms

(Des A. Arel. Litho)

1936 (17 Aug). P 11.
1	**1**	30c. blue	£650	£450

Issued first at Granada by the Junta de Defensa Nacional and after relief from the siege of Granada it was used in other parts of Nationalist Spain.

This stamp exists in blue and in green imperf on thin paper with blurred impression but these are thought to be proofs although used copies are known. Beware of forgeries.

The 30c. in red (perf or imperf), in bright green (perf) as also the 50c. brown and 75c. orange-yellow (both perf) are all bogus.

LOGRONO

(Province of Logroño)

(1)

1937 (6 Nov). Optd with T **1**, in blue.
1	**181**	1c. green	50	50
2	**143**	2c. chestnut (p 11½)	70	70
3	**179**	2c. chestnut	3·75	3·75
4	**182**	2c. red-brown	50	50
5	**183**	5c. olive-brown (*sideways*)	70	70
6		10c. yellow-green (*sideways*)	70	70
7	**184**	15c. black	1·25	1·50
8		20c. violet	3·50	3·50
9		30c. rose-lake	3·50	3·50
10		40c. orange	12·00	12·00
11		50c. deep blue	15·00	15·00
12		60c. yellow	20·00	20·00
13		1p. blue	26·00	26·00
1/13	Set of 13		80·00	80·00

Authorised by the Communications Commission of the State Technical Junta, on 11 April 1937.

MALAGA

(Province of Málaga)

(1)  (2)

(Optd by Juan Marra)

1937 (Feb–Mar). Optd as T **1**.

(a) POSTAGE
1	**66**	1c. green	20	20
2	**143**	1c. blue-green	20	20
		a. Red opt	50	50
3	**126**	2c. red-brown	11·00	11·00
		a. Red opt	47·00	47·00
4	**143**	2c. chestnut (p 11)	20	20
5		2c. chestnut (p 13½×13)	40	40
6	**144**	2c. chestnut	20	20
7	**126**	5c. chocolate (R.)	20	20
		a. Black opt	28·00	28·00
8	**128**	10c. yellow-green	11·00	11·00
		a. Red opt	11·00	11·00
9	**129**	10c. green	20	20
10	**130**	15c. blue-green (R.)	45	45
11	**131**	15c. blue-green (R.)	45	45
12	**127**	20c. violet (R.)	30	30
13	**133**	25c. deep lake	1·25	1·25
14	**132**	25c. deep lake	20	20
15	**136**	30c. carmine	20	20
16	**139**	30c. scarlet (*sideways*)	1·00	1·00
17	**138**	40c. deep ultramarine (R.)	20	20
18	**130**	50c. deep ultramarine (R.)	1·25	1·25
19	**138**	60c. yellow-green	75	75
20	**142**	1p. black (R.)	1·25	1·25

(b) EXPRESS LETTER
E21	E **145**	20c. red	75	75
1/E21	Set of 21		75·00	75·00

Authorised by decree of the Civil Governor on 11 February 1937.
Other stamps bearing a tryptych Málaga overprint as a salute to Generals Franco and Queipo de Llano and the Italian Consul Tranquillo-Bianchi were unofficial.

SPAIN / Civil War, 1936–39

(Optd by Juan Marra)

1937 (July). First Anniv of Nationalist Uprising. Optd with T **2**.

21	**183**	5c. olive-brown (R.) (*sideways*)	10	10
22		10c. yellow-green (*sideways*)	10	10
23	**184**	15c. black (R.)	10	10
24		30c. rose-lake	45	45
25		50c. deep blue	2·75	2·75
26		60c. yellow	1·20	1·20
27		1p. blue (R.)	55	55
21/27 Set of 7			4·75	4·75

Authorised by decree of the Provincial Civil Governor dated 5 July 1937.

MALLORCA

(Balearic Islands)

¡Viva España!
Mallorca
19 Julio
1936
(1)

Habilitado
0'05 ptas
(2)

1936 (25 July). Optd with T **1**.

1	**143**	1c. blue-green	1·90	1·90
2	**144**	2c. chestnut	1·90	1·90
3	**131**	15c. blue-green	8·50	8·50
4	**136**	30c. carmine	4·75	4·75

Authorised by decree of the Civil Governor of the Balearic Islands on 25 July 1936.

1937 (1 Jan). Surch with T **2**.

5	**143**	0.05p. on 1c. blue-green	3·25	3·25
6		0.05p. on 2c. chestnut	3·25	3·25
7		0.10p. on 1c. blue-green	3·25	3·25
8		0.15p. on 2c. chestnut	3·25	3·25

These provisionals were similarly authorised.

MELILLA

Melilla, on the north coast of Morocco, is administered as part of the province of Málaga, so Spanish stamps are used there.

Melilla
VIVA
ESPAÑA
17-7-1936
(1)

1936 (29 Oct). Optd with T **1**.

1	**133**	30c. carmine	42·00	42·00
2	**137**	30c. scarlet	4·75	4·75

Authorised by the military authority in Morocco.

MINORCA

(Balearic Islands)

ESPAÑA
Isla de Menorca
Sello Provisional
CORREOS
0'40
(1)

ESPAÑA
Isla de Menorca
Sello Provisional
CORREO AÉREO
1'40
(2)

1939 (13 Feb). Type-set. With black control figures on back. Imperf.

(a) POSTAGE

1	**1**	0,40p. black, *green*	12·50	12·50

(b) AIR

2	**2**	1,40p. black, *green*	26·00	26·00

Authorised by the Military Commander, Francisco Rovira, on 13 February 1939.

Minorca surrendered to the Nationalists on 8 February 1939. As only Republican stamps remained on the island and these had been demonetised in August 1937 it was necessary to print new stamps locally. Being type-set many errors are known.

ORENSE

(Province of Orense)

¡ VIVA
ESPAÑA !
(1)

¡VIVA
ESPAÑA!
+ 5 cts.
(2)

1936 (10 Oct). Optd with T **1**.

(a) POSTAGE

1	**143**	1c. blue-green (B.)	70	70
		a. Red opt	1·50	1·50
2		2c. chestnut (p 11½)	4·00	4·00
3	**144**	2c. chestnut	65	75
4	**126**	5c. chocolate (R.)	1·50	1·50
5	**129**	10c. green (B.)	2·75	2·75
		a. Red opt	15·00	15·00
6	**131**	15c. blue-green (R.)	2·75	2·75
7	**127**	20c. violet (B.)	2·75	2·75
8	**132**	25c. deep lake	4·00	4·00
9	**136**	30c. carmine (B.)	2·75	2·75
		a. Black opt	5·25	5·25
10	**138**	40c. deep ultramarine (R.)	4·25	4·25
11	**130**	50c. deep ultramarine (R.)	7·00	7·00
12	**138**	60c. yellow-green	5·50	5·50
		a. Red opt	16·00	16·00

(b) EXPRESS LETTER

E13	E **145**	20c. red (B.)	2·75	2·75
		a. Black opt	5·50	5·50
1/E13 Set of 13			37·00	37·00

1936 (10 Oct). CHARITY. Optd with T **2**, in blue.

(a) POSTAGE

13	**66**	+5c. on 10c. green	50	50
14	**143**	+5c. on 1c. blue-green	2·50	2·50
15		+5c. on 2c. chestnut (p 11½)	60	60
16	**144**	+5c. on 2c. chestnut	60	60
17	**126**	+5c. on 5c. chocolate	90	90
18	**129**	+5c. on 10c. green	90	90
19	**131**	+5c. on 15c. blue-green	1·25	1·25
20	**127**	+5c. on 20c. violet	90	90
21	**132**	+5c. on 25c. deep lake	1·50	1·50
22	**136**	+5c. on 30c. carmine	3·50	3·50
23	**147**	+5c. on 30c. carmine	45·00	45·00
24	**138**	+5c. on 60c. yellow-green	£210	£210

(b) EXPRESS LETTER

*(i) Optd with T **2**, in blue*

E25	E **145**	+5c. on 20c. red	1·50	1·50

*(ii) Optd with T **1** and **2**, in blue*

E26	E **145**	+5c. on 20c. red	1·60	1·60
13/E26 Set of 14			£225	£225

Both the above issues were authorised by the Civil Governor on 4 August 1937. The premium was for charitable work in the province.

PONTEVEDRA

(Province of Pontevedra)

The following issues are known to have been used on mail but the decree authorising them has not been traced.

¡VIVA ESPAÑA!
PONTEVEDRA
20 JULIO 1936
(1)

1937 (Apr–May). Optd with T **1**.

(a) POSTAGE
A. Black opt
B. Red opt

			A	B
1	**66**	1c. green	22·00	20·00
2	**143**	1c. blue-green	70	1·00
3		2c. chestnut (p 11½)	1·50	†
4		2c. chestnut (p 13½×13)	5·25	7·00
5	**144**	2c. chestnut	65	2·75
6	**126**	5c. chocolate	65	1·50
7	**129**	10c. green	65	2·50
8	**131**	15c. blue-green	1·00	1·50
9	**127**	20c. violet	3·25	4·50
10	**132**	25c. deep lake	80	4·50

SPAIN / Civil War, 1936–39

11	**133**	30c. carmine	2·00	†
12	**136**	30c. carmine	3·50	†
13	**138**	40c. deep ultramarine	1·25	2·00
14	**130**	50c. deep ultramarine	6·00	15·00
15	**138**	60c. yellow-green	3·00	6·25
16	**142**	1p. black	4·50	22·00
17	–	4p. magenta (768)	45·00	†
18	–	10p. brown (769)	45·00	†

(b) AIR

19	**145**	2p. dull blue	80·00	80·00

(c) EXPRESS LETTER

E20	E **146**	20c. red	2·50	†
1/E20 *Set of 20*			£175	

Same prices, unused or used.

CORREO AÉREO

¡Arriba España!   ¡Arriba España
PONTEVEDRA   PONTEVEDRA
18 Julio 1937   18 Julio 1937
II Año Triunfal   II Año Triunfal
(**2**)   (**3**)

1937 (18 July). First Anniv of Nationalist Uprising.

(a) POSTAGE. Optd with T **2**

20	**143**	1c. blue-green	70	70
		a. Red opt	2·75	2·75
21	**144**	2c. chestnut	1·25	1·25
22	**126**	5c. chocolate	75	75
23	**129**	10c. green (R.)	1·50	1·50
24	**127**	20c. violet (R.)	15·00	15·00
25	**132**	25c. deep lake	12·00	12·00
26	**136**	30c. carmine	2·00	2·00

(b) AIR. Variously optd as T **3**

27	**142**	1p. black	25·00	25·00
		a. Red opt	30·00	30·00
28	**148**	1p. black (R.)	£300	£300
29	**145**	2p. dull blue	75·00	75·00
		a. Red opt	75·00	75·00
20/29 *Set of 10 (cheapest)*			£350	£350

SAN SEBASTIAN

(Province of Guipúzcoa)

¡¡ARRIBA   DIOS
ESPAÑA!!   PATRIA
1936   y REY
                   1936
(**1**)   (**2**)

(Optd by D. Manuel Romeo)

1936 (15 Dec). Optd with T **1**.

1	**143**	1c. blue-green (R.)	65	65
		a. Blue opt	3·25	3·25
2		2c. chestnut (p 11½) (B.)	90	90
3		2c. chestnut (p 13½×13) (B.)	4·25	4·25
4	**144**	2c. chestnut (B.)	90	90
5	**127**	5c. sepia (R.)	5·25	5·25
6	**126**	5c. chocolate (R.)	90	90
7	**129**	10c. green (R.)	1·50	1·50
8	**131**	15c. blue-green (R.)	1·80	1·75
9	**127**	20c. violet (R.)	2·25	2·25
10	**132**	25c. deep lake (B.)	2·25	2·25
11	**135**	30c. carmine (B.) *(Opt inverted)*	33·00	33·00
12	**136**	30c. carmine (B.)	1·50	1·50
13	**138**	40c. deep ultramarine (R.)	4·25	4·25
14	**130**	50c. deep ultramarine (R.)	4·25	4·25
15	**138**	60c. yellow-green (R.)	9·50	9·50
		a. Blue opt	11·00	11·00
1/15 *Set of 15*			55·00	55·00

Authorised by local Falange Party. Also found on two 10c. fiscal stamps.

(Optd by J. Rodriguez)

1937 (5 Apr). Optd with T **2**.

(a) POSTAGE

16	**66**	1c. green	3·50	3·50
17	**143**	1c. blue-green (R.)	6·00	6·00
18	**126**	2c. red-brown	6·00	6·00
19	**143**	2c. chestnut (p 11½)	90	90
20	**144**	2c. chestnut	90	90
21	**126**	5c. chocolate (R.)	1·00	1·00
22	**129**	10c. green	1·25	1·25
23	**131**	15c. blue-green (R.)	2·00	2·00
24	**127**	20c. violet (R.)	1·75	1·75
25	**132**	25c. deep lake	2·00	2·00
26	**136**	30c. carmine	2·00	2·00
27	**138**	40c. deep ultramarine	3·00	3·00
28	**130**	50c. deep ultramarine (R.)	4·50	4·50
29	**140**	60c. slate-blue (R.)	19·00	19·00
30	**138**	60c. yellow-green (R.)	4·50	4·50

(b) EXPRESS LETTER

(i) Much wider opt

E31	E **145**	20c. red	4·50	4·50

(ii) Optd With T **2** *twice, side by side*

E32	E **145**	20c. red	6·00	6·00
16/E32 *Set of 17*			65·00	65·00

Authorised by the War Council of Guipúzcoa on 5 April 1937.

CORREO
AÉREO
(**3**)

SALUDO A FRANCO
13 SEPTIEMBRE
1936-1937
VIVA ESPAÑA
ARRIBA-ESPAÑA
SAN SEBASTIÁN
(**4**)

1937 (Apr). AIR. Optd with T **3**.

31	**145**	2p. dull blue (R.)	25·00	25·00
		a. Black opt	70·00	

1937 (13 Sept). Variously optd as T **4**.

(a) Nationalist issues

32	**181**	1c. green (R.)	40	40
33	**182**	2c. red-brown	40	40
34	**183**	5c. olive-brown (R.)	40	40
35		10c. yellow-green (V.)	50	50
36	**184**	15c. black (R.)	60	60
37		20c. violet (G.)	60	60
38		25c. lake	60	60
39		30c. rose-lake (II) (V.)	60	60
40		30c. rose-lake (III) (V.)	25·00	25·00
41		40c. orange (G.)	1·50	1·50
42		50c. deep blue (C.)	2·50	2·50
43		60c. yellow	3·50	3·50
		a. Green opt	19·00	19·00
44		1p. blue (R.)	5·75	5·75
45		4p. magenta (G.)	15·00	15·00
46		10p. blue (O.)	20·00	20·00
32/46 *Set of 15*			60·00	60·00

(b) Defensa de Junta issue

47	–	5c. grey-brown (862) (V.)	3·50	3·50
48	–	15c. blue-green (863) (C.)	3·50	3·50
		a. Orange opt	12·00	12·00
		b. Gold opt	5·50	5·50
49	**178**	30c. carmine (I) (G.)	5·50	5·50
50		30c. carmine (II) Bk.)	5·50	5·50

Authorised by the Civil Governor of Guipúzcoa by decree of 10 September 1937.

SANTA CRUZ DE TENERIFE

(Canary Islands)

Viva España
18 Julio
1936
(**1**)

1937 (10 Aug). Optd with T **1**.

1	**143**	1c. blue-green (R.)	90	90
		a. Black opt	3·00	2·25
2		2c. chestnut (p 11½)	10·50	10·50
3	**144**	2c. chestnut	1·00	1·00
4	**126**	5c. chocolate (R.)	3·00	3·00
5	**129**	10c. green (R.)	2·75	2·75
6	**132**	25c. deep lake	10·50	10·50
7	**138**	40c. deep ultramarine (R.)	2·50	2·50
8	–	10p. brown (769)	£250	£250
1/8 *Set of 8*			£290	£190

Authorised by the Technical Council of State. There was a second printing on 24 August 1937 in which the "J" of "Julio" is smaller and these are rare.

SPAIN / Civil War, 1936–39

SANTA MARIA DE ALBARRACIN

(Province of Teruel)

(1)

1937. Optd with T **1**.
1	143	1c. blue-green (R.)	2·50	2·50
2	144	2c. chestnut (B.)	2·50	2·50

Authorised by the Inspector-General of Posts.

SEGOVIA

(Province of Segovia)

(1)

(Optd by Mariano Salcedo)

1937 (31 Oct). Optd variously as T **1**.
1	181	1c. green	80	80
2	179	2c. chestnut	4·50	4·50
3	182	2c. red-brown	80	80
4	183	5c. olive-brown	1·50	1·50
5		10c. yellow-green	2·10	2·10
6	184	15c. black (R.)	2·25	2·25
7		20c. violet	6·50	6·50
8		25c. lake	6·50	6·50
9		30c. rose-lake	2·25	2·25
10		40c. orange	15·00	15·00
11		50c. deep blue (R.)	22·00	22·00
1/11 Set of 11			47·00	47·00

Authorised by the Civil Governor of the Province on 23 October 1937.

1937 (Nov). Large overprints showing arms in centre with "HOMENAGE al General VARELA DEFENSOR de SEGOVIA II Ano triunfal" and "30–5–37 31-10-37" applied over blocks of four stamps, in green.
12	185	15c. (×4) reddish brown	11·50	11·50
13	186	30c. (×4) rose-carmine	11·50	11·50
14	187	1p. (×4) red-orange and blue	11·50	11·50

Authorised by the Civil Governor of Segovia on 26 October 1937.

SEVILLE

(Province of Seville)

All the following were authorised by General Queipo de Llano.

(1)   (2)

1936 (31 July). Handstamped with T **1**.

(a) POSTAGE
1	143	1c. blue-green	30	30
2	144	2c. chestnut	30	30
3	126	5c. chocolate	30	30
4	129	10c. green	30	30
5	131	15c. blue-green	30	30
6	127	20c. violet	30	30
7	132	25c. deep lake	30	30
8	136	30c. carmine	30	30
9	137	30c. scarlet	1·60	1·60
10	138	40c. deep ultramarine	55	55
11	130	50c. deep ultramarine	1·60	1·60
12	138	60c. yellow-green	55	55
13	142	1p. black	3·00	3·00
14	–	4p. magenta (768)	9·50	9·50
15	–	10p. brown (769)	3·75	3·75

(b) AIR
| 16 | 145 | 2p. dull blue | 8·00 | 8·00 |

(c) EXPRESS LETTER
| E17 | E **145** | 20c. red | 1·60 | 1·60 |
| 1/E17 Set of 17 | | | 29·00 | 29·00 |

Another handstamp was used having a thicker "S" in "SEVILLA" and a squarer "S" in "ESPANA".

1936. Optd with T **2**.
17	143	1c. blue-green	30	30
18	144	2c. chestnut	30	30
19	126	5c. chocolate (R.)	30	30
20	129	10c. green	30	30
21	131	15c. blue-green (R.)	55	55
22	127	20c. violet (R.)	55	55
23	132	25c. deep lake	55	55
24	136	30c. carmine	55	55
25	137	30c. scarlet	5·75	5·75
26	138	40c. deep ultramarine (R.)	3·75	3·75
27	130	50c. deep ultramarine (R.)	3·75	3·75
28	138	60c. yellow-green	4·75	4·75
17/28 Set of 12			19·00	19·00

(3)   (4)   (5)

1937 (31 July). First Anniv of Nationalist Uprising. Optd with T **3**.

(a) Republican issues

(i) POSTAGE
29	143	1c. blue-green	20	20
		a. Red opt	30	30
30		2c. chestnut (p 11½)	40	40
31		2c. chestnut (p 13½×13) (B.)	80	80
32	144	2c. chestnut	40	40
		a. Blue opt	30	30
33	127	5c. sepia (R.)	25·00	25·00
34	126	5c. chocolate (R.)	60	60
35	129	10c. green (R.)	50	50
		a. Black opt	25·00	25·00
36	130	15c. blue-green (R.)	90	90
37	131	15c. blue-green (R.)	90	90
38	127	20c. violet (R.)	1·00	1·00
39	133	25c. deep lake (B.)	28·00	28·00
40	132	25c. deep lake	1·00	1·00
41	136	30c. carmine	50	50
		a. Blue opt	25·00	25·00
42	138	40c. deep ultramarine (R.)	1·25	1·25
43	130	50c. deep ultramarine (R.)	2·25	2·25
44	138	60c. yellow-green (R.)	1·50	1·50
45	142	1p. black (R.)	8·00	8·00
46	–	4p. magenta (768) (B.)	28·00	28·00
47	–	10p. brown (769) (G.)	28·00	28·00

(ii) EXPRESS LETTER
| E48 | E **145** | 20c. red (R.) | 90 | 90 |
| 29/E48 Set of 20 | | | £110 | £110 |

(b) Nationalist issues
48	181	1c. green (R.)	35	35
		a. Black opt	6·50	6·50
49	182	2c. red-brown (B.)	30	30
50	183	5c. olive-brown (R.) (sideways)	50	50
51		10c. yellow-green (R.) (sideways)	50	50
52	184	15c. black (R.)	70	70
53		20c. violet (R.)	70	70
		a. Blue opt	22·00	22·00
54		25c. lake (B.)	90	90
55		30c. rose-lake (B.)	90	90
56		40c. orange (B.)	90	90
57		50c. deep blue (R.)	1·50	1·50
58		60c. yellow (B.)	2·25	2·25
59		1p. blue (R.)	3·00	3·00
48/59 Set of 12			10·00	10·00

1937 (18 July–31 Oct). Handstamped as T **4**.
60	143	1c. blue-green	1·10	1·10
61	181	1c. green	1·00	1·00
62	143	2c. chestnut (p 13½×13)	2·50	2·50
63	144	2c. chestnut	85	85
64	182	2c. red-brown	50	50
65	183	5c. olive-brown (vert)	1·10	1·10
		a. Opt horiz	2·30	2·30

66		10c. yellow-green (vert)	1·10	1·10
		a. Opt horiz	2·40	2·40
67	184	15c. black	1·40	1·40
68		20c. violet	2·00	2·00
69		25c. lake	1·60	1·60
70		30c. rose-lake	1·60	1·60
71		40c. orange (Oct)	32·00	†
60/71 Set of 12			43·00	

1938 (10 Feb). Homage to General Queipo de Llano. Optd with T **5**.

72	181	1c. green (R.)	90	90
		a. Blue opt	2·50	2·50
73	182	2c. red-brown (B.)	90	90
74	184	15c. black (R.)	1·75	1·75
75		30c. rose-lake (B.)	1·75	1·75

TERUEL

(Province of Teruel)

CORREOS

¡Viva España!

TERUEL
Heróica y Leal
(1)

1937. Optd with T **1**.

1	143	1c. blue-green (R.)	2·50	2·50
2	144	2c. chestnut (B.)	2·50	2·50

Authorised by the Inspector-General of Posts.

VITORIA

(Province of Alava)

(1) (2) (3)

T **1**. Thin figures
T **2**. Thick figures with sloping serif to "1" and short curves to other figures
T **3**. Thick figures with more horizontal serif to "1" and longer curves to other figures.

All three types appeared in the sheet of fifty, there being 20 of T **1**, 11 of T **2** and 19 of T **3**.

1937. (7 Apr). Optd with T **1/3**.

A. T **1** or **3**
B. T **2**

(a) POSTAGE

			A	B
1	143	1c. blue-green	25	25
2	126	2c. red-brown	8·00	8·00
3	143	2c. chestnut (p 11½)	1·50	1·50
4		2c. chestnut (p 13½×13)	1·40	1·40
5	144	2c. chestnut	25	25
6	126	5c. chocolate (R.)	90	90
7	129	10c. green	25	25
8	131	15c. blue-green	25·00	25·00
9	127	20c. violet	3·00	3·00
10	132	25c. deep lake	25	25
11	136	30c. carmine	2·25	2·25
12	138	40c. deep ultramarine (R.)	2·75	2·75
13	130	50c. deep ultramarine	5·00	5·00
14	138	60c. yellow-green	6·00	6·00
15	142	1p. black	7·00	7·00
16	–	4p. magenta (768)	17·00	17·00
17	–	10p. brown (769)	28·00	28·00

(b) EXPRESS LETTER

E18	E **145**	20c. red	1·50	1·50
1/E18 Set of 18			£100	£100

Same prices, unused or used.
Authorised by the Communications Commission of the Technical Council of State on 30 March 1937.

SPAIN / Civil War, 1936–39 / British Post Offices in Spain

ZARAGOZA

(Province of Zaragoza)

(1)

(2)

1937 (18 Feb). Handstamped with T **1**.

1	143	1c. blue-green (C.)	75	75
		a. Black handstamp	6·00	6·00
2		2c. chestnut (p 11½)	1·50	1·50
3		2c. chestnut (p 13½×13)	1·50	1·50
4	144	2c. chestnut	1·75	1·75

Authorised by the Inspector-General of Communications. Other values are found with this handstamp but they were not authorised.

1937 (June). Optd with T **2**.

5	143	1c. blue-green (R.)	90	90
		a. Blue opt	2·75	2·75
6		2c. chestnut (p 11½) (B.)	90	90
7		2c. chestnut (p 13½×13) (B.)	3·50	3·50
8	144	2c. chestnut (B.)	2·25	2·25

Also authorised by the Inspector-General of Communications but not the higher values which are also found.

BRITISH POST OFFICES IN SPAIN

Little is known about the operation of British Packet Agencies in Spain, other than the dates recorded for the various postal markings in the G.P.O. Proof Books. The Agency at Corunna is said to date from the late 17th century. No. CC1 was probably issued in connection with the inauguration of the P. & O. service to Spain in 1843. The Spanish port of call was changed to Vigo in 1846 and the office at Corunna was then closed. Teneriffe became a port of call for the South American packets in 1817 and this arrangement continued until 1858.

> **CROWNED-CIRCLE HANDSTAMPS.** Under regulations circulated in December 1841, letters and packets forwarded through offices abroad to the United Kingdom or any of its territories were to be sent unpaid, the postage being collected on delivery. Where this was not possible, for example from a British colony to a foreign country or between two foreign ports, then a crowned-circle handstamp was to be applied with the postage, paid in advance, noted alongside in manuscript.
> The dates quoted are those on which the handstamp appears in the G.P.O. Record Books, but it seems to have been normal for the handstamps to be sent to the office concerned immediately following this registration.

CORUNNA

Crowned-circle Handstamp. As Type CC **1b** of British Post Offices in Cuba.
CC1   "PAID AT CORUNNA" (28.2.1842)
Although recorded in the G.P.O. Proof Books no example of No. CC1 on cover is known.

TENERIFFE (CANARY ISLANDS)

CC 7

CC 4

Crowned-circle Handstamps.
CC2   CC **7** in black (6.1.1851) .... *Price on cover* £3750
CC3   CC **4** in black (23.10.1857) .... *Price on cover* £3750
Nos. CC2/3 can be found used on covers from Spain to South America with the rate from Spain to Teneriffe paid in Spanish adhesive stamps.

Cape Juby

100 Céntimos = 1 Peseta

In June 1916 Spanish troops occupied Cape Juby, at the southern extremity of Morocco, where a British engineer named Mackenzie had established a commercial factory which he later sold to the Sultan of Morocco.

CABO JUBI 40 CENTIMOS (1)   **CABO JUBY** (2)

1916. Stamps of Rio de Oro, 1914, surch as T **1**.

1	12	5c. on 4p. rose-carmine (V.)	£250	27·00
		a. Surch in blue		
2		10c. on 10p. dull violet (R.)	55·00	27·00
3		15c. on 50c. brown (R.)	55·00	27·00
		a. Surch in green	50·00	27·00
4		40c. on 1p. dull lilac (R.)	90·00	37·00
		a. Surch in green	90·00	37·00

From 1917 to 1919 stamps of Rio de Oro (*see under* Spanish Sahara) and of Spanish Morocco were used in Cape Juby.

1919–29. *Stamps of Spain overprinted.*

1919. Optd with T **2** diagonally upwards. Control figures on back in blue.

5	38a	¼c. green (R.)	20	20
6	64	2c. sepia	20	20
		a. Opt double	36·00	36·00
		b. Opt double (Bk.+R.)	70·00	70·00
7		5c. deep green (R.)	70	45
		a. Opt inverted	48·00	70·00
		b. Opt double	36·00	36·00
8		10c. carmine	90	65
		a. Opt double	36·00	36·00
		b. Opt double (R.+Bk.)	70·00	70·00
9		15c. yellow	3·75	3·50
		a. Opt double	36·00	36·00
		b. Control figures in red	8·00	6·00
10		20c. bronze-green (R.)	24·00	23·00
11		25c. blue (R.)	3·50	1·80
		a. Opt double	36·00	36·00
12		30c. blue-green (R.)	3·50	1·80
13		40c. salmon	3·50	1·40
14		50c. blue (R.)	4·50	3·50
15		1p. rose-red	12·00	11·00
16		4p. plum (R.)	50·00	50·00
17		10p. orange	70·00	70·00
5/17 Set of 13			£160	£140

1919. EXPRESS LETTER. No. E307 optd as T **2**.

E18	E 53	20c. red	3·50	3·50
		a. Opt double	65·00	36·00
		b. Opt double (Bk.+R.)		

1922–23. Optd with T **2**.

18	66	1c. green (*imperf*) (R.) (1923)	28·00	18·00
18a	64	2c. bistre (359)	£350	
19		20c. bright violet (335)	£140	47·00

1925. Optd with T **2**.

19a	68	2c. deep yellow-green	£375	
20		5c. purple	5·50	4·25
21		10c. deep green	16·00	4·25
22		20c. violet	32·00	14·50

CABO–JUBY (3)   **CABO JUBY** (4)   **Cabo Juby** (5)

1926. Red Cross. T **70**/**1**, and similar types (colours changed), optd with T **3**.

(a) POSTAGE

23	70	1c. red-orange	17·00	17·00
24	–	2c. carmine	17·00	17·00
25	–	5c. sepia	4·25	4·25
26	–	10c. myrtle	2·10	2·10
27	70	15c. violet (V.)	1·50	1·50
28	–	20c. purple	1·50	1·50
29	71	25c. crimson	1·50	1·50
30	70	30c. olive-green	1·50	1·50
31	–	40c. ultramarine	50	50
32	–	50c. brown-lake	50	50
33	–	1p. orange-red	50	50
34	–	4p. bistre	1·90	1·90
35	71	10p. violet	4·50	4·50
23/35 Set of 13			49·00	49·00

(b) EXPRESS LETTER

E36	E 77	20c. ultramarine	4·50	4·50

1929. Seville and Barcelona Exhibitions stamps optd with T **4** (horiz (15, 25c.) or sideways (others)).

36	–	5c. carmine-lake (B.)	50	70
37	–	10c. green (R.)	50	70
38	83	15c. turquoise-blue (R.)	50	70
39	84	20c. violet (R.)	50	70
40	83	25c. carmine (B.)	50	70
41	–	30c. blackish brown (B.)	50	70
42	–	40c. blue (R.)	50	70
43	84	50c. red-orange (B.)	60	90
44	–	1p. greenish slate (R.)	24·00	34·00
45	–	4p. claret (R.)	35·00	55·00
46	–	10p. brown (B.)	35·00	55·00
36/46 Set of 11			90·00	£130

1934–48. *Stamps of Spanish Morocco overprinted.*

1934–36. Optd with T **5**.

(a) Stamps of 1928–32

47	11	1c. carmine ("Ct")	1·90	1·40
48		2c. violet (R.)	4·25	2·75
49		5c. blue (R.)	4·25	2·75
50		10c. green	10·50	8·25
51		15c. chestnut	25·00	18·00
52	12	25c. lake	4·25	2·75
53	–	1p. yellow-green	42·00	33·00
54	–	2p.50 bright purple	£100	70·00
55	–	4p. ultramarine (R.)	£120	55·00
47/55 Set of 9			£275	£200

*(b) Stamps of 1933–35 (as T **14**/**15**). P 14½×14 (vert) or 14×14½*

56		1c. scarlet	45	35
57		10c. blackish green (R.) (1936)	2·75	2·10
58		20c. greenish black (R.)	9·50	6·25
59		30c. brown-lake	9·50	6·25
60		40c. deep ultramarine (R.)	31·00	25·00
61		50c. red-orange	60·00	47·00
56/61 Set of 6			£100	80·00

(c) EXPRESS LETTER. No. E138

E62	E 12	20c. black (R.)	10·50	10·50

CABO JUBY (6) 16½ mm   **CABO JUBY** (7)

1935–36. Stamps of 1933–35 (as T **14**/**15**), optd with T **6**. (16½ mm)

(a) P 14½×14 (vert) or 14×14½

62		1c. scarlet (1936)	20	10
63		2c. green (R.)	60	50
64		5c. magenta	2·40	1·70
65		10c. blackish green (R.) (1936)	16·00	11·00
66		15c. yellow (B.)	5·50	4·25
67		20c. greenish black (R.) (1936)	5·50	4·25
68		25c. scarlet	70·00	47·00
69		1p. slate (R.)	10·50	7·00
70		2p.50 brown (B.)	37·00	27·00
71		4p. yellow-green (R.)	60·00	45·00
72		5p. black (R.)	50·00	36·00
62/72 Set of 11			£225	£170

(b) P 13½

73		25c. violet (R.)	5·25	5·25
74		30c. scarlet	5·25	5·25
75		40c. red orange	7·50	7·50
76		50c. ultramarine (R.)	15·00	15·00
77		60c. blue-green (R.)	20·00	20·00
78		2p. red-brown	£110	£110
73/78 Set of 6			£150	£150

(c) EXPRESS LETTER. No. E171

E79	E 16	20c. vermilion	5·25	5·25

1937. First Anniv of Civil War. Nos. 184/99 optd as T **6** (15½ mm).

(a) POSTAGE

79		1c. grey-violet	50	50
80		2c. red-brown	50	50
81		5c. magenta	50	50
82		10c. bright green	50	50
83		15c. blue	50	50
84		20c. maroon	50	50
85		25c. mauve	50	50
86		30c. red	50	50
87		40c. orange	1·50	1·50

CAPE JUBY

88	50c. ultramarine (R.)	1·50	1·50
89	60c. dull green	1·50	1·50
90	1p. bright violet	1·50	1·50
91	2p. greenish blue	£110	£110
92	2p.50 black (R.)	£110	£110
93	4p. sepia	£110	£110
94	10p. black (R.)	£110	£110
79/94 Set of 16		£400	£400

(b) EXPRESS LETTER. No. E200

E95	E **19**	20c. carmine	1·50	1·50

1938 (1 June). AIR. As Nos. 203/12 (colours slightly changed), optd (vert on 5c.) as T **6** (15½ mm).

95	5c. brown	20	20
96	10c. bright green	20	20
97	25c. scarlet	20	20
98	40c. light blue	3·75	3·75
99	50c. bright purple	20	20
100	75c. deep blue	20	20
101	1p. blackish brown	20	20
102	1p.50 bright violet	2·50	2·50
103	2p. brown-lake	5·50	5·50
104	3p. brownish black	15·00	15·00
95/104 Set of 10		25·00	25·00

1939 (1 May). As Nos. 213/6 (colours changed), optd as T **6** (15 mm).

105	5c. scarlet	55	55
106	10c. grey-green	55	55
107	15c. maroon	55	55
108	20c. light blue	55	55
105/108 Set of 4		2·00	2·00

1940. As Nos. 217/32, but without "ZONA" on back, optd as T **6** (16 mm).

(a) POSTAGE

109	1c. brown	15	15
110	2c. brown-olive (R.)	15	15
111	5c. grey-blue (R.)	15	15
112	10c. magenta	15	15
113	15c. grey-green (R.)	15	15
114	20c. violet (R.)	15	15
115	25c. sepia (R.)	15	15
116	30c. yellow-green	15	15
117	40c. slate-green (R.)	60	60
118	45c. vermilion	60	60
119	50c. orange brown	60	60
120	70c. light blue (R.)	2·00	2·00
121	1p. brown and indigo	4·25	4·25
122	2p.50 green and chocolate	12·50	12·50
123	5p. sepia and purple	12·50	12·50
124	10p. red-brown and olive-brown	35·00	35·00
109/124 Set of 16		60·00	60·00

(b) EXPRESS LETTER. As No. E233

E125	E **21**	25c. carmine-red	55	55

1942 (1 Apr). AIR. As Nos. 258/62, but without "Z" opt, inscr "CABO JUBY".

125	5c. deep blue	15	15
126	10c. orange-brown	15	15
127	15c. blackish green	15	15
128	90c. carmine-rose	55	55
129	5p. black	1·80	1·80
125/129 Set of 5		2·50	2·50

1944 (2 Oct). Nos. 269/82 (agricultural designs), optd with T **7**.

130	1c. light blue and chocolate	15	15
131	2c. light green and slate-green	15	15
132	5c. blackish green and chocolate (R.)	15	15
133	10c. red-orange and bright ultramarine	15	15
134	15c. light green and slate-green	15	15
135	20c. black and claret (R.)	15	15
136	25c. chocolate and light blue	15	15
137	30c. bright ultramarine & yellow-grn (R.)	15	15
138	40c. claret and chocolate	15	15
139	50c. red-brown and bright ultramarine	15	15
140	75c. bright ultramarine & yellow-grn (R.)	1·40	1·40
141	1p. chocolate and bright ultramarine	1·40	1·40
142	2p.50 bright ultramarine and black (R.)	4·00	4·00
143	10p. grey-black and salmon (R.)	27·00	27·00
130/143 Set of 14		32·00	32·00

1946 (Mar). Nos. 285/94 (craftsmen), optd with T **7**.

144	1c. brown and violet	25	25
145	2c. slate-violet and deep green (R.)	25	25
146	10c. ultramarine and red-orange	25	25
147	15c. green and blue	25	25
148	25c. blue and green	25	25
149	40c. brown and deep blue (R.)	25	25
150	45c. carmine and black	30	30
151	1p. deep blue and blackish green	2·20	2·20
152	2p.50 grey-green and red-orange (R.)	6·50	6·50
153	10p. grey-black and deep blue (R.)	20·00	20·00
144/153 Set of 10		27·00	27·00

1948 (1 Jan). As Nos. 307/317 (transport and commerce), but without "Z" on back, optd with T **7**.

154	2c. sepia and violet	25	25
155	5c. violet and claret	25	25
156	15c. blue-green and blue	25	25
157	25c. grey-green and black	25	25
158	35c. grey-black and blue	25	25
159	50c. violet and vermilion	25	25
160	70c. light blue and deep green	25	25
161	90c. grey-green and cerise	25	25
162	1p. violet and blue	35	35
163	2p.50 grey-green and brown-purple	2·00	2·00
164	10p. blue and black	6·00	6·00
154/164 Set of 11		9·25	9·25

Cape Juby was incorporated in Spanish Sahara in 1950. It was ceded to Morocco in 1958.

Cuba

1855. 8 Reales Plata Fuerte (strong silver reales) = 1 Peso
1866. 100 Céntimos = 1 Escudo
1871. 100 Céntimos = 1 Peseta
1881. 1000 Milesimas = 100 Centavos = 1 Peso

Cuba was discovered by Columbus on 27 October 1492, and was conquered for Spain by Diego Velásquez with about 300 men during 1511–13. From 1855 until 1873 joint issues were made for Cuba and Puerto Rico. During the period 1869 to 1879 some stamps of Cuba and Puerto Rico and of the separate issues for Cuba were also used in Fernando Poo.

PRINTERS. All the stamps of the Spanish Colony of Cuba were printed at the Government Printing Works, Madrid, *unless otherwise stated.*

A. CUBA AND PUERTO RICO

Queen Isabella of Spain, 1833–68

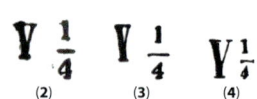

1

Y 1/4 (2) Y 1/4 (3) Y 1/4 (4)

(Dies eng J. P. Varela. Typo)

1855 (24 Apr–Sept). Bluish paper. Wmk Loops (T **10** of Spain). Imperf.

1	1	½r. blue-green	75·00	3·00
		a. Blackish green (13.9)	£130	13·50
2		1r. yellow-green	60·00	3·00
		a. Green	65·00	7·00
3		2r. deep carmine	£550	16·00
		a. Dull red (13.9)	£1200	31·00

Nos. 2*a* and 3 were also used in the Philippine Islands and are worth more cancelled "MANILA", "CAVITE" or some other Philippine town. These stamps handstamped "HABILITADO POR LA NACION" were only used in the Philippines. See after No. 10 of Philippines.

1855 (19 Nov). Surch in Havana by J. Toribio de Arazoza.

4	2	Y¼ on 2r. deep carmine	£850	£250
		a. Dull red	£900	£275
5	3	Y¼ on 2r. deep carmine	£1000	£350
		a. Dull red	£950	£550

Nos. 4, 5 and 12 were only used in Cuba.

1856. Yellowish paper. Wmk Crossed Lozenges (T **11** of Spain). Imperf.

6	1	½r. blue-green	9·75	1·20
7		1r. bright green	£1000	25·00
		a. Yellow-green	£750	22·00
8		2r. red	£250	20·00

1857–61. White paper. No wmk. Imperf.

9	1	½r. greenish blue	5·00	1·20
		a. Pale blue	6·25	1·50
		b. Left upper corner white		
		c. New cliche, missing pearl (1861)		
10		1r. bright green	5·00	1·20
		a. Deep green	5·00	1·20
		b. Yellow-green	5·00	1·20
11		2r. rose-red	22·00	5·00
		a. Orange-red	22·00	5·00

The missing pearl in the new cliche is the first pearl on the left of the second row of pearls in the top-left hand triangle between the frame and the circle. There are also other minor differences between the new and original cliches. 12 new cliches were substituted in the plate of 170.

The 2r. is known used from Santo Domingo.

(Litho Havana)

1860. OFFICIAL. As Type O **10** of Spain but without full points after "OFICIAL" and "ONZAS" or "LIBRA". Imperf.

O12	½o. black/*yellow*	—	70·00
O13	1o. black/*rose*	—	70·00
O14	4o. black/*green*	—	£300
O15	1l. black/*blue*	—	£750

Nos. O12/15 were used only in Cuba. The face values are expressed in onzas (ounces) or libra (pound), referring to the maximum weight for which each value could prepay postage.

Nos. O50/7 of Spain were also used, both in Cuba and Puerto Rico, from January 1858. Such use can only be identified by the town postmark, which was usually applied on the cover away from the stamp.

1860. Surch in Havana by J. Toribio de Arazoza.

12	4	Y¼ on 2r. rose red	£300	£120

Varieties exist, including (i) with the figure "1" of "¼" inverted, and (ii) with the fraction bar (which is not an ordinary bar but a numeral "1" lying on its left side) reversed.

5

6

(7)

(T **5/6** dies eng J. P. Varela. Typo)

1862 (Nov). Imperf.

13	5	¼r. black/*buff*	30·00	36·00

1864 (1 Jan). Imperf.

14	6	¼r. black/*buff*	23·00	32·00
15		½r. green	5·25	1·10
16		½r. green/*rose*	11·50	2·75
17		1r. dull blue/*pale brown*	5·00	1·10
		a. Bright blue/salmon	5·25	1·30
18		2r. red/*rose*	27·00	6·50
		a. Red/buff	32·00	8·00
		b. Vermilion	26·00	7·25

Nos. 13 and 14 were not used in Puerto Rico.

The ½r. is known used from Santo Domingo.

BISECTS. Many stamps issued from 1864 on exist bisected. Such use was not however officially authorised until 1888.

(T **7** die eng J. P. Varela. Typo)

1866 (1 Jan). New Currency. Dated 1866. Imperf.

19	7	5c. dull mauve	48·00	55·00
20		10c. blue	5·00	1·10
21		20c. green	2·40	1·10
22		40c. rose	15·00	10·50

66

(8)

9

1866 (Nov). No. 14 optd with T **8**.

23	6	¼r. black/*buff*	95·00	£110

A small quantity of No. 23 was first handstamped with a small "1866", as this was not easily visible the whole consignment was typographed with Type **8**.

1867 (1 Jan). Dated 1867. P 14.

24	7	5c. dull mauve	55·00	26·00
25		10c. blue	29·00	1·60
26		20c. green	18·00	2·50
27		40c. rose	18·00	11·50

The 10c. and 20c. are known imperf.

The currency change of 1866 did not take effect in Puerto Rico until 1868 so Nos. 19/27 were not used there.

(T **9** die eng J. P. Varela. Typo)

1868. Dated 1868. P 14.

28	9	5c. dull lilac	36·00	16·00
29		10c. blue	3·50	1·80
		a. Deep blue	3·50	1·80
30		20c. green	6·75	3·50
		a. Deep green	6·75	3·50
31		40c. rose	15·00	9·00

Provisional Government of Spain, 1868–70

HABILITADO
POR LA
NACION.

(10)

This overprint is generally diagonal, but exists in various positions.

1868–69. Optd with T **10**.

(a) Dated 1868

32	9	5c. dull lilac	60·00	36·00
33		10c. blue	60·00	36·00
34		20c. green	60·00	36·00
35		40c. rose	60·00	36·00

CUBA / Cuba and Puerto Rico / Separate Issues for Cuba

(b) Dated 1869

36	9	5c. rose		£140	38·00
37		10c. brown		60·00	36·00
38		20c. orange		50·00	36·00
39		40c. dull lilac		70·00	36·00

1869. Dated 1869. P 14.

40	9	5c. rose		38·00	16·00
41		10c. brown		3·50	1·80
42		20c. orange		6·25	2·30
43		40c. dull lilac		34·00	11·50

No. 40 was used locally in Havana and is not known used in Puerto Rico.

11   12

(T **11/12** dies eng E. Juliá. Typo)

1870. P 14.

44	11	5c. blue		£180	90·00
45		10c. green		2·50	90
		a. Deep green		2·50	90
46		20c. brown		2·75	90
		a. Pale brown		2·75	90
47		40c. rose		£200	41·00

The 5c. was not used in Puerto Rico.

King Amadeo of Spain, 1870–73

1871 (1 Feb). New Currency. Dated 1871. P 14.

48	12	12c. pale mauve		27·00	11·00
		a. Grey-lilac		32·00	23·00
49		25c. pale ultramarine		2·75	90
		a. Deep ultramarine		2·30	90
50		50c. green		2·30	90
		a. Deep green		3·25	1·40
51		1p. pale brown		33·00	8·00
		a. Brown		36·00	8·50

The thickness of paper varies in this issue.
All the values of this set are known imperf.
The 12c. was not used in Puerto Rico.

B. SEPARATE ISSUES FOR CUBA

From 1873 Cuba had its own stamps. Until 1877 these were overprinted with a monogram for use in Puerto Rico. These monogram overprints and further issues of Puerto Rico will be found listed under that territory.

13   14   15

1873 (Feb). P 14.

52	13	12½c. green		39·00	19·00
53		25c. pearl-grey		2·50	1·10
		a. Pale lilac		6·25	1·30
54		50c. brown		2·10	1·10
55		1p. chestnut		£325	55·00

The 25c. and 50c. are known imperf.

Spanish Republic, 1873-74

1874 (Feb). Dated 1874. P 14.

56	12	12½c. brown		28·00	14·00
57		25c. pale ultramarine		95	70
		a. Deep ultramarine		95	70
58		50c. indigo-lilac		1·80	85
		a. Grey		1·80	85
59		1p. carmine		£325	90·00
		a. Pale carmine		£325	90·00

The 1p. is known imperf.

King Alfonso XII of Spain, 1874-85

(Dies eng L. Plañol. Typo)

1875 (Jan). P 14.

60	14	12½c. mauve		1·00	1·50
		a. Lilac		6·00	1·60
61		25c. ultramarine		80	55

62		50c. green		80	55
63		1p. brown		8·50	5·50
		a. Deep brown		9·75	5·50

The 12½, 25 and 50c. are known imperf.

(Dies eng J. Gaicia Morago. Typo)

1876. P 14.

64	15	12½c. green		2·00	1·80
		a. Deep green		3·00	2·75
65		25c. mauve		5·50	35
		a. Grey-lilac		5·50	35
		b. Pearl-grey		90	35
66		50c. ultramarine		1·10	35
67		1p. black		13·00	7·25

The 50c. and 1p. are known imperf.

16   17   18

(T **16** die eng J. García Moragu. Typo)

1877. Dated 1877. P 14.

68	16	10c. yellow-green		35·00	
		a. Emerald-green		35·00	
69		12½c. grey-lilac		8·00	4·50
		a. Lilac		8·00	4·50
70		25c. blue-green		80	70
71		50c. black		80	70
72		1p. brown		38·00	16·00
		a. Deep brown		38·00	16·00

The 12½, 25 and 50c. are known imperf.

1878. Dated 1878. P 14.

73	16	5c. blue		90	55
		a. Deep blue		90	55
74		10c. black		£100	
75		12½c. grey-bistre		5·50	3·00
		a. Bistre-buff		5·50	3·00
76		25c. yellow-green		90	20
		a. Bluish green		90	20
77		50c. blue-green		90	20
		a. Deep blue-green		90	20
78		1p. carmine		19·00	5·75
		a. Rose		19·00	5·75

1879. Dated 1879. P 14.

79	16	5c. olive-black		90	35
80		10c. orange		£180	
81		12½c. aniline rose		90	35
82		25c. ultramarine		90	35
		a. Deep ultramarine		90	30
83		50c. grey		90	30
84		1p. olive-bistre		19·00	13·50

Stamps of T **16** imperforate are proofs or from trial sheets.

(T **17/18** dies eng E. Juliá. Typo)

1880. Dated 1880. P 14.

85	17	5c. green		80	45
86		10c. carmine		£110	
87		12½c. grey-lilac		80	40
88		25c. dull lavender		80	40
		a. Grey-blue		80	40
89		50c. sepia		80	40
90		1p. chestnut		5·25	3·00

1881. New Currency. Dated 1881. P 14.

91	17	1c. grey-green		90	30
92		2c. lake-rose		60·00	
93		2½c. grey-bistre		90	25
		a. Olive-bistre		90	25
94		5c. dull lavender		90	25
95		10c. brown		90	25
		a. Deep brown		90	25
96		20c. sepia		5·25	5·25

1882. P 14.

97	18	1c. green		90	35
98		2c. carmine-rose		2·40	35
99		2½c. grey-brown		4·25	1·50
100		5c. dull lavender		2·40	55
		a. Slate-violet		2·75	70
101		10c. olive-bistre		80	20
102		20c. brown		£120	40·00

See also Nos. 118/28.

383

CUBA / Separate Issues for Cuba

(19) (20) (21)
(22) (23)

1883. Stamps of the preceding issue optd or surch by "La Propaganda Literaria", Havana.

(a) With T **19**

103	**18**	5c. (R.)	2·50	4·25
104		10c. (B.)	7·25	8·75
105		20c.	£225	£200

(b) As T **20**

106	**18**	5 on 5c. (R.)	1·70	2·10
107		10 on 10c. (B.)	2·75	4·25
108		20 on 20c.	70·00	37·00
		a. Error. 10 on 20c.	85·00	85·00

(c) As T **21**

109	**18**	5 on 5c. (R.)	1·80	2·10
		a. "5" omitted	13·50	13·50
110		10 on 10c. (B.)	2·75	3·25
111		20 on 20c.	36·00	30·00
		a. Error. 10 on 20c.	90·00	90·00

(d) As T **22**

112	**18**	5 on 5c. (R.)	1·80	2·10
113		10 on 10c. (B.)	8·00	4·75
114		20 on 20c.	50·00	36·00
		a. Error. 10 on 20c.	90·00	90·00

(e) As T **23**

115	**18**	5 on 5c. (R.)	2·20	1·90
116		10 on 10c. (B.)	8·00	4·75
117		20 on 20c.	70·00	70·00
		a. Error. 10 on 20c.	90·00	85·00

Most of the above surcharges may be found *inverted* and *double*.
The various surcharges have been reprinted on the 20c., but are handstamped instead of machine-printed.

1883–88. P 14.

118	**18**	2½c. bistre	5·00	1·80
119		2½c. mauve (1884)	1·50	85
		a. *Bright mauve* (1885)	1·50	85
		b. *Ultramarine* (1886)	85·00	
120		2½c. chestnut	2·50	1·00
		a. *Pale brown* (1888)	2·30	80
121		20c. olive bistre	20·00	3·00
122		20c. brown lilac (1888)	20·00	4·25

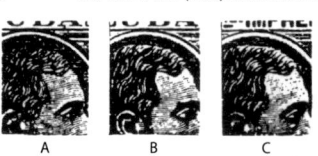

A B C D

The plate for T **18**, which was used for Philippine Islands, Puerto Rico, and Fernando Poo, as well as Cuba, was retouched three times. The second retouch is only known in Philippine stamps, but for convenience of reference we illustrate all the differences here.

A. Original state—The medallion is surrounded by a heavy line of colour, of nearly even thickness, touching the horizontal line below the inscription in the upper label; the opening in the hair above the temple is narrow and pointed. All the preceding stamps of T **18** are as A.

B. First retouch—The line above the medallion is thin, except at the upper right, and does not touch the horizontal line above it; the opening in the hair is slightly wider and a trifle rounded; the lock of hair above the forehead is shaped like a broad "V", and ends in a point; there is a faint white line below it, which is not found in the original state.

C. Second retouch—The opening is still wider and more rounded; the lock of hair does not extend as far down on the forehead, is very slightly rounded, instead of being pointed, and the white line below it is thicker.

D. Third retouch—The opening in the hair forms a semicircle; the lock above the forehead has only a slight wave, and the white line is broader than before.

T **18** *retouched. P 14.*
First retouch (B)

123	**18**	5c. grey	2·40	50
124		5c. dull lavender (1884)	2·40	50
125		10c. deep brown	2·40	85
		a. *Pale chestnut* (1886)	2·40	85
126		10c. blue (1888)	1·60	85

Third retouch (D)

| 127 | **18** | 1c. grey-green (1885) | £160 | 17·00 |
| 128 | | 5c. dull lavender (1887) | 27·00 | 2·75 |

King Alfonso XIII of Spain, 1886-1931

P **24** Alfonso XII   **24**   P **25**

(T **24** and P **24/5**. Dies eng E. Juliá. Typo)

1888. PRINTED MATTER. P 14.

P129	P **24**	½m. black	85	20
P130		1m. black	85	20
P131		2m. black	85	20
P132		3m. black	1·10	70
P133		4m. black	2·10	1·10
P134		8m. black	9·25	4·00
P129/134 Set of 6			13·50	5·75

1890. P 14.

135	**24**	1c. brown	25·00	13·00
136		2c. indigo	8·25	4·00
137		2½c. blue-green	11·50	7·25
138		5c. slate	95	90
139		10c. purple-brown	4·50	1·40
140		20c. dull purple	95	90
135/140 Set of 6			46·00	25·00

1890. PRINTED MATTER. P 14.

P141	P **25**	½m. red-brown	90	70
P142		1m. red-brown	90	70
P143		2m. red-brown	1·40	90
P144		3m. red-brown	1·40	90
P145		4m. red-brown	10·50	7·25
P146		8m. red-brown	10·50	7·25
P141/146 Set of 6			23·00	16·00

1891. P 14.

147	**24**	1c. olive-grey	9·00	5·00
148		2c. purple-brown	1·70	60
149		2½c. salmon	55·00	18·00
150		5c. blue-green	95	60
151		10c. dull rose	2·10	60
152		20c. blue	23·00	12·50
147/152 Set of 6			85·00	34·00

1892. PRINTED MATTER. P 14.

P153	P **25**	½m. dull lilac	35	25
P154		1m. dull lilac	35	25
P155		2m. dull lilac	35	25
P156		3m. dull lilac	2·30	35
P157		4m. dull lilac	4·50	2·10
P158		8m. dull lilac	10·50	5·00
P153/158 Set of 6			17·00	7·50

1894. P 14.

159	**24**	1c. blue	3·50	55
160		2c. aniline pink	44·00	13·00
161		2½c. lilac	3·25	30
		a. *Bright mauve*	2·75	30
162		20c. brown	27·00	13·50
159/162 Set of 4 *(cheapest)*			70·00	25·00

1894. PRINTED MATTER. P 14.

P163	P **25**	½m. aniline pink	20	10
P164		1m. aniline pink	70	20
P165		2m. aniline pink	70	20
P166		3m. aniline pink	2·40	90
P167		4m. aniline pink	4·50	1·10
P168		8m. aniline pink	9·00	4·50
P163/168 Set of 6			16·00	6·25

CUBA / Separate Issues for Cuba / British Post Offices in Cuba

1896–97. P. 14.
169	**24**	1c. dull purple	1·00	30
170		2c. lake	9·50	1·00
171		2½c. aniline pink	70	10
172		5c. indigo	60	10
173		10c. blue-green	2·50	20
174		20c. lilac	18·00	7·25
175		40c. chestnut (1897)	36·00	18·00
176		80c. chocolate (1897)	70·00	26·00
169/176	Set of 8		£120	48·00

Note after No. 84 also applies to stamps of T **24**.

1896. PRINTED MATTER. P. 14.
P177	P **25**	½m. blue-green	20	10
P178		1m. blue-green	20	10
P179		2m. blue-green	20	10
P180		3m. blue-green	2·50	80
P181		4m. blue-green	5·50	4·50
P182		8m. blue-green	10·50	7·25
P177/182	Set of 6		17·00	11·50

25

(Dies eng B. Maura. Typo)

1898. P. 14.
183	**25**	1m. chestnut	30	10
184		2m. chestnut	30	10
185		3m. chestnut	30	10
186		4m. chestnut	4·25	1·90
187		5m. chestnut	30	10
188		1c. plum	30	10
189		2c. blue-green	30	10
190		3c. deep brown	20	10
191		4c. orange	11·00	3·00
192		5c. aniline rose	90	10
193		6c. blue	30	10
194		8c. grey-brown	90	30
195		10c. vermilion	1·00	30
196		15c. olive-slate	4·25	30
197		20c. maroon	60	10
198		40c. mauve	2·75	30
199		60c. black	3·25	30
200		80c. chocolate	18·00	9·75
201		1p. yellow-green	18·00	9·75
202		2p. indigo	32·00	9·75
183/202	Set of 20		90·00	33·00

All values are known imperf.

Risings against Spanish rule led to wars of independence from 1868 to 1878 and 1895 to 1898. Following the unexplained sinking of the U.S. battleship Maine at Havana on 15 February 1898, a Spanish-American war began on 24 April. The war ended with the Treaty of Paris, 10 December 1898, by which Spain relinquished Cuba to the United States, in trust for the island's inhabitants.

Subsequent issues are listed in Part 15 (*Central America*) of this catalogue.

BRITISH POST OFFICES IN CUBA

The British Postal Agency at Havana opened in 1762, the island then being part of the Spanish Empire. A further office, at St. Jago de Cuba, was added in 1841.

Great Britain stamps were supplied to Havana in 1865 and to St. Jago de Cuba in 1866. They continued in use until the offices closed on 30 May 1877.

CROWNED-CIRCLE HANDSTAMPS. Under regulations circulated in December 1841, letters and packets forwarded through offices abroad to the United Kingdom or any of its territories were to be sent unpaid, the postage being collected on delivery. Where this was not possible, for example from a British colony to a foreign country or between two foreign ports, then a crowned-circle handstamp was to be applied with the postage, paid in advance, noted alongside in manuscript.

The dates quoted are those on which the handstamp appears in the G.P.O. Record Books, but it seems to have been normal for the handstamps to be sent to the office concerned immediately following this registration.

PRICES. Prices quoted for Great Britain stamps used abroad are for fine used examples with the cancellation clearly legible. Poor impressions of the cancellations are worth much less than the prices quoted.

HAVANA

CC **1b** Curved "Paid", serifed letters

CC **1c** Curved "Paid", sans-serif letters

CC **2** Straight "Paid"

Crowned-circle Handstamps.
CC1	CC **1b**	In black (13.11.1841) .... *Price on cover*	£1000
CC2	CC **1c**	In black (1848) .... *Price on cover*	£1000
CC3	CC **2**	In black (14.7.1848) .... *Price on cover*	£825

Z **1**

Z **2**

Queen Victoria stamps of GREAT BRITAIN cancelled "C 58" as Types Z **1/2**.

1865–77.
Z1	–	½d. rose-red (1870) (Plate Nos. 6, 12)	75·00
Z2	A	1d. rose-red (1864-79)	60·00
		Plate Nos. 86, 90, 93, 115, 120, 123, 144, 146, 171, 174, 208.	
Z3		2d. blue (1858-69) (Plate Nos. 9, 14, 15)	75·00
Z4	C	3d. rose (1867-73) (Plate No. 4)	£140
Z5	D	3d. rose (1873-76) (Plate Nos. 18, 19)	
Z6	B	4d. vermilion (1865-73) .... *From*	65·00
		Plate Nos. 7, 8, 10/14.	
Z7	D	4d. vermilion (1876) (Plate No. 15)	£300
Z8	B	6d. lilac (1865) (with hyphen) (Plate No. 5)	
Z9	D	6d. grey (1873-76) (Plate No. 1b)	
Z10		8d. orange (1876)	
Z11	C	9d. straw (1867)	£275
Z12		10d. red-brown (1867)	£300
Z13	B	1s. green (1865) (Plate No. 4)	£160
Z14	C	1s. green (1867-73) (Plate Nos. 4, 5, 7) ..... *From*	65·00
Z15	D	1s. grn (1873-77)	
		Plate Nos. 10, 12, 13. .... *From*	90·00
Z16	C	2s. blue (1867)	£275
Z17	–	5s. rose (1867-74) (Plate Nos. 1, 2)	£600

A. Wmk Large Crown.
B. Large uncoloured corner letters. Wmk Large Garter (4d.) or Emblems (roses, shamrock and thistle) (others).
C. As B. but wmk Spray of Rose.
D. Coloured corner letters. Wmk Large Garter (4d., 8d.) or Spray of Rose (others).

ST. JAGO DE CUBA

CC **1d** Z **3**

Crowned-circle handstamp.
CC4 CC **1d** In red (15.12.1841) .... *Price on cover* £6000

Queen Victoria stamps of GREAT BRITAIN cancelled "C 88" (Type Z **3***).*

1865–77.
Z18	–	½d. rose-red (1870–79) (Plate Nos. 4, 6, 14)	
Z19	A	1d. rose-red (1864–79) .... *From*	£150
		Plate Nos. 100. 105/6, 109, 111, 120, 123, 138, 144, 146/8, 171, 208.	
Z20		1½d. lake-red (1870–74) (Plate No. 3)	
Z21		2d. blue (1858–69) (Plate Nos. 9, 12/14)	£200
Z22	C	3d. rose (1867) (Plate No. 5)	
Z23	B	4d. vermilion (1865–73) .... *From*	£225
		Plate Nos. 9/14.	
Z24	D	4d. vermilion (1876) (Plate No. 15)	£600
Z25	C	6d. violet (1867–70) .... *From*	£450
		Plate Nos. 6, 8, 9.	
Z26		6d. buff (Plate No. 11)	
Z27	B	9d. straw (1865)	
Z27a	C	9d. straw (1867)	
Z28		10d. red-brown (1867)	£600
Z29		1s. green (1867–73) (Plate Nos. 4/6) ...... *From*	£450
Z30	D	1s. green (1873–77) (Plate Nos. 9/10, 12/13)....	
Z31	C	2s. blue (1867)	
Z32	–	5s. rose (1867) (Plate No. 1)	

For description of Types A to D see below No. Z17.

Elobey, Annobon and Corisco

100 Centimos = 1 Peseta

The islands of Annobon (in the Atlantic south of St. Thomas) and Elobey and Corisco (off the coast of Gabon) were acquired by Spain from Portugal in 1778.

PRINTERS. All the stamps of Elobey, Annobon and Corisco were printed at the Government Printing Works, Madrid, *unless otherwise stated.*

1 Alfonso XIII (**2**)

(Dies eng B. Maura. Typo)

1903 (June). Dated 1903. P 14.
1	**1**	¼c. rosine	85	60
2		½c. deep purple	85	60
3		1c. black	85	60
4		2c. brick-red	85	60
5		3c. myrtle-green	85	60
6		4c. blue-green	85	60
7		5c. dull lilac	85	60
8		10c. rose-lake	1·80	1·60
9		15c. orange	5·75	2·75
10		25c. slate-blue	10·00	7·25
11		50c. brown	12·00	12·50
12		75c. sepia	12·00	16·00
13		1p. orange-red	19·00	24·00
14		2p. deep brown	50·00	70·00
15		3p. slate-green	80·00	85·00
16		4p. maroon	£180	£120
17		5p. emerald	£200	£120
18		10p. grey-blue	£400	£225
1/18	*Set of 18*		£900	£600

1905. Dated 1905. P 14.
19	**1**	1c. rose	1·60	85
20		2c. deep purple	7·00	85
21		3c. black	1·60	85
22		4c. pale red	1·60	85
23		5c. myrtle-green	1·60	85
24		10c. blue-green	5·75	1·10
25		15c. dull lilac	7·00	6·00
26		25c. rose-lake	7·00	6·00
27		50c. dull orange	12·00	9·50
28		75c. deep blue	12·00	9·50
29		1p. chocolate	24·00	21·00
30		2p. sepia	27·00	29·00
31		3p. orange-red	27·00	29·00
32		4p. brown	£200	£110
33		5p. slate-green	£200	£110
34		10p. lake	£550	£350
19/34	*Set of 16*		£1000	£600

1906 (Nov). Nos. 19/22 surch locally as T **2**.
35	**1**	10c. on 1c. rose	18·00	10·00
		a. Surch inverted	22·00	12·50
		b. Surch double	22·00	12·50
		c. Value omitted	31·00	16·00
		d. Frame omitted	16·00	7·50
		e. Date and ornament omitted	32·00	27·00
		f. "15c." for "10c."	31·00	16·00
36		15c. on 2c. deep purple (R.)	12·50	10·00
		a. Frame omitted	21·00	15·00
		b. "25c." for "15c."	21·00	15·00
37		15c. on 2c. deep purple	21·00	11·50
38		25c. on 3c. black (R.)	12·50	10·00
		a. "15c." for "25c."	18·00	12·00
39		25c. on 3c. black	23·00	13·00
		a. "10c." for "25c."	36·00	26·00
		b. "15c." for "25c."	21·00	18·00

ELOBEY, ANNOBON AND CORISCO / FERNANDO POO

40		50c. on 4c. pale red	12·50	10·00
		a. Surch inverted	22·00	19·00
		b. Value omitted	36·00	28·00
		c. Frame omitted	18·00	17·00
		d. "10c." for "50c." (R.)	33·00	18·00
		e. "25c." for "50c."	34·00	19·00

3

(4)

(Dies eng B. Maura. Typo.)

1907 (1 Jan–May). P 14.
41	3	1c. deep purple	50	50
42		2c. black	50	50
43		3c. orange-red	50	50
44		4c. grey-green	50	50
45		5c. blue-green	50	50
46		10c. dull lilac (May)	6·25	6·75
47		15c. carmine-rose (May)	2·10	2·20
48		25c. orange-buff (May)	2·10	2·20
49		50c. blue (May)	2·10	2·20
50		75c. brown (May)	7·00	3·00
51		1p. sepia (May)	11·00	5·50
52		2p. vermilion (May)	15·00	19·00
53		3p. chocolate (May)	15·00	19·00
54		4p. bronze-green (May)	18·00	19·00
55		5p. lake (May)	25·00	19·00
56		10p. rose (May)	55·00	39·00
41/56	Set of 16		£140	£130

1908 (Apr)–**10**. Surch as T **4**.
57	3	05c. on 1c. deep purple (R.) (1910)	3·75	2·50
		a. Surch inverted	20·00	19·00
		b. Surch in black	14·00	6·25
58		05c. on 2c. black (R.) (1910)	3·75	2·50
		a. Surch inverted	18·00	17·00
		b. Surch in black	14·00	2·10
59		05c. on 3c. orange-red (1909)	4·00	2·50
		a. Surch inverted	18·00	18·00
60		05c. on 4c. grey-green (1909)	4·00	2·50
		a. Surch inverted	18·00	18·00
61		05c. on 10c. dull lilac	9·75	9·25
		a. Surch inverted	18·00	18·00
		b. Surch double	20·00	18·00
		c. Surch in red	25·00	10·00
		d. Surch double (Bk.+R.)		
62		26c. on 10c. dull lilac	37·00	21·00
		a. Surch inverted	21·00	18·00
57/62	Set of 6		55·00	36·00

Other errors exist including "PARA" omitted on all values.
05 c. surcharges on Nos. 47/56 were prepared but not issued.

(5)

1909. Fiscal stamps, inscr "POSESIONES ESPAÑOLAS DE AFRICA OCCIDENTAL", surch locally with T **5**.
63		10c. on 50c. green	27·00	18·00
64		10c. on 1p.25 lilac	41·00	22·00
65		10c. on 2p. brown	£160	£120
66		10c. on 2p.50 blue	£160	£120
67		10c. on 10p. brown	£170	£120
68		10c. on 15p. grey	£160	£120
69		10c. on 25p. red-brown	£160	£120

Very many errors exist in the above issue.

From 1909 to 1960 these islands were joined with Fernando Poo and Spanish Guinea as the Spanish Territories of the Gulf of Guinea, known from 1949 as Spanish Guinea (q. v.). In 1959 Annobon became part of the Spanish Overseas Province of Fernando Poo and Elobey and Corisco became part of the similar province of Rio Muni.

Fernando Poo

1868-93. Currencies stated below issues
1894. 1000 Milesimas = 100 Centavos = 1 Peso
1901. 100 Céntimos = 1 Peseta

SPANISH COLONY

The island of Fernando Poo, in the Gulf of Guinea, was discovered by the Portuguese sailor Fernão do Poo in 1472. It was acquired by Spain under a treaty of 1778. From 1827 to 1834 it was leased to the United Kingdom as a naval base from which to check the slave trade.

PRINTERS. All the stamps of Fernando Poo were printed at the Government Printing Works. Madrid, *unless otherwise stated.*

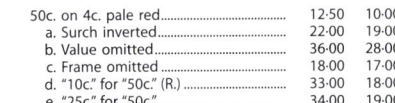
1 Isabella II

(Dies eng J. P. Varela. Typo)

1868 (1 July). P 14.
1	1	20c. brown	£800	£190

This stamp was in use up to December 1868, from which date, up to 1879, the stamps of Cuba were used in Fernando Poo.
Value expressed in *centimos de escudo*.

2 Alfonso XII (3)

(Dies eng E. Juliá. Typo)

1879 (1 July). P 14.
2	2	5c. grey-green	70·00	18·00
3		10c. rose	34·00	18·00
4		50c. blue	£120	18·00

Values expressed in *centimos de peseta*.

1882 (1 Jan)–**89**. P 14.
5	2	1c. grey-green	13·00	7·75
6		2c. rose	19·00	13·50
7		5c. lavender	60·00	18·00
8		10c. brown (1.7.89)	90·00	9·75

Values expressed in *centavos de peso*.

1884–93. Handstamped as T **3** in centimos de peseta.
A. In blue
9A	2	50c. on 1c. (1893)	£150	34·00
10A		50c. on 2c. (5.84)	41·00	10·50
11A		50c. on 5c. (1887)	£190	55·00

B. In black
9B	2	50c. on 1c. (1893)	£150	34·00
10B		50c. on 2c. (5.84)	41·00	10·50
11B		50c. on 5c. (1887)	£190	55·00

This handstamp may be found inverted and also double. There are two types of this handstamp.

1893–98. T **3**, on plain paper.
A. In blue
12A		50c. on blue	19·00	19·00

B. In black
12B		50c. on blue	19·00	19·00

In default of stamps this surcharge was also applied direct to envelopes, and thus is known on different coloured papers according to the envelope presented by the sender.

4 Alfonso XIII (5) (6)

387

FERNANDO POO

(Dies eng E. Juliá. Typo)

1894–97. New Currency. P 14.
13	**4**	⅛c. grey	33·00	5·50
14		2c. deep rosine	23·00	4·25
15		5c. blue-green (1.1.97)	23·00	4·25
16		6c. indigo-purple	20·00	5·50
17		10c. violet brown	£375	£110
		a. Deep brown	35·00	7·50
18		10c. pale lake (1895)	70·00	17·00
19		10c. chestnut (1896)	16·00	4·25
20		12½c. sepia	17·00	5·00
21		20c. indigo	17·00	5·00
22		25c. pale lake	33·00	5·00
13/16, 17a/22 Set of 10			£250	55·00

1896–98. Handstamped as T **5**, in blue.
23	**4**	5c. on ⅛c. grey	£130	43·00
		a. In black	80·00	17·00
		b. In red	85·00	23·00
24		5c. on 2c. deep rosine (8.98)	65·00	26·00
		a. In black	43·00	16·00
		b. In red	48·00	21·00
25		5c. on 6c. indigo-purple	£190	70·00
		a. In black	£190	70·00
		b. In red		
		c. In violet	£190	70·00
26		5c. on 10c. violet-brown (Blk.)	£190	70·00
		a. Deep brown (Blk.)	85·00	70·00
		ab. In blue	65·00	19·00
		ac. In red	65·00	19·00
		ad. In violet	65·00	19·00
27		5c. on 10c. chestnut	£190	43·00
		a. In black	£120	28·00
		b. In violet	£130	55·00
28		5c. on 12½c. sepia (8.98)	47·00	21·00
		a. In black	29·00	13·50
		b. In red	39·00	25·00
		c. In violet	35·00	12·00
29		5c. on 20c. indigo	£190	70·00
		a. In black	£120	46·00
		b. In red	£120	46·00
30		5c. on 25c. pale lake	£190	65·00
		a. In black	£120	37·00
		b. In violet	£130	38·00

Being handstamped the surcharge is found inverted, double, etc. in the above and following two issues.
There are three types of this handstamp.

7 (8)

HABILITADO

— PARA —

CORREOS
(9)

1896. Fiscal stamp T **7**, handstamped in blue, Imperf.
31	**8**	5c. on 10c. rose-red (1 Dec)	40·00	17·00
		a. In black	42·00	28·00
		b. In red	25·00	14·00
		c. In violet	£120	17·00
32	**9**	10c. rose-red (Oct)	40·00	17·00
		a. In black	45·00	31·00
		b. In red	90·00	55·00
		c. In violet	38·00	55·00

These handstamps exist inverted, double, vertical, etc.
No. 32 was also made available for postal use without handstamp in August 1896.

1897 (June)–**99.** Handstamped as T **6**, in blue.
33	**4**	5c. on ⅛c. grey (8.97)	37·00	19·00
		a. In black	£110	40·00
		b. In red	£110	28·00
34		5c. on 2c. deep rosine	37·00	19·00
		a. In black	18·00	16·00
		b. In red	18·00	16·00
35		5c. on 5c. blue-green (End 1897)	£180	60·00
		a. In black	£100	22·00
		b. In red	£110	20·00
36		5c. on 6c. indigo-purple (9.97)	26·00	38·00
		a. In black	25·00	18·00
		b. In red	20·00	14·00
		c. In violet	20·00	14·00
37		5c. on 10c. deep brown	£200	75·00
		a. In black	£120	25·00
38		5c. on 10c. pale lake	£400	£425
39		5c. on 10c. chestnut	£190	65·00
		a. In black	29·00	18·00
		b. In red		
		c. In violet	£190	65·00
40		5c. on 12½c. sepia (1.98)	80·00	31·00
		a. In black	48·00	8·00
		b. In red	48·00	12·00
41		5c. on 20c. indigo (2.99)	46·00	27·00
		a. In black	30·00	10·00
		b. In red	34·00	11·00
42		5c. on 25c. pale lake (End 1898)	45·00	31·00
		a. In black	48·00	18·00
		b. In red		

There are four types of this handstamp, one being without stop.

1898 (May)–**99.** Handstamped as T **3**, in blue.
43	**4**	50c. on ⅛c. grey	£350	£130
44		50c. on 2c. deep rosine	95·00	32·00
		a. In black	55·00	20·00
		b. In violet	65·00	45·00
45		50c. on 5c. blue-green (Bk.)	£250	90·00
46		50c. on 10c. deep brown	£225	90·00
		a. In black	£120	28·00
47		50c. on 10c. pale lake	£250	90·00
		a. In black	£120	28·00
48		50c. on 10c. chestnut	£225	90·00
		a. In black	£120	28·00
49		50c. on 12½c. sepia (1899)	£190	55·00
		a. In black	£110	18·00
50		50c. on 25c. pale lake (Bk.)	£225	80·00

Nos. 51/60 are vacant.

1898 (Oct). T **7**, dated 1898, handstamped as T **9** with value added, in black. Imperf.
61	15c. on 10c. blue-green	47·00	28·00
	a. Error. "HAEILITADO"	35·00	25·00
	b. In blue	47·00	28·00
	c. In red	£130	90·00

Exists inverted, double, vertical etc.

10

Fernando Póo 1899

Habilitado
para
Correos
15 Cent. de Peso.
(11)

1899 (June). Fiscal stamp, T **10**, handstamped as shown, in black with "CORREOS" in red, or with T **11**, in black.
62	10c. on 25c. blue-green	£130	80·00
63	15c. on 25c. blue-green	£200	£140

FERNANDO POO

1899. Fiscal stamp, T **10** handstamped diagonally as T **12**, in black.
| 64 | 25c. blue-green | £475 | £225 |

This is also known handstamped "1898" in large figures and also "1.899" in smaller figures.

1899. Fiscal stamp, T **10**, handstamped with T **13**, in red with manuscript signature in black.
| 65 | 15c. on 25c. blue-green | £3250 | £2250 |

(Dies eng B. Maura. Typo)

1899 (Sept). Dated 1899. P 14.
66	14	1m. chestnut	2·75	1·00
67		2m. chestnut	2·75	1·00
68		3m. chestnut	2·75	1·00
69		4m. chestnut	2·75	1·00
70		5m. chestnut	2·75	1·00
71		1c. indigo-purple	2·75	1·00
72		2c. blue-green	2·75	1·00
73		3c. deep brown	2·75	1·00
74		4c. orange	18·00	2·50
75		5c. rosine	2·75	1·00
76		6c. ultramarine	2·75	1·00
77		8c. grey-brown	10·50	1·00
78		10c. vermilion	7·25	1·00
79		15c. olive-slate	7·25	1·00
80		20c. maroon	20·00	2·50
81		40c. deep lilac	£140	44·00
82		60c. black	£140	44·00
83		80c. chocolate	£140	44·00
84		1p. yellow-green	£450	£200
85		2p. indigo	£450	£200
66/85 Set of 20			£1300	£500

1900. T **14** handstamped, in black.
86	5	5c. on 20c. maroon	£375	26·00
		a. In blue	£375	26·00
87	6	5c. on 20c. maroon	13·00	6·75
		a. In blue	18·00	10·00
		b. In violet	18·00	10·00
		c. In red		
88	3	50c. on 20c. maroon	16·00	6·75
		a. In blue	15·00	11·00
		b. In red	—	£120

1900. Dated 1900. P 14.
91	14	1m. black	4·25	1·00
92		2m. black	4·25	1·00
93		3m. black	4·25	1·00
94		4m. black	4·25	1·00
95		5m. black	4·25	1·00
96		1c. deep green	4·25	1·00
97		2c. dull lilac	4·25	1·00
98		3c. bright pink	4·25	1·00
99		4c. deep chocolate	4·25	1·00
100		5c. bright blue	4·25	1·00
101		6c. orange	4·25	4·25
102		8c. bronze-green	4·25	4·25
103		10c. lake	4·25	1·00
104		15c. indigo-purple	4·25	1·00
105		20c. brown	4·25	1·00
106		40c. orange-brown	10·00	4·50
107		60c. bright green	24·00	4·50
108		80c. deep blue	24·00	7·50
109		1p. red-brown	£130	60·00
110		2p. orange-vermilion	£225	£130
91/110 Set of 20			£425	£200

1900 (Sept). T **7**, dated 1900, handstamped, in black.

*(a) With T **6** and **12***
(i) "CORREOS" above value
| 111 | 7 | 5c. on 10c. blue | 85·00 | 35·00 |
| | | a. In red | £110 | 44·00 |

(ii) "CORREOS" below value
| 112 | 7 | 5c. on 10c. blue | 95·00 | 42·00 |

(iii) "CORREOS" twice, value between, diag
| 113 | 7 | 5c. on 10c. blue | £140 | 85·00 |
| | | a. In red | — | £140 |

*(b) With T **12**, diagonally*
114	7	10c. blue	50·00	19·00
		a. In red	32·00	8·25
		b. Optd twice, in red	65·00	19·00

These handstamps exist double, inverted etc. and fancy varieties of handstamp also exist, an entire sheet having been seen with different combinations on each row.
The 10c. blue also exists postally used without hand-stamp.

1900. T **7**, dated 1900, handstamped with T **8**, in black.
| 115 | 7 | 5c. on 10c. blue | £650 | £500 |
| | | a. In red | £950 | £650 |

1900 (Oct). Nos. 74 and 105 handstamped with T **3**, in black.
116	14	50c. on 4c. orange	20·00	10·50
		a. In violet	12·00	6·50
		b. In green	21·00	11·00
		c. In red	28·00	16·00
117		50c. on 20c. brown	28·00	8·25

These exist double, inverted, etc.

1900–01. Fiscal stamp T **14a** dated 1900 1901 handstamped in black.

*(a) With T **12** and **6***
| 118 | 5c. on 25c. brown | £1000 | £600 |
| | a. In red | £650 | £375 |

*(b) With T **12** and **5***
| 119 | 5c. on 25c. brown | £650 | £350 |
| | a. In red | £650 | £375 |

These exist double, inverted, etc.

1901 (Jan). New Currency. Dated 1901. P 14.
124	14	1c. black	2·75	1·70
125		2c. chestnut	2·75	1·70
126		3c. indigo-purple	2·75	1·70
127		4c. dull lilac	2·75	1·70
128		5c. vermilion	1·80	1·70
129		10c. brown	1·80	1·70
130		25c. blue	1·80	1·70
131		50c. claret	2·75	1·70
132		75c. sepia	2·20	1·70
133		1p. blue-green	65·00	15·00
134		2p. red-brown	41·00	22·00
135		3p. olive-green	41·00	30·00
136		4p. red	41·00	30·00
137		5p. myrtle-green	50·00	30·00
138		10p. pale orange	£110	90·00
124/138 Set of 15			£325	£200

For the above issue handstamped "Bata" see the note at the beginning of Spanish Guinea.

(T **15/17**. Dies eng B. Maura. Typo)

1902 (Jan). With blue control figures on back. P 14.
140	15	5c. deep green	2·75	50
141		10c. slate	2·75	50
142		25c. lake	6·75	1·40
143		50c. brown	17·00	5·00
144		75c. dull lilac	17·00	5·00
145		1p. rosine	21·00	8·25
146		2p. bronze-green	43·00	21·00
147		5p. pale red	65·00	48·00
140/147 Set of 8			£160	80·00

389

FERNANDO POO

1903 (Jan). Figures in blue on back. P 14.

154	**16**	¼c. indigo-purple	40	40
155		½c. black	40	40
156		1c. brick-red	40	40
157		2c. myrtle-green	40	40
158		3c. blue-green	40	40
159		4c. dull lilac	40	40
160		5c. rose-lake	55	40
161		10c. orange	70	55
162		15c. blue-green	3·00	1·90
163		25c. brown	3·00	3·00
164		50c. sepia	5·00	5·00
165		75c. rosine	20·00	9·75
166		1p. deep brown	26·00	18·00
167		2p. slate-green	39·00	25·00
168		3p. maroon	39·00	25·00
169		4p. slate-blue	47·00	43·00
170		5p. deep blue	70·00	50·00
171		10p. red-orange	£150	80·00
154/171	Set of 18		£375	£250

1905 (Jan). Dated 1905. Figures in blue on back. P 14.

172	**16**	1c. deep purple	50	50
173		2c. black	50	50
174		3c. orange-red	50	50
175		4c. myrtle-green	50	50
176		5c. blue-green	55	50
177		10c. dull lilac	2·00	95
178		15c. rose-lake	2·00	95
179		25c. dull orange	18·00	3·00
180		50c. blue-green	11·00	5·00
181		75c. chocolate	16·00	16·00
182		1p. sepia	18·00	16·00
183		2p. rosine	31·00	23·00
184		3p. brown	48·00	27·00
185		4p. slate-green	55·00	35·00
186		5p. lake	90·00	55·00
187		10p. deep blue	£140	80·00
172/187	Set of 16		£400	£250

1907 (Mar). Figures in blue on back. P 14.

188	**17**	1c. slate-black	20	20
189		2c. bright rose	20	20
190		3c. deep purple	20	20
191		4c. black	20	20
192		5c. orange-buff	20	20
193		10c. claret	1·70	90
194		15c. bronze-black	40	40
195		25c. brown	41·00	22·00
196		50c. blue-green	20	20
197		75c. orange-red	35	20
198		1p. dull blue	2·75	95
199		2p. chocolate	11·00	8·75
200		3p. dull rose	11·00	8·75
201		4p. dull lilac	11·00	8·75
202		5p. bronze-brown	11·00	8·75
203		10p. orange-brown	11·00	8·75
188/203	Set of 16		90·00	60·00

HABILITADO
PARA
05 CTMS
(**18**)

FERNANDO POO
(**19**)

1908. Handstamped with T **18**, in black.

204	**17**	5c. on 10c. claret	5·00	4·25
		a. In blue	12·50	7·75
		b. In red	21·00	9·50

Exists double, inverted, etc.

In 1909 Fernando Poo was joined with Elobey, Annobon and Corisco and Spanish Guinea as the Spanish Territories of the Gulf of Guinea, renamed Spanish Guinea in 1949. Except for the following issue of 1929, the stamps used in Fernando Poo from 1909 to 1960 were those listed as Spanish Guinea Nos. 101 onwards.

1929. Seville and Barcelona Exhibitions. Nos. 504/14 of Spain optd with T **19** (horiz (15, 25c.) or sideways (others)). P 11.

209	–	5c. carmine-lake (B.)	35	35
210	–	10c. green (R.)	35	35
		a. Perf 14	1·50	1·50
211	**83**	15c. turquoise-blue (R.)	35	35
212	**84**	20c. violet (R.)	35	35
213	**83**	25c. carmine (B.)	35	35
214	–	30c. blackish brown (B.)	35	35
215	–	40c. blue (R.)	95	95
216	**84**	50c. red-orange (B.)	2·10	2·10
217	–	1p. greenish slate (R.)	8·25	8·25
218	–	4p. claret (B.)	40·00	40·00
219	–	10p. brown (B.)	50·00	50·00
209/219	Set of 11		95·00	95·00

OVERSEAS PROVINCE OF SPAIN

On 30 July 1959 two Overseas Provinces of Spain in the Gulf of Guinea were created. (i) Fernando Poo, comprising that island and Annobon; and (ii) Rio Muni, comprising the mainland territory of that name, with Elobey and Corisco.

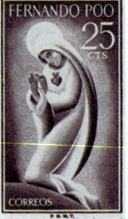

24 Woman at Prayer   **25** De Falla (composer)

(Des J. M. de Asua. Photo)

1960 (25 Feb). P 13×12½.

220	**24**	25c. violet-grey	35	20
221		50c. olive-brown	35	20
222		75c. purple-brown	35	20
223		1p. orange-red	35	20
224		1p.50 turquoise-green	35	20
225		2p. bright purple	35	20
226		3p. blue	3·25	1·00
227		5p. red-brown	40	20
228		10p. olive-green	50	25
220/228	Set of 9		5·50	2·40

(Des T. Miciano, R. Almagro, M. Tornero. Photo)

1960 (1 June). Child Welfare. T **25** and similar designs inscr "PRO-INFANCIA 1960". P 12½×13 (T **25**) or 13×12½ (others).

229	**25**	10c.+5c. brown-purple	60	60
230	–	15c.+5c. bistre-brown	60	60
231	–	35c. blackish green	60	60
232	**25**	80c. deep bluish green	60	60
229/232	Set of 4		2·20	2·20

Designs (De Falla's ballets): Vert—15c. Spanish dancer (*Love, the Magician*); 35c. Tricorne, stick and windmill (*Three-Cornered Hat*).

26 Sperm Whale   **27** "The Blessing"

(Des J. Olcina J. de Castro Photo)

1960 (23 Dec). Stamp Day. T **26** and similar horiz design inscr "DIA DEL SELLO 1960". P 12½×13.

233	**26**	10c.+5c. brown-lake	60	60
234	–	20c.+5c. blackish green	60	60
235	**26**	30c.+10c. olive-brown	60	60
236	–	50c.+20c. sepia	60	60
233/236	Set of 4		2·20	2·20

Design:—20, 50c. Natives harpooning humpback whale.

(Des V. Vila (T **27**), M. Salamanca (others). Photo)

1961 (21 June). Child Welfare. T **27** and similar vert design inscr "PRO-INFANCIA 1961". P 13×12½.

237	**27**	10c.+5c. lake	65	65
238	–	25c.+10c. slate-violet	65	65
239	**27**	80c.+20c. deep bluish green	70	70
237/239	Set of 3		1·80	1·80

Design:—25c. African kneeling before Cross.

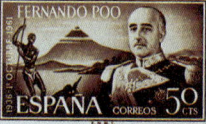

28   **29** Great Turtle

FERNANDO POO

(Des V. D. Urosa (25c.), T. Miciano (T **28**), V. S. Algora (70c.). Photo)

1961 (1 Oct). 25th Anniv of Gen. Franco as Head of State. T **28** and similar designs. P 13×12½ (vert) or 12½×13 (horiz).

240	–	25c. violet-grey	60	60
241	**28**	50c. olive-brown	60	60
242	–	70c. emerald	60	60
243	**28**	1p. orange-red	60	60
240/243 Set of 4			2·20	2·20

Designs: Vert—25c. Map; 70c. St. Isabel Cathedral.

(Des E. Cerra (T **29**). V. D. Urosa (others). Photo)

1961 (23 Nov). Stamp Day. T **29** and similar horiz design inscr "DIA DEL SELLO 1961". P 12½×13.

244	**29**	10c.+5c. rose-red	60	60
245	–	25c.+10c. plum	60	60
246	**29**	30c.+10c. brown-purple	60	60
247	–	1p.+10c. red-orange	60	60
244/247 Set of 4			2·20	2·20

Design:—25c., 1p. Native porters, palm trees and shore.

30 Spanish Freighter *Okume*

(Des A. B. Hernandez (T **30**), R. L. Prieto (50c.). Photo)

1962 (10 July). Child Welfare. T **30** and similar horiz design Inscr "PRO-INFANCIA 1962". P 12½×13.

248	**30**	25c. slate-violet	65	65
249	–	50c. olive-green	65	65
250	**30**	1p. chestnut	70	70
248/250 Set of 3			1·80	1·80

Design:—50c. Spanish freighter *San Francisco*.

31 Postman   **32** Native Shrine   **33** Sister and Child

(Des A. Balbuena (T **31**), J. Olcina. Photo)

1962 (23 Nov). Stamp Day. T **31** and similar design inscr "DIA DEL SELLO 1962". P 12½×13 (35c.) or 13×12½ (others).

251	**31**	15c. deep green	65	65
252	–	35c. magenta	65	65
253	**31**	1p. brown	70	70
251/253 Set of 3			1·80	1·80

Design: Horiz—35c. Mail transport.

(Des V. D. Urosa. Photo)

1963 (29 Jan). Seville Flood Relief. P 13×12½.

254	**32**	50c. olive brown	75	75
255	–	1p. reddish purple	75	75

(Des J. J. de Castro (T **33**), V. S. Algora (others). Photo)

1963 (1 June). Child Welfare. T **33** and similar design inscr "PRO-INFANCIA 1963". P 13×12½ (50c.) or 12½×13 (others).

256	–	25c. bright purple	65	65
257	–	50c. bluish green	65	65
258	–	1p. orange-red	70	70
256/258 Set of 3			1·80	1·80

Design: Horiz—25c., 1p. Two sisters.

34 Child and Arms   **35** Governor Chacon

(Des J. de Miguel. Photo)

1963 (12 June). "For Barcelona". P 12½×13.

259	**34**	50c. olive-brown	75	75
260	–	1p. carmine	75	75

(Des A. B. Vera (T **35**), V. Vila (50c.). Photo)

1964 (6 Mar). Stamp Day. T **35** and similar design inscr "DIA DEL SELLO 1963". P 13×12½ (50c.) or 12½×13 (others).

261	**35**	25c. deep violet blue	65	65
262	–	50c. olive-brown	65	65
263	**35**	1p. Venetian red	70	70
261/263 Set of 3			1·80	1·80

Design: Vert—50c. Orange blossom.

36 Canoe   **37** Ring-necked Francolin

(Des V. Vlla. Photo)

1964 (1 June). Child Welfare. T **36** and similar vert design inscr "PRO INFANCIA 1964". P 13×12½.

264	**36**	25c. reddish violet	65	65
265	–	50c. yellow-olive (Pineapple)	65	65
266	**36**	1p. brown-purple	70	70
264/266 Set of 3			1·80	1·80

(Des J. L. Bueno Fraile (T **37**), J. A. Prieto Dolores (25c., 1, 5p.), A. Blanco Varas (others). Photo)

1964 (1 July). Birds. T **37** and similar vert designs. P 13×12½.

267	**37**	15c. yellow-brown	35	25
268	–	25c. slate-violet	35	25
269	–	50c. yellow-olive	35	25
270	**37**	70c. green	35	25
271	–	1p. orange-brown	35	25
272	–	1p.50 turquoise-blue	35	25
273	**37**	3p. grey-blue	50	25
274	–	5p. dull purple	1·50	25
275	–	10p. blue-green	2·75	1·00
267/275 Set of 9			6·25	2·75

Birds:—25c., 1p., 5p. Mallard; 50c., 1p.50, 10p. Great blue turaco.

38 "The Three Kings"   **39** Native

(Des T. Miciano (T **38**), C. Tauler (others). Photo)

1964 (23 Nov). Stamp Day. T **38** and similar design. P 13×12½ (vert) or 12½×13 (horiz).

276	–	50c. bronze green	60	60
277	**38**	1p. orange-red	60	60
278	–	1p.50 deep green	60	60
279	**38**	3p. blue	1·70	1·70
276/279 Set of 4			3·25	3·25

Design: Vert—50c., 1p.50, King presenting gift to infant Jesus.

(Des T. Miciano and C. Tauler. Photo)

1965 (22 Feb). 25th Anniv of End of Spanish Civil War. T **39** and similar vert designs inscr "XXV ANOS DE PAZ". P 13×12½.

280	–	50c. indigo	65	65
281	–	1p. brown-red	65	65
282	–	1p.50 turquoise blue	70	70
280/282 Set of 3			1·80	1·80

Designs:—1p. "Agriculture" (fruit farming); 1p.50, "Education" (child writing).

FERNANDO POO / British Post Office at Fernando Poo

40 *Metopodontus savagei* (stag beetle)   **41** Pole Vaulting

(Des M. Salamanca and J. J. de Castro. Photo)

1965 (1 June). Child Welfare. Insects. T **40** and similar design. P 12½×13 (1p.) or 13×12½ (others).
283	50c. bronze-green	65	65
284	1p. rose-red	65	65
285	1p.50 new blue	70	70
283/285	Set of 3	1·80	1·80

Insect: Vert—50c., 1p.50, *Plectrocnemia cruciata* (squashbug).

(Des T. Miciano and A. Varas. Photo)

1965 (23 Nov). Stamp Day. T **41** and another design. P 12½×13 (horiz) or 13×12½ (vert).
286	**41**	50c. green	65	65
287	–	1p. chestnut	65	65
288	**41**	1p.50 blue	70	70
286/288	Set of 3		1·80	1·80

Design: Vert—1p. Arms of Fernando Poo.

42 European and African Women   **43** Greater White-nosed Monkey (*Cercopithecus nictitans*)

1966 (1 June). Child Welfare. T **42** and similar design. Photo. P 13×12½ (1p.50) or 12½×13 (others).
289	**42**	50c. myrtle-green	65	65
290		1p. brown-red	65	65
291	–	1p.50 blue	70	70
289/291	Set of 3		1·80	1·80

Design: Vert—1p.50, St. Isabel of Hungary.

(Des D. E. Cerra. Photo)

1966 (23 Nov). Stamp Day. T **43** and similar design. P 13.
292	**43**	10c. steel-blue and yellow	60	60
293		40c. bright blue and bistre-brown	60	60
294	**43**	1p.50 olive and orange-brown	60	60
295		4p. orange-brown and slate-green	70	70
292/295	Set of 4		2·30	2·30

Design: Vert—40c., 4p. Moustached monkey (*Cercopithecus cephus*).

44 Flowers   **45** African Linsang (*Poiana richardsoni*)

(Des T. Miciano. Photo)

1967 (1 June). Child Welfare. T **44** and similar vert floral design. P 13.
296	**44**	10c. cerise and dull green	60	60
297	–	40c. lake-brown and yellow-orange	60	60
298	**44**	1p.50 bright purple and light brown	60	60
299	–	4p. deep blue and yellow-green	70	70
296/299	Set of 4		2·30	2·30

1967 (23 Nov). Stamp Day. T **45** and similar designs. Photo. P 13.
300	1p. black and bistre	65	65
301	1p.50 red-brown and yellow-olive	65	65
302	3p.50 brown-purple and grey-green	95	95
300/302	Set of 3	2·00	2·00

Designs: Vert—1p.50, Western needle-clawed bushbaby (*Euoticus elegantulus*). Horiz—3p.50, Lord Derby's flying squirrel (*Anomalurus fraseri*).

46 Arms of San Carlos and Stamp of 1868   **47** Libra (Scales)

1968 (4 Feb). Stamp Centenary. T **46** and similar horiz designs. Photo. P 12½×13.
303	1p. chestnut and purple	65	65
304	1p.50 chestnut and deep blue	65	65
305	2p.50 chestnut and deep red-brown	95	95
303/305	Set of 3	2·00	2·00

Designs: Each with stamp of 1868—1p.50, Arms of Santa Isabel; 2p.50, Arms of Fernando Poo.

1968 (25 Apr). Child Welfare. Signs of the Zodiac. T **47** and similar horiz designs. Photo. P 13.
306	1p. magenta/*pale yellow*	65	65
307	1p.50 red-brown/*pale pink*	65	65
308	2p.50 deep violet/*pale greenish yellow*	95	95
306/308	Set of 3	2·00	2·00

Designs:—1p.50, Leo (Lion); 2p.50, Aquarius (Water-man).

On 12 October 1968 Fernando Poo was joined again to Rio Muni to form the independent Republic of Equatorial Guinea (see Part 12 (*Africa since Independence A–E*) of this catalogue). In 1973 Fernando Poo was renamed Macias Nguema Bryoga.

BRITISH POST OFFICE AT FERNANDO POO

The British government leased naval facilities from 1827 to 1834. A British Consul was appointed in 1849 and a postal agency was opened on 1 April 1858.

The use of Great Britain stamps was authorized in 1858, but a cancellation was not supplied until 1874. The office remained open until 1877.

CROWNED-CIRCLE HANDSTAMPS. Under regulations circulated in December 1841, letters and packets forwarded through offices abroad to the United Kingdom or any of its territories were to be sent unpaid, the postage being collected on delivery. Where this was not possible, for example from a British colony to a foreign country or between two foreign ports, then a crowned-circle handstamp was to be applied with the postage, paid in advance, noted alongside in manuscript.

The dates quoted are those on which the handstamp appears in the G.P.O. Record Books, but it seems to have been normal for the handstamps to be sent to the office concerned immediately following this registration.

Prices quoted for these handstamps are for examples used on cover during the pre-adhesive period.

PRICES. Prices quoted for Great Britain stamps used abroad are for fine used examples with the cancellation clearly legible. Poor impressions of the cancellations are worth much less than the prices quoted.

CC **4**   Z **1**

Crowned-circle Handstamp.
CC1   CC **4** In red (19.2.1859) .... Price on cover £5500

Queen Victoria stamps of GREAT BRITAIN cancelled with Type Z **1**.

1874–77.
Z1	A	4d. vermilion (1865-72) (Plate Nos. 13, 14)	£700
Z2	B	4d. vermilion (1876) (Plate No. 15)	
Z3		6d. grey (1874-76) (Plate Nos. 13/16) ..	£600

A. Large uncoloured corner letters.
B. Coloured corner letters.

Ifni

100 Céntimos = 1 Peseta

The enclave of Ifni, on the Atlantic coast of Morocco, was ceded to Spain on 26 April 1860. Before the issue of postage stamps, letters were franked by a rubber stamp and the signature of an official.

PRINTERS. All the stamps of Ifni were printed at the Government Printing Works, Madrid, *unless otherwise stated*.

TERRITORIO DE IFNI
(1)

1941–42. Stamps of Spain optd horiz with T **1**. Without imprint at foot.

1	181	1c. green (R.)	8·50	8·00
		a. Vert opt	39·00	23·00
2	182	2c. chestnut (B.)	8·50	8·00
		a. Vert opt	39·00	23·00
3	183	5c. sepia (R.)	1·10	75
4		10c. carmine (*shades*) (B.)	4·75	2·75
		a. Red opt	34·00	18·00
		b. Red and blue opt	44·00	27·00
5		15c. yellow-green (D) (R.)	1·10	70
6	196	20c. violet (R.)	1·10	70
7		25c. claret (R.)	1·10	70
8		30c. blue (R.)	1·10	70
9		40c. greenish slate (R.)	1·80	65
10		50c. slate (R.)	9·50	2·40
11		70c. deep blue (R.)	9·50	6·75
		a. With "SANCHEZ TODA" imprint (955)	75·00	50·00
12		1PTA black (R.)	9·50	6·75
13		2PTAS sepia (R.)	£130	45·00
14		4PTAS. rose (B.)	£375	£200
15		10PTS. brown (R.)	£1200	£500
1/15 Set of 15			£1600	£700

Covers are known between September 1941 and June 1942 bearing Spanish stamps either alone or in combination with stamps of the above set. In November 1942 stampless covers are found, postage paid being endorsed in manuscript and the pre-stamp cachet applied.

2 Nomadic Shepherds   **3** El Santuario   **4** Nomad Family

(T **2**/**4** des M. Bertuchl. Litho Rieusset, Barcelona)

1943. T **2**/**3** and similar vent designs. P 12½.

(a) POSTAGE. Inscr "CORREO"

16	**2**	1c. magenta and yellow-brown	20	20
17	–	2c. indigo and yellow-green	20	20
18	–	5c. violet-blue and claret	20	20
19	**2**	15c. green and blackish green	20	20
20	–	20c. lake-brown and violet	20	20
21	**2**	40c. violet and purple	25	25
22	–	45c. scarlet and purple-brown	30	30
23	–	75c. blue and indigo	30	30
24	**2**	1p. brown and scarlet	1·90	1·90
25	–	3p. deep green and violet-blue	4·50	4·50
26	–	10p. black and sepia	45·00	45·00
16/26 Set of 11			48·00	48·00

Designs:—2c., 20c., 45c., 3p. Arab rifleman; 5c., 75c., 10p. La Alcazaba.

(b) AIR. Inscr "CORREO AEREO"

27	**3**	5c. chocolate and claret	20	20
28	**3**	25c. sepia and yellow-green	20	20
29	**3**	50c. turquoise and indigo	30	30
30	–	1p. light blue and violet	30	30
31	**3**	1p.40 blue and grey-green	30	30
32	–	2p. orange-brown and purple	2·30	2·30
33	**3**	5p. violet and brown	3·25	3·25
34	–	6p. grey-green and blue	48·00	48·00
27/34 Set of 8			49·00	49·00

Design:—25c., 1p., 2p., 6p. Airplane over oasis.

(c) EXPRESS LETTER Inscr "URGENTE"

E35		25c. carmine and grey-green	1·50	1·50

Design:—La Alcazaba.

1947 (Feb). New value and design. P 10.

35	**4**	50c. black and purple-brown	18·00	85

IFNI (5)   Territorio de Ifni (6)   Territorio de Ifni (7)

1947 (29 Nov). AIR. Unissued stamps of Spain optd with T **5**.

36	195	5c. yellow (R.)	3·25	80
37		10c. blue-green (R.)	3·25	80

1948 (2 Aug). "El Cid" and Franco portrait stamps of Spain optd with T **6**, in red.

38	183	5c. sepia (899)	4·00	70
39	229	15c. yellow-green (1089)	4·00	70
40	201	90c. green (1024)	19·00	3·50
41	196	1PTA black (974)	35	20
38/41 Set of 4			25·00	4·50

See also Spanish West Africa for joint issues for Ifni and Spanish Sahara front 1949 to 1951.

1949 (9 Oct). Stamp Day and 75th Anniv of U.P.U. Spanish stamps optd with T **7**.

(a) POSTAGE

42	240	50c. red-brown (B.)	5·75	1·90
43		75c. ultramarine (R.)	5·75	1·90

(b) AIR

44	240	4p. blackish olive (R.)	6·25	1·90
42/44 Set of 3			16·00	5·25

1949 (10 Oct)–**50**. Stamps of Spain optd with T **6**.

(a) POSTAGE (10.10.49)

45	182	2c. chocolate (*p* 13×13½) (B.)	25	20
46	183	5c. sepia (902) (R.)	25	20
47		10c. carmine (903) (R.)	25	20
48		15c. grey-green (904) (R.)	25	20
49	196	25c. claret (1115) (R.)	25	20
50		30c. blue (965) (R.)	25	20
51	232	40c. brown (1097) (R.)	25	20
52		45c. rose-carmine (1098) (B.)	30	30
53	196	75c. slate (1120) (R.)	25	20
54	232	75c. indigo (1102) (R.)	55	20
55	201	90c. green (1024a) (R.)	55	30
56		1p.35 violet (1025a) (R.)	5·25	3·50
57	196	2PTAS sepia (976) (R.)	4·00	2·50
58		4PTAS rose (1025) (B.)	15·00	7·25
59		10PTAS brown (*p* 13) (R.)	37·00	22·00
45/59 Set of 15			60·00	34·00

(b) AIR (1.4.50)

60	195	25c. carmine-red (R.)	60	20
61		50c. purple-brown (R.)	70	20
62		1p. ultramarine (R.)	70	20
63		2p. green (R.)	4·00	90
64		4p. slate blue (R.)	11·00	4·25
65		10p. bright violet (R.)	15·00	8·75
60/65 Set of 6			29·00	13·00

(c) EXPRESS LETTER. No Imprint. P 10 (10.10.49)

E66	E **198**	25c. carmine-red (E1022) (B.)	30	20

Stocks of Spain 898a and 979 were perforated as indicated before overprinting as Nos. 45 and 59.

8 General Franco   **9** Lope Sancho de Valenzaela   **10** Woman and Dove

(Des M. Lois. Photo)

1950 (19 Oct). Child Welfare. P 13.

66	**8**	50c.+10c. sepia	55	35
67		1p.+25c. blue	18·00	8·25
68		6p.50+1p.65 blue-green	6·50	3·75
66/68 Set of 3			23·00	11·00

IFNI

(Des J. Nadel del Val. Photo)
1950 (23 Nov). AIR. Colonial Stamp Day. P 13×12½.
| 69 | **9** | 5p. blackish olive | 5·25 | 4·25 |

(Des T. Miciano. Recess)
1951 (22 Apr). AIR. Fifth Centenary of Birth of Isabella the Catholic. P 10.
| 70 | **10** | 5p. vermilion | 27·00 | 9·75 |

11 General Franco

(Des F. Hernández. Photo)
1951 (18 July). Visit of General Franco. P 12½×13.
71	**11**	50c. orange	55	60
72		1p. lake-brown	4·75	1·20
73		5p. blue-green	37·00	13·00
71/73 Set of 3			38·00	13·50

12 Fennec Fox   **13** Mother and Child   **14** Ferdinand the Catholic

(Des E. Serra and S. Quintana. Photo)
1951 (30 Nov). Colonial Stamp Day. P 13×12½.
74	**12**	5c.+5c. brown	1·00	75
75		10c.+5c. red-orange	1·10	80
76		60c.+15c. deep olive	2·10	1·50
74/76 Set of 3			3·75	2·75

(Des J. Blanco del Pueyo. Photo)
1952 (1 June). Child Welfare. P 13×12½.
77	**13**	5c.+5c. brown	80	60
78		50c.+10c. greenish black	80	60
79		2p.+30c. deep blue	3·75	3·00
77/79 Set of 3			4·75	3·75

(Des J. Nadal del Val. Photo)
1952 (18 July). AIR. Fifth Centenary of Birth of Ferdinand the Catholic. P 13×12½.
| 80 | **14** | 5p. brown | 34·00 | 9·75 |

15 Shag   **16**   **17** Addra Gazelle and Douglas DC-4 Airliner

(Des R. L. Prieto. Photo)
1952 (23 Nov). Colonial Stamp Day. P 13×12½.
81	**15**	5c.+5c. brown	65	65
82		10c.+15c. claret	70	70
83		60c.+15c. bronze-green	1·40	1·30
81/83 Set of 3			2·50	2·40

(Des T. Miciano. Photo)
1952 (10 Dec). Fourth Centenary of Death of Leo Africanus (geographer). P 13×12½.
84	**16**	5c. red-orange	65	65
85		35c. blackish olive	70	70
86		60c. brown	1·40	1·30
84/86 Set of 3			2·50	2·40

(Des T. Miciano. Photo)
1953 (1 Apr). AIR. P 13×12½.
87	**17**	60c. brown	35	30
88		1p.20 lake	35	30
89		1p.60 brown	45	40
90		2p. deep bright blue	3·00	55
91		4p. blackish green	1·70	70
92		10p. bright purple	9·50	3·25
87/92 Set of 6			14·00	5·00

18 Musician   **19** Fish and Jellyfish

(Des G. Calve and M. Cuervo. Photo)
1953 (1 June). Child Welfare. T **18** and similar horiz design inscr "PROINFANCIA 1953". P 12½×13.
93	**18**	5c.+5c. brown-lake	60	60
94	–	10c.+5c. bright purple	60	60
95	**18**	15c. deep olive	60	60
96	–	60c. brown	70	70
93/96 Set of 4			2·30	2·30
Design:—10, 60c. Two native musicians.

(Des T. Miciano and E. M. Gimeno. Photo)
1953 (23 Nov). Colonial Stamp Day. T **19** and similar horiz design inscr "DIA DEL SELLO COLONIAL 1953". P 12½×13.
97	**19**	5c.+5c. deep bright blue	95	60
98	–	10c.+5c. deep mauve	95	60
99	**19**	15c. deep green	95	60
100	–	60c. brown	1·20	70
97/100 Set of 4			3·75	2·30
Design:—10, 60c. Fish and seaweed.

20 Mediterranean Gull   **21** Asclepiad

(Des A. O. Urrutia, R. L. Prieto and J. Blanco del Pueyo. Photo)
1954 (22 Apr). T **20/1** and similar vert design. P 12½×13 (horiz) or 13×12½ (vert).
101	**20**	5c. red-orange	20	20
102	**21**	10c. brown-olive	20	20
103	–	25c. lake	20	20
104	**20**	35c. bronze-green	20	20
105	**21**	40c. deep purple	20	20
106	–	60c. deep brown	25	20
107	**20**	1p. brown	9·75	1·30
108	**21**	1p.25 carmine-red	30	20
109	–	2p. blue	40	20
110	**21**	4p.50 deep yellow-green	55	65
111	–	5p. greenish black	41·00	13·00
101/111 Set of 11			48·00	15·00
Design:—25c., 60c., 2p., 5p. Cactus.

22 Woman and Child   **23** Lobster

IFNI

(Des G. Calvo. Photo)

1954 (1 June). Child Welfare. T **22** and similar vert design inscr "PRO-INFANCIA 1954". P 13×12½.

112	**22**	5c.+5c. red-orange	50	50
113	–	10c.+5c. deep mauve	50	50
114	**22**	15c. bronze green	50	50
115	–	60c. brown	55	55
112/115 Set of 4			1·80	1·80

Design:—10, 60c. Woman and girl.

(Des R. A. Fabré and V. D. Urosa. Photo)

1954 (23 Nov). Colonial Stamp Day. T **23** and similar horiz design inscr "DIA DEL SELLO COLONIAL 1954". P 12½×13.

116	**23**	5c.+5c. orange-brown	80	50
117	–	10c.+5c. reddish violet	80	50
118	**23**	15c. bronze green	80	50
119	–	60c. brownish lake	95	55
116/119 Set of 4			3·00	1·80

Design:—10, 60c. Smooth hammerhead shark.

24 Ploughman and "Justice"   **25** Eurasian Red Squirrel

(Des E. M. Jimeno and V. D. Urosa. Photo)

1955 (1 June). Native Welfare. T **24** and similar horiz design inscr "PRO-INDIGENAS 1955". P 12½×13.

120	**24**	10c.+5c. bright purple	50	50
121	–	25c.+10c. lilac	50	50
122	**24**	50c. blackish olive	55	55
120/122 Set of 3			1·40	1·40

Design:—25c. Camel caravan and "Spain".

(Des J. J. P. Cobarro and J. L. B. Fraile. Photo)

1955 (23 Nov). Colonial Stamp Day. T **25** and similar horiz design inscr "DIA DEL SELLO COLONIAL 1955". P 12½×13.

123	**25**	5c.+5c. red-brown	50	50
124	–	15c.+5c. deep bistre	50	50
125	**25**	70c. green	55	55
123/125 Set of 3			1·40	1·40

Design:—15c. Squirrel holding nut.

26 Senecio antheuphorbium   **27** Arms of Sidi-Ifni and Drummer   **28** Feral Rock Pigeons

(Des V. Sánchez Algora (T **26**). F. Jiménez Ontiveros (others) Photo)

1956 (1 June). Child Welfare. T **26** and similar vert design inscr "PRO-INFANCIA 1956". P 13×12½.

126	**26**	5c.+5c. bronze green	50	50
127	–	15c.+5c. yellow-brown	50	50
128	**26**	20c. myrtle green	50	50
129	–	50c. deep brown	55	55
126/129 Set of 4			1·80	1·80

Design:—15, 50c. Limoniastrum ifniensis.

(Des E. M. Gimeno (5c.), T. Miciano (15c.), M. Sánchez Algora (70c.). Photo)

1956 (23 Nov). Colonial Stamp Day. T **27** and similar designs inscr "DIA DEL SELLO 1956". P 13×12½ or 12½×13 (70c.).

130		5c.+5c. sepia	50	50
131		15c.+5c. yellow-brown	50	50
132		70c. dull green	55	55
130/132 Set of 3			1·40	1·40

Designs: Vert—5c. Arms of Spain and Bohar reedbucks. Horiz—70c. Arms of Sidi-Ifni, shepherd and sheep.

(Des T. Miciano (T **28**), M. S. Algora (15c.). Photo)

1957 (1 June). Child Welfare Fund. T **28** and similar vert designs inscr "PRO INFANCIA 1957". P 13×12½.

133	**28**	5c.+5c. deep green & orange-brown	50	50
134	–	15c.+5c. purple brown and ochre	50	50
135	**28**	70c. brown and yellowish green	55	55
133/135 Set of 3			1·40	1·40

Design:—15c. Stock pigeon in flight.

29 Golden Jackal

30 Barn Swallows and Arms of Valencia and Sidi Ifni

(Des G. Sanchez (T **29**), M. S. Algora (others). Photo)

1957 (23 Nov). Colonial Stamp Day. T **29** and similar design inscr "DIA DEL SELLO 1957". P 12½×13 (T **29**) or 13×12½ (others).

136	**29**	10c.+5c. brown and bright purple	50	50
137	–	15c.+5c. blackish green & yellow-brown	50	50
138	**29**	20c. reddish brown & bright blue-green	50	50
139	–	70c. bistre-brown and bluish green	55	55
136/139 Set of 4			1·80	1·80

Design: Vert—15, 70c. Head of golden jackal.

(Des T. Miclano. Photo)

1958 (6 Mar). "Aid for Valencia". P 12½×13.

140	**30**	10c.+5c. chestnut	50	50
141		15c.+10c. brown-ochre	50	50
142		50c.+10c. olive-brown	55	55
140/142 Set of 3			1·40	1·40

31 Basketball   **32** Greater Spotted Dogfish

(Des J. J. P. Cobarro (T **31**), G. Sánchez Algora (others). Photo)

1958 (1 June). Child Welfare Fund. T **31** and similar vert design inscr "PRO-INFANCIA 1958". P 13×12½.

143	**31**	10c.+5c. orange-brown	50	50
144	–	15c.+5c. yellow-brown	50	50
145	**31**	20c. deep bluish green	50	50
146	–	70c. bronze green	55	55
143/146 Set of 4			1·80	1·80

Design:—15, 70c. Cycling.

(Des J. Cobarro (T **32**), M. Carrillo (25c.), T. Miciano (50c.). Photo)

1958 (23 Nov). Colonial Stamp Day. T **32** and similar designs inscr "DIA DEL SELLO 1958". P 13×12½ (25c.) or 12½×13 (others).

147		10c.+5c. Venetian red	50	50
148		25c.+10c. slate-purple	50	50
149		50c.+10c. olive brown	55	55
147/149 Set of 3			1·40	1·40

Designs: Vert—25c. Ray. Horiz—50c. Fishing boats.

IFNI

33 Ewe and Lamb   **34** Footballer

1959 (1 June). Child Welfare Fund. T **33** and similar designs inscr "PRO-INFANCIA 1959". P 12½×13 (10c., 70c.) or 13×12½ (others).
150	**33**	10c.+5c. deep chestnut	50	50
151	–	15c.+5c. brown	50	50
152	–	20c. deep bluish green	50	50
153	**33**	70c. yellow-green	55	55
150/153	Set of 4		1·80	1·80

Designs: Vert—15c. Native trader with mule; 20c. Mountain goat.

(Des T. Miclano (T **34**), L. Esteban (20c.), A. Boue (50c.). Photo)

1959 (23 Nov). Colonial Stamp Day. T **34** and similar vert designs inscr "DIA DEL SELLO 1959". P 13×12½.
154		10c.+5c. red-brown	50	50
155		20c.+5c. blackish green	50	50
156		50c.+20c. deep olive	55	55
154/156	Set of 3		1·40	1·40

Designs:—20c. Footballers; 50c. Javelin-thrower.

35 Dromedaries   **36** White Stork

(Des R. Almagro, J. M. de Asua, J. Olcina. Photo)

1960 (1 June). Child Welfare. T **35** and similar design inscr "PRO-INFANCIA 1960". P 13×12½.
157	**35**	10c.+5c. brown-purple	50	50
158	–	15c.+5c. bistre-brown	50	50
159	–	35c. blackish green	50	50
160	**35**	80c. deep bluish green	55	55
157/160	Set of 4		1·80	1·80

Designs:—15c. Wild boar; 35c. Red-legged partridges.

1960 (10 Oct). Birds. T **36** and similar designs. Photo. P 13×12½ (75c., 2p., 10p.) or 12½×13 (others).
161	**36**	25c. slate-violet	25	25
162	–	50c. olive-brown	25	25
163	–	75c. dull purple (31.10)	25	25
164	**36**	1p. vermilion	25	25
165	–	1p.50 deep turquoise (31.10)	25	25
166	–	2p. bright purple (31.10)	25	25
167	**36**	3p. grey-blue (31.10)	90	25
168	–	5p. red-brown (31.10)	1·60	55
169	–	10p. olive-green (31.10)	5·75	2·10
161/169	Set of 9		8·75	4·00

Birds: Horiz—50c., 1p.50, 5p. Eurasian goldfinches. Vert—75c., 2p., 10p. Eurasian sky larks.

37 Church of Santa Cruz del Mar   **38** High Jump

(Des J. Olcina, E. M. Jimeno. Photo)

1960 (29 Dec). Stamp Day. T **37** and similar design inscr "DIA DEL SELLO 1960". P 13×12½ (10c., 30c.) or 12½×13 (others).
170	**37**	10c.+5c. chestnut	50	50
171	–	20c.+5c. blackish green	50	50
172	**37**	30c.+10c. red-brown	50	50
173	–	50c.+20c. olive-brown	55	55
170/173	Set of 4		1·80	1·80

Design: Horiz—20, 50c. School building.

1961 (21 June). Child Welfare. T **38** and similar vert design inscr "PRO-INFANCIA 1961". Photo. P 13×12½ (vert) or 12½×13 (horiz).
174	**38**	10c.+5c. lake-brown	50	50
175	–	25c.+10c. slate-violet (Football)	50	50
176	**38**	80c.+20c. deep bluish green	55	55
174/176	Set of 3		1·40	1·40

39   **40** Camel and Truck

(Des J. Olcina (25c.), T. Miciano (T **39**), V. Sánchez Algora (70c.). Photo)

1961 (1 Oct). 25th Anniv of General Franco as Head of State. T **39** and similar designs. P 13×12½ (vert) or 12½×13 (horiz).
177	–	25c. violet-grey	50	50
178	**39**	50c. olive-brown	50	50
179	–	80c. emerald	50	50
180	**39**	1p. orange-red	55	55
177/180	Set of 4		1·80	1·80

Designs: Vert—25c. Map. Horiz—70c. Government building.

(Des E. M. Jimeno (T **40**), R. L. Prieto (others). Photo)

1961 (23 Nov). Stamp Day. T **40** and similar horiz design inscr "DIA DEL SELLO 1961". P 12½×13.
181	**40**	10c.+5c. brown-lake	50	50
182	–	25c.+10c. plum	50	50
183	**40**	30c.+10c. chocolate	50	50
184	–	1p.+10c. red-orange	55	55
181/184	Set of 4		1·80	1·80

Design:—25c., 1p. Freighter at wharf.

41 Admiral Jofre Tenorio   **42** Desert Postman   **43** "Golden Tower", Seville

(Des V. Vila. Photo)

1962 (10 July). Child Welfare. T **41** and similar vert design inscr "PRO-INFANCIA 1962". P 13×12½.
185	**41**	25c. slate-violet	50	50
186	–	50c. deep bluish green	50	50
187	**41**	1p. chestnut	55	55
185/187	Set of 3		1·40	1·40

Design:—50c. C. Fernandez-Duro (historian).

(Des J. J. de Castro (T **42**), A. Boué (35c.). Photo)

1962 (23 Nov). Stamp Day. T **42** and similar vert design inscr "DIA DEL SELLO 1962". P 13×12½.
188	**42**	15c. blue	50	50
189	–	35c. magenta	50	50
190	**42**	1p. claret	55	55
188/190	Set of 3		1·40	1·40

Design:—35c. Winged letter on hands.

(Des V. Sánchez Algora. Photo)

1963 (29 Jan). Seville Flood Relief. P 13×12½.
191	**43**	50c. green	60	60
192		1p. chestnut	60	60

IFNI

44 Moroccan Copper Butterfly and Flower

45 Child with Flowers

(Des S. H. Fernández (T **44**), J. A. P. Dolores (others). Photo)

1963 (6 June). Child Welfare. T **44** and similar vert design inscr "PRO-INFANCIA 1963". P 13×12½.

193	25c. blue	50	50
194	50c. green	50	50
195	1p. carmine	55	55
193/195 Set of 3		1·40	1·40

Design:—25c., 1p. Moroccan orange-tips.

(Des A. Boué. Photo)

1963 (12 June). "For Barcelona". P 12½×13.

196	**45**	50c. olive-green	60	60
197		1p. chocolate	60	60

46 *Steraspis speciosa*

47 Edmi Gazelle

(Des V. Vila (T **46**), T. Miciano (50c.). Photo)

1964 (6 Mar). Stamp Day. T **46** and similar vert design inscr "DIA DEL SELLO 1963". P 13×12½.

198	**46**	25c. grey-blue	50	50
199	–	50c. deep olive	50	50
200	**46**	1p. red-brown	55	55
198/200 Set of 3			1·40	1·40

Design:—50c. *Schistocerca gregaria*.

(Des C. R. de Galarreta (50c.), J. L. B. Fraile (others). Photo)

1964 (1 June). Child Welfare. T **47** and similar vert design inscr "PRO INFANCIA 1964". P 13×12½.

201	**47**	25c. bluish violet	50	50
202	–	50c. slate (Head of roe deer)	50	50
203	**47**	1p. orange-red	55	55
201/203 Set of 3			1·40	1·40

48 Cyclists Racing

49 Port Installation, Sidi Ifni

(Des E. M. Jimeno (1p.), J. Olcina (others). Photo)

1964 (23 Nov). Stamp Day. T **48** and similar horiz design inscr "DIA DEL SELLO 1964". P 12½×13.

204	**48**	50c. brown	50	50
205	–	1p. orange-red (Motorcycle racing)	50	50
206	**48**	1p.50 deep bluish green	55	55
204/206 Set of 3			1·40	1·40

1965 (22 Feb). 25th Anniv of End of Spanish Civil War. T **49** and similar designs inscr "XXV ANOS DE PAZ". Photo. P 13×12½ (vert) or 12½×13 (horiz).

207	50c. bronze-green	50	50
208	1p. red	50	50
209	1p.50 grey-blue	55	55
207/209 Set of 3		1·40	1·40

Designs: Vert—50c. Ifnian; 1p. "Education" (children in class).

50 *Eugaster fernandezi*

51 Arms of Ifni

1965 (1 June). Child Welfare. Insects. T **50** and similar horiz design. Photo. P 12½×13.

210	**50**	50c. purple	50	50
211	–	1p. rose-red (*Halter halteratus*)	50	50
212	**50**	1p.50 ultramarine	55	55
210/212 Set of 3			1·40	1·40

(Des R. Farré and C. Galarreta. Photo)

1965 (23 Nov). Stamp Day T **51** and similar design. P 13×12 (vert) or 12½×13 (horiz).

213	50c. red-brown	50	50
214	1p. vermilion	50	50
215	1p.50 greenish blue	55	55
213/215 Set of 3		1·40	1·40

Design: Vert—50c., 1p.50, Golden eagle.

52 de Havilland D.H.9C Biplanes

53 Maid Alice Moth (*Syntomis alicia*)

1966 (1 June). Child Welfare T **52** and similar design. Photo. P 12½×13 (2p.50) or 13×12½ (others).

216	1p. orange-brown	50	50
217	1p.50 new blue	50	50
218	2p.50 bluish violet	1·90	1·90
216/218 Set of 3		1·40	1·40

Design: Vert—1p., 1p.50, Douglas DC-8 jetliner over Sidi Ifni.

(Des D. E. Cerra. Photo)

1966 (23 Nov). Stamp Day. Insects. T **53** and similar horiz design. P 13.

219	**53**	10c. bronze green and red	50	50
220	–	40c. yellow-brown and blackish brown	50	50
221	**53**	1p.50 violet and yellow	50	50
222	–	4p. light blue and maroon	55	55
219/222 Set of 4			1·80	1·80

Design:—40c., 4p. African monarch (*Danais chrysippus*).

54 Coconut Palm

55 Bulk Carrier and Floating Crane

(Des E. M. Jimeno. Photo)

1967 (1 June). Child Welfare. T **54** and similar vert design. P 13.

223	**54**	10c. green and brown	50	50
224	–	40c. deep bluish green & orange-brown	50	50
225	**54**	1p.50 turquoise and sepia	50	50
226	–	4p. sepia and chestnut	55	55
223/226 Set of 4			1·80	1·80

Design:—40c., 4p. Cactus.

1967 (28 Sept). Inauguration of Port Ifni. Photo. P 12½×13.

227	**55** 1p. 50 chestnut and deep emerald	60	60

56 Skipper

57 Posting Letter

397

1967 (23 Nov). Stamp Day. T **56** and similar designs showing fish. Photo. P 13.

228	1p. bright green and blue	55	55
229	1p.50 slate-purple and yellow	55	55
230	3p.50 red and blue	80	80
228/230 Set of 3		1·70	1·70

Designs: Vert—1p.50, John Dory. Horiz—3p.50, Tub gurnard.

1968 (24 Apr). Child Welfare. Signs of the Zodiac. Horiz designs as T **47** of Fernando Poo. Photo. P 13.

231	1p. magenta/*pale yellow*	55	55
232	1p.50 red-brown/*pale pink*	55	55
233	2p.50 deep violet/*pale greenish yellow*	80	80
231/233 Set of 3		1·70	1·70

Designs:—1p. Pisces (Fishes); 1p.50, Aries (Ram); 2p.50, Sagittarius (Archer).

(Des T. Miciano. Photo)

1968 (23 Nov). Stamp Day. T **57** and similar horiz designs. P 12½×13.

234	1p. black and orange-yellow	50	50
235	1p.50 black, plum and greenish blue	50	50
236	2p.50 black, blue and bright green	55	55
234/236 Set of 3		1·40	1·40

Designs:—1p.50, Dove with letter; 2p.50, Magnifying glass and stamp.

On 30 June 1969 Ifni was returned to Morocco.

Mariana Islands

The Mariana Islands in the Western Pacific Ocean were discovered by Magellan in 1521 and became a Spanish possession in 1565. Guam, to the south, came under Spanish rule in 1688.

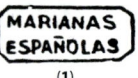

(1)

1899 (Sept). Stamps of Philippine Islands, 1898, handstamped with T **1** sideways, in blue-black.

S1	38	2c. blue-green	£650	£225
S2		3c. brown	£550	£180
S3		5c. rosine	£650	£225
S4		6c. blue	£4000	£2500
S5		8c. sepia	£350	£150
S6		15c. olive-slate	£1700	£1100

After the Spanish-american War of 1898, the United States acquired Guam. The handstamp was applied to Philippine Islands stamps for use in the islands which remained under Spanish rule until Germany purchased rights to a protectorate over them in 1899. German issues are listed in Part 7 (*Germany*) of this catalogue.

Philippines

1854. 20 Cuartos = 1 Real
8 Reales = 1 Peso Plata Fuerte
1864. 100 Céntimos = 1 Peso Plata Fuerte
1871. 100 Céntimos = 1 Escudo (= ½ Peso)
1872. 100 Céntimos = 1 Peseta (= 1/5 Peso)
1876. 1000 Milesimas = 100 Céntimos (or Centavos) = 1 Peso

The first European to discover the islands (which in 1542 were named the Philippines) was Magellan, who was killed there in 1521 in a fight with the natives. In 1565 Miguel Lopez de Legazpi made a settlement in Cebu and in 1571 he founded Manila. The Moros of Mindanao and the Sulu archipelago, who were Moslems, fiercely resisted all Spanish attempts at domination until 1878, when they had to capitulate. Elsewhere missionary friars developed a Catholic civilization amongst the Filipinos, who intermarried with Spaniards and Chinese.

Queen Isabella II of Spain
29 September 1833–30 September 1868

1 2 3

Two plates of the 5 cuartos

(a) Head on ground of fine lines.
(b) Head on ground of coarse lines, farther apart.

(Eng on copper. Recess Plana, Jorba y Cia, Manila)

1854 (1 Feb). Forty varieties on each plate. Imperf.
1	1	5c. orange-red (a)	£2500	£425
2		5c. orange-red (b)	£2500	£450
3		10c. carmine	£850	£300
		a. Pale rose	£900	£300
5	2	1r. pale blue	£950	£325
		a. "CORROS"	£4250	£1900
		b. Slate-blue	£1100	£350
		ba. "CORROS"	£4500	£2250
7		2r. bright green	£1300	£225
		a. Dull green	£1300	£250

Printed in sheets of 40 (5×8). The "CORROS" error occurs on position 26.

(Litho Plana, Jorba y Cia, Manila)

1855 (June). Inner circle broken by outer frame at top and bottom. Four varieties. Imperf.
9	3	5c. red	£2250	£475

(Litho Plana, Jorba y Cia, Manila)

1855 (Aug). Inner circle smaller and unbroken. One type only. Imperf.
10	3	5c. red	£12000	£1100

USE OF STAMPS OF CUBA AND PUERTO RICO. Nos. 2a and 3 of the combined issues for Cuba and Puerto Rico were also issued for use in the Philippines from 1 January 1856. They may be included in a collection of this country if they have an identifiable Philippines cancellation, the most common being Manila and Cavite. (Prices for used copies with identifiable Philippines postmarks: No. 2a, 1r. green/bluish, £130; No. 3, 2r. deep carmine/bluish, £170.)

Nos. 11/12 are vacant.

4 5 6

(T **4/6** Litho M. Perez y Hijo, Manila)

1859 (1 Jan). Four varieties. Imperf.
(a) Thick wove paper
13	4	5c. vermilion	24·00	7·75
		a. Scarlet	27·00	11·50
		b. Orange	32·00	17·00
14		10c. dull rose	24·00	23·00

(b) Thin paper
15	4	5c. vermilion	27·00	7·50

(c) Thick, rough, ribbed paper
16	4	5c. vermilion	75·00	23·00
		a. Pale red	75·00	23·00

1861. Imperf.
17	5	5c. vermilion	65·00	16·00

In T **5** the network is finer and the circle of pearls less clear than in T **4**.

1862 (Aug). Coarse network. Period after "CORREOS". Imperf.
18	6	5c. dull red	£180	75·00

7 8 9

(T **7/9** Litho M. Perez y Hijo, Manila)

1863 (Jan). Fine network. Colon after "CORREOS". Imperf.
19	7	5c. scarlet	21·00	7·50
20		10c. carmine	65·00	65·00
21		1r. rosy mauve	£1100	£650
22		2r. blue	£800	£550

The 10c. was made from the plate of the 5c., and the 2 reales from the plate of the 1 real.

1863 (Mar). Inscr in Roman type. Imperf.
23	8	1r. bottle-green	£450	£180
		a. Without stop before and after "CORREOS"	£450	
24		1r. grey-green	£250	£130
		a. Without stop before and after "CORREOS"	£250	

1863 (Oct). Inscr in block letters. Imperf.
25	9	1r. emerald-green	£170	55·00
		a. Yellow-green	£180	70·00

10

(Dies eng J. P. Varela. Typo Govt Ptg Works, Madrid)

1864 (1 Jan). New Currency. Imperf.
26	10	3^1/$_8$c. black/buff	5·25	2·75
27		6^2/$_8$c. green/pale rose	5·25	1·60
28		12^4/$_8$c. blue/flesh	10·50	1·30
29		25c. bright red/pale rose	21·00	7·50
30		25c. brown-red/white	16·00	4·75

The metric system was introduced in 1864, and the above four values were equal to the 5c. and 10c. and 1 and 2 reales of the preceding issue.

PROVISIONAL GOVERNMENT OF SPAIN
6 October 1868–15 June 1869

HABILITADO
POR LA
NACION.
11

1868 (Dec). Handstamped with T **11**.
31	10	3^1/$_8$c. black/buff	27·00	6·50
32		6^2/$_8$c. green/pale rose	27·00	6·50
33		12^4/$_8$c. blue/flesh	70·00	37·00
34		25c. brown-red	32·00	21·00

REGENCY
15 June 1869–30 December 1870
Regent, Marshal Francisco Serrano

(Duke de la Torre)

1870 (12 Apr). Nos. 24/5 handstamped with T **11**.
35	8	1r. grey-green	£250	55·00
36	9	1r. emerald-green	70·00	29·00

PHILIPPINES

King Amadeo of Spain (Duke of Aosta)
30 December 1870–12 February 1873

12

(Die eng E. Juliá. Typo Govt Ptg Works, Madrid)

1871 (Mar). New Currency. P 14.
37	**12**	5c. blue	85·00	9·00
38		10c. deep green	11·50	7·75
39		20c. brown	£100	55·00
40		40c. carmine	£130	27·00

1872 (24 Jan). Handstamped with T **11**.
(a) Nos. 19 and 21/22
41	**7**	5c. scarlet	£100	55·00
42		1r. rosy mauve	£950	£550
43		2r. blue	£800	£375

(c) Nos. 2a/3 of Cuba and Puerto Rico
44		1r. green/*bluish*	£275	£150
45		2r. deep carmine/*bluish*	£375	£150

13

(Dies eng H. Fernandez. Typo Govt Ptg Works, Madrid)

1872 (8 May–15 Oct). New Currency. P 14.
46	**13**	12c. rose (15 Oct)	20·00	7·50
47		16c. blue	£190	49·00
		a. Ultramarine	£200	75·00
48		25c. lilac-grey	15·00	6·25
		a. Grey	15·00	7·00
49		62c. pale mauve	46·00	13·00
50		1p.25 bistre-brown (15 Oct)	85·00	41·00
		a. Chestnut	85·00	41·00

The 12c. blue and the 62c. rose are colour trials.

FIRST SPANISH REPUBLIC
12 February 1873–31 December 1874

1873 (7 Oct). No. 18 handstamped with T **11**.
51	**6**	5c. dull red	£100	55·00

1874 (Jan). Nos. 5 and 14 handstamped with T **11**.
52	**2**	1r. bright blue	£3250	£1600
		a. "CORROS"		£3750
53	**4**	10c. dull rose	£140	80·00

14

(Die eng E. Juliá. Typo Govt Ptg Works, Madrid)

1874. P 14.
54	**14**	12c. grey	21·00	6·50
		a. Lilac-grey	21·00	6·50
55		25c. ultramarine	8·25	2·75
56		62c. rose	65·00	6·50
57		1p.25 brown	£350	95·00

King Alfonso XII of Spain
(House of Bourbon restored)
31 December 1874–25 November 1885

15   16

(Die eng J. Garcia Moragó. Typo Govt Ptg Works, Madrid)

1875–77. New Currency. Rosette on each side of "FILIPINAS" Value in centimos de peso. P 14.
58	**15**	2c. rose (Aug 1875)	3·00	1·10
59		2c. blue (Dec 1877)	£325	£130
60		6c. orange (Aug 1877)	15·00	3·50
61		10c. blue (Aug 1877)	4·00	1·10
62		12c. mauve (Jan 1876)	4·25	1·10
63		20c. deep purple-brown (Dec 1876)	27·00	4·50
64		25c. blue-green (Mar 1876)	32·00	1·10

1878–79. Without rosettes. Value in milesimas de peso, block lettering. P 14.
65	**16**	25m. black (Apr 1878)	4·25	65
66		25m. green (Jan 1879)	95·00	41·00
67		50m. dull purple (Jan 1878)	48·00	17·00
		a. Deep purple	48·00	27·00
68		(62½m.) 0.0625 lilac (Jan 1878)	£130	45·00
		a. Grey	85·00	27·00
69		100m. carmine (1879)	£160	65·00
70		100m. yellow-green (1879)	15·00	3·75
71		125m. blue (Jan 1878)	7·00	65
72		200m. rose (1879)	49·00	9·25
73		200m. dull claret (1879)	£475	£225
74		250m. brown (Sept 1879)	19·00	3·75

Many stamps of T **15/16** may be found imperforate but they are proofs or from trial sheets.

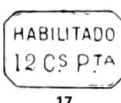

17

1877–79. Surch locally with T **17**.
75	**15**	12c. on 2c. rose (Aug 1877)	£160	40·00
		a. Surch inverted	£800	£375
		b. Surch double	£550	£350
76	**16**	12c. on 25m. black (Jan 1879)	£160	40·00
		a. Surch inverted	£850	£650
77		12c. on 25m. black (B.) (Jan 1879)	£300	£225
		a. Surch Inverted	£950	£650

18   19

1879 (Sept). Surch locally.
*(a) As T **18***
78	**16**	2c. on 25m. green	80·00	15·00
		a. Surch double	—	£130
79		8c. on 100m. carmine	55·00	10·00
		a. "CORRZOS" for "CORREOS"	—	£150
		b. "COREROS" for "CORREOS"	£140	75·00

*(b) As T **19***
80	**16**	2c. on 25m. green	£275	£110
		a. "CONVINIO" for "CONVENIO"	—	£110
81		8c. on 100m. carmine	£300	£110

No. 79b occurs on position 69.

20

> **PLATES OF TYPE 20**. The plate for Type **20**, the Alfonso XII portrait design without year dates at top, was also used for contemporary issues of Cuba, Fernando Poo and Puerto Rico. It was retouched three times and the illustrations and notes which follow should enable collectors to distinguish the types easily.

400

PHILIPPINES

Original state   First retouch

Second retouch   Third retouch

Original state. The medallion is surrounded by a heavy line of colour, of nearly even thickness, touching the horizontal line below the inscription in the upper label; the opening in the hair above the temple is narrow and pointed. Nos. 82/94 are all in this original state.

First retouch. The line above the medallion is thin, except at the upper right, and does not touch the horizontal line above it; the opening in the hair is slightly wider and a trifle rounded; the lock of hair above the forehead is shaped like a broad "V", and ends in a point; there is a faint white line below it, which is not found in the original state.

Second retouch. The opening is still wider and more rounded; the lock of hair does not extend as far down on the forehead, is very slightly rounded, instead of being pointed, and the white line below it is thicker.

Third retouch. The opening in the hair forms a semicircle; the lock above the forehead has only a slight wave, and the white line is broader than before.

(Die eng E. Juliá. Typo Govt Ptg Works, Madrid)

1880 (19 Apr)–**89**. Value in centimos de peso. P 14.

82	20	2c. crimson	2·10	2·30
		a. Dull rose	1·20	1·20
83		2½c. sepia	11·50	2·30
84		2⁴/₈c. ultramarine (Feb 1882)	1·20	2·30
85		5c. grey (19 July 1882)	1·20	2·30
		a. Lavender	1·80	2·75
87		6²/₈c. green (Mar 1882)	8·50	13·00
		a. Deep green	9·25	15·00
88		8c. chestnut	60·00	30·00
		a. Deep brown	60·00	30·00
89		10c. pale brown	4·75	2·30
		a. Brown-pink (Dec 1882)	4·75	2·30
90		10c. brown-purple (Dec 1882)	9·50	19·00
91		10c. green	£600	£350
92		12⁴/₈c. rosine (19 July 1882)	2·75	2·30
		a. Pale pink	2·75	2·30
93		20c. grey-brown (19 July 1882)	4·75	2·30
94		25c. deep brown (19 July 1882)	6·25	2·30

Type **20** retouched. P 14
First retouch (Nov 1883)

95	20	2⁴/₈c. dull blue	85	30
		a. Bright blue	85	30
		b. Deep ultramarine	85	30

Second retouch (1 Jan 1886)

96	20	2⁴/₈c. ultramarine	8·50	5·25

Third retouch. Value in milesimas de peso on 50m. (1887–89)

97	20	1c. grey-green (Jan 1888)	45	20
98		1c. brt yellow-green (1 May 1889)	70	20
99		50m. bistre (Apr 1887)	70	20
100		6c. brown (Jan 1888)	18·00	2·50

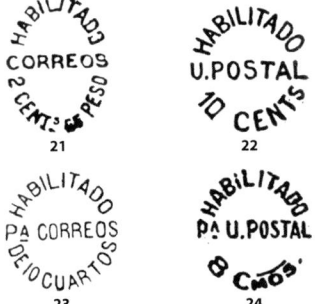

21   22

23   24

1881–**86**. Various stamps diversely surcharged at Manila.

I. POSTAGE STAMPS. Issues of 1880–89, T **20**

(a) Black surch

101	21	2c. on 2½c. sepia (June 1881)	5·75	
		a. Surch inverted	49·00	49·00
102	22	10c. on 2⁴/₈c. ultram (11 Sept 1886)	11·50	2·30
103	23	20c. on 8c. brown (22 Feb 1883)	15·00	5·25
		a. Surch inverted	16·00	14·50
		b. Surch double	16·00	16·00
104		1r. on 2c. dull rose (Oct 1883)	£150	65·00
105		2r. on 2⁴/₈c. ultramarine (4 June 1883)	9·50	2·75
		a. Surch inverted	60·00	39·00
		b. Surch double	50·00	39·00

(b) Green surch

106	24	8c. on 2c. crimson (4 June 1883)	11·50	2·75
		a. Surch inverted	23·00	18·00
		b. Surch double	27·00	24·00
107	23	10cuartos on 2c. crimson (Oct 1883)	7·00	2·10
		a. Surch inverted	15·00	15·00
		b. Surch double	36·00	36·00
		c. Surch double, one inverted	55·00	46·00
108		1r. on 2c. crimson (Oct 1883)	£160	55·00
		a. Surch double	95·00	46·00
109		1r. on 5c. lavender (22 Feb 1883)	9·50	4·00
		a. Surch inverted	33·00	21·00
		b. Surch double	33·00	21·00
110		1r. on 8c. brown (22 Feb 1883)	18·00	7·00
		a. Surch inverted	37·00	18·00
		b. Surch double	46·00	35·00

(c) Red surch

111	22	1c. on 2⁴/₈c. ultram (11 Sept 1886)	1·20	75
112	23	16cuartos on 2⁴/₈c. ultram (Oct 1883)	18·00	4·50
		a. Surch double	55·00	24·00
113		1r. on 2c. crimson (4 June 1883)	11·50	4·50
		a. Surch inverted	22·00	13·50
		b. Surch double	55·00	39·00
114		1r. on 5c. lavender (4 June 1883)	30·00	8·50
		a. Surch inverted	55·00	25·00

25   26

HABILITADO
PARA
CORREOS
27   28

II. FISCAL STAMPS. T **25** *inscr "DERECHO JUDICIAL" (Judicature Fees)*

(a) Black surch

115	21	2c. on 10cuartos bistre (Apr 1881)	41·00	26·00
		a. Surch inverted	50·00	55·00
116	26	2⁴/₈c. on 10cuartos bistre (Jan 1881)	5·75	1·30
		a. Surch inverted	37·00	37·00
117		2⁴/₈c. on 2r. blue (Jan 1881)	£300	£130
118		8c. on 2r. blue (Apr 1881)	16·00	4·25
119		8c. on 10c. brown	£325	£250
120	23	1r. on 10cuartos bistre (Jan 1882)	23·00	7·50
		a. Surch double	30·00	27·00
121		1r. on 1248c. lavender (Oct 1883)	15·00	7·00
		a. Surch inverted	55·00	49·00
		b. Surch double	80·00	80·00

(b) Blue opt

122	27	10cuartos bistre (Jan 1881)	£300	£130

(c) Yellow surch

123	23	16cmos. on 2r. blue (4 June 1883)	10·50	4·50

PHILIPPINES

		(d) Red surch or opt		
124	28	6²/₈c. on 12⁴/₈c. lavender (24 Feb 1885)	9·00	5·25
125	23	1r. on 12⁴/₈c. lavender (4 June 1883)	13·00	5·75
		a. Surch inverted	55·00	
		b. Surch double	60·00	
126	27	1r. green (Jan 1881)	£160	£120
		a. Surch inverted	£120	
		(e) Green surch		
127	23	1r. on 10cuartos bis (22 Feb 1883)	21·00	7·50
		*(f) Surch with two different values, T **26** and **23***		
128		8c. on 2r. on 2r. blue (R.) (Oct 1883)	26·00	13·00

29   **30**   **31**

*III. FISCAL STAMPS. T **29** and T **30** inscr "DERECHOS DE FIRMA" (Duty on Acknowledgments)*

		*(a) Yellow surch, T **24***		
129	29	2c. on 200m. green (Jan 1882)	9·00	4·50
		a. Surch inverted	17·00	19·00
		b. Surch double	34·00	29·00
		*(b) Red surch, T **23***		
130	29	1r. on 200m. green (4 June 1883)	£110	70·00
		a. Surch inverted	£100	£100
		b. Surch double	£120	£110
131		1r. on 1peso green (4 June 1883)	55·00	27·00
132	30	1r. on 10pesetas bis (4 June 1883)	80·00	41·00

*IV. TELEGRAPH STAMPS. Surch as T **23***

		(a) Red surch		
133	31	2r. on 250m. ultram (22 Feb 1883)	18·00	5·75
		a. Surch double	42·00	42·00
		(b) Black surch		
134	31	20c. on 250m. ultram (22 Feb 1883)	£550	£325
		a. Surch inverted	£120	£120
135		2r. on 250m. ultram (4 June 1883)	23·00	7·50
		(c) Surch with (a) and (b)		
136	31	1r. in *red* and 20c. in *black* on 250m. ultramarine (22 Feb 1883)	19·00	8·00
		a. Red surch inverted	9·50	7·25
		b. Red surch double	18·00	15·00
		(d) Yellow surch		
137	31	20c. on 150m. ultramarine	27·00	22·00

P **32**

(Die eng E. Juliá. Typo Govt Ptg Works, Madrid)

1886–89. PRINTED MATTER. P 14.

P138	P **32**	1m. rose (1 May 1889)	30	20
		a. Carmine	30	20
P139		18c. green (1 Jan 1886)	30	20
P140		2m. blue (1 May 1889)	30	20
P141		5m. brown (1 May 1889)	30	20
P138/141	*Set of 4*		1·10	70

32   **33**   **34**

1887 (Dec)–**88.** Various stamps surch with T **32** or **33** (No. 142), in magenta.

I. POSTAGE STAMPS

138	20	2⁴/₈c. on 1c. grey-grn (27 June 1888)	3·75	2·10
		a. Surch inverted	7·50	7·50
		b. Surch double	7·50	7·50
139		2⁴/₈c. on 5c. lavender (27 June 1888)	2·50	1·20
140		2⁴/₈c. on 50m. bistre (27 Feb 1888)	3·50	2·30
141		2⁴/₈c. on 10c. green (29 Aug 1888)	2·50	1·30
142		8c. on 2⁴/₈c. ultramarine	1·50	85
		a. Surch inverted	8·75	8·75
		b. Surch double	8·75	8·75

II. PRINTED MATTER STAMP

143	P **32**	2⁴/₈c. on 18c. green (29 Sept 1888)	85	30

III. FISCAL STAMPS

144	29	2⁴/₈c. on 200m. green (26 June 1888)	7·50	3·25
145		2⁴/₈c. on 20c. brown (29 Sept 1888)	20·00	9·00

IV. TELEGRAPH STAMP

146	34	2⁴/₈c. on 1c. bistre (27 June 1888)	1·50	1·10
		a. Surch double	7·50	7·50

35

1889 (7 June). Various provisional stamps used for postage. Surch "RECARGO DE CONSUMOS" (Extra Tax on Provisions), as T **35**.

*I. POSTAGE STAMPS. T **20***

147		2⁴/₈c. on 1c. green	20	20
		a. Surch inverted		
		b. Surch double	4·75	4·75
		c. Surch double, one inverted	7·25	7·25
148		2⁴/₈c. on 2c. crimson	15	15
		a. Surch inverted	4·75	5·25
		b. Surch double	5·00	5·50
149		2⁴/₈c. on 2⁴/₈c. ultramarine	10	10
		a. Surch inverted	3·75	3·75
150		2⁴/₈c. on 5c. lavender	15	15
		a. Surch inverted	5·75	6·00
151		2⁴/₈c. on 50m. bistre	15	15
		a. Surch inverted	5·50	5·50
152		2⁴/₈c. on 12⁴/₈c. rose	75	75

*II. TELEGRAPH STAMPS. T **34***

153		2⁴/₈c. on 1c. bistre	40	40
154		2⁴/₈c. on 2c. carmine	40	40
155		2⁴/₈c. on 2⁴/₈c. brown	15	15
		a. Surch double	6·00	6·75
156		2⁴/₈c. on 5c. blue	15	15
		a. Surch inverted	5·00	5·50
		b. Surch double	6·00	6·00
157		2⁴/₈c. on 10c. green	15	15
		a. Surch inverted	9·25	9·25
158		2⁴/₈c. on 10c. mauve	80	70
		a. Surch double	5·75	6·00
159		2⁴/₈c. on 20c. mauve	30	30
		a. Surch double	7·00	6·75

*III. PRINTED MATTER STAMP. Type P **32***

160		2⁴/₈c. on 18c. green	20	20
		a. Surch double	1·80	1·80

*IV. FISCAL STAMP. Inscr "DERECHO JUDICIAL" (central motif as for T **43** of Spain). Magenta surch*

161		1748c. on 5p. green	75·00	

In addition to the above, various telegraph and fiscal stamps without any surcharge were likewise used postally.

Varieties of many stamps from No. 101 to 161 are known with surcharges *sideways, omitted* (in pairs with normal), triple, etc. The surcharges in most cases also vary considerably in setting on the sheet.

King Alfonso XIII of Spain
17 May 1886–14 April 1931

36   P **37**

402

PHILIPPINES / Filipino Revolutionary Government

(Die eng E. Juliá. Typo Govt Ptg Works, Madrid)

1890 (1 Jan). Thin paper. P 14.

162	**36**	2c. lake	20	20
163		2⁴/₈c. deep blue	75	20
164		5c. slate-green	75	20
165		5c. indigo	75	20
166		8c. yellow-green	45	20
167		10c. blue-green	2·75	45
168		12⁴/₈c. pale yellow-green	45	20
169		20c. pale rosine	£140	70·00
170		25c. sepia	10·50	2·10
162/170 Set of 9			£140	65·00

(Die eng E. Juliá. Typo Govt Ptg Works, Madrid)

1890. PRINTED MATTER. P 14.

P171	P **37**	1m. deep purple (1 Jan)	20	20
P172		48c. deep purple (12 June)	20	20
P173		2m. deep purple (12 June)	20	20
P174		5m. deep purple (12 June)	20	20
		a. Imperf (pair)	55·00	55·00

1891 (20 Apr). Colours changed. P 14.

171	**36**	5c. blue-green	1·20	45
172		10c. lilac-rose	1·20	35
173		12⁴/₈c. deep yellow-green	30	20
174		20c. salmon	16·00	6·50
175		25c. indigo (thin paper)	2·20	85
171/175 Set of 5			19·00	7·50

1892 (1 Jan). Colours changed and new values. P 14.

176	**36**	1c. dull violet	1·40	45
177		2c. light violet	65	20
		a. Deep violet	65	20
178		2⁴/₈c. olive-grey	45	20
179		5c. sage-green	1·10	20
180		5c. violet-black*	£1100	£400
181		6c. brown-purple	45	20
182		8c. ultramarine	1·10	45
183		10c. light carmine	1·20	20
184		12⁴/₈c. orange	1·20	20
185		15c. cinnamon	1·40	45
186		20c. olive-sepia	3·50	55
		a. Greyish brown	3·50	55
187		25c. blue (*greyish paper*)	3·50	55
176/187 (except 180) Set of 11			14·50	3·25

Do not confuse this with No. 199.

1892 (1 Jan). PRINTED MATTER. Colours changed. P 14.

P188	P **37**	1m. pale green	3·25	85
P189		18c. pale green	1·50	30
P190		2m. pale green	4·00	85
P191		5m. pale green	£400	85·00

1893 (13 June). PRINTED MATTER. Colours changed. P 14.

P192	P **37**	1m. emerald-green	3·75	95
P193		18c. emerald-green	1·70	20
P194		2m. emerald-green	4·50	95

1894 (1 Jan)–95. Colours changed. Thick paper. P 14.

188	**36**	1c. rosine	27·00	11·50
		a. Carmine-lake (25 Apr 1895)	27·00	11·50
189		2c. carmine	30	20
190		2c. sepia	30	20
191		5c. pale-green	1·10	80
192		6c. orange-red	2·75	1·30
193		8c. brown-violet	1·30	45
194		10c. lake (*greyish paper*)	1·30	45
195		15c. rosine	3·00	1·30
196		20c. deep purple	32·00	11·50
188/196 Set of 9			60·00	25·00

1894 (1 Jan). PRINTED MATTER. Colours changed. Thick paper. P 14.

P197	P **37**	1m. olive-grey	35	35
P198		18c. red-brown	35	35
P199		2m. olive-grey	35	35
P200		5m. olive-grey	35	35

1896 (1 Jan). Colours changed. P 14.

197	**36**	1c. emerald	3·75	1·10
198		2c. ultramarine	45	25
199		5c. brown-violet	15·00	5·50
200		5c. bright blue-green	9·75	3·25
201		6c. rosine	9·75	5·50
202		10c. cinnamon	95	45
203		15c. blue-green	3·50	2·50
204		20c. orange	7·50	2·75
197/204 Set of 8			46·00	19·00

1896 (1 Jan). PRINTED MATTER. Colours changed. P 14.

P205	P **37**	1m. blue	45	20
P206		18c. blue	1·50	1·10
P207		2m. sepia	55	20
P208		5m. blue-green	4·25	2·50

1897. New values. P 14.

205	**36**	40c. deep purple	32·00	9·25
206		80c. carmine-lake	43·00	30·00

Imperforate stamps of Type **36** are from trial sheets.

37   38

1897. Surch as T **37**.

(a) In black

207	**36**	5c. on 5c. pale green	34·00	21·00
208		15c. on 15c. rosine	4·25	2·30
		a. Surch inverted	12·00	10·50
209		20c. on 20c. deep purple	30·00	17·00
		a. Surch inverted	34·00	34·00
210		20c. on 25c. sepia	21·00	14·00
		a. Surch inverted	14·50	14·50

(b) In violet

211	**36**	15c. on 15c. rosine	17·00	14·00

(c) In blue

212	**36**	5c. on 5c. pale green	7·50	4·25
213		15c. on 15c. cinnamon	6·50	3·75
		a. Surch inverted	12·50	11·50
214		20c. on 20c. greyish brown	10·50	6·50
		a. Surch inverted	14·50	14·50

(d) In red

215	**20**	5c. on 5c. lavender	8·50	4·00
		a. Surch in blackish red (mixed inks)		
216	**36**	5c. on 5c. sage green	6·50	4·00

Other surcharges in violet-black are known but are believed to be reprints.

(Dies eng B. Maura. Typo Govt Ptg Works, Madrid)

1898 (Jan). P 14.

217	**38**	1m. chestnut	20	20
218		2m. chestnut	20	20
219		3m. chestnut	20	20
220		4m. chestnut	13·00	2·50
221		5m. chestnut	20	20
222		1c. deep purple	20	20
223		2c. blue-green	20	20
224		3c. brown	20	20
225		4c. orange	21·00	15·00
226		5c. rosine	45	20
227		6c. blue	1·50	80
228		8c. sepia	70	20
229		10c. orange-vermilion	2·75	1·80
230		15c. olive-slate	2·50	1·20
231		20c. maroon	2·50	1·80
232		40c. dull lilac	1·50	1·20
233		60c. black	6·50	4·00
234		80c. red-brown	8·50	4·00
235		1p. yellow-green	30·00	19·00
236		2p. Prussian blue	43·00	23·00
217/236 Set of 20			£120	70·00

FILIPINO REVOLUTIONARY GOVERNMENT

The desire of the Filipinos for independence arose when Spain first became a republic in 1873. Dr. José Rizal became the propagandist of the movement, but in 1892 he was deported from Manila after founding the Liga Filipino for the betterment of the people. On 26 August 1896 a revolt began and Rizal, who took no part in it, was later shot by the Spaniards. In March 1897 Emilio Aguinaldo was elected President of a Philippine Republic. After the Spanish–American War broke out on 21 April 1898, Aguinaldo proclaimed the independence of the Philippines on 12 June and co-operated with the Americans. Following the cession of the islands to the United States he revolted against American rule until, after his capture in March 1901, he took an oath of allegiance.

In the following designs the letters "KKK" are the initials of the Katipunan secret political society, which plotted for independence. They were adopted as part of the emblems of the Filipino Revolutionary Government.

PHILIPPINES / Filipino Revolutionary Government / PUERTO RICO

39   **40** (lines below value)   **41** (no lines)

(Typo Litografía del Gómez, Santa Cruz)
1898–99. P 11½.

(a) POSTAGE
237	**39**	2c. red		2·75	2·75
238	**40**	2c. red		21·00	21·00
239	**41**	2c. red		30	95
		a. Imperf between (vert pair)		6·75	

R **42**   P **43**

(b) REGISTERED LETTER
R240	R **42**	8c. green		2·10	16·00
		a. Imperf (pair)		9·75	

(c) PRINTED MATTER
P241	P **43**	1m. black		75	1·10
		a. Imperf (pair)		2·75	

The stamps are inscribed for different classes of mail, but as no instructions were given as to their usage they were employed indiscriminately, 2c. and 50c. telegraph stamps and a 10c. revenue stamp (inscribed "RECIBOS") were issued and are known used postally.

There were also a number of local provisional issues made under the auspices of local governments of islands and towns.

The Spanish-American War, in which the Spanish fleet was destroyed off Manila, ended with the Treaty of Paris on 10 December 1898, by which Spain ceded the Philippines to the United States for $20,000,000. Military rule was followed by civil administration from 4 July 1901. Issues of the United States Administration are listed in Part 21 (*South-East Asia*) and Part 22 (*United States*) of this catalogue.

Puerto Rico

1873. 100 Céntimos = 1 Peseta
1881. 1000 Milesimas = 100 Centavos = 1 Peso

The island of Puerto Rico was discovered by Columbus in 1493 and became one of the earliest Spanish settlements in the Caribbean. The first town was founded there by Juan Ponce de Leon in 1508. The island remained loyal to Spain during the Wars of Independence in Latin America, and in 1897 moderate reformers obtained powers of self-government.

For issues of 1855 to 1871 see Cuba and Puerto Rico, under Cuba.

> **PRINTERS.** All stamps of Spanish Puerto Rico were printed at the Government Printing Works, Madrid, *unless otherwise stated*.

King Amadeo of Spain
30 December 1870-12 February 1873

1   (**2**)

1873–76. *Stamps of Cuba optd. P 14.*
1873. With T **2**.
1	**1**	25c. deep pearl-grey		55·00	1·60
		a. Lilac		60·00	3·25
3		50c. deep brown		£160	7·75
4		1p. chestnut		£350	32·00

SPANISH REPUBLIC
12 February 1873-31 December 1874

3   (**4**)   **5**

1874. With T **4**.
5	**3**	25c. deep ultramarine		55·00	3·50

King Alfonso XII of Spain
31 December 1874-25 November 1885

1875. With T **4**.
6	**5**	25c. deep ultramarine		35·00	4·25
7		50c. deep green		50·00	5·25
		a. Opt inverted		£190	£130
8		1p. brown		£190	28·00

6   (**7**)   (**8**)

1876.
*(a) With T **7***
9	**6**	25c. deep grey-lilac		5·00	3·25
10		50c. deep ultramarine		12·50	5·25
		a. Opt inverted		36·00	27·00
11		1p. black		70·00	23·00

404

PUERTO RICO

		(b) With *T* **8**		
12	6	25c. deep grey-lilac	50·00	2·10
13		1p. black	£110	30·00

Other varieties are known with these overprints double, sideways, and part of overprint omitted, etc.

(T **9/11**. Dies eng E. Juliá. Typo)

1877. P 14.
14	9	5c. brown	9·75	4·00
		a. Error. Carmine	£250	
15		10c. carmine	33·00	4·50
		a. Error. Brown	£250	
16		15c. blue-green	49·00	22·00
17		25c. ultramarine	19·00	3·25
18		50c. bistre	33·00	7·75
14/18 *Set of* 5			£130	37·00

1878. Dated 1878. P 14.
19	9	5c. drab	19·00	19·00
20		10c. brown	£300	£120
21		25c. blue-green	2·50	1·40
22		50c. ultramarine	7·50	3·00
23		1p. bistre	16·00	7·25
		a. Bronze-bistre	16·00	7·25
19/23a *Set of* 5			£300	£140

1879. Dated 1879. P 14.
24	9	5c. lake	18·00	9·50
25		10c. sepia	18·00	9·50
26		15c. olive-slate	18·00	9·50
27		25c. blue	6·25	2·75
28		50c. blue-green	18·00	9·50
29		1p. grey-lilac	85·00	42·00
24/29 *Set of* 6			£150	75·00

Stamps of T **9** *imperf* are proofs or from trial sheets.

1880. P 14.
30	10	¼c. blue-green	34·00	27·00
31		½c. rosine	8·50	3·50
32		1c. dull claret	16·00	15·00
33		2c. grey	8·50	6·25
34		3c. buff	8·50	6·25
35		4c. black	8·50	6·25
36		5c. grey-green	4·00	2·75
37		10c. carmine-lake	4·75	3·00
38		15c. yellow-brown	8·50	4·75
39		25c. lavender	4·00	2·20
40		40c. grey	17·00	2·20
41		50c. sepia	36·00	23·00
42		1p. olive-bistre	£130	29·00
30/42 *Set of* 13			£250	£120

1881. Dated 1881. New Currency. P 14.
43		½m. crimson	30	20
		a. Pale lake	45	40
45		1m. deep violet	30	20
46		2m. pale rosine	65	45
47		4m. bright green	1·10	35
48		6m. dull claret	1·10	70
49		8m. ultramarine	2·75	1·70
		a. Dull blue	4·50	2·30
50		1c. grey-green	4·50	1·70
51		2c. carmine-lake	5·75	4·75
52		3c. sepia	13·50	8·00
53		5c. lavender	4·25	45
54		8c. brown	4·25	2·20
55		10c. slate	65·00	13·50
56		20c. olive-bistre	70·00	25·00
43/56 *Set of* 13			£160	53·00

1882. Undated. P 14.
57	11	½m. pale rosine	30	20
		a. Salmon	55	35
58		1m. carmine-lake	30	20
59		2m. dull violet	30	20
		a. Mauve	45	25
60		4m. dull claret	30	20
61		6m. brown	60	20
62		8m. bright green	60	20
63		1c. grey-green	30	20
64		2c. carmine-lake	1·80	20
65		3c. yellow	5·75	3·50
		a. Error. 8c. yellow	£140	90·00
66		5c. lavender	23·00	2·30
67		8c. sepia	5·25	20
68		10c. blue-green	5·25	45
69		20c. slate	8·75	45
70		40c. olive-green	70·00	24·00
71		80c. olive-bistre	95·00	35·00
57/71 *Set of* 15			£200	60·00

1884–85. P 14.
73	11	½m. lake	45	35
74		1m. rosine	25	20
75		1m. salmon	25	20
76		3c. brown	3·50	75
		a. Error. 8c. brown	£110	£120
		b. Pale brown	4·50	90
		c. Error. 8c. pale brown	23·00	27·00
77		5c. lavender (*a*)	18·00	2·50
78		5c. lavender (*b*)	£100	5·00

(*a*), first retouch; (*b*) third retouch. For description of the differences see notes after No. 81 of Philippines.

King Alfonso XI of Spain
17 May 1886-14 April 1931

12 **13** Landing of Columbus **14**

(Dies eng E. Juliá. Typo)

1890. P 14.
80	12	½m. black	25	20
81		1m. blue-green	35	20
82		2m. pale lake	25	20
83		4m. olive-black	17·00	9·50
84		6m. deep green	60·00	25·00
85		8m. bronze-bistre	44·00	37·00
86		1c. cinnamon	25	20
87		2c. deep purple	1·50	1·40
88		3c. indigo	11·50	1·70
89		5c. deep purple	18·00	65
90		8c. ultramarine	24·00	3·00
91		10c. rosine	6·75	1·70
92		20c. red	7·75	6·50
93		40c. orange	£250	85·00
94		80c. yellow-green	£700	£275
80/94 *Set of* 15			£1000	£400

1891–92. Colours changed. P 14.
95		½m. olive-grey	20	20
96		1m. deep purple	20	20
97		2m. dull purple	20	20
98		4m. ultramarine	20	20
99		6m. green	20	20
100		8m. yellow-green	20	20
101		1c. green	85	20
102		2c. brown-rose	1·40	20
		a. Brown	2·00	45
103		3c. orange	1·40	20
104		5c. blue-green	1·40	20
105		8c. sepia	20	20
106		10c. pale lake	1·90	55
107		20c. deep lilac	3·50	75
108		40c. indigo	8·75	6·50
109		80c. orange-red	23·00	19·00
95/109 *Set of* 15			39·00	26·00

(Des P. B. Viala. Litho Boletin Mercantil de Puerto Rico)

1893 (19 Nov). 400th Anniv of Discovery of America by Columbus. P 12.
110	13	3c. deep green	£300	70·00
		a. Green	£300	70·00

1894 (1 Jan). Colours changed again. P 14.
111	12	½m. chocolate	20	20
112		1m. blue	20	20
113		2m. pale red	20	20
114		4m. cinnamon	20	20
115		1c. purple-brown	11·50	65
116		2c. deep lilac	4·25	65
117		3c. olive-grey	11·50	65
118		4c. indigo	3·00	65

PUERTO RICO / British Post Offices in Puerto Rico

119		5c. yellow-green	11·50	1·70
120		6c. orange	70	20
121		8c. deep purple	27·00	7·50
122		20c. rosine	3·25	65
		a. Bright rosine	3·25	65
123		40c. lake	17·00	17·00
111/123	Set of 13		90·00	30·00

1896–97. Further colour changes. P 14.

124	12	½m. deep purple	25	20
125		1m. sepia	25	20
126		2m. pale yellow-green	25	20
127		4m. blue-green	1·50	50
128		1c. claret	95	20
129		2c. chestnut	95	20
130		3c. blue	34·00	50
131		3c. claret-brown (1897)	30	20
132		4c. blue	1·00	20
133		5c. blue	30	20
134		6c. deep lilac	30	20
135		8c. rosine	4·50	2·10
136		20c. olive-grey	11·00	2·10
137		40c. pale red	11·00	2·10
138		80c. black (1897)	46·00	35·00
124/138	Set of 15		£100	40·00

Stamps of T **12** *imperf* are proofs or from trial sheets.

(Dies eng B. Maura. Typo.)

1898. P 14.

139	14	1m. chestnut	25	20
140		2m. chestnut	25	20
141		3m. chestnut	25	20
142		4m. chestnut	3·25	80
143		5m. chestnut	25	20
144		1c. deep purple	25	20
		a. Tête-bêche (pair)	£1800	
145		2c. blue-green	25	20
146		3c. deep brown	25	20
147		4c. orange	3·25	1·50
148		5c. aniline rose	25	20
149		6c. blue	25	20
150		8c. grey-brown	25	20
151		10c. vermilion	25	20
152		15c. olive-slate	25	20
153		20c. maroon	3·50	80
154		40c. deep lilac	2·50	2·20
155		60c. black	2·50	2·20
156		80c. chocolate	10·00	8·25
157		1p. pale green	25·00	18·00
158		2p. indigo	55·00	23·00
139/158	Set of 20		95·00	55·00

Some values are known imperforate but it is doubtful if they were ever issued.

Habilitado PARA 1898 y '99
(15)

IMPUESTO DE GUERRA
(W 16)

1898 (8 June–17 Oct). Handstamped with T **15** in carmine.

159	12	½c. purple	23·00	13·50
160		1m. sepia	1·80	1·80
161		2m. pale yellow-green	55	55
162		4m. blue-green	55	55
163		1c. claret	4·50	4·50
		a. Violet handstamp	7·25	7·25
164		2c. chestnut	80	1·20
165		3c. ultramarine	50·00	22·00
166		3c. brown	4·25	4·25
167		4c. sepia	1·00	1·00
168		4c. indigo	29·00	20·00
169		5c. ultramarine	1·00	1·00
170		5c. blue-green (104) (V.)	13·50	11·00
171		5c. yellow-green (119)	23·00	18·00
172		6c. deep lilac	1·00	65
173		8c. rosine	7·25	6·75
		a. Violet handstamp	1·70	1·30
		b. Carmine and violet handstamp	27·00	27·00
174		20c. olive-grey	1·70	1·70
175		40c. pale red	4·25	4·25
176		80c. black	50·00	32·00
159/176	Set of 18		£190	£130

Being handstamped, T **15** is found double, inverted, etc. Overprints "Habilitado 4 ctva.", "1898 PROVISIONAL 1899", or "HABILITADO-17OCTUBRE 1898" in a rectangle, in *red* or *black*, applied to stamps of Type **12**, were unauthorised. The date in the latter is that on which the Government of the United States formally took over the island of Puerto Rico.

1898. WAR TAX.

*(a) Handstamped with Type W **16**, in violet*

W177	12	1m. blue	3·50	2·30
W178		1m. sepia	9·00	6·50
		a. Red handstamp	11·00	9·00
W179		2m. pale red	17·00	11·00
W180		2m. pale yellow-green	9·00	6·50
		a. Red handstamp	11·00	9·00
W181		4m. blue-green	9·75	9·75
W182		1c. cinnamon	9·00	5·50
		a. Black handstamp	9·00	5·50
W183		1c. claret	15·00	14·00
W184		2c. deep purple	1·20	1·20
W185		2c. brown-rose	55	35
W186		2c. deep lilac	55	35
W187		2c. chestnut	50	45
W188		3c. orange	17·00	14·00
		a. Red handstamp		
W189		5c. blue-green	2·30	2·30
		a. Black handstamp	2·30	2·30
W190		5c. yellow-green	4·00	4·00
W191		8c. deep purple	26·00	22·00

*(b) Handstamped with Type W **16** and surch in addition, in violet*

W192	12	2c. on 2m. pale red	55	35
		a. Red handstamp	4·25	3·75
W192a		2c. on 3c. orange		
W193		2c. on 5c. blue-green	3·50	2·30
		a. Red handstamp	5·75	4·25
		b. Magenta handstamp	5·75	4·25
		c. Black handstamp	3·50	2·30
W194		3c. on 10c. rosine	3·00	2·20
W195		4c. on 20c. red (Bk.)	17·00	13·00
W196		5c. on ½m. chocolate	6·50	4·25
		a. Red handstamp	3·75	3·75
		b. Black handstamp	6·50	4·25
W197		5c. on 1m. deep purple	35	35
		a. Red handstamp	55	35
W198		5c. on 1m. blue (R.)	9·00	6·50
		a. Violet handstamp	3·50	3·50
W199	14	5c. on 1m. chestnut	9·00	6·50
W200	12	5c. on 5c. blue-green (R.)	9·00	5·75
		a. Magenta handstamp	15·00	11·00

Being handstamped, Type W **16** is found double, inverted, etc. These stamps, although primarily intended to denote a tax, were also used to pay postage during the early days of the occupation by United States' forces.

Puerto Rico was occupied by U.S. troops during the Spanish-American War and was ceded to the United States on 10 December 1898. Subsequent issues are listed in Part 22 (*United States*) of this catalogue.

BRITISH POST OFFICES IN PUERTO RICO

A British Postal Agency operated at San Juan from 1844. On 24 October 1872 further offices were opened at Aguadilla, Arroyo, Mayaguez and Ponce, with Naguabo added three years later. Great Britain stamps were used during 1865-66 and from 1873 to 1877. All the British Agencies closed on 1 May 1877.

PRICES. Prices quoted for Great Britain stamps used abroad are for fine used examples with the cancellation clearly legible. Poor impressions of the cancellations are worth much less than the prices quoted.

Z 1   Z 2

AGUADILLA

1873–77. Queen Victoria stamps of GREAT BRITAIN cancelled "F 84" as Type Z **1**.

Z1	–	1d. rose-red (1870) (Plate No. 6)	90·00
Z2	B	1d. rose-red (1864-79)	55·00
		Plate Nos. 119, 122, 139, 149, 156, 160.	
Z3		2d. blue (1858-69) (Plate No. 14)	
Z4	E	3d. rose (1867-73) (Plate Nos. 7/9)	

PUERTO RICO / British Post Offices in Puerto Rico

Z5	F	3d. rose (1873-76) (Plate No. 12)	
Z6	D	4d. vermilion (1865-73) (Plate No. 12/14)	65·00
Z7	F	4d. vermilion (1876) (Plate No. 15)	£300
Z7a		6d. pale buff (1872-73) (Plate No. 11)	
Z8		6d. grey (1874-76) (Plate Nos. 13, 14)	
Z9	E	9d. straw (1867)	£350
Z10		10d. red-brown (1867)	£350
Z11		1s. green (1867-73) (Plate Nos. 4/7) .... From	65·00
Z12	F	1s. green (1873-77) (Plate Nos. 8/12) .... From	75·00
Z13	E	2s. blue (1867)	£275

A. 1d. Letters in lower corners only.
B. 1d., 1d., 2d. Letters in all four corners.
C. Small uncoloured corner letters.
D. Large uncoloured corner letters. Wmk Large Garter (4d.) or Emblems (roses, shamrock and thistle) (others).
E. As D. but wmk Spray of Roses.
F. Coloured corner letters. Wmk Large Garter (4d., 8d.) or Spray of Roses (others).

ARROYO

1873–77. Queen Victoria stamps of GREAT BRITAIN cancelled "F 83" as Type Z **1** or Z **2**.

Z14	–	1d. rose-red (1870) (Plate No. 5)	60·00
Z15	B	1d. rose-red (1864-79)	55·00
		Plate Nos. 149/51, 156, 164, 174/5.	
Z16		1½d. lake-red (1870) (Plate Nos. 1, 3)	
Z17		2d. blue (1858-69) (Plate No. 14)	
Z18	E	3d. rose (1867-73) (Plate Nos. 5, 7, 10)	60·00
Z19	F	3d. rose (1873-76)	65·00
		Plate Nos. 11, 12, 14, 16, 18.	
Z20	D	4d. vermilion (1865-73) (Plate Nos. 12/14)	65·00
Z21	F	4d. vermilion (1876) (Plate No. 15)	£300
Z22	E	6d. chestnut (1872) (Plate No. 11)	65·00
Z23		6d. pale buff (1872) (Plate No. 11)	80·00
Z23a		6d. grey (1873) (Plate No. 12)	
Z24		6d. grey (1874-76) (Plate Nos. 13/15)	65·00
Z25		9d. straw (1867)	£300
Z26	E	10d. red-brown (1867)	£300
Z27	D	1s. green (1865) (Plate No. 4)	
Z28	E	1s. green (1867-73) (Plate Nos. 4/7)	65·00
Z29	F	1s. green (1873-77) (Plate Nos. 8/13)	75·00
Z30	E	2s. blue (1867)	£250
Z31		5s. rose (1867-74) (Plate No. 2)	

For description of Types B to F see below No. Z13.

MAYAGUEZ

1873–77. Queen Victoria stamps of GREAT BRITAIN cancelled "F 85" as Type Z **1**.

Z32	–	1d. rose-red (1870) (Plate Nos. 4/6, 8/11) From	55·00
Z33	B	1d. rose-red (1864-79) .... From	38·00
		Plate Nos. 76, 120/2, 124, 134, 137, 140, 146, 149/51, 154/7, 160, 167, 170/1, 174/6, 178, 180, 182, 185/6, 189.	
Z34		1½d. lake-red (1870-74) (Plate Nos. 1,3)	50·00
Z35		2d. blue (1858-69) (Plate Nos. 13/15)	50·00
Z36	E	3d. rose (1867-73) (Plate Nos. 7/10)	55·00
Z37	F	3d. rose (1873-76) (Plate Nos. 11/12, 14/19)	50·00
Z38	D	4d. vermilion (1865-73) (Plate Nos. 11/14)	50·00
Z39	F	4d. vermilion (1876) (Plate No. 15)	£300
Z40		4d. sage-green (1877) (Plate No. 15)	
Z41	E	6d. mauve (1870) (Plate No. 9)	
Z42		6d. buff (1872) (Plate No. 11)	80·00
Z43		6d. chestnut (1872) (Plate No. 11)	70·00
Z44		6d. grey (1873) (Plate No. 12)	£200
Z45	F	6d. grey (1874-80) (Plate Nos. 13/16)	50·00
Z46		8d. orange (1876)	£300
Z47	E	9d. straw (1867)	£225
Z48		10d. red-brown (1867)	£300
Z49		1s. green (1867-73) (Plate No. 417)	45·00
Z50	F	1s. green (1873-77) (Plate Nos. 8/12) ...... From	60·00
Z51	E	2s. blue (1867)	£180
Z52	–	5s. rose (1867-74) (Plate Nos. 1, 2)	

For description of Types B to F see below No. Z13.

NAGUABO

Z 3

1875–77. Queen Victoria stamps of GREAT BRITAIN cancelled with Type Z **3**.

Z53	–	1d. rose-red (1870-79) (Plate Nos. 5, 12, 14)	
Z54	B	1d. rose-red (1864-79) (Plate Nos. 159, 165)	£550
Z55	F	3d. rose (1873-76) (Plate Nos. 17, 18)	£850
Z56	D	4d. verm (1872-73) (Plate Nos. 13, 14) ..... From	£850
Z57	F	4d. vermilion (1876) (Plate No. 15)	
Z58		6d. grey (1874-76) (Plate Nos. 14, 15)	
Z59	E	9d. straw (1867)	
Z60		10d. red-brown (1867)	£1200
Z61	F	1s. green (1873-77) (Plate Nos. 11, 12)	
Z62	E	2s. dull blue (1867) (Plate No. 1)	£1200

For description of Types B to F see below No. Z13.

PONCE

1873–77. Queen Victoria stamps of GREAT BRITAIN cancelled "F 88" as Type Z **1**.

Z63	–	1d. rose-red (1870) (Plate Nos. 5, 10, 12)	55·00
Z64	B	1d. rose-red (1864-79) .... From	45·00
		Plate Nos. 120/4. 146, 148, 154, 156/8, 160, 167, 171, 174/5. 179, 186/7.	
Z65		1½d. lake-red (1870-74) (Plate No. 3)	£110
Z66		2d. blue (1858-69) (Plate Nos. 13, 14)	55·00
Z67	E	3d. rose (1867-73) (Plate Nos. 7/9)	
Z68	F	3d. rose (1873-76) (Plate Nos. 12, 16/19)	50·00
Z69	D	4d. vermilion (1865-73) .... From	55·00
		Plate Nos. 8/9, 12/14.	
Z70	F	4d. vermilion (1876) (Plate No. 15)	£300
Z71		4d. sage-green (1877) (Plate Nos. 15, 16)	£200
Z72	E	6d. buff (1872-73) (Plate Nos. 11, 12)	75·00
Z73		6d. chestnut (1872) (Plate No. 11)	65·00
Z74		6d. grey (1873) (Plate No. 12)	
Z75	F	6d. grey (1874-76) (Plate Nos. 13/15) ...... From	55·00
Z76	E	9d. straw (1867)	£275
Z77		10d. red-brown (1867)	£300
Z78		1s. green (1867-73) (Plate Nos. 4, 6, 7)	50·00
Z79	F	1s. green (1873-77) (Plate Nos. 8/13) ...... From	60·00
Z80	E	2s. blue (1867)	
Z81	–	5s. rose (1867-74) (Plate Nos. 1, 2) .... From	£500

For description of Types B to F see below No. Z13.

SAN JUAN

CROWNED-CIRCLE HANDSTAMPS. Under regulations circulated in December 1841, letters and packets forwarded through offices abroad to the United Kingdom or any of its territories were to be sent unpaid, the postage being collected on delivery. Where this was not possible, for example from a British colony to a foreign country or between two foreign ports, then a crowned-circle handstamp was to be applied with the postage, paid in advance, noted alongside in manuscript.
The dates quoted are those on which the handstamp appears in the G.P.O. Record Books, but it seems to have been normal for the handstamps to be sent to the office concerned immediately following this registration.
Prices quoted for these handstamps are for examples used on cover duirng the pre-adhesive period.

CC 1

1844. Crowned-circle Handstamp.
CC1   CC **1** In red or black (25.5.1844).......... Price on cover   £650
No. CC1 may be found on cover used in conjunction with Spanish colonial adhesive stamps paying the local postage.

Z 4   Z 5

407

PUERTO RICO / British Post Offices in Puerto Rico / RIO MUNI

Z 6

Queen Victoria stamps of GREAT BRITAIN cancelled "C 61" as Type Z **4**, Z **5** or Z **6** (latter with or without integral datestamp). **1865** to **1866** and **1873** to **1877**.

Z82	–	1d. rose-red (1870).. From	50·00	
		Plate Nos. 5, 10, 15.		
Z83	A	1d. rose-red (1857).		
Z84	B	1d. rose-red (1864-79) .... From	38·00	
		Plate Nos. 73/4, 81, 84, 90, 94, 100/2, 107, 117, 122, 124/5, 127, 130, 137/40, 145/6, 149, 153, 156, 159/60, 162/3, 169, 171/5, 179/80, 182, 186.		
Z85		1d. lake-red (1870-74) (Plate Nos. 1, 3).... From	65·00	
Z86		2d. blue (1858-69) (Plate Nos. 9, 13, 14) . From	38·00	
Z87	D	3d. rose (1865) (Plate No. 4)	90·00	
Z88	E	3d. rose (1867-73) (Plate Nos. 5/10) .... From	50·00	
Z89	F	3d. rose (1873-76) .... From	45·00	
		Plate Nos. 11/12, 14/18.		
Z90	D	4d. verm (1865-73) (Plate Nos. 7/14) .... From	50·00	
Z91	F	4d. vermilion (1876) (Plate No. 15)	£300	
Z92	D	6d. lilac (1865-67) (Plate Nos. 5, 6)............ From	75·00	
Z93	E	6d. lilac (1867) (Plate No. 6)	75·00	
Z94		6d. violet (1867-70) (Plate Nos. 6, 8/9) ..... From	70·00	
Z95		6d. buff (1872-73) (Plate Nos. 11, 12)	75·00	
Z96		6d. chestnut (1872) (Plate No. 11)	50·00	
Z97		6d. grey (1873) (Plate No. 12)		
Z98	F	6d. grey (1874-76) (Plate Nos. 13/15) ...... From	50·00	
Z99	C	9d. straw (1862)	£300	
Z100	D	9d. straw (1865)	£375	
Z101	E	9d. straw (1867)	£200	
Z102		10d. red-brown (1867)	£275	
Z103	D	1s. green (1865) (Plate No. 4)	£140	
Z104	E	1s. green (1867-73) (Plate Nos. 4/7)......... From	45·00	
Z105	F	1s. green (1873-77) (Plate Nos. 8/13) ..... From	60·00	
Z106	E	2s. blue (1867)	£130	
Z107	–	5s. rose (1867) (Plate Nos. 1, 2) .... From	£450	

For description of Types A to F see below No. Z13.

Rio Muni

100 Centimos = 1 Peseta

OVERSEAS PROVINCE OF SPAIN

On 30 July 1959 the colony of Spanish Guinea (q.v.) was divided into two Overseas Provinces of Spain, Fernando Poo and Rio Muni. The latter consisted of the mainland territory of Spanish Guinea, between Cameroun and Gabon, and the islands of Elobey and Corisco.

PRINTERS. All the stamps of Rio Muni were printed at the Government Printing Works, Madrid.

1 Native Boy reading Book   **2** Cactus   **3** Bishop Juan de Ribera

(Des D. Juan J. de Castro. Photo)

1960 (27 Apr). P 13×12½.
1	1	25c. violet-grey..................................	30	25
2		50c. olive-brown...............................	30	25
3		75c. dull purple.................................	30	25
4		1p. orange-red.................................	30	25
5		1p.50 turquoise-green...................	30	25
6		2p. bright purple..............................	30	25
7		3p. blue..	55	35
8		5p. red-brown...................................	1·30	45
9		10p. olive-green................................	2·30	70
1/9 Set of 9			5·25	2·75

(Des P. Gómez (T **2**), E. Jimeno (15c.), R. Prieto (35c.). Photo)

1960 (1 June). Child Welfare Fund. T **2** and similar vert designs inscr "PRO-INFANCIA 1960". P 13×12½.
10	2	10c.+5c. brown-purple............................	55	55
11	–	15c.+5c. bistre-brown..............................	55	55
12	–	35c. blackish green..................................	55	55
13	2	80c. deep bluish green...........................	65	65
10/13 Set of 4			2·10	2·10

Designs:—15c. Sprig with berries; 35c. Star-shaped flowers.

(Des T. Miciano, V. D. Urosa, M. Carillo. Photo)

1960 (29 Dec). Stamp Day. T **3** and similar vert designs. P 13×12½.
14	3	10c.+5c. brown-lake.................................	55	55
15	–	20c.+5c. blackish green..........................	55	55
16	–	30c.+10c. olive-brown............................	55	55
17	3	50c.+20c. bistre-brown...........................	65	65
14/17 Set of 4			2·10	2·10

Designs:—20c. Portrait of man (after Velázquez); 30c. Statue.

4 Mandrill with Banana

(Des T. Miciano (T **4**), M. Carillo (25c.). Photo)

1961 (21 June). Child Welfare. T **4** and similar vert design inscr "PRO-INFANCIA 1961". P 13×12½.
18	4	10c.+5c. brown lake.................................	55	55
19	–	25c.+10c. slate-violet (African elephant)...	55	55
20	4	80c.+20c. deep bluish green................	65	65
18/20 Set of 3			1·60	1·60

408

RIO MUNI

5

6 Statuette

(Des T. Miciano (T **5**), E. Jimeno (25c.), V. S. Algora (70c.). Photo)

1961 (1 Oct). 25th Anniv of Gen. Franco as Head of State. T **5** and similar horiz designs. P 12½×13.

21	–	25c. violet-grey	55	55
22	**5**	50c. olive-brown	55	55
23	–	70c. emerald	55	55
24	**5**	1p. orange-red	65	65
21/24 Set of 4			2·10	2·10

Designs:—25c. Map; 70c. Government building.

(Des M. Vicente (T **6**), V. S. Algora (others). Photo)

1961 (23 Nov). Stamp Day. T **8** and similar vert design. P 13×12½.

25	**6**	10c.+5c. brown-red	55	55
26	–	25c.+10c. purple	55	55
27	**8**	30c.+10c. olive-brown	55	55
28	–	1p.+10c. red-orange	65	65
25/28 Set of 4			2·10	2·10

Design:—25c., 1p. Figure holding offering.

7 Girl wearing Headdress

8 African Buffalo

(Des J. G. Arroyo (T **7**), A. Boulé (50c.). Photo)

1962 (10 July). Child Welfare. T **7** and similar vert design inscr "PRO-INFANCIA 1962". P 13×12½.

29	**7**	25c. bluish violet	55	55
30	–	50c. green (Native mask)	55	55
31	**7**	1p. chestnut	65	65
29/31 Set of 3			1·60	1·60

(Des J. Espinosa (T **8**), J. L. Bueno (35c.). Photo)

1962 (23 Nov). Stamp Day. T **8** and similar vert design inscr "DIA DEL SELLO 1962". P 13×12½ (35c.) or 12½×13 (others).

32	**8**	15c. olive	55	55
33	–	35c. bright purple (Gorilla)	55	55
34	**8**	1p. orange-red	65	65
32/34 Set of 3			1·60	1·60

9 Statuette

10 "Blessing"

11 Child at Prayer

(Des P. Gómez. Photo)

1963 (29 Jan). Seville Flood Relief. P 13×12½.

35	**9**	50c. green	55	55
36		1p. chestnut	65	65

(Des T. Miciano (50c.), J. J. de Castro (others). Photo)

1963 (1 June). Child Welfare. T **10** and similar vert design inscr "PRO-INFANCIA 1963". P 13×12½.

37		25c. deep violet (Priest)	55	55
38		50c. deep olive	55	55
39		1p. orange-red (Priest)	65	65
37/39 Set of 3			1·60	1·60

(Des A. Boué. Photo)

1963 (12 June). "For Barcelona". P 13×12½.

40	**11**	50c. bluish green	55	55
41		1p. red-brown	65	65

12 Copal Flower   13 Giant Ground Pangolin

(Des J. J. de Castro (50c.), V. Vila (others). Photo)

1964 (6 Mar). Stamp Day. T **12** and similar horiz design inscr "DIA DEL SELLO 1963". P 12½×13 (50c.) or 13×12½ (others).

42	**12**	25c. reddish violet	55	55
43	–	50c. turquoise (Cinchona blossom)	55	55
44	**12**	1p. carmine-lake	65	65
42/44 Set of 3			1·60	1·60

(Des V. S. Algora (50c.), S. H. Fernández (others). Photo)

1964 (1 June). Child Welfare. T **13** and similar horiz design inscr "PRO INFANCIA 1964". P 13×12½.

45	**13**	25c. deep violet	55	55
46	–	50c. yellow-olive (Chameleon)	55	55
47	**13**	1p. chestnut	65	65
45/47 Set of 3			1·60	1·60

(Des E. Jimeno (crocodile), J. Olcina (leopard), A. M. Fernández (rhinoceros). Photo)

1964 (1 July). Wild Life. Designs similar to T **13** but without "PRO INFANCIA" inscription. P 12½×13.

48		15c. yellow-brown	20	20
49		25c. violet	20	20
50		50c. yellow-olive	20	20
51		70c. green	20	20
52		1p. light red-brown	95	20
53		1p.50 turquoise-green	95	20
54		3p. deep blue	1·90	30
55		5p. brown	4·75	45
56		10p. green	8·50	1·20
48/56 Set of 9			16·00	2·75

Animals: Horiz—15c., 70c., 3p. Crocodile; 25c., 1p., 5p. Leopard; 50c., 1p.50, 10p. Black rhinoceros.

14 "Goliath" Frog

15 Woman

(Des J. A. Prieto (1p.), C. Tauler (others). Photo)

1964 (23 Nov). Stamp Day. T **14** and similar vert design. P 13×12½ (1p.) or 12½×13 (others).

57	**14**	50c. bronze-green	55	55
58	–	1p. crimson-lake (Helmeted guineafowl)	55	55
59	**14**	1p.50 deep bluish green	65	65
57/59 Set of 3			1·60	1·60

409

RIO MUNI

(Des T. Miciano and C. Tauler. Photo)

1965 (22 Feb). 25th Anniv of End of Spanish Civil War. T **15** and similar vert designs inscr "XXV ANOS DE PAZ". P 13×12½.
60	50c. emerald-green	55	55
61	1p. orange-red (Nurse)	55	55
62	1p.50 turquoise (Logging)	65	65
60/62 Set of 3		1·60	1·60

16 Goliath Beetle (*Goliathus goliathus*)

17 Leopard and Arms of Rio Muni

(Des S. H. Fernández and M. Salamanca. Photo)

1965 (1 June). Child Welfare. Insects. T **16** and similar horiz designs. P 12½×13.
63	**16**	50c. deep bluish green	55	55
64	–	1p. sepia (*Acridoxena hewaniana*)	55	55
65	**16**	1p.50 black	65	65
63/65 Set of 3			1·60	1·60

(Des C. Tauler and J. Espinosa. Photo)

1965 (23 Nov). Stamp Day. T **17** and similar design. P 13½×12 (vert) or 12×13½ (horiz).
66	50c. olive-grey	55	55
67	1p. sepia	55	55
68	2p.50 reddish violet	2·10	2·10
66/68 Set of 3		3·00	3·00

Design: Vert—50c., 2p.50, Common pheasant.

18 African Elephant and Grey Parrot

19 Water Chevrotain (*Hyemoschus aquaticus*)

1966 (1 June). Child Welfare. T **18** and similar horiz design. Photo. P 12½×13.
69	**18**	50c. olive-brown	55	55
70	–	1p. slate-lilac	55	55
71	–	1p.50 greenish blue	65	65
69/71 Set of 3			1·60	1·60

Design:—1p.50, African and lion.

(Des D. E. Cerra. Photo)

1966 (23 Nov). Stamp Day. T **19** and similar design. P 13.
72	**9**	10c. blackish brown and ochre	55	55
73	–	40c. deep brown and lemon	55	55
74	**19**	1p.50 deep slate-violet and carmine	55	55
75	–	4p. steel-blue and yellow-green	65	65
72/75 Set of 4			2·10	2·10

Design: Vert—40c., 4p. Giant ground pangolin (*Smutsia gigantea*).

20 Floss Flowers

21 Bush Pig (*Potamocherus porcus*)

(Des V. S. Algora. Photo)

1967 (1 June). Child Welfare. T **20** and similar vert floral design. P 13.
76	**20**	10c. lt yellow, olive-yellow and dp green	55	55
77	–	40c. green, black and magenta	55	55
78	**20**	1p.50 light red and new blue	55	55
79	–	4p. black and green	65	65
76/79 Set of 4			2·10	2·10

Designs:—40c., 4p. Ylang-ylang.

1967 (23 Nov). Stamp Day. T **21** and similar designs. Photo. P 13.
80	1p. chestnut and blackish brown	55	55
81	1p.50 bistre-brown and yellow-green	55	55
82	3p.50 light brown and emerald	1·10	1·10
80/82 Set of 3		2·00	2·00

Designs: Vert—1p.50, Potto (*Perodicticus potto*). Horiz—3p.50, African golden cat (*Profelis aurata*).

1968 (25 Apr). Child Welfare. Signs of the Zodiac. Horiz designs as T **47** of Fernando Poo. Photo. P 13.
83	1p. magenta/*pale yellow*	55	55
84	1p.50 red-brown/*pale pink*	55	55
85	2p.50 deep violet/*pale greenish yellow*	95	95
83/85 Set of 3		1·80	1·80

Designs:—1p. Cancer (crab); 1p.50, Taurus (bull); 2p.50, Gemini (twins).

On 12 October 1968 Rio Muni was again joined to Fernando Poo to form the independent Republic of Equatorial Guinea (see Part 12 (*Africa since Independence A-E*) of this catalogue).

SPANISH GUINEA

Spanish Guinea

100 Céntimos = 1 Peseta

SPANISH PROTECTORATE

The mainland territory of Spanish Guinea, also known as Rio Muni, was proclaimed a Spanish protectorate on 9 January 1885. In 1901 Nos. 124/38 of Fernando Poo were handstamped "Bata" (the name of the chief town) and the same stamps, except the 10c., were handstamped "HABILITADO PARA BATA" and value in a frame but these were not authorised.

PRINTERS. All stamps of Spanish Guinea were printed at the Government Printing Works, Madrid, *unless otherwise stated.*

1 Alfonso XIII (2)

(Dies eng B. Maura. Typo)

1902. With blue control figures on back. P 14.
1	1	5c. green	17·00	10·50
2		10c. slate	17·00	10·50
3		25c. lake	£120	80·00
4		50c. brown	£120	80·00
5		75c. deep lilac	£120	80·00
6		1p. rosine	£190	80·00
7		2p. bronze-green	£225	£180
8		5p. pale red	£375	£325
1/8 Set of 8			£1100	£750

1903. Fiscal stamps, inscr "POSESIONES ESPAÑOLAS DE AFRICA OCCIDENTAL", surch with T **2**. With blue or black control figures on back. Imperf.
9	10c. on 25c. black	£600	£225
	a. Red surch	£500	£200
	b. Violet surch	£850	£325
10	10c. on 50c. orange	£130	38·00
	a. Blue surch	£130	38·00
	b. Red surch	£225	70·00
11	10c. on 1p.25 rose	£850	£375
	a. Red surch	£950	£450
12	10c. on 2p. lake	£900	£550
	a. Blue surch	£1400	£850
13	10c. on 2p.50 brown	£1800	£900
	a. Blue surch	£1900	£950
14	10c. on 5p. olive-black	£1800	£900
	a. Red surch	£1900	£950
15	10c. on 10p. brown (R.)	£1200	£500
16	10c. on 15p. lilac (R.)	£950	£500
	a. Blue surch	£1200	£500
17	10c. on 25p. blue (R.)	£950	£750
	a. Blue surch	£1200	£750
18	10c. on 50p. violet-brown (R.)	£1200	£850
	a. Blue surch	£1400	£750
19	10c. on 75p. deep violet (R.)	£1400	£750
20	10c. on 100p. green (R.)	£1900	£850
	a. Blue surch	£2250	£1300

Many values exist with the surcharge inverted or double.

3 (4)

(Dies eng B. Maura. Typo)

1903. With blue control figures on back. P 14.
21	3	¼c. black	1·70	1·20
22		½c. blue-green	1·70	1·20
23		1c. claret	1·70	1·00
24		2c. slate-green	1·70	1·00
25		3c. chocolate	1·70	1·00
26		4c. red	1·70	1·00
27		5c. olive-black	1·70	1·00
28		10c. brown	2·75	1·20
29		15c. deep blue	10·00	9·75
30		25c. orange	10·00	9·75
31		50c. lake	18·00	22·00
32		75c. deep lilac	25·00	22·00
33		1p. emerald	41·00	33·00
34		2p. myrtle-green	41·00	33·00
35		3p. brick-red	£110	46·00
36		4p. blue	£140	75·00
37		5p. deep purple	£250	£110
38		10p. rosine	£425	£150
21/38 Set of 18			£1000	£475

1905. Dated 1905. With blue control figures on back. P 14.
39	3	1c. black	30	20
40		2c. green	30	20
41		3c. lake	30	20
42		4c. slate-green	30	20
43		5c. chocolate	30	20
44		10c. orange-red	1·70	95
45		15c. sepia	5·25	3·25
46		25c. chocolate	5·25	3·25
47		50c. deep blue	13·00	7·50
48		75c. dull orange	14·00	7·50
49		1p. lake	14·00	7·50
50		2p. deep lilac	30·00	17·00
51		3p. blue-green	80·00	40·00
52		4p. myrtle-green	80·00	49·00
53		5p. pale red	£130	60·00
54		10p. pale blue	£225	£160
39/54 Set of 16			£550	£325

1905 (17 Jan). Nos. 19/34 of Elobey, optd with T **4**, in violet or blue.
55	1	1c. rose	7·00	5·00
56		2c. deep purple	7·00	5·00
57		3c. black	7·00	5·00
58		4c. pale red	7·00	5·00
59		5c. myrtle-green	7·00	5·00
60		10c. blue-green	14·00	10·00
61		15c. dull lilac	26·00	15·00
62		25c. rose-lake	26·00	15·00
63		50c. dull orange	34·00	18·00
64		75c. deep blue	41·00	21·00
65		1p. chocolate	80·00	37·00
66		2p. sepia	£110	44·00
67		3p. orange-red	£160	75·00
68		4p. brown	£600	£200
69		5p. slate-green	£600	£200
70		10p. lake	£2500	£1000
55/70 Set of 16			£3750	£1500

The 1907 issue of Elobey exists with a lighter type of over-print similar to Type **4** in violet, blue, red or green.

5 (6)

(Dies eng B. Maura. Typo)

1907. With blue control figures on back. P 14.
71	5	1c. bronze-green	85	20
72		2c. dull blue	85	20
73		3c. deep lilac	85	20
74		4c. pale green	85	20
75		5c. lake	85	20
76		10c. bistre	4·50	1·90
77		15c. brown	3·25	1·10
78		25c. blue	3·25	1·10
79		50c. deep brown	3·25	1·10
80		75c. blue-green	3·25	1·10
81		1p. brown-orange	15·00	2·00
82		2p. purple-brown	19·00	9·25
83		3p. olive-black	19·00	9·25
84		4p. dull lake	24·00	19·00
85		5p. blue-green	24·00	24·00
86		10p. deep purple	34·00	28·00
71/86 Set of 16			£140	90·00

411

SPANISH GUINEA / Spanish Territories of the Gulf of Guinea

1908–09. Surch as T **6**.
87	5	05c. on 1c. bronze-green (R.)	5·50	3·00
88		05c. on 2c. dull blue (R.)	5·50	3·00
89		05c. on 3c. deep lilac	5·50	3·00
90		05c. on 4c. pale green	5·50	3·00
91		05c. on 10c. bistre	5·50	3·00
92		15c. on 10c. bistre	20·00	13·00
87/92 Set of 6			43·00	25·00

All values exist with surcharges in other colours and there are numerous errors such as double, inverted, omitted, etc. Nos. 77/86 also exist surcharged 05c. but these were not issued.

1909. Fiscal stamps, inscr "TERRITORIOS ESPAÑOLES DEL AFRICA OCCIDENTAL", surch with T **2**, in black. With or without control figures on back.
93	10c. on 50c. green	£100	75·00
	a. Red surch	£180	£120
	b. Violet surch	£180	£120
94	10c. on 1p.25 violet	£300	£180
95	10c. on 2p. brown	£750	£500
96	10c. on 5p. mauve	£750	£500
97	10c. on 25p. red-brown	£1100	£750
98	10c. on 50p. lake	£3750	£1800
99	10c. on 75p. rose	£3750	£1800
100	10c. on 100p. orange	£3750	£1800

SPANISH TERRITORIES OF THE GULF OF GUINEA

The following issues were for use on the mainland and in the islands of Fernando Poo, Elobey, Annobon and Corisco.

From 1949 the name of the colony was shortened to Spanish Guinea, except on the definitive issue of 1949–50 and the Air Mail and Express Letter stamps of 1951.

7　　　　(8)　　　　9

(Dies eng G. Carrascu and A. Morago. Typo)

1909. With blue control figures on back. P 14.
101	7	1c. brown	20	20
102		2c. rosine	20	20
103		5c. myrtle	1·50	20
104	7	10c. orange-vermilion	40	20
105		15c. black-brown	40	20
106		20c. deep reddish mauve	70	40
107		25c. indigo-blue	70	40
108		30c. chocolate	95	20
109		40c. lake	55	20
110		50c. indigo-lilac	55	20
111		1p. green	16·00	8·25
112		4p. orange	3·50	5·00
113		10p. salmon	3·50	5·00
101/113 Set of 13			26·00	19·00

1911. Handstamped with T **8**.
114	7	1c. brown (B.)	40	40
115		2c. rosine (G.)	40	40
116		5c. myrtle (R.)	1·70	55
117		10c. orange-vermilion	1·10	60
118		15c. black-brown (R.)	1·70	1·20
119		20c. deep reddish mauve	2·30	1·80
120		25c. indigo-blue (R.)	2·75	3·50
121		30c. chocolate (B.)	3·50	4·50
122		40c. lake (B.)	3·75	4·75
123		50c. indigo-lilac	6·75	7·75
124		1p. green (R.)	£100	39·00
125		4p. orange (G.)	28·00	29·00
126		10p. salmon (G.)	38·00	48·00
114/126 Set of 13			£170	£130

The first stamp of each row in the sheet was without date "1911" in the overprint. Value about four times normal.

This handstamp is known reading vertically downwards and also horizontally.

(Dies eng A. Morago. Typo)

1912. With blue control figures on back. P 13.
127	9	1c. black	20	20
128		2c. brown	20	20
129		5c. green	20	20
130		10c. red-orange	35	20
131		15c. dull claret	35	20
132		20c. red	60	20
133		25c. blue	35	20
134		30c. lake	5·75	3·00
135		40c. rose	4·00	1·70
136		50c. orange	3·00	70
137		1p. deep grey-lilac	4·00	2·10
138		4p. mauve	9·00	4·00
139		10p. blue-green	20·00	16·00
127/139 Set of 13			43·00	26·00

10　　　　(11)

(Dies eng A. Morago. Typo)

1914. With blue control figures on back. P 13.
140	10	1c. dull violet	20	20
141		2c. rose-carmine	20	20
142		5c. green	20	20
143		10c. vermilion	20	20
144		15c. purple	20	20
145		20c. brown	1·40	55
146		25c. deep blue	35	35
147		30c. yellow-brown	1·70	60
148		40c. blue-green	1·70	60
149		50c. lake	65	40
150		1p. vermilion	1·70	2·30
151		4p. dull claret	8·50	8·00
152		10p. grey-brown	12·50	14·50
140/152 Set of 13			27·00	25·00

Stamps of T **3** with an overprint of this date (1914) have been declared by the authorities to be bogus.

1917. Stamps of 1912 optd "1917" as in T **11**.
153	9	1c. black	£120	80·00
154		2c. brown	£120	80·00
155		5c. green	40	20
156		10c. red-orange	40	20
157	9	15c. dull claret	40	20
158		20c. red	40	20
159		25c. blue	20	20
160		30c. lake	40	20
161		40c. rose	70	40
162		50c. orange	35	20
163		1p. purple-brown	70	40
164		4p. violet	9·75	5·00
165		10p. blue-green	9·75	5·00
153/165 Set of 13			£250	£150

1918. Stamps of 1912 surch as T **11**.
166	9	5c. on 40c. rose	41·00	15·00
167		10c. on 4p. violet	41·00	15·00
168		15c. on 20c. red	80·00	26·00
169		25c. on 10p. blue-green	80·00	26·00
		a. Error. "52" for "25"	£500	£450

All values exist with "Génts" or "Cénst" for "Cénts".

12　　　　12a　　　　13

(Dies eng A. Mendiola. Typo)

1919. With blue control figures on back. P 13.
170	12	1c. dull violet	1·10	80
171		2c. rose-carmine	1·10	80
172		5c. vermilion	1·10	80
173		10c. purple	1·80	80
174		15c. brown	3·75	90
175		20c. blue	7·50	1·70
176		25c. green	3·75	1·70
177		30c. orange	1·70	1·70
178		40c. orange	4·75	1·70
179		50c. red	4·75	1·70
180		1p. violet	4·75	5·00
181		4p. claret	10·00	20·00
182		10p. brown	18·00	34·00
170/182 Set of 13			60·00	65·00

412

SPANISH GUINEA / Spanish Territories of the Gulf of Guinea

(Dies eng G. Carrascu and A. Morago. Typo)
1920. With blue control figures on back. P 13.

183	**12a**	1c. brown	20	20
184		2c. carmine	20	20
185		5c. green	20	20
186		10c. carmine	20	20
187		15c. orange	20	20
188		20c. yellow	20	20
189		25c. blue	70	40
190		30c. blue-green	49·00	25·00
191		40c. brown	60	35
192		50c. purple	1·70	40
193		1p. red-brown	1·70	40
194		4p. rose	5·50	6·25
195		10p. violet	11·00	13·00
183/195 Set of 13			65·00	42·00

(Des B. Maura. Dies eng J. E. Gisbert. Typo)
1922. With blue control figures on back. P 13.

196	**13**	1c. brown	70	35
197		2c. claret	70	35
198		5c. blue-green	70	35
199		10c. red	4·75	1·60
200		15c. orange	70	35
201		20c. mauve	3·00	1·40
202		25c. blue	5·75	1·70
203		30c. violet	4·75	1·80
204		40c. turquoise-blue	3·50	95
205		50c. rose	3·50	95
206		1p. myrtle-green	3·50	95
207		4p. red-brown	14·50	17·00
208		10p. yellow	28·00	33·00
196/208 Set of 13			65·00	55·00

14 Nipa House   GUINEA ESPAÑOLA (**15**)   GUINEA (**16**)

1924. Typo. With blue control figures on back. P 12½×13.

209	**14**	5c. blue and brown	20	20
210		10c. blue and green	20	20
211		15c. black and carmine	20	20
212		20c. black and violet	20	20
213		25c. black and vermilion	50	20
214		30c. black and orange	50	20
215		40c. black and blue	50	20
216		50c. black and claret	50	20
217		60c. black and brown	50	20
218		1p. black and violet	2·00	20
219		4p. black and light blue	4·75	2·50
220		10p. black and blue-green	10·50	5·00
209/220 Set of 12			18·00	8·50

1926. Red Cross. T **70**/1, and similar types of Spain (colours changed), optd with T **15**.

221	–	5c. sepia	13·50	13·50
222	–	10c. myrtle	13·50	13·50
223	**70**	15c. violet (V.)	3·00	3·00
224	–	20c. purple	3·00	3·00
225	**71**	25c. crimson	3·00	3·00
226	**70**	30c. olive-green	3·00	3·00
227	–	40c. ultramarine	65	65
228	–	50c. brown-lake	65	65
229	**71**	60c. grey-green	65	65
230	–	1p. orange-red	65	65
231	–	4p. bistre	2·50	2·50
232	**71**	10p. violet	9·00	9·00
221/232 Set of 12			48·00	48·00

1929. Seville and Barcelona Exhibitions. Spanish stamps optd with T **16** (sideways on 5, 10, 30, 40c., 1, 4, 10p.).

233	–	5c. carmine-lake (B.)	40	40
234	–	10c. green (R.)	40	40
235	**83**	15c. turquoise-blue (R.)	40	40
236	**84**	20c. violet (R.)	40	40
237	**83**	25c. carmine (R.)	40	40
238	–	30c. blackish brown (B.)	40	40
239	–	40c. blue (R.)	70	70
240	**84**	50c. red-orange (B.)	70	70
241	–	1p. greenish slate (R.)	13·00	13·00
242	–	4p. claret (B.)	27·00	27·00
243	–	10p. brown (B.)	50·00	50·00
233/243 Set of 11			85·00	85·00

17 Porter   **18** King Alfonso XIII and Queen Victoria

(Eng C. Delhom and J. L. Sánchez Toda. Recess)
1931 (Jan). T **17**/**18** and similar vert design. Blue control figures on back except on Nos. 244/5. P 14.

244	**17**	1c. deep bluish green	20	20
245		2c. brown	20	20
246		5c. brownish black	20	20
247		10c. green	20	20
248		15c. blue-black	20	20
249		20c. slate-lilac	20	20
250		25c. rose-red	20	20
251		30c. lake	35	20
252		40c. deep blue	1·00	70
253		50c. red-orange	2·50	1·70
254	**18**	80c. deep ultramarine	4·50	2·75
255		1p. black	7·75	6·25
256		4p. magenta	55·00	37·00
257		5p. deep brown	21·00	26·00
244/257 Set of 14			85·00	70·00

Design:—25c. to 50c. Native drummers.
See also Nos. 286/92 and 318/20.

REPUBLICA   República Española   HABILITADO 30 Cts.
ESPAÑOLA (**19**)   (**19a**)   (**20**)

1931 (June). Nos. 244/257 optd with T **19**.

258	**17**	1c. blue-green	20	20
259		2c. chocolate	20	20
260		5c. grey-black	20	20
261		10c. green	20	20
262		15c. greenish slate	20	20
263		20c. violet	20	20
264	–	25c. carmine	20	20
265		30c. lake	65	30
266	–	40c. indigo	4·75	65
267	–	50c. vermilion	18·00	8·50
268	**18**	80c. ultramarine	4·75	4·50
269		1p. black	16·00	5·50
270		4p. claret	36·00	36·00
271		5p. brown	28·00	17·00
258/271 Set of 14			£100	65·00

Nos. 244/57 also exist overprinted locally at Santa Isabel "REPUBLICA ESPAÑOLA" underlined diagonally downwards in black or violet.

1932 (July). Nos. 244/257 optd horiz with T **19a**.

272	**17**	1c. blue-green (R.)	20	20
273		2c. chocolate (R.)	20	20
274		5c. grey-black (R.)	20	20
275		10c. green (B.)	20	20
276		15c. greenish slate (R.)	20	20
277		20c. violet (R.)	70	20
278	–	25c. carmine (B.)	60	35
279	–	30c. lake (B.)	55	35
280	–	40c. indigo (R.)	4·50	1·00
281	–	50c. vermilion (B.)	17·00	5·00
282	**18**	80c. ultramarine (R.)	8·25	4·50
283		1p. black (R.)	17·00	4·50
284		4p. claret (B.)	55·00	39·00
285		5p. brown (B.)	65·00	39·00
272/285 Set of 14			£150	85·00

These were released in Madrid in July 1932 but not put on sale in Spanish Guinea until Aug–Sept 1933.

1934–36. No control figures on back. Recess. P 10.

286	**17**	1c. blue-green (1935)	13·00	20
287		2c. light brown (1935)	13·00	20
		a. Perf 14 (1936)	28·00	19·00
288		5c. blackish brown	2·00	20
289		10c. yellowish green	2·00	20
		a. Perf 14 (1936)	24·00	26·00
290		15c. deep bluish green	4·50	20
291	–	30c. rose-red (as 253)	5·50	20
292		50c. deep blue (as 253) (1935)	12·50	1·00
		a. Perf 14 (1936)	47·00	30·00
286/292 Set of 7			47·00	2·00

413

SPANISH GUINEA / Spanish Territories of the Gulf of Guinea

1937. Surch as T **20**.
293		30c. on 40c. (252)	5·50	3·25
	a.	Italic "3"	28·00	19·00
294		30c. on 40c. (266)	23·00	5·00
	a.	Italic "3"	55·00	28·00
295		30c. on 40c. (280)	85·00	26·00
	a.	Italic "3"	£160	75·00

Territorios Españoles del Golfo de Guinea **Habilitado 40 cts.**
(21)　　　(22)

1938 (5 July). Stamps of Spain optd with T **21**, horiz on T **183**, or vert on T **184** by B. Fournier, Burgos.
296	**183**	10c. yellow-green	2·40	75
297	**184**	15c. black (R.)	2·40	75
298		20c. violet	5·00	2·50
299		25c. lake	5·00	2·50
296/299 *Set of 4*			13·50	5·75

1939 (23 Sept). Surch with T **22**.
300	**18**	40c. on 80c. (268)	24·00	11·50
301		40c. on 80c. (282)	24·00	7·00

23　　　24　　　25

1939 (23 Sept). Fiscal stamps inscr "ESPECIAL MOVIL", optd as in T **23** or surch in addition (1p.). P 11.
302	**23**	5c. carmine	5·75	1·70
303	–	1p. on 15c. olive-green	21·00	6·75

Design:—No. 303, As T **23** but larger (23×29 mm).

1940–41. Fiscal stamps surch as in T **24**. P 11½.
(a) Surch reading down, in black (4.40)
304		5c. on 35c. yellow-green	6·75	2·40
305		25c. on 60c. yellow-brown	6·75	2·75
306		50c. on 75c. sepia	8·75	2·75

(b) Surch reading up, in red (15.5.41)
307		10c. on 75c. brown	8·75	2·75
308		15c. on 1p.50 violet	6·75	2·75
309		25c. on 60c. yellow-brown	11·50	3·75

1940 (May). Fiscal stamp optd as in T **25**. With control figures on back. P 13.
310	**25**	1p. yellow-bistre	£100	39·00

Habilitado para Correo Aéreo Intercolonial
Una Peseta
26 General Franco　　(27)

1940. P 11½. *(Des J. L. Sánchez Toda. Litho Fournier)*
311	**26**	5c. brown	4·50	1·10
312		40c. blue	5·75	1·10
313		50c. greenish grey	41·00	18·00
314		50c. green	8·00	1·10
311/314 *Set of 4*			55·00	19·00

The above exist perf 14 but were probably not issued thus.

1941. Fiscal stamps (23×30 mm) inscr "IMPUESTO SOBRE CONTRATOS". P 11.
(a) POSTAGE. Surch "HABILITADO/Correos/1 Pta"
315		1p. on 40p. green (15 May)	15·00	4·75

(b) POSTAGE. Surch "Habilitado para/Correos/Una Peseta"
316		1p. on 17p. carmine	50·00	16·00

(c) AIR. Surch as T 27
317		1p. on 17p. carmine (I) (18 May)	60·00	40·00
	a.	Type II (18 June)	45·00	25·00

The bar between "Intercolonial" and "Una Peseta" measures 9 mm in Type I and 6½ mm in Type II.

1941. As T **17**, etc., but litho. No control figures. P 10.
318	**17**	5c. olive-grey	3·00	20
319		20c. violet	3·00	20
320	–	40c. grey-green (as 252)	1·20	20

Habilitado
3 Pesetas　　**Golfo de Guinea.**
(28)　　　(29)

1942 (1 Feb). No. 319 surch with T **28**.
321	**17**	3p. on 20c. violet	14·50	2·30

1942 (23 June). Stamps of Spain optd.
(a) POSTAGE. Optd as T 29 but in two lines. P 9½×10½
322	**196**	1PTA. black (I) (R.)	60	20
	a.	Type II	19·00	14·00
323		4PTAS. rose	13·00	1·00

1p. In Type I the lines of overprint are spaced 2 mm apart and in Type II they are 3 mm apart.

(b) AIR. Optd with T 29
324	**195**	1p. bright blue (R.)	2·30	20

Territorios españoles del Golfo de Guinea.　　**Correo Aéreo Viaje Ministerial 10-19 Enero 1948**　　**Habilitado para quince cts.**
(30)　　(31)　　(32)

1943. Stamp of Spain optd with T **30**. P 9½×10½.
325	**196**	2PTAS. sepia (R.)	1·20	20

1948. AIR. Ministerial Visit. No. 323 optd in Santa Isabel with T **31**.
326	**196**	4p. rose	17·00	4·25

1949 (1 Sept). Nos. 322 and 325 surch in Santa Isabel as T **32**, in green.
327	**196**	5c. on 1PTA. black (I)	95	20
	a.	Type II	95	20
328		15c. on 2PTAS. sepia	95	20

33 Natives in Pirogue　　34 Count Argalejo and San Carlos Bay

(Des Tauler. Photo)

1949 (9 Oct). 75th Anniv of Universal Postal Union. P 12½×13.
329	**33**	4p. violet	4·75	3·00

(Des A. S. Fuentes. Photo)

1949 (23 Nov). AIR. Colonial Stamp Day. P 12½×13.
330	**34**	5p. grey-green	4·75	3·00

35 San Carlos Bay　　36 Manuel Iradier y Bulfy

(Des Nuñez de Celis. Photo)

1949 (1 Dec)–**50**. As T **35**. P 12½×13.
331	**35**	2c. yellow-brown	20	20
332	–	5c. reddish violet	20	20
333	–	10c. turquoise-blue	20	20
334	–	15c. blackish green	20	20
335	**35**	25c. red-brown	20	20
336	–	30c. yellow (1950)	20	20
337	–	40c. grey-olive	20	20
338	–	45c. claret	20	20
339	**35**	50c. brown-orange	20	20
340	–	75c. blue (1950)	20	20
341	–	90c. blue-green	30	20
342	–	1p. grey-black	1·90	20

SPANISH GUINEA / Spanish Territories of the Gulf of Guinea

343	35	1p.35 violet		7·50	2·40
344	–	2p. grey-brown		21·00	5·75
345	–	5p. magenta		29·00	17·00
346	35	10p. yellow-brown		£120	70·00
331/346 Set of 16				£160	90·00

Designs:—5c., 30c., 75c., 2p. Rapids on Benito River; 10c., 40c., 90c., 5p. Coast scene and Clarence Peak, Fernando Poo; 15c., 45c., 1p. Niepan, Benito River.

(Des C. T. Esmenola. Photo)

1950 (23 Nov). AIR. Colonial Stamp Day. P 13×12½.
347	36	5p. yellow-brown	7·50	2·75

37 Hands and Native   38 Mt. Mioco

(Des J. Nadal del Val. Photo)

1950 (1 Dec). Native Welfare Fund. P 13×13½.
348	37	50c.+10c. ultramarine	45	45
349	–	1p.+25c. blue-green	19·00	5·25
350	–	6p.50+1p.65 brown-orange	4·25	2·40
348/350 Set of 3			21·00	7·25

(Des Nuñez de Celis. Photo)

1951 (1 Mar). AIR. As T **38**. P 12½×13.
351		25c. brownish yellow	20	20
352	38	50c. magenta	20	20
353	–	1p. green	20	20
354	–	2p. blue	30	20
355	38	3p.25 reddish violet	95	20
356	–	5p. sepia	8·25	4·00
357	–	10p. scarlet	35·00	14·00
351/357 Set of 7			41·00	17·00

Designs:—25c., 2p., 10p. Benito Rapids; 1p., 5p. Santa Isabel Bay.

E **38** Fernando Poo

(Des Nuñez de Celis. Photo)

1951 (1 Mar). EXPRESS LETTER. P 12½×13.
E358	E 38	25c. carmine	30	25

38a Woman and Dove   **39** Leopard

(Des T. Miciano. Recess)

1951 (22 Apr). AIR. Fifth Centenary of Birth of Isabella the Catholic. P 10.
358	38a	5p. blue	24·00	14·00

(Des A. Varas. Photo)

1951 (23 Nov). Colonial Stamp Day. P 13×12½.
359	39	5c.+5c. brown	55	45
360	–	10c.+5c. red-orange	60	45
361	–	60c.+15c. deep olive	1·20	95
359/361 Set of 3			2·10	1·70

40 Native and Map   41 Native Man

(Des T. Miciano. Photo)

1951 (5 Dec). International West African Conference. P 12½×13.
362	40	50c. orange	45	45
363	–	5p. indigo	8·50	1·90

(Des M. C. Gil. Photo)

1952 (10 Mar). P 12½×13.
364	41	5c. lake-brown	70	40
365	–	50c. blackish olive	70	40
366	–	5p. deep violet	3·75	1·90
364/366 Set of 3			4·50	2·40

42 *Crinum giganteum*   43 Ferdinand the Catholic   44 Brown-cheeked Hornbills

(Des R. L. Prieto. Photo)

1952 (1 June). Native Welfare Fund. P 13×12½.
367	42	5c.+5c. brown	60	40
368	–	50c.+10c. greenish black	60	40
369	–	2p.+30c. deep blue	2·75	2·10
367/369 Set of 3			3·50	2·50

(Des R. L. Prieto. Photo)

1952 (18 July). AIR. Fifth Centenary of Birth of Ferdinand the Catholic. P 13×12½.
370	43	5p. chocolate	33·00	16·00

(Des L. Esteban. Photo)

1952 (23 Nov). Colonial Stamp Day. P 13×12½.
371	44	5c.+5c. brown	50	50
372	–	10c.+5c. brown-purple	50	50
373	–	60c.+15c. deep green	1·00	1·00
371/373 Set of 3			1·80	1·80

45 Native Musician   46 Native Woman and Dove

(Des T. Miciano and G. Calvo. Photo)

1953 (1 July). Native Welfare Fund. T **45** and similar horiz design inscr "PRO INDIGENAS 1953". P 12½×13.
374	45	5c.+5c. brown-lake	50	50
375	–	10c.+5c. bright purple	50	50
376	45	15c. olive-brown	50	50
377	–	60c. brown	55	55
374/377 Set of 4			1·80	1·80

Design:—10, 60c. Musician facing right.

(Des T. Miciano and A. Varas. Photo)

1953 (5 Sept). T **46** and another vert design. P 13×12½.
378	46	5c. orange-red	50	20
379	–	10c. bright reddish purple	50	20
380	–	60c. bistre-brown	50	25
381	–	1p. slate-lilac	2·10	25
382	–	1p.90 greenish black	4·75	1·20
378/382 Set of 5			7·50	1·90

Design:—1p., 1p.90, Native drummer.

415

SPANISH GUINEA / Spanish Territories of the Gulf of Guinea

47 *Tragocephala nobilis* (longhorn beetle)

48 Hunting with Bow and Arrow

(Des R. L. Prieto and J. L. Garcia Ruiz de Medina. Photo)

1953 (23 Nov). Colonial Stamp Day. T **47** and similar vert design inscr "DIA DEL SELLO COLONIAL 1953". P 13×12½.

383	47	5c.+5c. deep blue	50	50
384	–	10c.+5c. bright reddish purple	50	50
385	47	15c. blackish green	50	50
386	–	60c. bistre-brown	55	55
383/386 Set of 4			1·80	1·80

Design:—10, 60c. African giant swallowtail (butterfly).

(Des R. A. Fabré and E. S. González. Photo)

1954 (10 June). Native Welfare Fund. T **48** and similar horiz design inscr "PRO-INDIGENAS 1954". P 12½×13.

387	48	5c.+5c. lake	50	50
388	–	10c.+5c. lilac	50	50
389	48	15c. deep green	50	50
390	–	60c. brown	55	55
387/390 Set of 4			1·80	1·80

Design:—10, 60c. Native hunting elephant with spear.

49 Turtle

50 M. Iradier y Bulfy

(Des T. Miciano and J. E. Matamala. Photo)

1954 (23 Nov). Colonial Stamp Day. T **49** and similar horiz design inscr "DIA DEL SELLO COLONIAL 1954". P 12½×13.

391	49	5c.+5c. orange-red	50	50
392	–	10c.+5c. reddish purple	50	50
393	49	15c. deep myrtle green	50	50
394	–	60c. reddish brown	55	55
391/394 Set of 4			1·80	1·80

Design:—10, 60c. Barbelled houndshark.

(Des T. Miciano. Photo)

1955 (18 Jan). Birth Centenary of Iradier (explorer). P 12½×13.

395	50	60c. red-brown	40	40
396		1p. deep slate-violet	3·25	3·25

51 Native Priest

52 Footballers

(Des F. J. Ontiveros and E. M. Jimeno, Photo)

1955 (1 June). Centenary of Apostolic Prefecture in Fernando Poo. T **51** and similar vert design. P 13×12½.

397	51	10c.+5c. bright purple	50	50
398	–	25c.+10c. violet ("Baptism")	50	50
399	51	50c. brown-olive	55	55
397/399 Set of 3			1·40	1·40

(Des T. Miciano. Photo)

1955–56. AIR. P 13×12½.

400	52	25c. violet-grey (20.4.56)	35	25
401		50c. brown-olive (20.4.56)	35	25
402		1p.50 brown (20.4.56)	1·40	35
403		4p. carmine-rose (20.4.56)	5·00	80
404		10p. yellowish green (1.7.55)	2·75	1·20
400/404 Set of 5			8·75	2·50

53 El Pardo Palace, Madrid

54 Moustached Monkeys

1955 (18 July). Treaty of Pardo, 1778. Photo. P 12½×13.

405	53	5c. olive-brown	50	50
406		15c. brownish lake	50	50
407		80c. deep myrtle-green	55	55
405/407 Set of 3			1·40	1·40

(Des M. Sanchez Algora and L. Estaban. Photo)

1955 (23 Nov). Colonial Stamp Day. T **54** and similar design inscr "DIA DEL SELLO COLONIAL 1955". P 12½×13 (horiz) or 13×12½ (vert).

408	54	5c.+5c. brown-lake and brown	80	80
409	–	15c.+5c. brown-black and lake	80	80
410	54	70c. greenish blue and deep grey-green	1·10	1·10
408/410 Set of 3			2·40	2·40

Design: Horiz—15c. Talapoin and young.

55 *Orquidea*

56 Arms of Santa Isabel

57 Grey Parrot

(Des J. Ruiz de Medina (T **55**), T. Miciano (others). Photo)

1956 (1 June). Native Welfare Fund. T **55** and similar vert design inscr "PRO-INDIGENAS 1956". P 13×12½.

411	55	5c.+5c. bronze green	50	50
412	–	15c.+5c. brown-ochre	50	50
413	55	20c. deep bluish green	50	50
414	–	50c. deep brown	55	55
411/414 Set of 4			1·80	1·80

Design:—15, 50c. *Strophantus kombe*.

1956 (23 Nov). Colonial Stamp Day. T **56** and similar design inscr "DIA DEL SELLO 1956". Photo. P 13×12½ or 12½×13 (15c.).

415	56	5c.+5c. lake-brown	50	50
416	–	15c.+5c. violet-grey	50	50
417	56	70c. yellow-green	55	55
415/417 Set of 3			1·40	1·40

Design: Horiz—15c. Arms of Bata and natives.

(Des T. Miciano (T **57**), M. S. Algora (15c.). Photo)

1957 (1 June). Native Welfare Fund. T **57** and similar horiz design inscr "PRO-INDIGENAS 1957". P 13×12½ (vert) or 12½×13 (horiz).

418	57	5c.+5c. brown-purple	50	50
419	–	15c.+5c. brown-ochre	50	50
420	57	70c. deep yellow-green	55	55
418/420 Set of 3			1·40	1·40

Design:—15c. Grey parrot in flight.

58 "Flight"

59 African Elephant and Calf

SPANISH GUINEA / Spanish Territories of the Gulf of Guinea

(Des T. Miciano. Photo)

1957 (19 Sept). AIR. 30th Anniv of Spain-Fernando Poo Flight by "Atlántida" Seaplane Squadron. P 13×12½.

| 421 | 58 | 25p. sepia and yellow-bistre | 16·00 | 3·25 |

(Des T. Miciano (T **59**), V. Algora (others). Photo)

1957 (23 Nov). Colonial Stamp Day. T **59** and similar design inscr "DIA DEL SELLO 1957". P 12½×13 (T **59**) or 13×12½ (others).

422	59	10c.+5c. magenta	50	50
423	–	15c.+5c. brown-ochre	50	50
424	59	20c. deep bluish green	50	50
425	–	70c. green	55	55
422/425 Set of 4			1·80	1·80

Design: Vert—15, 70c. Elephant trumpeting.

60 Doves and Arms of Valencia and Santa Isabel

61 Boxing

(Des T. Miciano. Photo)

1958 (6 Mar). "Aid for Valencia". P 12½×13.

426	60	10c.+5c. chestnut	50	50
427	–	15c.+10c. brown-ochre	50	50
428	–	50c.+10c. deep brown-olive	55	55
426/428 Set of 3			1·40	1·40

(Des T. Miciano (T **61**), V. S. Algora (10c., 80c., 2p., 3p.), J. Escuin (15c., 2p.30). Photo)

1958 (10 Apr). Sports. As T **61**. P 12½×13 (5c., 15c., 1p., 2p.30) or 13×12½ (10c., 80c., 2p., 3p.).

429	61	5c. chocolate	25	25
430	–	10c. chestnut	25	25
431	–	15c. yellow-brown	25	25
432	–	80c. green	25	25
433	61	1p. orange-red	25	25
434	–	2p. reddish purple	40	25
435	–	2p.30 deep lilac	55	35
436	–	3p. blue	65	40
429/436 Set of 8			2·50	2·00

Designs: Vert—10c., 2p. Basketball; 80c., 3p. Running. Horiz—15c., 2p.30, Long jumping.

62 Missionary holding Cross

63 African Monarchs (*Danaus chrysippus*)

(Des T. Miciano (T **62**), V. Urosa (others). Photo)

1958 (1 June). Native Welfare Fund. T **62** and similar vert design inscr "1883 PRO-INDIGENAS 1958". P 13×12½.

437	62	10c.+5c. deep chestnut	50	50
438	–	15c.+5c. brown-ochre	50	50
439	62	20c. deep bluish green	50	50
440	–	70c. green	55	55
437/440 Set of 4			1·80	1·80

Design:—15, 70c. The Crucifixion.

(Des T. Miciano (T **63**), R. Prieto (25c.), V. Urosa (50c.). Photo)

1958 (23 Nov). Colonial Stamp Day. T **63** and similar vert designs inscr "DIA DEL SELLO 1958". P 13×12½.

441		10c.+5c. brown-red	50	50
442		25c.+10c. reddish violet	50	50
443		50c.+10c. deep olive	55	55
441/443 Set of 3			1·40	1·40

Designs:—25c., 50c. Different views of butterflies on plants.

64 Digitalis

65 Boy on "Penny-farthing" Cycle

1959 (12 June). Child Welfare Fund. T **64** and similar vert design inscr "PRO-INFANCIA 1959". Photo. P 13×12½.

444	64	10c.+5c. deep brown-red	50	50
445	–	15c.+5c. brown-ochre	50	50
446	–	20c. deep bluish green	50	50
447	64	70c. green	55	55
444/447 Set of 4			1·80	1·80

Design:—15, 20c. Castor bean (*different designs*).

(Des T. Miciano (T **65**), M. Carrillo (20c.), E. Jimeno (50c.). Photo)

1959 (23 Nov). Colonial Stamp Day. T **65** and similar vert designs inscr "DIA DEL SELLO 1959". P 13×12½.

448		10c.+5c. brown-red	50	50
449		20c.+5c. deep bluish green	50	50
450		50c.+20c. deep olive	55	55
448/450 Set of 3			1·40	1·40

Designs:—20c. Racing cyclists; 50c. Winning cyclist.

On 30 July 1959 Spanish Guinea was divided into the two Spanish Overseas Provinces of Fernando Poo and Rio Muni (see under these headings).

417

Spanish Morocco

100 Céntimos = 1 Peseta

Morocco, which had been the Roman province of Mauretania, was conquered by Moslem invaders from the east in 710. Arab and Berber forces crossed into Spain in 711 and by 719 reached the Pyrenees. Moorish dynasties ruled much of Spain until 1212 and the Moors were not finally expelled from Granada, their last stronghold there, until 1492. A long period of warfare between rival dynasties in Morocco followed. Morocco shut itself in a mediaeval civilisation and the area where the sultan's rule was obeyed steadily decreased.

In the 19th century European powers began to cast acquisitive eyes on Morocco. A Spanish invasion took place in 1859-60 and in 1904 secret conventions provided for the partition of Morocco between Spain and France. Germany also claimed interests, until in 1911 these were given up in exchange for the acquisition of part of French Congo.

On 30 March 1912 the Sultan of Morocco was forced to accept a French protectorate over all the country except for a Spanish zone of protection in the north (established by a Franco-Spanish agreement of 27 November 1912), and Tangier which was given a special status. Stamps issued by the French protectorate are listed in Part 6 (*France*) of this catalogue.

Stamps of Spain overprinted

(3) (4) (5)

1914 (22 July).

		(a) Optd as T **3** but smaller (14½×2½ mm)		
42	38a	¼c. green (R.)	20	20
		(b) Optd with T **3**		
43	64	2c. black-brown (R.)	20	20
44		5c. deep green (R.)	40	35
45		10c. red (B.)	40	35
46		15c. bright violet (R.)	1·90	1·30
47		20c. grey-green (R.)	2·75	2·40
48		25c. blue (R.)	2·75	1·90
49		30c. blue-green (R.)	5·75	3·25
50		40c. pink (B.)	11·50	4·75
51		50c. slate-blue (R.)	7·50	2·40
52		1p. carmine-lake (B.)	7·50	4·75
53		4p. plum (R.)	36·00	34·00
54		10p. orange (B.)	55·00	50·00
		EXPRESS LETTER		
E55	E **53**	20c. red (R.)	6·25	3·00
42/E55 Set of 14			£120	£100

All values except the 15c. and 20c. postage exist with the overprint inverted and most values with it double. All values except the ¼c. exist with inverted "S".

1915–16. Optd with T **4**.

		(a) POSTAGE		
55	38a	¼c. green (R.)	60	30
56	64	2c. black-brown (R.)	30	30
57		5c. deep green (R.)	70	30
58		10c. red (B.)	60	30
59		15c. bright violet (R.)	85	30
60		20c. grey-green (R.)	2·20	30
61		25c. blue (R.)	2·40	45
62		30c. blue-green (R.)	2·50	55
63		40c. pink (B.)	3·75	55
64		50c. slate-blue (R.)	6·50	45
65		1p. carmine-lake (B.)	8·50	55
66		4p. plum (B.)	50·00	34·00
67		10p. orange (B.)	65·00	50·00
		(b) EXPRESS LETTER		
E68	E **53**	20c. red (B.)	5·00	2·50
55/E68 Set of 14			£130	80·00

All values except the express stamp exist with the overprint inverted; all except the 50c. and express stamp are known with it double; all except the ¼c. and express stamp exist with the first "R" of "PROTECTORADO" inverted; all except the ¼c. are known with "Ñ" omitted. There are numerous other errors.

1916–21. Optd with T **5**.

68	38a	¼c. green (R.)	1·80	40
69	66	1c. green (R.) (1921)	2·10	20
70	64	2c. black-brown (R.)	1·80	40
71		5c. green (R.)	7·50	40
72		10c. red (B.)	9·75	40
73		15c. orange (B.) (1920)	10·50	40
74		20c. bright violet (R.) (1921)	14·50	20
75		25c. blue (R.)	31·00	5·00
76		30c. green (R.)	41·00	33·00
77		40c. rose (B.) (1921)	36·00	95
78		50c. blue (R.) (1921)	19·00	45
79		1p. claret (B.) (1921)	44·00	3·50
80		4p. plum (R.) (1921)	65·00	19·00
81		10p. orange (B.) (1921)	£160	£140
68/81 Set of 14			£400	£180

The 5, 10 and 15c. and 10p. exist with overprint inverted and the 2, 5, 10, 25 and 50c. with it double.

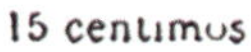

15 centimos 10 céntimos 10 cts.
(6) (7) (8)

1920.

(a) Nos. 60 and 62 bisected by horizontal perforation, and each half surch as T **6**, in red (prices are for complete stamps)

82	64	10c.+10c. on 20c. grey-green	5·75	2·75
83		15c.+15c. on 30c. blue-green	17·00	12·50

(b) No. E68, bisected by vertical perforation, and each half surch in black (prices are for complete stamps)

(i) With T **7**, vertically

84	E **53**	10c.+10c. on 20c. red	20·00	10·00

(ii) With T **7** and **8**

85	E **53**	10c.+10c. on 20c. red	£200	£120

(c) Telegraph stamps of Spain, 1912 (inscr "TELEGRAFOS"), with opt T **5**, authorized for use as postage stamps. P 13

86		5c. green	1·90	45
87		10c. blue	1·90	45
88		15c. lilac	1·90	60
89		30c. violet	3·25	55
		a. Bisected by perforation (15c.)		

(d) Postal Order stamps of Spain (inscr "GIRO") with opt T **4**, authorized for use as postage stamps. P 13½×13

91		5c. blue-green	4·75	1·90
92		10c. yellow-green	4·75	1·90

The 25c. red, 50c. orange, and 1p. lilac were also authorized for use as postage stamps, but as they represented rates for abroad, or on heavy letters and parcels, their use was small.

(9)

ZONA PROTECTORADO
ESPAÑOL

(10)

(e) Fiscals bisected and surch as in T **9**. P 11½

93		5c. on 5p. blue (R.)	11·50	2·30
94		5c. on 10p. green (R.)	65	20
95		10c. on 25p. grey-green (R.)	30	20
96		10c. on 50p. blue-grey (R.)	55	35
97		15c. on 100p. red (G.)	55	35
98		15c. on 500p. deep red (G.)	16·00	8·25
93/98 Set of 6			27·00	10·50

(f) Postage stamps with opt T **4**, bisected by diagonal or horizontal perforation, and used for half original values without further surch

99	64	Half of 2c. black-brown	—	14·00
100		Half of 30c. blue-green	—	14·00

1923–30. Optd as T **5**.

		(a) POSTAGE		
101	68	2c. deep yellow-green (R.) (1926)	1·00	20
102		5c. purple (R.)	1·00	20
103		10c. deep grey-green (R.) (1925)	4·50	20
		a. Deep green (R.) (1930)	7·50	20
105		15c. deep greenish blue (R.)	4·50	20
106		20c. violet (R.)	10·00	20

107		25c. carmine-red (B.) (1925)	20·00	2·00
108		40c. blue (R.)	20·00	6·50
109		50c. red-orange (B.) (1926)	50·00	11·50
110	69	1p. deep greenish slate (R.) (1926)	75·00	6·50

(b) EXPRESS LETTER

E111	E 53	20c. red (B.)	17·00	13·50
101/E111 *Set of 10*			£180	37·00

1926. Red Cross Fund. T **70** and similar vert types, optd with T **10**. Colours changed.

(a) POSTAGE

111		1c. reddish orange	11·00	11·00
112		2c. carmine	16·00	16·00
113		5c. sepia	5·50	5·50
114		10c. myrtle	5·50	5·50
115		15c. violet (V.)	1·00	1·00
116		20c. purple	1·00	1·00
117		25c. crimson	1·00	1·00
118		30c. olive-green	1·00	1·00
119		40c. ultramarine	20	20
120		50c. brown-lake	20	20
121		1p. orange-vermilion	20	20
122		4p. bistre	1·00	1·00
123		10p. violet	3·75	3·75

(b) EXPRESS LETTER

E124	E 77	20c. black and ultramarine	3·75	3·75
111/E124 *Set of 14*			46·00	46·00

11 Mosque of Alcazarquivir

12 Moorish Gateway, Larache

E **12** Moorish Courier

PROTECTORADO
MARRUECOS
(**13**)

(Des M. Bertuchi. Recess De La Rue)

1928–32. T **11**, **12** and similar designs. Without control figures. P 14.

(a) POSTAGE

124	11	1c. carmine-red ("Cs")	20	20
125		1c. carmine ("Ct") (1.10.32)	35	35
126		2c. violet	20	20
127		5c. blue	20	20
128		10c. green	20	20
129		15c. chestnut	45	20
130	12	20c. olive-green	45	20
131		25c. lake	45	20
132		30c. chocolate	1·80	20
133		40c. milky blue	2·50	20
134		50c. purple	4·75	20
135		1p. yellow-green	7·50	40
136		2p.50 bright purple	38·00	10·00
137		4p. ultramarine	33·00	6·25

(b) EXPRESS LETTER

E138	E **12**	20c. black	4·75	4·75
124/E138 *Set of 15*			85·00	21·00

Designs: Horiz—1p. Well at Alhucemas; 2p.50, Xauen; 4p. Tetuan.

1929. Seville and Barcelona Exhibitions. Nos. 502/14 of Spain optd in various horiz or vert settings as T **13**.

138	83	1c. turquoise-green (R.)	35	35
139	84	2c. yellow-green (R.)	35	35
140	–	5c. carmine-lake (B.)	35	35
141	–	10c. green (R.)	35	35
142	83	15c. turquoise-blue (R.)	35	35
143	84	20c. violet (R.)	35	35
144	83	25c. carmine (B.)	35	35
145	–	30c. blackish brown (B.)	95	95
146	–	40c. blue (B.)	95	95
147	84	50c. red-orange (B.)	95	95
148	–	1p. greenish slate (R.)	8·00	8·00
149	–	4p. claret (B.)	19·00	19·00
150	–	10p. brown (B.)	41·00	41·00
138/150 *Set of 13*			65·00	65·00

Spanish stamps with diagonal "MARRUECOS" overprint are listed under Spanish Post Offices in Tangier.

14 Xauen   **15** Market-place, Larache

(Des M. Bertuchi. Photo Waterlow)

1933–35. Pictorial designs as T **14/15**. Green control figures on back.

(a) P 14½×14 (vert) or 14×14½ (horiz)

151	14	1c. scarlet	20	20
152	–	2c. green	20	20
153	–	5c. magenta	20	20
154	–	10c. blackish green	40	40
155	–	15c. yellow	2·30	45
156	14	20c. greenish black	90	70
157	–	25c. scarlet	25·00	70
158	–	30c. brown-lake	9·25	50
159	15	40c. deep ultramarine	21·00	50
160		50c. red orange	55·00	13·00
161	–	1p. slate	23·00	50
162	–	2p.50 brown	38·00	13·00
163	–	4p. yellow-green	38·00	13·00
164	–	5p. black	50·00	13·00
151/164 *Set of 14*			£250	50·00

Designs: Horiz—2c., 1p. Xauen; 5c., 2p.50, Arcila; 25c., 5p. Sultan and bodyguard. Vert—10c., 30c. Tetuan; 15c., 4p. Alcazarquivir.

(b) New designs. P 13½ (1935)

165		25c. violet	1·30	35
166		30c. scarlet	21·00	35
167		40c. red-orange	10·50	45
168		50c. ultramarine	10·50	45
169		60c. blue-green	10·50	45
170		2p. red-brown	75·00	16·00
165/170 *Set of 6*			£120	16·00

Designs: Vert—25c., 40c., 60c. Wayside scene, Arcila. Horiz—30c., 50c., 2p. Forest, Ketama.

See also Nos. 177/83 and 213/32.

18-7-36

= 0'25 + 2'00 =

E **16** Moorish Courier

(**16**)

(Des M. Bertuchi. Photo Waterlow)

1935. EXPRESS LETTER. Green control figures on back. P 14½×14.

E171	E **16**	20c. vermilion	2·30	50

The 20c. sepia, as Type E **16**, lithographed, is an unissued printing made in Spain in 1940 in connection with a proposal that stamps for Morocco should be printed in Spain instead of in London.

1936. AIR. No. 157, surch with T **16**.

171		25c.+2p. on 25c. scarlet	32·00	9·75
		a. Surch in blue	75·00	33·00

🝔 **10 cts.** 🝔

(**17**)

1936. Nos. 131, 135/137 and E138 variously surch as T **17**.

172		1c. on 4p. ultramarine (B.)	35	20
173		2c. on 2p.50 bright purple (G.)	35	20
174		5c. on 25c. lake (R.)	20	20
175		10c. on 1p. yellow-green (G.)	12·50	5·75
176		15c. on 20c. black (B.)	10·00	3·25
172/176 *Set of 5*			21·00	8·50

SPANISH MOROCCO

(Des M. Bertuchi. Photo Waterlow)

1937 (1 June). Designs as T **14/15**. Without control figures. P 13½.

177	1c. green	20	20
178	2c. magenta	20	20
179	5c. orange	20	20
180	15c. violet	20	20
181	30c. scarlet	70	35
182	1p. ultramarine	7·25	45
183	10p. red-brown	£120	44·00
177/183	Set of 7	£120	41·00

MS183a 105×95 mm. Nos. 177/9 and 182: 1c., 2c., 5c., 1p. .... 21·00 21·00

MS183b 105×95 mm. Nos. 178/81: 2c., 5c., 15c., 30c. .... 21·00 21·00

Designs. Vert—1c., 15c., Caliph and Viziers; 30c. Tetuan; 1p. Arcila; 10p. Caliph on horseback. Horiz—2c. Bokoia; 6c. Alcazarquivir.

18 Legionaries

E **19** Moorish Courier

19 General Franco

(Des M. Bertuchi. Photo Waterlow)

1937 (17 July). First Anniv of Civil War As T **18** (inscr "17 JULIO 1936"). Without control figures. P 13½.

(a) POSTAGE

184	1c. grey blue	20	20
185	2c. red-brown	20	20
186	5c. magenta	20	20
187	10c. bright green	20	20
188	15c. blue	20	20
189	20c. maroon	20	20
190	25c. mauve	20	20
191	30c. red	20	20
192	40c. orange	20	20
193	50c. ultramarine	20	20
194	60c. dull green	20	20
195	1p. bright violet	20	20
196	2p. greenish blue	13·50	12·50
197	2p.50 black	13·50	12·50
198	4p. sepia	13·50	12·50
199	10p. black	13·50	12·50

(b) EXPRESS LETTER

E200	E **19**	20c. carmine	20	20
184/E200		Set of 17	50·00	47·00

Designs. Vert—1c. Sentry; 5c. Trooper; 10c. Volunteers; 15c. Colour bearer; 20c. A desert halt; 25c. Ifni mounted horsemen; 30c. Trumpeters; 40c. Cape Juby Camel Corps; 50c. Infantryman; 60c., 1p., 2p., 4p. Types of Sherifian Guards; 2p.50, Cavalryman. Horiz—10p. "Road to Victory".

1937–1939. Obligatory Tax for Disabled Soldiers. Photo. P 12½.

200	**19**	10c. sepia (1937)	60	20
201		10c. brown (1938)	60	20
202		10c. blue (1939)	60	20
200/202		Set of 3	1·60	55

Sheets (each 120×100 mm) containing blocks of four. Imperf (1939)

MS202a	sepia	4·75	2·75
MS202b	brown	4·75	2·75
MS202c	blue	4·75	2·75

20 Yellow-billed Stork over Mosque

E **21** Moorish Courier

(21)   (E 22)

(Des M. Bertuchi. Photo Waterlow)

1938 (1 July). AIR. As T **20** (airplanes or storks over various designs). P 13½.

203	5c. brown	20	20
204	10c. emerald-green	20	20
205	25c. scarlet	20	20
206	40c. blue	3·00	90
207	50c. magenta	20	20
208	75c. ultramarine	20	20
209	1p. sepia	20	20
210	1p.50 violet	90	65
211	2p. crimson-lake	65	20
212	3p. black	2·30	45
203/212	Set of 10	7·25	3·00

Designs: Vert—5c. Mosque de Baja, Tetuan; 25c. Straits of Gibraltar; 40c. Desert natives; 1p. Mounted postman; 1p.50, Farmers; 2p. Sunset; 3p. Shadow of airplane over city. Horiz—50c. Airplane over Tetuan; 75c. Larache.

(Des M. Bertuchi. Photo Waterlow)

1939 (1 May). Pictorial designs as T **14**. Without control figures. P 13½.

213	5c. orange	20	20
214	10c. bright green	20	20
215	15c. red-brown	55	20
216	20c. ultramarine	55	20
213/216	Set of 4	1·40	70

Designs: (inscr)—5c. "Carta de España"; 10c. "Carta de Marruecos"; 15c. "Larache"; 20c. "Tetuan".

1940. Pictorial designs as T **14** inscr "ZONA" on back. Photo. P 11½×11.

(a) POSTAGE

217	1c. brown	20	20
218	2c. brown-olive	20	20
219	5c. grey-blue	20	20
220	10c. magenta	20	20
221	15c. grey-green	20	20
222	20c. violet	20	20
223	25c. sepia	20	20
224	30c. yellow-green	20	20
225	40c. slate-green	2·10	20
226	45c. vermilion	85	20
227	50c. orange-brown	85	20
228	70c. light blue	85	20
229	1p. brown and indigo	2·75	20
230	2p.50 green and chocolate	32·00	5·50
231	5p. sepia and purple	2·75	35
232	10p. red-brown and olive-brown	28·00	10·50

(b) EXPRESS LETTER

E233	E **21**	25c. carmine-red	45	35
217/E233		Set of 17	65·00	17·00

Designs:—1c. Postman; 2c. Pillar box; 5c. Winter landscape; 10c. Alcazar street scene; 15c. Castle wall, Xauen; 20c. Palace sentry, Tetuan; 25c. Caliph on horseback; 30c. Market-place, Larache; 40c. Gateway, Tetuan; 45c. Gateway, Xauen; 50c. Street scene, Alcazarquivir; 70c. Post Office; 1p. Spanish War veterans; 2p.50, Flag bearers; 5p., 10p. Cavalry.

1940 (17 July). Fourth Anniv of Nationalist Uprising. Optd with T **21** (recess).

(a) POSTAGE. (Nos. 184/99)

233	1c. grey-blue	85	85
234	2c. red-brown	85	85
235	5c. magenta	85	85
236	10c. bright green	85	85
237	15c. blue	85	85
238	20c. maroon	85	85
239	25c. mauve	85	85
240	30c. red (P.)	85	85
241	40c. orange (P.)	1·40	1·40
242	50c. ultramarine	1·40	1·40
243	60c. dull green	1·40	1·40
244	1p. bright violet (P.)	1·40	1·40
245	2p. greenish blue (B.)	60·00	60·00
246	2p.50 black (P.)	60·00	60·00
247	4p. sepia (B.)	60·00	60·00
248	10p. black (C.)	60·00	60·00

(b) EXPRESS LETTER (No. E200). Surch also with Type E 22 (typo)

E249	E **19**	25c. on 20c. carmine	17·00	17·00
233/E249		Set of 17	£250	£250

420

SPANISH MOROCCO

22 Soldier on Horseback   **23** Larache

1941. Obligatory Tax for Disabled Soldiers. Litho. P 13½.
249	**22**	10c. green	5·00	20
250		10c. pink	5·00	20
251		10c. brown-red	5·00	20
252		10c. ultramarine	5·00	20
249/252		Set of 4	18·00	70

(Des M. Bertuchi. Litho Rieusset, Barcelona)

1941. As T **23** (views). P 11.
253	5c. brown and deep brown		20	20
	a. Perf 12½		30	20
254	10c. vermilion and carmine		20	20
255	15c. yellow-green and green		20	20
256	20c. light blue and ultramarine		60	20
257	40c. claret and purple		1·70	20
253/257	Set of 5		2·75	90

Designs: Vert—10c. Alcazarquivir; 15c. Larache market; 20c. Moorish house; 40c. Gateway, Tangier.
See also Nos. 263/4.

24 Mosque at Tangier   **25** General Franco

(Des M. Bertuchi. Litho Rieusset, Barcelona)

1942 (1 Apr). AIR. As T **24** (views). P 12½.
258	5c. deep blue	20	20
259	10c. orange-brown	20	20
260	15c. blackish green	20	20
261	90c. carmine-rose	20	20
262	5p. black	1·10	60
258/262	Set of 5	1·70	1·30

Designs: Vert—5c. Atlas mountain landscape; 15c. Velez fortress; 90c. Sanjurjo harbour; 5p. Straits of Gibraltar.

1942. As T **23**. P 12½.
263	10c. deep blue (Alcazarquivir)	20	20
264	40c. purple-brown (Larache market)	75·00	40

1943. Obligatory Tax for Disabled Soldiers. Litho. P 10.
265	**25**	10c. grey	10·50	20
266		10c. slate-blue	10·50	20
267		10c. grey-brown	10·50	20
268		10c. pale violet	10·50	20
265/268		Set of 4	39·00	70

See also Nos. 283/4 and 295/6.

26 Homeward Bound   **27** Dyers

(Des M. Bertuchi. Litho Rieusset, Barcelona)

1944 (2 Oct). As T **26** (agricultural designs). P 12½.
269	1c. light blue and chocolate	20	20
270	2c. light green and slate-green	20	20
271	5c. blackish green and chocolate	20	20
272	10c. red-orange and bright ultramarine	20	20
273	15c. light green and slate-green	20	20
274	20c. black and claret	20	20
275	25c. chocolate and light blue	20	20
276	30c. bright ultramarine and yellow-green	20	20
277	40c. claret and chocolate	20	20
278	50c. red-brown and bright ultramarine	55	20
279	75c. bright ultramarine and yellow-green	75	20
280	1p. chocolate and bright ultramarine	75	20
281	2p.50 bright ultramarine and black	8·75	3·25
282	10p. grey-black and salmon	14·50	8·50
269/282	Set of 14	24·00	12·50

Designs (35½×20 mm):—1c., 30c. Ploughing; 2c., 40c. Harvesting; 10c., 75c. Threshing; 15c., 1p. Vegetable garden; 20c., 2p.50, Gathering oranges; 25c., 10p. Shepherd and flock; 50c. T **26**.

1945. Obligatory Tax for Disabled Soldiers. As Nos. 265/8, but new colours. Photo. P 12.
283	**25**	10c. brown and magenta	12·50	20
284		10c. deep green and orange	12·50	20

(Des M. Bertuchi. Litho Rieusset, Barcelona)

1946 (Mar). As T **27** (craftsmen). Black control letter "Z" in circle on back. P 12½ (40c.) or 10 (others).
285	1c. brown and violet	30	20
286	2c. slate-violet and deep green	30	20
287	10c. ultramarine and red-orange	30	20
288	15c. green and blue	30	20
289	25c. blue and green	30	20
290	40c. brown and deep blue	30	20
291	45c. carmine and black	75	20
292	1p. deep blue and blackish green	1·00	20
293	2p.50 deep green and red-orange	2·75	70
294	10p. grey-black and deep blue	15·00	2·75
285/294	Set of 10	19·00	4·50

Designs:—1c., 10c., 25c. Potters; 15c., 45c. T **27**; 40c. Blacksmiths; 1p. Cobblers; 2p.50, Weavers; 10p. Metal workers.

1946. Obligatory Tax for Disabled Soldiers. As Nos. 265/8, but new colours. Litho. P 12.
295	**25**	10c. brown and ultramarine	12·50	20
296		10c. lilac and grey-black	12·50	20

28 Sanatorium   **29** Sanatorium

1946 (1 Sept). Anti-Tuberculosis Fund. As T **28**. Litho. P 11½×10½ or 10.
297	10c. green and red	30	20
298	25c. brown and red	30	20
299	25c.+5c. violet and red	30	20
300	50c.+10c. blue and red	40	20
301	90c.+10c. grey-brown and red	95	55
297/301	Set of 5	2·00	1·20

Designs: Vert—10c. Emblem and arabesque ornamentation; 25c.+5c. Mountain roadway; 50c.+10c. Fountain; 90c.+10c. Wayfarers.

1947 (1 Sept). Anti-Tuberculosis Fund. As T **29**. Litho. P 10.
302	10c. blue and red	30	20
303	25c. chocolate and red	30	20
304	25c.+5c. lilac and red	30	20
305	50c.+10c. blue and red	35	30
306	90c.+10c. sepia and red	1·00	75
302/306	Set of 5	2·00	1·50

Designs: Vert—10c. Emblem, mosque and palm tree; 25c.+5c. Hospital ward; 50c.+10c. Nurse and children; 90c.+10c. Arab swordsman.

30 Goods Train

(Des M. Bertuchi. Litho Rieusset, Barcelona)

1948 (1 Jan). As T **30** (forms of Transport and Commerce). Inscr "Z" in circle on back. P 10.
307	2c. sepia and violet	30	20
308	5c. violet and claret	30	20
309	15c. blue-green and blue	30	20
310	25c. grey-green and black	30	20
311	35c. grey-black and blue	30	20
312	50c. violet and vermilion	30	20

421

SPANISH MOROCCO

313	70c. light blue and deep green	30	20
314	90c. grey-green and cerise	30	20
315	1p. violet and blue	80	45
316	2p.50 grey-green and brown-purple	2·20	45
317	10p. blue and black	4·75	1·80
307/317 Set of 11		9·25	4·00

Designs:—5, 35c. Road transport; 15, 70c. Urban market; 25, 90c. Rural market; 50c; 1p. Camel caravan; 2p.50, Type **30**; 10p. *Arango* (freighter) at quay.

31 Emblem **32** Herald **33** Market Day

(Des M. Bertuchi. Litho Rieusset, Barcelona)

1948 (1 Oct). Anti-Tuberculosis Fund. As T **31**/2 (inscr "PRO TUBERCULOSOS"). P 10.

318	10c. emerald-green and red	30	20
319	25c. blue-green and red	2·20	1·10
320	50c.+10c. purple and red	30	20
321	90c.+10c. black and red	1·70	65
322	2p.50+50c. sepia and red	13·00	4·50
323	5p.+1p. violet and red	19·00	8·75
318/323 Set of 6		33·00	14·00

Designs: Vert—25c. Aeroplane over Sanatorium; 90c. Arab swordsman; 2p.50, Natives sitting in the sun; 5p. Aeroplane over Ben Karrich.

(Des M. Bertuchi. Litho Rieusset, Barcelona)

1949 (1 Jan). AIR. As T **33** (views). P 10.

324	5c. green and brown-purple	40	20
325	10c. magenta and black	40	20
326	30c. grey-green and ultramarine	40	20
327	1p.75 ultramarine and vermilion	40	20
328	3p. black and blue	40	20
329	4p. cerise and blackish green	85	20
330	6p.50 brown and green	2·50	30
331	8p. blue and magenta	4·25	75
324/331 Set of 8		8·50	2·00

Designs:—5c., 1p.75, Straits of Gibraltar; 10c., T **33**; 30c., 4p. Kebira Fortress; 6p.50, Arrival of the mail plane; 8p. Galloping horseman.

34 Caliph on Horse-back **35** Emblem

(Des M. Bertuchi. Photo Rieusset, Barcelona)

1949 (15 May). Caliph's Wedding Celebrations. T **34** and similar type inscr "15 MAYO-15 JUNTO 1949/BODA DE S.A.I. JALIFA".

(a) POSTAGE. P 10

| 332 | **34** | 50c.+10c. bright carmine | 40 | 20 |

(b) AIR. inscr "CORREO AEREO". P 11

| 333 | | 1p.+10c. greenish black | 1·10 | 40 |

Design:—1p. Wedding crowds in Palace grounds.

CONTROL NUMBERS. Nos. 334 to 429, except Nos. 398/9, and the corresponding Express Letter stamps have black or grey control numbers on the back.

(Des M. Bertuchi. Litho Rieusset, Barcelona)

1949 (1 Oct). Anti-Tuberculosis Fund. As T **35**. P 10.

334	5c. yellow-green and red	30	20
335	10c. violet-blue and red	30	20
336	25c. black and red	75	30
337	50c.+10c. brown and red	45	20
338	90c.+10c. green and red	1·40	30
334/338 Set of 5		3·00	1·10

Designs: Vert—10c. Road to recovery; 25c. Palm tree and tower; 50c. Flag and followers; 90c. Moorish horseman.

36 Postman, 1890 E **37** Air Mail, 1935 **37** Morabito

(Des M. Bertuchi. Litho Rieusset, Barcelona)

1950 (15 Feb). 75th Anniv of Universal Postal Union. T **36** and similar vert designs. P 11.

(a) POSTAGE

339	**36**	5c. ultramarine and purple-brown	30	20
340	–	10c. grey-brown and ultramarine	30	20
341	–	15c. emerald-green and blackish green	30	20
342	–	35c. black and mauve	30	20
343	–	45c. bright purple and carmine	30	20
344	**36**	50c. purple-brown and emerald-green	30	20
345	–	75c. ultramarine and deep blue	30	20
346	**36**	90c. carmine and blackish green	30	20
347	–	1p. grey-green and purple-brown	30	20
348	–	1p.50 ultramarine and carmine	75	20
349	–	5p. purple-brown and black	1·50	20
350	–	10p. ultramarine and mauve	40·00	28·00

Designs:—5, 50c. Type **38**; 10c., 1p. Hunters and hounds; 5p. Fishermen; 10p. Carabo (fishing boat).

(b) EXPRESS LETTER

| E351 | E **37** | 25c. black and rose-carmine | 40·00 | 28·00 |
| 339/E351 Set of 13 | | | 75·00 | 50·00 |

Designs:—10, 45c., 1p. Mounted postman; 15c., 1p.50, Mail coach; 35, 75c., 5p. Mail van; 10p. Steam mail train.

(Des M. Bertuchi. Litho Rieusset, Barcelona)

1950 (1 Oct). Anti-Tuberculosis Fund. Vert designs as T **37**. P 10.

351	5c. black and red	30	20
352	10c. blue-green and red	55	20
353	25c. blue and red	1·40	40
354	50c.+10c. brown and red	55	20
355	90c.+10c. green and red	1·40	40
351/355 Set of 5		3·75	1·30

Designs:—5c. Arab horseman; 10c. Fort; 25c. Sanatorium; 50c. Gathering at Fountain of Life.

38 Hunting **39** Emblem

(Des M. Bertuchi. Litho Rieusset, Barcelona)

1951 (1 Jan). Horiz designs as T **38**. P 10½×10.

356	5c. magenta and brown	30	20
357	10c. grey and carmine	30	20
358	50c. sepia and green	30	20
359	1p. claret and bluish violet	85	20
360	5p. bluish violet and deep claret	1·30	20
361	10p. deep claret and grey-green	4·50	55
356/361 Set of 6		6·75	1·40

(Des M. Bertuchi. Litho Rieusset, Barcelona)

1951 (1 Oct). Anti-Tuberculosis Fund. As T **39** (vert designs inscr "PRO TUBERCULOSOS 1951"). P 12.

362	5c. green and carmine	20	20
363	10c. violet-blue and carmine	20	20
364	25c. black and carmine	75	50
365	50c.+10c. chocolate and carmine	20	20
366	90c.+10c. pale blue and carmine	35	20
367	1p.+5p. slate-blue and carmine	10·00	4·00
368	1p.10+25c. blackish brown Er carmine	3·75	2·30
362/368 Set of 7		14·00	6·75

Designs: Vert—10c. Natives and children; 25c. Airplane over Nubes; 50c. Moorish horsemen; 90c. Riverside fortress; 1p. Brig Heman Cones; 1p.10, Airpane over caravan.

SPANISH MOROCCO

40 Mounted Riflemen

E **41** Moorish Courier

(Des M. Bertuchi. Litho Rieusset, Barcelona)

1952 (15 Mar). Horiz designs as T **40**. P 11.

(a) POSTAGE

369	5c. lake-brown and deep blue	20	20
370	10c. magenta and sepia	20	20
371	15c. emerald and black	20	20
372	20c. reddish purple and deep green	20	20
373	25c. light blue and scarlet	20	20
374	35c. orange and grey-olive	20	20
375	45c. pale scarlet and scarlet	20	20
376	50c. deep green and rose-red	20	20
377	75c. bright blue and purple	20	20
378	90c. reddish purple and violet-blue	20	20
379	1p. lake-brown and deep blue	20	20
380	5p. blue and scarlet	1·70	35
381	10p. black and green	2·75	50

(b) EXPRESS LETTER

E382	E **41**	25c. carmine and crimson	20	20
369/E382 Set of 14			6·25	3·00

Designs:—10c. Grooms leading horses; 15c. Parade of horsemen; 20c. Peasants on highway; 25c. Monastic procession; 35c. Native band; 45c. Moorish tribesmen; 50c. Natives overlooking roof tops; 75c. Inside a tea-house; 90c. Wedding procession; 1p. Pilgrims on horseback; 5p. Storyteller and audience; 10p. Natives talking.

41 Road to Tetuan

42 Natives at Prayer

(Des M. Bertuchi. Photo Rieusset, Barcelona)

1952 (1 Sept). AIR. Tetuan Postal Museum Fund. T **41** and similar horiz designs. P 11.

382	2p. blue and black	40	20
383	4p. scarlet and black	75	20
384	8p. deep green and black	1·20	25
385	16p. purple-brown and black	7·25	1·40
382/385 Set of 4		8·75	1·80

Designs:—4p. Moors watching airplane; 8p. Horseman and airplane; 16p. Shadow of airplane over Tetuan.

(Des M. Bertuchi. Photo Rieusset, Barcelona)

1952 (1 Oct). Anti-Tuberculosis Fund. T **42** and similar vert designs. P 11.

386	5c. grey-green and carmine-red	70	65
387	10c. sepia and carmine-red	70	65
388	25c. blue and carmine-red	1·40	85
389	50c.+10c. black and carmine-red	70	65
390	60c.+25c. grey-green and carmine-red	2·75	1·40
391	90c.+10c. brown-purple & carmine-red	2·75	1·40
392	1p.10+25c. reddish violet & carm-red	9·00	3·50
393	5p.+2p. black and carmine-red	20·00	10·00
386/393 Set of 8		34·00	17·00

Designs: Vert—10c. Beggars outside doorway; 25c. Airplane over cactus; 50c. Natives on horseback; 60c. Airplane over palms; 90c. Hilltop fortress; 1p.10 Airplane over agaves; 5p. Mounted warrior.

43 Sidi Saidi

(**44**)   (**45**)   **46**

(Des M. Bertuchi. Photo Rieusset, Barcelona)

1953 (15 Mar). AIR. T **43** and similar vert designs showing aeroplane over views. P 11.

394	35c. crimson and blue	20	20
395	60c. deep green and carmine-lake	20	20
396	1p.10 black and blue	25	20
397	4p.50 brown and carmine-lake	95	35
394/397 Set of 4		1·40	85

Designs:—35c. Carabo (fishing boat); 1p.10, La Yunta (ploughing); 4p.50, Fortress, Xauen.

1953 (1 Sept). AIR. No. *208* surch.

398	**44**	50c. on 75c. ultramarine	45	20
399	**45**	50c. on 75c. ultramarine	45	20

(Des M. Bertuchi. Photo Rieusset, Barcelona)

1953 (1 Oct). Anti-Tuberculosis Fund. Vert designs as T **32**, but inscr "PRO TUBERCULOSOS 1953". P 9½ or 10.

400	5c. bluish green and cerise	35	30
401	10c. purple and cerise	35	30
402	25c. green and cerise	1·60	85
403	50c.+10c. violet and cerise	35	30
404	60c.+25c. bistre-brown and cerise	3·75	1·60
405	90c.+10c. greenish black and cerise	1·10	55
406	1p.10+25c. chocolate and cerise	6·25	2·75
407	5p.+2p. deep blue and cerise	25·00	12·50
400/407 Set of 8		35·00	17·00

Designs:—5c. Herald; 10c. Moorish horseman; 25c. Aeroplane over Ben Karrich; 50c. Mounted warrior; 60c. Aeroplane over sanatorium; 90c. Moorish horseman; 1p.10, Aeroplane over sea; 5p. Arab swordsman.

(Des M. Bertuchi. Litho Rieusset, Barcelona)

1953 (15 Nov). P 10.

408	**46**	5c. scarlet	20	20
409		10c. grey-green	20	20

47 Water-carrier

E **48** Moorish Courier

(Des M. Bertuchi. Photo Rieusset, Barcelona)

1953 (15 Dec). 25th Anniv of First Pictorial Stamps of Spanish Morocco. T **47** and similar vert designs inscr "1928 1953". P 10.

(a) POSTAGE

410	35c. purple and green	45	20
411	50c. bluish green and vermilion	45	20
412	90c. orange and deep blue	45	20
413	1p. green and deep olive-brown	45	20
414	1p.25 magenta and slate-green	45	20
415	2p. blue and purple	70	25
416	2p.50 orange and deep grey-green	1·80	25
417	4p.50 deep bluish green and magenta	9·50	60
418	10p. black and green	12·50	1·40

(b) EXPRESS LETTER

E419	E **48**	25c. magenta and deep blue	25	20
410/E419 Set of 10			24·00	3·25

Designs:—35c., 1p.25, Mountain women; 50c., 2p.50, T **47**; 90c., 2p. Mountain tribesmen; 1p., 4p.50, Veiled Moorish women; 10p. Arab dignitary.

(Des M. Bertuchi. Photo Rieusset, Barcelona)

1954 (1 Nov). Anti-Tuberculosis Fund. Vert designs as T **32** inscr "PRO TUBERCULOSOS 1954". P 10.

419	5c. turquoise-green and cerise	25	25
420	5c.+5c. purple and cerise	25	25
421	10c. sepia and cerise	25	25
422	25c. blue and cerise	25	25
423	50c.+10c. deep green and cerise	95	70
424	5p.+2p. black and cerise	12·50	7·75
419/424 Set of 6		13·00	8·50

Designs:—5c. (419), Convent; 5c. (420), White stork on tower; 10c. Moroccan family; 25c. Airplane over Spanish coast; 50c. Father and child; 5p. Chapel.

48 Saida Gate   E **49** Tangier Gate   **49** Celebrations

(Des M. Bertuchi. Litho Rieusset, Barcelona)
1955 (1 Feb). Views as T **48**. P 11.
(a) POSTAGE

425	–	15c. emerald and black	20	20
426	48	25c. purple-brown and black	20	20
427	–	80c. bright blue and black	20	20
428	48	1p. magenta and black	25	20
429	–	15p. deep turquoise-green and black	3·75	1·40

(b) EXPRESS LETTER

E430	E **49**	2p. reddish violet and black	20	20
425/E430 *Set of 6*			4·25	2·20

Designs: Vert—15c., 80c. Queen's Gate; 15p. Ceuta Gate.

(Des M. Bertuchi. Recess (15p.), photo (others) Govt Ptg Wks, Madrid)
1955 (8 Nov). Thirtieth Anniv of Caliph's Accession to the Throne. T **49** and similar veil' designs inscr "1925 1955". P 13×12½.

430	**49**	15c. brown-olive and yellow-brown	40	40
431	–	25c. lake and purple	40	40
432	–	30c. slate-green and brown-black	40	40
433	**49**	70c. green and deep bluish green	40	40
434	–	80c. yellow-brown and brown-olive	40	40
435	–	1p. red-brown and deep blue	40	40
436	**49**	1p.80 blackish violet and black	40	40
437	–	3p. grey and blue	40	40
438	–	5p. brown and blackish blue-green	3·25	1·50
439	–	15p. green and red-brown	8·00	5·00
430/439 *Set of 10*			13·00	8·75

Designs:—25c., 80c., 3p. Caliph's portrait; 30c., 1p., 5p. Procession; 15p. Coat-of-arms.

The independence of Morocco was recognised by Spain on 7 April 1956 and the Spanish protectorate then terminated. Ceuta and Melilla remained under Spanish sovereignty. Stamps of independent Morocco are listed in Part 13 (*Africa since Independence F-M*) of this catalogue.

Spanish Post Offices In Morocco and Tangier

100 Céntimos = 1 Peseta

A. MOROCCO

There were Spanish Post Offices in Arzila, Casablanca, Larache, Mazagan, Mogador, Rabat, Saffi, Tangier and Tetuan. From 1867 to 1903 unoverprinted Spanish stamps were used. Stamps of 1860 can be found cancelled with Army Post Office marks although military post was free.

Stamps of Spain overprinted

(1)   (2)

1903–09. Optd with T 1.

(a) Thick yellowish paper

1	**38a**	¼c. green (R.)	3·75	2·40

(b) Ordinary white paper (1909)

2	**38a**	¼c. green (R)	70	35

1903–09. Optd with T 2.

3	**52**	2c. brown (R.)	1·70	1·70
4		5c. deep green (R.) (1903)	1·90	90
		a. Opt in blue	80·00	70·00
5		10c. rose-red (B.) (1903)	2·50	35
6		15c. violet (R.)	3·25	95
7		20c. olive-black (R.)	12·50	4·50
8		25c. blue (R.) (1903)	1·00	95
9		30c. bluish green (R.)	7·50	4·50
10		40c. rose (R.)	13·50	7·50
11		50c. greenish blue (R.)	7·50	7·25
		a. Error of colour. Deep green (R.)	£550	
12		1p. claret (B.)	28·00	10·50
13		4p. plum (R.)	65·00	18·00
14		10p. orange (B.)	38·00	45·00
3/14 *Set of 12*			£160	90·00

All values exist with "L" omitted and some values with overprint inverted or double.

1908. Handstamped "TETUAN" in black, blue or violet.

15	**38a**	¼c. green	14·50	5·75
16	**52**	2c. brown	60·00	19·00
17		5c. deep green	75·00	33·00
18		10c. rose-red	80·00	36·00
19		15c. violet	80·00	36·00
20		20c. olive-black	£250	£200
21		25c. blue	£120	60·00
22		30c. bluish green	£275	£110
23		40c. olive-bistre	£375	£200
15/23 *Set of 9*			£1200	£625

1908. Nos. 2/5 and 7/8 handstamped as above.

24	**38a**	¼c. green	24·00	15·00
25	**52**	2c. brown	£200	£110
26		5c. deep green	£190	60·00
27		10c. rose-red	£190	60·00
28		20c. olive-black	£425	£200
29		25c. blue	£160	60·00
24/29 *Set of 6*			£1100	£450

1909–10. Optd with T **2**.

30	**64**	2c. black-brown (R.)	1·60	40
31		5c. deep green (R.)	6·25	40
		a. Opt inverted	80·00	70·00
32		10c. red (B.)	8·25	40
		a. Opt inverted	70·00	55·00
33	**64**	15c. bright violet (R.)	13·00	1·00
34		20c. grey-green (R.)	25·00	1·60
35		25c. blue (R.)	£160	
36		30c. blue-green (R.)	8·50	1·00
37		40c. pink (B.)	8·50	1·00
38		50c. slate-blue (R.)	13·50	12·50

39		1p. carmine-lake (B.)	31·00	25·00
40		4p. plum (R.)	£140	
41		10p. orange (B.)	£140	
30/34, 36/39 Set of 9			£100	39·00

The 25c., 4p. and 10p. were not issued. All values exist with "L" omitted and some values with overprint inverted or double.

By a Franco-Spanish agreement of 27 November 1912, a Spanish protectorate was established in the north of Morocco (see Spanish Morocco). After the appearance of Nos. 45/54 for the Spanish Protectorate in 1914, the use of Nos. 30/41 was restricted to Tangier.

For other stamps of this type with the same overprint, see under Spanish Post Offices in Tangier.

B. TANGIER

The first Spanish Post Office in Tangier was established in 1861.

Tangier was given a special status, outside the protectorates, by the Franco-Spanish agreement of 27 November 1912. The Tangier Convention, ratified by the U.K., France and Spain on 14 May 1924, provided for government of Tangier by an international commission.

Nos. 30/41 of Spanish Post Offices in Morocco were exclusively used in Tangier from 27 November 1914.

Stamps of Spain overprinted

1921–27. Optd with T **2** of Spanish Post Offices in Morocco ("CORREO ESPAÑOL MARRUECOS").

1	66	1c. green (R.) (1927)	30	20
2	64	2c. bistre (359) (Fl.) (1927)	£500	
3		15c. yellow (B.)	2·00	20
4		20c. bright violet (R.)	3·25	20

1923–33. Optd as above.

5	68	2c. deep yellow-green (R.) (1928)	7·75	25
6		5c. purple (B.)	7·75	25
7		5c. carmine (Bk.)(1928)	7·75	25
8		10c. deep grey-green (R.)	9·50	25
		a. Deep green (R.) (1928)	9·50	25
10		20c. violet (R.) (1926)	14·00	2·75
11		50c. red-orange (R.) (1930)	65·00	19·00
12	69	10p. brown (B.) (1933)	4·25	9·75
5/12 Set of 7			£100	29·00

```
CORREO ESPAÑOL         TANGER       MARRUECOS
   TANGER
     (1)                 (2)            (3)
```

1926. Red Cross Fund T **70** and similar vertical types, optd with T **1**. Colours changed.

(a) POSTAGE

13		1c. reddish orange	10·50	10·50
14		2c. carmine	10·50	10·50
15		5c. sepia	5·00	5·00
16		10c. myrtle	5·00	5·00
17		15c. violet (V.)	1·90	1·90
18		20c. purple	1·90	1·90
19		25c. crimson	1·90	1·90
20		30c. olive-green	1·90	1·90
21		40c. ultramarine	40	40
22		50c. brown-lake	40	40
23		1p. orange-vermilion	95	95
24		4p. bistre	95	95
25		10p. violet	5·00	5·00

(b) EXPRESS LETTER

E26	E **77**	20c. black and ultramarine	5·00	5·00
13/E26 Set of 14			46·00	46·00

POSTAL UNION CONGRESS STAMPS.—Two hundred sets of T **66, 68, 69** and E **89** of Spain in the following values, and overprinted with type **2** of Spanish Post Offices in Morocco in the colours indicated, were presented in booklets to delegates to the Ninth Postal Union Congress held in London, 1929, but were otherwise unissued. All except the 1c. and 2c. are numbered on the back A, 000.000. 1c. (B.), 2c. (B.), 5c. purple (R.), 5c. crimson (B.), 10c. green (B.), 15c. (R.), 20c. (B.), 25c. (Die I) (B.), 30c. (R.), 40c. (R.), 50c. (B.), 1p. (R.), 4p. (B.), 10p. (B.), 20c. (No. E522) (B.).

1929. Seville and Barcelona Exhibitions. Nos. 504/14 optd as T **2** horizontally (T **83/4**) or sideways (others).

27	–	5c. carmine-lake (B.)	40	40
28	–	10c. green (R.)	40	40
29	83	15c. turquoise-blue (R.)	40	40
30	84	20c. violet (R.)	40	40
31	83	25c. carmine (B.)	40	40
32	–	30c. blackish brown (R.)	40	40
33	–	40c. blue (R.)	1·10	1·10
34	84	50c. red-orange (B.)	1·10	1·10
35	–	1p. greenish slate (R.)	11·50	11·50
36	–	4p. claret (R.)	32·00	32·00
37	–	10p. brown (R.)	46·00	46·00
27/37 Set of 11			85·00	85·00

1930–32. King Alfonso XIII type optd with T **2** of Spanish Post Offices in Morocco.

38	97	10c. yellow-green (R.)	3·75	55
39		15c. blue-green (R.) (1932)	£190	2·00
40		20c. bright violet (R.)	4·25	85
41		30c. deep lake (B.) (1931)	4·50	2·00
42		40c. deep blue (I) (1932)	17·00	11·00
38/42 Set of 5			£200	15·00

1933. Stamps without control figures optd with T **3**.

(a) Imperf

43	143	1c. blue-green	20	20

(b) P 11½

44	143	2c. chestnut	20	20
45	127	5c. sepia	20	20
46	128	10c. yellow-green	20	20
47	130	15c. blue-green	20	20
48	127	20c. violet	20	20
49	132	25c. deep lake	20	20
50	133	30c. carmine	75·00	9·25
51	138	40c. deep ultramarine	40	20
52	130	50c. orange	1·00	20
53	138	60c. yellow-green	1·00	20
54	142	1p. black	1·00	40
55	–	4p. magenta	2·75	3·75
56	–	10p. brown	3·75	9·25
43/56 Set of 14			80·00	22·00

1933. EXPRESS LETTER. Optd with T **3**. P 10.

E57	E **145**	20c. red	1·80	55

During the Spanish Civil War, 1936–39, two Spanish post offices were open in Tangier. One was controlled by the Nationalist régime and the other by the Republican government in Madrid. Nos. 58/125 were issued by the Republican post office until it was taken over by the Nationalists in 1940.

```
TANGER        Correo      Correo
              Español     Español
               Tanger     Tanger
  (4)           (5)
```

1937–38. Optd with T **4**.

(a) Imperf

58	143	1c. blue-green	60	20

(b) P 11½

59	143	2c. chestnut	60	20
60	127	5c. sepia (R.)	60	20
61	128	10c. yellow-green	60	20
62	130	15c. blue-green (R.)	70	20
63	127	20c. violet (R.)	70	65
64	132	25c. deep lake	70	65
65	136	30c. carmine	70	20
66	138	40c. deep ultramarine	1·90	90
		a. Perf 14	9·50	
67	130	50c. orange	5·50	90
68	142	1p. black	10·00	5·00
69	–	4p. magenta	£375	
70	–	10p. brown	£375	

1938. Optd as T **5**.

(a) Reading up

71	143	5c. brown (R.)	2·00	1·00
		a. Opt reading down	2·40	1·90
72		10c. yellow-green (R.)	2·00	1·00
		a. Opt reading down	3·25	2·00
73		15c. blue-green (R.)	2·00	1·00
		a. Opt reading down	2·40	1·90
74		20c. violet (R.)	2·00	60
		a. Opt reading down	2·40	2·40
75		25c. magenta (B.)	2·00	60
76		30c. carmine (B.)	7·50	3·50
		a. Opt reading down	19·00	14·00
77	160a	40c. rose (B.)	3·50	1·70
78		45c. carmine (B.)	1·40	40
79		50c. blue (R.)	1·40	40
80		60c. blue (R.)	3·50	1·70

SPANISH POST OFFICES IN MOROCCO AND TANGIER / Tangier

(b) Horiz

81	**145**	2p. blue (780) (B.)		23·00	9·50
		a. Opt inverted		85·00	
82	–	4p. magenta (768) (B.)		23·00	9·50
		a. Opt inverted		70·00	
71/82 *Set of 12*				65·00	28·00

The 25c. and 40c. to 4p. exist with double overprint. All values except the 2p. exist without accent in "Tanger" and the 5c. to 20c. exist with "Tanget" for "Tanger".

CORREO AÉREO

Correo Aéreo   CORREO   AÉREO

TÁNGER   TÁNGER   TÁNGER
(6) (Lines 10½ mm apart)   (7)   (8) (Lines 16½ mm apart)

1939. AIR. Optd locally from plates made in Paris.

(a) With T 6

83	**143**	25c. magenta		1·10	55
		a. "aÉREO"		8·50	2·75
		b. Lines 13 mm apart		4·25	4·25
		c. Opt inverted		12·50	12·50
84	**160a**	50c. blue		1·10	55
		a. "aÉREO"		8·50	3·00
		b. Lines 13 mm apart		4·25	4·25
		c. Opt inverted		12·50	12·50

(b) With T 7

85	**145**	2p. blue (780)		9·00	3·25
		a. "aÉREO"		47·00	47·00
		b. Lines 13 mm apart		28·00	28·00

(c) With T 8

86	**142**	1p. black (767) (R.)		1·10	55
		a. "aÉREO"		8·50	3·25
		b. Lines 14½ mm apart		5·75	5·75
		c. Opt inverted		12·50	12·50
		d. Optd in black		31·00	
87	–	4p. magenta (p 10) (768c)		9·00	3·25
		a. "aÉREO"		47·00	47·00
		b. Lines 14½ mm apart		28·00	28·00
		c. Perf 11½		31·00	
88	–	10p. top brown (p 10) (769a)		65·00	41·00
		a. "aÉREO"		£160	£160
		b. Lines 14½ mm apart		95·00	95·00
83/88 *Set of 6*				80·00	44·00

All values exist with double overprint.

Vía Aérea Tanger   Tanger
(9)   (10)

1939. Optd locally with T 9.

89	**143**	5c. brown		70	40
90		10c. yellow-green		70	40
91		15c. blue-green		70	40
92		20c. violet		70	40
93		25c. magenta		70	40
94		30c. carmine		70	40
95	**160a**	40c. rose		70	40
96		45c. carmine		70	40
97		50c. blue		1·90	1·50
98		60c. blue		1·10	40
99	**142**	1p. black (767)		1·50	75
		a. Opt in red		£160	
100	**145**	2p. blue (780)		25·00	17·00
101	–	4p. magenta (p 10) (768c)		25·00	17·00
102	–	10p. brown (769)		25·00	17·00
89/102 *Set of 14*				75·00	50·00

All values except the 2p. exist with the overprint inverted and all except the 2 and 4p. with it double. All except the 10p. are known with "T" inverted.

1939. AIR. Optd locally with T 10 horiz or sideways (up or down) on 10p.

(a) On postage stamps

103	**143**	5c. brown		1·10	95
104		10c. yellow-green		1·10	95
105		15c. blue-green		1·00	85
106		20c. violet		1·00	85
107		25c. magenta		1·00	85
108		30c. carmine		1·90	1·00
109	**160a**	40c. rose		50·00	
110		45c. carmine		45	
111		50c. blue		£100	
112		60c. blue		13·00	10·50
113	**142**	1p. black (p 10) (767c)		33·00	
		a. Opt in red		47·00	34·00
114	–	4p. magenta (p 10) (768c)		55·00	30·00
115	–	10p. brown		£160	

(b) On Express Letter stamp

116	E **145**	20c. red		3·50	1·70

The 40c., 50c. and 10p. may not have been used; the 2p. was prepared but not issued.
All values except Nos. 113a and 114/5 exist with the overprint inverted and all except Nos. 109, 111, 113a and 114/5 with it double.

Correo   Correo Aéreo
Tánger   Tánger
(11)   (12)

1939. Various fiscal types inscr "DERECHOS CONSULARES ESPAÑOLES" optd locally with T **11**. P 14 or 11½ (5p. 10p.).

117		50c. rose		22·00	22·00
		a. Opt double, one inverted		50·00	50·00
118		1p. rose		5·75	5·75
		a. Opt double, one inverted		50·00	50·00
119		2p. rose		5·75	5·75
		a. Opt double, one inverted		50·00	50·00
120		5p. carmine and green		6·25	6·25
		a. Opt double, one inverted		50·00	50·00
121		10p. carmine and violet		29·00	29·00
		a. Opt double		85·00	85·00
		b. Opt double, one inverted		95·00	95·00
117/121 *Set of 5*				60·00	60·00

All values exist without accent in "Tánger" and all are known with "C" omitted.

1939. AIR. The same types in different colours optd locally with T **12**. P 14 or 11½ (10p.).

122		1p. ultramarine		75·00	75·00
		a. Opt double, one inverted		95·00	95·00
123		2p. ultramarine		75·00	75·00
		a. Opt double, one inverted		95·00	95·00
124		5p. ultramarine		10·50	10·50
		a. Opt double, one inverted		95·00	95·00
125		10p. ultramarine		10·50	10·50
		a. Opt double, one inverted		95·00	95·00

The 5p. and 10p. exist without accent in "Tánger" and they are also known with "C" omitted.

In 1940 a number of stamps were overprinted "Correo Aéreo TANGER" and surcharged with new values. They were produced by officials at the Republican Consulate, who stayed on there after the war ended, but the stamps were not issued.

On 14 June 1940 Tangier was occupied by troops of the Khalifa, the Sultan's representative in the Spanish Zone, and on 4 November a decree extended that Zone to include Tangier. The International Administrationn was restored on 11 October 1945.

13 Palm Tree   14 Old Map of Tangier   15 Moroccan Woman

(Photo (1c., 2c.), recess (others). Govt Ptg Wks, Madrid)
1948 (16 Feb)–51. As T **13/15**. P 12½×13 (1c., 2c., 10c., 20c.). P 9½×10½ (others).

126	–	1c. emerald-green (12.6.51)		20	20
127	–	2c. red-orange (12.6.51)		20	20
128	**13**	5c. purple (1.8.49)		20	20
129	–	10c. blue (12.6.51)		20	20
130	–	20c. purple-brown (12.6.51)		20	20
131	**13**	25c. green ('50)		20	20
132	**14**	30c. greenish grey		40	20
133	–	45c. rose-carmine		40	20
134	**15**	50c. claret		40	20
135	–	75c. deep blue		85	20
136	–	90c. green		65	20
137	**14**	1p. 35 vermilion		2·75	45
138	**15**	2p. violet		5·00	45
139	–	10p. blue-green (1.8.49)		6·25	95
126/139 *Set of 14*				16·00	3·75

Designs:—1c., 2c. Head facing right; 10c., 20c. Head facing left; 45c., 10p. Street scene; 75c., 90c. Bearded Moor's head facing left.

16 Douglas DC-3   **E 17** Courier

(Recess Govt Ptg Wks, Madrid)

1949 (1 Aug)–**50**. AIR. T **16** and similar types. P 11 or 11½ (25c.).
140	–	20c. purple-brown (24.11.50)	40	20
141	**16**	25c. orange-red	40	20
142	–	35c. green	40	20
143	–	1p. violet (24.11.50)	1·40	20
144	**16**	2p. blue-green	2·30	40
145	–	10p. slate-purple	4·25	1·70
140/145 Set of 6			8·25	2·50

Designs: Horiz—20c., 1p. Lockheed Constellation airliner and map; 35c., 10p. Boeing.

(Recess Govt Ptg Wks, Madrid)

1949 (1 Aug). EXPRESS LETTER. P 13.
E146	E **17**	25c. scarlet	90	45

On 29 October 1956 international rule in Tangier ended and the zone was returned to Morocco. The Spanish post offices were not closed down until 30 April 1957.

Spanish Sahara

100 Céntimos = 1 Peseta

In 1436 Portuguese explorers discovered a bay on the north-west coast of Africa, opposite the Canary Islands, which they mistakenly named Rio de Oro (River of Gold), because the inhabitants traded in gold dust from lands to the south. On 9 January 1885, after Lieut. Emilio Bonelli had explored the area, and made pacts of friendship with the local shaikhs, Spain proclaimed a protectorate over the Rio de Oro coast between Capes Bojador and Blanco. France opposed Spanish expansion into the interior, but the boundaries of the protectorate were agreed by Franco-Spanish conventions of 1900, 1904 and 1912. Until 1901, when it became a Spanish colony, Rio de Oro was administered by the Captain-General of the Canary Islands.

PRINTERS. All the stamps of the Spanish Sahara were printed at the Government Printing Works, Madrid, *unless otherwise stated.*

King Alfonso XIII of Spain
17 May 1886–14 April 1931

A. RIO DE ORO

From 1901 to 1905 King Alfonso XIII stamps of Spain, Nos. 293/6 and 299, were used without overprint in Rio de Oro.

1   (2)

(Dies eng B. Mauro. Typo)

1905 (Dec). Blue control figures on back. P 14.
1	1	1c. emerald	4·75	4·50
2		2c. brown-lake	4·75	4·50
3		3c. greenish black	4·75	4·50
4		4c. deep chocolate	4·75	4·50
5		5c. orange-red	4·75	4·50
6		10c. sepia	4·75	4·50
7		15c. chocolate	4·75	4·50
8		25c. deep blue	£120	55·00
9		50c. myrtle-green	60·00	23·00
10		75c. violet	60·00	31·00
11		1p. chestnut	41·00	12·50
12		2p. dull orange	£140	85·00
13		3p. deep lilac	90·00	31·00
14		4p. blue-green	90·00	31·00
15		5p. dull blue	£120	65·00
16		10p. red	£275	£200
		a. Pale brown	£275	£200
1/16 Set of 16			£950	£500

1906. Handstamped with T **2**, in carmine.
17	1	15c. on 25c. deep blue	£300	£190

HANDSTAMP ERRORS. Types **2**, **4**, **8/10** and the handstamp on Type **6** occur inverted, double, double with one inverted and omitted in pairs with normal.

1907
10
Cens
3   (4)

(Dies eng B. Maura. Typo)

1907. Blue control figures on back. P 14.
18	3	1c. claret	4·25	3·75
19		2c. bronze-black	4·25	3·75
20		3c. brown	4·25	3·75
21		4c. dull red	4·25	3·75
		a. Deep red	4·25	3·75
22		5c. bronze-brown	4·25	3·75
23		10c. chocolate	4·25	3·75
24		15c. slate-blue	4·25	3·75

427

SPANISH SAHARA / Rio de Oro

25		25c. bronze-green	19·00	3·75
26		50c. deep purple	19·00	3·75
27		75c. brown	19·00	3·75
28		1p. orange-buff	28·00	3·75
29		2p. deep lilac	7·00	3·75
30		3p. blue-green	7·00	3·75
		a. Error. 4p. blue-green	£475	£325
31		4p. dull blue	12·00	7·50
32		5p. dull red	12·00	7·50
33		10p. blue-green	12·00	19·00
18/33 Set of 16			£150	75·00

No. 30a came about because a cliché of the 4p. had been included in the plate of the 3p.

1907. Handstamped with T **4**, in red.

34	1	10c. on 50c. myrtle-green	£160	41·00
35		10c. on 75c. violet	£120	41·00

1908. Handstamped as T **4**, but dated 1908.

36	1	2c. on 2p. dull orange (V.)	95·00	41·00
37	3	10c. on 50c. deep purple (R.)	32·00	6·25

On No. 36 the date in the handstamped overprint is sometimes 11 or 12 mm in length.

1908. Handstamped with T **2**.

38	3	15c. on 25c. bronze-green (C.)	38·00	6·75
39		15c. on 75c. brown (V.)	50·00	13·00
40		15c. on 1p. orange-buff (V.)	50·00	13·00
41		15c. on 1p. orange-buff (G.)	50·00	13·00
42		15c. on 1p. orange-buff (C.)	50·00	13·00

6   **7**

1908. Fiscal stamp handstamped locally as in T **6**. Imperf.

(a) With control number on back

43	6	5c. on 50c. green (*shades*) (C.)	£225	95·00
44		5c. on 50c. green (*shades*) (V.)	£375	£140

(b) Without control number

45	6	5c. on 50c. green (*shades*) (C.)	£110	47·00
46		5c. on 50c. green (*shades*) (V.)	£140	75·00

(Dies eng G. Carrascu and A. Morago. Typo)

1909 (1 Mar). Blue control figures on back. P 14.

47	7	1c. salmon	95	65
48		2c. brownish orange	95	65
49		5c. grey-green	95	65
50		10c. orange-vermilion	95	65
51		15c. blue-green	95	65
52		20c. black-purple	2·50	1·10
53		25c. indigo-blue	2·50	1·10
54		30c. crimson	2·50	1·10
55		40c. chocolate	2·50	1·10
56	7	50c. deep purple	4·50	1·10
57		1p. black-brown	6·25	5·25
58		4p. rosine	7·50	8·00
59		10p. claret	17·00	14·00
47/59 Set of 13			45·00	32·00

(8)   **(9)**   **(10)**

1910. Handstamped locally as T **8**.

60	1	10c. on 5p. dull blue (Bk.)	22·00	14·00
61		10c. on 5p. dull blue (R.)	£120	70·00
62		10c. on 10p. red (Bk.)	21·00	12·50
63		10c. on 10p. red (V.)	£190	95·00
64		10c. on 10p. red (G.)	£190	95·00
65		15c. on 3p. deep lilac (Bk.)	21·00	12·50
66		15c. on 4p. blue-green (Bk.)	21·00	12·50
		a. Error. "10c." for "15c."	£950	£325

1911–13. Stamps of T **3** handstamped locally.

67	9	2c. on 4p. dull blue (R.)	16·00	13·00
68		5c. on 10p. blue-green (V.)	41·00	13·00
69	10	10c. on 2p. deep lilac	20·00	14·00
70		10c. on 3p. blue-green (1913)	£250	80·00
71	2	15c. on 3p. blue-green (1913)	£250	36·00
72		15c. on 5p. dull red	16·00	15·00

11   **12**   **1917**
(13)

(Dies eng A. Morago. Typo)

1912. Blue control figures on back. P 13.

73	11	1c. rose	35	20
74		2c. lilac	35	20
75		5c. green	35	20
76		10c. red	35	20
77		15c. orange-brown	35	20
78		20c. brown	35	20
79		25c. blue	35	20
80		30c. deep lilac	35	20
81		40c. blue-green	35	20
82		50c. claret	35	20
83		1p. red	7·75	20
84		4p. lake	8·50	7·50
85		10p. grey-brown	13·50	12·50
73/85 Set of 13			30·00	21·00

(Dies eng A. Morago. Typo)

1914. Blue control figures on back. P 13.

86	12	1c. black-brown	40	20
87		2c. purple	40	20
88		5c. green	40	20
89		10c. vermilion	40	20
90		15c. orange-red	40	20
91		20c. lake	40	20
92		25c. deep blue	40	20
93		30c. blue-green	40	20
94		40c. orange	40	20
95		50c. brown	40	20
96		1p. dull lilac	9·50	3·75
97		4p. prose-carmine	12·50	3·75
98		10p. dull violet	12·50	11·50
86/98 Set of 13			35·00	19·00

1917. Stamps of 1912 optd with T **13**.

99	11	1c. rose	18·00	1·70
		a. Opt inverted	26·00	4·75
100		2c. lilac	18·00	1·70
		a. Opt inverted	25·00	4·75
101		5c. green	3·25	1·70
		a. Opt inverted	12·50	4·25
102		10c. red	3·25	1·70
		a. Opt inverted	12·50	4·25
103		15c. orange-brown	3·25	1·70
		a. Opt inverted	12·50	4·25
104		20c. brown	3·25	1·70
105		25c. blue	3·25	1·70
		a. "9117"	£190	
106		30c. deep lilac	3·25	1·70
		a. "9117"	£190	
107		40c. blue-green	3·25	1·70
		a. "9117"	£190	
108		50c. claret	3·25	1·70
		a. "9117"	£190	
109		1p. red	18·00	11·00
		a. "9117"	£190	
110		4p. lake	31·00	14·50
		a. "9117"	£190	
111		10p. grey-brown	55·00	24·00
		a. "9117"	£190	
99/111 Set of 13			£150	60·00

14   **15**   **16**

428

(Dies eng A. Mendiola. Typo)

1919. Blue control figures on back. P 13.

112	**14**	1c. brown		1·00	70
113		2c. purple		1·00	70
114		5c. green		1·00	70
115		10c. red		1·00	70
116		15c. orange-red		1·00	70
117		20c. orange		1·00	70
118		25c. blue		1·00	70
119		30c. blue-green		1·00	70
120		40c. orange		1·00	70
121		50c. brown		1·00	70
122		1p. dull lilac		7·50	7·25
123		4p. rose-carmine		12·50	14·00
124		10p. dull violet		18·00	24·00
112/124 *Set of 13*				43·00	47·00

(T **15/16**. Dies eng J. E. Gisbert. Typo)

1920. Blue control figures on back. P 13.

125	**15**	1c. purple		90	65
126		2c. rose		90	65
127		5c. red		90	65
128		10c. purple		90	65
129		15c. grey-brown		90	65
130		20c. green		90	65
131		25c. orange		90	65
132		30c. blue		5·75	6·25
133		40c. orange		3·25	3·00
134		50c. purple		3·25	3·00
135		1p. blue-green		50·00	3·00
136		4p. red		9·50	7·00
137		10p. brown		24·00	20·00
125/137 *Set of 13*				90·00	42·00

(Des B. Maura. Dies eng J. E. Gisbert. Typo)

1921. Blue control figures on back. P 13.

138	**16**	1c. yellow		90	60
139		2c. red-brown		90	60
140		5c. blue-green		90	60
141		10c. red		90	60
142		15c. myrtle-green		90	60
143		20c. turquoise-blue		90	60
144		25c. deep blue		90	60
145	**16**	30c. rose		1·70	1·70
146		40c. violet		1·70	1·70
147		50c. orange		1·70	1·70
148		1p. mauve		5·75	2·75
149		4p. claret		16·00	11·00
150		10p. brown		24·00	25·00
138/150 *Set of 13*				50·00	43·00

Rio de Oro was renamed Spanish Sahara in 1924.

B. LA AGÜERA

La Agüera, on the peninsula of Cape Blanco, was occupied by Spanish troops as a site for a military air base on the projected air route to South America.

LA AGÜERA
(1)   **2**

1920 (June). T **15** of Rio de Oro optd with T **1**. Control figures in blue on back.

1	1c. blue-green		2·75	2·75
2	2c. dull brown		2·75	2·75
3	5c. dull green		2·75	2·75
4	10c. orange-red		2·75	2·75
5	15c. yellow		2·75	2·75
6	20c. pale violet		2·75	2·75
7	25c. deep blue		2·75	2·75
8	30c. chocolate		2·75	2·75
9	40c. pink		2·75	2·75
10	50c. turquoise		9·00	9·00
11	1p. brown-lake		18·00	18·00
12	4p. deep purple		50·00	50·00
13	10p. orange		£110	£110
1/13 *Set of 13*			£190	£190

(Dies eng G. Carrascu and A. Morago. Typo)

1923 (June). Control figures in blue on back. P 13.

14	**2**	1c. turquoise-blue		1·70	1·10
15		2c. deep green		1·70	1·10
16		5c. blue-green		1·70	1·10
17		10c. red		1·70	1·10
18		15c. red-brown		1·70	1·10
19		20c. yellow		1·70	1·10
20		25c. deep blue		1·70	1·10
21		30c. deep brown		1·70	1·10
22		40c. rose-red		2·40	1·60
23		50c. purple		6·75	5·00
24		1p. magenta		14·00	10·50
25		4p. violet		41·00	30·00
26		10p. orange		65·00	46·00
14/26 *Set of 13*				£130	90·00

La Agüera was incorporated in Spanish Sahara in 1924.

C. SPANISH SAHARA

The name of the colony was changed from Rio de Oro to Spanish Sahara in 1924. In 1958 it was made an Overseas Province of Spain.

SAHARA ESPAÑOL   SAHARA
1 Tuareg and   (2)   (3)
Camel

1924. Typo. With blue control figures on back. P 13.

1	**1**	5c. blue-green		3·00	1·10
2		10c. grey-brown		3·00	1·10
3		15c. turquoise-blue		3·00	1·10
4		20c. violet		3·00	1·60
5		25c. vermilion		3·00	1·60
6		30c. red-brown		3·00	1·60
7		40c. dull blue		3·00	1·60
8		50c. orange		3·00	1·60
9		60c. purple		3·00	1·60
10		1p. claret		16·00	9·00
11		4p. deep brown		75·00	44·00
12		10p. purple		£170	£140
1/12 *Set of 12*				£250	£190

The 15c. to 10p. values also exist without control figures on back, perf 10 but they were not issued.

1926. Red Cross. T **70/1** and similar types of Spain, optd with T **2**.

13	–	5c. sepia		12·50	12·50
14	–	10c. myrtle		12·50	12·50
15	**70**	15c. violet (V.)		3·50	3·50
16	–	20c. purple		3·50	3·50
17	**71**	25c. crimson		3·50	3·50
18	**70**	30c. olive-green		3·50	3·50
19	–	40c. ultramarine		30	30
20	–	50c. brown-lake		30	30
21	**71**	60c. grey-green		30	30
22	–	1p. orange-red		30	30
23	–	4p. bistre		3·50	3·50
24	**71**	10p. violet		8·75	8·75
13/24 *Set of 12*				47·00	47·00

1929. Seville and Barcelona Exhibitions. Nos. 504/14 of Spain optd as T **3**, horiz (T **83/4**) or sideways (others).

25	–	5c. carmine-lake (B.)		30	30
26	–	10c. green (R.)		30	30
27	**83**	15c. turquoise-blue (R.)		30	30
28	**84**	20c. violet (R.)		30	30
29	**83**	25c. carmine (B.)		30	30
30	–	30c. blackish brown (B.)		30	30
31	–	40c. blue (R.)		75	75
32	**84**	50c. red-orange (B.)		75	75
33	–	1p. greenish slate (R.)		4·25	4·25
34	–	4p. claret (B.)		31·00	31·00
35	–	10p. brown (B.)		60·00	60·00
25/35 *Set of 11*				90·00	90·00

SPANISH REPUBLIC
14 April 1931–1 April 1939

República   SAHARA
Española   ESPAÑOL
(4)   (5)

SPANISH SAHARA / Spanish Sahara

1931–34. Optd with T **4**.

A. Optd reading upwards (1931)

36A	**1**	5c. blue-green (R.)	95	95
37A		10c. grey-green (R.)	95	95
38A		15c. turquoise-blue (R.)	95	95
39A		20c. violet (R.)	95	95
40A		25c. vermilion (B.)	1·10	95
41A		30c. red-brown (R.)	1·10	95
42A		40c. dull blue (B.)	5·00	1·50
43A		50c. orange (B.)	5·00	3·25
44A		60c. purple (B.)	5·00	3·25
45A		1p. claret (B.)	5·00	3·25
46A		4p. deep brown (B.)	65·00	38·00
47A		10p. purple (B.)	£120	70·00
36A/47A Set of 12			£190	£110

B. Horizontal Optd (10.32–34)

36B		5c. blue-green (R.)	1·50	1·20
		a. Blue surch (1934)	5·75	4·75
37B		10c. grey-green (R.)	1·50	1·20
		a. Blue surch (1934)	5·75	4·75
38B		15c. turquoise-blue (R.)	1·50	1·20
		a. Blue surch (1934)	5·75	4·75
39B		20c. violet (R.)	1·50	1·20
		a. Blue surch (1934)	5·75	4·75
40B		25c. vermilion (B.)	1·70	1·40
41B		30c. red-brown (R.)	1·70	1·40
42B		40c. dull blue (B.)	8·00	6·50
		a. Blue surch (1934)	5·75	4·75
43B		50c. orange (B.)	8·00	6·50
44B		60c. purple (B.)	8·00	6·50
45B		1p. claret (B.)	8·00	6·50
46B		4p. deep brown (B.)	85·00	70·00
47B		10p. purple (B.)	£160	£130
36B/47B Set of 12			£250	£200

Another printing in 1932 had the overprint reading vertically downwards. Prices approximately as for horizontal overprints.

NATIONALIST GOVERNMENT

1941. Stamps of Spain optd with T **5** (sideways on 2c.).

47a	**181**	1c. green (R.)	2·75	2·75
47b	**182**	2c. red-brown (B.)	2·75	2·75
48	**183**	5c. sepia (R.)	75	75
49		10c. carmine (R.)	2·75	2·75
		a. Red opt	20·00	9·75
50		15c. yellow-green (R.)	75	75
51	**196**	20c. violet (R.)	75	75
52		25c. claret (R.)	2·00	1·80
53		30c. blue (R.)	2·00	2·00
54		40c. greenish slate (R.)	75	75
55		50c. slate (R.)	9·75	2·75
56		70c. blue (R.)	6·75	4·00
57		1PTA. black (R.)	31·00	6·00
58		2PTAS. sepia (R.)	£180	£140
59		4PTAS. rose (B.)	£400	£325
60		10PTS. brown (R.)	£1200	£550
47a/60 Set of 15			£1700	£950

The air stamps, Nos. 942/7 of Spain, were also issued in Madrid overprinted as Type **5** but they have not been seen used and it is doubtful whether they were sent out to Spanish Sahara.

6 Dorcas Gazelles   **7** Ostriches   E **8** Camel Troop

(Des M. Bertuchi. Photo Rieusset, Barcelona)

1943. Photo. P 12½.

(a) POSTAGE. Inscr "CORREO" as T 6

61	**6**	1c. magenta and brown	20	20
62	–	2c. indigo and green	20	20
63	–	5c. violet-blue and cerise	20	20
64	**6**	15c. emerald and slate-green	20	20
65	–	20c. purple-brown and reddish violet	20	20
66	**6**	40c. violet and reddish purple	20	20
67	–	45c. scarlet and maroon	30	30
68	–	75c. blue and indigo	30	30
69	**6**	1p. chocolate and scarlet	1·30	1·30
70	–	3p. slate-green and deep violet-blue	2·40	2·40
71	–	10p. black and sepia	41·00	41·00
61/71 Set of 11			42·00	42·00

Designs: Vert—2c., 20c., 45c., 3p. Camel caravan; 5c., 75c., 10p. Camel troops.

(b) AIR. Inscr "CORREO AEREO" as T 7

72	**7**	5c. purple-brown and cerise	20	20
73	–	25c. brown-olive and yellow-green	20	20
74	**7**	50c. blue-green and indigo	20	20
75	–	1p. light blue and violet	20	20
76	**7**	1p.40 deep blue and bronze-green	20	20
77	–	2p. yellow-brown and deep magenta	1·40	1·40
78	**7**	5p. reddish violet and bistre-brown	2·40	2·40
79	–	6p. deep green and light blue	42·00	42·00
72/79 Set of 8			42·00	42·00

Design: Vert—25c., 1p., 2p., 6p. Aeroplane and camels.

(c) EXPRESS LETTER

E80	E **8**	25c. carmine and deep grey-green	1·40	1·40

See also Spanish West Africa for joint issues for Ifni and Spanish Sahara from 1949 to 1951

8 Boy carrying Lamb   **9** Diego de Herrera

(Des J. Nadal del Val. Photo)

1950 (20 Oct). Child Welfare Fund. P 13×12½.

80	**8**	50c.+10c. brown	35	35
81		1p.+25c. claret	16·00	16·00
82		6p.50+1p.65 deep blue-green	8·50	8·50
80/82 Set of 3			22·00	22·00

(Des S. Quintana. Photo)

1950 (23 Nov). AIR. Colonial Stamp Day. P 12½×13.

83	**9**	5p. violet	4·50	4·50

9a Woman and Dove   **9b** General Franco

(Des T. Miciano. Recess)

1951 (22 Apr). AIR. 500th Birth Anniv of Isabella the Catholic. P 10.

84	**9a**	5p. green	37·00	18·00

(Des F. Hernández. Photo)

1951 (18 July). Visit of General Franco. P 12½×13.

85	**9b**	50c. orange	60	60
86		1p. lake-brown	75	75
87		5p. blue-green	48·00	48·00
85/87 Set of 3			44·00	44·00

10 Dromedary and Calf   **11** Native Woman   **12** Morion, Sword and Banner

(Des T. Miciano. Photo)

1951 (23 Nov). Colonial Stamp Day. P 13×12½.

88	**10**	5c.+5c. brown	55	55
89		10c.+5c. orange	60	60
90		60c.+15c. deep olive	1·20	1·20
88/90 Set of 3			2·10	2·10

SPANISH SAHARA / Spanish Sahara

(Des J. Nadal del Val. Photo)

1952 (1 June). Child Welfare Fund. P 13×12½.
91	**11**	5c.+5c. brown	65	65
92	–	50c.+10c. greenish black	65	65
93	–	2p.+30c. deep blue	3·75	3·75
91/93	Set of 3		4·50	4·50

(Des J. L. L. Pavia. Photo)

1952 (18 July). AIR. Fifth Birth Centenary of Ferdinand the Catholic. P 13×12½.
| 94 | **12** | 5p. brown | 38·00 | 14·00 |

13 Head of Ostrich **14** "Geography" **15** Woman Musician

(Des Allende. Photo)

1952 (23 Nov). Colonial Stamp Day. P 13×12½.
95	**13**	5c.+5c. brown	55	55
96	–	10c.+5c. deep claret	60	60
97	–	60c.+15c. bronze-green	1·90	1·90
95/97	Set of 3		2·75	2·75

(Des R. L. Prieto. Photo)

1953 (2 Mar). 75th Anniv of Royal Geographical Society. P 13×12½.
98	**14**	5c. red-orange	55	55
99	–	35c. blackish green	55	55
100	–	60c. brown	65	65
98/100	Set of 3		1·60	1·60

(Des J. Blanco del Pueyo and T. Miciano. Photo)

1953 (1 June). Child Welfare Fund. T **15** and similar vert design inscr "PRO-INFANCIA 1953". P 13×12½.
101	**15**	5c.+5c. brown-red	55	55
102	–	10c.+5c. bright purple	55	55
103	**15**	15c. blackish olive	55	55
104	–	60c. brown	65	65
101/104	Set of 4		2·10	2·10

Design:—10, 60c. Native man musician.

16 **17** Hurdlers

(Des V.D. Urosa and J. Blanco del Pueyo. Photo)

1953 (23 Nov). Colonial Stamp Day. T **16** and similar horiz design. P 12½×13.
105	**16**	5c.+5c. violet	55	55
106	–	10c.+5c. green (Two fishes)	55	55
107	**16**	15c. bronze green	55	55
108	–	60c. orange (Two fishes)	65	65
105/108	Set of 4		2·10	2·10

(Des T. Miciano. Photo)

1954 (1 June). Child Welfare Fund. T **17** and similar design. P 12½×13 (horiz) or 13×12½ (vert).
109	**17**	5c.+5c. chestnut	55	55
110	–	10c.+5c. reddish violet	55	55
111	**17**	15c. deep green	55	55
112	–	60c. brown	65	65
109/112	Set of 4		2·10	2·10

Design: Vert—10, 60c. Native runner.

18 Atlantic Flyingfish **19** E. Bonelli

(Des F. F. Vigara and T. Miciano. Photo)

1954 (23 Nov). Colonial Stamp Day. T **18** and similar horiz design. P 12½×13.
113	**18**	5c.+5c. red	55	55
114	–	10c.+5c. purple	55	55
115	**18**	15c. bronze green	55	55
116	–	60c. red-brown	65	65
113/116	Set of 4		2·10	2·10

Design:—10. 60c. Gilthead Seabream.

(Des M. S. Algora and T. Miciano. Photo)

1955 (1 June). Birth Centenary of Bonelli (explorer). T **19** and similar horiz design inscr "1954 CENTENARIO BONELLI". P 12½×13.
117	**19**	10c.+5c. bright purple	55	55
118	–	25c.+10c. reddish violet	55	55
119	**19**	50c. brown-olive	65	65
117/119	Set of 3		1·60	1·60

Design:—25c. Bonelli and felucca.

20 Scimitar Oryx **21** Antirrhinum ramosissimum

(Des J. J. P. Cobarro and A. Boué. Photo)

1955 (23 Nov). Colonial Stamp Day. T **20** and similar horiz design inscr "DIA DEL SELLO COLONIAL 1955". P 12½×13.
120	**20**	5c.+5c. brown	55	55
121	–	15c.+5c. deep olive-bistre	55	55
122	**20**	70c. deep green	65	65
120/122	Set of 3		1·60	1·60

Design:—15c. Scimitar oryx's head.

(Des R. Lozano Prieto. Photo)

1956 (1 June). Child Welfare Fund. T **21** and similar vert design inscr "PRO-INFANCIA 1956". P 13×12½.
123	**21**	5c.+5c. bronze green	55	55
124	–	15c.+5c. yellow-brown	55	55
125	**21**	20c. blue-green	55	55
126	–	50c. deep brown	65	65
123/126	Set of 4		2·10	2·10

Design:—15, 50c. Sesuvium portulacastrum (wrongly inscr "Sesiviun").

22 Arms of Aaiun, and Native on Camel

(Des V. S. Algora (T **22**), T. Miciano (15c.) Photo)

1956 (23 Nov). Colonial Stamp Day. T **22** and similar design inscr "DIA DEL SELLO 1956". P 12½×13 or 13×12½ (15c.).
127	**22**	5c.+5c. black and deep lilac	55	55
128	–	15c.+5c. green and ochre	55	55
129	**22**	70c. bistre-brown and yellow-green	65	65
127/129	Set of 3		1·60	1·60

Design: Vert—15c. Arms of Villa Cisneros, and native chief.

23 Dromedaries **24** Golden Eagle **25** Head of Striped Hyena

SPANISH SAHARA / Spanish Sahara

(Des M. S. Algora (T **23**), T. Miciano (15, 80c.),
E. M. Jimeno (others). Photo)

1957 (10 Apr). T **23** and similar designs. P 13×12½.
130	**23**	5c. deep lilac	35	35
131	–	15c. brown-ochre (Ostrich)	35	35
132	–	50c. olive-brown (Dorcas gazelle)	40	35
133	**23**	70c. yellow-green	1·10	40
134	–	80c. bluish green (Ostrich)	1·10	40
135	–	1p.80 magenta (Dorcas gazelle)	1·40	75
130/135 Set of 6			4·25	2·40

(Des V. Dominguez (T **24**), C. Bentabol (15c.). Photo)

1957 (1 June). Child Welfare Fund. T **24** and similar vert design inscr "PRO-INFANCIA 1957". P 13×12½.
136	**24**	5c.+5c. red-brown	55	55
137	–	15c.+5c. yellow-brown	55	55
138	**24**	70c. green	65	65
136/138 Set of 3			1·60	1·60

Design:—15c. Tawny eagle in flight.

(Des E. Jimeno (T **25**), M.S. Algora (others) Photo)

1957 (23 Nov). Colonial Stamp Day. T **25** and similar design inscr "DIA DEL SELLO 1957". P 13×12½ (T **25**) or 12½×13 (others).
139	**25**	10c.+5c. reddish purple	55	55
140	–	15c.+5c. brown-ochre	55	55
141	**25**	20c. blackish green	55	55
142	–	70c. bronze green	65	65
139/142 Set of 4			2·10	2·10

Design: Horiz—15, 70c. Striped hyena.

26 White Stork and Arms of Valencia and Aaiun   **27** Cervantes

(Des M. S. Algora. Photo)

1958 (6 Mar). Aid for Valencia. P 12½×13.
143	**26**	10c.+5c. chestnut	55	55
144	–	15c.+10c. ochre	55	55
145	–	50c.+10c. olive-brown	65	65
143/145 Set of 3			1·60	1·60

(Des T. Miciano (T **27**), E. Sánchez (15c.), M. S. Algora (20c.). Photo)

1958 (1 June). Child Welfare Fund. T **27** and similar designs inscr "PRO-INFANCIA 1958". P 13×12½ (T **27**) or 12½×13 (others).
146	**27**	10c.+5c. dp orange-grn & chestnut	55	55
147	–	15c.+5c. dp bronze-grn & brn-orge	55	55
148	–	20c. blue-green and brown	55	55
149	**27**	70c. dp greenish blue & yellow-green	65	65
146/149 Set of 4			2·10	2·10

Designs: Vert—15c. Don Quixote and Sancho Panza on horseback. Horiz—20c. Don Quixote and the lion.

28 Hoopoe Lark   **29** Lope de Vega (author)   **30** Grey Heron

(Des M. S. Algora (T **28**), T. Miciano (25c.), C. R. de Galarreta (50c.). Photo)

1958 (23 Nov). Colonial Stamp Day. T **28** and similar designs inscr "DIA DEL SELLO 1958". P 12½×13 (25c.) or 13×12½ (others).
150		10c.+5c. Venetian red	55	55
151		25c.+10c. reddish violet	55	55
152		50c.+10c. deep olive	65	65
150/152 Set of 3			1·60	1·60

Designs: Horiz—25c. Hoopoe lark feeding young. Vert—50c. Fulvous babbler.

1959 (1 June). Child Welfare Fund. T **29** and similar vert designs. P 13×12½.
153	**29**	10c.+5c. dp olive-green & orge-brn	55	55
154	–	15c.+5c. deep brown & yellow-brown	55	55
155	–	20c. sepia and light green	55	55
156	**29**	70c. black-green and light emerald	65	65
153/156 Set of 4			2·10	2·10

Designs:—Characters from Lope de Vega's comedy *The Star of Seville*: 15c. Spanish lady; 20c. Caballero.

(Des M. Carillo (T **30**), T. Miciano (50c., 1p.50, 5p.), M. S. Algora (75c., 2p., 10p.). Photo)

1959 (15 Oct). Vert bird designs as T **30**. P 13×12½.
157	**30**	25c. slate-violet	30	20
158	–	50c. bronze-green	30	20
159	–	75c. sepia	30	20
160	**30**	1p. orange-red	30	20
161	–	1p.50 blue-green	40	20
162	–	2p. bright purple	95	20
163	**30**	3p. blue	1·00	25
164	–	5p. chestnut	1·90	30
165	–	10p. olive-green	11·50	5·00
157/165 Set of 9			15·00	6·00

Birds:—50c., 1p.50, 5p. European sparrow hawk; 75c., 2p., 10p. Herring gull.

31 Saharan Postman   **32** F. de Quevedo (writer)

(Des J. de Castro (T **31**), J. Arroyo (20c.), A. Boué (50c.). Photo)

1959 (23 Nov). Colonial Stamp Day. T **31** and similar vert designs inscr "DIA DEL SELLO 1959". P 13×12½.
166		10c.+5c. brown and brown-red	55	55
167		20c.+5c. brown and green	55	55
168		50c.+20c. deep slate-blue & olive-brn	65	65
166/168 Set of 3			1·60	1·60

Designs:—20c. Postman tendering letters; 50c. Camel postman.

(Des C. de Galarreta and T. Miciano. Photo)

1960 (1 June). Child Welfare. T **32** and similar designs inscr "PRO INFANCIA 1960". P 12½×13 (T **32**) or 13×12½ (others).
169	**32**	10c.+5c. brown-purple	55	55
170	–	15c.+5c. bistre-brown	55	55
171	–	35c. blackish green	55	55
172	**32**	80c. deep bluish green	65	65
169/172 Set of 4			2·10	2·10

Designs: Vert (representing Quevedo's works)—15c. Winged wheel and hourglass; 35c. Man in plumed hat wearing cloak and sword.

33 Leopard   **34** Houbara Bustard   **35** Cameleer and Plane

(Des A. M. Fernandez, J. Olcina, E. Cerra. Photo)

1960 (29 Dec). Stamp Day. T **33** and similar vert designs inscr "DIA DEL SELLO 1960". P 13×12½.
173		10c.+5c. magenta	55	55
174		20c.+5c. blackish green	55	55
175		30c.+10c. chocolate	55	55
176		50c.+20c. olive-brown	65	65
173/176 Set of 4			2·10	2·10

Designs:—20c. Fennec fox; 30c. Golden eagle defying leopard; 50c. Red fox.

SPANISH SAHARA / Spanish Sahara

(Des T. Miciano and M. Jimeno. Photo)
1961 (18 Apr). T **34** and similar vert design. P 13×12½.
177	**34**	25c. slate-violet	20	20
178	–	50c. olive-brown	20	20
179	**34**	75c. dull purple	20	20
180	–	1p. vermilion	20	20
181	**34**	1p.50 bluish green	20	20
182	–	2p. magenta	80	25
183	**34**	3p. deep blue	1·00	35
184	–	5p. red-brown	1·20	40
185	**34**	10p. yellow-olive	3·50	1·90
177/185 Set of 9			6·75	3·50

Design:—50c., 1p., 2p., 5p. Feral rock pigeon.

(Des T. Miciano. Photo)
1961 (16 May). AIR. P 13×12½.
186	**35**	25p. sepia	3·75	1·90

36 Dorcas Gazelles   **37**

(Des V. Vila (25c.), R. L. Prieto (others). Photo)
1961 (21 June). Child Welfare. T **36** and similar vert design inscr "PRO-INFANCIA 1961". P 13×12½.
187	**36**	10c.+5c. carmine-red	55	55
188	–	25c.+10c. slate-violet	55	55
189	**36**	80c.+20c. deep bluish green	65	65
187/189 Set of 3			1·60	1·60

Design:—25c. One dorcas gazelle.

(Des R. L. Prieto (25c.), V. S. Algora (70c.), T. Miciano (others). Photo)
1961 (1 Oct). 25th Anniv of General Franco as Head of State. T **37** and similar vert designs. P 13×12½ (vert) or 12½×13 (horiz).
190	–	25c. violet-grey (Map)	55	55
191	**37**	50c. olive-brown	55	55
192	–	70c. emerald (Aiun Chapel)	55	55
193	**37**	1p. orange-red	65	65
190/193 Set of 4			2·10	2·10

38 A. Fernández de Lugo   **39** *Neurada procumbres linn*   **40** Hoefler's Butterflyfish

(Des T. Miciano. Photo)
1961 (23 Nov). Stamp Day. T **38** and similar vert design inscr "DIA DEL SELLO 1961". P 13×12½.
194	**38**	10c.+5c. deep orange-red	55	55
195	–	25c.+10c. plum	55	55
196	**38**	30c.+10c. chocolate	55	55
197	–	1p.+10c. orange-red	65	65
194/197 Set of 4			2·10	2·10

Portrait:—25c., 1p. D de Herrera.

1962 (26 Feb). T **39** and similar vert floral designs. Photo. P 13×12½.
198	**39**	25c. slate-violet	20	20
199	–	50c. sepia	20	20
200	–	70c. deep emerald	20	20
201	**39**	1p. orange-red	20	20
202	–	1p.50 blue-green	40	20
203	–	2p. bright purple	1·20	25
204	**39**	3p. slate-blue	2·20	40
205	–	10p. brown-olive	5·00	1·90
198/205 Set of 8			8·75	3·25

Designs:—50c., 1p.50, 10p. *Anabasis articulata moq*; 70c., 2p. *Euphorbia resinifera*.

(Des V. D. Urosa (50c.), J. Olicina (others). Photo)
1962 (10 July). Child Welfare. T **40** and similar horiz design inscr "PRO-INFANCIA 1962". P 12½×13 (50c.) or 13×12½ (others).
206	**40**	25c. deep violet	55	55
207	–	50c. bronze-green (Grouper)	55	55
208	**40**	1p. chestnut	65	65
206/208 Set of 3			1·60	1·60

41 Goats

(Des F. Galindo (35c.), M. S. Algora (others). Photo)
1962 (23 Nov). Stamp Day. T **41** and similar horiz, design inscr "DIA DEL SELLO 1962". P 12½×13.
209	**41**	15c. yellow-green	55	55
210	–	35c. reddish purple (Sheep)	55	55
211	**41**	1p. chestnut	65	65
209/211 Set of 3			1·60	1·60

42 Seville Cathedral   **43** Cameleer and Camel   **44** Dove in Hands

(Des P. G. Gomez. Photo)
1963 (29 Jan). Seville Flood Relief. P 12½×13.
212	**42**	50c. olive-brown	55	55
213	–	1p. chestnut	65	65

(Des V. Vila. Photo)
1963 (1 June). Child Welfare. T **43** and similar vert design inscr "PRO-INFANCIA 1963". P 13×12½.
214	–	25c. deep violet	55	55
215	–	50c. deep grey	55	55
216	–	1p. orange-red	65	65
214/216 Set of 3			1·60	1·60

Design:—25c., 1p. Three camels.

1963 (12 June). "For Barcelona". Photo. P 13×12½.
217	**44**	50c. deep bluish green	55	55
218	–	1p. chestnut	65	65

45 John Dory (*Zeus faber*)

(Des V. S. Algora (T **45**), J. J. de Castro (50c.) Photo)
1964 (6 Mar). Stamp Day. T **45** and similar design inscr "DIA DEL SELLO 1963". P 13×12½ (50c.) or 12½×13 (others).
219	**45**	25c. deep reddish violet	55	55
220	–	50c. deep olive	55	55
221	**45**	1p. Venetian red	65	65
219/221 Set of 3			1·60	1·60

Design: Vert—50c. Plain bonito (*Sarda unicolor*).

SPANISH SAHARA / Spanish Sahara

46 Striped Hawk Moth

47 Mounted Dromedary and Microphone

(Des T. Miciano (50c.) P. G. Gomez (others). Photo)

1964 (1 June). Child Welfare. T **46** and similar design. P 13×12½ (50c.) or 12½×13 (others).

222	**46**	25c. deep violet	55	55
223	–	50c. black-olive	55	55
224	**46**	1p. orange-red	65	65
222/224 Set of 3			1·60	1·60

Design: Vert—50c. Goat moths.

(Des J. J. de Castro (T **47**), T. Miciano (50c., 1p.50, 3p.), M. S. Algora (70c., 2p., 10p.). Photo)

1964 (30 Sept). T **47** and similar vert designs. P 13×12½.

225	**47**	25c. purple	30	30
226	–	50c. olive-brown	30	30
227	–	70c. green	30	30
228	**47**	1p. brown-purple	30	30
229	–	1p.50 turquoise	30	30
230	–	2p. deep bluish green	30	30
231	–	3p. deep blue	30	30
232	–	10p. lake	1·80	95
225/232 Set of 8			3·50	2·75

Designs:—50c., 1p.50, 3p. Flute-player; 70c., 2p., 10p. Woman drummer.

48 Barbary Ground Squirrel's Head

49 Doctor tending Patient, and Hospital

(Des J. L. Bueno (1p.), E. M. Jimeno (others). Photo)

1964 (23 Nov). Stamp Day. T **48** and similar design. P 13×12½ (vert) or 12½×13 (horiz).

233		50c. olive-brown	55	55
234		1p. brown-lake	55	55
235		1p.50 deep green	65	65
233/235 Set of 3			1·60	1·60

Design: Vert—50c., 1p.50, Eurasian red squirrel eating.

1965 (22 Feb). 25th Anniv of End of Spanish Civil War. T **49** and similar designs inscr "XXV AÑOS DE PAZ". Photo. P 12½×13 (1p.) or 13×12½ (others).

236		50c. olive-brown	55	55
237		1p. brown-red	55	55
238		1p.50 blue	65	65
236/238 Set of 3			1·60	1·60

Designs: Vert—50c. Saharan woman; 1p.50, Desert Installation and cameleer.

50 Anthia sexmaculata

51 Handball

1965 (1 June). Child Welfare. Insects. T **50** and similar design. Photo. P 12½×13 (50c., 1p.50) or 13×12½ (others).

239	**50**	50c. slate-blue	55	55
240	–	1p. blue-green	55	55
241	**50**	1p.50 yellow-brown	55	55
242	–	3p. indigo	65	65
239/242 Set of 4			2·10	2·10

Insect: Vert—1, 3p. Blepharopsis mendica.

(Des A. Varas and E. Jimeno. Photo)

1965 (23 Nov). Stamp Day. T **51** and similar vert design. P 13×12½.

243	**51**	50c. crimson	55	55
244	–	1p. reddish purple	55	55
245	**51**	1p.50 Prussian blue	65	65
243/245 Set of 3			1·60	1·60

Design:—1p. Arms of Spanish Sahara.

52 Bows of *Rio de Oro*

53 Big-eyed Tuna (*Parathunnus obesus*)

1966 (1 June). Child Welfare. T **52** and similar horiz design. Photo. P 12½×13.

246	**52**	50c. olive-green	55	55
247	–	1p. chocolate	55	55
248	–	1p.50 blue-green	65	65
246/248 Set of 3			1·60	1·60

Design:—1p.50, Freighter *Fuerta Ventura*.

1966 (23 Nov). Stamp Day. T **53** and similar designs. Photo. P 13.

249	**53**	10c. steel-blue & pale greenish yellow	55	55
250	–	40c. bluish grey and salmon	55	55
251	**53**	1p.50 chocolate & pale sage-green	55	55
252	–	4p. dull purple and yellow-green	65	65
249/252 Set of 4			2·10	2·10

Design: Vert—40c., 4p. Ocean sunfish (*Mola mole*).

54 Fig

55 Quay, Aaiun

(Des J. J. Castro. Photo)

1967 (1 June). Child Welfare. T **54** and similar vert floral design. P 13.

253	**54**	10c. orange-yellow and indigo	55	55
254	–	40c. purple and bright green	55	55
255	**54**	1p.50 greenish yellow and myrtle-green	55	55
256	–	4p. yellow-orange and new blue	65	65
253/256 Set of 4			2·10	2·10

Design:—40c., 4p. Lupin.

1967 (28 Sept). Inauguration of Sahara Ports. T **55** and similar horiz design. Photo. P 12½×13.

257		1p.50 chocolate and new blue	55	55
258		4p. ochre and new blue	85	85

Design:—4p. Port of Villa Cisneros.

56 Ruddy Shelduck

56a Scorpio (Scorpion)

1967 (23 Nov). Stamp Day. T **56** and similar designs. Photo. P 13.

259		1p. chestnut and emerald	55	55
260		1p.50 magenta and black	55	55
261		3p.50 brown-lake and grey-brown	65	65
259/261 Set of 3			1·60	1·60

Designs: Vert—1p.50, Greater Flamingo. Horiz—3p.50, Rufous scrub robin.

1968 (25 Apr). Child Welfare. Signs of the Zodiac. T **56a** and similar horiz designs. Photo. P 13.

262		1p. magenta/*pale yellow*	55	55
263		1p.50 red-brown/*pale pink*	55	55
264		2p.50 deep violet/*pale greenish yellow*	65	65
262/264 Set of 3			1·60	1·60

Designs:—1p.50, Capricorn (goat); 2p.50, Virgo (virgin).

SPANISH SAHARA / Spanish Sahara

57 Dove, and Stamp within Posthorn

58 Head of Dorcas Gazelle

(Des C. Tauler. Photo)

1968 (23 Nov). Stamp Day. T **57** and similar veil designs. P 13×12½.
265	1p. deep blue and bright purple	55	55
266	1p.50 blackish green and bright green	55	55
267	2p.50 blue and orange	65	65
265/267 Set of 3		1·60	1·60

Designs:—1p.50, Postal handstamp, stamps and letter; 2p.50, Saharan postman.

(Des E. Carra. Photo)

1969 (1 June). Child Welfare. T **58** and similar diamond-shaped designs. P 13.
268	1p. brown and black	45	45
269	1p.50 brown and black	45	45
270	2p.50 brown and black	70	70
271	6p. brown and black	1·20	1·20
268/271 Set of 4		2·50	2·50

Designs:—1p.50, Dorcas gazelle tending young; 2p.50, Dorcas gazelle and camel; 6p. Dorcas gazelle leaping.

59 Woman beating Drum

59a Fennec Fox

(Des T. Miciano (50c., 2p.), S. Algora (1p.50, 25p.). Photo)

1969 (23 Nov). Stamp Day. T **59** and similar designs. P 13.
272	50c. lake-brown and light bistre	40	40
273	1p.50 deep bluish green and lt olive-green	45	45
274	2p. slate-blue and yellow-brown	55	55
275	25p. brown and pale green	2·40	2·40
272/275 Set of 4		3·50	3·50

Designs:—Vert—1p.50, Man playing flute. Horiz—2p. Drum and mounted cameleer; 25p. Flute.

1970 (1 June). Child Welfare. Diamond-shaped designs as T **59a**. Photo. P 13.
276	50c. ochre and dull blue	45	45
277	2p. brown and dull blue	50	50
278	2p.50 yellow-ochre and dull blue	65	65
279	6p. yellow-ochre and dull blue	1·20	1·20
276/279 Set of 4		2·50	2·50

Designs:—2p. Fennec fox walking; 2p.50, Head of fennec fox; 6p. Fennec fox family.

60 *Grammodes boisdeffrei* (moth)

(Des D. E. Cerra. Photo)

1970 (23 Nov). Stamp Day. T **60** and similar diamond-shaped designs. Multicoloured. P 12½.
280	50c. Type **60**	45	45
281	1p. Type **60**	50	50
282	2p. African monarch (*Danaus chrysippus*) (butterfly)	55	55
283	5p. As 2p.	80	80
284	8p. Spurge hawk moth (*Celerio euphorbiae*)	1·50	1·50
280/284 Set of 5		3·50	3·50

61 Dorcas Gazelle and Arms of El Aaiun

E 62 Despatch-rider

1971 (1 June). Child Welfare. T **61** and similar designs. Photo. P 13.
285	1p. multicoloured	45	45
286	2p. deep olive and brown-olive	55	55
287	5p. cobalt, red-brown and grey	65	65
288	25p. bronze green, greenish grey and greenish blue	2·20	2·20
285/288 Set of 4		3·50	3·50

Designs: Horiz—2p. Tourist Inn, Aaiun; 5p. Assembly House, Aaiun. Vert—25p. Smara Mosque.

1971 (6 Sept). EXPRESS LETTER. Photo. P 13.
E289	E **62**	10p. bronze-green and rose-red	1·70	1·70

63 Trumpeter Finch (*Rhodopechys githaginea*)

64 Seated Woman

1971 (23 Nov). Stamp Day. T **63** and similar designs showing birds. Multicoloured. Photo. P 12½.
290	1p.50 Type **63**	45	45
291	2p. Type **63**	45	45
292	5p. Cream-coloured courser (*Cursorius cursor*)	85	85
293	24p. Lanner falcon (*Falco biarmicus*)	2·50	2·50
290/293 Set of 4		3·75	3·75

1972 (18 Feb). Saharan Nomads. T **64** and similar vert designs. Photo. P 13.
294	1p. agate, pale rose and dull blue	35	30
295	1p.50 grey-black, pale lilac & pur-brn	35	30
296	2p. slate-black, pale cinn & bottle-green	35	30
297	5p. maroon, stone and greenish blue	35	30
298	8p. deep lilac, greenish grey and black	70	30
299	10p. dp turquoise-bl, brownish grey and black	70	30
300	12p. multicoloured (10.4)	70	55
301	15p. multicoloured (10.4)	80	55
302	24p. multicoloured (10.4)	1·90	1·40
294/302 Set of 9		5·50	3·75

Designs:—1p.50, 2p. Squatting nomad; 5p. Type **64**; 8p., 10p. Head of nomad; 12p. Woman with bangles; 15p. Nomad with rifle; 24p. Woman displaying trinkets.

435

SPANISH SAHARA / Spanish Sahara

65 Tuareg Woman

66 Mother and Child

1972 (1 June). Child Welfare. T **65** and similar vert design. Multicoloured. Photo. P 13.
303		8p. Type **65**	1·00	1·00
304		12p. Tuareg elder	1·20	1·20

1972 (23 Nov). Stamp Day. T **66** and similar vert design. Multicoloured. Photo. P 13.
305		4p. Type **66**	80	80
306		15p. Nomad	1·30	1·30

67 Sahara Desert

68 Villa Cisneros

1973 (1 June). Child Welfare. T **67** and similar horiz design. Multicoloured. Photo. P 13.
307		2p. Type **67**	70	70
308		7p. City Gate, El Aaiun	1·20	1·20

1973 (23 Nov). Stamp Day. T **68** and similar multicoloured design. Photo. P 13.
309		2p. Type **68**	70	70
310		7p. Tuareg (*vert*)	1·20	1·20

69 U.P.U. Monument, Berne

70 Archway, Smara Mosque

1974 (May). Centenary of Universal Postal Union. Photo. P 13.
311	**69**	15p. multicoloured	1·70	1·70

1974 (1 June). Child Welfare. T **70** and similar vert design. Multicoloured. Photo. P 13.
312		1p. Type **70**	55	55
313		2p. Villa Cisneros Mosque	85	85

71 Eagle Owl (*Bubo desertorum*)

72 "Espana" Emblem and Spanish Sahara Stamp

1974 (23 Nov). Stamp Day. T **71** and similar diamond-shaped design. Multicoloured Photo. P 12½.
314		2p. Type **71**	55	55
315		5p. Lappet-faced vulture (*Torgos tracheliotus*)	85	85

1975 (4 Apr). España 75 International Stamp Exhibition, Madrid. Photo. P 13.
316	**72**	8p. yellow-olive, greenish blue and black	1·20	1·20

73 Desert Conference

74 Tuareg Elder

1975 (1 June). Child Welfare. T **73** and similar horiz design. Multicoloured. Photo. P 13.
317		1p.50 Type **73**	55	55
318		3p. Desert oasis	85	85

1975 (7 Nov). Photo. P 13.
319	**74**	3p. brown-purple, pale green and black	70	70

The Spanish government announced on 23 May 1975 that it was ready to give independence to Spanish Sahara and opened negotiations with Morocco, Mauritania, Algeria and Polisario (the Popular Front for the Liberation of Saguia el Hamra and Rio de Oro).

Precipitated by the 'Green March' of 6 November 1975, when King Hassan of Morocco led 350,000 civilians into Spanish Sahara in a peaceful demonstration, a tripartite agreement was announced on 14 November 1975, providing for the transfer of power in the territory to the Moroccan and Mauritanian governments by 28 February 1976. Morocco quickly consolidated its position by occupying, in December 1975 and January 1976, most of the principal towns.

Spanish troops were withdrawn by 26 February 1976. The country was divided between Morocco (receiving the northern two-thirds) and Mauritania (receiving the southern third). The border was delineated under a convention signed in Rabat on 14 April 1976. It ran east from the Atlantic coast north of Dakhla (formerly Villa Cisneros) to a point south of Bir Enzaran, then turned south-east towards the Mauritanian town of Zourrate.

Polisario resisted the agreements and at midnight on 27/28 February 1976 it proclaimed the Saharan Arab Democratic Republic and formed a government, which some countries have recognized. Guerrilla warfare has ensued throughout the former Spanish Sahara (since its partition often termed Western Sahara).

On 5 August 1979 Mauritania signed a peace treaty with Polisario and withdrew from the territory it had annexed in the south as Tiris el Gharbia. Morocco occupied its capital, Dakhla, on 11 August and assumed control of the whole area by mid-month. Tiris el Gharbia was renamed Oued Eddahab (Arabic for Rio de Oro) and became a province of Morocco.

Issues inscribed "SAHARA OCC.", denominated in pesetas, were printed in Cuba for the Frente Polisario and exist cancelled-to-order. There is however no evidence of a postal service in those parts of the interior desert beyond the Moroccan defensive lines.

Spanish West Africa

100 Céntimos = 1 Peseta

The following stamps were issued in 1949-51 for use both in Ifni and Spanish Sahara.

1 Native

2 Isabella the Catholic

(Des S. Quintana and Goico. Photo Govt Ptg Works, Madrid)
1949 (9 Oct). 75th Anniv of Universal Postal Union. P 13×12½.
| 1 | 1 | 4p. slate-green | 3·75 | 3·75 |

(Des Tauler. Photo Govt Ptg Works, Madrid)
1949 (23 Nov). AIR. Colonial Stamp Day. P 13×12½.
| 2 | 2 | 5p. yellow-brown | 3·00 | 3·00 |

3 Tents

4 Palm Trees by Lake Tinzarrentz

5 Camels and Irrigation

6 Camel Transport

7 Desert Camp

8 Camel Train

9 Four Camels

E **10** Port Tilimenzo

(Des Nuñez de Celis. Photo Govt Ptg Works, Madrid)
1950 (5 June)–**51**. P 12½×13.
(a) POSTAGE

3	3	2c. yellow-brown	20	20
4	4	5c. reddish violet	20	20
5	5	10c. turquoise-blue	20	20
6	6	15c. olive-black	20	20
7	3	25c. red-brown	20	20
8	4	30c. yellow	20	20
9	5	40c. olive	20	20
10	6	45c. claret	20	20
11	3	50c. brown-orange	20	20
12	4	75c. blue	25	20
13	5	90c. blue-green	25	20
14	6	1p. grey-black	25	20
15	3	1p.35 violet	70	55
16	4	2p. sepia	1·40	1·20
17	5	5p. magenta	21·00	4·75
18	3	10p. yellow-brown	45·00	30·00
3/18		Set of 16	65·00	35·00

(b) AIR (1 Mar 1951)

19	7	25c. brownish yellow	20	20
20	8	50c. magenta	20	20
21	9	1p. green	30	20
22	7	2p. blue	75	25
23	8	3p.25 reddish violet	1·70	1·70
24	9	5p. sepia	22·00	5·75
25	7	10p. scarlet	46·00	31·00
19/25		Set of 7	65·00	35·00

(c) EXPRESS LETTER (1 Mar 1951)

| E26 | E **10** | 25c. carmine | 40 | 40 |

ANDORRA / French Post Offices

Andorra

This small state in the Pyrenees, which uses both French and Spanish currency, has two nominal heads of state—the French President and the Spanish Bishop of Urgel, the Co-princes. A new constitution adopted in 1993 made the co-princes a single constitutional monarchy and instituted a parliament. Andorra now conducts its own affairs, with consultation on foreign matters that affect France or Spain.

French and Spanish stamps were probably first used in Andorra in 1877. During the 1880s, French interest in Andorra increased and the earliest known postmark is a French style circular datestamp "ANDORRE-VAL D'ANDORRE" of 15 October 1882. The U.P.U. allocated Andorran postal administration to Spain; however, in 1887, France organized a courier service (using contemporary French stamps) which, in improved form, existed from 1892 to 1931. No postmarks were available, but datestamps of French telegraph offices in Andorra occur on cover. The Spanish P.O. in Andorra opened on 1 January 1928 and the French Postal Service commenced on 16 June 1931.

A set of 12 stamps produced in 1890 showing the Arms and inscribed "REPUBLICA DE ANDORRA" and postage dues inscribed "Multa/ANDORRA" are bogus. Souvenir sheets and other items inscribed "VEGUERIA EPISCOPAL/SERVEI D'EMISSIONS" were issued by the parish authorities but served no postal function.

Ordinary internal mail is carried free, but registration and other special facilities are charged.

I. FRENCH POST OFFICES

1931. 100 Centimes = 1 Franc
2002. 100 Cents = 1 Euro

French stamps are not valid for use in Andorra.

PRINTERS. All the following were printed at the Government Printing Works, Paris (from 1970 at Périgueux).

IMPERFORATE STAMPS. Most issues of the 1944–51 series and from 1961 exist imperforate from limited printings.

(F **1**)

(F **2**)

1931 (16 June). Contemporary types of France optd.

(a) Optd with Type F **1**

F1	11	½c. (R.) on 1c. slate (No. 379)	1·10	6·50
		a. Opt double	£4000	
F2		1c. greenish slate	1·20	1·70
		a. Opt double	£2500	
F3		2c. claret	1·60	8·00
F4		3c. orange	2·10	4·25
F5		5c. green	3·25	8·25
F6		10c. lilac	5·25	10·00
F7	18	15c. lake-brown	9·00	9·75
F8		20c. magenta	14·50	15·00
F9		25c. ochre-brown	12·50	17·00
F10		30c. green	12·50	15·00
F11		40c. ultramarine	13·50	23·00
F12	15	45c. violet	26·00	31·00
F13		50c. vermilion	18·00	20·00
F14		65c. sage green	37·00	41·00
F15		75c. magenta	42·00	46·00
F16	18	90c. scarlet	55·00	70·00
F17	15	1f. blue	60·00	70·00
F18	18	1f.50 blue	65·00	80·00

(b) Optd with Type F **2**

F19	13	2f. red and blue-green	60·00	90·00
F20		3f. deep mauve and carmine	£110	£150
F21		5f. deep blue and buff	£150	£250
F22		10f. sage green and red	£325	£450
F23		20f. magenta and green	£425	£500
F1/23	Set of 23		£1300	£1700

1931 (16 June)–**32**. POSTAGE DUE. Postage Due stamps of France optd with Type F **1**.

(a) Type D **11**

FD24	5c. blue	2·10	5·75
FD25	10c. brown	2·10	4·50
FD26	30c. pale carmine	1·10	5·25
FD27	50c. dull claret	2·10	5·75
FD28	60c. green	26·00	55·00
FD29	1f. lake-brown/*straw*	2·10	7·00
FD30	2f. deep mauve	17·00	41·00
FD31	3f. magenta	4·25	9·75
FD24/31 *Set of 8*		50·00	£120

(b) Type D **43**

FD32	1c. grey-olive (1932)	3·25	5·75
FD33	10c. carmine	6·25	14·00
FD34	60c. red	31·00	48·00
FD35	1f. deep bluish green (21.3.32)	95·00	£140
FD36	1f.20 on 2f. greenish blue (No. D471)	90·00	£160
FD37	2f. bistre-brown (21.3.32)	£180	£275
FD38	5f. on 1f. purple (No. D472)	95·00	£130
FD32/38 *Set of 7*		£450	£700

PAPER AND SHADE VARIETIES. Numerous printings were made of many definitives from No. F24 to F184, resulting in paper and/or gum varieties and minor shades. Only major differences are listed.

F **3** Our Lady's Chapel, Meritxell

F **4** St. Anthony's Bridge

F **5** St. Michael's Church, Engolasters

F **6** Valley of Sant Julia

F **7** Andorra la Vella

(Des and eng. A. Delzers (F **3**), J. Piel (F **4**), G. Hourriez (F **5**),
H. Chaffer (F **6**), A. Mignon (F **7**). Recess)

1932 (16 June)–**43**. P 13.

F24	F **3**	1c. slate	75	2·75
F25		2c. reddish violet	1·10	2·30
F26		3c. brown	1·20	2·50
F27		5c. deep bluish green	95	2·75
F28	F **4**	10c. reddish lilac	1·80	3·25
F29	F **3**	15c. vermilion	2·75	3·50
F30	F **4**	20c. bright magenta	13·50	17·00
F31	F **5**	25c. brown	5·75	7·50
F32	F **4**	25c. lake-brown (11.37)	13·50	34·00
F33		30c. emerald	3·75	4·50
F34		40c. ultramarine	10·50	9·25
F35		40c. blackish brown (16.6.39)	1·60	4·00
F36		45c. vermilion	15·00	29·00
F37		45c. deep blue-green (16.6.39)	7·50	22·00
F38	F **5**	50c. claret	16·00	17·00
		a. Brown-purple	£140	£140
F39	F **4**	50c. bright violet (16.6.39)	7·50	20·00
F40		50c. yellow-green (1.1.41)	2·10	10·50
F41		55c. deep reddish violet (6.38)	32·00	70·00
F42		60c. yellow-brown (6.38)	2·10	7·50
F43	F **5**	65c. deep turquoise-green	70·00	75·00
F44	F **4**	65c. slate-blue (1.38)	19·00	33·00
F45		70c. red (12.7.39)	2·40	5·75
F46	F **5**	75c. bright violet	11·50	12·50
F47	F **4**	75c. ultramarine (16.6.39)	5·25	17·00
F48		80c. deep green (6.38)	28·00	70·00
F49	F **6**	80c. blue-green (1.1.41)	1·70	6·25
F50		90c. carmine	9·50	9·25
F51		90c. myrtle green (16.6.39)	7·50	15·00
F52		1f. deep bluish green	34·00	23·00
F53		1f. vermilion (5.38)	32·00	34·00
F54		1f. royal blue	1·40	3·50
F55		1f.20 bright violet (8.7.42)	1·30	6·50
F56	F **3**	1f.25 magenta (6.33)	65·00	80·00
F57		1f.25 carmine (16.6.39)	8·00	20·00
F58	F **6**	1f.30 sepia (1.1.41)	1·70	6·50
F59	F **7**	1f.50 royal blue	26·00	37·00
F60	F **6**	1f.50 rosine (1.1.41)	1·10	6·50

438

ANDORRA / French Post Offices

F61		1f.75 violet (6.33)	£110	£140
F62		1f.75 deep blue (4.38)	60·00	75·00
F63		2f. dull claret	10·50	23·00
F64	F 3	2f. carmine (1.1.41)	2·10	8·50
F65		2f. deep green (8.7.42)	1·20	8·50
F66		2f.15 deep reddish violet (4.38)	60·00	90·00
F67		2f.25 ultramarine (12.7.39)	10·50	30·00
F68		2f.40 vermilion (8.7.42)	1·40	6·50
F69		2f.50 black (12.7.39)	12·50	36·00
F70		2f.50 ultramarine (1.1.41)	2·75	10·50
F71	F 6	3f. chestnut	25·00	41·00
F72	F 3	3f. red-brown (1.1.41)	2·20	7·00
F73		4f. deep blue (8.7.42)	1·60	6·25
F74		4f.50 violet (8.7.42)	2·10	8·25
F75		5f. brown	1·80	7·00
F76	F 7	10f. reddish violet	2·40	7·00
		a. Purple	13·00	30·00
F78		15f. royal blue (8.7.42)	1·60	4·00
F79		20f. carmine	2·10	3·75
		a. Red	7·50	8·25
F81	F 4	50f. greenish blue (15.3.43)	3·00	9·25
F24/81 Set of 56			£700	£1100

Nos. F24/9 optd "ELECTIONS/SEPTEMBRE/1933" were unauthorized productions.

FD 7   (F 8)   F 9

1935 (Aug). POSTAGE DUE. Typo. P 14×13½.
FD82	FD 7	1c. grey-olive	4·25	9·25

1935 (25 Sept). No. F38 surch with Type F 8.
F82	F 5	20c. on 50c. claret	16·00	29·00
		a. Brown-purple	£120	£130
		b. Surch double	£7500	

(Eng A. Ouvré. Recess)

1936 (Dec)–**42**. P 14×13.
F83	F 9	1c. black (3.37)	55	3·25
F84		2c. light blue	55	3·25
F85		3c. brown (1.37)	55	3·25
F86		5c. rose-carmine (1.37)	40	3·25
F87		10c. dull ultramarine (3.37)	40	3·25
		a. Deep blue (1942)	6·00	6·00
F88		15c. deep mauve	3·25	5·25
F89		20c. green (3.37)	40	3·25
F90		30c. dull vermilion (5.38)	75	7·00
		a. Red (1941)	7·00	7·00
F91		30c. brownish black (2.12.42)	1·50	6·50
F92		35c. deep bluish green (4.38)	60·00	90·00
F93		40c. lake-brown (8.7.42)	1·10	6·25
F94		50c. deep blue-green (8.7.42)	1·20	6·50
F95		60c. greenish blue (8.7.42)	1·60	6·50
F96		70c. bright violet (8.7.42)	1·60	6·50
F83/96 Set of 14			65·00	£140

FD 10   FD 11 Wheat Sheaves

1937–**41**. POSTAGE DUE. Typo. P 14×13½.
FD97	FD 10	5c. light blue	7·50	16·00
FD98		10c. brown (1941)	5·25	30·00
FD99		2f. bright mauve (1941)	11·50	16·00
FD100		5f. orange (1941)	25·00	40·00
FD97/100 Set of 4			45·00	90·00

(Des P. Gandon. Die eng H. Cortot. Typo)

1943 (25 Oct)–**46**. POSTAGE DUE. P 14×13½.
FD101	FD 11	10c. blackish brown	55	3·50
		a. Sepia	65	2·10
FD102		30c. bright mauve	1·90	2·75
FD103		50c. myrtle green	1·40	3·25
FD104		1f. ultramarine	2·10	4·75
FD105		1f.50 rosine	5·75	14·50
FD106		2f. greenish blue	2·10	5·25
FD107		3f. brown-red	2·50	9·75
FD108		4f. violet (22.10.45)	5·25	15·00
FD109		5f. bright magenta	4·25	14·50
		a. Imperf (pair)	£600	
FD110		10f. red-orange (22.10.45)	5·75	15·00
FD111		20f. olive-brown (27.5.46)	8·00	22·00
FD101/111 Set of 11			36·00	£100

For design as Type D **11** but inscr "TIMBRE-TAXE", see Nos. FD143/52 and FD185/8.

F **10**   F **11** Church of St. John of Caselles

F **12** House of the Valleys   F **13** Andorra la Vella

F **14** Councillor Jaume Bonell

(Des R. Louis (F **10**). Lucas (F **13**), A. Ouvré (others).
Eng J. Piel (F **10**), A. Ouvré (others). Recess)

1944 (14 Aug)–**51**.

(a) P 14×13
F97	F **10**	10c. violet	20	4·00
F98		30c. carmine	20	4·00
F99		40c. deep blue	40	4·00
F100		50c. dull vermilion	20	4·50
		a. Indian red (1950)	2·10	4·50
F101		60c. black	40	4·00
F102		70c. bright mauve	30	5·75
		a. Horiz pair, one imperf, one perf 3 sides	£2750	
F103		80c. myrtle green	20	5·75
F104		1f. dull ultramarine (28.3.49)	1·10	2·40
		a. Deep blue (1950)	2·75	3·00

(b) P 13
F105	F **11**	1f. brown-purple (6.11.44)	20	6·25
F106		1f.20 blue (6.11.44)	20	6·25
F107		1f.50 vermilion (6.11.44)	20	6·25
F108		2f. deep bluish green (6.11.44)	20	4·00
F109	F **12**	2f.40 rosine (6.11.44)	20	4·00
F110		2f.50 rosine (27.5.46)	4·25	10·50
F111		3f. sepia (6.11.44)	60	2·75
		a. Agate (1947)	11·00	11·00
F112	F **11**	3f. vermilion (9.7.51)	4·25	5·75
F113	F **12**	4f. ultramarine (6.11.44)	55	6·25
F114		4f. deep turquoise-green (26.7.48)	1·10	7·50
F115	F **11**	4f. blackish brown (28.3.49)	2·30	10·50
F116	F **13**	4f.50 brownish black (6.11 .44)	60	5·75
F117	F **12**	4f.50 greenish blue (8.3.47)	5·25	20·00
F118	F **13**	5f. ultramarine (6.11.44)	55	6·25
F119		5f. deep bluish green (27.5.46)	1·40	6·50
F120	F **12**	5f. bright emerald (28.3.49)	3·25	11·50
F121		5f. deep lilac (9.7.51)	4·25	8·00
F122	F **13**	6f. carmine (1.11.45)	55	3·75
		a. Carmine-red (1947)	4·50	4·50
F123		6f. brown-purple (26.7.48)	55	5·75
F124	F **12**	6f. emerald (9.7.51)	3·25	7·50
F125	F **13**	8f. indigo (4.12.48)	1·60	8·00
F126	F **12**	8f. lake-brown (28.3.49)	1·10	3·50
F127	F **13**	10f. deep bluish green (6.11.44)	40	5·75
F128		10f. ultramarine (27.5.46)	1·60	1·80
F129		12f. vermilion (26.7.48)	1·40	7·50
F130		12f. blue-green (1.2.49)	1·60	5·75
F131	F **14**	15f. deep magenta (6.11.44)	65	6·50
F132	F **13**	15f. carmine-red (1.2.49)	85	3·50
F133		15f. deep reddish brown (9.7.51)	7·50	4·50
F134	F **14**	18f. blue (26.7.48)	3·25	12·00
F135	F **13**	18f. scarlet (9.7.51)	12·50	26·00

ANDORRA / French Post Offices

F136	F **14**	20f. blue (6.11.44)	1·10	6·50
F137		20f. deep reddish violet (26.7.48)	3·25	10·00
F138		25f. rose-red (27.5.46)	3·75	10·50
F139		25f. ultramarine (1.2.49)	2·10	8·50
F140		30f. royal blue (9.7.51)	21·00	29·00
F141		40f. deep green (27.5.46)	3·25	9·25
F142		50f. deep purple-brown (6.11.44)	1·80	4·25
		a. *Chocolate* (1945)	11·00	9·25
F97/142 *Set of 46*			95·00	£300

No. F102a. caused by the last vertical row in the sheet being imperforate, should be collected as listed to distinguish the error from pairs from the limited printing of imperforate sheets.

1946–59. POSTAGE DUE. As Type FD **11**, but inscr "TIMBRE-TAXE". Typo. P 14×13½.

FD143		10c. sepia (25.9.46)	1·10	7·25
FD144		1f. deep ultramarine (13.10.7)	1·30	4·00
		a. *Bright blue* (959)	3·75	2·30
FD145		2f. greenish blue (13.10.47)	1·40	4·00
FD146		3f. red-brown (13.10.47)	2·75	6·00
FD147		4f. violet (13.10.47)	3·75	7·25
FD148		5f. bright rose-carmine (13.10.47)	2·10	5·75
FD149		10f. orange (3.10.47)	3·75	7·50
FD150		20f. olive-brown (3.10.47)	7·50	13·00
FD151		50f. deep green (2.10.50)	60·00	55·00
FD152		100f. green (3.4.53)	£110	£160
FD143/152 *Set of 10*			£170	£250

See also Nos. FD185/8.

F **15** Chamois and Pyrenees   F **16** Les Escaldes

(Des and eng G. Barlangue. Recess)

1950 (10 Feb). AIR. P 13.
F143   F **15**   100f. indigo.................... £110   £110

(Des A. Decaris. Eng C. Hertenberger (1 to 5f.), A. Frères (6 to 12f.). C. P. Dufresne (15 to 25f.), A. Decaris (30 to 500f.). Recess)

1955 (15 Feb)–58. Type F **16** and similar designs. P 13.
(a) POSTAGE

F144		1f. slate-blue	20	2·75
F145		2f. green	55	2·10
F146		3f. bright scarlet	65	2·10
F147		5f. chocolate	65	2·10
F148		6f. deep bluish green	2·20	2·75
F149		8f. lake	2·40	3·25
F150		10f. bright reddish violet	4·25	2·75
F151		12f. indigo	2·30	2·10
F152		15f. vermilion	3·00	2·30
F153		18f. turquoise-blue	2·75	3·75
F154		20f. deep violet	3·25	2·30
F155		25f. blackish brown	3·50	4·00
F156		30f. deep bright blue	26·00	34·00
F157		35f. greenish blue (13.8.57)	13·50	14·50
F158		40f. deep green	35·00	55·00
F159		50f. carmine	4·25	4·50
F160		65f. reddish violet (27.1.58)	9·50	29·00
F161		70f. light brown (13.8.57)	9·25	22·00
F162		75f. violet-blue	45·00	90·00
F144/162 *Set of 19*			£150	£250

(b) AIR. Inscr "POSTE AERIENNE"

F163		100f. deep green	10·50	15·00
F164		200f. carmine	21·00	23·00
F165		500f. deep blue (13.3.57)	85·00	90·00

Designs: Horiz—6 to 12f. Santa Coloma Church; 30 to 75f. Les Bons village. Vert—1 to 5f. Type F **16**; 15 to 25f. Gothic cross, Andorra la Vella; 100 to 500f. East Valira River.

New currency.
100 (old) francs = 1 (new) franc

F **21**   F **22** Gothic Cross, Meritxell

(Des R. Louis; die eng A. Barre, Typo (Type F **21**). Des and eng C. Mazelin (Type F **22**), P. Gandon (60c. to 1f.), C. Durrens (2 to 10f.). Recess)

1961 (17 June)–**82**. Type F **21** and horiz views as Type F **22**. Creamy paper. P 14×13½ (Type F **21**) or 13 (others).

(a) POSTAGE

F166	F **21**	1c. grey, dp blue and slate-purple (16.5.64)	65	1·60
F167		2c. yell-orge, black and orange (16.5.64)	65	1·60
		a. *Reddish orange and black* (1974)*	3·00	3·50
F168		5c. pale green, black and emerald	40	1·60
		a. *Bright green, black and emerald* (1980)	3·00	3·50
F169		10c. rose, black and red	45	45
		a. *Salmon, black and red* (1971)	2·30	2·30
F170		12c. greenish yellow, deep reddish purple and emerald (16.5.64)	2·20	2·75
		a. *Lemon, maroon and emerald* (1966)	2·20	4·50
F171		15c. new blue, black and blue	75	1·60
		a. *Light blue and black* (1966)*	1·90	1·80
		b. *Light blue, black and new blue* (1972)	3·00	3·00
F172		18c. rose, black and brt mauve (16.5.64)	1·40	3·25
F173		20c. bistre-yellow, reddish brown and orange-yellow	80	55
		a. *Yellow and reddish brown* (1964)*	2·10	1·30
F174	F **22**	25c. pale blue, violet and emerald	1·10	1·10
F175		30c. brown-purple, lake and green	1·10	80
F175a		40c. bronze green and orange-brown (24.6.65)	1·30	2·00
F176		45c. blue, indigo and yellow-green	21·00	34·00
F176a		45c. olive-brown, deep slate-blue and deep violet (13.6.70)	1·30	2·75
F177		50c. sepia, purple, green and olive-brown	2·75	2·75
F177a	–	60c. dp brown & orange-brown (24.6.65)	1·60	2·10
F178	–	65c. brown-olive, turq-bl and chocolate	23·00	55·00
F179	–	85c. dp violet, maroon, purple and magenta	23·00	40·00
F179a	–	90c. blue-green, bright blue and yellow-brown (28.8.71)	1·60	3·50
F180	–	1f. indigo, sepia and turquoise	2·75	2·75
		a. *White paper* (1970)	3·50	3·50
F166/180 *Set of 19*			80·00	£140

(b) AIR

F181	–	2f. brown-olive, brt scarlet & mar	2·20	2·30
		a. *Grey-olive, bright scarlet and maroon* (1976)	4·50	4·50
		b. *Brown-olive, bright scarlet and deep reddish purple (white paper)* (1980)	4·50	4·50
F182	–	3f. brown-pur, dp bl and blackish green	2·40	2·50
		a. *White paper* (1982)	7·50	5·75
F183	–	5f. orange, bright purple and lake	4·00	4·00
F184	–	10f. dp green & turq-bl (25.4.64)	6·00	5·50
		a. *Deep green and greenish blue (white paper)* (1982)	16·00	16·00
F181/184 *Set of 4*			13·00	13·00

Designs:—60c. to 1f. Engolasters Lake; 2f. to 10f. Inclès Valley.
*On Nos. F167a, F171a and F173a the colour of the frame matches the colour of the shield background.

1961 (19 June). POSTAGE DUE. As Nos. FD143/52 but new values and colours.

FD185	FD **11**	5c. carmine	4·25	8·25
FD186		10c. orange-red	9·50	17·00
FD187		20c. olive-brown	13·50	29·00
FD188		50c. blackish green	26·00	47·00
FD185/188 *Set of 4*			48·00	90·00

F **23** "Telstar" Satellite and part of Globe

(Des C. Durrens. Eng P. Béquet. Recess)

1962 (29 Sept). First Trans-Atlantic Television Satellite Link. P 13.
F185   F **23**   50c. reddish violet and bright blue........   1·60   2·75

440

ANDORRA / French Post Offices

F **24** "La Sardane" (dance)

(Des and eng C. Durrens (20c.). A. Decaris (others). Recess)

1963 (24 June). Andorran History (1st issue). Type F **24** and larger horiz designs inscr "1963". P 13.

F186	20c. reddish purple, magenta and olive-green	3·75	6·50
F187	50c. lake and slate-green	6·75	12·50
F188	1f. deep bluish green, blue and red-brown	9·50	21·00
F186/188	Set of 3	18·00	36·00

Designs: 48½×27 mm—50c. Charlemagne crossing Andorra. 48×27 mm—1f. Foundation of Andorra by Louis the Debonair.

F **25** Santa Coloma Church and Grand Palais, Paris

F **26** Virgin of Santa Coloma

(Des and eng J. Comber. Recess)

1964 (18 Jan). PHILATEC 1964 International Stamp Exhibition, Paris. P 13.

| F189 | F **25** | 25c. green, brown-purple and sepia | 1·60 | 3·25 |

(Des and eng Decaris. Recess)

1964 (25 Apr). Andorran History (2nd issue). Horiz designs as Nos. F187/8 inscr "1964". P 13.

F190	60c. dp bluish green, chestnut and brown	11·50	32·00
F191	1f. blue, sepia and orange-brown	16·00	32·00

Designs: 48½×27 mm—60c. "Napoleon re-establishes the Andorran Statute, 1806"; 1f. "Confirmation of the Co-Government, 1288".

1964 (15 June)–**71**. POSTAGE DUE. Designs as Nos. D1650/6 of France, but inscr "ANDORRE". P 14×13½.

FD192	5c. red, myrtle grn and bright purple (26.4.65)	55	4·25
	a. Red, green and bright purple (1965)	3·25	4·25
FD193	10c. blue, green and bright purple (26.4.65)	85	4·25
FD194	15c. red, light green and brown	95	4·25
	a. Red, myrtle green and brown (1978)	4·25	4·25
FD195	20c. purple, lt green and blue-green (15.3.71)	1·10	4·25
FD196	30c. blue, blue-green and brown	85	2·50
FD197	40c. yellow, cerise & bl-grn (15.3.71)	2·10	2·75
FD198	50c. carmine, myrtle green and ultramarine (26.4.65)	1·70	1·70
FD192/198	Set of 7	7·25	22·00

(Des and eng C. Durrens. Recess)

1964 (25 July). Red Cross Fund. P 13.

| F192 | F **26** | 25c.+10c. red, green and blue | 21·00 | 38·00 |

F **27** "Syncom", Morse Key and Pleumeur-Bodou Centre

F **28** Andorra House, Paris

F **29** Chair-lift

(Des and eng A. Decaris. Recess)

1965 (17 May). International Telecommunications Union Centenary. P 13.

| F193 | F **27** | 60c. violet, light blue and crimson | 4·75 | 8·00 |

(Des and eng P. Béquet. Recess)

1965 (5 June). Opening of Andorra House, Paris. P 13.

| F194 | F **28** | 25c. orange-brown, olive-brown and blue | 1·10 | 2·30 |

(Des and eng J. Combet. Recess)

1966 (2 Apr). Winter Sports. Type F **29** and similar design. P 13.

F195	25c. myrtle-green, brn-pur and new blue	1·30	3·25
F196	40c. sepia, bright blue and crimson	2·10	4·00

Design: Horiz—40c. Ski-lift.

F **30** Satellite "FR 1"

F **31** Europa "Ship"

(Des and eng C. Durrens. Recess)

1966 (7 May). Launching of Satellite "FR 1". P 13.

| F197 | F **30** | 60c. new blue, emer and myrtle-green | 2·10 | 4·25 |

(Des G. and J. Bender. Eng J. Combet. Recess)

1966 (24 Sept). Europa. P 13.

| F198 | F **31** | 60c. brown | 3·50 | 6·25 |

F **32** Cogwheels

F **33** "Folk Dancers" (statue)

F **34** Telephone and Dial

(Des O. Bonnevalle. Eng R. Cami. Recess)

1967 (29 Apr). Europe. P 13.

F199	F **32**	30c. deep indigo and light blue	4·25	5·75
F200		60c. brown-red and bright purple	5·50	10·50

(Des and eng P. Béquet (after Viladomat). Recess)

1967 (29 Apr). Centenary (1966) of the New Reform. P 13.

| F201 | F **33** | 30c. myrtle-green, olive-grn and slate | 1·50 | 3·50 |

(Des and eng J. Combet. Recess)

1967 (29 Apr). Inauguration of Automatic Telephone Service. P 13.

| F202 | F **34** | 60c. black, violet and carmine | 1·60 | 3·75 |

F **35** Andorran Family

F **36** "The Temptation"

(Des and eng A. Decaris. Recess)

1967 (23 Sept). Institution of Social Security. P 13.

| F203 | F **35** | 2f.30 lake-brown and purple-brown | 8·50 | 18·00 |

441

ANDORRA / French Post Offices

(Des and eng J. Combet. Recess)

1967 (23 Sept). 16th-Century Frescoes in House of the Valleys (1st series). Type F **36** and similar vert designs. P 13.

F204	25c. Venetian red and black	1·10	2·75
F205	30c. bright purple and deep reddish violet..	1·20	3·50
F206	60c. greenish blue and deep blue	1·60	4·50
F204/206	Set of 3	3·50	9·75

Designs: Frescoes—30c. "The Kiss of Judas"; 60c. "The Descent from the Cross".
See also Nos. F210/12.

F **37** Downhill Skiing

F **38** Europa "Key"

(Des and eng J. Combet. Recess)

1968 (27 Jan). Winter Olympic Games, Grenoble. P 13.

| F207 | F **37** | 40c. purple, yellow-orange and red .... | 1·40 | 3·75 |

(Des H. Schwarzenbach. Eng P. Béquet. Recess)

1968 (27 Apr). Europa. P 13.

| F208 | F **38** | 30c. new blue and deep slate | 5·25 | 8·50 |
| F209 | | 60c. reddish violet and brown | 8·50 | 14·00 |

(Des and eng J. Combet. Recess)

1968 (12 Oct). 16th-Century Frescoes in House of the Valleys (2nd series). Horiz designs similar to Type F **36**. P 13.

F210	25c. bronze-green and myrtle-green	95	3·25
F211	30c. plum and chocolate	1·20	4·75
F212	60c. chocolate and lake	2·10	6·50
F210/212	Set of 3	3·75	13·00

Frescoes:—25c. "The Beating of Christ"; 30c. "Christ Helped by the Cyrenians"; 60c. "The Death of Christ".

F **39** High Jumping   F **40** Colonnade

(Des and eng G. Bétemps. Recess)

1968 (12 Oct). Olympic Games. Mexico. P 13.

| F213 | F **39** | 40c. red-brown and new blue | 2·10 | 3·75 |

(Des L. Gasbarra and G. Belli. Eng P. Béquet. Recess)

1969 (26 Apr). Europa. P 13.

| F214 | F **40** | 40c. slate, greenish blue and deep cerise | 9·50 | 11·50 |
| F215 | | 70c. brown-red, olive and indigo | 13·00 | 22·00 |

F **41** Canoeing

F **42** "The Apocalypse"

1969 (2 Aug). World Kayak-Canoeing Championships, Bourg-St. Maurice. P 13.

| F216 | F **41** | 70c. grey-blue, blue and myrtle-green | 2·10 | 5·25 |

(Des and eng J. Combet. Recess)

1969 (27 Sept). European Water Charter. Vert design similar to T **639** of France. P 13.

| F217 | 70c. black, greenish blue and ultramarine .... | 5·25 | 9·75 |

(Des and eng J. Combet. Recess)

1969 (18 Oct). Altar-screen, Church of St. John of Caselles (1st series). "The Revelation of St. John". Type F **42** and similar vert designs, showing further sections of the screen. Dated "1969". P 13.

F218	30c. brown-red, dp reddish violet and brown	1·10	2·10
F219	40c. bistre-brown, purple-brn & slate	1·60	2·75
F220	70c. bright purple, lake & carmine-red	2·10	3·50
F218/220	Set of 3	4·25	7·50

Designs:—40c. Angel "clothed with cloud, with face as the sun, and feet as pillars of fire" (Rev. 10); 70c. Christ with sword and stars, and seven candlesticks.
See also Nos. F225/7, F233/5 and F240/2.

F **43** Handball Player

F **44** "Flaming Sun"

(Des and eng G. Bétemps. Recess)

1970 (21 Feb). Seventh World Handball Championships, France. P 13.

| F221 | F **43** | 80c. new blue, chocolate and indigo . | 2·75 | 5·25 |

(Des L. le Brocquy. Eng G. Bétemps. Recess)

1970 (2 May). Europa. P 13.

| F222 | F **44** | 40c. yellow-orange | 9·50 | 8·00 |
| F223 | | 80c. bluish violet | 12·00 | 13·00 |

F **45** Putting the Shot   F **46** Ice Skaters

(Des and eng G. Bétemps. Recess)

1970 (11 Sept). First European Junior Athletic Championships, Paris. P 13.

| F224 | F **45** | 80c. maroon and new blue | 2·75 | 5·50 |

(Des and eng J. Combet. Recess)

1970 (24 Oct). Altar-screen, Church of St. John of Caselles (2nd series). Vert designs as Type F **42**, but dated "1970". P 13.

F225	30c. reddish violet, purple-brn and cerise	1·50	2·50
F226	40c. myrtle-green and violet	1·60	2·75
F227	80c. rose, indigo and deep olive	3·25	4·00
F225/227	Set of 3	5·75	8·25

Designs:—30c. Angel with keys and padlock; 40c. Angel with pillar; 80c. St. John being boiled in cauldron of oil.

(Des and eng P. Forget. Recess)

1971 (20 Feb). World Ice Skating Championships, Lyon. P 13.

| F228 | F **46** | 80c. reddish violet, bright purple and red | 3·00 | 4·75 |

F **47** Capercaillie

F **48** Europa Chain

ANDORRA / French Post Offices

(Des J. Combet. Photo (No. F229). Des and eng Combet. Recess No. F230)

1971 (24 Apr). Nature Protection. T **47** and similar vert design. P 13.
F229	F **47**	80c. multicoloured	4·75	6·25
F230	–	80c. chocolate, myrtle-grn and new blue	4·75	6·25

Design:—No. F230, Brown bear.

(Des H. Haflidason. Eng G. Bétemps. Recess)

1971 (8 May). Europe. P 13.
F231	F **48**	50c. rose-red	10·50	12·50
F232		80c. turquoise-green	16·00	20·00

(Des and eng J. Combet. Recess)

1971 (18 Sept). Altar-screen, Church of St. John of Caselles (3rd series). Vert designs similar to Type F **42**, but dated "1971". P 13.
F233		30c. emerald, olive-brown and myrtle-green	1·80	4·50
F234		50c. olive-brown, red-orange & lake	2·40	5·25
F235		90c. new blue, plum & blackish brown	3·75	7·00
F233/235	Set of 3		7·25	15·00

Designs:—30c. St. John in temple at Ephesus; 50c. St. John with cup of poison; 90c. St. John disputing with pagan philosophers.

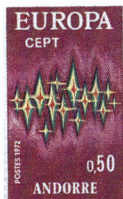 

F **49** "Communications" F **50** Golden Eagle

(Des Pierrette Lambert after P. Huovinen. Photo)

1972 (29 Apr). Europe. P 13.
F236	F **49**	50c. multicoloured	10·00	10·50
F237		90c. multicoloured	15·00	18·00

(Des and eng P. Forget. Recess)

1972 (27 May). Nature Protection. P 13.
F238	F **50**	60c. olive, bluish green and purple	4·75	6·25

F **51** Rifle-shooting F **52** General De Gaulle

(Des and eng G. Bétemps. Recess)

1972 (8 July). Olympic Games. Munich. P 13.
F239	F **51**	1f. plum	3·25	4·50

(Des and eng J. Combet. Recess)

1972 (16 Sept). Altar-screen, Church of St. John of Caselles (4th series). Vert designs as Type F **42** but dated "1972". P 13.
F240		30c. bright purple, slate and greenish olive	1·40	2·30
F241		50c. grey and ultramarine	1·70	2·75
F242		90c. slate-green and greenish blue	2·75	4·00
F240/242	Set of 3		5·25	8·25

Designs:—30c. St. John in discussion with bishop; 50c. St. John healing a cripple; 90c. Angel with spear.

(Des and eng P. Béquet. Recess)

1972 (23 Oct). Fifth Anniv of Gen. De Gaulle's Visit to Andorra. Type F **52** and similar vert design. P 13.
F243		50c. deep ultramarine	3·50	5·75
	a.	Horiz strip. Nos. F243/4 plus label	8·50	14·00
F244		90c. brown-lake	4·75	7·75

Design:—90c. Gen. De Gaulle in Andorra la Vella, 1967.
Nos. F243/4 were issued together in horizontal pairs with intervening label showing Andorra's arms.
See also Nos. F434/5.

F **53** Europa "Posthorn" F **54** "Virgin of Canolich" (wood-carving)

(Des Pierrette Lambert, after L. Anisdahl. Photo)

1973 (28 Apr). Europa. P 13.
F245	F **53**	50c. multicoloured	10·00	10·50
F246		90c. multicoloured	10·50	21·00

(Des and eng P. Forget. Recess)

1973 (16 June). Andorran Art. P 13.
F247	F **54**	1f. lilac, greenish blue and drab	3·00	4·25

F **55** Lily F **56** Blue Tit F **57** "The Virgin of Pal"

(Des Pierrette Lambert. Photo)

1973 (7 July). Pyrenean Wild Flowers. (1st series). Type F **55** and similar vert designs. Multicoloured. P 13.
F248		30c. Type F **55**	1·10	3·25
F249		50c. Columbine	2·10	4·50
F250		90c. Wild pinks	1·60	3·50
F248/250	Set of 3		4·25	10·00

See also Nos. F253/5 and F264/6.

(Des H. Heinzel. Photo)

1973 (27 Oct). Nature Protection. Birds. Type F **56** and similar vert design. Multicoloured. P 13.
F251		90c. Type F **56**	2·75	5·25
F252		1f. Lesser spotted woodpecker	3·00	5·75

See also Nos F259/60.

(Des Pierrette Lambert. Photo)

1974 (6 Apr). Pyrenean Wild Flowers (2nd series). Vert designs as Type F **55**. Multicoloured. P 13.
F253		45c. Iris	55	4·00
F254		65c. Tobacco plant	65	4·50
F255		90c. Narcissus	1·40	4·75
F253/255	Set of 3		2·30	12·00

(Des and eng A. Decaris. Recess)

1974 (27 Apr). Europa. Church Sculptures. Type F **57** and similar vert design. Multicoloured. P 13.
F256		50c. Type F **57**	17·00	11·50
F257		90c. "The Virgin of Santa Coloma"	23·00	18·00

F **58** Arms of Andorra F **59** Letters crossing Globe

ANDORRA / French Post Offices

(Des and eng P. Béquet. Recess)
1974 (24 Aug). Co-Princes' Meeting, Cahors. P 13.
F258 F **58** 1f. ultramarine, reddish violet and reddish orange .... 1·40 5·75

(Des H. Heinzel. Photo)
1974 (21 Sept). Nature Protection, Birds. Vert designs as Type F **56**. Multicoloured. P 13.
F259 60c. Chaffinch .... 4·25 7·00
F260 80c. Bullfinch .... 4·25 7·00

(Des and eng P. Béquet. Recess)
1974 (5 Oct). Centenary of Universal Postal Union. P 13.
F261 F **59** 1f.20 brn-lake, slate & yell-brn .... 2·30 4·25

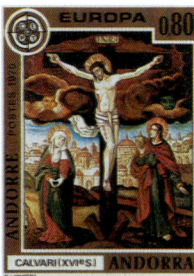

F **60** "Calvary"

(Des Pierrette Lambert. Photo)
1975 (26 Apr). Europa. Type F **60** and similar multicoloured designs showing paintings from La Cortinada Church. P 11½×13 (vert) or 13×11½ (horiz).
F262 80c. Type F **60** .... 8·50 15·00
a. Black (inscr and face value) omitted £14000
F263 1f.20 "Coronation of St. Martin" (horiz) ..... 10·50 23·00

(Des Pierrette Lambert. Photo)
1975 (10 May). Pyrenean Flowers (3rd series). Vert designs as Type F **55**, but inscribed "ANDORRE-ANDORRA". P 13.
F264 60c. multicoloured .... 65 3·25
F265 80c. multicoloured .... 1·80 4·00
F266 1f.20 lemon, rose and deep green .... 1·30 3·50
F264/266 Set of 3 .... 3·50 9·75
Designs:—60c. Gentian; 80c. Anemone; 1f.20, Colchicum.

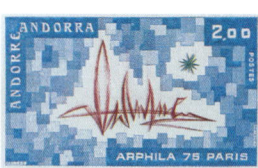 

F **61** "Arphila" Motif F **62** Pres. Pompidou (Co-prince of Andorra)

(Des Odette Baillais. Eng G. Bétemps. Recess)
1975 (7 June). Arphila 75 International Stamp Exhibition, Paris. P 13.
F267 F **61** 2f. carm-lake, greenish blue and emerald .... 2·00 4·50

(Des and eng J. Pheulpin. Recess)
1975 (23 Aug). President Pompidou of France Commemoration. P 13.
F268 F **62** 80c. black and deep violet .... 1·10 3·25

F **63** "La Pubilla" and Emblem F **64** Skier

(Des H. Sainson. Eng J. Pheulpin. Recess)
1975 (8 Nov). International Women's Year. P 13.
F269 F **63** 1f.20 black, deep reddish purple and new blue .... 2·10 3·75

(Des and eng P. Forget. Recess)
1976 (31 Jan). Winter Olympic Games, Innsbruck. P 13.
F270 F **64** 1f. bl-blk, ol-green and greenish blue .... 1·60 3·50

F **65** Telephone and Satellite F **66** Catalan Forge

(Des and eng M. Monvoisin. Recess)
1976 (20 Mar). Telephone Centenary. P 13.
F271 F **65** 1f. deep yell-grn, black and bright carmine .... 1·60 3·75

(Des Pierrette Lambert. Eng M. Monvoisin. Recess)
1976 (8 May). Europa. Type F **66** and similar horiz design. P 13.
F272 80c. dull pur-brn, vio-bl & slate-grn .... 4·25 4·50
F273 1f.20 carmine-red, bottle grn & blk .... 5·25 5·75
Design:—1f.20, Andorran folk-weaving.

F **67** Thomas Jefferson F **68** Ball-trap (clay-pigeon) Shooting

(Des and eng R. Quillivic. Recess)
1976 (3 July). Bicentenary of American Revolution. P 13.
F274 F **67** 1f.20 slate-grn, ol-brn & bl-grn .... 1·40 3·50

(Des and eng C. Haley. Recess)
1976 (17 July). Olympic Games, Montreal. P 13.
F275 F **68** 2f. bistre-brown, reddish violet and green .... 2·10 4·00

F **69** New Chapel F **70** Apollo (*Parnassius apollo*)

(Des and eng J. Pheulpin. Recess)
1976 (4 Sept). New Chapel of Our Lady, Meritxell. P 13.
F276 F **69** 1f. yellow-green, maroon and orange-brown .... 1·20 3·25

(Des H. Heinzel. Photo)
1976 (16 Oct). Nature Protection. Butterflies. Type F **70** and similar vert design. Multicoloured. P 13.
F277 80c. Type F **70** .... 3·25 6·50
F278 1f.40 Camberwell beauty (*Euvanessa antiopa*) .... 4·00 7·00

ANDORRA / French Post Offices

F 71 Stoat   F 72 Church of St. John of Caselles   F 73 Book and Flowers

(Des H. Heinzel. Photo)

1977 (2 Apr). Nature Protection. P 13.
F279   F 71   1f. brownish grey, black and chalky blue............... 2·40   3·75

(Des Huguette Sainson. Eng M. Monvoisin (1f.), Cécile Guillame (1f.40). Recess)

1977 (30 Apr). Europa. Type F 72 and similar vert design. P 13.
F280   1f. purple, dp yellow-green and deep turquoise-blue.............. 6·75   5·75
F281   1f.40 indigo, yellow-olive & ultram...... 11·00   7·00
Design—1f.40, St. Vicens Château.

(Des and eng C. Durrens. Recess)

1977 (11 June). First Anniv of Institute of Andorran Studies. P 13.
F282   F 73   80c. red-brown, slate-green and royal blue............ 1·20   2·75

F 74 St. Roma   F 75 General Council Assembly Hall

(Des and eng P. Béquet. Recess)

1977 (23 July). Reredos of St. Roma's Chapel, Les Bons. P 12½×13.
F283   F 74   2f. multicoloured............ 2·75   3·50

(Des and eng C. Haley (1f.10). P. Gandon (2f.). Recess)

1977 (24 Sept). Andorran Institutions. Type F 75 and similar design. P 13.
F284   1f.10 dull scarlet, brt blue & chocolate .... 2·75   4·00
F285   2f. sepia and deep carmine.............. 2·75   4·00
Design: Vert—2f. Don Guillem D'Arény Plandolit.

F 76 Eurasian Red Squirrel   F 77 Escalls Bridge

(Des and eng J. Pheulpin. Recess)

1978 (18 Mar). Nature Protection. P 13.
F286   F 76   1f. purple-brown, blue-green and brown-olive .... 1·30   2·75

(Des and eng C. Andréotto. Recess)

1978 (8 Apr). 700th Anniv of Parity Treaties (1st issue). P 13.
F287   F 77   80c. deep yellow-green, reddish brown and deep turquoise-blue.   85   2·75
See also No. F292.

F 78 Church at Pal   F 79 "Virgin of Sispony"

(Des Pierrette Lambert. Eng Marie-Noëlle Goffin (1f.), E. Lacaque (1f.40). Recess)

1978 (29 Apr). Europa. Type F 78 and similar design. P 13.
F288   1f. chocolate, deep yellow-green and scarlet.............. 7·00   5·75
F289   1f.40 indigo, greenish blue and scarlet .... 11·50   7·50
Design: Vert—1f.40, Charlemagne's House.

(Des and eng P. Béquet. Recess)

1978 (20 May). Andorran Art. P 12½×13.
F290   F 79   2f. multicoloured.................. 2·10   3·50

F 80 Tribunal Meeting

(Des and eng C. Haley. Recess)

1978 (24 June). Tribunal of Visura. P 13×12½.
F291   F 80   1f.20 multicoloured............... 1·80   2·75

F 81 Treaty Text

(Des and eng J. Combet. Recess)

1978 (2 Sept). 700th Anniv of Parity Treaties (2nd issue). P 13×12½.
F292   F 81   1f.70 agate, green and deep carmine..   1·30   2·75

F 82 Chamois   F 83 Rock Ptarmigans   F 84 Early 20th Century Postman and Church of St. John of Caselles

(Des and eng P. Béquet. Recess)

1979 (24 Mar). Nature Protection. P 13.
F293   F 82   1f. deep brown, light brown and blue............ 85   2·40

445

ANDORRA / French Post Offices

(Des Pierrette Lambert after H. Heinzel. Photo)
1979 (7 Apr). Nature Protection. P 13.
F294   F 83   1f.20 multicoloured...................   1·70   3·25

(Des and eng E. Lacaque. Recess)
1979 (28 Apr). Europa. Type F 84 and similar vert design. P 13.
F295   1f.20 slate-black, bistre-brown and deep
       bluish green ....   3·25   4·75
F296   1f.70 purple-brown, yellow-grn & mar ...   5·25   5·75
Design:—1f.70, Old French post office, Andorra.

F 85 Wall Painting, Church of St. Cerni, Nagol
F 86 Boy with Sheep 

(Des and eng G. Bétemps. Recess)
1979 (12 June). Pre-Romanesque Art. P 12½×13.
F297   F 85   2f. olive-green, rose-pink and agate   1·60   2·75

1979 (7 July). International Year of the Child. Photo. P 13.
F298   F 86   1f.70 multicoloured...................   1·30   2·75

F 87 Co-princes Monument (Luigiteruggi)
F 88 Judo 

(Des and eng C. Haley. Recess)
1979 (29 Sept). Co-princes Monument. P 13.
F299   F 87   2f. blackish-grn, brn-ol and brown-
              red ....   1·60   3·25

(Des Huguette Sainson. Eng Cécile Guillame. Recess)
1979 (24 Nov). World Judo Championships. Paris. P 13.
F300   F 88   1f.30 black, dull ultramarine and blue.   1·10   2·75

F 89 Cal Pal, La Cortinada
F 90 Cross-country Skiing 

(Des and eng Marie-Noelle Goffin. Recess)
1980 (26 Jan). P 13.
F301   F 89   1f.10 deep brown, Prussian blue and
              deep green   85   2·40

(Des and eng J. Jubert. Recess)
1980 (9 Feb). Winter Olympics, Lake Placid. P 13.
F302   F 90   1f.80 ultramarine, dull ultramarine
              and bright crimson ....   1·50   3·25

F 91 Charlemagne
F 92 Pyrenean Lily 
F 93 Dog's-tooth Violet 

(Des and eng P. Gandon. Recess)
1980 (26 Apr). Europa. Type F 91 and similar vert design. P 13.
F303   1f.30 agate, chestnut and lake-brown ......   2·10   3·50
F304   1f.80 dull yellowish grn & lake-brn ....   2·75   4·00
Design:—1f.80, Napoleon.

(Des Pierrette Lambert. Photo)
1980 (17 May). Nature Protection. P 13.
F305   F 92   1f.30 multicoloured   85   2·40

(Des Pierrette Lambert. Photo)
1980 (21 June). Nature Protection. P 13.
F306   F 93   1f.10 multicoloured   95   2·50

F 94 Cyclists
F 95 House of the Valleys 

(Des and eng C. Haley. Recess)
1980 (30 Aug). World Cycling Championships. P 13.
F307   F 94   1f.20 reddish violet, deep magenta
              and reddish brown....................   1·20   2·50

(Des and eng Cécile Guillame. Recess)
1980 (6 Sept). 400th Anniv of Restoration of House of the Valleys
(meeting place of Andorran General Council). P 13.
F308   F 95   1f.40 red-brown, deep reddish violet
              and yellow-green ....   1·20   2·50

F 96 Wall Painting, Church of St. Cerni, Nagol

(Des and eng E. Lacaque. Recess)
1980 (25 Oct). Pre-Romanesque Art. P 13×12½.
F309   F 96   2f. multicoloured ....   1·70   3·25

F 97 Shepherds' Huts, Mereig
F 98 Bear Dance (Encamp Carnival) 

(Des and eng Marie-Noëlle Goffin. Recess)
1981 (21 Mar). Architecture. P 13.
F310   F 97   1f.40 dp brown & dp grey-blue ....   1·10   1·70

ANDORRA / French Post Offices

(Des and eng J. Delpech. Recess)

1981 (16 May). Europa. Type F **98** and similar horiz design. P 13.
F311   1f.40 black, dp turq-grn & dp ultram............... 1·60   2·30
F312   2f. black, deep ultramarine and scarlet....... 2·10   3·50
Design:—2f. El Contrapas (dance).

F **99** Bonelli's Warbler (*Phylloscopus bonelti*)

F **100** Fencing

(Des H. Heinzel. Photo)

1981 (20 June). Nature Protection. Birds. Type F **99** and similar vert design. Multicoloured. P 13.
F313   1f.20 Type F **99** .... 1·10   2·75
F314   1f.40 Wallcreeper (*Tichodroma muraria*)........... 1·30   2·75

(Des and eng R. Quillivic. Recess)

1981 (4 July). World Fencing Championships, Clermont-Ferrand. P 13.
F315   F **100**   2f. ultramarine and black....................... 1·30   2·75

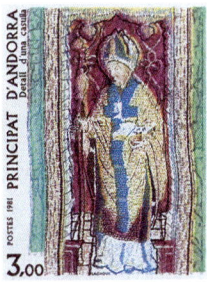

F **101** Chasuble of St. Martin (miniature)

F **102** Fountain, Sant Julia de Loria

(Des and eng E. Lacaque. Recess)

1981 (5 Sept). Art. P 12½×13.
F316   F **101**   3f. multicoloured .... 1·80   2·75

(Des and eng Marie-Noëlle Goffin. Recess)

1981 (17 Oct). International Decade of Drinking Water. P 13.
F317   F **102**   1f.60 grey-blue and deep brown .... 1·10   2·50

F **103** Symbolic Disabled

F **104** Scroll and Badge (creation of Andorran Executive Council, 1981)

(Des Odette Baillais. Eng Cécile Guillame, Recess)

1981 (7 Nov). International Year of Disabled Persons. P 13.
F318   F **103**   2f.30 deep turquoise-blue, red and brown-olive .... 1·50   2·75

(Des and eng R. Quillivic. Recess)

1982 (8 May). Europa. Type F **104** and similar horiz design. P 13.
F319   1f.60 indigo, yellow-brown & red-orge............. 2·10   2·75
F320   2f.30 indigo, black and red-orange................. 2·75   3·25
Design:—2f.30, Hat and cloak (creation of Land Council, 1419).

F **105** Footballer running to Right

F **106** 1f.25 Stamp, 1933

(Des and eng R. Quillivic. Recess)

1982 (12 June). World Cup Football Championship, Spain. Type F **105** and similar vert design, each blackish brown and orange-vermilion. P 13.
F321   1f.60 Type F **105** .... 1·30   2·40
       a. Horiz strip. Nos. F321/2 plus label............ 3·50   5·50
F322   2f.60 Footballer running to left..................... 1·90   2·75
Nos. F321/2 were issued together in horizontal pairs with intervening label showing Andorra's arms.

(Eng C. Jumelet. Recess)

1982 (21 Aug). First Official Exhibition of Andorran Postage Stamps. Sheet 143×94 mm. P 13.
MSF323   F **106**   5f. black and rosine .... 2·75   4·00

F **107** Wall Painting, La Cortinada Church

(Des and eng E. Lacaque. Recess)

1982 (4 Sept). Romanesque Art. P 13×12½.
F324   F **107**   3f. multicoloured..................... 1·60   4·75

F **108** Wild Cat (*Felix sylvestris sylvestris*)

F **109** Dr. Robert Koch

(Des Pierrette Lambert. Eng C. Haley (1f.80), Cécile Guillame (2f.60). Recess)

1982 (9 Oct). Nature Protection. Type F **108** and similar horiz design. P 13.
F325   1f.80 olive-black, blackish grn & slate............... 1·60   3·75
F326   2f.60 sepia and bronze green...................... 1·40   4·00
Design:—2f.60, Scots pine (*Pinus sylvestris*).

(Des and eng C. Andréotto. Recess)

1982 (13 Nov). Centenary of Discovery of Tubercle Bacillus. P 13.
F327   F **109**   2f.10 deep rose-lilac.................... 1·40   2·75

F **110** St. Thomas Aquinas

F **111** Montgolfier and Charles Balloons over Tuileries, Paris

447

ANDORRA / French Post Offices

(Des and eng E. Lacaque. Recess)
1982 (4 Dec). St. Thomas Aquinas Commemoration. P 13.
F328 F 110   2f. sepia, lake-brown and slate .... 1·30   2·75

(Des and eng J. Gauthier. Recess)
1983 (26 Feb). Bicentenary of Manned Flight. P 13.
F329 F 111   2f. bronze green, rosine and
              blackish brown .... 1·30   2·75

F **112** Silver Birch F **113** Mountain Cheesery
(*Betula pendula*)

(Des Pierrette Lambert. Eng P. Albuisson. Recess)
1983 (16 Apr). Nature Protection. Type F 112 and similar horiz design. P 13.
F330   1f. crimson, sepia and deep dull green ...... 1·50   3·75
F331   1f.50 blackish olive, Prussian bl & sep .... 1·60   4·00
Design:—1f.50, Brown trout (*Salmo trutta*).

(Des Odette Baillais (1f.80), P. Canturri and Odette Baillais (2f.60). Eng Cécile Guillame. Recess)
1983 (7 May). Europa. Type F 113 and similar horiz design. P 13.
F332   1f.80 deep dull purple and bright violet ..... 2·40   3·75
F333   2f.60 rosine, magenta and purple .... 2·75   4·00
Design:—2f.60, Catalan forge.

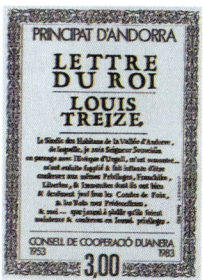

F **114** Royal Edict of Louis XIII   F **115** Early Coat of Arms

(Des and eng J. Combet. Recess)
1983 (14 May). 30th Anniv of Customs Co-operation Council. P 13.
F334 F **114**   3f. black and slate .... 2·00   5·50

(Des and eng Cécile Guillame. Recess)
1983 (3 Sept)–**90**. Inscr "POSTES". P 13.
F335 F **115**   5c. olive-green and brown-red .... 1·10   2·30
F336   10c. deep grey-green and deep olive 1·10   2·30
F337   20c. reddish violet and bright
                  magenta .... 1·10   2·30
F338   30c. deep reddish pur and reddish
                  violet .... 1·10   2·30
F339   40c. dull ultramarine and ultramarine 1·10   2·30
F340   50c. grey-black and vermilion .... 1·10   2·30
F341   1f. lake and brown-lake .... 1·10   2·30
F342   1f.90 emerald (28.3.87) .... 3·75   4·75
             a. Booklet pane. Nos. F342×2 and
                F345×6 (28.3.87) .... 14·50
F343   2f. bright rose-red and lake-brown .. 1·50   1·60
F344   2f.10 emerald (12.5.90) .... 1·50   2·75
F345   2f.20 vermilion (28.3.87) .... 1·10   3·75
F346   2f.30 vermilion (12.5.90) .... 1·40   3·75
F347   3f. deep turq-green and maroon
                  (1.12.84) .... 1·60   4·00
F348   4f. brt orge and dp yell-brn
                  (19.4.86) .... 3·25   6·25
F349   5f. sepia and brown-red .... 2·10   5·75
F350   10f. Indian red and blackish brown
                  (9.2.85) .... 4·25   6·25
F351   15f. green and myrtle green
                  (19.4.86) .... 6·25   9·00
F352   20f. blue and deep brown (1.12.84) .. 8·00   9·25
F335/352 *Set of* 18 .... 38·00 65·00
Nos. F342 and F345 were issued only in booklets.
For design as Type F 115 but inscribed "LA POSTE" see Nos. F446/9.

No. F353 is vacant.

F **116** Wall Painting,   F **117** Plandolit
La Cortinada Church   House

(Des and eng E. Lacaque. Recess)
1983 (24 Sept). Romanesque Art. P 12½×13.
F354 F **116**   4f. multicoloured .... 2·10   4·00

(Des and eng C. Andréotto. Recess)
1983 (15 Oct). P 13.
F355 F **117**   1f.60 deep brown and deep bluish
                  green .... 1·10   1·70

F **118** Snowflakes and   F **119** Pyrenees and Council
Olympic Torch   of Europe Emblem

(Des and eng R. Quillivic. Recess)
1984 (18 Feb). Winter Olympic Games, Sarajevo. P 13.
F356 F **118**   2f.80 vermilion, blue and deep
                  turquoise .... 1·70   2·75

(Des and eng Cécile Guillame. Recess)
1984 (28 Apr). Work Community of Pyrenees Region. P 13.
F357 F **119**   3f. new blue and sepia .... 1·80   3·25

F **120** Bridge   F **121** Sweet Chestnut
                    (*Castanea sativa*)

(Des and eng J. Larrivière. Recess)
1984 (5 May). Europa. P 13.
F358 F **120**   2f. emerald .... 3·75   4·00
F359   2f.80 lake .... 4·75   5·25

(Des Pierrette Lambert. Eng P. Albuisson. Recess)
1984 (7 July). Nature Protection. Type F 121 and similar horiz design. P 13.
F360   1f.70 deep green, deep brown and deep
       claret .... 1·30   3·75
F361   2f.10 myrtle green and deep brown .... 1·60   4·00
Design:—2f.10, Walnut (*Juglans regia*).

F **122** Centre Members   F **123** "St. George" (detail of
                            fresco, Church of St. Cerni,
                            Nagol)

448

ANDORRA / French Post Offices

(Des and eng G. Bétemps. Recess)
1984 (7 Sept). Pyrenean Cultures Centre, Andorra. P 13.
F362 F **122** 3f. ultramarine, yellow-orange and rosine .... 1·80 3·50

(Des and eng P. Béquet. Recess)
1984 (17 Nov). Pre-Romanesque Art. P 12½×13.
F363 F **123** 5f. multicoloured .... 2·75 4·00

F **124** Sant Julia Valley

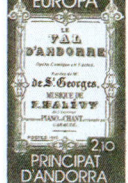
F **125** Title Page of *Le Val d'Andorre* (comic opera)

(Des and eng R. Coatantiec. Recess)
1985 (13 Apr). P 13.
F364 F **124** 2f. grey-green, brown-olive and orange-brown .... 1·50 2·75

(Des and eng J. Combet. Recess)
1985 (4 May). Europa. Type F **125** and similar vert design. P 13.
F365 2f.10 dull green .... 3·75 4·00
F366 3f. bistre-brown and blackish brown .... 4·75 5·25
Design:—3f. Musical instruments within frame.

F **126** Teenagers holding up Ball

F **127** Mallard (*Anas platyrhynchos*)

(Des and eng Cécile Guillame. Recess)
1985 (8 June). International Youth Year. P 13.
F367 F **126** 3f. scarlet and deep brown .... 1·60 3·25

(Des Odette Baillais. Photo)
1985 (3 Aug). Nature Protection. Type F **127** and similar horiz design. Multicoloured. P 13.
F368 1f.80 Type F **127** .... 1·40 3·50
F369 2f.20 Goldfinch (*Carduelis carduelis*) .... 1·70 4·00

F **128** St. Cerni and Angel (fresco, Church of St. Cerni, Nagol)

FD **129** Holly Berries

(Des and eng E. Lacaque. Recess)
1985 (14 Sept). Pre-Romanesque Art. P 12½×13.
F370 F **128** 5f. multicoloured .... 2·30 4·00

(Des Marie-Noëlle Goffin. Eng Marie-Noëlle Goffin (50c., 1, 2, 4, 5f.). C. Durrens (others). Recess)
1985 (21 Oct). POSTAGE DUE. Fruits. Type FD **129** and similar vert designs. P 13.
FD371 10c. scarlet and deep green .... 1·70 2·75
FD372 20c. deep brown and slate-blue .... 1·70 2·75
FD373 30c. bronze green and bright crimson .... 1·70 2·75
FD374 40c. deep brown and black .... 1·70 2·75
FD375 50c. bronze green and deep reddish violet .... 1·70 2·75
FD376 1f. emerald and royal blue .... 1·70 2·75
FD377 2f. carmine-vermilion and orange-brown .... 1·80 3·00
FD378 3f. maroon and deep green .... 2·10 3·50
FD379 4f. brown-olive and violet-blue .... 2·75 3·75
FD380 5f. deep olive and scarlet .... 3·25 4·25
FD371/380 *Set of 10* .... 18·00 28·00
Designs:—20c. Wild plum; 30c. Raspberry; 40c. Dogberry; 50c. Blackberry; 1f. Juniper; 2f. Rose hip; 3f. Elder; 4f. Bilberry; 5f. Strawberry.

F **130** 1979 Europa Stamp

F **131** Ansalonga

(Des and eng E. Lacaque. Recess)
1986 (22 Mar). Inauguration of Postal Museum. P 13.
F381 F **130** 2f.20 deep brown and myrtle green .... 1·40 3·25

(Des Marie-Noëlle Goffin. Recess)
1986 (3 May). Europa. Type F **131** and similar horiz design. P 13.
F382 2f.20 black and bright blue .... 4·25 4·50
F383 3f.20 black and yellow-green .... 5·25 5·50
Design:—3f.20 Pyrenean chamois.

F **132** Players

F **133** Angonella Lakes

(Des G. Bétemps. Litho)
1986 (14 June). World Cup Football Championship, Mexico. P 13.
F384 F **132** 3f. green, black and dull blue-green 2·10 3·50

(Des Huguette Sainson. Photo)
1986 (28 June). P 13.
F385 F **133** 2f.20 multicoloured .... 1·40 2·75

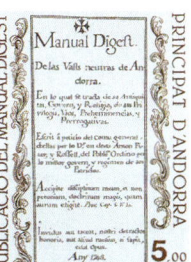
F **134** Title Page of *Manual Digest*, 1748

F **135** Dove with Twig

449

ANDORRA / French Post Offices

(Des and eng C. Durrens. Recess)
1986 (6 Sept). *Manual Digest*. P 13.
F386   F **134**   5f. blue-black, brown-ol and red-brown .... 2·75   4·00

(Des and eng P. Forget. Recess)
1986 (27 Sept). International Peace Year. P 13.
F387   F **135**   1f.90 turquoise-blue and indigo............. 1·30   2·75

F **136** St. Vincent's Chapel, Enclar   F **137** Arms

(Des Luquet. Recess)
1986 (18 Oct). P 13.
F388   F **136**   1f.90 ol-sep, brownish blk and deep olive........... 1·30   2·75

(Des A. Rouhier. Litho)
1987 (27 Mar). Visit of French Co-prince (French president). P 12½×13.
F389   F **137**   2f.20 multicoloured............ 2·00   4·00

F **138** Meritxell Chapel   F **139** Ransol

(Des and eng J. Jubert. Recess)
1987 (2 May). Europa. Type F **138** and similar horiz design. P 13.
F390   2f.20 reddish purple & bright crimson .... 5·25   4·50
F391   3f.40 bluish violet and bright blue................... 7·50   6·25
Design:—3f.40, Ordino.

(Des Huguette Sainson. Photo)
1987 (15 June). P 13.
F392   F **139**   1f.90 multicoloured................. 1·50   3·50

F **140** Horse   F **141** Arualsu (fresco, La Cortinada Church)

(Des F. Guiol. Photo)
1987 (4 July). Nature Protection. Type F **140** and similar horiz design. Multicoloured. P 13.
F393   1f.90 Type F **140** .... 1·70   4·25
F394   2f.20 Isabel (*Graellsia isabellae*) (moth)............ 2·00   4·50

(Des and eng E. Lacaque. Recess)
1987 (5 Sept). Romanesque Art. P 12½×13.
F395   F **141**   5f. multicoloured................... 3·00   4·25

F **142** Walker with Map by Signpost   F **143** Key

(Des and eng C. Andréotto. Recess)
1987 (19 Sept). Walking. P 13.
F396   F **142**   2f. dp dull purple, brown-olive and deep green........... 1·40   2·75

(Des J.-P. Veret-Lemarinier. Litho)
1987 (17 Oct). La Cortinada Church Key. P 13.
F397   F **143**   3f. multicoloured.................. 1·70   3·50

F **144** Arms   F **145** Bronze Boot and Mountains

(Des and eng J. Jubert. Recess)
1988 (6 Feb)–**93**. Booklet stamps. P 13.
(a) Inscr "POSTES"
F398   F **144**   2f.20 bright scarlet .... 1·40   2·75
       a. Booklet pane. No. F398×5........ 7·25
F399   2f.30 bright scarlet (7.4.90) .... 1·60   4·50
       a. Booklet pane. No. F399×5........ 8·25
(b) Inscr "LA POSTE"
F400   F **144**   2f.50 bright scarlet (19.10.91) .... 1·70   4·50
       a. Booklet pane. No. F400×5........ 8·75
F401   2f.80 scarlet (7.8.93) .... 1·80   4·25
       a. Booklet pane. No. F401×5........ 9·25
F398/401 Set of 4........................... 5·75   14·50

Nos. F402/6 are vacant.

(Des Pierrette Lambert. Photo)
1988 (13 Feb). Archaeology. P 13.
F407   F **145**   3f. multicoloured.................. 1·70   3·75

F **146** Players   F **147** Enclar Aerial

(Des and eng P. Forget. Recess)
1988 (19 Mar). Rugby. P 12½×13.
F408   F **146**   2f.20 black, orange-yell and turquoise-green............. 1·40   4·50

(Des and eng C. Andréotto. Recess)
1988 (30 Apr). Europa. Transport and Communications. Type F **147** and similar vert design, each blue-green, sepia and deep ultramarine. P 13.
F409   2f.20 Type F **147** .... 3·75   4·00
F410   3f.60 Hand pointing to map on screen (tourist information) .... 4·75   5·75

ANDORRA / French Post Offices

F **148** Les Escaldes　　F **149** Ansalonga Pass
Hot Spring

(Des and eng R. Quillivic. Recess)
1988 (14 May). P 13.
F411　F **148**　2f.20 turquoise-blue, chestnut and
yellowish green .... 1·40　2·75

(Des Eve Luquet. Recess)
1988 (11 June). P 13.
F412　F **149**　2f. deep grey-blue, blackish green
and deep olive............................ 1·20　2·75

F **150** Pyrenean　　F **151** Fresco, Andorra La Vella Church
Shepherd Dog

(Des F. Guiol. Photo)
1988 (2 July). Nature Protection. Type F **150** and similar vert design.
Multicoloured. P 13.
F413　　2f. Type F **150** .... 1·90　4·50
F414　　2f.20 Hare .... 2·00　4·50

(Des and eng E. Lacaque. Recess)
1988 (3 Sept). Romanesque Art. P 13×12½.
F415　F **151**　5f. multicoloured................................ 3·00　4·00

F **152** Birds　　F **153** Pal

(Des J.-M. Folon. Litho)
1989 (1 Jan). Bicentenary of French Revolution. P 13.
F416　F **152**　2f.20 blue-violet, black and scarlet-
vermilion................................ 1·50　2·75

(Des and eng P. Albuisson. Recess)
1989 (4 Mar). P 13.
F417　F **153**　2f.20 bright violet and deep blue.......... 1·50　2·75

F **154** The Strong Horse　　F **155** Wounded Soldiers

(Des P. Arquer. Eng P. Béquet. Recess and photo)
1989 (29 Apr). Europa. Children's Games. Type F **154** and similar horiz
design, each blackish brown and cream. P 13.
F418　　2f.20 Type F **154** .... 3·25　3·50
F419　　3f.60 The Handkerchief................................ 4·25　4·75

(Des and eng C. Andréotto. Recess)
1989 (6 May). 125th Anniv of International Red Cross. P 13.
F420　F **155**　3f.60 reddish brown, black and bright
scarlet .... 2·10　3·50

F **156** Archaeological　　F **157** Wild Boar
Find and St. Vincent's
Chapel, Enclar

(Des Pierrette Lambert. Photo)
1989 (3 June). Archaeology. P 13.
F421　F **156**　3f. multicoloured................................ 1·60　3·50

(Des F. Guiol. Eng P. Albuisson. Recess)
1989 (16 Sept). Nature Protection. Type F **157** and similar horiz
design. P 13.
F422　　2f.20 black, yellowish green and lake-brown　1·60　3·50
F423　　3f.60 blk, yellowish green and deep bluish
green .... 2·10　4·50
Design:—3f.60, Palmate newt.

F **158** Retable of St. Michael
de la Mosquera, Encamp

(Des Odette Baillais. Eng P. Béquet. Recess)
1989 (14 Oct). P 13×12½.
F424　F **158**　5f. multicoloured................................ 3·25　5·50

F **159** La Marginéda Bridge　　F **160** Llorts Iron Ore Mines

(Des and eng Eve Luquet. Recess)
1990 (24 Feb). P 13.
F425　F **159**　2f.30 dp vio-bl, bistre-brn and
turquoise-blue.............................. 1·60　2·75

(Des and eng C. Durrens. Recess)
1990 (21 Apr). P 12½×13.
F426　F **160**　3f.20 multicoloured................................ 2·10　3·25

F **161** Exterior of Old Post　　F **162** Censer, St. Roma's
Office, Andorra La Vella　　Chapel, Les Bons

(Des and eng Marie-Noëlle Goffin. Recess)
1990 (5 May). Europa. Post Office Buildings. Type F **161** and similar
horiz design. P 13.
F427　　2f.30 carmine-red and black .... 4·25　5·25
F428　　3f.20 blue-violet and scarlet............................ 6·25　7·00
Design:—3f.20, Interior of modern post office.

451

ANDORRA / French Post Offices

(Des J.-P. Veret-Lemarinier. Eng G. Bétemps. Recess and photo)

1990 (23 June). P 12½×13.
F429   F **162**   3f. multicoloured .... 2·10   3·25

F **163** Wild Roses   F **164** Tobacco-drying Sheds, Les Bons

(Des Huguette Sainson. Eng G. Bétemps. Recess and photo)

1990 (7 July). Nature Protection. Type F **163** and similar multicoloured design. P 13×12½ (2f.30) or 12½×13 (3f.20).
F430   2f.30 Type F **163** .... 1·60   3·25
F431   3f.20 Otter (horiz) .... 2·10   3·50

(Des and eng P. Forget. Recess)

1990 (15 Sept). P 12½×13.
F432   F **164**   2f.30 yellow, black and carmine-red..... 1·60   2·75

F **165** Part of Mural from Santa Coloma Church   F **166** Coin from St. Eulalia's Church, Encamp

(Des L. Arquer. Eng E. Lacaque. Recess)

1990 (6 Oct). P 12½×13.
F433   **165**   5f. multicoloured .... 2·75   3·75

(Des and eng P. Béquet. Recess)

1990 (23 Oct). Birth Centenary of Charles de Gaulle (French statesman). As Nos. F243/4 but values changed. P 13.
F434   2f.30 bright violet-blue .... 2·10   3·25
         a. Horiz strip. Nos. F434/5 plus label............ 4·75   7·00
F435   3f.20 bright scarlet .... 2·50   3·50
Design:—3f.20, As No. F244.
Nos. F434/5 were issued together in horizontal pairs se-tenant with intervening label showing Andorran arms.

(Des Odette Baillais. Litho)

1990 (27 Oct). P 13.
F436   F **166**   3f.20 multicoloured .... 2·10   3·25

F **167** Chapel of Sant Roma Dels Vilars   F **168** Emblem and Track

(Des and eng Eve Luquet. Recess)

1991 (9 Mar). P 13.
F437   F **167**   2f.50 dp dull bl, bl-blk and bottle green .... 1·60   2·75

(Des Odette Baillais. Photo)

1991 (6 Apr). Fourth European Small States Games. P 13.
F438   F **168**   2f.50 multicoloured .... 1·50   2·75

F **169** Television Satellite   F **170** Bottles

(Des and eng R. Coatantiec. Recess)

1991 (27 Apr). Europa. Europe in Space. Type F **169** and similar multicoloured design. P 13×12½ (2f.50) or 12½×13 (3f.50).
F439   2f.50 Type F **169** .... 4·25   4·50
F440   3f.50 Globe, telescope and eye (horiz) .... 7·50   8·00

(Des J.-P. Veret-Lemarinier. Photo)

1991 (11 May). Artefacts from Tomb of St. Vincent of Enclar. P 13.
F441   F **170**   3f.20 multicoloured .... 1·80   2·75

F **171** Sheep   F **172** Players

(Des Huguette Sainson. Eng J. Rajewicz. Recess)

1991 (22 June). Nature Protection. Type F **171** and similar horiz design. P 13.
F442   2f.50 light brown, greenish blue and black.... 2·10   4·50
F443   3f.50 reddish brown, deep magenta and black .... 2·20   4·75
Design:—3f.50, Pyrenean cow.

(Des and eng J. Gauthier. Recess)

1991 (14 Sept). World Pétanque Championship, Engordany. P 13.
F444   F **172**   2f.50 greenish black, bistre and crimson .... 1·80   2·75

F **173** Mozart, Quartet and Organ Pipes   F **174** "Virgin of the Remedy of Sant Julià and Sant Germà"

(Des Pierrette Lambert. Eng P. Albuisson. Recess)

1991 (5 Oct). Death Bicentenary of Wolfgang Amadeus Mozart (composer). P 13.
F445   F **173**   3f.40 blue, blue-black and turq-blue.... 2·20   3·25

(Des and eng Cécile Guillame. Recess)

1991 (26 Oct)–**96**. As Type F **115** but inscr "LA POSTE". P 13.
F446   F **115**   2f.20 emerald .... 1·40   4·00
F447   2f.40 emerald (7.8.93) .... 3·00   4·50
F448   2f.50 vermilion .... 1·60   4·00
F449   2f.70 emerald (17.4.96) .... 2·75   4·00
F450   2f.80 vermilion (7.8.93) .... 2·75   4·00
F451   3f. vermilion (17.4.96) .... 2·75   4·00
F446/451 Set of 6 .... 13·00   22·00

Nos. F452/4 are vacant.

(Des and eng G. Bétemps. Recess)

1991 (16 Nov). P 12½×13.
F455   F **174**   5f. multicoloured .... 3·25   3·75

ANDORRA / French Post Offices

F **175** Slalom

F **176** St. Andrew's Church, Arinsal

(Des L. Arquer. Litho)

1992 (8 Feb). Winter Olympic Games, Albertville. Type F **175** and similar vert design. Multicoloured. P 13.
F456	2f.50 Type F **175**	2·40	2·75
	a. Horiz strip. Nos. F456/7 plus label	5·50	6·25
F457	3f.40 Figure skating	2·75	3·25

Nos. F456/7 were issued together in horizontal pairs *se-tenant* with intervening label bearing the games emblem.

(Des and eng Eve Luquet. Recess and photo)

1992 (21 Mar). P 12½×13.
F458	F **176**	2f.50 black and buff	1·80	2·20

F **177** Navigation Instrument and Columbus's Fleet

F **178** Canoeing

(Des and eng P. Forget. Recess and photo)

1992 (25 Apr). Europa. 500th Anniv of Discovery of America by Columbus. Type F **177** and similar horiz design. Multicoloured. P 13.
F459	2f.50 Type F **177**	4·75	4·50
F460	3f.40 Fleet, Columbus and Amerindians	7·50	5·75

(Des C. Andréotto. Litho)

1992 (6 June). Olympic Games, Barcelona. Type F **178** and similar multicoloured design. P 13.
F461	2f.50 Type F **178**	1·90	2·30
	a. Horiz strip. Nos. F460/1 plus label	4·25	5·00
F462	3f.40 Shooting	2·20	2·50

Nos. F461/2 were issued together in horizontal pairs *se-tenant* with intervening label bearing the games emblem.

F **179** Globe Flowers

F **180** "Martyrdom of St. Eulalia" (altarpiece, St. Eulalia's Church, Encamp)

(Des Odette Baillais (2f.50). F. Guiol (3f.40). Litho)

1992 (4 July). Nature Protection. Type F **179** and similar multicoloured design. P 13.
F463	2f.50 Type F **179**	1·70	2·40
F464	3f.40 Griffon vulture (horiz)	2·30	2·75

(Des Pierrette Lambert. Photo)

1992 (12 Sept). P 13.
F465	F **180**	4f. multicoloured	2·40	2·75

F **181** "Ordino Arcalis 91" (Mauro Staccioli)

F **182** Grau Roig

(Des and eng P. Béquet (F466), C. Durrens (F467). Recess)

1992 (13 Oct–14 Nov). Modern Sculpture. Type F **181** and similar multicoloured design. P 12½×13½ (F466) or 13×12½ (F467).
F466	5f. Type F **181**	3·25	3·50
F467	5f. "Storm in a Teacup" (Dennis Oppenheim) (horiz) (14.11)	3·25	3·50

(Des F. Guiol (F470, F472), C. Andréotto (others). Litho)

1993 (13 Mar). Ski Resorts. Type F **182** and similar vert designs. Multicoloured. P 13.
F468	2f.50 Type F **182**	1·60	2·30
	a. Strip of 3. Nos. F468/9 and F471	5·75	
F469	2f.50 Ordino	1·60	2·30
F470	2f.50 Soldeu el Tarter	1·60	2·30
	a. Strip. Nos. F470 and F472 plus label	4·25	5·25
F471	3f.40 Pal	2·30	2·75
F472	3f.40 Arinsal	2·30	2·75
F468/472	Set of 5	8·50	11·00

Nos. F468/9 and F471 were issued together in *se-tenant* strips of three within the sheet; Nos. F470 and F472 were issued together *se-tenant* with intervening label showing "Ski Andorra" logo.

F **183** "Estructures Autogeneradores" (Jorge du Bon)

F **184** Common Blue (*Polyommatus icarus*)

(Des and eng Eve Luquet; recess (2f.50). Des J.-P. Veret-Lemarinier; litho (3f.40))

1993 (15 May). Europa. Contemporary Art. Type F **183** and similar design. P 12½×13 (2f.50) or 14 (3f.40).
F473	2f.50 slate-blue, greenish blue and deep violet	2·20	3·25
F474	3f.40 multicoloured	2·40	3·50

Design: Horiz—3f.40, "Fisicromia per Andorra" (Carlos Cruz-Diez).

(Des Bové (2f.50), L. Blasco (4f.20). Litho)

1993 (26 June). Nature Protection. Butterflies. Type F **184** and similar vert design. Multicoloured. P 13.
F475	2f.50 Type F **184**	2·10	3·25
F476	4f.20 Nymphalidae	3·00	4·00

F **185** Cyclist

F **186** Smiling Hands

453

ANDORRA / French Post Offices

(Des C. Andréotto. Litho)
1993 (19 July). Tour de France Cycling Road Race. P 13.
F477   F **185**   2f.50 multicoloured .... 2·20   3·50

(Des F. Ribó and M. Portell. Litho)
1993 (18 Sept). Tenth Anniv of Andorran School. P 13.
F478   F **186**   2f.80 multicoloured .... 2·50   3·50

F **187** "A Pagan Place"   F **188** Cross-country Skiing
(Michael Warren)

(Des and eng Eve Luquet (No. F479). Des J.-P. Veret-Lemarinier;
eng P. Bequet (F480). Recess)
1993 (16 Oct–6 Nov). Modern Sculpture. Type F **187** and similar vert
design. P 12×13.
F479   5f. black and bright blue .... 3·50   3·00
F480   5f. multicoloured (6.11) .... 3·50   3·00
Design:—No. F480, "Pep, Lu, Canòlic, Ton, Meritxell, Romà, Anna,
Pau, Carles, Eugènia... and Others" (Erik Dietman).

(Des F. Guiol. Litho)
1994 (19 Feb). Winter Olympic Games, Lillehammer, Norway. P 13.
F481   F **188**   3f.70 multicoloured .... 2·20   2·50

F **189** Constitution   F **190** AIDS Virus
Monument

(Des E. Armengol (2f.80), Laura Martinez Agell (3f.70). Litho)
1994 (14 Mar). First Anniv of New Constitution. Type F **189** and
similar vert design. P 13.
F482   2f.80 multicoloured .... 1·90   2·00
        a. Horiz strip. Nos. F482/3 plus label............ 4·50   5·75
F483   3f.70 black, yellow and magenta .... 2·40   3·50
Design:—3f.70, Stone tablet.
Nos. F482/3 were issued together in horizontal pairs se-tenant with
intervening label showing Andorran arms.

(Des J. Jubert (2f.80), J.-P. Cousin (3f.70). Litho)
1994 (7 May). Europa. Discoveries and Inventions. Type F **190** and
similar horiz design. Multicoloured. P 13.
F484   2f.80 Type F **190** .... 2·50   2·50
F485   3f.70 Radio mast .... 3·00   3·00

F **191** Competitors' Flags and   F **192** Horse Riding
Football

(Des J.-P. Veret-Lemarinier. Litho)
1994 (18 June). World Cup Football Championship, U.S.A. P 13.
F486   F **191**   3f.70 multicoloured .... 2·50   2·75

(Des M. Palau (F487). Raquel Ambatlle (F488),
F. Ribó (F489), J. Perona (F490). Litho)
1994 (9 July). Tourist Activities. Type F **192** and similar vert designs.
Multicoloured. P 13.
F487   2f.80 Type F **192** .... 1·90   1·90
        a. Horiz strip. Nos. F487/8 plus label.......... 4·00   4·00
F488   2f.80 Mountain biking .... 1·90   1·90
F489   2f.80 Climbing .... 1·90   1·90
        a. Horiz strip. Nos. F489/90 plus label........ 4·00   4·00
F490   2f.80 Fishing .... 1·90   1·90
F487/490 Set of 4 .... 6·75   6·75
Nos. F487/8 and F489/90 respectively were issued together in
horizontal pairs se-tenant with intervening label bearing the emblem
of the Ministry of Tourism and Sport.

F **193** Scarce Swallowtail   F **194** "26 10 93"
(*Iphiclides podalirius*)

(Des D. Grau. Litho)
1994 (3 Sept). Nature Protection. Butterflies. Type F **193** and similar
horiz design. Multicoloured. P 13.
F491   2f.80 Type F **193** .... 2·50   2·75
F492   4f.40 Small tortoiseshell (*Aglais urticae*) .... 3·75   4·00

(Des F. Ribó. Litho)
1994 (22 Oct). Meeting of Co-Princes. P 13.
F493   F **194**   2f.80 multicoloured .... 1·70   2·00

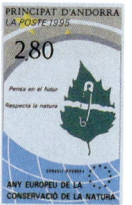 

F **195** Emblem   F **196** Globe, Goal and Player

1995 (25 Feb). European Nature Conservation Year. Litho. P 13.
F494   F **195**   2f.80 multicoloured .... 1·90   2·10

(Des A. Lavergne. Litho)
1995 (22 Apr). Third World Cup Rugby Championship, South Africa.
P 13.
F495   F **196**   2f.80 multicoloured .... 1·90   2·10

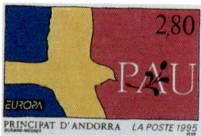 

F **197** Dove and Olive Twig   F **198** Emblem
("Peace")

(Des M. Durand-Mégret. Litho)
1995 (29 Apr). Europa. Peace and Freedom. Type F **197** and similar
horiz design. Multicoloured. P 13.
F496   2f.80 Type F **197** .... 2·50   2·75
F497   3f.70 Flock of doves ("Freedom") .... 2·75   3·00

(Des Odette Baillais. Litho)
1995 (13 May). 15th Anniv of Càritas Andorrana (welfare
organization). P 13.
F498   F **198**   2f.80 multicoloured .... 1·90   2·30

ANDORRA / French Post Offices

F **199** Caldea Thermal Baths, Les Escaldes-Engordany
F **200** National Auditorium, Ordino

(Des J. Xandri. Litho)

1995 (17 June). P 13.
F499 F **199** 2f.80 multicoloured .... 1·90 2·30

(Des M. Balaguer. Eng R. Coatantiec. Recess)

1995 (8 July). P 13.
F500 F **200** 3f.70 black and buff .... 2·50 2·75

F **201** "Virgin of Meritxell"
F **202** Brimstone (*Gonepteryx rhamni*)

(Des F. Torres. Litho)

1995 (9 Sept). P 14×13½.
F501 F **201** 4f.40 multicoloured .... 2·75 3·00

(Des P. Porta (2f.80). C. Forcada (3f.70). Litho)

1995 (23 Sept). Nature Protection. Butterflies. Type F **202** and similar multicoloured design. P 13.
F502   2f.80 Type F **202** .... 2·50 2·75
F503   3f.70 Marbled white (*Melanargia galathea*) (horiz) .... 3·00 3·25

F **203** National Flag over U.N. Emblem
F **204** National Flag and Palace of Europe, Strasbourg

(Des D. Trouillet. Litho)

1995 (21 Oct). 50th Anniv of United Nations Organization. Type F **203** and similar vert design. Multicoloured. P 13.
F504   2f.80 Type F **203** .... 2·50 2·75
       a. Strip. Nos. 1504/5 plus label .... 5·50 6·00
F505   3f.70 Anniversary emblem over flag .... 2·75 3·00
Nos. F504/5 were issued together *se-tenant* with an intervening label showing the Andorran flag.

(Des R. Dessirier. Litho)

1995 (4 Nov). Admission of Andorra to Council of Europe. P 13.
F506 F **204** 2f.80 multicoloured .... 1·90 2·00

F **205** Emblem
F **206** Basketball

1996 (27 Jan). Fourth Borrufa Trophy Skiing Championship. Litho. P 13.
F507 F **205** 2f.80 multicoloured .... 1·90 2·00

(Des F. Ribó. Litho)

1996 (27 Jan). P 13.
F508 F **206** 3f.70 rosine, black and greenish yellow .... 3·00 3·75

F **207** Children
F **208** European Robin

1996 (17 Feb). 25th Anniv of Our Lady of Meritxell Special School. Litho. P 13.
F509 F **207** 2f.80 multicoloured .... 1·90 2·10

(Des Pierrette Lambert. Litho)

1996 (23 Mar). Nature Protection. Type F **208** and similar horiz design. Multicoloured. P 13.
F510   3f. Type F **208** .... 2·50 3·00
F511   3f.80 Great tit .... 3·00 3·25

F **209** Cross, St. James's Church, Engordany
F **210** Ermessenda de Castellbò

(Des E. Cardús. Litho)

1996 (20 Apr). Religious Objects. Type F **209** and similar multicoloured design. P 13.
F512   3f. Type F **209** .... 2·50 2·75
F513   3f.80 Censer, St. Eulalia's Church, Encamp (horiz) .... 2·75 3·00

(Des E. Cardús. Litho)

1996 (4 May). Europa. Famous Women. P 13.
F514 F **210** 3f. multicoloured .... 2·50 2·75

F **211** Canillo
F **212** Chessmen

1996 (8 June). Booklet stamp. No value expressed. Self-adhesive. Litho. Die-cut (straight edge×wavy edge).
F515 F **211** (3f.) multicoloured .... 2·50 2·75
The stamps are peeled from the booklet cover and cannot therefore be collected as separate panes.

(Des A. Rouhier. Litho)

1996 (8 June). Chess. P 13.
F516 F **212** 4f.50 bright scarlet, black and new blue .... 3·00 3·25

F **213** Cycling, Running and Throwing the Javelin
F **214** Singers

455

ANDORRA / French Post Offices

(Des J.-P. Veret-Lemarinier. Litho)
1996 (29 June). Olympic Games, Atlanta. P 13.
F517   F **213**   3f. multicoloured .... 1·90   2·00

(Des M. Deu and A. Lavergne. Litho)
1996 (14 Sept). Fifth Anniv of National Youth Choir. P 13.
F518   F **214**   3f. multicoloured .... 1·90   2·00

F **215** Man and Boy with Animals
F **216** St. Roma's Chapel, Les Bons

(Des S. Mas. Eng C. Durrens. Recess)
1996 (26 Oct). Livestock Fair. P 12½×13.
F519   F **215**   3f. orange-yellow, lake and black...... 1·90   2·00

(Des J. Xandri (F520), J. Duro (F521). Litho)
1996 (16 Nov). Churches. Type F **216** and similar vert design. Multicoloured. P 13½×13.
F520   6f.70 Type F **216** .... 4·00   4·25
F521   6f.70 Santa Coloma .... 4·00   4·25

F **217** Mitterrand
F **218** Parish Emblem
F **219** Volleyball

(Des L. Briat. Litho)
1997 (4 Jan). François Mitterrand (President of France and Co-prince of Andorra, 1981–95) Commemoration. P 13.
F522   F **217**   3f. multicoloured .... 1·90   2·00

(Des Odette Baillais. Litho)
1997 (22 Feb). Parish of Encamp. Booklet stamp. No value expressed. Self-adhesive. Die-cut (straight edge×wavy edge).
F523   F **218**   (3f.) deep turquoise-blue............... 1·90   2·00
The stamps are peeled directly from the booklet cover and cannot therefore be collected as separate panes.

(Des C. Bonnehon. Litho)
1997 (22 Mar). P 13.
F524   F **219**   3f. multicoloured .... 1·90   2·00

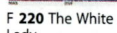

F **220** The White Lady
F **221** Swallow approaching Nest

(Des S. Mas and A. Lavergne. Litho)
1997 (10 May). Europa. Tales and Legends. P 13.
F525   F **220**   3f. multicoloured .... 2·50   2·75

(Des Pierrette Lambert. Litho)
1997 (31 May). Nature Protection. P 13.
F526   F **221**   3f.80 multicoloured .... 1·90   2·00

F **222** Mill and Saw-mill, Cal Pal
F **223** Monstrance, St. Iscle and St. Victoria's Church

(Des A. Lavergne. Litho)
1997 (13 Sept). Tourism. Type F **222** and similar horiz design showing paintings by Francesc Galobardes. Multicoloured. P 13.
F527   3f. Type F **222** .... 2·50   2·75
F528   4f.50 Mill and farmhouse, Solé (horiz)............. 3·00   3·25

(Des F. Ribó. Litho)
1997 (25 Oct). Religious Silver Work. Type F **223** and similar vert design. Multicoloured. P 13.
F529   3f. Type F **223** .... 2·50   2·75
       a. Horiz strip. Nos. F529/30 plus label........ 10·50 11·00
F530   15f.50 Pax, St. Peter's Church, Aixirivall.......... 7·50   8·00
Nos. F529/30 were issued in horizontal se-tenant pairs together with an intervening label.

F **224** The Legend of Meritxell
F **225** St. Michael's Chapel, Engolasters

(Des S. Mas. Litho)
1997 (22 Nov). Legends. Type F **224** and similar vert designs. Multicoloured. P 13.
F531   3f. Type F **224** .... 1·90   2·10
           a. Horiz strip of 3. Nos. F531/3 .... 7·00
F532   3f. The Seven-armed Cross .... 1·90   2·10
F533   3f.80 Wrestlers (The Fountain of Esmelicat) .. 3·00   3·25
F531/533 Set of 3 .... 6·00   6·75
Nos. F531/3 were issued together in horizontal se-tenant strips of three stamps within the sheet.

(Des Odette Baillais. Litho)
1997 (28 Nov). International Stamp Exhibition, Monaco. P 13.
F534   F **225**   3f. multicoloured .... 1·90   2·10

F **226** Harlequin juggling Candles
F **227** Super Giant Slalom
F **228** Arms of Ordino

(Des J.-P. Cousin. Litho)
1998 (3 Jan). Birthday Greetings Stamp. P 13.
F535   F **226**   3f. multicoloured .... 1·90   2·10

ANDORRA / French Post Offices

(Des G. Coda. Litho)
1998 (14 Feb). Winter Olympic Games, Nagano, Japan. P 13.
F536 F **227** 4f.40 multicoloured .... 3·25 3·50

(Des J.-P. Cousin. Litho)
1998 (7 Mar). Booklet stamp. No value expressed. Self-adhesive. Die-cut (straight edge×wavy edge).
F537 F **228** (3f.) multicoloured .... 1·90 2·10
The stamps are peeled directly from the booklet cover and cannot therefore be collected as separate panes.

F **229** Altarpiece and Vila Church

(Des E. Cardús. Litho)
1998 (28 Mar). P 13.
F538 F **229** 4f.50 multicoloured .... 3·25 3·50

F **230** Emblem and Cogwheels   F **231** Chaffinch and Berries

(Des F. Ribó. Litho)
1998 (11 Apr). 20th Anniv of Rotary International in Andorra. P 13.
F539 F **230** 3f. multicoloured .... 1·90 2·10

(Des G. Duval. Litho)
1998 (2 May). Nature Protection. P 13.
F540 F **231** 3f.80 multicoloured .... 3·00 3·25

F **232** Players   F **233** Treble Score and Stylized Orchestra

(Des J.-P. Veret-Lemarinier. Litho)
1998 (6 June). World Cup Football Championship, France. P 13.
F541 F **232** 3f. multicoloured .... 1·90 2·10

(Des Clara Vives. Litho)
1998 (20 June). Europa. National Festivals. Music Festival. P 13.
F542 F **233** 3f. multicoloured .... 1·90 2·10

F **234** River

F **235** Chalice

(Des J. Pujal. Litho)
1998 (4 July). Expo '98 World's Fair, Lisbon, Portugal. P 13.
F543 F **234** 5f. multicoloured .... 3·75 4·25

(Des F. Ribó. Litho)
1998 (19 Sept). Chalice from the House of the Valleys. P 13.
F544 F **235** 4f.50 multicoloured .... 3·25 3·75

(F **236**)   F **237** Andorra, 1717

1998 (14 Nov). French Victory in World Cup Football Championship. No. F541 optd with Type F **236** in deep ultramarine.
F545 F **232** 3f. multicoloured .... 3·75 4·25

(Des J. Xandri (3f.), F. Ribó (15f.50). Litho)
1998 (14 Nov). Relief Maps. Type F **237** and similar multicoloured design. P 13½×13 (3f.) or 13×13½ (15f.50).
F546   3f. Type F **237** .... 1·90 2·10
F547   15f.50 Andorra, 1777 (horiz) .... 9·75 10·50

F **238** Museum   F **239** Front Page of First Edition

(Des E. Cardús. Litho)
1998 (19 Nov). Inauguration of Postal Museum. P 13.
F548 F **238** 3f. multicoloured .... 1·90 2·10

(Des J. Xandri. Litho)
1998 (5 Dec). 250th Anniv of *Manual Digest*. P 13.
F549 F **239** 3f.80 multicoloured .... 3·00 3·25

F **240** Arms of La Massana   F **241** House and Recycling Bins

(Des J.-P. Cousin. Litho)
1999 (16 Jan). Booklet stamp. No value expressed. Self-adhesive. Die-cut (straight edge×wavy edge).
F550 F **240** (3f.) multicoloured .... 1·90 2·10
The stamps are peeled directly from the booklet cover and cannot therefore be collected as separate panes.

(Des T. Struve. Litho)
1999 (13 Mar). "Green World". Recycling of Waste. P 13.
F551 F **241** 5f. multicoloured .... 3·75 4·25

F **242** Vall de Sorteny

(Des J. Riba. Litho)
1999 (10 Apr). Europa. Parks and Gardens. P 13.
F552 F **242** 3f. multicoloured .... 1·90 2·10

457

ANDORRA / French Post Offices

F **243** Council Emblem and Seat, Strasbourg
F **244** "The First Mail Coach"

(Des G. Coda. Litho)
1999 (5 May). 50th Anniv of Council of Europe. P 13.
F553   F **243**   3f.80 multicoloured .... 3·00   3·25

(Des S. Mas. Litho)
1999 (15 May). P 13.
F554   F **244**   2f.70 multicoloured .... 1·70   1·90

F **245** Footballer and Flags
F **246** St. Michael's Church, Engolasters, and Emblem

(Des A. Seyrat. Photo)
1999 (9 June). Andorra–France Qualifying Match for European Nations Football Championship. P 12½.
F555   F **245**   4f.50 multicoloured .... 3·50   4·00

(Des A. Lavergne. Litho)
1999 (2 July). Philexfrance 99 International Stamp Exhibition, Paris, France. P 13×13½.
F556   F **246**   3f. multicoloured .... 1·80   2·00

F **247** Winter Scene
F **248** Emblem and "50"

(Des A. Seyrat. Litho)
1999 (10 July). Paintings of Pal by Francesc Galobardes. Type F **247** and similar multicoloured design. P 13½×13 (F557) or 13×13½ (F558).
F557   3f. Type F **247** .... 1·80   2·00
F558   3f. Summer scene (horiz) .... 1·80   2·00

(Des P. Moles. Litho)
1999 (24 July). 50th Anniv of International Photographic Art Federation. P 13.
F559   F **248**   4f.40 multicoloured .... 2·75   3·00

F **249** Rull House, Sispony

(Des S. Mas. Litho)
1999 (4 Sept). P 13.
F560   F **249**   15f.50 multicoloured .... 7·25   8·00

F **250** Chest with Six Locks

(Des E. Cardús. Litho)
1999 (9 Oct). P 13.
F561   F **250**   6f.70 multicoloured .... 3·25   3·50

F **251** Angels   F **252** Revellers

(Des J. Xandri. Litho)
1999 (27 Nov). Christmas. P 13.
F562   F **251**   3f. multicoloured .... 1·80   2·00

(Des M. Pujol. Litho)
2000–3 Jan). Year 2000. P 13×13½.
F563   F **252**   3f. multicoloured .... 1·80   2·00

F **253** Arms of La Vella
F **254** Snowboarder

(Des J.-P. Cousin. Litho)
2000 (26 Feb). Booklet stamp. No value expressed. Self-adhesive. Die-cut (straight edge×wavy edge).
F564   F **253**   (3f.) multicoloured .... 1·80   2·00
   The stamps are peeled directly from the booklet cover and cannot therefore be collected as separate panes.

(Des F. Ribó. Litho)
2000 (17 Mar). P 13.
F565   F **254**   4f.50 greenish blue, chestnut and black .... 2·75   3·00

F **255** Emblem
F **256** Campanula cochlearifolia

(Des J. Xandri. Litho)
2000 (1 Apr). Montserrat Caballé International Opera Competition, Saint Julià de Lòria. P 13×13½.
F566   F **255**   3f.80 yellow and ultramarine .... 2·30   2·50

ANDORRA / French Post Offices

(Des J. Guardiola. Litho)
2000 (15 Apr). P 13.
F567   F **256**   2f.70 multicoloured .... 1·80   2·00

F **257** "Building Europe"   F **258** Church (Canòlic Festival)

(Des J.-P. Cousin. Litho)
2000 (9 May). Europa. P 13½×13.
F568   F **257**   3f. multicoloured .... 2·50   2·75

(Des S. Mas. Litho)
2000 (27 May). Festivals. Type F **258** and similar square design. Multicoloured. P 13.
F569   3f. Type F **258** .... 1·80   2·00
           a. Horiz strip. Nos. F569/70 plus label .... 3·75   4·25
F570   3f. People at Our Lady's Chapel, Meritxell (Meritxell Festival) .... 1·80   2·00
Nos. F269/70 were issued in horizontal se-tenant pairs together with an intervening label.

F **259** Sparrow   F **260** Hurdling   F **261** Goat, Skier and Walker

(Des P. Moles. Litho)
2000 (7 July). P 13.
F571   F **259**   4f.40 multicoloured .... 2·75   3·00

(Des A. Lavergne. Litho)
2000 (9 Sept). Olympic Games, Sydney. P 13.
F572   F **260**   5f. multicoloured .... 3·00   3·50

(Des P. Moles. Litho)
2000 (27 Sept). Tourism Day. P 13.
F573   F **261**   3f. multicoloured .... 1·80   2·00

F **262** Flower, Text, Circuit Board and Emblems   F **263** Stone Arch and Flag

(Des J. Pujal. Litho)
2000 (6 Oct). EXPO 2000 World's Fair, Hanover, Germany. P 13.
F574   F **262**   3f. multicoloured .... 1·80   2·00

(Des J. Xandri. Litho)
2000 (4 Nov). European Community. P 13½×13.
F575   F **263**   3f.80 multicoloured .... 2·30   2·50

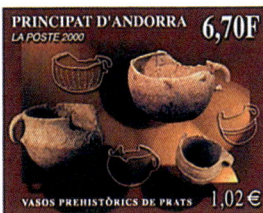 

F **264** Pottery   F **265** Drawing

(Des M. Pujol. Litho)
2000 (16 Dec). Prehistoric Pottery. P 13×13½.
F576   F **264**   6f.70 multicoloured .... 3·25   3·50

(Des F. Ribó and A. Seyrat. Litho)
2000 (22 Dec). 25th Anniv of National Archives. P 13.
F577   F **265**   15f.50 multicoloured .... 7·25   8·00

F **266** Arms of Saint Julia de Lòria   F **267** Ski Lift

(Des J.-P. Cousin. Litho)
2001 (19 Jan). Booklet stamp. No value expressed. Self-adhesive. Die-cut (straight edge×wavy edge).
F578   F **266**   (3f.) multicoloured .... 1·80   2·00
The stamps are peeled directly from the booklet cover and cannot therefore be collected as separate panes.

(Des J. Xandri. Photo)
2001 (10 Feb). Canillo Àliga Club. P 13.
F579   F **267**   4f.50 multicoloured .... 2·75   3·00

F **268** Decorative Metalwork   F **269** Legend of Lake Engolasters

(Des F. Sánchez. Litho)
2001 (17 Feb). Casa Cristo Museum. P 13½×13.
F580   F **268**   6f.70 multicoloured .... 3·25   3·50

(Des S. Mas. Litho)
2001 (23 Mar). Legends. Type F **269** and similar vert design. Multicoloured. P 13.
F581   3f. Type F **269** .... 1·80   2·00
           a. Horiz strip. Nos. F581/2 plus label .... 3·75   4·25
F582   3f. Lords before King (foundation of Andorra) .... 1·80   2·00
Nos. F581/2 were issued together in horizontal se-tenant strips of two stamps with intervening label.

ANDORRA / French Post Offices

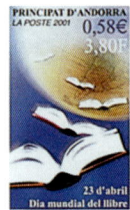

F **270** Globe and Books F **271** Water Splash F **272** Raspberry

F **277** Hotel Pla F **278** Cross

(Des J. Xandri. Litho)

2001 (23 Apr). World Book Day. P 13.
F583   F **270**   3f.80 multicoloured .... 2·30   2·50

(Des E. Fayolle. Litho)

2001 (28 Apr). Europa. Water Resources. P 13.
F584   F **271**   3f. multicoloured .... 2·50   2·75

(Des G. Duval (F585), P. -Y. Schmitt (F586). Litho)

2001 (12 May). Type F **272** and similar multicoloured design. P 13.
F585   3f. Type F **272** .... 2·30   2·50
F586   4f.40 Jay (horiz) .... 3·00   3·50

(Des F. Ribó. Photo)

2001 (12 Oct). P 13.
F591   F **277**   15f.50 black, deep violet and bright green .... 7·75   8·75

(Des J. Riba. Litho)

2001 (17 Nov). Grossa Cross (boundry cross at the crossroads between Avinguda Meritxell and Carrer Bisbe Iglesias). P 13½.
F592   F **278**   2f.70 multicoloured .... 1·60   1·70

New Currency
100 Cents = 1 Euro

F **273** Profiles talking   F **274** Post Offices Trumpeter

F **279** State Arms   F **280** The Legend of Meritxell

(Des J. Xandri. Litho)

2001 (16 June). European Year of Languages. P 13.
F587   F **273**   3f.80 multicoloured .... 2·75   3·25

(Des J. Peguero. Litho)

2001 (7 July). Jazz Festival, Escaldes-Engordany. P 13.
F588   F **274**   3f. multicoloured .... 2·30   2·50

(Des A. Seyrat. Photo)

2002 (2 Jan)–**03**. P 13.
(a) With face value
F593   F **279**   1c. multicoloured 30   35
F594   2c. multicoloured 30   35
F595   5c. multicoloured 30   35
F596   60c. multicoloured (15.1.07) .... 1·90   2·10
(b) No value expressed
(i) Ordinary gum. P 13
F598   F **279**   (46c.) multicoloured (green) (29.11.03).. 2·30   2·50
F599   (46c.) multicoloured (red) .... 2·30   2·50
(ii) Size 17×23 mm. Self-adhesive gum. Die-cut
F599a F **279**   (52c.) multicoloured (red) (31.3.07) .... 1·70   1·90
F593/F599 Set of 7 .... 8·25   9·00

Nos. F598/9 were sold at the rate for inland letters up to 20 grammes.

No. 599a was die-cut all round to simulate perforations and was issued in booklets of 20 (3×2, 2×2) stamps.

Numbers have been left for additions to this series.

F **275** Kitchen

2002 (2 Jan)–**09**. Legends. Designs as Nos. F525, F531/3 and F581/2 and new designs but with values in new currency as Type F **280**. Multicoloured. P 13.
F600   10c. Type F **280** 55   60
F601   20c. Wrestlers (The Fountain of Esmelicat) ... 55   60
F602   41c. The Piper (Le joueurde cornmuse) (27.9) .... 1·40   1·60
F603   45c. Legend of Saint Vincent Castle (15.5.04) .... 1·40   1·60
F604   48c. Port Rat (12.2.05) .... 2·10   2·30
F604a   48c. The Cave of Ourse (8.4.06).......... 1·40   1·60
F604b   49c. The Testament of the Ilop (26.2.07).... 1·40   1·60
F604c   50c. El tresor de la font del Manegó (10.3.08) .... 1·40   1·60
F605   50c. The Seven-armed Cross .... 1·40   1·60
F605a   51c. The Devils of Aixirivall (Les Diables d'Aixirivall) (7.3.09) .... 1·40   1·60
F606   75c. Le joueur de cornemuse .... 2·10   2·30
F606a   90c. Legende du pin de la Marginedo .... 2·75   3·00
F610   €1 Lords before King (foundation of Andorra) .... 2·75   3·00
F611   €2 Legend of Lake Engolasters .... 5·50   6·25
F612   €5 The White Lady .... 12·50   14·00
F600/612 Set of 15 .... 35·00   40·00

(Des P. Canturri. Litho)

2001 (10 Aug). P 13.
F589   F **275**   5f. multicoloured .... 3·00   3·50

F **276** Chapel

(Des Odette Baillais. Litho)

2001 (7 Sept). 25th Anniv of Chapel of Our Lady, Meritxell. P 13.
F590   F **276**   3f. multicoloured .... 2·30   2·50

Numbers have been left for additions to this series.

460

ANDORRA / French Post Offices

F 281 Pedestrians on Crossing   F 282 Skier

(Des Anna Poyal. Litho)
2002 (25 Jan). Schools' Road Safety Campaign. P 13½×13.
F615   F 281   69c. multicoloured ....   2·50   2·75

(Des Odette Ballais. Litho)
2002 (2 Feb). Winter Olympic Games, Salt Lake City, U.S.A. P 13.
F616   F 282   58c. multicoloured ....   1·90   2·10

F 283 Hotel Rosaleda   F 284 Water Droplet and Clouds

(Des F. Galobardes. Litho)
2002 (16 Mar). P 13.
F617   F 283   46c. multicoloured ....   1·70   1·80

(Des J. Xandri. Litho)
2002 (22 Mar). World Water Day. P 13.
F618   F 284   67c. multicoloured ....   2·10   2·30

F 285 Clown   F 286 Myrtle

(Des P. Canturri. Litho)
2002 (10 May). Europa. Circus. P 13.
F619   F 285   46c. multicoloured ....   2·50   2·75

(Des G. Duval. Litho)
2002 (6 July). P 13.
F620   F 286   46c. multicoloured ....   1·70   1·80

F 287 Seated Nude (Josep Viladomat)   F 288 Mountains from Tunnel Entrance

(Des F. Ribó and A. Seyrat. Litho)
2002 (24 Aug). P 13½×13.
F621   F 287   €2.36 multicoloured ....   6·50   7·00

(Des P. Moles and A. Seyrat. Litho)
2002 (31 Aug). Completion of the Envalira Road Tunnel between Andorra and France. P 13.
F622   F 288   46c. multicoloured ....   1·70   1·80

F 289 Mural (detail) (Santa Coloma Church, Andorra la Vella)   F 290 Arms of Escaldes-Engordany

(Des E. Cardús. Litho)
2002 (16 Nov). P 13.
F623   F 289   €1.02 multicoloured ....   3·25   3·50

(Des A. Seyrat. Photo)
2003 (18 Jan). Arms. Booklet stamps. No value expressed. Self-adhesive. Imperf×wavy edge.
F624   F 290   (46c.) multicoloured ....   1·90   2·10
No. F624 was sold at the rate for inland letters up to 20 grammes.

F 291 State Arms   F 292 Les Bons

(Des S. Mas. Litho)
2003 (8 Feb). Legends. "Légende du pin de la Margineda". Vert design as Type F 280. P 13.
F625   69c. multicoloured ....   1·90   2·10

(Des J. Xandri and A. Seyrat. Litho)
2003 (14 Mar). Tenth Anniv of Constitution. P 13×13½.
F626   F 291   €2.36 multicoloured ....   6·50   7·00

(Des F. Galobardes and A. Seyrat. Litho)
2003 (31 Mar). Architecture. P 13.
F627   F 292   67c. multicoloured ....   2·50   2·10

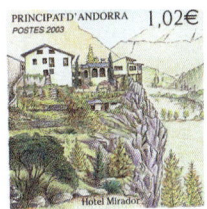 

F 293 Hotel Mirador   F 294 Man, Dog and Sheep

(Des P. Canturri and A. Seyrat. Litho)
2003 (12 Apr). P 13.
F628   F 293   €1.02 multicoloured ....   3·25   3·50

(Des S. Mas and A. Seyrat. Litho)
2003 (19 May). Europa. Poster Art. P 13.
F629   F 294   46c. multicoloured ....   2·50   2·75

461

ANDORRA / French Post Offices

F **295** Dancers and Fire   F **296** Cyclist and Map

(Des P. Canturri and A. Seyrat. Litho)
2003 (23 June). Fires of St. John the Baptist Festival. P 13.
F630   F **295**   50c. multicoloured .... 1·90   2·10

(Des Odette Ballais. Litho)
2003 (5 July). Centenary of Tour de France (cycle race). P 13.
F631   F **296**   50c. multicoloured .... 1·90   2·10

F **297** Pole Vault   F **298** *Grexia sparassis crispa*

(Des F. Ribó. Litho)
2003 (8 Aug). World Athletics Championships, Paris. P 13.
F632   F **297**   90c. multicoloured .... 2·75   3·25

(Des F. Ribó. Litho)
2003 (13 Sept). P 13.
F633   F **298**   45c. multicoloured .... 1·30   1·40

F **299** Red Currant   F **300** Telephone, Satellite and Globe

(Des F. Ribó. Litho)
2003 (13 Sept). P 13.
F634   F **299**   75c. multicoloured .... 2·50   2·75

(Des E. Cardús and A. Seyrat. Litho)
2003 (30 Oct). Centenary of First Telephone in Andorra. P 13.
F635   F **300**   50c. multicoloured .... 1·90   2·10

F **301** "Maternity" (Paul Gauguin)   F **302** St. Anthony's Market

2003 (29 Nov). Litho. P 13.
F636   F **301**   75c. multicoloured .... 2·75   3·00

(Des P. Canturri. Litho)
2004 (17 Jan). P 13.
F637   F **302**   50c. multicoloured .... 1·90   2·10

F **303** Children   F **304** Hotel Valira

(Des A. Montané. Litho)
2004 (22 Mar). P 13.
F638   F **303**   50c. multicoloured .... 1·90   2·10

(Des F. Galobardes. Litho)
2004 (19 Apr). P 13.
F639   F **304**   €1.11 multicoloured .... 3·50   3·75

F **305** Woman and Andorra Sign   F **306** Madriu-Perafita-Claror Valley

(Des F. Ribó. Litho)
2004 (7 May). Europa. Holidays. P 13.
F640   F **305**   50c. yellow-orange, orange-red and black .... 2·10   2·30

(Des F. Ribo. Litho)
2004 (28 June). UNESCO World Heritage Site. P 13.
F641   F **306**   75c. multicoloured .... 2·50   2·75

F **307** Poblet de Fontaneda   F **308** Runner and Swimmer

(Des S. Mas. Litho)
2004 (5 July). P 13.
F642   F **307**   50c. multicoloured .... 1·90   2·10

(Des H. Galeron. Litho)
2004 ((9 Nov)). Olympic Games, Athens 2004. P 13.
F643   F **308**   90c. multicoloured .... 3·00   3·25

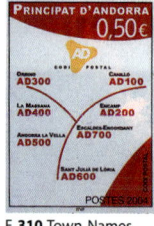

F **309** "Pont de la Margineda" (sketch)   F **310** Town Names and Post Codes

2004 (2 Oct). Art. Margineda Bridge by Joaquim Mir (Spanish artist). Type F **309** and similar horiz design. Multicoloured. Litho. P 13.
F644   €1 Type F **309** .... 3·00   3·25
         a. Horiz strip. Nos. F644/5 plus label ...... 9·00   9·75
F645   €2 "Pont de la Margineda" (painting) ...... 5·75   6·25
Nos. F644/5 were issued in horizontal strips of two stamps separated by a label showing "Self-Portrait" by Joaquim Mir.

ANDORRA / French Post Offices

2004 (23 Oct). Introduction of Postal Codes. Litho. P 13½.
F646 F **310** 50c. orange-vermilion, black and lemon.................................... 1·90 2·10

F **311** Emblem

F **312** Children's Nativity

(Des Nadal. Litho)
2004 (8 Nov). Tenth Anniv of Entry into Council of Europe. P 13½.
F647 F **311** €2.50 multicoloured........................ 7·75 8·50

(Des F. Ribo. Litho)
2004 (4 Dec). Christmas. P 13½.
F648 F **312** 50c. black, lake-brown and olive-bistre.................................... 1·90 2·10

F **313** Three Kings visiting Child

F **314** Mountains and Lake

(Des S. Mas. Litho)
2005 (5 Jan). P 13½.
F649 F **313** 50c. multicoloured......................... 1·90 2·10

(Des A. Tena. Litho)
2005 (22 Jan). World Heritage Site. Madriu-Claror-Perafita Valley. P 13½.
F650 F **314** 50c. multicoloured......................... 1·90 2·10

F **315** Tengmalm's Owl (*Aegolius funereus*)

F **316** Bottle, Glass, Jug and Fruit

(Des Cardus. Litho)
2005 (14 Feb). P 13½.
F651 F **315** 90c. multicoloured......................... 2·75 3·25

(Des C. Mas. Litho)
2005 (7 May). Europa. Gastronomy. P 13×13½.
F652 F **316** 55c. multicoloured......................... 2·00 2·20

F **317** Marksman

F **318** Mountain Hut, Bordes d'Ensegur

(Des Xandri. Litho)
2005 (28 May). Small States of Europe Games. Sheet 151×70 mm containing Type F **317** and similar vert designs. Each black and magenta. P 13½.
MSF653 53c. Type F **317**; 55c. Runner; 82c. Swimmer; €1 Diver.. 9·00 9·50

2005 (11 June). Litho. P 13½.
F654 F **318** €2.50 multicoloured....................... 8·00 8·75

F **319** Motorcycle

F **320** "Prats de Santa Coloma" (Joaquim Mir)

2005 (4 July). Litho. P 13½.
F655 F **319** 53c. sepia, grey brown and black........ 1·60 1·70

2005 (10 Aug). Art. Litho. P 13½.
F656 F **320** 82c. multicoloured......................... 2·75 2·75

F **321** Hostel Calones

F **322** Lorry in Snow (Josep Alsina)

(Des P. Canturri. Litho)
2005 (10 Sept). P 13½.
F657 F **321** €1.98 multicoloured....................... 6·25 6·50

(Des F. Ribo. Litho)
2005 (28 Oct). Photography. P 13½.
F658 F **322** 53c. multicoloured......................... 1·70 1·80

F **323** Emblem

F **325** Ursus arctos

F **324** "Adoration of the Shepherds" (A. Viladomat)

(Des J. Peguero. Litho)
2005 (5 Nov). Centenary of Rotary International. P 13½.
F659 F **323** 55c. multicoloured......................... 1·90 2·00

2005 (7 Dec). Christmas. P 13½.
F660 F **324** €1.22 multicoloured....................... 4·00 4·25

463

ANDORRA / French Post Offices

F **326** Alpine Skier

F **326a** Tobacco Leaves

(Des J. Xandri. Litho)
2006 (16 Jan). Fauna. Type F **326** and similar multicoloured design. P 13½.
F661   53c. Type F **326** .... 1·70   1·80
F662   53c. Rupicapra pyrenaica (vert) .... 1·70   1·80

(J.-P. Veret-Lemarinier. Litho)
2006 (6 Feb). Winter Olympic Games, Turin. Type F **326** and similar vert design. Multicoloured. P 13½.
F663   55c. Type F **326** .... 1·70   1·80
          a. Pair. Nos. F663/4 plus central label .... 4·25   4·50
F664   75c. Cross country skier .... 2·30   2·50
     F663/4 were issued in horizontal *se-tenant* strips of two stamps surrounding a central stamp size label inscribed for the games.

F **327** Napoleon

(Des F. Ribo. Litho)
2006 (4 Mar). Tobacco Museum, Sant Julià de Lòria. P 13½.
F665   F **326a**   82c. multicoloured .... 2·75   2·75

(Des F. Ribo. Litho)
2006 (27 Mar). Bicentenary of Napoleon's Decree restoring Statute of Co-Principality. P 13½.
F666   F **327**   53c. blue, azure and black .... 1·70   1·80

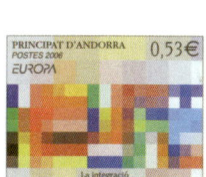
F **328** Coloured blocks

F **329** Sorteny Valley Nature Reserve

(Des E. Cardus. Litho)
2006 (9 May). Europa. Integration. P 13½.
F667   F **328**   53c. multicoloured .... 2·00   2·10

(Des A. Montané. Litho)
2006 (10 June). P 13½.
F668   F **329**   55c. multicoloured .... 1·90   2·00

F **330** Pablo Casals

F **331** Model T Ford

(Des C. Drochon. Litho)
2006 (29 July). 130th Birth Anniv of Pablo Casals (cellist). P 13½.
F669   F **330**   90c. multicoloured .... 3·00   3·25

(Des F. Ribo. Litho)
2006 (4 Sept). P 13½.
F670   F **331**   85c. multicoloured .... 2·75   3·00

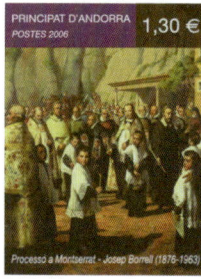
F **332** "Montserrat Procession" (Josep Borrell)

F **333** Reredos (retable), Sant Marti de la Cortinada, Ordino

2006 (4 Nov). P 13½.
F671   F **332**   €1.30 multicoloured .... 4·25   4·50

2006 (2 Dec). P 13½.
F672   F **333**   54c. multicoloured .... 1·90   2·00

F **334** Marmot (*Marmota marmota*)

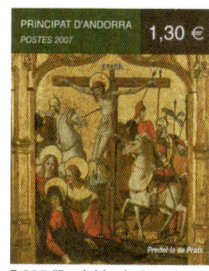
F **335** "Predel la de Prats" (Master of Canillo)

(Des J. Xandri)
2007 (22 Jan). Fauna. Type F **334** and similar multicoloured design. P 13½.
F673   54c. Type F **334** .... 1·90   2·00
F674   60c. Eurasian red squirrel (*Sciurus vulgaris*)
           (horiz) .... 2·00   2·10

(Des J. Xandri)
2007 (17 Mar). P 13½.
F675   F **335**   €1.30 multicoloured .... 4·25   4·50

F **336** Heart enclosing Rose

F **337** Salute

2007 (23 Apr). Saint George. P 13½.
F676   F **336**   86c. multicoloured .... 3·00   3·25
     No. F676 was perforated in a heart shape, enclosed in an outer perforated square.

(Des E. Cardus)
2007 (7 May). Europa. Centenary of Scouting. P 13½.
F677   F **337**   54c. multicoloured .... 1·90   2·00

ANDORRA / French Post Offices

F **338** Virgin, Meritxell

F **339** 'Pinette'

(Des Sergi Mas)

2007 (2 June). Twinning of Meritxell and Sabart. T F **338** and similar vert design. Multicoloured. P 13½×13.
F678   54c. Type F **338** .... 1·90   2·00
     a. Strip. Nos. F678/9 plus label   4·25
F679   54c. Virgin, Sabart .... 1·90   2·00
  Nos. 678/9 were issued in horizontal *se-tenant* strips of two stamps surrounding a central stamp size label.

(Des Francesc Rilbó.)

2007 (10 July). P 13.
F680   F **339**   60c. multicoloured .... 2·00   2·10

F **340** Players

F **341** Vall del Comapedrosa

(Des Bruno Ghiringhelli. Litho)

2007 (1 Sept). Rugby World Cup, France. P 13.
F681   F **340**   85c. multicoloured .... 2·75   3·00
  No. F681 was perforated in an ellipse enclosed in an outer perforated square.

2007 (8 Oct). P 13.
F682   F **341**   €3.04 multicoloured .... 10·00   10·50

F **341a** Prehistoric Family

F **342** Cave Dwellers

(Des Francesc Ribo)

2007 (5 Nov). Pre-Historic Sites. El Cedre. P 13½×13.
F683   F **341a**   85c. multicoloured .... 3·00   3·25

(Des Francesc Ribo)

2007 (12 Nov). Pre-Historic Sites. La Barma de la Marginada. P 13½×13.
F684   F **342**   60c. multicoloured .... 2·00   2·10

F **343** Altarpiece, Sant Marti de la Cortinada

F **344** *Vulpes vulpes* (red fox)

2007 (3 Dec). Christmas. P 13.
F685   F **343**   54c. multicoloured .... 1·90   2·00

(Des Xandri)

2008 (28 Jan). Fauna. Type F **344** and similar multicoloured design. P 13.
F686   54c. Type F **344** .... 2·00   2·10
F687   60c. *Sus scrofa* (wild boar) (vert) .... 2·20   2·30

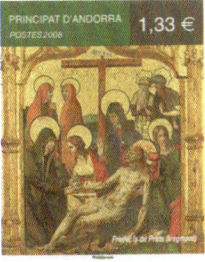 

F **345** Predella, Altar of St. Michael de Prats Church

F **346** Cartercar, 1906

(Des Xandri)

2008 (14 Apr). Easter. P 13½×13.
F688   F **345**   €1.33 multicoloured .... 5·00   5·25

(Des Stéphanie Ghinéa)

2008 (5 May). P 13½×13.
F689   F **346**   65c. multicoloured .... 2·75   2·75

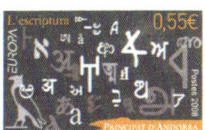 

F **347** Symbols of Writing

F **348** Rowing

(Des Enric Cardús)

2008 (17 May). Europa. The Letter. P 13½.
F690   F **347**   55c. multicoloured .... 2·30   2·40

(Des Joan Xandri)

2008 (16 June). Olympic Games, Beijing. Sheet 210×60 mm containing T F **348** and similar horiz designs. Multicoloured. P 13×13½.
MSF691   55c.×4, Type F **348**; Running; Swimming; Judo .... 8·25   8·50
  The stamps of No. **MS**F691 were not for sale separately.

F **349** *Narcissus poeticus*

F **350** Vall d'Incles (Incles valley)

(Des Stéphanie Ghinéa and André Boos)

2008 (18 June). P 13½×13.
F692   F **349**   55c. multicoloured .... 2·30   2·40

(Des TENA)

2008 (5 July). P 13×13½.
F693   F **350**   €2.80 multicoloured .... 10·50   11·00

F **351** Men

F **352** Valley

465

ANDORRA / French Post Offices

(Des Francesc Ribo)
2008 (1 Sept). 75th Anniv of Male Suffrage. P 13×13½.
F694 F **351** 55c. multicoloured .... 2·30 2·40

(Des Tena)
2008 (6 Oct). Sustainable Development. P 13×13½.
F695 F **352** 88c. multicoloured .... 3·75 4·00

F **353** El roc d'Enclar

F **354** St. Mark and St. Mary (alterpiece (reredos))

(Des Francesc Ribo)
2008 (8 Nov). P 13½×13.
F696 F **353** 85c. multicoloured .... 3·50 3·75

2008 (13 Dec). P 13×13.
F697 F **354** 55c. multicoloured .... 2·75 2·75

F **355** Louis Braille

F **356** *Equus mulus* (mule)

(Des and eng Andre Lavergne. Recess and embossed)
2009 (24 Jan). Birth Bicentenary of Louis Braille (inventor of Braille writing for the blind). P 13.
F698 F **355** 88c. new blue and brown .... 4·00 4·00

(Des Joan Xandri. Litho)
2009 (14 Feb). Domestic Animals. Type F **356** and similar multicoloured design. P 13.
F699   55c. Type F **356** .... 2·30 2·40
F700   65c. *Bos taurus* (cow) (horiz) .... 2·50 2·50

F **357** Penguins

F **358** Predel la de Prats (detail)

(Des and Yves Beaujard. Recess and litho)
2009 (27 Mar). Preserve Polar Regions and Glaciers. Sheet 143×120 mm containing Type F **357** and similar multicoloured design. P 13×13½.
MSF701 56c. Type F **357**; 85c. Polar ice .... 6·25 6·50

2009 (20 Apr). Litho. P 13½.
F702 F **358** €1.35 multicoloured .... 6·00 6·25

F **359** Nebula

F **360** Renault Voiturette, 1898

(Des Cardus. Litho)
2009 (4 May). Europa. Astronomy. P 13.
F703 F **359** 56c. multicoloured .... 2·50 2·50

2009 (18 May). First Car manufactured by Renault. P 13½×13.
F704 F **360** 70c. multicoloured .... 3·00 3·25

F **361** *Sant Joan de Caselles* (Maurice Utrillo)

(Des and eng Yves Beaujard. Recess and litho)
2009 (25 May). Art. P 13×13½.
F705 F **361** 90c. multicoloured .... 4·00 4·00

F **362** Cercle dels Pessons

F **363** Cyclist

(Des Tena. Litho)
2009 (15 June). P 13.
F706 F **362** €2.80 multicoloured .... 11·50 12·00

(Des Xandri. Litho)
2009 (13 July). Tour de France (cycle race). P 13.
F707 F **363** 56c. multicoloured .... 2·50 2·50

F **364** Allegory

F **365** Santa Coloma Church

F **366** The Nativity

(Des Mas)
2009 (5 Oct). 40th Anniv of Circle of Arts and Letters. P 13.
F708 F **364** 51c. multicoloured .... 2·40 2·40

(Des Ribo)
2009 (9 Nov). Romanesque Art in Andorra. P 13.
F709 F **365** 85c. multicoloured .... 3·75 3·75

466

2009 (14 Dec). Christmas. P 13.
F710   F **366**   56c. multicoloured .... 2·50   2·50

F **366a** Arms   F **367** Athlete

2010 (1 Jan). State Arms. Background colour given. P 13.

(a) With face value

F710	F **366a**	1c. multicoloured (pale lemon)........	20	25
F711		5c. multicoloured (cobalt)	25	30
F712		10c. multicoloured (bright yellow-orange)..	55	60
F713		20c. multicoloured (lavender)	55	60
F714		50c. multicoloured (olive-bistre)........	1·40	1·60

(b) No value expressed

F715		(60c.) multicoloured (aquamarine).....	2·40	2·50
F710/715 Set of 6			5·25	5·75

Nos. F710/F715 are as Nos. F **279** but with different inscriptions.

(Des Cardus)

2010 (23 Jan). Winter Olympic Games, Vancouver. P 13.
F716   F **367**   85c. multicoloured .... 3·75   3·75

 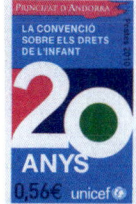

F **368** Casamanya Peak   F **369** Anniversary Emblem

(Des Tena)

2010 (15 Feb). Mountains. P 13.
F717   F **368**   €2.80 multicoloured .... 11·50   12·00

2010 (2 Mar). 20th Anniv of Convention on Rights of the Child. UNICEF. P 13.
F718   F **369**   56c. multicoloured .... 2·50   2·50

STAMP BOOKLETS

The following checklist covers, in simplified form, booklets issued by French Post Offices in Andorra. It is intended that it should be used in conjunction with the main listings and full details of panes and stamps listed there are not repeated.

Prices are for complete booklets

Booklet No.	Date	Contents and Cover Price	Price
SB1	28.3.87	Early Coat of Arms (Type F **115**) 1 pane, No. F342a (17f.).........	15·00
SB2	6.2.88	Arms (Type F **144**) 2 panes, No. F398a (22f.).........	15·00
SB3	7.4.90	Arms (Type F **144**) 2 panes, No. F399a (23f.).........	18·00
SB4	19.10.91	Arms (Type F **144**) 2 panes, No. F400a (25f.).........	19·00
SB5	7.8.93	Arms (Type F **144**) 2 panes, No. F401a (28f.).........	20·00
SB6	10.6.96	Canillo (Type F **212**) 1 pane, No. F515x10..................	26·00
SB7	22.2.97	Encamp (Type F **218**) 1 pane, No. F523x10 (30f.).........	20·00
SB8	7.3.98	Ordino (Type F **228**) 1 pane, No. F537x10 (30f.).........	20·00
SB9	16.1.99	La Massana (Type F **240**) 1 pane, No. F550x10 (30f.).........	20·00
SB10	26.2.00	La Vella (Type F **253**) 1 pane, No. F564x10 (30f.).........	19·00
SB11	19.1.01	Saint Julia de Lòria (Type F **266**) 1 pane, No. F578x10..................	19·00
SB12	18.1.03	Arms (Type F **290**) 1 pane, F624x10 (€4.60)..........	20·00
SB13	15.1.07	Arms (Type F **279**) 1 pane, F599ax20 (€10.40)........	18·00

II. SPANISH POST OFFICES

1928. 100 Centimos = 1 Peseta
2002. 100 Cents = 1 Euro

From 1 January to 27 March 1928 Andorra used unoverprinted Spanish stamps: Types **66**, Crown (1c.), **68**, Alfonso XIII (2c., 5c. purple, 5c. carmine. 10c. carmine, 10c. green, 15, 20, 25, 30, 40, 50c.), **69**, Alfonso XIII (1, 4, 10p.) and Express Letter E **53**, Pegasus (20c. rose). These forerunners can only be distinguished from the same stamps used in Spain by the cancellation; however, few genuinely used Andorran items have been identified. Examples with first day postmarks are known but these are believed to have been manufactured some months later.

From 1939 Spanish stamps have occasionally been sold in Andorra when Andorran stamps have not been available. Spanish stamps brought into Andorra by individuals have also been accepted for paying postage at Andorran Spanish post offices.

PRINTERS. All the following were printed at The Government Printing Works, Madrid.

CORREOS

⊷ CORREOS ⊶   CORREOS

ANDORRA   A N D O R R A
   (1)   (E 2)

1928 (28 Mar). Types of Spain (King Alfonso XIII), optd with T **1**.

A. P 12×11½ (comb)

2A	68	5c. carmine	17·00	17·00
3A		10c. deep green (R.)	10·50	10·50
5A		15c. deep greenish blue (R.)...	26·00	26·00
6A		20c. violet (R.)	25·00	25·00
7A		25c. carmine-red	8·50	8·50
8A		30c. blackish brown (R.)........	29·00	29·00
9A		40c. blue (R.)	34·00	34·00
10A		50c. red-orange	37·00	37·00
12A	69	4p. lake	£180	£180
13A		10p. brown	£250	£250

B. P 13×12½ (comb)

1B	68	2c. deep yellow-green (R.).....	1·70	2·30
2B		5c. carmine	2·30	2·75
3B		10c. deep green (R.)	3·50	4·00
5B		15c. deep greenish blue (R.)...	3·50	4·00
6B		20c. violet (R.)	3·75	4·25
8B		30c. blackish brown (R.)........	£275	£350
10B		50c. red-orange	£400	£450
11B	69	1p. deep greenish slate (R.)...	34·00	36·00
12B		4p. lake	£350	£350

C. P 14 (line)

1C	68	2c. deep yellow-green (R.).....	29·00	34·00
2C		5c. carmine	£550	£650
3C		10c. deep green (R.)	40·00	46·00
		a. Deep grey-green (R.)	£225	
5C		15c. deep greenish blue (R.)...	90·00	£100
6C		20c. violet (R.)	85·00	£170
8C		30c. blackish brown (R.)........	55·00	70·00
9C		40c. blue (R.)	70·00	80·00
10C		50c. red-orange	£350	£400
11C	69	1p. deep greenish slate (R.)...	£400	£500
12C		4p. lake	£350	£450
13C		10p. brown	£600	£650

All except No. 1 have blue control figures on back; stamps numbered "A000,000" are specimens. Stamps perforated other than those listed and 25, 30 and 50c. with inverted overprint come from imperf overprinted sheets stolen from the printing works with false control numbers, gum and perforations added. Stamps from the stolen sheets with perforations similar to the issued stamps can be identified by the letter "A" in the control number; in the genuine numbers the top of the "A" is flat, in the fakes it is pointed.

Overprints in the wrong colour are forgeries. Forged overprints in the correct colour can often be identified by the control number which on the genuine stamps consists of "A000." followed by three figures.

1928 (28 Mar–July). EXPRESS LETTER. Type E **53** of Spain (Pegasus), optd with Type E **2**. P 14.

E14		20c. red (without figs)...........	£110	£140
E15		20c. rose (blue figs on back) (July)........	70·00	90·00

2 House of the Valleys   **3** General Council of Andorra   E **4** Lammergeier over Pyrenees

467

ANDORRA / Spanish Post Offices

(Des P. Galindo. Eng C. Delhom (T **3**), J. L. Sanchez Toda (others). Recess).

1929 (25 Nov)–**38**. As T **2** (various designs) and **3**. Blue control figures on back of all except No. 14.

A. P 14 (line) (1929)

14A	2	2c. yellow-green	2·00	2·30
		c. Perf 13×12½	46·00	
15A	–	5c. claret	3·75	4·00
16A	–	10c. green	3·75	4·00
		c. Perf 13×12½	£130	
17A	–	15c. slate blue *to* slate-green	5·50	5·75
18A	–	20c. violet	5·50	6·25
		c. Perf 13×12½	70·00	
19A	–	25c. carmine	11·50	14·00
20A	2	30c. blackish brown	£150	£160
21A	–	40c. deep blue	11·50	8·00
22A	–	50c. red-orange	11·50	7·00
		c. Perf 13×12½	£130	
23A	3	1p. greenish slate	23·00	29·00
24A	–	4p. magenta	£110	£100
25A	–	10p. deep brown	£130	£130
		c. Perf 13×12½	£200	

B. P 11½ (1931–38)

14B	2	2c. yellow-green	5·75	7·00
15B	–	5c. claret	10·50	16·00
16B	–	10c. green	9·25	11·50
17B	–	15c. slate blue *to* slate-green	16·00	18·00
18B	–	20c. violet	18·00	23·00
19B	–	25c. carmine	14·00	17·00
20B	2	30c. blackish brown	£170	£190
21B	–	40c. deep blue	16·00	14·00
22B	–	50c. red-orange	£550	
23B	3	1p. greenish slate	34·00	40·00
24B	–	4p. magenta		

Designs:—5, 40c. Church of St. John of Caselles; 10, 20, 50c. Sant Julia de Loria; 15, 25c. Santa Coloma Church.

Dates of issue for perf 11½: 2 to 25c. 1931; 30c. 1932; 40c. 1935; 1p. 1938.

*50c. and 4p. perf 11½ with control number "A000,000" are specimen stamps.

In 1929 the peseta values were unofficially reprinted, in issued and different colours, from the original dies on show at the Barcelona Exhibition. The reprints exist imperf; comb perf 14 and perf 11½ and with forged cancellations.

Other imperf, imperf between, comb perf 14, and perf 14 stamps without control numbers (except 2c.) come from imperf sheets stolen from the printing works. Stamps from these sheets also exist perf 11½ and with forged control numbers.

See also Nos. 26/40.

1929 (25 Nov). EXPRESS LETTER. Blue figures on back. Recess. P 14.

E26	E **4**	20c. scarlet	34·00	40·00
		a. Perf 13×12½	£275	£325

No. E26 also exists perf 11½ with control number "A000,000"; this is a specimen stamp.

See also No. E41.

> A set of stamps inscribed "CORREU AERI/SOBRETAXA" was privately produced in 1932 for a proposed Andorra—Barcelona air service. The stamps also exist overprinted "FRANQUICIA DEL CONSELL" and "MUESTRA".

1935–42. As Nos. 14/25 but without control figures and some colours changed. P 11½.

26	2	2c. chestnut (1937)	1·40	2·30
27	–	5c. sepia (1936)	2·10	2·75
		a. Blackish brown	3·50	4·00
28	–	10c. yellow-green (1938)	£110	£130
29	–	10c. blue-green (1942)	10·50	8·00
		a. Perf 11	£650	£650
30	–	15c. blue-green (1937)	5·75	7·00
31	–	15c. yellow-green (1938)	7·00	7·50
32	–	20c. violet (1939)	6·25	6·25
33	–	25c. carmine (1937)	2·75	3·50
34	2	30c. bright rose-red (1935)	2·75	4·00
35	–	40c. blue (1942)	£700	£750
36	2	45c. carmine-red (1937)	2·30	2·75
37	–	50c. red-orange (1938)	5·75	7·00
38	2	60c. blue (1937)	4·50	5·75
		b. Perf 11	£350	£400
39	3	4p. bright purple (1942)	46·00	50·00
40	–	10p. brown (1942)	70·00	75·00
		a. Perf 11	£550	£550
26/40 Set of 15			£900	£950

All values exist perf 14; these are fake perforations made from imperf sheets.

1937. EXPRESS LETTER. Without control figures. P 11½.

E41	E **4**	20c. red	8·00	10·50

7 Councillor Manuel Areny Bons   **8** Arms   **9** Market Place, Ordino

 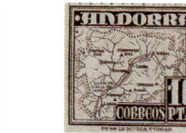

10 Shrine near Meritxell Chapel   **11** Map

1948 (16 Feb)–**53**. Photo (2, 5, 10c.), recess (others). P 12½×13 (2, 5, 10, 25c.), 10½×10 (4, 10p.) or 9½×10½ (others).

41	–	2c. olive (12.6.51)	1·10	1·70
42	–	5c. orange (8.1.53)	1·10	1·70
43	–	10c. deep blue (8.1.53)	1·10	1·70
44	**7**	20c. deep reddish purple	10·50	7·00
45	–	25c. yellow-orange (8.1.53)	7·00	3·50
46	**8**	30c. blackish green	23·00	11·50
47	–	50c. green	34·00	15·00
48	**10**	75c. indigo	33·00	10·00
49	**9**	90c. claret	17·00	11·50
50	**10**	1p. orange-vermilion	29·00	15·00
51	**8**	1p.35 deep violet	11·50	11·50
		a. Deep reddish lilac	23·00	17·00
52	**11**	4p. ultramarine (8.1.53)	34·00	29·00
53	–	10p. purple-brown (12.6.51)	65·00	34·00
41/53 Set of 13			£250	£150

Design: 2c. to 10c. Edelweiss (frame as T **7**).

E **12** Eurasian Red Squirrel (after Dürer) and Arms   **12** Andorra La Vella

1949 (13 Aug). EXPRESS LETTER. Recess. P 10.

E54	E **12**	25c. orange-vermilion	7·00	8·00

1951 (12 June). AIR. Recess. P 11.

54	**12**	1p. deep purple-brown	40·00	26·00

13 St. Anthony's Bridge   **14** Daffodils (*N. pseudonarcissus*)

1963 (20 July)–**64**. T **13** and similar designs. Recess. P 13.

55		25c. bistre-brown and grey-black	25	30
56		70c. olive-black and deep grey-green	35	55
57		1p. deep rose-lilac and grey-lilac	90	1·50
		a. Blackish lilac and indigo	1·10	1·70
58		2p. deep reddish violet and deep reddish lilac	1·10	1·70
59		2p.50 maroon and dull claret (29.2.64)	90	1·40
60		3p. slate-green and black (29.2.64)	1·10	1·60
61		5p. brown-purple and agate (29.2.64)	3·50	3·75
62		6p. deep rose-red & blackish brown (29.2.64)	4·50	4·00
55/62 Set of 8			11·50	13·50

Designs: Vert—70c. Anyos meadows (wrongly inscr "AYNOS"); 1p. Canillo; 2p. Santa Coloma Church; 2p.50, Andorran arms; 6p. Virgin of Meritxell. Horiz—3p. Andorra la Vella; 5p. Ordino.

1966 (10 June). Pyrenean Flowers. T **14** and similar vert designs. Recess. P 13.

63	50c. blue and slate-blue	55	1·10
64	1p. maroon and yellow-brown	1·10	1·30
65	5p. slate-blue and blue-green	3·25	3·50
66	10p. slate-purple and violet	1·70	2·75
63/66	Set of 4	6·00	7·75

Designs:—1p. Carnation (*Dianthus caryophyllus*); 5p. Narcissus (*N. poeticus*); 10p. Anemone (*Pulsatilla vernalis*) (*wrongly inscribed* "HELEBORUS CONI").

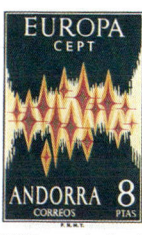 

15 "Communications"   **16** Encamp Valley

1972 (2 May). Europa. Photo. P 13.

67	**15**	8p. multicoloured	£150	£140

Forgeries exist, printed by lithography instead of photogravure.

1972 (4 July). Tourist Views. T **16** and similar multicoloured designs. Photo. P 13.

68	1p. Type **16**	1·00	1·20
69	1p.50 La Massana	1·10	1·20
70	2p. Skis and snow-cape, Pas de la Casa	2·10	2·40
71	5p. Lake Pessons (horiz)	2·30	2·40
68/71	Set of 4	5·75	6·50

17 Volleyball   **18** St. Anthony's Auction

1972 (26 Aug). Olympic Games, Munich, T **17** and similar multicoloured design. Photo. P 13.

72	2p. Type **17**	50	55
73	5p. Swimming (horiz)	70	75

1972 (5 Dec). Andorran Customs. T **18** and similar multicoloured designs. Photo. P 13.

74	1p. Type **18**	35	35
75	1p.50 "Les Caramelles" (choir)	35	35
76	2p. Nativity play (Christmas)	55	60
77	5p. Giant cigar (vert)	90	1·00
78	8p. Carved shrine. Meritxell (vert)	1·10	1·20
79	15p. "La Marratxa" (dance)	3·00	3·25
74/79	Set of 6	5·75	6·00

The 2p. is inscribed "NAVIDAD 1972".

19 "Peoples of Europe"   **20** "The Nativity"

1973 (30 Apr). Europa. T **19** and similar horiz design. Photo. P 13.

80	2p. black, red and blue	55	60
81	8p. red, pale brown and black	1·70	1·90

Design:—8p. Europa "Posthorn".

1973 (14 Dec). Christmas. Frescoes from Meritxell Chapel. T **20** and similar vert design. Multicoloured. Photo. P 13.

82	2p. Type **20**	55	60
83	5p. "Adoration of the Kings"	1·70	1·90

 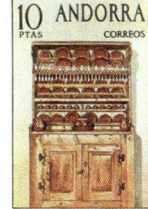

21 "Virgin of Ordino"   **22** Oak Cupboard and Shelves

1974 (29 Apr). Europa. Sculptures. T **21** and similar vert design. Multicoloured. Photo. P 13.

84	2p. Type **21**	2·75	3·00
85	8p. Cross	4·00	4·25

1974 (30 July). Arts and Crafts. T **22** and similar vert design. Multicoloured. Photo. P 13.

86	10p. Type **22**	2·75	3·00
87	25p. Crown of the Virgin of the Roses	6·25	6·75

23 Universal Postal Union Monument, Berne   **24** "The Nativity"

1974 (9 Oct). Centenary of Universal Postal Union. Photo. P 13.

88	**23**	15p. multicoloured	3·50	3·75

1974 (4 Dec). Christmas. Carvings from Meritxell Chapel. T **24** and similar horiz design. Multicoloured. Photo. P 13.

89	2p. Type **24**	1·10	1·20
90	5p. "Adoration of the Kings"	3·50	3·75

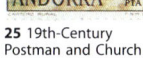

25 19th-Century Postman and Church of St. John of Caselles   **26** "Peasant with Knife"

1975 (4 Apr). España 75 International Stamp Exhibition, Madrid. Photo. P 13.

91	**25**	3p. multicoloured	55	60

1975 (28 Apr). Europa. 12th-century Romanesque Paintings from La Cortinada Church. T **26** and similar vert design. Multicoloured. Photo. P 13.

92	3p. Type **26**	2·75	3·00
93	12p. "Christ"	5·75	6·25

27 Cathedral and Consecration Text   **28** "The Nativity"

1975 (4 Oct). 1100th Anniv of Urgel Cathedral Consecration. Photo. P 13.

94	**27**	7p. multicoloured	3·50	3·75

ANDORRA / Spanish Post Offices

1975 (2 Dec). Christmas. Paintings from La Cortinada Church. T **28** and similar horiz design. Multicoloured. Photo. P 13.
95	3p. Type **28**		55	60
96	7p. "Adoration of the Kings"		1·10	1·20

29 Copper Cauldron   **30** Slalom Skiing

1976 (3 May). Europa. T **29** and similar multicoloured design. Photo. P 13.
97	3p. Type **29**		70	75
98	12p. Wooden marriage chest (horiz)		2·10	2·30

1976 (9 July). Olympic Games, Montreal. T **30** and similar multicoloured design. Photo. P 13.
99	7p. Type **30**		70	75
100	15p. Canoeing (horiz)		2·10	2·30

31 "The Nativity"   **32** Ansalonga

1976 (7 Dec). Christmas. Carvings from La Massàna Church. T **31** and similar horiz design. Multicoloured. Photo. P 13½×13.
101	3p. Type **31**		40	45
102	25p. "Adoration of the Kings"		2·50	2·75

1977 (2 May). Europa. T **32** and similar horiz design. Multicoloured. Photo. P 13.
103	3p. Type **32**		70	75
104	12p. Xuclar		2·10	2·30

33 Boundary Cross   **34** Map of Andorran Post Offices

1977 (2 Dec). Christmas. T **33** and similar vert design. Multicoloured. Photo. P 13×12½.
105	5p. Type **33**		55	60
106	12p. St. Michael's Church, Engolasters		2·50	2·75

1978 (31 Mar). 50th Anniv of Spanish Post Offices. Sheet 105×149 mm containing T **34** and similar vert designs. Multicoloured. Photo. P 13½×13.
MS107	5p. Type **34**; 10p. Postman delivering letter, 1928; 20p. Spanish Post Office, Andorra la Vella, 1928; 25p. Andorran arms	2·75	3·00

35 House of the Valleys   **36** Crown, Mitre and Crook

1978 (2 May). Europa. T **35** and similar horiz design. Multicoloured. Photo. P 13½×13.
108	5p. Type **35**		55	75
109	12p. Church of St. John of Caselles		1·40	2·30

1978 (7 Sept). 700th Anniv of Parity Treaties. Photo. P 13½×13.
110	**36**	5p. multicoloured	85	1·50

37 "Holy Family"   **38** Young Woman's Costume

1978 (5 Dec). Christmas. T **37** and similar vert design showing frescoes in St. Mary's Church, Encamp. Multicoloured. Photo. P 13.
111	5p. Type **37**		40	45
112	25p. "Adoration of the Kings"		95	1·10

1979 (14 Feb). Local Costumes. T **38** and similar vert designs. Multicoloured. Photo. P 13×13½.
113	3p. Type **38**		30	30
114	5p. Young man's costume		40	45
115	12p. Newly-weds		70	75
113/115	Set of 3		1·30	1·40

39 Old Post Bus   **40** Drawing of Boy and Girl

1979 (30 Apr). Europa. T **39** and similar horiz design. Recess. P 13½×13.
116	5p. bronze-green & indigo/*pale yellow*		70	75
117	12p. dp lilac & brown-lake/*pale yellow*		1·40	1·50

Design:—12p. Pre-stamp letters.

1979 (18 Oct). International Year of the Child. Photo. P 13½×13.
118	**40**	19p. greenish blue, bright rose-red and black	1·40	1·50

41 Agnus Dei, Santa Coloma Church   **42** Père d'Urg

1979 (28 Nov). Christmas. T **41** and similar vert design. Multicoloured. Photo. P 13×13½.
119	8p. Santa Coloma Church		40	45
120	25p. Type **41**		95	1·10

1979 (27 Dec). Bishops of Urgel. Co-princes of Andorra (1st series). T **42** and similar horiz designs. Recess. P 13½×13.
121	1p. indigo and reddish brown		30	30
122	5p. crimson and slate-violet		40	45
123	13p. deep brown and deep green		85	90
121/123	Set of 3		1·40	1·50

Designs:—5p. Joseph Caixal; 13p. Joan Benlloch.
See also Nos. 137/8, 171, 182 and 189.

ANDORRA / Spanish Post Offices

43 Antoni Fiter i Rosell   **44** Skiing

1980 (28 Apr). Europa, T **43** and similar vert design. Photo. P 13×13½.
124		8p. reddish brown, yellow-ochre and greenish black	40	45
125		19p. blackish brown, sage green and greenish black	1·70	1·80

Design:—19p. Francesc Cairat i Freixes.

1980 (23 July). Olympic Games, Moscow. T **44** and similar horiz designs. Photo. P 13½×13.
126		5p. dp greenish blue, carm-red & blk	30	30
127		8p. multicoloured	40	45
128		50p. multicoloured	1·50	1·70
126/128 Set of 3			2·00	2·20

Designs:—8p. Boxing; 50p. Shooting.

45 Nativity   **46** Santa Anna Dance

1980 (12 Dec). Christmas. T **45** and similar horiz design. Multicoloured. Litho. P 13½×13½ (10p.) or 13½×13 (22p.).
129		10p. Type **45**	40	45
130		22p. Epiphany	95	1·10

1981 (7 May). Europa. T **46** and similar horiz design. Multicoloured. Photo. P 13½×13.
131		12p. Type **46**	70	75
132		30p. Festival of the Virgin of Canolich	1·40	1·50

47 Militia Members   **48** Handicapped Child learning to Write

1981 (2 July). 50th Anniv of People's Militia. Photo. P 13½×13.
133	**47**	30p. slate-green, deep grey and black	1·40	1·50

1981 (8 Oct). International Year of Disabled Persons. Photo. P 13½×13.
134	**48**	50p. multicoloured	2·10	2·30

49 "The Nativity"   **50** Arms of Andorra

1981 (3 Dec). Christmas. Carvings from Encamp Church. T **49** and similar horiz design. Multicoloured. Photo. P 13½×13.
135		12p. Type **49**	70	75
136		30p. "The Adoration"	1·40	1·50

1981 (17 Dec). Bishops of Urgel, Co-princes of Andorra (2nd series). Horiz designs as T **42**, Recess. P 13½×13.
137		7p. deep reddish purple and deep blue	40	45
138		20p. brown and bottle green	95	1·10

Designs:—7p. Salvador Casañas; 20p. Josep de Boltas.

1982 (17 Feb–Sept). With "PTA" under figure of value.

(a) Size 22×26½ mm. Photo. P 13
139	**50**	1p. magenta	30	30
140		3p. orange-brown	30	30
141		7p. orange-red	30	30
142		12p. brown-lake	30	30
143		15p. ultramarine	40	45
144		20p. blue-green	70	75
145		30p. rosine	70	75

(b) Size 25×31 mm. Recess. P 13×12½
146	**50**	50p. slate-green (30.9.82)	1·70	1·90
147		100p. deep blue (30.9.82)	3·00	3·50
139/147 Set of 9			7·00	7·75

See also Nos. 203/6.

Nos. 148/53 are vacant.

51 The New Reforms, 1866   **52** Footballers

1982 (12 May). Europa. T **51** and similar horiz design. Multicoloured. Photo. P 13×13½ (14p.) or 13½×13 (33p.).
154		14p. Type **51**	95	1·10
155		33p. Reform of the Institutions, 1981	1·80	2·00

1982 (13 June). World Cup Football Championship, Spain. T **52** and similar horiz design. Multicoloured. Litho. P 13½×13.
156		14p. Type **52**	1·40	1·50
		a. Horiz strip. Nos. 156/7 plus label	4·50	4·75
157		33p. Tackle	2·75	3·00

Nos. 156/7 were issued in *se-tenant* pairs with intervening half stamp-size label showing the Championship emblem.

53 Arms and 1929 1p. Stamp   **54** Spanish and French Permanent Delegations Buildings

1982 (21 Aug). National Stamp Exhibition. Recess. P 13½×13.
158	**53**	14p. black and yellow-green	1·40	1·50

1982 (7 Sept). Anniversaries. T **54** and similar vert designs. Recess. P 13×13½.
159		9p. red-brown and deep blue	40	45
160		23p. deep blue and red-brown	70	75
161		33p. black and yellow-green	1·10	1·20
159/161 Set of 3			2·00	2·20

Designs:—9p. Type **54** (centenary of Permanent Delegations); 23p. "St. Francis feeding the Birds" (after Ciambue) (800th birth anniv of St. Francis of Assisi); 33p. Title page of *Relacio sobre la Vall de Andorra* (birth centenary of Tomas Junoy (writer)).

55 "Virgin and Child" (statue, Andorra la Vella Parish Church)   **56** Building Romanesque Church

471

1982 (9 Dec). Christmas. T **55** and similar horiz design. Multicoloured. Photo. P 13×13½ (14p.) or 13½×13 (33p.).
162		14p. Type **55**	70	75
163		33p. Children beating log with sticks	2·10	2·30

1983 (7 June). Europa. T **56** and similar horiz design. Photo. P 13½×13.
164		16p. yellow-green, brown-purple and black	70	75
165		38p. olive-bistre, light blue and black	2·10	2·30

Design:—38p. 16th-century water-mill.

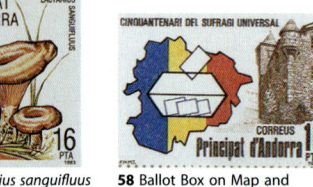

57 *Lactarius sanguifluus*
58 Ballot Box on Map and Government Building

1983 (20 July). Nature Protection. Photo. P 13½×12½.
166	**57**	16p. multicoloured	70	75

1983 (6 Sept). 50th Anniv of Universal Suffrage in Andorra. Recess and litho. P 13½×13.
167	**58**	10p. multicoloured	70	75

59 Mgr. Cinto Verdaguer
60 Jaume Sansa Nequi

1983 (6 Sept). Centenary of Mgr. Cinto Verdaguer's Visit. Recess and litho. P 13½×13.
168	**59**	50p. multicoloured	2·10	2·30

1983 (20 Oct). AIR. Jaume Sansa Nequi (Vegueria-Episcopal) Commemoration. Recess. P 13×13½.
169	**60**	20p. blackish brown and yellow-brown	70	75

  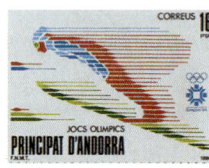

61 Wall Painting, Church of St. Cerni, Nagol
62 Ski Jumping

1983 (24 Nov). Christmas. Photo. P 13½.
170	**61**	16p. multicoloured	70	75

1983 (7 Dec). Bishops of Urgel, Co-princes of Andorra (3rd series). Horiz design as T **42**. Recess. P 13½×13.
171		26p. brown and carmine lake	1·40	1·50

Design:—26p. Joan Laguarda.

1984 (17 Feb). Winter Olympics, Sarajevo. Litho. P 13½×14.
172	**62**	16p. multicoloured	95	1·10

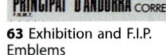 

63 Exhibition and F.I.P. Emblems
64 Bridge

1984 (27 Apr). España 84 International Stamp Exhibition, Madrid. Photo. P 13½×13.
173	**63**	26p. multicoloured	1·40	1·50

(Des J. Larrivière. Recess)

1984 (15 May). Europa. P 13½×13.
174	**64**	16p. reddish brown	70	75
175		38p. blue	2·10	2·30

 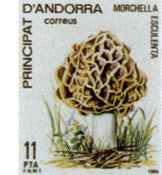

65 Hurdling
66 Common Morel (*Morchella esculenta*)

1984 (9 Aug). Olympic Games, Los Angeles. Litho. P 14.
176	**65**	40p. multicoloured	2·10	2·30

1984 (27 Sept). Nature Protection. Photo. P 13½×12½.
177	**66**	11p. multicoloured	4·25	7·50

67 Pencil, Brush and Pen
68 The Holy Family (wood carvings)

(Des P. S. Gonzalez. Photo)

1984 (25 Oct). Pyrenean Cultures Centre, Andorra. P 13×13½.
178	**67**	20p. multicoloured	85	90

(Des J. Prieto Dolores. Photo)

1984 (6 Dec). Christmas. P 13½×13.
179	**68**	17p. multicoloured	70	75

69 Mossen Enric Marfany and Score
70 Beefsteak Morel (*Gyromitra esculenta*)

1985 (3 May). Europa. T **69** and other vert design. Recess. P 13½.
180		18p. deep green, purple and reddish brown	95	1·10
181		45p. reddish brown and bottle green	1·80	2·00

Design:—45p. Musician with viola (fresco detail, La Cortinada Church).

1985 (13 June). AIR. Bishops of Urgel, Co-princes of Andorra (4th series). Horiz design as T **42**. Recess. P 13½.
182		20p. orange-brown and brown-ochre	70	75

Design:—20p. Ramòn Iglesias.

1985 (19 Sept). Nature Protection. Phosphorescent paper. Photo. P 13×12½.
183	**70**	30p. multicoloured	1·40	1·50

ANDORRA / Spanish Post Offices

71 Pal

72 Angels (St. Bartholomew's Chapel)

1985 (7 Nov). Phosphorescent paper. Recess. P 13×13½.
184 **71** 17p. deep blue and bright blue................ 70 75

1985 (11 Dec). Christmas. Phosphorescent paper. Photo. P 13½×13.
185 **72** 17p. multicoloured............................. 70 75

73 Scotch Bonnet (*Marasmius oreades*)

74 Sun, Rainbow, Lighthouse and Fish

1986 (10 Apr). Nature Protection. Phosphorescent paper. Photo. P 13×12½.
186 **73** 30p. multicoloured............................. 1·40 1·50

1986 (5 May). Europa. T **74** and similar vert design, each blue, dull vermilion and deep green. Phosphorescent paper. Recess. P 13×13½.
187   17p. Type **74**................................... 1·40 1·50
188   45p. Sun and trees on rocks.................... 2·10 2·30

1986 (11 Sept). Bishops of Urgel, Co-princes of Andorra (5th series). Horiz designs as T **42**. Phosphorescent paper. Recess. P 13½×13.
189   35p. deep blue and yellow-brown.............. 1·40 1·50
Design:—35p. Justi Guitart.

 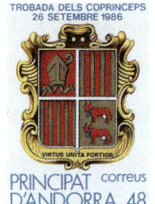

75 Bell of St. Roma's Chapel, Les Bons

76 Arms

1986 (11 Dec). Christmas. Litho. P 14.
190 **75** 19p. multicoloured.......................... 70 75

PHOSPHORESCENT PAPER. From No. 191 all stamps are printed on phosphorescent paper.

1987 (27 Mar). Meeting of Co-princes. Photo. P 14×13½.
191 **76** 48p. multicoloured.......................... 1·40 1·50

  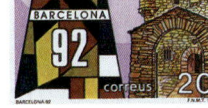

77 Interior of Chapel

78 Emblem and House of the Valleys

1987 (15 May). Europa. Meritxell Chapel. T **77** and similar vert design. Recess. P 13½×14 (19p.) or 14×13½ (48p.).
192   19p. reddish brown and deep blue............. 70 75
193   48p. deep blue and reddish brown............. 1·40 1·50
Design:—18p. Exterior of Chapel.

1987 (20 July). Olympic Games, Barcelona (1992). Sheet 122×86 mm containing T **78** and similar horiz design. Multicoloured. Photo. P 13½×14.
MS194 20p. Type **78**; 50p. Torch carrier and St. Michael's Chapel, Fontaneda, bell tower.............. 5·50 6·00

 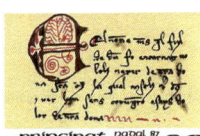

79 Cep (*Boletus edulis*)

80 Extract from *Doctrina Pueril* by Ramón Llull

1987 (11 Sept). Nature Protection. Photo. P 13×12½.
195 **79** 100p. multicoloured......................... 3·50 3·75

1987 (18 Nov). Christmas. Litho. P 13½×14.
196 **80** 20p. multicoloured.......................... 70 75
       a. Imperf (pair)....................................

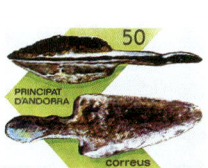 

81 Copper Lance Heads

82 Early 20th-century Trader and Pack Mules

1988 (25 Mar). Archaeology. Photo. P 13½×14.
197 **81** 50p. multicoloured.......................... 1·70 1·80

1988 (5 May). Europa. Communications. T **82** and similar vert design, each deep grey-blue and scarlet. Recess. P 14×13½.
198   20p. Ancient road, Les Bons.................... 70 75
199   45p. Type **82**...................................... 2·10 2·30

83 Pyrenean Mountain Dog

84 Commemorative Coin

1988 (26 July). Nature Protection. Litho. P 14×13½.
200 **83** 20p. multicoloured.......................... 1·40 1·50

1988 (27 Oct). 700th Anniv of Second Parity Treaty. Photo. P 14×13½.
201 **84** 20p. black, greenish slate and olive-bistre... 70 75

 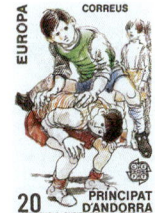

85 Church of St. John of Caselles

86 Leap-frog

473

ANDORRA / Spanish Post Offices

1988 (30 Nov). Christmas. Litho. P 13½×14.
202   **85**   20p. multicoloured 70   75

1988 (2 Dec). As T **50** but without "PTA" below figure of value.
(a) Size 22×26½ mm. Photo. P 13
203   **50**   20p. blue-green 70   75
(b) Size 25×31 mm. Recess. P 13×12½
204   **50**   50p. slate-green .... 2·10   2·30
205   100p. deep blue .... 3·75   4·25
206   500p. deep brown .... 12·50   13·50
203/206 *Set of 4* .... 17·00   19·00

Nos. 207/9 are vacant.

1989 (8 May). Europa. Children's Games. T **86** and similar multicoloured design. Recess and litho. P 14×13½ (20p.) or 13½×14 (45p.).
210   20p. Type **86** .... 1·40   1·50
211   45p. Girl trying to pull child from grip of other children (horiz) .... 2·10   2·30

87 St. Roma's Chapel, Les Bons

88 Anniversary Emblem

1989 (20 June). P 13½×14.
212   **87**   50p. black, turquoise-green and blue.... 2·10   2·30

1989 (26 Oct). 125th Anniv of International Red Cross. Litho. P 14×13½.
213   **88**   20p. multicoloured 70   75

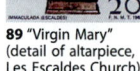
89 "Virgin Mary" (detail of altarpiece, Les Escaldes Church)

90 Old French and Spanish Post Offices, Andorra La Vella

1989 (1 Dec). Christmas. Photo. P 14×13½.
214   **89**   20p. multicoloured 70   75

(Des J. Prieto. Photo)

1990 (8 May). Europa. Post Office Buildings. T **90** and similar multicoloured design. P 13½×14 (20p.) or 14×13½ (50p.).
215   20p. Type **90** 70   75
216   50p. Modern Spanish post office, Andorra La Vella (vert) .... 2·10   2·30

91 *Gomphidius rutilus*

92 Plandolit House

(Des J. Garcia. Photo)

1990 (21 June). Nature Protection. P 13×12½.
217   **91**   45p. multicoloured .... 2·10   2·30

(Des J. Garcia. Eng A. Sánchez. Recess)

1990 (17 Oct). P 13×12½.
218   **92**   20p. red-brown and orange-yellow 70   75

93 Angel, La Massana Church

94 Throwing the Discus

(Des J. Suárez. Photo)

1990 (26 Nov). Christmas. P 14×13½.
219   **93**   25p. reddish brown, stone and lake 85   90

(Des P. Sánchez. Photo)

1991 (29 Apr). European Small States Games. T **94** and similar horiz design. Multicoloured. P 13½×14.
220   25p. Type **94** 95   1·10
221   45p. High jumping and running .... 1·80   2·00

95 "Olympus 1" Satellite

96 Parasol Mushroom (*Macrolepiota procera*)

(Des M. Plaza Torralba. Litho)

1991 (10 May). Europa. Europe in Space. T **95** and similar multicoloured design. P 14×13½ (25p.) or 13½×14 (55p.).
222   25p. Type **95** .... 2·10   2·30
223   55p. Close-up of "Olympus 1" telecommunications satellite (horiz)........ 3·50   3·75

(Des A. Millán Olagaray. Photo)

1991 (20 Sept). Nature Protection. P 13×12½.
224   **96**   45p. multicoloured .... 2·10   2·30

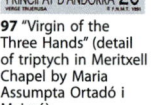
97 "Virgin of the Three Hands" (detail of triptych in Meritxell Chapel by Maria Assumpta Ortadó i Maimó)

98 Woman fetching Water from Public Tap

1991 (29 Nov). Christmas. Photo. P 14×13½.
225   **97**   25p. multicoloured .... 1·40   1·50

(Des P. Sánchez. Photo)

1992 (14 Feb). P 13½×14.
226   **98**   25p. multicoloured .... 1·40   1·50

ANDORRA / Spanish Post Offices

99 Santa Maria   **100** White-water Canoeing

(Des M. Escobar and J. Angel. Photo)

1992 (8 May). Europa. 500th Anniv of Discovery of America by Columbus. T **99** and similar design. P 14×13½ (27p.) or 13½×14 (45p.).
227		27p. multicoloured	2·10	2·30
228		45p. reddish brown, scar-verm and dull orange	2·75	3·00

Design: Horiz—45p. Engraving of King Ferdinand from map sent by Columbus to Ferdinand and Queen Isabella the Catholic.

(Des J. Prieto. Photo)

1992 (22 July). Olympic Games, Barcelona. P 13½×14.
229	**100**	27p. multicoloured	1·40	1·50

101 Benz "Velo", 1894   **102** "Nativity" (Fra Angelico)

(Des M. Escobar. Eng J. M. Mata. Recess and litho)

1992 (10 Sept). National Motor Car Museum, Encamp. P 13½×14.
230	**101**	27p. multicoloured	1·40	1·50

1992 (18 Nov). Christmas. Photo. P 14×13½.
231	**102**	27p. multicoloured	1·40	1·50

103 Chanterelle (*Cantharellus cibarius*)   **104** "Upstream" (J. A. Morrison)

(Des J. Suárez. Photo)

1993 (25 Mar). Nature Protection. P 13½×14.
232	**103**	28p. multicoloured	1·40	1·50

1993 (20 May). Europa. Contemporary Art. T **104** and similar multicoloured design. P 13½×14 (28p.) or 14×13½ (45p.).
233		28p. Type **104**	1·40	1·50
234		45p. "Ritme" (Angel Calvente) (vert)	2·10	2·30

105 Society Emblem on National Colours   **106** Illuminated "P" (Galceran de Vilanova Missal)

(Des S. Más. Photo)

1993 (23 Sept). 25th Anniv of Andorran Arts and Letters Circle. P 14×13½.
235	**105**	28p. multicoloured	1·40	1·50

(Des P. Sánchez. Recess and litho)

1993 (25 Nov). Christmas. P 14×13½.
236	**106**	28p. multicoloured	1·40	1·50

107 National Colours   **108** Sir Alexander Fleming and Penicillin

(Des P. Sánchez. Photo)

1994 (14 Mar). First Anniv of New Constitution. Sheet 105×78 mm. P 14×13½.
MS237	**107**	29p. multicoloured	2·10	2·30

(Des J. Suárez. Photo)

1994 (9 May). Europa. Discoveries. T **108** and similar horiz design. P 13½×14.
238		29p. multicoloured	1·40	1·50
239		55p. new blue and black	2·75	3·00

Design:—55p. Test tube and AIDS virus.
First Day Covers are dated 6 May but the stamps were not placed on sale in Andorra until the 9th.

109 *Hygrophorus gliocyclus*   **110** "Madonna and Child" (anon)

(Des P. Sánchez. Photo)

1994 (27 Sept). Nature Protection. P 13½×14.
240	**109**	29p. multicoloured	1·40	1·50

(Des P. Sánchez. Photo)

1994 (29 Nov). Christmas. P 14×13½.
241	**110**	29p. multicoloured	1·40	1·50

111 Madriu Valley (south)   **112** Sun, Dove and Barbed Wire

(Des J. Angel. Photo)

1995 (23 Mar). European Nature Conservation Year. T **111** and similar horiz design. Multicoloured. P 13½×14.
242		30p. Type **111**	85	90
243		60p. Madriu Valley (north)	1·90	2·10

(Des M. Salamanca and A. Millán. Photo)

1995 (8 May). Europa. Peace and Freedom. P 13½×14.
244	**112**	60p. green, orange and grey-black	2·10	2·30

475

ANDORRA / Spanish Post Offices

113 "Flight into Egypt" (altarpiece, St. Mark and St. Mary's Church, Encamp)

114 Palace of Europe, Strasbourg

(Des P. Sánchez. Photo)
1995 (8 Nov). Christmas. P 14.
245   **113**   30p. multicoloured .... 1·40   1·50

(Des J. Suárez. Photo)
1995 (10 Nov). Admission of Andorra to Council of Europe. P 13½×14.
246   **114**   30p. multicoloured .... 1·40   1·50

115 *Ramaria aurea*

116 Isabelle Sandy (writer)

(Des M. Escobar. Photo)
1996 (30 Apr). Nature Protection. T **115** and similar horiz design. Multicoloured. P 13½×14.
247   30p. Type **115** .... 1·40   1·50
248   60p. Black truffles (*Tuber melanosporum*) .... 2·30   2·50

1998 (7 May). Europa. Famous Women. Photo. P 14×13½.
249   **116**   60p. multicoloured .... 2·75   3·00

117 Old Iron

118 "The Annunciation" (altarpiece, St. Eulalia's Church, Encamp)

1996 (12 Sept). International Museums Day. Photo. P 14.
250   **117**   60p. multicoloured .... 2·10   2·30

(Des P. Sánchez. Photo)
1996 (26 Nov). Christmas. P 13½×14.
251   **118**   30p. multicoloured .... 1·40   1·50

119 Drais Velocipede, 1818

120 The Bear and The Smugglers

(Des M. Plaza. Photo)
1997 (28 Apr). Bicycle Museum. T **119** and similar horiz design. Multicoloured. P 13½×14.
252   32p. Type **119** 95   1·10
253   65p. Michaux velocipede, 1861 .... 1·90   2·10

(Des S. Mas. Photo)
1997 (6 May). Europa. Tales and Legends. P 14×13½.
254   **120**   65p. multicoloured .... 2·75   3·00

121 Dove and Cultural Symbols

122 Catalan Crib Figure

(Des P. Sánchez. Photo)
1997 (30 Sept). National United Nations Educational, Scientific and Cultural Organization Commission. P 14.
255   **121**   32p. multicoloured 70   75

(Des J. Suárez. Photo)
1997 (25 Nov). Christmas. P 14.
256   **122**   32c. multicoloured 70   75

 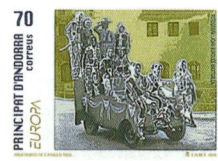

123 Giant Slalom

124 Harlequins of Canillo

1998 (23 Feb). Winter Olympic Games, Nagano, Japan. Photo. P 13½×14.
257   **123**   35p. multicoloured 70   75

(Des J. Plaza. Photo)
1998 (24 Apr). Bicycle Museum (2nd series). Horiz designs as T **119**. Multicoloured. P 13½×14.
258   35p. Kangaroo bicycle, Great Britain, 1878 95   1·10
259   70p. The Swallow, France, 1889 .... 1·90   2·10

(Des J. Suárez. Photo)
1998 (22 May). Europa. National Festivals. P 13½×14.
260   **124**   70p. multicoloured .... 2·10   2·30

 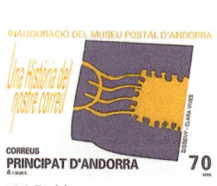

125 Front Page of First Edition and Landscape

126 Emblem

(Des P. Sánchez. Photo)
1998 (30 Sept). 250th Anniv of *Manual Digest*. P 14×13½.
261   **125**   35p. multicoloured 70   75

(Des Clara Vives. Photo)
1998 (19 Nov). Inauguration of Postal Museum. P 13½×14.
262   **126**   70p. dull violet and orange-yellow .... 2·10   2·30

ANDORRA / Spanish Post Offices

127 St. Lucia Fair

128 Mules

(Des J. Suárez. Photo)
1998 (26 Nov). Christmas. P 13½×14.
263　127　35p. multicoloured .... 1·40　1·50

(Des M. Plaza. Photo)
1999 (29 Jan). Bicycle Museum (3rd series). Multicoloured designs as T **119**. P 14×13½ (35p.) or 13½×14 (70p.).
264　　　35p. Salvo tricycle, 1878 (vert) .... 95　1·10
265　　　70p. Rudge tricycle, Coventry, England....... 1·90　2·10

(Des J. Suárez. Photo)
1999 (18 Feb). Postal History. P 13½×14.
266　128　35p. black and light brown .... 1·40　1·50

129 Palace of Human Rights, Strasbourg

130 Vall d'Incles National Park, Canillo

(Des P. Sánchez. Photo)
1999 (29 Apr). 50th Anniv of Council of Europe. P 13½×14.
267　129　35p. multicoloured .... 1·40　1·50

(Des M. Plaza. Photo)
1999 (6 May). Europa. Parks and Gardens. P 13½×14.
268　130　70p. multicoloured .... 2·10　2·30

131 Full House, Sispony

132 Angel (detail of altarpiece, St. Serni's Church, Canillo)

(Des J. Suárez. Photo)
1999 (22 Sept). P 13½×14.
269　131　35p. multicoloured .... 1·40　1·50

(Des J. Suárez. Recess)
1999 (10 Nov). Christmas. P 14×13½.
270　132　35p. reddish brown and orange-brown .... 1·40　1·50

133 Santa Coloma Church

134 "Building Europe"

(Des M. Plaza. Photo)
1999 (12 Nov). European Heritage. P 14×13½.
271　133　35p. multicoloured .... 1·40　1·50

(Des J.-P. Cousin. Photo)
2000 (11 May). Europa. P 14×13½.
272　134　70p. multicoloured .... 2·75　3·00

135 Angonella Lakes, Ordino　136 Casa Lacruz

(Des M. Plaza. Photo)
2000 (29 June). P 13½×14.
273　135　35p. multicoloured .... 1·40　1·50

(Des J. Rincón. Photo)
2000 (20 July). 131st Birth Anniv of Josep Cadafalch (architect). P 13½×14.
274　136　35p. multicoloured .... 1·40　1·50

137 Dinner Service　138 Hurdling

(Des J. Suárez. Photo)
2000 (27 July). D'Areny-Plandolit Museum. P 14×13½.
275　137　70p. multicoloured .... 2·10　2·30

(Des P. Sánchez. Photo)
2000 (29 Sept). Olympic Games, Sydney. P 14×13½.
276　138　70p. multicoloured .... 2·10　2·30

139 United Nations Headquarters, Strasbourg　140 Gradual, St. Roma, Les Bons

(Des J. Suárez. Photo)
2000 (3 Nov). 50th Anniv of United Nations Declaration of Human Rights. P 13½×14.
277　139　70p. multicoloured .... 2·10　2·30

(Des M. Plaza. Photo)
2000 (14 Nov). 25th Anniv of National Archives. P 14×13.
278　140　35p. multicoloured .... 70　75

141 "Quadre de les Animes" (Joan Casanovas)　142 Rec del Solà

477

ANDORRA / Spanish Post Offices

(Des P. Sánchez. Photo)
2000 (22 Nov). Christmas. P 14×13½.
279   141   35p. multicoloured 70   75

(Des J. Ricón. Photo)
2001 (10 Mar). Natural Heritage. P 14×13½.
280   142   40p. multicoloured .... 1·20   1·40

143 Roc del Metge (thermal spring), Escaldes-Engordany
144 Casa Palau, Sant Julià de Lòria

2001 (16 May). Europa. Water Resources. Photo. P 14.
281   143   75p. multicoloured .... 2·10   2·30

2001 (20 June). Photo. P 14.
282   144   75p. multicoloured .... 2·10   2·30

145 Part of Sanctuary, Meritxell
146 Building

(Des J. Suárez. Photo)
2001 (7 Sept). 25th Anniv of Chapel of Our Lady, Meritxell. P 14.
283   145   40p. multicoloured .... 1·40   1·50

(Des J. Suárez. Photo)
2001 (20 Sept). Tenth Anniv of National Auditorium, Ordino. P 14.
284   146   75p. multicoloured .... 2·10   2·30

147 Angel (detail of altarpiece, Church of St. John of Caselles)
148 State Arms

2001 (20 Nov). Christmas. Litho. P 13½×14.
285   147   40p. multicoloured .... 1·40   1·50

New Currency
100 Cents = 1 Euro

2002 (2 Jan)–**07**. P 13.
286   148   25c. dull orange 70   75
286a   27c. new blue (2.1.04) 70   75
286b   28c. deep blue (28.1.05) 85   90
286c   29c. olive sepia (1.3.06) 85   90
286d   30c. rose carmine (19.1.07) 85   90
287   50c. crimson .... 1·40   1·50
288   52c. olive-yellow (2.1.04) .... 1·50   1·70
289   53c. dull yellow-green (28.1.05) .... 1·50   1·70
289a   57c. bright blue (1.3.06) .... 1·70   1·80
289b   58c. grey-black (19.1.07) .... 1·70   1·80
290   77c. pale orange (2.1.04) .... 2·20   2·40
291   78c. magenta (28.1.05) .... 2·20   2·40
286/291 Set of 12 .... 14·50   16·00
Numbers have been left for additions to this series.

149 Alpine Accentor (*Prunella collaris*)
150 Emblem

2002 (27 Mar). Native Birds. T **149** and similar horiz design. Multicoloured. P 13½×14.
300   25c. Type **149** 95   1·10
301   50c. Snow finch (*Montifringilla nivalis*) .... 1·90   2·10

2002 (5 Apr). International Year of the Mountain. P 13½×14.
302   **150**   50c. multicoloured .... 2·10   2·30

151 Tightrope Walker
152 Casa Fusilé, Escaldes-Engordany

2002 (9 May). Europa. Circus. P 13½×14.
303   **151**   50c. multicoloured .... 14·00   15·00

2002 (14 June). Architectural Heritage. T **152** and similar vert design. Multicoloured. Photo. P 14.
304   €1.80 Type **152** .... 5·50   6·00
305   €2.10 Farga Rossell Iron Museum, La Massana ..... 6·25   6·75

153 Pinette Minim
154 Plaça Benlloch, Areny-Plandolit

2002 (8 Oct). History of the Motor Car (1st series). T **153** and similar multicoloured design. P 14.
306   25c. Type **153** 95   1·10
307   50c. Rolls Royce Silver Wraith .... 1·90   2·10
See also Nos. 317/18 and 324/5.

2002 (26 Nov). Christmas. P 14.
308   **154**   25c. multicoloured .... 1·40   1·50

155 Painted Medallion
156 Sassanat Bridge

2002 (28 Nov). Cultural Heritage. Romanesque Murals from Santa Coloma Church, Andorra la Vella. T **155** and similar vert designs. Photo. P 14.
309   25c. Type **155** 70   75
       a. Strip of 3. Nos. 309/11 .... 4·50
310   50c. Part of damaged fresco showing
              seated figure .... 1·40   1·50
311   75c. Frieze .... 2·10   2·30
309/311 Set of 3 .... 3·75   4·00
Nos. 309/11 were issued together in *se-tenant* strips of three stamps within the sheet.

ANDORRA / Spanish Post Offices

2003 (27 Feb). Photo. P 13½×14.
312   156   26c. multicoloured .... 1·40   1·50

157 State Arms

158 Man drinking, Donkey and Market Stalls

2003 (14 Mar). Tenth Anniv of Constitution. Photo. P 13½×14.
313   157   76c. multicoloured .... 2·75   3·00

2003 (24 Apr). Europa. Poster Art. P 14×13½.
314   158   76c. multicoloured .... 2·75   3·00

159 Northern Wheatear (*Oenanthe oenanthe*)

160 Multicoloured Stripes

2003 (11 June). Native Birds. Photo. P 14.
315   159   50c. multicoloured .... 1·40   1·50

(Des J. Duró. Photo)

2003 (28 July). Tenth Anniv of Andorras, Membership of United Nations. P 14.
316   160   76c. multicoloured .... 2·75   3·00

161 Carter (1908)

162 Roadside Cross, Andorra la Vella

2003 (15 Oct). History of the Motor Car (2nd series). T **161** and similar multicoloured design. Photo. P 14.
317   51c. Type **161** .... 1·70   1·80
318   76c. Peugeot (1928) (horiz) .... 2·50   2·75

2003 (20 Nov). Christmas. Photo. P 14.
319   162   26c. multicoloured .... 1·40   1·50

163 "Fira del Bestiar" (Joaquim Mir)

164 "L'Escorxador" (Joaquim Mir)

2004 (20 Feb). Photo. P 14.
320   163   27c. multicoloured .... 1·10   1·20

2004 (18 Mar). Photo. P 14.
321   164   52c. multicoloured .... 1·90   2·10

165 Coaches and Skiers in Snow

166 Chaffinch (*Fringilla coelebs*)

2004 (29 Apr). Europa. Holidays. Photo. P 14.
322   165   77c. black .... 2·75   3·00

2004 (15 June). Native Birds. Photo. P 14.
323   166   27c. multicoloured .... 1·10   1·20

167 Simca 508 C (1939)

168 Map showing Postal Districts

2004 (15 Oct). History of the Motor Car (3rd series). T **167** and similar horiz design. Photo. P 14.
324   €1.90 Type **167** .... 6·50   7·25
325   €2.19 Messerschmitt KR 1 (1955) .... 7·25   8·00

2004 (25 Oct). Introduction of Postal Codes. Photo. P 14.
326   168   52c. orange, deep magenta and black . 2·10   2·30

169 Stars and Flag as Jigsaw Pieces

170 Nativity

2004 (10 Nov). Tenth Anniv of Entry into Council of Europe. P 14.
327   169   52c. multicoloured .... 2·10   2·30

2004 (22 Nov). Christmas. Photo. P 14.
328   170   27c. multicoloured .... 1·10   1·20

171 Madriu-Perafita-Claror Valley

172 "Endless" (Mark Brusse)

479

ANDORRA / Spanish Post Offices

(Des F. Ribo. Litho)
2005 (7 Mar). UNESCO World Heritage Site. Photo. P 14.
329   **171**   28c. multicoloured ....   1·10   1·20

2005 (14 Mar). P 14.
330   **172**   53c. multicoloured ....   2·20   2·40

173 Glass, Flowers, Jug and Tureen
174 Cyclist

2005 (15 Apr). Europa. Gastronomy. Photo. P 13×13½.
331   **173**   78c. multicoloured ....   3·00   3·50

2005 (20 May). Small States of Europe Games. Photo. P 14.
332   **174**   €1.95 lake brown and black ....   5·50   6·00

175 Shrine
176 Dipper (*Cinclus cinclus*)

2005 (15 June). 25th Anniv of Caritas Andorra (humanitarian organization). Photo. P 14.
333   **175**   28c. multicoloured ....   1·10   1·20

2005 (11 July). Native Birds. Photo. P 14.
334   **176**   €2.21 multicoloured ....   6·25   6·75

177 The Nativity (Sergei Mas)
178 Skiers

2005 (2 Nov). Christmas. Photo. P 14.
335   **177**   28c. multicoloured ....   1·10   1·20

2006 (15 Feb). Winter Olympic Games, Turin. Photo. P 14.
336   **178**   29c. multicoloured ....   1·40   1·50

179 "Ruta del Hierro" (sculpture) (Satora Sato)
180 Stylized People of Many Colours and Abilities

2006 (10 Apr). Cultural Heritage. Photo. P 14.
337   **179**   78c. multicoloured ....   2·50   2·75

2006 (16 May). Europa. Integration. Photo. P 14.
338   **180**   57c. multicoloured ....   2·20   2·40

181 Grey Partridge (*Perdix perdix*)
182 Scrabble Letters

2006 (6 June). Natural Heritage. Photo. P 14.
339   **181**   €2.39 multicoloured ....   8·25   9·00

2006 (8 Sept). Fulbright Scholarships. Photo. P 14.
340   **182**   57c. multicoloured ....   2·20   2·40

183 Head Containing World Map
184 Nativity

2006 (2 Oct). 60th Anniv of UNESCO and Tenth Anniv of CNAU. Photo. P 14.
341   **183**   €2.33 multicoloured ....   8·00   8·75

2006 (2 Nov). Christmas. Photo. P 14.
342   **184**   29c. multicoloured ....   1·20   1·20

185 "Encamp 1994" (F. Galobardes)
186 Doves and Emblem

2007 (12 Feb). Cultural Heritage. Photo. P 14.
343   **185**   30c. multicoloured ....   1·20   1·20

2007 (23 Apr). Europa. Centenary of Scouting. Photo. P 14.
344   **186**   58c. multicoloured ....   2·30   2·50

187 "La Familia Jordino" (sculpture by Rachid Khimoune)
188 Capercaillie (*Tetrao urogallus*)

2007 (21 May). Cultural Heritage. The Iron Route (historical trail). Photo. P 14.
345   **187**   €2.43 multicoloured ....   8·50   9·00

2007 (4 July). Natural Heritage. Photo. P 14.
346   **188**   €2.49 multicoloured ....   8·75   9·25

189 *Casa de la Vall* (Francesc Galobardes)   **190** *Stylized Figures*

2007 (10 Sept). Cultural Heritage. Photo. P 14.
347   **189**   78c. multicoloured .... 3·00   3·25

2007 (15 Oct). 25th Anniv of Andorra Red Cross. Photo. P 14.
348   **190**   30c. bright carmine and black .... 1·20   1·20

191 Lamb kneeling before Infant Jesus (painting by Sergi Mas)   **192** *Gypaetus barbatus* (Lammergeier or bearded vulture)

2007 (2 Nov). Christmas. Photo. P 14.
349   **191**   30c. multicoloured .... 1·20   1·20

2008 (24 Jan). Natural Heritage. P 14.
350   **192**   31c. multicoloured .... 1·40   1·50

193 *Carro Vortiu* (sculpture by Jordi Casamajor)   **194** Flag and Ballot Box

2008 (24 Jan). Cultural Heritage. P 14.
351   **193**   60c. multicoloured .... 2·50   2·75

2008 (12 Mar). 15th Anniv of Constitution. P 14.
352   **194**   31c. multicoloured .... 1·80   2·10

195 Envelope   **196** Adam, Eve and Graph

2008 (23 Apr). Europa. The Letter. P 14.
353   **195**   60c. greenish blue and black .... 2·75   3·00

(Des Claude Marty)

2008 (14 May). 25th Anniv of National Science Society. P 14.
354   **196**   78c. new blue and black .... 3·75   4·00

ANDORRA / Spanish Post Offices

197 Fluvi (exhibition mascot)   **198** Games Emblem

2008 (13 June). Zaragoza 2008 International Water and Sustainable Development Exhibition. Sheet 105×79 mm. P 14.
MS355   **197**   €2.60 multicoloured .... 10·50   11·50

2008 (8 July). Olympic Games, Beijing. P 14.
356   **198**   60c. multicoloured .... 2·75   3·00

199 Vall del Comapedrosa   **200** *Sispony* (Carme Massana)

2008 (15 Sept). Natural Heritage. P 14.
357   **199**   €2.44 multicoloured .... 9·25   10·00

2008 (13 Oct). Cultural Heritage. P 13.
358   **200**   31c. multicoloured .... 1·60   1·80

201 Midnight Mass   **202** Narcissus

2008 (11 Nov). Christmas. P 13.
359   **201**   31c. multicoloured .... 1·60   1·80

2009 (17 Jan). Natural Heritage. Flora. Self adhesive. Die-cut perf 13½.
360   **202**   32c. multicoloured .... 1·60   1·80

203 '25'   **204** Merce Rodoreda

2009 (9 Feb). 25th Anniv of Escola Andorrana. P 14.
361   **203**   62c. multicoloured .... 2·75   3·00

(Des A. Bernad)

2009 (6 Mar). Merce Rodoreda (Catalan writer) Commemoration. P 14.
362   **204**   78c. black .... 3·50   3·75

205 Emblem   **206** Figures and Stars

MACHINE LABELS

1996 (16 Sept). Mountains. Self-adhesive. Face values in pesetas. Values from 1p. to 9999p. in 1p. steps.
Fixed Values: 16.9.96 60p., 87p., 114p., 140p.
 1.1.97 65p., 94p., 123p., 151p.

2001 (28 Dec). Mountains. Self-adhesive. Face values in euros. Values from 1c. to 99.99.
Fixed values: 28.12.01 50c., 75c., €1.16, €1.63.

2009 (6 Apr). 60th Anniv of Council of Europe. P 14.
363 205 32c. multicoloured .... 1·60 1·80

2009 (23 Apr). Europa. Astronomy. P 14.
364 206 62c. multicoloured .... 2·75 3·00

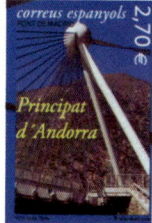 

207 Bridge Strut   **208** Eurasian Sparrowhawk

2009 (18 May). Pont de Madrid (bridge designed by Carlos Fernandez Casado). Sheet 106×80 mm. P 14.
MS365 207 €2.70 multicoloured .... 12·00 13·00

2009 (10 Sept). Natural Heritage. *Accipiter nisus*. P 14.
366 208 €2.47 multicoloured .... 9·25 10·00

209 El Tarter (Francesc Galobardes)   **211** Iris

2009 (8 Oct). Cultural Heritage. T **209** and similar horiz design. Multicoloured. P 14.
367 62c. Type **209** .... 2·75 3·00
368 78c. *Contrallum a Canillo* (Carme Massana). 3·50 3·75

No. 369 and T **210** are vacant.

2010 (12 Jan). Flora. Self-adhesive. Die-cut wavy edge.
370 211 34c. multicoloured .... 1·70 1·90

212 Jacint Verdaguer   **213** Central Section

2010 (8 Feb). 165th Birth Anniv of Jacint Verdaguer i Santaló (Catalan poet). Recess. P 14.
371 212 64c. black .... 2·75 3·00

2010 (5 Mar). Pont de Paris (bridge designed by Carlos Fernández Casado). P 14.
372 213 €2.75 multicoloured .... 12·00 13·00

INDEX

African Colonies (Portuguese Colonies and Overseas Territories) 195
Aguadilla (British Post Offices in Puerto Rico) 406
Andorra (French) 438
Andorra (Spanish) 467
Angola 100
Angola (Portuguese Congo) 111
Angra (Azores) 126
Annobon 386
Antequera (Civil War) 371
Arroyo (British Post Offices in Puerto Rico) 407
Avila (Civil War) 372
Azores 113
Azores (Angra) 126
Azores (British Post Office on São Miguel) 127
Azores (Horta) 126
Azores (Ponta Delgada) 127
Azores (Stamp Booklets) 126

Baena (Civil War) 372
Bilbao (Civil War) 372
Biscay, Navarra, Guipuzcoa and Avala (Carlist Issues) 371
British India Post Office at Damão (Portuguese India) 214
British Post Office at Fernando Poo (Fernando Poo) 392
British Post Office at St. Vincent (Cape Verde Islands) 134
British Post Office in Macao (Macao) 160
British Post Office in Madeira (Madeira) 170
British Post Office on São Miguel (Azores) 127
British Post Offices in Cuba (Cuba) 385
British Post Offices in Cuba (Havana) 385
British Post Offices in Cuba (St. Jago de Cuba) 386
British Post Offices in Puerto Rico (Aguadilla) 406
British Post Offices in Puerto Rico (Arroyo) 407
British Post Offices in Puerto Rico (Mayaguez) 407
British Post Offices in Puerto Rico (Naguabo) 407
British Post Offices in Puerto Rico (Ponce) 407
British Post Offices in Puerto Rico (San Juan) 407
British Post Offices in Spain 379
British Post Offices in Spain (Canary Islands) 379
British Post Offices in Spain (Corunna) 379
British Post Offices in Spain (Teneriffe) 379
Burgos (Civil War) 372

Cadiz (Civil War) 373
Canary Islands (British Post Offices in Spain) 379
Canary Islands (Civil War) 374, 377
Cape Juby 380
Cape Verde Islands 128
Cape Verde Islands (British Post Office at St. Vincent) 134
Carlist Issues 371
Carlist Issues (Biscay, Navarra, Guipuzcoa and Avala) 371
Carlist Issues (Catalonia) 371
Carlist Issues (Valencia) 371
Catalonia (Carlist Issues) 371
Civil War (Antequera) 371
Civil War (Avila) 372
Civil War (Baena) 372
Civil War (Bilbao) 372
Civil War (Burgos) 372
Civil War (Cadiz) 373
Civil War (Canary Islands) 374, 377
Civil War (Durango) 375
Civil War (Granada) 375
Civil War (Logrono) 375
Civil War (Malaga) 375
Civil War (Mallorca) 376
Civil War (Melilla) 376
Civil War (Minorca) 376
Civil War (Orense) 376
Civil War (Pontevedra) 376
Civil War (San Sebastian) 377
Civil War (Santa Cruz de Tenerife) 377
Civil War (Santa Maria de Albarracin) 378
Civil War (Segovia) 378
Civil War (Seville) 378
Civil War (Teruel) 378, 379
Civil War (Vitoria) 379
Civil War (Zaragoza) 379
Civil War, 1936-39 371
Corisco 386
Corunna (British Post Offices in Spain) 379
Cuba 382
Cuba (British Post Offices in Cuba) 385
Cuba (Cuba and Puerto Rico) 382
Cuba (Separate Issues for Cuba) 383
Cuba (Spanish Republic) 383
Cuba and Puerto Rico (Cuba) 382

Design Index (Portugal) 93
Design Index (Spain) 366
Durango (Civil War) 375

East Timor (United Nations Transitional Administration in East Timor) 229
Elobey 386
Elobey, Annobon and Corisco 386

Fernando Poo 387
Fernando Poo (British Post Office at Fernando Poo) 392
Fernando Poo (Overseas Province of Spain) 390
Fernando Poo (Spanish Colony) 387
Filipino Revolutionary Government (Philippines) 403
First Republic (Spain) 235
First Spanish Republic (Philippines) 400
Fiscal Stamps Used for Postage (Spain) 365
French Andorra (Stamp Booklets) 467
French Andorra 438
Funchal (Madeira) 162

General Issues (Portuguese Colonies and Overseas Territories) 195
Granada (Civil War) 375

Havana (British Post Office in Cuba) 385
Horta (Azores) 126

Ifni 393
Inhambane (Mozambique) 182

Kionga (Mozambique) 183

La Agüera (Spanish Sahara) 429
Logrono (Civil War) 375
Lourenço Marques (Mozambique) 183

Macao 134
Macao (British Post Office in Macao) 160
Macao (Machine Labels) 160
Macao (Stamp Booklets) 160
Machine Labels (Macao) 160
Machine Labels (Portugal) 84
Machine Labels (Spain) 362
Madeira 161, 162
Madeira (British Post Office in Madeira) 170
Madeira (Funchal) 162
Madeira (Stamp Booklets) 170
Malaga (Civil War) 375
Mallorca (Civil War) 376
Mariana Islands 398
Mayaguez (British Post Offices in Puerto Rico) 407
Melilla (Civil War) 376
Minorca (Civil War) 376
Morocco (Spanish Post Offices in Morocco and Tangier) 424
Mozambique 171
Mozambique (Inhambane) 182
Mozambique (Kionga) 183
Mozambique (Lourenço Marques) 183
Mozambique (Mozambique Company) 185
Mozambique (Nyassa Company) 191
Mozambique (Portuguese Republic) 173
Mozambique (Quelimane) 193
Mozambique (Tete) 193
Mozambique (Zambezia) 193
Mozambique Company 185

Naguabo (British Post Offices in Puerto Rico) 407
Nationalist Government (Spanish Sahara) 430
Nyassa Company (Mozambique) 191

Orense (Civil War) 376
Overseas Province of Spain (Fernando Poo) 390
Overseas Province of Spain (Rio Muni) 408

Philippines 399
Philippines (Filipino Revolutionary Government) 403
Ponce (British Post Offices in Puerto Rico) 407
Ponta Delgada (Azores) 127
Pontevedra (Civil War) 376
Portugal 1
Portugal (Design Index) 93
Portugal (Machine Labels) 84
Portugal (Republic) 6
Portugal (Stamp Booklets) 91
Portuguese Colonies and Overseas Territories 195
Portuguese Colonies and Overseas Territories (Africa Colonies) 195
Portuguese Colonies and Overseas Territories (General Issues) 195
Portuguese Congo (Angola) 111
Portuguese Guinea 196
Portuguese Guinea (Portuguese Republic) 197
Portuguese India 204
Portuguese India (British India Post Office at Damão) 214
Portuguese India (Portuguese Republic) 208
Portuguese Republic (Mozambique) 173
Portuguese Republic (Portuguese Guinea) 197
Portuguese Republic (Portuguese India) 208
Portuguese Republic (St. Thomas and Prince Islands) 216
Portuguese Republic (Timor) 225
Postal Tax Stamps (Spain) 365
Puerto Rico 404
Puerto Rico (Aguadilla) 406
Puerto Rico (Arroyo) 407
Puerto Rico (British Post Offices in Puerto Rico) 406

483

Index

Puerto Rico (Mayaguez)	407
Puerto Rico (Naguabo)	407
Puerto Rico (Ponce)	407
Puerto Rico (San Juan)	407
Puerto Rico (Spanish Republic)	404

Quelimane (Mozambique)	193

Republic (Portugal)	6
Rio de Oro (Spanish Sahara)	427
Rio Muni	408
Rio Muni (Overseas Province of Spain)	408

San Juan (British Post Offices in Puerto Rico)	407
San Sebastian (Civil War)	377
Santa Cruz de Tenerife (Civil War)	377
Santa Maria de Albarracin (Civil War)	378
Segovia (Civil War)	378
Seville (Civil War)	378
Separate Issues for Cuba (Cuba)	383
Spain	231
Spain (British Post Offices in Spain)	379
Spain (Design Index)	366
Spain (Fiscal Stamps Used for Postage)	365
Spain (Machine Labels)	362
Spain (Postal Tax Stamps)	365
Spanish (Andorra)	467
Spanish Colony (Fernando Poo)	387
Spanish Guinea	411
Spanish Guinea (Spanish Protectorate)	411
Spanish Guinea (Spanish Territories of the Gulf of Guinea)	412
Spanish Morocco	418
Spanish Post Offices in Morocco and Tangier	424
Spanish Post Offices in Morocco and Tangier (Morocco)	424
Spanish Post Offices in Morocco and Tangier (Tangier)	425
Spanish Protectorate (Spanish Guinea)	411
Spanish Republic (Cuba)	383
Spanish Republic (Puerto Rico)	404
Spanish Republic (Spanish Sahara)	429
Spanish Sahara	427, 429
Spanish Sahara (La Agüera)	429
Spanish Sahara (Nationalist Government)	430
Spanish Sahara (Rio de Oro)	427
Spanish Sahara (Spanish Republic)	429
Spanish Territories of the Gulf of Guinea (Spanish Guinea)	412
Spanish West Africa	437
St. Jago de Cuba (British Post Office in Cuba)	386
St. Thomas and Prince Islands	214
St. Thomas and Prince Islands (Portuguese Republic)	216
Stamp Booklets (Azores)	126
Stamp Booklets (French Andorra)	467
Stamp Booklets (Macao)	160
Stamp Booklets (Madeira)	170
Stamp Booklets (Portugal)	91

Tangier (Spanish Post Offices in Morocco and Tangier)	425
Teneriffe (British Post Offices in Spain)	379
Teruel (Civil War)	378, 379
Tete (Mozambique)	193
Timor	223
Timor (East Timor)	229
Timor (Portuguese Republic)	225

United Nations Transitional Administration in East Timor (East Timor)	229

Valencia (Carlist Issues)	371
Vitoria (Civil War)	379

Zambezia (Mozambique)	193
Zaragoza (Civil War)	379

Dear Catalogue User,

As a collector and Stanley Gibbons catalogue user for many years myself, I am only too aware of the need to provide you with the information you seek in an accurate, timely and easily accessible manner. Naturally, I have my own views on where changes could be made, but one thing I learned long ago is that we all have different opinions and requirements.

I would therefore be most grateful if you would complete the form overleaf and return it to me. Please contact Lorraine Holcombe (lholcombe@stanleygibbons.co.uk) if you would like to be emailed the questionnaire.

Very many thanks for your help.

Yours sincerely,

Hugh Jefferies,
Editor.

Questionnaire

2011 Portugal & Spain Catalogue

1. **Level of detail**
   Do you feel that the level of detail in this catalogue is:
   a. too specialised ○
   b. about right ○
   c. inadequate ○

2. **Frequency of issue**
   How often would you purchase a new edition of this catalogue?
   a. Annually ○
   b. Every two years ○
   c. Every three to five years ○
   d. Less frequently ○

3. **Design and Quality**
   How would you describe the layout and appearance of this catalogue?
   a. Excellent ○
   b. Good ○
   c. Adequate ○
   d. Poor ○

4. How important to you are the prices given in the catalogue:
   a. Important ○
   b. Quite important ○
   c. Of little interest ○
   d. Of no interest ○

5. Would you be interested in an online version of this catalogue?
   a. Yes ○
   b. No ○

6. Do you like the new format?
   a. Yes ○
   b. No ○

7. What changes would you suggest to improve the catalogue? E.g. Which other indices would you like to see included?

   ....
   ....
   ....
   ....

8. Which other SG catalogues do you buy?

   ....
   ....
   ....
   ....

9. Would you like us to let you know when the next edition of this catalogue is due to be published?
   a. Yes ○
   b. No ○

   If so please give your contact details below.
   Name: ....
   Address: ....
   ....
   ....
   ....
   Email: ....
   Telephone: ....

10. Which other Stanley Gibbons Catalogues are you interested in?
    a. ....
    b. ....
    c. ....

Many thanks for your comments.

Please complete and return it to: Hugh Jefferies (Catalogue Editor)
Stanley Gibbons Limited, 7 Parkside, Ringwood, Hampshire BH24 3SH, United Kingdom
or email: lholcombe@stanleygibbons.co.uk to request a soft copy

Portugal & Spain Catalogue

From Stanley Gibbons, THE WORLD'S LARGEST STAMP STOCK

Priority order form – Four easy ways to order

Phone: 020 7836 8444 Overseas: +44 (0)20 7836 8444
Fax: 020 7557 4499 Overseas: +44 (0)20 7557 4499
Email: lmourne@stanleygibbons.co.uk
Post: Lesley Mourne, Stamp Mail Order Department, Stanley Gibbons Ltd, 399 Strand, London, WC2R 0LX, England

Customer Details

Account Number ....
Name ....
Address ....
....
Postcode .... Country ....
Email ....
Tel No. .... Fax No. ....

Payment details

Registered Postage & Packing £3.60

○ Please find my cheque/postal order enclosed for £ ....
Please make cheques payable to Stanley Gibbons Ltd.
Cheques must be in £ sterling and drawn on a UK bank

○ Please debit my credit card for £ .... in full payment.
  ○ Mastercard ○ VISA ○ Diners ○ AMEX ○ Switch

  Card Number
  CVC Number   Issue No (Switch)
  Start Date (Switch & Amex)   /   Expiry Date   /

Signature .... Date ....

Portugal & Spain Catalogue

From Stanley Gibbons, THE WORLD'S LARGEST STAMP STOCK

Condition (mint/UM/used)	Country	SG No.	Description	Price	Office use only
				POSTAGE & PACKING £3.60	
				GRAND TOTAL	

Minimum price. The minimum catalogue price quoted in 10p. For individual stamps, prices between 10p and 95p are provided as a guide for catalogue users. The lowest price charged for individual stamps or sets purchased from Stanley Gibbons Ltd is £1.

Please complete payment, name and address details overleaf

Give your collection the home it deserves

Frank Godden albums are a labour of love, with each individual album beautifully handmade to an unmistakable and unmatchable quality.

All leaves are now made to the internationally recognised standard for archival paper, the type that is used and recommended by all major museums.

Revered throughout the philatelic world for their supreme quality and craftsmanship, Frank Godden albums are built to last a lifetime and to offer you a lifetime of enjoyment.

If you are passionate about your collection, then Frank Godden provides the home it deserves.

Whether you are looking for the best quality albums, exhibition cases, protectors, leaves or interleaving, you can find whatever you are looking for at Stanley Gibbons, the new home of Frank Godden.

For more information, visit **www.stanleygibbons.com/frankgodden**

Stanley Gibbons Publications
7 Parkside, Christchurch Road, Ringwood, Hampshire, BH24 3SH
Tel: +44 (0)1425 472 363 | Fax: +44 (0)1425 470 247
Email: orders@stanleygibbons.co.uk

www.stanleygibbons.com

NEW LOOK
FOR OUR 399 STRAND STORE

The New 399 Strand
More space | Better displays
Interactive information | A better shop for you

**Come and experience it for yourself!
The new look home of stamp collecting**

Following months of renovations in advance of the London 2010 show, the new look 399 Strand has officially re-opened its doors to provide you with an exciting new shopping and browsing experience.

The retail area has been expanded to allow you much more space, better, clearer displays and to allow dedicated seating areas for stamp viewing and helpful, interactive information points. The famous stamp counter will remain and the shop will continue to offer an unrivalled range of philatelic items, coupled with the expertise you expect from our dedicated team of philatelic specialists.

399 Strand – The only choice for valuations, auctions, investments, gifts and a range of premium collectibles.

We look forward to seeing you!

Thousands of high quality modern issues added to stock following the acquisition of N&M Haworth in August 2010. **Visit us in store to find out more.**

Est 1856
STANLEY GIBBONS

399 Strand, London WC2R 0LX | Tel: +44 (0)20 7836 8444
Email: orders@stanleygibbons.co.uk

www.stanleygibbons.com

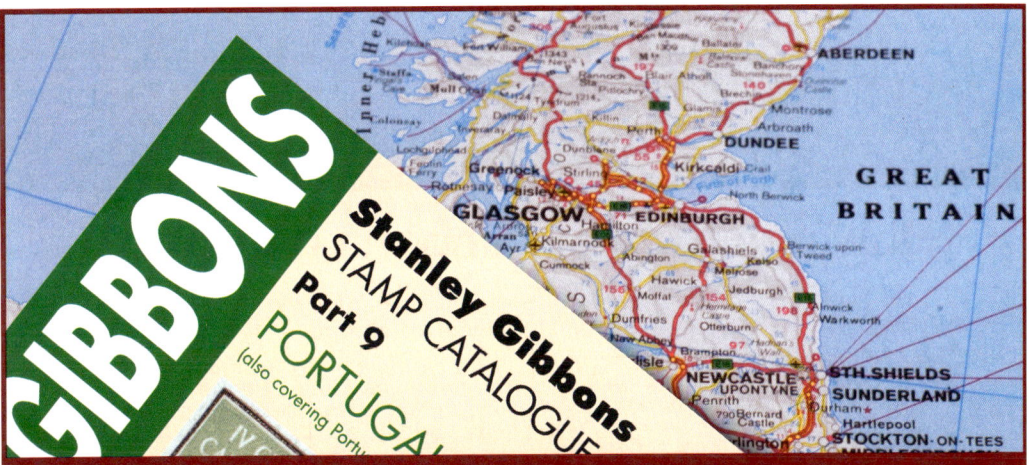

Our buying roadshow could be coming to a town near you

We hold regular roadshows throughout the year, covering the whole of the United Kingdom.

- Free verbal appraisals
- Put forward material for future auctions
- Excellent prices paid for selected Great Britain and Commonwealth
- Our team will be happy to examine anything remotely philatelic

So, if you were thinking of selling that single rare stamp, a part of your collection or the whole thing, then speak to our expert team first at Stanley Gibbons Ltd on +44(0)20 7836 8444 or auctions@stanleygibbons.co.uk

For a list of our forthcoming roadshows, visit **www.stanleygibbons.com/auctions**

Stanley Gibbons Auction Department
399 Strand, London, WC2R 0LX
Contact Steve Matthews or Ryan Epps on Tel: +44 (0)20 7836 8444
Fax: +44 (0)20 7836 7342 | Email: auctions@stanleygibbons.co.uk
www.stanleygibbons.com/auctions

How can Stanley Gibbons help you?

Our History

Stanley Gibbons started trading in 1856 and we have been at the forefront of stamp collecting for more than 150 years, making us the world's oldest philatelic company. We can help you build your collection in a wide variety of ways – all with the backing of our unrivalled expertise.

399 Strand, London, UK - Recently Refurbished!

'...I only wish I could visit more often...' JB, December 09

Our world famous stamp shop is a collector's paradise. As well as stamps, the shop stocks albums, accessories and specialist philatelic books. Plan a visit now!

Specialist Stamp Departments

When purchasing high value items you should definitely contact our specialist departments for advice and guarantees on the items purchased. Consult the experts to ensure you make the right purchase. For example, when buying early Victorian stamps our specialists will guide you through the prices – a penny red SG 43 has many plate numbers which vary in value. We can explain what to look for and where, and help you plan your future collection.

Stanley Gibbons Publications

Our catalogues are trusted worldwide as the industry standard, see the facing page for details on our current range. Keep up to date with new issues in our magazine, Gibbons Stamp Monthly, a must-read for all collectors and dealers. It contains news, views and insights into all things philatelic, from beginner to specialist.

Completing the set

When is it cheaper to complete your collection by buying a whole set rather than item by item? Use the prices in your catalogue, which lists single item values and a complete set value, to check if it is better to buy the odd missing item, or a complete set.

Auctions and Valuations

Buying at auction can be great fun. You can buy collections and merge them with your own - not forgetting to check your catalogue for gaps. But do make sure the condition of the collection you are buying is comparable to your own.

Stanley Gibbons Auctions have been running since the 1900's. They offer a range of auctions to suit both novice and advanced collectors and dealers. You can of course also sell your collection or individual rare items through our public auctions and regular postal auctions. Contact the auction department directly to find out more - email auctions@stanleygibbons.co.uk or telephone 020 7836 8444.

Condition

Condition can make a big difference on the price you pay for an item. When building your collection you must keep condition in mind and always buy the best condition you can find and afford. For example, ensure the condition of the gum is the same as issued from the Post Office. If the gum is disturbed or has had an adhesion it can be classed as mounted. When buying issues prior to 1936 you should always look for the least amount of disturbance and adhesion. You do have to keep in mind the age of the issue when looking at the condition.

The prices quoted in our catalogues are for a complete item in good condition so make sure you check this.

Ask the Experts

If you need help or guidance, you are welcome to come along to Stanley Gibbons in the Strand and ask for assistance. If you would like to have your collection appraised, you can arrange for a verbal evaluation Monday to Friday 9.00am – 4.30pm. We also provide insurance valuations should you require. Of course an up-to-date catalogue listing can also assist with the valuation and may be presented to an insurance agent or company.

Stanley Gibbons Publications

7 Parkside, Christchurch Road, Ringwood, Hants. BH24 3SH Tel: +44 (0)1425 472363 Fax: +44 (0)1425 470247
Email: orders@stanleygibbons.co.uk